Conflict Resolution:
Contributions of the
Behavioral Sciences

Conflict Resolution:

Contributions of the

Behavioral Sciences

Clagett G. Smith, editor

UNIVERSITY OF NOTRE DAME PRESS
NOTRE DAME   LONDON

Library of Congress Catalog Card Number: 72-159274

Manufactured in the United States of America by
NAPCO Graphic Arts, Inc., Milwaukee, Wisconsin

But we shall also do our part to build a world of peace where the weak are safe and the strong are just. We are not helpless before the task or hopeless of its success. Confident and unafraid, we labor on—not toward a strategy of annihilation but toward a strategy of peace.

John F. Kennedy

Commencement Address at the American University, June 10, 1963

LIST OF CONTRIBUTORS

ALLPORT, GORDON W.
> Deceased, Formerly Department of Psychology, Harvard University

BOULDING, KENNETH
> Institute of Behavior Science, University of Colorado

BROWN, JUDSON
> Department of Psychology, State University of Iowa

CLAUDE, INIS L., JR.
> Department of Political Science, University of Michigan

COSER, LEWIS A.
> Department of Sociology, State University of New York at Stony Brook

DENTON, FRANK H.
> The Rand Corporation

DEUTSCH, MORTON
> Department of Psychology, Columbia University

DYNES, RUSSELL R.
> Department of Sociology and Disaster Research Center, Ohio State
> University

ETZIONI, AMITAI
> Department of Sociology, Columbia University

FISHER, ROGER
> Harvard Law School, Harvard University

FROMM, ERICH
> Patricio Sanz, Mexico City

GALTUNG, JOHAN
> International Peace Research Institute, Oslo, Norway

GAMSON, WILLIAM A.
> Department of Sociology, University of Michigan

GLAGOLEV, I.
> Institute for World Economy and International Relations, Academy
> of Sciences, Moscow

GORYAINOV, M.
> Institute for World Economy and International Relations, Academy
> of Sciences, Moscow

GUETZKOW, HAROLD
> Department of Sociology and Political Science, Northwestern Uni-
> versity

HAUSER, PHILIP M.
> Population Research Center, University of Chicago

HAYDON, THOMAS
> Mental Health Research Institute, University of Michigan

HIMES, JOSEPH S.
> Department of Sociology and Anthropology, University of North
> Carolina

HOROWITZ, IRVING LOUIS
 Department of Sociology, Rutgers University

JANIS, IRVING L.
 Department of Psychology, Yale University

JEFFRIES, VINCENT
 Department of Sociology, San Fernando Valley State College

KATZ, DANIEL
 Department of Psychology, University of Michigan

KELMAN, HERBERT C.
 Department of Social Relations, Harvard University

KLINGBERG, FRANK L.
 Department of Government, Southern Illinois University

LEVI, WERNER
 Department of Political Science, University of Hawaii

MACK, RAYMOND W.
 Department of Sociology, Northwestern University

MORRIS, RICHARD T.
 Department of Sociology, University of California–Los Angeles

OSGOOD, CHARLES E.
 Institute of Communications Research, University of Illinois

PATCHEN, MARTIN
 Department of Sociology, Purdue University

PETTIGREW, THOMAS F.
 Department of Social Relations, Harvard University

PHILIPS, WARREN
 Department of Political Science, University of Hawaii

PILISUK, MARC
 School of Social Welfare, University of California–Berkeley

QUARANTELLI, E. L.
 Department of Sociology and Disaster Research Center, Ohio State
  University

RUMMEL, R. J.
 Department of Political Science, Yale University

SCHURMANN, FRANZ
 Department of History, University of California–Berkeley

SHUBIK, MARTIN
 Department of Administrative Sciences, Yale University

SMOKER, PAUL
 Department of Political Science, Northwestern University

SNYDER, ROBERT C.
 Department of Political Science, Northwestern University

STAGNER, ROSS
 Department of Psychology, Wayne State University

TANTER, RAYMOND
 Department of Political Science, University of Hawaii

WRIGHT, QUINCY
 Department of Foreign Affairs, University of Virginia

ZAWODNY, J. K.
 Department of Political Science, University of Pennsylvania

ZINNES, DINA A.
 Department of Government, Indiana University

CONTENTS

Preface   xiii

Introduction   xv

PART ONE: THEORETICAL APPROACHES TO THE STUDY OF CONFLICT   1
RAYMOND W. MACK AND RICHARD C. SNYDER
   The Analysis of Social Conflict—Toward an Overview
   and Synthesis   3
MORTON DEUTSCH
   Conflict and Its Resolution   36
LEWIS A. COSER
   Social Conflict and the Theory of Social Change   58
IRVING LOUIS HOROWITZ
   Consensus, Conflict and Cooperation: A Sociological Inventory   66

PART TWO: CONFLICT SYSTEMS   79
  A. Intrapersonal Conflict
    DANIEL KATZ
     Current and Needed Psychological Research in
     International Relations   81
    JUDSON S. BROWN
     Principles of Intrapersonal Conflict   88
    ROSS STAGNER
     Personality Dynamics and Social Conflict   98
    IRVING L. JANIS
     Problems of Theory in the Analysis of Stress Behavior   110

  B. Interpersonal Conflict
    MARTIN PATCHEN
     Decision Theory in the Study of National Action:
     Problems and a Proposal   119
    MARTIN SHUBIK
     On the Study of Disarmament and Escalation   130
    WILLIAM A. GAMSON
     A Theory of Coalition Formation   146
    ROGER FISHER
     Fractionating Conflict   157

  C. Intergroup Conflict
    JOSEPH S. HIMES
     The Functions of Racial Conflict   170
    THOMAS F. PETTIGREW
     Social Psychology and Desegregation Research   180

RICHARD T. MORRIS AND VINCENT JEFFRIES
Class Conflict: Forget It!   190

RUSSELL R. DYNES AND E. L. QUARANTELLI
The Absence of Community Conflict in the Early Phases
of Natural Disasters   200

DANIEL KATZ
Group Process and Social Integration: A System
Analysis of Two Movements of Social Protest   205

IRVING L. JANIS AND DANIEL KATZ
The Reduction of Intergroup Hostility:
Research Problems and Hypotheses   219

D. Conflict and Societal Processes

RAYMOND TANTER
Dimensions of Conflict Behavior Within and
Between Nations, 1958–60   233

R. J. RUMMEL
Dimensions of Conflict Behavior within Nations, 1946–59   254

FRANZ SCHURMANN
On Revolutionary Conflict   261

JOHAN GALTUNG
A Structural Theory of Aggression   272

MARC PILISUK AND THOMAS HAYDEN
Is There a Military-Industrial Complex Which
Prevents Peace?: Consensus and Countervailing
Power in Pluralistic Systems   294

E. Internation Conflict

   1. Conflict Phenomena

      WERNER LEVI
      On the Causes of War and the Conditions of Peace   318

      FRANK H. DENTON AND WARREN PHILLIPS
      Some Patterns in the History of Violence   327

   2. Economic Considerations

      PHILIP M. HAUSER
      Demographic Dimensions of World Politics   339

   3. Political Strategy and Decision-Processes

      QUINCY WRIGHT
      The Escalation of International Conflicts   349

      DINA A. ZINNES
      An Analytical Study of the Balance of Power Theories 364

      PAUL SMOKER
      Nation State Escalation and International Integration 380

      J. K. ZAWODNY
      Unconventional Warfare   393

      HAROLD GUETZKOW
      Isolation and Collaboration: A Partial Theory of
      Inter-nation Relations   398

   4. Social Psychological Processes

      DANIEL KATZ
      Nationalism and Strategies of International
      Conflict Resolution   416

4. Social Psychological Processes—Continued

HERBERT C. KELMAN
Societal, Attitudinal and Structural Factors in
International Relations 445

PART THREE: THE RESOLUTION OF INTERNATIONAL CONFLICT:
APPROACHES, STRATEGIES, AND POLICY RECOMMENDATIONS 457

FRANK L. KLINGBERG
Predicting the Termination of War: Battle Casualties
and Population Losses 459

LEWIS A. COSER
The Termination of Conflict 486

KENNETH E. BOULDING
The Prevention of World War III 492

I. GLAGOLEV AND M. GORYAINOV
Some Problems of Disarmament Research 498

INIS L. CLAUDE, JR.
United Nations Use of Military Force 503

CHARLES E. OSGOOD
Graduated Unilateral Initiatives for Peace 515

ERICH FROMM
The Case for Unilateral Disarmament 526

GORDON W. ALLPORT
Guide Lines for Research in International Co-operation 535

AMITAI ETZIONI
Strategic Models for a De-Polarizing World 542

Index-Bibliography 551

PREFACE

This book is one of a series of works of the Program in Non-Violence of the University of Notre Dame. Thanks are due for its generous support under the leadership of Father Maurice Amen, even though the editor is solely responsible for its contents.

This book was undertaken in response to a felt need of my students at the Universities of Wisconsin and Notre Dame. Its emphasis and directions can be traced to my Michigan heritage, and to the encouragement and stimulation, however indirect, of Professors Daniel Katz, Kenneth E. Boulding, and Anatol Rapaport. Its thrust is compounded by the impetus from the works of Professors Morton Deutsch and Amitai Etzioni of Columbia University.

Above all, this book is the direct work of the many contributors who generously agreed to have their papers included. The editor is grateful for the opportunity to be able to disseminate their endeavors. Finally, thanks are due to my wife Mary who not only assisted in the demands of preparing this volume for publication but also provided the initial encouragement for its undertaking.

Clagett G. Smith
University of Notre Dame
May, 1971

INTRODUCTION

Through the ages man has attempted to cope with the problem of achieving peace within himself and with others. In the current era alienation, lack of identity, and role conflicts are everyday facts of life, urban centers are torn with racial strife, and the threat of total nuclear destruction remains imminent. The issue of the control of conflict, especially in its violent manifestations, constitutes the crisis of our very existence. In contrast to previous generations, traditional attitudes of pessimism and powerlessness over our destiny are being replaced by those of ambivalence and even hope. In view of the tremendous and sometimes awesome achievement of the physical sciences and their technological applications, some feel that perhaps, through science, man, who has brought these problems into existence, may develop some measure of control over them before it is too late.

Academically, the ground of optimism is the knowledge explosion which has come to pervade, or at least become focused upon, the phenomenon of conflict through the efforts of an increasing number of scholars in the various social science disciplines. An era of speculation is being replaced by an objective stance: traditional issues are being redefined into more viable ones, and empirical research is increasing in an exponential fashion. With the establishment of such research institutes as the Center for Conflict Resolution at Michigan, the Peace Research Institute in Norway, Studies of International Conflict and Integration at Stanford, the Center for Policy Research at Columbia, and the U.S. Arms Control and Disarmament Agency, such endeavors have been translated into organized research efforts. For the editor there are grounds for encouragement and even excitement at what has become a fervor of activity. However, for the serious practitioner and the interested student these efforts still represent the periphery of the social and behavioral sciences. While the relevance of the behavioral sciences in particular is no longer an issue, the problem of the dissemination of this research and theorizing to permit stocktaking, assessment, and application is badly needed. The present volume represents an attempt to compile and integrate some of the key studies to encourage such evaluation and utilization.

The component objectives of this volume are as follows: (1) to present the more recent conceptualizations in conflict theory, (2) to compile studies of conflict phenomenon at various systems levels to benefit not only the student of international relations but those concerned with intergroup relations and interpersonal phenomenon, and (3) in the light of such research and theorizing, to present some of the more imaginative, yet operational, recommendations for the resolution or management of conflict.

Certain biases are implicit in our approach. First is that of the multilevel analysis of conflict phenomenon. Consistent with the approach of Deutsch and the premise of Mack and Snyder, it is asserted that studies of conflict can in the long run benefit most from a multidiscipline approach. It is affirmed that conflict phenomena are indeed partially in the minds of men but also are implicated in larger systems and structural contexts. As a con-

sequence, our outline includes conflict systems at different analytical levels, ranging from the personality, interpersonal, and intergroup to that of the configuration of nation-states. It is based on the assertion that, first, conflict phenomena at a particular level deserve inquiry in their own right in contrast to the rather exclusive emphasis heretofore on international relations. Thus the student or practitioner of various disciplines and persuasions may find cerain portions of this volume particularly relevant to their interests and concerns. Second, if not more important, it is assumed that, in view of the current level of research and theorizing on conflict, such multilevel approaches may reveal certain uniformities and principles characteristic of all conflict systems. By undertaking such an inventory, it may facilitate the development of general conflict theory and encourage integrative approaches. Some may assert that such an approach is premature; others may object to the reductionism or avenues of analogic reasoning implicit in such an inquiry. Hopefully, the compilation will assist the reader in drawing his own conclusions concerning the efficiency of this approach. Its feasibility remains open to question. If it is partially confirmed, with due emphasis placed on new emergent properties at higher levels, conflict theory will be advanced that further.

Second, the approach attempts to select studies which have definite conceptual implications yet remain tied to empirical research. As will become apparent, the emphasis is on conceptual, or "think pieces," which are linked to general behavioral theory. To this end, the major papers of this nature attempt an integration of models of conflict with general theory, where conflict systems are not anomalous phenomenon but represent continuities with other social processes. As a consequence, theory concerned with "normal social processes" becomes a point of departure without neglecting the unique properties of conflict systems. However, as will become apparent, the empirical relevance of such models and approaches is highlighted by our selection. Deutsch's article based on laboratory research represents one end of the continuum, while Etzioni's formulation in terms of the depolarization occurring in the international arena illustrates the ubiquity of theory development based on actual characteristics of conflict phenomenon.

Finally, a third bias is the emphasis on the operational, the feasible—on findings and research by which a practitioner or policy maker can achieve some leverage. The more humanistically oriented, the theorist, or the student may object to such "tough-minded" approaches. However, through this emphasis upon workable approaches and procedures, especially regarding aspects of conflict of manageable proportions, solutions may become more apparent in a realistic sense. Cryptically stated, the studies are operationally oriented whereby the pitfalls of philosophical speculation and traditional theorizing not directed by disciplined empirical inquiry are avoided. Yet this is not to say that the research-based papers are not imaginative. A reading of such redirections of inquiry suggested by Katz, Osgood, Pettigrew, Zinnes, and Etzioni, to name a few, capitalize on extant knowledge but go much further, forcing a recentering from the traditional assumptions or fallacies which have impeded research efforts to date.

In initiating this volume we felt that behavioral science theorizing, the orientation implicit in a multilevel analysis, and operational approaches were definitely neglected in the literature. It remains for the reader to judge the efficiency of such approaches. In terms of this orientation three guide-

lines were followed in selecting material for inclusion. First, studies of conflict phenomena from a variety of different settings were included which had general implications for conflict theory. Hopefully, the material will have relevance for a number of disciplines, for selections were made with a view that a member of one discipline can understand that of another discipline. More specifically, the material was selected to interest the individualistically oriented, the student of intergroup relations, or one from international relations, yet common parallels and principles would remain in primary focus.

Second, the emphasis is on research initiated from 1958 onward, wherein behavioral science approaches represent a major criterion of selection. Yet the basis of their selection for inclusion is not simply their specific validity, but their more broader empirical implications. In the attempt to include the most recent developments it is hoped that their continuity with previous research and theorizing will not be overlooked.

Finally, the emphasis on the operational and feasible in the management, redirection, or resolution of conflict is highlighted in the final section which contains recommendations for the resolution of conflict, yet this approach permeates the other sections. However, such an emphasis is far from being nonhumanistic or nonidealistic. The material may provide grounds for encouragement that realistic tactics and strategies can become available for actual social action and policy making.

In line with the objectives of this work, Part I is concerned with more recent theoretical approaches in the study of conflict, wherein the emphasis is on integrative and synthetic approaches furnished against the backdrop of traditional social science theory. Conflict in all its varieties and manifestations is pursued in Part II, which successively deals with intrapersonal and interpersonal conflict, intergroup conflict, societal processes, and finally internation conflict. The concern with international conflict attempts to provide as broad a basis as possible by presenting economic considerations, political strategy and decision processes, and social-psychological approaches. Part III deals with approaches, strategies, and policy recommendations concerning the resolution of international conflict. These include arms control and disarmament strategies, factors involved in reducing international tensions, and the social-structural considerations for world peace in the foreseeable future.

C. G. S.

Part One

Theoretical Approaches to the Study of Conflict

THE ANALYSIS OF SOCIAL CONFLICT—
TOWARD AN OVERVIEW AND SYNTHESIS *

RAYMOND W. MACK and RICHARD C. SNYDER[1]

I. Introduction

It is clearly evident from the citations and bibliography presented elsewhere in this issue that a vast literature on social conflict has accumulated. Even allowing for a high degree of selectivity, the list of relevant writings is imposing. Over the years, research suggestions and problem- or policy-oriented proposals have grown in number and sophistication. Action programs designed to reduce or eliminate conflict have been subjected to critical appraisal. Attention has been focused on a wide variety of conflict and conflict situations: intrapersonal, interpersonal, interorganizational, and intergroup. In particular, war and peace, labor and management, personality, interest groups, race, ethnology, and ideology have been central topics of conflict analysis. There is, of course, a differential distribution of research and writing among the major categories of social conflict, but none has been totally neglected.

As preceding pages amply reveal, such a broad area of research and analysis is marked by diverse approaches and purposes and by the usual methodological problems and disagreements. To a certain extent this is both natural and in some sense welcome. On the other hand, it has been remarked (11; 12, chap. i) that a priori postures toward social conflict have delayed, if not prevented, the acquisition of systematic, socially applicable knowledge. The view of conflict as completely and always "bad" and the attribution of war to "herd instincts" are cases in point. Given the pervasiveness of conflict phenomena

and the diversity of approaches to inquiry, it is legitimate to ask whether the apparent intellectual disorder reflects an inherently incoherent focus of social analysis—a focus artificially created by a label—or whether the disparateness of data and interpretations is due in part to interdisciplinary compartmentalization, to academic individualism, or to rapid growth, with its consequent inattention to direction.

Obviously, "conflict" is for the most part a rubber concept, being stretched and molded for the purposes at hand. In its broadest sense it seems to cover everything from war to choices between ice-cream sodas or sundaes. At any rate, the distinctions between conflict and non-conflict are fuzzy at best and at worst are not made at all. There is also a persistent tendency to regard *all* conflict as bad, as susceptible to *complete elimination*, given "good will," "understanding," and so on, and as basically different from "co-operation." The conflict—co-operation dichotomy has been pushed to the point where one is defined in terms of the absence of the other. Relatively little effort has been made to specify analytically different properties of conflict as a generic phenomenon and to differentiate explicitly between conflict and closely related concepts. Systematic and fruitful classification of conflict and conflict situations has only just begun. Variables cited to account for conflict tend to be many in number and to be unrelated or unrelatable in many instances. With several notable exceptions to be noted later, the identification and evaluation of basic propositions have been neglected. For criticism of the present state of the "sociology of conflict" and of theoretical and other inadequacies see Bernard (3), Hager (22), Coser (12, chap. i), Sheppard (35), and Sorensen (38). Inadequate conceptualization and theorizing have had important consequences. First, generalization across disciplinary or subject-matter

* Reprinted by permission from the author and publisher from the *Journal of Conflict Resolution*, 1957, *1*: 212–248.

[1] Fellow, Center for Advanced Study in the Behavioral Sciences, 1956–57. The stimulation and facilities provided in such generous measure by the Center helped in the preparation of this study and are gratefully acknowledged.

lines has been slow to develop and, where it does appear, is often implicit. Second, it has been difficult to link propositions systematically. Third, research has not always been guided by hypotheses of acceptable power and significance. Fourth, no well-rounded body of case materials based on comparative types, unifying concepts, and general hypotheses has developed.

In the absence of some sort of framework of conflict analysis—related concepts, definitions, models, questions, hypotheses, etc.— it becomes difficult to choose rationally between alternative approaches: the sociological versus the social-psychological, the "conflict is functional" versus "conflict is dysfunctional," the causes of conflict (e.g., war) versus the conditions of non-conflict (e.g., peace), "peoples" versus "governments" research, the "human-relations" approach versus the "power-relations" approach, and so on. So, too, it becomes difficult to transfer relevant knowledge from one arena of social conflict to another.

Despite the accumulation of experience and writing, certain basic queries remain unanswered. Only a few need be set forth here. Why do serious situations sometimes *not* develop into violent conflict while not so serious ones do? Why do some conflicts rather quickly run a natural course while others do not? What kinds of group attachments to which men are susceptible (in particular situations) are closely related to well-delineated lines of cleavage in society? What is the effect of size of groups on intergroup conflict? Does increased social mobility increase or decrease social conflict? Is desire to convert others to a set of beliefs more conducive to intense conflict than desire for scarce resources? Do differing value commitments have greater conflict potential when the corresponding behavior patterns are not brought into face-to-face confrontation than when they are? Under what conditions are psychological mechanisms crucial to the emergence of conflict? Why do some forms of group identification accompany intergroup conflict while others do not? Under what conditions do differing needs, demands, and aspirations, combined with appraisals of interaction situations, produce conflict behavior? Such questions

suggest either gaps in knowledge and/or the ineffective organization of existing knowledge (8).

For the foregoing reasons, we wish to argue the need for further intellectual stocktaking—for a propositional survey and assessment and for more precise conceptualization. We shall only attempt to suggest in simplified form the general lines along which this might be carried out. The essays which comprise the heart of this symposium exemplify a significant trend in this direction. We shall push some of the implications a step further. Needless to say, the acquisition of new knowledge will depend primarily on empirical research. For a recent critical evaluation of conflict research, the reader should consult the very useful UNESCO volume, *The Nature of Conflict: Studies on the Sociological Aspects of International Tensions* ("Tensions and Technology Series" [1957]). This volume represents a different kind of intellectual stocktaking and stands in complementary relationship to the present essay.

II. Basic Propositions

A reasonably thorough scanning of the literature reveals that the materials for an orderly and general index of propositions on social conflict are available. Coser has reformulated and analyzed sixteen of Simmel's propositions concerning intergroup conflict (12, chaps. ii–ix). Williams has presented one hundred and two propositions dealing with racial, ethnic, and religious conflict (39). Indeed, the latter has provided a model which might well be copied for other areas of conflict. Cooper has reviewed the psychological literature on war (11). Jackson has discussed eight major propositions regarding international mediation (23, pp. 126–70). Chase summarizes the findings and principles from several branches of social science which bear on sixteen levels of conflict—from two persons to the East-West crisis (7). Rose offers twenty-one hypotheses on effective industrial mediation devices (33). Dubin (*JCR*, 1957, *1*: 179) has built his analysis of industrial conflict around five central propositions, together with twenty-five corollaries.

Listing propositions could easily be an empty exercise. Why is a propositional survey useful, and what are the necessary rules for constructing it? To begin with, it is universally recognized that a body of knowledge about anything consists primarily of a set of existential propositions which are in varying degrees verified. A necessary step in stocktaking is, therefore, the pinpointing of major generalizations. Once they are made explicit and rendered in propositional form, critical assessment is possible. A series of questions can and should be put to any set of propositions: What evidence can be mobilized in support or disproof? Which are educated guesses? Which are generally agreed to or disagreed from by qualified experts? Which need further testing and/or reformulation? Which represent cumulative, consistent observations?

In order to avoid an almost infinite list of propositions based on indiscriminate choice, criteria are required. Williams (39, p. 50) suggests three: (1) those of potential importance for understanding social conflict and for application to policy problems; (2) those which offer the most promise of fruitfully guiding empirical research; and (3) those of most probable validity. These criteria direct initial attention to propositions which are of sufficient generality to provide a framework for more particular propositions (lower order of generality), which highlight the necessary and sufficient causes of social conflict, which provide a basis for linking different kinds of social conflict (e.g., industrial and international), and which can be ordered into a theory having explanatory and predictive power.

Some examples (paraphrased) drawn from the literature will illustrate, omitting for the moment the question of verification and qualification:

Proposition 1: *Intragroup harmony tends to reduce intergroup friction* (industrial relations) (24, p. 201).

Proposition 2: *Certain personality characteristics germane to particular national groups are conflict-instigating* (international relations) (27).

Proposition 3: *The more totalitarian a group, organization, or society, the greater the likelihood that its leaders will be aggressive* (general) (18, p. 33).

Proposition 4: *The more compartmentalized and restricted are the claims of a particular faith to define and regulate religious values, the less likely is religious group membership to be divisive* (religious conflict) (40, p. 15).

Proposition 5: *The more fixed the size of the "pie" to be divided, the more intense the conflict* (industrial relations) (26, p. 230).

Proposition 6: *Violence is more likely when a minority group is not content to accept the designation of low rank by majority groups and when it attempts to redefine the situation to permit its assimilation or equal ranking* (racial conflict) (14, p. 420).

Proposition 7: *The main source of persistence of intergroup hostility is the interlocking and mutual reinforcement of realistic and unrealistic conflict elements* (general) (39, p. 41).

Proposition 8: *As unions gain power, the duration of strikes decreases* (industrial relations) (35, p. 337).

Proposition 9: *Conflict with outgroups increases internal cohesion* (general) (12, p. 88).

Proposition 10: *Warlike attitudes may be expressions of deep-lying personality factors laid down in child-rearing* (international relations) (18, p. 34).

Proposition 11: *If the power of two parties is not grossly unequal, agreement is more likely when both are least rigid in their positions* (industrial and international relations) (23, p. 137).

Proposition 12: *The major source of international tension resides between, rather than within, nations* (international relations) (9, p. 17).

Proposition 13: *Far from being necessarily dysfunctional, a certain degree of conflict is an essential element in group formation and the persistence of group life* (general) (12, p. 31).

Proposition 14: *Religious conflict persists because of the need to preserve or protect one's power position* (religious conflict) (21, p. 40).

Proposition 15: *Conflict between groups becomes institutionalized* (general) (this issue, p. 187).

These fifteen propositions, drawn more or less randomly from a larger sample, differ markedly from one another. Nevertheless, they are all focused on social conflict, and, to the extent that they are sustained by adequate evidence, they are not trivial. On the other hand, if the list were increased tenfold, the resulting revelation would be counterbalanced by an impression of confusion and incompleteness. For as soon as the process of ordering and evaluating the propositions began, it would be noticed that no explicit scheme of classification is present beyond the mere reference to the social conflict arena to which each was originally applied, that essential terms are undefined, and that the conditions under which the various propositions are alleged to hold true are not specified. Also the crucial question of relevant, acceptable, and sufficient evidence of proof or disproof is ignored. It is our contention that these problems, together with the application of Williams' criteria, are not susceptible of self-evident solutions. Propositions stated as they are above are literally imbedded in an invisible context.

There are, of course, a number of classification devices which might be employed, among them the one mentioned in our earlier introduction (intrapersonal, intergroup, interorganizational, international, etc.) and the one implied by the identifications in parentheses following each proposition above (industrial, racial, religious, etc.). Williams classifies his propositions roughly according to conflict types, sources, and responses. The UNESCO study referred to earlier in effect discusses research findings in terms of two broad classes of approaches—the sociological and the psychological. However, there may be advantages in considering a somewhat different kind of classificatory scheme. One advantage is that of juxtaposing propositions drawn from observations in different areas of social conflict. If certain propositions on, say, industrial relations and international relations remain in completely separate categories, possible connections (logical and empirical) may be overlooked. Or if aspects of conflict analysis are not distinguished, propositions cannot be ordered and examined effectively.

Classification is one problem. Another is definition. Proposition 7, for example, hinges significantly on the respective definitions of realistic and unrealistic conflict. In Proposition 11, what does "power of two parties" actually mean? What is involved in the institutionalization of conflict as stated in Proposition 15? Does conflict itself have a common meaning throughout? Still another problem is the condition under which the propositions hold true. One implication of Proposition 4 is that persons of certain faiths may have a minimal involvement in their religion and that they may share non-religious values with others whose religious values conflict with their own, offsetting religious-value conflict. Proposition 2 seems to imply either that citizens exert a great deal of influence on war decisions or that policy-makers all share certain general personality characteristics.

Propositions must also be compared and related to one another. Often propositions are flatly contradictory—or so it seems. Two pairs of examples drawn from international and religious conflict will illustrate:

Proposition 16: *Ideational and symbological conflicts are more important than economic or political conflicts in straining international relations* (5, p. 107).

Proposition 17: *Change in the relative power position of nations is the source of tension leading to conflict* (9, p. 20).

Proposition 18: *Religious intergroup conflict is most likely to develop when there are no cross-pressures at work within the individual* (10, p. 45).

Proposition 19: *Intensity of positions taken in religious conflict is a function of guilt and insecurity feelings over having taken such positions* (8, p. 64).

Obviously, sufficient pertinent data would be needed to judge the relative validity of these competing propositions or to reconcile them. But, more than that, it would be necessary to probe the fundamental nature of conflict as well as types of conflict and conflict situations.

Knowledge is advanced by linking propositions. Here are three propositions which may be integrated into a more inclusive one:

Proposition 20: *Social conflicts are primarily realistic conflicts of power* (12, p. 52).

Proposition 14: *Religious conflict persists because of the need to preserve or protect one's power position* (21, p. 40).

Proposition 17: *Change in the relative power position of nations is the source of tension leading to conflict* (9, p. 20).

Proposition 21 (combining 20, 14, 17): *Social conflict is normally accompanied by a felt or actual discrepancy in the power relations of the parties.*

Many of the propositions which are current in the literature of a particular field ought to be analyzed to discover whether, in fact, they have greater generality. Jackson (23), as already indicated, has explored the possibility of applying principles drawn from industrial mediation to the problem of mediation between nations. As Williams (40, p. 12) points out in the case of ethnic and racial conflict, the propositions applicable to these kinds of intergroup conflict have not been shown to be equally applicable to religious conflict. However, it is more than idle speculation to inquire whether the "cross-pressures" proposition (No. 18) is, in fact, generalizable to international conflict. Is international conflict lessened when nationals are subject to conflicting loyalties either within their nation or across national frontiers? Similarly, take these propositions:

Proposition 22: *If an adversary's strength could be measured prior to engagement in conflict, antagonistic interests might be adjusted without conflict.*

Does this apply to *all* kinds of social conflict?

Proposition 23: *Misunderstandings and misuse of words often contribute to lessen-*

ing conflict between labor and management (26, p. 233).

If this is true, and, to the extent that it is true, would it hold for international conflict? Again it should be emphasized that more than empirical data is needed to answer these questions. Some way of putting industrial and international conflict on a comparable basis for the purposes at hand is also required.

III. The Problem of Conceptualization and Choices of Major Variables

Having argued that the classification, ordering, and evaluation of basic propositions require prior intellectual operations, we shall now explore a tentative framework of analysis which might aid in these pursuits.

Definitions and Distinctions

Unless the phenomena denoted by the term "conflict" are limited and differentiated, the concept becomes too inclusive. On the whole, it is easier to begin by specifying what is not considered to be conflict. A review of the literature reveals certain distinctions which are apparently agreed upon or at least commonly made. *Competition* is not regarded as conflict or a form of conflict, though it may be an important source of the latter (12, p. 134; 26, p. 230; 38, p. 263; 44, p. 198). Competition involves striving for scarce objects (a prize or a resource usually "awarded" by a third party) according to established rules which strictly limit what the competitors can do to each other in the course of striving; the chief objective is the scarce object, not the injury or destruction of an opponent per se. A football game played normally according to the rules is competition *until* one or more players begin to assault one another in a manner forbidden by the rules; then it becomes a conflict.

Though closely related to conflict, the following are also considered differentiable: *antagonistic interests* (12, p. 135); *misunderstandings* (2, p. 118); *aggressiveness* (2; 12, p. 58); *hostility or hostile sentiments* (39, pp. 42–43; 12, p. 37); *desire or intention to oppose* (26, p. 233); *social cleavages* (e.g., along class lines) (8, p. 64); *logical irreconcilability of goals or interests* (44, pp. 193–94); *tensions* (44); and *rivalry* (44). The attitudes, behaviors, and states of affairs signified by these terms *may* be among the underlying sources of conflict. Or such factors *may* accompany or intensify conflict. But it seems generally agreed that none of the terms is a proper synonym for conflict, nor are the factors denoted singly or in combination sufficient preconditions of social conflict. However, there is no general agreement as to whether any one or more is a necessary precondition for conflict to arise or continue. On the other hand, the potential relevance of the factors is clear. These problems can be clarified by confronting the nature, sources, and conditions of conflict.

Properties of Conflictful Behaviors and Conflict Relationships

We shall not attempt a formal definition of conflict. Rather, a set of properties will be suggested which *in toto* will constitute a model for identifying and characterizing conflict phenomena and situations. Without claiming to be exhaustive, we shall insist that the essential elements are included and that conflict does not exist if the empirical conditions implied by properties 1–5 are not present. For the moment we shall avoid the awkward problem of the relationship between subjective (i.e., from the standpoint of the actor or actors) and objective (i.e., from the standpoint of an observer) perspectives. The following formulation is not original; we have attempted to synthesize and somewhat formalize the contributions of the papers in this volume and other sources:

1. *Conflict requires at least two parties or two analytically distinct units or entities* (i.e., actor, organism, group, individual, collectivity, etc.).
    a) Social conflict is, by definition, an interaction relationship between two or more parties.
    b) One-party conflict (intrapersonal or individual conflict) may be viewed as *either* individual-environment or actor-nature conflict (in which case the

parties may be human and non-human entities), *or* the individual in conflict with himself (conflict of two or more needs and values).
    c) "Games against nature" as provided in some formulations of game theory can be regarded as social conflict, but other forms of one-party conflict can be regarded as socially significant non-social conflict.
    d) A minimum "contact" (not necessarily face-to-face) and "visibility" are implied (39, pp. 42–43).
2. *Conflict arises from "position scarcity" and "resource scarcity"* (2, p. 112).
    a) Position scarcity is a condition in which an object cannot occupy two places at the same time, an object cannot simultaneously serve two different functions, a role cannot be simultaneously occupied or performed by two or more actors, and different prescribed behaviors cannot be carried out simultaneously.
    b) Resource scarcity is a condition in which the supply of desired objects (or states of affairs) is limited so that parties cannot have *all* they want of anything.
    c) Different underlying value judgments may condition the demand or need for scarce resources and positions.
    d) Hence mutually exclusive and/or mutually incompatible values and opposed values are inevitable characteristics of conflict.
3. *Conflictful behaviors are those designed to destroy, injure, thwart, or otherwise control another party or other parties, and a conflict relationship is one in which the parties can gain (relatively) only at each other's expense* (26, p. 230).
    a) The key is the intent of action and the object of action.
    b) Gains for one party result either from a net loss to the other party or from one party's having less of what he wants than he would have had in the absence of opposition.
    c) Many tactics and techniques may be manifest in conflictful behaviors which are not necessarily always identified with conflict per se.

d) Expressive behaviors, such as anger, hostility, shouting, aggressiveness, may or may not accompany conflictful behavior.

4. *Conflict requires interaction among parties in which actions and counteractions are mutually opposed* (26, 44).

   a) Conflict cannot exist without action.

   b) The action-reaction-action sequence must embody the pursuit of exclusive or incompatible values.

   c) Threats are actions.

5. *Conflict relations always involve attempts to gain control of scarce resources and positions or to influence behavior in certain directions; hence a conflict relationship always involves the attempt to acquire or exercise power or the actual acquisition or exercise of power* (35).

   a) Power is defined as control over decisions (i.e., disposition of scarce resources and positions) and as the basis of reciprocal influence between or among parties (i.e., control over behaviors).

   b) Conflict reflects power strains (i.e., the need or desire to achieve or change control), and opposed actions are directed to changing or preserving existing power relations (i.e., control over objects and behaviors).

6. *Conflict relations constitute a fundamental social-interaction process having important consequences* (17, p. 183).

   a) Conflict is not a breakdown or cessation of social interaction.

   b) The conflict process has important functions for the parties and for the larger social system of which it is a part.

   c) Conflict has a cost dimension.

7. *A conflict process or relation represents a temporary tendency toward disjunction in the interaction flow between parties* (37, p. 230).

   a) Disjunction results from the presence of mutually incompatible tendencies which disrupt the normal or persistent patterns of behavior, norms, and expectations of the parties and their responses to each other.

8. *Conflict relations do not represent a breakdown in regulated conduct but rather a shift in the governing norms and expectations.*

   a) Disjunctive tendencies do not continue to the point where the interaction is completely disrupted because the conflict process is subject to its own rules and limits.

If the foregoing provides a basis for at least a crude distinction between conflict and non-conflict, it does not go far enough. Thus far we have indicated that there must be *parties* and *a particular kind of interactional relationship between parties*. But there are kinds and forms of conflict relations; there are sources of conflict; various conditions affect the nature and duration of conflict; conflict has certain functions or consequences; and, finally, conflict always occurs in an environmental context which transcends the conflict relationship itself.

Types of Conflict

We shall mention some major distinctions only briefly. One obvious distinction is implied in Postulate 1: conflict *within* persons (intraparty) and conflict *between* persons or groups. Both meet the criteria set forth, and respective analogies can be pursued usefully. For example, persons undergoing psychotic conflict can quite literally destroy themselves. However, the primary emphasis in this volume is on social conflict, which, by definition, is interactional. Perhaps the most significant question is the impact of intrapersonal conflict on social conflict—a problem to which we shall return later.

An important and familiar distinction is between *realistic* and *non-realistic* conflict (12, p. 49; 39, p. 40). Realistic conflict is characterized by opposed means and ends, by incompatibility of values and interests. Non-realistic conflict arises from the need for tension release, from deflected hostility, from historical tradition, and from ignorance or error. The two types differ in origin and in the ultimate motivation behind opposed action. In realistic conflict, wants and needs seem to be, or become, incompatible because of other factors, that is, resource and position scarcity. But non-realistic conflict, for example, would be continued opposed action between nations whose actual conflicting interests had long since been reconciled. Propositions 2 and 16, listed above, clearly are based on the alleged existence of much non-realistic conflict among nations. Proposition 7 states a relation between the two types—an important generalization which might be lost in the absence of the distinction. Along similar lines Kerr (26, p. 234) draws a distinction between *real* and *induced* conflict, the latter being cases where representatives of conflicting groups have ends to be gained (e.g., their own prestige) apart from the ends in dispute between groups. This would be the situation if labor-union leaders precipitated a conflict with management in order to strengthen their hold over the union membership. Coser differentiates *basic cleavages*—conflict over the very nature of a consensual framework within which individuals and groups have hitherto operated —and conflicts over means and subordinate ends within a consensual framework (12, p. 73). This parallels Simpson's distinction between *non-communal* and *communal* conflicts, respectively (36, p. 17). An illustration of a basic cleavage—non-communal type of conflict would be the American Civil War. The opposite type would be exemplified by a conflict between an income tax and a sales tax, assuming general agreement to levy taxes of some kind.

An implicit distinction is usually drawn between *institutionalized* and *non-institutionalized* conflict. The former is characterized by explicit rules, predictable behavior, and continuity, as in the case of collective bargaining. Most racial conflict is, on the other hand, non-institutionalized. *Disorganized* conflict, as in the case of a riot (regardless of organized effort to initiate it), may take place within an institutional framework or not, the former being illustrated by an unauthorized, partially supported strike. Organized conflict, such as a war between armies, is obviously different from a spontaneous border clash between irregular armed units. *Extreme* (35, p. 324), *aggressive* (26, p. 232), and *violent* (12, p. 88) conflict are also differentiated from *non-violent*, *"diplomatic"* conflict—chiefly on the basis of coercive means versus persuasive means and on the assumption that, in the former, destruction or crippling of one of the parties is highly possible.

It appears useful to separate *primary, face-to-face conflicts* from *secondary, mediated conflicts*. Generally speaking, the rank and file of labor and the rank and file of management do not face each other in a conflict relation. Rather, chosen representatives speak for well-organized collectivities. On the other hand, in a town meeting or a legislature or in racial or ethnic contacts, conflict relations are, for the most part, direct. Closely related is another set of opposite types: *personal subjective conflict* and *impersonal objective* conflict. A conflict between husband and wife would fit the first category, and a conflict between two lawyers, each representing a client, would fit the second. A difference between *conflicts of right* and *conflicts of interest* may be noted. A conflict of right concerns the application of agreed standards to specified actions; a conflict of interest concerns the changing of old standards or the introduction of new standards—roughly, the distinction is between judicial and legislative conflict. This distinction applies to industrial, international, racial, and ethnic conflict.

Opposed values have been specified as inevitable concomitants of conflict, but any preliminary typology should include mention of types of conflict which are predominantly value conflicts per se. *Ideological conflict* is characterized by a clash of "conceptions of the desirable" (28, p. 391) and prescriptive norms and beliefs which do or should govern particular behaviors. For purposes of this analysis, ideologies can be classified as relatively open and relatively closed in terms of the extent to which alien or opposed values and belief can or will be accommodated or absorbed. Ideological conflict can be further classified according to the significance of the clash of absolute values, i.e., no "higher values" exist to mediate "lower values," and thus one set must triumph, or there must be benevolent neutrality. Conflict of religious dogmas exemplifies this, as well as certain conflicting political ideologies. Religious conflict is likely to be intense where conversion from one faith to another is required or where one faith regards another as "infidel"; but the same would hold true of non-religious ideologies.

Cultural conflict is a term used so broadly that it often includes all other types and even subsumes "social." Presumably, of course, conflicts between cultures, depending on the nature of the contacts, might well include conflicting ideologies, religions, interests, rights, and all the other types suggested above. A breakdown of cultural conflict into component elements, then, would be facilitated by a typology and by the basic conceptualization of conflict. Frazier has pointed out that initial contacts between races and cultures are essentially biological (19, p. 46). At this stage, conflict is biological in the sense that the two parties do not regard each other as human; no common moral order prevails to restrain conduct or otherwise regulate behavior. It seems likely in view of wide differences in the circumstances under which racial and cultural contacts lead to intermarriage and general acculturation that there is a primitive psychological factor at work too. At any rate, the analysis of contemporary conflict between races and cultures ought to recognize the fundamental importance of initial psychobiological contacts and the persistent attitudes which they generate (19, chaps. i, ii, xvii).

The foregoing is obviously only the beginning of a typology. For the moment we shall allow the bases of the classification to remain implicit. As we develop the analysis, new types will be added, and classificatory bases will be made explicit.

Underlying Sources of Conflict

Properties 1–5 set forth above may be viewed as a set of analytic preconditions of conflict, but, as formulated, they say nothing about the empirical content in particular cases. For example, position and resource scarcity is one of the necessary preconditions of conflict; yet we have to look elsewhere for the factors which produce, or account for, a specific pattern of scarcity. Underlying sources are those empirical phenomena which may result in the existence of the five preconditions of conflict. Perhaps the line between sources and preconditions

will seem arbitrary and difficult to draw. The distinction seems required, nonetheless, because the presence or persistence of underlying source factors does not necessarily mean that conflict, as defined, will arise. An observer is often embarrassed to discover that conflict does not arise despite the apparent indication of important source factors effectively at work in the social situation. Or conflict may arise in the absence of certain source factors. If the parties cannot "reach" each other by opposed action or if initiative is not assumed by at least one of the parties, a conflict interaction is impossible. Conversely, the decisions of one or more parties may, in effect, define a position or resource scarcity which an observer would find did not exist by his objective standards.

Most social scientists now accept the principle of multiple causality; hence there is no one basic source of conflict. In view of the preoccupation with the evil consequences of conflict, it is not surprising that the literature on causation overbalances the rest (7, chaps. i, iv; 11; 24; 42). Indeed, so far as particular areas of conflict are concerned, underlying sources have been rather thoroughly catalogued. It is fairly easy merely to list the most significant sources of, say, war (42). The central problem is, of course, to determine the particular combination of underlying source factors in a given situation which does result in the analytic preconditions. In general, the catalogues of conflict sources which are available do not, for the most part, provide the observer with more than a list of alternative possibilities which he would want to explore in any single instance. Above all, there is little guidance as to patterns of combination which produce conflict and to the conditions under which they are formed. The latter point suggests that difficulties are further compounded because the combination of sources and the translation of these into the preconditions may be influenced by non-source factors, which is one reason why we shall discuss conditions of conflict in the next section.

Emphasis on the sources of conflict has not been due solely to the scientist's attempt to answer the question of why conflict arises. Because of preoccupation with conflict as a costly social problem, sources are natural foci for reforms and changes which will supposedly reduce or eliminate conflict. If the source of conflict is a psychological state called "tension," tension reduction is an indicated strategy. If the source is ignorance, as in the case of some non-realistic conflict, education will eliminate or minimize the "cause" of such conflict. And so on. Now there is impressive evidence that a direct approach to the removal or adaptation of sources per se is not necessarily an effective way to curb conflict. Freeman (20, p. 86) argues that race itself may not be the "proper first object" of concern in controlling racial conflict and goes on to suggest that the key may be in the behavioral patterns exhibited in the *generic* phenomena of conflict—which means putting racial conflict in a broader framework of the sort being outlined here. One of Simmel's basic propositions, as reformulated by Coser (12, p. 55) is that hostile or aggressive impulses do not account for social conflict. Williams (39, p. 40) insists that factors producing conflict are not necessarily those most important for control purposes. It is interesting to compare Wright's analysis of theories of causes of wars (42) with Cottrell's five models of a peaceful world (13). In the former, conditions of peace turn out to be the inverse of sources of war (in the theories he reviews); in the latter, the requisites of peace (nonviolent conflict relations) are derived from quite different bases.

While it is true that the specific sources of, say, industrial conflict and international conflict are quite different, it is also true that generalized sources and types of sources may be identified. A generalized source is one which is not peculiar to any one arena or kind of conflict. Insofar as "tensions" are, in fact, a source of conflict, they may be either general personality conditions which can be focused on a range of particular situations, or they can be closely connected with only certain interaction relationships. Tensions between unions and managements may arise from the shrinking pie to be divided between them, or tensions from other sources may induce the demands

which are made upon the existing pie. Presumably, the latter might also be expressed in ethnic or religious or other intergroup conflict. The search for underlying sources in the first case carries one only as far as the size of the pie; in the second, it requires a much wider range of inquiry. Two questions arise. First, how deep should the search for underlying factors (this usually involves personality dynamics) be pushed? Second, are there certain basic motive patterns or facts of social life which might serve to account partially for a variety of conflict relations? Some explanations of conflict are based on the alleged consequences of what might be called "psychoanalytic mechanisms," such as Proposition 1 cited earlier (18, p. 34; 27). Some are somewhat closer to the surface, as it were, being rooted in psychological variables, such as inferiority feelings or hostility and the like (39, chap. i). Still others are more sociological in nature, i.e., discontents over income, job conditions (26, p. 230). More or less in accord with these three levels of sources, two writers (34, p. 25) have asserted that three primary motives underlie intergroup conflict: (*a*) desire for acquisition of scarce values (political or power conflict); (*b*) desire to convert others (ideological conflict); and (*c*) desire to prevent contact with inferiors (racist conflict). On the surface at least, there is no common agreement on the first question, namely, Should the search for source factors be pushed to the psychoanalytic level? But the lack of agreement is due partly to the failure to make consistent distinctions among types of, and parties to, conflict and to link sources explicitly with conditions and contexts. Furthermore, the problem of psychological and sociological levels of explanation should not obscure an integrative question: Under what social conditions do psychological mechanisms operate as sources of conflict?

On the second question, it seems generally agreed that scarcity of desired objects, states of affairs, and resources in nature and culture, the division of labor in organized society, and social differentiation lead inevitably to potentially conflictful cleavages and antagonistic interests. It is (or seems to be) further agreed that these factors, as well as more deeply psychological ones, contribute to a reservoir of "free-floating" aggression, hostility, and tension which, in turn, *may* lead to conflictful behaviors. This is illustrated by the mechanisms of projection and displacement which may be focused on any object or group (industrial, international, ethnic, etc.) in a conflict situation. Hence two general categories of sources emerge: those centering on interactional relationships, e.g., a conflict over land between cattle grazers, and those centering on certain internal characteristics of parties or intrapersonal (personality dynamics) factors, e.g., the frustration-aggression hypothesis. Propositions embodying explanations for the rise of conflict, which can be grouped according to these two categories, will be discussed in the next two sections. One utility of the distinction between realistic and non-realistic conflict now becomes clear. Realistic conflicts are presumed to have their origin primarily in interactional factors; non-realistic conflicts are presumed to be accountable for primarily in terms of non-interactional factors. Thus industrial conflict is inherent in the institutional situation in which labor and management interact: both cannot make the same decisions separately, their roles give rise to different values, total income from a given business is limited and cannot satisfy maximum demands by each side, and so on (26, p. 230). Religious conflict, in contrast, is inherent in the private nature of religious experience, in the nature of religious values as substitutes for other social values, and in the manner of transmission of religious beliefs (10, p. 49).

Concern over the origins of conflict draws attention to potential responses to conflict situations and to the decisions which result in moving from a desire to oppose to acts of opposition. In ascertaining why some situations lead to actual conflict interaction while others do not, it is necessary to identify certain crucial foci of analysis. Responses or decisions may result in the origination of conflict interaction, in withdrawal from a potential conflict situation, in a change from non-violent to violent or extreme conflict, or in accommodation to a stable conflict rela-

tionship. These outcomes, more often than not, depend on choices. Therefore, the conditions which affect such choices must be probed, and similar cases which have different outcomes must be compared. Two possible foci will be mentioned here. First, in the case of secondary, mediated intergroup conflict, Deutsch's decision-making and communications approach would seem particularly useful. His approach suggests, for example, that a central question concerning the outbreak of war is: Under what conditions do foreign policy-makers decide, in effect, that all viable alternatives have been reduced to one? Is it possible to identify a "point of no return" in a conflict relation progressing toward war? What effect do the nature, flow, and interpretation of information have on the foreclosure of alternatives? Analyzing war decisions along these lines represents a much more fundamental approach than the listing of causes of war or the attribution of single, overpowering motives to nations. A second focus of analysis is more appropriate for individual responses to primary, mediated intergroup conflict. One lead is supplied by the cross-pressures hypothesis (Proposition 18), which indicates that conflict potential is dampened if individuals are pulled in opposite directions by their group affiliations or incompatible values. On the other hand, one of two contradictory pulls may triumph over the other. Thus Brown's approach-avoidance analysis may yield some hypotheses regarding the circumstances under which conflicting stimuli will produce either of two responses. Though it is an obvious example, we can cite cases where individuals are not necessarily prevented from discriminatory acts against minorities by their religious values which prescribe the Golden Rule. Clearly, in this situation the minority member does not represent an ambiguous stimulus—as would be true if the discriminatory individual saw him as both an undesirable inferior and a human being deserving of equal treatment. The converse of the cross-pressures hypothesis is that group conflicts are more likely to develop and to be intense when there is no conflict within the individual. Basically, in this situation the stimulus is unambiguous, and the "approach" response tendency is the stronger.

It is noteworthy that these two general approaches—and there are others which focus on decisions and responses—require simultaneous attention to psychological and sociological variables. The behavior of decision-makers is to be viewed as a resultant of such factors as individual perceptions and institutionalized information flows. The behavior of individuals responding to conflict or possible conflict is to be viewed as a resultant of competitory response tendencies and the nature of stimuli in the social environment.

Conditions of Conflict

The main reason for analyzing the accompanying conditions of conflict separately is that particular sources which result in the analytic preconditions do not account for the origin, form, intensity, duration, reduction, or resolution of conflict. This can be demonstrated by Dahlke's (14, pp. 421–24) analysis of race riots, which, he argues, are highly probable when (*a*) the period is one of change and mobility; (*b*) the minority group has an outstanding trait or characteristic which can become a basis for negative assessments; (*c*) lawful authorities assign the minority group a subordinate status; (*d*) one or more major associations or organizations direct the attack against the minority; (*e*) the press and other media have been minority-baiting; and (*f*) suitable personnel (students and marginal workers) are available for initiating action.

Clearly, the notion of conditions opens up a wide range of relevant factors. In calling attention to the analytic separation of these factors, we mean only to say that certain elements inherent in the nature of parties to conflict, in the interaction relationships between parties, and in the social context will often account for the origin, form, intensity, duration, limits, and resolution of conflict. Conditions are not, then, a special category of factors but a way of viewing the impact of the elements to be discussed in succeeding sections.

To illustrate in a preliminary fashion, we list sample propositions:

Proposition 24: *Mediation increases the possibility of resolving conflict when parties are small* (33, p. 194).

Proposition 25: *Realistic conflict need not be accompanied by hostility and aggressiveness* (12, p. 58).

Proposition 26: *It is more difficult to mediate controversy where costs of aggressive conflict are high* (26, p. 239).

Proposition 27: *Social conflict cannot be integrative and functional in the absence of community* (36, p. 42).

Proposition 28: *Ideological conflict is more intense and the parties thereto are more intransigent because of objectification of issues and lack of inhibitions on personal attacks* (12, p. 115).

Proposition 29: *A high degree of intimacy between the parties, as contrasted with a high degree of functional interdependence, will intensify conflict* (12, p. 67).

In addition, two other conditioning factors are of importance. Our specification of the essential properties of conflict relations stressed the power component. To the extent that conflict is over the nature of the respective roles of the parties in decision-making with respect to mutual interests, the form, intensity, and duration of the conflict will depend on the length of time it takes to test the power relationship conclusively and the means available to each party for exerting control. Intensity will also be affected by the cruciality of the decision-making functions at issue. A long war, a long strike, or a long bargaining period may indicate roughly an equal power equation or the failure to find adequate indexes of power. Another condition of great importance is the amount of information available to, and interpreted correctly by, the parties to conflict. Bernard (this issue, p. 111) has graphically portrayed the potential impact of this factor.

The Social Context of Conflict

The conditions discussed above were those primarily confined to the parties and to their relationship. However, it is axiomatic that conflict occurs in, affects, and in turn is affected by, a surrounding environment. Conflict must be re-searched and analyzed against the background of the total social system in which it occurs (39, p. 47). Once again, all we can hope to do here is outline the crucial considerations by means of illustrative propositions.

Social change affects conflict in a number of ways. Changes are constantly shifting the bases of potentially antagonistic interests and the relative power positions of individuals and groups. As the value potentiality of the social environment shifts, new demands, new frustrations, and new incompatibilities arise. Population growth, invention, urbanization, mobility—indeed, all the changes which result in and are resultants of greater social complexity—affect the sources of conflict, the nature and number of parties to conflict, the instrumentalities of conflict, the issues of conflict, modes of settlement, and so on (10; 14; 17, p. 179; 22; 26; 29, pp. 3–22; 30; 35; 39, pp. 43 ff.). The same general point applies to international conflict, which has its own social context:

Proposition 30: *Important alternations in the balance of forces as between societies occurs as a result of profound changes internal to one or more societies* (9, p. 19).

Social organization will determine the number and kinds of parties to conflict within any society. In a complex industrial urban society realistic conflict will tend to be carried on by highly organized groups having diverse memberships and specialized representatives and negotiators. In a less complex communal society, there will tend to be more direct, face-to-face interpersonal conflict. Social differentiation (status, occupational roles, power positions, etc.) will tend to define lines of consensus and cleavage, to lead to the formation of groups and groupings which are foci of consensus and cleavage. In a recent book, *Race and Culture Contacts in the Modern World,* Frazier organizes his analysis around the ecological, economic, political, and social organization. The impact of the social context on racial conflict is clearly shown. For example, economic racial conflict does not arise where the division of labor is based on objective standards of competitive success (p. 331). Whyte's study, *Pattern for Industrial Peace,* is concerned with a more immediate context of conflict: the relation between company structure and labor-management relations. Changes in organization are correlated with three stages of development: from disorganized conflict to organized conflict to organized co-operation.

Interinstitutional strain, as in the case of religious and political institutions in the United States, may create intrapersonal conflict (religious versus secular values) and/or intergroup conflict over such issues as public aid to parochial schools (40, pp. 12–20). Coser (12, p. 77) and Williams (40, p. 12) have argued that a "loosely organized society" with many crisscrossing pressures and influences on individuals and groups reduces the possibility of single, rigid, and intense conflicts which divide the whole society or a large segment of it and also provides stability despite extensive conflict. Thus a multiplicity of potential or actual conflict situations, combined with shared values which cut across lines of cleavage, prevents any one conflict situation or kind of conflict (e.g., religious) from dominating the relations of sizable groups and large numbers of individuals. Closely related to this is Simmel's notion of safety-valve institutions which channel hostility and drain off residual conflict responses (12, pp. 41–44).

This suggests another significant aspect of the social context of conflict. Normally, no matter how serious a conflict exists between particular groups and individuals, there will always be *disinterested* or neutral, but nonetheless affected, outsiders (or, indirectly, "third" parties). If conflict completely divides a local, national, or international community, which means in effect that there are no outsiders, solutions become very difficult indeed. This is partly because there are no available neutral conciliators or mediators and partly because no one has a vested interest in the cessation of conflict (25, p. 297). The pressure for liquidation or control of social conflict from disinterested but affected bystanders is one of the primary limits on its duration, extension, and intensity. Both labor and management in the United States have been compelled to recognize a "public interest," and one of the functions of the United Nations is to mobilize world-wide public pressure on disputants.

The availability and permissibility of the instrumentalities of conflict are obviously dependent on the social environment. Firearms are strictly controlled in most societies as a means for settling interpersonal conflict. In many Latin-American countries military rebellion is a recognized mode of carrying on political conflict. It took many years for the strike to be sanctioned as a proper instrument in industrial conflict. There has been a long history of attempts to establish legitimate and illegitimate uses of war as an instrument of national policy.

One of the major problems of the social order at all levels of society is the control of violent conflict. Hence one of the tasks of public policy, social engineering, and scientific study of human behavior is to determine what kinds of social arrangements are conducive to non-violent conflict (31).

Proposition 31: *The more integrated into the society are the parties to conflict, the less likely will conflict be violent* (26, p. 243).

But, as important as violent conflict is as a basic form or type, the problem is, in fact, much broader. Order and conflict (all types) are persistent states of any social system. While to an extent they are, or appear to be, opposites, both can and must exist side by side. Furthermore, the relationship between them will determine the degree of social stability. Basically, the stability-instability balance will be a resultant of the success or failure of the normative order in regulating conflicts of interest (30, pp. 139–40). Conflict induces a constant pressure of factual situations on the normative order. In turn, conflict is in some manner controlled by social norms. As already remarked, social change—its rate and direction—is an ultimate source of conflict because, as the factual social order undergoes transition, new incompatibilities and antagonistic interests arise. The relevant regulatory norms either will accommodate (permit) acceptable "solutions" or will be modified (or perhaps consistently violated) to take account of the actual power relations between the parties.

If we are interested in generalizing propositions about social conflict from one area of behavior to another, it is obviously necessary to compare relevant social contexts (23, chap. i; 26, p. 235). To the extent that the social environments of industrial and international conflict differ, *some* propositions will not hold for both. For example, it is unclear whether the international social environment has yet produced a reservoir of mediators and conciliators such as exist in most complex industrial societies. Perhaps one of the reasons that the propositions from racial and ethnic intergroup conflict do not apply to religious conflict is that the social context even in a single society is different. Thus far in the United States, for example, there has been clear separation between religious and political institutions (church and state), while racial and ethnic factors permeate family, educational, economic, and political institutions.

The Functions of Conflict

Since preoccupation with conflict often centers on its most violent, abhorrent, and socially costly forms, it is likely that the average reader will regard *all* conflict as universally bad. Proposition 13, listed above, boldly states the contrary view. There is no way of evaluating this proposition unless the functions and consequences of conflict are systematically examined. It is noteworthy that most contemporary social scientists lay stress on the constructive consequences of conflict relations (7, 12, 22, 24, 26, 29, 36, 38). Coser (12, chaps. ii, viii) has summarized sociological thinking on this point with particular reference to social groups. Dubin's five central propositions (p. 179) constitute a broader thesis: intergroup conflict is a fundamental institutionalized social process which determines the direction of social change and, in effect, defines social welfare. Though most of his analysis is drawn from experience in industrial relations, the propositions have wider applicability.

It is unnecessary to review the whole range of functions served by social conflict. Several major propositions will suffice:

Proposition 32: *Conflict sets group boundaries by strengthening group cohesiveness and separateness* (12).

Proposition 33: *Conflict reduces tension and permits maintenance of social interaction under stress* (26, p. 232; 12, chap. iii).
Proposition 34: *Conflict clarifies objectives* (29, p. 16).
Proposition 35: *Conflict results in the establishment of group norms* (24, pp. 196–97).
Proposition 36: *Without conflict, accommodative relations would result in subordination rather than agreement* (38, p. 263).

The foregoing is a brief reminder that there are important positive social functions served by conflict. Evidence discussed by writers in support of Propositions 32–36 would tend to support the more general Proposition 13 presented earlier. This perspective does not, of course, imply that conflict is not often dysfunctional and very costly. One of the most difficult problems in conflict analysis is to arrive at a method for determining the dividing line between constructive functions and dysfunctions. Clearly, the question of the cost of social conflict involves different relevant criteria. It may seem a macabre joke to emphasize the constructive consequences of conflict in an age of nuclear weapons or in the face of the three-year Kohler strike in Kohler, Wisconsin. On the other hand, no scholar, reformer, critic, or politician has ever denied that conflict is an all-pervasive fact of human life, nor does anyone deny that society persists in spite of violent and costly conflict. As a matter of fact, the functional and dysfunctional aspects of conflict are opposite sides of the same coin.

As a crude first approximation to a meaningful distinction, it might be suggested that conflict is, *on balance,* dysfunctional to the extent that its positive functions are impaired or neutralized under certain conditions. For example, the normal course of a realistic conflict may under some circumstances generate, instead of relieve, hostility or tension. Indeed, a realistic conflict may be transformed into a non-realistic conflict, which may, in turn, undermine institutionalized modes of resolving realistic conflict and also raise costs far beyond what is proportionate to any advantages accruing to the parties or affected bystanders. A long strike which results in obscuring objectives, in an almost total breakdown of interaction and mutual dependence, in hostility which becomes unrelated to the goals of the parties, and in confusion of actual power relations is dysfunctional and wasteful. Functional conflict encourages collaboration and a more efficient division of labor between parties because of heightened consciousness of purpose and strengthening of positions taken. It is one of the characteristics of dysfunctional conflict that it is difficult to say, as time goes on, what the conflict is about.

Violence at the international level is often accompanied by a tragic lack of reliable knowledge about the objectives and power potentials of the respective contenders and by inadequacy of machinery through which the positive functions of conflict can be realized. In terms of the whole thesis being developed here, the most abhorrent and costly social conflicts should be viewed not as abrupt breaks in "order" and "co-operation" but as transitions or abrupt shifts from one kind of conflict relationship to another. However, it is quite likely that predominantly dysfunctional conflict will lead to a cessation of interaction at some point.

While socially useful and socially undesirable consequences of conflict can and should be kept separate, it is probably true that they go together. From some vantage points at least, it is difficult to imagine any conflict having only one kind of consequence. Therefore, part of the problem of differentiation of the functional and dysfunctional aspects of conflict is the identification of conditions under which dysfunctional consequences can be minimized. A fundamental research question is, then, How and why do the dysfunctional consequences come to predominate?

Summary

Though the framework for conflict analysis outlined so far has centered on the concept, types, sources, conditions, context, and functions of conflict, it is clear from the brief comment and propositions that such aspects cannot be discussed without mentioning the connection between relevant party characteristics and the conflict relationship, the nature of conflict interaction itself, and the problem of conflict resolution and control. We shall therefore develop the framework one step further in the next two sections by considering two major foci of conflict analysis—party characteristics and interaction. Since the problem of conflict resolution and control has already been touched upon, we shall continue to refer to it where it naturally fits our scheme instead of treating it separately.

IV. The Parties to Conflict: Implications of Nature, Number, and Internal Characteristics

The term "party" here will be taken to include individual actors, culture, coalition, social class, personality, nation, organization, organism, system, or group. Party refers to analytic units, regardless of level of generality, *between* which, or in some cases *within* which, conflict takes place. It is assumed that each of these unit types may be viewed operationally as an abstraction of certain observable tendencies and actions of persons and of certain relationships.

Identification and Establishment

This raises the question of identification, which often is not self-evident or given in the particular situation. At the same time, we have proposed that one of the preconditions of a conflict relationship is visibility of parties to each other. Logically, this implies that if the parties are *not subjectively* identifiable, conflict, as defined, cannot exist, though potentially it may be likely if and when identification does take place. It is one of the notable caprices of social conflict that parties may be misidentified, i.e., an individual or group may be *assumed* to be the opponent in a clash of mutually incompatible goals or values when objectively such is not the case at all. As a matter of fact, one of the major features of a sequence of preconflict-conflict-postconflict actions and reactions may be a process of establishing visibility and/or changing identifications of parties. Matters are further complicated by the social context, which may

include, as noted, bystander or neutral elements which are affected but not technically involved. The line between party and nonparty may be a fine one indeed. Sympathy strikes, for example, would seem to be instances of where unions not parties to a particular conflict become, in effect, by their correlated action parties to another (and new) conflict. And, if the sympathy strike occurs in a highly integrated industry, the sympathy strike may actually add a party to the original conflict.

The problem of the identity of parties to conflict is not just a methodological exercise. An observer's identification and the participants' identification may or may not coincide. What may appear to be a realistic conflict between labor and management may, in fact, be what has been called an "induced" conflict, i.e., one between officials on both sides. Thus another of our earlier distinctions is useful and points to phenomena which may not be self-evident. For example, political party conflict is often the induced kind. Once the distinction is made, its base seems obvious, but the implications are perhaps not so obvious. Not only is diagnosis of the *sources* of such conflicts likely to be in error (or at least incomplete), but the conditions and effective modes of resolution may be quite different. One general hypothesis might be: *Induced conflict is likely to be more intense than realistic conflict because of the coincidence of group and personal values.* A second general hypothesis might be: *Induced conflicts arise more from imbalance or ambiguity of power relations, whereas realistic conflicts arise more from incompatibility of objectives.* A third general hypothesis might be: *Induced conflicts are not readily susceptible to normal mediation procedures.*

In the sphere of international affairs, an observer might argue that, in a given case, governments are the real parties, whereas, subjectively, whole nations may be perceived as parties. Apart from the fact that in the social world it is the latter which really counts, actors in conflict situations attempt to manipulate the nature and number of parties. Diplomats and foreign policymakers may attempt to *delimit* severely the parties to international conflict by separating the government from the people of a foreign nation: "Our quarrel is not with you but with your leaders." Conversely, governmental leaders may attempt deliberately to *extend* either the number or size of opposing parties by saying to a whole population: "This conflict directly involves your welfare, and you had better restrain your leaders or else." The practice of equating group interests and general welfare represents (among other things) an attempt to enlarge the size or change the constituency of one party. It might be supposed that the enlargement-through-changed-identification tendency, where manifest in a monolithic or highly stratified social context, would cause conflict to spread. The establishment of visible and recognized parties is thus part of the conflict process. The following proposition will illustrate:

Proposition 37: *The early stages of conflict are often carried on with the object of establishing the intergroup nature of conflict* (24, p. 195).

A proportionately large number of strikes at the beginning of the organized labor movement supports the conclusion that one of the primary objectives was recognition of the union as a party in industrial conflict. As one writer has pointed out, conflicts do not necessarily presuppose *established* and *coherent groups* (24). On the other hand, a party to conflict may be created by the search for an "enemy" and by another party —provided, of course, that there is conflictful interaction, once the latter has been found.

Number of Parties

We have been concentrating on conflict involving two or more parties, and we have already drawn a distinction between conflict involving a single entity (see Brown's essay, p. 135) and conflict between parties or entities of whatever number. Comments here would not, of course, apply to the former.

Actually, little seems to be known about the effect on social conflict of the sheer number of parties. On a common-sense basis it would seem that the larger the number of parties to a conflict, the more complex the power relations and the more ambiguous the incompatibility of values. Several tentative hypotheses may be suggested:

1. *The larger the number of parties, the more difficult it will be to discover a common solution, in which all parties can achieve at least some gain over previous power positions.*
2. *The larger the number of parties, the less intense will be the non-realistic components of the conflict relationship.*
3. *There is a persistent tendency to reduce multiple-party conflict to two-party conflict via coalitions and blocs.*

If one of the functions of conflict is the clarification of goals and the exploration of common aims, this will depend on the distribution of reliable information among parties and the potential existence of an area of value compatibility. An increase in the number of parties enhances the chance of communications failure and reduces the range of alternative solutions acceptable to all parties. On the other hand, a large number of parties will tend to diffuse hostility and antagonism because more outlets or objects are provided. The tendency to reduce the number of parties to conflict is obviously due to the need to make power more effective and to arrive at a clear-cut definition of power relations which is somewhat stable. Diffuse power relations are notoriously unstable. The general hypothesis would be: *Social conflict tends toward bipolarization of power relations and to centralize the bases of effective power.* This tendency is clearly reflected in the formation of coalitions.

Internal Characteristics of Parties

The problem here is a dual one: the determination of relevant characteristics and the linking of these to clearly differentiated units of analysis. If we keep in mind what has been said previously, it is possible to suggest a crude check list of characteristics. Naturally, since it is not at all clear a priori what range of internal characteristics is relevant to particular types of conflict situations, any list must be derived in part from the postulated properties of conflict, in part from hypothesized relationships between characteristics of parties and aspects of conflict, and in part from further empirical investigation. The following dimensions might serve as a point of departure: *motives, values, and attitudes; beliefs, perceptual frameworks, and information; degree of internal organization and intraparty relationships; size; strength; and extraparty factors having internal implications.* Each of these kinds of characteristics deserves considerable exposition, but only brief illustration is possible here.

1. It has already been indicated that some observers (for example, Propositions 1, 2, and 10 above) attribute the source of conflict to motivational, value, and attitudinal factors and that other observers have linked these same party characteristics to the conditions of conflict (for example, Proposition 16 above). To take one arena, there are numerous psychoanalytic hypotheses bearing on international conflict and war (18), of which the following are additional examples:

Proposition 38: *Persons with character disorders have a predilection for public positions, and the public has a predilection for electing such persons* (11, p. 9).
Proposition 39: *Intrapersonal conflict between aggressive impulses and socially sanctioned moral norms of behavior leads to projection of aggression on external groups* (31).

In general, these hypotheses involve a causal connection between personality dynamics or psychological mechanisms operating at the individual actor level and some aspect of intergroup conflict. Individual attitudes or general personality characteristics are cited to account for, say, national policies leading to conflict or a war decision. More specifically, the implications of Brown's analysis of intrapersonal conflict for intergroup conflict are at issue.

We have noted earlier that the broad issue of the desirability of pushing intergroup conflict analysis to this depth of motivation is unsettled. There is agreement, implicitly or explicitly, that conflict should be viewed in the context of the needs, beliefs, perceptions, values, and attitudes of individuals and groups. However, there also seems to

be agreement (*a*) that hostility, aggression, or particular personality disorders are not necessarily concomitants of conflict and (*b*) that realistic or objective conflict may itself induce prejudice, unfavorable stereotypes, and hostility. The latter point implies that the relationship between party characteristics and conflict interaction is reciprocal, not unilateral. More than this, not all individual responses are destructive; constructive responses can be conflict-inducing. Thus ethnocentricity may be functional in the sense of being a factor in group survival and cooperation, while at the same time it is a potential source or condition of conflict. Even were such not the case, counterhypotheses to the ones cited are present in the literature:

Proposition 40: *The source of international tension resides between, rather than within, nations* (9, p. 20).
Proposition 41: *Belligerents in recent wars have not enjoyed greater sexual, economic, or prestige frustrations, . . . nor have they been more viciously manipulated by their leaders than have nonbelligerents* (9).

There are two important points to be considered in evaluating or verifying propositions of this kind. First, the nature of the analytic unit which is to be denoted as the party to conflict becomes crucial. Is a nation, as a group, to be thought of in terms of its whole population or only in terms of the officials who act in its behalf? Proposition 2 seems to include all members of a nation, including policy-makers, and hence flies in the face of much evidence that official decisions are the result of rational processes. Proposition 38, on the other hand, hypothesizes a link between personality factors affecting masses of individuals in society and the selection of officials who have "character disorders" which presumably influence national policies. Propositions 2 and 38 both typically assume complete identity or homogeneity of motives, values, attitudes, and perceptions among citizens and between citizens and policy-makers and also ignore the organizational setting in which governmental decisions are made. Now it is perfectly conceivable that rational policy-makers may feel bound to act on the basis of a public opinion, which, in turn, is formed by underlying non-rational or irrational personality factors. Thus the aggressive tendencies of the people as a whole *could* lead to a conflict policy formulated by policy-makers who were not themselves subject to these tendencies. However, this is quite a different proposition.

Similarly, is a labor union, as a party to conflict, to be designated as the entire membership or as the union leaders? Kerr's distinction between real and induced conflict implies that the latter is related to characteristics of union and management officials and not to characteristics of union membership and a company viewed as collectivities. Nor would we expect to apply a psychoanalytic hypothesis concerning individual behavior to a complex organization or a system in Boulding's terminology without the significant qualification that in each case we referred to certain individuals whose behavior was the focus of analysis. It is perfectly permissible to speak of organizational or system goals, ideology, information, and so on, as long as the properties of such entities are not confused with those of individual actors considered as total personalities.

Second, motivation, values, and attitudes as party characteristics must be related to a specific situation, to a particular conflict interaction context. As one writer has put it (1, chap. i), we must do more than specify a psychological mechanism which is unrelated to an objective state of affairs; rather, we must seek emotional predispositions which cause individuals to perceive and react to real conflict situations.

A somewhat different perspective on the relationships between individual characteristics and intergroup relations is offered by Guetzkow in his *Multiple Loyalties: Theoretical Approach to a Problem in International Organization* (6). One of the basic propositions which emerges from this study is:

Proposition 42: *Citizen loyalty to the nation and citizen loyalty to some kind of supranational organization are not incompatible, provided that the latter is perceived to meet new or independent needs* (6, pp. 39–40).

Behind this proposition is a more general one to the effect that multiple loyalties may or may not produce conflict within the individual, thus leading him to withdraw one set of loyalties in favor of another or to be caught in indecisiveness. In a preliminary test of the proposition, Guetzkow used UNESCO survey data and compared multiplists (those citizens with both national and supranational loyalties), patriots (those citizens with exclusive loyalty to the nation), and the alienated (those whose loyalties were primarily supranational). Results were then correlated with such indexes as education, economic status, age, and attitude toward the future. The larger problem being explored here is, of course, the impact of loyalty to one group or set of values on the relations of groups or sets of values. Does loyalty to one preclude loyalty to others? Does loyalty to one group necessarily enhance the possibility of group conflict because multiple loyalties cannot be held by the individual? Guetzkow's thesis appears to represent the positive side to the cross-pressures thesis noted above: cross-pressures mitigate against exclusive loyalties and hence reduce conflict potential; but, to the extent that multiple loyalties can be accommodated, mutually exclusive loyalties to different groups or values need not induce conflict within the individual and may foster intergroup collaboration.

The role of values in conflict analysis can be highlighted by a reminder that value incompatibility is, by definition, an element in conflict. Hence the examination of the respective values (preferred state of affairs, standards of conduct, criteria of choice among goals and actions, etc.) of opposing parties is inescapable. More specifically, ideological and religious conflict should be mentioned in this connection. Very often opposed values can be compromised or partially accommodated, but often they cannot. Ideological conflict may be marked by the fact that a basic value of one party (e.g., freedom of speech in a free society) requires the absolute denial of a basic value of another party (e.g., an official ideology in a totalitarian society). Religious conflict may be marked not only by a clash of ultimate values but by a commitment to conversion of those of different faith. Proposition 4 calls attention to the general problem of the relation between the claims of a faith or an ideology to define and regulate religious and political values and the intensity and resolution of conflict. In general, the more inclusive or broader the claim, the less susceptible is the conflict to some form of resolution. The conditions under which religious and other values tend to become inclusive or the conditions under which incompatible value commitments can be held without inducing conflictful behavior are thus extremely important.

2. Propositions 2, 4, 10, and 19 refer to traits shared by so many individual members of a group that the behavior of the group as a whole is alleged to reflect them. But none of them states anything about intraparty relations or the nature and degree of organization among individual members or components. Another dimension of party characteristics concerns these factors. These propositions, two of which have been cited previously, will illustrate:

Proposition 43: *Conflict between the Soviet Union and the United States is to be understood partly in terms of institutional rivalry* (15, p. 31).

Proposition 1: *Intragroup harmony and solidarity reduce intergroup friction* (24, p. 201).

Proposition 9: *Conflict with outgroups increases internal cohesion* (12, p. 73).

Proposition 44: *Conflict between loosely organized groups (i.e., members are only peripherally involved in group activities or loyalty) is less intense* (12, pp. 68–69).

Proposition 45: *As organizations become more bureaucratic, nonrealistic conflict decreases, induced conflict increases* (26, p. 235).

Proposition 46: *Internal political structures which effectively channel and accommodate discontent are less likely to exhibit external aggressiveness* (32, pp. 196–97).

The range of factors suggested is, of course, extensive, even in this small selected set of propositons. Perhaps the most critical point is obvious enough: there is a basic reciprocal functional relationship between the structure and internal dynamics of any group and intergroup conflict interaction. In analyzing these functional relationships, it is once again necessary to bear in mind that propositions will differ, depending on whether we are discussing unorganized individuals as comprising a group, leader-follower, or citizen-policy-maker relations; a heterogeneous political organization; a complex bureaucracy; a total political or social system; or a particular set of institutions. In the absence of additional research, it is difficult to tell whether there is a limited number of strategic aspects of intraparty organization which yield hypotheses of broad generality. At first glance, the existing literature seems to suggest at least three related aspects: (1) degree of internal cohesion and intimacy; (2) degree of centralization of internal control, including group representatives or a bureaucracy; and (3) degree and exclusiveness of commitment to group or organizational values.

Intraparty organization and relations may or may not contribute to either the inducement of conflict or its resolution and control. Familiar propositions fall roughly into two categories—positive and negative. Positive ones are associated with the general view of conflict as a fundamental interaction process which serves needed social functions. Negative ones stress the role of intraparty characteristics in the origin, intensification, and enlargement of conflict. Obviously, this reflects the fact that internal cohesion, centralization of control, and exclusiveness of commitment to group values may be empirically either functional or dysfunctional. On the one hand, for example, all three aspects are functional in the sense that clarification of opposed goals and mobilization of power are facilitated. On the other hand, dysfunctional consequences may follow—needless intensification, enhancement of non-realistic factors, and enlargement of conflict beyond the parties whose interests are really at stake.

What is more important, perhaps, is that the three aspects point to the "management of forces" which conflict requires. The quality of leadership and morale become significant in the instigation and maintenance of conflict relations. No analysis of social conflict would be adequate without due attention to leadership as a party characteristic. This is implied at several points in the foregoing scheme, particularly in connection with motivational elements and induced conflict. It is easier to grant the importance of leadership than to specify what an orderly and bounded inquiry would entail. Leadership is too ambiguous a concept. At a minimum, it would be desirable to formulate a set of leadership roles and role functions and to relate these to types, sources, context, conditions, and consequences of conflict.

One kind of leadership role might be that of the intellectual. Among other things, the intellectual leader is one who uses and creates ideas, and one consequence is to objectify conflict. Earlier we hypothesized that depersonalization or objectification tended to intensify conflict, to neutralize certain limits on modes of resolution. Joining these propositions and assuming each to be true to some extent, we emerge with a general hypothesis: *Effective intellectual leadership tends to intensify social conflict.* Empirical investigation would be required to confirm or refute this statement and to ascertain the conditions under which it holds. Provided that data are available, it would be interesting to compare conflict situations in which intellectual leadership was present with those in which it was either negligible or absent.

Another relevant internal characteristic of parties to conflict follows naturally from the discussion of management of conflict. Dubin has suggested the need for a typology of organizations and groups in terms of the centrality of conflict in their activities. Clearly, a conspiratorial group (e.g., the Communist party) or an organized interest group (e.g., the National Association of Manufacturers) is much more conflict-oriented than is a company like General Motors. One would expect that the former types would pay much more attention to the "management of forces" and to the relationship between internal organization and conflict interaction. In general, it might be

expected that the more central conflict is to the operations of a group or organization, the more highly developed will be the techniques of conflict waging. For groups and organizations whose missions are not primarily conflict-directed, conflict avoidance or quicker resolution might be expected.

3. The size and strength of parties are two further dimensions. Implications of these gross variables may be in some sense obvious, but propositions embodying them are much less numerous. A well-known relationship between party size and conflict has been observed in the case of interethnic and interracial opposition. In general, it is said that, as a minority group increases in size, conflict is intensified or arises in the first instance. Where the Negro population is small relative to whites in southern communities, conflict over segregation is less intense. High intensity seems to be correlated with a 60-40 or near 50-50 ratio, though the exact numerical proportion has not been ascertained. Religious conflict appears less serious or non-existent where, say, Protestants are almost completely surrounded by Catholics and vice versa. Rose argues that mediation increases the possibility of resolving conflict when the parties are small (33, p. 194). Coser observes that small parties tend to make themselves rigid and inelastic, to withstand pressure toward dissolution, and also tend to absorb the whole individual person in group commitment (12, p. 98). Hence smaller groups may engage in more intense conflict relations and may be much more intransigent regarding resolution. The content or issues of conflict may be affected by group size: the larger the group, the lower the common denominator of group goals.

Party strength has several ramifications and is related to a fundamental property of conflict interaction already discussed, namely, the power relation. Paradoxically, the need for and accomplishment of a readjustment of power relations is both a source of conflict (21) and a function of conflict (Dubin, p. 191). A further paradox is that in some cases the readjustment of power relations requires, or aims at, the complete destruction or crippling of an opposing party, and, in other cases, the weakening of one of the parties beyond a certain point is a distinct disadvantage to the other. Power is an object of conflict and a conditioner of conflict: relative weaknesses may lead to conflict, and the comparative strength of parties will partially determine the new power relation which emerges from conflict. Previous distinctions will be helpful here, among them the differentiation of institutionalized and non-institutionalized conflict.

In the case of institutionalized conflict where continuity of interaction and regularized rules or expectations are essential, the conflicting parties have a vested interest in each other's strength (24, p. 201). There is considerable evidence that industrial conflict has become much more stabilized as unions have grown stronger. Proposition 8 (35, p. 337) above suggests that, as unions gain power, the duration of strikes is decreased. Furthermore, the enforcement of rules of conduct and mutual obligations which result from conflict interaction depend heavily on a minimum self-control (i.e., power to control internal decisions) by the two parties involved. In the case of non-institutionalized conflict, these considerations probably do not apply. Indeed, it may well be that it is precisely the lack of vested interest in continuity and stability which accounts for the instability and inconclusiveness of much non-institutionalized conflict.

Another facet of the party-strength factor relates to sources of conflict. This is epitomized in the following proposition already mentioned:

Proposition 17: *Changes in the relative power positions of nations are the source of tension leading to international conflict* (9, p. 20).

Although applied to phenomena of international conflict, the proposition would appear to apply to most intergroup conflict, except perhaps where groups are unorganized individuals or where conflict is religious in nature. We should also draw a distinction between the recognized and the unrecognized power of groups, that is, a factual change in the power status of one party which is not accepted as a condition of interaction by an opposing party. As noted earlier, the establishment of recognized parties may be the key factor in the initial phase of conflict. Group weakness, on the other hand, may induce conflict where the capacity for enduring frustration of group wants or needs is low (4, pp. 215–16).

Obviously, one of the primary conditions of conflict interaction is the respective influence that two parties can bring to bear on each other in the attempt to control outcomes or otherwise direct behavior along intended lines. Factors range from the capacity to endure threatened deprivation to the capacity to inflict damage, from bargaining skill to flexibility of requirements. The central underlying problem is the identification and measurement of the bases of effective reciprocal influence in conflict interaction. More scholarly effort has been expended on the analysis of potential power and on the calculation of gross power factors available to conflicting parties than on the determination of why under particular conditions a bargain is closer to the desired optimum result of one party than the other, or why one party yields more control over joint decision-making to the other. Conflict analysis clearly joins another strategic focus of analysis—social power. Conceivably, the overemphasis on the more dramatic forms of conflict resolution, such as force or financial superiority, has tended to obscure this broader connection. This is an added reason for the explicit postulation of the significance of the power relation in social conflict.

4. Finally, we come to extraparty factors which affect the links between intraparty characteristics and conflict interaction. The concept of context is once again relevant. Three propositions, drawn from different areas of social conflict, will indicate the general point:

Proposition 18: *Religious intragroup conflict is most likely to develop and to be intense when there are no cross-pressures at work within the individual* (10, p. 46).

Proposition 47: *To the extent that workers and unions are integrated into the gen-*

eral society, the propensity to strike is decreased (35, p. 337).

Proposition 48: *The higher the level of prosperity, the less intense the conflict between ethnic and racial majorities and minorities.*

Proposition 18 implies that when individuals are affected by shared values which offset or run counter to religious values which put them into opposition with others, religious conflict will be less likely to develop. For example, the Catholic and Protestant businessmen who share certain goals and prescribed behaviors are less susceptible to conflict on religious grounds than are Catholics and Protestants who do not share these goals and behaviors. Proposition 47 states, in effect, that when parties to industrial conflict are accorded roughly equal status, privileges, and opportunities, there is a tendency to avoid violent conflict. Proposition 48, a very familiar thesis, calls attention to the fact that psychological mechanisms and opposed interests are unlikely under conditions where the majority group does not regard improvement in the status of a minority group as a direct threat to its access to material goods which are becoming scarcer because of a decline in economic activity.

One basic question concerning conflict at the group, society, and international levels is: What social arrangements conduce to non-violent or non-aggressive conflict? On the basis of present evidence, the answer is not at all clear. Another basic question concerns the relations of major social conflicts to one another. Williams (41, p. 531) has remarked on the canceling-out or non-cumulative incidence of conflict in American society. Coser (12, pp. 68–69) has alerted us to the significance of the degree of individual involvement in a single conflict group. A hypothesis worth examining might be formulated as follows: *The larger the number of conflicts in any particular context, the less likely that any one will become all-inclusive with respect to persons, groups, energies, and resources.* Wright (44, pp. 202, 203) suggests, on the other hand, that there is a tendency for all international conflict to become total and

absolute. Under what conditions is either or both true?

Summary

In the preceding section we have attempted to outline some of the major aspects of the problem of exploring connections between a set of typical characteristics of parties to conflict and the pattern of conflict interaction. It is essential to emphasize again that propositions which properly fall under this heading must be evaluated in the light of the conceptual elements set forth in Section III. Thus certain propositions are relevant for one type of conflict but not for others. Propositions bearing on the sources or functions of conflict will not necessarily apply to the conditions of conflict. Again, the unit of analysis may introduce significant qualifications for the range of empirical phenomena covered by a particular proposition. As discussed immediately above, the context of conflict gives rise to propositions. Therefore, there is good reason initially to take any proposition involving a party characteristic and conflict interaction and relate it systematically to types, units, contexts, functions, sources, or conditions of conflict. Finally, the breakdown of this section into number, establishment and identification, and characteristics of parties to conflict also offers another basis for classifying conflicts.

V. Conflict as an Interaction System

Conflict has been characterized as a basic social-interaction process, and the tendency toward some degree of institutionalization has been noted. The conflict relation has been postulated as existing in a social context and as embodying a power component. Hence it is not a long step to viewing conflict as a system in the general sense employed by Boulding. Two elements of any conflict system—parties and issues—have been discussed, and a third—the power relation—has been touched upon at several points. In view of this background, we shall confine ourselves to a limited number of additional elements and to a short commentary on each. Various elements of conflict systems are, of course, related to one another and to factors mentioned earlier.

Modes of Resolution

There is a variety of methods for resolving or controlling conflict—many more than can be mentioned here. Arbitration, mediation (more often than not used synonymously with conciliation), negotiation, inquiry, legislation, judicial settlement, informal consensus (meeting of minds through discussion), the market, violence or force, authoritative command, and varieties of voting procedures are familiar ones. A range of techniques is implied in the phrase "intergroup therapy": interracial housing, co-operative living experiments, education for tolerance, interfaith movements, and so on. When "bargaining" and "negotiation" are not used in a specific technical sense, as in the case of collective bargaining in industry or diplomatic negotiation, these terms apply to many conflict situations. For each mode there are particular types—compulsory versus voluntary arbitration, conciliation recommendations which are not binding versus those which are, majority vote versus unanimity, and so on. Essentially, modes may be regarded as a set of rules for handling the need for resolution or accommodation. Different rules produce different results in different situations, and the rules themselves are a frequent conflict issue. Furthermore, some modes are appropriate for some conflict systems and not others. Voting between an equal number of representatives of labor and management would nearly always be indecisive, while arbitration is hardly a suitable mode of settlement for conflict among political parties. These trivial examples illustrate an important point, namely, that modes of resolution are fundamentally related to the nature of conflict. Evidence indicates that proposed modes of resolution are often inappropriate. Thus no amount of "better understanding through better communication" by iself is going to resolve a genuine power conflict. Mediation cannot function effectively if conflict is between unorganized groups, because mediation requires representatives who can speak authoritatively enough for each group that agreements become binding. At any rate, conflict systems can and

should be characterized according to their predominant mode (or combination of modes) of resolution. Basically, Dahl and Lindblom have analyzed the handling of political and economic conflict in terms of basic social processes in their *Politics, Economics, and Welfare.*

Given the growing significance of interorganizational conflict or conflict between highly organized groups, mediation deserves special attention. This mode probably now dominates or is coming to dominate the area of collective bargaining and is becoming more frequent in the area of international relations. Experience has accumulated to the point where observers are beginning to generalize about it and to hypothesize the conditions under which it is or is not successful. The works of Rose (33) and Jackson (23), cited previously, exemplify this. Jackson has analyzed eight propositions which, he argues, hold for both industrial and international relations; two are repeated here:

Proposition 49: *Public debate is occasionally an aid in the mobilization of public interest, but extended public debate by the parties tends to harden their views.*

Proposition 50: *Techniques for getting parties together on agreement, once mediation has started, are very similar in international and labor fields.*

Such propositions must be evaluated in the light of similarites and differences between the two areas of conflict (23, pp. 119ff.; 26, p. 235). However, it appears true that data have not been systematically related to the specified conditions under which mediation is successful, nor do we have a sufficient number of detailed case studies of the process. Nonetheless, there is substantial agreement among experts on the conditions of successful mediation. It is agreed on all sides that the personal qualifications and professional skills of the mediator are essential to mediation success. Something might be gained from a comparison of the model qualities of an industrial mediator, which can be found in the literature, with the attributes and skills of Dr. Ralph Bunche and Secretary-General Hammarskjöld, who have functioned effectively as mediators for the United Nations. The progress of mediation at the international level would seem to be heavily dependent on an available group of knowledgeable and trusted mediators. Experience with this problem within societies might be revealing for future developments in international organization. Moreover, Kerr's (26, p. 236) distinction between tactical and strategic mediation may be useful. Rather than being aimed at basic solutions to major issues, Kerr sees tactical mediation as resulting in reduced irrationality, removal of non-rational conflict elements, creation of possible new solutions, and assistance in the graceful retreat of parties from overly rigid positions. Various agencies and processes within the United Nations, many hidden from public view, should be examined as manifestations of tactical mediation. Observations based on industrial mediation (16, pp. 72 ff.) indicate definite phases to the conflict resolution process. The initial phase is likely to be one of strong language and positions of apparent inflexibility—a phase the layman is probably most familiar with and which he either mistakes for the general tenor of the whole process or assumes to be irrelevant. This spectacular phase, unless seen in the light of a sequential set of phases, may be very misleading. In more general terms, the ceremonial aspect of conflict resolution through mediation turns out to be functional, and its abolition, which many equate with the "solution" to conflict, would have serious consequences for the likelihood of eventual agreement. However, if conflict becomes entirely or predominantly ceremonial, complexity and rigidity of rules may be the reason (26, p. 236).

In considering conflict resolution, the distinction between violent (or aggressive) and non-violent modes provides another way of classifying systems. Wars, strikes, riots, armed rebellions, and physical assaults are all violent or aggressive modes. From many points of view the chief problem is to channel conflict resolution into non-violent, non-aggressive modes. Some writers blame the seriousness of human conflict on ultimate weapons available (1), and violent modes have been in some respects overemphasized as the essence of conflict systems. The over-emphasis on violent modes has, of course, been a reflection of their cost, overtness, and dramatic impact, but it has had the effect of obscuring the relation between non-violent and violent modes, of inspiring superficial solutions, and of divorcing modes of resolution from the underlying nature of conflict interaction. A general hypothesis can be stated as follows: *The possibility of aggressive conflict or employment of violence tends to set a terminal point to controversy.* A related general hypothesis is: *The more destructive the means available to both parties to a conflict, the less likely is it that the ends for which conflict is waged can be served if such means are used.* At first glance, these tentative propositions may be an affront to the reader who is thinking of frequent wars and strikes and who reads and hears threats among superpowers possessing nuclear weapons. Obviously, these hypotheses imply important conditions and qualifications. The first implies a common interest in joint survival and some degree of functional interrelatedness between the parties. The second implies a rough equality of capacity to administer destruction and the absence of values which decree total elimination of one or both parties. Serious though these qualifications are, they help to sharpen the questions to be asked of empirical evidence.

Several familiar reminders are appropriate here. In the evolution from individual or group self-help to the monopoly of the instrumentalities of force in the hands of government, it is essential to note that violent modes of conflict settlement did not disappear but were *institutionalized,* i.e., their employment was subject to restrictive conditions and other modes of resolution were made available. The same thing can be said of strikes: as mediation and other modes of resolution of industrial conflict have grown in significance, the strike was *not* abolished but was related to the other modes in the collective-bargaining system in such a way as to curb its use without removing it as an incentive to agreement. It hardly seems likely that mediation could have developed if strikes had been abolished. Similarly, it may be seriously questioned whether international mediation would develop merely because nuclear weapons were abolished. Many disarmament solutions neglect the central function of violent modes: to make bargaining more conclusive and more effective. Attempts by conflicting parties to control violent modes can be interpreted as a recognition that the utility of aggressive conflict has become severely limited.

The necessity to relate the nature of conflict situations to modes of resolution can be seen in another connection. There is, of course, a substantial literature on bargaining generally and on effective strategies in "social games."[2] For the most part, attention is focused on descriptions of bargaining and games of strategy and on prescriptions for rational behavior where opposing parties are making choices under conditions of uncertainty. We should say in passing that, although this type of analysis employs formal mathematical or economic models which, as yet, have had relatively little empirical application to a wide range of social conflicts, very useful insights into the nature of conflict have been forthcoming. The title of a new book by H. Duncan Luce and Howard Raiffa, to be published this year by John Wiley and Sons, is "Conflict, Collusion, and Conciliation"—a thorough discussion of what in our language we have called "modes of resolution" (i.e., solutions) for certain kinds of social conflicts or "games." Propositions derived from game theoretical analysis can be used as guides to empirical research. However, the main point here is that, along with other key assumptions, it is assumed that bargaining can and should lead to an intersection of demands by parties to conflict such that both "win" (see Braithwaite, *Theory of Games as a Tool for the Moral Philosopher*), and

there are strategies in social games which will yield optimum results (this may involve minimizing losses) to the opponents under given conditions. Psychologists, on the other hand, have been concerned with situations in which there is ambivalence toward alternative states of affairs or outcomes and in which conflict is intensified precisely because plus and minus values either do not cancel out or cannot be "resolved" by the choice of a particular value or combination of values. This suggests that value conflict, in the sense of ideological conflicts mentioned above, requires a different type of mode of resolution from those prescribed in bargaining strategies or game theory. For the latter kind of conflict, some sort of value integration seems required, that is, conflicting goal values are converted into instrumental values serving a superordinate goal value. For example, two independent nations may not be able to reach a mutually satisfactory trade bargain because any alternative point of mutually beneficial agreement may have other negatively valued (including non-economic adverse consequences) aspects. But, by organizing themselves into a single trade unit (economic union), trade relations may subserve a higher value, such as a more advantageous all-round division of labor between them or closer political ties.

We have only sketched some of the implications of modes of resolution for conflict systems. What is needed is a systematic comparison of the consequences of various modes with respect to types, sources, conditions, and functions of conflict. The next step is to test the applicability of resulting propositions across the major areas of social conflict.

Power Relations

In a previous section we discussed party strength as a factor in the general relationship between party characteristics and conflict interaction. Clearly, however, power is a relational concept, and it is the nature and distribution of power among the parties *and* relative to the issues of conflict which are significant. Accommodation to preconflict changes in comparative party strength and clarification of mutual control over

[2] See, e.g., M. Shubik (ed.), *Readings in Game Theory and Political Behavior* (New York: Doubleday, 1954); J. D. Williams, *The Compleat Strategyst* (New York: McGraw-Hill Book Co., 1954); O. Morgenstern, "The Theory of Games," *Scientific American*, CLXXX (1949), 22 ff.; J. Bernard, "The Theory of Games as a Modern Sociology of Conflict," *American Journal of Sociology*, LIX (1954), 411–24; N. W. Chamberlain, *A General Theory of Economic Process* (New York: Harper & Bros., 1955), chaps. vi–ix.

decisions have also been established as functions of the conflict relation. Thus the power-relations component of any conflict system consists of the respective bases of effective influence on which the parties can operate *and* the allocation of control over decisions which occur during the interaction. There seems to be no inherent reason why, empirically, the bases of influence and distribution of control over behavioral choices cannot be identified and measured with some degree of precision whether the parties are unorganized groups or individuals or bureaucracies. As remarked previously, this task is not easy, and such knowledge as we have has not been codified in these terms.

If we can assume for a moment that power relations have been at least crudely defined, two characteristic patterns might serve to differentiate conflict systems: (1) *diffuseness* and *specificity* and (2) *stability* and *instability*. In most situations it is likely that these concepts represent a continuum rather than mutually exclusive polar opposites. Diffuseness-specificity implies a distinction between a system characterized by a broad range of effective bases of influence and ambiguity of control over decisions, as against a system embodying a narrow range of effective bases of influence and definite prescriptions for control over decisions. This dimension appears to be related to other variables—the number of parties and internal organization. Interracial or inter-ethnic conflict would appear, in general, to manifest multiple parties and lack of centralized relations within parties. Face-to-face relations among parties are likely to cover a number of life-situations and hence to offer several possible influence relationships. In contrast, labor-management conflict is predominantly characterized by centralized interaction and formal allocation of decision-making power.

An unstable power relation is one in which no durable resolution of power conflicts or establishment of regular joint decision-making patterns is possible (or has been achieved) and/or in which there is no accepted means of measuring the power balance. The perishable nature of coalitions is probably related to the difficulty of stabilizing power relations under certain conditions. Instability accompanies shifting agenda of issues, i.e., the relationship must accommodate a large number of issues generally unpredictable in advance and rapid changes in internal characteristics of parties. When the bases of effective influence are primarily of a subtle psychological kind rather than force or economic bargaining, indexes of power are difficult to determine. This seems to be true of, say, party conflict in the French Chamber of Deputies and of contemporary international politics.

What are the implications of the power factor for the problem of resolution and control of conflict? For one thing, to the extent that the function of conflict is the clarification and stabilization of power relations, modes of resolution which omit or cannot basically affect these relations are likely to be ineffective (35). It is not only that opposed goals are at stake in conflict situations but that control over the choices governing alternative goals and means is also at stake. "Human-relations" approaches which attempt exclusively to create a sense of common goals while by-passing the joint decision-making phase may therefore be wide of the mark in many situations.

The difficulty of estimating power in advance of a concrete test is undoubtedly a major obstacle in preventing conflict or in reducing the likelihood of extreme conflict (12, p. 35). Hence the problem of social conflict resolution may be viewed in a dual aspect: the necessity to devise advance measurements of power outcomes and the substitution of small-scale (i.e., discussion or vote) methods for large-scale (i.e., a strike or war) methods in trials of power. In effect, the parties to conflict need to know beforehand whether a better decision can be reached via one mode of resolution than by another. A straw vote, an advisory court opinion, and a mediation process are all examples of ways of avoiding premature or mistaken trials whose possibly adverse consequences cannot be avoided, once they occur. Misinformation or guesses concerning conflict outcomes tend to result in situations in which all parties lose or in which interaction is completely disrupted and therefore must be painfully re-established.

No one knows how often parties to conflict have allowed themselves to be boxed in and driven to actions they themselves acknowledged to be undesirable.

Despite the universal common-sense recognition of the need for face-saving and graceful retreats when ultimate tests of power are bound to be adverse or inconclusive, we know little about the effective detection and accommodation of this stage in a conflict interaction. In areas of disorganized social conflict typified by diffuse and unstable power relations, the possibility of dysfunctional interaction is much greater, especially in the case of unrealistic conflict.

Nature and Degree of Institutionalization

The foregoing comments lead to another dimension of conflict systems. Institutionalization of conflict generally means continuity of interaction; regularized procedures for handling changes in conditions, goals, and power; interdependence of parties; and the creation of new norms (24). Out of institutionalized conflict come new social policies. As conflict is partially resolved at various stages through time, certain issues disappear, and a common law governing formerly disputed matters is built up. Ways of measuring power relations and correcting imbalances without aggressive conflict or violence are developed. Institutionalization requires the combination of conflict and co-operation, since rules and procedures cannot function in the absence of voluntary obedience or enforcement through sanctions (29, p. 17). Even war, the ultimate in conflict, is co-operative to the extent necessary to permit communication between enemies and administration of mutually advantageous rules. Thus the frequent rigid dichotomy between harmony and opposition, co-operation and conflict, is very misleading. As Sumner pointed out, co-operation can be antagonistic and can result from bribed interdependence. In any event, institutionalized conflict and co-operation go together. Co-operation does not imply an absence of conflict or vice versa.

Non-institutionalized conflict or conflict interaction having a low degree of institutionalization is marked by chronic recurrence of unsettled issues, by an absence of agreed procedures for review of relations, and by discontinuity of interaction or drastic shifts in the mode of resolution. This type of system is correlated, if not causally linked, with diffuse and unstable power relations. Hypothetically, a higher degree of institutionalization is similarly linked to more specific and stable power relations. A general hypothesis, which could be tested empirically, is: *The higher the degree of institutionalization, the greater the consistency and balance of strength of the parties to conflict.* The pressures of functional interdependence between parties and the need to preserve predictable conflict relations result in modes of resolution which stop short of the complete destruction or crippling of one of the parties. Indeed, it is no accident that wars, for example, seem to be terminated while there is still an entity for the victor to deal with, some minimal organization to make possible a new formulation of the now altered power relation.

There are noteworthy differences in the nature of institutionalization of conflict. The conflict relation may be autonomous in the sense that the parties voluntarily establish an informal social control of their interactions. Or a conflict relation may be regulated by legal norms enforced from outside the conflict system. Industrial collective bargaining in Great Britain is an expression of the former and collective bargaining in the United States is an expression of the latter. International conflict is for the most part a mixture, with predominate emphasis on autonomy. The growth and success of industrial bargaining suggest that the appropriate social context of conflict can permit autonomous conflict resolution as exemplified by experience in Great Britain.

Another pattern of institutionalization relates to centralization and decentralization of conflict systems. In general, political institutionalization is centralized with respect to some area of jurisdiction (or political unit), while the institutionalization of economic conflict, in free societies at least, is more decentralized. Centralized institutionalization of conflict is exemplified by national legislation, a local ordinance binding on all members of the community, or by an authoritative Supreme Court decision. Decentralized institutionalization is exemplified by the market. Hence social policies which accommodate conflicting goals, demands, and needs may evolve from a central decision-making agency which lays down rules and determines power relations or from the cumulative impact of a number of separate bargains whether between individuals or firms or between consumers and producers. One of the most familiar and persistent problems of political economy is, of course, the relative merits of these two general patterns of conflict systems. Progressive income taxation and redistribution of purchasing power through sliding-scale wage or income provisions represent two different approaches to one aspect of social welfare.

There is good reason to assume, in the absence of strong evidence to the contrary, a persistent tendency toward institutionalization of social conflict. From the foregoing, three directions of this tendency can be inferred. First, particular institutionalization for particular kinds of conflict may evolve. Second, institutionalization may be based on the support of existing machinery in the social context outside a given conflict system. Third, these two patterns may be combined. Conflict which is essentially disorganized, unrealistic, characterized by diverse modes of resolution, diffuse and unstable power relations, and, on balance, more dysfunctional than functional, tends to lead to institutionalization through mechanisms operating in the social context —usually a centralized institution. Conflict which manifests the opposite properties tends to lead to autonomous, decentralized, and more particularistic institutionalization. Racial conflict would probably fall into the first category and industrial conflict clearly into the second. The conditions leading to a combination are not immediately clear. Presumably, the general character of the culture and social organization would be controlling, but such a statement is not very specific. A major subject for inquiry is the set of factors which affect the degree and form of institutionalization.

It is difficult to escape the conviction that the resolution and control of social conflict are intimately related to the nature and degree of institutionalization. Superficially, it would appear that conflict relations are functional and stable (i.e., predictable and subject to semiautomatic adjustment to new conditions) to the extent that *appropriate* institutionalization exists. The fact that wars and strikes are institutionalized in an important sense in no way undercuts the argument that it is the institutionalization of other modes and the relationship of various modes within an institutional framework which are crucial.

Direct, Unmediated Systems Versus Mediated Representational Systems

Another aspect of conflict systems which can be analytically differentiated is closely bound up with the previous dimension. Again, intuitive observation suggests a sizable difference between much interpersonal and unorganized group conflict, on the one hand, and organized intergroup or interorganizational conflict, on the other. The model for the latter, which would cover a large sector of social conflict, can be indicated briefly:

1. The relationships among two sets of representatives or bargainers and the relationships among each set of bargainers or representatives
   a) The values and perceptions of the representatives or bargainers
2. The nature of the membership or constituency represented
   a) The values and perceptions of the memberships
   b) Degree of unity and kinds of relations among members
3. The relationship between representatives or bargainers and the membership or constituency
   a) Nature and consequences of authority relationship
   b) Nature and function of leadership
4. The role of the mediator or mediating agencies (if present)
   a) Qualities and effectiveness of mediation
   b) Relationship of mediating function to the social context

5. Interrelation of bargaining or representational system to social context
   a) Institutional links (e.g., sanctions)
   b) Non-institutional links (e.g., interested publics)

This model, though highly general and though it includes no basis for deriving links among the five sets of variables, does offer a possibly fruitful method of organizing and classifying propositions which then could be connected in the description and explanation of a conflict system which conformed to the underlying assumptions. Furthermore, direct unmediated systems could be analyzed in terms of the presence or absence of the five components. Nor is there any reason why the other characteristics of conflict systems discussed above could not be incorporated in the model as well as the party characteristics, also discussed above. It should be noted that the model is not restricted to formal mediation as a mode of resolution. If non-institutionalization and institutionalization imply a continuum, then the closer to the non-institutionalization end a particular system is, the less likely is the system to conform to the specifications of the model.

System Limitations and Boundaries

Finally, we come to the limitations on conflict, a subject best left to this point because so much of what has been said bears on it. Since conflict has been so often associated with social instability, waste, destruction, random outbursts of violence, and long-drawn-out-struggles, it is easy to equate conflict with a breakdown of control or to underestimate its limits. But social conflict behavior is rarely, if ever, random and without limitations.

One of the properties of any system is that it is boundary-maintaining. That is, for the purposes at hand, an observer can usually discover empirical distinctions between the related parts which comprise the system and other phenomena which are either unrelated or, from the observer's standpoint, unimportant. Thus the parties to conflict and the conflict interaction (including its components) can be empirically separated from what was earlier called the

"social context." The social context consists of non-system factors which the observer *does* think are important. Apart from system boundaries (or limits) in this sense, the other meaning of limitation on conflict concerns those factors (inside or outside the system) which tend to affect the intensity, duration, enlargement, and mode of resolution of the conflict interaction process. As presented by Boulding, the proper way to connect system and non-system boundaries and limitations is by a concept of an "open system," i.e., one which is characterized by internal changes in relationships among constituent parts *and* one which is susceptible to influences from outside its boundaries. Implicitly, at least, many propositions on conflict are based on a closed system or on an ever expanding system or on a system which manifests only disequilibrium as its essential property. There is ground for distrusting all three as approaches to the study of conflict.

Major limitations on conflict can be listed briefly. Intrasystem limits are (1) functional interdependence between parties, (2) regulation through institutionalized norms and procedures, (3) the need for continued communication between parties, (4) conflict cost, (5) availability and feasibility of certain modes of resolution, (6) inertia and organizational inefficiency of parties, (7) ignorance or misunderstanding, and (8) avoidance taboos. Most of these are self-evident on the basis of the preceding discussion. Thus the implications of conflict cost as a limitation on conflict are rather obvious. It may be that some conflict systems have as their outstanding feature the desire of one or both parties to inflict maximum disorder on the conflict relationship—subversion or a rebellion would be examples. Nonetheless, in conflict systems having predominantly highly institutionalized non-violent modes of resolution, there is a limit on tolerable disorder. The restoration of order following a disruption of normal interaction places a burden on each party. The contractual spacing of conflict resolution, e.g., a one-year or more union-management agreement, confirms this natural limitation. Even during a steel strike, a union will assign some of its members to keeping open-hearth furnaces banked.

The last three limitations have not been mentioned before. Party weakness has been mentioned as a source of conflict under some conditions, but inertia and organizational inefficiency may also limit conflict. Many social conflicts become less intense or die out altogether because one or both parties simply run out of sustained drive. Conflict relations may be emotionally satisfying and substantively rewarding, but they are also burdensome. Sustained conflict, if vigorously waged, puts a great premium on energy and resources, neither of which is unlimited in supply. Ignorance and misunderstanding are normally cited as sources and conditioners of conflict. However, it is not always recognized that these same factors may also prevent or minimize conflict. How much more conflict would there be if individuals and groups really thoroughly and correctly understood each other's motives, words, and deeds? Kerr argues (26, p. 233): "In fact, misunderstanding and the misuse of words have probably made a substantial contribution to industrial peace." Diplomatic language, often dismissed as double talk, makes possible "planned misunderstandings" which keep tensions down and provide opportunity for clarification prior to ultimate or aggressive measures. Avoidance taboos, a term mostly employed by social anthropologists, denote behavioral restraints which have not been broadly examined as a limiting factor in conflict. Everyone is aware of "things which are just not said or done," regardless of provocation. Such restraints, if operative at enough key junctures of interpersonal and intergroup relations, may be a much more powerful limitation on conflict than is realized. Religious conflict in the contemporary United States is undoubtedly restrained by avoidance taboos.

Limitations arising outside any conflict system can be classified as follows: (1) shared cultural and social values which neutralize or dominate conflicting values; (2) institutional sanctions against certain kinds of power relations and modes of resolution; (3) third parties interested in control or resolution; (4) crisscrossing of other conflict systems which prevents enlargement or bipolarization around any single system; and (5) "cross-pressures" which create ambivalences within parties.

To the extent that there are "natural limits" to conflict, the lesson for the problem of resolution and control would seem to be this: *Social strategies designed to keep conflict functional and to prevent violent or aggressive conflict ought to be based in part on deliberate attempts to capitalize on natural limits.* This may involve giving up notions of "abolishing" conflict, of "final" resolutions, and may direct attention to less obvious control devices. Avoidance taboos, for example, may be easier to inculcate and enforce than centralized political controls. Clarification and invigoration of existing common values may be more feasible than finding formulae for reconciling some conflicting values.

Summary

Counting parties and issues, seven properties of conflict systems have been outlined. Aside from providing categories to locate and relate descriptive and causal propositions, this part of the analytic framework has other potential uses. Given a particular conflict system and given X empirical content of categories 1 through 7, an observer might be able to hypothesize about the sources, conditions, functions, context, and type of conflict. Or, for example, if there are multiple parties (category 1), if the issue is one of political power (category 2), if power relations are diffuse and unstable (category 3), if the conflict is relatively non-institutionalized (category 5), if the conflict is direct and immediate (category 6), and if limitations (internal and external) are either absent or minimal, then an observer might predict a violent mode of resolution (category 4).

VI. Conclusion

When all is said and done, there is no substitute for more reliable and systematic knowledge produced by soundly conceived and executed research. The kind of analysis attempted here can aid in posing significant questions, in exposing areas of ignorance, and in generating testable hypotheses. Furthermore, an explicit framework provides a way of codifying existing unfunded common-sense knowledge and research findings. We also feel that detailed studies will be more cumulative if it is possible to compare meaningfully cases and situations from a wide range of social conflicts. Meanwhile, the search for a limited number of major variables, the formulation of bold hypotheses, cross-field generalizations, and typification have their place in conflict analysis.

REFERENCES

1. Andrzejewski, S. *Military Organization and Society.* London: Routledge, 1954.
2. Bernard, Jessie. *Journal of Conflict Resolution,* I (1957), 111.
3. _____. "Where Is the Modern Sociology of Conflict?" *American Journal of Sociology,* LVI (1950), 11–16.
4. Boasson, C. "The Relevance of Research to the Problems of Peace." In *Research for Peace,* pp. 215–16. Oslo: Institute for Social Research, 1954.
5. Boulding, K. "Economic Issues in International Conflict," *Kyklos,* VI (1953), 99–115.
6. Center for Research on World Political Institutions. Publication No. 4. Princeton: Princeton University, 1955.
7. Chase, S. *Roads to Agreement.* New York: Harper & Bros., 1951.
8. Chein, I. "Research Needs," *Journal of Social Issues,* XII (1956), 57–66 (for an appraisal of the lack of knowledge concerning religious conflict).
9. Chertok, E. "Sources of International Tension," *Bulletin of the Research Exchange on the Prevention of War,* III (1955), No. 17.
10. Coleman, J. "Social Cleavage and Religious Conflict," *Journal of Social Issues,* XII (1956), 45.
11. Cooper, J. B. "Psychological Literature on the Prevention of War," *Bulletin of the Research Exchange on the Prevention of War,* III (1955), 2–15.
12. Coser, L. *The Functions of Social Conflict.* Glencoe, Ill.: Free Press, 1956.
13. Cottrell, W. F. "Research To Establish Conditions for Peace," *Journal of Social Issues,* XI (1955), 13–20.
14. Dahlke, O. "Race and Minority Riots: A Study in the Typology of Violence," *Social Forces,* XXX (1952), 420.
15. Davis, A. K. "Conflict between Major Social Systems," *Social Forces,* XXX (1951), 31.
16. Douglas, A. "The Peaceful Settlement of Industrial and Intergroup Conflict," *Journal of Conflict Resolution,* I (1957), 72 ff.
17. Dubin, R. *Journal of Conflict Resolution,* I (1957), 179.
18. Farber, M. "Psychoanalytic Hypotheses in the Study of War," *Journal of Social Issues,* XI (1955), 33.
19. Frazier, E. F. *Race and Culture Contacts in the Modern World.* New York: Alfred Knopf, 1957.
20. Freeman, F. D. "Theory and Strategy of Action in Race Relations," *Social Forces,* XXX (1951), 86.
21. Glock, C. Y. "Issues That Divide: A Postscript," *Journal of Social Issues,* XII (1956), 40.
22. Hager D. J. "Introduction: Religious Conflict," *Journal of Social Issues,* XII (1956), 3–11.
23. Jackson, E. *Meeting of Minds.* New York: McGraw-Hill Book Co., Inc., 1952.
24. Kahn-Freund, D. "Intergroup Conflicts and Their Settlement," *British Journal of Sociology,* V (1954), 201.
25. Kecskemeti, P. *Meaning, Communication, and Value.* Chicago: University of Chicago Press, 1952.
26. Kerr, C. "Industrial Conflict and Its Mediation," *American Journal of Sociology,* LX (1954), 230.
27. Klineberg, O. *Tensions Affecting International Understanding.* New York: Social Science Research Council, 1950.
28. Kluckhohn, C. "Values and Value-Orientations in the Theory of Action: An Exploration in Definition and Classification." In Parsons, Talcott, and Shils, E. A. (eds.), *Toward a General Theory of Action.* 1951.
29. Kornhauser, A., Dubin, R., and Ross, A. M. *Industrial Conflict.* New York: McGraw-Hill Book Co., 1954.
30. Lockwood, D. "Some Remarks on 'the Social System,'" *British Journal of Sociology,* VII (1956), 134–45.
31. Parsons, T. "Certain Primary Sources and Patterns of Aggression in the Social Structure of the Western World." In Bryson, L., *et al., Conflicts of Power in Modern Culture.* 1947.
32. Rickman, J. "Psychodynamic Notes," In Cantril, H. (ed.), *Tensions That Cause Wars.* 1950.
33. Rose, A. "Needed Research on the Mediation of Labor Disputes," *Personnel Psychology,* V (1952), 196–99.
34. Rose, A. M., and Rose, C. B. "Intergroup Conflict and Its Mediation," *International Social Science Bulletin,* VI (1954), 25.
35. Sheppard, H. "Approaches to Conflict in American Sociology," *British Journal of Sociology,* V (1954), 324–42.
36. Simpson, G. *Conflict and Community: A Study in Social Theory.* New York: T. S. Simpson, 1937.
37. Singer, K. "Resolution of Conflict," *Social Research,* VI (1949), 230.
38. Sorensen, R. C. "The Concept of Conflict in Industrial Sociology," *Social Forces,* XXIX (1951), 263–67.
39. Williams, R. M., Jr. *The Reduction of Intergroup Tensions.* New York: Social Science Research Council, 1947.
40. _____. "Religion, Value-Orientations, and Intergroup Conflict," *Journal of Social Issues,* XII (1956), 15.

41. _____. *American Society*. New York: Alfred A. Knopf, 1950.
42. Wright, Q. *A Study of War*. 2 vols. Chicago: University of Chicago Press, 1942.
43. _____. "Criteria for Judging the Relevance of Researches on the Problems of Peace." In *Research for Peace*, pp. 68–82. Oslo: Institute for Social Research, 1954.
44. _____. "The Nature of Conflict," *Western Political Quarterly*, IV (1951), 198.

CONFLICT AND ITS RESOLUTION*

MORTON DEUTSCH

The other day, in the garden of a friend's house, my five-year-old son and his chum were struggling over a water hose. Each wanted to use it first to water the flowers. Both were tugging at it in an effort to get it away from the other, and both were crying. Each was very frustrated and neither was able to use the hose to sprinkle the flowers as he had desired. After reaching a deadlock in their tug-of-war, they began to punch one another and call each other names. The escalation of the conflict to physical violence led to the intervention of a powerful third party (an adult), who suggested an interesting game to determine who would use the hose first. The boys, each somewhat frightened by the violence of the struggle, were relieved to agree to the suggestion. They got absorbed in the game of trying to find a small object I had hidden, and they obediently followed the rule that the winner would have a first turn of two minutes with the hose. They soon tired of the water hose and began to pick blackberries, which they threw provocatively at a ten-year-old who responded to their ineffectual sallies with an amused tolerance.

Even a simple episode of this sort suggests many questions, questions which are of pertinence to conflicts of all sorts: intrapersonal, interpersonal, intragroup, intergroup, and international. Thus one might inquire about the participants in the conflict, how their individual characteristics (their strength, their cognitive resources, their personalities, their emotional state, etc.) and their prior relationship with one another affected the development and course of the dispute. One might expect, for instance, that if the disputants were men

rather than boys, the resort to physical violence would have been less likely. If so, would this be because violence is more painful and dangerous among men than among boys and hence the social and personal restraints against adults punching one another are likely to be stronger? Or could it be that violence is less likely because of the greater intellectual resourcefulness of adults? Also, it seems reasonable to assume that girls would be less likely to punch one another than boys. If so, how is it possible to socialize or otherwise indoctrinate people so that certain forms of waging conflict are so alien to their concept of themselves that they become "unthinkable" methods of conflict?

Or one may ask about the issue in conflict, its motivational significance and its phrasing. Was there anything about the possession or nonpossession of a water hose which might have been of particular emotional significance to the quarrelers? A Freudian might stress the phallic symbolism and the intensity of the rivalrous and anxious feelings a boy of five years is likely to have about possessing a big and powerful water sprinkler. Also, the issue might have been phrased so that its magnitude was large or small, so that the legitimate claims of both or of only one were recognized. Thus, the issue may be defined as all-or-none (the hose becomes one boy's exclusive possession and under his sole control) or as one in which "I use the hose for two minutes and then you can use it for two minutes."

Or one may inquire into the broader social environment within which the conflict occurs. For example, was conflict more likely because neither child had clear territorial rights (both were visitors in an unfamiliar locale)? Did the known presence of an interested and significant audience (parents) affect the course of conflict in particular ways? What modes of intervention by a third party are likely to be most

* Paper presented on September 5, 1965 at the meetings of the American Psychological Association. Preparation of this paper was facilitated by work in connection with a National Science Foundation Grant, GS-302, and a contract with the Office of Naval Research, NONR-4294. Reprinted by permission of the author.

effective in resolving a conflict of a given type? What characteristics of the third party, including his relationship to the parties in conflict, determine how acceptable his intervention will be? I doubt if the two five-year-olds would have been much influenced by a cease and desist order from a four-year-old. Yet, it is not unknown for a physically powerless third party to help prevent the conflict of more powerful parties from escalating into violent forms. What are the characteristics of third parties which aid in resolving conflict and what characteristics for its deadlock and interminable conflict?

Variables Affecting the Course of Conflict

There are many other questions which can be raised about this episode of conflict. As I have indicated earlier, I believe such questions have relevance to conflict at different levels, from the intrapersonal to the intranational. Whether the conflict under scrutiny is between union and management or between nations or between a husband and wife or between children, it is useful to know something about:

(a) The characteristics of the parties in conflict (their values and motivations; their aspirations and objectives; their physical, intellectual, and social resources for waging or resolving conflict; their beliefs about conflict, including their conceptions of strategy and tactics; and so forth);

(b) Their prior relationship to one another (their attitudes, beliefs, and expectations about one another, including the beliefs about the other's view of oneself, and particularly the degree of polarization which has occurred on such evaluations as "good-bad," "trustworthy-untrustworthy");

(c) The nature of the issue giving rise to the conflict (its scope, its rigidity, its motivational significance, its formulation, its periodicity, etc.);

(d) The social environment within which the conflict occurs (the facilities and restraints, the encouragements and deterrents it provides with regard to the different strategies and tactics of waging or resolving conflict, including the nature of the social norms and institutional forms for regulating conflict);

(e) The interested audiences to the conflict (their relationships to the parties in conflict and to one another, their interests in the conflict and its outcomes, their characteristics);

(f) The strategy and tactics employed by the parties in the conflict (in assessing one another's utilities, disutilities, and subjective probabilities; in changing one another's utilities, disutilities, and subjective probabilities; in influencing the other's conceptions of one's own utilities and disutilities through tactics which vary along such dimensions as legitimacy-illegitimacy, the relative use of positive and negative incentives such as promises and rewards or threats and punishments, freedom of choice-coercion, the openness and veracity of communication and sharing of information, the degree of credibility, the degree of commitment, the types of motives appealed to, and so on);

(g) The consequences of the conflict to each of the participants and to other interested parties (the gains or losses relating to the immediate issue in conflict, the precedents established, the internal changes in the participants resulting from engaging in conflict, the long-term effects on the relationship between the parties involved, the reputation that each party develops in the eyes of the various interested audiences).

I have sketched out this outline of some of the variables involved in conflicts involving different types of units—individuals, groups, organizations, and nations. This demonstration is not meant to imply that the mechanisms or capabilities of acquiring information, making decisions, and acting are similar in the different types of units. I shall not commit the "group mind" fallacy. Yet I will not ignore the fact that nations as well as individuals have the capacity to act even though each unit cannot do the same kinds of things: a nation can declare war, a man cannot; a man can hide himself, a nation cannot. Individuals, groups, and nations—having the capacity to act, each may do so stupidly if it lacks relevant information before it acts.

The Functions of Conflict

I stress the legitimacy of employing similar concepts to discuss conflict between different types of units to justify the approach to the question which is at the heart of this essay. My inquiry is into the conditions which determine whether a conflict will be resolved with constructive or destructive consequences. My approach is to examine different levels of conflict to see whether or not there are some central notions which can throw light on varied situations of conflict and, then, to investigate these notions in laboratory experiments. I cannot claim any originality for either the inquiry or the approach; both are common to many scholars working in the field of conflict and conflict resolution. Nor, as you will see, may I assert that my investigations have as yet given any definitive answers.

The central question underlying my investigation assumes that conflict is potentially of personal and social value. Conflict is a pervasive and inevitable aspect of life. Its pervasiveness suggests that conflict is not necessarily destructive or lacking in pleasure. Conflict has many positive functions. It prevents stagnation, it stimulates interest and curiosity, it is the medium through which problems can be aired and solutions arrived at; it is the root of personal and social change. Moreover, conflict is often part of the process of testing and assessing oneself and, as such, may be highly enjoyable as one experiences the pleasure of the full and active use of one's capacities.

I stress the positive functions of conflict, and I have by no means provided an exhaustive listing of such functions, because many discussions of conflict cast it in the role of the villain, as though conflict *per se* were the cause of psychopathology, social disorder, war. A superficial reading of such theories as Gestalt theory with its focus on good form, psychoanalytic theory with its emphasis on the "pleasure principle," field theory with its stress on tension reduction, and dissonance theory with its preoccupation with dissonance reduction would seem to suggest that the psychological utopia would be a conflict-free existence. Yet it is apparent that most of us seek out conflict in competitive sports and games, or by going to the theatre or reading a novel, or by attending to the news, or in the teasing interplay of intimate encounters, or in our intellectual work. Fortunately none of us have to face the prospect of a conflict-free existence. It cannot be eliminated nor even suppressed for very long.

The Query

The question, I repeat, is not how to eliminate or prevent conflict but rather how to make it productive or, minimally, how to prevent it from being destructive. There are inherent ambiguities in this question because of the ambiguity of such value-laden terms as "destructive" and "productive." One may well ask, Cannot a conflict be productive for the victor and destructive for the vanquished? And isn't it possible for a conflict to be productive in relation to certain values but destructive in relation to others? However, my concern is with conflict situations where it is possible for there to be an outcome of mutual satisfaction and mutual net gain for the participants, and I am interested in the conditions which lead to this mutually positive outcome rather than either to an outcome of mutual dissatisfaction and loss or to an outcome in which one party gains while the other party loses. It is, of course, easier to identify and measure satisfactions-dissatisfactions and gains-losses in simple laboratory conflict situations than it is in the complex conflicts of groups in everyday life. Yet even in these complex situations, it is not impossible to compare outcomes roughly in terms of their outcomes: e.g., in some instances union-management negotiations may lead to a prolonged strike with considerable loss and ill will resulting to both parties; in other instances it may lead to a mutually satisfying agreement where both sides obtain something they want.

I have limited my discussion to conflict situations in which positive outcomes for all the participants are possible. That is to say, I am not dealing with situations of "pure" conflict—the zero sum game—in which inevitably one side loses what the other gains. My interest is in "impure" conflict, where there is a mixture of cooperative and competitive interests. In other words, in situations where a variety of outcomes are possible: mutual gain, mutual loss, gain for one and loss for the other. Thus, my initial query can be restated as an investigation of the conditions under which the participants will evolve a cooperative relationship or a competitive relationship in a situation which permits either. I would stress here that my elimination of pure conflict situations is not very limiting. There are very few situations, particularly if the situation is repetitive or if the participants are involved in many different situations together, which are so rigidly structured that inevitably one's gains must come from the other's losses. It is, of course, true that the participants may define a situation which permits mutual gain as one of pure conflict and respond to one another in a purely competitive manner.

The Symptoms of Cooperative and Competitive Processes of Conflict Resolution

The reformulation of my query permits me to apply my theory of cooperation and competition to characterize two processes of interrelationships in dealing with conflict: a cooperative process and a competitive process. In effect, I am stating that the development of a cooperative or competitive relationship will be manifest not only in the outcomes but also in the processes of dealing with the conflict. Elsewhere, I have described in detail the social psychological differences between a cooperative and competitive process and presented the results of experimental study of these processes (Deutsch, 1949a, 1949b, 1962). I shall not repeat this description here. However, I wish to highlight the following differences between the two processes by considering them in their strict forms:

1. Communication

(a) A cooperative process is characterized by open and honest communication of relevant information between the participants. Each is interested in informing as well as being informed by the other.

(b) A competitive process is characterized by either lack of communication or misleading communication. It also gives rise to espionage or other techniques which attempt to obtain information about the other that the other is unwilling to communicate. Each is interested in obtaining information about the other and in providing discouraging or misleading information to the other.

2. Perception

(a) A cooperative process tends to increase sensitivity to similarities and common interests, while minimizing the salience of differences. It stimulates a convergence or conformity of beliefs and values.

(b) A comparative process tends to increase sensitivity to differences and threats, while minimizing the awareness of similarities. It stimulates the sense of complete oppositeness: "You are bad, I am good." It seems likely that competition produces a stronger bias toward misperceiving the other's neutral or conciliatory actions as malevolently motivated than the bias induced by cooperation to see the other's actions as benevolently intended.

3. Attitudes toward one another

(a) A cooperative process leads to a trusting, friendly attitude and it increases the willingness to respond helpfully to the other's needs and requests.

(b) A competitive process leads to a suspicious, hostile attitude and it increases the readiness to exploit the other's needs and to respond negatively to the other's requests.

4. Task orientation

(a) A cooperative process leads to a definition of the conflicting interests as a mutual problem to be solved by collaborative effort. It facilitates the recognition of the legitimacy of each other's interests and of the necessity of searching for a solution which is responsive to the needs of each side. It tends to limit rather than expand the scope of conflicting interests. It enables the participants to approach the mutually acknowledged problem in a way which utilizes their special talents and enables them to substitute for one another in their joint work so that duplication of effort is reduced. Influence attempts tend to be limited to processes of persuasion. The enhancement of mutual power becomes an objective.

(b) A competitive process stimulates the view that the solution of the conflict can only be of the type that is imposed by one side on the other. The enhancement of one's own power and minimization of the other's power becomes an objective. It leads to a minimization of the legitimacy of the other side's interests in the situation and tends to expand the scope of the issues in conflict, so that the conflict becomes a matter of general principle rather than a confrontation confined to a particular issue at a given time and place. The expansion of the conflict increases its motivational significance to the participants and intensifies their emotional involvement in it; these, in turn, may make a limited defeat less acceptable or more humiliating than mutual disaster. Duplication of effort, so that the competitors become mirror-images of one another, is more likely than division of effort in the competitive process. Influence attempts tend to employ coercive processes.

This sketch of some aspects of competitive and cooperative processes suggests that each process tends to be self-confirming, so that the experience of cooperation will induce a benign spiral of increasing cooperation, while competition will induce a vicious spiral of intensifying competition. Indeed, this is likely to some extent, but there are restraints which usually operate to limit the spiralling of both types of processes. Not the least of these restraints arise from the fact that a person or group is usually involved in many situations and relationships simultaneously, and his other involvements and relationships usually restrain what might be termed an obsessive intensification of any particular relationship.

A Paradox?

I have now characterized the central social psychological manifestations of the cooperative and competitive approaches to the resolution of conflicting interests. I have also suggested that it may be fruitful to think of the mutually destructive consequences of conflict as resulting from a competitive process of conflict resolution, while the mutually constructive consequences emerge from the cooperative process. It is now time to turn back to our basic query, In a situation of conflict what conditions determine which process will dominate? But before I turn back to it, I must face an apparent contradiction in my presentation so far. Earlier I indicated that conflict has positive individual and social functions, and yet now I state that a competitive process of conflict resolution is likely to be destructive. There are several points to be made. First of all, conflict is not confined to competitive processes; controversy over the means to achieve a mutually desired objective is a common part of cooperation. Conflict of this sort is not competitive so long as the cooperators are motivated to select the best means to their mutual objective rather than the one which they advocated initially. There is no reason to think of this kind of conflict as not being constructive. Second, competition is not inevitably destructive to both sides. Often one side is more powerful, or more determined, or more resourceful than the other, and it may be able to impose its initially preferred solution to the conflict. It is, of course, possible that the defeat of an individual, group, or nation in a conflict may be constructive for others besides the immediate victor and occasionally it is so even for the defeated party. In my view, for example, the legislative victories of the civil rights advocates will be of ultimate value to many who have bitterly opposed equal rights. Finally, it seems reasonable to speculate that much of the pleasure of competition arises when it occurs in a cooperative encounter: when there is a cooperative interest in having a mutually enjoyable competition rather than a primary interest in defeating the other.

I turn back now to a consideration of the conditions which give rise to one rather than another process of conflict resolution. In an attempt to arrive at some broad generalizations, I shall examine conflict at several different levels: the intrapersonal, interpersonal, and intergroup.

Intrapersonal Conflict

The pervasive character of intrapsychic conflict is indicated in the distinguished roster of psychological theorists who have concerned themselves with it. A partial listing would include Freud and all the other psychoanalytically oriented theorists, as Pavlov, Lewin, Hull, Guthrie, Miller, Brown, Heider, Festinger, and the various decision-theorists. I shall not attempt to summarize the work of these various theorists but will, nevertheless, draw freely from their contributions.

If we ask what are some of the conditions which determine whether an intrapersonal conflict will be easy or difficult to resolve, research results indicate that a conflict is harder to resolve when

(a) the competing alternatives are negatively rather than positively valued (a choice between aversions or fears is more difficult to make than a choice between pleasures or desires);

(b) the competing alternatives are each internally conflicted, so that each alternative is both desired and feared more than when the alternatives are both of the same sign;

(c) the competing alternatives are strong or important rather than weak or unimportant (an intense or large conflict is more difficult to resolve than a small one);

(d) the more equal in strength and salience the competing tendencies are;

e) the more the choice of one positively valued alternative precludes the future attainment of the competing positively valued alternatives, and the less substitutable one is for the other.

These results are useful, and I believe they are applicable to the conflicts between persons as well as within persons. However, they do not shed much light on the conditions under which intrapersonal conflict has pathological or fruitful consequences.

The model underlying these results is a mechanical one of impersonal forces pushing and pulling an impersonal object which is subject to stress as a result of the opposing forces. Such a model, in essence, envisages the agents in conflict as *lifeless* rather than as active, purposeful systems that take one another into account as they engage in conflict and its resolution. (Parenthetically, let me note that my bias is to anthropomorphize, to use the images of life, in dealing with living processes rather than to physicomorphize and employ the inanimate images of physics.)

The literature dealing with psychopathology suggests that intense psychic conflict is likely to have pathological consequences when it elicits anxiety, when it is unconscious, and when the individual in conflict lacks ego strength. Let us examine each of these notions for their core meanings.

Anxiety.

The term "anxiety" is used in many different ways, but it is commonly distinguished from fear on the basis that fear comes from without while anxiety comes from within. As Sartre (1945, p. 29) has written: "A situation provokes fear if there is a possibility of my life being changed from without; my being provokes anguish to the extent that I distrust myself and my own reactions in the situation. The artillery preparation which precedes the attack can provoke fear in the soldier who undergoes bombardment but anguish is born in him when he tries to foresee the conduct with which he will face the bombardment, when he asks himself if he is going to be able to 'hold up.'" Fear, then, is an expectation of external danger of misfortune, while anxiety is an expectation of internal danger or damage to one's conception of one's self.

Psychic conflict elicits anxiety when a defeat of one or another of the competing intrapsychic tendencies would lead to a damaging change to one's self-concept. Thus, consider the conflict of a deeply religious and amorous man whose wife is sexually rejecting and whose religion strictly forbids extramarital intercourse. If he "holds up" to his religious conception of himself and fails to live up to his conception of himself as a sexually desirable male, his view of himself as a man may be impaired. On the other hand, if he conforms to his view of himself as a sexually potent male by involving himself in extramarital affairs, his conception of himself as a person of moral character may be damaged. Only if he is able to work out a solution to his conflict which preserves both images of himself—e.g., by helping his wife to change—would anxiety be avoided. But, of course, even this solution may be inconsistent with his view of himself as a victim of circumstance.

A "win-lose" intrapsychic conflict of this sort where victory for one of the conflicting tendencies implies defeat for the other not only leads to anxiety because of the anticipated damage to one's self conception but may also lead to all the usual manifestations of the competitive process of conflict resolution as one intrapsychic tendency tries to defeat the other: mutual suspicion, mutual derogation, accentuation of imcompatibility, expansion of the scope of conflict, etc. In addition, the process of intrapsychic communication may be hampered and distorted. Making the conflict unconscious is one form of such distortion of communication.

Unconscious conflict.

The notion of unconscious conflict contains within it the paradox of self-deception: the paradox of the deceiver and the deceived being the same person. This paradox is resolvable by assuming that the self is an organization with many subsystems and that although the subsystems may be able to communicate with one another, they do not necessarily have the power to inspect each other. Either or both sides to a conflict may attempt to deny the existence of the other side or to misrepresent the other side or to deny its own existence or to misrepresent itself. Thus, some women will pretend to experience no sexual pleasure during the sexual act to prove to themselves that they are only doing it as a self-sacrifice for the man's pleasure.

It is not surprising that the dialogue of non-recognition, concealment, distortion, and misrepresentation between conflicting aspects of the self may resemble the dialogue between people in an intense struggle. The internal dialogue is, as George Herbert Mead pointed out many years ago, often an internalization of the experienced relationship between oneself and a significant other. The tactics of self and other deception are both neatly catalogued in the so-called mechanisms of defense: denial, projection, repression, displacement, reaction, formation, undoing, isolation, regression, and so on. By the reaction-formation of frigidity a woman can conceal her sexual obsession from herself or from her sexual partner; by "isolation" a person can make a hostile feeling seem insignificant and accidental to himself or to another; by repression one can conceal from oneself or from another the nature of one's intentions; and so on. If the tactics of misleading communication are similar in intrapsychic and interpersonal conflicts, it seems likely that a study of such tactics in interpersonal conflict would provide useful insights into intrapsychic dynamics. For example, isn't "bluffing," which is a widely used tactic in interpersonal conflict, also a widely used mechanism of defense (or more appropriately a mechanism of offense)? Isn't, in fact, the term "mechanism of defense" too confining? Are we not dealing with mechanisms or tactics of conflict which include both "aggressive" and "defensive" forms of deception?

The connection between self-deception (or unconsciousness) and the pathology of psychic conflict resides in the likelihood that the distortions may prevent the discovery that the original conflict is no longer present and that the expected self-disapproval for certain kinds of actions or thoughts will not occur. Self-deception may also hinder the development of a cooperative conflict resolution which would permit gratification for both of the once-opposed tendencies. For example, a woman who denies her sexual interest in men to prove her respectability to herself may be unable to affirm her interest again even when it is respectable to do so because she has become committed to her denial (to express interest would be to deny her original denial).

Thus, self-deception is elicited by anxiety, a threat to a central conception of oneself. But it seems reasonable to suppose that individual vulnerability to such threats varies and, further, that anxiety does not inevitably kindle an unbridled, no-holds-barred competitive process of conflict resolution. The psychoanalysts have used the term "ego strength" to refer to both the individual's invulnerability to threats to his self-esteem and to his ability to cope with conflict-induced anxiety without resort to an inner tooth-and-nail struggle. A "strong ego" enables the individual to cope with external difficulties and serves to regulate and integrate diverse internal processes into a coordinated, cooperative system.

What are the characteristics of a "strong ego"? Erik Erikson (1964) in his paper "Human Strength and the Cycle of Generations" has given us a useful list: hope, will, purpose, competence, fidelity, love, care, and wisdom. Many other theorists have made attempts to characterize the related concept of mental health (see Jahoda, 1958). However, neither Erikson nor others have yet specified in any detail the conditions under which these virtues develop. Perhaps the safest quick generalization is that ego strength develops from experiences of a moderately high degree of success in coping with a moderately difficult and demanding environment. In other words, an individual needs the experience of coping successfully with external conflict, but he also needs the experience of coping successfully with failure. For him to have such experiences, the developing individual needs a social environment which is responsive but not enslaved by his needs, which can trust his capabilities and place realistic demands upon them, and which provides a basis for identification with effective models for coping with difficulties and conflict. I would like to stress the importance of the opportunity to learn effective techniques of conflict resolution through the observation of how conflict is actually resolved in one's social environment. It seems likely that personal styles of resolution of psychic and interpersonal conflict often reflect an internalization of the techniques of conflict resolution observed and experienced in one's social environment. I suspect that styles of conflict resolution can be cultivated systematically through special techniques of training. If this is so, it may well

be that many of the pathological consequences of conflict could be prevented through carefully planned educational efforts.

More is known about the conditions which breed ego weakness than ego strength. Such conditions include a social environment which lacks the virtues Erikson has described, massive exposure to failure and derogation, overprotection and lack of exposure to conflict and difficulty, the loss of status, the prolonged experience of internal conflict, the prolonged experience of powerlessness and helplessness, isolation and lack of contact with social reality, and fatigue, intoxication, and illness. Ego weakness, for any of these reasons, is likely to make the individual more vulnerable to threat to his self-esteem and is more likely to stimulate a competitive process of conflict resolution, self-deception, and the conditions which perpetuate the conflict.

It would be a mistake, however, to assume that only those people lacking in ego strength are vulnerable to the pathological consequences of conflict. It is well to note that there are certain kinds of conflict which have no reasonable solution and to which almost anyone entrapped in one will fall prey. Consider this horrible example from the long list of Nazi crimes. A Jewish mother is told by a Nazi guard to select which of her two children is to be killed, and if she refuses to make the choice both will be killed. There is no constructive solution to such a conflict except to outlaw it. This type of conflict involves not merely being "damned if you do and damned if you don't" but being damned by oneself. In less extreme form, this type of conflict is not uncommon in pathogenic families. Thus, a child may be confronted with the choice of believing that his perception of reality is distorted (and accepting the view of his parents) or believing that he is the child of untrustworthy parents. His choice may be limited to these alternatives by the way his parents phrase the conflict.

Bateson, (Bateson, Jackson, Haley, and Weakland, 1956 and 1964) has referred to a similar form of pathogenic conflict, the "double-bind," which he posits as underlying the genesis of schizophrenia. He indicates that this type of conflict is characterized by a primary negative injunction, a secondary negative injunction conflicting with the first (and, like the first, enforced by punishments which threaten survival), and a tertiary negative injunction prohibiting the victim from escaping the field. In addition, there are injunctions against recognizing the nature of the incongruity or of calling it to the attention of the parents in any way. A child is caught in a "double-bind" if his mother responds negatively to his affectionate gestures and yet condemns him if he is not affectionate to her as she denies her inconsistency and punishes the child for his audacity in recognizing her inconsistency.

Let me summarize this section on intrapersonal conflict in terms of some propositions which may apply to interpersonal and intergroup conflict as well as intrapersonal conflict:

1. Conflict over negatives is more difficult to resolve cooperatively than conflict over positives.

2. Conflict over large issues is more difficult to resolve cooperatively than conflict over small issues.

3. Conflict between parties that mutually perceive themselves to be equal in power and legitimacy is more difficult to resolve cooperatively than when there is a mutual recognition of differential power and legitimacy.

4. Conflict which threatens the self-esteem of the parties involved is more difficult to resolve cooperatively than conflict which does not threaten self-esteem.

5. Self-esteem is more likely to be threatened by conflict if a party to the conflict has little rather than much basis for self-confidence or if he is plagued by existing conflict or difficulty rather than successful in coping with his problems.

6. Conflict which is resolved by a more powerful tendency suppressing or repressing a weaker one often leads to more energy being employed to maintain the repression and to the return of the repressed in disguised forms.

7. Some conflicts are inherently patho-logical and can best be handled by preventing their occurrence.

Intergroup Conflict

I shall turn now to intergroup conflict. There are, of course, many different types of intergroup conflict: gang fights, religious conflict, race conflict, class conflict, industrial conflict, and so on. I shall focus on class conflict and industrial conflict, because of their interrelation, and because they seem to provide useful parallels with other forms of intergroup conflict.

Karl Marx presented one of the most fully developed theories of social conflict in his theory of class conflict. His theory, in effect, assumes that class conflict must inevitably give rise to a competitive process which will spiral into an increasing intensity of conflict until a revolutionary change occurs in the power relations of the conflicting classes. His theory posits that class conflict arises because there is a category of persons who possess effective private property (ownership of capital or the means of production) which is assumed to be the basis of power, and another category of persons who have no such property or power and who must, as a consequence, hire themselves out as wage laborers to those who own capital. The inherent conflict of interest with regard to the distribution of the fruits of production gives rise to classes, as individuals within one category engage in a common struggle against individuals from another category. As the struggle proceeds, "the whole society breaks up more and more into two great hostile camps, two great, directly antagonistic classes: bourgeoisie and proletariat." The classes polarize, so that they become internally more homogeneous and more and more sharply distinguished from one another in wealth and power. The initial power advantage of the ruling class is used to augment its power vis-à-vis the working class, leading to a progressive impoverishment of the working class and the swelling of its ranks by the impoverishment of groups (the petit bourgeoisie, the small industrialist, the farmer) that were marginal between the two classes. The increasing intensity of the conflict and class homogenization leads the enlarging oppressed proletariat to unite in effective action to overthrow the ruling minority.

The Marxian theory of class conflict seems to be a perfectly reasonable description of what might have happened if class conflict were to have followed the dynamics of a strictly competitive process of conflict resolution. But class conflict did not turn into such a process. It is of interest to consider what prevented this development and, hence, reduced the possibility of violent conflict resolution.

Marx's theory of the political and economic development of capitalist society was incorrect in several major respects (Dahrendorf, 1959). The growth of capital did not occur at labor's expense nor did it lead to its pauperization as he predicted. Rather, it helped to increase the productivity of labor, which resulted in a general improvement of living standards. Thus, gains by both sides have lessened the intensity of conflict. Second, the nature of economic and technological development in industrial society did not produce an increasing homogeneity within the so-called bourgeosie and proletariat as Marx assumed. Rather, it led to an increasing heterogeneity within each class and some blurring of class distinctions in their common roles as "consumers" and "citizens." Within the bourgeosie there is not only the distinction between owners or shareholders and managers; there are many different types of owners and managers. Moreover, the meaning of "capital" itself became more differentiated: there is ownership or control of the physical means of production, of different kinds of knowledge and expertise, of the techniques of persuasion, of the techniques of violence, and so on. Similarly, there is the development of different forms of labor, requiring different skills and training, rather than the predicted leveling of workers into an undifferentiated, unskilled uniformity. Thus, differences within and similarities between classes restrained the polarization process. Third, unlike Marx's prediction that social mobility would primarily be downwards from the bourgeosie and petit bourgeosie to the working class, social mobility has been up as well as down.

The continuous expansion of industry has required the recruitment of many workers to managerial positions. The possibility of upward mobility from class to class interfered with the development of allegiances to one's class of origin. Fourth, for reasons which are partly economic, partly educational, partly technological, and partly the outcome of struggle by various interest groups competing for the allegiances of large audiences, the status of citizenship has been endowed with a growing array of rights, and this has to some extent led to the dissociation between political power and industrial power. This has also served to reduce the polarization of conflict by enabling economic gains to be obtained through the political process rather than through direct confrontation. In addition, it has led to the institutionalization of patterns of conflict regulation which serve to limit the destructiveness of conflict when it occurs. Finally, conflict within industry has been progressively institutionalized through the development of procedures for collective bargaining, mediation, and arbitration, so that it is conducted under an increasingly wide area of shared norms by both sides to the conflict. This institutionalization not only reduces the likelihood of destructive conflict but gives them a common interest in maintaining the institutionalized system of rules for dealing with conflict.

This analysis of why class conflict did not develop into the intensely competitive process predicted by Marx's theory suggests some general propositions.

1. Any attempt to introduce a change in the existing mode of relationship between two parties is more likely to be accepted if each expects some net gain from the change than if either side expects that the other side will gain at its expense. Some such proposition underlies the approach of Gandhi and of Martin Luther King to inducing social change.

2. Conflict is more likely to be resolved by a competitive process when each of the parties in conflict are internally homogeneous but distinctly different from one another in a variety of characteristics (class, race, religion, political affiliation, group memberships) than when each is internally

heterogeneous and they have overlapping characteristics. One of the possible virtues of the American two-party system is that the heterogeneity within each party makes interparty warfare unlikely.

3. More generally, the more coincidental conflicts there are in other areas between two parties the less likely a conflict in any given area will be resolved cooperatively; the more cooperative relationships there are in other areas the less likely it is that they will resolve a conflict in any given area by a competitive process. Sherif's studies (Sherif *et al.*, 1961) of the effects of the introduction of supraordinate goals in the Robbers Cave Experiment is a good illustration.

4. A competitive process of conflict resolution is less likely the more exchange of memberships there is between the two groups.

5. The institutionalization and regulation of conflict increases the likelihood of a cooperative process of conflict resolution.

6. Conflict is more likely to be regulated effectively when the parties in conflict are each internally coherent and stable rather than disorganized or unstable.

7. Conflict is more likely to be regulated effectively when neither of the parties in conflict see the contest between them as a single contest in which defeat, if it occurs, would be total and irreversible with respect to a central value.

8. The experience or anticipation of a hopeless outcome of conflict such that nothing of value is preserved makes the effective regulation of conflict less likely.

9. Conflict is less likely to be regulated effectively if the rules for engaging in conflict are seen to be biased and are thus, themselves, the subject of conflict.

So far my discussion has centered on unregulated conflict and the conditions under which it is likely to move in the direction of a competitive process in which the outcomes are determined by a power struggle or in the direction of a cooperative process in which the outcomes are determined by joint problem-solving. However, it is evident that conflict is often regulated by institutional forms (e.g., collective bargaining, the judicial system), social roles (mediators, conciliators, referees, judges, policemen), social norms ("fairness," "justice," "equality," "nonviolence," "integrity of communication," etc.), rules for conducting negotiations (when to initiate and terminate negotiations, how to set an agenda, how to present demands, etc.), and specific procedures ("hinting" versus "explicit" communication, public versus private sessions, etc.) These societal forms may be aimed at regulating how force may be employed (as in the code of a duel of honor or in certain rules of warfare), or it may be an attempt to ascertain the basic power relations of the disputants without resort to a power struggle (as is often the case in the negotiations of collective bargaining and international relations), or it may be oriented toward removing power as the basis for determining the outcome of conflict (as is often the case in judicial processes).

With regard to regulated conflict, it is pertinent to ask what are the conditions which make it likely that the regulations will be adhered to by the parties in conflict? In a duel of honor, when would a duelist prefer to die rather than cheat? These questions, if pursued along relevant intellectual lines, would lead to an examination of different forms of rule violation and social deviance, their genesis and control. Such an investigation is beyond the scope of this essay. However, it seems reasonable to assert that adherence to the rules is more likely when the rules are known, unambiguous, consistent, and not biased; the other adheres to the rules; violations are quickly known by significant others; there is significant social approval for adherence and significant social disapproval for violation; adherence to the rules has been rewarding in the past; one would like to be able to employ the rules in the future.

It is also relevant to ask about the conditions under which the regulations will be effective. For example, under what conditions will the institution of collective bargaining between union and management result in industrial peace rather than industrial warfare? Let me quote from a monograph on the *Causes of Industrial Peace* which lists the conditions which have led to peaceful settlement of disputes under collective bargaining.

1. There is a full acceptance by management of the collective bargaining process and of unionism as an institution. The company considers a strong union an asset to management.
2. The union fully accepts private ownership and operation of the industry; it recognizes that the welfare of its members depends upon the successful operation of the business.
3. The union is strong, responsible, and democratic.
4. The company stays out of the union's internal affairs; it does not seek to alienate the workers' allegiance to their union.
5. Mutual trust and confidence exist between the parties. There have been no serious ideological incompatibilities.
6. Neither party to bargaining has adopted a legalistic approach to the solution of problems in the relationship.
7. Negotiations are "problem-centered"— more time is spent on day-to-day problems than on defining abstract principles.
8. There is widespread union-management consultation and highly developed information-sharing.
9. Grievances are settled promptly, in the local plant whenever possible. There is flexibility and informality within the procedure.

In brief, negotiations involving conflicts of interest are more likely to have acceptable outcomes for the parties involved to the extent that they take place in a context of cooperative relations between the conflicting parties. But not all negotiating processes are so benign; negotiations may deadlock and break off because of misunderstandings, faulty communications, the development of hostile attitudes, the inability to discover a mutually satisfying solution, and so on. How can a malignant process of this sort be aborted or undone? How can a third party intervene therapeutically?

If one examines the role of the mediator in industrial disputes, the role of the psychotherapist doing conjoint therapy with husbands and wives having marital problems, or the role of the human relations consultant in intergroup conflicts of various sorts, certain common functions can be identified:

1. Helping to remove the blocks and distortions in the communication process so that mutual understanding may develop. This often entails serving as a translator as well as a stimulator of communication.
2. Helping to reduce the tension between the two sides through careful listening, blunting and narrowing the issue in conflict, reducing stereotypes and black-white conceptions, finding areas of agreement, reducing the sense of threat, and so on.
3. Helping to establish norms for rational interaction such as the desirability of mutually satisfying agreement, open communication, mutual respect, use of persuasion rather than coercion.
4. Helping to determine what kinds of solutions are possible. Thus, do the aspirations of the conflicting parties have to be changed or can the problem be redefined so that the different aspirations can both be realized?
5. Helping to make a workable agreement acceptable to the parties in conflict. This may entail efforts to change the factual or value premises of one or both parties, to establish the conditions under which retreat is possible without loss of face, to help focus discussion on a likely settlement, and so on.
6. Helping to make the negotiators and the agreement which is arrived at seem prestigeful and attractive to interested audiences, especially the groups represented by the negotiators.

These are useful functions a mediator can perform to prevent strife, but how does this role get established and accepted? Elmore Jackson's (1952) survey of mediation in his book *Meeting of Minds* suggest that mediation is likely to develop when there are powerful third parties, such as a strong public, with an interest in preventing strife because of the damage it does to the community or because of the harm it does to the parties in conflict. The available evidence suggests that the mediation process is likely to be sought out or accepted willingly by parties in conflict when the process has become known as being impartial, non-coercive, the servant of the parties in conflict rather than other interested parties, and successful in preventing strife.

Interpersonal Conflict

I now turn to the experimental work by myself and my associates on interpersonal conflict. Since much of this work has been published, I shall not describe our methodology nor results in any detail. Our research has employed three different two-person games, in each of which it is possible for the players to have outcomes of mutual gain, mutual loss, or gain for one and loss for the other. The question underlying our research is the question underlying this paper, namely, what determines whether people will resolve a situation of conflict in such a way so that there is mutual gain or not.

Our first answer is a self-evident one: if people have a pre-existing cooperative orientation toward one another, they are likely to resolve a conflict of interest by a cooperative process; if they have a prior competitive orientation, they are likely to resolve it by a competitive process. An individualistic orientation will lead to one or the other process as a function of other determinants.

We have elicited the different orientations by a variety of procedures: (1) by the normative definitions of the situation that we have induced, (2) by the pay-off structures we have used, (3) by the beliefs about the other we have induced, and (4) by selecting people with given personality characteristics. We have also helped mold the course of interaction between players who were induced to have an initial individualistic orientation by (5) the size of the problem confronting them, (6) the threat capabilities with which they were provided, (7) by the communication facilities and training they were given, (8) by the inspection procedures they were allowed, and (9) by the behavioral strategies they were exposed to from accomplices of the experimenter.

Normative Definitions.

In our first experimental work with the Prisoners Dilemma game many years ago (Deutsch, 1958, 1960) we induced different motivational orientations by employing the prestige of the experimenter to define for the subjects what the appropriate relationship would be for them to have with one another. A *cooperative relationship* was induced by defining the other player as a partner and by characterizing each player's objective as "You want to win as much money as you can for yourself . . . and you also want your partner to win too." An *individualistic orientation* was elicited by instructions which stressed mutual indifference to one another's fate as one pursued one's own objective: "You're not out to help him and you're not out to beat him. You simply want to win as much money as you can for yourself and you don't care what happens to him." A *competitive orientation* was produced by statements such as, "Your motivation should be to win as much money as you can for yourself and to do better than the other person. You want to make rather than lose money but you also want to come out ahead of the other person."

The results of this experiment are clear-cut. The mutually cooperative orientation elicited highly predictable trusting and trustworthy behavior and honest communication (when communication was permitted) which resulted in mutual gain; the mutually competitive orientation led to suspicious and exploitative behavior and no communication or hostile or misleading communication (when communication was allowed) which resulted in mutual loss; the individualistic orientation generally led to results that were more or less similar to the competitive orientation depending upon the adequacy of interpersonal communication.

In the summer of 1965 we had adolescents from New York City high schools play the game of "chicken" in our laboratory. We have adapted our Acme-Bolt trucking game (Deutsch and Krauss, 1960, 1962) to this purpose. In our laboratory game of chicken each of the two players are paid a certain fee for taking his truck from a starting point to a destination minus the cost of the trip, which is a function of how long the trip takes. Both players must use the same road, but they go in opposite directions and a large section of the road is only one lane in width. The players can see the position of both trucks at all times. Each player can lock his truck into forward gear, if he so chooses, so that he can no longer stop or reverse his truck. That is, he can commit himself irreversibly to going forward. If he does so, his commitment is immediately made known to the other subject by a signalling device. If the trucks collide on the one lane section, the trial is over and each player is penalized the number of cents which is equal to the time spent since the beginning of the trial. The subjects play the game for 20 trials.

In an experiment that we have recently completed (Deutsch and Lewicki, in preparation) the subjects played the game under either of two instructions: "chicken" instructions or "problem-solving" instructions. The "chicken" instructions identified the game as a game of "chicken," and the subjects were told that it separates people into two groups, "those who give in under pressure and those who do not." The "problem-solving" instructions identified the game as involving "social problem-solving," and the subjects were told that it separates people into two groups, "those who can arrive at a solution to a problem that will bring maximum benefits to both of the players, and those who cannot work out this solution." In both conditions the subjects were told that "it's important for you to earn as much money as you can and to lose as little as possible in the game." The subjects played for real money, in amounts which were not insignificant to them.

The results are striking. The "chicken" instructions resulted in substantial mutual loss for nine of ten pairs. The modal pair had somewhat more than ten collisions during the twenty trials. In contrast, the "problem-solving" instructions resulted in substantial mutual gain for all but three pairs, with the modal pair having less than four collisions during the twenty trials. I have no doubt that we could intensify our in-

structions and produce even more marked differences.

The results of these experiments are clear: either a cooperative, problem-solving orientation or a competitive struggle to conflict resolution can be elicited by the normative context within which the conflict is placed by the experimenter. We have not investigated the normative assumptions about conflict resolution which people bring with them to the laboratory. However, although there is a bias toward a competitive orientation in games, it seems likely that there are cultural variations which may incline some people to define a game of chicken as a conflict and others as a mutual problem.

Pay-off Structure.

Robert Krauss (in press) has employed the Acme-Bolt trucking game to show that the pay-off structure of the game can lead to a cooperative process of conflict resolution. When, for example, subjects know that they will benefit economically if the other profits and suffer if the other has losses, they are more likely to develop a cooperative orientation than if they benefit from the other's losses and suffer if the other gains. His study has shown that a cooperative reward structure as compared with a competitive one produces less use of threat and aggression, more friendly attitudes, and more mutual gain. Similar results have been obtained in a study by Hornstein and myself (Hornstein and Deutsch, 1967) using a different experimental game, called the "allocation game." In this game subjects could allocate their effort among the production of three products: an individualistic product which was worth a certain amount no matter what the other player did, a cooperative product which was worth a small amount if the other player did not produce a matching product and a considerable larger amount if the other player did, and a competitive product which could be used to attack the other player and to obtain a certain amount of money from him. In this experiment we studied the effects of having or not having the cooperative alternative available, the effects of variations in the relative strengths of the incentives for engaging in the different kinds of behavior, and the effect of different inspection procedures for obtaining information about the activities of the other person. There are many fascinating results to this study, but I shall limit myself to those that are relevant at this point.

First, it is evident that the availability of a means of cooperating not only permits cooperation but also reduces the likelihood of competition. Moreover, our results indicate that the availability of a means of cooperation reduces competitive behavior disproportionately more than individualistic behavior. The results also indicate that the pay-off values associated with the various forms of behavior very much influence the likelihood of this selection: when a relatively low pay-off is associated with competitive behavior, it is less likely to be selected. The kind of behavior which is selected, however, is associated with other actions such as an attack or the use of inspection procedures. Relatively high pay-offs for cooperative behavior stimulate both cooperative behavior and the use of inspection procedures that verifies and supports further cooperative behavior; relatively high pay-offs for competitive behavior stimulate competitive behavior and attack which verifies and supports further competitive behavior.

The Induction of Perceived Similarity.

In my discussion of the symptoms of cooperative and competitive processes I pointed out that a distinguishing symptom is that cooperation leads to an accentuated perception of similarity in values among cooperators, while competition leads to an emphasis on differences and oppositeness. It seems likely that the causal arrow can lead from the perception of similarity or dissimilarity to a cooperative or competitive process as well as *vice versa*. Krauss (in press), in the experiment to which I referred previously, has demonstrated this to be the case. He had his subjects fill out an opinion inventory dealing with basic moral and political values, and then he gave them the inventory presumably filled out by the other person with whom they were to play the Acme-Bolt game. However, they actually received an inventory filled out by

the experimenter which was very similar or dissimilar to the opinions the subject had expressed. It is evident that perceived similarity was more likely to evoke a cooperative process and perceived dissimilarity more likely to evoke a competitive process of conflict resolution.

In a somewhat different context, one of my former co-workers, James Farr, demonstrated that in the Prisoner's Dilemma game two subjects were more likely to cooperate if they both had developed negative relations with a third person (a stooge who had been trained to be obnoxious). This was especially so if the disliked person could profit from the losses of either of the two players (see Deutsch, 1958). Joseph Margolin, a former student, has done a somewhat related study (see Deutsch, 1958), which indicates that a subject is likely to develop cooperative or competitive relations with another person depending upon whether or not this person has the same or opposite relationship with a third person that the subject has with that person. Thus, if the subject is in a competitive or negative relationship with Person "A" and he sees that Person "B" is in a competitive or negative relationship with "A," the subject is likely to develop a cooperative relationship with "B."

Personality Characteristics.

In various of our studies we have found small but significant correlations between personality variables and the game playing behavior of the subjects. And like several other investigators, we have found that women are often more competitive than men. However, we have not systematically paired people with given personality characteristics in such a way as to develop any real understanding of what kinds of personality pairing are likely to lead to one or another process of conflict resolution.

In passing, I might note that Ravich, a psychiatrist, Bert Brown and myself (Ravich, Deutsch and Brown, 1965) have been investigating different forms of pathological conflict resolution processes in married couples. Married couples, who are in psychotherapy with Dr. Ravich, have been playing our Acme-Bolt bargaining game. Our experience with about 50 couples suggests that the stereotyped processes of dealing with conflict that characterize these troubled couples is reflected in the way they handle the conflict situation of the bargaining game. The various details of the game process—whether or not they arrive at a profitable solution, how soon they arrive at it, who proposes it, how equally rewards are distributed, how the distribution is determined, how stable is the solution, who yields when there is a need to back up, and so forth—seem to reflect their characteristic ways of dealing with marital conflict. Not only is the game of potential diagnostic value but it seems to have the therapeutic value of objectifying the process of conflict in such a way that many of the couples are enabled to view their daily conflicts in terms which have similar meaning because they are based on a similar imagery.

In the preceding pages I have discussed some of the determinants of whether a cooperative or competitive orientation to conflict resolution will develop. Now I shift focus slightly and consider what determines the course of interaction in a conflict situation between people who are individualistically oriented. I consider such factors as problem size, threat capabilities, communication facilities and skills, inspection procedures, and behavioral strategies.

Problem Size.

Roger Fisher (Fisher, 1964) in a brilliant paper entitled "Fractionating Conflict" has pointed out that "issue control" may be as important as "arms control" in the management of conflict. His thesis is the familiar thesis that small conflicts are easier to resolve than large ones. However, he also points out that the participants may have a choice in defining the conflict as a large one or small one. Conflict is enlarged by dealing with it as a conflict between large units rather than small units (e.g., as a conflict between two individuals of different races or as a racial conflict), as a conflict over a substantive issue rather than a small one (e.g., over "being treated fairly" or "being treated unfairly on a particular occasion"), as a conflict over a principle rather than the application of a principle, as a conflict whose solution establishes large rather than small substantive or procedural precedents.

We (Deutsch, Canavan, and Brown, in preparation) have conducted a simple test of the proposition that small-sized conflicts are easier to resolve than large-sized conflicts. In the Acme-Bolt trucking game it is possible to vary the length of the one-lane path. As one increases the length of the one-lane path, the size of the conflict between the players increases; it becomes more of a handicap to wait and let the other player go through first. We ran an experiment in which the size of the one-lane section of the 20-unit main path was set so as to be either 4 units, 10 units, or 18 units long. The results support the proposition quite strongly. The players in the "4-unit" conflict resolve their conflict with less deadlock and struggle, with less use of threat, and with greater mutual gain than do the players in the "10-unit" conflict; the players in the "10-unit" conflict are, in turn, more efficacious than those in the "18-unit" conflict. There is, however, considerable more variability in the outcomes of different pairs in the largest-sized conflict than in the two smaller ones. (I note that my statements of comparisons are based on the adjusted data which correct for the relative time advantages of the players in the smaller-sized conflicts.)

Threat Capabilities.

Some of our experiments have been concerned with the effects of threat upon conflict resolution. There are many different questions that can be asked about threat: How does the likelihood that threats will be made vary with the absolute and relative threatening power of the parties in conflict? With the kind of relationship between the parties? What determines the comprehensibility and credibility of a threat and one's willingness to carry it through? Under what conditions will a threat be effective in controlling the behavior of the other, under what conditions will it increase conflict, under what conditions will it be irrelevant? And so on. Our research has dealt with only a very limited aspect of these questions.

In one set of experiments (Deutsch and Krauss, 1960 and 1962) we were concerned with the effects of giving the subjects an instrument that each could use at his own initiative in an attempt to intimidate the other. We made two basic assumptions. First, since the instrument was, so to speak, a low-calibre weapon, it was likely to be used during the course of conflict (if the subjects were not cooperatively oriented to one another). Second, its use would make the conflict more difficult to resolve cooperatively because it would enhance the competitive interests of the players by introducing a contest over the right to intimidate that would turn the conflict into a competitive struggle for self-esteem. The results of our experiments are consistent with these assumptions: the subjects did use the weapons if they were available, and their use made it more difficult for them to work out a cooperative solution to the conflict of interest confronting them.

An experiment by Hornstein (1965), using a different game and a different type of threat, suggests that an available threat is less likely to be used when subjects are equal in threat-power and their threat-power is either very high or very low than if their threat-power is equal but of middling intensity. His results help to qualify our findings and suggest that the threats employed in the Deutsch-Krauss experiments were of significant but not of devastating intensity. They also quite strongly indicate that the use of threat does hamper the development of cooperative agreement.

Communication Facilities and Training.

In a number of experiments, with both the Prisoners Dilemma game (Deutsch 1958 and 1960; Loomis, 1959) and the Acme-Bolt game (Deutsch and Krauss, 1962; Krauss and Deutsch, 1966), we have studied the effects of having or not having communication facilities. A consistent finding is that cooperatively oriented pairs of subjects don't need such facilities to work out effective agreements in such simple games and competitively oriented subjects cannot use them effectively or with honest intent. It is also apparent that while individualistically oriented subjects may benefit from the opportunity to communicate with one another, many do not know how to use

the opportunity effectively. They often restrict themselves to communicating their desire or their intent, without indicating the complementing relationship between the behavior one desires from the other and the behavior one intends toward the other.

Loomis (1959), using the Prisoners Dilemma game, has demonstrated that a communication is likely to be effective in inducing cooperation the more completely it contains all of the following basic elements: (1) a statement of expected behavior from the other, (2) a statement of intended behavior toward the other, (3) a statement of the sanctions that will be employed if one's cooperative expectations are violated, and (4) a statement of the conditions under which the other can return to "grace" after having violated cooperative expectations.

Krauss and Deutsch (in press) have similarly shown that subjects who are tutored by the experimenter to make fair proposals ("a proposal which is reasonable and acceptable both to yourself and to the other person . . . which is both fair to yourself and which you would be willing to accept if you were in her shoes") are more able to overcome the deleterious effects of possessing weapons than those who are not indoctrinated into this social norm of "fairness" or "equity" as a basis for communication. It is of interest to note that both untutored and tutored communication seemed to be utilized more effectively by the subjects if it were allowed only after they had experienced a series of deadlocked trials than if communication were initiated prior to the experience of deadlock. The experience of deadlock appeared to serve as an incentive to use the communication opportunity effectively. However, it seems clear that drawing the lessons of experience explicitly helped the subjects to use them more aptly.

The Effects of Inspection Procedures.

Hornstein and I (Hornstein and Deutsch, 1967) recently finished a study in which we studied the effects of different inspection procedures upon the development of cooperation in the allocation game. We compared "no inspection" with "periodic mandatory inspection" (which was made by the experimenter and announced to both players), "voluntary-symmetric inspection" (which could be initiated by either player for a small cost at any time), and "voluntary-asymmetric inspection" (which could be initiated by only one of the players). The inspector in all instances was the experimenter, and he gave precise and reliable information. Our hypothesis was that inspection would facilitate cooperation and inhibit competition because it would enable the players to reveal to one another their cooperative efforts and prevent them from concealing their competitive efforts. The results support the hypothesis. There was most competition, least cooperation, and the smallest joint pay-off in the "no inspection" condition. Also, it is evident that as the relative economic value of competitive activity increased, the requests for inspections decreased. The differences among the different forms of inspection are small and yield to no simple explanation.

The Effects of Different Behavior Strategies.

Leonard Solomon (1960), in his doctoral dissertation, studied the effects upon the subject's behavior in the Prisoners Dilemma of three different behavioral strategies followed by the other subject who was serving as an accomplice of the experimenter: (1) an *unconditionally benevolent* strategy which required the accomplice to choose cooperatively no matter what the naive subject did, (2) a *conditionally benevolent* strategy which required the accomplice to match the subject's behavior, and (3) an *unconditionally malevolent* strategy which required the accomplice to make a competitive choice no matter what the subject did. Solomon's results indicated that the conditionally benevolent strategy produced most cooperation and most favorable attitudes toward the accomplice, while neither the unconditionally benevolent nor unconditionally malevolent strategy induced much cooperation.

Recently, we used an extended form of the allocation game in which the subjects could on each trial engage in individualistic, cooperative, or altruistic behavior or they could produce aggressive weapons or defensive weapons, or they could attack or disarm. The behavior of the subjects was announced to one another after each trial. The game was played for sixty trials. We (Deutsch, Epstein, and Canavan, in preparation) used this game to study the effects of a number of different behavioral strategies: (1) *Turn the other cheek*. The accomplice made a cooperative move on the first trial, an altruistic move on the second trial, and cooperative moves thereafter except that he would respond to attacks or threats by altruistic moves. (2) *Reactive defensiveness*. The accomplice made cooperative moves on the first three trials and reciprocated the subject's behavior thereafter except that he responded self-protectively rather than with counterthreats or counterattacks when the subject threatened or attacked. He also responded with cooperative moves if the other behaved defensively or disarmed. (3) *Reactive hostility*. The accomplice made a cooperative move on the first trial and thereafter responded threateningly to any noncooperative move and cooperatively to any cooperative or altruistic or disarm move. He counterattacked when attacked. (4) *Reformed sinner*. During the first 15 trials the accomplice threatened or attacked on every trial; on the sixteenth trial he disarmed. Thereafter he followed consistently a "turn the other cheek" strategy or a "reactive defensiveness" strategy.

Over a period of sixty trials the results comparing the first three strategies indicate that the reactive hostility strategy produces the lowest joint outcomes for both the subject and the accomplice; the reactive defensive strategy leads to the highest joint outcomes and the highest outcome for the accomplice; "turn the other cheek" yields the highest outcome for the subject. There is a sizeable discrepancy between the outcomes of the subject and the accomplice only in the "turn the other cheek" strategy condition.

It is of interest to note that the "turn the other cheek" strategy is considerably more effective if one has initially been a sinner. Shortly after his saintly transformation to "turn the other cheek," the accomplice does better, the joint outcomes are better, and the discrepancy in outcome between the subject and the accomplice is reduced as compared with the condition where the accomplice is a saint from start to finish. On the other hand, the sinner who reforms and adopts a reactive defensive strategy does not do as well as the other type of reformer nor does he do as well as the accomplice who follows a reactive defensive strategy all the way through.

These results suggest several conclusions: neither a punitive nor a rewarding response to noncooperative behavior is most effective in eliciting mutually rewarding cooperation. The latter leads to exploitation unless it has been preceded by a convincing display of aggressive potential. The former makes it difficult to perceive one's cooperative intention as one is engaging in threatening and aggressive behavior to deter noncooperation. On the other hand, a strategy which does not reciprocate hostility but nevertheless does not allow it to be rewarding seems to be effective in eliciting cooperative behavior so long as it is also generously responsive to the other's cooperative behavior.

These results bear tangentially on a problem which I have ignored so far in this essay: the problem of assymmetry in orientation between two parties in conflict. Suppose one person has a cooperative orientation and the other a competitive orientation to conflict resolution? It seems evident from our results and the results of other investigators (Solomon, 1960; Shure and Meeker, 1964) that a naive and blind goodwill, which leads to an inflexible benevolence on the part of the cooperatively oriented party, will often lead to exploitation by the competitively oriented and will encourage the continuation of such exploitation. It is also apparent that a punitive strategy of reactive hostility is not effective.

But what do you do if you want to induce a competitor or even an enemy to cooperate? Elsewhere (Deutsch, 1964) I have outlined a strategy for producing change in an adversary. This strategy is similar to the strategy of reactive defensiveness which was so effective in inducing cooperation among our subjects. Its key notions are "firmness" and "friendliness": a firm resistance to efforts by the other to exploit and to gain an unwarranted competitive victory combined with a continuing, friendly, and generous willingness to cooperate to obtain mutual gain.

Conclusions and Implications

I started this essay with the assumption not only that one could speak in the same terms about conflict at different levels—intrapsychic, interpersonal, intergroup, and international—but that it is useful to do so. My hunch was that one could obtain some insights into intrapsychic conflict by studying interpersonal conflict, that the understanding of international conflict would be fostered by an examination of intergroup conflict, and so on. This hunch, which grew out of extensive readings in the different disciplines dealing with the various forms of conflict, assumes that there are some general principles which can be used to characterize conflict and the processes of conflict resolution which are applicable in a wide variety of contexts.

In the course of my discussion of different types of conflict I have attempted to list some general propositions relating to the restricted query of this essay, namely, what are the determinants which lead to a cooperative rather than competitive process of conflict resolution? It is well to recognize that my query has been restricted and that I have not dealt with many important aspects of conflict, especially the strategy and tactics of waging conflict. My concern has been with the conditions leading to mutual agreement and mutual satisfaction rather than with the conditions leading to one-sided victory.

My major points may be summarized as follows:

1. There are two major types of conflict resolution processes: cooperative and competitive. Although neither type is found in its pure form, without the presence of the other, one type or another will usually predominate and will give rise to characteristic manifestations in communication, attitudes, perception, task orientation, and outcomes. Each process tends to be self-confirming and self-perpetuating, so that each tends to persist despite a change in its originating conditions. This is so because the communi-

cation patterns, attitudes, perception, task orientation, and outcomes which are evoked by a given process tend to elicit the very same process which evokes them. Hence, one way of eliciting a cooperative process is to attempt to induce the communication patterns, attitudes, and so forth which help to support such a process.

2. There are several major, interrelated types of factors which help to determine which type of conflict resolution process will dominate:

(a) The size (scope, importance, centrality, etc.) and rigidity of the issue in conflict: the greater the size and rigidity the more difficult it will be to resolve cooperatively. Many determinants of conflict size could be listed. For example, an issue which bears upon self-esteem or change in power or status is likely to be more important than an issue which does not. Illegitimate threats or attempts to coerce are likely to increase the size of the conflict. Similarly, some determinants of issue rigidity can be identified. Thus, an issue is more rigid if it permits no substitute satisfactions and there is only enough for one party. "Victory over the other" is a rigid issue.

(b) The relative strength and salience of the existing cooperative and competitive links between the conflicting parties: the stronger and more salient the cooperative bonds are, the less likely it is that they will engage in a competitive process. The total strength of the cooperative bonds would be a function of the number of bonds and the strength or importance of each bond. There are obviously many different types of bonds that could be enumerated: superordinate goals, mutually facilitating interests, common allegiances and values, linkage to a common community, and so on.

It is evident that the size of conflict and relative strength of cooperative bonds must be considered jointly in making predictions. Conflict is likely to be resolved cooperatively in situations where the parties have less at stake in a conflict than they have in the ongoing relationship between them or in the community which has generated rules and procedures for regulating conflict.

(c) The expectation that the outcome of one process or another will be more un-

satisfactory or less valuable than the other. Many factors influencing such an expectation could be listed: the prior experience of success and failure with the two processes, the relative power of the parties involved, the skills the parties have in each of the two processes, and so on.

(d) The internal cohesiveness of each of the parties in conflict: cooperative conflict resolution is less likely when either of the parties is characterized by internal dissension or factionalism. Internal conflict may stimulate external conflict as a tactic to increase cohesiveness, or it may lead to an instability that makes it difficult to work out a durable agreement, or it may tempt the other side to take advantage of internal weakness.

(e) The attitudes, strength, and resources of interested and relevant third parties. For example, a conflict is more likely to be resolved cooperatively if powerful, prestigeful third parties encourage such a resolution and help to provide resources (institutions, facilities, personnel, social norms, and procedures) to expedite discovery of a mutually satisfactory solution.

Implications

Are there any implications in any of this for the acute problems of conflict that confront us in South Vietnam, race relations, and the revolutionary struggles throughout the underdeveloped areas? I think it is obvious that there are many, and in previous papers (Deutsch 1962, 1965) I have enumerated some. I shall not attempt to enumerate them here.

Instead let me comment that many of the intense conflicts are between those groups who have possession of authority and the conventional means of social and political influence and those groups who are excluded from such authority and influence. These are the kinds of conflicts which a Marxian might identify as having many of the dynamics of class struggles. However, as the failure of Marx's prediction suggests, it is not inevitable that such conflict be destructive. Class conflict, as our earlier analysis indicated, took a benign form because there was substantial improvement in the standard of living rather than an impoverishment of those lacking in power; the development of a relatively open society with the possibility of considerable upward mobility for those born in lower status families; there was a sharing of effective power as the status of citizen became endowed with more and more rights; there was increasing differentiation rather than homogenization within groups as a complex economy required more varied skills; there was the development of institutions, social norms, and procedures to restrain the use of arbitrary power and to regulate conflict.

May it not be possible for a change from the malignant to benign processes of conflict resolution to occur if those groups who have authority and conventional power learn the lessions implicit in the failure of Marx's predictions? Particularly, if they learn to realize that power and prosperity are like information in some respects: it does not necessarily get lost by being given to those who lack it. I emphasize this point because to me the critical issue in South Vietnam, in racial conflict, and in revolutionary struggles relates to how the groups in power can share some of their power and prosperity with those groups who have been excluded from power without experiencing a vital loss or a humiliation. Related questions are how groups that have been excluded from power can learn to prevent the abuse and misuse of power as they obtain access to it and how can they learn to resist the temptation to humiliate and obtain revenge upon those who in the past excluded them from power.

Let me briefly consider the situation in South Vietnam. It is a civil war in which the opposing sides are each receiving substantial military and other assistance from other governments. North Vietnam is aiding the Vietcong, a group that unofficially governs about two-thirds of the country, and the United States is aiding the official government of South Vietnam. Our aid seems to be of more massive proportions. There is reason to suspect that both sides in the civil war have become so beholden to their foreign sponsors that neither could function effectively in the war without the assistance of their sponsors. It is generally recognized that the official government of South Vietnam would soon collapse without American support; there is some dispute as to whether the Vietcong would similarly collapse without the support of North Vietnam.

The United States has actively been seeking to obtain a negotiated solution of the conflict and has put forth some proposals for negotiation. North Vietnam has also stated a four-point formula for peace but, for reasons which are not clear, is not apparently eager for negotiations. To persuade North Vietnam that negotiations would be more desirable than continued war, we began to harass North Vietnam with bombing raids and we increased our military involvement in the war in the hope of convincing them that they could not obtain their objectives by force.

Our proposals for negotiations and the North Vietnam peace-formula are similar except in one crucial respect. We want the government we sponsor in South Vietnam to be considered the legitimate power in South Vietnam and we wish to define the Vietcong purely as North Vietnam; North Vietnam would like the National Liberation Front to be considered as the legitimate power in South Vietnam, and the government we sponsor as our agent. How do we get out of such an impasse? It seems to me that we have to recognize that the Vietcong cannot be excluded from participation in legitimated power and authority in South Vietnam no more than it would be sensible to exclude other groups from such power.

Our resistance to adopting such a view seems to lie in the fear of some vital loss of power. Our reasoning appears to be: if the Vietcong is recognized as a legitimate participant in power, South Vietnam will soon have a Communist-dominated government; if this happens it will fall under the control of North Vietnam; this will lead to Communist control of Southeast Asia; which, in turn, would threaten the independence of the Philippines and Australia; and so on. Implicitly, we have defined the conflict in the widest terms, so that anything that benefits the other side will be seen as a major setback to our interests. Yet this need not be the case. France gained rather than lost when Algeria gained its independence. Similarly, we might gain if we recognized that a strong, independent government in South Vietnam will require the support of the Vietcong and that close relations between North and South Vietnam may be to our interest.

However, I think it is difficult enough to recognize a gain in what is often considered to be a defeat, but it takes extraordinary courage and wisdom to do so when the other party to the conflict is attempting to deny any mutual interests and is intent on inflicting a humiliation. This appears to be the intent of the Vietcong and North Vietnam. If indeed this is their intent, we shall need extraordinary wisdom to allow ourselves to ask how such an intent could have been developed and what can we do to change the assumptions underlying it. And we shall need extraordinary courage to disregard such an intent and to act responsibly in terms of the interests of the Vietnamese people, our own interests, and the interests of preventing World War III.

BIBLIOGRAPHY

Bateson, G., Jackson, D., Haley, J., and Weakland, J. Toward a theory of schizophrenia. *Behavioral Science*, 1956, *1*, 251–264.

Bateson, G., Jackson, D., Haley, J., and Weakland, J. A note on the double bind. *Family Process*, 1963, *2*, 34–51.

Dahrendorf, R. *Class and class conflict in industrial society*. Stanford: Stanford University Press, 1959.

Deutsch, M. A theory of cooperation and competition. *Human Relations*, 1949, *2*, 129–151. (a)

Deutsch, M. An experimental study of the effects of cooperation and competition upon group process. *Human Relations*, 1949, *2*, 199–231. (b)

Deutsch, M. Trust and suspicion, *Journal of Conflict Resolution*, 1958, *2*, 265–279.

Deutsch, M. The effect of motivational orientation upon trust and suspicion. *Human Relations*, 1960, *13*, 123–139.

Deutsch, M. Cooperation and trust: Some theoretical notes. In M. R. Jones (ed.), *Nebraska Symposium on Motivation*. Lincoln, Nebraska: University of Nebraska Press, 1962, 275–320.

Deutsch, M. Producing change in an adversary. In R. Fisher (ed.), *International Conflict and Behavioral Science: The Craigville Papers*. New York: Basic Books, 1964.

Deutsch, M. A psychological approach to international conflict. In G. Sperrazzo (ed.), *Psychology and International Relations*. Washington, D.C.: Georgetown University Press. 1965, 1–20.

Deutsch, M., Canavan, D. M., and Brown, B. The effect of problem-size upon bargaining. In preparation.

Deutsch, M. and Krauss, R. M. The effects of threat upon interpersonal bargaining. *Journal of Abnormal and Social Psychology*, 1960, *61*, 181–189.

Deutsch, M. and Krauss, R. M. Studies of interpersonal bargaining. *Journal of Conflict Resolution*, 1962, *6*, 52–76.

Deutsch, M. and Lewicki, R. J. The game of "chicken": some experimental studies. In preparation.

Erickson, E. H. *Insight and responsibility*. New York: W. W. Norton, 1964.

Fisher, R. Fractionating conflict. In R. Fisher (ed.), *International Conflict and Behavioral Science: The Craigville Papers*. New York: Basic Books, 1964, 91–110.

Hornstein, H. A. The effects of different magnitudes of threat upon interpersonal bargaining. *Journal of Experimental Social Psychology*, 1965, *1*, 282–293.

Hornstein, H. and Deutsch, M. The tendencies to compete and to attack as a function of inspection, incentive and available alternatives. *Journal of Personal Social Psychology*, 1967, 5: 311–318.

Jackson, E. *Meetings of Minds*. New York: McGraw-Hill, 1952.

Jahoda, M. *Current Concepts of Positive Mental Health: A Report to the Staff Director Jack R. Ewalt*, 1958. New York: Basic Books, 1958.

Krauss, R. M. and Deutsch, M. Communication in interpersonal bargaining. In Press. *J. Pers. Soc. Psychol.*

Krauss, R. M. Structural and attitudinal factors in interpersonal bargaining. In press.

Loomis, J. L. Communication and the development of trust. *Human Relations*, 1959, *12*, 305-315.

Marx, K. *Capital, the Communist Manifesto and other Writings*. M. Eastman (ed.). New York: The Modern Library, 1932.

National Planning Association. *Causes of Industrial Peace Under Collective Bargaining*. Washington, D.C.: National Planning Association, 1953.

Ravich, R., Deutsch, M., and Brown, B. An Experimental Study of Decision-Making and Marital Discord. Paper delivered, February, 1965, Meeting of Association for Research in Psychiatry.

Sartre, J.-P. *Being and Nothingness: An Essay on Phenomenological Ontology*. New York: Philosophical Library, 1956, p. 29.

Sherif, M. *Intergroup Conflict and Cooperation: the Robbers Cave Experiment*. Norman, Oklahoma: University Book Exchange, 1961.

Shure, G. H. and Meeker, R. J. *The Effectiveness of Pacifist Strategies in Bargaining Games*. Paper read at American Psychological Association, Los Angeles, August, 1964.

Solomon, L. The influence of some types of power relationships and game strategies upon the development of interpersonal trust. *Journal of Abnormal and Social Psychology*, 1960, *61*, 223–230.

SOCIAL CONFLICT AND THE THEORY OF SOCIAL CHANGE*

LEWIS A. COSER

This paper attempts to examine some of the functions of social conflict in the process of social change. I shall first deal with some functions of conflict *within* social systems, more specifically with its relation to institutional rigidities, technical progress and productivity, and will then concern ourselves with the relation between social conflict and the changes *of* social systems.

A central observation of George Sorel in his *Reflections on Violence* which has not as yet been accorded sufficient attention by sociologists may serve us as a convenient springboard. Sorel wrote:

We are today faced with a new and unforeseen fact—a middle class which seeks to weaken its own strength. The race of bold captains who made the greatness of modern industry disappears to make way for an ultracivilized aristocracy which asks to be allowed to live in peace.

The threatening decadence may be avoided if the proletariat hold on with obstinacy to revolutionary ideas. *The antagonistic classes influence each other in a partly indirect but decisive manner.* Everything may be saved if the proletariat, by their use of violence, restore to the middle class something of its former energy.[1]

Sorel's specific doctrine of class struggle is not of immediate concern here. What is important for us is the idea that conflict (which Sorel calls violence, using the word in a very special sense) prevents the ossification of the social system by exerting pressure for innovation and creativity. Though Sorel's call to action was addressed to the working class and its interests, he conceived it to be of general importance for the total social system; to his mind the gradual disappearance of class conflict might well lead to the decadence of European culture. A social system, he felt, was in need of con-

flict if only to renew its energies and revitalize its creative forces.

This conception seems to be more generally applicable than to class struggle alone. Conflict within and between groups in a society can prevent accommodations and habitual relations from progressively impoverishing creativity. The clash of values and interests, the tension between what is and what some groups feel ought to be, the conflict between vested interests and new strata and groups demanding their share of power, wealth and status, have been productive of vitality; note for example the contrast between the 'frozen world' of the Middle Ages and the burst of creativity that accompanied the thaw that set in with Renaissance civilization.

This is, in effect, the application of John Dewey's theory of consciousness and thought as arising in the wake of obstacles to the interaction of groups. 'Conflict is the gadfly of thought. It stirs us to observation and memory. It instigates to invention. It shocks us out of sheeplike passivity, and sets us at noting and contriving . . . . Conflict is a *sine qua non* of reflection and ingenuity.'[2]

Conflict not only generates new norms, new institutions, as I have pointed out elsewhere,[3] it may be said to be stimulating directly in the economic and technological realm. Economic historians often have pointed out that much technological improvement has resulted from the conflict activity of trade unions through the raising of wage levels. A rise in wages usually has led to a substitution of capital investment for labour and hence to an increase in the volume of investment. Thus the extreme mechanization of coal-mining in the United

---

* Reprinted by permission of the author and publisher from *The British Journal of Sociology*, 1957, 8: 197–207.

[1] George Sorel, *Reflections on Violence*, ch. 2, par. 11.

[2] John Dewey, *Human Nature and Conduct*, N.Y., The Modern Library, 1930, p. 300.

[3] Lewis A. Coser, *The Functions of Social Conflict*, Glencoe, Ill.; London, Routledge and Kegan Paul, 1956.

States has been partly explained by the existence of militant unionism in the American coalfields.[4] A recent investigation by Sidney C. Sufrin[5] points to the effects of union pressure, 'goading management into technical improvement and increased capital investment'. Very much the same point was made recently by the conservative British *Economist* which reproached British unions for their 'moderation' which it declared in part responsible for the stagnation and low productivity of British capitalism; it compared their policy unfavourably with the more aggressive policies of American unions whose constant pressure for higher wages has kept the American economy dynamic.[6]

This point raises the question of the adequacy and relevancy of the 'human relations' approach in industrial research and management practice. The 'human relations' approach stresses the 'collective purpose of the total organization' of the factory, and either denies or attempts to reduce conflicts of interests in industry.[7] But a successful reduction of industrial conflict may have unanticipated dysfunctional consequences for it may destroy an important stimulus for technological innovation.

It often has been observed that the effects of technological change have weighed most heavily upon the worker.[8] Both informal and formal organization of workers represent in part an attempt to mitigate the

insecurities attendant upon the impact of unpredictable introduction of change in the factory.[9] But by organizing in unions workers gain a feeling of security through the effective conduct of institutionalized conflict with management and thus exert pressure on management to increase their returns by the invention of further cost-reducing devices. The search for mutual adjustment, understanding and 'unity' between groups who find themselves in different life situations and have different life chances calls forth the danger that Sorel warns of, namely that the further development of technology would be seriously impaired.

The emergence of invention and of technological change in modern Western society, with its institutionalization of science as an instrument for making and remaking the world, was made possible with the gradual emergence of a pluralistic and hence conflict-charged structure of human relations. In the unitary order of the medieval guild system, 'no one was permitted to harm others by methods which enabled him to produce more quickly and more cheaply than they. Technical progress took on the appearance of disloyalty. The ideal was stable conditions in a stable industry.'[10]

In the modern Western world, just as in the medieval world, vested interests exert pressure for the maintenance of established routines; yet the modern Western institutional structure allows room for freedom of conflict. The structure no longer being unitary, vested interests find it difficult to resist the continuous stream of change-producing inventions. Invention, as well as its application and utilization, is furthered through the ever-renewed challenge to vested interests, as well as by the conflicts

[4] Cf. McAlister Coleman, *Men and Coal*, N.Y., Farrar and Rinehart, 1943.

[5] *Union Wages and Labor's Earnings*, Syracuse, Syracuse Univ. Press, 1951.

[6] Quoted by Will Herberg, 'When Social Scientists View Labor,' *Commentary*, Dec. 1951, XII, 6, pp. 590–6. See also Seymour Melman, *Dynamic Factors in Industrial Productivity*, Oxford, Blackwell, 1956, on the effects of rising wage levels on productivity.

[7] See the criticism of the Mayo approach by Daniel Bell, 'Adjusting Men to Machines,' *Commentary*, Jan. 1947, pp. 79–88; C. Wright Mills, 'The Contribution of Sociology to the Study of Industrial Relations,' *Proceedings of the Industrial Relations Research Association*, 1948, pp. 199–222.

[8] See, e.g., R. K. Merton, 'The Machine, The Workers and The Engineer,' *Social Theory and Social Structure*, Glencoe, Ill., 1949, pp. 317–28; Georges Friedmann, *Industrial Society*, Glencoe, Ill., 1956.

[9] For informal organization and change, see Roethlisberger & Dickson, *Management and the Worker*, Cambridge, 1939, especially pp. 567–8; for formal organization, see Selig Perlman, *The Theory of the Labor Movement;* on general relations between technology and labour, see Elliot D. Smith and Richard C. Nyman, *Technology and Labor*, New Haven, Yale Univ. Press, 1939.

[10] Henri Pirenne, *Economic and Social History of Medieval Europe*, London, Routledge and Kegan Paul, 1949, p. 186.

between the vested interests themselves.[11]

Once old forms of traditional and unitary integration broke down, the clash of conflicting interests and values, now no longer constrained by the rigidity of the medieval structure, pressed for new forms of unification and integration. Thus deliberate control and rationalized regulation of 'spontaneous' processes was required in military and political, as well as in economic institutions. Bureaucratic forms of organization with their emphasis on calculable, methodical and disciplined behaviour[12] arose at roughly the same period in which the unitary medieval structure broke down. But with the rise of bureaucratic types of organization peculiar new resistances to change made their appearance. The need for reliance on predictability exercises pressure towards the rejection of innovation which is perceived as interference with routine. Conflicts involving a 'trial through battle' are unpredictable in their outcome, and therefore unwelcome to the bureaucracy which must strive towards an ever-widening extension of the area of predictability and calculability of results. But social arrangements which have become habitual and totally patterned are subject to the blight of ritualism. If attention is focused exclusively on the habitual clues, 'people may be unfitted by being fit in an unfit fitness',[13] so that their habitual training becomes an incapacity to adjust to new conditions. To quote Dewey again: 'The customary is taken for granted; it operates subconsciously. Breach of wont and use is focal; it forms "consciousness".'[14] A group or a system which no longer is challenged is no longer capable of a creative response. It may subsist, wedded to the eternal yes-

terday of precedent and tradition, but it is no longer capable of renewal.[15]

'Only a hitch in the working of habit occasions emotion and provokes thought.'[16] Conflict within and between bureaucratic structures provides the means for avoiding the ossification and ritualism which threatens their form of organization.[17] Conflict, though apparently dysfunctional for highly rationalized systems, may actually have important latent functional consequences. By attacking and overcoming the resistance to innovation and change that seems to be an 'occupational psychosis' always threatening the bureaucratic office holder, it can help to insure that the systems do not stifle in the deadening routine of habituation and that in the planning activity itself creativity and invention can be applied.

We have so far discussed change within systems, but changes of systems are of perhaps even more crucial importance for sociological inquiry. Here the sociology of Karl Marx serves us well. Writes Marx in a polemic against Proudhon:

Feudal production also had two antagonistic elements, which were equally designated by the names of *good side* and *bad side* of feudalism, without regard being had to the fact that it is always the evil side which finishes by overcoming the good side. It is the bad side that produces the movement which makes history, by constituting the struggle. If at the epoch of the reign of feudalism the economists, enthusiastic over the virtues of chivalry, the delightful harmony between rights and duties, the patriarchal life of the towns, the prosperous state of domestic industry in the country, of the development of industry organized in corporations, guilds and fellowships, in fine of all which constitutes the beautiful side of feudalism, had proposed to themselves the problem of eliminating all which cast a shadow upon this lovely picture—serfdom,

[11] See W. F. Ogburn, *Social Change*, N.Y.: B. W. Huebsch, 1923, for the theory of 'cultural lag' due to 'vested interests.'

[12] Cf. Max Weber, 'Bureaucracy,' *From Max Weber*, Gerth and Mills, ed., pp. 196–244. For the pathology of bureaucracy, see R. K. Merton, 'Bureaucratic Structure and Personality,' *Social Theory and Social Structure*, op. cit., pp. 151–60.

[13] Kenneth Burke, *Permanence and Change*, N.Y., New Republic, 1936, p. 18.

[14] John Dewey, *The Public and Its Problems*, Chicago, Gateway Books, 1946, p. 100.

[15] This is, of course, a central thesis of Arnold Toynbee's monumental *A Study of History*, O.U.P.

[16] John Dewey, *Human Nature and Conduct*, op. cit., p. 178.

[17] See, e.g., Melville Dalton, 'Conflicts Between Staff and Line Managerial Officers,' *Am. Soc. R.*, XV (1950), pp. 342–51. The author seems to be unaware of the positive functions of this conflict, yet his data clearly indicate the 'innovating potential' of conflict between staff and line.

privilege, anarchy—what would have been the result? All the elements which constituted the struggle would have been annihilated, and the development of the bourgeoisie would have been stifled in the germ. They would have set themselves the absurd problem of eliminating history.[18]

According to Marx, conflict leads not only to ever-changing relations within the existing social structure, but the total social system undergoes transformation through conflict.

During the feudal period, the relations between serf and lord (between burgher and gentry) underwent many changes both in law and in fact. Yet conflict finally led to a breakdown of all feudal relations and hence to the rise of a new social system governed by different patterns of social relations.

It is Marx's contention that the negative element, the opposition, conditions the change when conflict between the subgroups of a system becomes so sharpened that at a certain point this system breaks down. Each social system contains elements of strain and of potential conflict; if in the analysis of the social structure of a system these elements are ignored, if the adjustment of patterned relations is the only focus of attention, then it is not possible to anticipate basic social change. Exclusive attention to wont and use, to the customary and habitual bars access to an understanding of possible latent elements of strain which under certain conditions eventuate in overt conflict and possibly in a basic change of the social structure. This attention should be focused, in Marx's view, on what evades and resists the patterned normative structure and on the elements pointing to new and alternative patterns emerging from the existing structure. What is diagnosed as disease from the point of view of the institutionalized pattern may, in fact, says Marx, be the first birth pang of a new one to come; not wont and use but the break of wont and use is focal. The 'matters-of-fact' of a 'given state of affairs' when viewed in the light of Marx's ap-

proach, become limited, transitory; they are regarded as containing the germs of a process that leads beyond them.[19]

Yet, not all social systems contain the same degree of conflict and strain. The sources and incidence of conflicting behaviour in each particular system vary according to the type of structure, the patterns of social mobility, of ascribing and achieving status and of allocating scarce power and wealth, as well as the degree to which a specific form of distribution of power, resources and status is accepted by the component actors within the different subsystems. But if, within any social structure, there exists an excess of claimants over opportunities for adequate reward, there arises strain and conflict.

The distinction between changes *of* systems and changes *within* systems is, of course, a relative one. There is always some sort of continuity between a past and a present, or a present and a future social system; societies do not die the way biological organisms do, for it is difficult to assign precise points of birth or death to societies as we do with biological organisms. One may claim that all that can be observed is a change of the organization of social relations; but from one perspective such change may be considered re-establishment of equilibrium while from another it may be seen as the formation of a new system.

A natural scientist, describing the function of earthquakes, recently stated admirably what could be considered the function of conflict. 'There is nothing abnormal about an earthquake. An unshakeable earth would be a dead earth. A quake is the earth's way of maintaining its equilibrium, a form of adjustment that enables the crust

[18] Karl Marx, *The Poverty of Philosophy*, Chicago, Charles H. Kerr & Co., 1910, p. 132.

[19] For an understanding of Marx's methodology and its relation to Hegelian philosophy, see Herbert Marcuse, *Reason and Revolution*, N.Y., O.U.P., 1941.

Note the similarity with John Dewey's thought: 'Where there is change, there is of necessity numerical plurality, multiplicity, and from variety comes opposition, strife. Change is alteration, or "othering" and this means diversity. Diversity means division, and division means two sides and their conflict.' *Reconstruction in Philosophy*, N.Y., Mentor Books, 1950, p. 97. See also the able discussion of the deficiencies of Talcott Parsons' sociological theories by David Lockwood, *B.J.S.*, June, 1956.

to yield to stresses that tend to reorganize and redistribute the material of which it is composed . . . . The larger the shift, the more violent the quake, and the more frequent the shifts, the more frequent are the shocks.'[20]

Whether the quake is violent or not, it has served to maintain or reestablish the equilibrium of the earth. Yet the shifts may be small changes of geological formations, or they may be changes in the structural relations between land and water, for example.

At what point the shift is large enough to warrant the conclusion that a change *of* the system has taken place, is hard to determine. Only if one deals with extreme instances are ideal types—such as feudalism, capitalism, etc.—easily applied. A system based on serfdom, for example, may undergo considerable change within—*vide* the effects of the Black Death on the social structure of medieval society; and even an abolition of serfdom may not necessarily be said to mark the end of an old and the emergence of a new system, *vide* nineteenth-century Russia.

If 'it is necessary to distinguish clearly between the processes *within* the system and processes of change *of* the system,' as Professor Parsons has pointed out,[21] an attempt should be made to establish a heuristic criterion for this distinction. We propose to talk of a change *of* system when all major structural relations, its basic institutions and its prevailing value system have been drastically altered. (In cases where such a change takes place abruptly, as, for example, the Russian Revolution, there should be no difficulty. It is well to remember, however, that transformations of social systems do not always consist in an abrupt and simultaneous change of all basic institutions. Institutions may change gradually, by mutual adjustment, and it is only over a period of time that the observer will be able

to claim that the social system has undergone a basic transformation in its structural relations.) In concrete historical reality, no clear-cut distinctions exist. Change *of* system may be the result (or the sum total) of previous changes *within* the system. This does not however detract from the usefulness of the theoretical distinction.

It is precisely Marx's contention that the change from feudalism to a different type of social system can be understood only through an investigation of the stresses and strains *within* the feudal system. Whether given forms of conflict will lead to changes in the social system or to breakdown and to formation of a new system will depend on the rigidity and resistance to change, or inversely on the elasticity of the control mechanisms of the system.

It is apparent, however, that the rigidity of the system and the intensity of conflict within it are not independent of each other. Rigid systems which suppress the incidence of conflict exert pressure towards the emergence or radical cleavages and violent forms of conflict. More elastic systems, which allow the open and direct expression of conflict within them and which adjust to the shifting balance of power which these conflicts both indicate and bring about, are less likely to be menaced by basic and explosive alignments within their midst.

In what follows the distinction between strains, conflicts and disturbances within a system which lead to a re-establishment of equilibrium, and conflicts which lead to the establishment of new systems and new types of equilibria, will be examined.[22]

---

[20] Waldemar Kaemfert, 'Science in Review,' *New York Times,* July 27, 1952.

[21] Talcott Parsons, *The Social System,* London, Tavistock Publications: 1951, p. 481.

I owe much to Prof. Parsons' treatment of this distinction despite a number of major disagreements with his theory of social change.

[22] The concept of *equilibrium* is of great value in social science provided it is used, as by Schumpeter, as a point of reference permitting measurement of departures from it. 'The concept of a state of equilibrium, although no such state may ever be realized, is useful and indeed indispensable for purposes of analyses and diagnosis, as a point of reference' (Joseph A. Schumpeter, *Business Cycle,* N.Y., McGraw-Hill, 1939, p. 69). But certain types of sociological functionalism tend to move from this methodological use of the concept to one which has some clearly ideological features. The ideal type of equilibrium, in this illegitimate use, becomes a normative instead of a methodological concept. Attention is focused on the maintenance of a system

Such an examination will be most profitably begun by considering what Thorstein Veblen[23] has called 'Vested Interests.'[24]

Any social system implies an allocation of power, as well as wealth and status positions among individual actors and component sub-groups. As has been pointed out, there is never complete concordance between what individuals and groups within a system consider their just due and the system of allocation. Conflict ensues in the effort of various frustrated groups and individuals to increase their share of gratification. Their demands will encounter the resistance of those who previously had established a 'vested interest' in a given form of distribution of honour, wealth and power.

To the vested interests, an attack against their position necessarily appears as an attack upon the social order.[25] Those who derive privileges from a given system of allocation of status, wealth and power will perceive an attack upon these prerogatives as an attack against the system itself.

However, mere 'frustration' will not lead to a questioning of the legitimacy of the position of the vested interests, and hence to conflict. Levels of aspiration as well as feelings of deprivation are relative to institutionalized expectations and are established through comparison.[26] When social systems have institutionalized goals and values to govern the conduct of component actors, but limit access to these goals for certain members of the society, 'departures from institutional requirements' are to be expected.[27] Similarly, if certain groups within a social system compare their share in power, wealth and status honour with that of other groups *and* question the legitimacy of this distribution, discontent is likely to ensue. If there exist no institutionalized provisions for the expression of such discontents, departures from what is required by the norms of the social system may occur. These may be limited to 'innovation' or they may consist in the rejection of the institutionalized goals. Such 'rebellion' 'involves a genuine transvaluation, where the direct or vicarious experience of frustration leads to full denunciation of previously prized values.'[28] Thus it will be well to distinguish between those departures from the norms of a society which consist in mere 'deviation' and those which involve the formation of distinctive patterns and new value systems.

What factors lead groups and individuals to question at a certain point the legitimacy of the system of distribution of re-

which is somehow identified with the ethically desirable (see Merton's discussion of this ideological misuse of functionalism in *Social Theory and Social Structure*, op. cit., pp. 38 ff. and 116–17; see also my review of Parsons' Essays, *American Journal of Sociology*, 55, March 1950, pp. 502–4). Such theorizing tends to look at all behaviour caused by strains and conflict as 'deviancy' from the legitimate pattern, thereby creating the perhaps unintended impression that such behaviour is somehow 'abnormal' in an ethical sense, and obscuring the fact that some 'deviant' behaviour actually serves the creation of new patterns rather than a simple rejection of the old.

[23] See especially *The Vested Interests and the State of the Industrial Arts*, N.Y., 1919.

[24] Max Lerner ('Vested Interests,' *Encyclopaedia of the Social Sciences*, XV, p. 240) gives the following definition: 'When an activity has been pursued so long that the individuals concerned in it have a prescriptive claim to its exercise and its profit, they are considered to have a vested interest in it.'

[25] Veblen has described this aptly: 'The code of proprieties, conventionalities, and usages in vogue at any given time and among any given people has more or less of the character of an organic whole; so that any appreciable change in one point of the scheme involves something of a change or readjustment of other points also, if not a reorganization all along the line. . . . When an attempted reform involves the suppression or thoroughgoing remodeling of an institution of first-rate importance in the conventional scheme, it is immediately felt that a serious derangement of the entire scheme would result. . . . Any of these innovations would, we are told, "shake the social structure to its base," "reduce society to chaos," . . . etc. The aversion to change is in large part an aversion to the bother of making the readjustment which any given change will necessitate' (*The Theory of the Leisure Class*, N.Y., The Modern Library, pp. 201–3).

[26] See Robert K. Merton and Alice S. Kitt, 'Contributions to the Theory of Reference Group Behaviour' for a development of the concept of 'relative deprivation' (originally suggested by Stouffer *et al.* in *The American Soldier*) and its incorporation into the framework of a theory of reference groups.

[27] This whole process is exhaustively discussed by Merton in his paper on 'Social Structure and Anomie,' *Social Theory*, op. cit.

[28] Ibid., p. 145.

wards, lies largely outside the scope of the present inquiry. The intervening factors can be sought in the ideological, technological, economic or any other realm. It is obvious, moreover, that conflict may be a result just as much as a source of change. A new invention, the introduction of a new cultural trait through diffusion, the development of new methods of production or distribution, etc., will have a differential impact within a social system. Some strata will feel it to be detrimental to their material or ideal interests, while others will feel their position strengthened through its introduction. Such disturbances in the equilibrium of the system lead to conditions in which groups or individual actors no longer do willingly what they have to do and do willingly what they are not supposed to do. Change, no matter what its source, breeds strain and conflict.

Yet, it may be well to repeat that mere 'frustration' and the ensuing strains and tensions do not necessarily lead to group conflict. Individuals under stress may relieve their tension through 'acting out' in special safety-valve institutions in as far as they are provided for in the social system; or they may 'act out' in a deviant manner, which may have serious dysfunctional consequences for the system, and bring about change in this way. This, however, does not reduce the frustration from which escape has been sought since it does not attack their source.

If, on the other hand, the strain leads to the emergence of specific new patterns of behaviour of whole groups of individuals who pursue 'the optimization of gratification'[29] by choosing what they consider appropriate means for the maximization of rewards, social change which reduces the sources of their frustration may come about. This may happen in two ways: if the social system is flexible enough to adjust to conflict situations we will deal with change *within* the system. If, on the other hand, the social system is not able to readjust itself and allows the accumulation of conflict, the 'aggressive' groups, imbued with a new system of values which threatens to

split the general consensus of the society and imbued with an ideology which 'objectifies' their claims, may become powerful enough to overcome the resistance of vested interests and bring about the breakdown of the system and the emergence of a new distribution of social values.[30]

In his *Poverty of Philosophy*, Marx was led to consider the conditions under which economic classes constitute themselves:

Economic conditions have first transformed the mass of the population into workers. The domination of capital created for this mass a common situation and common interest. This mass was thus already a class as against capital, but not for itself. It is in the struggle . . . that the mass gathers together and constitutes itself as a class for itself. The interests which it defends become class interests.[31]

With this remarkable distinction between class *in itself* and class *for itself* (which unfortunately he didn't elaborate upon in later writings though it informs all of them—if not the writings of most latter-day 'marxists'), Marx illuminates a most important aspect of group formation: group belongingness is established by an objective conflict situation—in this case a conflict of interests;[32] but only by experiencing this antagonism, that is, by becom-

[29] T. Parsons, *The Social System,* op. cit. p. 498.

[30] R. K. Merton, *Social Theory and Social Structure,* op. cit., pp. 42–3 and 116–17.

[31] Karl Marx, *The Poverty of Philosophy,* op. cit., pp. 188–9.

[32] This makes it necessary to distinguish between realistic and non-realistic conflict: social conflicts that arise from frustration of specific demands and from estimates of gains of the participants, and that are directed at the presumed frustrating object, may be called realistic conflicts. Non-realistic conflicts, on the other hand, are not occasioned by the rival ends of the antagonists, but by the need for tension release of one or both of them. Some groups may be formed with the mere purpose of releasing tension. Such groups 'collectivize' their tensions, so to speak. They can, by definition, only be disruptive rather than creative since they are built on negative rather than positive cathexes. But groups of this kind will remain marginal; their actions cannot bring about social change unless they accompany and strengthen realistic conflict groups. In such cases we deal with an admixture of non-realistic and realistic elements mutually reinforcing each other within the same social movements. Members who join for the mere purpose of tension release are often used for the 'dirty work' by the realistic conflict groups.

ing aware of it and by acting it out, does the group (or class) establish its identity.

When changes in the equilibrium of a society lead to the formation of new groupings or to the strengthening of existing groupings that set themselves the goal of overcoming resistance of vested interests through conflict, changes in structural relations, as distinct from simple 'maladjustment,' can be expected.

What Robert Park said about the rise of nationalist and racial movements is more generally applicable:

They strike me as natural and wholesome disturbances of the social routine, the effect of which is to arouse in those involved a lively sense of common purpose and to give those who feel themselves oppressed the inspiration of a common cause. . . . The effect of this struggle is to increase the solidarity and improve the morale of the 'oppressed' minority.[33]

It is this sense of common purpose arising in and through conflict that is peculiar to the behaviour of individuals who meet the challenge of new conditions by a group-forming and value-forming response. Strains which result in no such formations of new conflict groups or strengthening of old ones may contribute to bringing about change, but a type of change that fails to reduce the sources of strain since by definition tension-release behaviour does not involve purposive action. Conflict through group action, on the other hand, is likely to result in a 'deviancy' which may be the prelude of new patterns and reward sys-

tems apt to reduce the sources of frustration.

If the tensions that need outlets are continually reproduced within the structure, abreaction through tension-release mechanisms may preserve the system but at the risk of ever-renewed further accumulation of tension. Such accumulation eventuates easily in the irruption of destructive unrealistic conflict. If feelings of dissatisfaction, instead of being suppressed or diverted are allowed expression against 'vested interests,' and in this way to lead to the formation of new groupings within the society, the emergence of genuine transvaluations is likely to occur. Sumner saw this very well when he said: 'We want to develop symptoms, we don't want to suppress them.'[34]

Whether the emergence of such new groupings or the strengthening of old ones with the attendant increase in self-confidence and self-esteem on the part of the participants will lead to a change *of* or *within* the system will depend on the degree of cohesion that the system itself has attained. A well-integrated society will tolerate and even welcome group conflict; only a weakly integrated one must fear it. The great English liberal John Morley said it very well:

If [the men who are most attached to the reigning order of things] had a larger faith in the stability for which they profess so great an anxiety, they would be more free alike in understanding and temper to deal generously, honestly and effectively with those whom they count imprudent innovators.[35]

[33] Robert E. Park, 'Personality and Cultural Conflict,' *Publications of the Am. Soc. Soc.,* 25, 1931, pp. 95–110. See p. 107.

[34] Wm. G. Sumner, *War and Other Essays,* p. 241.
[35] John Morley, *On Compromise,* London, Macmillan & Co., 1917, p. 263.

CONSENSUS, CONFLICT AND COOPERATION:
A SOCIOLOGICAL INVENTORY* †

IRVING LOUIS HOROWITZ

ABSTRACT

The purpose of this study is to explain the growth and popularity of consensus theory in present day sociology. It seeks to explore shortcomings in the current employment of the concept of consensus, and in so doing to explain the continued relevance of conflict theory for sociological research. The final aim is to logically distinguish consensus and conflict from the general theory of cooperation—particularly to show that consensus and cooperation do not mutually entail each other. The equation of consensus to social structure and conflict to social dynamics is subjected to criticism on the grounds that such a dichotomization prevents the effective development of a sociological theory of change and process.

Few words in the vocabulary of contemporary sociology appear as soothing or as reassuring as consensus. The chain of agreeable associations of the term symbolize the final mating of the science of sociology and a theory of social equilibrium. What stands in need of investigation is the price paid for this essentially recent turn in sociological theory. Specifically it must be asked whether the movement away from traditional theories of conflict and conflict resolution represents a genuinely new stage in the secularization of social science or is in fact a narrowing down of the field brought about by social pressures.

Whatever its meaning, the notion of consensus is an impressively stated although inadequately explored reference point in present day sociology. The resilient strength of consensus theories stems in part from some vague sense that they are connected to functionalism. For those skeptical of this fusion of consensus and function, analysis of the issues is blunted by the plethora of definitions the unwary examiner is greeted with. The fact is that there is an absence of consensus in sociological theory as to just what does and does not constitute consensus or a consensual matrix.

There are at least seven shadings of

meaning which currently attaches to the term consensus beyond the common-sense usage of the word as a proper synonym for agreement between people. First and perhaps most commonly, sociologists define consensus as "adjustment of social dissension." This usage is borrowed from the present psychoanalytic definition of normality as social adjustment and neurosis as the absence of adjustment.[1] The second view has its point of departure in role theory. Consensus is seen as an accord between role behavior and role expectation.[2] The third position, while having a point of contact with an adjustment approach to consensus, lifts it out of the individual realm into a cultural framework. "Where an opinion is very widely held and cuts across all groups in society" there you have consensus.[3] The fourth theory sees our term as affiliated to hedonistic impulse, as "possible only when two or more parties want to maintain a relationship which each regards as in its own interest."[4] A cognate definition is offered by the same writer in

---

[1] J. O. Hertzler, *American Social Institutions: A Sociological Analysis* (Boston: Allyn and Bacon, 1961), p. 63.

[2] Neal Gross, "The Sociology of Education," *Sociology Today: Problems and Prospects*, ed. by R. K. Merton, L. Broom, L. S. Cottrell, Jr. (New York: Basic Books, 1959), p. 140.

[3] Leonard Broom and Philip Selznick, *Sociology: A Text with Adapted Readings* (Evanston, Ill.: Row, Peterson & Co., 1958, second edition), p. 278.

[4] Arnold W. Green, *Sociology: An Analysis of Life in Modern Society* (New York: McGraw-Hill Book Co., 1960, third edition), p. 65.

---

* Reprinted by permission of the author and publisher from *Social Forces*, 1962, *41*: 177–188.

† First prepared and presented for the ninth annual meeting of the New York State Sociological Association held at Hobart & William Smith Colleges, Geneva, New York, 1962.

terms of game theory. "Two parties or groups are playing to gain a maximum, but they are prepared to settle for less within the recognized limits."[5] The sixth account identifies consensus with the curbing of hedonistic impulse and instinct, and with the Durkheim notion of solidarity and social cohesion generally.[6] Our last author sees consensus in its barest atomic terms as a sharing of perspectives, as "nothing more or less than the existence on the part of two or more persons, of similar orientations toward something."[7]

Examining these definitions dispassionately, and leaving aside the truth content of each, it is difficult to understand why the concept of consensus has aroused such intense sociological interest. No logical unravelling of the above definitions will explain why consensus, barely a meaningful word in the sociological lexicon of previous decades, is now viewed as a fully matured theory. An accounting of the term is therefore required on extra philological grounds. The expanding uses and abuses of consensus theory overshadows the existing definitional ambiguities.

Consensus theory is now employed to settle a wide range of sociological problems. What is most frequently encountered is the identification of consensus with functional efficiency, and no less with the social requisites of political democracy.[8] In its simplest form, the bivariate equation is that increase in the amount of social consensus yields an increase in functional efficacy and democratic polity; while inversely, decrease in the amount of social consensus creates social disorganization and dysfunction. On a broader front, advocates of consensus theory see this as a new turn in sociology—away from the knotty issue of how conflicts arise and are settled to the spatially and temporally more durable issue of how men cooperate with one another. By defining the core of social action in terms of two functional references: (a) the maintenance of a pattern of orientation, and (b) the definition of the meaning of one or more situational objects, consensus comes to be equated with social equilibrium.[9]

Before proceeding to the substance of my remarks, an historical observation is in order. It is clear that the early development of sociology from Marx to Simmel takes as its point of departure the idea that society is best understood as a selective and collective response to the needs of social interaction in a nonequilibriated world. This involved a rejection, conscious or otherwise, of the idea that society is best understood as a contractual or informal agreement made between equals to secure common goals. As such, the Roman Empire for Simmel is not a union of the general will with particularized wills, but rather an illustration of the efficiency, the functionality of political superordination, of what he terms Caesaristic types of rule. Thus what consensus exists is for Simmel the "tendency of domination by means of leveling." This apparent consensual apparatus is but *disguised* superordination. In discussing Philip the Good of Burgundy, he notes that "legal differences were created exclusively by the arbitrary pleasure of the ruler. They thus marked all the more distinctly the common, unalterable subordination of his subjects."[10]

Similarly for Marx, the economic system called capitalism does not come into existence in consequence of the clamor of public opinion, or to express the general will (although those who do come to power exercise such rationalizations) but simply to satisfy the historical process which brings a social class to power. The welding of such power to a new social class is the purpose of the State, which in turn enters the historical picture as the central agency of coercion

[5] Arnold W. Green, *ibid.*, p. 67.

[6] Ely Chinoy, *Society, An Introduction to Sociology* (New York: Random House, 1961), pp. 344–46.

[7] Theodore Newcomb, "The Study of Consensus," *Sociology Today, op. cit.,* p. 279.

[8] Seymour M. Lipset, "Political Sociology," *Sociology Today, op. cit.,* p. 114.

[9] Talcott Parsons, *The Social System* (Glencoe: The Free Press, 1951), p. 507. This same view is even more forcefully developed in "The Point of View of the Author," *The Social Theories of Talcott Parsons,* ed. by Max Black (Englewood Cliffs, New Jersey: Prentice Hall, 1961). p. 327.

[10] Georg Simmel, "Subordination under an Individual," *The Sociology of Georg Simmel,* edited and translated by K. H. Wolff (Glencoe: The Free Press, 1950), pp. 201–207.

while posing as the agency of social consensus.

The *practical* struggle of these particular interests, which constantly *really* run counter to the communal and illusory communal interests, makes *practical* intervention and control necessary through the illusory "general interest" in the form of the state. The social power, i.e., the multiplied productive force, which arises through the cooperation of different individuals as it is determined within the division of labor, appears to these individuals, since their cooperation is not voluntary but natural, not as their own united power, but as an alien force existing outside them, of the origin and end of which they are ignorant, which they thus cannot control.[11]

Consensus is thus the idealization of coercion.

The roots of conflict theory reach back in time to Hobbes and the formation of the modern nation-State, Marsilius of Padua in the medieval world, and Thrasymachus, Socrates and Plato in ancient Greek society. In essence, the position holds that social organization does not flow from the consensus of *vox populi,* but from the contradictory yet interrelated needs and designs of men. It is interesting to note that the debate between Thrasymachus and Socrates in *The Republic* concerning the nature of justice (the dialogue on power versus virtue) at no point assumes society to be the consequence of popular will or common agreement. Nonetheless, it cannot be said that the history of social and political theory has been a one-sided acceptance of conflict theory and its underlying power thesis as the only explanation of social structure and social action. Such an assertion would have to discount the bulk of writings from Aristotle's "golden mean" to Dewey's "common faith." Thus the history of conflict and consensus has been a dialogue between exclusive frames of reference seeking to explain the same phenomenon—human cooperation.

From the point of view of sociological

history, however, it is pertinent to bear in mind its close affiliation with conflict theorists: Marx on *Klassenkampf,* Gumplowicz on *Rassenkampf,* Mosca's ruling and ruled classes, and Simmel on *Superordnung* and *Unterordnung.* Only now, with sociology in the full passion of its empiricist revolt against European systems of sociology and social philosophy, has a strenuous effort been made to overcome theories of conflict —what has come to be termed "crisis ideologies." Part of this cleansing process has been the promotion of consensus theory. With this promotion has come the inevitable search for new sociological hero images. The brilliant social historian deToqueville in particular has been elevated in current estimates.[12]

The rallying point in deToqueville is the comment that "a society can exist only when a great number of men consider a great number of things from the same point of view; when they hold the same opinions upon many subjects, when the same occurrences suggest the same thoughts and impressions to their minds."[13] Here then seems to be the historical progenitor of the new theory of consensus, and the repudiation of those political sociologies which seek to define social structure in terms of holders and seekers of power, of the ability to command and to coerce. We must now focus attention on current efforts to convert deToqueville's insight into a theory.

Perhaps the most widespread axiom of consensus theory holds that it is a necessary condition for social structure.[14] The social structure has come to be defined as excluding those patterns of human action which are spontaneous and unstructured. Social

---

[11] Karl Marx and Friedrich Engels, *The German Ideology,* in *Basic Writings on Politics and Philosophy: Marx and Engels,* ed. by L. S. Feuer (Garden City: Doubleday and Co., 1959), pp. 255–256, also p. 253.

[12] Seymour M. Lipset, *Political Man: The Social Bases of Politics* (Garden City: Doubleday and Co., 1960), pp. 26–28, 65–66. Lipset's continual juxtaposition of deToqueville and Marx is a strong indication that the differences between consensus and conflict theories involve something more than scientific requirements. Indeed, he has made them ideological poles: consensus representing democracy and conflict representing authoritarianism.

[13] Alexis deToqueville, *Democracy in America,* trans. by H. Reeve (New York: Century and Co., 1899), v. I, p. 398.

[14] cf. Robert E. Park, "Reflections on Communication and Culture," *The American Journal of Sociology,* XLIV (1939), 191–205.

structure is said to consist in a "set of statuses" defined by relatively stable relationships between people. What follows is a mechanical notion of the relation of consensus and conflict as structured and unstructured modes of behavior respectively. Consensus involves objectification of position, group cohesion, collective representations, common traditions, and rules for inducting and indoctrinating new members; while conflict is seen as external to social structure, as spontaneity, impulsive action, lack of organization, intuitive response to immediate situations. In short, consensus differs from conflict as organization differs from deviance.[15] Thus to discuss social structure is by definition not to examine conflict situations, and of course, the pernicious *vice versa*, to examine conflict situations is to discuss something extraneous to social structure.

To place conflict outside the framework of social structure, or to go beyond that and see conflict as necessarily destructive of the social organism, is to place a definite premium on social equilibrium. It strongly implies that a society can be changed only by apocalyptic or spontaneous methods. The identification of consensus with social structure reinforces the stereotyped view that change does not emanate from the Establishment and, keeping within the boundaries it informally sets, is deviant in relation to social order as such. Consensus theory thus tends to become a metaphysical representation of the dominant ideological matrix. It rests on a principle of "general interests" which every member of society is supposed to imbibe if he wishes to avoid the onus of being a deviant or an unconnected isolate. The sociology of small groups has been especially active in pushing this view; the implication being that a condition of social conflict necessarily is a world of deviants and isolates quite incapable of attending to problems of functional survival.[16] The possibility that differing goal orientations are consonant with a single

functional agency is too rarely entertained.[17]

A social structure might well be considered as precisely a dynamic balance of disharmonious parts and therefore subject to endless change and redefinition. If we start from the position of real societies it is evident that conflict situations are intrinsic and organic to social structure. Considered in this manner, the group, the community, or the nation, is the particularized area of social activity in which conflicts arise and are resolved. Coser, following Simmel, has shown that conflict is intrinsic to social structure. Indeed, the form of society is itself defined by the quality and types of conflict situations tolerated if not openly sanctioned.

Types of conflict and types of social structure are not independent variables. Internal social conflicts which concern goals, values or interests that do not contradict the basic assumptions upon which the relationship is founded tend to be positively functional for the social structure. Such conflicts tend to make possible readjustment of norms and power relations within groups in accordance with the felt needs of its individual members or sub-groups.[18]

Briefly then, only when social function is narrowly defined as social equilibrium can a sociological theory of conflict be viewed as an overt or hidden menace to the social system.

A series of considerations which are increasingly being adduced to demonstrate the singular advantages of consensus theory over conflict theory relates to the difficulties of a social examination of unstable relations. Three factors in particular are pointed out: (a) the transitory nature of conflict situations, that is the actual behavior of a mass in an extreme situation, such as civil war or revolution, is so short lived and capricious that predicting conclusions or consequences of conflict situations is impossible; (b) the necessity for dealing with

[15] Kurt Lang and Gladys E. Lang, *Collective Dynamics* (New York: Thomas Y. Crowell Co., 1961), pp. 13–14.

[16] Theodore Newcomb, "The Study of Consensus," *Sociology Today, op. cit.*, p. 284.

[17] Gideon Sjoberg, "Contradictory Functional Requirements and Social Systems," *Journal of Conflict Resolution*, IV (1960), 198–208; also see, Eugene Litwak, "Models of Bureaucracy which permit Conflict," *The American Journal of Sociology*, LXVII (1961), 177–184.

[18] Lewis A. Coser, *The Functions of Social Conflict* (Glencoe: The Free Press, 1956), pp. 151–152.

conflict situations in their natural social environment has as its corollary the absence of controlled experiments such as one finds in strictly delineated types of research; (c) the consequent necessity of presenting evaluations in terms of second and third hand materials such as newspaper reports, autobiographical sketches, and historical studies of unique events—all of which clearly involve the sociological researcher in commitments beyond the empirical confines of the sampling situation.[19]

The scrutiny of this series of objections reveals a transparency and shallowness that poses a serious threat to sociological research as such. The criteria of scientific analysis have never been reducible to the simplicity of an investigatory context. What the above objections fail to take account of is the need for a criterion of significance, of the importance of any specific undertaking to the general growth of sociological knowledge. While it is correct that conflict situations, even of major proportions, are generally of "short" duration (at least in relation to the consequences), this is not a serious objection either to the empirical study of conflict situations, or more to the point, of a causal analysis of the genesis and sources of such situations. Sheer brevity of the conflict situation in relation to the consensual consolidation which may follow only indicates that certain sampling devices are ineffectual to resolve certain kinds of social events. To reason that any step beyond the borders of current methodological safeguards is to step beyond sociology as such is sheer casuistry; justifying the deep fears of many scholars in cognate social sciences that sociologists are too interested in domination and too little interested in cooperation.

The objection to the study of conflict situations because such situations have no well defined contours or boundaries is equally transparent. For this is very nearly always the case of the anthropologist in relation to a given culture. Would it seriously be contended that the "natural" set-

ting of anthropological research makes it a lesser social science? The surest guarantee against provincialism and ethnocentrism would be a greater effort by sociologists to develop techniques of study suitable to this "natural" social setting. The failure to do so has too frequently placed the sociologist in the position of offering questionnaires devised for particular situations as uniformly (if not universally) valid in other cultural and social settings. The natural setting within which conflict arises, far from being an obstacle, should provide a powerful incentive to move beyond the highly structured but hardly universal, world of the small group. That this opportunity has not been seized is more a reflection of the limits of the "opinion leaders" among sociologists than a true delimiting of the legitimate boundaries of sociology.

The pernicious notion that the sociologist somehow has a unique tool of investigation that entitles him to ignore or downgrade the value of journalistic reports or historical surveys is insupportable on scientific grounds. Criteria for sound analysis are fairly constant throughout the spectrum of the social and historical sciences. The same questions can be asked about newspaper clippings as about questionnaires. Lasswell has done just that in his *Language of Politics*.

Can we assume that a scholar read his sources with the same degree of care throughout this research? Did he allow his eye to travel over the thousands upon thousands of pages of parliamentary debates, newspapers, magazines and other sources listed in his bibliography or notes? Or did he use a sampling system, scanning some pages superficially, though concentrating upon certain periods? Was the sampling system for the *Frankfurter Zeitung*, if one was employed, comparable with the one for the *Manchester Guardian*? Were the leaflets chosen simply because they were conveniently available to the scholar, or were they genuinely representative of the most widely circulated propaganda leaflets?[20]

These are, to be sure, correctly framed sociological questions. But they carry no im-

---

[19] A fuller catalogue of objections to the study of conflict situations is contained in Kurt Lang and Gladys Lang, *op. cit.*, pp. 545–53.

[20] Harold D. Lasswell, "Why be Quantitative," in *Reader in Public Opinion and Communication*, enlarged edition, edited by Bernard Berelson and Morris Janowitz (Glencoe: The Free Press, 1953), p. 267.

plication that results are inferior if they are gathered from one source and not another. There is a difference between *resolving* a case for a position on the basis of news reports and *employing* such reports in attempting to arrive at some position.

To equate the worth of a theory (such as consensus theory *or* conflict theory) with ease of study, is a sophistical device which leads to a situation in which only those things are studied for which data already exists—which may help to account for that fantastic sameness and duplication of research efforts in present day small-group sociology. The greatest sociological requirement is precisely to fashion methods adequate to the tasks of studying problems of social order in a world of conflicting interests, standards, and values. Social order must itself be defined, and no less define, the larger universe of social change. The sociologist can hardly run the risk of being surprised by events of common currency in consequence of a theory of society bewitched by order and befuddled by change.

The faith in consensus theory as operationally more worthwhile than conflict theory often takes the form of a deep respect for the amazing complexity of social organization in industrial economies: the automation of production, the automation of human responsibilities, the precision of "chain of command" and "line" matrices, and the auto-regulative capacities of man in mass society to continually adjust to (and make adjustments in) bureaucratic procedures. The Parsonian school of sociology in particular seems impressed with the regularities which obtain between organization and society as such. Here the dilemma lies in equating organization to consensus. The stress and strain of organizational life gives rise to a definition of social action as that auto-regulative mechanism which adjusts for such "alienative" factors.

Such a view suffers from the master problem in traditional laissez-faire economics; namely, the assumption that automatic marketing "laws" somehow operate over and above the actual desires and ends of men. To meet the laissez-faire implications in the theory of social consensus, certain functionalists have developed a theory of

the "safety-value," such that organizations "provide substitute objects upon which to displace hostile sentiments as well as means of abreaction of aggressive tendencies."[21] But this sub-theory only reinforces the "metaphysical pathos" surrounding the theory of social organization since, far from being challenged, the assumption of institutional omnipotence and omniscience is reinforced. One is forced to conclude that the "clever" organization can even program small scale conflict situations in order to guarantee the consensual apparatus as a whole.

The wide uses of consensus theory, particularly as a replacement for conflict theory, shows a close historical and analytical connection to the displacement of the language of social class with an alternate langauge of social status. It is a shift in viewing industrial society as susceptible to many and varied forms, to a vision of the industrial complex as growing omnipotent with time. Essentially, the Weberian theory of bureaucracy is a pessimistic vision, a view of organization as once and for all superceding production as the master social agency. In the theory of bureaucracy, the question of which class or group of classes holds the reins of power is secondary, since the "basic" bureaucratic factor continues to grow whatever economic organization might obtain. Bureaucracy comes to be viewed as omnipotent, subject to temporary setbacks but never to any real or sizeable defeat. If such is the case, then consensus theory is indeed no less omnipotent than the organizational procedures from which it derives its originating impulse.

Consensus theory has led to such a stress on continuities and similarities in the life of an industrial complex that all real differences between democracy and autocracy, ruling and being ruled, exploiting and being exploited, are eliminated—in theory at least. The "natural history of society" technique, which sees everything in terms of functional identities, has made a universe in which only grey cats and clever hounds exist. Political systems are reduced to "quantifiable" terms of how decisions are arrived

[21] Lewis A. Coser, *op. cit.*, pp. 155–156.

at in system A or system B. The fusion of Michels and Weber being urged upon us, a fusion between "iron laws" of oligarchy and bureaucracy respectively, is not a resolution of the crisis in consensus theory, but a symptom of that crisis.[22] Since everything is reduced to administrative techniques, goals of any specific organization vanish into functional identifications, and the individual is left with an impotence that derives from being a part of an association that has a consensual life over and above the person. Consensus becomes the ideological celebration of the corporate personality, possessing a reality which transcends human society as such.

The mystique of consensus theory is evident in the work of many students of complex organization. Here we are met with the impermeable and impenetrable sovereignty of total specialization: the narcotizing effect of role-sets, the functional value of constraint and persuasion, decision-making machinery, etc. The paradox is that consensus theory, far from acting as a bulwark of democratic social theory (as it starts out to be), is the very reverse. It is a theory not for reaching agreements, but one which states that harmony is intrinsic to the organization of the bureaucratic life: a harmony which exists over and above the actual accords reached by men. And such must consensus theory remain since any serious theory of agreements and decisions must at the same time be a theory of disagreements and the conditions under which decisions cannot be reached. Yet consensus theorists, starting from the metaphysical "need" for consensus as universal, can only talk about absolute and relative consensus, complete or partial integration but never about conflict as a means of expressing genuine social needs and aspirations.[23]

On this point, Gouldner has put matters rightly by pointing out that

Instead of telling men how bureaucracy might be mitigated, they insist that it is inevitable. Instead of explaining how democratic patterns may, to some extent, be fortified and extended, they warn us that democracy cannot be perfect. Instead of controlling the disease, they suggest that we are deluded, or more politely, incurably romantic, for hoping to control it. Instead of assuming responsibilities as realistic clinicians, striving to further democratic potentialities wherever they can, many social scientists have become morticians, all too eager to bury men's hopes.[24]

In this connection it is interesting to note Parsons' restructuring of Merton's paper on "Social Structure and Anomie." Parsons writes that "what Merton calls 'conformity' is clearly what we here mean by the equilibriated condition of the interactive system without conflict on either side or alienative motivations."[25] But if we employ a pattern-variable scheme which admits of an equation between "rebellion" and "alienation," and "conformity" and "equilibrium," we are a priori ruling out the possibility that a condition of rebellion is consonant with equilibrium at any level, and correspondingly, that extreme states of consensus might create social or personal disequilibrium. If this formula is seriously entertained, I find it hard to fathom Parsons' sensitivity to the charge that his is a conservative doctrine that sees social change as deviant to social order, and as a phenomenon which is possible only when the "control mechanisms of the social system" break down. Paradoxically, these remarks by Parsons are made in connection with the necessity for theory of change.[26]

The entire concept of deviant behavior itself rests on a faith that consensus is in every situation observable and functionally relevant; a statement which cannot pass inspection. From the point of view of established consensus as to the sanctity of private property, an act of juvenile vandalism might be measured in the same way as an

[22] Seymour M. Lipset, "Political Sociology," *op. cit.*, pp. 89–91.

[23] See in particular, Chester I. Barnard, *The Functions of the Executive* (Cambridge: Harvard University Press, 1938); James D. Mooney and Alan C. Reiley, *The Principles of Organization* (New York: Harper & Co., 1939); Talcott Parsons, "Suggestions for a Sociological Approach to the Theory of Organizations," *Administrative Science Quarterly*, I (1956), 63–85; Philip Selznick, "Foundations of the Theory of Organization," *American Sociological Review*, XIII (1948), 25–35.

[24] Alvin W. Gouldner "Metaphysical Pathos and the Theory of Bureaucracy," *American Political Science Review*, 49 (1955), pp. 506–507.

[25] Talcott Parsons, *op. cit.*, pp. 257–259.

[26] Talcott Parsons, *op. cit.*, pp. 320–321.

act of political rebellion, e.g., the physical damage involved in the "Freedom Riders" actions. But from the point of view of the goals sought, what is meant by consensus needs to be spatially and temporally stipulated; and no less, the difference between means and ends must itself be considered as a factor existing over and beyond the supposed functional damage the social order sustains. Too often, deviance is ambiguously formulated so as to cover extremely different situations; i.e., a departure from the rules on the part of an isolated member of a group, and no less, defiance of group rules from those external to the specific referential set.

It cannot be stated as a theoretical first principle that consensus carries an implication of social equilibrium, or for that matter, that conflict entails disequilibrium. There is a distinction to be made between types and levels of conflict, especially between conflicts *over* the basis of consensus, and those conflicts arising *within* the consensual apparatus. There are, to draw an analogy from game theory, conflicts programmed for continuation of the game (such as parliamentary debates), and there are those programmed to end the game through a change of the rules as such (such as *coup d'états*). In neither case is a theory of conflict tied to social disorganization or to deviance from norms. This is not to say that conflict situations do not contain possibilities of social disorganization. Of course they do. For example, the absence of a formal constitution over an extended period of time can create political chaos and turmoil. But likewise, a perfect constitution, preparing the ground for every sort of contingency, can have a boomerang effect and heighten the stress situation by a failure to arrive at common standards of belief and action. In short, both consensus and conflict are phenomena which may promote or retard social cooperation or political cohesion.

Simmel caught the authentic spirit of the relation of conflict to social cooperation when he noted that

If a fight simply aims at annihilation, it does approach the marginal case of assassination in which the admixture of unifying elements is almost zero. If, however, there is any consideration, any limit to violence, there already exists a socializing factor, even though only as the qualification of violence. One unites in order to fight, and one fights under the mutually recognized control of norms and rules.[27]

It must therefore be noted that conflict, no less than consensus operates within the social structure, within the system of mutually established laws, norms, and values.

There is a powerful strain in social psychology which sees the entire socialization process as one of "learning" appropriate responses and role-sets, when to act in terms of formal rules and when it is permissible or even preferable to act on the basis of the informal rule structure. To this is added a whole series of dualisms: when to acquiesce in the ascriptive process and when performance elements ought to be emphasized; when to behave in accordance with reference group associations and when to act in terms of membership group affiliations. In this fashion, consensus theory slips gently beyond the boundaries of scientific description into a guide for the perplexed, and into a metaphysics of what ordinary society has come to know as the double-standard. Consensual definitions of normal and deviant behavior is directly related to a conformist standpoint since the ability to perform the multiplicity of roles in a universe of contrasting formal and informal rules is precisely what characterizes one as "socialized" or not.

The spectacle of witnessing socialization defined in terms of consensus is that learned responses becomes a euphemism for gamed responses; playing the game in such a way that formal obedience to the rule system is never challenged since there are always those shifting and shifty informal rules to fall back upon in times of stress. Those who do not accept such a reified parceling of society are unscientific; and people concerned with the *right* as well as the *real* are described as pariahs, deviants, abnormals, marginals, and now even clerics.[28] It must be added that the multiple definitions of

[27] Georg Simmel, *Conflict*, pp. 25–26. Quoted in Lewis A. Coser, *op. cit.*, p. 121.

[28] S. M. Lipset and Neil Smelser, "Change and Controversy in Recent American Sociology," *The British Journal of Sociology*, XII (1961), 41–51.

consensus, connected as they are to game-playing and organizational performance, is the perfect completion of the legitimated bifurcation of values and actions, beliefs and behavior. In this form, consensus is reduced to a "rites of passage" faith, with a powerful onus cast on any "rights of man" faith, i.e., on any position which asserts the need or the value of conflict as a fundamental problem-resolving tool. Consensus theory has reduced itself to "thinking together."[29] Whether this proves an adequate replacement for the old-fashioned idea of thinking for one's self remains to be demonstrated.

If consensus and conflict occupy the same social universe and logically imply one another, what is the basis for suggesting the empirical superiority of conflict theory as an analytical tool? Fundamentally, it is the impossibility of describing any but the most permissive and tolerant communities in terms of consensus matrices. While conflict theory, with its openness to problems of coercion, pressure groups, social classes, political myths, cultural clashes, racial strife, etc., more nearly approximates the going issues in *Gesellschaft* relationships. In short, from a descriptive point of view, conflict theory covers a wider and more profound range of questions. From a prescriptivist position it is, to be sure, better for men to settle their differences on the basis of free agreement rather than external pressures. But this is an entirely different level of sociological analysis, the level of what kind of decisions make for human cooperation. In any event, consensus theorists cut themselves off from this avenue of thought because of their uniform faith in a descriptivist sociology. They are thus reduced to platitudinous statements that not enough attention has been given to the consensus apparatus in group relations. However, even admitting the validity of this claim, this does not carry with it a mandate to consider consensus as either a more virtuous—or what is more significant, a more practiced—

form of arranging social affairs than custom, myth or even coercion.

The present turn to consensus theory is a change in direction of subjectivism, of elevating individual criteria and auto-evaluations concerning status and prestige to the level of objective fact. In the "Warner tradition" for example the definition of social class is reduced to what the community consensus says a class is.[30] The abandonment of serious consideration of the sociology of knowledge, to the forms of ideological distortions of social reality, leads to the naive and calamitous identification of truth with what popular consensus claims as true. This return to a culture and counting theory of truth reinforces the tendency to equate the function of science with a description of the mythic properties in thought. In this way, the manipulative aspects of a social science replace the traditional quest for discovery of social laws.

Consensus theory has a narrowing effect on the conduct of sociological science as such. Consensual units are too frequently seen in terms of small group and small community relation, such as Newcomb's Bennington College dormitory students, Warner's Yankee City, Kaufman's Oldland, or Hollingshead's Elmtown. In this sense, consensus theory has a self-fulfilling prophetic dimension, in that what is examined already presupposes a high degree of social cohesion and interaction.[31] Precisely in the larger social and national

---

[29] Edward Gross, "Symbiosis and Consensus as Integrative Factors in Small Groups," *American Sociological Review*, XXI (1956), 174–179.

[30] W. Lloyd Warner and Paul S. Lunt, *The Social Life of a Modern Community—Yankee City Series*: Vol. I (New Haven: Yale University Press, 1941), p. 82, et. passium. For a brilliant critique of anthropological subjectivism, see Ruth Rosner Kornhauser, "The Warner Approach to Social Stratification," in *Class, Status and Power: A Reader in Social Stratification*, edited by Reinhard Bendix and Seymour Martin Lipset (Glencoe: The Free Press, 1953), pp. 224–255. See also C. Wright Mills, "The Social Life of a Modern Community—An Evaluation," in *Power, Politics and People: The Collected Papers of C. Wright Mills*, edited by Irving L. Horowitz (New York: Oxford University Press, 1963), pp. 40–54.

[31] This is not to imply that conflict situations, and thus conflict theory, is inoperative at small group levels. Quite the contrary, the most significant literature of this genre has shown a marked concern with conflict and conflict resolution as the essence of group interaction. See, for example, Arthur J.

units are such unifying agencies and symbols absent. Immigration waves, differences in cultural, racial and ethnic backgrounds, sectional, caste and class antagonisms, these types of situations stand in continual need of a sociological theory of conflict and conflict resolution; one which makes no assumptions as to the auto-regulative or equilibriated conditions of a specific social system. To declare, as a legion of small group sociologists have, that the only viable avenue of scientific study open to the sociologist is the group, since only in group relations can the study of consensus be presently undertaken, is not to prove the worth of consensus but only to demonstrate the extent to which larger units of social research have been hastily and needlessly surrendered to other social sciences.

That even the original intent of consensus theory, to establish a measurement of what public opinion maintains as true or desirable at any given point, has been subverted, has been forcefully made clear by the elitist corruption of consensus to signify what "prestige judges" think consensus to be.[32] The pretense that consensus is somehow intrinsically more democratic than conflict theory is about as sound as the "theory" that clean-shaven men are kindlier than bearded men. As Leonard Reissman has well pointed out, consensus theorists "create an uncomfortable suspicion about what consensus means and how valid is the use of prestige judges as a research technique. There is something unexplained that badly needs elucidation when a measure can turn up eleven or more distinguishable classes in a community with a total population of some 1200." In a later

section Reissman notes the central weakness of consensual definitions of social class. "There is the tendency, although not an inevitable one, to consider behavior as the result of the value system of class rather than as the effect of, say, economic factors, social power, education, or political forces. The crux of class distinction, thereby, becomes one of values, which in turn become the presumed causes of class difference in behavior."[33] It must thus be concluded, not that status factors are inoperative as independent variables, but rather that such a conclusion is not necessarily arrived at by a theory of consensus. Shifts in modes of behavior from class to prestige lines can be more readily and accurately gauged on historical grounds than on pseudo-psychological grounds of the instinctual need for togetherness and social acceptance.

Why then has the great shift from conflict theory to consensus theory taken place at this juncture in American sociology? Several hypotheses suggest themselves. First, that as American society becomes more democratic, more easy-going, the search for the consensual basis becomes more pronounced. This seems to be the viewpoint adopted by Lipset. However, his view of the end of ideology seems not so much a consequence of an expanding democratic temper, as it is simply a reflection of domestic affluence, and the large share of the United States inhabitants benefitting from the affluent society.[34]

A much more powerful line of reasoning has been suggested by Morris Janowitz, when he indicates that technical bureaucracies and team-member proficiency has tended to usurp the older power of formal authority as distinct from science. Which is to say that the older situation of science as isolated from policy making has disintegrated. With this, authority shifts from outright reliance on domination to a wider utilization of manipulation, on demonstrated managerial skills, operational proficiencies, and the capacity to develop

Vidich and Joseph Bensman, *Small Town in Mass Society: Class Power and Religion in a Rural Community* (Garden City: Doubleday-Anchor Books, 1960); Judith R. Kramer and Seymour Leventman, *Children of the Gilded Ghetto: Conflict Resolutions of Three Generations of American Jews* (New Haven: Yale University Press, 1961); and Kenneth Wilson Underwood, *Protestant and Catholic: Religious and Social Interaction in an Industrial Community* (Boston: The Beacon Press, 1957).

[32] Harold Kaufman, *Prestige Classes in a New York Rural Community* (Ithaca: Cornell University Agricultural Experiment Station, March 1944), Memoir 260, p. 46.

[33] Leonard Reissman, *Class in American Society* (Glencoe: The Free Press, 1959), pp. 127 and 175.

[34] Seymour M. Lipset, *Political Man*, pp. 403–417; see also in this connection, Daniel Bell, *The End of Ideology* (Glencoe: The Free Press, 1960).

positive organizational loyalties. Therefore, in such a context, consensus comes to be the decisive pivot upon which the success or failure of the manipulative society hangs.[35]

But perhaps the most powerful reason for the shift to consensus theory is the "enlightened" recognition that mass terror is not as powerful an instrument for extracting economic and political loyalties as mass persuasion. The entire theoretical edifice of small group theory comes to rest on the idea that the formal sanctioning of force is less potent a factor in individual or group motivation than the informal sanctions of the immediately involved reference-set. The belief in consensus as a stratagem is well articulated by Frank when he writes:

The idea has spread that employers were wasting human energy by the traditional authoritarian ways of imposing their decisions on their employees. Psychologists—collaborating with engineers and economists and, more recently, anthropologists—have made many studies concerned with the impact of physical aspects of the workplace, such as lighting, color of walls and machines, temperature and humidity; with working conditions, such as hours, shifts, rest periods, piece rates, and especially relations of foreman and supervisors to their groups. Such studies helped to articulate a new view of corporate life.[36]

But what, it must be asked, is the content of this new view of corporate life? Is it a theory of the corporation or simply a technique of mass persuasion and manipulation? Is it a sociological statement of the nature of the corporate structure, or the uses by the corporate structure of sociological statements? The promotion of consensus as a theory has had as its asking price the conversion of sociology from a science to a tool of policy. A policy which, moreover, fails to reach the goal of harmony.[37] As White recently indicated, "There is nothing new in manipulated opinion and engineered consent. . . . Even the sheer bulk of distortion is not altogether new, merely more refined. What is new is the acceptability, the mere taken-for-grantedness of these things."[38]

I want to terminate my remarks with a plea for sharper logical and linguistic distinctions, specifically to point out that the issue of human cooperation, while related to consensus and conflict, has a quite unique dimension and operational range. It must be pointed out that a decision in favor of consensus theory is not automatically a decision on behalf of cooperation. It is simply a decision to examine social structure to the partial or total exclusion of social dynamics; a decision to act as if breaks with tradition, shifts in the culture complex, disruption of moral patterns, can be described as marginal in character. There is indeed a kind of safety in the continuing, the prolonged, the enduring. But this safety gratuitously cloaking itself in the mantle of the secularization of science is nothing but the abdication of the field of social change, and hence an abandonment of the on-going problems confronting those most directly concerned with achieving human cooperation at group, regional, national, or international levels.

The functional successes of any given social structure should not define the limits of sociological discourse. For we may find ourselves celebrating our social order one day, and another the next—and in precisely the same "functional-structural" terms. The central task of sociology is explanation and prediction, each in terms of the other, and no theory which identifies consensus with the social order as such can fail to come upon hard times.

What then is the difference between consensus and cooperation? There seem to be

[35] Morris Janowitz, *Sociology and the Military Establishment* (New York: Russell Sage Foundation, 1959), pp. 27–38. Janowitz' remarks are confined to the military. Responsibility for enlarging the scope and context of his argument is mine.
[36] Lawrence K. Frank, "Psychology and the Social Order," in *The Human Meaning of the Social Sciences,* edited by Daniel Lerner (New York: Meridian Books, Inc., 1959), p. 230.
[37] David Riesman, Nathan Glazer, Revel Denney, *The Lonely Crowd: A Study of the Changing American Character* (Garden City: Doubleday Anchor Books, 1954), pp. 306–307.
[38] Howard B. White, "The Processed Voter and the New Political Science," *Social Research,* XXVIII (1961), 150.

three distinguishable factors to be identified. First: consensus stands for agreement internally, i.e., in terms of shared perspectives, agreements on the rules of association and action, a common set of norms and values. Cooperation for its part makes no demands on role uniformity but only upon procedural rules. Cooperation concerns the settlement of problems in terms which make possible the continuation of differences and even fundamental disagreements. Thus one can legitimately speak of cooperation between labor and management, while one speaks on the degree of consensus each side brings to bear at the bargaining table. Second: consensus is agreement on the content of behavior, while cooperation necessitates agreement only on the form of behavior. We speak of consensus if all members of the Women's Christian Temperance Union agree to abstain from drinking alcoholic beverages. But we speak of cooperation when agreement is reached on the forms allowed for drinking and the forms allowed for curbing the intake of liquor. As the "Prohibition Era" dramatically showed, the substitution of consensus for cooperation did not lead to a new morality but simply to chaos. Third: cooperation concerns toleration of differences, while consensus demands abolition of these same differences. If a game theory analogy be preferred, the distinction between cooperation and consensus might be stated in the following terms: consensus programs the termination of the game by insisting on the principle of unity and unilateral victory, whereas cooperation is pluralistic because it programs the continuation of the game by maintaining and insisting upon the legitimacy of differences.

What is required at this juncture is a more adequate sociological theory of cooperation; a stipulation of the conditions of that minimum set of beliefs about man and his social universe that is consonant with continued survival and growth. Such a theory of cooperation would insist on the need for maintaining life although leaving open the question of what to do with it;

the need to secure the material and cultural needs of men although differing on the sort of social system best able to meet such needs. Beyond this, there is a need for a theory of conflict, a programming of conflict, that would allow people to shift and choose their conceptions of what constitutes progress, pleasure, etc., and the institutionalization of avenues of action to implement these conceptions. Consensus theory has done nothing to melt the present freezing of attitudes on either a national or international scale. Nor will it, unless sociologists show a willingness to expand their collective vision of the social universe beyond the confines of a dormitory or a hospital ward.

The unity required to evolve such a sociological theory of cooperation is methodological rather than systematic. It requires us to approach ideas and attitudes concerning cooperation as hypotheses whose truth content must be measured by the degree with which they can be correlated to objective circumstances. This is something quite different than placing men in a Procrustean bed of pattern variables which may or may not hold for previous or future generations —or, for that matter, for the present one. The methods of sociology do not exclude decisive choices in favor of specific objectives. It does caution us against ignoring alternative conceptual frameworks on the basis of their unpopularity or marginality. The concept of cooperation is essentially the programming of common standards in a world of conflicting interests and even different notions as to what constitutes interests. Precisely because a general theory of cooperation would offer no transcendental commitments to the eternal righteousness of any existing social order, it can place itself in the service of men. It would do well for sociology to perform a decisive role in the structuring of a theory of cooperation, both for the general values this would help establish and for a way to settle some long standing ambiguities in sociological research.

Part Two
Conflict Systems

A. Intrapersonal Conflict

CURRENT AND NEEDED PSYCHOLOGICAL RESEARCH IN INTERNATIONAL RELATIONS[*]

DANIEL KATZ

Six related areas of current and needed psychological research can be identified in the field of international relations[1]: (1) the differing strategies of dealing with group conflict and the effects of these strategies upon conflict resolution—the area of social action; (2) the basis of aggression and violence in the individual personality —the individual motivational approach; (3) national imagery, the image people hold of other countries as well as of their own country—the area of cognitive structures; (4) the role of public opinion in the outbreak of war and the role of public opinion with respect to disarmament and nuclear warfare—the social process approach; (5) the psychological basis of national sovereignty and national involvement—the area of social structure; (6) the social and psychological conditions conducive to the development of international structures— additional social structural considerations.

[*] Reprinted by permission of the author and publisher from *Journal of Social Issues*, 1961, *17*: 69–78.

[1] The author is indebted to his colleagues at the Center for Research on Conflict Resolution of the University of Michigan for many of the research suggestions listed in these pages. He is also grateful to two mimeographed reports commissioned by the Institute for International Order, presently to be published, which cover in much more comprehensive fashion the task attempted in this paper: one by Ithiel de Sola Pool entitled "Research on Communication and Values in Relation to War and Peace," the other by Richard C. Snyder and James H. Robinson on "National and International Decision Making." Three other sources should be called to the attention of the interested reader: The new quarterly digest, *Current Thought on Peace and War*, published by the Institute for International Order, New York City; the reviews of current research on conflict resolution which appear in the *Journal of Conflict Resolution* and the UNESCO volume of 1957, *The Nature of Conflict*, published by the International Sociological Association.

Strategies of Conflict Resolution

The first area of needed research concerns the strategies of conflict resolution in terms of their effects upon counter strategies and, in the final analysis, upon world peace. Since this topic has received considerable attention in the other papers in this symposium in their analysis of deterrence, non-violence, threat and counterthreat I will add only one comment about this general area of action research. Psychology, and the other behavioral sciences, have thus far missed a critical opportunity in their neglect of research on the applications of Gandhian philosophy to the resolution of group conflict. The strategy of non-violence has helped to change the history of the east and is presently helping to change the pattern of race relations in America. The basic aspects of Gandhian philosophy of non-violence, of non-deceit, of sacrificial devotion to humanitarian values, of refusal to justify the means by the end are not only rich in their social psychological implications but are feasible objectives for research study (Janis and Katz, 1959). We need not waste time in regretting the neglected opportunities for systematic field studies of such events as the Alabama bus strike or the sit-in techniques at segregated lunch counters. The movement for racial equality, employing techniques of non-violence, may only be in its beginning. Opportunity does knock more than once.

Personal Basis of Aggression

Perhaps psychologists have focused more upon the second area of research, that of the personal basis of aggression, than upon any other. The neo-Freudians have called attention to the relationship between adult aggression and the frustrations and repression of hostilities in the socialization process. The impact of the volume, *The Authoritarian Personality* is still being felt in research conducted both here and abroad (Adorno *et al.*, 1950; Christiansen, 1959). The studies in the field of personal aggression have been ably reviewed by Elton McNeil (1959) in a recent number of the *Journal of Conflict Resolution.*

Interesting as these contributions are, I believe they are not central to an explanation of violent conflict between nations. They help in our understanding of why violence is part of the behavioral repertoire of human beings but they have nothing to say about particular forms of group action which involve the use of violence. Conflict between nations cannot be equated to conflict between individuals. Too many other variables are involved in international conflict to consider it as the sum of the aggressive tendencies of individual citizens. The properties of a social system are not found by the simple addition of the properties of individual component members. These properties are the result of the complex interaction of people engaged in the many role relationships of national systems and sub-systems. In other words, our actions in the roles we play in a social system are limited and determined by the role requirements of the system and are not the direct reflection of our own personality needs and desires.

Those who cling to a personality explanation of international strife, and yet realize that few wars are desired consciously or unconsciously by the great majority of people on either side, find refuge in emphasizing the personality dynamics of the top leaders in the national structure. The final decision to push the fatal button may be made by one man just as the final decision to drop an atomic bomb on Hiroshima was made by President Truman. Granted that we need to know the character structure of key role incumbents for a full understanding of group action, we also need to know the role demands which are made upon top leaders. And we need to know the social requirements at any one period which exert a selective influence upon the type of leaders who are likely to move up-

ward in the military and governmental structure. Nazi Germany was less the psychopathology of Hitler than it was a set of social and economic conditions and an institutional structure of irresponsibility for "the little people."

National Imagery

Personality factors do contribute, however, to our third area of study, namely, the way in which people see their own nation and other nations. The nation as the major geographical and political unit of social life provides an easy organizational focus about which cognitive structures readily develop—structures which characteristically have dimensions of hostility and friendliness and strength and weakness (Boulding, 1959). The image of one's own country is generally one of a peace loving strong nation while other countries may be perceived as chauvinistic and aggressive. The nature of such images and their determinants has been a continuing interest in social psychology. Buchanan and Cantril (1953) in their UNESCO study reported that people develop a particular image of another nation to give cognitive substance to their fears or hopes induced by information about the other country's threatening or friendly actions. Older stereotyped conceptions furnish the raw material for the organization of such images. The same investigators found that an international frame of reference was part of a broader set of values which asserted the belief in the changeability of human nature. Harold Isaacs of MIT is currently investigating the reciprocal images of Americans and Africans and attempting to discover how these mutual images affect the course of American-African relations. In preparation at the present time is a volume under the sponsorship of SPSSI edited by Herbert Kelman which will center on the role of national images in international behavior.

A number of studies have dealt with the effects of contact with other peoples upon national imagery. Increases in international understanding are assumed to be related to a more realistic and less stereotyped conception of another people and such changes are supposed to come about through more contact and communication. The many programs for the exchange of scholars, students, technicians and other personnel proceed upon this assumption. In fact these activities have been recently upgraded in our State Department with a new Bureau On Intercultural Activities, the head of which has become an Assistant Secretary in the Department. In general the many studies of the effects of these exchanges report a positive outcome of intercultural exchanges, but the results are not so overwhelming in this direction as to dismiss *The Ugly American* as sheer fantasy. E. Reigrotski and N. Anderson (1959) did find favorable effects of cultural exchange in extensive samples of people who were followed up in Belgium, France, Holland and Germany. But, as in the case of racial prejudice, sheer contact is not the crucial variable in the improvement of attitudes of the groups involved. Selltiz, Hopson and Cook (1956) interviewed 348 foreign students in 35 American universities and colleges, shortly after their arrival, and again five months later. These investigators found no relationship between the amount of personal interaction with Americans and favorable attitude change. The focus for future studies on this problem should be upon the conditions under which contact and interaction produce various effects. We already know from the studies that have been done and from related research more than we put into practice, namely, that the expectations which people bring from their native country are significant (Morris, 1956); that assessment of needs and providing appropriate experience is even more important (Watson and Lippitt 1958); and that the basic conditions of cooperation or competition are central considerations. We have Sherif's study (1958) of attitudes toward out-groups in a boy's camp which is relevant here, but tends to be forgotten. After conflict and competition between two gangs of campers had been fostered, the boys were brought together under the pleasant circumstances of a picnic. Instead of a change in attitudes resulting, the old hostile attitudes persisted and

the boys merely used the food provided for the picnic as missiles to hurl against one another. It took a situation in which superordinate goals were created, one in which the boys could perceive a community of interest, before favorable attitudes between the two gangs were established.

Public Opinion

Though favorable images of another nation may exist, it is still possible to mobilize public opinion against its rulers. In World War II we concentrated more upon the creation of an unfavorable image of German rulers than of the German people than we did in World War I. The study of the role of public opinion in the outbreak of hostilities is currently receiving some attention, in that in democracies public opinion affects the national decision-making processes, either as a factor which is manipulated by leaders, or as an influence which guides leaders in national policy-making.

Proposals have been made by Quincy Wright (1957) and by Stuart Dodd (1959) for a barometer of public opinion the world over, which would indicate areas of tension in time for constructive action to be taken. Moreover, national leaders are often inadequately informed of the developing opinion in another nation and so are poorly equipped to deal with it. Walter Lippmann, for one, believes that we, not only, were slow to assess public opinion in Cuba but are still not adequately informed about the climate of opinion in some other Latin American countries. The significant dimensions of opinions in other cultures could profit by more thorough psychological research and Robert Hefner has begun a non-parametric type of factor analysis to get at common and unique dimensions of international attitudes in different cultures.

The determinants of public opinion relating to international relations is also worthy of further investigation. W. Maurer has suggested the importance of studying the gatekeepers of information about foreign affairs, the small number of foreign correspondents, whose reports furnish the bulk of our knowledge of what is going on in various parts of the world. Ithiel Pool (1960) points out that all United States reportage from India, apart from embassy circles, comes through the correspondents of the *Associated Press,* the *United Press, Time, Life* and the *New York Times* who form the better part of the American full-time press corps in New Delhi. In similar fashion, the news from most capitals of the world comes from a handful of men. Pool suggests a study, not only of the qualifications of correspondents, but of how far they can rise above the limited perspective of their clientele to a frame of reference of citizens of the world. This research might parallel that of Chadwick Alger of Northwestern who is studying the secretariat staffs of international organizations to see what effects their international roles have upon their values and attitudes.

Though it is important to develop our knowledge about the role of public opinion in international crises, it is also necessary to recognize that the next war may be set off by accident or design, through the pressing of buttons, without the mediation of any opinion process. It becomes critical, then, to study opinions and attitudes about nuclear weapons and disarmament, about war and peace. In the past few years British and Scandanavian public opinion has become aroused about the use of atomic weapons. The British have moved a long way back to the notion of conventional weapons rather than atomic weapons as a deterrent. In 1958 the Norwegian Labor Party, the party in power, had a grass roots rebellion on its hands over the issue of entrusting Germany with atomic weapons. In Germany itself similar attitudes against the use of nuclear weapons are appearing. Studies are needed both in the United States and other nations of the conditions under which people will become sufficiently aroused about nuclear destruction to demand constructive action from their leaders. Political leaders in our country seem much more afraid of the charge that their party has been guilty of some weakening of the national defense than of brinkmanship.

In general, large scale shifts in attitudes to support protective actions against disas-ter follow rather than precede disaster, as witness the history of legislation to guard the public against fires, epidemics, and other hazards. What is necessary to create psychological salience of possible impending disaster? Who were the people in England and other European countries who changed their attitudes toward nuclear disarmament? Why did they change?

National Structure

The fifth area of national structure and national sovereignty has received little study from psychologists. Though national structure is of primary concern to other social scientists we need more psychological understanding of such questions as: Why is the national structure, with its remoteness from the daily life of the individual, so potent a determinant of his behavior with respect to critical matters? What is the nature of legitimate authority in terms of the perceptions, attitudes and habits of people? It is currently popular for sociologists to invoke Max Weber's (1947) old concept of legitimacy but what are its psychological dimensions? What accounts for the varying degrees to which people in different countries see themselves as nonparticipators in decisions about war and peace? Two aspects of our highly developed institutional structure may be of interest here. The first has to do with the socialization process which makes us amenable to assuming any role in adult life which the group setting demands with a consequent divorcing of any deep feeling of personal responsibility for the consequences of our role performance. Cohen and Brehm (1960) gave school children the onerous task of writing essays in favor of shorter summer vacations for stated prizes. Most of the subjects complied and those who received the higher prizes changed their own attitudes on the subject less than those who received smaller prizes and yet went ahead with the task. In other words, the heavy reward meant that they assumed the role with little cognitive dissonance since it was a role forced upon them by the amount of the reward. In similar fashion many adults turn out shoddy work on their jobs, write advertising copy that verges on the fraudulent or engage in any number of other activities to which they do not apply their own canons of private morality. Many students of the contemporary social scene believe that we have gone too far in making a virtue of role conformity in and of itself and so permitting the individual complete irresponsibility for his role performances. What we need, however, is not moral sermonizing about the evils of institutions but theoretical analysis, research study and social inventions which will preserve the advantages of bureaucratic role structure and yet improve desirable social outcomes.

A second relevant aspect of social structure is the weakness of clearly defined areas of role responsibility for integrating the organizational parts both for policy making and policy implementation. The impersonality of role structures, the doctrine of checks and balances, the lack of an appropriately informed public for decision validation makes it both difficult to assess blame and to institute corrective action. The feedback mechanisms for the correction of foreign policy seem to operate insensitively and ineffectively. Again the problem is not hopeless. Social institutions are man-made inventions which can be improved by their creators. What is needed is the recognition that they are man-made, that they are devices for satisfying human purposes and that their alteration should be studied objectively and scientifically. It is my thesis in short that our emphasis should not be upon changing people as if they operated in a social vacuum but upon changing role systems and other social devices. This still means changing people but it also means a differing emphasis in social change.

Another related series of questions would deal with the meaning of national sovereignty to different sub-groups in our population and other populations. Kenneth Boulding in this connection has suggested a study of people who give up their national membership in one country to become naturalized citizens of another. To what extent is national sovereignty a concept which gives emotional gratification in its verbal expression but is unrelated to specific attitudes of subscribing to an international order? For example, the Gallup release of August 6 of last year reported that 72 per cent of the American people approved of a UN army of sufficient size to deal with small wars throughout the world. Yet if the question had been about yielding national sovereignty the results might have been far different. On the other hand, as people we are apparently not as involved emotionally in national concepts as we once were. Our national honor seems less sensitive than it once was; instance the lack of national reaction to the trial of Powers and his less than patriotic stance; instance the reaction to the attack upon our airmen in the Congo. It may be that nationalism like religion is taking on new dimensions.

Still another aspect of research on national structure concerns its organization as a system for the maintenance of conflict as a heritage from the historical origins of the state (Coser, 1958). Are national leaders mistaken in their conception that to achieve and maintain political leadership they must give priority to protecting their people from dangers from without? What is the psychology of such sub-structures as the military and defense departments, the veterans' organizations, and other types of special interest groups? Our total economy and our way of life is geared to armaments and defense with over half of our 80 billion dollars budget going for these purposes. How could we conceivably disarm?—especially when we consider we can afford such sums more easily than the Soviet Union? Is this the reason for our lack of staff preparation for disarmament conferences? Benoit of Columbia and Boulding of Michigan are studying the economic consequences of disarmament. A related study should be made of the psychological consequences of disarmament as it affects specific dislocations in our way of life.

International Structure

The sixth area of needed research is the obverse of national involvement, namely, the psychological factors productive of growth of international structures. What are the effects of non-political structures which cut across national systems with respect to science, the arts, religion and humanitarian causes? What factors will foster their growth? What can be done to strengthen the international political structure of the UN? A recent report by the *Commission to Study the Organization of Peace,* headed by Arthur Holcombe (1960), has a series of specific proposals aimed at this objective. For example, the scholars writing this report suggest reconstructing the Security Council to make it a center for negotiation and enlarging the role of the Secretary General so that among other things he will be included in summit conferences. If these and similar proposals are sound, how can they gain adequate consideration by our policy makers, and how can operational research aid in the process?

Kenneth Boulding has advanced the hypothesis that the major factor in the negotiation of conflicts between organized groups is not a guarantee about the keeping of an agreement but the setting up of machinery for the adjudication of subsequent claims and grievances. Thus, labor and management got nowhere, so long as they centered on getting a settlement which either party could be trusted to keep. But they made great progress when the emphasis shifted to include machinery for the hearing of grievances which might arise. Can research substantiate this hypothesis between organized groups within the nation?

Thorough research is critically needed on some of the amazing developments in the direction of international cooperation. European countries with centuries of hostility, distrust and hatred are beginning to cooperate in the European common market which dislocates some of their citizens and which means some giving up of national sovereignty. Studies of this process by European social scientists with some collaboration from Americans constitute a genuine priority in the international field. It is of interest in this connection to note that Lloyd Free's study (1959) of one hundred members of Parliament in each of seven countries, supplemented by other leadership interviews, reports ardent support for the integration of Italy into the European community in Italian official and elite circles with four out of ten parliamentary leaders stating that the most important problem facing Europe is European unification. The difficulty of studying international relations has led Harold Guetzkow (1959) to a series of simulation experiments in which teams are set up to represent nations in interaction with different team members assigned to different national roles in keeping with the Rand research on gaming. The hope is that such simulation models may lead to clarification of theories about international relations.

Incompatible Values

Finally, the basic issue of peaceful coexistence and its psychological assumptions must be faced. Can there be economic and ideological competition on the one hand between the Russian and Western systems, and yet cooperation in the control and prevention of war? The Russian leaders maintain that the answer is in the affirmative but our own leaders question their sincerity. The psychological problem is whether or not mechanisms can be worked out to accommodate incompatible values. In the United States we have a history of toleration and of accommodation for incompatible religious values, even for such extreme groups as the Amish whose religious values color so much of their everyday beliefs and habits. In some countries there has been a peaceful coexistence between a socialistic labor movement and a capitalistic management in spite of Marxian predictions about the inevitable overt conflict. European countries have tolerated Communist parties in the body politic, though not without cost. We need more theoretical formulation of the accommodation of incompatible or conflicting value systems, and research to discover how and why such accommodation does work wherever it occurs (Wright *et al.,* 1954). For as C. Wright Mills (1960) puts it, "Before the world is made safe again for American capitalism or Soviet communism or anything else, it had better be made safe for human life."

REFERENCES

1. Adorno, Theodor W., Frenkel-Brunswik, Else, Levinson, Daniel J., and Sanford, R. Nevitt. *The Authoritarian Personality*. New York: Harper & Bros., 1950.
2. Boulding, Kenneth E. National images and international systems. *Journal of Conflict Resolution*, 1959, *3*, 121–131.
3. Buchanan, William and Cantril Hadley. *How Nations See Each Other*. Urbana: University of Illinois Press, 1953.
4. Christiansen, Bjorn. *Attitudes Toward Foreign Affairs as a Function of Personality*. Oslo: Oslo University Press, 1959.
5. Cohen, Arthur R. Attitudinal consequences of induced discrepancies between cognitions and behavior. *Public Opinion Quarterly*, 1960, *24*, 297–318.
6. Coser, Lewis. *The Functions of Social Conflict*. Glencoe, Illinois: Free Press, 1956.
7. Dodd, Stuart C. A proposed barometer of international tensions. *Journal of Conflict Resolution*, 1959, *3*, 430–434.
8. Free, Lloyd A. *Six Allies and a Neutral*. Glencoe, Illinois: Free Press, 1959.
9. Guetzkow, Harold. A use of simulation in the study of international relations. *Behavioral Science*, 1959, *4*, 183–191.
10. Holcombe, Arthur et al. Report of the Commission to Study the Organization of Peace, 1960.
11. Janis, Irving L. and Katz, Daniel. Reduction of intergroup hostility. *Journal of Conflict Resolution*, 1959, *3*, 80–100.
12. McNeil, Elton B. Psychology and aggression. *Journal of Conflict Resolution*, 1959, *3*, 195–293.
13. Mills, C. Wright. The balance of blame. *The Nation*, June 1960, *190*, 530.
14. Morris, Richard T. National status and attitudes of foreign students. *Journal of Social Issues*, 1956, *12*, 20–25.
15. Pool, Ithiel de Sola. *Research On Communication and Values in Relation to War and Peace*. New York: Institute of International Order, 1960.
16. Reigrotski, Erich and Anderson, Nels. National stereotypes and foreign contacts. *Public Opinion Quarterly*, 1959, *23*, 515–528.
17. Sherif, Muzafer. Superordinate goals in the reduction of intergroup conflict. *American Journal of Sociology*, 1958, *63*, 349–356.
18. Selltiz, Claire, Hopson, Anna L., and Cook, Stuart W. The effects of situational factors on personal interaction between foreign students and Americans. *Journal of Social Issues*, 1956, *12*, 33–44.
19. Watson, Jeanne and Lippitt, Ronald. Cross-cultural experience as a source of attitude change. *Journal of Conflict Resolution*, 1958, *2*, 61–66.
20. Weber, Max. *The Theory of Social and Economic Organization*. New York: Oxford University Press, 1947.
21. Wright, Quincy. Project for a world intelligence center. *Journal of Conflict Resolution*, 1957, *1*, 93–97.
22. Wright, Quincy, Cottrell, W. Fred, Boasson, Charles, and Gullvag, Ingemund. *Research for Peace*. Institute for Social Research, Oslo, Norway, 1954.

PRINCIPLES OF INTRAPERSONAL CONFLICT*

JUDSON S. BROWN

It is difficult to escape the conclusion that, from the very dawn of life, living organisms have been constantly subjected to the disrupting effects of conflicting tendencies to action. Whenever and wherever they have moved, the forces inciting them to action have been opposed by other agencies demanding either alternate responses or the cessation of action; for even the simplest movement cannot be executed unless the friction and inertia of bodily members are overcome; and no movement can long continue if the chemical products of fatigue are allowed to accumulate or if competing muscular contractions are not inhibited. For the individual organism, then, conflict is an inevitable consequence of an inherent capacity to act in any manner and especially of the ability to perform a multiplicity of acts.

It is with these intrapersonal conflicts, arising from competitions among incompatible tendencies to act, that the present paper is concerned. Its specific aim is to review in brief, and in some cases to enlarge upon, a selected group of explanatory principles that have proved valuable in the analysis of intra-individual conflict behavior.

A Basic Paradigm for Intrapersonal Conflict

A fundamental paradigm to which all intrapersonal conflicts can perhaps be reduced is shown in Figure 1. Here S designates a stimulus complex or pattern of cues having a high probability, when presented to an organism, of evoking two different and incompatible responses, R_1 and R_2. In any specific situation, the tendency (T_1) for S to elicit R_1 may be stronger than the tendency (T_2) to evoke R_2, or the reverse may

* Judson S. Brown, "Principles of Intrapersonal Conflict," *Journal of Conflict Resolution*, Vol. 1, No. 2 (1957), pp. 135–153. Reprinted by permission of the author and the publisher. The beginning of this article is omitted.

be true, or the two may be equal; and, when equal, they may be strong or weak. When

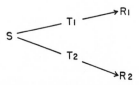

FIG. 1. Basic conflict paradigm. S is a stimulus complex capable of arousing two tendencies (T_1 and T_2) to perform antagonistic responses (R_1 and R_2). For simplicity, it has been assumed that only two antagonistic reactions are involved.

one of the antagonistic tendencies becomes strong enough to modify the behavior-determining action of the other, the paradigm illustrates conflict, as it has been described above. But if one of the tendencies is too weak to modify the action of its competitor, the paradigm is descriptive of commonplace, unambivalent behavior. Here and in what follows, unambivalent behavior refers to actions that can be satisfactorily explained by the invocation of a single dominant tendency, with minor disrupting effects of weakly antagonistic tendencies being ignored.

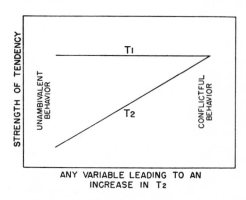

FIG. 2. Diagrammatic representation of relationships characterizing the continuum between unambivalent behavior and conflictful behavior.

An attempt has been made, by means of the diagram in Figure 2 to summarize the critical elements . . . of conflict and to expand the fundamental paradigm for conflict. In this diagram the base line represents any variable, such as frequency or intensity of punishment, that might lead to an increase in the strength of T_2. For simplicity, the strength of T_1 is assumed to remain constant. Now if, as the diagram shows, T_2 increases from a very low value at the left up to equality with T_1 at the right, the difference between the strengths of the two tendencies is reduced, and the effects of competition should become greater. On the present view, a marked inequality in the strengths of the tendencies is characteristic of unambivalent behavior, and equality is typical of conflictual behavior.

Varieties of Conflicts

Of recent years, psychologists have rather commonly classified conflicts into three major groups: (1) spatial conflicts, (2) discrimination-induced conflicts, and (3) temporal conflicts. If tendencies are present both to approach and to retreat from a given point in space, the conflict is identified as *spatial.* Conflicts arising from pressures to avoid objects on the left as well as on the right or from tendencies to approach two spatially separated goals would also be described by the adjective "spatial." *Discrimination-induced* conflicts are marked by the requirement that a difficult discrimination must be made between quite similar cues. As we have seen, this was the method used by Pavlov to produce experimental neuroses in his dogs. The third group, the *temporal* conflicts, includes those in which the degree of equality of competitory tendencies varies as a function of nearness in time to a particular event. These temporal conflicts have never been critically analyzed, and a preliminary attempt will be made to alleviate this deficiency in a later section of this paper. The central point to be stressed, however, in connection with these varieties of conflict is that, *in essence, they are simply three different techniques for manipulating the stimulus complex of our simple paradigm.* Shifting an organism's position in space cannot possibly affect its tendencies to action unless that shift produces a change in stimuli. Space, as such, can have

no causal efficacy with respect to behavior. Nor, for that matter, can the passage of time. . . . In the case of conflicts arising where difficult discriminations are required, it is evident that the relative strengths of the competing tendencies are changed through the experimenter's manipulations of the positive and negative stimuli.

Spatial Conflicts

Up to this point, as a consequence of an attempt to reduce the problem of conflict to its barest essentials, the discussion has been couched in extremely general terms. To increase the intelligibility of a subsequent treatment of temporal conflicts and to illustrate concretely the type of analysis that currently seems most fruitful, we turn now to a brief review of some typical spatial conflicts. The type of analysis to be followed is essentially identical with that of Miller, whose treatment rested on a foundation laid down by Lewin and Hull.

In a *spatial approach-avoidance conflict* . . . the organism is both attracted to and repelled from a specific region in his environment, and conflict increases as the antagonistic tendencies approach equality. For any practical analysis of such conflicts, however, information as to the manner in which the tendencies might normally be expected to vary with distance from the point of reward and punishment is an important prerequisite. Previous research and theory provide strong support for the idea that in a wide variety of situations the numerical values of both approach and avoidance tendencies increase as the organism moves nearer to the goal, with the avoidance tendency rising more rapidly than the approach. Figure 3 represents these assumptions in a purposely oversimplified form. Here the solid line denotes the approach tendency, and the dashed lines are weak, moderate, and strong avoidance tendencies. If, for the moment, we consider only the approach and the moderate avoidance tendencies, it will be apparent that their intersection near the center marks the region of maximum conflict. With departures from equality in either direction, the situation tends, increasingly, to evoke unambivalent behavior. If the individual is placed at the

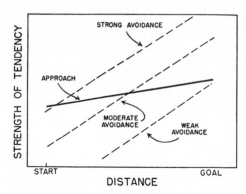

FIG. 3. Schematic diagram representing a single approach gradient (*soild line*) and three avoidance gradients (*dashed lines*) of differing over-all strengths. The gradients have been drawn as straight lines merely to simplify exposition.

starting position, he should approach in an unambivalent manner toward the goal, since the avoidance tendency is relatively weak at the starting point. Or, if placed in the situation near the goal, where the tendencies are also unequal, the subject should exhibit unambivalent avoidance. Let us assume, for the moment, however, that the avoidance subtracts from the approach at the left and the approach subtracts from the avoidance on the right. On this assumption, both approach and avoidance reactions would become weaker as the center is neared, and the subject would remain at the point of intersection of the gradients so long as their values remain unchanged. Reasoning in this manner, one arrives at an acceptable account of such conflict-situation behavior as going partway forward toward an ambivalent goal object or retreating partway and then pausing.

If the height of the avoidance gradient is reduced (lower dashed line) through the extinction of fear or if the positive gradient is elevated, the locus of conflict will be shifted toward the goal. This will produce an expansion in a goalward direction of the region of unambivalent approach in which the positive tendency is dominant. Throughout a greater proportion of the distance from the start, therefore, the behavior will be free of competition, and the goal may actually be reached without excessive slowing down or hesitation. Conversely, either an increase in the negative gradient (upper dashed line) through intensified punishment or a decrease in the positive tendency following satiation will shift the intersection toward the left. This will expand the region throughout which unimpeded avoidance should occur and will lessen the likelihood of the organism's ever reaching the goal.

As to the resolution of this type of conflict, under the restriction that the intersection of the gradients occurs between the starting point and the goal, the following may be said. Whenever the individual behaves by avoiding when the negative tendency is clearly dominant or by approaching when the positive is pre-eminent, he is inevitably sucked into the maelstrom of conflict. Behavior is self-regulating in this situation, but, since the position of equilibrium is conflictful, it can best be described as a kind of pernicious homeostasis. Because of this self-balancing aspect, an approach-avoidance conflict can never be resolved unless the values of the tendencies are markedly altered. Perhaps this self-regulatory feature of behavior in ambivalent situations accounts for the relative inescapability of such conflicts and for their stubborn resistance to therapeutic amelioration.

In a *spatial avoidance-avoidance conflict*, an individual in attempting to avoid one threatening object, must move toward another that is equally threatening. On the assumption that the strength of the tendency to avoid each object decreases with distance, the situation would be marked by relationships like those of Figure 4. Here again, for purposes of simplification, the avoidance gradients have been drawn as straight lines of essentially equal slopes, with their intersection falling halfway between the two fear-arousing regions. Subtracting one tendency from the other yields the dashed-line gradients to the right and left on the upper surfaces of the cross-hatched areas. The left-hand one of these is the net tendency to avoid the region at the left, and the right-hand one is the net tendency to escape from the right.

From our preceding analysis it should now be obvious that, at the extreme ends of this spatial array, behavior will be unambivalent, and unimpeded avoiding reactions

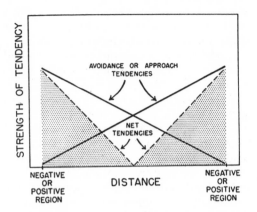

FIG. 4. Schematic diagram of gradients in the strength of tendencies either to avoid or to approach two spatially separated goals. The dashed-line gradients denote the net tendencies obtainable by algebraically summating the overlapping gradients.

will take place. But the occurrence of such avoidance drives the organism into the central region, where the tendencies are equal, and conflict results. If barriers are present ·to prevent the individual from leaving the situation, conflict must continue. Again, the regulatory mechanism is pernicious, since behavior consistent with the dictates of the tendencies always leads back to a region of conflict. Under these conditions, conflict can be alleviated by drastically reducing the strength of one or both tendencies. If the object at the right is no longer feared, the corresponding gradient would be eliminated, and behavior throughout the entire space between the two negative regions would qualify as unimpeded avoidance behavior with respect to the left-hand object. In the absence of restrictive barriers, of course, an individual can resolve or reduce the conflict by moving away from both feared objects at the same time. By moving far enough, the tendencies, though still theoretically equal, would be too weak to operate effectively in the production of any behavior.

The diagram of Figure 4 may also be used to illustrate the relevant variables in an *approach-approach conflict*. Here the two points of reinforcement are equally desirable objects, and the solid-line gradients represent increasing positive tendencies

to approach each. The dashed-line gradients now denote the net tendencies to approach either side. In an environment where these relations hold, the organism can never undergo prolonged conflict. In contrast with the approach-avoidance and avoidance-avoidance kinds of conflict, the behavioral homeostatic mechanism in this case has benign rather than pernicious consequences. Regardless of the individual's position, if he responds in accordance with the demands of the tendencies, he will always progress from a region of relative equality and conflict to a region of conflictless inequality. Even if he were placed precisely at the point where the tendencies are equal, any slight change in the stimulus conditions would upset the momentary balance, and he would tend to move toward one or the other goal. The approach-approach conflict is thus self-resolving, whereas the others are self-perpetuating. Presumably, such self-resolving conditions would never lead to neurotic tendencies, and clinical experience probably bears this out.

Under the circumstances of everyday living, however, it is doubtful whether pure approach-approach conditions such as these ever exist. In nearly every case, the choice of one goal generates an avoidance tendency due to the fact that the other goal may have to be relinquished. As Godbeer and Miller have shown, such double approach-avoidance conflicts are not readily resolved. By and large, these double approach-avoidance conflicts reduce to a kind of avoidance-avoidance paradigm, and they need not, therefore, be considered further here.

Discrimination Conflict

Conflict arising when an individual is required to perform difficult discriminations are amenable to theoretical analyses (3) that parallel, in many respects, those we have discussed in connection with spatial conflicts. Suppose, for example, that a subject has been trained to push a lever forward when a high-frequency tone is sounded and to refrain from responding when a low-frequency tone is sounded. Now, if on successive trials, the pitch of the high tone is progressively reduced and the pitch of the low one is raised, the accuracy of the subject's performance will decline, and, as the two tones approach equality, he may exhibit symptoms of indecision and conflict. Clearly, this discrimination situation differs from those we have already described as spatial, since the subject neither approaches nor avoids a spatial region and since the conflict-inducing stimuli, being under the experimenter's control, are not altered appreciably by the subject's behavior.

In interpreting discrimination-induced conflicts such as these, it is convenient to invoke the *principle of stimulus generalization*. According to this principle, after a response has been associated with one stimulus, other stimuli similar to the first will also elicit the same response without further training. Moreover, the greater the similarity between the old and the new cues, the higher the probability that the new ones will elicit the same response as the old.

The application of this concept of stimulus generalization to our hypothetical discrimination problem with the high and low tones is illustrated in **Figure 5**. Here the

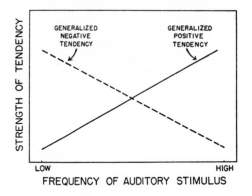

FIG. 5. Generalized tendencies to respond and to refrain from responding as a function of distance on a frequency dimension.

abscissa represents the tonal continuum ranging from the low to the high tone used in the problem. And the ordinate, as before, represents the strengths of the reaction tendencies. The solid-line gradient on the right indicates, in accord with stimulus generalization, that the tendency to respond by pushing the lever is strongest at the point

where training has been conducted (high tone) but is present in appreciable degree at all other points on the dimension. Similarly, the dashed line depicts the generalized tendency to refrain from responding to the low tone.

If the actual relationships were as shown in this figure, it would follow that if either the high tone or the low tone were presented, no conflict would result, since the generalized tendencies to make the incompatible responses are minimal at those (unambivalent) points. But tones near the middle of the dimension would tend to elicit both positive and negative generalized responses. And the closer the stimuli approached the middle of the dimension, the more equal would the competing tendencies become and the stronger the conflict.

With respect to the resolution of discrimination-induced conflicts, it is clear from Figure 5 that an increase or decrease in the height of either gradient will increase the disparity between the strengths of the two tendencies at certain points on the dimension and thus reduce conflict at those points. This can be accomplished by retraining, by extinction procedures, by changing the nature of the stimuli, or by alterations in the individual's motivational level.

Temporal Conflicts

As has been indicated, conflicts may arise from changes in an organism's temporal nearness to any event that elicits competing tendencies to action. There are almost no experimental studies of temporal conflicts in the psychological literature, however, and even in Miller's (21) extensive review only a sentence or two is devoted to them. In view of this relative neglect of what may be an important area, it is interesting to see whether a meaningful analysis of temporal conflicts can be achieved within the general conceptual framework employed here.

To extend the principles of conflict from the spatial and similarity dimensions to the dimension of time we must begin by asking whether it is realistic to suppose that both positive and negative tendencies change systematically as a consequence of stimulus variations attending the passing of time.

That is, are there positive and negative gradients in time?

Positive temporal gradients. The presence of a positive temporal gradient would be implied by the observation that the tendency to perform a periodically evoked response increases with nearness to the moment at which the response has usually been elicited and rewarded. Such observations have indeed been made in the case of both classically conditioned (27) and instrumentally conditioned responses (31). Moreover, human subjects, when required to make simple manual movements to a regularly recurring signal, exhibit progressively shorter reaction times as the customary time for the appearance of the signal is approached (25). These data are paralleled by such commonplace observations as that of the mounting excitement shown by children with the approach of Christmas. There appear to be adequate grounds, therefore, for supposing that after a response has been reinforced at regular intervals the strength of the tendency to make that response will increase as the usual time of its elicitation approaches. This is clearly analogous to the approach gradient described previously for spatial conflict situations.

Negative temporal gradients. It is also reasonable to believe that the strengths of tendencies to avoid or to fear an expected noxious or painful event increase with nearness to that event. If one arranges to have a wisdom tooth extracted at some time in the future, the dread of pain is relatively mild when the appointment is made. But, as the fateful hour draws close, fear mounts increasingly. Everday observations of this kind are supported by experimental data from studies by Brown (2) and by Rigby (29). These investigators have shown that rats' fears of a painful shock become intensified as the customary time for being shocked grows near.

Incidentally, much of the process of socialization in children seems to be directed toward extending their gradients of fear in time. If the child's fear is not aroused until the actual moment of punishment, the fear cannot function as a deterrent to the performance of socially tabooed acts. One must learn to fear parental displeasure long before the strap descends if disapproved actions are to be inhibited. To achieve a disciplined society, anxieties concerning the punishments to be expected for robbery, arson, rape, and the like must be aroused long before the penitentiary doors swing open.

Having decided, then, that both positive and negative temporal gradients may reasonably be assumed to exist under specific conditions of learning and reinforcement, the next question is how conflicts, if any, develop or decline through time. A number of different possibilities suggest themselves here, and we shall consider each of them briefly.

Thwarted-avoidance conflict. One variety of temporal conflict which might be called *thwarted-avoidance conflict,* is characterized by the fact that, as time passes, a noxious state of affairs comes nearer and nearer, but escape is prevented by physical barriers. The convicted murderer awaiting certain death in the electric chair provides a grim but realistic example. For such an unfortunate individual, dread of the coming traumatic episode increases with time, but all avoidance responses are thwarted by strong barriers.

A comparable situation, more directly analogous to the kinds of conflicts we have already considered, exists where the restraints against escape are social or cultural rather than physical. Thus the tradition that one's honor must be maintained at any cost might force one to engage in a duel having a high probability of leading to death. Such conditions existed for Gary Cooper in the movie High Noon, as you may recall. The time-induced conflict here involves an increasing fear of death as the dueling hour approaches and a competitive fear of social disgrace or ostracism. Assuming the fear of dishonor to remain constant, the conflicting tendencies may be represented by the solid-line gradient and either of the dashed-line gradients in the sketch of Figure 6. If the fear of dishonor is greater than the weak fear of death, the duel will actually be carried out. But if the over-all strength of the tendency to fear death is increased, the gradients will cross at an earlier point in time. The period of maximum conflict will then occur sooner, and the individual may well escape entirely from the situation. There are also, of course, various factors that would operate to increase the strength of the tendency to carry out the feared act and to decrease the anticipation of trauma. Primitive tribesmen, when going to war, commonly fortify themselves by specialized rituals involving singing, dancing, and appeals to the gods for supernatural aid. Even civilized man knows that alcohol may sometimes function to alleviate or obliterate fears of impending pain. The relationships diagrammed in Figure 6, though superficially different from

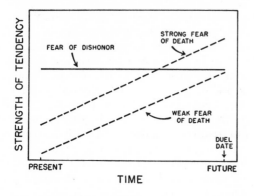

FIG. 6. Competing tendencies involved in thwarted-avoidance temporal conflict.

some we have considered, are comparable in many respects to those of spatial avoidance-avoidance conflicts. Time moves in only one direction, however, and hence the difference between the competitive tendencies must always decrease (up to the point of equality), and conflict or frustration must always increase.

Thwarted-approach conflict. Conflictful situations also exist in which, for assorted reasons, *one simply cannot perform a given response until a certain period of time has elapsed.* In some localities, eager young couples cannot become legally united until a "cooling-off" period of several days has elapsed following the purchase of the marriage license. And many of us often find that we must wait until the arrival of a salary check at the end of the month to buy a much wanted, but expensive, article.

In these and in similar instances the tendency to perform the thwarted act increases with time. But time cannot be hurried, and its very stodginess is often frustrating and irritating. Social rules and taboos, of course, are the primary factors providing the restraints, but the restraints are inextricably geared to the flow of time.

A diagrammatic representation of the reactive and restraining tendencies in a conflict of this type would be essentially identical with the previous sketch. For example, let the line labeled "fear of dishonor" in Figure 6 represent the strength of the restriction against marrying, and let the temporal base line represent the "cooling-off" period. If the lower of the two dashed-line gradients is taken to indicate the strength of the young couple's tendency to get married, it follows that conflict should increase with nearness to the deadline. And, so long as the restriction or fear of punishment is stronger than the positive desire, the couple will wait until the approved time. But if, as a consequence of biological or social incentives or goads, the tendency to consummate the marriage becomes excessively strong, the period of maximal conflict will occur during the waiting period, and the lovers may rush off to a Gretna Green to get married more quickly.

This situation also resembles, to a degree, the spatial approach-avoidance conflict. In the thwarted-approach paradigm the strength of the inhibiting tendency is greater than the positive tendency up to the point of equality, and hence the response is prevented from occurring until that point is reached or passed. In the spatial approach-avoidance, however, the positive tendency exceeds the negative at the more remote distances from the goal, and the response will tend to occur up to the point of equality, but not beyond.

Temporal approach-avoidance conflicts. An attractive possibility in considering temporal conflicts is that there might exist situations which could best be described by appeal to positive and negative gradients of the sort already utilized in spatial approach-avoidance behavior. For example, when the amorous swain, under the influence of a full moon and other stimulants, proposes marriage the positive aspects of an imagined life with his inamorata are doubtless preeminent. As the succeeding days of the engagement period pass, however, the potentially negative aspects of marriage—loss of freedom, family responsibilities, and financial burdens—may loom larger and larger. The result may be—and often is, apparently—that the period just before the wedding becomes especially conflictful. And in extreme cases, when the avoidance becomes stronger than the approach, the bride may be left standing at the altar.

To explain such behavior it might be assumed that the strength of the tendency to avoid marriage increases at a more rapid rate with nearness to the event than do the more positive aspects. Assuming, further, that the positive and negative tendencies summate algebraically, it follows that the likelihood of getting married decreases, but conflict increases, with nearness to the nuptial day. Perhaps this is co-ordinate with the common notion that long engagements are less likely to lead to marriage than short ones.

Apparently, the only published experimental study of a temporal approach-avoidance conflict is that by Rigby (29). As has already been observed, he obtained gradients in the amplitudes of both approach and avoidance responses as a function of nearness to an event that was both rewarding and punishing. He was unable, however, to support the suggestion that the avoidance gradient might be steeper than that for approach. Such experimental verification will be needed if further attempts to extend the theory into temporal dimensions are to prove fruitful.

It is also possible to describe, within the general outline of the temporal conflict paradigm, situations analogous to the approach-approach and avoidance-avoidance scheme we have already considered. Since these have not been previously described, a brief analysis of them appears justified.

Conflict as a function of temporal nearness to an approach-approach situation. In this type of conflict the passage of time brings an organism increasingly close to a situation in which strong incompatible approaching responses will be simultaneously evoked. Suppose, for example, that equally attractive movies are announced a week in advance at two different theaters. On the day when these productions are actually being shown, the situation is identical with the simple approach-approach type of conflict. But when the "coming attractions" are announced, the tendencies to approach both theaters, though equal, should be extremely weak or non-existent. As the days go by, the two tendencies should increase in strength and reach their maximum at the instant of final decision when the moviegoer is standing between the two theaters with his money in his hand. In these circumstances the moviegoer is, in a manner of speaking, drawn into the presence of cues to competing actions by the passage of time. Ordinarily, there is nothing he can do either to hasten or to delay the appearance of the movies. Time flows past the motionless individual, and in so doing brings to him events capable of arousing incompatible proclivities to respond.

An attempt to diagram these relations is reproduced in Figure 7. Here the back wall of a three-dimensional structure represents, in its left-right dimension, the spatial separation of the two positive goals, i.e., the movie theaters. The height of any point on that wall indicates the strength of the tendency to approach, and the lines ABC and DBE represent identical intersecting approach gradients. To this spatial wall there is added another dimension, that of time. This is shown as extending outward from the wall toward the viewer. Finally, it is assumed that the approach tendencies spread out into this new dimension in such a way as to form two conical surfaces. The plane of intersection of these cones is indicated by the letters BFG and the dotted shading. Our attention centers on this plane. If, when the movies are announced, the movie fan is at the space-time point G, the strength of the tendencies to approach either theater are equal but negligible. As the days go by, the back surface of the figure may be thought of as moving forward

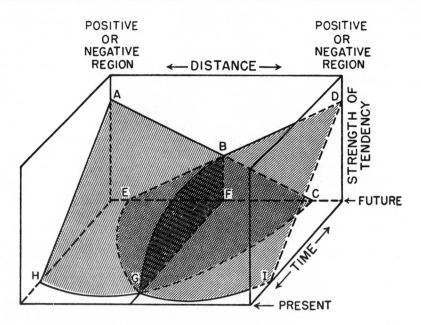

FIG. 7. A tridimensional space-time structure designed to represent changes in the strengths of competing tendencies as a function of temporal nearness to either an approach-approach or an avoidance-avoidance conflict situation.

toward the moviegoer. Consequently, the strengths of the two competitive tendencies increase simultaneously in a manner indicated by the changing height of the curved line GB above the floor of the structure. At the final instant of decision, the subject is at point F, and both tendencies are maximally strong, having a value corresponding to the length of line BF.

The behavioral consequences to be predicted from this analysis depend on one's theory of whether variations in the absolute strengths of two equal positive tendencies do, indeed, lead to modified actions. Approach-approach conflicts are presumably always self-resolving unless covert avoidance tendencies are also present. Ease of conflict resolution may not, therefore, be affected by variations in the absolute strengths of two competing positive tendencies. But it is quite possible that degree of emotional arousal and hence drive level would increase as the time for decision approaches. It is also clear that if the slopes of the gradients varied with changes in their absolute heights at the point of intersection, differences in the speed of conflict

resolution might be predicted. Thus, if the gradients were very flat at the crossing point, we would expect a definite reaction toward one of the two alternatives to have a longer latency than if the gradients rose steeply on each side of the junction.

Conflict as a function of temporal nearness to an avoidance-avoidance situation. Consider now the case of an infantryman who is told that in exactly one hour he must charge forward from his relatively safe dugout into the face of strong enemy fire or remain and struggle with enemy forces advancing from the rear. Both these alternatives are undesirable, and at the zero hour he will be enmeshed in a strong avoidance-avoidance situation. But until that hour arrives he is temporally remote from both these fear-producing possibilities. When the gravity of the situation first becomes clear, his fears may be aroused, but, since he is still somewhat remote from the crucial moment, the conflict should not be exceptionally strong. As time passes, however, he finds himself in the presence of cues which, to an ever increasing degree, elicit incompatible avoidance reactions and stronger and stronger fears.

The principal variables in this type of spatiotemporal conflict may be represented by a geometrical figure like the one we have just seen. Thus in Figure 7 the lines ABC and DBE may be taken to represent the strengths of the tendencies to avoid the two enemy forces situated at the two negative regions on either side. When the dilemma is presented, the soldier may be thought of as located somewhere near G on the line GF. With each tick of the clock, however, point F comes closer, and the absolute strengths of the (equal) negative tendencies increase along the line GB.

Since the flow of time is unidirectional, the soldier in this example cannot back up along the line FG toward G and thereby effect a simultaneous reduction in the strengths of both negative tendencies. By and large, escape is impossible and one might predict that the degree of emotional arousal would become magnified with nearness to the "moment critique," that the level of motivation should increase, and that the frequency and magnitude of oscillations might change. Precisely which of these alternatives would be predicted would depend upon the specific assumptions one makes as to the shapes of the avoidance gradients. Curvilinear gradients would lead to different predictions than linear gradients.

It would also be possible to describe conflicts which are a function of temporal nearness to double approach-avoidance situations. As we have previously noted, however, such types of competition reduce essentially to the avoidance-avoidance type, and a separate analysis of them seems unnecessary.

REFERENCES

2. Brown, J. S. "A Note on a Temporal Gradient of Reinforcement," *Journal of Experimental Psychology*, XXV (1939), 221–227.

3. _____. "Factors Determining Conflict Reactions in Difficult Discriminations," *ibid.*, XXXI (1942), 272–297.

21. Miller, N. E. "Experimental Studies of Conflict." In Hunt, J. McV. (ed.), *Personality and the Behavior Disorders*. New York: The Ronald Press Company, 1944.

25. Mowrer, O. H. "Preparatory Set (Expectancy): Some Methods of Measurement." *Psychological Monographs*, Vol. LII, No. 2 (1940) (whole No. 233).

27. Pavlov, I. P. *Conditioned Reflexes.* Translated by G. V. Anrep. London: Oxford University Press, 1927.

29. Rigby, W. K. "Approach and Avoidance Gradients and Conflict Behavior in a Predominantly Temporal Situation," *Journal of Comparative and Physiological Psychology.* XLVII (1954), 83–89.

31. Rosenbaum, G. "Temporal Gradients of Response Strength with Two Levels of Motivation," *Journal of Experimental Psychology*, XLI (1951), 261–267.

PERSONALITY DYNAMICS AND
SOCIAL CONFLICT*[1]

ROSS STAGNER

"Wars begin in the minds of men" asserts the UNESCO charter. This is, of course, a view widely held outside of our profession as well as within it. Mr. George F. Kennan, distinguished analyst of foreign policy, has also stressed the psychological determinants of American activities. In 1954 he wrote, "It is precisely these subjective factors—factors relating to the state of mind of many of our own people—rather than the external circumstances, that seem to constitute the most alarming component of our situation. It is such things as the lack of flexibility in outlook, the stubborn complacency about ourselves and our society, the frequent compulsion to extremism, the persistent demand for absolute solutions . . . it is these things in the American character that give added gravity to a situation which would in any case be grave enough" (Kennan, 1954, p. 32).

We may appropriately enough note that Mr. John Foster Dulles, whose rigidity Kennan was implicitly criticizing, had in 1938 taken a stand on the same basis as Kennan. Dulles wrote, "there has been a grave misconception of the nature of peace. Peace has been identified with the status quo, stability with rigidity" (Dulles, 1939, p. ix). And elsewhere he stated, "The human race craves certainty and precision . . . . It treats the world as a basket in which are placed packages, each wrapped, labeled and tied in its separate container . . ." (Dulles, 1939, p. 156). "The ambitious and dynamic powers bitterly resent a dominant world philosophy under which peace and international morality are equated with the preservation of rigidities which for long operated, as they believe, to protect selfish-

ness and to prolong inequities" (Dulles, 1939, pp. 162–163).

Some readers may suspect that I have chosen this quotation from our late Secretary of State because of his emphasis on the craving for certainty and related rigidity. This suspicion is justified. I want to deal with problems of social conflict in the framework of a homeostatic conception of human nature, and an emphasis on perception as a major process. Let me remind you of only a few basic assumptions which will assume considerable importance in the analysis.

A Homeostatic Conception of Human Nature

According to this view, the dominant principle in the behavior of living organisms is the maintenance of certain vital constancies of the internal environment—that is, the steady states of oxygen, food, water, and other essentials for survival. In the service of these constancies man creates a predictable environment, in the physical world, by way of agriculture, housing, economic systems, and the like; in his personal world by way of the perceptual constancies. He learns to adapt to the changing aspects of physical reality, *distorting* sensory inputs to correspond to the most probable physical object. He creates a *constant* perceptual environment, and as far as possible he stabilizes the physical and social milieu within which he lives. Some individuals even come to value the ideological environment which they associate with survival, and mobilize energy to resist change in this structure of institutions, beliefs, and values (Stagner, 1961, pp. 69–86).

The specific application of this thesis which I shall propose in this paper is that man comes to value his nation, or other social group, as an essential part of his environment, and mobilizes energy to pro-

* Reprinted by permission of the author and publisher from *Journal of Social Issues*, 1961, *17*: 28–44.
[1] This paper, in essentially its present form, was delivered as the Presidential Address to the American Psychological Association's Division of Personality and Social Psychology on September 2, 1960.

tect it. Further, as a part of this process, he distorts the input of information in such a fashion as to protect valued aspects of his social environment, and these distortions contribute in no small degree to the intensity and bitterness of social conflicts. The rigidity referred to by Messrs. Kennan and Dulles is a key aspect of this distortion.

In this connection it is important, I think, to clarify a source of confusion which sometimes creeps into discussions of homeostasis. Man needs a *predictable environment,* a stable milieu, within which he can function. But this is not to say that he wants to make the same responses over and over. It is not uniformity of behavior, but an environment within which he can anticipate the consequences of behavior, which is essential.

In an agrarian civilization, man's need for such a stable environment was largely met by the uniformity of physical laws, the weather and the seasons, plants and lower animals. But as men multiplied and lived closer together, their very spontaneity and unpredictability as individuals compelled the creation of bureaucracy as a device for imposing some order upon chaos —for improving the stability of the milieu. Strong men imposed rules on their fellows to obtain predictability; but the strong man did not expect to, and generally did not, conform to the rules. As Dalton (1959) has pointed out, the efficient executive is one who knows when to ignore or circumvent rules. And unquestionably man will go on trying to evade bureaucratic controls, just as he has always sought to master the limitations imposed by physical and biological laws.

Ethnocentrism

It was over 60 years ago that Hobson, a British social scientist, wrote, "The actual direct efficient forces in history are human motives." Yet, despite sporadic efforts, psychologists as a group have contributed relatively little to the understanding of social conflict.

Some efforts, of course, have been made in this direction. SPSSI established in 1936 a Committee on War and Peace. In recent years, the American Psychological Association has created a committee to study the place of psychology in the maintenance of world peace. I should like to urge all of you to cooperate with this committee with suggestions, with questions, with research proposals.

I would like to hark back for just a moment to the work of the SPSSI Committee on War and Peace, whose labors were rudely interrupted by Pearl Harbor. A major conclusion had early been reached by this committee, on the basis of a careful study of the writings of historians, economists, and political scientists—viz., that the major psychological factor involved in the occurrence of international war was the attitude complex called "nationalism" (Stagner et al., 1942). The political scientists, for example, stressed the phenomenon of sovereignty; disputes could not be settled peacefully because nations recognized no higher authority to which they could be submitted. Blackstone's famous Commentaries referred to sovereignty as "the supreme irresistible, absolute, uncontrolled authority." Clearly persons who hold such a view cannot tolerate the notion of yielding to a court of justice; equally clearly there is an element here of psychotic delusions of grandeur. Similarly, in economic discussions of war stress was placed on a struggle for competitive advantage, with ruthless disregard for the welfare of other nations, through policies of economic nationalism (Stagner et al., 1942).

The defining features of nationalism are generally considered to be two in number: an exaggerated glorification of the nation, its virtues, its benefactions, its right to superiority; and an exaggerated denigration of nations perceived as being in opposition, these nations generally being seen as bad, cruel, vicious and untrustworthy.

When we look at this description, we readily observe that a similar pattern appears in other forms of social conflict. During the religious wars in Europe 300 years ago, a comparable glorification of one's in-group and vilification of the out-group were common; and anti-Semitism in this country shows this pattern in less bizarre form. The white supremacists of our southern states, and in extreme the Afrikaners of South Africa, hold similar delusions of racial grandeur and of the inferiority of colored races. Partisans of labor unions and of industrial owners do not show quite the same extremes of grandeur and hostility, but certainly many of them suggest that all virtue is on their side, all stupidity, violence, or greed on the other. It seems, therefore, that this bi-polar attitude of grandeur and evil is a psychological feature of all social conflicts. It is unfortunate that we have no generally accepted term for labeling this pattern. Ethnocentrism is undoubtedly the most appropriate term, but it has become identified with religious and racial prejudice. I shall use ethnocentrism to identify this general trend toward group-centeredness, and nationalism for its specific form in international conflict, on which I shall focus.

The central problem, from the point of view of personality theory, is how the motives and perceptions of individuals influence their decisions on social issues. Psychoanalytic writers on these problems, such as Glover, Hopkins, Durbin and Bowlby, and Alix Strachey, have tended to emphasize the decisive influence of motivation, frequently in the form of a "death instinct." In opposition, I wish to stress the perceptual approach to these questions.

Hostility as a Critical Factor in Social Conflicts

Let me first deal with the argument that the decisive consideration in major social conflicts is the level of aggressive drive or hostility. I propose to argue that this is not an important consideration, and indeed that it can, in some degree, be ignored as both a theoretical and a practical problem.

As a theoretical problem aggression has mainly been conceptualized in one of two ways: first, as an instinctive drive, as in the nineteenth century "instinct of pugnacity" associated with the names of McDougall and James; and its modern variant, the "death instinct" proposed by Freud and still advocated by some orthodox analysts. Secondly, aggression has been conceptualized as a derivative of frustration—largely

in a means-end relationship, proposed by John Dollard and the Yale School, and also in a tension-release formulation by Norman Maier (Dollard *et al.*, 1939; Maier, 1949).

A hereditary conception of aggression leads nowhere with regard to social conflict. If man is born with a given potential for aggression, we must apparently assume that in the course of his life he will act out this potential in some form. But aggression, as even the Freudians agree, may be channeled into face-to-face hostility, into competitive behavior, and even into work, or it may be vented in group competition and conflict of a non-violent nature. Thus the theory cannot logically lead to any kind of prediction about the occurrence of violent social conflict, whether between nations, or classes, or races.

A similar conclusion must be reached with respect to the frustration-aggression hypothesis. This view is somewhat more directly relevant to problems of social interaction because it carries an important, sometimes unstated, assumption that the preferred outlet for aggression will be an attack on the frustrating agent. This would suggest that, if large numbers of individuals find themselves being frustrated by, let us say, communist tactics, they will become hostile to communists. The inadequacy of this approach is suggested by the fact that most of the applications of the theory to social problems make use of displaced aggression, as in the famous study of southern lynchings, in which it appeared that a drop in the price of cotton led to more aggressive outbursts. But opposed to this we have the observation of criminologists that crimes of violence for the entire population increase in times of prosperity, not in times of depression. It thus appears that the crucial question is not, what led to the increase in aggressive acts? The question must be phrased: what variables determine the direction to be taken in expressions of hostility? It seems likely that the groups perceived as "bad" and therefore suitable for attack, and preferably "weak," hence not in a position to retaliate, will be the objects of aggression.

As a practical problem neither an instinctivist nor an environmentalist theory of aggression has much value from the point of view of blunting or disarming social conflicts. Both the Freudians and the Yale School advocate reducing frustrations to a socially tolerable minimum, especially for young children; but this seems to be based on concern for the mental health of the individual more than for social health.

As a concrete example, let me say that many people suppose the level of hostile tension experienced by the leaders of the Soviet Union to be a factor of great importance as regards the possible outbreak of World War III. It is assumed that these men may allow, or even order, acts which will precipitate a nuclear war. But does the level of aggression have anything to do with such a decision? On the hereditary assumption, we must conclude that their tension levels are already determined and what we do is irrelevant. If we look at the problem in terms of a frustration theory, we must certainly conclude that the men in the Kremlin are not hungry, they are not cold and wretched, and they have tremendous gratifications for any drive toward power which may motivate them. Can we suppose, then, that their *personal* level of frustration is relevant to a decision on international policy? I think not.

There is, of course, the theory of leader behavior expressed variously by Plato, by Machiavelli, and by more recent advisors to rulers: if your people are aggressive, encourage them to hate a foreign enemy, thus displacing their hatred from yourself. But even on this kind of theorizing, it must be clear that the crucial consideration becomes this: what are the perceptual factors determining the *direction* of aggression? The level of aggressive tension then becomes a remote rather than an immediate factor—not to be ignored, but not open to practical manipulation if we seek to reduce the probability of organized violence.

In opposition to those views of social conflict which stress drive, therefore, I want to talk about the decisive role of perception. Essentially, what I shall say is that for both theoretical and practical reasons, we should focus on how members of groups perceive other groups, and their goals and their tactics. To quote Kenneth Boulding (1959,

p. 120), "the people whose decisions determine the policies and actions of nations do not respond to the 'objective' facts of the situation, whatever that may mean, but to their 'image' of the situation."

The Decisive Role of Perception

Perception can operate in the service of creating a predictable environment in at least three ways. First, it can magnify certain information inputs, giving them greater weight; and secondly, the obvious corollary, it can diminish the importance of other cues. Finally, actual distortions may occur in quality and magnitude. The phenomena of size constancy, for example, require that the individual differentiate among cues of apparent size, and weight them in such a fashion as to give the closest approximation to the assumed "real object."

Perception in social affairs shows the same attributes. The real virtues of our nation are magnified; our sins are blocked out. The evils of the enemy are exaggerated, and his virtues ignored. Finally, cues indicative of behavior contrary to our expectations are often distorted to support the rigid percepts already organized. The great British statesman, Edmund Burke, said a long time ago, "We can never walk surely but by being sensible of our blindnesses." We must recognize our tendency to exclude certain information from consciousness. Another early insight on this topic comes from the Greek historian, Thucydides, who commented that, "Different eyewitnesses give different accounts of the same events, speaking out of partiality for one side or the other, or else from imperfect memories." Since memory distortions seem to obey the same dynamic principles as perceptual distortions, it appears that most erroneous reports stem from dynamic influences within the personalities of the reporters.

But let us not assume that only reporters and historians are guilty of partiality. Diplomats, presidents, and prime ministers likewise have their blind spots, their distortions, their misperceptions. So does the famous "man in the street." Each tends to see reality only in the manner which is compatible with his own motives and past experiences.

I propose this assertion as a starting point for my discussion of social conflict: social conflicts are rational if we grant the accuracy of the way in which the participants perceive the issues. It is easy enough for the detached observer to see the irrationality of both sides, let us say, in the Spanish-American War of 1898, in the 1959 steel strike, or in the religious wars of three hundred years ago. But if we learn to look at the matters in controversy as they were seen by the participants, it becomes clear that perceptual distortion was a fundamental process. Once given these misperceptions, given a distorted reality, the behavior of the participants was reasonable.

I shall propose, in other words, that the behavior of the Communist is rational once we grant his way of perceiving western democracy; the behavior of the white supremacist is rational if we accept his way of perceiving the Negro; the behavior of the steelworkers' union is rational if we grant this way of perceiving the companies' proposals in changes in work rules, and so on.

This view, in effect, says that it is inappropriate for psychologists to label other people as "good" or "bad," even if we do it in fancy terms like authoritarian aggression, autistic hostility, unresolved Oedipus complexes and the like. I suggest that the problem of psychological theory is not to pin labels on those persons who hold attitudes with which we disagree, but to analyze the processes by which certain distorted perceptions become established and to consider ways in which these ways of seeing reality might be modified.

Such an approach does not eliminate any occasion for concern with needs, desires, emotions and conflicts. It does shift the focus of theoretical exploration from the motivational state itself to the effects of motivation on perceiving—recognizing, of course, that any distinction between the two processes is logical, not functional.

We must be concerned not solely with the processes of perceptual distortion and rigidity, but also with content. Many perceptual distortions are strictly interpersonal and have no social implications. Some relate to

religious, racial or industrial conflicts, others to national problems. I should like to illustrate my remarks primarily with reference to questions of international hostility.

Whittlesey (1942) reproduced a propaganda map issued by Nazi Germany early in the campaign against Czechoslovakia. It visualized that small nation as a dagger aimed at the heart of Germany, with bombers readily capable of saturating the German nation. What it ignored was the much greater extent to which Czechoslovakia was at the mercy of Germany, a fact which became apparent in 1938. One need not assume that the German author was aware of this distortion; consider the excitement in the USA today over the situation in Cuba, which is even less capable of mounting an assault on our country. Looked at from the other side, note that Americans approve strongly of the ring of air bases we have built around Russia, many of which are as close to that nation as Cuba is to ours.

The perceptual distortion here arises from the fact that we perceive our nation and its purposes as good and pure, hence our bases are no threat to anyone. Russia, on the other hand, is obviously bad, cruel and untrustworthy, hence Russian bases are a great menace to world peace. Please do not interpret my remarks as implying that a Russian base in Cuba would be innocent and virtuous; what I do want to observe is that objectively similar events look quite different when viewed through nationalistic spectacles.

We should also remember that a policy of secrecy is no monopoly of the Soviet Union. Just after World War II our futile efforts to keep the A-Bomb secret aroused antagonism even among our allies. It was undoubtedly perceived as extremely threatening by the Russians—as, indeed, we find their secrecy so alarming that we risk air flights over their territory to penetrate the curtain. Perhaps such efforts at secrecy are always interpreted as threats because of the phenomenon which Else Frenkel-Brunswik christened "intolerance of ambiguity"—the very common mechanism which treats an unclear situation as potentially dangerous. The individual who is extremely anxious is likely to show this intolerance of ambiguity in extreme form. This, clinicians tell us, leads to both perceptual rigidity and behavioral rigidity. It gives rise to the sharp polarization of good and bad which is so characteristic of nationalism, and to the inflexibility deplored by Mr. Kennan and Mr. Dulles.

The significance of this intolerance of ambiguity as regards foreign policy questions can readily be illustrated by a report by Lane (1955). In the Korean War of 1950–53, clear-cut choices were represented by "get out of Korea entirely" or by "bomb China and Manchuria," whereas an ambiguous policy was represented by "keep on trying to get a peaceful settlement." In a national sample, the high authoritarian cases chose either of the clear-cut choices much oftener than the middle choice; the low authoritarian cases avoided the extreme policies.

Perhaps this is a good point at which to say that I consider such findings to be important regardless of one's emphasis on leaders or on the general population as determinants of policy. Leaders have personalities too, and there is every reason to believe that they can be impatient, can seek for and push the quick, clear-cut alternative, can shy away from policies which appear weak and vacillating. Similarly, the populace can prod the government in certain directions. Our concern with perceptual dynamics is thus not tied to either alternative view of policy determination.

Rigidity on the part of a dominant group is perceived by others as an arbitrary frustration, and so gives rise to exceptionally strong hostility. The inflexible policy of *Apartheid* in South Africa is arousing violence on the part of the natives. Despite the examples of Algeria, Cyprus, and other former colonies, the Afrikaners cling blindly to their delusion that tyranny can work. Few of us will have doubts as to the tragic violence so elicited.

I have noted above the tendency to personalize the nation, to deal with it as a hero or as a villain. Sometimes the personalization is in terms of a specific individual: Churchill, Stalin, DeGaulle, Eisenhower, sometimes in terms of a mythical personage such as Uncle Sam. While psychologists have often deplored this because of the obvious distortion involved, I think we must accept it as inevitable. After all, our patterns of cognition are derived from experience—unless we wish to accept some Kantian absolutes. Since our experience of active agents has almost exclusively been with people, it is scarcely possible that we would think of nations except in a personalized way. Certainly it is easier to build myths of grandeur and virtue about a nation-hero than about the oddly assorted characters we see on the bus going to work. And it is easier to project vicious, violent attitudes onto a foreign leader than onto the total foreign population which, even the relatively naive citizen realizes, must be much like ourselves. It is also true that the leader of a nation is more dangerous than the average citizen. By the demands of his social role, he must be more defensive of national honor, more suspicious of national enemies, more alert to exaggerate trivial actions into major threats. Should he underestimate a foreign danger he would be derelict in his duty. But by his actions he tends to magnify these delusions of persecution which are so widely held among the citizens.

The dilemma of the two World Powers today is that each is afraid to give up the ability to destroy the other. The best escape route available today seems to be this: the control of these destructive devices must be placed in other hands, so that Russia and the USA can withdraw gracefully from their hazardous positions. I think this is entirely possible; we have done little to explore the techniques for accomplishing it. Creative thinking along this line is urgently needed. C. E. Osgood (1959) has offered an intriguing suggestion in his recent article, "On winning the real war with communism."

The solution, according to the political scientists, calls for giving to an international force a monopoly on the instruments of violence. We clearly dare not allow sovereignty—with its concomitant right to unlimited violence—to the small countries of the world. As in the days of our own Wild West—at least as portrayed on TV—we must have a Wyatt Earp or Matt Dillon who will deny to small nations the right to shoot up the town. But such a plan can work only if the USA and the USSR will support it. Our picture of the Communists, and theirs of us, make such cooperation difficult.

The legal authority must not only have a monopoly of violence, but he must also be perceived as impartial. This calls for a body of law, a set of rules acceptable to the contesting parties, which he enforces. Labor unions would not give up what they considered the sovereign right to violence until law enforcement was less purely a defense of managerial rights. Religious wars continued until both Protestants and Catholics came to perceive the government as an impartial arbiter. Can we turn to international law as a body of doctrine which could provide this framework of impartiality? Unfortunately, nobody today knows just what international law is. Clearly we shall not be able to provide for peaceful settlement of national disputes until we get some legal framework within which the participants can expect to receive justice.

Some Principles of Perception

Before taking up the problem of what can be done to foster such a development let me return to the question of theory for a moment. I said that personification of the nation, while it is a distortion of reality, seems inevitable. In terms of the conceptualization I am offering, the individual's awareness of his nation is qualitatively similar to his perception of another person. This suggests that we may utilize the same principles of perception which have become well-accepted in our observations of physical objects and in face-to-face personal relations.

There are two possible approaches to this problem. One places emphasis on stimulus generalization or perceptual equivalence. That is, one may simply generalize from perceptions of persons to a percept of the nation as a person. This is known as the *generalization hypothesis*. A second approach stems from psychoanalytic theory and involves the notion that emotions such as hostility may be repressed as regards persons near at hand, but are expressed toward foreign groups or personified nations. Christiansen (1959) has suggested that this be called the *latency hypothesis*, since its distinctive feature is that latent emotions are directed toward out-groups.

The empirical evidence, as collected both in this country and abroad, seems to favor the generalization hypothesis. An excellent study, within the limits of attitude scales and questionnaires, has recently been published in Norway by Christiansen (1959). He finds that persons who report aggressive behavior toward their fellows also endorse aggressive policies toward other nations by Norway. Persons reporting generally cooperative behavior endorse less aggressive policies. Those inclined to be self-critical and intropunitive are likely to assume that Norway may have committed errors in international dealings, whereas the extrapunitive individual usually assumes that Norway was right and the other nation guilty. I reported somewhat parallel findings on American subjects 20 years ago (Stagner, 1944a), and other researchers, e.g., Harry Grace (1949) have confirmed this.

The latency hypothesis, on the other hand, would predict a negative correlation between manifest behavior toward close associates and preferred behavior toward foreign nations, racial minorities, etc. This follows from the fact that the displaced emotion, either affection or hostility, leaves its opposite to govern behavior and perception. Thus the boy who resolves his Oedipus complex by repressing hostility to his father will presumably show affection and positive attitudes at home, but will project bad, tyrannical characteristics onto the evil rulers of foreign nations.

Limited evidence favoring the latency hypothesis is reported by Christiansen using the Blacky Pictures and the Rosenzweig P-F test as devices for getting at latent emotions. On the whole he confesses to disappointment that the evidence is not clear-cut. Similar, slightly favorable evidence has been reported by Krout and Stagner (1939), by Lasswell (1930) and others. No one has reported strong support for this point of view.

The complexity of the problem is exaggerated by variations in what may be called the range of stimulus generalization. This is important in connection with the role of reference groups in defining "good" and "bad" nations or social groups. The anthropologists tell us that isolated cultures quite commonly hold to the view that "only we are human." The Hebrews' perception of the Gentiles, like the Greek view of the barbarians, illustrates this. Growing up in an ethnocentric culture, we become alert to trivial cues which identify the in-group, but which enable us to label and reject the out-group. Various studies suggest that anti-Semites are more accurate at detecting Jewish facial characteristics than are their more tolerant peers. Whether this alleged sensitivity can hold up realistically is unimportant. The individual *believes* that he can perceive major differences between his fellows and the out-group; his gradient of generalization, and his responses of friendship and cooperation, are thus limited in scope. There is reason to believe, however, that some individuals are unable to perceive these allegedly differentiating cues, and thus may generalize responses of acceptance to humans beyond the in-group. These persons may manifest the cognitive style which George Klein (1951) has called "levelling"; i.e., they tend to iron out differences and to see *all* humans as basically similar.

A second factor which appears to play a part in the choice of such reference groups is also perceptual-cognitive in character. Helen Peak and her students (Peak *et al.,* 1960) have been working with a cognitive style which they call *opposition.* Each of us, I am sure, knows one or more persons who have a consistent tendency to "see the other side" of any issue. They enjoy playing the devil's advocate; and often enough they are not playing. In contrast to this, of course, we have the response-set of *acquiescence,* which has received so much attention in the aftermath of the "Authoritarian Personality" and F-scale studies. A distribution of cases on a hypothetical continuum from extreme acquiescence to extreme opposition would, of course, reveal a skew toward the acquiescent end. And this confirms everyday experience; most children within a nation grow up to accept the nation's leaders as a reference group. But occasionally we get individuals who insist upon looking at the other side, who are not convinced that the policies of their nation are always just, the leaders necessarily paragons of virtue and wisdom. Such critics may become mere cranks and chronic objectors; they may, indeed, find some foreign reference group which is more acceptable. But another common outcome is that they choose an idealistic reference group, and perhaps contribute to the development of a body of advocates of an internationalist position. Peak cites some evidence to indicate that oppositionists are also "levellers"; they would thus be more likely to perceive all human beings as basically alike.

I assume that I need not expand on the application of this idea to parallel social conflicts. How did the Reformation start? Because some people rejected the leaders of the Catholic Church. How did feudalism begin its decline? When some individuals saw the possibility of rejecting feudal leaders and organizing a different social structure. Men such as Martin Luther, John Calvin, Descartes, and Spinoza were undoubtedly characterized by the tendency to ponder automatically the opposite of statements posed to them. (This does not suggest that such men reacted favorably to questioning of their own dogmas. On the contrary, such persons are often quite intolerant of "opposite thinking" when it is focused on their views.)

Given these facts regarding the ways in which decision-makers may act on biased information, and the psychological processes which lead to biasing, one must ask: what can we do about it? The physical scientists have already made it possible for all men to *die* together. The task of the social scientists is to seek ways by which we can *live* together.

In this paper, I can only suggest a line of approach. Let me mention a couple of suggestions which seem quite futile, and some which appear to have promise.

First of all, I see no point in the recommendation, offered in all seriousness by some psychoanalysts, that government leaders ought to be analyzed. Can we imagine a megalomaniac like Hitler, on the threshold of power, taking off a few years to be analyzed? Can we suppose the United Nations would demand that a Prime Minister come in for psychotherapy? Or that he would obey? I think not.

Secondly, I see little value in communications which focus on the horrors of war, and the devastation which would result from atomic war. It is clear that past decision-makers have in general found war and violence distasteful, but these alternatives have seemed to them less painful than the situations facing them. That is, if the Communist perceives capitalism as a deadly menace, he must eventually come to the point at which he will risk nuclear war because he is so hostile to the bad capitalist nations; the citizen of a capitalist nation must also come to such a point when he perceives communism as an intolerable threat.

Turning to the positive side, I would stress first the importance of *diluting sovereignty* by building up groups and institutions of a supranational character. As we cede a little bit of sovereignty to the International Postal Union, we get used to the idea that our nation cannot act in a completely unilateral manner, without regard to other nations and their rights. More spectacular and more beneficial, of course, is the UN venture in the Congo. This enables people all over the world to get used to the idea that force might be removed from nationalistic controls and used for the welfare of the entire human race.

We need a much larger staff of persons who are agents of such supranational agencies. Ernst Haas (1958), in his recent book, *The Uniting of Europe,* shows the major contributions of the European Coal and Steel Community to developing an internationalist point of view. He speaks of the "spill-over" process, i.e., that men whose duty it is to run the ECSC organization efficiently find themselves forced to expand international cooperation in areas peripheral to the organization itself. I am reminded here of the observations reported by Melville Dalton (1959), describing industrial managers who, in their quest for personal power, go beyond assigned roles (treaties?) to activate new functions. Dalton's findings support Haas; they indicate that the creation of a few more supranational structures like ECSC may help tremendously in the task defined by Haas as "redirecting the loyalties and expectations of political actors" from one level of government (the national) to another (the European).

A more frequent suggestion is that we exchange more visitors with other countries. While this can be hardly undesirable, I think the benefits may easily be exaggerated. Unless personal motives become engaged in the perception of other persons and other nations, the effects are likely to be minimal.

We should keep in mind the rigidity of perceptual constancy, and the effectiveness of perceptual defense. Mere communication without involvement has little effect. A recent proposal by the well-known semanticist, S. E. Hayakawa (1960), for example, argues that we could make progress toward peace simply by listening, i.e., by inviting Russian speakers over and letting them state their case, if we were allowed to do likewise. It seems to me unlikely that this would have any effect.

The French have a phrase, *le dialogue des sourds*—the dialogue of the deaf—to refer to the fact that two people may talk to each other without either hearing what the other is trying to communicate. Clearly such dialogues make up a major portion of what passes for social communication. Consider, for example, the Negro-White colloquy in the southern United States. The Negro is talking about education to fit him for job opportunities, the opening up of these opportunities, the chance to participate in economic and political affairs. The White speaks of violence, immorality and other social problems. Neither listens to what the other has to say. We have had, of course, a more dramatic instance of the same kind in the recent interchanges between the USA and the Soviet Union over disarmament. The Russians speak in favor of complete disarmament, the Americans ask about controls and inspections. Since all of you are familiar with the defects of the Russian argument, let me point out a weakness in our own approach. The Russians propose that reports of violations of arms agreements go to the UN Security Council; we object that this would enable them to veto any resolution of condemnation. This utterly misses the point that we have been trying frantically, via U-2, RB-47, and heaven knows what other devices, to get information from inside Russia. If a UN inspection team reported a violation, does it matter who is condemned? We would have obtained vital information; effective counteraction must be taken by the United States, not by the UN.

Unless we take account of the different realities perceived by ourselves and the Russians, increased communication may lead only to increased *misunderstanding*. Let me cite a very simple case. The Yalta agreements provided for "free democratic elections" in Poland, Czechoslovakia, and other satellite nations. Ultimately we learned that these were to be "free and democratic" as in Russia, i.e., the voter was free to vote for the Communist slate or not to vote. The Russians were not hypocritical; the words did not convey the same "reality" to them as to us.

I hope I am making my point clear. I am trying to say that perceptual distortions and perceptual rigidities block communication between groups in conflict. Further, man's craving for a stable, predictable environment tends to force ambiguous data into the existing perceptual structure. All of you remember the Irishman who, when told that Ireland was neutral in the last war, said, "Yes, I know we are neutral, but who are we neutral against?" Thus many Americans assumed that a neutral India must be against us. Fortunately, it has become more clear in recent months that India is neutral against communism; however, this is not the crux of the matter. The psychological phenomenon here takes the form of a demand for a clearly-structured environment, one with a minimum of ambiguities. It has variously been discussed by Osgood (1955) as a need for congruity, by Festinger (1957) in terms of consonance and dissonance, and by Newcomb (1953)

as a case of symmetry of meaning. Osgood points out that if an approved source, say ex-President Eisenhower, issues a statement favorable to a disapproved object, such as communism, incompatible responses are activated, and conflict occurs. Congruity is achieved by becoming less favorable to Eisenhower or more favorable to communism. However, there is another solution which is often adopted; this is to refuse, in effect, to receive the communication. The technique effectively blocks channels and makes possible the "dialogue of the deaf."

Let me say just a word about the role of *consciousness* in adaptation. Studies of subliminal perception make it clear that the organism can utilize information fed in under conditions operationally defined as unconscious, i.e., when the subject could not report verbally that he had received the information (Miller, 1939). But such utilization is at a very low level of efficiency. Material of which one is consciously aware can be used more effectively in guiding behavior; Norman Maier (1931) has shown that problem-solving goes on more expeditiously when the experimenter calls attention to significant cues. Finally, we have the widespread belief of clinicians that the resolution of a neurotic conflict requires that all of the significant components of the conflict become available to consciousness. If we are on firm ground in our assertion that social conflicts must be resolved—as they were initiated—in the minds of men, then it follows that men must become conscious of aspects of the social conflict which heretofore they have refused to see. Whether non-directive or directive psychotherapy is appropriate here we cannot say at this moment, but my prediction is that a vigorously directive approach will be necessary for effective treatment.

Is an attempt to understand the Russians, and to seek ways in which we might establish peaceful co-existence, a sign of national weakness? I do not think so. I am reminded of the fact that, 300 years ago, suggestions of religious tolerance were denounced as evidence of moral weakness. Today we consider religious *intolerance* a sign of moral decay. I think we may reach a point at which the delusions of national pride and national persecution will be looked upon with the same tolerance—when they no longer threaten us with the holocaust of nuclear war.

How Can Our Civilization Survive?

The illusory nature of perceived reality, our tendency to build up a dream-world based on wishful thinking, was brilliantly described by Matthew Arnold:

"The world, which seems
To lie before us like a land of dreams,
So various, so beautiful, so new,
Hath really neither joy, nor love, nor
light . . . ."

Unconsciously we have deceived ourselves into the belief that we can have more chromium on our cars and fewer teachers in our schools; that we can afford the luxuries of nationalism and race prejudice, and dispense with the sacrifices of comfort and ego-expansion needed to resolve these social conflicts. But repression means wandering the dark, denying ourselves the information essential to a problem solution. To complete Arnold's familiar passage,

"We are here, as on a darkling plain
Swept with confused alarms of struggle
and flight
Where ignorant armies clash by night."

This is the problem facing social psychologists; to devise methods by which we can break the darkness, enlighten the ignorant armies. At all levels of society there are psychological barriers to clear understanding of the social conflicts which plague us. Can we marry the skills and insights of social and clinical psychologists to aid this clarification? This is the specific version, for our profession, of the great question facing the West today: how can our civilization survive?

REFERENCES

1. Boulding, Kenneth E. National images and international systems. *Journal of Conflict Resolution,* 1959, *3,* 120–131.
2. Christiansen, Bjorn. *Personality and Attitudes Toward Foreign Policy.* Oslo: University of Oslo Press, 1959.
3. Dalton, Melville. *Men Who Manage.* New York: John Wiley & Sons, 1959.
4. Dollard, John et al. *Frustration and Aggression.* New Haven: Yale University Press, 1939.
5. Dulles, John Foster. *War, Peace and Change.* New York: Harper & Bros., 1939.
6. Durbin, E. F. M., and Bowlby, John. *Personal Aggressiveness and War.* New York: Columbia University Press, 1939.
7. Festinger, Leon. *A Theory of Cognitive Dissonance.* Evanston, Ill.: Row, Peterson and Co., 1957.
8. Grace, Harry A. *A Study of the Expression of Hostility in Everyday Professional, and International Verbal Situations.* New York: Columbia University, 1949.
9. Haas, Ernst B. *The Uniting of Europe.* Stanford: Stanford University Press, 1958.
10. Hayakawa, Samuel I. Formula for Peace: Listening. New York Times Magazine, July 31, 1960, 10–12.
11. Janis, Irving L. Decisional conflicts: a theoretical analysis. *Journal of Conflict Resolution,* 1959, *3,* 6–27.
12. Kennan, George F. The illusion of security. *Atlantic Monthly,* August 1954, 31–34.
13. Klein, George S. The personal world through perception. In Robert R. Blake and Glenn Ramsey (eds.), *Perception: an Approach to Personality.* New York: Ronald Press, 1951.
14. Krout, Maurice H. and Stagner, Ross. Personality development in radicals: a comparative study. *Sociometry,* 1939, *2,* 31–46.
15. Lane, Robert E. Political personality and electoral choice. *American Political Science Review,* 1955, *49,* 173–190.
16. Lasswell, Harold D. *Psychopathology and Politics.* Chicago: University of Chicago Press, 1930.
17. Levinson, Daniel J. Authoritarian personality and foreign policy. *Journal of Conflict Resolution,* 1957, *1,* 37–47.
18. Maier, Norman R. F. Reasoning in humans. II. The solution of a problem and its appearance in consciousness. *Journal of Comparative Psychology,* 1931, *12,* 181–194.
19. _____. *Frustration.* New York: McGraw-Hill Book Co., 1949.
20. Miller, James G. Discrimination without awareness. *American Journal of Psychology,* 1939, *52,* 562–578.
21. Newcomb, Theodore M. An approach to the study of communicative acts. *Psychological Review,* 1953, *60,* 393–404.1.
22. Osgood, Charles E. Suggestions for winning the real war with communism. *Journal of Conflict Resolution,* 1959, *3,* 295–325.
23. Osgood, Charles E. and Tannenbaum, Percy. The principle of congruity in the prediction of attitude change. *Psychological Review,* 1955, *62,* 42–55.
24. Peak, Helen et al. Opposite structures, defenses, and attitudes. *Psychological Monographs,* 1960, *74,* No. 8.

25. Stagner, Ross. Studies in aggressive social attitudes. I. *Journal of Social Psychology,* 1944a, *20,* 109–120.

26. _____. Studies in aggressive social attitudes. III. *Journal of Social Psychology,* 1944b, *20,* 129–140.

27. _____. *Psychology of Personality* (3rd. ed.) New York: McGraw-Hill Book Co., 1961.

28. Stagner, Ross, Brown, Junius F., Gundlach, Ralph H., and White, Ralph K. Analysis of social scientists' opinions on the prevention of war. *Journal of Social Psychology,* 1942, *15,* 381–394.

29. Strachey, Alix. *The Unconscious Motives of War.* New York: International Universities Press, 1957.

30. Whittlesey, Derwent. *German Strategy of World Conquest.* New York: Farrar & Rinehart, Inc., 1942.

PROBLEMS OF THEORY IN THE ANALYSIS OF STRESS BEHAVIOR*

The Recognized Need for Systematic Research

Whenever social scientists address themselves to the scientific problems of studying community disasters, there is one general notion that is almost certain to be emphasized. It is usually expressed in terms of orienting research toward working out a "general theory of disaster" or developing a consistent "conceptual schema," or constructing "comprehensive behavioral models." What the point essentially boils down to is this: there is an obvious need for general theoretical categories and constructs that will help to delineate central problems of disaster behavior that should be investigated.

It is noteworthy that despite protracted discussions of this need in numerous scientific conferences held during the past decade, very little progress has been made. Productive research workers and dignitaries representing the various social science disciplines have repeatedly been brought together to discuss research on the human aspects of disaster. Usually the participants are keenly aware of the grave importance of such research, particularly when the conference has been arranged at the behest of military or government officials who feel appalled by forecasts of the catastrophic potentialities of A-bombs, H-bombs and other new weapons.

After attending several such conferences, one begins to notice that the content of the discussion follows a rather predictable pattern. First, there is likely to be general agreement among the participants that applied research which tries to answer purely practical questions ought to be given less priority in the future than more basic research which aims at understanding the

general principles and conditions of disaster responses. Everyone is likely to approve of the notion that this goal can be furthered by carrying out well planned field studies in communities that are stricken by earthquakes, floods, tornadoes or other large-scale disasters.

On this subject, one hears some candid comments from those conferees who are familiar with the existing field data. They usually say that investigators are no longer justified in going into disaster areas simply to see what kind of behavior goes on, that a great deal of descriptive information is already available on the varieties and range of disaster reactions, and that now we ought to concentrate on finding out why certain effects occur. A resolution is then forthcoming to the effect that from now on field research should concentrate on well-defined problems and hypotheses that will orient the observations toward finding causal factors. At this point, the conferees begin to talk about the way in which the definition, selection, and appraisal of research problems could be facilitated by developing sound theoretical categories which will highlight the significant variables. Finally, someone will speak, more or less eloquently, to the point that no one discipline can embrace more than a small sector of the human aspects of a large scale disaster and that in order to arrive at a comprehensive theoretical framework we shall ultimately have to use a thoroughly interdisciplinary approach in which the conventional subdivisions of the social sciences are more or less ignored.

Perhaps it is out of a combination of rational conviction and polite recognition of the presence of academic colleagues from a number of different university departments that this final notion is not only hastily approved but is also often taken to imply that a comprehensive theory can

* Reprinted by permission of the author and publisher from *Journal of Social Issues,* 1954, *10*: 12–25.

somehow readily be produced if only a properly constituted team will get down to work on it. In any case, once a consensus is reached concerning the future value of an interdisciplinary approach, the conferees seem to feel a sense of closure, and the conference moves rapidly toward adjournment.

Thus, what mainly comes out of such conferences is general agreement that field research on the human aspects of disaster should be encouraged, that such research should be directed toward testing general hypotheses and that the hypotheses ought to be grounded in social science theory.

As a conferee who has whole-heartedly participated on a number of occasions in arriving at just such a consensus, I have begun to wonder if perhaps these conferences mainly serve a ceremonial function. It seems that despite our sincere and emphatically worded resolutions, there continue to be rather large gaps and chasms in those places where our disaster theory is supposed to be.

It is true that in recent years a number of theoretical contributions have been made which may help to illuminate one or another aspect of disaster behavior. Nevertheless, anyone familiar with the recent empirical literature in this field will probably agree that theory is lagging far behind the rapidly accumulating body of descriptive facts. As yet little advance has been made in the direction of developing any kind of theoretical framework that systematically covers the effects that disasters are known to have on individuals, organizations, and communities. Field studies of large scale disaster have received little or no impetus toward transforming their operations from a hit or miss "fishing expedition" into hypothesis-oriented research. In fact, there is still relatively little field research that amounts to much more than a somewhat sophisticated form of journalistic reportage supplemented by a few quantitative data showing the percentage of interviewees who made various statements about what they saw and how they felt and acted during the disaster.

The "Disasterology" Myth

Perhaps it is useful to raise the question as to why there continues to be a relative dearth of theoretical formulations which generate testable hypotheses despite a relative abundance of well-trained social scientists who agree that such formulations should be given high priority. One source of inhibition, I suspect, is that many of those who are qualified to work on theoretical aspects of disaster research have an exaggeratedly high level of aspiration and cannot easily escape the discouraging anticipation that one's attempts will fail to measure up to the mark. In part this may stem from a somewhat distorted conception of the need for a multi-disciplinary approach. The widespread recognition of this need seems to have contributed to the expectation that anyone who is working on theoretical aspects of disaster behavior ought to try to integrate the facts, concepts and theoretical models stemming from all of the relevant disciplines. Somehow the notion seems to have grown up that the field of disaster research offers a touchstone to a truly interdisciplinary social science and that we are actually on the threshold of a major theoretical breakthrough.

At several conferences where this inspirational notion seemed to be in the air, I have noticed that it quickly evaporated as soon as any question was raised as to the actual content of disaster theory. As the various specialists in the human sciences talk about the way in which disaster research ties in with their own theoretical interests, the myth that we are about to witness the birth of a comprehensive socio-politico-psychological science of disasterology is quickly replaced by the sober realization that we are in the presence of a large number of uncoordinated inquiries concerning the disparate effects of a complex set of unusual stresses on individuals, families, informal groups, social classes, organized communities, political and economic hierarchies—inquiries that we permit ourselves to package together mainly because they all have something to do with practical social problems which arise at approximately the same time in localities where a tornado or bombing or some other disruptive force has destroyed many people and buildings.

Consider, for example, a sociologist whose scientific curiosity is stimulated by instances where a minority ethnic group does not respond to official warnings and evacuation directives, despite the fact that most of them heard and understood the official messages issued via the local radio stations. Perhaps the sociologist's study of such instances leads him to the discovery that practically all recommendations from outside authorities, including even emergency messages, tend to go unheeded by this group unless there are certain signs of explicit endorsement on the part of their local leaders. The formulation of theoretical propositions pertaining to this aspect of disaster behavior might require an analysis of pre-established group norms, leadership roles, and patterns of intragroup communication. Such an analysis would certainly take account of numerous non-disaster phenomena—for instance, the way these same people respond to election campaigns, to Community Chest and Savings Bond drives, and to numerous other authoritative appeals or demands that are issued through the mass media and through the special channels of communication which reach the members of this group.

A political scientist, on the other hand, may have a keen theoretical interest in certain phenomena which cut across an entirely different sector of leadership problems within both disaster and non-disaster situations. Perhaps his special concern has to do with the way in which an administrative hierarchy reacts and readjusts to the loss of certain key leaders who may suddenly abandon a critical power position as a result of injury in a disaster, accidental death, acceptance of a new leadership role in another locale, or any of a dozen other different causes. The theoretical concepts that are brought to bear on this problem might help to explain why certain sorts of decisions are made promptly and why other decisions are left pending during the administrative crisis that occurs when a certain type of organizational structure

must continue to operate despite the loss of a top level leader.

One could hardly expect the same set of concepts to have any particular application to the sort of leadership problems with which a social psychologist is concerned when he studies the emergence of spontaneous neighborhood leaders who temporarily direct the rescue and relief activities of disaster survivors. Nor would an adequate theory of emergent leadership necessarily be of direct use to the psychiatrist or clinical psychologist who is trying to work out theoretical assumptions that will help us to understand the differences in personality make-up between those civic leaders who are likely to recover rapidly from harrowing danger experiences and those who are apt to develop chronic traumatic neuroses.

It is certainly valuable to take an occasional comprehensive look at the ramified effects of large scale disasters for the special purpose of trying to discern hitherto unnoticed interrelationships. But we should realize that many of the theoretical issues and hypotheses considered under the general heading of disaster research cannot be expected to hang together in the sense that they will be illuminated by a common set of explanatory concepts and principles. It seems to me that we must resign ourselves to a rather piecemeal development of general hypotheses and theoretical assumptions. We must be content with any isolated bits of explanatory theory—"miniature" theories as they are sometimes called—which increase our understanding in depth of one or another limited aspect of disaster behavior. Moreover, it would be unrealistic to assume that theories pertaining to disaster phenomena are somehow going to push far ahead of our present social science knowledge. Rather, we must expect the theoretical developments in disaster research to grow directly out of the current theoretical concepts and hypotheses with which research workers in each of the various disciplines are preoccupied.

Contemplation of the messianic hope for an Einsteinian type of general field theory—to integrate major propositions and tested "miniature" theories from all the various human sciences—should not lull us into overlooking the cruel fact that right now there are not very many such verified hypotheses waiting around to be integrated with each other. The successful use of an interdisciplinary approach will probably often be confined to instances where the same or overlapping behavioral phenomena are being investigated from somewhat different standpoints by research workers from bordering disciplines. For such phenomena, more complete explanatory propositions than are currently available might emerge from deliberate attempts at theoretical cross-fertilization through a careful examination of the similarities and differences in the explanatory concepts used by specialists who approach the common problem with somewhat different frames of reference. But there are undoubtedly also many important theoretical tasks which will require a more or less intra-disciplinary approach in order to increase our understanding of certain of the psychological, sociological, economic, or political effects of community disasters.

Psychological Research on Disaster Behavior

Having renounced the high ambition of trying to work out a sweepingly comprehensive theory and having also resolved to ignore the potential sins of intradisciplinarianism, the writer now feels much more comfortable about revealing the limited scope of the theoretical problems which occupy his interest. Like many other psychologists, the writer is inclined to view disaster research as a source of valuable observations on the way in which people cope with extreme situations and as an especially promising site for studying the strengths and weaknesses of the human personality which determine adaptive and maladaptive reactions to stress. Of particular importance is the opportunity to supplement laboratory and clinical observations on stress behavior with studies of large numbers of persons who display one or another form of temporary emergency reaction which deviates from their normal behavior patterns. These emergency reactions are commonly referred to by such terms as personal disorganization, impulsive emergency action, emotional stress, panic, and demoralization.

It should be noted that psychological phenomena of this type can also be studied in a variety of extreme situations other than large-scale physical disasters—in financial depressions where people face extreme economic insecurity; in personal disasters such as those involving loss of health, status, prestige, or the breaking of affectionate ties; in emotionally traumatic accidents where a person undergoes a narrow escape from death; in concentration camps where men are subjected to severe deprivations or are constantly threatened with punishment and torture.

Insofar as the central problems of psychological analysis involve isolating the causal factors which account for the way people react to threat or danger stimuli, one can expect that the most crucial tests of general propositions will require controlled experiments in which basic determinants derived from theoretical analysis can be varied systematically. Probably the most cogent experimental evidence will come from those studies in which the subjects are exposed to actual conditions of threat or danger, such as can be found in any large hospital or clinic where people are subjected to distressing medical and dental treatments. Although plenty of practical difficulties would have to be overcome, there are no insurmountable obstacles to prevent at least some of the psychological research carried out in community disasters from being designed as controlled experiments. For instance, by comparing the stress behavior of an experimental group that had been given prior training, information or warnings with that of an equivalent control group that had not, it would be possible to obtain fairly precise information on cause-and-effect relationships.

In general, the theorist who is concerned primarily with psychological aspects of stress behavior will be inclined to examine community disasters from the standpoint of specifying the stresses to which people are subjected and delineating the various types of emergency responses which these stresses produce. Most of the stresses can be viewed as arising in three major types of danger situations which characterize every large-scale disaster:

1) *Threat* situations in which people perceive objective signs of impending danger or receive explicit warnings that some kind of danger might be approaching, at a time when the immediate environment is still free from the physical impact of the danger;

2) *Danger impact* situations in which people are actually confronted with physical danger in their immediate environment such that one's chances of escaping injury or death are at least partly contingent upon the speed and efficiency of one's protective actions.

3) *Danger victimization* situations, usually occurring immediately after the actual impact of the danger has subsided or terminated, in which people perceive the variety and magnitude of the losses sustained by themselves and by others with whom they are emotionally identified—destruction of one's home, bereavement, mutilation, etc. When these situations occur in community disasters, the emotional effects of perceiving one's personal losses are often complicated by the occurrence of new threats to the community, particularly those involving impending deprivations—e.g., anticipation of unrelieved hunger, inadequate shelter, health hazards.

One of the major tasks of psychological theory, then, is to analyze the three types of danger situations with respect to describing the causal factors or determinants that account for the predominance of one or another type of reaction.

Patterns of Emotional Behavior

If theoretical analysis is to be oriented toward helping us arrive at hypotheses concerning causal factors in stress behavior, a logical first step in the inquiry would be to raise the question: what are the dominant reactions that need to be accounted for?

Perhaps the most useful way to begin is to classify the clinical varieties of emotional behavior that have been most frequently noted in studies of the way people react when exposed to wartime bombing attacks, large-scale natural disasters, and a variety of personal disasters in which individuals undergo threats of injury, near-miss accidents, or some form of profound personal loss. Tentatively, we can single out at least five different reaction patterns which have been frequently described as typical emotional responses to danger:

1. *Apprehensive avoidance:* This form of reaction is perhaps the most common of all emergency behavior in situations where danger is perceived to be rapidly approaching or actually at hand. The pattern includes the usual physiological, motor and subjective symptoms of acute fear accompanied by overt actions that are oriented toward escaping from the apparent locus of the danger. Long after the objective dangers have subsided, however, some persons continue to display intense fear, flight tendencies, or a "jittery" alertness to minor signs of threats that are ordinarily disregarded.

2. *Stunned immobility:* This is usually a reaction of relatively short duration during and immediately following a sudden experience of danger impact. The outstanding features are the relative absence of both motor and mental activity coupled with some degree of disorientation. Usually the acute "freezing" reaction subsides after a few minutes, but sometimes people wander about for hours in a distracted, dazed state that resembles sleep walking.

3. *Apathy and depression:* In the wake of practically every large-scale disaster there seems to be a widespread reaction of lethargy and pessimism, especially among those individuals who experience the traumatic impact of the danger or who are most severely victimized. Outstanding symptoms are depressive mood and lethargy, characterized by abnormally low level of energy output, absence of initiative in performing any kind of work, lack of interest in normal social activities, constriction of attention, and so on. Sometimes the overall reaction corresponds to what psychiatrists describe as a mild reactive depression. Although relatively few suicides occur and suicidal thoughts do not seem to be very prevalent, depressive attitudes are frequently expressed by those who show a

marked apathy reaction (e.g., "What's the use of bothering about anything anymore?").

4. *Docile dependency:* Without necessarily being lethargic or depressed, many disaster victims are apt to show an unusual lack of independent action, coupled with a marked tendency to cling to authoritative persons and to become more or less passive followers. These tendencies are particularly noticeable during the period when disaster victims first become aware of their losses and throughout the early phases of community recovery, when the help of every able-bodied person is needed for rescue and relief work. In extreme form, the reaction pattern consists of almost automatic obedience to the demands of persons in leadership roles, coupled with a child-like seeking for attention and direction from others. Essentially the same tendencies seem to be present in milder forms among those who simply wait around until someone tells them what to do. Without direct encouragement from leaders, people in this emotional state carry out assigned tasks in an almost automatic, perfunctory way, without seeking out the information they need to perform the task correctly. Sometimes their emotional docility is such that they will blindly follow a directive that is obviously inappropriate or mistaken. One of the important social consequences of the docile dependency reaction is that it greatly reduces the chances that administrative errors can be rapidly noted and corrected through employee's suggestions and complaints and other forms of feedback that normally can be counted on when gross errors are made.

5. *Aggressive irritability:* Symptoms of aggression become highly visible among a population that is recovering from a disaster, particularly after the most urgent rescue and relief operations are over. The readiness to give vent to angry resentment, and heated condemnation, particularly of local officials, is perhaps the most widely noted manifestation. More subtle expressions of aggressive irritability may take the form of deliberate non-compliance with official regulations, a high degree of sensitivity to possible slights or inequalities in the distribution of scarce supplies, and a suspicious unfriendly attitude toward "outsiders." The dominant emotional mood often seems to involve a sort of self-protective withdrawal: "I've been through hell and from now on I intend to watch out strictly for number one—for me and mine."

For each of the five reaction patterns, marked individual differences have been observed. Some persons show a predominance of only one type with very little tendency to display any of the others. Nevertheless, it should be borne in mind that these various reaction patterns are not mutually exclusive; the same persons may show several of the reactions at different stages or time periods during a danger episode. Occasionally the same individual will show all five reactions in a definite sequence, the first during the brief period of maximal threat, the second during the period of danger impact, the third and fourth shortly after the obvious signs of danger have disappeared, and the last during the subsequent post-danger recovery period.

All five patterns have this in common: irrespective of the particular actions that are taken and the subjective feelings that accompany them, there is some degree of loss in mental efficiency. Depending upon how intense the reaction is, a variety of "ego functions" will be impaired to a greater or lesser degree. Each of the reaction patterns can at least temporarily interfere with the person's ability to perceive reality correctly, to appraise the safe and dangerous features of his environment, to plan realistically for the future, to control one's socially unacceptable impulses, to take account of the consequences of alternative courses of action, and so on. From the standpoint of the economic and social welfare of the community, a high incidence of sustained emotional reactions of any one of the five types would constitute a serious problem especially because of the resulting inefficiency in rescue and relief activities and the decline in overall work productivity

The Analysis of Determinants

Having briefly delineated a number of dominant emotional patterns, we are now able to describe more specifically the kinds of research problems which require theoretical analysis. For the present, one of the main tasks is that of formulating hypotheses about the conditions under which each of the various types of emotional reactions occurs, specifying the determinants which increase (or decrease) the intensity and duration of the reaction.

One set of determinants to be considered involves the particular characteristics of the danger stimuli which are perceived and experienced by the individual. In general, the available evidence shows that the most severe and prolonged emotional reactions occur among those persons who are subjected to the highest degree of personal involvement in danger—for example those who are knocked down by the blast of an explosion or who barely escape being killed in a collapsing building. (3, 5, 9, 13, 15) But we still need to know much more about the specific ways in which various types of near-miss experiences give rise to temporary and prolonged emotional disturbance and create chronic traumatic neuroses. Among the major exposure variables which warrant detailed investigation both through experimental laboratory work and field studies, are the following: 1. Degree of warning and alertness (e.g., time interval between warning signals and exposure to danger; activity in progress at the onset of danger.) 2. Degree of injury inflicted by danger stimuli (e.g., amount of pain, perceived severity of the injury; part of the body incapacitated.) 3. Perceptible routes of escape (e.g., perceived barriers to successful flight from danger stimuli; signs of entrapment.) 4. Availability of rescue and aid (e.g., time interval between onset of injury, entrapment or suffering and the arrival of rescue personnel.)

Direct personal involvement may also take the form of the loss or the threatened loss of emotionally cathected persons or objects; for instance, the death of a parent, injury or illness among members of the family, or total destruction of the home. Obviously, the various forms of victimization will require detailed comparative investigation.

Still another important set of situational determinants has to do with the social context of the danger situation. The intensity of emotional reactions will depend to some extent upon whether or not one is surrounded by one's family or by the members of some other psychologically *protective group*—irrespective of whether the presence of these other people actually does decrease one's own chances of survival. Similarly the mere knowledge that trusted *leaders* are somewhere in the neighborhood or will be in a position to mitigate impending dangers may have a markedly dampening effect upon emotional excitement. The reassuring (or non-reassuring) *official communications* which emanate from authority figures and the *informal communications* from other sources—including *rumors* spread by fellow disaster victims—can have a strong influence on increasing or decreasing emotional tension.

Thus, on the basis of the existing research literature, we are able to single out a number of important sets of *situational* determinants which are known to have some effect on emotional reactions, but whose causal role is by no means fully understood at present. On the same basis, there are also numerous categories of *predispositional* determinants to be taken into account. These would include such factors as: 1) previously established ideologies and attitudes concerning the divine or natural causes of disasters; 2) previously formed expectations concerning the ways in which danger situations can be averted or mitigated; 3) self-conception of one's social role in the emergency situation; 4) degree of identification or affiliation with primary groups that are threatened by the danger; 5) social status with respect to chances of receiving aid, relief, and preferential treatment; 6) amount of prior training in relevant protective strategies and tactics for dealing with the danger situation; 7) personality characteristics, such as strength of dependency needs and chronic level of anxiety with respect to body integrity.

We are already at the stage where detailed hypotheses can be formulated concerning the way that these and other predispositional characteristics may be related to observable individual differences in the form and magnitude of emotional responses among people who are exposed to roughly the same kind of situational stress.

Use of Theoretical Constructs

Research on the influence of situational and predispositional factors can be viewed as providing answers to two main questions. First, at times when people are exposed to threats or to actual danger, what *events or circumstances* make them more likely to react one way rather than another? Second, when circumstances are such that a sizable percentage of exposed individuals do react in a particular way, *who* are the ones that are especially likely to show the reaction? When working on questions of this sort it is sometimes helpful to speculate about what must be going on in a person's mind that would explain why certain circumstances and certain predisposing characteristics make him behave the way he does. As is generally recognized, such speculations can sometimes furnish the main ingredients of an explanatory theory—provided, of course, that the concepts are properly refined by means of logically coherent assumptions and definitions from which unambiguous predictions can be made concerning observable behavioral events. Thus, we may expect that some of the current speculations about the way people perceive, think, imagine, and feel during catastrophes may furnish the substance of theoretical constructs. Such constructs could ultimately form the nuclei for constructing miniature theories concerning perceptual, cognitive or motivational processes which are assumed to mediate various observable relationships.

Already a number of theoretical advances seem to be in the making which ought to help explain emotional behavior under stress conditions. For instance, some aspects of reactions to external danger signals and to fear-arousing communications seem to be at least partly accounted for by propositions derived from behavior-theory postulates which assume that fear or anxiety operates as a learned drive. Central notions in this theory are that a) the intense emotional state aroused by danger cues will motivate varied escape behavior—including thinking, planning, fantasy and other symbolic reactions as well as overt activity, and b) whatever response terminates or greatly reduces the intensity of the emotional state will be reinforced and hence will tend to become the dominant reaction. These assumptions seem to offer an explanation for certain kinds of adaptive and maladaptive behavior in response to fear stimuli. (Cf. Dollard and Miller [2], pp. 62–168, and Hovland, Janis and Kelley [4], pp. 56–98).

Another recent line of theoretical development derives from psychoanalytic propositions concerning denial, isolation, and related mechanisms of defense. Of particular relevance to disaster behavior are those psychodynamic hypotheses concerning: a) how people defend themselves against anxiety in the face of impending danger through reliance upon group identification and beliefs of personal invulnerability, and b) the way relatively minor events during actual danger episodes produce a disproportionately intense emotional impact by shattering the individual's defensive beliefs. (Cf. Grinker and Spiegel [3], pp. 130ff., Rado [12], Schmideberg [13]).

Perhaps it is not premature to begin searching for some new sources of hypothetical constructs and theoretical assumptions concerning the nature of human stress behavior so as to supplement those already in use. In so doing, however, we are apt to overlook or discard some of the most promising theoretical leads if we always live up to that special kind of ambition which demands that a theoretical analysis should employ only those constructs and postulates which have already been sharply formulated, are already in the process of being vigorously tested, and, in brief, are scientifically quite respectable. When working on relatively unexplored problems of human behavior, we ought to allow ourselves to work with dirty hands for a while provided that we sincerely promise our scientific conscience to try to work out operational definitions and otherwise clean up the mess afterwards if it does turn out that relaxing our standards of purity enables us to get our hands on some real pay dirt.

There are numerous theoretical concepts which, although somewhat vaguely formulated in discussions of phenomena quite remote from disaster behavior, may nevertheless furnish the basis for important theoretical advances. For instance, concepts such as "reference groups," "internalization of role assignments," and "emotional regression" ought to be carefully examined as potential theoretical leads for explaining the effects of specified determinants and for tying together seemingly unrelated reactions to environmental stress.

In addition to modifying our quality ambitions, we shall also have to curtail our quantity ambitions. Here we return to the theme stated at the outset of this paper: we shall probably end up with very little productive theory and research if, in appraising theoretical constructs, we insist upon using as one of our main criteria the total number of different propositions to which the construct could potentially be applicable. Consider, for example, the conflict-theory postulates which psychologists have worked out on *approach-avoidance* and *avoidance-avoidance conflicts*. Although developed mainly on the basis of controlled experiments in which animals and human subjects have been exposed to relatively simple dilemmas, the theory is rapidly being extended to more complicated aspects of human motivational conflicts. Such extensions may prove to be of considerable relevance for explaining the way a person behaves when disaster circumstances suddenly place him in an emotionally disturbing conflict between his anxious desire, as a father, to search for his family and his sense of duty, as a conscientious local official, to begin immediately to carry out his disaster control assignment. Similarly, the way in which a person conforms to neighbors' urgent demands for help as well as to official emergency rules and regulations is often determined by sharp conflicts between fear of personal loss on the one hand and social conformity motives on the other. Thus, conflict theory may prove to be a valuable source of testable propositions concerning various sorts of emotional dilemmas that arise in danger situations, even though it may fail to have any bearing whatsoever on some of the most important general propositions concerning the conditions under which strong reactions of apprehensive avoidance and of stunned immobility occur.

It is certainly to be hoped that someday we shall be in the enviable scientific position of being able to set up extremely catholic standards for constructing theory,

so that we shall be warranted in living up to extremely high quality and quantity ambitions. In the meantime, we ought to feel elated with any new theoretical concept and any new piece of evidence that helps us to arrive at a warranted generalization concerning one or more determinants of any given reaction variable. Such generalizations are, of course, essential building blocks of the science of human behavior. They are the stuff that our dreams of theory should be made of.

REFERENCES

1. Carr, L. J., "Disaster and the sequence-pattern concept of social change," *American Journal of Sociology*, 1932, *38*, 207.
2. Dollard, J., and Miller, N. E., *Personality and Psychotherapy*. New York: McGraw-Hill, 1950.
3. Grinker, R. R., and Spiegel, J. P., *Men Under Stress*. Philadelphia: Blakiston, 1945.
4. Hovland, C. I., Janis, I. L., and Kelley, H. H., *Communication and Persuasion*. New Haven: Yale Univ. Press, 1953.
5. Janis, I. L., *Air War and Emotional Stress*. New York: McGraw-Hill, 1951.
6. Janis, I. L., *Proposals for Field Research on the Psychological Impact of Peacetime Disasters*. Report for Rand Corporation, Crisis and Disaster Study, (Mimeo.) 1949, 60pp.
7. Killian, L. M., "The significance of multiple-group membership in disaster," *American Journal of Sociology*, 1952, *57*, 309–14.
8. Leighton, A., "Psychological factors in major disasters," *Medical Projects Reports*, University of Rochester, 1951.
9. National Research Council (Div. of Med. Sci.) and Walter Reed Army Medical Center, *Symposium on Stress*. Washington: Army Medical Service Graduate School, 1953.
10. Postman, L., and Bruner, J. S., "Perception under stress," *Psychological Review*, 1948, *55*, 314–323.
11. Powell, J. W., and Rayner, Jeannette, "Progress notes: disaster investigation," Report for Army Chemical Center, Md., (Mimeo.) 1952.
12. Rado, S., "Pathodynamics and treatment of traumatic war neurosis (traumataphobia)," *Psychosomatic Medicine*, 1942, *43*, 362–368.
13. Schmideberg, Mellita, "Some observations on individual reactions to air raids," *International Journal of Psychoanalysis*, 1942, *23*, 146–176.
14. Tyhurst, J. S., "Individual reactions to community disaster: the natural history of psychiatric phenomena," *American Journal of Psychiatry*, 1950–51, *107*, 764–769.
15. Wallace, A. F. C., *Human Behavior in Extreme Situations: A Survey of the Literature and Suggestions for Further Research*. Report for Committee on Disaster Studies, National Research Council. (Mimeo.) 25pp.

B. Interpersonal Conflict

DECISION THEORY IN THE STUDY OF NATIONAL ACTION: PROBLEMS AND A PROPOSAL*

MARTIN PATCHEN

A theoretical analysis of national decision-making and internation influence in terms of decision theory has been made recently by several political scientists, including Singer (1963), Glenn Snyder (1960), and Russett (1963). In fact, theoretical analysis in the language of decision theory seems increasingly widespread among political scientists and other social scientists concerned with international affairs.

This paper discusses a number of difficulties in the use of decision theory for actual research on national decision-making. It also discusses a modification of the decision-theory approach which may make easier the actual measurement of theoretical variables relevant to decision-making.[1]

The Use of Decision Theory to Study International Influence

First, let us look at the way in which decision theory has been used by students of international relations. Conceptualization of the behavior of national decision-makers in terms of decision theory is expressed by Singer in the following words:

Having examined the varieties of influence situations, we should notice one other consideration prior to evaluating the range of techniques available to the influencer in these situations. This is the influencee's decisional calculus: the abstract dimensions upon which he

(i.e., those individuals who, alone or together, act on behalf of the target nation) weighs a range of conceivable outcomes in any influence situation. For every outcome which any decision-maker can conceive of as possible, there are at least two such dimensions. The degree to which he likes or dislikes the prospect is called the *utility* or *disutility,* and the likelihood which he assigns to its ever occurring is called the *probability*. Both of these are, of course, subjective variables: preferences and predictions of the influencee.

In the abstract, the combined judgments which the influencee makes along both of these dimensions will determine his contingent expectations and thus his response to the influence attempt [1963, p. 424].

A widely used hypothesis of decision theory states that people will maximize their expected utility. Expected utility of action 1 is represented by the equation:

$$EU_1 = (U_a \times P_a) + (U_b \times P_b) \ldots + (U_n \times P_n)$$

where: EU = expected utility

$U_a, U_b, \ldots, U_n$ are the subjective utilities[2] of the possible outcomes *(a, b, . . . n)* of action 1.

$P_a, P_b, \ldots, P_n$ are the subjective probabilities of each of the possible outcomes *(a, b, . . . n)* occurring as a result of action 1.

According to the maximization hypothesis, a decision-maker will choose action 1 over action 2 when $EU_1 > EU_2$.

* Reprinted by permission of the author and publisher from *Journal of Conflict Resolution*, 1965, *9*: 164–176.
[1] I am indebted to Jerald Bachman, Dorwin Cartwright, Ward Edwards, Clinton Fink, Bruce Russett, J. David Singer, and Glenn Snyder for helpful comments on earlier drafts of this paper. Of course, the author alone is responsible for the views presented.

[2] Since the term "utility" refers to subjective value, the term subjective utility is, strictly speaking, redundant. However, since the subjective nature of the variables is important for this discussion, it is hoped that the redundancy will be tolerated for the sake of greater clarity.

This "maximization of expected utility" principle has been used by Singer to account for national reactions to threats and to promises of reward.[3] Glenn Snyder and Russett use this decision theory approach to analyze the success of attempts by one nation to deter aggression by another nation. These analyses have so far been of a discursive rather than an empirical type. While no one has (to my knowledge) actually attempted to measure specific utilities and probabilities in an international situation, several writers have used utility-probability notions as a general guide for their empirical work.[4]

Decision theory has an appealing theoretical elegance when applied to the discipline of international relations, which has lacked rigorous theory. Moreover, it seems intuitively to fit what we know about national decision-making fairly well. Presidents and premiers do sit down with their advisers and weigh alternatives, consider possible outcomes of action, implicitly or explicitly assign utilities to these outcomes, and try to assess the probabilities that various outcomes will follow a given action.

Yet there have been reservations and doubts raised about the usefulness of decision theory for understanding the actions of national decision-makers. Two major issues have been raised. The first concerns the quesiton of how "rational" decision-makers actually are. The second concerns the operational problems of trying to measure the decision-makers' subjective utilities and subjective probabilities. As we shall see, these issues are interrelated.

The Question of Rationality in Decision-Making

Concerning the assumption of "rationality" in decision-making, some cautions come from the same political scientists who have made use of decision theory as a theoretical model. Singer suggests that under certain circumstances—e.g., under conditions of threat and anxiety—decision-makers may not act "rationally," i.e., will not try to maximize the product of utility and probability (Singer, 1963, pp. 428–30).

Glenn Snyder also acknowledges that national decision-makers may act "irrationally," noting that: "Irrationality may take the form either of failing to act in accordance with one's best estimate of costs, gains, and probabilities, or of faulty calculation of these factors in the light of the evidence available" (G. Snyder, 1960, p. 174).

The source of some of the "irrationality" of behavior is suggested in a comment by Morton Deutsch. In discussing the assumptions behind the theory of stable deterrence, he says: "Behavior, particularly in a time of high tension and crisis, is more likely to be determined by anxiety, stereotypes, self-esteem defense maneuvers, and social conformity pressures, than by simple rational estimates of economic loss and gain" (Deutsch, 1961, p. 64).

A number of investigators have been explicitly concerned with whether people do in fact make choices "rationally"—i.e., in accord with the utility multiplied by the probability of each outcome. These investigators have noted the intrusion of personality and other "nonrational" factors. Brim and his associates (1962) studied choices made by parents among ways of handling child-raising problems (e.g., not doing homework; masturbation). They report that their subjects did generally choose in accordance with the "maximization of expected utility (utility × probability)" hypothesis. However, certain subjects did not choose "rationally"—i.e., in accord with their indicated utilities and probabilities—in selecting a course of action for the masturbation problem. The authors suggest that this is because these people are more "emotional" about the masturbation problem. The Brim study also indicates some association—though not a powerful one—between "rationality" of choice and such personality factors as belief in the predictability of life. In addition, this study indicates that decisions made by groups are more likely to approximate the utility-

---

[3] A number of different types of decision models have now been developed. For a review of these, see Edwards (1961).

[4] See, for example, Alan Whiting's book on the Chinese decision to enter the Korean war (Whiting. 1960, p. ix).

probability model than are decisions made by individuals.

Scodel, Ratoosh, and Minas (1959) found in a laboratory study of gambling choices that people who differ in need for achievement and in fear of failure will choose different combinations of payoff and probability. For example, people with high need for achievement chose bets of intermediate probability (and moderate payoff) more often than did those with low need for achievement.

Further suggestion of the importance of "irrational" factors in choice behavior comes from the work of French and his associates. In analyzing coercive power, this group conceptualized the "induction force" exerted on an individual in terms of the "valence" of the punishment for nonconformity and in terms of the probability that punishment will follow conformity or nonconformity. They state that the strength of the coercive power (induction force) depends upon the magnitude of the negative valence of the threatened punishment multiplied by the perceived probability that the person can avoid the punishment by conformity (French and Raven, 1959, p. 157). Substitute the word "utility" for the word "valence"—a substitution which retains the essential meaning—and the formulation is now closely similar to that of decision theory. But for French and his coworkers, following Lewin, this is only half the story. The other half is the "resistance force." French and Raven state: "The direction of the resultant force on P will depend on the relative magnitude of the induced force set up by the act of O, and the resisting force in the opposite direction which is generated by that same act" (p. 152).

The nature of this resistance force is indicated by some of its operational measures —e.g., agreement or disagreement with statements like, "I thought the superior's evaluation was unfair" and "I resented the threat of being fired." In empirical studies of coercive power and of coercive power compared to reward power, French, Morrison, and Levinger (1960) and Zipf (1958) find resistance to be an important factor in reducing conformity to influence. But the concept of resistance stands outside the valence-probability framework used to conceptualize the induction force. It therefore appears, in the work of French and his associates, to have the status of an interfering "irrational" factor.

Data on the use of threat, reported by Deutsch and Krauss (1962), seem closely related to the "resistance" phenomenon studied by French's group.

Now what are the implications of these data on "irrational" factors for the use of decision theory? It may be noted first that the term "rational" as applied to various influences on decision-making may be misleading. There is really nothing less sensible, or reasonable, about trying to increase one's sense of self-esteem, or to reduce one's feeling of anxiety, than there is about trying to increase the territorial size of one's country. In this respect both kinds of motivation are equally rational.

Secondly, it is not necessary that behavior be rational, in the sense of trying to maximize practical benefits, in order to be describable by the hypothesis that people tend to maximize expected utility. It is possible for the theorist to consider, for example, outcomes like personal prestige, satisfaction of revenge motives, self-respect, etc., in the same conceptual terms as the practical outcomes of a decision. Each of these nonpragmatic outcomes may have a certain subjective utility and a certain subjective probability of resulting from a given decision.

Consciousness of Utilities

There is, however, a very crucial difference between the nonpragmatic outcomes and the pragmatic ones. This difference is that the utility and the subjective probability of the nonpragmatic motives are often totally or partially unconscious. They are not calculated and considered in the same way that pragmatic outcomes are.

For example, in Zipf's experiment, the persons who had, in effect, to decide how hard to work undoubtedly considered quite consciously the value of the money rewards or fines and their probabilities. It is very doubtful if these subjects consciously considered the utility and probability of such outcomes as "hurting the boss," maintaining their own self-respect, and expressing their anger—i.e., the expected utility of "resistance." It is this difference in the conscious calculation of utilities and probabilities that is the important difference between what has been called the "rational" and the "irrational" in decision-making.

Those who have attempted to understand international events in terms of decision theory have recognized that decision-makers are interested in more than pragmatic gains like military and trade advantages. But they have limited their analysis to situations in which any nonpragmatic motives are considered in a deliberate and fully conscious manner. Thus Glenn Snyder writes:

> . . . "rationality" may be defined as choosing to act in the manner which gives best promise of maximizing one's value position, on the basis of a sober calculation of potential gains and losses and the probabilities of enemy actions. This definition is broad enough to allow the inclusion of such 'emotional' values as honor, prestige, and revenge, as legitimate ends of policy. It may be perfectly rational, in other words, to be willing to accept some costs solely to satisfy such emotions; but if such emotions inhibit a clear-eyed view of the consequences of an act, they may lead to irrational behavior [1960, pp. 173–174].

It is clear from the phrase "sober calculation" in this passage and from many other passages in Snyder's article that, while nonpragmatic utilities can have a place in the analysis, this place is that of consciously calculated ends.

While Singer does not systematically consider the theoretical place of such utilities as honor, prestige, and revenge, he appears also to restrict his analysis to the conscious, problem-solving aspect of decision-making. Thus he sees a decision theory analysis as losing its applicability where the "problem-solving capacity" of the decision-maker is impaired, as under great stress.

Russett notes the possible importance to the defender of "intangible" values such as prestige and self-esteem, but states: "A defender's decision whether to pursue a 'firm' policy that risks war will depend upon his calculation of the value and probability of

various outcomes" (p. 106). Again the nonpragmatic values are limited to the part which they play in conscious calculation.

While much of the decision-making of national leaders is undoubtedly based on conscious calculation of relevant factors, the experimental studies on decision-making cited above caution us not to overlook the role of less conscious factors. It is difficult to obtain direct evidence concerning the relative importance of conscious versus partly-conscious motives for national decision-makers. But it is not hard to imagine partly-conscious motives being important in some international situations.

Take, for example, the value of maintaining self-esteem which, on the basis of experimental evidence, Deutsch considers important in accounting for resistance to threat. A Khrushchev or a Johnson may coldly calculate the advantages to his nation's prestige, but does he really consciously assess the possible effects on his own self-esteem of a successful or unsuccessful move? And how about the potential effects of a foreign policy move on his own political fortunes? If he were suitably Machiavellian, he might indeed be able to include this fully in his calculations. But will a Khrushchev or a Johnson or a de Gaulle fully admit to himself that he may be willing to take some gamble with the lives of his countrymen rather than face a serious political setback? It seems likely that such considerations of personal aggrandizement remain rather shadowy and semiconscious on the fringes of his mind. The point is not that the decision-maker is completely unaware of such motives. It is rather that, because such motives are less socially desirable than others, the decision-maker may not be aware of the magnitude of their importance to him. One could go on to make similar arguments about the at least partially unconscious role that other factors may play—such as personal anger, personal anxiety, and the need for achievement.

Partly-Conscious Motives and Decision Theory

If, in fact, partly-conscious motives may play an important part in some national decisions, can such motives be handled by a decision theory analysis? In terms of the applicability of decision theory, e.g., of the hypothesis that people tend to maximize expected utility—the answer is yes.

The presence of unconscious or partly-conscious motives does not make invalid the decision-theory hypothesis. As Friedman and Savage (1948) point out, it is no more necessary for the decision-maker to consciously maximize all relevant utilities and probabilities than it is for the expert billiard player to be aware of the mathematical equations which describe his choice of angles and speeds on the billiard table. In both cases, it is sufficient that the observer is able to account for the behavior in these theoretical terms—not that the actor himself be able to explain his behavior in those terms.

However, the presence of partly-conscious motives does present formidable difficulties for decison theory as a tool for research into and measurement of decision processes. These methodological difficulties introduced by the presence of partly-conscious motives complicate what are already serious practical difficulties of measuring subjective utility and subjective probability.

Problems of Research and Measurement Using Decision Theory

To illustrate the methodological problems attendant on use of decision theory, let us consider the circumstances surrounding Khrushchev's decision to break up the "summit conference" which met in Paris on May 16, 1960. The reader will recall that, shortly after a Khrushchev "goodwill" visit to the United States, the Soviets shot down a U-2 spy plane over Russian territory. This occurred on May 1, 1960. A frank and unusual admission by President Eisenhower that our planes were in fact flying over Russia for spying purposes brought a barrage of outraged attack on this US policy by the Russians. Khrushchev then went to Paris only long enough to demand an apology from President Eisenhower for the U-2 flights. Not obtaining such an apology, he left the conference and withdrew his country's invitation to President Eisenhower to visit the USSR. Such, in brief outline, are the well-known facts of the U-2 affair and its immediate aftermath.

Among the questions which may be asked about these events are the following: (1) Why did Khrushchev decide to precipitate a break-up of the long-awaited summit conference? (2) Could we have predicted what Khrushchev was likely to do, prior to his actual action in Paris?

Let us consider how one would approach these problems of explanation and prediction using a decision theory (utility–probability) framework. Presumably the researcher could distinguish the most relevant outcomes of alternative actions in the situation—e.g., increased threat of war, Khrushchev retaining his hold on the Soviet government, embarrassment of Eisenhower, defending Soviet "honor," etc. One would then attempt to find out what the utility of each relevant outcome was to the decision-maker (Khrushchev) as well as his subjective probability that each possible outcome would follow a given course of action. Appropriate formulas which combined these utilities and probabilities would then tell us what move to expect Khrushchev to make.

How could we have known what Khrushchev's utilities and subjective probabilities were?[5] At the time at which the decisions in question were being made, it is plain that those outside the Politburo could not obtain this information from Mr. Khrushchev himself. In fact, therefore, we could not have used the utility-probability approach to predict his action in advance of occurrence. This is a very serious practical deficiency of the decision theory approach. However, ten or twenty years later perhaps, one might gain access to relevant Russian government records, including what Khrushchev said at the crucial time. Perhaps one might also be able to obtain a fairly candid retrospective interview with Khrushchev and with other people who were involved in the decision-making meeting. Such a post-facto analysis of decision-making, though not using decision theory,

---

[5] For the sake of simplicity, this discussion assumes that it was Khrushchev and not a group of persons who made the crucial decisions. The actual historical facts may be somewhat different.

has been made for such important decisions as the US decision to resist aggression in Korea (R. Snyder and Paige, 1958) and for the decisions of European leaders in the days just before World War I (e.g., Zinnes *et al.*, 1961).

However, even if one could get decision-makers to cooperate fully with the researchers, it is far from certain that one could find out from them the real subjective utilities of relevant outcomes. The reason is, as discussed previously, that the true utility of some outcomes may not be fully conscious.

To return again to the example of the U-2 affair, suppose that we had transcripts of everything Khrushchev said to his associates concerning the action he might take at the Paris summit conference. It is unlikely that he would have admitted that personal prestige had a high utility for him in the circumstances. It is still less likely that he would state that a desire to express his anger at Eisenhower, to "get even" with him for an alleged personal "doublecross," had a high utility for him. If such outcomes of breaking up the summit conference did have high utility for Khrushchev, this high utility—especially for the outcome of revenge—may not have been fully conscious or fully expressed to colleagues.

To adequately measure subjective utility and subjective probability we would have to make use of the more sophisticated methods which are beginning to be developed for this purpose (e.g., Davidson and Suppes, 1957; Suppes and Walsh, 1959). The effort to measure utility has usually involved some procedure whereby persons choose between different options. For example, in the notable Davidson and Suppes approach to utility measurement, the situation faced by the subject may be diagrammed as follows:

	Option 1	Option 2
$p = 0.5$	x	u
$p = 0.5$	y	v

The entries in the table (x, y, u, v) represent possible outcomes. If the subject chooses Option 1, he has an even chance of getting either x or y. If he chooses Option 2, he has an even chance of getting u or v. Davidson and Suppes demonstrate that where the subject is indifferent between the two options, i.e., chooses each 50 percent of the time, then the difference in utility between x and v is equal to the difference in utility between y and u.

In their empirical studies, Davidson and Suppes had subjects choose between options which involved different sums of money and different classical phonograph records. Using the utility values obtained by this method, along with measured subjective probability values, the authors are fairly successful in predicting further choice behavior. Evidently, then, their measurement of the utility of simple outcomes in laboratory situations is reasonably good.

Now suppose we wanted to use this general method to assess the relative utility to Khrushchev of various outcomes, such as personal political failure and war, at the time of the 1960 summit conference. We might wish to present him with options of the following kind:

	Option 1 Go ahead with summit	Option 2 Break up summit
$p = 0.5$	No change in personal position now; no war within 10 years.	Personal success now; war within 10 years.
$p = 0.5$	Personal failure now; no war within 10 years.	No change in personal position now; no war within 10 years.

By getting Khrushchev to make meaningful choice among a series of such options, we might theoretically be able to obtain reasonably good measures of the relative utility to him of various outcomes.

There are, however, a number of obvious problems in obtaining such choices. First, one would hardly expect to get Khrushchev to submit to such testing during the time period that the options are most meaningful (i.e., prior to the summit conference). But even if one could, the choice between options such as illustrated would be hypothetical and not real. This is because the real outcomes among which Khrushchev chooses contain many additional suboutcomes, each having its own utility. For example, wrecking the summit conference might not only risk war; it might also help maintain Khrushchev's leadership in Russia, keep the Chinese in check, embarrass Eisenhower, etc. When presented with the necessarily simplified and hypothetical options shown above, Khrushchev might not express his real preference. To admit that he really preferred Option 2 would be to admit that he gives greater weight to personal success than to the lives of millions of his countrymen. This would be a difficult admission to make even to himself. Similar problems of the candidness of preference would apply if Khrushchev were retrospectively choosing among these options ten years after the event.

In short, because of the practical difficulties both of data collection and of the partly-conscious nature of some motives, it would be exceedingly difficult to measure the subjective utilities which help determine actual national decisions—either before such decisions are made or afterward. If this is true, it may help explain why, despite the popularity of decision theory ideas, no serious attempts have been made to apply the utility-maximization principle to the study of actual decisions.

A Possible Alternative Approach to Decision-Making

It may be that the motivational theory proposed by Atkinson[6]—one which is in many ways similar to decision theory— provides a more useful theoretical guide to research in this area. Atkinson has proposed and offered some experimental evidence (Atkinson, 1957, 1958) in support of the proposition that:

Aroused motive to perform act X = f(Motivational disposition $\times$ Incentive $\times$ Expectancy)

Motivational disposition represents a relatively permanent disposition (personality trait) to value incentives (rewards or punishments) of a certain kind.

Incentive is the magnitude of the specific

[6] Atkinson's theoretical model is in the mainstream of psychological work, having strong similarities and explicit connections to the work of Lewin, Tolman, and Rotter, as well as to decision theory.

reward or potential satisfaction offered should the expected consequence of act X occur. Incentives vary in the extent to which they satisfy a particular motivational disposition.

Expectancy is indicated by the probability that the performance of act X will have a certain consequence.

(In his most recent work, Atkinson [1964, p. 279] discussed the need to add a Habit variable to the motivational equation. Habit is concerned with such things as whether the response is one which the person has performed frequently, and which therefore has prominence in his repertoire.)

The key difference between this formulation and that of decision theory is that the "utility" term of decison theory is split into two parts. One part, motivational disposition, is concerned with enduring needs and values of the actor; the other part, incentive, is concerned with aspects of the environment which are relevant to satisfying these needs or values. Motivational disposition $\times$ Incentive $=$ Utility (Atkinson, 1961). Both theoretical models treat the factor of probability (or expectancy) in similar fashion.

Now in what ways does this modification help in solving the research and measurement problems which we have discussed? It may be useful first to see how we could use the $M \times I \times E$ model to understand our illustration—Khrushchev's decision to precipitate a breakup of the summit conference. The theory directs our attention away from the wholly subjective variables of Khrushchev's utilities to more situationally-based variables—the incentives facing him. We would therefore attempt to assess the *situation* faced by Khrushchev in terms of the incentives and probabilities existing for him.

Assessing Incentives and Probabilities

The variables of incentive and probability in the Atkinson formula are not wholly objective. It is the actor's perception of the incentives and probabilities which will determine his behavior. Nevertheless, it may be possible to handle this problem in an adequate way without getting involved in the difficulties associated with trying to obtain subjective data. A possible solution is to analyze the situation in terms of the information which is available to the decision-maker. Thus, in trying to predict Khrushchev's action at the 1960 summit, we would attempt to determine what information is available to him concerning matters such as the likely US response to various actions; the likely Chinese response to various actions; the likely response of "world opinion," etc. What concessions concerning Berlin has the US indicated it will agree to, or not agree to, if the summit meets? What have the Chinese said in their government publications about how they would interpret a Russian meeting with Eisenhower in the face of the U-2 affair? Whom are the governments of neutral countries blaming for the possible collapse of the summit talks?

Not all of the information available to Khrushchev was available to us at the time of his decision to break up the summit conference, and some of it may never be known to us. For example, we do not know what other members of the Soviet Politburo may have told him about the probable domestic repercussions of going ahead with the summit. However, the US government did know at the time a great deal about the situation faced by Khrushchev and the information available to him. We knew the contents of the diplomatic exchanges between Washington and Moscow and between the other Western capitals and Moscow. We knew that the Chinese press was opposing Russian–Western accommodation; that an international conference of Communist parties, at which Russia would try to maintain her control over the world Communist movement, was to meet soon; that the leaders and press of "neutral" nations were urging on Khrushchev a certain course; from ambassadors and intelligence sources, we may even have known something of what was going on behind the scenes in the Kremlin. On the basis of this objective, even though incomplete, information about the situation as it impinged on Khrushchev, we could have attempted systematically to assess the incentives and probabilities which accompanied each of several courses of action open to him. We

could also have assessed the "availability" of various response patterns on the basis of Khrushchev's previous behavior.

This proposed research strategy is similar in some ways to that proposed by Fink. After expressing some doubt about the current feasibility of measuring subjective factors, Fink says:

One approach which does not depend so directly on the motivational model starts with the postulate that the behavioral outcome of the deterrence situation is determined by the total pattern of communicative influence attempts (threats, promises, and suasion) directed at A's decision-makers after A threatened to attack P. It can be assumed that some of these messages will be favorable to the attack, and that others will oppose it; it can also be assumed that some countries will not attempt to influence A in a particular case, thus by default communicating permissiveness. It can also be assumed, that the impact of each message will be a function of the power of its sender; thus each message can be weighted according to some index of the sender's power, and a weighted sum of favorable, unfavorable, and permissive messages can be obtained. A's response can be predicted from the ratio of the total strength of unfavorable messages to the total strength of favorable messages, perhaps modified by the total amount of permissiveness present in the situation. The link between these factors and the motivational model is contained in the assumption that M_o [A's motive *not* to attack P] is positively correlated with the total strength of unfavorable messages, and that M_a [A's motive to attack P] is increased by the occurrence of favorable messages and perhaps by the presence of permissiveness [Fink, 1965, p. 64].

The present proposal is similar to that of Fink in suggesting the possible advantages of relatively objective data. It differs from Fink's in proposing that all objective information confronting the decision-maker (direct messages plus other information) be considered and that these be analyzed in terms of incentives and probabilities relevant to different actions, rather than in terms of favorableness or unfavorableness toward those actions. This type of analysis, while probably more difficult than what Fink suggests, has the advantage of being directly connected to a motivational theory.

Assessing Motivational Dispositions

A further important methodological problem in using the Atkinson theoretical approach is that of measuring the motivational dispositions of the decision-maker. How strong was Khrushchev's motive for personal political tenure, as compared to his motive to avoid war, or to "get even" with Eisenhower? The incentives and probabilities which we might isolate from situational information have greatest meaning in relation to these and other motives.

The problems of getting good motivational measures—especially for noncaptive subjects—are very great. Yet it may prove possible to get such measures on the basis of objective information. One approach is to analyze projectively verbal materials—such as informal interviews, speeches, articles, letters, etc. A second, and perhaps more promising, method is to analyze conditions of reward and punishment in a person's past history which are known to contribute to various motives. For example, we might be able to assess the strength of Khrushchev's motivation to avoid war on the basis of our knowledge of his past experience with war. Did he suffer personally in the past wars? Did he lose a son? Did he witness horrible scenes? His motivation for personal success and achievement might be assessed from knowledge of the learning conditions of his own childhood, if such information is available; or if it is not, one could rely on knowledge of the child-raising practices of the Ukranian peasant society from which he came.[7]

One can attempt to validate measures of motives obtained by such indirect methods against more direct measures like questionnaire responses or behavioral choices.[8] Thus, using subjects like college sopho-

mores, one might attempt to validate an indirect measure of strength of motivation for personal success, derived from analysis of past learning conditions, against more direct questionnaire, projective, and behavioral data. Such an indirect and validated motivational measure could then be applied to the assessment of actual world leaders like Khrushchev. It may be noted that validation of objective measures of utility appear to be less feasible. Whereas motivational dispositions (e.g., to achieve, to express anger) are usually of a fairly general nature and relevant to most people, utilities are concerned with outcomes specific to given individuals. Since the utilities with which Khrushchev might have been concerned (e.g., keeping control of the world Communist movement) were specific to his own life situation, measures of these could not be validated with data obtained from other people.

Laboratory and Simulation Studies

In addition to its advantages over decision theory for measurement in practical situations, use of the Atkinson $M \times I \times E$ model appears to offer some strategic advantages for laboratory studies. One advantage is that one is led to study separately the effect on decision-making of systematic variations in situational rewards and punishment (incentives) and of internalized motives and values (motivational dispositions). A decision theory model, by encompassing both motive and incentive in the concept of utility, directs our attention away from separate consideration of situational and personal factors.

In this context, the $M \times I \times E$ model seems more appropriate for the exciting new work on simulation of international relations. Simulation may prove useful for understanding the behavior of national decision-makers and even for predicting such behavior in advance. A major theoretical and methodological problem in much simulation work is to "match" the simulation participants with real national decision-makers (e.g., Hermann and Hermann, 1962). Such a matching on motivational dispositions fits smoothly into the $M \times I \times$

---

[7] Jerald Bachman has pointed out to the author that if the researcher could measure incentives and probabilities existing for the decision-maker in a number of past choice situations, he could then infer from actual choices made (and the $M \times I \times E$ formula) what the strength of the motivational dispositions were.

[8] That childhood learning conditions may be clearly related to adult motives is demonstrated by work on the achievement motive (see McClelland *et al.*, 1953).

E theoretical framework, but is not explicitly taken into account in a utility-probability framework. Furthermore, for simulation to be a valid method of understanding the real world, "essential" features of the real world must be represented in the simulation. The $M \times I \times E$ theoretical approach provides a possible theoretical rationale for isolating these essential features—i.e., in terms of the incentives and probabilities in the situation. It may prove useful to conceptualize the situation in terms of these variables, thus linking our conceptualization of the situation directly to a motivational theory.

Summary and Conclusions

This paper has considered problems in the use of decision theory as a theoretical tool for predicting and explaining the behavior of national decision-makers.

First, some evidence indicating the possible importance of nonpragmatic, so-called "irrational" factors in decision-making was reviewed. The significance of the unconscious or partly-conscious nature of many nonpragmatic motives was indicated. It was pointed out that writers who use decision theory to explain national decision-making have tended not to take account of utilities which are not deliberately considered and weighed by the decision-maker. It was argued that while decision theory could incorporate partly-conscious motives into its theoretical framework, there are formidable operational problems of measuring partly-conscious utilities. These measurement problems complicate already serious operational problems encountered by a decision theory analysis—problems of gaining access to the data required to assess the subjective variables of utility and probability.

An alternative, though similar, analytic approach was proposed which makes use of Atkinson's theory of motivation. The variables of motivational disposition, incentive, and expectancy in this theory are also ultimately subjective variables. However, it was argued that they are easier to estimate by objective methods than is the variable of utility. Other advantages of the

research strategy proposed are that it enables us to analyze separately the effects of situational and personal variables and that it may be of more help in simulation studies.

What has been proposed is a rather general research strategy. To test its effectiveness, considerable work would have to be done on some of the operational problems mentioned—especially the assessment of incentives, probabilities, and motivational dispositions from objective data. It may turn out that the measurement problems using such a theory are also too great for this approach to be of practical use. Or further work may reveal the need for revision of the theory or use of a better theory. However, it appears that work in this general direction—of using theories whose variables appear fairly susceptible to measurement and of separating situational from subjective factors—promises greater eventual payoff in explanation and prediction than does the decision theory approach which is currently so popular.

REFERENCES

Atkinson, J. W. "Motivational Determinants of Risk-Taking Behavior," *Psychological Review*, 64 (1957), 359–72.

———. "Toward Experimental Analysis of Human Motivation in Terms of Motives, Expectancies and Incentives." In J. W. Atkinson (ed.), *Motives in Fantasy, Action and Society*. Princeton: D. Van Nostrand, 1958.

———. "A New Premise for Research in Motivation." December, 1961 (unpublished).

———. *An Introduction to Motivation*. Princeton, N.J.: Van Nostrand, 1964.

Brim, O. G., et al. *Personality and Decision Processes*. Stanford: Stanford University Press, 1962.

Davidson, D., and P. Suppes, in collaboration with S. Siegel. *Decision-Making: An Experimental Approach*. Stanford: Stanford University Press, 1957.

Deutsch, M. "Some Considerations Relevant to National Policy," *Journal of Social Issues*, 17 (1961), 57–68.

Deutsch, M., and R. M. Krauss. "Studies of Interpersonal Bargaining," *Journal of Conflict Resolution*, 6, 1 (March 1962), 52–76.

Edwards, W. "Behavioral Decision Theory." In *Annual Review of Psychology*, Vol. 12. Palo Alto: Annual Reviews, Inc., 1961.

Fink, C. F. "More Calculations About Deterrence," *Journal of Conflict Resolution*, 9, 1 (March 1965), 54–65.

French, J. R. P., Jr., and B. Raven. "The Bases of Social Power." In D. Cartwright (ed.), *Studies in Social Power*. Ann Arbor: University of Michigan Press, 1959.

French, J. R. P., Jr., H. W. Morrison, and G. Levinger. "Coercive Power and Forces Affecting Conformity," *Journal of Abnormal and Social Psychology*, 61 (1960), 93–101.

Friedman, M., and L. J. Savage. "The Utility Analysis of Choices Involving Risk," *Journal of Political Economy*, 56 (1948), 279–304.

Hermann, C. F., and M. G. Hermann. "The Potential Use of Historical Data for Validation Studies of the Inter-nation Simulation." Unpublished paper, Dept. of Political Science, Northwestern University, Aug. 1962.

McClelland, D., *et al. The Achievement Motive*. New York: Appleton-Century-Crofts, 1953.

Russett, B. M. "The Calculus of Deterrence." *Journal of Conflict Resolution*, 7, 2 (June 1963), 97–109.

Scodel, A., P. Ratoosh, and J. S. Minas, "Some Personality Correlates of Decision-Making under Conditions of Risk," *Behavioral Science*, 4 (1959), 19–28.

Singer, J. D. "Inter-Nation Influence: A Formal Model," *American Political Science Review*, 57 (1963), 420–430.

Snyder, G. II. "Deterrence and Power," *Journal of Conflict Resolution*, 4, 2 (June 1960), 163–78.

Snyder, R. C., and G. D. Paige. "The United States Decision to Resist Aggression in Korea," *Administrative Science Quarterly*, 3 (1958), 341–79.

Suppes, P., and K. Walsh. "A Non-Linear Model for the Experimental Measurement of Utility," *Behavioral Science*, 4 (1959), 204–11.

Whiting, A. S. *China Crosses the Yalu: The Decision to Enter the Korean War*. New York: Macmillan, 1960.

Zinnes, D. A., R. C. North, and H. E. Koch, Jr. "Capability, Threat, and the Outbreak of War." In J. N. Rosenau (ed.), *International Politics and Foreign Policy*. New York: Free Press of Glencoe, 1961.

Zipf, S. G. "An Experimental Study of Resistance to Influence." Unpublished doctoral dissertation, University of Michigan, 1958.

ON THE STUDY OF DISARMAMENT AND ESCALATION[*][1]

MARTIN SHUBIK

1. Introduction

Disarmament and escalation must both be considered in the overall context of a national defense policy, and in particular in their relation to deterrence.

In the course of the last twenty years there has been a considerable growth in methods and theories concerning different aspects of human behavior. In particular, in situations involving conscious choice under conditions of possible conflict or cooperation there has been a development in political science, mathematical economics, programming, psychology, simulation, gaming, and game theory.

For several years an expectation was built up that game-theoretical models would make an immediate operational contribution to the applied art and hoped-for science of weapons control. The diplomat, the general, and the social scientist, when confronted with the ill-defined and the uncontrollable, have often hoped for a "powerful witch-medicine" to solve their problems. A common modern formula for the powerful witch medicine contains a game-theoretic model and a large digital computer. Unfortunately, neither the growth of methodology nor technology by itself can solve problems which require a deep substantive knowledge. This does not mean that the new methodologies and technologies do not have an important role to play in the construction of worthwhile theories; it merely stresses the proposition that although they may be of considerable use, they may be necessary but are not sufficient for such a development.

The actions involved in disarming may

be viewed as a series of moves in a game in extensive form. With due care this model of the process may be of use in analysis; however, it is a belief put forward here that formal game theory and utility theory as they exist at this time are of limited use in the study of disarmament (or rearmament). They do help considerably in defining problem areas, in the separation of variables, and in the analysis of parts of the overall problem of disarmament; however, much care must be taken in the application and interpretation of any formal mathematical model.

2. Mathematical Models and Institutions: What Is the Game?

What is the game? Who are the players? What are the payoffs? These are all well-defined concepts for chess or checkers or even for some relatively simple economic situations. However, when the situation involves the nation-state and an intermix of diplomatic and military affairs these concepts become extremely difficult to define.

In order to be able to answer such questions as "What is the game?" we must be in a position to model institutions in relatively complete detail in mathematical terms. This, in my considered opinion, leads to the development of a reasonable taxonomy for institutions in terms of features such as viability, flexibility, threat power, and so forth. This taxonomy must take into account specifically at least the following features:

(1) *Who are the players?* In the application of mathematical formalisms to human affairs, who or what do we take as the fundamental unit? Do we regard the nation-state as the player; its representatives; the leaders of the armed forces; the political parties; or some aggregation of "the man in the street"? Is it meaningful to talk about "France wants" or "Germany believes"?

[*] Reprinted by permission of the author and publisher from *Journal of Conflict Resolution*, 1968, 12:83–101.
[1] Originally written under MATHEMATICA Contract No. ACDA/ST-80 for the Arms Control and Disarmament Agency, Washington, D.C.

What is the interrelationship between formal and informal organizations? How does this interrelationship become manifested in the viability of the organizations; in the ability to bargain and to maneuver? The player in chess is the individual; his reaction times, perceptions, and data-processing abilities are difficult to measure but at least are more or less well defined. It is easy to write down a general formal statement saying, "Let us consider the United States and the Soviet Union as two players. . . ."; it is not so easy to defend the proposition that it was worth while to do so.

(2) *How is utility evaluated?* Closely tied in with the problem of defining and describing the actual player is that of defining the value of the payoffs, the utility function or the preference ordering of the player for possible states of the system. This splits into two parts. The first is a conceptually straightforward matter which involves describing the states of the system. It nevertheless calls for a high degree of conceptualization and empirical work in order to provide an appropriate level of aggregation for the problem at hand. The second is more complex. On the assumption that the description of the outcomes is given, it is still necessary to evaluate them. How do we construct value functions for a society? It is difficult enough trying to construct a representation of the preference system of the single individual, let alone that of a whole society.

The whole problem of evaluation and value is central to many social sciences and to philosophical discussions of society. It may be presumptuous to believe that we may assign much more than an ordering for the preferences in a society considered as an aggregate for more than a few broad alternatives.

(3) *What do the payoff matrices mean?* The payoff matrix, much beloved as an explanatory device by those engaged in operations research, decision theory, and conversational or formal game theory, can be of considerable use as an aid to analysis if used with extreme care when applied to international affairs. However, the accuracy and order that it brings to some tactical problems, cost studies, and relatively well

formulated economic choices, is usually a spurious accuracy when applied to problems of diplomacy, war, and dealings between nations.

Often in a formal game-theoretic model a description will be given: "Let there be two players each with a set of strategies S_1 and S_2. Let s_1 and s_2 be specific strategies pertaining respectively to Players 1 and 2. We may define two payoff functions P_1 (s_1, s_2) and P_2 (s_1, s_2) which may be described in the form of two payoff matrices which specify the payoffs to each player as a function of the strategies both employ."
The matrices would be of the following form (shown for the first payoff function):

	1	2	—	s_2	—	m
1				—		
2				—		
—				—		
s_1	—	—	—	$P_1(s_1,s_2)$	—	—
n				—		

As a formal description of a well-defined game the above represents a great step forward in our abilities to mathematize certain reasonably well understood social processes. I stress "reasonably well understood" because implicit in this formulation are the assumptions that: (1) the players are well-defined entities; (2) they know what their strategies are; (3) they know what the outcomes from their strategies are; and (4) they are able to assign values to these outcomes.

The social scientist looking for illustrative examples or for situations with which to experiment has been attracted to a very special, attractive, easy to exposit, and highly misleading special case of the formulation given above. These are the matrix games in which each player is limited to two strategies. Unless they are used with extreme care it is my contention that the 2×2 examples can do a great deal more harm than good.

There is little doubt that the 2×2 examples may provide several paradigms of considerable value. They are, however, in general, valuable in the negative sense; i.e., not as a portrayal of reality, but as a demonstration of what can go wrong with our concepts of rationality, competition, cooperation, and so forth even when applied to highly oversimplified situations. In the following sections some of the more important examples will be examined.

	Attack	Maintain status quo
If attacked, defend	−10, −10	0, 0
If attacked, do not defend	−5, 5	0, 0

The above example might be used to initiate an analysis of the strategic situation faced in the Berlin blockade. As a device to teach the lesson that it may pay to pre-commit oneself to the defense even at the risk of a war, because the effect of a threat may be sufficient to deter the enemy, the matrix serves its purpose. On the other hand it may be misleading in the extreme because there may be many other strategies, far more important than the two noted, which do not appear in the analysis; furthermore, the numbers assigned to the outcomes, although they may be suggestive, may easily be suggestive of the wrong thing. They may lull us into believing that we have some reasonably good evaluations of the different overall worths of these outcomes.

	Keep course	Veer
Keep course	−5, −5	2, −2
Veer	−2, 2	0, 0

Another example which has been talked about in what I think of as "folktale game theory" is the game of Chicken, illustrated above. In the canonical form of this game we may consider two leather-jacketed California high school dropouts, each armed with a souped-up old car, driving toward each other on a superhighway, each with one pair of the wheels of his car on the line in the middle of the road. The first one to veer from the collision course is deemed to be "Chicken" and loses the game. Of course, if neither veers, they crash and may both lose their lives but maintain their honor.

This game teaches the general proposition that if you value your life more highly than your honor, sometimes it pays to be chicken. However, if—as could easily be the case in many political situations—the individuals were on collision courses but regarded their honor as more valuable than

their lives, a different lesson could be learned. In my estimation, the main things that can be learned from the study of Chicken (especially if combined with some empirical work) are some deeper insights into the behavior patterns of a subculture in south Californian society.

Diplomacy and international negotiations may easily be among the most important and complex occupations of men. Any aid that simple mathematical models can render can be of considerable worth, but simple, homely analogies can mislead and obscure with the wrong abstraction and false aggregation.

(4) *What are the moves?* What are the moves in the game and how is the passing of time portrayed? Both of these are of critical importance in any attempt to describe a lengthy process such as escalation or international trade negotiations. In the formal study of n-person games of finite length a distinction has been made between games in *normal* or *strategic* form and games in *extensive form* (Luce and Raiffa, 1957, p. 48). In the former each player has only one move; that is his strategy. The strategy is a complete plan which takes care of all contingencies until the end of the game. It is a master outline, which contains instructions as to how to act in every eventuality.

The extensive-form description of the game gives a blow-by-blow commentary on what is going on at every point; it includes a listing of the information conditions prevalent every time an individual has to make a choice, as well as a listing of all alternatives at every point in the game. When the phenomenon being studied is basically static and when both players are in a position to carry out all the calculation, sorting, and selection necessary to consider their alternatives, it can be shown that the two formulations of the game are equivalent. An immediate implication of this is that, although the order of moves is important, the length of time taken does not enter explicitly as a consideration. This is because much of game theory is best suited to portray static phenomena. This is not necessarily bad. Much of the success in the development of economic theory has been in the fruitfulness of statics and comparative statics. Processes such as disarmament do not appear to fall in this category. Even though the first attempts to construct theory may be crude, it appears that dynamic elements are needed.

Timing, time limits, time pressures, and speed in the processing and obtaining of information appear to be of critical importance in many aspects of diplomatic affairs. It is quite difficult to reflect these features in a matrix game, and relatively difficult to do so in a game in extensive form unless the appropriate modifications are made. It is a safe bet to state that a useful mathematical theory dealing with disarmament or escalation will make use of models of games of indefinite length. In these games, furthermore, it may quickly become desirable to model explicitly the role of timing.

(5) *What knowledge do players have of each other's values?* Even if we assume that the individual countries, sides, or players know their own value systems, very often they may be quite ill-informed about the goals of their opponents or competitors. As will be discussed below, signalling systems to inform or deceive the other side are one of the most important features in the design of disarmament procedures. Lack of knowledge, or lack of clarity about one's own goals and strategic possibilities (man, the nation, or an institution viewed as an adaptive organism functioning under incomplete information), are manifested in several forms when we attempt to describe a process in terms of a matrix game. Below, three different matrices are displayed. If we wish to adopt a rigid and unimaginative approach to modeling we might assume that all three examples present the same mathe-

	1	2	3
1	a_{11}	a_{12}	a_{13}
2	a_{21}	?	a_{23}
3	a_{31}	a_{32}	a_{33}

	1	2	3
1	a_{11}	a_{12}	?
2	a_{21}	a_{22}	?
3	?	?	?

	1	2	—	?
1	a_{11}	a_{12}		?
2	a_{21}	a_{22}		?
—				
?	?	?		?

matical problem and can all be patched up by the invocation of some magical formula such as "put in a subjective probability-utility estimate for all blanks." Often the important aspect of the problem is the obtaining of the estimate; hence this advice is of little worth unless it is made more specific. The first case above, where there is a hole (or a few holes) in an otherwise well defined matrix, might easily arise from a situation which is well understood; however, there are a few gaps in technological or economic knowledge. Given the details of the actual problem it might be very reasonable to "patch the holes" by fairly straightforward averaging or extrapolation. The second case is a presentation of a situation in which both sides are aware of a new strategy or technology but they do not yet have any reasonable set of evaluation procedures or any body of experience to guide them in assigning value. The third case is the worst; here the individuals are not even aware of the opportunities available to them in their environment. They do not know that certain things are technologically or socially feasible at this time; there are possibilities which may be seen by others which have not come to their attention and about which they do not even have any concepts. In order to handle this type of situation we need theories of search, viability, and survival.

The comments here are not meant to imply that the use of the strategic form in studying of international affairs is *per se* bad; they are merely meant to specify some important *caveats*.

(6) *What is the coding problem?* Probably the most critical source of misunderstanding and misapplication of game-theoretic and other mathematical models to problems of negotiation and international affairs is caused by a fundamental semantic confusion. This confusion can be best characterized as centering around the definition of the word *threat*. More generally it is based on the lack of an adequate calculus to handle language as moves in a game. In the formal development of game theory the concept of "move" is clear. The analogy with chess is useful. Here the actual physical movement of a chessman has a direct mathematical equivalent. In chess, further-

more, both players know all the rules; the contract is implicitly, rigidly, and completely enforced throughout the game. In tournaments this detail even includes the exclusion of unsporting talk designed to "ploy" the opponent. In negotiations, moves cannot be so easily described. We may wish to consider verbal statements as moves. We might even deem it to be necessary to include the "tone" and manner in which the statements were made. " 'If you cross that line, I shall kill you,' he said icily" may have a considerably different import from " 'If you cross that line, I shall kill you,' he said, nervously fingering the trigger."

Do you wish to consider statements as contrasted to physical acts as moves in games of the type we are interested in? In the case of negotiations the answer is emphatically yes! But how are we to do this? Should we contemplate limiting ourselves to a special restricted vocabulary? What is the relation to be between words and deeds? How are we to handle the "cry wolf" situations? In other words, what sort of correlation (or degree of belief) are we to attach to (1) words expressing intent to perform a certain act in the future and (2) the eventual performance of the act? Neither game theory nor, for that matter, any other theory handles this problem in a completely satisfactory manner.

Possibly the most valuable and at the same time the most confused and misleading contribution of the work of Schelling (1960) is based upon the implicit appreciation of the difference between words and actions in negotiations. In a strictly formal game-theoretic context, if we wished to introduce words as moves, the assumption of the rigid enforceability of contract would imply that, if a player states that "Berlin will be defended if attacked" or "an atomic bomb will be dropped if missile bases are not withdrawn by the end of the month," that is what is going to happen. If the contingency arises, then the words will be translated into the deed.

As soon as we modify the assumption of perfect contract, we must consider attaching a measure of degree of belief to any verbal move. Actually things are even worse than that. Physical acts may themselves become symbols in a communication system. Thus the bombing of some targets in North Vietnam may be done more because it is an addendum to the discourse than because it is a physical act of violence. When is an act of violence an act of violence, and when is it a symbol? When are troops in action participating in a police action, a symbolic war, or a real war?

The recent but still unpublished work of Aumann and Maschler, based upon some ideas of Harsanyi, is an important contribution to understanding the role of signalling, bluffing, and taking advantage of the situation in conditions where the players may be misinformed about each others' goals. This will be discussed further below. Here it suffices to say that this work is a direct extension of classical well-defined game theory with fully enforceable contract (i.e., completely specified rules) and no difficulty in defining moves. One somewhat disconcerting feature is that this formulation turns games which might be objectively zero-sum games into non-zero-sum situations.

The role of individuals and the role of words spoken at a bargaining table in their effect on history and the course of nations have been and still are topics for considerable investigation in many different ways. We may ask both behavioristic and normative questions such as: How does phrasing affect the course of negotiation? or: Should we not try to design negotiation procedures so that the effect of personality is minimized? However, if we wish to construct formal mathematical models of the process, care should be taken to make explicit how the problem of language has been handled.

(7) *Coalitions, countries and institutions.* In general when historians, statesmen, or managers discuss negotiations, coalitions, treaties, mergers, understandings, and alliances they are all highly conscious of the specific institutions involved and the details of the dynamics and administrative mechanisms which bring about whatever results are forthcoming. At this stage of theory-building most mathematizations have treated coalitions in as "institution-free" a manner as possible. Thus, for example, the von Neumann and Morgenstern theory for *n*-person games leaves out all of the dynam-

ics and costs of coalition-formation or organization-building, thereby limiting itself to a sufficiently simplified description of society to permit the erection of a general static theory. It is my contention that this is a highly valuable approach to much of economics and possibly some other behavioral sciences, but is nowhere near as valuable an approach to the study of negotiations, escalation, arms races, or other aspects of diplomatic affairs. When we wish to discuss multilateral dealings it is imperative that we make explicit how dependent our models and theorizing are upon specific institutional detail.

3. The Prerequisites of the System and What Is a Solution?

The first tasks to be tackled in the study of disarmament or escalation are to decide whether there is any problem that merits being studied; and if there is, then to be able to describe and specify the problem. After that we are left with the tasks of deciding upon what constitutes a solution to the problem and how to obtain the solution.

Let us assume that it is important to consider disarmament schemes. What features or properties do we regard as desirable for such processes? To whom do I refer when I employ the word "we"? Do I mean the behavioral scientists concerned with the problem and their value systems, or the President of the United States, or in some ill-defined sense the people of the United States or NATO? As a crude answer to this question it is assumed that the suggested criteria arise from logical considerations and are offered normatively as those which the consensus of political opinion in a civilized country should be willing to accept.

(1) *Feasibility.* The observation that it is necessary to check to see if a scheme is feasible may appear to be trivial and platitudinous. Unfortunately, although it is probably both, checking is still necessary and often very hard to carry out, since many disciplines may be involved. Thus a scheme that may be acceptable diplomatically may not satisfy the constraints of internal politics, the limits of current tech-

nology, or the conditions imposed by the internal social structure.

Very often the formal prerequisites of a system may be easily and accurately stated in mathematical terminology. A series of prerequisites which are mutually consistent and complete can serve to provide us with a solution concept for what we require from a system. Currently there exist several dozen solution concepts for n-person game theory. Each one of them may be examined for the implications of the axioms needed to define it. One of the most useful services that formal mathematical theory can render to the study of human affairs comes in attempts to axiomatize and specify the properties required of any system.

(2) *Optimality.* Whatever system is adopted for whatever purpose, if we have a measure of worth, then we will be in a position to define efficiency. *Ceteris paribus,* it is usually deemed to be desirable to achieve one's goals as efficiently as possible. This prerequisite is not as trivial as it may appear inasmuch as the *ceteris paribus* conditions may not be easy to define. When uncertainty is involved, for example, *ex post* and *ex ante* conditions may not match. If conditions of peace prevail for a long period various people may argue that weapons which were built and then became obsolescent without being "used" were a waste of money and inefficient. This, of course, depends upon the definition of the word "use."

(3) *Decentralization.* When a process involves the coordination of groups of allies and/or action by many different institutions within the same country, a certain level of decentralization may be deemed to be a desirable property. The definition of decentralization poses many difficult problems. When it is applied to systems designed to control the distribution and use of items such as atomic warheads, it becomes clear that the need to understand the nature of decentralization is not based solely upon academic curiosity.

(4) *Equity.* Even in international negotiations, lip-service is paid to the principles of equity. These are often combined with considerations of power. Thus it may be claimed that a treaty is equitable if the

relative powers of the negotiators are taken into account. The concepts of power and equity are basic in the study of both political science and law. In game theory there are several solution concepts which may be regarded as attempts to axiomatize "fair division processes" or, to be more precise, the final outcome of a fair division process (e.g., the work of Nash and Shapley; Luce and Raiffa, 1957, chs. 9–12; Harsanyi, 1962).

Undoubtedly static solution concepts are inadequate for many reasons, some of which are discussed immediately below; however, under the principle of dividing difficulties, it appears to be a worthwhile research strategy to try to examine the meaning and implications of equity criteria in as simple a set of models as possible. For example, if we do so we are immediately able to isolate a critical group of problems involving individual and group utilities. They concern the assumptions we are willing to make on the measurability and comparability of values. In the study of welfare economics fifty years ago and earlier it was assumed more or less without question that interpersonal comparisons of welfare could be made. With the growth of modern economic theory and experimentation it has become unfashionable, at least in economic theory, to consider interpersonal comparisons. The mere fact that some *in vitro* experiments in a laboratory, using undergraduates, prisoners, or buck privates as experimental subjects, may confound a hypothesis concerning interpersonal comparability of values does not mean that *in vivo*, as a good first approximation, we may not be able to show that interpersonal comparisons *are* made.

A remark that is often seen in newspapers in articles discussing Western and Eastern relations is that the Eastern countries place a relatively low value on individual human life. It may well be that such a statement is arrant nonsense and is not taken seriously by responsible officials, or it may be that it is believed by almost all of the generals in the Pentagon. The analysis of remarks such as this constitutes useful research and a useful application of research inasmuch as it may aid those engaged in day-to-day operations to avoid the pitfalls caused by basic misconceptions.

In sum, there are at least three major problem areas which need to be investigated even if we limit ourselves to static, complete-information, rationalistic models of valuation. They are:

(1) The aggregation of individual values to form a meaningful, operational national value system.

(2) The construction of a cardinal rather than an ordinal representation of these values; i.e., the construction of a metric with which to measure the relative importance of goals.

(3) The comparison of the scales of measurement between different countries.

If we wish to consider process, the dynamics of bargaining undoubtedly must reflect changes in value systems; shifts in the levels of information and belief; the growth or decay of trust; changes in the perceptions of the bargainers and their feelings of security or insecurity. Many of these features call for the construction of models and the carrying out of investigations which properly belong to many different behavioral sciences. For example, many game-theoretic concepts of solution make use of the axiom of the independence of irrelevant alternatives. The definition of what is an irrelevant alternative calls for much more sophisticated sociological, political, and psychological concepts than are current in any work performed to date in utility theory or in game theory.

(5) *The minimal increment of trust.* The successful design of a disarmament system calls for the construction of a viable self-policing system. Given whatever levels of faith and trust there may exist between the parties, the system in itself must provide a high degree of guarantee that the expected gains to one and damage to the other due to double-cross are sufficiently small that it is easy for all to perceive that a policy of double-crossing does not pay.

The minimal increment of trust is a feature specifically relevant to giving structure to dynamic models of disarmament or escalation processes. Models with this feature are naturally formulated in terms of differential or difference equations as stress is given to the speed and rate of change of speed in negotiation.

It is evident that the level of trust or suspicion between nations may change as a body of experience is built up. Learning and reinforcement and, for that matter, teaching have roles in the process. There are myriads of *ad hoc* models which can be constructed to reflect learning, teaching, and changes in the level of trust. The three criteria which can be used to select a few models to investigate are: (1) relevance as indicated by empirical investigations, (2) our ability to model the relevant aspects of behavior adequately as indicated by the results of experimentation or other investigations, and (3) mathematical tractability.

To sum up so far: There are many theories of games in existence. Each one is based upon a solution concept for how individuals do behave or should behave under conditions involving an intermix of conflict and parallelism of interest. Most of the theories deal only with statics. A few relatively simple games of indeterminate length have been analyzed and a small literature exists on games to be played in extensive form (see Dresher *et al.,* 1957); however, a successful theory which can be applied to the dynamics of international bargaining (be it game-theoretical, political, or other) has not yet been constructed.

Behavioral scientists can probably be of little direct use to the design of negotiation procedures, at least in the way that aerodynamic engineers are of use in the design of aircraft. Their analysis may be of considerable use in supplying *caveats* which can be spotted from the study of oversimplified models and which also apply to the world in all its complexity. Their advice as wise men who have thought at length about the problem at hand may be of great worth; but a body of formal theory does not yet exist for them to apply.

The methodology of the behavioral sciences and especially mathematical model-building has grown considerably in the past few years. Thus, although the appropriate theory may not exist, the methods for constructing it are far more adequate now than even a decade ago. In this section it has been suggested that a highly useful research approach to the problem of disarmament or escalation is to attempt to isolate and analyze the features that we wish to include as part of a solution. Many game-theory solution concepts can be obtained as axiomatizations of lists of desiderata. An approach to political problems and to the dynamics of bargaining in the same spirit, in order to construct the appropriate solution concepts, appears to be worthwhile.

The use of simple analogies, oversimplified gaming exercises, and broad discursive articles on the solution of the burning problems of the day all indeed have their place in human affairs and in the framing of policy; but they should not be confused with the construction and validation of a body of theory.

4. Some Formal Problems in Game and Utility Theory

Negativistic remarks are often easier to make than to present a constructive approach to the problem at hand. In this section it is suggested that there are many research projects which could be of direct value as steps toward the eventual construction of a theory of disarmament or escalation. Sometimes complex phenomena are, in fact, complicated, and cannot be explained simply and concisely to the layman, even by those who understand them completely. Satisfactory simple theories are often the end product of a lengthy process of search and attempts at synthesis.

The major premise presented here is that the phenomenon of international bargaining and arms control is so complex that, at this stage in the development of the behavioral sciences, we are far from producing a satisfactory general theory. Work needs to be done utilizing the approaches of many different behavioral and physical sciences. Until several bodies of knowledge have been erected upon a considerably firmer basis than they now have, it is unlikely that a satisfactory general theory can be synthesized.

The remarks here are restricted primarily to the uses of utility theory and game theory. These are only a few of the disciplines required; the omission of the others is not meant to imply that these two topics are deemed to be most important to the understanding of negotiations. It is suggested, however, that they are among the more important subjects.

The investigations suggested can be described under four major categories:

(a) Static Theory: Model Building
(b) Static Theory: Solutions and Analysis
(c) Dynamic Game Theory: Model Building
(d) Dynamic Game Theory: Solutions and Analysis

In categories (a) and (c), questions such as what is the game, what are the moves, who are the players, what is the state of information, and what are the goals must be formulated and answered. These questions are related to but preliminary to mathematical analysis and belong more to behavioral science than to mathematics.

Limiting ourselves to statics, two broad programs for research suggest themselves immediately:

(1) *Players and aggregation.* How do we represent countries, institutions, and people as players in the game? How are preferences to be aggregated? What properties are required of a community preference scheme? This problem has a long history in economic theory and poses several fundamental difficulties, as is shown in the work of Arrow (1951).

(2) *Lack of information concerning the rules.* This deals with the problems already noted in (5) of section 2. How do we expect an individual to behave in a "game against nature"? What assumptions are deemed to be reasonable to cover gaps in his understanding of his own preferences or knowledge of the environment?

On the assumption that it is both possible and fruitful carefully to define a set of games relevant to the study of international affairs, restricting ourselves to statics, there are several programs concerning solution which merit investigation.

(3) *Solution concepts: properties and axioms.* In Section 3 different solution concepts were discussed. As we are far from possessing a monolithic theory, it appears to be reasonable to attempt to do a systema-

tic study of alternative solutions. It is probably here that the uses of game theory show at their best. Every attempt to axiomatize equity, power, efficiency, and so forth has encountered difficulties. Yet frequently the examination of the difficulties has served to separate out variables and isolate problems. The type of abstract thought exemplified by the variety of game-theory solution concepts could be applied directly to the analysis of the misconceptions which often surround early attempts to find out what the problem is.

Of the problems amenable to this type of analysis, two examples may be given: (1) The role of the status quo in bargaining procedures. What should be taken as the initial point in a bargain? When equity is being considered, from what basis is this to be measured? (2) The role of continuity and precedent in bargaining. Are they desirable properties and how should they be interpreted?

(4) *The theory of teams.* If analysis is to proceed in depth it is highly desirable to be in a position to divide difficulties. There is little doubt that it is important to be able to characterize an organization as a single player. Even if we abstract from the conflict problem between negotiators and assume that utilities or value systems are well defined, and even if we set aside all sociological and sociopsychological problems, there still remain two important areas for investigation. They can be characterized as the team problem under uncertainty and the command and control problem. We address the first here. One very simplified view of an organization is that all individuals have exactly the same goal. There is total unanimity in their aims. This, of course, abstracts from the possibility that although many may be in harmony with the organization they work with, individuals do have lives and motivations apart from the institutions with which they associate. Accepting the abstraction as a reasonable approximation to some important aspects of organizations, we may consider that the organization operates under conditions of uncertainty and that different parts of the organization receive different messages and information about their en-

vironment. In order to coordinate operations, messages have to be sent between the
various subsections of the organization.
However, the cost of sending messages may
be an important consideration. The theory
of teams deals with the design of optimum
organizations and message-transmission systems. The pioneering work has been done
by Jacob Marschak (1955) and Radner. It
must be noted that they make a further
abstraction: messages are assumed to be
numerical, hence the coding and semantic
problems which usually confront human
communication systems are excluded.

(5) *Command and control.* Let us now
assume away the problems caused by uncertainty and the costs of transmitting information and, instead, consider an organization as a collection of individuals with
possibly different value systems who are
interlinked by a set of formal constraints.
It is evident that the standard organization
charts are unsatisfactory as a method for
portraying the command and control structure within an organization. Recently Lloyd
Shapley (1962) suggested a mathematical
characterization for command and control
based upon work in cooperative game theory. His work on this topic has so far consisted primarily of producing a language
to express the complicated patterns of command and control which exist in large
organizations. There are no major theorems
and no general theory. Nevertheless this
work is an important first step toward the
construction of a body of knowledge which
may later enable us to consider organizations as individual players.

(6) *Games with three or more players.*
Our present lack of understanding of bilateral bargaining is sufficiently profound to
indicate that research ought probably to
concentrate on the development of a theory
of bilateral bargaining, possibly extending
the investigation to three players. Current
experience suggests that almost every solution concept applied to general games with
three or more players is either relatively
unsatisfactory, owing to its basic assumptions, or else has little resolving power and
is highly complex. If investigations are
limited to games based upon considerations
of economic theory, certain interesting lim-

iting results for a large number of players
have been obtained (Shapley and Shubik,
forthcoming). However, the relevance of
these results to bargaining and international negotiations is hard to perceive.

There is little doubt that an adequate
understanding of bargaining, negotiations,
and processes such as disarmament and
escalation depend upon the development of
a dynamic theory. A few attempts have
been made to develop theories of games
played in extensive form and games of
indefinite length (Dresher *et al.,* 1957).
Three areas for research are suggested
which involve a high degree of modeling
and mathematical analysis.

(7) *Games of economic and political
survival.* Shubik (1959, ch. 10) and Shubik
and Thompson (1959) have suggested and
studied a type of game called a game of
economic survival, in which the player has
considerations both of profit and of survival
within a dynamic process of indefinite
length. One immediate consequence of this
game is that certain solution concepts
which were well defined for a static finite
analysis are no longer well defined. In particular, the famous Prisoner's Dilemma—
with its paradoxical solution in the form of
an equilibrium point which is disastrous to
all sides—has many other solutions. Shubik
(1964, pp. 61–70) has suggested that this
type of game-theory analysis can be applied
to political situations, and a class of games
called games of political survival can be
usefully defined.

The Prisoner's Dilemma in its one-period
version is illustrated below:

$$10, 10 \qquad -1, +15$$
$$+15, -1 \qquad 0, \ 0$$

A cursory inspection indicates that the individually rational act for each player is to
select his second strategy, since that strategy
dominates the first in every entry. Against
the first strategy of his opponent a player
has a choice of gaining 10 or 15 and he
prefers the latter. Against the second strategy he has a choice of −1 or 0 and he prefers the latter. If both players apply this
logic, they each will use their second strategy and obtain the payoffs of 0, 0. If both

had used their first strategy, they would have obtained 10 each.

If we consider this game to be played for an indefinite length of time, with (say) a fixed probability of termination after any play, then it can be shown that there may exist strategies containing threats which are great enough to enforce adherence to a jointly optimal outcome during each trial.

(8) *Dynamic games and games of timing.* Richardson (1960) many years ago presented several interesting differential-equation models of arms races, and Dalkey (1965) has recently studied models of escalation with consideration given to timing. Models of this type are useful in carrying out investigations of the importance in the size of step taken in disarmament or escalation processes.

(9) *Quasi-cooperative solutions.* As has been noted above, the various solution concepts which have been defined for static analysis do not necessarily generalize in a satisfactory manner to dynamic situations. Economists have been aware of the difficulties of obtaining worthwhile solution concepts for bargaining in the context of oligopolistic competition (e.g., Zeuthen, 1930; Stackelberg, 1934; and Fellner, 1949; see also Cyert and March, 1963). The fact that a situation is of indefinite length means that long-term enforcement mechanisms may be of some effect. This leads to the possibility of defining quasi-cooperative solutions in which the level of cooperation is brought about by the signaling and enforcement mechanisms available in the period-by-period structure of the game.

(10) *Games with Bayesian players.* The recent work of Harsanyi (1966) and Aumann and Maschler (1966) has produced some interesting games with which one is able to obtain deeper insight into the concepts of bluffing, signaling, and the use and value of information in games played over many periods. The basic idea behind this investigation is that the players may not know each other's value systems. During the game it may or may not be desirable and feasible to disclose one's value system to one's competitor in such a manner that he believes what he is being told. These games use purely numerical data, but even at this level a connection is made be-

tween "words and deeds" in the sense that the strategies disclosed during the play may be deliberately designed so that the wrong inference is drawn by one's opponent concerning the structure of one's own preferences.

(11) *Coding; words, deeds, and numbers.* Although the work noted in (10) above represents an important step forward in the analysis of information in competitive processes, there is a serious gap between formal numerical game models and bargaining processes in which words play a role. There are many different disciplines which can be brought to bear on attempting to code the language of diplomacy and negotiation as moves and deeds in the game. Game theory and utility theory by themselves, however, are not suited for this investigation.

5. A Critique of Gaming and Some Suggestions

In the past few years, two important methods have been added to the ways of studying conflict. They are gaming and simulation. Although the words are often used interchangeably, in the context here they are distinguished. Gaming is used to refer to exercises (training or experimentation) which involve the use of human beings playing their own roles or simulating the roles of others within an environment selected or controlled and created by those in charge of the exercises. Simulation as used here refers to the operation of computer models of systems in order to study their dynamics. Typically the output from a simulation of the type considered here is a set of time series or a set of state variables describing the condition of the system at the end of the period being simulated.

Gaming can be further characterized as either "environment rich" or "environment poor," "free" or "rigid." In the "rich" or "free" case, the rules of the game are not necessarily fully specified; they may be modified during the play. Many real or simulated details may be introduced into the environment and the problems of experimental or other operational control over the game become considerable. In the "environment poor" or "rigid" case, the environment is rigidly controlled and it is possible to run simple experiments. The danger with these, however, is that for certain aspects of human behavior the poverty of the experimental environment may kill the phenomenon to be studied.

Simulations, by the very nature of computer operations, have to at least be consistent and complete if they are to run. This, by itself, may be of considerable use inasmuch as it imposes a fairly heavy discipline on a model-builder to satisfy those requirements. Beyond that limitation, however, simulations have been constructed with routines ranging all the way from representations of well-validated fact to pure fancy.

Simulations give the experimenter leeway to investigate systems so complex that he would not have a hope of analyzing them by other means. The danger is that even the output of the simulations may become too complex to interpret. The difficulties caused by complexity are twofold. One is with respect to mathematical and logical analysis; the other has to do with the realism and relevance of the model as a representation of the phenomenon for which it is the simulator. Some of the most "unrealistic" simulations may have been the most enlightening as research tools. For example, the "wars" of Dalkey are of sufficient simplicity that no one would be foolish enough to interpret his "black box" as a rich model of reality; however, the game processes involved are such that they could not be easily analyzed by other means. Simulations of the variety of TEMPER[2] run into the danger so succinctly stated to this writer by Herman Kahn, who said that he did not mind using simulation so long as he knew the sign to be attached to the effect of a change in variable. For example, before we try to simulate US policy in a Vietnamese village, it would be desirable to know if the expenditure of more money in that village would improve the situation or cause a deterioration.

With due care, it is probable that large-scale gaming exercises and simulations could both be of use in studying pro-

[2] Acronym for "Technological, Economic, Military and Political Evaluation Routine," a computer model of the Cold War devised and programmed for the Joint War Games Agency by Raytheon.

cesses such as escalation and disarmament. That is an open question and no attempt will be made to supply an answer here. I believe, however, that a considerable contribution to the body of knowledge needed for the understanding of bargaining and negotiation processes can be made by controlled gaming experiments and small simulations. They undoubtedly will not answer burning questions and will not be "realistic," but they can provide insights and build up basic theory. The literature on gaming is now quite large; rather than mention any specific reference, several bibliographies may be cited: Riley and Young, 1957; Shubik, 1960; and Shubik, 1964, which includes a bibliography of bibliographies.

A set of problems which are relevant and appear to be amenable to study by means of environment-poor experimental games are those which deal with the "degree of trust" between players and the deterioration of trust under conditions of stress. Much study has been made of the Prisoner's Dilemma game, both as a single-shot game and a many-period situation. The general auction game has scarcely been studied, yet it offers both a structured and more flexible format for a game which still has the dominance properties of the former game.

Consider a game in which each player is to name an integer from 1 to 10. If they both name the same integer, each obtains a payoff, say in dollars, which is half the number he named. If they name different numbers, the individual who names the lowest number obtains that payoff and the other obtains zero. The matrix is given below:

	1	2	3	4	5	6	7	8	9	10
1	½	1	1	1	1	1	1	1	1	1
2	0	1	2	2	2	2	2	2	2	2
3	0	0	³⁄₂	3	3	3	3	3	3	3
4	0	0	0	2	4	4	4	4	4	4
5	0	0	0	0	⁵⁄₂	5	5	5	5	5
6	0	0	0	0	0	3	6	6	6	6
7	0	0	0	0	0	0	⁷⁄₂	7	7	7
8	0	0	0	0	0	0	0	4	8	8
9	0	0	0	0	0	0	0	0	⁹⁄₂	9
10	0	0	0	0	0	0	0	0	0	5

An examination of the tenth row shows that it is dominated by the ninth row for the first player (the same would hold true if we had also drawn the payoff matrix for the second player). If we look at the reduced matrix obtained by excluding the two dominated strategies (i.e., the tenth row and column) we find that the ninth strategies are dominated by the eighth, and so on, until we are left with both players using their first strategies and obtaining a payoff of $\frac{1}{2}$ each. This is a more continuous version of the Prisoner's Dilemma.

It is possible to investigate the strategic form of playing games which consist of repeated plays of this particular subgame by having the players relay messages, proposals, and threats in numerical form (with a specific word format if need be for readability). These messages can be sent with or without a guarantee by the experimenter that they must be adhered to. A particularly interesting set of one-person games which can be used to study the decay of trust can be run by using a dummy player as one of the participants. Consider, for example, the following game set-up. The player receives a message from his competitor: "I will play 10 as long as I observe that you play 10; if you ever depart from playing 10, on the first occasion I will play 1, k times; on the second occasion after these k periods, I will play 1, $2k$ times and so forth." Before he has received this message he is instructed by the referee (and if need be shown the apparatus) that there is a fault in communications purposely introduced by the referee, but only known to the opponent *after* he has sent his message. The fault is such that there is a probability distribution that when the opponent selects as a move in the subgame the number n, this number is transmitted to the referee as the number $n-m$ (or 1, whichever is the higher).

The result of this flaw in communications is such that if the player tries to follow his jointly optimal policy of playing 10, every now and then he will lose because of the transmission error. As he builds up his experience, given that he has been told the error distribution function, he must judge whether or not his opponent is staying honest or—under the guise of lack of control—is subtly "chiseling."

False two-person non-zero-sum games where one of the players is a dummy under the control of the experimenter offer considerable possibilities for the study of the building or the breakdown of trust.

In summary, I believe that there is much basic important groundwork to be done utilizing small "unrealistic" simulations and experimental games. They need to be supported as basic research. The uses of large complex simulations and environment-rich games may possibly have some immediate operational value; in general, however, they appear to be inordinately expensive and require more talent and skill to validate their use than is available or has been forthcoming so far.

6. The Crucial Role of the Concept of Threat

In much of the literature on negotiation and bargaining the concept of threat is often discussed. This word is used more or less technically in many other disciplines such as law, psychiatry, or history. In all uses there appears to be a common underlying basis, yet in all cases the word is used somewhat differently.

An understanding of the meaning of threat appears to be basic to making headway with the problem of coding and the interlinking of words with physical acts. The importance of the problem has been emphasized by the lack of success of game theory in dealing with it. In the game-theory analyses which have dealt with threat, it is treated as nothing more or less than a part of a consciously formulated strategy which contains a firm commitment (completely enforceable by the rules of the game) to carry out some act which will lead to a nonoptimal outcome for all parties unless the others restrict their choice of moves to a set specified by the player. As part of a strategy it is much like any other contingent statement.

If we are willing to consider the possibility of measuring preferences or comparing value systems, then it becomes possible to introduce concepts of optimal threat in terms of the relative marginal costs of inflicting damage, or as a damage exchange-rate measure. This measure can and has been used to fix the "zero point" in various bargaining schemes. In other words, each player is presumed to use his optimal threat in order that the basis from which any bargain will be worked out will reflect the degree of peril with which each is confronted.

It is important to note that, although game theory requires some very restrictive assumptions in order to specify threat, even with these assumptions there are several difficulties which have not been overcome. First we state the assumptions and then discuss the difficulties.

Assumptions: (1) It is possible to obtain a measure for the preferences of each player (and, in some cases, to compare preferences).

(2) The players are completely informed about each other's value systems.

(3) All of their decision processes are conscious, explicit, complete, and not subject to errors of omission or miscalculation.

(4) All messages sent are completely understood in all of their meanings (i.e., there is no coding problem).

(5) All agreements are completely enforceable.

All these conditions are still not sufficient to explain how or why a player should select a threat. The von Neumann and Morgenstern theory for cooperative games is based on the calculation that the worth to be ascribed to any coalition is that which it can obtain if those excluded from the coalition try to minimize its payoff. However, this assumption is pessimistic in the extreme and in some cases is unrealistic almost to the point of modeling paranoid behavior. It gives no consideration whatsoever to the cost to the other side in carrying out its threat. If the costs of inflicting damage are far greater to the threatener than the costs of the damage inflicted, he may not carry out his threat.

Other threat conditions which may appear to be more reasonable and have been considered are based on the difference in the cost of damage, or on the assumption that if cooperation is not forthcoming each will attempt noncooperatively to maximize his own welfare. In many situations the application of these different ways for selecting threat will result in highly different threat outcomes. If these outcomes are to be used as initial points or as a natural zero from which to calculate equitable arbitration schemes, it is necessary to specify conditions which justify selecting one as more reasonable than the others. In human affairs in general and in international affairs in particular, where statements of intent are not binding, we are forced to consider problems other than those which have been covered by game-theory analysis to date.

It is possible that any stranger walking down the street at any time could run amok, pull a knife, and start to attack passersby. At any time, however, there is a degree of belief concerning the dangers present in the immediate environment. It is the analysis of this degree of belief and the mechanisms which bring it about and change it that will help to cast light on the implicit and explicit role of threat. Usually we do not behave as though we expect to be attacked by any passerby; in some situations we do. When does it become reasonable to state that China's threat to commence a thermonuclear war is serious and plausible, given a certain US policy, and when should we assume that it is mere braggadocio?

Some important open questions concerning normative or behavioristic approaches to conflict and threat are: Can human beings and nations be taught to be non-aggressive? Is the use of force to "solve" situations involving a conflict of interests always bad? In the sociology of human affairs does war have a positive role? What are the alternatives to war? What are the mechanisms for individuals and nations to release their aggressions? Formal mathematical analysis has little of value to contribute to the understanding of sentences such as "Is that a threat or a promise?"— yet social psychology and psychiatry do provide insights.

In diplomacy, many have maintained that protocol plays an important role. The actual form of the negotiations serves as a signaling device and contains much information for all parties. In zoological studies different formal patterns for intraspecies and interspecies fighting behavior have been observed (Eibl-Eibesfeldt, 1963). Many animals appear to conform to their own codes or "international laws" on fighting and "weapons control." Thus, for example, the oryx-antelope does not use its horns to gore another oryx when engaged in an intraspecies fight, but uses them when fighting other species.

How are the codes constructed? What are the conditions under which individuals feel threatened or feel secure? Deeper insight into the processes of the formation of codes and the conditions for their violation appears to be a precondition for being able to describe the scenario within which negotiations, disarmament procedures, or escalations take place.

Among the disciplines in which the word "threat" has been used more or less technically are zoology, history, law, psychiatry, political science, military science, diplomacy, economics, game theory, social psychology, sociology, and anthropology. In each instance there is the relationship between intent and behavior to be considered; the roles of acts, symbolic acts, and symbols need to be elucidated.

At this time it appears that an interdisciplinary exchange of views, definitions, and insights on the concept of threat would serve to isolate problems and variables and provide a broader and sounder basis for work in individual disciplines. Such an interchange could make the task of mathematical modeling far less *ad hoc* and at the same time possibly provide a mathematical basis for examining the implications of observations from the different disciplines.

7. Concluding Remarks

The interchange of ideas and insights between those responsible for policy and those engaged in research in the behavioral or physical sciences can be of great operational value. The wise use of wise men has always offered a way to cope with the uncertainties that face decision-makers. Yet the problems of research are far different from those of application. Game theory,[3]

[3] For a compendium of masterful misapplications and misinterpretations of game theory, see Wohlstetter (1964).

utility theory, and the behavioral sciences in general are research-oriented and not application-oriented. In most instances the body of accepted and tested theory is too small to provide more than general guidelines and *caveats* for those interested in application.

It could be of considerable worth to society, I think, to support basic research in topics from which theories of bargaining and negotiation will eventually arise. In the process of doing so, two products are obtained. The first is the new theory and basic research; the second is a body of trained, intelligent individuals who have considered in depth various aspects of the problems relevant to the negotiation process. The presence of experts who know the limitations as well as the strength of their theories is a valuable asset to the decision-maker seeking advice.

REFERENCES

Arrow, K. J. *Social Choice and Individual Values.* New York: Wiley, 1951.

Aumann, R., and M. Maschler. "Independent Preferences: An Area of Applicability of Utility Theory to Disarmament," and "Game Theoretic Aspects of Gradual Disarmament." MATHEMATICA Report, Contract No. ACDA/ST-80. June 1966.

Cyert, R. L., and J. G. March. *A Behavioral Theory of the Firm.* New York: Prentice-Hall, 1963.

Dalkey, N. C. "Solvable Nuclear War Models," *Management Science*, 2, 9 (July 1965), 783–91.

Dresher, M., A. W. Tucker, and P. Wolfe (eds.). *Contributions to the Theory of Games*, Vol. III. Princeton, N.J.: Princeton University Press, 1957.

Eibl-Eibesfeldt, I. "Aggressive Behavior and Ritualized Fighting in Animals." In J. H. Masseoman (ed.), *Violence and War.* New York: Greene and Stratton, 1963, pp. 8–17.

Fellner, W. *Competition Among the Few.* New York: Knopf, 1949.

Harsanyi, J. C. "Measurement of Social Power in N-Person Reciprocal Power Situations," *Behavioral Science*, 7, 1 (Jan. 1962), 81–91.

———. "The Use of Utility Theory and Game Theory in the Analysis of Arms Control and Disarmament Problems," and "A Game-Theoretical Analysis of Arms Control and Disarmament Problems." MATHEMATICA Report, Contract No. ACDA/ST-80. June 1966.

Luce, R. D., and H. Raiffa. *Games and Decisions.* New York: Wiley, 1957.

Marschak, J. "Elements of a Theory of Teams," *Management Science*, 1, 2 (1955), 127–37.

Richardson, L. F. *Arms and Insecurity*. Chicago: Quadrangle Books, 1960.

Riley, V., and J. R. Young. "Bibliography on War Gaming," Operations Research Office, Chevy Chase, Md., April 1957.

Schelling, T. C. *The Strategy of Conflict*. Cambridge, Mass.: Harvard University Press, 1960.

Shapley, L. S. "Single Games: An Outline of the Descriptive Theory," *Behavioral Science*, 7, 1 (Jan. 1962), 59–66.

_____ and M. Shubik. Unpublished manuscript on N-person game theory. RAND Corporation (forthcoming).

Shubik, M. *Strategy and Market Structure*. New York: Wiley, 1959.

_____. "Bibliography on Simulation, Gaming, Artificial Intelligence and Allied Topics," *Journal of the American Statistical Association*, 55 (Dec. 1960), 736–51.

_____ (ed.). *Game Theory and Related Approaches to Social Behavior*. New York: Wiley, 1964.

_____ and G. L. Thompson. "Games of Economic Survival," *Naval Research Logistics Quarterly*, 6 (1959).

von Stackelberg, H. *Marktform und Gleichgewicht*. Berlin: J. Springer, 1934.

Wohlstetter, Albert. "Sin and Games in America." In M. Shubik (ed.), *Game Theory and Related Approaches to Social Behavior*. New York: Wiley, 1964, pp. 209–25.

Zeuthen, F. *Problems of Monopoly and Economic Warfare*. London: G. Routledge, 1930.

A THEORY OF
COALITION FORMATION[*][†]

WILLIAM A. GAMSON

Coalition formation is a pervasive aspect of social life. This paper presents a theory of coalition formation with a statement of conditions and assumptions. While applicable to groups of varying sizes, it is shown to be consistent with Caplow's theory of coalitions in the triad. It successfully handles the experimental results of Vinacke and Arkoff. Finally, the applicability of various work in n-person game theory is discussed with the conclusion that, in its present state, it fails to provide a basis for a descriptive theory of coalitions.

Many novelists as well as political scientists have been fascinated by the intrigues that mark political life. When these intrigues involve not only individuals but also nations we have the stuff of history. This paper deals in a general way with a subject that has been treated specifically by historians and journalists for centuries.

In every historian's description of a revolution, in every political biographer's description of the ascent of his subject, there is a more or less explicit account of the coalitions and alliances which furthered the final outcome. Few areas exhibit less external uniformity. "Politics makes strange bed fellows" we say to express our bewilderment at some new coalition which belies our expectations from past knowledge of the participants.

There are three separate streams of work which have been concerned with the theme. The sociological tributary flows primarily from Simmel,[1] and has focused, in particular, on the relatively simple and manageable three-person group. The triadic relationship has been explored in a series of experimental and theoretical papers by Mills, Strodtbeck, Caplow, and Vinacke and Arkoff.[2]

A second tradition has grown entirely since the end of the Second World War following the publication of von Neumann and Morgenstern's *Theory of Games and Economic Behavior* in 1944.[3] Articles by Shapley and Shubick and by Luce and Rogow on *a priori* power distributions, the von Neumann-Morgenstern "solution" to n-person games and the notion of psi-stability are relevant examples.[4] Both the small group and the mathematical literature will be discussed in detail following the presentation of the theory.

[*] The author is indebted to Dorwin Cartwright of the Research Center for Group Dynamics and Anatol Rapoport of the Mental Health Research Institute for their critical comments and suggestions. This paper was completed under a grant from the Social Science Research Council.

[†] Reprinted by permission of the author and publisher from *American Sociological Review*, 1961, 26:373–382.

[1] Georg Simmel, "Significance of Numbers for Social Life" in A. Paul Hare, Edgar F. Borgatta, and Robert F. Bales, editor, *Small Groups*, New York: Knopf, 1955.

[2] T. M. Mills, "Coalition Pattern in Three Person Groups," *American Sociological Review*, 19 (December, 1954), pp. 657–667. F. L. Strodtbeck, "Family as a Three Person Group," *American Sociological Review*, 19 (February, 1954), pp. 23–29. T. Caplow, "A Theory of Coalitions in the Triad," *American Sociological Review*, 21 (August, 1956), pp. 489–493 and "Further Development of a Theory of Coalitions in the Triad," *American Journal of Sociology*, 64 (March, 1959), pp. 488–493. W. E. Vinacke and A. Arkoff, "Experimental Study of Coalitions in the Triad," *American Sociological Review*, 22 (August, 1957), pp. 406–415.

[3] J. von Neumann and O. Morgenstern, *Theory of Games and Economic Behavior*, Princeton, New Jersey: Princeton University Press, third edition, 1953.

[4] L. S. Shapley and M. Shubick, "Method for Evaluating the Distribution of Power in a Committee System," *American Political Science Review*, 48 (September, 1954), pp. 787–792. R. D. Luce and A. A. Rogow, "A Game Theoretical Analysis of Congressional Power Distributions for a Stable Two-Party System," *Behavior Science*, 1 (April, 1956), pp. 83–96. The fine book by R. D. Luce and H. Raiffa, *Games and Decisions*, New York: John Wiley, 1957, contains excellent summaries of work in the theory of games of relevance to social scientists.

The third body of work comes from historians and journalists and is primarily descriptive. Not only do these accounts capture much of the drama of coalition formation, but they also serve as a valuable reference point for a theory with descriptive rather than strictly normative ambitions. The accounts of the French National Assembly by Lerner and Aron[5] and by Leites[6] and descriptions of the rise of Hitler and Stalin highlight the dimensions of a theory of coalitions.

Coalitions are temporary, means oriented, alliances among individuals or groups which differ in goals. There is generally little value consensus in a coalition and the stability of a coalition requires *tacit neutrality* of the coalition on matters which go beyond the immediate prerogatives. This makes the pursuit of power itself, i.e., control over future decisions, an ideal basis for coalition formation since it is an instrument for the achievement of widely ranging and even incompatible goals. Two members may realize their mutual goal antagonisms but such decisions lie in the future and the present alliance may make both better able to achieve a wide range of goals not all of which will be incompatible. Power is the currency of politics.

The Theory

Some Definitions. A *decision* is a selection among alternatives. When there are several participants, the selection of any given alternative will distribute rewards among them in a particular fashion. The reward which accrues to any participant or group of participants from a decision is the *payoff*. The payoff may include influence on future decisions.

In any decision, there exists a weight associated with each participant involved such that some critical quantity of these weights is necessary for the decision to be made. We shall call these weights *resources*. They vary with the situation, from military force and industrial capacity in a war to votes in a parliamentary situation to verbal

[5] D. Lerner and R. Aron, *France Defeats EDC*, New York: Frederick A. Praeger, 1957.

[6] N. Leites, *On the Game of Politics in France*, Rand Corporation: Unedited Advance Copy, 1958.

and logical ability in a court of law. One may be able to influence the decision more than his resources would warrant through his strategic position. In fact, this "influence of position" is a primary focus of the theory. The *rules of the game* provide the manner in which the decision may be made; this includes specification of the resources which are relevant to the decision.

A *social unit* is any individual or group which for the duration of the decision follows the same coalition strategy. It might be a state delegation to a political convention, a voting bloc in the United Nations, or an association of retail stores. A *coalition* is the joint use of resources by two or more social units. Once formed, a coalition will frequently meet the definition of a social unit from the period of formation until the decision has been made. A *winning coalition* is one with sufficient resources to control the decision. The *decision point* is the minimum proportion of resources necessary to control the decision.

Conditions of the Theory. A *full-fledged coalition situation* is one in which the following conditions are present:

1. There is a decision to be made and there are more than two social units attempting to maximize their share of the payoffs.

2. No single alternative will maximize the payoff to all participants.

3. No participant has dictatorial powers, i.e., no one has initial resources sufficient to control the decision by himself.

4. No participant has veto power, i.e., no member *must* be included in every winning coalition.

The first two of these conditions imply that each of the participants has some stake in the outcome—we are not dealing with a null game—and the situation is competitive. Together with condition three, we are assured that a full-fledged coalition situation is an essential game.[7] The portion of condi-

[7] An *inessential* game, write Luce and Raiffa, *op. cit.*, p. 185, is one in which "no coalition of players is more effective than the several players of the coalition operating alone . . . For every disjoint R and S, V(RUS) = V(R) + V(S) . . . Any game which is not *inessential* is called *essential.*" We will call a game strictly essential if the players operating alone always get zero payoff.

tion one which states that more than two social units are involved can easily be derived from the last two conditions. In a one-man group, the participant has dictatorial powers and, in any dyad, either one member is a dictator or each possesses a veto power.

While the first three conditions merely remove trivial situations from consideration, condition four places much more severe limits on the generality of the theory. Many interesting situations involving *blocking* coalitions are excluded by this condition for reasons which will become apparent shortly.

However, if the decision point is 50 per cent or less, condition three implies condition four. Then, condition four would be violated if and only if some member controlled more than 50 per cent of the resources; but if this were true, then this member would be a dictator and condition three would be violted.

Parameters of the Theory. To predict who will join with whom in any specific instance, the model requires information on the following:

1. *The initial distribution of resources.* We must know, of course, what the relevant resources are for any given decision and, at some starting point, how much of these resources each participant controls.

2. *The payoff for each coalition.* Every alternative coalition is a partition of the players into classes, and for every such partition we must know the total rewards for each class. In Game Theory, the *characteristic function* of a game is calculated by computing the payoff to any subset of players on the assumption that the complementary set of players will form a coalition. In short, it is postulated that the players assume that every game will reduce to a two-person game. This sometimes gives an unrealistically conservative value for a coalition.

We shall include partitions into more than two classes of players in calculating the payoffs. The same subset may receive one payoff when the complementary set is partitioned in one manner and an entirely different payoff when it is partitioned in a second way. To illustrate, a coalition may be losing and have an estimated payoff of

zero if we assume that its opponents will combine but it may be winning on the contrary assumption.

The function which we require appears more complicated than the characteristic function. However, since the theory specifies that only one coalition wins and the payoff to all non-members is zero, in practice we need know only the payoff associated with each possible winning coalition.[8]

Since the rewards will frequently include anticipations of future events, the payoff must reflect differences in the probability of achieving future rewards. To illustrate, the payoff for a coalition at a political convention should reflect the various probabilities that the coalition's candidate will be elected. The payoff for a coalition would be the *expected value* of future decisions—the total payoff from such decisions multiplied by the probability of the coalition's achieving them.

3. *Non-utilitarian strategy preferences.* We must have a rank ordering (with ties allowed) of each participant's inclination to join with every other player *exclusive of that player's control of the resources.* The sources of this non-utilitarian preference will vary depending on the situation: in a small committee, the primary source would probably be interpersonal attraction. In a political convention, we would expect the relative similarity of others' ideology and beliefs to be the principal determinant.

4. *The effective decision point.* The rules of the game will frequently specify an amount of resources *formally* necessary to control the decision. Yet an amount of resources less than the formal amount may be sufficient to control the decision for all practical purposes. This may occur through considerations which prevent a potentially winning opposition from uniting or through a "band-wagon effect."

For example, in a political convention when a candidate reaches a certain number of votes, close to but still short of a majority, the opposition will "stampede." The

[8] Thus, the complete payoff function for any particular game maps every possible coalition into some single value—zero if the coalition is losing and some positive but variable value if the coalition is winning.

decision point in which we are interested is the *effective* rather than the *formal* decision point, although there will be many situations in which these are identical.

If we know the payoff for each coalition, then we can logically deduce the effective decision point. However, in practice the construction of the payoff matrix is dependent on our prior knowledge of this value. In other words, to specify the complete payoff function we must know both whether a coalition has sufficient resources to be winning and how much it will receive. Since separate information is required, we have handled this as an additional constant, but it is not a genuinely independent one.

Additional Definitions and Assumptions: A *minimal winning coalition* is a winning coalition such that the defection of any member will make the coalition no longer winning. The *cheapest winning coalition* is that minimal winning coalition with total resources closest to the decision point. A *payoff class* is a set of payoffs of which the lowest is no more than K per cent less than the highest. The value of K is something which must be determined empirically for a given coalition situation. It specifies, in effect, how large a difference in payoff there must be to make a difference.

The theory applies to full-fledged coalition situations in which we assume the following to be true:

Assumption One: The participants have the same (but not necessarily perfect) information about the initial distribution of resources and the payoff to any coalition.

Assumption Two: Participants do not distinguish between payoffs in the same payoff class.

Assumption Three: Every participant has a rank ordering of non-utilitarian preferences for joining with the other players.

These assumptions and the conditions of the full-fledged coalition situation define the class of games to which the theory is applicable. We can now state the empirical hypotheses of the theory, starting with the general hypothesis:

Any participant will expect others to demand from a coalition a share of the payoff proportional to the amount of resources which they contribute to a coalition.

Any participant, A, estimates the *payoff to himself* from a prospective coalition as a product of the *total payoff* to that coalition and A's expected *share* of that total. The total payoff is known to A and the general hypothesis specifies the share which A will expect to give to others. Thus, A can assign to any prospective coalition a personal payoff value—his proportion of the resources in the coalition multiplied by the total payoff for that coalition.

These values can be assigned to payoff classes of which A will prefer the highest. He does not recognize payoff differences between coalition strategies (prospective coalitions) in the same payoff class. Within any class, he will pursue that coalition strategy whose members have the highest mean rank on his scale of non-utilitarian preferences.

When a player must choose among alternative coalition strategies where the total payoff to a winning coalition is constant, he will maximize his payoff by maximizing his share. The theory states that he will do this by maximizing the ratio of his resources to the total resources of the coalition. Since his resources will be the same regardless of which coalition he joins, the lower the total resources, the greater will be his share. Thus, where the total payoff is held constant, he will favor the *cheapest winning coalition*.

As an illustrative example, let us say that A has 30 per cent of the resources, B has 19 per cent, C has 30 per cent, and D has 21 per cent where the decision point is 51 per cent. For A, the minimal winning coalitions which he must consider are AC and AD. In the former, he will expect $\frac{1}{2}$ of the payoff, while in the latter he expects to get approximately $\frac{3}{5}$. If they differ in payoff as well, $\frac{1}{2}$ of payoff AC may be higher than $\frac{3}{5}$ of payoff AD. If these two figures are in the same payoff class, then he will choose to join with the one which he ranks higher on non-utilitarian strategy preference.

Finally, a coalition will form if and only if there are *reciprocal strategy choices* between two participants. To illustrate, let us assume that X's desired coalition in some three-person game is XY, that Y's is XY or YZ, and that Z's favored coalition is XZ. Only X and Y have *reciprocal strategy choices*, i.e. require the other in their *pre-*

ferred coalition, and, thus, the coalition XY is predicted by the theory.

The model envisions the process of coalition formation as a step-by-step process where the participants join two at a time. Once a coalition has been formed, the situation becomes a new one—that is, there is a fresh distribution of resources—and, in the new coalition situation, the original strategies may or may not be appropriate. *If a coalition which forms was predicted by the theory, then each player's original strategy will remain the same.* Thus, if W's preferred coalition was WXY in some game, then if X and Y join, W will still *necessarily* prefer the strategy WXY. If, however, a coalition forms which is an "error" in terms of the theory, the strategy requirements for some players *may* change. Thus, if player W planned to join with X and Y but Y and Z joined, W might now prefer the group YZ to X.

evaluation of the experimental evidence.[9] He specified eight types of coalition situations based on the initial distribution of resources. Table 1 reproduces the eight types with Caplow's predicted coalition for the continuous situation.

To make our theory applicable to the Caplow situations, we must assume (1) that all winning coalitions have the same payoff, (2) that there are no differences in non-utilitarian strategy preferences, and (3) that the decision point is a simple majority of the resources. It is clear, then, that the prediction from our model will be simply the *cheapest winning coalition* in the applicable situations.

Four of the eight types in Table 1 do not meet the conditions for a full-fledged coalition situation. Types Four and Six represent a dictator situation, and Caplow's prediction for these *inessential* games is also that no coalition will form. Types Seven

TABLE 1
PREDICTED COALITIONS IN TRIADS OF VARYING INITIAL STRENGTH

Type No.	Distribution of Resources	Predicted Coalition	
		Caplow	Gamson
1	A=B=C	any	any
2	A>B, B=C, A<(B+C)	BC	BC
3	A<B, B=C	AB or AC	AB or AC
4	A>(B+C), B=C	none	none
5	A>B>C, A<(B+C)	BC or AC	BC
6	A>B>C, A>(B+C)	none	none
7	A>B>C, A=(B+C)	AB or AC	Inapplicable
8	A=(B+C), B=C	AB or AC	Inapplicable

We can now explain why we have excluded games in which some member possesses veto power, i.e., in which condition four of the full-fledged coalition situation is violated. The bargaining situation which is essential for the general hypothesis to be correct is one in which every participant has alternatives. Where one member has veto power, there is no alternative to his inclusion; he could no longer be expected to demand only a proportional share of the payoff.

Coalitions In the Triad

Caplow has published two papers on a theory of coalition in the triad including an

and Eight fail to meet our fourth condition that no member have veto power for in each of these A must be included in any winning coalition.

In Type One, any coalition will have the same total resources and thus, under the previous assumptions that other things are equal, any coalition would have equal probability. In Type Two, B and C will form a winning coalition, and since A is greater than either B or C, the coalition BC must be cheaper than either AB or AC. Therefore, our prediction for Type Two agrees with Caplow's.

In Type Three, where A's position is

[9] Caplow, 1956, *op. cit.*

ideal for the role of *tertius gaudens,* the coalitions AB and AC are equal in strength and both are cheaper than the coalition BC. Once again, our prediction corresponds to Caplow's.

Type Five is the only situation in which the two theories differ in their consequences. Caplow finds the following assumptions equally plausible[10]: "The 'chooser' in a triad seeks the maximum advantage or minimum disadvantage of strength relative to his coalition partner" or, "The 'chooser' in a triad seeks to maximize the strength of the coalition in relation to the excluded member." He reasons that the weak man, C, in a Type Five situation, would be sought as a coalition partner by both of the others and could choose on either basis.

Our theory clearly implies the first of these two assumptions. C will prefer the coalition BC to the coalition AC because he expects that the stronger A will demand a larger share of the payoff in accordance with his superior resources. The coalition BC is, of course, the cheapest coalition.

Caplow has discussed several experimental studies of triads with the conclusion that they lend some support to his analysis although designed with other purposes in mind. For example, Mills discovered that a subject who was the "odd man" (A) in a Type Three situation tended very slightly to make more efforts to disrupt the coalition between the equals than the subject placed in A's role in a Type Two situation.[11] Caplow concludes that "we would expect less resistance to the 'inevitable' coalition of BC in Type Two than to the improbable, and, therefore, unstable coalition of BC in Type Three."[12]

The most crucial and significant evidence on coalitions in the triad comes from Vinacke and Arkoff who, stimulated by Caplow's first paper, designed an experiment to test the first six of his situations.[13] This experiment is certainly a test of our theory as well, given the earlier predictions of Table 1. Furthermore, in testing the Type Five

[10] Caplow, 1959, *op. cit.*
[11] Mills, *op. cit.*
[12] Caplow, 1956, *op. cit.*
[13] Vinacke and Arkoff, *op. cit.*

situation, it provides a comparison at the only point where our predictions differ.

The experimenters had subjects play a parchesi game in which each player's moves were weighted by a numbered counter which he drew from a hopper at the beginning of the game. The weights on these counters represented the six different initial distributions of resources specified by Caplow's theory. Table 2 gives the weights for each situation. Thirty triads played each game three times with the order arranged to vary systematically the position of the situation in each series.

Vinacke and Arkoff suggested a "game theory" prediction for each of these situations as well, which we shall call the Strict Rationality Theory. They reason that the strictly rational player must realize in a situation such as Type Five that any pair will win, and that if he fails to form a coalition, he can expect his opponents to do so. This reasoning will hold whether one has a weight of two, three, or four, and there is no reason to expect, on rational grounds, that any coalition will form with greater frequency than any other. In fact, this

TABLE 2

VINACKE AND ARKOFF DESIGN FOR EXPERIMENTAL TEST OF SIX CAPLOW SITUATIONS

Type No.	Description	Weights		
		A	B	C
1	A=B=C	1	1	1
2	A>B, B=C, A<(B+C)	3	2	2
3	A<B, B=C	1	2	2
4	A>(B+C), B=C	3	1	1
5	A>B>C, A<(B+C)	4	3	2
6	A>B>C, A>(B+C)	4	2	1

reasoning holds for the first three types as well. In the non-essential types four and six, there is nothing to be gained by forming a coalition and the prediction is that none will take place.

This experiment, then, gives us a chance to compare its results with three different theoretical predictions—Caplow's, Strict Rationality, and our own. In Table 3 we compare these predictions with the actual results of the experiment.

In situations one, four, and six, where

there are no differences between theories, each is supported. Coalitions do not usually occur in the latter two situations, and in situation one, they seem to occur approximately at random.

In situations two and three, the results provide negative evidence for the strict rationality predictions and positive evidence for the other two theories. Apparently, the ability to perceive the necessity for a coalition in these situations is more difficult from certain positions than from others. "It is harder," Vinacke and Arkoff write, "for an initially stronger member to reach the conclusion that the relative strengths are irrelevant than for the other one or two to arrive at this interpretation. In effect, the weaker members can immediately understand the necessity for forming a coalition, whereas the stronger member must go through more complex reasoning to do so."

tion; furthermore, his share of the winnings was larger than his strength might seem to warrant mainly because there was competition for him, *because the other players saw him as weaker, hence more readily to be induced into partnership.*"[14]

Willerman draws similar conclusions from his study of coalitions in a fraternity council.[15] ". . . Distribution of control within the coalition was isomorphic with the relative status and resources of the members outside of the coalition. However, there seem to be occasions when the strategic position of a member gives him power out of proportion to his rank order of status or resources."

There is apparently some basis for the assumption that the size of the demands which a participant will make reflects the proportion of resources which he controls— or, at least, will affect what others will *ex-*

TABLE 3

RESULTS OF VINACKE-ARKOFF EXPERIMENT WITH THREE THEORETICAL PREDICTIONS

Predicted	1 A=B=C	2 A>B, B=C, A<(B+C)	3 A<B, B=C	4 A>(B+C), B=C	5 A>B>C, A<(B+C)	6 A>B>C, A>(B+C)
Caplow	any	BC	AB or AC	none	AC or BC	none
Strict rationality[a]	any	any	any	none	any	none
Gamson	any	BC	AB or AC	none	BC	none
Actual						
AB	33	13	24	11	9	9
AC	17	12	40	10	20	13
BC	30	64	15	7	59	8
Total	80	89	79	28	88	30
No coalition	10	1	11	62	2	60
Probability[b]	NS	.01	.01	NS	.01	NS

[a] These are also the predictions made by Caplow for the "episodic" situation.
[b] From Vinacke and Arkoff: Chi Square with two degrees of freedom.

Situation five is perhaps the most crucial since each theory makes a different prediction for the outcome. While Caplow predicts that either of the coalitions AC or BC are equally likely, the cheapest coalition BC actually takes place three times as frequently as the alternative!

This confirmation is interpreted by Vinacke and Arkoff in a manner which echoes the general hypothesis of our theory: ". . . the weakest member was found to be most often a member of the winning coali-

pect him to demand. In a situation where participants meet with each other sequentially rather than simultaneously, these expectations of others' bargaining demands become even more crucial.

In short, the small group studies of coalitions in the triad uniformly support the

[14] *Ibid.*, emphasis mine.
[15] B. Willerman, *A Final Report: Research on Cohesive and Disruptive Tendencies in Coalition Type Groups,* University of Minnesota. Mimeographed, 1957.

theory presented here. While Caplow's predictions are in most cases consistent with the predictions from our theory under the special case where payoffs and non-utilitarian strategy preferences are held constant, in one crucial difference, the results of Vinacke and Arkoff support the prediction made here.

Mathematical Literature

The mathematical theory of games of strategy as it presently exists is a rich source of ideas, but it can only provide orientations in situations of the type with which we are concerned here. This is true for several reasons. The most powerful mathematical developments of the theory are in the area of two-person, zero-sum games. The theory of games involving many players is, to quote Abraham Kaplan, "in a very unsatisfactory state."[16]

We do not object to the theory of games on the grounds that its assumptions are "unrealistic." They are, at least, clearly stated and we may substitute more plausible ones if we can find some which are workable. Luce and Raiffa write: ". . . it is crucial that social scientists recognize that game theory is not *descriptive* but rather (conditionally) *normative*. It states neither how people do behave nor how they should behave in an absolute sense, but how they should behave if they wish to achieve certain ends."[17] Our own object is descriptive but a normative theory often provides a useful starting point for a descriptive theory.

One attempt to handle the problem of the n-person game is the von Neumann-Morgenstern "solution" theory.[18] A *solution* generally consists of a *set of imputations* (an imputation is an n-tuple giving the pay-

off to each player and satisfying certain conditions) having the following two properties: (1) no imputation in the set *dominates* any other imputation, and (2) every imputation not in the set is dominated by one in the set.[19]

I shall illustrate this with a solution to the three-man game: (1/2, 1/2, 0), (1/2, 0, 1/2), (0, 1/2, 1/2). No imputation among the three dominates another since only one player could improve his position by switching from one to another. Any particular imputation in the solution such as (0, 1/2, 1/2) is dominated by imputations outside of the set—for example, (1/6, 2/3, 1/6), but this, and in fact any imputation outside of the solution set, is dominated by a member of the solution (in this case by 1/2, 0, 1/2).

Luce and Raiffa argue that a "solution must be interpreted as a description of a set of possible payments, any of which might arise if the players choose strategies and form collusive arrangements as they 'should.'" This would seem to offer some promise for our purposes in spite of the fact that the emphasis is on distribution of payoffs. An imputation where some values are positive and others are zero defines an implicit coalition between the positive entries.

Unfortunately, we are not given a single imputation as a solution but rather a set of these, and furthermore, a set in which all possible coalitions are allowed. As if this difficulty were not sufficient, the solution to the three-man game given above is not the only solution; in fact, there is an infinity of solutions. "In their theory," write Luce and Raiffa, ". . . freedom to cooperate leads to vast numbers of 'solutions' with no criteria to select among them. They are forced . . . to the *ad hoc* assumption that in practice there exist social standards which determine *the* solution which actually occurs, but no attempt is made to exhibit a theory of these standards."

There has been an attempt by Vickrey[20] to narrow down the number of solutions to

[16] In M. Shubik, *Readings in Game Theory and Political Behavior,* Garden City, New York: Doubleday, 1954.

[17] Luce and Raiffa, *op. cit.*

[18] This is discussed in relatively non-technical fashion in Luce and Raiffa, *op. cit.* In a sense, we are proposing in this paper a new definition of solution for certain classes of n-person essential games, but because of the specific meaning of "solution" in the von Neumann-Morgenstern sense, we have refrained from using the word.

[19] For a formal definition of imputation and domination, see Luce and Raiffa, *op. cit.*, p. 193 and p. 201.

[20] *Ibid.*, p. 213.

be considered. "Roughly, a solution is called *strong* if the sequence—(1) an imputation in the solution, (2) a change to a non-conforming imputation, and (3) a return to an imputation in the solution—*always* means that at least one of the players participating in the original deviation ultimately suffers a net loss. Thus, a strong solution has an inherent stability not possessed by other solutions, and so it might be expected to occur rather than one of the weaker solutions."

It turns out, encouragingly, that the *only* strong solution for the three-person game is the symmetric one given earlier: (1/2, 1/2, 0), (1/2, 0, 1/2), (0, 1/2, 1/2). Since none of these imputations dominates any other, again extra-theoretical reasons will determine which imputation in the set is chosen.

Vinacke and Arkoff[21] present data on the division of spoils made by their subjects which allow us to examine the frequency with which the strong solution did occur. In the Type One situation where all players had an equal share of the resources originally, the final imputation was a member of the solution set 60 per cent of the time, but in the Type Three situation (A < B, B = C) only 39 per cent of the time. Many of these may have occurred on those occasions (19 per cent) in which the two strong, equally powerful members joined.

We may tentatively conclude that where the initial distribution of resources *differs* among the three members of the triad, not only are the various imputations in a solution set *not* equally probable, but the tendency to divide the rewards symmetrically is considerably less than when participants have equal power.

A second mathematical concept, that of psi-stability, would seem to be more appropriate for our purposes since here a game is described by both an imputation and a coalition structure. The basis of this notion, which has been developed by Luce,[22] is that a pair—an imputation and a given coalition structure—is stable when no *admissible* change in the coalition structure is immediately profitable.

An important addition here is the recognition that from any given coalition structure, every possible coalition is not admissible. The concept of non-utilitarian strategy preferences developed earlier is, in part, an attempt to define the admissible changes between any two stages of the process of coalition formation.

The implications of psi-stability for the theory presented here are less important than one might hope. First, we are concerned primarily with the process of coalition formation rather than coalition stability. Although problems of stability can frequently be translated into the terms of the theory, essentially the game is over when a winning coalition has been formed for a particular decision, and the next decision involves a new game.[23] Secondly, psi-stable pairs, like solutions, are not generally unique and the problem of how to select just *one* still exists.

A full-fledged coalition situation is a strictly essential game and it is not difficult to see that any losing coalition will be psi-unstable. However, in the full-fledged triadic situation, any two-man coalition will meet the conditions of psi-stability regardless of the initial distribution of resources. If our aim is uniqueness, we are no better off here than under solution theory. Attempts by Milnor[24] to describe n-person games in terms of "reasonable outcomes" involve the same type of difficulties ascribed to solution and psi-stability theory.

Shapley[25] gives a method for evaluating the worth of an n-person game for any player that should help us to determine the relative bargaining positions of the several players in a game. He lists three *apparently* weak conditions and then shows that these uniquely determine an evalua-

[21] Vinacke and Arkoff, *op. cit.*

[22] R. D. Luce, "A Definition of Stability for N-Person Games," *Annals of Mathematics*, 59 (May, 1954), pp. 357–366.

[23] This is not a criticism of Luce since coalition stability is obviously an important problem in its own right. Eventually, a satisfactory theory of coalitions should be able to handle both coalition formation and stability.

[24] Described in Luce and Raiffa, *op. cit.*

[25] L. S. Shapley, "A Value for N-Person Games," *Annals of Mathematics Studies*, 28 (1953), pp. 307–317.

tion function. Ultimately, he arrives at an explicit formula for calculating the value for a player, i. "It amounts," to quote Luce and Raiffa, "to a weighted sum of the incremental additions made by i to all the coalitions of which he is a member." In the full-fledged triadic situation, the values are 1/3 for each player. This suggests the symmetric solution.

In an article by Shapley and Shubik,[26] the authors attempt to apply the Shapley value to certain "simple" games (in a *simple* game, every coalition has as its payoff either one or zero, i.e. it is either winning or losing). They argue that the value gives an *a priori* estimation of relative power in many committee or parliamentary situations. An individual's power is given by the index, P/N, where N is the total number of permutations among the players and P is the number of permutations in which his resources are *pivotal* in turning a losing coalition into a winning one. Luce and Rogow[27] applied this to an analysis of coalitions between the President and the parties in the two houses of Congress.

The calculations involved in the Shapley-Shubik power index are relatively simple to make, especially when the N is small. In the triad, there are 3! or six permutations, and in the full-fledged coalition situation each person will be pivotal twice, giving rise to the earlier figure of 1/3.

Suppose, however, we did not assume that resources are used as a bloc. Instead of asking which person is pivotal in the permutation, we might ask which resource unit is pivotal. Referring back to Table 3, we can see that for the Type One situation, the Shapley value remains as 1/3. However, for Type Two, there are 7! permutations instead of 3!. Any given resource unit will be pivotal in 6! ways since the other six units can be permuted that many ways while it remains fixed in the pivotal spot. It follows that A's three resource units will be pivotal 3 x 6! times while B and C will have the pivotal unit in 2 x 6! ways each. The resultant Shapley values are 3/7, 2/7,

2/7, respectively or exactly proportional to the share of resources.

Finally, suppose we make the assumption that within any coalition, a player can expect to share in the payoff proportionally to his Shapley value. It then follows that one will maximize his share in a simple game if he can maximize his power relative to the other members of his winning coalition. In short, we are led to predict that the cheapest coalition will form!

It is certainly possible to question the assumptions by which we used the Shapley value to yield the predictions of our theory. Why should the resource rather than the player be considered the unit and why should the Shapley value determine the proportion of payoff within a coalition? Certainly these are not Shapley's assumptions and his analysis strongly suggests the symmetric solution to the triadic situation, but it is interesting to note that we can reach the same theoretical predictions by this slightly different pathway.

Summary

We have presented a theory of coalition formation to apply to a full-fledged coalition situation defined by four conditions. It is intended to apply where several parties are competitively attempting to determine a decision and in which no participant has either dictatorial or veto powers. The theory requires information on the initial distribution of resources, the payoff for each coalition, the non-utilitarian strategy preferences, and the effective decision point. Three additional assumptions further defined the situation to which the model applies.

Our general hypothesis stated that participants will expect others to demand from a coalition a share of the payoff which is proportional to the amount of resources which they are contributing to it. Each participant will estimate the value of any coalition strategy as the total payoff to a coalition multiplied by his share. He estimates this latter figure by the ratio of his resources to the total resources of the coalition. Every player will pursue strategies in the highest

[26] Shapley and Shubik, *op. cit.*
[27] Luce and Rogow, *op. cit.*

payoff class, but among alternative strategies in the same class, he will choose that one which maximizes his non-utilitarian strategy preference.

A coalition will form between two players if and only if there are reciprocal choices of coalition strategy between them. Thus, the model envisions the process of coalition formation as a step-by-step process until by successive pairing, the decision point has been reached.

The theory was compared with Caplow's predictions for coalitions in the triad and we found that in the special case where payoffs and non-utilitarian strategy preferences are constant, the two theories make identical predictions with one exception. In an experimental test by Vinacke and Arkoff, the results supported Caplow's and our own theory where they were opposed to the predictions of a strict rationality theory. At the one point where Caplow's theory differed from the one presented here, Vinacke and Arkoff's evidence supported the latter.

In examining the mathematical literature, we found that the von Neumann-Morgenstern solution theory was inadequate for our purposes because of its profusion of solutions for many games. An attempt by Vickrey to limit these somewhat by defining a *strong* solution still left the crucial difficulty of determining which member of a set of imputations would actually occur. The concept of psi-stability also left the unique specification of a coalition to extra-theoretical determination.

Finally, we explored the Shapley value and showed that it still suggests the equal probability of coalitions despite initial differences in resources. However, by the addition of two not unreasonable assumptions, it will lead to the same predictions as the theory presented here.

FRACTIONATING CONFLICT*

ROGER FISHER

The problem of avoiding war is usually seen as one of establishing an alternative means of settling the important questions over which countries fight. Cures are designed not to alter the character of the dispute but to provide a substitute for armed conflict. Governments are urged to adjudicate or arbitrate those issues over which they would otherwise go to war.

Looked at in this way, the possibility of international adjudication or arbitration seems remote. The issues for which the United States, for example, would go to war are large and important; they include national survival, freedom, democracy, and our way of life. It seems unlikely that the United States will ever be prepared to refer such an issue to the International Court of Justice or let it be decided by any group of neutrals. Wherever a country believed that so much was at stake in a controversy that nuclear war was preferable to losing, it would almost certainly believe that too much was at stake to be entrusted to a court. Little issues can be adjudicated, but big issues appear to be different.

Dangers Inherent In Over-All Confrontation

If we look at the relations between two hostile countries, we find that each international incident tends to be perceived as part of a large total confrontation, nation-to-nation. Rather than being considered as a small isolated event, each issue is seen as, and thus tends to become, an integral part of an over-all contest between freedom and Communism, or between colonialism and independence, or between NATO and the Warsaw Pact powers. In particular, the relations between the United States and the Soviet Union are perceived and described as a Cold War—a major all-out

* Reprinted by permission of the author and publisher from Fisher, Roger (editor), *International Conflict and Behavioral Sciences: The Craigville Papers* (New York: Basic Books, 1964), pp. 91–110.

contest which is like a war except that there is no shooting.

When all incidents are considered part of a big dispute, the relationship is precarious. All eggs are in one basket. Similar situations occur between individuals when relations become on an *ad hominem* basis. Not what is said but who said it becomes important. The merits of particular issues are lost in one big over-all controversy. Statements, proposals, offers, and concessions are judged not by their content but by their source. Little controversies are pictured, understood, and dealt with as—and hence become—integral parts of a big controversy.

If we look at the relations between countries where there is the least possibility of war, we find that issues are more often dealt with separately. As problems come up they are formulated as small matters, each to be considered and negotiated in terms of what is most immediately relevant.

The danger inherent in big disputes and the difficulty of settling them suggests that, rather than spend our time looking for peaceful ways of resolving big issues, we might better explore the possibility of turning big issues—even issues like Hitler and Communism—into little ones. Each side plays a part in determining the scope of a controversy. It is well recognized that moves made in the bargaining and negotiating process often increase the stakes, raising the controversy from a small one to a big one. It is also well recognized that on occasion part of a dispute can be settled, leaving the balance unresolved. But a change in the size of a conflict is usually the unintended by-product of action taken for some other reason. This paper focuses attention on the sizing of disputes. It considers the conscious formulation of issues in conflict, and the advantages and disadvantages of breaking up big issues into little ones. Viewed from this perspective, adjudication appears not as a process for settling big conflicts, but rather as one that is valuable because it tends to fragment conflict situations by cutting off and serving up for decision one small issue at a time.

To suggest that what is now seen as a major conflict should often be dealt with as a number of small ones is not to assert that the smaller issues have a greater objective reality than the large one. A detached observer from Mars might conclude that a useful way to understand current Soviet-United States relations is to consider "Communism" and "democracy" locked in political combat; each move is part of a single large conflict. It could also be true that many moves on the part of the Soviet Union are taken by Communist leadership as part of a master plan for a Communist world. Fractionating such a conflict will not make existing differences disappear. It will affect not the diagnosis but the prescription for dealing with issues on a day-to-day basis.

Issues between people and between governments do not have objective edges established by external events. These problems of life lie in a seamless web of interrelated facts and circumstances. People and governments can choose which congeries of events shall be considered as a unit for the purpose of working out relations with others. Related events may be joined together for some purposes and treated separately for other purposes. Ideological, national, racial, and religious differences may be "fundamental," but may nonetheless be treated either as relevant or as irrelevant to economic questions that come up daily for decision.

A few examples show that the United States does have a choice in defining issues. In August, 1961, a civil aviation agreement between the United States and the Soviet Union was negotiated. The United States might have signed the agreement, treating it as a separate matter. We chose, however, to decline to sign it, and considered the matter related to Berlin. Sometimes, as has been the case with cultural exchange agreements, we agree to treat a particular problem between us and the Soviet Union as a matter that can be settled independently of other outstanding issues.

Another way in which an issue can be fractionated was illustrated after Brazil ex-propriated an American-owned telephone company in 1962. There were suggestions in Congress that if Latin America treated the United States in this way, we should give no further aid to the Alliance for Progress. The president, however, at a press conference defined the dispute as one between the governor of a province and a single American company over the form and amount of compensation due. A potentially big issue was turned into a small one. The way in which a government defines a dispute obviously does make a difference.

In short, this paper is not concerned with debating whether major conflicts of interest exist between countries; it is concerned with dealing with them. It does not suggest that any one country has complete control over the formulation of international conflict issues, but that it has a measure of control. It does not suggest that it is always wise to fractionate conflict into little issues, but that it is often wise to do so. Actions affecting the size of an issue should be undertaken consciously, with the advantages and disadvantages in mind. The formulation of issues in dispute between our country and another should not be undertaken accidentally or emotionally. Defining an issue in big terms—for example, defining issues in South Vietnam or Berlin in terms of freedom versus Communism—may satisfy the human desire for clear, simple black-and-white choices. But it may be as ineffective as arguing military policy in terms of whether one is for peace or for war.

Within the last few years, it has been recognized that bigger military weapons do not necessarily mean better ones. Study of the complex questions involved in determining the military restraint which a country should exercise has developed the field of arms control. It is obvious that with international disputes, as with weapons, the bigger does not necessarily mean the better. Yet little study has been devoted to the criteria and methods by which a country should formulate and expand or contract issues in controversy. Arms are used only over issues. Perhaps more important than the field of arms control is the field of "issue control."

Criteria of Success

The way in which a country wishes to carry on a dispute must be judged in light of the nation's objectives. The foreign policy objectives of the United States can be roughly divided into two categories. The first covers our substantive social goals: we want to preserve the freedom, equality, and prosperity that we have and to extend such values to other people throughout the world. We are concerned with both defending and advancing the American position when it is in conflict with the social objectives of other governments. These goals are implicit in such phrases as "defending America from Communism" and "winning the Cold War."

The second major category of foreign policy objectives lies in the field of international procedure, the process by which conflicts between nations are resolved. Here again, our objectives are both defensive and offensive. We want to protect America from the dangers involved in the present method of adjusting international differences and to develop better methods of dealing with situations in which one country's goals collide with those of another. The second category of foreign policy objectives is implicit in such phrases as "avoiding war," "ending the arms race," and "developing a world rule of law."

In short, the United States' basic objectives are: first, to win each dispute with another country and, second, to avoid war and develop a fair way of settling such disputes—objectives which are somewhat inconsistent. While the United States would like to win *each* dispute, it is not seeking a world in which any one country wins *every* dispute. Internationally, as well as domestically, our government is simultaneously interested in winning each case and in promoting the rule of law—a regime in which the government does not always win. It is interested in winning disputes and in settling them peacefully. No absolute priority can be established between these two objectives; both need to be kept in mind in each dispute. It is against these objectives that the process of formulating and fractionating conflict issues must be judged.

There are, perhaps, an infinite number of ways in which international issues might be sliced. For a first approximation, it may be useful to consider five dimensions which measure the size of a conflict issue:
(1) The parties on each side of the issue;
(2) The immediate physical issue involved;
(3) The immediate issue of principle;
(4) The substantive precedent which settlement will establish;
(5) The procedural precedent which settlement will establish.

With respect to each of these, there is a certain amount of choice as to how big or small the issue is made. Although these variables are not wholly independent, they will serve as a basis for exploring different ways in which conflict issues may be increased or decreased in size.

Parties On Each Side Of the Issue

Objectively, there is no single correct definition of the parties on each side of a dispute. Each party is often free to define one or both sides in the way that best suits its interests. For example, if a Polish fishing vessel has damaged a trans-Atlantic cable, the party on the "left-hand" side of the dispute might be taken as the helmsman of the ship, the captain of the ship, the department of the Polish government concerned with regulating fishing, the Polish government, the Soviet government, Khrushchev, or "the Communists." The party on the "right-hand" side might be considered to be the private company owning the cable, the United States, or the West.

In traditional international law, the nation is considered as the proper unit to represent the interests of a citizen who is injured. In some circumstances, the nation is held responsible for wrongs committed by its citizens. Thus history as well as nationalism support the present tendency to attribute to the Soviet Union and the United States positions taken by individuals or groups within each nation. If an editorial writer in *Pravda* criticizes the New York Stock Exchange, it is likely to be reported in American newspapers under the headline SOVIET UNION ATTACKS WEST. Similarly, if a retired United States Air Force general makes provocative remarks, Soviet spokesmen are likely to treat them as official statements of the United States government.

Disputes between people ruled by different governments need not be treated as intergovernmental disputes. Disputes between groups in different states within the United States are rarely treated as interstate disputes. Among nations, even actions by government officials are often deliberately treated as though the government itself were not involved. When the first secretary of the United States embassy in Moscow is accused of spying, the charge is directed against him as an individual. He is declared *persona non grata,* and when he leaves the country the dispute is usually treated as closed.

There are advantages in downgrading a dispute and in treating it as one between individuals, or at least as one in which the other government is not involved. As long as disputes are considered in this way, there is little chance of war. Part of the strong emotional outburst by the Soviet Union over the U2 incident in 1960 was apparently due to President Eisenhower's insistence that the flights were official governmental action, not unauthorized conduct on the part of the Central Intelligence Agency.

Treating disputes as cases between individuals or groups rather than nations has the further virtue of establishing crosscutting conflicts. In such conflicts, the opponents in one controversy are not identical with the opponents in another. If a number of different disputes divide the same two nations or the same two groups of nations along a common boundary, the conflict situation becomes aggravated. But if the lines of one conflict cross those of other conflicts, divisions become less sharp, people begin to recognize some common interests. On the international scene today, Yugoslavia and Poland have helped this country understand that our disputes with the Soviet Union and our disputes with Communism are not always the same thing. By identifying more accurately our opponent in certain Far East situations as "China" rather than as "Communism," we may find that we have reduced the size of our opponent and also that on occasion we have an ally in the Soviet Union. We may be able to identify our opponent still more narrowly on some occasions as a particular guerrilla leader and further increase our chances of establishing crosscutting conflicts.

On our own side, we can insist that some matters are nongovernmental. The New York World's Fair Committee asked the White House whether the Peking government should be invited to exhibit at the 1964 fair. A White House decision that the Peking government should *not* be invited turned a possible nongovernmental matter into a governmental one. The issue would have been downgraded if either the committee or the White House had decided that it was a matter for decision by the committee.

There are often, however, conveniences in treating a single government as the responsible opponent in what would otherwise be a mass of unrelated problems. A simple over-all solution may be possible only by considering matters on a government-to-government basis. Using one dispute as leverage on another, as discussed below, often requires a preliminary step—that of treating as governmental two disputes which otherwise would be considered to involve different groups or individuals.

Defining the parties to a dispute is thus a basic way of making disputes bigger or smaller.

Immediate Physical Issue Involved

Any particular conflict can be thought of as having a certain minimum size in factual or physical terms. This is measured by the inconsistency between the physical events desired by the two adversaries. If two men want to sit at the same time on a particular chair that will only hold one, a conflict is defined which can hardly be further reduced.

If the Soviet Union wants to keep a certain number of soldiers in Cuba and if we want them to have a smaller number, these facts set a certain minimal physical size to the conflict issue. It is possible to take action which makes the issue larger, and it is possible to take steps which will reduce the issue back to its physical dimensions, but often there is a minimum size below which it cannot be reduced. The apparent minimum size of a conflict can often be broken up by spreading it over a time scale. For example, assume that one country wants to increase the number of authorized border-crossing places by twenty, and the neighboring country is opposed. The issue might be broken down to consider whether one new crossing place should be opened this month, leaving open the question of the rest.

There are two ways of expanding the physical size of an issue: first, by defining more broadly the subject matter in dispute; second, by bringing in different subjects which are related only because the parties are the same.

By rational extension, almost anything can be related to anything else. The question for each party is whether it would prefer to deal with issues separately or together. Should it seek agreement on a portion of a problem and be willing to postpone consideration of other aspects, or should it insist that nothing will be agreed upon until all of a defined subject matter is settled? For example, countries can agree on co-operative development of weather satellites as a separate issue or insist that the subject is intimately connected with military satellites and that a single agreement must cover both aspects of the problem. The question of releasing prisoners from the April 1961 landing on Cuba could be treated as a special issue (in fact, each prisoner could be considered separately), or it could be treated as part of a single over-all political dispute between the United States and Cuba.

It seems clear that if a subject is too narrowly defined, there will be little possibility of a bargain. The narrower the point, the more likely it is that a change will benefit one party only. It would seem desirable to expand the subject until it is large enough for a bargain which benefits each, if not to the same extent, at least to some degree. As a general rule, enlargement of the issue beyond that point is unwise. If either party tries to get a still greater benefit, it runs the risk of cutting off its nose to spite its face. It is impossible to settle all matters simultaneously. The argument for settling disputes in small units so long as a bargain is

possible is comparable to the argument for free trade versus state trading. It is possible that by state trading a nation, using its full economic leverage to make large bargains, will do better on a particular occasion. As a general rule, however, it will probably do better under a system in which individual trades are made wherever a bargain can be reached.

The Technique of Coupling Issues

The immediate issue under discussion between two sides may be expanded by coupling one dispute with another. Here the connection is made not by broadening the definition of the subject matter but by recognizing that two matters involve the same parties. The considerations involved in coupling one dispute with another deserve more study. If the joining of problems is made as an offer, the process seems constructive, facilitating agreement: "I will let you have what you want in the X dispute if you will let me have what I want in the Y dispute." Without such bargaining, it may be difficult to settle either dispute. If the proposed solution of the X dispute will benefit the other side by, say, sixty "utility units" but cost us twenty, we will suffer a net loss and hence have no incentive to accept the solution unless some other matter is thrown in—a matter in which we benefit by twenty units or more. Coupling disputes in this way may increase the chances of agreement.

Even here, however, shifting the nature of the dispute—from a narrow subject matter to one in which the only common denominator is the parties involved—tends to bring up all possible issues in the relationship and may do more harm than good. It encourages the unfortunate "over-all confrontation" described earlier. The joining of issues as leverage or bargaining currency, even when constructively looking toward a negotiated agreement, tends to shift the focus away from the merits of a problem and to put relative bargaining power in issue.

One way to improve the relationship between two adversaries may be to treat different subjects as separate issues. At roughly every other stage in the escalating process, each party has that option and should be aware of it.

In international negotiation, it may be difficult to couple apparently unrelated disputes. A large part of international negotiation is conducted in public view; governments are under some compulsion to justify their conduct. As national positions are increasingly expressed in terms of principle, it becomes increasingly unacceptable to engage in unprincipled bargaining. Coupling the Cuban problem with the Berlin dispute might make it objectively easier to draft an agreement benefiting both the Soviet Union and the United States. But both countries operate under political inhibitions that tend to make such a trade unacceptable, particularly when the interests of third states are involved.

Pressure in a Dispute

It seems important to distinguish talking about an additional issue by way of a counteroffer, as discussed above, from taking action on an otherwise unrelated matter by way of pressure. When pressure produces counterpressure, the escalating process is much like that by which limited hostilities grow into all-out war. As is the case with limited war, the more unrelated the action of one country is to the action taken by the other, the more difficult it is to find a boundary to the conflict.

In such a process, it is also difficult to keep a limited objective in view. Although no shot may be fired, the situation becomes warlike, particularly in that the aims become unclear. The pressure is no longer being applied for a specific and limited purpose. Relations between the United States and China have broadened out in this way. The United States is applying pressure on a country that is now widely regarded as its enemy. But we are not sure what we want that pressure to accomplish or what China would have to do in order to yield to it. In effect, our pressure is for unconditional surrender, an objective so broad that it becomes impossible to attain by negotiation or otherwise.

When pressure, though substantively unrelated, is applied for a narrow, specific objective, the dispute in one sense remains quite small. This was the case in Laos when the United States suspended economic aid and brought substantial pressure on the government. The pressure was directed at causing the government to accept the specific terms of a particular agreement on the neutralization of Laos.

An unrelated matter may also be brought in by way of reprisal or punishment: "I am doing this to you since you did that to me." Such action may provide grist for future disputes but does not seem to be part of the process of formulating an international issue. Punishment, which functions as a lesson for the future, should apparently be distinguished from actions which broaden a dispute. The latter are taken or threatened in order to induce a change in an adversary's immediate position.

The Immediate Issue of Principle

The size of a dispute is determined not only by the parties and physical issues involved but by the issue of principle which each side considers to be at stake. To some extent the immediate issue of principle can be considered apart from the problem of the precedent which a settlement may establish. The position which a country takes in a particular controversy is usually not an *ad hoc* position applicable only to those circumstances; it generally reflects broad political and moral principles of wide applicability. A major difficulty in settling a dispute lies in the fact that it is often seen in terms of principle, and on matters of principle countries are usually unwilling to yield.

To be strong and effective, a country apparently needs principles and needs to adhere to them. Principles can be flexible, however, and the extent to which they are involved in a particular controversy can be limited in two ways. The first is by recognizing that we can be loyal to our principles without insisting that our opponents be disloyal to theirs. To arouse the maximum support of our own people, we often identify a dispute as a conflict of principle, in which one principle or the other must yield. We do this also as a form of commital strategy in which we strengthen our negotiating position by tying our own hands and making it harder to back down. If we wish to win a controversy, it would seem wiser to say that the solution we seek is not only consistent with our principles but is also consistent with those of our adversary—at least if properly construed and applied. By insisting that our adversary can come along without abandoning his principles, we make it easier for him to do so. In this way a country can remove an issue of principle from a controversy without in any sense abandoning its principles. If another country is prepared to accept a physical solution which we regard as consistent with our principles, no principle of ours requires that it first accept some generalized statement of what it is doing.

In many instances, an issue is defined differently for several different audiences. Each government may tell its own people that a particular issue is an important step in furthering its national goals and is an application of strongly-held national principles. At the same time, it may be explaining to its adversary that the particular matter can be settled pragmatically without regard to differences of principle. While explaining to the American people that the Antarctic Treaty was furthering the principle of complete inspection for any disarmament agreement, the United States government could point out to the Soviet Union that it could accept this practical solution without abandoning any matter of principle.

The Application of Principle

The second way of limiting the extent to which principle is involved in a controversy is to recognize the difference between principle and the application of principle. In almost every dispute, there are conflicting principles involved. In a lawsuit, each side urges that a different principle should be the controlling one. A resolution of the dispute does not necessarily mean that either principle need be abandoned; it often means that, at this point, a particular accommodation between them has to be worked out, leaving both principles intact. The United States government rarely argues a case in the Supreme Court except to further some principle in which it believes. To

lose a case, as the government often does, is rarely to abandon its principles or to be disloyal to them. Litigation may simply determine that, in this case, the principle does not properly apply. The same determination can be reached through negotiation; to do so is not to be disloyal to principle.

Recognizing where possible that a dispute involves a question of the *application* of principle rather than the central principle itself should make it possible to decrease the stakes. Nonetheless, in every controversy, a certain minimum amount of principle is involved; it cannot be further reduced. This is probably best identified in terms of the precedent which will necessarily be established by resolution of the controversy. The size of a controversy may be measured in terms of both the substantive and procedural precedents which its resolution will set.

Substantive Precedent Which Settlement Would Establish

In almost every conflict each side is thinking not only of how much it would lose immediately if it yielded a point, but of how much it would lose by way of precedent. Similarly, a country may press a position, not for the immediate consequences, but with the hope of establishing a precedent for the future.

A nation's concern in international affairs over the problem of precedent is substantial. Even those who contend that the precedents embodied in international law are wholly ineffective are often the first to contradict themselves by saying that the United States must not yield on a point because it would set a dangerous precedent which would be difficult or impossible to overcome. Those who contend that the Soviet Union respects no rules are often those who also insist that the United States must press certain propositions as precedents for the future. A precedent is a piece of a rule. There can be no doubt that it has some effect. The impact of a precedent depends upon its *strength* and its *scope*. To the extent that these can be controlled, the size of the matter in conflict can be changed.

A precedent no doubt has some strength.

Even without an implied promise to be consistent, governments, like people, find it much easier to do what they have done before. A precedent is a fact which cannot be undone by accompanying the action with a statement that it is not a precedent. The fact demonstrates to oneself as well as to others what actions one is prepared to take under particular circumstances. Also, basic fairness tends to require that different people be treated in the same way under the same circumstances. A highly bureaucratic government like that of the Soviet Union is particularly bound by precedent on small matters—those which top authority is too busy to decide and which lower bureaucrats have no authority to decide.

The scope of a precedent is always somewhat ambiguous. In political affairs as in the legal system, ambiguity permits a nice accommodation between consistency and flexibility as new circumstances arise. The minimum scope of a precedent is determined by that which cannot reasonably be distinguished from it. Additional scope may be established by what is said before and during the resolution of an issue. The language used by one or both sides may turn a simple case into a test case. Significant possibilities exist for limiting the size of a conflict by limiting the precedent. Apparently either party to a controversy can, by itself, limit the substantive scope of the precedent that will be established. It takes two to make an agreement, but either one can create a dispute. If the parties agree that a controversy is a test case which will decide a broad category of issues, the scope of the precedent is thereby enlarged. But if the parties disagree as to the scope of the precedent, it is thereby reduced. For if the yielding party truly considers a particular settlement unique, it will ignore it when other questions come up. It will not have been effectively bound by the precedent, whatever the other party contends.

For several days in the fall of 1962, Russian guards for the war memorial were allowed to enter West Berlin in armored cars instead of buses. Later the United States told the Russian guards to revert to transportation by bus, which they did. The United States was not effectively tied up by the armored car precedent because it distinguished the circumstances. The armored cars were allowed during a period of rioting. Once the rioting had stopped, the cases were different.

Procedural Precedent Which Settlement Would Establish

Since international substantive issues can usually be distinguished from each other, greater concern is generally expressed over the broad procedural aspects of a precedent. The United States is constantly being warned against establishing the precedent of giving up something for nothing or of yielding to threats of force. We are told that particular issues are not so important in themselves but because a line must be drawn somewhere. We hear that appeasement does not work; that once concessions are made, further concessions are almost inevitable.

A close relationship exists between the substantive issue involved and the procedural precedent established by reaching an agreement. To the extent that a settlement is substantively sound, it can be justified "on its merits"; the fact that concessions were made will have limited effect. If both parties have made some concessions, the effects are likely to be in balance. If one party has made all the concessions, the Munich situation obtains. The effects of such a concession need to be examined in terms of their influence on each party and on third states. The lessons learned from Munich deserve more study than they have received.

The first lesson—that a country may not succeed in pacifying another by yielding to its purportedly last demands—has been thoroughly absorbed. In fact, appeasement has become such a bad word that there is little attempt to identify situations in which it might be politically effective. The fact that a particular concession may not accomplish its purpose has, however, little to do with the precedent established.

The second lesson of Munich is that the party to whom the concession has been given may think that a procedural precedent has been established and may seek further concessions in the same way. Having discovered that the British would not fight over one issue, Hitler apparently assumed that they would not fight over a comparable issue. Third states may have reached the same conclusion.

The third lesson of Munich, however, is that Hitler was wrong. Governments, like individuals, are tolerant to a degree. They will co-operate with others on a give-and-take basis, but unless concessions are reciprocal, it is less likely, rather than more, that additional concessions will be made. Each concession a country makes diminishes the number of its citizens who perceive the other country's demands as legitimate. Finally it becomes clear that further concessions will accomplish nothing. Instead of weakening .British will, the yielding at Munich tended to stiffen the subsequent British determination to resist. Of course, if a country gives up territory or arms of substantive importance, it may become weaker through concessions. The Munich example, however, suggests that the effect of a procedural precedent on a country that yields has been widely exaggerated. It suggests that the famous "slippery slope" goes uphill, not down.

Fractionation and the Peaceful Settlement Of Disputes

When considering only the "procedural" objective of the United States—to avoid war and to improve the method of settling international differences—it appears that the practice of fractionating conflict issues is definitely to our interest. Separating issues into their smallest components and dealing with them one at a time reduces the risk of war significantly. No country is likely to fight over what it perceives as a small issue. It is only when a country fears that it might lose a great deal, or hopes to gain a great deal, that it will go to war.

When issues are considered separately and in terms of their smallest size, the process of settling disputes should be peaceable. But some disputes may not be settled. Unlike judicial settlement, negotiation requires scope for bargaining. Ideally, one country should yield on a dispute about which its adversary cares more than it does,

confident that on some subsequent occasion the process would be reversed. But realistically, the chance of settling an issue when one party's gain means another party's loss seems to be increased either by enlarging the substantive issue until it includes enough ground so that a settlement will benefit each or by coupling it with another issue in which the position of the parties is reversed.

Fractionating conflict should avoid the stalemate that comes from a nation-to-nation confrontation in which neither country feels that it can make any concession without losing part of an over-all war. To the extent that issues are decided separately there is an increased chance that they are decided on their merits, that is, in light of their particular facts and circumstances. In this sense, agreements reached might be objectively better. Piecemeal settlement also recognizes that everything cannot be done at once and permits progress in certain areas while other matters are being worked out.

Thus, one technique of lessening the risk of war and improving the process of international settlement is to separate and reduce the size of issues. Apparently this technique ought to be pursued unless significantly better results can be obtained by the contrary technique of enlarging and coupling issues. Fractionating conflict can help in coping with disputes peaceably, but how does it stand up in terms of our companion objective—winning disputes?

Fractionation and the Winning Of Disputes

No general statement, of course, can be made that either fractionating a conflict issue or enlarging it will always be better for a country from the point of view of winning the matter in dispute. Sometimes a country will gain a point by coupling one issue with another, or by enlarging it in terms of a broader subject matter or in terms of principle. On other occasions, it will do better to treat the issue in its narrowest possible context. Some tentative guides as to when one strategy or the other will help to obtain a substantive payoff can perhaps be formulated.

Coupling one issue with another may be useful as a form of pressure. If one country has sufficient power for effective arm-twisting, the desired substantive result may be accomplished. Such substantive gain must be weighed against the procedural loss which deciding disputes on the basis of superior power involves. There are other limitations on the pressure technique. Usually, a country must possess superior power and be willing and able to use it to make the method effective. When dealing with an opponent who has the opportunity to escalate a conflict issue by throwing in counter-leverage and counterthreats, the tactic can backfire. It is not at all clear that the consequence of raising the ante will result in winning the original dispute.

Even when one country of superior power is applying pressure in large quantities, the effectiveness of that pressure is likely to depend upon keeping the issue on which it is focused small. The effectiveness of pressure is a function of the difference between how much the pressure currently hurts and how much it would hurt to yield on the issue involved. Economic sanctions against Cuba or Mississippi or South Africa, for example, would be more effective if it were made clear that they would stop upon the attainment of an identified, limited objective, than if pressure were directed against "Communism" or against "discrimination." The effectiveness of pressure is increased by keeping the objective narrow and making it easy for the adversary to back down.

The coupling technique may also be a useful way of winning one dispute at the expense of another. If an issue that is likely to be lost anyway is on the table, a country may be able to retrieve something by coupling that dispute with one on which the adversary might yield. If an issue that a country strongly desires to win is on the table, perhaps it can be bought by coupling it with a "loser."

Similarly, expanding the subject matter under dispute may make it possible to work out an agreement in which we win something. Negotiating the allocation of a single radio frequency between several countries would be difficult. There would be more

likelihood of success if the subject were broadened to include enough frequencies so that each country would get at least one. Finally, if it is already clear that one side is going to win in a particular conflict situation, the larger the terms in which the issue can be defined, the more that side will win.

These instances indicate that fractionating a conflict situation—insisting that the issues be dealt with separately and in their narrowest possible scope—may not always be the wisest strategy. However, they do not cover the most frequent occasions on which countries tend to insist that big issues are involved.

Escalation As a Defensive Technique

Perhaps the most important proposition developed in this preliminary consideration of the field of issue control is that a country which defines an issue in large terms has adopted a negative strategy. An issue is often defined broadly as a deliberate defensive maneuver. Rather than treat the transit of men and materials from West Germany to West Berlin as a group of narrow, pragmatic questions, the United States has defined the problem in terms of freedom versus Communism. The West has insisted that any interference with its access to Berlin would be serious enough to justify a war—including, perhaps, a nuclear war.

This tactic of issue escalation was deliberately adopted as a form of commital strategy. It makes the West less willing to yield. By turning an issue into a test case, by insisting that what is involved is not a small and unique event but a major principle, a country makes backing down more difficult. In addition, citizens, allies, and friends can more easily be rallied to fight for a big, clear-cut principle than for a particular case. In seeking to preserve the status quo, a country insists that any change would be catastrophic. The technique is common in domestic as well as international politics. In an effort to stop a threatened change, groups will argue that the proposed measure is the first step toward socialism or totalitarianism, or that it threatens the entire American way of life. Internationally, the United States has sometimes taken the position that recognition of a government is not simply a question of deciding what authority is in fact in charge, but involves the larger question of approval of the regime. Those opposed to the admission of Red China to the United Nations insist that the issue is a large one of principle, not a small one of credentials.

Insisting that a small change from the status quo would bring disastrous consequences is a defensive move, a kind of rearguard action, slowing down the pace of change. It retards the loss of a substantive point, but is unlikely to be wholly successful in preserving the status quo. The United States can insist that any interference with our right of access to Berlin will be viewed as grounds for war. This may slow down the slice-by-slice "salami tactics" of the Soviet Union, but it can hardly stop them. To insist that a small change would be a justification for war does not by itself make it so. An additional five- or ten-minutes delay on a convoy of trucks to Berlin, or the addition of one more inspector to the routine, does not mean the end of freedom or democracy, whatever we may say. If the slices are thin enough and are taken slowly enough, the prophesied doom does not in fact materialize. The country which defines small issues and presses forward on them is likely to make headway which its adversary, by insisting that large principles are at stake, may delay but is unable to stop.

Escalation As an Offensive Strategy

If increasing the size of an issue has little long-run promise as a defensive strategy, it has even less promise as an offensive technique. If a party desires to alter the status quo, defining an issue as one involving a large subject matter or big principles tends to make success less likely. Almost inevitably, change from the status quo must be brought about incrementally. Even those who have the power to bring about major changes and would like to do so must face the question of where to begin. A group which defines its action program as "for peace" is likely to be as ineffective as if it were for virtue and against sin. If one is to be effective in domestic politics, he must

combine the public support which broad issues and principles can arouse with the pursuit of narrowly defined goals.

It would seem equally important for a government which wishes to alter the behavior of another government to define its immediate goal in narrow and specific terms, to break up the big issues into smaller ones, and to press for these separately. At this writing, the United States is carrying on a dispute with Cuba over major issues. The Cuban government is pursuing policies which we would like to change; the United States has been applying increasing pressure on Cuba to that end. While broadening the pressure, we have, consciously or unconsciously, broadened our demands at the same time. We have stated our goals in such terms as "a free and democratic Cuba"—a goal which, like "peace" and "ending the arms race" is admirable, but too broad as a focus for effective action. We are interested in particular issues—for example, the removal of Soviet weapons from this hemisphere, no armed subversion in other countries, respect for international law, free elections. By asking for more than we need and more than we really want, and by lumping all our demands into one big issue, we make our case an extremely hard one to win. Furthermore we rally and unify the opposition. In seeking "to topple the Castro regime," we are defining the issue in the largest possible terms, as we did in seeking unconditional surrender during World War II. The British experience in seeking "to topple Nasser" is instructive. By defining an issue in all-or-nothing terms, we tend to make sure that we get nothing unless we are prepared to exert the force required to get all. Having declared that the choice is between Communism and freedom, little victories look like compromises with Communism. In this context it is difficult for us to apply the "salami tactics" of moving forward slice by slice.

Escalating a matter into a large issue of principle appears to be somewhat effective as a defensive strategy; at least it can gain time. It would seem generally unwise as a strategy to pursue in areas in which we would like to change the status quo.

Fractionating issues, on the other hand,

seems almost invariably the best tactic for a country seeking to bring about change. And in a world in which change is inevitable, the best defense is probably a good offense. The situation anywhere could always be better. The best way to preserve and advance our values would seem to be to press constantly for *small* improvements in all areas. Ironically, those who take a "tough" position in international affairs are usually against breaking up the issues; they unwittingly inhibit action which could bring about changes they desire. Routine insistence upon the big issue would seem a prescription for an unsuccessful defense of the status quo.

The Southern Example

Within an organized society the legal system facilitates the fractionating process; domestic experience may nonetheless be useful in illustrating its virtues. In the South today, a fundamental and major conflict exists between differing views that are strongly held. Leaders of the Negro community and proponents of the conservative Southern point of view see the conflict in terms of broad principles—and they are correct. Each side also has a problem of strategy. Without in any way abandoning their over-all objective or their principle of full and equal rights, Negro leaders, by and large, have proceeded by fractionating the conflict issues and moving step by step. Small issues have been raised: including Negroes on a particular jury list, allowing Negroes to register to vote in a particular county, admitting Negro students to a particular school, and serving Negroes at bus terminals and restaurants.

On most occasions, the White Citizens Councils and others opposed to integration have adopted the strategy of escalating the issue into broad political terms. They insist that what is involved in this case is a choice beween the Southern way of life and mongrelization of the races. This strategy may have caused some delay, but it has not served the White Citizens Councils well. The freedom riders and others have experienced substantial success by pursuing the salami tactics of one slice at a time. At almost no point has the loss of a particular slice been painful enough to cause a united uprising of the opposition.

If one were advising the conservative Southerner on the strategy he ought to take, one might well suggest that he fractionate the issues and proceed with his own salami tactics. For example, starting with the established base that a purely social club may exclude from membership whomever it pleases, one might proceed through a series of incremental cases; the country club that owns land; the country club where members live on the club property; the "residential" club where only members may use the swimming pool and take lessons at the private school; the two or three blocks which form a residential club, and so on. How successful such a series of cases might be in limiting the consequences of the racial covenant and school integration decisions is an open question. But the strategy appears to have far greater promise of success than the "big issue" strategy currently being pursued.

Conclusion

Internationally, it is more difficult to force a decision on the little issues. The lack of compulsory jurisdiction for the International Court of Justice means that we have no institutionalized method of bringing up and disposing of one case at a time. The virtues of adopting and pressing for a small specific objective, however, go far beyond the legal machinery. In international politics as in domestic politics, the strategy of separating out small and immediate issues and dealing with them one at a time would seem likely to advance our social and substantive goals.

Instead of identifying every issue as a part of a Cold War to be dealt with as a single major conflict, it would seem wiser to insist that each issue, whether or not it reflects basic and fundamental differences, be dealt with independently on its merits. By separating out the Antarctic problem, and dealing with it outside the context of the Cold War, the United States accomplished in the Antarctic Treaty a significant victory for its own objectives. By urging the United Nations to deal with the Middle East and Congo problems in terms of what the particular circumstances required we advanced our objectives of strengthening the United Nations and world order more than we would have had we cast these problems as part of an East-West conflict.

If the United States continues to press, in the United Nations and elsewhere, on many small and separate issues—issues in which our position makes more practical sense than the position of our opponents—we have a fair chance of prevailing. If the issues are small, no one defeat will be serious enough to cause any country to pick up its chips and go home. By dealing with issues in their narrow and immediate factual context, there is a greater chance that the position of other countries will be determined by the merits of the problem rather than by broad ideological points of view. To the extent that our position has merit, and to the extent that countries normally opposed to us are persuaded to pay less attention to ideological differences, we may find that the opposition has been lessened and divided. In Berlin, Cuba, the United Nations, Latin America, and elsewhere, we would seem well advised, in applying whatever political, economic, or military pressure we deem appropriate to the situation, to define immediate objectives which are limited and precise. The salami can be sliced either way.

Fractionating conflict would thus seem to be a promising strategy not only for reducing the risk of war but also for promoting victory for our values. This does not mean that such a strategy is opposed to the real interests of any other country. As we need to be reminded so often, the world is not a zero-sum game where victory for some automatically means defeat for others. If we examine all the detailed social objectives of any two countries, including the United States and the Soviet Union, we find an enormous area of overlap. Each believes that the people should have better schools, better health, better highways, better homes, a chance to benefit from the experience of others, and so forth. However basic and significant other disagreements may be, in perhaps 90 per cent of the detailed factual issues our interests are not in conflict. In this area, measures can be taken which benefit us both. As long, however, as most issues are dealt with in terms of a nation-to-nation conflict, common interests will be lost in the major conflict which precludes agreement. It would seem that only by dividing up the issues and considering them separately in small units will we be able to find and to work together in those areas where we have common goals and common interests and thus obtain the optimum accommodation possible.

C. Intergroup Conflict

THE FUNCTIONS OF
RACIAL CONFLICT*†

JOSEPH S. HIMES

ABSTRACT

Social conflict is revealed as both natural and functional in human society. Conflict is called "realistic" when rationally determined means are used to achieve culturally approved ends. In the field of Negro struggle, legal redress, political pressure and mass action meet these defining criteria of realistic conflict.

This study examines some of the social functions of conflict as here defined. It is asked: does realistic conflict by Negroes have any system-maintaining and system-enhancing consequences for the larger American society? The analysis revealed that realistic racial conflict (1) alters the social structure, (2) extends social communication, (3) enhances social solidarity, and (4) facilitates personal identity.

When one contemplates the contemporary American scene, he may be appalled by the picture of internal conflict portrayed in the daily news. The nation is pictured as torn by dissension over Vietnam policy. The people are reported being split by racial strife that periodically erupts into open violence. Organized labor and management are locked in a perennial struggle that occasionally threatens the well-being of the society. The reapportionment issue has forced the ancient rural-urban conflict into public view. Religious denominations and faiths strive against ancient conflicts of theology and doctrine toward unification and ecumenism. Big government is joined in a continuing struggle against big industry, big business, big finance, and big labor on behalf of the "public interest."

The image created by such reports is that of a society "rocked," "split" or "torn" by its internal conflicts. The repetition of such phrases and the spotlighting of conflict suggest that the integration, if not the very existence of the society is threatened. It is

thus implied, and indeed often stated that the elimination of internal conflict is the central problem for policy and action in the society.

These preliminary remarks tend to indicate that there is widespread popular disapproval of social conflict. In some quarters the absence of conflict is thought to signify the existence of social harmony and stability. According to the human relations theme, conflict, aggression, hostility, antagonism and such devisive motives and behaviors are regarded as social heresies and therefore to be avoided. Often the word conflict is associated with images of violence and destruction.

At the same time, in contemporary sociology the problem of social conflict has been largely neglected. As Coser, Dahrendorf and others have pointed out, this tendency issues from preoccupation with models of social structure and theories of equilibrium.[1] Conflicts are treated as strains, tensions or stresses of social structures and regarded as pathological. Little attention is devoted to the investigation of conflict as a functional social process.

---

* Presidential address delivered at the annual meeting of the Southern Sociological Society, New Orleans, April 8, 1966. I am indebted to Professors Ernst Borinski, Lewis A. Coser, Hylan G. Lewis, and Robin M. Williams, Jr., for their critical reading of this manuscript.

† Reprinted by permission of the author and publisher from *Social Forces*, 1966, *45*:1–10.

[1] Lewis A. Coser, *The Functions of Social Conflict* (Glencoe, Illinois: The Free Press, 1956), p. 20; Ralf Dahrendorf, *Class and Class Conflict in Industrial Society* (Stanford: Stanford University Press, 1959), chap. 5.

However, some of the earlier sociologists employed social conflict as one central element of their conceptual systems. Theory and analysis were cast in terms of a process model. Conflict was viewed as natural and as functioning as an integrative force in society.

To Ludwig Gumplowicz and Gustav Ratzenhofer conflict was the basic social process, while for Lester F. Ward and Albion W. Small it was one of the basic processes. Sumner, Ross, and Cooley envisaged conflict as one of the major forces operating to lace human society together.[2] Park and Burgess employed social conflict as one of the processual pillars of their sociological system.[3]

At bottom, however, the two analytic models of social organization are really not inconsistent. Dahrendorf argues that consensus-structure and conflict-process are "the two faces of society."[4] That is, social integration results simultaneously from both consensus of values and coercion to compliance. Indeed, in the present study it is observed that the two sources of social integration are complementary and mutually supporting.

Coser has led the revival of sociological attention to the study of social conflict. In this task he has injected the very considerable contributions of the German sociologist Georg Simmel into the stream of American sociological thought. Ralf Dahrendorf, among others, has made further substantial contributions to the sociology of social conflict. One latent consequence of this development has been to sensitize some sociologists to conflict as a perspective from which to investigate race relations. Thus race relations have been called "power relations" and it has been proposed that research should be cast in terms of a "conflict model."[5] This approach is consistent with Blumer's thesis that race prejudice is "a sense of group position" and that empirical study involves "a concern with the relationship of racial groups."[6]

In the present discussion the term racial conflict is used in a restricted and specific sense.[7] By racial conflict is meant rational organized overt action by Negroes, initiating demands for specific social goals, and utilizing collective sanctions to enforce these demands. By definition, the following alternative forms of conflict behavior are excluded from the field of analysis.

1. The aggressive or exploitative actions of dominant groups and individuals toward minority groups or individuals.

2. Covert individual antagonisms or affective compensatory or reflexive aggressions, and

3. Spontaneous outbursts or nonrationalized violent behavior.

As here treated, racial conflict involves some rational assessment of both means and ends, and therefore is an instance of what Lewis Coser has called "realistic conflict."[8]

---

[2] William Graham Sumner, *Folkways* (Boston: Ginn, 1906); Edward Alsworth Ross, *The Principles of Sociology* (New York: Century, 1920); Charles Horton Cooley, *Social Process* (New York: Charles Scribner's Sons, 1918), and *Social Organization* (New York: Charles Scribner's Sons, 1909).

[3] Robert E. Park and Ernest W. Burgess, *Introduction to the Science of Sociology* (Chicago: University of Chicago Press, 1924).

[4] Dahrendorf, *op. cit.*, pp. 157–165. Arthur I. Wastow makes the same point in his concepts of "church," "state," and "government" as models of social integration. See *From Race Riot to Sit-In, 1919 and the 1960s: A Study in the Connections Between Conflict and Violence* (New York: Doubleday & Co., 1966).

[5] Lewis M. Killian and Charles M. Grigg, *Racial Crisis in America* (Englewood Cliffs, New Jersey: Prentice-Hall, 1964), p. 18 ff.; H. M. Blalock, Jr., "A Power Analysis of Racial Discrimination," *Social Forces*, 39 (October 1960), pp. 53–59; Ernst Borinski, "The Sociology of Coexistence—Conflict in Social and Political Power Systems," unpublished, pp. 6–7; Wilson Record, *Race and Radicalism* (Ithaca: Cornell University Press, 1964); Ernst Borinski, "The Litigation Curve and the Litigation Filibuster in Civil Rights Cases," *Social Forces*, 37 (December 1958), pp. 142–147.

[6] Herbert Blumer, "Race Prejudice as a Sense of Group Position," in J. Masuoka and Preston Valien (eds.), *Race Relations* (Chapel Hill: The University of North Carolina Press, 1961), p. 217.

[7] In much authoritative literature the concept conflict in racial relations is used in various other ways. See for example, George Simpson and J. Milton Yinger, *Racial and Cultural Minorities* (New York; Harper & Row, 1965), chap. 4; Killian and Grigg, *op. cit.*; Leonard Broom and Norval D. Glenn, *Transformation of the Negro American* (New York: Harper & Row, 1965), esp. chaps. 3 and 4.

[8] Coser, *op cit.*, pp. 48–55.

Because of the calculating of means and ends, racial conflict is initiating action. It is a deliberate collective enterprise to achieve predetermined social goals. Of necessity, conflict includes a conscious attack upon an overtly defined social abuse.

Merton has pointed out that groups sometimes resort to culturally tabooed means to achieve culturally prescribed ends.[9] Under such circumstances one might assume that if legitimate means were available, they would be employed. But, Vander Zanden has observed, "Non-violent resistance is a tactic well suited to struggles in which a minority lacks access to major sources of power within a society and to the instruments of violent coercion."[10] He goes on to add that, "within the larger American society the Negro's tactic of non-violent resistance has gained a considerable degree of legitimacy."[11] Three principal manifestations of Negro behavior fit this definition of racial conflict.

1. Legal redress, or the calculated use of court action to achieve and sanction specific group goals. Legal redress has been used most often and successfully in the achievement of voting rights, educational opportunities and public accommodations.

2. Political action, or the use of voting, bloc voting and lobby techniques to achieve legislative and administrative changes and law enforcement.

3. Non-violent mass action, or organized collective participation in overt activity involving pressure and public relations techniques to enforce specific demands.

This paper examines some of the social functions of conflict as here defined. It is asked: Does realistic conflict by Negroes have any system-maintaining and system-enhancing consequences for the larger American society? To this question at least four affirmative answers can be given. Realistic racial conflict (1) alters the social structure, (2) enhances social communica-

tion, (3) extends social solidarity and (4) facilitates personal identity. Because of space and time limitations, considerations of societal dysfunctions and goal achievements are omitted.

Structural Functions

H. M. Blalock has noted that within the American social structure race relations are power relations.[12] Thus, realistic social conflict is an enterprise in the calculated mobilization and application of social power to sanction collective demands for specific structural changes. Yet, because of minority status, Negroes have only limited access to the sources of social power. Robert Bierstedt has identified numbers, resources and organization as leading sources of power.[13] Of these categories, resources which Bierstedt specifies as including money, prestige, property and natural and supernatural phenomena, are least accessible to Negroes.

Perforce then, realistic racial conflict specializes in the mobilization of numbers and organization as accessible sources of power. Thus a boycott mobilizes and organizes numbers of individuals to withhold purchasing power. A demonstration organizes and mobilizes numbers of individuals to tap residual moral sentiments and to generate public opinion. Voter registration and bloc voting mobilize and organize numbers of citizens to influence legislative and administrative processes. Legal redress and lobby techniques mobilize organization to activate legal sanctions or the legislative process.

The application of mobilized social power in realistic racial conflict tends to reduce the power differential between actors, to restrict existing status differences, and to alter the directionality of social interaction. First, in conflict situations, race relations are defined unequivocally in power terms. Sentimentality and circumlocution are brushed aside. The power dimension is brought into central position in

[9] Robert K. Merton, *Social Theory and Social Structure* (Glencoe, Illinois: The Free Press, 1957), pp. 123–149.

[10] James W. Vander Zanden, "The Non-Violent Resistance Movement Against Segregation," *American Journal of Sociology*, 68 (March 1963), p. 544.

[11] *Ibid.*, p. 544.

[12] Blalock, *op. cit.*, pp. 53–59.

[13] Robert Bierstedt, "An Analysis of Social Power," *American Sociological Review*, 15 (December 1950), pp. 730–738. Bierstedt argues that numbers and organization as sources of social power are ineffectual without access to resources.

the structure of interaction. The differential between conflict partners along this dimension is thus reduced. The power advantage of the dominant group is significantly limited. In this connection and perhaps only in this connection, it may be correct to liken embattled Negroes and resisting whites to "armed camps."

Second, alteration of the power dimension of interracial structure tends to modify status arrangements. In the traditional racial structure, discrimination and segregation cast whites and Negroes in rigid and separate orders of superiority and inferiority. The limited and stylized intergroup contacts are confined to a rigid and sterile etiquette. However, in realistic conflict initiating actors assume, for they must, a status coordinate with that of the opposition.[14]

Status coordination is one evident consequence of power equalization. Moreover, it is patently impossible to make demands and to sanction them while acting from the position of a suppliant. That is, the very process of realistic conflict functions to define adversaries in terms of self-conception as status equals. Martin Luther King perceives this function of realistic conflict in the following comment on the use of non-violent action and deliberately induced tension.[15]

Non-violent direct action seeks to create such a crisis and foster such a tension that a community which has constantly refused to negotiate is forced to confront the issue. It seeks so to dramatize the issue that it can no longer be ignored.

That is, social power is used to bring interactors into status relations where issues can be discussed, examined and compromised. There are no suppliants or petitioners and no condescending controllers in a negotiation relationship. By the very nature of the case, interactors occupy equal or approximately equal positions of both status and strength.

Third, power equalization and status coordination affect the interactional dimension of social structure. The up and down

flow of interaction between super- and subordinates tends to level out in relations between positional equals. That is, rational demands enforced by calculated sanctions cannot be forced into the molds of supplication and condescension.

The leveling out of social interaction is inherent in such realistic conflict mechanisms as sit-ins, freedom rides, bloc voting, voter registration campaigns and boycotts. Thus, for example, the interruption of social interaction in a boycott implies an assumption of status equality and the leveling of interaction. The relationship that is interrupted is the up and down pattern inherent in the status structure of inequality. No relationship is revealed as preferable to the pattern of supplication and condescension. Whether such structural functions of realistic conflict become institutionalized in the larger social system will depend on the extent of goal achievement of the total Negro revolution. That is, structural consequences of conflict may be institutionalized through the desegregation and nondiscrimination of education, employment, housing, recreation and the like. Changes in these directions will provide system-relevant roles under terms of relatively coordinate status and power not only for the conflict participants, but also for many other individuals. Developments in these directions will also be influenced by many factors and trends apart from the process of realistic racial conflict.

We may now summarize the argument regarding the structural functions of realistic racial conflict in a series of propositions. Realistic conflict postulates race relations as power relations and undertakes to mobilize and apply the social power that is accessible to Negroes as a minority group.

In conflict, the traditional interracial structure is modified along three dimensions. The power differential between interactors is reduced; status differentials are restricted; and social interaction tends to level out in directionality. Whether these structural consequences of realistic conflict become institutionalized in the general social system will depend on the extent and duration of goal achievement in the larger social structure.

---

[14] Thomas F. Pettigrew, *A Profile of the Negro American* (Princeton: D. Van Nostrand Co., 1964), p. 167.

[15] Martin Luther King, *Why We Can't Wait* (New York: Harper & Row, 1963), p. 81.

Communicational Functions

It is widely claimed that Negro aggression interrupts or reduces interracial communication. Whites and Negroes are thought to withdraw in suspicion and hostility from established practices of communication. The so-called "normal" agencies and bridges of intergroup contact and communication are believed to become inoperative. Such a view of conflict envisages Negroes and whites as hostile camps eyeing each other across a "no man's land" of antagonism and separation.

It is true that racial conflict tends to interrupt and reduce traditional communication between whites and Negroes. But traditional interracial communication assumes that communicators occupy fixed positions of superiority and inferiority, precludes the consideration of certain significant issues, and confines permitted interchanges to a rigid and sterile etiquette. "The Negro," write Killian and Grigg, "has always been able to stay in communication with the white man and gain many favors from him, so long as he approached him as a suppliant and as an inferior, and not as a conflict partner."[16]

It will be evident that intergroup communication under such structural conditions is both restricted in content and asymmetrical in form. However, our analysis indicates that realistic conflict functions to correct these distortions of content and form and to extend the communication process at the secondary mass media level.

First, realistic racial conflict heightens the individual level and extends the social range of attention to racial matters. Individuals who have by long custom learned to see Negroes only incidentally as part of the standard social landscape, are brought up sharply and forced to look at them in a new light. Persons who have been oblivious to Negroes are abruptly and insistently confronted by people and issues which they can neither avoid nor brush aside. Many individuals for the first time perceive Negroes as having problems, characteristics and aspirations that were never before recognized, nor at least so clearly recognized.

Racial conflict thus rudely destroys what Gunnar Myrdal aptly called the "convenience of ignorance."[17]

In *Freedom Summer,* Sally Belfrage gives a graphic personal illustration of the attention-arresting function of realistic racial conflict.[18] In the most crowded and hottest part of an afternoon the daughter of one of Greenwood's (Mississippi) leading families walked into the civil rights headquarters. In a lilting southern voice she asked to everybody in general: "I jus' wanted to know what y'all are up to over here."

At the same time the "race problem" is brought into the focus of collective attention by realistic conflict. Negroes as well as their problems and claims insist upon having both intensive and extensive consideration. To support this contention one has only to consider the volume of scientific, quasi-scientific and popular literature, the heavy racial loading of the mass media, and the vast number of organizations and meetings that are devoted to the racial issue.

Further, realistic racial conflict tends to modify both the cognitive and affective content of interracial communication. Under terms of conflict whites and Negroes can no longer engage in the exchange of standardized social amenities regarding safe topics within the protection of the status structure and the social etiquette. Communication is made to flow around substantive issues and the calculated demands of Negroes. Communication is about something that has real meaning for the communicators. It makes a difference that they communicate. In fact, under terms of realistic conflict it is no longer possible to avoid communicating. Thus Martin Luther King argued that non-violent mass action is employed to create such crisis and tension that a community which has refused to negotiate is forced to confront the issue.[19]

In conflict the affective character of communication becomes realistic. The communicators infuse their exchanges of cognitive meanings with the feelings that, within the

16 Killian and Grigg, *op. cit.,* p. 7.

17 Gunnar Myrdal, *An American Dilemma* (New York: Harper & Bros., 1944), pp. 40–42.
18 Sally Belfrage, *Freedom Summer* (New York: The Viking Press, 1965), p. 48.
19 King, *op. cit.,* p. 81.

traditional structure, were required to be suppressed and avoided. That Negroes are permitted, indeed often expected to reveal the hurt and humiliation and anger that they formerly were required to bottle up inside. Many white people thus were shocked to discover that the "happy" Negroes whom they "knew" so well were in fact discontented and angry people.

Thus the cognitive-affective distortion of traditional interracial communication is in some measure at least corrected. The flow of understanding and affection that was permitted and encouraged is balanced by normal loading of dissension and hostility. The relationship thus reveals a more symmetrical character of content and form.

Finally, attrition of primary contacts between unequals within the traditional structure and etiquette is succeeded, in part at least, by an inclusive dialogue at the secondary communication level. The drama of conflict and the challenges of leaders tend to elevate the racial issue in the public opinion arena. The mass media respond by reporting and commenting on racial events in great detail. Thus millions of otherwise uninformed or indifferent individuals are drawn into the public opinion process which Ralph H. Turner and Lewis M. Killian have analyzed as defining and redefining the issue and specifying and solving the problem.[20]

Much obvious evidence reveals the secondary communication dialogue. Since 1954 a voluminous scientific, quasi-scientific and popular literature on the race issue has appeared. Further evidence is found in the heavy racial loading of newspapers, magazines, television and radio broadcasting and the motion pictures. The race problem has been the theme of numerous organizations and meetings at all levels of power and status. From such evidence it would seem reasonable to conclude that few if any Americans have escaped some degree of involvement in the dialogue over the race issue.

We may now summarize the argument briefly. Realistic racial conflict tends to reduce customary interracial communication between status unequals regarding trivial matters within the established communication etiquette. On the other hand, conflict tends to extend communication regarding significant issues with genuine feelings and within noncustomary structures and situations. At the secondary level both the volume of communication and the number of communicators are greatly increased by realistic conflict. These observations would seem to warrant the conclusion that communication within the general social system is extended by realistic racial conflict.

Solidarity Functions

A corollary of the claim that racial conflict interrupts communication is the assertion that conflict also is seriously, perhaps even radically disunifying. Struggles between Negroes and whites are thought to split the society and destroy social solidarity. It is at once evident that such a claim implies the prior existence of a unified or relatively unified biracial system. Notwithstanding difference of status and condition, the racial sectors are envisaged as joined in the consensus and structure of the society.

A judicious examination of the facts suggests that the claim that racial conflict is seriously, perhaps even radically disunifying is not altogether correct. On the one hand, the image of biracial solidarity tends to be exaggerated. On the other, realistic racial conflict serves some important unifying functions within the social system.

As Logan Wilson and William Kolb have observed, the consensus of the society is organized around a core of "ultimate values."[21] "In our own society," they assert, "we have developed such ultimate values as the dignity of the individual, equality of opportunity, the right to life, liberty, and the pursuit of happiness, and the growth of the free personality."

Far from rejecting or challenging these ultimate values, the ideological thrust of realistic racial conflict affirms them.[22] That

[20] Ralph H. Turner and Lewis M. Killian, Collective Behavior (Englewood Cliffs, New Jersey: Prentice-Hall, 1957), chaps. 11 and 12.

[21] Logan Wilson and William L. Kolb, Sociological Analysis (New York: Harcourt, Brace & Co., 1949), p. 513.

[22] Pettigrew, op. cit., p. 193.

is, the ultimate values of the society constitute starting points of ideology and action in racial conflict. As Wilson Record and others have observed, Negro protest and improvement movements are thoroughly American in assumption and objectives.[23]

This fact creates an interesting strategic dilemma for the White Citizens Councils, the resurgent Ku Klux Klan and similar manifestations of the so-called "white backlash." The ideology of racial conflict has preempted the traditional high ground of the core values and ultimate morality. The reactionary groups are thus left no defensible position within the national ethos from which to mount their attacks.

One consequence of realistic racial conflict, then, is to bring the core values of the society into sharp focus and national attention. People are exhorted, even forced to think about the basic societal tenets and to consider their meaning and applications. A dynamic force is thus joined to latent dedication in support of the unifying values of the society. Thus, as Coser has observed, far from being altogether disunifying, realistic conflict functions to reaffirm the core and unifying values of the society.[24] In other words the "two faces of society" are seen to be complementary and mutually supporting.

The primacy of core values in realistic racial conflict is revealed in many ways. Martin Luther King places the ultimate values of the society at the center of his theoretic system of non-violent mass action.[25] In his "Letter from Birmingham Jail" he refers to "justice," "freedom," "understanding," "brotherhood," "constitutional rights," "promise of democracy" and "truth." See how he identifies the goal of racial freedom with the basic societal value of freedom. "We will reach the goal of freedom in Birmingham and all over the nation, because the goal of America is freedom."[26]

One impact of realistic racial conflict is upon interpretation of core values and the means of their achievement. Thus, the issue is not whether or not men shall be free and equal, but whether these values are reserved to white men or are applicable to Negroes as well. Or again, the phrases "gradualism" and "direct action" depict an important point of disagreement over means to universally affirmed ends. But, it may be observed that when men agree on the ends of life, their quarrels are not in themselves disunifying.

Further, the very process of realistic racial conflict is intrinsically functional. Participants in the conflict are united by the process of struggle itself. The controversy is a unique and shared social possession. It fills an interactional vacuum maintained in the traditional structure by limited social contacts and alienation.

At the same time, as Coser has argued, a relationship established by conflict may lead in time to other forms of interaction.[27] It is conceivable that Negroes and whites who today struggle over freedom and justice and equality may tomorrow be joined in cooperation in the quest of these values.

Conflict is also unifying because the object of struggle is some social value that both parties to the conflict wish to possess or enjoy. The struggle tends to enhance the value and to reveal its importance to both actors. A new area of consensus is thus defined or a prior area of agreement is enlarged. For example, that Negroes and whites struggle through realistic conflict for justice or freedom or equality tends to clarify these values for both and join them in the consensus regarding their importance.

"Simultaneously," as Vander Zanden observes, "within the larger American society the Negro's tactic of non-violent resistance has gained a considerable degree of legitimacy."[28] That is, conflict itself has been defined as coming within the arena of morally justifiable social action. The means as well as the ends, then, are enveloped within the national ethos and serve to enhance societal solidarity. In this respect realistic racial conflict, like labor-management conflict, tends to enter the "American way of life" and constitutes another point of social integration.

[23] Record, *op. cit.*; Pettigrew, *op. cit.*; Broom and Glenn, *op. cit.*

[24] Coser, *op. cit.*, pp. 127–128.

[25] King, *op. cit.*, pp. 77–100.

[26] *Ibid.*, p. 97.

[27] Coser, *op. cit.*, pp. 121–122.

[28] Vander Zanden, *op. cit.*, p. 544.

Many years ago Edward Alsworth Ross pointed out that nonradical conflicts may function to "sew" the society together.[29]

Every species of conflict interferes with every other species in society . . . save only when lines of cleavage coincide; in which case they reinforce one another. . . . A society, therefore, which is ridden by a dozen oppositions along lines running in every direction may actually be in less danger of being torn with violence or falling to pieces than one split just along one line. For each new cleavage contributes to narrow the cross-clefts, so that one might say that society is sewn together by its inner conflicts.

In this sewing function, realistic racial conflict is interwoven with political, religious, regional, rural-urban, labor-management, class and the other persistent threads of struggle that characterize the American social fabric. What is decisive is the fact that variously struggling factions are united in the consensus of the ultimate societal values. The conflicts are therefore nonradical, crisscrossing and tend to mitigate each other.

The proposition on the solidarity function of realistic racial conflict can now be formulated briefly. The claims that racial conflict is disruptive of social solidarity, though partially true, tends to obscure other important consequences. Conflict not only projects the combatants into the social consensus; it also acts to reaffirm the ultimate values around which the consensus is organized. Moreover, conflict joins opposing actors in meaningful interaction for ends, whose importance is a matter of further agreement. From this perspective and within a context of multifarious crisscross-

ing threads of opposition, realistic racial conflict is revealed as helping to "sew" the society together around its underlying societal consensus. We now turn to a consideration of certain social-psychological consequences of realistic racial conflict.

Identity Functions

The fact is often overlooked that realistic racial conflict permits many Negroes to achieve a substantial measure of identity within the American social system. This function of racial conflict is implied in the foregoing analyses of communication and solidarity. However, the analysis of the identity function of racial conflict begins with a consideration of the alienation of the American Negro people. Huddled into urban and rural slums and concentrated in menial and marginal positions in the work force, Negroes are relegated to inferior and collateral statuses in the social structure. Within this structural situation discrimination prevents their sharing in the valued possessions of the society. Legal and customary norms of segregation exclude them from many meaningful contacts and interactions with members of the dominant group.

Isolated and inferior, Negro people searched for the keys to identity and belonging. The social forces that exclude them from significant participation in the general society also keep them disorganized. Thus identity, the feeling of belonging and the sense of social purpose, could be found neither in membership in the larger society nor in participation in a cohesive racial group. Generation after generation of Negroes live out their lives in fruitless detachment and personal emptiness. In another place the alienation of Negro teenagers has been described as follows.[30]

The quality of Negro teenage culture is conditioned by four decisive factors: race, inferiority, deprivation and youthfulness. Virtually every experience of the Negro teenager is filtered through this complex qualifying medium; every act is a response to a distorted perception of the world. His world is a kind of nightmare, the

[29] Ross, op. cit., pp. 164–165. Dahrendorf, op. cit., pp. 213–215, argues that conflicts tend to become "superimposed," thus threatening intensification. "Empirical evidence shows," he writes, "that different conflicts may be, and often are, superimposed in given historical societies, so that the multitude of possible conflict fronts is reduced to a few dominant conflicts . . . . If this is the case, (class) conflicts of different associations appear superimposed; i.e., the opponents of one association meet again—with different titles, perhaps, but in identical relations—in another association." (Pp. 213–214.) Such an argument, however, fails to recognize that conflicts may superimpose along religious, regional, ethnic or other fronts and thus mitigate the strength of the class superimposition.

[30] Joseph S. Himes, "Negro Teen Age Culture," Annals, 338 (November 1961), pp. 92–93.

creation of a carnival reflection chamber. The Negro teenager's culture, his customary modes of behavior, constitute his response to the distorted, frightening, and cruel world that he perceives with the guileless realism of youth.

Yet the search for identity goes on. It takes many forms. In the Negro press and voluntary organizations it is reflected in campaigns for race pride and race loyalty. One sector of the Negro intelligentsia invented the "Negro history movement" as a device to create a significant past for a "historyless" people. For the unlettered and unwashed masses the church is the prime agent of group cohesion and identity. The National Association for the Advancement of Colored People and other militant organizations provide an ego-enhancing rallying point for the emancipated and the aggressive. The cult of Negro business, escapist movements like Father Divine's Heaven, and nationalist movements like Marcus Garvey's Universal Negro Improvement Association, and the Black Muslims provide still other arenas for the Negro's search for identity.

Despite this variegated panorama of effort and search, the overriding experience of Negroes remains isolation, inferiority and the ineluctable sense of alienation. Whether involved in the search or not, or perhaps just because of such involvement, individuals see themselves as existing outside the basic American social system. Vander Zanden puts it this way: "By virtue of his membership in the Negro group, the Negro suffers considerably in terms of self-esteem and has every incentive for self-hatred."[31] Thus self-conception reflects and in turn supports social experience in a repetition of the familiar self-fulfilling prophecy.

In this situation, collective conflict had an almost magical although unanticipated effect upon group cohesion and sense of identity among Negroes. Group struggle, as Coser and others have pointed out, functions to enhance group solidarity and to clarify group boundaries.[32] The separations among collective units are sharpened and the identity of groups within a social sys-

tem is established. In the course of conflict collective aims are specified, defined and communicated. Cadres of leaders emerge in a division of labor that grows clearer and more definite. Individuals tend to find niches and become polarized around the collective enterprise. All participants are drawn closer together, both for prosecution of the struggle and for common defense.

As the racial conflict groups become more cohesive and organized, the boundaries with other groups within the American social system become clearer. The distinction between member and nonmember is sharpened. Individuals who stood indecisively between groups or outside the fray are induced or forced to take sides. The zones of intergroup ambiguity diminish. Internally, the conflict groups become more tightly unified and the positions of members are clarified and defined more precisely.

Further, conflict facilitates linkage between the individual and his local reference group as the agent of conflict. The individual thus achieves both a "commitment"[33] and a "role" as a quasi-official group representative in the collective struggle. Pettigrew writes:[34]

Consider the Student Non-Violent Coordinating Committee (SNICK), . . . The group is cohesive, highly regarded by Negro youth, and dedicated entirely to achieving both personal and societal racial change. Recruits willingly and eagerly devote themselves to the group's goals. And they find themselves systematically rewarded by SNICK for violating the 'Negro' role in every particular. They are expected to evince strong racial pride, to assert their full rights as citizens, to face jail and police brutality unhesitatingly for the cause. . . . Note, . . . that these expected and rewarded actions all publicly commit the member to the group and its aims.

In the general racial conflict system individuals may act as leaders, organizers and specialists. Some others function as sit-

---

[31] Vander Zanden, *op. cit.*, p. 546.
[32] Coser, *op. cit.*, p. 34.

[33] Amitai Etzioni employs the concept "commitment" to designate one dimension of cohesiveness and operational effectiveness in complex organizations. See his *Complex Organizations: A Sociological Reader* (New York: Henry Holt Co., 1961), p. 187; and *A Comparative Study of Complex Organization* (Glencoe, Illinois: The Free Press, 1961), pp. 8–22.
[34] Pettigrew, *op. cit.*, pp. 165–166.

inners, picketers, boycotters, demonstrators, voter registration solicitors, etc. Many others, removed from the areas of overt conflict, participate secondarily or vicariously as financial contributors, audience members, mass media respondents, verbal applauders, etc.

In the interactive process of organized group conflict self-involvement is the opposite side of the coin of overt action. Actors become absorbed by ego and emotion into the group and the group is projected through their actions. This linkage of individual and group in ego and action is the substance of identity.

Paradoxically, the personal rewards of participation in conflict groups tend to support and facilitate the larger conflict organization and process. Edward Shils and Morris Janowitz have noted this fact in the functions of primary groups in the German Army in World War II.[35] That is, for the individual actor the sense of identity is grounded and sustained by gratification of important personal needs.

In the case of realistic racial conflict, group-based identity functions to facilitate sociopsychic linkage between the individual and the inclusive social system. It was shown above that racial conflict is socially unifying in at least two ways. First, the conflict ideology identifies parties to the conflict with the core values of the social heritage. Thus sit-inners, and demonstrators and boycotters and all the others in the drama of racial conflict conceive themselves as the latter-day warriors for the freedom, justice and equality and the other moral values that are historically and essentially American. For many Negroes the sense of alienation is dispelled by a new sense of significance and purpose. The self-image of these embattled Negroes is consequently significantly enhanced.

Second, the conflict process draws organized Negroes into significant social interaction within the inclusive social system. Some of the crucial issues and part of the principal business of the society engage Negroes of all localities and stations in life. Though often only vicariously and by projection, life acquires a new meaning and quality for even the poorest ghetto dweller and meanest sharecropper. The sense of alienation is diminished and the feeling of membership in the inclusive society is enhanced.

We may now formulate the argument as follows. Intense alienation kept alive the Negro's quest for identity and meaning. Miraculously almost, realistic racial conflict with its ideological apparatus and action system functions to alleviate alienation and to facilitate identity. Conflict enhances group solidarity, clarifies group boundaries and strengthens the individual-group linkage through ego-emotion commitment and overt action. In-group identity is extended to the larger social system through the extension of communication, the enlargement of the network of social interactions and ideological devotion to national core values. It may be said, then, that through realistic racial conflict America gains some new Americans.

[35] Edward A. Shils and Morris Janowitz, "Cohesion and Disintegration in the Wehrmacht in World War II," *Public Opinion Quarterly*, 12 (Summer 1948), p. 281.

SOCIAL PSYCHOLOGY AND
DESEGRATION RESEARCH[*][1]

THOMAS F. PETTIGREW

What one hears and what one sees of southern race relations today are sharply divergent. Consider some of the things that occur in interviews with white Southerners.

"As much as my family likes TV," confided a friendly North Carolina farmer, "we always turn the set off when they put them colored people on." But as the two of us were completing the interview, a series of famous Negro entertainers performed on the bright, 21-inch screen in the adjoining room. No one interrupted them.

A rotund banker in Charleston, South Carolina, was equally candid in his remarks: "Son, under no conditions will the white man and the black man ever get together in this state." He apparently preferred to ignore the government sponsored integration at his city's naval installation, just a short distance from his office.

Another respondent, this time a highly educated Chattanooga businessman, patiently explained to me for over an hour how race relations had not changed at all in his city during the past generation. As I left his office building, I saw a Negro policeman directing downtown traffic. It was the first Negro traffic cop I had ever seen in the South.

The South today is rife with such contradictions; social change has simply been too rapid for many Southerners to recognize it. Such a situation commands the attention of psychologists—particularly those in the South.

There are many other aspects of this sweeping process that should command our professional attention. To name just two, both the pending violence and the stultifying conformity attendant with desegregation are uniquely psychological problems. We might ask, for instance, what leads to violence in some desegregating communities, like Little Rock and Clinton, and not in others, like Norfolk and Winston-Salem? A multiplicity of factors must be relevant and further research is desperately needed to delineate them; but tentative early work seems to indicate that desegregation violence so far has been surprisingly "rational." That is, violence has generally resulted in localities where at least some of the authorities give prior hints that they would gladly return to segregation if disturbances occurred; peaceful integration has generally followed firm and forceful leadership.[2]

Research concerning conformity in the present situation is even more important. Many psychologists know from personal experience how intense the pressures to conform in racial attitudes have become in the present-day South; indeed, it appears that the first amendment guaranteeing free speech is in as much peril as the fourteenth amendment. Those who dare to break consistently this conformity taboo must do so in many parts of the South under the intimidation of slanderous letters and phone calls, burned crosses, and even bomb threats. Moreover, this paper will contend that conformity is the social psychological key to analyzing desegregation.

It is imperative that psychologists study these phenomena for two reasons: first, our psychological insights and methods are needed in understanding and solving this, our nation's primary internal problem; second, this process happening before our eyes offers us a rare opportunity to test in the

[*] Reprinted from *American Psychologist*, 1961, *16*, 105–112, by permission of author and publisher, The American Psychological Association.

[1] This paper was given as an invited address at the Annual Meeting of the Southeastern Psychological Association, Atlanta, Georgia, March 31, 1960. The author wishes to express his appreciation to Gordon W. Allport of Harvard University, E. Earl Baughman of the University of North Carolina, and Cooper C. Clements of Emory University for their suggestions.

[2] Clark (1953) predicted this from early border-state integration, and a variety of field reports have since documented the point in specific instances.

field the psychological concomitants of cultural stress and social change. Thus I would like in this paper to assess some of the prospects and directions of these potential psychological contributions.

Role of Social Science in the Desegregation Process to Date

The role of social science, particularly sociology and psychology, in the desegregation process has been much publicized and criticized by southern segregationists.[3] Many of these critics apparently think that sociology is synonymous with socialism and psychology with brainwashing. In any event, their argument that we have been crucially important in the Supreme Court desegregation cases of the fifties is based largely on the reference to seven social science documents in Footnote 11 of the famous 1954 *Brown vs. Board of Education* decision. It would be flattering for us to think that our research has has such a dramatic effect on the course of history as segregationalists claim, but in all truth we do not deserve such high praise.

In making their claim that the 1954 decision was psychological and not legal, the segregationists choose to overlook several things. The 1954 ruling did not come suddenly "out of the blue"; it was a logical continuation of a 44-year Supreme Court trend that began in 1910 when a former private in the Confederate Army, the liberal Edward White, became Chief Justice (Logan, 1956). When compared to this backdrop, our influence on the 1954 ruling was actually of only footnote importance. Furthermore, the language and spirit of the 1896 *Plessy vs. Ferguson,* separate-but-equal decision, so dear to the hearts of segregationists, were as immersed in the jargon and thinking of the social science of that era as the 1954 decision was of our era. Its 1896, Sumnerian argument that laws cannot change "social prejudices" (Allport, 1954, pp. 469–473) and its use of such social Darwinism terms as "racial instincts" and "natural affinities" lacked only a footnote to make it as obviously influenced by the then current social science as the 1954 ruling.

A final reason why we do not deserve the flattering praise of the segregationists is our failure to make substantial contributions to the process since 1954. The lack of penetrating psychological research in this area can be traced directly to three things: the lack of extensive foundation support, conformity pressures applied in many places in the South that deter desegregation research, and the inadequacy of traditional psychological thinking to cope with the present process. Let us discuss each of these matters in turn.

A few years ago Stuart Cook (1957) drew attention to the failure of foundations to support desegregation research; the situation today is only slightly improved. It appears that a combination of foundation fears has produced this situation. One set of fears, as Cook noted, may stem from concern over attacks by southern Congressmen on their tax free status; the other set may stem from boycotts carried out by some segregationists against products identified with the foundations. In any case, this curtailment of funds is undoubtedly one reason why social scientists have so far left this crucial process relatively unstudied. Recently, however, a few moderate sized grants have been made for work in this area; hopefully, this is the beginning of a reappraisal by foundations of their previous policies. And it is up to us to submit competent research proposals to them to test continually for any change of these policies.

It is difficult to assess just how much damage has been done to desegregation research in the South by segregationist pressures. Probably the number of direct refusals to allow such research by southern institutions outside of the Black Belt has actually been small. More likely, the greatest harm has been rendered indirectly by the stifling atmosphere which prevents us from actually testing the limits of research opportunities. Interested as we may be in the racial realm,

---

[3] For instance, once-liberal Virginius Dabney (1957, p. 14), editor of the *Richmond Times-Dispatch,* charged that "the violence at Little Rock . . . never would have happened if nine justices had not consulted sociologists and psychologists, instead of lawyers, in 1954, and attempted to legislate through judicial decrees."

we decide to work in a less controversial area. Perhaps it is less a matter of courage than it is of resignation in the face of what are thought to be impossible barriers. If these suspicions are correct, there is real hope for overcoming in part this second obstacle to desegregation research.

In some situations, there should be little resistance. In racially integrated veterans' hospitals, for instance, much needed personality studies comparing Negro and white patients should be possible. In other situations, the amount of resistance to race research may be less than we anticipate. Since Little Rock, many so-called "moderates" in the South, particularly businessmen, have become more interested in the dynamics of desegregation. This is not to say that they are more in favor of racial equality than they were; it is only to suggest that the bad publicity, the closing of schools, and the economic losses suffered by Little Rock have made these influential Southerners more receptive to objective and constructive research on the process. It is for this reason that it is imperative the limits for the southern study of desegregation be tested at this time.

Finally, psychological contributions to desegregation research have been restricted by the inadequacy of traditional thinking in our discipline. More specifically, the relative neglect of situational variables in interracial behavior and a restricted interpretation and use of the attitude concept hinder psychological work in this area.

The importance of the situation for racial interaction has been demonstrated in a wide variety of settings. All-pervasive racial attitudes are often not involved: many individuals seem fully capable of immediate behavioral change as situations change. Thus in Panama there is a divided street, the Canal Zone side of which is racially segregated and the Panamanian side of which is racially integrated. Biesanz and Smith (1951) report that most Panamanians and Americans appear to accommodate without difficulty as they go first on one side of the street and then on the other. Likewise in the coal mining county of McDowell, West Virginia, Minard (1952) relates that the majority of Negro and white miners follow

easily a traditional pattern of integration below the ground and almost complete segregation above the ground. The literature abounds with further examples: southern white migrants readily adjusting to integrated situations in the North (Killian, 1949), northern whites approving of employment and public facility integration but resisting residential integration (Reitzes, 1953), etc. Indeed, at the present time in the South there are many white Southerners who are simultaneously adjusting to bus and public golf course integration and opposing public school integration. Or, as in Nashville, they may have accepted school integration but are opposing lunch counter integration.

This is not to imply that generalized attitudes on race are never invoked. There are some Panamanians and some Americans who act about the same on both sides of the Panamanian street. Minard (1952) estimated about two-fifths of the West Virginian miners he observed behave consistently in either a tolerant or an intolerant fashion both below and above ground. And some whites either approve or disapprove of all desegregation. But these people are easily explained by traditional theory. They probably consist of the extremes in authoritarianism; their attitudes on race are so generalized and so salient that their consistent behavior in racial situations is sometimes in defiance of the prevailing social norms.

On the other hand, the "other directed" individuals who shift their behavior to keep in line with shifting expectations present the real problem for psychologists. Their racial attitudes appear less salient, more specific, and more tied to particular situations. Conformity needs are predominantly important for these people, and we shall return shortly to a further discussion of these conformists.

One complication introduced by a situational analysis is that interracial contact itself frequently leads to the modification of attitudes. A number of studies of racially integrated situations have noted dramatic attitude changes, but in most cases the changes involved specific, situation-linked attitudes. For example, white department store employees become more accepting of Negroes in the work situation after equal status, integrated contact but not necessarily more accepting in other situations (Harding & Hogrefe, 1952). And *The American Soldier* studies (Stouffer, Suchman, DeVinney, Star, & Williams, 1949) found that the attitudes of white army personnel toward the Negro as a fighting man improve after equal status, integrated contact in combat, but their attitudes toward the Negro as a social companion do not necessarily change. In other words, experience in a novel situation of equal status leads to acceptance of that specific situation for many persons. Situations, then, not only structure specific racial behavior, but they may change specific attitudes in the process.

One final feature of a situational analysis deserves mention. Typically in psychology we have tested racial attitudes in isolation, apart from conflicting attitudes and values. Yet this is not realistic. As the desegregation process slowly unfolds in such resistant states as Virginia and Georgia, we see clearly that many segregationist Southerners value law and order, public education, and a prosperous economy above their racial views. Once such a situation pits race against other entrenched values, we need to know the public's hierarchy of these values. Thus a rounded situational analysis requires the measures of racial attitudes in the full context of countervalues.[4]

A second and related weakness in our psychological approach is the failure to exploit fully the broad and dynamic implications of the attitude concept. Most social psychological research has dealt with attitudes as if they were serving only an expressive function; but racial attitudes in the South require a more complex treatment.

In their volume, *Opinion and Personality*, Smith, Bruner, and White (1956) urge a more expansive interpretation of attitudes. They note three attitude functions. First, there is the *object appraisal* function; attitudes aid in understanding "reality" as it is defined by the culture. Second, attitudes can play a *social adjustment* role by con-

tributing to the individual's identification with, or differentiation from, various reference groups. Finally, attitudes may reduce anxiety by serving an expressive or *externalization* function.

Externalization occurs when an individual . . . senses an analogy between a perceived environmental event and some unresolved inner problem . . . [and] adopts an attitude . . . which is a transformed version of his way of dealing with his inner difficulty (pp. 41–44). (Reprinted with permission of John Wiley & Sons, Inc.)

At present the most fashionable psychological theories of prejudice—frustration-aggression, psychoanalytic, and authoritarianism—all deal chiefly with the externalization process. Valuable as these theories have been, this exclusive attention to the expressive component of attitudes has been at the expense of the object appraisal and social adjustment components. Moreover, it is the contention of this paper that these neglected and more socially relevant functions, particularly social adjustment, offer the key to further psychological advances in desegregation research.[5]

The extent to which this psychological concentration on externalization has influenced the general public was illustrated recently in the popular reaction to the swastika desecrations of Jewish temples. The perpetrators, all agreed, must be juvenile hoodlums, or "sick," or both. In other words, externalization explanations were predominantly offered.[6] Valid though these explanations may be in many cases, is it not also evident that the perpetrators were accurately reflecting the anti-Semitic norms of their subcultures? Thus their acts and the attitudes behind their acts are socially adjusting for these persons, given the circles in which they move.

Much less the public, some sociologists,

---

[4] A popular treatment of this point has been made by Zinn (1959).

[5] Though this paper emphasizes the social adjustment aspect of southern attitudes toward Negroes, the equally neglected object appraisal function is also of major importance. Most southern whites know only lower class Negroes; consequently their unfavorable stereotype of Negroes serves a definite reality function.

[6] Such explanations also serve for many anti-Semitic observers as an ego-alien defense against guilt.

too, have been understandably misled by our overemphasis on externalization into underestimating the psychological analysis of prejudice. One sociologist (Rose, 1956) categorically concludes:

There is no evidence that . . . any known source of "prejudice" in the psychological sense is any more prevalent in the South than in the North (p. 174).

Two others (Rabb & Lipset, 1959) maintain firmly:

the psychological approach, as valuable as it is, does not explain the preponderance of people who engage in prejudiced behavior, but do *not* have special emotional problems (p. 26).

Both of these statements assume, as some psychologists have assumed, that externalization is the only possible psychological explanation of prejudice. These writers employ cultural and situational norms as explanatory concepts for racial prejudice and discrimination, but fail to see that conformity needs are the personality reflections of these norms and offer an equally valid concept on the psychological level. To answer the first assertion, recent evidence indicates that conformity to racial norms, one "known source of prejudice," is "more prevalent in the South than in the North." To answer the second assertion, strong needs to conform to racial norms in a sternly sanctioning South, for instance, are *not* "special emotional problems." Psychology is not just a science of mental illness nor must psychological theories of prejudice be limited to the mentally ill.

Conformity and Social Adjustment In Southern Racial Attitudes

Evidence of the importance of conformity in southern attitudes on race has been steadily accumulating in recent years. The relevant data come from several different research approaches; one of these is the study of anti-Semitism. Roper's (1946, 1947) opinion polls have twice shown the South, together with the Far West, to be one of the least anti-Semitic regions in the United States. Knapp's (1944) study of over 1,000 war rumors from all parts of the country in 1942 lends additional weight to this finding. He noted that anti-Semitic stories constituted 9% of the nation's rumors but only 3% of the South's rumors. By contrast, 8.5% of the southern rumors concerned the Negro as opposed to only 3% for the nation as a whole. Consistent with these data, too, is Prothro's (1952) discovery that two-fifths of his white adult sample in Louisiana was quite favorable in its attitudes toward Jews but at the same time quite unfavorable in its attitudes toward Negroes. But if the externalization function were predominant in southern anti-Negro attitudes, the South should also be highly anti-Semitic. Externalizing bigots do not select out just the Negro; they typically reject all out-groups, even, as Hartley (1946) has demonstrated, out-groups that do not exist.

Further evidence comes from research employing the famous F Scale measure of authoritarianism (Adorno, Frenkel-Brunswik, Levinson, & Sanford, 1950). Several studies, employing both student and adult samples, have reported southern F Scale means that fall well within the range of means of comparable nonsouthern groups (Milton, 1952; Pettigrew, 1959; Smith & Prothro, 1957). Moreover, there is no evidence that the family pattern associated with authoritarianism is any more prevalent in the South than in other parts of the country (Davis, Gardner, & Gardner, 1941; Dollard, 1937). It seems clear, then, that the South's heightened prejudice against the Negro cannot be explained in terms of any regional difference in authoritarianism. This is not to deny, however, the importance of the F Scale in predicting individual differences; it appears to correlate with prejudice in southern samples at approximately the same levels as in northern samples (Pettigrew, 1959).

The third line of evidence relates conformity measures directly to racial attitudes. For lack of a standardized, nonlaboratory measure, one study defined conformity and deviance in terms of the respondents' social characteristics (Pettigrew, 1959). For a southern white sample with age and education held constant, potentially conforming respondents (i.e., females or church attenders) were *more* anti-Negro than their counterparts (i.e., males or nonattenders of church), and potentially deviant respondents (i.e., armed service veterans or political independents) were *less* anti-Negro than their counterparts (i.e., nonveterans or political party identifiers). None of these differences were noted in a comparable northern sample. Furthermore, Southerners living in communities with relatively small percentages of Negroes were less anti-Negro than Southerners living in communities with relatively large percentages of Negroes, though they were *not* less authoritarian. In short, respondents most likely to be conforming to cultural pressures are more prejudiced against Negroes in the South but not in the North. And the percentage of Negroes in the community appears to be a fairly accurate index of the strength of these southern cultural pressures concerning race.

Thus all three types of research agree that comformity to the stern racial norms of southern culture is unusually crucial in the South's heightened hostility toward the Negro.[7] Or, in plain language, it is the path of least resistance in most southern circles to favor white supremacy. When an individual's parents and peers are racially prejudiced, when his limited world accepts racial discrimination as a given way of life, when his deviance means certain ostracism, then his anti-Negro attitudes are not so much expressive as they are socially adjusting.

This being the case, it is fortunate that a number of significant laboratory and theoretical advances in the conformity realm have been made recently in our discipline. Solomon Asch's (1951) pioneer research on conformity, followed up by Crutchfield (1955) and others, has provided us with a wealth of laboratory findings, many of them suggestive for desegregation research. And theoretical analyses of conformity have been introduced by Kelman (1958, 1961), Festinger (1953, 1957), and Thibaut and Kelley (1959); these, too, are directly appli-

[7] Similar analyses of South African student data indicate that the social adjustment function may also be of unusual importance in the anti-African attitudes of the English in the Union (Pettigrew, 1958, 1960).

cable for desegregation research. Indeed, research in southern race relations offers a rare opportunity to test these empirical and theoretical formulations in the field on an issue of maximum salience.

Consider the relevance of one of Asch's (1951) intriguing findings. Asch's standard situation, you will recall, employed seven pre-instructed assistants and a genuine subject in a line judgment task. On two-thirds of the judgments, the seven assistants purposely reported aloud an obviously incorrect estimate; thus the subject, seated eighth, faced unanimous pressure to conform by making a similarly incorrect response. On approximately one-third of such judgments, he yielded to the group; like the others, he would estimate a 5-inch line as 4 inches. But when Asch disturbed the unanimity by having one of his seven assistants give the correct response, the subjects yielded only a tenth, rather than a third, of the time. Once unanimity no longer existed, even when there was only one supporting colleague, the subject could better withstand the pressure of the majority to conform. To carry through the analogy to today's crisis in the South, obvious 5-inch lines are being widely described as 4 inches. Many Southerners, faced with what appears to be solid unanimity, submit to the distortion. But when even one respected source—a minister, a newspaper editor, even a college professor—conspicuously breaks the unanimity, *perhaps* a dramatic modification is achieved in the private opinions of many conforming Southerners. Only an empirical test can learn if such a direct analogy is warranted.

Consider, too, the relevance of recent theoretical distinctions. Kelman (1958, 1961), for example, has clarified the concept of conformity by pointing out that three separate processes are involved: *compliance, identification,* and *internalization.* Compliance exists when an individual accepts influence not because he believes in it, but because he hopes to achieve a favorable reaction from an agent who maintains surveillance over him. Identification exists when an individual accepts influence because he wants to establish or maintain a satisfying relationship with another person

or group. The third process, internalization, exists when an individual accepts
influence because the content of the behavior itself is satisfying; unlike the other
types of conformity, internalized behavior
will be performed without the surveillance
of the agent or a salient relationship with
the agent. It is with this third process that
Kelman's ideas overlap with authoritarian
theory.

We have all witnessed illustrations of
each of these processes in the acceptance by
Southerners of the region's racial norms.
The "Uncle Tom" Negro is an example of
a compliant Southerner; another example
is furnished by the white man who treats
Negroes as equals only when not under the
surveillance of other whites. Identification is
best seen in white Southerners whose resistance to racial integration enables them to
be a part of what they erroneously imagine
to be Confederate tradition. Such identifiers are frequently upwardly mobile people who are still assimilating to urban
society; they strive for social status by identifying with the hallowed symbols and
shibboleths of the South's past. Southerners
who have internalized the white supremacy
dictates of the culture are the real racists
who use the issue to gain political office, to
attract resistance group membership fees,
or to meet personality needs. Southerners
with such contrasting bases for their racial
attitudes should react very differently toward desegregation. For instance, compliant
whites can be expected to accept desegregation more readily than those who have
internalized segregationist norms.

On the basis of this discussion of conformity, I would like to propose a new concept: *the latent liberal.* This is not to be
confused with the cherished southern notion of the "moderate"; the ambiguous term
"moderate" is presently used to describe
everything from an integrationist who
wants to be socially accepted to a racist
who wants to be polite. Rather, the latent
liberal refers to the Southerner who is
neither anti-Semitic nor authoritarian but
whose conformity habits and needs cause
him to be strongly anti-Negro. Through the
processes of compliance and identification,
the latent liberal continues to behave in a
discriminatory fashion toward Negroes even
though such behavior conflicts with his
basically tolerant personality. He is at the
present time *illiberal* on race, but he has
the personality potentiality of becoming
liberal once the norms of the culture
change. Indeed, as the already unleashed
economic, legal, political, and social forces
restructure the South's racial norms, the
latent liberal's attitudes about Negroes will
continue to change. Previously cited research suggests that there are today an
abundance of white Southerners who meet
this latent liberal description; collectively,
they will reflect on the individual level the
vast societal changes now taking place in
the South.

Some Suggested Directions For Future Psychological Research On Desegregation[8]

We are in serious need of research on
the Negro, both in the North and in the
South. Most psychological research in this
area was conducted during the 1930s and
directed at testing racists' claims of Negro
inferiority. But the most sweeping advances
in American Negro history have been made
in the past generation, requiring a fresh new
look—particularly at the Negro personality.

Two aspects of this research make it complex and difficult. In the first place, the
race of the interviewer is a complicating
and not as yet fully understood factor. Further methodological study is needed on
this point. Moreover, special problems of
control are inherent in this research. Not
only are there some relatively unique variables that must be considered (e.g., migration history, differential experience with
the white community, etc.), but such simple factors as education are not easy to
control. For instance, has the average graduate of the southern rural high school for
Negroes received an education equal to the
average graduate of such a school for
whites? No, in spite of the South's belated
efforts to live up to separate-but-equal education, available school data indicate that
the graduates have probably not received

[8] For other suggestions, see the important analysis of desegregation by Cook (1957).

equivalent educations. Yet some recent research on Negro personality has been based on the assumption that Negro and white education in the South are equivalent (e.g., Smith & Prothro, 1957).

Fortunately, the Institute for Research in the Social Sciences at the University of North Carolina has embarked on a large study of many of these content and methodological problems. It is to be hoped that their work will stimulate other efforts.

Some of the most valuable psychological data now available on desegregation have been collected by public opinion polls. But typically these data have been gathered without any conceptual framework to guide their coverage and direction.

For example, one of the more interesting poll findings is that a majority of white Southerners realize that racial desegregation of public facilities is inevitable even though about six out of seven strongly oppose the process (Hyman & Sheatsley, 1956). The psychological implications of this result are so extensive that we would like to know more. Do the respondents who oppose desegregation but accept its inevitability have other characteristics of latent liberals? Are these respondents more often found outside of the Black Belt? Typically, we cannot answer such questions from present poll data; we need to build into the desegregation polls broader coverage and more theoretical direction.

The third direction that psychological research in desegregation could usefully take concerns measurement. Save for the partly standardized F Scale, we still lack widely used, standardized field measures of the chief variables in this realm. Such instruments are necessary both for comparability of results and for stimulation of research; witness the invigorating effects on research of the F Scale, the Minnesota Multiphasic Inventory, and the need achievement scoring scheme. Mention of McClelland's need achievement scoring scheme should remind us, too, that projective and other indirect techniques might answer many of these measurement requirements—especially for such sensitive and subtle variables as conformity needs.

Finally, the definitive interdisciplinary

case study of desegregation has yet to be started. Properly buttressed by the necessary foundation aid, such a study should involve comparisons before, during, and after desegregation of a wide variety of communities. The interdisciplinary nature of such an undertaking is stressed because desegregation is a peculiarly complex process demanding a broad range of complementary appproaches.

Any extensive case project must sample three separate time periods: before a legal ruling or similar happening has alerted the community to imminent desegregation, during the height of the desegregating process, and after several years of accommodation. Without this longitudinal view, desegregation as a dynamic, ongoing process cannot be understood. This time perspective, for instance, would enable us to interpret the fact that an overwhelming majority of Oklahoma whites in a 1954 poll sternly objected to mixed schools, but within a few years has accepted without serious incident integrated education throughout most of the state (Jones, 1957).

A carefully selected range of communities is required to test for differences in the process according to the characteristics of the area. Recent demographic analyses and predictions of the South's school desegregation pattern (Ogburn & Grigg, 1956; Pettigrew, 1957; Pettigrew & Campbell, 1960) could help in making this selection of communities. Comparable data gathered in such a selected variety of locations would allow us to pinpoint precisely the aspects of desegregation unique to, say, a Piedmont city, as opposed to a Black Belt town.

Compare the potential value of such a broad research effort with the limited case studies that have been possible so far. Low budget reports of only one community are the rule; many of them are theses or seminar projects, some remain on the descriptive level, all but a few sample only one time period, and there is almost no comparability of instruments and approach. A comprehensive case project is obviously long overdue.

This has been an appeal for a vigorous empirical look at southern race relations. Despite segregationists' claims to the contrary, social psychological contributions to desegregation research have been relatively meager. There are, however, grounds for hoping that this situation will be partly corrected in the near future—particularly if psychologists get busy.

Foundations appear to be re-evaluating their previous reluctance to support such research. And we can re-evaluate our own resignation in the face of barriers to conduct investigations in this area; the tragedy of Little Rock has had a salutary effect on many influential Southerners in this respect.

Recognition of the importance of the situation in interracial behavior and the full exploitation of the attitude concept can remove inadequacies in the traditional psychological approach to the study of race. In this connection, an extended case for considering conformity as crucial in the Negro attitudes of white Southerners was presented and a new concept—the latent liberal—introduced. One final implication of this latent liberal concept should be mentioned. Some cynics have argued that successful racial desegregation in the South will require an importation of tens of thousands of psychotherapists and therapy for millions of bigoted Southerners. Fortunately for desegregation, psychotherapists, and Southerners, this will not be necessary; a thorough repatterning of southern interracial behavior will be sufficient therapy in itself.

REFERENCES

Adorno, T. W., Frenkel-Brunswik, Else, Levinson, D. J., & Sanford, N. *The authoritarian personality*. New York: Harper, 1950.

Allport, G. W. *The nature of prejudice*. Cambridge, Mass.: Addison-Wesley, 1954.

Asch, S. E. Effects of group pressure upon the modification and distortion of judgments. In H. Guetzkow (Ed.) *Groups, leadership and men*. Pittsburgh: Carnegie, 1951.

Biesanz, J., & Smith, L. M. Race relations of Panama and the Canal Zone. *Amer. J. Sociol.*, 1951, 57, 7–14.

Clark, K. B. Desegregation: An appraisal of the evidence. *J. soc. Issues*, 1953, 9, 1–76.

Cook, S. W. Desegregation: A psychological analysis. *Amer. Psychologist*, 1957, 12, 1–13.

Crutchfield, R. S. Conformity and character. *Amer. Psychologist*, 1955, 10, 191–198.

Dabney, V. The violence at Little Rock. *Richmond Times-Dispatch*, 1957, 105, September 24, 14.

Davis, A., Gardner, B., & Gardner, Mary. *Deep South*. Chicago: Univer. Chicago Press, 1941.

Dollard, J. *Caste and class in a southern town*. New Haven: Yale Univer. Press, 1937.

Festinger, L. An analysis of compliant behavior. In M. Sherif & M. O. Wilson (Eds.), *Group relations at the crossroads*. New York: Harper, 1953.

Festinger, L. *A theory of cognitive dissonance*. Evanston, Ill.: Row, Peterson, 1957.

Harding, J., & Hogrefe, R. Attitudes of white department store employees toward Negro co-workers. *J. soc. Issues*, 1952, 8, 18–28.

Hartley, E. L. *Problems in prejudice*. New York: King's Crown, 1946.

Hyman, H. H., and Sheatsley, P. B. Attitudes toward desegregation. *Scient. Amer.*, 1956, 195, 35–39.

Jones, E. City limits. In D. Shoemaker (Ed.), *With all deliberate speed*. New York: Harper, 1957.

Kelman, H. C. Compliance, identification, and internalization: Three processes of attitude change. *J. conflict Resolut.*, 1958, 2, 51–60.

Kelman, H. C. *Social influence and personal belief*. New York: Wiley, 1961.

Killian, L. W. Southern white laborers in Chicago's West Side. Unpublished doctoral dissertation, University of Chicago, 1949.

Knapp, R. H. A psychology of rumor. *Publ. opin. Quart.*, 1944, 8, 22–37.

Logan, R. W. The United States Supreme Court and the segregation issue. *Ann. Amer. Acad. Pol. Soc. Sci.*, 1956, 304, 10–16.

Milton, O. Presidential choice and performance on a scale of authoritarianism. *Amer. Psychologist*, 1952, 7, 597–598.

Minard, R. D. Race relations in the Pocahontas coal field. *J. soc. Issues*, 1952, 8, 29–44.

Ogburn, W. F., & Grigg, C. M. Factors related to the Virginia vote on segregation. *Soc. Forces*, 1956, 34, 301–308.

Pettigrew, T. F. Demographic correlates of border-state desegregation. *Amer. sociol. Rev.*, 1957, 22, 683–689.

Pettigrew, T. F. Personality and sociocultural factors in intergroup attitudes: A cross-national comparison. *J. conflict Resolut.*, 1958, 2, 29–42.

Pettigrew, T. F. Regional differences in anti-Negro prejudice. *J. abnorm. soc. Psychol.*, 1959, 59, 28–36.

Pettigrew, T. F. Social distance attitudes of South African students. *Soc. Forces*, 1960, 38, 246–253.

Pettigrew, T. F., & Campbell, E. Q. Faubus and segregation: An analysis of Arkansas voting. *Publ. opin. Quart.*, 1960, 24, 436–447.

Prothro, E. T. Ethnocentrism and anti-Negro attitudes in the deep South. *J. abnorm. soc. Psychol.*, 1952, 47, 105–108.

Rabb, E., & Lipset, S. M. *Prejudice and society*. New York: Anti-Defamation League of B'nai B'rith, 1959.

Reitzes, D. C. The role of organizational structures: Union versus neighborhood in a tension situation. *J. soc. Issues*, 1953, 9, 37–44.

Roper, E. United States anti-Semites. *Fortune,* 1946, 33, 257–260.

Roper, E. United States anti-Semites. *Fortune,* 1947, 36, 5–10.

Rose, A. M. Intergroup relations vs. prejudice: Pertinent theory for the study of social change. *Soc. Probl.,* 1956, 4, 173–176.

Smith, C. U., & Prothro, J. W. Ethnic differences in authoritarian personality. *Soc. Forces,* 1957, 35, 334–338.

Smith, M. B., Bruner, J. S., & White, R. W. *Opinion and personality.* New York: Wiley, 1956.

Stouffer, S. A., Suchman, E. A., DeVinney, L. C., Star, Shirley A., Williams, R. M., Jr. *Studies in social psychology in World War II.* Vol. 1. *The American soldier: Adjustment during army life.* Princeton: Princeton Univer. Press, 1949.

Thibaut, J. W., & Kelley, H. H. *The social psychology of groups.* New York: Wiley, 1959.

Zinn, H. A fate worse than integration. *Harper's,* 1959, 219, August, 53–56.

CLASS CONFLICT: FORGET IT!*

RICHARD T. MORRIS AND VINCENT JEFFRIES

ABSTRACT

This discussion is based upon a secondary analysis of data collected in the Los Angeles Riot Study in 1965, with a sample of 583 interviews collected from six Los Angeles area communities. The general logic of analysis is to discover whether class awareness is related to objective class position, whether class awareness is necessary for the development of class consciousness, and whether class consciousness is related to class action involving class conflict. There is an attempt to measure class awareness by asking for subjective class placement, objective position, the importance of class, and the clarity of class lines. Class consciousness is indicated by answers to questions as to the degree of class dissatisfaction and antagonism, beliefs about mobility chances, personal alienation, and work alienation. Class action is indicated by the Goldwater-Johnson vote in the 1964 presidential election. The findings are that people can place themselves in classes, fairly objectively, that they disagree whether classes are important or clearly demarcated, that class awareness does not seem to affect class dissatisfaction, and that class dissatisfaction is not clearly related to class action.

During the last few years there has been a renewed and lively interest in the possibility, not to say the desirability, of class conflict in the United States. The New Left, under its various names and versions, very often has as one of its planks an advocacy of some sort of class conflict to change the present structure of this society. Certainly there are all kinds of conflict in progress, between blacks and whites, students and universities, hawks and doves, between nations, but do any of these represent class conflict in any sense of that word? It is our contention, as will be more fully argued below, that in order to describe conflict as class conflict, there must be class consciousness and class ideology. The findings which are presented in this paper indicate that there is very little evidence that such consciousness exists on any broad scale in our society.

The authors recently completed a secondary analysis of data we collected in the Los Angeles Riot Study in 1965.[1] This study was focused mainly on white reactions to the "riots," but it did include some ques-

tions on class. We used the sample of 583 interviews collected from six communities in Los Angeles County. Like all secondary analyses, our argument here suffers badly from unasked or badly-asked questions for the purposes at hand, i.e., to discover whether there is any evidence of class consciousness or class conflict, incipient or actual, in our sample.

Morris and Murphy in their "Paradigm for the Study of Class Consciousness"[2] suggest that in order to have class conflict or class action of other kinds, there must be class consciousness present, and in turn, in order for class consciousness to develop, there must be existent some form of class awareness.

Class action was defined as behavior undertaken by an individual or group on behalf of the interests of the class, in order to maintain, protect or improve the position of that class. It may consist of political activity, cooperation or conflict with other classes, passive acceptance or resistance, legal or illegal actions, etc., at the expense, or not, of the other classes. Class conflict is one form of class action which involves a struggle for power or goods, in which one side wins and the other loses, or there

* Reprinted by permission of the authors and publisher from *Sociology and Social Research*, 1970, 54, 306–320.

[1] Richard T. Morris and Vincent Jeffries, *The White Reaction Study*. Los Angeles Riot Study, Institute of Government and Public Affairs, University of California, Los Angeles, June 1, 1967, 43 pp. (mimeographed).

[2] Richard T. Morris and Raymond J. Murphy, "A Paradigm for the Study of Class Consciousness," *Sociology and Social Research*, 50, (April, 1966), 297–313.

TABLE 1
STUDIES OF SUBJECTIVE CLASS PLACEMENT
USING CLOSED CATEGORIES

	Centers[4] 1945	Gross[5] 1950	Kahl & Davis[6] 1953		Haer[7] 1957	The Present Study 1965	
Upper Class	3	2	5		5	3	
Upper Middle Class			19			22	
Middle Class	43	42	12	43	53	50	77
Lower Middle Class			12			5	
Working Class	51	45	47		37	16	
Lower Class	1	3	3			2	
DK	1	2			1	1	
Don't Believe (Or no classes)	1	5	2				
Other		2			5		
N	1097	935	219		320	583	

is an ultimate stalemate and a continuing struggle.

Class consciousness was defined as an identification with and commitment to class interests and ideology. Class awareness was defined in the paradigm as the perception of discrete ranked economic categories, and the ability to place self and others in the various classes, as distinct from status awareness which involves the perception of continuous economic status ranges.

Finally, in order for the class action, the class consciousness, or the class awareness, to be "real" instead of "false," it must be determined whether these perceptions, beliefs and behaviors are related to objective positions in the social structure: in the current analysis, in terms of education, income, and occupation.

These ideas, of course, do not depart very far from the classic Marxist distinction between a class-in-itself and a class-for-itself, wherein the members of a class become aware of their position vis a vis other classes, develop a sense of identity, and of their proper role in changing or preserving the present class system.

First, as evidence of class awareness, we asked the old question, "If you were to use one of these names for your social group, to which one would you belong?" In this study, we spread out the varieties of "middle" to avoid the usual pile-up.[3]

It is interesting to note the shrinkage of working class identification and the growth of middle class identification, from 1945 to 1965, in studies which all used a version of Center's closed categories.

It seems that our respondents were able to

[3] Cf. Richard Centers, *The Psychology of Social Classes.* (Princeton, New Jersey: Princeton University Press, 1949). His format contains the original four categories, with an undifferentiated middle class. Also cf. Joseph A. Kahl and James A. Davis, "A Comparison of Indexes of Socio-Economic Status," *American Sociological Review*, 20 (1955), 317–25. The authors split the middle class into upper middle, middle, and lower middle as we have done.

[4] Richard Centers, *op. cit.*, 77.

[5] Neal Gross, "Social Class Identification in the Urban Community," *American Sociological Review*, 18 (August, 1953), 398–404.

[6] Joseph A. Kahl and James A. Davis, *op. cit.*, 321.

[7] John L. Haer, "Predictive Utility of Five Indices of Social Stratification," *American Sociological Review*, 2, (October, 1957), 116. It might be argued, as indeed it was, when this paper was presented, that Leggett's study in 1960, of Detroit blue-collar workers shows a reversal in this trend of reduced working class identification over the years and what it implies about reduced class consciousness. We should remember, however, that his sample consisted of 375 blue-collar workers, 75 per cent of whom were union members, and most were ethnic. Furthermore, each respondent was counted as class conscious if he answered any one of eleven questions in the right way. Even so, 14 per cent of the white respondents were classified as "class indifferents." John C. Leggett, "Economic Insecurity and Working-Class Consciousness," *American Sociological Review*, 29 (April, 1964), 226–34.

TABLE II
THE RELATION BETWEEN OBJECTIVE POSITION
AND SUBJECTIVE PLACEMENT,
IN PERCENTAGES

A. *Income and Subjective Class Placement*

	U/UM Per cent	M Per cent	LM/W/L Per cent	Per cent
Income L ($0-4999)	12	43	45	100
M ($5000-$8999)	11	58	31	
H ($9000 & over)	42	51	8	
				(N = 556)

(P .001, gamma .58)

B. *Occupation and Subjective Class Placement*

	U/UM Per cent	M Per cent	LM/W/L Per cent	Per cent
Blue Collar	10	51	40	100
Clerical-Sales	29	50	12	
Managerial	32	50	18	
Professional	46	44	10	
				(N = 254)

(Small N due to the fact that only the employed are included)
(P .001, gamma .45)

C. *Education and Subjective Class Placement*

	U/UM Per cent	M Per cent	LM/W/L Per cent	Per cent
Less than HS graduate	5	51	44	100
HS graduate	17	53	30	
Some college	34	53	14	
Graduate or Grad. School	48	49	4	
				(N = 552)

(P .001, gamma .54)

place themselves in classes (only 1 per cent "don't know"). Recognizing all of the usual criticisms of this methodology, i.e., if people are given class names, they will dutifully assign themselves to one of these categories whether or not they normally think of themselves, or behave, in class terms, we did find that the subjective class placements are significantly related to other variables.

First, despite the artificial nature of the question asking for self-placement in a class, and the large proportion who say they are in the middle, we still find a strong relationship between a person's objective position and his subjective placement in the class structure.

These findings still leave room for a vari-

ety of interpretations: should we say that *fully* 45 per cent of the low income group, 40 per cent of the blue-collar group, and 44 per cent of the high school drop-outs identify themselves as lower middle, working or lower class, or should we say *only* 40–45 per cent of the lower classes so identify themselves, with a larger proportion saying they are middle (49–51 per cent).[8]

The Marxian notion of class consciousness includes an awareness of the importance of classes in the historical process and in the life history of individuals. As class

[8] Cf. Herbert Hyman, *Survey Design and Analysis* (New York: The Free Press, a Division of The Macmillan Co., 1955), 126–28.

consciousness develops, class comes to be perceived as the dominant social fact. The following two questions served as indicators of this facet of class awareness:

"Do you think that class differences are very important in this country?"; "Is it easy to tell who is in what class?" In both cases, the decision provided a fairly even split. For the first question, 47 per cent said Yes, 51 per cent No, and 2 per cent did not answer; while for the second question the split was 44 per cent Yes, 54 per cent No, and 2 per cent no answer.

The answers to how important classes are, and whether or not it's easy to tell what class a person is in, are not related to the objective indicators. For example, 52 per cent of the low income group say that class differences are important, and 48 per cent of the high income group say so. Forty-five per cent of the low income group say it's easy to tell who is in what class and 43 per cent of the high income group say it is easy to tell. The same pattern is found with occupation and education. One might think that in Marxian terms, the lower income and occupational groups would believe that class is more important and obvious. Although this is where much of Marx's concern is concentrated, he also points out that the bourgeois groups are highly aware of class and its importance, and that this consciousness is useful in bolstering their position. The Glantz[9] and Jones[10] studies also seem to show that, if anything, the business classes in American have more consistency in their loyalty, allegiance, and affiliation to class interests than do the working classes. In any case, there is not much difference here between the lower groups in education, occupation, or income, and the upper groups, when we consider their attitudes about the salience or visibility of class differences. Fully half of the lower class think that class differences are important and clear.

In addition to a rational awareness of the importance of class, Marx believed that

class consciousness involved an emotional sense of injustice, exploitation, and antagonism toward other classes. Again we are limited by the shortcomings of secondary analysis. If one set out to construct a set of questions which attempted to discover the presence of class ideology, he would certainly pick better questions than those which follow. These measures consist of two pairs of questions which to some extent involve class dissatisfaction and antagonism. The first pair contains the question: "A lot of people in this country have things they don't deserve." (34 per cent agree, 61 per cent disagree and 5 per cent did not answer). The second question is: "Do you think there are any groups or kinds of people in this country who are trying to get ahead at the expense of people like you?" (48 per cent agree, 49 per cent disagree, 3 per cent did not answer.) The two questions are significantly correlated with each other at the .001 level.

We felt that these two questions involve some sort of ideas about class dissatisfaction or division and that they seem to be statements of suspicion or antagonism toward other classes. We would first have to demonstrate, however, that the "people" or "groups" referred to are class groupings of some kind. In answer to the question, "What people?" for those who agreed on the two questions ("don't deserve" and get ahead at my expense, respectively), the distributions are as follows: 60 per cent-60 per cent answered in terms of the "Haves" (the rich, the powerful, etc.) 26 percent-20 percent in terms of the "Have nots" (the poor, those on relief, etc.) and 13 per cent-21 per cent in terms of minorities (Negroes, Jews, etc.). Fully (only?) 80-85 per cent of the respondents who have such feelings are replying in class terms.

Neither one of these questions was related to subjective class position, nor were they related to the "awareness" items of the importance or clarity of class.

Insofar as these two questions are any fair measure or even indirect indicators of the presence of class ideology, our initial hypothesis that class awareness is necessary in order to have class consciousness, is not borne out, as shown in Table III.

[9] Oscar Glantz, "Class Consciousness and Political Solidarity," *American Sociological Review*, 23 (1958), 375–82.

[10] Alfred W. Jones, *Life, Liberty and Property*. (Philadelphia: Lippincott, 1941).

TABLE III

PER CENT CLASS AWARNESS AND CLASS
DISSATISFACTION

"Class differences are important":	important	*not* *important*
A lot of people in this country have things they don't deserve:	yes 40	32
	no 60	68
		(N=542)
People are trying to get ahead at my expense:	yes 53	48
	no 48	52
		(N=526)

These findings are in the right direction, i.e., people who think class differences are important are more apt to believe in class antagonism, but the differences are so small that they may be due to chance.

The second pair of questions deal with beliefs about mobility. We viewed these questions as possible indicators of structural dissatisfaction or discontent, in that a person who feels that it is difficult to move up through the structure may be expressing a criticism of that structure. To view it in another way, Marx considered a belief in high upward mobility as part of the bourgeois ideology which helps maintain the position of the ruling class, and enables them to coopt the most prominent and energetic men of the working class.

The questions used were: "Is it easy to move from one class to another?" and "Would you say that any person who has ambition and talent could move from the bottom to the top?" (These two questions are related to each other at the .001 level).

We might expect people at the bottom of the structure to be more apt to disagree with these statements, and those at the top to agree. There is very little difference, however, between the subjective classes in their attitudes toward the possibility of mobility. For example, on the question of people with ambition and talent moving from the bottom to the top, 90 per cent of the low subjective class say "yes," whereas only 83 per cent of the high subjective class

say "yes." Findings are similar for objective indicators of class position, as shown in Table V, using income and occupation as measures. The Horatio Algers are still in good supply at the bottom of the social structure. The mobility questions are related, however, to the perceived importance of class. Those who think classes are important are more apt to see difficulties in mobility.

The concept of alienation is central to Marx's ideas of the human condition produced by the capitalist system of production. Man becomes alienated from his work, his fellow man, and the social institutions of capitalism. Our measures of social alienation deal with estrangement from others, and from the institution of government. The first question is "The way things are today in the world, people can't count on really getting to know each other very well." 46 per cent agree with this statement and 54 per cent disagree. The second question is as follows: "The average citizen can have an influence on the way the government is run." 70 per cent agree with this statement and 26 per cent disagree. Both of these questions are related to subjective class at the .02 and .01 level, with those in the lower classes being more alienated. The patterns of relationship with the importance of class and clarity of class are as expected, i.e., those who believe in the importance and clarity of class are more alienated, but the per cent differences are small and not statistically significant.

Another facet of alienation is that of an alienation from work. Man fulfills himself and expresses his creative potential through work. In the capitalist system of production, Marx believed, man is deprived of this basic need. Work is monotonous and routinized, the worker becomes a "mere appendage to the machine" and work is "avoided like the plague" whenever circumstances permit. Under these conditions the worker becomes alienated from his work, and this alienation is a major factor in the development of class consciousness. We included a pair of questions to measure some of these facets of work alienation. The first asks: "If you had the opportunity to retire right now, would you prefer to do that or would you

TABLE IV
PER CENT WHO SHOW 'CLASS' DISSATISFACTION

	Class Awareness Items						
Items Showing Class Dissatisfaction	Subjective Class			Class Differences Important		It's easy to Tell What Class	
	U/UM	M	LM/W/L	Yes	No	Yes	No
A lot of people have things they don't deserve	37	36	34	40	32	38	35
Some people trying to get ahead at my expense	45	51	54	53	48	53	47
Difficult to move from one class to other	39	41	49	57	***30	56	***31
Ambitious cannot move from bottom to top	17	13	10	19	****8	13	13
Can't get to know each other	35	49	*50	50	42	50	42
Average citizen cannot have influence on government	18	25	**37	30	22	29	24
Prefer to retire now	24	31	38	28	31	26	33
Cannot try out ideas on job	21	33	39	32	31	35	29

* P.02, ** P.01, *** P.001

(Ns vary between 540 and 560 for all comparisons except for the last two work alienation questions where they drop to 260-270, due to the fact that only the employed were asked these questions.

prefer to keep working at your present job?" 28 per cent answering said that they would retire now and the rest would go on working. The second question asks: "Does your job really give you a chance to try out ideas on your own?" 62 per cent say "yes," 30 per cent say "no." Neither of these items were related in statistically significant way to subjective class position or to the importance or clarity of class, but the differences generally are in the expected direction, i.e., more work alienation at the bottom of the subjective class structure.

A summary of these findings is shown in Table IV.

The over-all pattern is fairly consistent, although there are some exceptions and in many cases the differences are small and not statistically significant. In general, those who place themselves at the bottom of the class structure are more apt to be dissatisfied, and those who think class differences are clear and important are more apt to be dissatisfied.

Here again, the fully-only interpretation plagues us. There are a large number of small differences which seem to indicate that subjective class position and class awareness determine class attitudes, but should we point to this pattern as evidence of a possible relationship, or should we deny the whole thing as statistically insignificant? The pattern is present but faint. There is no evidence for any massive dissatisfaction at the bottom of the structure which might result in a serious class cleavage or disruption. It should be recalled that we are discussing white respondents only—the situation with blacks may be different.

When we relate objective class position to the eight dissatisfaction items, the same general, weak pattern emerges (and is also found with education).

It is interesting to note that five of the six

TABLE V
PER CENT WHO SHOW 'CLASS' DISSATISFACTION

| | Income | | | | Occupation | | |
	9 & over	5-9	under 5	Prof.	Mgr.	Cler.	Blue
A lot of people have things they don't deserve	30	37	*46	36	33	24	47
Some people trying to get ahead at my expense	48	53	49	37	55	53	58
Difficult to move from one class to another	39	45	42	32	34	39	39
Ambitious cannot move from bottom to top	15	11	10	17	8	8	8
Can't get to know each other	39	46	**57	36	46	40	46
Average citizen cannot have influence on government	22	25	*35	16	21	14	**37
Prefer to retire now	29	26	44	17	29	36	*40
Cannot try out ideas on job	24	36	49	11	11	46	**46

* P.02, ** P.01, *** .001

(Ns vary between 540 and 560 for all comparisons except for the last two work alienation questions where they drop to 260-270, due to the fact that only the employed were asked these questions.)

statistically significant differences are in the area of alienation. Perhaps Marx was right and Fromm was wrong, if our questions on alienation are any good measure of what Marx was talking about. Fromm makes the point that although Marx believed that alienation would be most acute in the working class, in Fromm's opinion the white collar classes should be most alienated.[11]

Our final step is to see whether class position (objective and subjective) and the various elements of class consciousness which we have previously considered are related to class conflict. Our indicator of class conflict is the choice of Lyndon Johnson or Barry Goldwater for president in the 1964 elections. While this vote is a far cry from a class revolution, Lipset has advanced a number of strong arguments for considering voting behavior as an expression of class interests and conflict. Lipset presents data to show that the lower classes throughout the world tend to support liberal par-

ties, e.g., those which advocate such policies as a minimum wage, graduated income tax and government control of business. In contrast, the upper classes throughout the world are consistent in their support of more conservative parties which oppose policies such as those previously mentioned, and in general support policies which would help to maintain the privileged position of the upper classes. These voting patterns are interpreted by Lipset as arising from economic self interest.[12]

In the case of Johnson vs. Goldwater, such class issues were particularly sharp, given their respective policies on economic and "welfare state" issues. We thus expected that the class conscious blue-collar workers would be more likely to vote for Johnson than those who are not class conscious, while the class conscious managerial and

[11] Erich Fromm, *Marx's Concept of Man*. (New York: Unger, 1961), 56–7.

[12] Seymour Martin Lipset, "Elections: The Expression of the Democratic Class Struggle," in Reinhard, Bendix and S. M. Lipset, Eds., *Class, Status and Power*, (New York: The Free Press, a Division of The Macmillan Co., 1966), 413–28.

professional should be more likely to vote for Goldwater than those occupying similar positions but who are not class conscious.

TABLE VI
SUBJECTIVE AND OBJECTIVE CLASS POSITION RELATED TO VOTE AND PARTY

	Per cent Goldwater Vote	Per cent Republican Vote
1. Occupation		
Professional	46	53
Managerial	65	63
Sales & Clerical	35	47
Blue Collar	25	29
	(N—195) P.01	(N—206) P.01
2. Subjective Class		
Upper		
Upper Middle	37	58
Middle	33	44
Lower Middle		
Working		
Lower	18	21
	(N—541) P.01	(N—474) P.001

* The reciprocal in each case represents the Johnson vote, or per cent Democrat.

tween these three objective measures of class, but it is interesting to note that although the managers are almost on the same level of income as the professionals, they fall far behind them on education.

The relationship between the class dissatisfaction items and the vote is shown in Table VIII.

Again the pattern is faint but clear, class dissatisfaction is related to a reduction in the Goldwater vote, except on the item of 'someone getting ahead at your expense.' Here, agreement with this item increases the Goldwater vote significantly.

To show the combined effects of objective position, as measured by occupation, and class dissatisfaction upon the vote, we ran occupation against vote, controlling for dissatisfaction.

Here we can only show a very confused picture. Work alienation (retire now, cannot try own ideas) reduces the Goldwater vote appreciably among professionals and managers, but has no effect or very small effect among the clericals and the blue collar workers. The reduction of the Goldwater vote shown in Table IX is largely

TABLE VII
PER CENT OCCUPATION RELATED TO INCOME AND EDUCATION

	Income						
	L	M	H	Less than HS	HS Grad	Some Coll	Coll grad & grad sch
Professional	1	23	76	6	9	23	62
Managerial	13	16	71	11	29	40	20
Sales & Clerical	14	31	55	10	31	46	13
Blue Collar	20	44	36	34	44	16	5
		(N—255) P.011			(N—245) P.001		

Table VI shows that both objective (occupation) and subjective class are related to the Goldwater vote and party affiliation in the expected direction.

We can get a better idea of what these occupational groupings mean, if we first see how they are related to income and education, which is shown in Table VII.

We see the usual high correlation be-

due to differences in the upper occupations, not the lower. The lower classes are more work-alienated, but this does not affect their voting behavior as much as it does the upper classes.

Agreement with the statement that someone is trying to get ahead at their expense increases the Goldwater vote substantially at every occupational level. The only ques-

TABLE VIII

PER CENT GOLDWATER VOTE

Items showing 'Class' Dissatisfaction	Satisfied	Dissatisfied	Amount of Difference
A lot of people have things they don't deserve	31	28	− 3
Some people get ahead at my expense	*25	36	+11
Difficult to move from one class to another	*34	24	−10
Ambitious cannot move from bottom to top	31	23	− 8
Can't get to know each other	29	31	+ 2
Average citizen cannot have influence on government	**31	17	−14
Prefer to retire now	35	24	−11
Cannot try out ideas on job	**37	20	−17

* P.02, ** P.01, *** P.001

(Ns vary between 540 and 560 for all comparisons except for the last two work alienation questions where they drop to 260-270, due to the fact that only the employed were asked these questions.)

tion that has a powerful effect on the blue collar vote is the one on mobility. Those who say it is difficult to move from one class to another are much less likely to vote for Goldwater. There is also an interesting pattern on the 'some people don't deserve' item and the 'ambitious cannot move' item, where the professionals vote less for Goldwater if they agree with these items, while the managers vote more for Goldwater when they agree. Each group is presumably expressing its own interpretation in terms of opposite political interests.

The most noticeable pattern which might be considered indicative of the effects of class consciousness in voting is found among professionals. Table VIII shows that for seven of the ten measures of consciousness, the Goldwater vote decreases for professionals who give the class consciousness response.

In summary, from the point of view of one looking for signs of class consciousness and class conflict, there is a faint track indeed, and it seems to lead to the top of the structure rather than to the bottom. People can place themselves in classes when asked to do so. An increasingly large number place themselves in the middle, and smaller proportions identify with the working class. They disagree, however, as to whether classes are important or clearly demarcated. Neither does their class position, either subjectively or objectively, seem to have much to do with their class dissatisfaction. Those at the bottom are more optimistic about the chances of moving to the top than anyone else. Finally even though class *position* is related, class dissatisfaction seems to have little effect on voting behavior or party membership. What effects there are seem to be working at the top of the structure and not among the blue-collar workers. Is this class conflict in the classical sense? Forget it.

TABLE IX

PER CENT GOLDWATER VOTE, BY OCCUPATION, CONTROLLING
FOR CLASS DISSATISFACTION AND
SUBJECTIVE CLASS POSITION

Objective Position	Without Controls	Class Differences are Important	Easy to tell who in what Class	Don't Deserve	Get ahead at Expense	Not Easy to Move	Ambitious Cannot Move	Can't get to know others	Cannot Influence Government	Would Retire Now	Cannot Try Ideas at Work	Subjective Class U-UM	M	LM-W-L
Professional	46	23	33	39	67	41	27	50	63	22	20	44	56	25
Managerial	65	69	71	73	67	64	100	69	71	50	50	90	50	67
Clerical & Sales	35	36	17	45	41	32	0	33	20	29	29	38	30	50
Blue Collar	25	28	11	25	28	9	25	29	38	27	26	17	32	11
	P=.01	P=.02	P=.001	NS	P=.02	P=.02	P=.05	NS	NS	NS	NS	P=.02	NS	P=.05
	(195)	(92)	(78)	(64)	(95)	(69)	(22)	(81)	(36)	(58)	(49)	(56)	(101)	(34)

THE ABSENCE OF COMMUNITY CONFLICT IN THE EARLY PHASES OF NATURAL DISASTERS[*][†]

RUSSELL R. DYNES AND E. L. QUARANTELLI

It is possible to assert that a severe stress situation, such as a natural disaster, creates community conflict or, at the very least, amplifies existing cleavages within the community. Several supporting reasons are often provided for such an assertion. Given the sudden destruction of existing community resources which occurs, competition is assumed to shift toward conflict. The opportunities for the assessment of blame in such situations is seen as leading to scapegoating.[1] The fluidity of the situation which is created is seen as lending itself to opportunism and selfishness.

Such an assertion of conflict and the evidence adduced to support it, however logical, has not proven to be generally true. Community conflict is usually absent in the emergency period following natural disaster, nor are there indications that cleavages which existed prior to the event are amplified during that time period. This has been the observation of the Disaster Research Center at The Ohio State University in its field studies of over seventy different community disasters.[2] Our consistent finding confirms reports of earlier disaster researchers.[3]

The lack of observed community conflict immediately subsequent to a disaster event leads to explaining its absence. We would like to suggest a number of reasons for lack of conflict. While these reasons are specific to communities affected, by disaster events, they also may provide insight into more general and perhaps more "normal" community processes. The following six dimensions seem to minimize conflict in the post-disaster emergency environment.

1. *The precipitating event is outside the community system.* Since disaster comes from outside the community system and the agent can generally be perceived and specified, the event cannot be easily used to amplify existing community conflict. Many other types of community crises are situations where the threats arise within the community or in which it becomes difficult to isolate and to identify the agent involved.[4] Disasters usually provide an external object or physical consequences toward which overt action can be directed. Other crises, however, are often vague, so that action possible in response is not clear. Vague threats generate vague anxieties or aggravate unresolved community conflicts.

2. *A consensus on a hierarchy of values quickly emerges within the community.* The development of an emergency consensus places high priority on the activities

[*] The research on which this article is based was partly supported by PHS Grant 5 R01 MH 15399-02 from the Center for Studies of Mental Health and Social Problems, Applied Research Branch, National Institute of Mental Health. An earlier version of this paper was presented at the 1969 annual meeting of the American Sociological Association in San Francisco, California.

[†] Reprinted by permission of the authors.

[1] Different points of view about this are discussed in Thomas E. Drabek and E. L. Quarantelli, "Blame in Disaster: Another Look, Another Viewpoint," in *Dynamic Social Psychology*, ed. by Dwight Dean (New York: Random House, 1969), pp. 604–618.

[2] For a description of the early work of the Center see Russell R. Dynes, J. Eugene Haas, and E. L. Quarantelli, "Administrative, Methodological and Theoretical Problems of Disaster Research," *Indian Sociological Bulletin* 4 (July 1967): 215–227. See also the January-February 1970 issue of the *American Behavioral Scientist*, which is exclusively devoted to reports of research conducted by the Center.

[3] Charles E. Fritz, "Disaster," in *Contemporary Social Problems: An Introduction to the Sociology of Deviant Behavior and Social Disorganization*, ed. by Robert K. Merton and Robert A. Nisbet (New York: Harcourt Brace Jovanovich, 1961).

[4] There is a discussion of this in Allen H. Barton, *Communities in Disaster: A Sociological Analysis of Collective Stress Situations* (Garden City, N. Y.: Doubleday and Company, 1969). See also James Coleman, *Community Conflict* (New York: Free Press, 1967).

which benefit the "total community" and low priority to segmental "selfish" interests.[5] This contrasts with other community crises, such as civil disturbances, which are manifestations of open conflict between different parties in the locality.[6]

3. *Emergency period problems require immediate and apparent actions.* The problems created by a disaster are immediate and imperative—rescue, debris clearance, etc.—and the actions necessary to solve them are apparent.[7] In most other community problems community members will have different and conflicting definitions of the nature of the problems and of the way they should be solved. In such situations needs often are unfulfilled and "partial" solutions are inadequate. But in disasters needs tend to be so obvious and the immediate solution so compelling that any community action produces an immediate payoff.

4. *Disasters produce a "present" orientation which minimizes previous memories of and future opportunities for conflict.* In normal community life people are preoccupied with the past and the future, as well as with the present. They worry about past conflicts with others and their future ability to meet responsibilities and goals. Disaster, however, provides a temporary liberation from these worries. Worries about the past and the future are unrealistic when judged with the realities of the present. People then concentrate attention on the immediate day-to-day, if not hour-to-hour, needs.[8] During the emergency this perspective tends to speed up the decision-making processes and to provide a degree of satisfaction in acting directly and to see accomplishments quickly.

5. *Disasters reduce status differences.* Existing social distinctions tend to be "minimized" in the emergency period in the sense that all groups and statuses within the community may be indiscriminately affected. Since danger comes from "outside" to affect "all" community members, this produces a temporary breakdown in class, ethnic, and other status distinctions.[9] A general democratization of social life is created by the fact that danger, loss, and suffering became a public phenomenon. In other crises people can point out discriminating injustices. Even in most accidents or life crises the victim often feels discriminated against since there are others who have been spared. And the necessity to explain why a particular person or class of individuals has been singled out for special punishment or suffering can heighten existing community conflict.

6. *Disasters also tend to strengthen community identification.* They do so and hence minimize community conflict by creating (a) a dramatic event in the life history of the community, (b) support to primary groups, and (c) wide opportunity for participation in community relevant activities.

(a) Some people have compared disasters to drama which grips peoples' imaginations, heightens the sense of importance of human action, and facilitates collective identification. This is a valid observation. Such events become important in the collective memories of a community and provide major reference points by which other events become compared and rated.[10] Since a disaster is such a public event, all those who have shared in it are brought together by their common participation in such a dramatic experience.

(b) Disasters tend to strengthen primary group life within the community during the emergency. This has also been observed by others. Fritz, for example, notes that such disorganization as occurs in disasters is dis-

---

[5] This is discussed in Russell R. Dynes, *Organized Behavior in Disaster: Analysis and Conceptualization,* Disaster Research Center Monograph Series (Columbus: Disaster Research Center, The Ohio State University, 1969).

[6] See E. L. Quarantelli and Russell R. Dynes, "Property Norms and Looting: Their Patterns in Community Crises," *Phylon* (in press).

[7] For a case study illustrating this see Daniel Yutzy with William A. Anderson and Russell R. Dynes, *Community Priorities in the Anchorage, Alaska Earthquake, 1964,* Disaster Research Center Monograph Series (Columbus: Disaster Research Center, The Ohio State University, 1969).

[8] This is well illustrated in E. S. Marks *et al.,* "Human Reactions in Disaster Situations," unpublished report, photographed (Chicago: National Opinion Research Center, University of Chicago, 1954).

[9] Fritz, "Disaster," p. 682.

[10] Dynes, Haas, and Quarantelli, "Problems of Disaster Research," p. 215.

ruption of secondary-group life.[11] He observes that a disaster

except momentarily, . . . does not disorganize primary-group life. On the contrary, this is strengthened, and this in turn constitutes the nucleus out of which the society can once again reconstitute itself and develop a new complexity of organization. It should be noted, however, that the primary-group life under disaster is more pristine and more widely based than in ordinary social life. It is not simply a withdrawal into the pre-existing primary groups of family, neighborhood, clique, or friendship; the quality of interaction within these groups and in the entire community of survivors approximates more closely the characteristics of intimate, personal, informal, sympathetic, direct, spontaneous, and sentimental interaction set forth in the concept of the primary group.

Fritz attributes this to the fact that disaster victims are able to confirm that others are basically like themselves.

That people respond in like manner to the fears, dangers, deprivations, and anxieties posed by the disaster, largely regardless of previous station in life, is greatly reassuring—especially for those who have previously felt marginal, detached, isolated, or uncomfortably different from others. The "outsider" becomes an "inside"; the "marginal man" a "central man." People are able to perceive, with a clarity never before possible, a set of underlying basic values to which all people subscribe. They come to see that collective action is necessary for these values to be maintained. Individual and group goals and means become merged inextricably. This merging of individual and societal needs provides a feeling of belongingness and a sense of unity rarely achieved under normal circumstances.

(c) Disasters also provide wide opportunities for participation in activities for the "good" of the community. While initially there is considerable anxiety generated for the welfare of family members, other kin, and relatives, much rescue activity is directed toward those whose tie is that of need and of community membership. After the initial rescue activity, there are subsequent opportunities for participation in organizational activities, either as a volun-

teer or as an organizational member.[12] Such activities are centered on emergency tasks created by the disaster; so many of the elements of community conflict which existed prior to the event are no longer relevant. Prior to the disaster event, day-to-day activities are carried out in conditions of opposing community interests and in situations which often engender hostility, not cooperation.

Participation in disaster activities is also carried out under conditions which give a person great latitude or choice in the determination of what and how certain things should be done. Earlier rules which may be felt as restrictive, previous procedures which encourage routine, as well as standardized situations which encourage repetition, tend to disappear. A person is confronted with a fluid situation where the old rules and procedures do not apply. The premium tends to be on adaptation and innovation. Others with whom the person is involved are faced with similar situations, not different ones, so interests become common rather than conflicting. Too, the efforts of each individual are easy to evaluate, and therefore a person can easily see his own contribution to the "good" of the community. This, in turn, strengthens his own identification with the community. The person has become a contributing member—a person with something to offer who can now show concrete and positive accomplishments.

While such enhancement of community morale has its positive consequences, there is another side of the coin which tends to complicate the community's relationships with "outside" help and with extra-community organizations. The increase in solidarity within the community is accompanied by an increase in hostility toward outsiders. This is true even when they come to give aid. This reduced tolerance has certain distinctive features. First, it does not apply to all who are outsiders in a geographical sense, since in particular situations members of nonlocality based organizations are welcomed. Second, the determination of

---

[11] The following quotations are taken from Fritz, "Disaster," p. 690.

[12] This is well illustrated in Louis Zurcher, "Social-Psychological Functions of Ephemeral Roles: A Volunteer Work Crew in Disaster," *Human Organization* 27 (Winter 1968): 281–297.

"who" is an outsider is not necessarily re-lated to whether the individual is perform-ing a useful function during the emergency period. Personnel from organizations who play critical roles in the emergency period are often the target of direct hostility. In effect, the determination of "who" is an outsider seems to be based primarily on the appearance that they share the sentiments of the insiders. For example, the Salvation Army workers who seem to express sympa-thy and share the "feelings" of local com-munity victims are often considered insiders, while Red Cross workers who maintain a more professional stance are often consid-ered outsiders.[13]

The dimensions just mentioned—external threat, the development of an emergency consensus, the need to respond to immedi-ate problems, a present time orientation, the leveling of social distinctions, the ex-pansion of opportunities to participate, the strengthening of community identity, and the generation of hostility toward outsiders —have been sometimes and partially con-ceptualized in the disaster literature as creating a "therapeutic community."[14] This seems a useful way of thinking about the phenomenon. The process is therapeutic at both the individual and social level in its nature and its effect, in the sense that it

1. tends to resolve and ameliorate pre-existing personal and social conflicts that could endanger the continuity of social life;

2. tends to attenuate or prevent disorgan-izing individual and social responses which could emerge in conditions of danger, loss, and deprivation;

3. tends to reduce or prevent self-aggres-sive and antisocial behavior arising from the losses imposed by the disaster;

4. tends to remotivate individuals within the community system to devote their ener-gies to socially constructive and regenera-tive tasks.

There is another aspect of the function of this "therapeutic" community which is of particular importance in reference to the subsequent pattern of community organiza-

tions. Turner has suggested that some de-gree of consensus on values within a com-munity is necessary in order for an effective division of labor to develop to achieve the tasks created by the impact.[15] Upon impact, the existing division of labor within the community becomes disorganized, since it is ineffective for the new tasks which have been created. But prior to the development of a new and more effective division of labor within the community, agreement on prior-ities has to be achieved. This consensus, then, is necessary for the reestablishment of the division of labor.

Turner has also suggested that the enact-ment of solidarity within the community during the emergency period is necessary since each person in the developing division of labor must neglect other essential tasks in order to perform his own. Consequently, he needs assurance that the neglected tasks will be performed by others. The enactment of solidarity during the emergency period reaffirms for community members the impor-tance of their contribution to the total group effort and, in turn, motivates them to contribute. Thus a period of enactment of community consensus is necessary to recreate the continued assurance of agree-ment on the priority of values. Once this assurance is "given," then a new division of labor can emerge. Until this assurance is "given," the adaptations necessary, in the form of a new and appropriate division of labor, will not be made. In other words, these evidences of solidarity are not just an interesting phenomenon associated with the disaster but a necessary condition for the development of a new division of labor to cope with the new situation.

One final note of caution should be added. The effects of solidarity with a disas-ter impacted community is primarily char-acteristic of the emergency period. Several students have commented on the reemer-gence of conflict at some later time period. Moore, for example, has described a brick-bat phase during the recovery in which old factionalism was awakened and scapegoats

[13] Ellwyn Stoddard, "Some Latent Consequences of Bureaucratic Efficiency in Disaster Relief," *Human Organization* 28 (Fáll 1969): 177–189.

[14] Fritz, "Disaster."

[15] Ralph H. Turner, "Types of Solidarity in the Reconstituting of Groups," *Pacific Sociological Review* 10, No. 2 (Fall 1967): 60–68.

were sought.[16] Others have commented on the emergence of new conflicts which, in some cases, were more severe in their consequences than pre-disaster conflict.[17] Our

own longitudinal studies indicate that some major community divisions can reemerge over time as a consequence of a disaster.[18] However, in general, the evidence points to increased solidarity within the community, and this is most evident during the emergency phase.

[16] Harry E. Moore, *Tornadoes Over Texas: A Study of Waco and San Angelo in Disaster* (Austin: University of Texas, 1958), pp. 315–316.

[17] F. L. Bates, C. W. Fogleman, V. J. Parenton, R. H. Pittman, and G. S. Tracy, *The Social and Psychological Consequences of a Natural Disaster: A Longitudinal Study of Hurricane Audrey* (Washington: National Academy of Sciences, National Research Council, 1963).

[18] See Russell R. Dynes and E. L. Quarantelli, "Community Conflict: Its Presence and Its Absence in Natural Disasters," unpublished paper.

GROUP PROCESS AND SOCIAL INTEGRATION: A SYSTEM ANALYSIS OF TWO MOVEMENTS OF SOCIAL PROTEST*

DANIEL KATZ

Social psychology as the area which lies between individual psychology and the social sciences has in the past been polarized toward psychology. The focus has been upon an understanding of the individual as he functions in social settings with limited investigation of those social settings. The study of small groups has pushed beyond this framework but not very far. Group process is generally examined as personal interaction divorced from social context. In fact, the major advances in social psychology since its gradual emergence as a discipline of its own in the late twenties and early thirties have been the growth of an experimental or laboratory social psychology and the accumulation of findings about the nature of small groups. Both types of contributions have been of such substantial character that social psychologists are no longer marginal men in departments of psychology. Indeed the introductory text in psychology which does not utilize fairly heavily the findings of social psychological research is the exception. And the success of these approaches will reinforce continued work along similar lines with potentially valuable outcomes. Nonetheless, it is my thesis that the significant area for the social psychology of the future lies not in a continuation of these main streams of research directed at the individual and small group isolated from social context. Rather, it lies in a social psychological analysis of social structure and the study of societal process. This is the area which led to the creation of SPSSI when psychologists became concerned with economic justice, industrial conflict, social cleavages based upon economic and racial differentials and war and peace. And it was to these problems which Kenneth Clark

(1965) addressed himself in a discussion of social power just a year ago in his Lewin Memorial talk.

The overriding concern of social psychology with the individual and the small group can be seen in the conventional accounts of its historical development. These accounts trace its origins in the United States to the work of McDougall representing the individual approach of the biological evolutionists and to the work of E. A. Ross reflecting the social interaction doctrines of French sociologists. This is correct but it ignores a persisting though minor stream of influence, namely the theorists concerned with social structure and social change, such as Durkheim, Marx and Weber. The French sociological contributions of Tarde and LeBon which were the basis of Ross' approach were not as much sociological as applications of concepts of French abnormal psychology to social problems. The true societal doctrines coming from Durkheim and Weber were much slower in affecting social psychology and even today are fragmented in their impact. Thus, we have seen the utilization of such concepts as norms and roles, social stratification, anomie, legitimacy, power, norms of reciprocity and interdependence—but generally as fairly isolated concepts.

Societal Process

The social psychology of the future, moreover, can well devote itself to the problems of societal process as well as group process, to the patterning of individuals which make up social structure as well as the cognitive structures of the individual. In the larger sense we have won the fight at the small group level. We know a great deal about how individuals are tied into the small group through processes of

* Reprinted by permission of the author and publisher from *Journal of Social Issues*, 1967, 23: 3–22.

participation, of socio-metric attraction, of mutual social reinforcement, of shared objectives. This has been the thrust of the group dynamics movement for the past twenty-five years. The work of the Tavistock researchers has demonstrated, moreover, that some of the individual processes of participation in a meaningful work cycle hold for the small group as well as for the personality under given conditions (Rice, 1958; Trist, 1963), a finding foreshadowed by the earlier work of Lewis and Franklin (1944) and Horwitz (1954) on the group Zeigarnik and more recently extended to the level of aspiration concept by Zander and Medow (1963). Much of course remains to be done in mopping up operations at the small group level and even more in applying these findings in many appropriate group settings. But there has been little major advance in the work on group process in recent years save for the move toward its use in therapeutic fashion for working through problems of defensive reactions of group members toward one another.

The major problems we face, however, need new approaches, new concepts and new research. We have too long neglected the nature of social systems and the dynamics of their functioning. We have made little progress in studying the role relationships which constitute social systems and with the relationships of subgroups to the larger societal framework. We have been remiss in applying ourselves to an understanding of social movements and conflicts between organized groups. The general reason given is that these problems belong to the other social sciences. But since social systems exist only as patterns of human behavior, they are an appropriate field of study for social psychologists. Artifacts or products of a society can be studied at a superorganic level, but the actual production of such artifacts in the complex actions of people can be studied at the social psychological level. Our constructs for such a study need to be social system concepts so that we are directed toward the relevant aspects of collective and reciprocal behaviors. The variables to be observed and measured are still psychological. The concep-

tualizations we use, however, should be such as to guide us to the appropriate interdependent behavior. Otherwise we are likely to employ a direct and misleading equivalent of a group outcome in searching for individual patterns of belief and action. Wars are made in the minds of men but this statement can be deceptive if it equates the declaration or prosecution of a war with the aggressive impulses of the members of the warring nation. The nation is not an aggregate of similarly-minded aggressive individuals acting in parallel but a complex organization of many criss-crossing cycles of social behavior (Allport, 1962).

Two Movements of Social Protest

Let us look at two movements of social protest in our society as examples of the relevance of social structure and system forces for an understanding of social phenomena—the civil rights movement and the protests against the war in Vietnam. From the conventional approach of individual psychology, they seem very similar. They have both been led by much the same type of people, largely those outside the basic power structure of the society: small groups of student activists, part of the academic and intellectual world, some Church groups and some members of the Negro community. The power groups of industry and business, organized labor and the organizations representing the professions of law, medicine and education have not been conspicuously arrayed in support of either of these movements. In addition to the overlapping personnel and overlapping group membership behind the two trends, there has been a similarity in their dedication to values of egalitarianism, humanitarianism, democracy and nonviolence. They are alike in their appeals to the American public and in their tactics for achieving their objectives.

They have one other major similarity which is more at the system than at the individual level. They both have the advantage that the values which justify their thrust are part of the value system of the larger society. In other words, they have legitimacy in the broader sense of the term in that they are sanctioned by the accepted ideology of society. The opposition in contrast has had great difficulty in finding a rationale to justify its position. The doctrine of racism furnishes little support for the opposition to Civil Rights in a political democracy of a multiethnic character recently involved in an all-out war against Nazi Germany. Such a racist ideology appeals only to very limited sectors of the society. The legal doctrine of interposition in its absurd legalism was merely a delaying tactic. The plea for nongovernment intervention on issues of civil rights makes little sense in a bureaucratic society committed to legislation as a means of solving problems. In brief, the discriminatory practices of our society had going for them some local laws, much internalized prejudice and specific economic advantage to certain subgroups, but no ideological legitimacy. In passing, it might be mentioned that there are those who see some danger in the slogan of black power in that it opens an ideological door to the rightists which had been slammed shut in their faces.

In similar fashion the protestors against the Vietnam war had the legitimizing values of the society on their side. Democracy demands the right of self determination of small as well as large nations. It does not justify the intervention of large powers in small nations merely because of their power. Our societal values are not consistent with the support of a military junta whose leaders fought on the side of the French rather than their own people in expelling colonial rule. Nor do they countenance the killing and wounding of women and children in an undeclared war. The United States, as Kenneth Boulding has commented, has all the advantages in the conflict in economic might, technological strength, military weapons and fire power, everything in short but legitimacy. This is one reason why American intervention in Vietnam has been so unpopular abroad even among our allies and so unenthusiastically received at home. There is, of course, the ideological justification of combatting communism but why communism has to be combatted in this particular way has not been clear either to American or to world opinion. The legiti-

macy for the conflict that does exist is more at the pragmatic level growing out of the dynamics of the conflict itself.

I have distinguished between legitimizing values at the societal level as a system force as against the individual values of the members of a protest movement. Individual values are internalized in the personality. System ideology is the set of values accepted as appropriate general guides for the behavior of members of the system. These values may or may not be internalized by a majority of system members and certainly are not internalized in their entirety. When a social system collapses, its ideology often collapses which would not be true if there were a one-to-one correspondence between personal and system values.

System Level Differences

Though the Civil Rights movement and the antiwar cause resemble one another in personnel, in individual motivation, in group tactics and in the system values utilized, the similarities of the two movements pretty well ends there. Their differences at the system level are great. The Civil Rights movement is basically consistent with the forces in our societal structure and is moving in the same direction as these forces. The antiwar movement opposes some of the dominant trends in the national system. Though the same individual motivations and sometimes the same individuals are found in the two movements, their progress and their effectiveness are radically different. It is necessary, then to consider the nature of the social system which affect these outcomes.

American society is basically an organizational, or bureaucratic, technological society in which role systems based upon rules and functional requirements have replaced traditional authority and absolutistic standards. Three characteristics of bureaucratic structure are relevant to our discussion: its growth or maximization dynamic, its conflict-reducing mechanisms to achieve an integrated system and the functional nature of its legitimizing values.

The dynamic of a bureaucratic system, once it is established, is to maximize its input-output ratio of energy to place it in a more powerful position with respect to other systems and to its environment (Yuchtman, 1966). It will ingest resources outside its boundaries, it will seek to control its external environment, it will grow until checked by outside forces (Katz and Kahn, 1966). With all our attempts to control monopolistic growth, our industrial enterprises have grown bigger and bigger. With all out talk about curbing the size of the federal government, its payroll and its activities, it continues to grow in size and in function. It is much more difficult in a bureaucratic structure to eliminate a subsystem once established than to add two new ones.

The dynamic of maximization is related to the second characteristic of bureaucratic systems, the development of mechanisms for reducing internal conflict. Cleavages within the system impair its effectiveness in competition with other systems. Conflicts about interests, privileges and ideas are met basically by compromises and mutual concessions and by not permitting all of the dissident voices representation in decision making. The general pattern for conflict reduction is the narrowing of channels for their expression so that many divergent views are reconciled or silenced at lower levels in the structure. A small unit has to resolve differences among members so that it speaks with one voice in its own subsystem and not with a multitude of opinions. Within the subsystem the unit differences have to be compromised so that the subsystem represents but one position to the higher levels in the structure. This pattern means that many conflicts are handled at lower levels. Though the final position of a large subsystem has the power of the entire subsystem behind it, this position is already a compromise of generalities which has blunted the sharpness of the conflicting interests and factions. The example par excellence of this pattern is the two-party system. By the time the wishes of the many interest and factional groups have been filtered up through the hierarchical structure, the party line is not far from dead center. The many competing groups are not represented directly and formally in the

Congress, the top decision-making political body. Many conflicts have thus been compromised and Congress has an easier task of reaching decisions. A multi-party system with proportional representation, on the other hand, gives more adequate representation to divergent interest and ideological factions but it has the disadvantage of making it more difficult to achieve national unity (Valen and Katz, 1964). The general trend in bureaucratic structures is toward the pattern achieved by the two-party system in getting agreement at various levels so that many sharp conflicts are absorbed along the line.

Restricted Communication—A Necessity

Ashby (1952) in his brilliant system analysis gives some of the reasons why this is so. Stability of the system would take infinitely long to achieve if all the elements in the system were in full contact and communication. All the variables of all the subsystems would have to be satisfied at once— a highly unlikely event. If, however, communication is restricted among subsystems, or they are temporarily isolated, then each subsystem can achieve its own stability. With restricted communication, success can accumulate from successive trials whereas in the single suprasystem success is all-or-none. An overall system can move toward equilibrium through sufficient connectedness of its subsystems so that the operation of one can activate another and enough separation so that each can reach agreement within itself. Equilibrium can be approached in the system as a whole, but no complex suprasystem would ever have equilibrium in all its subsystems at the same time.

To the general Ashby description of subsystem and suprasystem we should add the concept of hierarchical levels. The need to reach some agreement at each succeeding level further structures and restricts the full interplay of communication and conflicting forces.

One reason why group process is inadequate for the study of social systems is that it deals with genuine group consensus through group discussion and decision-making. This can only be realistically applied at the very lowest level in social structures, for the moment the decision of the local group is carried by its representatives to a higher level, we are dealing with a political process of compromise and majority rule. At the next higher level, the representatives are no longer free to work through to a full agreement as individuals. They are role representatives of their local groups as well as members of the higher group in the structure. They must take back something to their constituents and hence they bargain and trade and finally reach some compromise rather than the integrated solution of group process. The dynamics differ from small group process and the outcomes differ.

Bureaucratic System—A Process of Progressive Agreement

In brief, the bureaucratic system handles conflict by a process of progressive agreement among subunits at each level of the structure. Many dissident voices are lost long before the final decision-making circles are reached. The structure is built to accommodate conflict, to mute its expression and to redefine clashing positions on clear-cut issues as moderate stands on ambiguous generalities.

There are also more direct mechanisms of repression as in the denial of the franchise to certain groups or the use of complex machinery to make difficult the participation of many people even at the local level.

Another device for slowing down change within a bureaucratic system comes from the character of the managerial and administrative roles. These roles are built around procedures for getting things done and not around the analysis of substantive issues. The administrator's major task is to keep things moving, to seek enough compromise to prevent the machinery from breaking down, in short to be an expert on procedure not on content. Thus the head of the poverty program was selected because of his administrative skills not because of his understanding of the poverty problem. In his administrative role the official takes his cues about general policy from those above him

in the structure. Basic changes in the system, however, require issue-oriented rather than procedure-oriented managers, i.e. men with genuine knowledge and understanding of the change objectives.

A third characteristic of bureaucratic structures is the functional nature of their legitimizing values. The system is unified not only through devices for handling internal conflict but also through the values which reflect the functional interdependence of the people in the system. These values, moreover, do not represent transcendental principles based upon divine revelation or an absolutistic morality. They have to relate to the functioning of the system to supply both cognitive structure and ideological justification for its activities. The essential justification for the assumption of roles is not that the role itself is morally correct, but that it is necessary for the operation of the system.

The process of building a social structure begins in early socialization and it takes on specification with adult socialization into given social systems. Individuals begin early to learn that family, school and social groupings all have expectations, rewards and sanctions for many specific roles in which the justification of the required behavior is not necessarily carried by the nature of the activity itself. There is a divorce from the meaning of the activities as desirable in and of themselves, and the goals which they are expected to accomplish. To be a good group member means that the individual accepts his role assignments as part of the rules of the game.

The justification for the assumption of roles lies in the rewards to the individual for being a member of the system. The system values then must be capable of translation into pragmatic programs. This is further emphasized by the technological character of our organizational society in which the criterion is constantly employed: Does it work? Finally, this system has the congruent property of a democratic ideology. Since people are required to assume many roles, since they are to be interchangeable for many purposes save where there is a high degree of specificity for an important role, their essential equality with respect to system demands and opportunities for participation becomes important. To utilize manpower resources effectively implies that surplus meanings of such characteristics as ethnic group membership, sex or hair color are irrelevant. And, as we move away from transcendental and traditional principles as the source of morality, an egalitarian democratic philosophy geared to the privileges and rights of all individuals becomes the common ground for the commitment of all citizens to their society.

The Civil Rights Movement—Extending Preexisting Trends

To return, then, to a consideration of the two liberal movements, I would call attention to some of the system forces which have been working to accord a different reception to the Civil Rights issue than to the antiwar cause. The racial cleavage in our society, deepened by economic stratification, has been under attack by liberals for more than a century. But it was not until World War II that the problem of racial integration was seriously considered in the perspective of national unity. Negroes were needed in defense industry, in governmental services and in the armed forces. It was no accident that some of the first moves toward integration were made in the armed forces and, moreover, in combat units at the front. And at home wartime agencies were directed to give employment to all qualified personnel. Shortly after the war President Truman issued the order authorizing integration throughout the armed forces. The realization grew, moreover, that in a world where the majority of the people were nonwhite and where millions of people in the areas uncommitted in the conflict between the United States and Russia were nonwhite, assigning third-class citizenship to American Negroes was not a wise policy. Nor was it a wise policy in an economy with little need for unskilled labor to deprive citizens of education and training for the economic needs of the nation.

Against this background, the Civil Rights movement utilized two other system forces

to achieve some of its initial successes. It obtained legitimacy in the narrow sense of legal sanctions by pushing for new interpretations and enforcement of existing laws of the land. The discriminatory practices of generations were clearly inconsistent with the legal basis of our political system. The precedent had been set by President Truman in his executive order making discrimination in the armed services illegal. Mention already has been made of the larger legitimacy of the movement in gearing into the values of a democratic society. The economics of the system in effectively using its manpower was thus not the sole cause of the changes brought about, but when economics, law and ideology are all on the same side, something is going to give.

Why, then, has the Negro revolution been so slow in achieving its objectives if the changes involved are so consistent with the general trends in the national system? The reason is that in addition to change forces pushing the system to maximizing its character there are also built-in maintenance forces representative of the older equilibrium. There are defenses in depth which slow down the change process. Subsystems with some power of their own operate in any large structure and can be resistant for limited periods to changes initiated in other parts of the system. We had an interesting example of the problem of change and the steady state of a system last semester when Selective Service put into effect the old device of draft deferment based upon standing in college or in national tests. This policy hit those groups with poorest academic preparation the hardest and can nullify the moves to open up channels for the training of Negroes for professional positions.

In other words, the overall system is not a single homogeneous structure. Subsystems exist such that political democracy does not have a corresponding parallel in economic structures with full equality of opportunity. The political system has been more open to change with the greatest advances occurring in this domain with the enfranchisement of Negroes and growing acquisition of equal legal rights. In the economic and social sectors, however, the built-in defenses in depth have been much more resistant to change.

Mechanisms for Dealing with Internal Conflict

More specifically, however, we need to take account of the mechanisms of a bureaucratic society for dealing with internal conflict. The most common devices are those of compromise and of indirect ways of meeting the conflict. Compromise has been conspicuous as in the gradualism doctrine, in the concessions made by nationwide employers, and in the agreements reached at the community level. The difficulty with the compromise technique is that its outcome is partially dependent upon the power of the bargaining group. This method places a premium upon the mobilization of threat of economic and political sanctions. As the integration movement has mobilized power to exact concessions, it has had considerable success but progress has not been great. The majority group still has the power of superior numbers, superior resources and an entrenched position in the social hierarchy. Moreover, if the struggle is confined to mobilization of black power rather than generalized to embrace broad values, it produces repercussions in certain sectors of the white population. Nevertheless, such power mobilization is an important if not the most important means for continuing progress with respect to civil rights.

The common mechanism for reducing conflict is the attenuation of its representation in decision-making centers. In a two-party system the Negroes are limited in their influence to the old A. F. of L. technique of rewarding friends and punishing enemies and generally this has to be done within a single party structure. The attempt to secure direct representation through a party of their own in Mississippi achieved some purposes but not the avowed objective. The system is so set up as to accommodate minority groups without integrating them. There were no institutional channels through which the Civil Rights movement could directly affect decision-making circles, apart from the judicial system. Thus they have taken to the streets and to demonstrations as well as to the use of economic boycotts and voter registration drives. The effectiveness of these tactics has been in part a matter of the power mobilized and in part a matter of making visible to important sectors of the American public the unjustified practices of discrimination.

Another way of damping the fire of an underprivileged group is through the many established blocks to their rise in the various power and prestige structures. Negroes have been successful in law and medicine but more within their own community than within the larger society. They have achieved some break-throughs in the political system. In the world of finance and industry, however, there has been less progress. They have lacked the training, the resources for commiting themselves to such careers, the social background, and the personal associations necessary to move into the economic sector in leadership roles.

Integration has been achieved at the political level so that great advances have been made in the citizenship rights of voting and equality before the law. Opportunities for schooling have been opened up in law though not always in practice. One would predict in terms of system forces that the greatest progress will continue to be in the political domain with full enfranchisement of Negro citizens, with equal legal rights, with equal access to public institutions and with increasing numbers of Negroes achieving positions of importance in the political structure. Where discrimination is reinforced by economic stratification, change will be much slower. Relative to past economic standards there will be improvement but relative to the rising standards of the white population, the improvement will not seem significant. The general economic upgrading of the national population has been proceeding rapidly and the person just entering the race may have great difficulty catching up to the accelerated pace.

In brief, then, the Civil Rights movement has achieved much as it has interacted with other system forces, received their support and helped to give them more adequate definition. It has not revolutionized the social system but has pushed it toward greater consistency. The threatened revolution has been contained within the system.

The Protest Movement—Opposing Preexisting Trends

The protest movement against the Vietnam war and the peace movement in general have the major difficulty of opposing some of the dynamic trends in the national system. The maximization dynamic is expressed in the extension of national interests and national power. There is the push to utilize our influence and power, for as we are now reminded, we have to assume our responsibilities in the world. Moreover, the major forces which challenge our international position come from the expansion of communism. And the assumption is that it is better to meet this challenge at distant points from our own shores which means protecting weaker nations less capable of resisting than the U.S.

Secretary of State Dean Rusk has acknowledged our military commitments to 40 nations around the globe. He denied that this represented a policy of *pax Americana* but there are those who interpreted this as diplomatic language. Such language needs to be understood in the context in which it appears. Since World War II we have been engaged in a continuing process of extending our psychological boundaries beyond our geographical borders. Conflicts with other expanding systems are bound to occur. These conflicts do not inevitably mean war but the immediate past suggests that we need to do more to take advantage of the degrees of freedom, to seek counter forces in the social situation, for the maintenance of world peace.

The facts are that Vietnam is only one instance of the collisions between the U.S. and other nations in Asia. Before Vietnam there was Laos; before Laos, Korea. After South Vietnam, there may be North Vietnam, Laos, Cambodia, Korea, and even China. In addition to our fighting forces in Vietnam, we have military bases in other parts of east Asia. The other day the press reported that we now have 27,000 troops in Thailand and are presently expanding our four military bases there by a new complex costing almost $100,000,000. Nor does the present conflict seem to be a function of the warlike personalities of our national leaders. Recall that in 1964 the American people chose between two slates of candidates, the trigger-happy Goldwater and his equally belligerent running-mate, Miller, and the consensus-seeking Johnson and the liberal Humphrey. Remember, too, it was supposed to be a choice not an echo. I am contending, then, that the decisions in national leadership roles are in good measure determined by system forces and that the conventional interpretation of these requirements in the Asian situation was an escalation of warlike measures. I am also arguing that such decisions were not inevitable and that there was enough range of interpretation of the situation and of appropriate national policy, for an *unusual* national leadership to have followed a different course. National interests, national prestige, national honor as well as the struggle against communism could have been defined in other ways. Though the dice were loaded, the players could have discarded them.

National Leaders—What Degree of Freedom?

The degree of freedom of movement for national leaders is greater at an early stage in international relations. Once, however, the decisions are made to utilize the military power of the nation, then it is extremely difficult at later stages to reverse the policy. At the early stage the problem is one of progressive commitment, i.e., what look like small steps in the beginning become binding decisions for more complete involvement. The decision to furnish aid to an anti-Communist government, the use of American military as advisers rather than as participants, the partial involvement of limited forces, and then greater and greater escalation were not necessarily thought through in advance as the desirable policy. One step led to another. To break out of this pattern of progressive commitment requires unusual qualities of statesmanship at the national level. The present and the preceding three administrations were all involved in this pattern though there are indications that the Kennedy administration if it had continued might have been more resourceful in arresting the trend. A statesmanlike leadership would have to rise above some of the relevant central subsystems in the national structure specifically the Department of State, the CIA, the Defense Department, the National Security Council and the Joint Chiefs of Staff. These subgroupings concerned with problems of national interest, prestige and power develop narrow conceptions of their goals and the means for achieving them. There are doves as well as hawks in these groups but the system tends to select more hawks than doves and to damp dovelike voices. Moreover, these agencies are already locked into a limited set of strategy alternatives dictated in part by their own responses to the moves of the international opponent and the subsequent reactions of the opposition.

The protest movement against our involvement in Vietnam was not effective in influencing the policy of the Administration as it moved from one critical decision to another. The protestors lacked organized power. The academic community did not speak with a single voice. Moreover, the voices were those of individuals not of organized groups of strength. There were no easily identifiable blocks of voters like Negroes or labor union members to support the movement. The pacifist organizations were courageous but tiny. The members of Congress who furnished the one source of leverage and who gave additional legitimacy to the movement received little support from the mass media. They were not able to contend with the strong executive-legislative combination of forces arrayed against them. Nor was there a peace lobby in Washington to compete with the lobbies representing business and industry interested in defense expenditures.

Once embarked upon the policy of military intervention and limited escalation, the system forces are even stronger in resisting a change toward peaceful alternatives. Even without a formal declaration of war, the use of American armed forces and the resulting casualty lists produce a situation in which the national membership character of the people becomes salient. The nation state becomes more than ever the dominant social structure. The state is the formal organized system to which all other structures are legally subservient. It functions as the final arbiter of decisions within the society when conflicts cannot be resolved at other levels. It has a monopoly on physical force for implementing these decisions.

The Arousal of National Roles

This is the formal description at the level of political science. What does it mean psychologically? It means that when national roles are aroused they take precedence over any other social role the individual can play as a member of his family, his church, his profession, his work organization, etc. National sovereignty also means that every organized group in the society must function as an arm of the state in times of national emergency if so ordered. This is most obvious when industries are nationalized in wartime but there are less thorough manifestations as when organizations cooperate with the government in not employing citizens whose loyalty is under suspicion. In times of peace, national roles are latent roles so that the average citizen spends most of his time in activities of making a living, being a member of his family, engaging in leisure time activities, etc. Apart from observing laws and voting, he gives little time or thought to his citizenship rights and obligations. The national state and his membership as an American citizen are remote considerations. But when the emergency of possible war or actual international conflict arises, national roles take priority over other roles. The basic institutional pattern that has been built into the members of the society through the socialization process and which has indirectly mediated the relationship of their activities to need satisfaction, now takes over. As a member of the national system the individual must either assume his national roles or leave the system. And there are no places to go save prison or exile.

Even an undeclared war provides the conditions for the arousal of national roles. One aspect of such arousal is the restriction of freedom of movement at all levels in the structure. Other roles are no longer open choices. And the definition of the national role assumes clearer structure with the decisions of national leaders. These leaders themselves lose freedom of movement. Not only are they committed by their previous decisions in their own eyes, but these decisions have activated expectations throughout the structure which further lock them into a given pattern of behavior. And, as leaders guiding the nation in an international conflict, they are more vulnerable to criticism from their political opponents if they do not play their roles in a militant manner ostensibly supportive of national interest. Freedom of movement is also reduced for groups and individuals with respect to actions and words opposing national policy. People not happy about the war and its escalation now take the position that we should get it over with in some fashion rather than complete withdrawal. The function of public opinion in affecting national policy becomes weak and negligible.

The solution to the war in Asia of a complete withdrawal of our armed forces, though logical, is unrealistic. It neglects not only the dynamics of the arousal of national roles but also the expansionist push of the American power system in Asia. We have established military bases in Asian countries other than Vietnam and have committed ourselves to fighting the spread of communism on the Asian continent. The pattern of commitment is not the same, however, for the administration and for the American people. The objectives of the administration go beyond the successful prosecution of the undeclared war. If it were to be won, or if some favorable peace could be negotiated, the conflict could readily flare up again either in Thailand, Laos or Cambodia. The American people, however, at the present time would be satisfied with the settlement of the Vietnam war.

Discouraging as the prospects are for a peaceful settlement in Vietnam and for a permanent peace in Asia, there are factors which conceivably can work toward international stability in this part of the world. For one thing, the American people after Korea and after Vietnam may be more reluctant to support further military intervention so far from our shores. Consistent with the interpretation is the fact that the motivational basis for national involvement has seen some change in the development of our bureaucratic society during the past forty years.

Symbolic, Normative or Instrumental Involvement

Individuals can be tied into a bureaucratic system in one of three ways or some combination of them: symbolic, normative, or instrumental involvement (Katz, 1965). Symbolic attachment refers to emotionally held attitudes in which the symbols represent absolute values and have a life of their own. They are not the means to an end but are ends in themselves. Emotional conditioning in childhood to symbols of the nation such as the flag, the national anthem or national heroes are one basis for symbolic commitment. Normative involvement on the other hand does not imply internationalization of the sanctity of given symbols but rather the acceptance of specific legitimate requirements of the system necessary for system membership. Thus one meets the demands of one's role because he wants to stay in the system not because he is emotionally attached to signs representing its abstract values. Finally, functional involvement has to do with commitment to the system because its demands are instrumental to his needs. The union member may be committed to his union because it is a group means for dealing with his needs. Such a functional attachment is not limited to bread-and-butter matters. It can also be related to his own values which find meaningful realization in group action which advance his beliefs and attitudes. I am thus trying to differentiate between an ideological commitment of a functional character where values get translated into specific programs of action as against symbolic attachment to nonoperational goals.

In the Vietnam war the man who enlists because his heart quickens at the sight of the flag shows symbolic commitment. The man who accepts his call to the service primarily because this is the requirement for the American male of certain ages is demonstrating normative commitment. The underprivileged youth who sees in armed service a way of getting an education and technical training is an example of functional commitment. So, too, would be the man who enters the service because he feels that democratic values are threatened by communism in Asia and armed intervention is necessary to prevent a communist takeover.

With the development of a bureaucratic society there has been a relative decline in symbolic commitment to national roles and a rise in normative and functional commitment. The great majority of the men in our armed forces are there not so much because of the considerations of national honor as because they received the notice from their draft boards. Bureaucratic society, emphasizing as it does the authority of rules rather than of tradition, is carried much more by role readiness and functional interdependence than by the internalization of emotional symbols. This is a relative matter, moreover, and suggests a different emphasis in the mix of motivational patterns in the history of our nation (Katz, Kelman & Flacks, 1963).

An Implication: More Freedom of Action

What are the implications of this analysis if we still find ourselves in war? What difference does it make if men carry out their military obligations on a different motivational basis than in World War I, as long as the end result is the same? I believe it does make a difference for these reasons: With greater functional and normative involvement there is more freedom of action than with symbolic commitment. Functional and normative nationalism can lead to other than military paths to objectives. It can lead to international negotiation and cooperation in situations in which symbolic patriotism would demand war.

National leaders often operate as if symbolic commitment were still the dominant way in which people were tied to the nation. Thus they sometimes perceive less freedom for action than they really have. They may assume that a conciliatory series of moves will mean political suicide because people will feel that national honor and interests are imperiled. The political opposition can be depended upon to try to arouse patriotic sentiments to discredit such soft policies. Though there are people who still are readily moved by slogan appeals of a superpatriotic character, they are not as numerous or as powerful as is often assumed. Both public opinion polls and election returns show that flag waving by those out of office does not necessarily defeat the incumbent.

Eighty-Eight Per Cent of Population for Negotiation

In late February and early March of this year Sidney Verba and a group of social scientists at Stanford University in cooperation with the National Opinion Research Center conducted a nation-wide survey on opinions toward the war in Vietnam (1966). This survey differed from the Gallup Poll in that it dug more deeply into the complex of attitudes toward the war. Its major findings indicated that people have very mixed feelings about the war and that there is more of a potential in American public opinion for *deescalation* than for *escalation*. In the first place, there are very few real hawks or doves. Only six per cent of the national sample take consistent positions in favor of escalation and opposed to deescalation. Fourteen per cent are consistent doves. In the second place, the great majority (some 88%) are willing to negotiate with the Vietcong and would support (some 70%) a UN-negotiated truce in Vietnam. "A 52 per cent majority would be willing to see the Vietcong assume a role in a South Vietnam coalition government and a 54 per cent majority favor holding free elections in South Vietnam, even if the Vietcong might win". In the third place, "the majority of American citizens have reservations about continuing the war when faced with its possible costs. The study asked whether people wanted to continue fighting in Vietnam if it meant cutting back various Great Society programs (such as aid to education and medicare), increasing taxes, and imposing economic controls. On every count majorities were registered in opposition".

Though 60 per cent would continue the war if it required calling up the National Guard, only 40 per cent would want to continue if it meant full-scale mobilization. And only 38 per cent would be in favor of a continuation of the conflict if it meant that several hundred American soldiers would be killed each week. Though the people are evenly divided about having a half a million troops in South Vietnam, a majority oppose steps of escalation such as bombing the cities of North Vietnam, fighting a ground war in China, or the use of atomic weapons. Finally, in spite of press reports, it is not true that the opposition to President Johnson on the war comes mainly from those who are in favor of a more vigorous prosecution of the conflict. The opposition is 2 to 1 from the other side; those who favor deescalation.

It is true, however, that 81 per cent of the people would disapprove of an immediate withdrawal of American troops if the Communists were to take over.

Vietnam—A Functional Commitment

I have cited these findings at some length because they come from the most thorough study we have had of American public reaction to the war. Moreover, they indicate that there is more freedom for our political leaders to follow other alternatives than escalation of the conflict than political leaders themselves seem to assume. People are concerned about winning the war in Vietnam but they are against continuing the war if it means genuine sacrifice. Thus their commitment is more functional than symbolic, in that a symbolic commitment calls for pursuance of policy no matter what the cost. Symbolic commitment in its absolutistic character emphasizes national sovereignty and opposes internationalism.

Functional involvement finds no difficulty in accepting an international arrangement consistent with broadly defined national goals. In a recent Michigan study we found that the functionally committed person wanted to strengthen the UN, the symbolically wanted to withdraw from it; the functionally committed were willing to abide by decisions of the World Court, the symbolically committed were not, and in general the symbolically committed favored a more aggressive stance toward communist countries than did the functionally involved.

The European community was achieved not because nations gave up their identity but because they had a functional basis to their nationalism (Haas, 1958). DeGaulle with his symbolic attachment has set back the clock with respect to furthering European integration.

Clear recognition by national leaders of the functional involvement of the American in the national structure and an application of the same logic would call for a realistic assessment of the gains and costs for alternative strategies in southeast Asia. The U.S. has the weapons and the manpower to conquer South Vietnam and for that matter, North Vietnam. The costs, however, would be huge in the death and devastation visited upon the civilians in those countries, in American lives, in the diversion of funds from the building of the Great Society at home. The extension of the war to North Vietnam and the destruction of that country, moreover, brings us perilously close to the next step, the use of atomic weapons. Even if all of Vietnam were conquered, the price of holding it would be high. It would require economic rehabilitation of both countries and a continuing large force of American troops to resist communist infiltration from the surrounding areas. Moreover, the objective of defeating Communism would not necessarily be achieved. To many of the uncommitted people in Asian countries, the escalation of the war would seem to them to validate the communist claims about the nature of American imperialistic might. We are judged not by our final objectives but by means we use to achieve them. The means are the visible proof in the opinion of other countries of what we are trying to do, rather than some idealized statement of what we assert is our objective. Finally, the basic answer to the spread of communism lies only partially in superior fire power. It also lies in superior ideology as that ideology can be implemented in securing a better way of life for the masses of people.

To Reverse the Spiral of Escalation . . .

Alternatives to our present policy in Vietnam must be considered in terms of a realistic step which would move toward deescalation of the war. The spiral of escalation is difficult but not impossible to reverse. In international conflict it receives two positive types of feedback: one from the counter-moves of the opponent, the other the internal feedback from the aroused nationalism of the people. Both cycles of feedback interact. But the aroused nationalism of the American people about the Vietnam war has not reached the proportions of intensity which means we have passed the point of no return. The majority of people would welcome a cessation or reduction of the war even if it did not mean the unconditional surrender of the Vietcong and the North Vietnamese. The external cycle is more difficult to predict but since the limited period of the cessation of bombing we have not experimented with specific moves of deescalation. We have increasingly seen the conflict in purely military terms.

I have given considerable emphasis to the role of national leadership and some of the factors affecting decision making at high levels. Another structural aspect of this concerns the information and ideas which the system furnishes for decision making. Here the nation suffers from the lack of an adaptive subsystem concerning foreign policy which would have the functions of research and intelligence to provide an accurate assessment of the world situation, an analysis of the effects of our policies, and a thoughtful consideration of alternative strategies. For the internal economy we have moved in the direction of such a subsystem with the President's Council of Economic Advisers. In the international field, however, we rely upon the State Department and the CIA which are action rather than intelligence agencies. From the point of view of furnishing information and ideas, these agencies are redundant systems. They operate to filter out new information and new ideas. They are closed information loops which receive and process the answers predetermined by their limited questions and their restricted coding sets. They operate in such fashion as to maintain rather than break out of the locked-in patterns of past strategy (Schlesinger, 1965). Exceptional presidents in the past have been able to by-pass these conventional structures in the determination of foreign policy. What is required as a reliable basis for system functioning in international relations is some governmental restructuring to provide an adequate adaptive subsystem available to national leadership. National decision making, then, would not be imprisoned by its own closed information circuits, would not have to repeat past errors, and could consider alternatives to atomic destruction. The apparent success of brinksmanship in the past is a poor guide for the future. Time has a way of running out on us as individuals. It can also run out for social systems.

REFERENCES

Allport, F. H. A structuronomic conception of behavior: individual and collective. *Journal of Abnormal and Social Psychology*, 1962, 64, 3–30.

Ashby, W. R. *Design for a brain*. New York: Wiley, 1952.

Clark, K. Problems of social power and social change. *Journal of Social Issues*, 1965, 21, 4–20.

Haas, E. B. *The uniting of Europe*. Stanford: Stanford University Press, 1958.

Horwitz, M. The recall of interrupted group tasks. *Human Relations*, 1954, 7, 3–38.

Katz, D. Nationalism and strategies of international conflict resolution. In H. C. Kelman (Ed.), *International Behavior*. New York: Holt, Rinehart & Winston, 1965, 354–390.

Katz, D., Kelman, H., and Flacks, R. The national role: some hypotheses about the relation of individuals to nation in America today. Peace Research Society, *Papers I*, Chicago Conference, 1963.

Katz, D., and Kahn, R. L. *The social psychology of organizations*. New York: Wiley, 1966.

Lewis, H. B. and Franklin, M. An experimental study of the ego in work. *Journal of Experimental Psychology*, 1944, 34, 195–215.

Rice, A. K. *Productivity and social organization.* London: Tavistock Publications, 1958.

Schlesinger, A. M., Jr. *A thousand days.* Boston: Houghton, Mifflin, 1965.

Trist, E. L., Higgin, C. W., Murray, H., and Pollock, A. B. *Organizational choice.* London: Tavistock Publications, 1963.

Valen, H. and Katz, D. *Political Parties in Norway.* London: Tavistock Publications, 1964.

Verba, S., et al. Public opinion and the war in Vietnam. 1966. (mimeo).

Yuchtman, E. The study of organizational effectiveness. Unpublished doctoral dissertation, University of Michigan, 1966.

Zander, A. and Medow, H. Individual and group levels of aspiration. *Human Relations*, 1963, 16, 89–105.

THE REDUCTION OF INTERGROUP HOSTILITY: RESEARCH PROBLEMS AND HYPOTHESES*

IRVING L. JANIS and DANIEL KATZ

It is a startling fact that almost the last area to be investigated empirically by the social sciences is the area of the constructive forces in human nature and society which make for the reduction of intergroup conflict. Research attention has focused upon the destructive tendencies in human conduct—upon antisocial action, hostility, distorted perceptions, irrational fears, authoritarian personality structure, and a wide variety of psychopathological disorders. Concern with positive forces has not reached the point of stimulating systematic investigation, perhaps because of the antinormative position of present-day scientists, most of whom feel inclined to leave such matters to philosophers and social reformers. Yet an adequate social science must study the social norms and ethical principles by which men live.

Naess (1958) has suggested that an analysis of ethical principles with respect to the psychological processes they implicate and the social conditions which maximize their effectiveness may be the most important next step for social science, from the point of view both of improving its theoretical adequacy and of contributing to the problem of social survival. His systematization of the ethical code of Mahatma Gandhi includes an explicit statement of testable hypotheses. Most of these hypotheses take the form of predicting that certain types of social action will have the long-run effect of achieving the humanistic aims of a nonviolent political movement while, at the same time, reducing the probability of hostile attacks from rival groups. Similar hypotheses can be extracted from the writings of John Dewey, William James, and other philosophers who have emphasized that the means one employs in a social struggle

* Reprinted by permission of the authors and publisher from *Journal of Conflict Resolution*, 1959, 3:85–100.

determine the ends that will ultimately be achieved. Additional hypotheses that may warrant reformulation and investigation probably can be extracted from writings on ethics by other modern philosophers such as B. Croce, L. T. Hobhouse, G. E. Moore, J. Royce, B. Russell, and A. E. Taylor.

Our main purpose in this paper is to examine some of the new and promising areas of research in the field of social psychology that are suggested by various ethical propositions concerning methods of reducing intergroup hostility and enhancing mutual adherence to a shared set of ethical norms. First, we shall call attention to some of the key variables that might be investigated and the types of research method that might be employed. Then we shall formulate a series of sample hypotheses that are offered for their suggestive value, illustrating some of the basic theoretical issues in contemporary psychology to which a systematic research program on intergroup conflict could contribute a great deal of pertinent evidence.

Some Key Variables

A major set of problems requiring both theoretical analysis and rigorous empirical investigation is that of evaluating the social and psychological consequences of the positive ethical means employed by any social movement, organization, or group to achieve socially desirable goals in its struggle against rival groups. A large-scale program of research would be needed to determine under what conditions the various ethical means (independent variables) have the intended or unintended effects (dependent variables).

Examples of independent variables

An excellent source of various ethical procedures that are illustrative of the means to be investigated is the analysis of

219

the Gandhian ethical system prepared by Naess (1958). Most of the normative propositions and hypotheses which specify the forms of conduct that will achieve the ultimate ethical goals can be restated in terms of means-consequence relationships. As examples, we have selected eight norms, all of which are here formulated as procedures or policies of social struggle which are means for attaining the various humanitarian ends. Although loosely defined at present, these means can be readily translated into operational terms and investigated as independent variables in systematic research studies:

1. *Refraining* from any form of verbal or overt *violence* toward members of the rival group
2. Openly *admitting* to the rival group one's plans and intentions, including the considerations that determine the tactics one is employing in the current struggle as well as one's longer-range strategic objectives
3. *Refraining* from any action that will have the effect of *humiliating* the rival group
4. Making visible *sacrifices* for one's cause
5. Maintaining a consistent and persistent set of *positive activities* which are explicit (though partial) realizations of the group's objectives
6. Attempting to initiate direct personal *interaction* with members of the rival group, oriented toward engaging in *friendly verbal discussions* with them concerning the fundamental issues involved in the social struggle
7. Adopting a consistent attitude of *trust* toward the rival group and taking overt actions which demonstrate that one is, in fact, willing to act upon this attitude
8. Attempting to achieve a high degree of *empathy* with respect to the motives, affects, expectations, and attitudes of members of the rival group

Besides the foregoing list, many additional examples of positive means could be culled from Gandhi's ethical code (1942–49), from Dewey's *Human Nature and Conduct* (1922), and from other ethical writings which also contain propositions concerning the positive and negative social consequences of using alternative ethical procedures.

Dependent variables

The effectiveness of the positive means can be assessed in relation to the following outcomes, which constitute the dependent variables to be investigated:

1. A reduction in the incidence and intensity of acts of violence
2. An increase in the willingness of the rival group to engage in arbitration and to overcome the obstacles that interfere with peaceful settlement of disputes
3. Favorable attitude changes among members of the rival group toward the group behaving according to ethical principles
4. Greater motivation on the part of group members to continue working toward the attainment of humanitarian and social welfare goals
5. Greater success of the group in achieving its specific humanitarian objectives
6. Favorable attitude changes among members of the group in the direction of greater commitment to peaceful settlement of disputes with all rival groups
7. Favorable attitude changes among spectators of the struggle (i.e., people who are unaffiliated with either of the contending groups) in the direction of being more attracted to the group using positive ethical means, placing greater reliance in their public communications, and thereby becoming more influenced in the direction of accepting their policies and objectives

In general, the predictions would be that the positive means such as those listed here would, singly or in combination, lead to favorable outcomes as specified by the seven dependent variables. But, in addition to these global predictions, a number of much more refined hypotheses would need to be tested in order to determine the intervening processes which mediate the predicted effects. In the course of investigating the social and psychological consequences of any one of the various means, it will probably turn out that there are a number of different component factors involved that must be separated and investigated as independent variables. For example, the policy of openly admitting one's intentions and plans to a rival group might give rise to three quite separate effects.

1. Revealing material that is ordinarily kept secret may influence the rival's attitude concerning the *moral status* of the acting group (e.g., they may become suspicious that something more important is being kept secret, or they may become much more respectful of the sincerity of the group).

2. Revealing tactical plans that will handicap the acting group may influence the rival's attitudes concerning the *strength* of the acting group (e.g., admission of one's plans may be perceived as signs of weakness and ineptness in conducting the struggle or as signs of an exceptionally powerful movement that is capable of being successful without resorting to secrecy).

3. Predicting in advance the deprivations that will be inflicted upon the rivals may have the effect of increasing or decreasing the magnitude of frustration and the intensity of the aggressive impulses aroused when the deprivations subsequently materialized.

Thus investigating positive ethical means may lead to the discovery of a number of different mediating processes, some of which may tie in with broad sectors of theory and research in the human sciences.

Implicit in the foregoing discussion is the expectation that objective evaluations of the consequences of the positive ethical means will include careful investigation of the *unfavorable* outcomes as well as the favorable ones. Obviously, the research would have to be carried out in such a way as to detect readily any instance in which the outcome was the reverse of that specified in the foregoing list of favorable outcomes. In this connection it will be necessary to specify a number of additional dependent variables, representing other types of adverse outcomes. For example, a certain type of positive ethical means may prove to be extremely frustrating to the members who are committed to using it and incline some of them to become defensively *apathetic* and to *disaffiliate* themselves from the group. In some cases the intrapersonal conflicts engendered by prolonged suppression of aggressive impulses might conceiv-

ably engender a marked increase in *anxiety* or other *symptoms of emotional tension*. In the long run, consistent adherence to certain of the positive means might result in a marked change in the composition of the membership, with a preponderance of masochistic and other *deviant personalities* being attracted to it.

To detect such unfavorable consequences, the research investigator would need to be alert to any indications of unintended effects that arise in the course of carrying out empirical investigations. Comparisons of instances of favorable outcomes with those of unfavorable outcomes should provide valuable evidence concerning the conditions under which the use of various positive means does and does not lead to the intended effects.

Conditioning Factors

One major set of conditions determining favorable versus unfavorable outcomes has to do with the *combination* of positive means that are employed by the group. For example, admission of one's own plans and refraining from violence may be interpreted as weakness and perceived as relatively ineffective unless accompanied by visible sacrifices for one's own cause and a program of persistent, clear activity demonstrating the group's objectives. Moreover, the use of one means, such as refraining from violence, may strengthen the commitment to the group goal, and this intervening psychological change may facilitate the effective execution of other means, such as making visible sacrifices for one's cause. Thus it will be necessary to study the independent variables in combination and in interaction as well as singly.

The nature of the group struggle is another conditioning factor in the operation of these variables. At least three dimensions of group struggle must be taken into account.

The first dimension is the degree of conflict of interest relative to the community of interest between competing groups. It is generally assumed that non-violent means and positive ethical practices are more applicable to factions within the same institution, since they have so much in common, than to rival nations, where the conflict of interest is high. Nevertheless, it is conceivable that the suicidal character of modern methods of violent group conflict has made this distinction less important, since the common interest in survival has become increasingly clear. In any case, it may be possible to discover auxiliary means of making common interests salient to rival nations and thereby increasing the chances of success for limiting international clashes to non-violent conflicts.

A second dimension concerns the psychological closeness of the group conflict to the people involved. The dynamics of enmity between close personal associates and distant peoples may be different. The distance between competing nations makes their struggle less intense on a personalized basis than that between rival factions in the same political party. On the other hand, the more remote, the fewer the reality checks and hence the easier it is for autistic perception, projected fantasies, and hostile distortions to play their role.

A third related dimension has to do with the degree of institutionalization of the channels, or means, of conducting group and national competition and conflict. Violent means of resolving personal and group conflicts may be a direct reflection of the personal aggression of the protagonists, as in frontier community violence, which is an anticipation of legal institutions. But more commonly at the group level, practices have become institutionalized so that there is no one-to-one correspondence between the warlike actions of a nation and the warlike character of its people (Kelman, 1955). Most wars are probably fought not because the great majority want to fight but because they accept the legitimacy of the process which has led them into war. All these considerations suggest the need for taking into account the nature of the group struggle in studying the effectiveness of ethical forms of social action. In a final section some aspects of the institutionalization of aggression will be discussed.

Closely related to research on limiting conditions is another field of investigation comprising the study of psychological and social conditions which facilitate the willingness of group members to use the positive ethical principles referred to as the "independent variables." In other words, it is also necessary as part of a systematic program of research to consider the use of the positive means as *dependent* variables and to find out the predisposing factors which enable individuals and groups to limit themselves to positive ethical policies in their struggles with opposing groups.

Methods and Techniques

We envisage three phases for the development, refinement, and testing of hypotheses about the peaceful resolution of intergroup conflicts. They need not constitute a discrete temporal sequence, since there is much to be gained from an overlap in the timing of the phases.

The first phase would consist of the use of existing data at two levels: documentary evidence and primary-source data. The former would call for comparative case studies of *historical instances* of social and political struggles in which the given action policies were and were not employed—e.g., studies of various radical, pacifist, religious, and nationalist movements whose social effects can be appraised from available documentary evidence. Primary-source data could be drawn from *interview and questionnaire studies* bearing on industrial conflict situations and factional disputes within social movements, military organizations, political parties, and schools. Of particular relevance would be data on the correlates of different demands and practices on the part of supervisors, union officials, military officers, political leaders, and teachers. This stage of the investigation would furnish some preliminary testing of hypotheses but would serve mainly for the more precise formulation of significant variables and their interrelationships.

The second phase would consist of field studies of *current* and *developing instances* of social and political struggles in which the given action policies are and are not being employed—e.g., collecting systematic interview data in the United States southern communities where Negro organizations are attempting to bring about desegregation.

The emphasis here would be upon specifying the relevant types of data in advance, whereas in the first phase the studies would be limited by the data which happen to be available. Again this stage could contribute both to the testing and to the reformulation of hypotheses.

The final or experimental phase would consist of field and laboratory experiments. The second phase gives better control over the collection of relevant data than the first, but adequate control of the operative variables requires the use of experimental techniques.

Field experiments, which involve the use of controlled experimental techniques in natural settings, have the advantage that the necessary controls can be taken into account in advance of the investigation. They also have the merit of dealing with the full power of social variables as they occur in a real community setting. Such experiments could be devised, for example, in connection with the program of a social or political group in which alternative action policies are carried out in equivalent towns. (E.g., the co-operation might be obtained of a research-minded national organization which is currently engaging in a social or poltical struggle within many different communities throughout the country. Certain local chapters in one designated set of communities might be asked to use a given action policy, whereas other chapters in an equivalent set of communities might be asked to use a contrasting action policy. The effects could be ascertained by interviewing representative samples within the two sets of communities and by using behavioral indexes such as incidence of overt violence on the part of rival groups, increases or decreases in membership of the competing groups, etc.)

Laboratory experiments of the type employed in current research on group dynamics could investigate some of the variables of interest in contrived settings, but the manipulations would be relatively weak. The advantage of this method would be the possibility of isolating single variables and varying their strength fairly precisely, although within limited ranges. The most efficient use of this method would probably be to deal with very specific questions which might arise from field experiments about the properties of a given variable.

Sample Hypotheses and Problems

This section will be devoted largely to presenting a series of hypotheses concerning the psychological processes which mediate the anticipated favorable and unfavorable effects of using various violent and non-violent procedures in intergroup conflicts. We shall present (1) some general propositions concerning the influence of instrumental actions on group goals and the role of leadership in using means consistent with the goals; (2) some of the major psychological changes that might account for the "corrupting" effects of using violent means; (3) a number of additional explanatory hypotheses bearing on the converse process—the "constructive" effects of abstaining from violence; and (4) hypotheses concerning the attitude changes produced by positive ethical means which involve consistently treating the members of opposing groups as potential allies.

A final section will consider the problem of the consequences of the institutionalization of violence.

Influence of Instrumental Actions on Group Goals

That individuals and groups can be involved in antisocial practices in the interests of desirable social goals and still maintain these goals in relatively pure fashion is a doctrine for which there is little psychological support. Once people act in a certain manner, they tend to develop beliefs and attitudes to make the behavior part of their value system. Thus psychologists have long talked about mechanisms becoming drives or instrumental activities becoming functionally autonomous (Allport, 1937). An important factor in the doctrine that the end justifies the means is the separation this imposes in fact between means and ends. John Dewey and other writers have emphasized that an expedient means chosen without regard for the goal sought will not be an intrinsic part of an integrated pattern of means-end activity. It becomes increasingly difficult for the person himself, as well as those who observe his actions, to identify the goal which he is seeking from the instrumental means he employs. When an individual devotes his major energies to using expedient means, he will tend to see the justification of his behavior not in what he actually does every day but in the great goal which lies somewhere beyond. And, of course, it is relatively easy to justify one's morality by goals which are remote and which permit little reality testing. Concrete everyday activities, however, do not permit easy rationalization when they have to be considered on their own merits. It may be just as important, therefore, for a group to tie its ethical standards to means as to ends, since the means can be checked and observed more readily than the goals.

The central point of what has just been said is that repeated behavior of an anti-social character, though originally in the interests of altruistic social goals, will probably lead to the abandonment of those goals as directing forces for the individual. This proposition applies to the leaders as well as the followers within any group or organization.

Persons in positions of leadership, of course, play the major role in proposing and executing the ethical policies that are used in any social struggle and in inducing the rest of the membership to adopt them. The leaders of groups with humanitarian goals may be able to execute certain of their functions more effectively if they adopt expedient means on an opportunistic basis. But, in the long run, opportunistic leaders will probably be less effective in moving their followers toward achieving the ulti-mate objectives of their organization than leaders who insist upon using means that are perceived by the members as being con-sistent with humanitarian goals. This prin-ciple has been recognized by those political and social movements which attempt to maintain a fictitious divorce between their ideology and their opportunistic methods by assigning different people to the two functions. Such groups sometimes try to keep their ethical ideology "pure" by not invoking it for every opportunistic measure.

There are at least four different consid-erations which make it likely that the long-run losses will offset the short-run gains whenever the leader of an altruistic move-ment indorses expedient means that are not consistent with the group's ultimate objec-tives. (1) If leaders justify bad means for good ends, it will create perceptual ambigu-ity for their followers. Many followers are not steeped in the ideology of the move-ment, and it is difficult for them to distin-guish in many instances the means from the end. (2) They will have less confidence in the sincerity of a leader who is not prepared to sacrifice for the cause. His espousing of expediency may be interpreted by the mem-bers as indicating that he is taking the easy way and is not sufficiently devoted himself to take the harder route to his objectives. (3) To restore confidence, the leader is likely to resort to aggressive behavior to-ward his opponents, to impute to them an exaggerated evil intent, and even to advocate violence toward them. (4) Even a single opportunistic practice by a leader sets a precedent and makes subsequent opportun-ism easier for the leader and his followers to accept. Since the principle has already been compromised once, further compro-mise will do little additional harm.

Thus, on the one hand, confidence in the leader's sincerity is likely to be undermined by his use of opportunistic methods, and, on the other hand, the goals of the group become obscured for the members when-ever their leaders succeed in inducing them to accept expedient means which are obvi-ously inconsistent with the group's objec-tives. When the expedient means involve the use of violence against opposing groups, these tendencies will tend to be accentuated. We turn now to some additional hypotheses which specify the psychological changes that occur within any participant who en-gages in hostile actions against people who are opposing the program or ideology of his group.

"Corrupting" Effects of Using Violent Means

Why and under what conditions would the use of violent means be expected to have extremely adverse effects on the indi-vidual participants in a social movement or organization? More specifically, what psychological changes within each participant might account for the following two consequences of the use of a violent means for the alleged purpose of attaining socially desirable goals: (a) an increase in the probability that such means will be used again in the future when similar, and perhaps even less demanding, occasions arise, and (b) a decrease in the probability that the group will work toward the achievement of socially desirable goals (i.e., violent means "corrupt" the ends)?

One obvious answer might be that a violent means will tend to corrupt the ends because it promotes counteraggression on the part of the group's opponents, and this creates a need to use more and more violence, ending up by engaging all the energies of the group in a violent struggle with the rivals instead of enabling positive actions to be taken toward the attainment of the long-run social goals. But even when we set aside the possibility of evoking counteraggression, there are at least three other psychological processes that may come into play, any one of which could have the effect of "corrupting" the members of a group that participates in the use of violent means:

1. Even when the violent means is socially sanctioned, the users may react with some degree of guilt (as a consequence of earlier moral training or as a consequence of generalization from nonsanctioned forms of violence). Guilt reactions may take the form of (a) high anticipation of being punished by the target group; (b) preoccupation with the question of whether or not the action was correct; and (c) effective disturbances, which may range from completely conscious feelings of guilt to vague feelings of uneasiness with no awareness of the source of the disturbance. One of the typical ways in which people attempt to reduce or counteract such guilt reactions is to attribute evil and immoral intentions to the target toward which their violence had been directed. Such attributions may enable a guilt-ridden person to justify the violent action to himself and to others; it may also involve a projection mechanism which operates as an unconscious technique for warding off guilt (Flugel, 1945). The perception of the target as being extremely threatening and evil would have the double effect of (a) increasing the tendency to attack violently again in an effort to weaken the target, (b) decreasing one's willingness to work out compromises with the target group, and (c) altering the conception of humanitarian objectives in such a way as to exclude members of the target group.

2. Participating in any violent action may have the effect of weakening the internal superego controls which are the product of normal socialization. Superego controls are often based on exaggerated conceptions and partially unconscious fantasies about the possible consequences of performing the forbidden act. In psychotherapy a characteristic sequence of changes occurs when patients overcome anxiety or guilt reactions in the sexual sphere or in connection with socially aggressive behavior. After they have once "tested out" the new (non-inhibited) mode of action, they are left with less exaggerated conceptions and fantasies about the consequences of such behavior. Thus the inhibition tends to be gradually extinguished. The same sort of process seems to go on among combat soldiers whose inhibitions about killing the enemy begin to lessen after the first time they are induced to perform the disturbing act of shooting at enemy soldiers. A similar learning process may go on in connection with each instance of group-sanctioned violent action such that the person's automatic superego controls are lessened and he becomes capable of indulging in more and more extreme forms of violence.

3. Social contagion effects may occur within a group or organization such that when a highly respected leader or member of the group uses a violent means under highly "justified" circumstances, other members of the group become less inhibited about engaging in similar acts of violence. This contagion may be partly the product of learning that the violent means is not disapproved, if it is used without criticism by the standard-bearers of morality within the group. Unconscious processes of identification may also facilitate the contagion effect. While, in the first instances, violence is applied by group leaders only after care-

ful judgment, in subsequent instances the followers will be much more ready to indulge in violence without such a careful appraisal of whether or not it is justified. Thus the attitude may gradually develop that violent means are acceptable and even desirable, provided only that they are used in the service of the group's cause.

Constructive Effects of Abstaining From Violence

The next question is the converse of the one just discussed: Why and under what conditions would *abstaining* from the use of sanctioned violent action be expected to have positive effects—e.g., decreasing the probability that violent means will be used in the future, increasing the probability that the group will work toward achieving its original humanitarian goals, and increasing members' adherence to the positive social objectives and moral standards which the group sponsors?

Some of the answers to this question may involve the same psychological mechanisms and social contagion effects specified in the preceding section. However, there may also be some processes that are of a different character, and for this reason we feel that the question of the constructive effects of non-violent action should be considered separately from the question of the "corrupting" effects of violent action. In the discussion which follows, we shall indicate additional mechanisms that may come into play when members of a group adhere to a group decision to abstain from using violent means under conditions where such means are considered to be an acceptable or expected form of behavior.

In many persons, participation in sanctioned violence may serve as a means of reducing conscious and unconscious fears of being passively manipulated by others or of being exposed to damaging attacks and deprivations at the hands of one's rivals. To the extent that such fears are based on misconceptions or exaggerated fantasies about the magnitude of the danger, a given act of abstaining from sanctioned violence may involve a process of *emotional relearning* (similar to that referred to in the preceding section in connection with the lower-

ing of superego control). In this instance, however, the process would be equivalent to that which goes on when a hyperaggressive patient undergoes psychotherapy. Sooner or later he tries out a passive, non-aggressive way of responding to the therapist and discovers that the dangers of passivity which he had so greatly feared do not actually materialize. Similarly, when the members of a group adhere to a group decision to behave in a conciliatory rather than a hostile way, their anticipations about the dangerous consequences of non-violence may be brought more into line with reality. If their fear of being passive is thereby reduced to some extent, they will no longer be so strongly motivated to engage in violence on future occasions when confronted with a choice between violent and non-violent means of struggle against their opponents.

Guilt mechanisms may also play an important role in the internalization of non-violent norms. Insofar as any act of violence (whether sanctioned or not) generates some degree of guilt, at least a slight degree of emotional tension would be experienced by the average group member whenever he *anticipates* engaging in a future act of violence. A reduction in emotional tension might occur if, at the time when the group member is experiencing anticipatory guilt, a communication from a group leader or an expression of group consensus conveys the idea that the group's goals can be better achieved by abstaining from violence and by using an effective form of non-violent action instead. The decision to accept the recommendation would be reinforced by the *reduction of anticipatory guilt*. The reward value of the decison might be enhanced if the ideology of the group included the norm that violence is a morally inferior form of action which should be avoided as much as possible. Even if only lip service is given to this norm, the group member may experience a heightening of self-esteem in addition to guilt reduction if he anticipates that others in his group will approve of his decision to abstain from violence. If each act of abstention is rewarded in this way, a new attitude will gradually tend to develop such that the person becomes increasingly more predisposed to decide or vote in favor of non-violent means. Perhaps under these conditions, good moral "practice makes perfect."

Attitude Changes Produced by Treating Opponents as Potential Allies

Many of the positive ethical means to which we have referred involve more than merely abstaining from violence. Among the examples which we have cited are such means as displaying an attitude of trust toward the members of opposing groups, maintaining friendly personal interactions with them, and seeking to understand their motives and attitudes by deliberately empathizing with them. Although somewhat different rationales for the various positive means have been put forth by their proponents, all of them seem to point in the general direction of replacing a hostile, competitive, antagonistic approach by a policy of treating opponents as potential friends or allies. The hypotheses which follow pertain to the use of any positive ethical means or combination of such means, provided that they are employed on the basis of adhering to this general policy.

Just as in the case of using violent means, *social contagion* effects may occur when positive ethical means are used. But the factors which facilitate the contagion may be somewhat different. Because hostility and violent aggressive action is a very elementary impulsive form of reaction to people who interfere with the attainment of important group objectives, many persons may remain unaware of alternative ways of dealing with opponents and of overcoming the frustrations engendered by their opposition. Thus, whenever violent group action is regarded as the socially accepted mode of response to this type of frustration, many members of the group may gain sudden enlightenment if a respected leader or sub-group calls attention to the possibility of using an alternative approach. If the group decides to try out the proposed alternatives, even if its success remains ambiguous, those members of the group who have a relatively low need for aggression may also learn that the new means is less energy-consuming and less disagreeable than the traditional means. In this way, a process of

acculturation may take place whereby a social technique evolved through the intelligence and ingenuity of others comes to be adopted by people who had formerly accepted, more or less unthinkingly, a general policy of dealing with opponents in a hostile manner.

Other psychological changes may also mediate the effects of adopting, on a tentative basis, the use of positive ethical means. Whenever a member of a group accepts a group decision to use an *unconventional* friendly approach to rivals, he is likely to feel it necessary to justify the fact that he is deviating from the expected course of action (e.g., "Why am I willing to allow these people to provoke us so much without our hating and punishing them?"). The need for such justification may sometimes arise from exposure to cross-pressures resulting from conflicting (pro-hostility) norms held by other groups with which one is affiliated. Or the need for justifying may come from internalized standards—e.g., awareness that one is deviating from the ego ideal associated with sex role ("Am I a sissy?"). In any case, the need to justify the policy of treating opponents as potential allies would motivate the person (a) to take account of the positive attitudes and human qualities of the rivals; (b) to minimize the hostile intentions of the rivals; and (c) to predict that the friendly positive approach will be more successful than an antagonistic approach would be. Thus the effort to justify an act of friendly treatment may lead to cognitive restructurings and a shift in motivational pressures, which could contribute to two types of attitude change: (1) reduced hostility toward the rival group and (2) more favorable evaluations of the desirability of using positive means in general.

Nor are the beneficial effects of non-violence confined to the members of the group pursuing this policy. As group members take into consideration the positive attitudes of members of the out-group and stop reacting toward them as if they were deadly enemies, the out-group itself is under less pressure to be defensively aggressive. Thus the opponents may be influenced to engage in fewer acts of provocative hostility, and, in the long-run, some of their leaders and part of the membership may even become motivated to live up to the other group's view of them as potential allies.

Some Further Consequences and Causes of Institutionalized Aggression

In the preceding discussion we have considered in some detail the psychological mechanisms which may account for the corrupting effects of violence and the constructive effects of abstaining from violence. In this section attention will be given to further consequences of the operation of these basic mechanisms and to supplementary social-psychological processes which make institutionalized aggression the persistent problem of organized society. Though our major concern is with socially sanctioned aggression, it is important for theoretical reasons to differentiate between personal hostility and institutionalized forms of aggression with respect to both causes and effects. The recipient and the initiator of social aggression may be affected differentially if the violence is a sanctioned institutional practice or if it is the release of personal aggression. The two violent actions may be alike in physical character, but they are not necessarily perceived, experienced, or reacted to as the same. Personal aggression may be felt by the recipient as more of an attack upon his ego than the institutional action; it may lead to personalized resentment, more immediate resort to counteraggression, and perhaps less long-term effect. Institutionalization may leave the individual no easily identifiable target of a personal nature for counteraggression; it may confront the individual with sufficient force that he has no way of striking back. It may lead to displaced aggression against a convenient scapegoat, to intropunitiveness, to apathetic acceptance, or to repressed hostility. These consequences can occur in response to personal acts of aggression, but they are less likely to occur where the personal target is easily identifiable and where countermeasures are within the grasp of the individual.

Our major problem today is not protection against the hostile elements among us as individuals capable of violence. Our major problem is with institutionalized

forms of violence, as in conflicts between organized groups and nations. Such institutionalized aggression is accentuated by the presence of hostile people in certain situations, but the correlation between the amount of intensity of group conflict and the amount of latent hostility would not be high save under very special conditions. There are situations, however, in which the interaction of the two—personal hostility and institutional aggression—is of far-reaching significance, as in the opportunities which institutional channels may offer for the expression of latent hostility.

There are three psychological dangers in the institutionalization of violence which are worthy of special investigation: (1) the release of latent hostilities under conditions of social sanction of violence, (2) the apathetic condoning of any institutionally approved practice, and (3) the perpetuation and intensification of institutional violence.

1. *The release of latent hostilities under conditions of the sanctioning of violence.* In Western society the antisocial nature of acts of aggression is communicated to children very early in the socialization process. Aggressive acts toward others are repeatedly censured and punished. If there is lack of understanding by parent and child in this process and continued frustration of the child, there may be repression, but retention, of the hostility. As a result, the adult will be burdened with strong latent hostility which comes into continual conflict with his superego standards. These standards are reinforced by perception of the social norms of the group which proscribes personal acts of violence. The presence of others and the presence of authority represent the stimulus situation which inhibits the aggressions of the individual. But, then, a curious reversal occurs. In certain contexts acts of violence are legitimized and sanctioned by groups and institutions. In times of war almost all sources of authority within each nation assert that it is noble and proper to kill for one's country. The social support for the antisocial action generally has three elements: the justification of a moral purpose, the justification of legitimacy, and the justification that others ap-

prove. Since the traditional inhibitor of violence has been the social environment, violence can assume intense and bizarre forms when the inhibitor is transformed into the facilitator. This is the classic theory of crowd behavior (Martin, 1920). But whereas in the crowd the social support is limited and temporary, in organized groups the support is more extensive and continuing. Thus within the areas where aggression is socially sanctioned, individuals can resolve their conflicts by indulging their worst impulses and by attaining social recognition and reward for so doing.

One danger in the social sanctioning of violence is that the release of hostility will go far beyond the bounds of what is sanctioned. Supposedly appropriate force is invoked on an objective and impersonal basis to accomplish the group's purpose. In practice, however, the way is open for abuses of various sorts. To the extent that latent hostility does exist in the members of the group and their leaders, there will be a tendency to push beyond the necessary force to accomplish the group goal because leaders directly and followers vicariously enjoy the opportunity to release repressed impulses. An extreme illustration would be the use of terror by the German Nazis to maintain power for the Nazi party, which was then pushed to the point of attempts to exterminate entire groups and alleged races. The classic argument against the use of corporal punishment in the schools is the possibility of sadism when the punisher can use aggression disguised as socially approved and necessary discipline. In a preceding section it was indicated that the use of violence leads to further violence through weakening the internal superego controls. The inhibition against the expression of aggression becomes extinguished. This is especially true in the area of institutional aggression, where social support makes it easy to violate the basic social prohibitions. Such social support makes it possible to rationalize away guilt feelings and makes similar violence easier in the future.

We are really dealing in these examples with an interaction of institutional and personal aggression. Our contention is that people may perceive and react differently to personal, as against institutional, violence. The former is more identifiable and leads to more personalized resentment, since it is felt to be a direct attack upon the self. The latter induces in its victims more displacement and more generalized hostility. Frequently, however, in the case of sanctioned violence which permits the expression of latent hostility we have a pattern combining both types of aggression. The chances are that this combination will be perceived by its victims as the most unjust of all aggression. There is a tendency to personalize actions which are in any way injurious to the self. In this instance, however, the afflicted individual is right, since there is personal animus in his punisher. But, unlike purely personal aggression, there is no recourse to any form of counteraggression, since the punishment is legal and proper. Moreover, the victim has limited opportunity for even verbally blowing off steam against his opponent. The result is often intense generalized hatred. Where the situation becomes completely intolerable, it may result in identification with the aggressor.

This combination of institutional violence and personal aggression is one reason why group conflicts become intensified over time and become difficult of solution, even when there is a good objective basis for solution. The scars left by a strike in which both company and union have used force are of this character. The company guards given free rein to their destructive impulses may have abused their power in a manner which the strikers never forget. And the strong-arm squad of the union may have acted similarly toward strike breakers. Both sides feel that the other side has taken advantage of a group struggle to perpetuate a personal outrage. Some of the bitterest memories of World War II are not of massive destruction by heavy artillery and bombers but the use of the cloak of military necessity for the expression of personal sadism.

2. *The apathetic condoning of institutional practices.* Another danger lies in the passive acceptance of any violence perpetrated by one's own group or even by a rival group if it has some legal sanction. This is a differ-

ent response from vicarious indulgence in one's own impulses toward violence and has not received adequate attention. Since the act of force is institutionally sanctioned, it is perceived by many as an objective event. There is no sense of personal outrage, even if the action is directed at deviant group members. This passive acceptance of violence sanctioned by the group, which would otherwise be regarded as basically wrong, is often the result of a compartmentalization in thinking and attitude. It is related to psychological factors mentioned in our previous discussion of the means-end problem, which also involves a compartmentalization such that the individual is not compelled to face up to consequences of his behavior. When this compartmentalization is carried to an extreme, it means that there is one morality for the individual and a completely different morality for the group. Since the group standard can be justified by very remote goals, any action which the group leaders suggest must be accepted. When the German people passively accepted the violence perpetrated in Nazi concentration camps, it was probably not because of their higher level of latent hostility or sadism but because of their compartmentalization of morality. What was legal and sanctioned by the authorities was right, whether or not it was consistent with their own personal standards of morality.

In general, people as group members will condone actions by group representatives which they will not approve of for themselves as individuals. In time the punishments used against individual members by the group will tend to be brought into line with the punishments approved of by members in their personal lives. Brutal forms of physical punishment tend to be dropped from public institutions after they are no longer approved of in interpersonal relations. But in the area of group actions in relation to other groups we permit types of behavior that we do not countenance among individuals. Though such a dual set of standards can be defended, the danger is that the justification comes to rest not on practice and its consequences but on a social myth which asserts the unques-

tioned prerogative of the institution qua institution. The corrupting effect of such condoning of institutional aggression can be seen in war and postwar periods when encroachments are made on individual and civil liberties. Self-seeking politicians under some cloak of governmental authority can carry such threats to an extreme and still secure the acquiescence of many people, since such institutional attacks against our enemies, external and internal, are assumed to be their legitimate function.

3. *The perpetuation and intensification of institutional violence.* Personal aggression, lacking institutional supports, is sporadic and variable. When violence becomes an accepted part of the practice of an organization, it not only is perpetuated but tends to grow much like other parts of the organization. This perpetuation and intensification of institutional aggression comes about in three ways: (a) the setting-up of specialized roles, (b) role adaptation, or the effects of taking roles upon personalities, and (c) role selection, or the tendency toward a fit between unusual roles and personality types.

a) By creating special roles, organizational structures do not rely upon chance factors for the performance of various functions but make such performance the systematic work of trained experts. In addition to the motivation intrinsic to the role, the institution enlists a variety of organization motivations such as monetary rewards, promotion or upgrading, group acceptance, etc. Moreover, in any sector of an organization people occupying given roles tend to make their role functions as important as possible, partly because of self-interest in their careers, partly for the encouragement of morale, and partly because of the psychological prominence of their own tasks compared to others they know less about. The armed forces or the FBI is like any other part of a bureaucratic structure in seeking bigger appropriations and more personnel.

b) In the earlier discussion of the effects of instrumental actions upon group goals it was pointed out that such actions affect the value system of the individual. Role behavior, like any other form of behavior, leads to its rationalization. Personal values are brought into line with the individual's action. What he does, he may do as his job, but after a time he sees this as necessary, important, and desirable. Even in those cases where the role is not originally congenial to the personality pattern of its occupant, remaining in the role results in modification of the personality. To be a member of a combat force and to hold pacifist values produces intense internal conflict. If the individual cannot readily escape from the behavioral demands of a role, he will tend to accept the rationalization provided by the organization in order to dull the sharp edges of the conflict. In time, this acceptance undermines old values and builds up a new value system. Thus role adaptation means not only carrying out the required behavior but justifying it as a desirable course of action. Every occupational and professional group develops an ideology which is supportive of its practices to the extent of occasional idealization of its functions. In the same fashion the military, police, and custodial vocations develop values consonant with their behavior.

c) There is a tendency toward a fit between unusual institutional roles and basic personality patterns. The general notion of the fit between bureaucratic roles and personality has probably been overdone, but there is a good deal of truth in the thesis when we are dealing with unusual roles which call for atypical patterns of motivation and behavior. The censor of pornographic literature may sometimes be suspected of enjoying his duty. When an institution permits violence as part of its function, people will be attracted to this role who derive satisfactions from the nature of the work. Thus there is a self-selection process for brutal roles. In the police forces of some American cities, among prison guards, and in the strong-arm squads of some labor unions there will be individuals who gravitate to and remain in these roles (when there are equally well-paid positions open to them elsewhere) who are of a special personality type. Before the professionalization of American police forces there were many cities in which it was not always easy to distinguish between the member of the third-degree squad and the criminal he was bringing to justice.

Institutional support for roles of violence can be a corrupting factor within an organization far more than is generally realized. Even though not all roles of violence are filled by persons with strong needs to discharge sadistic or hostile impulses, such personalities can readily dominate their part of the organization. Less congenial personalities for these roles will tend to drop out over time. The more brutal individuals will remain and, through their continuity in the organization and their greater motivation, will set the pattern of accepted practice. Moreover, their mutual reinforcement of one another may intensify brutal practices and perpetuate them. The history of some concentration camps illustrates this trend. Brutal practices in prisons and among police forces have been difficult to uproot because it would mean the wholesale dismissal of large groups of people—those guilty of flagrant violations and those who are virtual accomplices in such violations.

Summary

The purpose of this paper was to show the applicability of the research methods of behavioral science to problems of group conflict and interpersonal hostility. The particular frame of reference employed is that of social psychology. Applications from the concepts and techniques of this field are made to certain aspects of the use of violence and of constructive methods in achieving group goals. A section on methods, moreover, outlines both a general strategy for research investigation and the more specific techniques called for at the tactical level. Some of the normative propositions from Arne Naess's analysis of the Gandhian ethical system are examined as the basis for empirical studies. Particular attention is given to the effects of the use of violence and of abstaining from violence in terms of the psychological processes involved. The concluding part of the paper discusses factors making for perpetuation and intensification of institutionalized aggression.

REFERENCES

Allport, G. W. *Personality: A psychological interpretation.* New York: Henry Holt & Co., 1937.

Dewey, J. *Human nature and conduct.* New York: Henry Holt & Co., 1922.

Flugel, J. C. *Man, morals, and society.* London: Duckworth, 1945.

Gandhi, M. K. *Non-violence in peace and war.* Vols. I, VIII, XI. Ahmedabad, 1942–49.

Kelman, H. C. Societal, attitudinal, and structural factors in international relations, *J. Soc. Issues,* 1955, *9*:42–56.

Martin, E. D. *The behavior of crowds.* New York: Harper & Bros., 1920.

Naess, Arne. A systematization of Gandhian ethics of conflict resolution. *J. Conflict Resolut.,* 1958, *2*:140–155.

D. Conflict and Societal Processes

DIMENSIONS OF CONFLICT BEHAVIOR
WITHIN AND BETWEEN NATIONS, 1958-60[*][1]

RAYMOND TANTER

This is a replication of a study by Rudolph J. Rummel (1963). The goals of that study were to determine the dimensions of variation in the domestic and foreign conflict behavior of nations, to locate nations on these dimensions, and to employ these dimensions in order to discover the relationship between both forms of conflict behavior. The goals of the replication are to obtain additional evidence relative to the dimensions of conflict behavior and the relationship between domestic and foreign conflict behavior. Data have been collected across eighty-three nations for 1958, 1959, and 1960 on the same twenty-two measures of conflict behavior used in the previous study. Similarly, these data are to be intercorrelated and factor analyzed, and multi-

* Reprinted by permission of the author and publisher from *Journal of Conflict Resolution*, 1966, *10*:41–64.

[1] Prepared in connection with research supported by the National Science Foundation, Grant NSF-GS224. The data were collected as part of the Dimensionality of Nations Project supported by that foundation, the Carnegie Seminar supported by the Carnegie Corporation, and the International Development Research Center (IDRC) at Indiana University, supported by the Ford Foundation.

The author wishes to thank Fred Riggs, formerly acting director of the IDRC, and Rudolph Rummel, principal investigator of the Dimensionality of Nations Project, Yale University, for making this study possible. Professor Rummel has aided in the preparation of the research design phase of this study in order to assure continuity from his study (Rummel, 1963) to the present one. I am also quite grateful for his comments on my interpretation of the results, and in reading earlier drafts; any errors, however, are mine. In addition, I am grateful to Milton Hobbs, Harold Guetzkow, J. David Singer, and Dean Pruitt for their comments, and to the Indiana and Northwestern University Research Computing Centers for the generous provision of their facilities.

ple regression is to be used to examine the relationship between domestic and foreign conflict behavior.

Theory

Many of the generalizations about international conflict behavior have been discovered through the use of historical analysis. For example, Richard Rosecrance concludes that through time there is a tendency for international instability to be associated with the domestic insecurity of elites (Rosecrance, 1963, p. 304). Two other students of international relations, Ernst Haas and Allen Whiting, suggest an explanation for the relationship between internal and external conflict behavior. They contend that groups seeking self-preservation may be driven to a foreign policy of conflict. The authors reason that the elites become fearful of losing their domestic positions during periods of rapid industrialization and widespread social change; they then try to displace the attention of the disaffected population onto some outside target. But the authors suggest that this form of self-preservation rarely leads to war (Haas and Whiting, 1956, pp. 61–62).

In addition to Rosecrance and Haas and Whiting, Quincy Wright suggests that there is a general relationship between internal and external conflict behavior. Interspersed in his two volumes of *A Study of War* (1942) are propositions such as the following:

By creating and perpetuating in the community both a fear of invasion and a hope of expansion, obedience to a ruler may be guaranteed. A system of world politics resting upon a balance of power contributes to the integration of each power by maintaining among the peoples the fear of war as well as the hope of dominance [Vol. II, p. 1016]. Rulers have forestalled internal sedition by starting external wars [Vol. I, p. 140]. There is no nation in which war or preparations of war have not to some degree or at some time been used as an instrument of national stability and order [Vol. I, p. 254]. In later stages of the Napoleonic Wars, Napoleon began to appreciate the value of war as an instrument of internal solidarity [Vol. II, p. 725]. Governments have often started war because it appeared to them a necessary or convenient means of establishing, maintaining, or expanding the power of the government, party, or class within the nation [Vol. II, p. 727].

Hopefully, this study will provide a systematic examination of the propositions of such theorists as Rosecrance, Haas and Whiting, and Wright. From a systematic examination and a series of *replications,* it may be possible to construct a general theory of intra- and internation conflict behavior. (See below, pp. 58 *ff.,* for a further discussion of such theories.)

Replication

Increasing the number of observations or trials in a particular design is referred to in the literature on the logic of experimentation as increasing the replications. Increasing the replications generally increases the confidence that the findings are not the result of chance factors (Edwards, 1954, p. 273). One frequently comes across references to the need for replication in the literature on research methods. For example, Katz asserts that the history of social psychology shows the significance of the replication of findings in that many of the original propositions have not been confirmed by later studies (Katz, 1953, p. 64). Moreover, Sidman contends that the most appropriate empirical test of the reliability of data is provided by replication (Sidman, 1960, p. 70).

Replication is especially suggested when there is disagreement with a well-established finding, the number of replications warranted being a function of the extent to which the previous findings were firmly established (Sidman, 1960, p. 78). As regards quantitative studies, the finding that there is very little relationship between domestic and foreign conflict behavior (Sorokin, 1937; Rummel, 1963) contrasts with other findings of a negative relationship (Huntington, 1962) and a positive relationship (McKenna, 1962). On the other hand, most of the nonquantitative works support the hypothesis of a positive relationship (Haas and Whiting, 1956; Rosecrance, 1963).[2] The quantitative studies where the generalization was not based on the collected data (such as Wright, 1942) also support the finding of a positive relationship.

The quantitative studies where the generalization was based on the data meet a minimum criterion for replication, e.g., the standardization of the specifications for data. And as Katz points out, "Only when we attain the level of standardizing our specifications for data can we see the extent to which reported findings are true generalizations" (Katz, 1953, p. 64). Moreover, the ability to replicate scientific inquiry depends largely upon an explicit statement of the research design decisions such as data collection and analysis procedures.

Population

To be included in this study, nations had to be sovereign for at least two years and have a population equal to or greater than 800,000 in 1958. As a result of more nations being able to meet these criteria for 1958 than for 1955, the population size increased to eighty-three from the seventy-seven in the 1955–57 study (see Appendix II for the list of nations). Intragroup replication would entail the use of the exact sample employed in the prior study. As with the Rummel study, however, the total *population* is being used. Consequently,

[2] The way some of these propositions are stated, however, it is almost possible to interpret them as suggesting a negative relationship. This interpretation, though, does not fit in with the context in which the propositions appear. With the introduction of a time lag between the occurrence of domestic and foreign conflict behavior, the theories of Coser (1956) and Simmel (1955) suggest a negative relationship.

sampling restrictions of this sort are not applicable.[3]

Data Sources and Coding Reliability

The New York Times Index, Deadline Data on World Affairs, Britannica Book of the Year, and *Facts on File* were used as sources of data for the twenty-two conflict behavior measures. The first two sources, however, proved to be far more productive of data than the others. Consequently, most of the data reported in this study were derived from *The New York Times Index* and *Deadline Data,* the others being consulted for an overview.

It may be argued that the cross-reference system of one of the primary data sources, *The New York Times Index,* is such that any reliability tests would have to be conducted over *all* the nations by two or more coders in order to test for the agreement between coders for a subset of nations. That position, however, is valid only as regards foreign conflict behavior measures. That is, when there is conflict between two countries, parts of the conflict behavior are recorded under each country involved as well as in other places. For example, as regards the United States, the bulk of its international activity is recorded under topic headings other than "United States." Although some of these cross-references are given in the *Index,* a large part of them are not. Consequently, only by going through all the nations can one be confident that he is obtaining most of the information on foreign conflict as regards a subset of the countries. For domestic conflict, however, the information is generally contained under the country heading. With these caveats in mind, reliability tests were conducted on the domestic measures. To assure maximum continuity in the codings for the 1955–57 and 1958–60 data, to discover the consistency of the author's codings at different points in time, and to ascertain the extent to which other coders would agree with the author's codings, three partial reliability tests were conducted.

A random sample of five nations from the 1955–57 data reported by Rummel were recoded by the author as regards the nine measures of internal conflict behavior. Agreement ranged from 85 to 100 percent, with purges and major government crises being the variables on which there was least agreement. Since the author did the large portion of the 1958–60 coding, he recoded a random sample of ten nations three months after the initial codings were made. In only two cases were there discrepancies. A third reliability test consists of the author recoding the five nations for 1958–60 that were initially coded by two assistants. Perfect agreement was found for these five. Although these partial reliability tests indicate that *some* of the data are reliable, there may be coding errors in the data which might bias the conclusions.

Systematic Error in the Data Sources

Censorship may result in a systematic understatement of the conflict behavior of a given country in the sources. Accordingly, a three point censorship scale for 1958 is derived from the Inter-American Press Survey of 1958[4] and the Survey of the World's Press by the International Press Institute[5], and for 1959[6] and 1960[7] from Associated Press Surveys of World Press Freedom. Values for each year were then summed across the three years for each nation so that those with high censorship had low scores.

Lack of world interest in a country may also result in an understatement of its conflict behavior. World interest may be operationalized as the number of embassies or legations *in* each country for 1959. The assumption is that this value for each nation reflects world interest in that nation. Although there are obvious exceptions to this assumption, such as the values for East Germany and China, the assumption appears to be valid for most other nations. A second measure of world interest is derived from one of the data sources—*Deadline Data on World Affairs.* It is the num-

[3] See Sidman (1960), p. 73, regarding intragroup and intergroup replication, and pp. 46*ff.*, as regards the concept of generality.

[4] *New York Times,* March 29, 1959.
[5] *New York Times,* April 13, 1959.
[6] *New York Times,* January 3. 1960.
[7] *New York Times,* January 1, 1961.

ber of index cards per country in the card file itself.

These three error measures are included in the correlation and factor analysis. If censorship has no correlation with the conflict behavior measures, then systematic bias as tapped by the censorship measure does not distort the conclusions. Negative correlation of censorship and the conflict behavior measures is not crucial because one can assume the direction of systematic bias to be under- instead of overstatement. Aside from possible exaggeration by the press, one would not expect nations to overstate the number of riots and revolutions it has. So if censorship is negatively correlated with riots, it might be inferred that the correlations between riots and the other conflict behavior measures would undergo little change even if censorship were suppressing knowledge of such incidents. Positive correlations between the censorship and the conflict behavior measures indicate that censorship in a nation could be distorting the results; positive correlation, however, is a necessary but not sufficient condition for such systematic error to distort the results of this study.

A high positive correlation between the world interest measures and the conflict behavior measures might mean that lack of world interest in some countries could be causing their conflict behavior to go unreported. Positive correlation, however, is a necessary but not sufficient condition for such systematic error to distort the conclusions. (In the Rummel study [1963] the direction of the correlation between the world interest measure and the conflict behavior measures was inadvertently stated as negative for systematic error to distort the results.)

Results[8]

In order to determine how well the 1958–60 data reflect a longer period, the

[8] Biomedical (BIMD) Computer Program 24 was used to test for outliers, and a visual test of linearity from the cross tabulation of each variable with every other. Outliers greater than three standard scores from the mean were "brought in" through transformation. No curvilinearity was found which might distort the conclusions.

data were compared and correlated with Rummel's 1955–57 data.[9] Table 1 contains the correlations of the 22 measures of conflict behavior for both 1955–57 and 1958–60. In the upper left hand corner of the matrix the domestic variables are intercorrelated with themselves; the values to the left are the 1958–60 correlations. The fact that all the correlations for each period are positive indicates a remarkable degree of similarity in the direction of the relationships. Out of a total of 36 correlations for each period there are 10 which are greater than or equal to .50. In other words, 28 percent of the domestic correlations for each period are $\geqslant$ .50.

This stability of the ratio of high correlations to the total for the domestic variables, however, is not found for the foreign variables. (The foreign variables for each period are located in the bottom right hand side of the matrix; the 1955–57 values are to the right of the diagonal while 1958–60 values are to the left). Out of a total of 78 correlations 23, or 29 percent, are $\geqslant$ .50 for the 1955–57 period, while only nine, or 12 percent, are $\geqslant$ .50 for the 1958–60 period. The direction of the relationships, however, argues for similarity between the periods. There are only two negatives for 1958–60 and three for 1955–57.

The other portions of the matrix, the correlations of domestic with foreign variables for both periods, are much more similar, although the negative range is greater in the earlier period. (The domestic-foreign intercorrelations for 1955–57 are in the upper right hand corner of the matrix, while those for 1958–60 are in the lower left hand corner). An analysis of the percentage of correlations that fall

[9] In addition, Richardson's data (1960) for thirty nations on war from 1825–1945 were correlated with 1958–60 data on war, war and military action, and number killed due to all foreign conflict; Harry Eckstein's data (Eckstein, 1962) for 1946–59 on total violence, internal warfare, and a coup are correlated with 1958–60 measures for seventy nations; and Raymond Cattell's correlations (Cattell, 1949) for five measures of conflict behavior were compared with similar correlations from 1958–60. The results indicate that the 1958–60 data are not unique to that period and appear to be moderately general to longer time periods.

within certain intervals argues for a similarity across both periods. This type of analysis does not tell one *which* variables have similar intercorrelations over both periods. An example of correlations be- tween intra- and international characteristics that are similar across periods is furnished by "riots" and "anti-foreign demonstrations." The 1955–57 correlation is .36, and for 1958–60 it is .38. One of the most

TABLE 1

CORRELATION MATRIX, 1955–57 AND 1958–60 [a]

Measures [b]	1	2	3	4	5	6	7	8	9	10	11	12	13	14	15	16	17	18	19	20	21	22	23	24	25
1. Assass		28	45	35	31	45	19	(51)	33	23	28	01	03	16	-09	15	15	19	06	28	20	18	29	08	21
2. Strike	38		24	29	46	(56)	(50)	(57)	(51)	20	-01	-01	14	13	07	-04	01	-06	01	-09	07	04	03	-03	00
3. Gu-War	49	36		09	17	13	33	20	(52)	00	00	-23	-08	17	-11	-10	-10	-10	-11	-11	-09	-04	06	-03	-07
4. Gvtcrs	43	42	(55)		30	36	38	41	20	21	29	10	28	-01	05	09	11	-05	05	-11	13	13	12	05	22
5. Purges	29	04	25	24		42	49	36	(57)	24	13	08	32	18	24	26	30	17	24	13	27	34	12	-21	03
6. Riots	(51)	(55)	34	41	25		32	(69)	(53)	36	16	19	18	26	08	15	08	12	13	02	21	19	29	05	19
7. Revolu	31	20	(65)	42	(51)	30		23	(62)	05	-04	-11	03	12	-11	-04	12	-04	07	-12	04	12	-02	-08	-06
8. Demons	46	(54)	32	44	19	(73)	19		45	38	26	29	14	26	28	36	16	20	23	21	35	21	47	-07	30
9. D-Kill	(51)	33	(67)	46	41	47	(69)	39		16	-04	00	-03	25	16	05	02	07	14	-06	12	22	18	-22	-01
10. F-Dmst	29	28	27	12	17	38	26	22	31		(53)	39	36	14	29	(50)	33	25	39	22	46	35	42	05	18
11. Negsan	23	00	20	14	20	17	10	13	13	21		47	33	05	33	(64)	35	24	45	38	48	30	(57)	03	33
12. Protst	04	15	05	-01	07	29	-01	24	04	27	39		19	09	47	(66)	39	(51)	(63)	46	(69)	(52)	(60)	-10	29
13. Sevdip	08	19	27	28	05	23	19	21	11	22	20	02		-08	12	38	(54)	07	15	23	39	31	04	-15	-08
14. Er-Amb	05	27	10	08	-03	17	-13	18	-08	19	36	(54)	09		10	12	-08	01	24	11	11	02	24	-14	13
15. Er-Les	27	11	10	08	11	16	-01	15	04	16	32	20	13	25		(50)	13	33	43	15	45	32	42	-23	34
16. Threat	10	01	07	-08	06	20	-05	18	07	42	(55)	(59)	13	42	22		(62)	(55)	(68)	(55)	(81)	(63)	(72)	-19	25
17. Milact	05	03	05	06	19	12	06	10	12	17	30	39	05	28	07	47		38	45	(54)	(65)	(72)	19	-09	07
18. War	00	-06	-05	01	03	01	-02	02	02	-06	21	22	08	25	-09	24	(51)		32	37	(56)	(77)	19	-10	20
19. Trpmvt	14	01	01	-07	19	40	02	24	07	30	24	49	11	23	22	42	26	22		30	(62)	(53)	(74)	-13	07
20. Mobili	00	04	07	00	31	05	04	03	14	25	30	36	16	38	04	48	43	41	37		44	38	(51)	15	33
21. Accusa	18	-07	17	07	32	19	16	18	12	25	47	(64)	12	40	29	(62)	49	38	39	44		(70)	19	-17	09
22. F-Kill	34	06	30	21	25	24	23	15	27	25	40	30	13	22	32	39	49	41	(53)	38	(70)		44	-27	09
23. Cards	03	10	05	-02	12	30	-05	31	09	28	35	(77)	-02	(53)	22	(67)	38	23	(55)	43	(63)	33		00	28
24. Censor	-03	19	-09	02	-28	17	-16	13	-13	21	-27	00	14	07	-18	-16	-37	-22	06	-09	-41	-26	00		39
25. D-Emby	01	34	04	06	-02	44	-17	40	-02	22	02	(52)	-02	37	21	21	01	34	15	14	-08	(57)	28	39	

[a] To the right of the principal diagonal of the matrix are the 1955–57 correlations, N=77; to the left are the 1958–60 correlations, N=83. Product moment coefficients of correlation are used throughout this study. Parenthesis indicates correlations ≥.50. Correlations are rounded off and multiplied by 100. No significance tests are given throughout this study because the entire universe under investigation is being analyzed.

[b] See Appendix I for full names of the variables as well as their definitions.

similar correlations across both periods, at the international level, is that between accusations and mobilizations, which is .46 for 1955–57 and .44 for 1958–60; one of the least stable is the correlation at the intranational level between purges and general strikes: .46 in 1955–57 and .04 in 1958–60.

The variability in Table 1 in the correlation of purges with general strikes might be partially explained by the very low correlation of 1955–57 purges with 1958–60 purges in Table 2. Out of 22 correlations, eight (36 percent) are ⩾.50. The variables which have the most similar intercorrelations generally appear to be those that happen most often, or those in which coding is not much of a problem (e.g., accusations, threats, riots).

Dimensions of Foreign Conflict Behavior

Table 3 gives the results of the factor analyses of the foreign conflict behavior measures for 1955–57 and 1958–60. The orthogonally rotated matrix is given.[10]

---

[10] Mesa 3 computer program is used for the factor analysis. Principal components technique is used with unities in the diagonal of the correlation matrix (see Rummel, 1963, ch. 3, for a detailed discussion of the research design decisions). Since the eigenvalue (sum of squares) of the unrotated fourth factor of the 1958–60 data is equal to only .95, only three factors are extracted and rotated orthogonally and obliquely. The criterion for the *number of significant factors* to extract and to which rotation is to be started is the same for the 1955–57 and 1958–60 studies. This criterion is the number of factors whose eigenvalues are ⩾1.00. An eigenvalue is the root of a characteristic equation.

Rotation is carried out in order to obtain a more stable solution, e.g., one that is not entirely dependent upon each particular variable in the analysis.

Orthogonal rotation is the fitting of factors to variables with the restriction that the correlation between the factors is zero. Hence, independence among the factors is forced on the data. The varimax criterion (Kaiser, 1958) is used to rotate orthogonally to simple structure, e.g., the maximization of low loadings.

Oblique rotation allows the factors to become correlated if such correlations actually exist among the factors.

The criterion for accepting either rotation is the extent to which simple structure is achieved. The number of variable loadings in the ±.10 hyperplane

In the orthogonally rotated solution of the 1958–60 data, a *diplomatic* dimension

TABLE 2
CORRELATIONS BETWEEN 1955–57 AND 1958–60 DATA[a]

Measures	Correlations[b]
1. Assass	24
2. Strike	33
3. Gu-War	(65)
4. Gvtcrs	36
5. Purges	05
6. Riots	(69)
7. Revolu	(55)
8. Demons	44
9. D-Kill	(55)
10. F-Dmst	38
11. Negsan	47
12. Protst	(57)
13. Sevdip	08
14. Er-Amb	14
15. Er-Les	38
16. Threat	(66)
17. Milact	43
18. War	41
19. Trpmvt	(58)
20. Mobili	15
21. Accusa	(71)
22. F-Kill	48

[a] Each value for a 1955–57 measure is correlated with the corresponding values for 1958–60; $N=74$. Parenthesis indicates correlations ⩾.50.

[b] Egypt, Syria, and Yemen were originally included in the 1955–57 study but were excluded, along with the UAR for 1958–60, in the calculations of these correlations.

is used to indicate the degree of simple structure. Hence, the solution which has the largest number of near-zero loadings will be accepted.

Loadings are correlations with factors for the unrotated and orthogonally rotated solutions. The values in the oblique matrices are pattern values which are coordinates rather than correlations.

The *communality*, h^2, of a variable is the sum of the squares of the loadings across the factors for the unrotated and orthogonally rotated solutions.

Percent of Total Variance under each column in the factor matrix is that portion of the variance in all the variables which that factor extracts. It is the sum of the squares in the factor column divided by the total number of variables.

Percent of Common Variance is the percent of variance that a factor has divided by the total variance extracted by all factors.

emerges first.[11] It is defined by the variables with high loadings, such as protests, threats, and accusations. (The higher the loading, the more the variable is associated with the factor, e.g., a set of highly related variables. The range of the loading is from +1.00 to −1.00, as is the range for the product moment correlation coefficients if the univariate distributions are similar). This dimension represents a nonviolent type of foreign conflict behavior similar to that which emerged as the second factor in the 1955–57 study. The 1955–57 measures that are mainly correlated with the *diplomatic* dimension are expelling or recalling ambassadors, expulsion of lesser officials, and

[11] The orthogonally rotated solution is selected over the oblique because the former meets more adequately the simple structure criterion. (The ±.10 hyperplane of the orthogonal solution contains more low variable loadings than the oblique solution has low pattern values.)

troop movements. The *diplomatic* dimensions from both periods pull together rationally calculated activities of a nonviolent nature, that is, diplomatic moves short of the use of force which are intended to influence other nations.

The second orthogonally rotated factor of the 1958–60 data is a *war* dimension. The variables with high loadings are war, military action, foreign killed, and mobilization. This dimension is comparable to the first factor which emerged from the 1955–57 data. Mobilization, war, and number killed best define the 1955–57 *war* dimension. The *war* dimensions in both periods pull together activities which index the preparation for war, war itself, and its consequences.

The third rotated factor of the 1958–60 data has anti-foreign demonstrations and severance of diplomatic relations as the only high loadings. This factor might be

TABLE 3[d]

FACTOR ANALYSIS OF FOREIGN CONFLICT MEASURES[a]: ORTHOGONALLY ROTATED FACTOR MATRIX, 1955–57 DATA WITH 1958–60 DATA[b]

Measures	Diplomatic		War		Belligerency		Communality (h^2)	
	T_1	R_2	$T_2{}^c$	$R_1{}^c$	T_3	R_3	T	R
1. F-Dmst	34	42	03	13	(64)	(63)	52	60
2. Negsan	(58)	41	22	20	26	(64)	46	62
3. Protst	(79)	49	26	(62)	−06	22	70	67
4 Sevdip	−06	−17	09	13	(82)	(82)	68	71
5. Er-Amb	(67)	(66)	18	−16	−05	−08	49	47
6. Er-Les	(59)	(60)	−29	33	21	08	47	48
7. Threat	(70)	43	35	(65)	23	48	66	84
8. Milact	28	−14	(74)	(65)	02	(57)	63	77
9. War	02	15	(83)	(85)	−09	−10	70	75
10. Trpmvt	46	(59)	32	47	26	28	38	64
11. Mobili	34	−08	(58)	(60)	19	35	48	49
12. Accusa	(67)	35	46	(70)	09	41	66	79
13. F-Kill	21	10	(76)	(87)	23	19	67	80
% Common variance	43.3	24.6	37.7	46.2	18.9	29.1	100.0	100.0
% Total variance	25.2	16.3	21.8	30.7	10.1	19.3	57.9	66.4
Intraclass correlation coefficient	.68		.67		.67			

[a] Parenthesis indicates loadings ≥.50.

[b] Decimals omitted from all loadings.

[c] Signs reversed.

[d] Factors labelled "T" are Tanter's 1958–60 orthogonally rotated factors. Factors labelled "R" are Rummel's 1955–57 orthogonally rotated factors (Rummel, 1963. p. 13).

labelled a *belligerency* dimension which is similar to the third factor of the earlier period. The 1955–57 *belligerency* dimension is defined by a cluster containing severance of diplomatic relations, anti-foreign demonstrations, military action of a limited nature, and negative sanctions. Some of the activities on the *belligerency* dimension in both periods are of an "emotional" nature as opposed to the "rational" nature characteristic of the activities on the *diplomatic* dimension.

Three dimensions of foreign conflict behavior describe both the 1955–57 and the 1958–60 data: *war, diplomatic,* and *belligerency* dimensions. (The degree of similarity—intraclass correlations—between the equivalent dimensions for each period is discussed in the section on *Comparisons of Dimensions from 1955–57 and 1958–60.*

Dimensions of Domestic Conflict Behavior

Table 4 gives the results of the factor analysis of the domestic conflict behavior measures for 1955–57 and 1958–60. The orthogonally rotated solution is given.[12] Upon orthogonally rotating the two factors for 1958–60 to a more stable solution, two distinct dimensions emerge, the first of which might be called a *turmoil* dimension. Demonstrations, riots, strikes, assassinations, and crises have high loadings and thus define the dimension. A similar dimension can be found in the rotated matrix of the 1955–57 data. The *turmoil* dimension for the earlier period is also defined by demonstrations, riots, crises, assassinations, and strikes.

The second 1958–60 orthogonally rotated factor pulls together a cluster of activities such as revolutions, domestic killed, guerrilla war, and purges. These activities are generally associated with organized conflict behavior of a highly violent nature.

This factor might thus be labelled an *internal war* dimension. The *internal war* dimension of the 1958–60 data subsumes the *revolutionary* and *subversive* dimensions of 1955–57. The *revolutionary* dimension pulled together overt, organized conflict behavior, while the *subversive* dimension was defined by activities of a covert organized nature.

Domestic conflict behavior for 1958–60 may thus be separated into two independent scales—a disorganized spontaneous *turmoil* dimension and an organized violent *internal war* dimension. Since both dimensions account for almost equal amounts of the total variance in the rotated solution, they may be considered equally important in describing domestic conflict behavior during the 1958–60 period.[13]

Comparison of Dimensions from 1955–57 and 1958–60

In order to obtain a more precise description of the degree of similarity between the dimensions which emerge from the two time periods, the intraclass coefficient of correlation is calculated (cf. Robinson, 1959, p. 25). Since the product moment coefficient converts raw data to standard scores, it does not take into account differences in origins, means, and variances; for the variance of a variable in standard form is unity, while the mean is zero. Consequently, the product moment only measures *changes* in one variable which are associated with *changes* in another variable. The intraclass coefficient, however, is sensitive to differences in origins, means, and variances; and as these differences increase, the coefficient decreases (Haggard, 1958, p. 30).

Table 5 compares the foreign and domestic dimensions between the two time periods; also given are the correlations between representative variables which index

---

[12] Since the eigenvalue of the third factor of the 1958–60 data is only .84, only two factors are extracted and rotated orthogonally and obliquely. The orthogonal solution is selected over the oblique because the number of loadings and pattern values in the ±.10 hyperplane for each solution is the same (4). And since the orthogonal solution is the simplest, it is selected.

[13] The inference as to degree of organization was based upon an inspection of background information on the conflict events in question. This tentative distinction should not lead us to ignore such facts as that some of the riots were highly organized. A further study is planned where the degree of organization will be coded systematically to see whether organization varies with type of conflict behavior.

TABLE 4[d]

FACTOR ANALYSIS OF DOMESTIC CONFLICT MEASURES[a]: ORTHOGONALLY ROTATED FACTOR MATRIX, 1955–57 DATA WITH 1958–60 DATA[b]

Measures	Turmoil		Revolutionary	Internal war	Subversive	Communality (h^2)	
	T_1	R_1	R_2[c]	T_2	R_3[c]	T	R
1. Assass	(59)	(59)	−03	41	(66)	52	78
2. Strike	(79)	(52)	(60)	06	05	63	63
3. Gu-War	35	−04	28	(74)	(90)	66	90
4. Gvtcrs	(53)	(60)	21	47	−04	50	41
5. Purges	01	32	(71)	(68)	03	46	60
6. Riots	(83)	(79)	31	21	09	73	73
7. Revolu	09	09	(85)	(89)	13	80	75
8. Demons	(86)	(85)	17	10	19	75	79
9. D-Kill	37	23	(75)	(78)	42	74	79
% Common variance	50.8	39.0	37.6	49.2	23.4	100.0	100.0
% Total variance	32.7	27.7	26.7	31.7	16.6	64.4	70.8
Intraclass correlation coefficient	.74		.45	.12			

[a] Parenthesis indicates loadings $\geqslant$.50.
[b] Decimals omitted from all loadings.
[c] Signs reversed.
[d] Factors labelled "T" are Tanter's 1958–60 orthogonally rotated factors. Factors labelled "R" are Rummel's 1955–57 orthogonally rotated factors (Rummel, 1963, p. 12).

the dimensions for each period. The correlations for the representative variables indicate that the two war measures are the most similar forms of foreign conflict behavior across the whole 1955–60 time span ($r = .64$). The most similar of the domestic representative variables is guerrilla war ($r = .65$). In terms of dimensions, however, the *turmoil* dimension is the most similar for the two periods. Moroever, the *internal war* dimension of 1958–60 is more similar to the 1955–57 *revolutionary* dimension that it is to the 1955–57 *subversive* dimension.

Relationship between Domestic and Foreign Conflict Behavior

The relationship between domestic and foreign conflict behavior is discovered by first factor analyzing all the conflict behavior measures together and then by regressing upon one another the variables which best index both forms of conflict behavior.

Table 6 contains the results of the merged factor analysis; the obliquely rotated solution is given.[14] Upon rotation to the more invariant oblique solution, domestic and foreign conflict behavior become clearly separate. In no case do any domestic measures have pattern values $\geqslant$.50 on the same factor on which a foreign measure is $\geqslant$.50.

The first factor in the oblique matrix is the *turmoil* dimension. The second factor is the *diplomatic* dimension and is defined by the communications variables as well as expulsion of ambassadors. In addition to these measures of diplomatic activity, however, the two error measures of world interest also help to define this dimension.

[14] Seven factors are extracted in contrast with the six-factor solution of the 1955–57 study because the eigenvalue of the seventh factor of the present work is 1.002 (see footnote 10). The oblique is selected over the orthogonal solution on the basis of simple structure criteria. The ±.10 hyperplane contains sixteen more loadings in the oblique than are found in the orthogonal solution.

TABLE 5

CORRELATIONS OF 1955–57 AND 1958–60 DIMENSIONS AND REPRESENTATIVE VARIABLES[d]

Dimensions correlated	Intraclass correlation coefficient	Representative variables correlated	Product moment correlation coefficient
Foreign:[a]		Foreign:[c]	
1955–57 *War* with		1955–57 F-Kill[e] with	
1958–60 *War*	.67	1958–60 War	.64
1955–57 *Diplomatic* with		1955–57 Er-Amb with	
1958–60 *Diplomatic*	.68	1958–60 Protst	.21
1955–57 *Belligerency* with		1955–57 Sevdip with	
1958–60 *Belligerency*	.67	1958–60 Sevdip	.08
Domestic:[b]		Domestic:[c]	
1955–57 *Subversion* with		1955–57 Gu-War with	
1958–60 *Internal War*	.12	1958–60 Gu-War	.65
1955–57 *Revolutionary* with		1955–57 Revolu with	
1958–60 *Internal War*	.45	1958–60 Gu-War	.38
1955–57 *Turmoil* with		1955–57 Demons with	
1958–60 *Turmoil*	.74	1958–60 Demons	.44

[a] $n = 13$ variables loaded on orthogonally rotated factors.
[b] $n = 9$ variables loaded on orthogonally rotated factors.
[c] $N = 74$ nations.
[d] A representative variable is one which has the highest loading on a particular factor and the lowest loadings with the remaining factors in the matrix.
[e] See Appendix I for full names of the variables as well as their definitions.

As previously mentioned, negative correlation or lack of correlation between censorship and the conflict behavior measures is no cause for alarm. A second error measure—cards per nation in *Deadline Data*—has to be analyzed in a different manner. There is a high positive pattern value of cards (.82) on the *diplomatic* dimension, where protests also show a value of .82 and expulsion of ambassadors .72; and there are high positive correlations of cards with protests (.77) and cards with expulsion of ambassadors (.55). This indicates that the level of world interest in a nation is associated with the tendency for its protests and expulsions of ambassadors to be reported.

The high correlation and mutually high pattern values of protests and the "cards" measure of world interest is likewise found

for the other measure of world interest—the number of embassies or legations in a country. The latter measure has a .52 correlation with protests and a pattern value of .73 on the *diplomatic* dimension (see Tables 1 and 6).

The similar manner in which the world interest measures act with the protest variable indicates that the two world interest measures are tapping the same thing. The small difference between the two may come from the fact that the cards in *Deadline Data* measure the extent of interest that the *editors* manifest in particular nations, while the number of embassies or legations in a country may reflect the degree of interest other *nations* have in that country.

On the basis of the relationships between protests and expulsion of ambassadors on the one hand, and the world interest error

TABLE 6c

FACTOR ANALYSIS OF DOMESTIC AND FOREIGN CONFLICT MEASURES[a]: SEVEN FACTOR SOLUTION

Measures	Oblique biquartimin pattern matrix[b]						
	F_1 Turmoil	F_2 Diplomatic	F_3 Int. War	F_4 War	F_5	F_6	F_7
1. Assass	(64)	−31	18	12	31	02	18
2. Strike	(70)	18	07	−02	−09	09	−23
3. Gu-War	28	01	(66)	−08	07	20	−24
4. Gvtcrs	(53)	−03	37	08	03	11	−40
5. Purges	−05	09	(76)	−02	02	−19	06
6. Riots	(77)	09	14	07	−02	−01	28
7. Revolu	05	−07	(91)	−10	−12	06	−08
8. Demons	(81)	14	06	09	02	−09	05
9. D-Kill	35	−07	(76)	05	−13	−03	02
10. F-Dmst	04	11	22	−14	03	(53)	(52)
11. Negsan	−08	19	03	16	(62)	25	−01
12. Protst	05	(82)	03	09	14	−13	04
13. Sevdip	01	−15	−03	06	10	(83)	05
14. Er-Amb	08	(72)	−16	11	22	12	−34
15. Er-Les	13	14	−11	−27	(82)	01	−07
16. Threat	−14	46	−04	22	34	22	27
17. Milact	04	21	01	(74)	02	−08	01
18. War	06	06	−16	(91)	−21	−02	−04
19. Trpmvt	14	22	−06	25	01	05	(68)
20. Mobili	−27	47	22	36	−15	22	07
21. Accusa	−11	49	22	31	38	−09	02
22. F-Kill	17	−10	08	(79)	04	12	27
23. Cards	06	(82)	04	11	10	−17	13
24. Censor	20	09	−28	−33	−45	42	30
25. D-Emby	41	(73)	−15	−20	−13	17	03

[a] Parenthesis indicates pattern values $\geqslant .50$.

[b] Decimals omitted from all loadings. The oblique rotation is a part of the Mesa 3 computer program. It consists of the class of analytical solutions called *oblimin*, developed by John B. Carroll at Harvard. The *biquartimin* solution is selected over the *quartimin* or *covarimin* because the quartimin solution is generally biased toward factor axes which are too highly correlated, while the covarimin is almost invariably biased toward factor axes which are too orthogonal (cf. Harmon, pp. 324–34).

[c] Correlations between factors for oblique rotation are cosines of the angles between the factors rather than the intraclass correlations based upon the pattern values. Correlations $> .25$ are: $r_{F_1F_6} = .26$; $r_{F_2F_7} = .28$; $r_{F_3F_4} = .26$; $r_{F_3F_5} = .26$; $r_{F_4F_5} = .27$.

measures on the other, propositions about these conflict measures should be qualified to this extent: the data of nations in which there is little interest *may not* be included in the correlations from which the propositions are inferred. But an alternative explanation is also plausible. The correlation of the cards measure of world interest with diplomatic behavior *may* be due to increased interest when there is diplomatic conflict. Also, the more important nations

have more interactions with other nations, and this may give them more opportunities for protest as well as more foreign newspapers in which their activities are reported.

Besides the *turmoil* and *diplomatic* dimensions, other factors in the oblique matrix of Table 6 may be interpreted. These are *internal war* (factor 3) and international *war* (factor 4). The merged factor analysis seems to show a lack of relationship between domestic and foreign

TABLE 7

PREDICTIONS OF 1955–57 FOREIGN CONFLICT BEHAVIOR[a]: INDEPENDENT VARIABLES—TURMOIL,
REVOLUTIONARY, SUBVERSION

Dependent variable	Year	Standard deviation	Standard error	Multiple R	R^2
War	1955–57	2.40	2.36	.26	.07
Diplomacy	1955–57	1.49	1.46	.26	.07
Belligerency	1955–57	1.00	.97	.31	.10

[a] $N = 77$ (Rummel, 1963, p. 20).

conflict behavior. This relationship may be investigated more precisely by using multiple regression.

Multiple Regression[15]

Both forms of conflict behavior for 1958–60 are regressed upon one another to discover the relationship between them at one cross section in time. In addition, the 1958–60 data are regressed on the 1955–57 data in order to discover the relationship between domestic and foreign conflict behavior with a time lag.

The independent foreign variables for the 1955–57 study are the *war, diplomatic,* and *belligerency* dimensions. The values of the variables used in regression in the Rummel study are the factor scores each nation has on each of the six factors extracted. These scores were estimated by adding together the standard scores of variables which have a loading ⩾.50 on a particular dimension and no loading ⩾.40 on another dimension within the matrix (Rummel, 1963, pp. 15–16).

[15] Multiple regression is a method by which the variation in a single dependent variable is related to the variation in several independent variables. Whereas factor analysis is the appropriate method for ascertaining the *interdependency* among variables, multiple regression is appropriate for discovering *independence-dependence* relationships. The rationale for factor analyzing prior to the regression analysis is to select conflict behavior variables for regression which best index the dimensions and which are relatively independent of one another. For example, one text asserts that, "The more highly the independent variables are interrelated among themselves, the less reliably can the net regression of X_1 upon any of them be determined" (Ezekiel and Fox, 1959, pp. 283–84).

The variables used in the prediction of domestic conflict behavior for 1958–60 are measures of conflict behavior which measure the dimensions, rather than the dimensions themselves. These measures are called representative variables. They are selected on the basis of having the highest loading on the orthogonally rotated dimensions, but no other high loadings in the matrix.

Thus the variables for the 1958–60 domestic dimensions are anti-government demonstrations and revolutions, which measure the *turmoil* and *internal war* dimensions respectively. The representative variables for the foreign dimensions are war, protests, and severance of diplomatic relations, which measure the *war, diplomatic,* and *belligerency* dimensions respectively.

In the time lag regressions of 1958–60 data on 1955–57 data, representative variables rather than factor scores for 1955–57 were employed as independent variables. Thus, the representative variables for the 1955–57 domestic dimensions are anti-government demonstrations, revolutions, and guerrilla warfare, which index the *turmoil, revolutionary,* and *subversive* dimensions respectively. The representative variables for the 1955–57 foreign dimensions are foreign killed, expulsion or recall of ambassadors, and severance of diplomatic relations, which measure the *war, diplomatic,* and *belligerency* dimensions respectively.

Representative variables were selected rather than factor scores because the substantive meaning of the variable is clear, whereas the meaning of factor scores is not so readily apparent. In addition, the theoretical significance of the representative variables can be readily discovered through a series of replications. But it is

TABLE 8

PREDICTIONS OF 1958–60 FOREIGN CONFLICT BEHAVIOR[a]: INDEPENDENT VARIABLES—
ANTI-GOVERNMENT DEMONSTRATIONS AND REVOLUTIONS

Dependent variable	Year	Standard deviation	Standard error	Multiple R	R^2
Wars	1958–60	.75	.76	.03	.00
Severance of diplomatic relations	1958–60	.15	.15	.26	.07
Protests	1958–60	.35	.35	.24	.06

[a] $N = 83$.

considerably more difficult to ascertain the theoretical significance of dimensions because the exact composition of the dimension is unique to each study.

Table 7 gives the results of the predictions of 1955–57 foreign from 1955–57 domestic conflict behavior dimensions carried out by Rummel (1963, p. 20). Only eight percent of the total variance in foreign conflict behavior is explained by domestic conflict behavior.[16] The small difference in the values for the standard deviation and the standard error indicates the failure of the domestic dimensions to predict changes in the foreign dimensions.

1958–60, which is somewhat lower than the eight percent found for the 1955–57 data.

Table 9 gives the results of the prediction of the 1955–57 domestic from the 1955–57 foreign conflict behavior dimensions. Almost eight percent of the total variance in the domestic dimensions is explained by the foreign dimensions. This is remarkably similar to the seven percent of the total variance in the 1958–60 domestic which is predicted by the 1958–60 foreign basic variables. Table 10 contains these results.

From the two sets of regressions for the 1955–57 and 1958–60 cross sections, there

TABLE 9

PREDICTIONS OF 1955–57 DOMESTIC CONFLICT BEHAVIOR[a]: INDEPENDENT VARIABLES—
WAR, DIPLOMACY, BELLIGERENCY

Dependent variable	Year	Standard deviation	Standard error	Multiple R	R^2
Turmoil	1955–57	2.43	2.31	.37	.14
Revolutionary	1955–57	1.73	1.70	.27	.07
Subversive	1955–57	1.00	1.01	.14	.02

[a] See Rummel, 1963, p. 20. $N = 77$.

Table 8 contains the results of the prediction of the 1958–60 foreign from the 1958–60 domestic conflict behavior variables. Only about four percent of the total variance in foreign conflict behavior is explained by the domestic measures for

[16] The percent of total variance for the dependent variables is calculated by summing down the R^2 column, dividing the result by the number of dependent variables, and multiplying by 100 (Rummel, 1964, p. 20).

appears to be only a small relationship between domestic and foreign conflict behavior. This apparent lack of relationship at one point in time may be investigated further by means of time lag regressions.

Time Lag Regressions

The 1955–57 foreign predicts 22.3 percent of the variance in the foreign variables for 1958–60 (Table 11). But only

TABLE 10

PREDICTIONS OF 1958–60 DOMESTIC CONFLICT BEHAVIOR[a]: INDEPENDENT VARIABLES—WAR,
PROTESTS, AND SEVERANCE OF DIPLOMATIC RELATIONS

Dependent variable	Year	Standard deviation	Standard error	Multiple R	R^2
Anti-government demonstrations	1958–60	.36	.35	.32	.10
Revolutions	1958–60	.27	.27	.20	.04

[a] $N = 83$.

half as much variance (11.7 percent) in the 1958–60 foreign is explained by the 1955–57 domestic (Table 12).

TABLE 11

PREDICTIONS OF 1958–60 FOREIGN CONFLICT BEHAVIOR: INDEPENDENT VARIABLES—1955–57 NUMBER KILLED IN FOREIGN CONFLICT BEHAVIOR, EXPULSION OR RECALL OF AMBASSADORS, AND SEVERANCE OF DIPLOMATIC RELATIONS[a]

1958–60 Dependent variable	Standard deviation	Standard error	Multiple R	R^2
Protest	.35	.33	.40	.16
War	.68	.52	.66	.43
Severance of diplomatic relations	.16	.15	.28	.08

[a] The independent variables are representative variables from the 1955–57 study (Rummel, 1963, p. 13). $N = 74$.

TABLE 12

PREDICTIONS OF 1958–60 FOREIGN CONFLICT BEHAVIOR: INDEPENDENT VARIABLES—1955–57 ANTI-GOVERNMENT DEMONSTRATIONS, REVOLUTIONS, AND GUERRILLA WARFARE[a]

1958–60 Dependent variable	Standard deviation	Standard error	Multiple R	R^2
Protest	.35	.32	.42	.18
War	.68	.69	.12	.01
Severance of diplomatic relations	.16	.14	.40	.16

[a] These independent variables are representative variables from the 1955–57 study (Rummel, 1963, p. 13). $N = 74$.

Table 13 contains the results of the prediction of 1958–60 domestic by 1955–57 domestic variables. The domestic conflict behavior of the 1955–57 period explains 27.5 percent of the total variance of the 1958–60 domestic.

The 1955–57 foreign, however, cannot

TABLE 13

PREDICTIONS OF 1958–60 DOMESTIC CONFLICT BEHAVIOR: INDEPENDENT VARIABLES—1955–57 ANTI-GOVERNMENT DEMONSTRATIONS, REVOLUTIONS, AND GUERRILLA WARFARE[a]

1958–60 Dependent variable	Standard deviation	Standard error	Multiple R	R^2
Anti-government demonstrations	.38	.34	.44	.19
Revolutions	.26	.22	.60	.36

[a] These independent variables are representative variables from the 1955–57 study (Rummel, 1963, p. 12). $N = 74$.

TABLE 14

PREDICTIONS OF 1958–60 DOMESTIC CONFLICT BEHAVIOR: INDEPENDENT VARIABLES—1955–57 FOREIGN KILLED, EXPULSION OR RECALL OF AMBASSADORS, AND SEVERANCE OF DIPLOMATIC RELATIONS[a]

1958–60 Dependent variable	Standard deviation	Standard error	Multiple R	R^2
Anti-government demonstrations	.38	.38	.16	.03
Revolutions	.26	.25	.37	.14

[a] These independent variables are representative variables from the 1955–57 study (Rummel, 1963, p. 12). $N = 74$.

predict the 1958–60 domestic variables. The results in Table 14 show that only 8.5 percent of the variance in the 1958–60 domestic is explained by the 1955–57 foreign variables.

From the time lag regressions one may conclude that there is a *moderate relationship* between domestic conflict behavior at one time and the same behavior at a later point in time. Similarly, there is a *moderate relationship* between foreign conflict behavior at the two points in time. In the absence of the time lag, only seven percent and 4.3 percent of the variance are explained by the 1958–60 foreign and domestic measures respectively. With the introduction of the lag, the explained variance increases to 8.5 and 11.7 percent. Although this is still a very small amount of variance on which to make a generalization, there seems to be some relationship between domestic and foreign conflict behavior with a time lag.[17]

Discussion and Summary

Dimensions of Domestic Conflict Behavior

One finding that appears to emerge from the 1958–60 data is that the structure of domestic conflict behavior is slightly different from that found in 1955–57. The internal war dimension combines the 1955–57 *subversion* and *revolutionary* dimensions; the *turmoil* dimension, however, is found in both periods.

The correlation matrix of Table 1 illustrates the changes in shared variance that revolutions and guerrilla war have which may result in their separation in the 1955–57 study and their merger in this study. The correlation of the two for the 1955–57 data is only .33, while for 1958–60 it is .65. In addition to the fact of an increase in shared variance from the 1955–57 pe-

riod, the absolute magnitudes and means for revolutions and guerrilla war have also increased. During 1955–57 ($N = 77$) there were 17 codings for the presence of guerrilla warfare and 44 revolutions with means of .21 and .57 respectively; on the other hand, during 1958–60 ($N = 83$), there were 58 codings for the presence of guerrilla warfare and 83 revolutions with means of .70 and 1.00 respectively.

Although 1958–60 domestic conflict behavior has a slightly different structure in comparison with the earlier period, foreign conflict behavior bears a remarkable similarity across the two points in time.

Dimensions of Foreign Conflict Behavior

The dimensions of 1958–60 foreign conflict behavior appear to reflect a strong similarity of structure with the 1955–57 dimensions with respect to the *type* of variables which define the clusters as well as to the magnitude and *pattern* of the loadings themselves. For example, the *war, diplomatic,* and *belligerency* dimensions do emerge from the 1958–60 data and the intraclass correlations are relatively high (see Table 7).

The previously mentioned change in the ratio of high to total correlations among the foreign measures in Table 1 might account for the slightly weaker loadings and consequent smaller amount of explained variance for the 1958–60 data. Not only are the correlations among the foreign variables lower than in the earlier period; the intensity of conflict behavior appears to have decreased also. The most extreme change can be seen in one of the measures of intensity—number killed due to foreign conflict behavior. The total for 1955–57 is 51,123 with a mean value of 664, while for 1958–60 the total is 974 with a mean of 11.74.

Hence, foreign conflict behavior appears to be slightly less correlated and somewhat less intense during the 1958–60 period, but nonetheless it compares quite well with the earlier period as regards the dimensions of conflict behavior.

---

[17] The range of the multiple R is $\geqslant 0 \leqslant + 1.0$. Thus R cannot be negative. In order to see whether the time lag resulted in any negative relationships between domestic and foreign conflict behavior, reference was made to the zero order correlations. None of the negative correlations was greater than $r = - .08$.

Relations Between Domestic and
Foreign Conflict Behavior

The merged factor analysis and the regression of both forms of conflict behavior on one another suggest only a small relationship between the two. A stronger relationship was expected on the basis of the theories of scholars such as Lewis Coser and Georg Simmel:

(1) The unity of a group is frequently lost when it does not have an opponent (Simmel, 1955, p. 97).

(2) Hostilities preclude the group boundaries from disappearing and they are frequently consciously cultivated to guarantee existing conditions (Simmel, 1955, p. 97).

(3) If a group with basic consensus regarding its preservation engages in outside conflict, internal cohesion is likely to be increased (Coser, 1956, pp. 92–93).

(4) Groups may look for enemies to help maintain and/or increase internal cohesion (Coser, 1956, p. 104).

(5) Exaggeration of the danger of an enemy serves to maintain group structure when it is threatened by internal dissension (Coser, 1956, p. 106).

Whereas Simmel and Coser agree as to the tendency for between-group relations to be largely a result of within-group relations, the experimental data of Muzafer Sherif and his colleagues suggest otherwise. Their general thesis is that inter-group attitudes and behavior are determined *primarily* by the nature of relations between groups and *not primarily* by the pattern of relations and attitudes within groups themselves (Sherif *et al.*, 1961, p. 38; italics in original). They conclude, however, that when friendliness already characterizes between-group relations, harmonious in-group relations probably contribute to solutions of mutual problems between groups (Sherif *et al.*, 1961, p. 200).

The theories and findings of Coser, Simmel and Sherif are based upon small groups. Thus, expectations at the national and international levels on the basis of their propositions should be qualified. The finding in this study of a small relationship between domestic and foreign conflict behavior, especially with a time lag, can be

viewed more clearly in the perspective of other empirical studies at the national and international levels.

Another theorist, Samuel Huntington, contends that a decrease in the frequency of interstate conflict is likely to increase the frequency of domestic violence.[18] He thus admits that some relationship exists between the internal and external conflict behavior of nations, but he asserts that it does not follow that external peace stimulates internal conflict or that there is any *necessary* relationship between the two. Furthermore, he admits that in this century the data appear to suggest a general relation between the inhibition of external war and the prevalence of internal war (Huntington, 1962, pp. 40–41). This agrees with Rummel's cross-sectional finding of a small inverse relationship between subversion and foreign conflict behavior (Rummel, 1964, p. 47); but little evidence is provided for Huntington's hypothesis in the present study.

Rummel also found a consistently positive relationship between domestic conflict behavior other than subversion and the *diplomatic* and *belligerency* dimensions. In the cross sectional correlations of Table 1 the highest correlations between domestic and foreign variables are between riots and troop movements (.40), and riots and anti-foreign demonstrations (.38). Since anti-foreign demonstrations help to define the *belligerency* dimension, and the riots variable does not appear on the *internal war* dimension, this study provides evidence in favor of a small positive relationship between domestic conflict behavior other than *subversion* and one of the variables which

[18] Although Huntington's hypotheses deal with the relationship between internal and external conflict behavior, he appears to have the international system as the unit of focus rather than the individual nations. In order for the propositions from the 1955–57 and 1958–60 studies to be comparable to Huntington's, one would have to sum each variable across all the nations and then examine the relationship between domestic and foreign conflict behavior at the *system* level. The design of this study, however, uses the *nation* as the unit, and examines the internal and external relationship across each nation.

helps to define the *belligerency* dimension.

Another facet of the relationship between the *diplomatic* dimension and domestic conflict behavior is suggested by Joseph McKenna (1962). McKenna suggests some internal effects of diplomatic behavior. He contends that diplomatic protests may function to assure domestic interests that the government is active on their problems and to provide propaganda for home consumption so that the general public may become aroused in support of the official policy toward the state to whom the protest is directed. More generally, he contends that the purpose of foreign policy is to influence external events so that domestic values are maintained and furthered (McKenna, 1962, p. 20; p. 26). Three of his findings bear directly on the theme of this study. He finds that the nations to whom United States protests were directed most frequently were characterized by revolution and other forms of domestic turmoil. Secondly, protest to major powers was less likely than to minor powers because the internal stability of the former probably minimized the number of offensive incidents directed at United States citizens. Thirdly, resistance to American demands was motivated by the domestic politics of the recipient (McKenna, 1962, p. 20; pp. 38–40; p. 201). The first two propositions suggest a positive relationship between domestic and foreign conflict behavior. Thus, he suggests a positive relationship between protests, on the *diplomatic* dimension, and revolution and/or turmoil. But, in the present study, the highest correlation between protests and a domestic variable is that with riots (.29), and in the oblique biquartimin matrix of the merged factor analysis, riots and revolutions appear on factors different from protests (cf. Tables 1 and 6).

The studies of Sorokin (1937) and Richardson (1960) may also be relevant to interpreting the findings in the present study. Sorokin visually examines data through seventeen centuries, 525 A.D. to 1925, and finds a small association between unsuccessful external wars and internal disturbances. As with the present study, he concludes that the presence or absence of general war and internal disturbances are fairly independent of one another (Sorokin, 1937, p. 487; p. 492).

From 1820 to 1945, Richardson finds 112 mainly internal as compared with 137 mainly external fatal quarrels (Richardson, 1960, p. 186).[19] Even though he is primarily interested in the relationship between deadly quarrels and such variables as the rate of armaments increase, trade, language differences, contiguity, and other nonconflict variables, he does allude to the possible relationship between intranation solidarity and external threats (Richardson, 1960, p. 156). But a proposition about such a relationship does not emerge from his data, nor does he subject one to systematic test.

Implications of Findings For Theory Construction

The principal finding of a small relationship between domestic and foreign conflict behavior may have implications for theory-building. There may be no "simple" relationship between domestic and foreign conflict behavior, but there may be a causal relationship which is being obscured by other phenomena. That is, the relationship may be mediated by a third variable such as the personality characteristics of the national decision-makers as is suggested by Haas and Whiting (1956, pp. 61–62).

Evidence against the "third variable" interpretation for *aggregate* data, however, is provided by the Dimensionality of Nations Project of which the present work is a substudy. The 22 domestic and foreign conflict behavior measures were included in a factor analysis of 236 national and international characteristics across 82 nations. A domestic and a foreign conflict behavior dimension came out *separate* from one another as well as from economic development, political orientation, and Catholic culture dimensions. The fact that domestic

[19] A fatal quarrel is a war in which a nation was involved which resulted in more than 3,163 deaths, e.g., more than $\log_{10}$ (deaths) = 3.5. Richardson contends that there is ambiguity as regards the classification of some forms of fatal quarrels; consequently, he categorizes them in three groups: mainly internal, mixed, and mainly external (1960, ch. 2; pp. 186–87).

and foreign conflict behavior dimensions remain separate within the larger context adds evidence that they are unrelated to other aggregate data at one point in time. Thus, having *controlled* for such things as the level of development, political orientation, and Catholic culture, the domestic and foreign conflict behavior dimensions remain separated. (Cf. Rummel, Guetzkow, Sawyer, and Tanter, *Dimensions of Nations,* forthcoming, 1966).

The "third variable" interpretation, however, may be valid for individual level characteristics as distinct from aggregate data. It may prove theoretically useful to inquire into the nature of the decision-maker's characteristics in order to see whether the relationship between domestic and foreign conflict behavior would increase. For example, the decision-making scheme presented by Richard Snyder and Glenn Paige (1958) might be relevant for suggesting third variables that mediate between the domestic and foreign conflict behavior relationship.

Summary

The goal of this study was to replicate an earlier work (Rummel, 1963) in order to obtain additional evidence relative to the dimensions of conflict behavior and the relationship between domestic and foreign conflict behavior. Data were collected across eighty-three nations on nine domestic and thirteen foreign measures of conflict behavior for 1958, 1959, and 1960. From a factor analysis of these data there emerged two domestic dimensions—*turmoil,* and *internal war*—and three foreign dimensions—*war, diplomatic,* and *belligerency.*

The *turmoil* dimension compares favorably with a similar dimension derived from the 1955–57 data, while the *internal war* dimension subsumes the *revolutionary* and *subversive* dimensions from the 1955–57 study. The threee 1958–60 foreign dimensions are quite similar to the three derived from the 1955–57 foreign measures.

From a factor analysis of domestic and foreign conflict behavior, the domestic measures separated themselves from the foreign variables, implying only a small relationship between the two. This rela-
tionship was investigated still further with multiple regression. Representative variables were selected on the basis of high correlation with the dimensions. Representative variables which indexed domestic and foreign dimensions were regressed upon each other to discover the relationship between domestic and foreign conflict behavior. The regression yielded a small relationship between domestic and foreign conflict behavior that increased with a time lag.

Three error variables were used to discover the extent to which systematic bias might distort the conclusions. Two of these, number of cards per nation in *Deadline Data* and number of embassies or legations in a country, were found to correlate highly with the protest variable and also to have high pattern values on the *diplomatic* dimension. It was concluded that the level of world interest in a nation is related to the tendency for a nation's protests and (to a lesser extent) its expulsion of ambassadors to be reported. Hence, propositions about these two conflict measures should be qualified to the extent that the data of nations in which little interest is expressed *may not* be included in the correlations from which the propositions are inferred.

Propositions

The following generalizations are offered on the basis of an analysis of domestic and foreign conflict behavior for 1958–60:

(1) The 1958–60 domestic conflict behavior of nations varies along two uncorrelated dimensions of equal importance—*turmoil* and *internal war.* The *turmoil* dimension is quite similar to the 1955–57 *turmoil* dimension, and the *internal war* dimension subsumes the 1955–57 *revolutionary* and *subversive* dimensions.

(2) The 1958–60 foreign conflict behavior of nations varies along three uncorrelated dimensions of the following order of importance: *diplomatic, war,* and *belligerency,* which compares favorably with the 1955–57 foreign dimensions.

(3) The variation in acts or occurrences of 1958–60 domestic conflict behavior are generally highly related in a manner similar to that for 1955–57.

(4) The variation in acts or occurrences of 1958–60 foreign conflict behavior are generally highly related, but not as highly related as that for 1955–57.

(5) There is a small relationship between 1958–60 domestic and foreign conflict behavior which increases with a time lag.

(6) Five representative variables measure the dimensions of domestic and foreign conflict behavior for 1958–60: anti-government demonstrations (*turmoil*); revolutions (*internal war*); protest (*diplomatic*); war (*war*); and severance of diplomatic relations (*belligerency*). These compare favorably with the representative variables for 1955–57: anti-government demonstrations (*turmoil*); revolutions (*revolutionary*); guerrilla warfare (*subversion*); foreign killed (*war*); expulsion or recall of ambassadors (*diplomatic*); and severance of diplomatic relations (*belligerency*).

(7) Level of world interest in a nation is associated with the tendency for its protests and expulsions of ambassadors to be reported.

Appendix I

Definitions of Conflict Behavior Measures

The criteria by which the conflict behavior measures were chosen and brief definitions of the measures themselves are the same as those used in the 1955–57 study.

Measures of Conflict Behavior

With respect to the methods and goals of this study, any act or occurrence chosen to index conflict behavior must: (1) be capable of empirical delimitation; (2) be an act or occurrence of sufficient interest to be generally reported—that is, data must be available; (3) be applicable to all countries (e.g., "colonial violence," if made a measure, would not be applicable to those countries without colonies) if spurious factors are not to result; (4) be as diverse as possible to cover the greatest possible range of conflict behavior; and (5) be an act of or within, or an occurrence with respect to, seven or more countries (this is to prevent the correlations from being dependent on too few such happenings and, therefore, to reduce the role of aberrations on what are meant to be general conclusions).

On the basis of these criteria, nine measures of domestic and thirteen measures of foreign conflict were chosen for this study. The domestic conflict measures and a brief definition of the conflict act or occurrence are as follows:

1. *Number of assassinations:* any politically motivated murder or attempted murder of a high government official or politician.

2. *Number of general strikes:* any strike of 1,000 or more industrial or service workers that involves more than one employer and that is aimed at national government policies or authority.

3. *Presence or absence of guerrilla warfare:* any armed activity, sabotage, or bombings carried on by independent bands of citizens or irregular forces and aimed at the overthrow of the present regime.

4. *Number of major government crises:* any rapidly developing situation that threatens to bring the downfall of the present regime—excluding situations of revolt aimed at such an overthrow.

5. *Number of purges:* any systematic elimination by jailing or execution of political opposition within the ranks of the regime or the opposition.

6. *Number of riots:* any violent demonstration or clash of more than 100 citizens involving the use of physical force.

7. *Number of revolutions:* any illegal or forced change in the top government elite, any attempt at such a change, or any successful or unsuccessful armed rebellion whose aim is independence from the central government.

8. *Number of anti-government demonstrations:* any peaceful public gathering of at least 100 people for the primary purpose of displaying or voicing their opposition to government policies or authority, excluding those demonstrations of a distinctly anti-foreign nature.

9. *Number of people killed in all forms of domestic violence:* any deaths resulting directly from violence of an intergroup nature, thus excluding deaths by murder and execution.

The measures of foreign conflict definitions are as follows:

1. *Number of anti-foreign demonstrations:* any demonstration or riot by more than 100 people directed at a particular foreign country (or group of countries) or its policies.

2. *Number of negative sanctions:* any non-violent act against another country—such as boycott, withdrawal of aid—the purpose of which is to punish or threaten that country.

3. *Number of protests:* any official diplomatic communication or governmental statement, the

purpose of which is to complain about or object to the policies of another country.

4. *Number of countries with which diplomatic relations severed:* the complete withdrawal from all official contact with a particular country.

5. *Number of ambassadors expelled or recalled:* any expelling of an ambassador from, or recalling for other than administrative reasons an ambassador to, a particular country—this does not involve expulsion or recall resulting from the severance of diplomatic relations.

6. *Number of diplomatic officials of less than ambassador's rank expelled or recalled:* replace "ambassador" by "officials of lesser . . . rank" in above definition.

7. *Number of threats:* any official diplomatic communication or governmental statement asserting that if a particular country does or does not do a particular thing it will incur negative sanctions.

8. *Presence or absence of military action:* any military clash of a particular country with another and involving gunfire, but short of war as defined below.

9. *Number of wars:* any military clash for a particular country with another and in which more than .02 percent of its population are militarily involved in the clash.

10. *Number of troop movements:* any rapid movement of large bodies of troops, naval units, or air squadrons to a particular area for the purpose of deterring the military action of another country, gaining concessions, or as a show of strength.

11. *Number of mobilizations:* any rapid increase in military strength through the calling up of reserves, activation of additional military units, or the de-mothballing of military equipment.

12. *Number of accusations:* any official diplomatic or governmental statement involving charges and allegations of a derogatory nature against another country.

13. *Number of people killed in all forms of foreign conflict behavior:* the total number of deaths resulting directly from any violent interchange between countries.

See Appendix I in the 1955–57 study (Rummel, 1963) for more extensive definitions.

Appendix II

List of Nations

Afghanistan	Argentina
Albania	Australia
Austria	Korea (Rep. of)
Belgium	Lebanon
Bolivia	Liberia
Brazil	Libya
Bulgaria	Mexico
Burma	Nepal
Cambodia	Netherlands
Canada	New Zealand
Ceylon	Nicaragua
Chile	Norway
China	Outer Mongolia
Republic of China	Pakistan
Colombia	Panama
Costa Rica	Paraguay
Cuba	Peru
Czechoslovakia	Philippines
Denmark	Poland
Dominican Republic	Portugal
Ecuador	Rumania
El Salvador	Saudi Arabia
Ethiopia	Spain
Finland	Sweden
France	Switzerland
Germany (DDR)	Thailand
Germany (Fed. Rep.)	Turkey
Greece	Union of South Africa
Guatemala	USSR
Haiti	UK
Honduras	USA
Hungary	Uruguay
India	Venezuela
Indonesia	Yugoslavia
Iran	Laos
Iraq	N. Vietnam
Irish Republic	S. Vietnam
Israel	Morocco
Italy	Sudan
Japan	Tunisia
Jordan	UAR
Korea (Dem. Rep.)	

REFERENCES

Carroll, J. B. "Biquartimin Criterion for Rotation to Oblique Simple Structure in Factor Analysis," *Science*, 126, 3283 (Nov. 1957), 1114–15.

Cattell, R. "The Culture Patterns Discoverable in the Syntal Dimensions of Existing Nations," *Journal of Social Psychology*, 32 (1950), 215–53.

———. "The Dimensions of Culture Patterns of Factorization of National Characters," *Journal of Abnormal and Social Psychology*, 44 (1949), 443–69.

——— *et al.* "An Attempt at More Refined Definition of the Cultural Dimensions of Syntality in Modern Nations," *American Sociological Review*, 17 (1951), 408–21.

Coser, Lewis A. *The Functions of Social Conflict.* Glencoe, Ill.: Free Press, 1956.

Eckstein, H. "The Incidence of Internal Wars, 1946–59." Appendix I of *Internal War: The Problem of Anticipation,* report submitted to Research Group in Psychology and the Social Sciences, Smithsonian Institution, January 15, 1962.

———— (ed.). *Internal War.* New York: Free Press, 1964.

Edwards, A. L. "Experiments: Their Planning and Execution." In G. Lindzey (ed.), *Handbook of Social Psychology.* Cambridge, Mass.: Addison Wesley, 1954, 259–88.

Ezekiel, M., and K. A. Fox. *Methods of Correlation and Regression Analysis.* New York: Wiley, 1959.

Haas, E. R., and A. S. Whiting. *Dynamics of International Relations.* New York: McGraw-Hill, 1956.

Haggard, Ernest A. *Intraclass Correlation and the Analysis of Variance.* New York: Dryden Press, 1958.

Harmon, H. *Modern Factor Analysis.* Chicago: University of Chicago Press, 1960.

Huntington, S. P. "Patterns of Violence in World Politics." In S. P. Huntington (ed.), *Changing Patterns of Military Politics.* New York: Free Press, 1962, 17–50.

Kaiser, H. F. "The Applications of Electronic Computers to Factor Analysis," *Education and Psychological Measurement,* 19 (1959), 413–20.

————. "The Varimax Criterion for Analytic Rotation in Factor Analysis." *Psychometrika,* 23, 3 (Sept. 1958), 187–200.

Katz, D. "Field Studies." In H. Festinger and D. Katz (eds.), *Research Methods in the Behavioral Sciences.* New York: Dryden Press, 1953, 56–97.

McKenna, Joseph C. *Diplomatic Protest in Foreign Policy.* Chicago: Loyola University Press, 1962.

Richardson, Lewis F. *Statistics of Deadly Quarrels.* Pittsburgh, Pa.: Boxwood Press, 1960.

Rosecrance, Richard N. *Action and Reaction in World Politics.* Boston: Little, Brown, 1963.

Rummel, R. J. "The Dimensions of Conflict Behavior Within and Between Nations," *General Systems Yearbook,* 8 (1963), 1–50.

————. "Testing Some Possible Predictors of Conflict Behavior Within and Between Nations," Proceedings of the Peace Research Conference, Nov. 18–19, 1963.

————. "Dimensions of International Relations in the Mid-1950s." Forthcoming, 1966.

————, Harold Guetzkow, Jack Sawyer, and Raymond Tanter. *Dimensions of Nations.* Forthcoming, 1966.

Sherif, M., *et al, Intergroup Conflict and Cooperation: The Robbers Cave Experiment.* Norman: University of Oklahoma Institute of Group Relations, 1961.

Sidman, M. *Tactics of Scientific Research.* New York: Basic Books, 1960.

Simmel, Georg. *Conflict and the Web of Intergroup Affiliations.* Glencoe, Ill.: Free Press, 1955.

Snyder, R., and G. Paige. "The United States Decision to Resist Aggression in Korea: The Application of an Analytical Scheme," *Administrative Science Quarterly,* 3 (1958), 341–78.

Sorokin, P. *Social and Cultural Dynamics,* Vol. III. New York: American Book, 1937.

Wright, Quincy. *A Study of War.* Chicago: University of Chicago Press, 1942.

————. "The Nature of Conflict," *Western Political Quarterly,* 4 (June 1951), 193–209.

DIMENSIONS OF CONFLICT BEHAVIOR
WITHIN NATIONS, 1946-59[*] [1]

R. J. RUMMEL

Introduction

Conflict behavior within nations may take a number of forms. There may be riots, demonstrations, coups, social revolutions, guerrilla warfare, assassinations, general strikes, and so on. Any one of these forms may occur by itself or in conjunction with others. When a number of conflict acts take place together within a nation, such as riots, demonstrations, and general strikes, we can speak of a cluster of conflict behavior. If such behavior is generally found to cluster together for all nations, then we might speak of a *dimension* of conflict behavior.

The identification of such dimensions within an empirical domain constitutes one of the first stages of scientific analysis. To discover dimensions helps to reduce a large number of phenomena to major patterns of covariation—to suggest labels by which such phenomena can be parsimoniously conceptualized, and to provide handles by which they might be analyzed and manipulated. Within the social sciences, research has been pursued for decades by those interested in identifying empirical dimensions in their domains. The primary tool of these investigations has been factor analysis,[2] a method for determining the major clusters of variation—dimensions—among phenomena of concern.

The goal of this paper is to apply this method to conflict behavior within countries from 1946 to 1959 in an attempt to delineate their major dimensions and to compare the results with those of similar studies.

Methodology

The data used were collected by Harry Eckstein (1962) from the *New York Times Index* on twelve kinds (measures) of domestic conflict for 113 countries for 1946–59: internal warfare, turmoil, rioting, large-scale terrorism, small-scale terrorism, mutinies, coups, plots, administrative actions, quasi-private violence, total number of unequivocal acts of violence (UE), and total number of unequivocal plus equivocal acts of violence (UE + E). A thirteenth measure, extended violence, derived from his tables was also used. (See Appendix for definitions.)

The data generally have negative exponential distributions, with more than a majority of nations for each measure having zero values. UE and UE + E measures were normally distributed.

To test for the effect and existence of systematic data error on the analysis, a preliminary correlation matrix and factor analysis through oblique (biquartimin) rotation was computed for Eckstein's *raw* data on thirteen measures of conflict behavior in addition to three measures of error.[3] The results, along with a discussion of the error measures, are filed with the American Documentation Institute (see footnote 1).

This preliminary error analysis of the data indicated that sources of systematic

[*] Reprinted by permission of the author and publisher from *Journal of Conflict Resolution*, 1966, *10*: 65–73.

[1] Prepared in connection with research supported by the National Science Foundation, contracts NSF-G24827 and NSF-GS-536. I am indebted to Richard Chadwick, Raymond Tanter, and Dina Zinnes for comments on a prior draft.

Ed. Note: An extended version of this paper has been deposited with the American Documentation Institute. Order Document No. 8691 from the Chief, Photoduplication Service, Library of Congress, Washington 25, D.C., Auxiliary Publication Project, remitting $1.75 for microfilm (35mm) or $2.50 for photocopies.

[2] For an overview of methodological and empirical factor analysis studies, see the bibliography contained in Harman (1960).

[3] See Rummel (1965) for a methodological discussion of assessing error in this fashion. For other applications of the methodology, see Rummel (1963) and Tanter (1964a).

error in the Eckstein data, as indexed in the above measures, generally would have only a random error effect, *if any*, on the results of correlating and factoring the data (Rummel, 1965). They might cause the correlations among the data to be lower than they should be, but they would not create distortion of the factor structure.

Results

The subsequent *substantive* analysis was carried out on the thirteen conflict behavior measures with all, except the normally distributed UE and UE + E data, log transformed.[4] The correlation matrix is on file in the extended version of this paper (see footnote 1). The unrotated and rotated factors are given here in Table 1. Orthogonal and oblique factor matrices are shown for comparison.[5]

A comparison of the orthogonal and oblique factor rotations in Table 1 shows little difference in loadings between them and no change in interpretation. That such should be expected is indicated by the low correlation (given in footnote d of the table) between the oblique factors. This low correlation and absence of change in interpretation from orthogonal to oblique rotations argues that we are dealing here with relationships that have an orthogonal structure—that is, dimensions which are *independent* of one another.

Turning to an interpretation of these independent dimensions based on the orthogonally rotated matrix given in Table 1, the first factor is seen to delineate a cluster of relationships among mutinies (.73),[6] coups (.85), and plots (.83). The UE (.55) and UE + E (.61) measures and administrative actions (.57) have lesser loadings. The nature of the highly loaded variables suggests that this is a *revolution* dimension involving rebellion, planned or carried out, against government authority. Although administrative action is not very highly loaded on this factor (a loading of .57 means that the factor accounts for 32.5 percent of its variance), it has its highest loading of the three factors on the *revolution* factor.

Revolutionary conflict behavior takes place independently of the relationships evidenced by factor 2. Warfare, or guerrilla warfare (see definitions in Appendix), and extended violence (.78 and .83, respectively) mainly define this factor. Large-scale terrorism (.46) has a low but still appreciable loading. The nature of this factor seems to be one of *subversion*, that is, attempts to undermine the strength of the government and to cause defection of the people through unconventional warfare and terrorism. This conflict behavior for 113 countries, 1946–59, takes place independently of revolution—of direct attempts to overthrow the government.

The *revolution* and *subversion* dimensions represent planned conflict behavior. The third dimension, on the other hand, delimits a kind of spontaneous conflict behavior. Riots (−.74), turmoil (−.54), small-scale terrorism (−.66), quasi-private violence (−.59), and the two summation measures, UE (−.75) and UE + E (−.74), are the variables mainly involved in this cluster.[7] Such conflict behavior appears to represent a *turmoil* dimension, a dimension of unplanned, uncoordinated violence which generally occurs unrelated to revolutionary and subversive behavior.

---

[4] With negative exponential distributions, the problem was to pull in extreme values at the right tail.

[5] The biquartimin criteria were used for the oblique rotation. As a check, the covarimin and quartimin solutions were also calculated. Although these different oblique solutions resulted in small changes in loadings, the interpretation of the factor patterns remained the same in each case.

[6] Since we are discussing the orthogonal results, the loadings given in parentheses may be considered as the *correlation* of the particular measure with the dimension.

[7] The author is indebted to Raymond Tanter and Richard Chadwick for independently pointing out that UE and UE + E are necessarily related to each other. Tanter further suggested that since they are summary measures, they are necessarily related to riots as well. As a consequence of this large shared variance, they might result in spurious factors; such would most likely be the case with the factor being discussed. To check the possibility of spurious factors, the author reanalyzed the data for all except the UE and UE + E measures. The new factor structure came out largely the same with each factor maintaining the identical interpretation.

TABLE 1

FACTOR MATRICES OF 1946–59 CONFLICT BEHAVIOR TRANSFORMED DATA[a]

Variable	Unrotated factors[b]				Orthogonally rotated factors[c]			Oblique factors, P matrix[d]		
	1	2	3	h2	1	2	3	1	2	3
1. UE	(.94)	.11	−.15	.92	(.55)	.25	(−.75)	(.76)	(.52)	.21
2. Warfare	.41	(.61)	.35	.67	.22	(.78)	−.12	.16	.19	(.77)
3. Turmoil	.36	.21	−.36	.31	−.02	.11	(−.54)	(.55)	−.05	.11
4. Riots	(.82)	.01	−.27	.74	.44	.08	(−.74)	(.74)	.41	.05
5. Large-scale terrorism	(.55)	.40	−.03	.46	.21	.46	−.45	.47	.17	.45
6. Small-scale terrorism	(.75)	.05	−.22	.61	.41	.12	(−.66)	(.66)	.37	.09
7. Mutinies	(.61)	−.09	.47	.60	(.73)	.26	−.03	.04	(.72)	.21
8. Coups	(.63)	−.31	.49	.73	(.85)	.07	.01	−.01	(.85)	.01
9. Plots	(.75)	−.36	.25	.75	(.83)	−.04	−.25	.24	(.83)	−.10
10. Admin. actions	(.56)	−.41	−.03	.49	(.57)	−.25	−.31	.30	(.57)	−.29
11. Quasi-private	.15	.05	(−.65)	.45	−.26	−.20	(−.59)	(.58)	−.28	−.18
12. Extended violence	.06	(.81)	.25	.72	−.18	(.83)	−.01	.05	−.20	(.84)
13. UE + E	(.96)	.01	−.16	.94	(.61)	.15	(−.74)	(.75)	(.57)	.11
Percent common variance:	40.7	12.6	11.0	64.3	26.8	13.7	23.8			
Sum of squares:								3.14	3.33	1.74

[a] Loadings ≥|.50| are given in parentheses.

[b] N = 113. Principal components technique with unities in the principal diagonal of the correlation matrix. Calculations of unrotated and orthogonally rotated factor matrices carried out on the Northwestern University IBM 709, using the University of Chicago Mesa 2 factor analysis program.

[c] Kaiser's varimax criterion employed for the rotation and only factors with eigenvalues ≥1.0 rotated.

[d] Factor pattern matrix of the biquartimin criterion. Factor correlations (cosines) are $r_{12} = .05$, $r_{13} = −.05$, $r_{23} = .10$. Computations carried out on the Indiana University IBM 709, using a revised version of John Carroll's "IBM 709–7090 Program for Generalized Analytic Rotation Solution in Factor Analysis." The biquartimin solution reported here took 60 major cycles at a precision level for the criterion of 0.1 × 10⁻⁴, and 308 iterations at an iteration accuracy of 0.1 × 10⁻⁵.

Comparison with Other Studies

The delineation of these three dimensions does not suffice. They must be compared with the results of other analyses—linked with similar studies so that our convergence upon reliable dimensions of domestic conflict behavior may be assessed.

Two similar studies have been done of domestic conflict behavior.[8] The first (Rummel, 1963) factored, and rotated orthogonally, 1955–57 domestic conflict behavior data for 77 nations[9] on nine measures:

[8] Other studies (Tanter, 1964b; Rummel, 1965a) have been completed, but too late for their results to be included. The findings, however, further confirm the conclusions of this paper. See footnote 12 below.

[9] Only nations that exchanged ambassadors and had a population greater than 750,000 were included.

assassinations, general strikes, guerilla warfare, major government crises, purges, riots, revolution, demonstrations, and number killed in all domestic conflict. (See Appendix I of the Tanter article in this issue for their definitions.) Most of the data came from *The New York Times Index,* although *Facts on File, Keesing's Contemporary Archives, Britannica Book of the Year,* and *New International Yearbook* were also consulted. Systematic error from censorship or lack of interest of the press in a nation was checked by including two measures of this error in a factor analysis of the data. They were found to have low correlations with the data and to load highly on a factor by themselves.

The orthogonal rotation of the 1955–57 data resulted in three dimensions, which—in terms of overlapping definitions—have the same meaning as those found in the

TABLE 2

COMPARISON OF THE OBLIQUE FACTOR MATRICES FOR THE ECKSTEIN, RUMMEL, AND TANTER DATA[a]

Eckstein variables	Rummel-Tanter variables	Oblique P factor matrices[b]								
		E_1	R_1	T_1	E_2	R_2	T_3	E_3	R_a	T_2
1. UE		(76)			(52)					
	9. Killed		32				(80)		43	(72)
13. UE + E		(75)			(57)					
2. Warfare								(77)		
12. External violence	3. Guerrilla war						35	(84)	(91)	(91)
5. Large-scale terrorism				47				45		
6. Small-scale terrorism	1. Assassinations	(66)	(63)	(52)	37				(65)	32
3. Riots		(74)			41					
	6. Riots		(82)	(87)		36				
4. Turmoil		(55)								
7. Mutinies					(72)					
8. Coups	7. Revolution				(85)	(87)	32			(82)
9. Plots					(83)					
10. Admin. actions	5. Purges	30	38		(57)	(73)	(87)			
11. Quasi-private	——	(58)								
	2. Gen. strikes		(57)	(70)			(63)	–31		
	4. Major govt. crises		(62)	32						(60)
	8. Demonstrations		(88)	(90)						

100 × (sum of squares/number of variables): 24.0, 31.0, 27.8; 25.6, 29.7, 12.2; 13.4, 16.5, 28.2

Factor (cosines) correlations: $E_{12} = .05$, $R_{12} = -.12$, $T_{13} = .03$
$E_{13} = -.05$, $R_{13} = -.03$, $T_{12} = .35$
$E_{23} = .10$, $R_{23} = -.09$, $T_{23} = .17$

[a] Only loadings $\geqslant |.30|$ are given. Those $\geqslant |.50|$ are shown in parentheses.
[b] E = Eckstein data factors given in Table 1. R = previously unpublished biquartimin solution for factors published in Rummel (1963). Major cycles for the R-factors were 20; iterations were 1,131. T = factors taken from computer output graciously made available to the author by Raymond Tanter. Analysis was on 1958–60 data for 83 nations. Major cycles were 10; iterations were 199. The R and T oblique factors were calculated on the Indiana University 709 using the same program employed for the Eckstein data oblique factors and the same precision levels.

Eckstein data. They too were labeled *revolution, subversion,* and *turmoil* dimensions.

A second study (Tanter, 1964a; and see Tanter's article in the present issue of this journal) involved replicating the analysis of the 1955–57 conflict behavior data. The factor analysis and rotation of Tanter's 1958–60 data delineated the same *turmoil* dimension as found in the 1946–59 and 1955–57 data. The revolution and subversion dimensions of these earlier data, however, were found by Tanter to merge into one dimension—an *internal war* dimension. Nonetheless, the distinction between planned behavior (*revolutionary* and *subversive* behavior) and spontaneous, uncoordinated behavior (*turmoil*) was found to hold.

The three findings for the three sets of data, 1946–59, 1955–57, and 1958–60, are given in Table 2. The measures used are reordered and combined according to similarity in definitions.[10] Tanter's unpublished

[10] Table 4 of the extended version of this paper, on file with the ADI (see footnote 1), similarly orders and compares the results of the orthogonal solutions.

three-factor rotations are shown for better comparison rather than the two dimensions included in his 1964a study.

The first set of similar factors in Table 2 are the *turmoil* dimensions, E_1, R_1, and T_1. The very close congruence between the high loadings of R_1 and T_1 can be seen. Their congruence with E_1 is also apparent although it is less evident because of the different measures being used. Considering the set of three factors, riots (.74) and turmoil (.55) are loaded on E_1, riots on R_1 and T_1 (.82 and .87, respectively). Small-scale terrorism has a high loading on E_1 (.66) and assassinations on R_1 (.63) and T_1 (.52). None of the three has a high loading for revolutions, purges, or guerrilla war-like measures. UE and UE + E, on the other hand, have high loadings (.76 and .75, respectively), while domestic killed has no loadings $\geq |.50|$ for R_1 and T_1. If one considers the cells defined by the vertical and horizontal lines in Table 2, and the presence or absence of loadings $\geq |.50|$ within each cell, then for the six cells in which loadings can appear for all three factors, the correlation (loadings $< |.50| = 0$, loadings $\geq |.50| = 1$)[11] between E_1 and R_1 and between E_1 and T_1 is .78 in both cases. For the nine measures for which mutual loadings can occur for both R and T, the correlation between R_1 and T_1 is .80. Consequently, one can conclude that the same *turmoil* dimension has been extracted from the three sets of data.

Considering the second set of factors in Table 2, the E_2 and R_2 factors are the *revolution* dimensions previously discussed. The congruence between the two is quite high; their correlation coefficient, calculated in the same manner as those above, is 1.0—a perfect correlation. T_3, however, is a dissimilar dimension. Its correlation with E_2 is .45; with R_2 it is .30.

The third set of factors constitutes the *subversion* dimension for E_3 and R_3. The congruence between E_3 and R_3 is not as close as for the *revolution* dimensions, but still quite close, with a correlation of .63. In this set of factors, again, the T dimension has the least congruence. The correlation of T_2 with E_3 is .45; with R_3 it is .06.

These low correlations of T_3 and T_2 with the *revolution* and *subversion* dimensions is due to the fact that T_2 combines elements of both, and to the specificity of T_3 to purges (.87). Note the much lower percent (12.2) of sum of squares for T_3 compared to those for E_2 and R_2 (25.6 and 29.7, respectively). Tanter quite rightly points out in his study that a two-factor rotation is, accordingly, the correct one for his data. The *internal war* dimension he found, in addition to the *turmoil* dimension, was essentially a combination of the T_2 and T_3 factors given in Table 2. The greater congruence of this 1958–60 *internal war* dimension with a combination of the *revolution* and *subversion* dimensions for 1946–59 and 1955–57 can be seen by combining the E_2–E_3, R_2–R_3, and T_3–T_2 loadings.[12] The correlation between E_2–E_3 and T_3–T_2 is then 1.0; between R_2–R_3 and T_3–T_2 it is .32—an overall improvement over the separate correlations of T_3 and T_2 with the E and R dimensions.

Conclusions and Propositions

Before tying together the results of the last section, it should be noted, first, that the three studies compared involved data collected independently of each other. Secondly, while Eckstein's data were collected from one source, *The New York Times Index,* the 1955–57 data were collected from several additional sources, such as *Facts on File,* and the 1958–60 data were collected from yet an additional source, *Deadline Data.* Thirdly, it might

[11] Calculating the correlation between loadings dichotomized into high and low avoids the problem of misleading pattern correlation which may result from correlating the loadings themselves. For example, while the magnitude of the loadings on one factor may be quite high and those on the other factor quite low, if their patterns of loadings are the same the correlation between them may be perfect.

[12] For example, for purposes of calculating the correlation, the two E_2 and E_3 dimensions are combined into one $E_2 - E_3$ dimension in this fashion: if either (or both) has a high loading $\geq |.50|$, the combined dimension is given a high loading; if both have a low loading, the combined dimension is given a low loading.

be mentioned that although there is about a 20 percent overlap in years between the Eckstein data for 1946–59 and the 1955–57 and 1958–60 sets of data, the latter two sets are for quite different periods. The overlap with the Eckstein data still allows considerable room for different correlations and a different factor structure to appear as a result of the relations among the 80 percent of non-overlapping data, *were the relations different*. Finally, evaluation of the results should take cognizance of the tests for systematic error that were made on *each* set. In no case were measures of *censorship* or *world interest in a nation* related to the findings in a way indicating possible distortion of the dimensions delineated.

Considering these points with regard to the comparisons of the three studies, the conclusion is that insofar as post-World War II domestic conflict behavior is concerned, *turmoil* is a major dimension—one that should be taken into account in a typology or empirical study of domestic conflict.

Moreover, it also appears clear that the kind of spontaneous behavior represented by *turmoil* has little relationship to the organized, cooperative kind of behavior represented by the *revolution-subversion* or the *internal war* dimensions. This spontaneous-planned distinction is clear in the results also. The independence between the two argues that different sufficient conditions or causes must be sought for *turmoil*, on the one hand, and *revolution* and *subversion*, on the other.[13]

What is not unambiguous is whether the planned conflict behavior constitutes two dimensions, as found in the 1946–59 and 1955–57 data, or one as found for 1958–60. Tanter has explored this ambiguity by doing a factor analysis (Tanter, 1964b) of the combined 1955–60 data. In this study, the *turmoil* and *internal war* dimensions

were extracted also, further emphasizing the independence between spontaneous and planned behavior, but underlining the ambiguity as to whether the planned behavior constitutes one or two dimensions. Further research on different sets of data is certainly needed to approach a decision on this question.[14]

Some propositions are suggested on the basis of the results given and comparisons made above.

(1) Domestic conflict behavior is highly structured in terms of independent clusters of activities.

(2) A spontaneous kind of conflict behavior, or *turmoil,* is a major dimension of domestic conflict behavior.

(3) Independently of a turmoil dimension, domestic conflict behavior also involves planned behavior represented by *revolution* and *subversion* dimensions, or their combination into one *internal war* dimension.

Appendix

Definitions of 1946–59 Eckstein Conflict Behavior Measures

(1) *UE:* This is the total number of incidents of unequivocal violence which occurred during 1946–59.

(2) *Warfare:* "This category includes both civil and guerrilla warfare, which have not been separately counted because of the frequent inadequacy of the source. Like external wars, both are characterized by a high degree of organization of the opponents, the continuity of fighting, the presence of operational planning, and the existence of territorial control, extended or discontinuous, by the insurgents."

(3) *Turmoil:* "Simultaneous, continuous rioting of considerable duration in two or more distinct geographic areas."

(4) *Rioting:* "Relatively unorganized and spontaneous short-term incidents, typically involving police contingents and an unintegrated

---

[13] The findings indicate, for example, that the correlation between *turmoil* and *revolution* dimensions is near zero. Consequently, if any variable x correlates near 1.0 with either *turmoil* or *revolution* dimensions, then its correlation with the other dimensions will be near zero.

[14] The Rummel (1965b) study compared twelve factor analyses of data that included some measures of domestic conflict. Using Ahmnavaara's transformation method of factor comparison, it was found that *turmoil* appeared by itself unambiguously in all studies. Although not always distinct from each other as dimensions, *subversion* also appeared in all studies and *revolution* in eleven out of twelve.

mass whose objectives are somewhat modest. Frequently, however, the actual instigators are highly organized extremist groups."

(5) *Large-Scale (L.S.) Terrorism:* "Large-scale terrorism (L.S.) is the systematic use of intimidation and harassment by assassination and/or sabotage by relatively small but cohesive groups."

(6) *Small-Scale (S.S.) Terrorism:* "Small-scale (S.S.) terrorism distinguishes the above from the more undisciplined and discontinuous use of terror, and includes the occasional assassination or bomb-plant."

(7) *Mutiny:* "Violence on the established order by groups which are part of its own instruments of force, such as the police, military, etc."

(8) *Coup:* "Violence or the threat of it by one or more parts of the power elite against other parts, i.e., Lasswell and Kaplan's 'palace revolution'."

(9) *Equivocal Plots:* "These are equivocal either because they are exposed while in an early conspiratorial stage (and thus are not violent), or because the alleged plot may be only a pretext by which the government seeks to eliminate its political competitors."

(10) *Administrative Action:* "The removal of political opposition through the use of the formal administrative apparatus, as in Soviet-type purges, police round-ups or raids."

(11) *Quasi-Private:* "Cases which are equivocal internal wars because the violence was not initially directed at the government, or which appear not to be anti-government because of insufficient information. The Index gave a very high number of such cases for South Africa, but these so-called intertribal disputes are very often genuine internal wars."

(12) *Extended Violence:* This measure is derived from Harry Eckstein's indication of the existence of extended violence, such as a prolonged civil war, through a double asterisk attached to the particular nation in his data table.

(13) *UE + E:* This is the total number of incidents of unequivocal (UE) and equivocal violence which occurred during 1946–1959.

"The equivocal-unequivocal distinction is one between cases of clear-cut internal wars and cases which are ambiguous for these reasons: 1) effective countermeasures by the incumbent power holders minimized or precluded actual violence, e.g., abortive insurrections or coups; 2) cases for which the Times Index coverage was so inadequate that the presence of violence was difficult to determine; 3) cases which took the form of police or administrative actions which may or may not have involved outright violence, e.g., police roundups of political opponents, or Soviet-type purges; 4) the violence was apparently not directed at the incumbents in the first instance, and cases of intertribal disputes."

All quotes are from Eckstein (1962, Appendix I).

REFERENCES

Eckstein, Harry. "The Incidence of Internal Wars, 1946–59." Appendix I of *Internal War: The Problem of Anticipation*, a report submitted to the Research Group in Psychology and the Social Sciences, Smithsonian Institution, Washington, D.C., January 15, 1962.

Harman, Harry. *Modern Factor Analysis*. Chicago: University of Chicago Press, 1960.

Rummel, Rudolph J. "Dimensions of Conflict Behavior Within and Between Nations," *General Systems Yearbook*, 8 (1963), 1–50.

———. "Dimensions of Error in Cross-National Data in the Mid-1950's." Dimensionality of Nations Project, Yale University, 1965a (mimeographed).

———. "A Field Theory of Social Action and of Political Conflict Within Nations." *General Systems Yearbook*, 10 (1965b).

Tanter, Raymond. "Dimensions of Conflict Behavior Within and Between Nations, 1958–60." Doctoral dissertation, Indiana University, 1964a.

———. "Dimensions of Conflict Behavior Within Nations, 1955–60: Turmoil and Internal War." Prepared for delivery before the Peace Research Conference, University of Chicago, November 16–17, 1964b.

———. "Dimensions of Conflict Behavior Within and Between Nations, 1955–60." *Peace Research Society Papers*, 3, 1965.

ON REVOLUTIONARY CONFLICT*

FRANZ SCHURMANN

Years ago an excellent French film entitled *Le Triomphe de la Médecine,* with the great actor Louis Jouvet, juxtaposed two philosophies of medicine: Is health a temporary deviation from sickness, or sickness a temporary deviation from health? Jouvet espoused the first philosophy to a beaten-down old doctor who followed the second. Without arguing the philosophies, Jouvet simply compared the results. The old doctor had a failing practice because no one ever got sick. Jouvet built an ultra-modern hospital and got half of the population in sick beds. *C'est seulement une question de philosophie.*

It is apparent that men throughout the world are tearing each other apart in conflict and that the threat of conflict is growing. With Vietnam and the now resumed Soviet-American arms race, the threat of major war has risen since the halcyon days of peaceful co-existence. With rebellions in advanced capitalist countries now joined to the endemic social discontent of poor countries, the threat of domestic conflict has escalated in almost every country of the world. Americans in particular have become fearful of growing waves of violence and express that fear in powerful political movements calling for "law and order." Only a few years ago most Americans accepted harmony, consensus, integration, and equilibrium as the normal state of mankind from which there were periodic deviations. Our foremost theoretical sociologist, Talcott Parsons, integrated these values in an intricate body of sociological theory. His theory even explained physical sickness necessitating hospitalization as "deviance" from the norm. Our foremost political sociologist, S. M. Lipset, lauded the stability of an American political system that allowed conflict within a firm framework of consensus. President L. B.

Johnson made consensus a key assumption of his politics. Given this philosophy of essential harmony, a system could tolerate a broad range of conflict, eventually finding means of resolution to restore a dynamic equilibrium.

Today many Americans betray a view of the world in which war, not peace, is the norm; in which the urge to rebel, not the desire to conform, is the norm. When Jouvet, in his funereal suit, came to the sturdily healthy French mountain town, he took an ox-like yokel into his office, showed him an anatomical chart, aroused his suspicions about aches and pains, and ushered him, broken in body and spirit, from his office. Was the yokel sick before he went into Jouvet's office? Detractors of the triumph of medicine would say: No, Jouvet was a diabolical *meneur,* an "outside agitator," who brainwashed the simpletons of the village to stampede them into sick beds. Friends of the triumph of medicine would say: Of course he was sick, as were others. If people lived healthily to the age of 100 before, who knows that they could still do so without the crutch of modern medicine. The argument is pointless, for the key fact is that after the yokel left Jouvet's office, *he was sick* and so were many of his fellow citizens.

I

Anthropologists in the Durkheimian tradition have long known that man develops a world view with which to order his perceptions and judgments. Through these logics of cosmic, social, and human behavior, man develops a sense of reality and gives constancy to his life. Suspicious by nature, he invests his world view with a higher authority, notably God. Like all such logics, this world view must have some simple assumptions (a few primitives and axioms) on which to construct more elaborate structures of belief and action. In ancient China, for example, philosophers clashed bitterly over whether man was fun-

* Reprinted by permission of the author and publisher from *Journal of International Affairs,* 1969, *23:* 36–53.

damentally good or evil. The Legalists, accepting man's evil nature, furnished the ideology for China's first empire: a disciplined, militarily and bureaucratically organized, conquest state. Like Thomas Hobbes later, the Legalists saw man in an incessant state of insecurity, where reason and its disciplined products were the only ways to create a viable social order. The totalitarian state they created in the third century B. C. gave concrete form to their logic. For them, constancy was the product of reasoned effort. The Legalists' view was a generalization of China's condition in the centuries preceding their founding of the empire: war, rebellion, and chaos coupled with the development of philosophy, technology, and organization.

When the Chinese switched their world view from Legalism to Confucianism, they showed their yearning for a stable world and their discontent with the organizational totalitarianism of the first empire. The Confucianists, espousing man's goodness, inherited the old empire and gave it a stability it lacked by generating a ruling class of power, prestige, and wealth. Confucianism became the religion of China and remained so for two millenia. It taught that a good society comes about only through a learned elite, who in return for its authority, would wisely manage the passionate and disorderly people. Like their Roman counterparts, the rulers of the Han Empire organized vast areas of Eastern Asia, developed technology, and created great wealth. They performed well for two millenia, and Confucianism was accepted as doctrinal by the people. When they ceased to perform, they sought only to preserve their power and privileges, while continuing to preach harmony. The Chinese Revolution, which began in this century, finally destroyed them, and with them their world view.

The Chinese today have broken with the Confucianist past. Mao Tse-tung preaches the uninterrupted revolution "which sees the world in ceaseless and perpetual flux, with no final and definitive harmony attainable even under Communism."[1] For Mao,

all conflict is revolutionary, since uninterrupted revolution is the condition of man from the contending forces of world history to the perpetual struggle in his soul. The Chinese say man can only master his fate if he recognizes his condition. To believe in the illusion of harmony is a sure road to self-destruction. Let Westerners not forget that these views are close to Christianity: man is conceived in original sin; his redemption comes either through painful work (Catholicism) or through the arbitrary grace of God (Protestantism). A Western world view is the passion of Christ: suffering in the service of man, violent death at an early age. The Chinese have lately propagated their own passions: the self-sacrificing tales of Norman Bethune treating the wounded of the Red Army and the youthful death of the soldier Lei Feng in routine service to the people.

While the Chinese thus have taken on a Western world view (perhaps Marxism is a Christian heresy, as Arnold Toynbee suggests), we in the West have evolved a very different world view, one seeing harmony and not struggle as the condition of man. In the United States, this world view is expressed in our dominant ideology, "liberalism." Characteristically, liberalism has an economic foundation. Neo-Keynesian doctrine and practice have substituted views of macroeconomic equilibrium through governmental regulation for the classic view of the "invisible hand" guiding the market. We have come to believe that stability is possible because we have found the means to overcome the destructive effects of the business cycle. It is, therefore, not surprising that our dominant general sociology teaches notions of "the social system," and our dominant political sociology teaches that our politics are based on commonly accepted "central values." And even where sociologists suggest a greater stress on conflict, it is on conflict within consensus.[2] The

---

[1] Stuart Schram, *Mao Tse-Tung* (Pelican, 1966), pp. 222–223.

[2] See Talcott Parsons, *The Social System* (The Free Press, 1951); Seymour Martin Lipset, *The First New Nation: The United States in Historical and Comparative Perspective* (Basic Books, 1963); Lewis Coser, *The Functions of Social Conflict* (The Free Press, 1956).

strength of liberalism's world view is revealed in the slogan "integration," implying that even the seemingly most insoluble social problem—the gap between black and white citizens—could eventually be resolved by giving blacks a real stake in the established order.

Even the Soviet Union has gradually changed its world view. The Soviets state that essential unity prevails in their society. Their reasoning is Marxist. Marx wrote that the source of all class power is property. Property is a legal, hence social relationship, and, therefore, a class relationship. As long as there are classes in society, there will be class struggle. It ends when the oppressed seize and destroy the property system. For the Soviets, class struggle ended when the workers and peasants seized the property of the capitalist and feudal classes (except for recurring struggle against counter-revolutionaries, the latest instance being Czechoslovakia). Since the peasants are an emerging working class (becoming so as the industrial mode of production spreads to agriculture), only one class remains in Soviet society. Thus the working class is the ruling class, which in Marxian fashion generates state power to assure its domination. When Mao Tse-tung admitted there were still contradictions in Chinese society, N. S. Khrushchev retorted (to American newsmen) that there are none in Soviet society. In fact, Khrushchev proclaimed, the Soviet Union was moving into the stage of communism. The full development of industry and its extension to all Soviet society would produce affluence and replace the scarcity that had necessitated a dictatorship of the proletariat. The Soviets admitted that revolutionary pressures continue within the capitalist and feudal worlds. But since those pressures so often aroused the ire of imperialism and threatened the security of the world's first workers state, the Soviets lost their enthusiasm for them. They argued that "peaceful co-existence" between capitalism and socialism is the fundamental framework within which all change must take place. The Chinese bitterly accuse the Soviets of elevating the policy of peaceful co-existence to a basic ideological principle.

Paradoxically, while the Chinese have become "Christians," the Americans and the Soviets have become "Confucians," for the Confucians traditionally saw harmony, not struggle, as the condition of man, society, and the cosmos. Who is right? *Est-ce que c'est seulement une question de philosophie?*

II

What makes conflict revolutionary? Why is it not a mere dispute among men over specific grievances? The question is not academic, for increasingly in our own country we have conflict where one side of the confrontation sees it as an eruption of specific grievances and the other sees it as something so deep that only a great transformation can resolve it. While the former seek to narrow down the areas of dispute to arbitrable dimensions, the latter escalate grievances, making violent confrontation inevitable. At Berkeley this phenomenon appeared in the great Free Speech controversy of Autumn, 1964. The F. S. M. disputed the power and authority of the administration. The administration perceived early the revolutionary nature of the movement and sought to repress it. It held to the notion that "outside agitators," "professional radicals," or non-students infiltrating from neighboring Telegraph Avenue, were stirring up the basically peaceful students. If one could only eliminate these *meneurs,* to use a term from what the Chinese call the "French Revolution" of 1968, by some kind of surgical strike, then all would be fine again. The administration struck during the Thanksgiving lull and suspended the protest leaders. Two weeks later it faced revolution on the campus. As in *Le Triomphe de la Médecine,* we cannot say the campus was sick before the F. S. M., but once the F. S. M. was there, the campus was sick—and to this day remains sick.

To attempt an explanation of revolutionary conflict, let us recall Marx's theory of revolution. For Marx, the key social relationships in society prevailed in the primary means of production, which in capitalist society were the factories. The capitalists who owned and controlled these means of production found themselves in an ever-worsening contradiction with the working class, for as the rate of profit declined, they intensified their exploitation of the working class, pressing it bit by bit below the subsistence level. Yet the declining rate of profit was the product of an even more fundamental contradiction within the ruling mode of production. While capitalism needed market freedom to assure economic and technological growth, it also needed property controls to assure its domination over the means of production and those who labored. As a result, the working class suffered increasing oppression as well as exploitation. Revolution arises when the workers, in their growing consciousness, see that there is no way out of their misery except a total transformation of the entire system. Their misery is the product of an insoluble contradiction within the system itself. We know, of course, that Marx's prediction of the intensifying misery of the working class and the declining rate of profit have not come true. As the Baran-Sweezy and Gorz arguments indicate, consumption and affluence, not production and poverty, pose the key problems in our society. Nevertheless, let us not forget Marx's basic teaching on revolution: that revolution, the transformation of an entire system, occurs when a class of men see no other way out of their misery than revolution.

Marx saw human misery not only in the exploitation of men, robbing them of the value they produce, but also in their oppression, putting them in chains of servitude. The German word for oppression, *unterdrückung*, pressing under, vividly suggests man being driven into the ground. A ruling class adds oppression to exploitation because it must assure itself stable conditions within which to exploit; thus, men must be prevented from protesting lest they disturb the process of production. To exercise oppression, the ruling class uses the instruments of the superstructure, notably state power, which it controls. Oppression is thus the political counterpart of economic exploitation. Marx's theory of political economy saw both as products of the same basic contradiction. In the advanced industrial countries, however his argument on exploitation has become ever weaker. With the enormous acceleration of production, the

social range of consumption has been rapidly widening. The working classes and even "the poor" have become major consumers. Note, for example, the rapidly expanding market of black consumers in the United States. While some scholars have seen these new economic facts as bases for the integration of the working class into modern industrial societies, others, such as the Marxist scholar André Gorz, have shifted their attention from exploitation to oppression. Gorz begins his analysis of the work situation with a discussion on oppression where men are "mutilated, stunted in knowledge and responsibility."

. . . no matter what price [the worker] receives for selling his liberty, that price will never be high enough to make up for the dead loss which he suffers in qualitative and human terms; even the highest pay will never restore to him control over his professional life and the liberty to determine his own condition.

Gorz, in effect, argues that the dehumanization that inevitably arises out of the capitalist mode of production is the modern form of oppression. Gorz concludes: "the cultural battle for a new conception of man, of life, education, work, and civilization, is the precondition for the success of all other battles for socialism because it establishes their meaning."[3]

Marx, I believe, would have been unhappy with Gorz's approach, not so much because it implies spiritual rather than material misery, but rather because it substitutes the here-and-now building of a new society for direct political struggle with the agents of oppression and exploitation, the ruling classes of society. Marx's bitter critique of the Utopians was precisely over the question of whether the violent destruction of capitalism or the building of a new society within the confines of the old should have priority in the revolutionaries' struggle. Marx believed that only after the enemy was destroyed could one proceed to build a new society. That was Lenin's view, and it is Mao Tse-tung's.

As one of the world's great teachers and practitioners of revolution, Mao Tse-tung

[3] André Gorz, *Strategy for Labor* (Beacon, 1965), pp. 37, 132.

has much to say about revolutionary conflict. He fully shares Marx's notion that revolution occurs when men see no other way out of their misery than a transformation of the entire system. Mao is an apostle of violent class struggle, which he sees in its initial stages as often assuming the form of a "hurricane." He openly welcomed the black power movement in the United States as a "hurricane"; the Chinese so greeted the "French Revolution" of 1968. His most famous statement on revolutionary hurricane was written in 1927:

The present upsurge of the peasant movement is a colossal event. In a very short time, in China's central, southern, and northern provinces, several hundred million peasants will rise like a mighty storm, like a hurricane, a force so swift and violent that no power, however great, will be able to hold it back. They will smash all trammels that bind them and rush forward along the road to liberation.[4]

Even though he struggled in a backward agricultural country so different from the advanced industrial West, Mao has developed certain ideas about class struggle which may be relevant for developed societies. I believe that Mao puts far greater stress on oppression than on exploitation. From his earliest writings, Mao has denounced oppressive conditions in society: peasants driven into the ground by landlords and officials, women driven to suicide because of forced marriage, poor peoples tyrannized by colonialists and imperialists, ordinary people bossed by men in power. Now, with the Cultural Revolution, he has indicated that the Chinese Communist Party was spawning a new ruling class "thwarting, spurning, attacking the children of the working people."[5] Mao has been less concerned with the economic question of extracting wealth from producers. He has shown a remarkable propensity to divorce

economics from politics during the Cultural Revolution. Despite periodic attacks on "economism" and on re-emerging private property, he has allowed the technical-administrative bureaucracy of the Chinese government to continue managing the Chinese economy along lines set in earlier years. The result has been remarkably little damage to the economy, considering the turbulence of the Cultural Revolution. Just as oppression is a more serious problem than exploitation, so Mao has always elevated the political over the economic struggle.[6] What then is this political struggle against oppression which, for Mao, is revolutionary struggle?

Mao is classically Marxian when he sees all struggle as class struggle. No one reading Mao can fail to sense his deep intuitive thinking in class terms. He explains all great conflict from struggles within man's soul to competition between countries in class terms. For Mao, man's identity is formed by his social environment, and the key to his environment is class difference. As a son, he is already subject to a class enemy, his father. As a man, he will always find himself in conditions of subjection to higher social, therefore class, power. Mao sees the black power movement in the United States as class struggle. He regards Soviet revisionism as the result of a new ruling class, which has emerged in the Soviet Union, and seeks a capitalist restoration. Mao appears to believe that the mere existence of class differences means power differences, where one class will necessarily assume power over others. Conversely, he believes that power differences will result in the generation of ruling classes as had allegedly been happening in China before the Cultural Revolution. I have always accepted as a simple definition of power the control over men and resources for the achievement of someone's goals. Mao would agree, I believe, and add: it is always men in some collective, i.e., class, form who exercise this control. Such control in itself is oppressive, for it places trammels on men. Man can never liberate himself from these

[4] "Report on an Investigation of the Peasant Movement in Hunan" (March, 1927), *Selected Works*, Vol. I, pp. 23–24.
[5] See the "Supplement" in the second edition of my book *Ideology and Organization in Communist China* (University of California Press, 1968), and my forthcoming article in *The Monthly Review*, "Lessons of the Chinese Revolution."

[6] See Stuart R. Schram, *The Political Thought of Mao Tse-Tung* (Frederick A. Praeger, 1963), p. 83.

trammels unless he smashes the entire class through which such control is exercised over individual men. Mao thus holds an essentially political view of oppression; it is control by some men over others. What necessarily makes the political struggle against oppression revolutionary is the realization that oppression can only be eliminated by destroying an entire ruling class. This means for Mao, as a Marxist, the transformation of society.

Mao would say that conflict becomes revolutionary when men begin to see it in class terms. Mao is rather flexible in his notion of class. Since he has quietly dropped Marx's economics in favor of his politics, Mao has seen a much broader range of class differences in human society. The ruling classes in China were the imperialists (and reactionaries), bureaucratic capitalists, and landlords; the ruled classes were workers, peasants, and intellectuals. Unlike classic Marxists, who hedged about intellectuals because of their unclear relationship to means of production, Mao explicitly regards them as a distinct class, not only in China, but elsewhere. Given his stress on "particular" as well as "universal" factors in societies, he willingly admits all kinds of classes. If pressed, I believe he would say that the blacks, or more generally the poor, in the United States constitute a class—in his pronouncements on the subject he distinguishes them from the workers. The Chinese unhesitatingly hailed the class alliance of students, workers, and peasants during the "French Revolution" of 1968. A Maoist rule of political struggle would be: always put the issues in terms of class struggle, but be sure that the classes are real, concrete, and "particular." Given Mao's deep philosophical belief that all conflicts are in fact class conflicts, this rule of struggle merely makes manifest what is latent. For Mao, revolutionaries must generalize every concrete issue of struggle to a specific class of men who are the source of oppression.

III

Karl Mannheim once wrote that ideological thinking arises when men systematically come to distrust each other. They evolve holistic beliefs to explain others' actions and generalize these beliefs to a class of men in the same station.[7] However sharp that distrust was in the beginning, ideology deepens it into an unbridgeable chasm. At this point hostile classes exist, juxtaposed to each other in growing enmity. Liberals in the United States and "Marxist-Leninists" in the Soviet Union look with horror on radicalism which preaches fundamental revolutionary rather than specific resolvable conflict. The traditionally tolerant liberals, although ready to concede many if not all the grievances of the rebels, accuse the ideological radicals of wanting to propel the country into bloody internecine war. They concede white Americans are infected with racism, but argue that the black racism preached by the militants can only lead to a final holocaust. The "Marxist-Leninists" pressure the reformist Czech leaders to quash their free press, lest it incite the Czech people to counter-revolution. They had already quashed the sparks of freedom of speech in the Soviet mass media out of this same fear. We are, of course, back to the *question de philosophie*. The American and Soviet proponents of the essential harmony of society believe that their respective radicals are merely blind trouble-makers, who know not what disasters they will bring upon all. Yet their fears betray an even deeper conviction that the radicals may be right—that mankind may be in a fundamental Hobbesian state of war, which only carefully built structures of reason can keep suppressed. This is true of those Soviets who well remember the reign of terror on which their present system was built. It is also true of American liberals who in the decades since Roosevelt have helped to build governmental power structures, which brought economic stability and social peace to the country. Seeing Nixon and Wallace challenge them from the right, they pleaded for support from the dissidents out of fear that these structures might disintegrate. Both Soviets and

[7] Karl Mannheim, *Ideology and Utopia* (Harcourt, Brace, and Company, 1940), pp. 54 ff.

Americans share the fear that only a fragile arrangement between the two super-powers is preventing a nuclear holocaust.

Is ideology the criminal that incites class conflict and revolutionary struggle? Daniel Bell would say yes. I suspect Mao Tse-tung would agree, but not about why. Bell suggests the destructive ideology of class conflict. Mao sees ideologies of power and authority as the criminals. Societies must undergo cultural revolutions so that men can extirpate the vestiges of authoritarian ideologies from their souls. These authoritarian ideologies, which Mao sees in the way Marx saw ideology, are instruments of ruling class domination. For Mao all ideologies are doctrines of power and authority which preach the subjugation of men[8] and the domination of one class over another.

Let us recall that the oppression of the black race in America is based on an ancient and profound myth that whites are born to exercise power and authority. In contrast to Latin America, where blacks and Indians are regarded simply as irremediably poor, the United States has produced a class ideology of white superiority: all whites are innately superior to all blacks. Let us also recall another major area of inequality: the absolute and sharp difference between all students and all professors in all of our universities. The ideology supporting this class difference is based on the belief that teaching is the sole prerogative of professors and learning of students. In an age when the production of knowledge has become so important, the technological and organizational inputs in the production process are even more important than capital, land, and labor (as John Kenneth Galbraith argues in his *The New Industrial State,* monopoly over teaching becomes an issue of power and authority relating to the entire society). Wherever class differ-

ences are important, one will find that "social mobility" is a sensitive and carefully controlled process. [Think of all the trouble a black man must go through to be accepted as white ("passing"). Think of all the trouble a student must go through to become a professor (he too must pass, again and again).]

Black liberation and student revolt have been the two areas of conflict in America which appear revolutionary. But nowhere in society have class differences been as sharp as in the ghettos and the schools. In industry the difference between blue- and white-collar workers has all but vanished. Unions have power and authority and have convinced the workers that they can bargain effectively with management. In housing, ethnic discrimination, except against non-whites, has virtually disappeared. Even in the army, egalitarian tendencies have grown since the 1940's; officers and enlisted men increasingly look alike. But in prisons the class differences between convicts and guards remain clear, and none would dispute that convicts are a permanently revolutionary class. In our lower schools we find the same sharp class difference between teachers and students as in the universities, with the ideology of age prerogatives reinforcing the distinctions. Considering the growing turmoil in these schools, which is not just racial, the rising amount of juvenile delinquency, and other signs of rebellion among the very young, it would be well to consider the lower schools as the site of another source of major conflict in American society. During the Cultural Revolution, fifteen- and sixteen-year-old Red Guards played a major role in pulling revered Party leaders from their pedestals of power.

Mao would say that the blacks, the students, the convicts, and the young in school are all classes, not just because of some innate common characteristic, but because they are in a dialectical relationship, a "contradiction," with a class of men who exercise power and authority. Blacks are not just black because they are black, but also because they are not white. The Soviets would snort at this Maoist class analysis as nonsense, for only property produces

---

[8] I have always been interested in why the Chinese always refer to "the thought of Mao Tse-tung" and never "Maoism." I now suspect it is because an "-ism" connotes some doctrine externally imposed on man, while "thought" connotes an autonomous, free consciousness within the individual. See my *Ideology and Organization in Communist China* (University of California Press, 1966).

classes; these are just *prosloiki*, "strata" of the population. American sociology, with its "structural-functionalism," teaches that society is divided into many and changing strata, all somehow functionally interrelated. Mao proposes: wherever there is a body of men collectively exercising power and authority, there is a ruling and a ruled class; there is class struggle, and therefore, revolution, manifest or latent.

S. M. Lipset has argued that equality and achievement are central values of the American system. Yet his research on stratification has led him to believe that differential status is a mark of all societies. Open access to high status positions and an institutionalized circulation of changing élites assure democracy.[9] One could call this a theory of democratic élitism. Such democratic élitism is not as contradictory to equality as it sounds. Achievement implies success, and success is a scarce commodity. But equality means that all men have the same access to success, like runners at the beginning of a race. Blacks, Lipset would argue, have or should have the same chance to rise to the top as whites, as should students to become professors. While he would accept the higher status (= élite status) of professors as part of the natural order of society (equality and achievement are both therein enshrined), he would sharply reject racism as a central value of the American system. It is a vestige from a pre-modern, feudal social order, Lipset would say. American liberalism, as evident in the Kerner Commission Report, rejects racism. Lipset would accept the élitism of the universities and reject that of white racism because one accepted the equality of access to success while the other did not. To attain inequality by achievement is "American"; to achieve it by ascription, by which sociologists mean status given through birth, is un-American. Lipset's central values should be supplemented with a corollary axiom,

that in America equality plus achievement leads to legitimate inequality. If inequality is thus built into the system as much as equality and achievement, then why, in a free society such as America, should people not seek inequality through their own criteria? Since an apparently very large body of white Americans feels that the black man is innately inferior, why then is not this form of ascription a central value? For Lipset to concede this would force him to recognize a deep split within American society which supposedly is a single social system governed by universally shared common values.

The values of equality and achievement imply that all Americans are first and foremost individuals, to be judged socially only by their individual attainments. Yet white racism is a class ideology, for it brands the black man a member of a particular class even before he is born. Though the blacks so obviously exist as a class in American society, liberals are reluctant to concede them chances to succeed as a class—though they are willing to give them all the chances to succeed as individuals, at least verbally. Liberals say: we shall bury this myth of white superiority by treating all black men as individuals. They say: let us multiply the number of blacks in universities, but we must not set up black colleges. Let us bring them into our élites as individuals. When many black men exercise power and authority over white men (within the framework of our system), white men shall learn to respect them. But suppose we do have many blacks in our political élites, as we have increasingly in government, the army, and the police. Will it destroy the myth or simply convince many whites that they are living under semi-black occupation where those whom they consider inferior have temporarily arrogated power unto themselves? Those who supported Wallace apparently believed the latter. Will it convince the army of black poor in ghettos that something fundamental has changed in their condition? Considering that blacks hate black police as much as white police, it hardly seems likely.

American liberals and Soviet "Marxist-Leninists" believe that the fundamental

[9] Seymour Martin Lipset, *The First New Nation, op. cit.; Political Man* (Doubleday, 1960), pp. 404–417; and Reinhard Bendix, *Social Mobility in Industrial Society* (University of California Press, 1959), pp. 1 ff.

questions of power and authority have been resolved in their respective societies. They recognize that enormous tasks remain: to create full abundance and affluence, to extend citizenship to all men, to alleviate the sufferings of individuals. But both believe they live in a just political order. They believe that their respective societies are governed by benevolent élites, formed by democratic selection, and that no political order could do much better. Both believe strongly that the remaining class differences in their societies must and will be finally expunged. They clearly reject the notion that élites constitute classes and further reject the notion that élites could give rise to revolutionary conflict within their societies. For either country to revert to class politics, as Czechoslovakia intended with its projected political reforms, is disaster. For American liberals the black power movement, which seeks to mobilize the entire black race into a political force, portends ominous consequences.

Let us return to our *question de philosophie*. Mao would have an answer. As long as there are élites in society, whether at the highest levels of national or the lowest levels of local power and authority, there will be an actual or an emerging ruling class. This ruling class (or classes) will propagate ideologies to secure its domination. These ideologies unite the mass of the oppressed into an identifiable ruled class. Such a situation is latently revolutionary. If Mao has seen *Le Triomphe de la Médecine,* he might have said: of course, the yokel was sick, precisely because he was the yokel. It was he, not the mayor or priest, whom his fellow citizens shoved into Jouvet's examination room to become a guinea pig for Jouvet's promise of "free medicine."

IV

Conceding that the juxtaposition of classes defines a latently revolutionary situation, how does it become manifestly revolutionary? This question is more poignant considering the "several Watts," and "several Berkeleys" in America (and the pros-

pect of more), and the "French Revolution" of ten million workers and students in Spring, 1968. In China, the Maoists claimed they unleashed the full fury of the Cultural Revolution after Liu Shao-ch'i, the "Chinese Khrushchev," attempted to stifle the student movement by what were in effect, goon squads of the Party (May-June, 1966). During F. S. M. in Berkeley the revolutionary drama erupted after the Administration tried to blunt the movement by expelling the leaders. In France, May-June, 1968, revolutionary student fury erupted after the C. S. R.'s, the government riot police, unleashed the violence of their *matraques* against the students and onlookers. On April 4, 1968, blacks throughout the United States erupted in riots and looting after Martin Luther King had been assassinated.

History reveals many instances where repressive counter-revolutionary acts against a potentially revolutionary movement led to violent uprisings. When Chiang Kai-shek and his henchmen murdered every Communist they could lay their hands on, Mao Tse-tung sparked the Autumn Harvest uprising, which though put down, led to the resurrection of Chinese Communism as a powerful political-military force. Kornilov's attempted counter-revolutionary coup of July, 1917, aroused a revolutionary wave against him and the liberal government, paving the way for the Bolshevik seizure of power in October. As Trotsky said, "Kornilov's uprising gave the radicalization of the masses a big push forward." Batista's killings (reportedly 20,000 during the years 1946–58) of dissidents led to the formation of a powerful urban revolutionary movement, which along with the guerrilla warfare in the Sierra Maestra, brought Fidel Castro Ruz to power.

There is an endless list of the armed rebellions which have succeeded acts or processes of repressive violence committed by rulers against the ruled. Would there be a Vietnam war today if Diem had not sent in his police and military to "secure control" of the villages in 1956 to save them from the Communist threat? No matter how voluminous the lessons of history, rulers seem forever to believe that a quick, strong, surgical strike will relieve them of their tormentors.[10]

What is it in these acts of repression and counter-revolution that triggers violent counter-actions? Frantz Fanon, who has written so eloquently about the violence which the wretched of the earth unleash, has said about armed rebellions:

... news of the repression comes to the country districts in a grossly exaggerated form; the tale runs that the leaders are arrested, that machine-gunning is rife, that the town is running with the blood of Negroes, or that the settlers are bathing in Arab blood. Thereupon the accumulated, exacerbated hatred explodes. The neighboring police barracks is captured, the policemen are hacked to pieces, the local school-master is murdered, the doctor only gets away with his life because he was not home, etc. Pacifying forces are hurried to the spot and the air force bombards it. Then the banner of revolt is unfurled, the old warriorlike traditions spring up again, the women cheer, the men organize and take up positions in the mountains, and guerrilla warfare begins.[11]

Two elements in Fanon's description of the armed rebellion are compelling. First, news of the repression spreads like wildfire in mythic form. People believe they have seen a dramatic act, which at last revealed the true feelings of the rulers toward the ruled—a hatred so deep, that given an excuse, the rulers will murder the ruled. Second, the perception of this mythic drama unleashes an explosion of long-accumulating hatred. Mao Tse-tung would call it a hurricane. They mythic drama of repression suggests the importance of ideology in class struggle. Whatever the specific form of their ideologies, ruling classes usually present themselves as the friends, benefactors, and protectors of the ruled. The French in Algeria, whom Fanon described,

declaimed: "You Arabs too are French." The Americans are in Vietnam to fight for the freedom of the South Vietnamese. The Soviets entered Czechoslovakia to defend the Czech people against counter-revolution. Yet when people perceive their reality as oppression, they begin to experience unbearable "cognitive dissonance."[12]

Suddenly, perhaps momentarily, the rulers remove their masks, and reveal their hatred for the oppressed. If the act of repression strikes at a revered leader, the symbolic importance of the mythic drama is enhanced. When Martin Luther King was assassinated, blacks immediately saw it as a conspiracy of white racists, and exploded by rioting. Their anger erupted into counter-violence, often out of all proportion to the initial violence, but not out of proportion to the depth of the oppression they felt.

Est-ce que c'est une quéstion de philosophie? In the small French mountain village, people for years had believed the ideology of health propagated by the beaten-down old doctor. Then, suddenly, they saw the yokel stumbling, broken in body and spirit, from Jouvet's examination room. True, Jouvet had broken him, but the mythic drama of his breakdown spread throughout the village and convinced the villagers of their true condition: they were not healthy as they had been told for so long, but terribly sick. Jouvet's procedure thereafter may suggest certain policies for rulers afraid of their oppressed. He built a magnificent hospital and gave the village one of the finest medical systems in France.

---

[10] As Gordon A. Craig writes about Berlin in 1848: "perhaps the most significant characteristic of military thinking, once the news from Paris had been received, was a stubborn insistence that the remorseless employment of military force was the only means of preventing a repetition of the Paris experience in Berlin." The military moved and Berlin exploded. *The Politics of the Prussian Army* (Oxford University Press, 1964), p. 93 ff.

[11] Frantz Fanon, *The Wretched of the Earth* (Grove Press Incorporated, 1966), p. 93.

[12] See "Attitudes," *International Encyclopedia of Social Science*, Volume I, p. 463. This suggests that ruling classes, determined to keep the oppressed in subjection, might do better with an openly repressive ideology. That appears to be the approach of the Afrikaners in South Africa, who look with glee at America's racial troubles, while vaunting their own law and order. However, while "liberal" ideologies deny that the oppressed form a class, repressive ideologies like that of the Afrikaners openly accept the oppressed as a distinct class. Mao would argue that when a class develops true class consciousness, a latently revolutionary situation arises. The "cognitive dissonance" leading to armed rebellions forges a class struggle which repressive ideologies create in a different way. The result is the same, as the Afrikaners will surely discover one day.

V

Conflict becomes revolutionary when one class of people comes to believe that there is no solution to their oppressive misery except the destruction of the class which oppresses them. In its most terrible form this conflict is genocide where the class differences are racial. It may become class liquidation where differences are social. In a world inflamed with nationalist passions, the spectre of genocide always haunts us. In the last two centuries, there were numerous instances of class liquidation: the destruction of the French aristocracy during the French Revolution, the liquidation of the bourgeoisie and landed aristocracy during the Russian Revolution, the killing of millions of landlords during the Chinese Revolution. The great humanist, Alexis de Tocqueville, found it difficult to understand why the French Revolution erupted. Despite its economic difficulties, pre-1789 France was one of the most prosperous and progressing countries in Europe; much of the political system instituted by the revolution had already been built. De Tocqueville concluded:

Readers of this book who have followed carefully my descriptions of eighteenth century France will have noticed the steady growth amongst the people of two ruling passions. . . . One of these, the more deeply rooted and longstanding, was an intense, indomitable hatred of inequality. This inequality forced itself on their attention, they saw signs of it at every turn; thus it is easy to understand why the French had for so many centuries felt a desire, inveterate and uncontrollable, utterly to destroy all such institutions as had survived from the Middle Ages. . . . The other ruling passion, more recent and less deeply rooted, was a desire to live not only on an equal footing but also as free men.[13]

For de Tocqueville the issues of this revolutionary conflict were equality and freedom. Equality demands that the status differences which separate men be erased. Freedom demands that the power and authority which some men exercise over others

be destroyed. Mao Tse-tung suggests and many examples from history demonstrate that people perceive the source of their inequality and servitude as another class of men which oppresses them.

When a revolutionary stage begins in a country, it must be accepted as the condition of life. Gone for a long time will be the days of tranquility in public and private life. What will come under these conditions —revolution, counter-revolution, or reform —can never be planned for. Accepting the reality of revolution as the condition of life means accepting permanent uncertainty. Few people wish bloodshed and violence, though many are willing to die for justice. There is always great temptation for rulers to resort to swift repressive acts or even the more awesome instrument of counter-revolution, which in our times has meant fascism. For if the revolutionary process is to be peaceful, then the central problems which generate revolutionary conflict, élitism and ruling classes, must be resolved.

Thomas Jefferson suggested that a country undergo revolution once every twenty years to prevent the rise of new aristocracies. Mao Tse-tung has a similar idea behind his policy of periodic rectification movements. Power and authority generate élites that become ruling classes. The élite governing China's first empire developed the gentry as a ruling class. While this gentry was recruited openly from society, it constituted nevertheless a distinct class which monopolized China's power, prestige, and wealth. It ruled for two millenia because people accepted inequality and servitude as the natural condition of life. But when people cried for equality and freedom, the gentry was destroyed.

Not only have the values of freedom and equality reached all parts of the world, but élites and ruling classes seem ever less capable of fulfilling the high leadership expectations demanded of them. In their weakness they resort to oppression to assure their domination. Wherever such élitism exists, it will produce revolutionary conflict. Whenever élites out of weakness and desperation resort to repressive violence, they invite revolution.

[13] Alexis de Tocqueville, *The Old Regime and the French Revolution* (Doubleday, 1955), pp. 207–208.

A STRUCTURAL THEORY OF AGGRESSION[*][†]

JOHAN GALTUNG

1. Introduction

This theoretical essay is concerned with the conditions of aggression. We shall define aggression somewhat vaguely as 'drives towards change, even against the will of others.'[1] The extreme forms of this phenomenon are crimes, including homicide, between individuals; revolutions, including elimination, between groups; and wars, including genocide, between nations. These forms make aggression negative and problematic, a cause of concern and prevention. But one can also turn the coin and look at the other face: aggression as the driving force in history, as the motivational energy that moves mountains. However, we shall be mainly concerned with aggression in its extreme forms where it becomes a drive to hurt and harm others because they stand in the way of one's own self-assertion, and not look at the good causes this may serve in the aggressors' own minds. Aggression in this sense is pervasive, important and catastrophic, with modern technology as a multiplier. It should be studied at its roots, at the very points where it emerges.

The postwar period has seen relatively little research into this problem of origin, and much research into how to control aggression, for instance the tremendous effort that has gone into arms control and disarmament research. It is as if the apocalyptic display of aggression during World War II has had a paralyzing effect. But at the slogan level we find two of the United Nations' specialized agencies sometimes making use of rather simplistic theories of aggression. For the UNESCO, war starts 'in the minds of men' and for the FAO, 'in the empty barrel.' The former theory has found no support in contemporary psychology if the word 'starts' is taken in the sense of 'always originates.' But whatever the external conditions leading to aggression are, they probably have to pass through the minds of men[2] and precipitate as perceptions with a high emotive content before they are acted out as aggression. It should also be noticed that what psychology can say today is not that war cannot originate in the minds of men, but that there is no necessity why it should do so. Hostile aggression is no inseparable part of the innate structure of the 'minds of men,' but added to it from the outside, e.g. through special socialization processes.

Lord Boyd Orr's dictum about hunger serves, like the dictum about the minds of men, to direct attention to a possible side-effect of the worthy activities of the UNESCO and the FAO. To spread knowledge and food are positive activities in themselves—if in addition they can be shown to have a war-preventive effect they may be even more hallowed. But the number of examples that will come to everybody's mind of hungry individuals and nations that have not aggressed against anybody, not to mention the myriad of individuals and nations with full stomachs and barrels in store who have, makes one wonder if the correlation between hunger and aggression, if positive at all (which we doubt) is high enough to be of much significance.

[*] This is a revised version of a paper presented during spring and summer 1964 at the Circolo Turati, Milano, Facoltà delle scienze politiche, Università di Torino, Polemological Institute, University of Groningen, Danish Conflict Research Society in Copenhagen, the study group in conflict and peace research, Lund University, the study group under the Scandinavian Summer University in Aarhus, and at a plenary session of the Scandinavian Summer University in Bergen, here published as PRIO publication no. 1–1. Deep gratitude is expressed for all the good ideas received during these discussions—particularly to Mr. Bengt Höglund of the study group in Lund. The study is an outcome of a grant from the Aquinas Foundation, New York, and from the Norwegian Research Council for Science and the Humanities, and serves as a theoretical basis for a series of empirical investigations.

[†] Reprinted by permission of the author and publisher from *Journal of Peace Research*, 1964, *1*: 95–119.

The difficulty with these theories, like the Dollard frustration theory, is that they are non-structural; they do not take the social context sufficiently into consideration. The first theory sees man as a self-sufficient unit; he is his own cause. It does not correspond to our feeling that position in the social structure does matter. Granted the importance of individual characteristics, it is at least as unlikely that the chance of aggression for a given individual is independent of social positon as it is that all individuals in the same position should display exactly the same tendency towards aggression.

The second theory locates aggression at the places in the social structure where hunger is found; in that sense it is a structural theory. Its sufficiency is rather in terms of the very limited aspect of the social structure it considers. Hunger may supply motivational energy, but it must be combined with a position in the social structure that gives a view to better life situations and resources. This is where the minds of men enter: a theory of aggression should combine the idea of frustration with the idea of perceiving aggression as a possible way out of the frustrating situation.

We now turn to the construction of a theory of that kind.

2. The Hypothesis About Rank-disequilibrium

Imagine that we have a system of elements that are *actors* in the traditional social science sense of having goals and being capable of directing actions towards them, and that they interact with each other.[3] Concretely, we are thinking of three such types of systems: the system of *individuals* found in a group and particularly in a nation; the system of *groups* found in a nation if the groups are so homogenized and organized that they can be seen as actors, and the *nations* in an international system. However, we shall prefer to proceed with the general theory for a while without making references to these three interpretations, and only return to them at length later on.

Even under these very general conditions it seems difficult to find counter-examples to the following: 1) There will be a *division of labor* in the sense that the elements will not carry out the same tasks all the time; 2) The elements will tend to be *ranked* according to a number of criteria evaluating their position in the system; and 3) The relative position of the elements according to these criteria will have a certain *stability*. All we are saying by this is that *stratification* seems to be a universal phenomenon. The distance from 'high' to 'low' can be reduced, the consequences of stratification can be alleviated, but it cannot be declared to be non-existent. If one wants an egalitarian society where everybody has the same rank this must be arrived at by such techniques as making an element that is low in one context high in another context (compensation) or letting individuals who have high ranks in one period have low ranks in the next period (rotation). It cannot be done by abolishing differential ranking as such. For as long as there is interaction there will tend to develop a certain cultural similarity, and as soon as this is the case the element that has more of, or is closer to, or is more in agreement with the values of the system will rise high, and the elements that have little of these values and seem to be far from realizing them—whether it is might and glory, power, intelligence, money, beauty, health—will stay low in the system.

Thus, an interaction system is a multi-dimensional system of stratification, where those who have and those who have not, those who have more and those who have less, find, are given, or are forced into their positions. For the sake of simplicity, let us deal with these criteria of rank in terms of two positions only—high and low. We shall refer to them as *topdog* and *underdog* positions (T and U). Thus, an element in a system with five rank criteria, will have a profile, say TUTTU, the interpretation of which depends on what kind of system and what kind of dimensions we are referring to. It may, for instance, stand for 'high on power, low on income, high on occupation, high on education, low on ancestry' (for individuals or groups) or 'high on military power, low on income *per capita,* high on industrialization, high on educational level, low on past glory' (for nations), and one may discuss how likely the configuration is. But two configurations are beyond doubt: the complete topdog, TTTTT, and the complete underdog, UUUUU, are both well-known occurrences in any social system, individual or national. We shall refer to these two as 'equilibrated positions,' since the ranks of the elements in these positions are in equilibrium with each other; they are equivalents.

With five dimensions and two positions on each there are 32 possible configurations, or in general 2^n combinations when n dimensions are used in the analysis. The theoretical problem is now: *where in the system, for what social types, is aggression most likely to accumulate and express itself?* For common sense as well as social experience make us doubt that aggression is randomly distributed on the configurations or social positions.

With the conceptual apparatus developed so far there are three possible answers: aggression will mainly come from the elements equilibrated at the top (the complete topdog), mainly from the elements equilibrated at the bottom (the complete underdog), or mainly from the elements in rank-disequilibrium, i.e. the elements with some positions high and some positions low. We shall examine the three possibilities.

The complete topdog has already obtained what the system has to offer in terms of rewards, but this by itself will not prevent 'much from wanting more.' Colonial wars and slavery were typical examples of aggression from the top, although closer analysis perhaps may reveal that they were also efforts made by nations and individuals close to the top, but short on one or two dimensions, to achieve the configuration of the complete topdog.

Then it may be argued that the complete topdog is always in a state of aggression relative to, for instance, the complete underdog. The reward structure of society is a built-in transfer of value from underdog to topdog where the latter inevitably gets more than his due through a process of accumulation. Where there is stratification there will also be exploitation. But however important this may be, it is not aggression in our sense. Aggression involves a desire for change, and as long as the topdogs are only soaking from the structure what is their institutional 'right' this cannot be defined as aggression (but possibly as exploitation). They may encounter aggression from positions lower down in the structure with more aggression, but that is reactive aggression which again is different from what we are investigating: the points where aggression can be studied *in statu nascendi.*

A number of authors have argued that this is not where the complete underdog is located. For imagine that it was: in that case feudal structures like the slave society[4] or classical Indian caste society[5] would not have been stable, but would have shown a much shorter lifetime. What was typical of these societies was not so much the differences between high and low—those differences are also found in 'modern' social structures—but the almost complete correlation between the rank-dimensions. If a person was high in one context relative to another person, this was also the case in a number of other contexts. Nevertheless, or precisely for that reason, the structures did exhibit a remarkable stability—until, we think, some mobility was permitted so that disequilibrated positions appeared.

James C. Davies[6] has summarized much of the thinking around the social basis of revolutions:

> On the basis of de Tocqueville and Marx, we can choose one of these ideas or the other, which makes it hard to decide just when revolutions are more likely to occur—when there has been social and economic progress or when there has been regress. It appears that both ideas have explanatory and possibly predictive value, if they are juxtaposed and put in the proper time sequence.[7]

The theories of Marx, de Tocqueville and Davies are all dynamic. Marx located the source of revolution low down in the society, in the proletariat, and predicted revolutions after a period of deterioration and exploitation. Davies uses the study by Za-wadzki and Lazarsfeld[8] against this view, and uses this description of the situation of the complete underdog:[9]

> . . . preoccupation with physical survival, even in industrial areas, is a force strongly militating against the establishment of the community-sense and consensus on joint political action which are necessary to induce a revolutionary state of mind. Far from making people into revolutionaries, enduring poverty makes for con-cern with one's solitary self or solitary family at best and resignation or mute despair at worst.

This theme recurs very often in studies of periods or places under depression,[10] or in the concentration camp studies.[11] Most of these studies focus on the moral or mental state of the complete underdog, however, or the low level of social organi-zation, and often forget the much simpler and more obvious factor that the underdog is deprived of the resources that make revo-lutions possible: ideas, visions, acquaint-ances, weapons, social experience, empathy, courage necessary to imagine oneself as a ruler, etc. What the underdog does not have he can get, but he gets it, we believe, precisely by changing one of his U statuses into a T status and converting that status into a resource for the dissolution of his disequilibrium.

To de Tocqueville aggression was tied to an amelioration of the situation:[12] 'Nations that have endured patiently and almost un-consciously the most overwhelming oppres-sion often burst into rebellion against the yoke the moment it begins to grow lighter.' De Tocqueville would have found solid support for his thesis in the present Negro revolt in the United States; it seems to con-firm his thesis both in space (particularly in the North) and time (increasing rapidly with increasing desegregation).

Davies combines the two perspectives and produces a neat little theory where revolu-tions are supposed to occur when a popula-tion is exposed to a de Tocqueville-effect followed by a Marx-effect, i.e., an improve-ment accompanied by a revolution of rising expectations followed by a crisis and dete-rioration in the level of need satisfaction so that one gets 'an intolerable gap between what people want and what they get.' That is when the revolutions occur, and he gives a number of well-reasoned illustrations but no statistical data to corroborate his thesis.

However good these theories, singly or in Davies's juxtaposition, are in predicting *when,* they do not predict or explain *where* in the social structure the revolutions or other activities of aggression are likely to arise. Davies's answer might be: exactly in the positions exposed to the Davies-effect. But it would hardly be difficult to show that the complete underdog has often been exposed to the ups and downs caused by economic fluctuations and changing styles of exploitation without resorting to any vio-lence, whereas other sectors of the society may be extremely sensitive to the slightest downward trend. The Davies theory may locate revolutions in time, like the Dollard theory, but neither theory locates them in social space.

We then turn to our hypothesis which is very simple:

Aggression is most likely to arise in social positions in rank-disequilibrium. In a sys-tem of individuals it may take the form of crime, in a system of groups the form of revolutions, and in a system of nations the form of war. But these extreme forms of aggression are unlikely to occur unless 1) other means of equilibration towards a complete topdog configuration have been tried, and 2)) the culture has some practice in violent aggression.[13]

We shall now present extensive comments on this hypothesis. Thus, to take up one point immediately: in another paper[14] we have discussed this problem from a differ-ent angle. In a world consisting mainly of complete topdog and complete underdog positions there will be nobody present to bridge the gap between the two. Hence, a conflict between the TTTTT and the UUUUU, would not be alleviated by the presence of mixed combinations that could serve partly as communication bridges, partly as a reservoir of neutrals who could be brought in as mediators and in general dampen the conflict (the classical theory of 'criss-cross'). A shortcoming of this theory is its neglect of aggressive needs located in the unbalanced combinations. Thus, the theory we are presenting here is in a sense complementary to the other theory: for the classical criss-cross theory, disequilibrated combinations will fulfill an aggression-binding function whereas for the present structural theory of aggression disequilibrium is a reservoir of aggression.

Since the predictions that follow from these two theories are contradictory there is an obvious need for a meta-theory. Just to indicate one possible line of thought: it is possible that the criss-cross theory presupposes 1) a high degree of system integration in order for the communication and mediation effects to be present and 2) good chances for the disequilibrated combinations to become equilibrated in a legitimate way. If the degree of system integration is low, as in the international system, and many mobility channels are blocked, the aggression effect will probably predominate over the criss-cross effect. We suggest this as a fascinating topic of future theoretical and empirical research.

3. The Theory About How Disequilibrium Works

The thesis is very simple and the theory behind it is also simple. It rests on a comparison between the social situation of, say, a TU and a UU, in our terminology. There are three such differences that seem to be decisive in this context.

a. *Disequilibrium Means Differential Treatment*

We have assumed that rank matters in the sense that the elements are treated according to their rank. An element in a TU position will be constantly reminded of his objective state of disequilibrium by the differential treatment he is exposed to. This will force a correspondence between his objective situation and his subjective perception of it—unless he cuts out interaction in one direction or the other. If he does so, he is actually living in a world with only one rank-dimension. But if he does not, disequilibrium will be a part of his phenomenological existence, and the idea of rectification may occur. However, we do not have to presuppose, for the sake of the theory, that an ideology of rectification has to be fully developed, or even perceived at all—only that the objective existence of disequilibrium will cause an instability in the life-style of the person or the nation, and cause what is often referred to as an 'unstable self-image.'

In more sociological terms, the crux of the matter is the high probability that the disequilibrated TU will use TT as his reference group even if UU is his membership group, whereas a complete underdog, UU, may not even dare to think in terms of TT as a reference group; the complete topdog will be beyond his imagination. The absolute deprivation of the UU may be higher, but the TU has relative deprivation built into his position. The destabilizing effect of this discrepancy will produce a mobility pressure, and the thesis is then that if there are no open channels of mobility, rectification of the disequilibrium will be carried out by other means. In this process two other aspects of the disequilibrium situation are of major importance.

b. *Disequilibrium Means Resources*

We have commented on the effects on the TU of having one foot in either camp, for instance, of being white and poor, as nation or as individual. Obviously, the position in the top camp not only creates the motivation towards equilibration, but also some of the resources that will come in handy in the struggle. The *nouveau riche* may be green, but he is nevertheless rich and the stories about him are about his efforts to obtain balance by converting money into culture and prestige. The small, overcrowded but economically developed nation has in its economic potential the possibility for conversion into military power with subsequent territorial expansion. The member of the intellectual proletariat may be low on almost everything, and yet have in his intellectual maturity, knowledge and academic discipline, invaluable tools that can be converted into power, high-ranking occupations and income. And the 'white' but 'poor' nation may draw on its kinship with white and rich nations to gain influence and recognition, as is the case with many Latin-American nations.

c. *Disequilibrium Means Self-righteousness*

Our culture seems to be more dominated by themes of balance and adequacy than by the theme of compensation. We have no empirical backing for this, but there seem to be more cases of people and nations saying 'considering our high rank on X it is right and proper that we should also have a high rank on Y, because that corresponds to what is due to us' than of people and nations saying 'considering my low ranks everywhere I think I am entitled to some compensation on at least one dimension.' Claims must be justified not only in the eyes of the others but also in the eyes of the claimants themselves; they must feel they are right to the point of self-righteousness. In the kind of achievement-oriented world in which we live, claims will be based on achievement rather than on lack of achievement—in the latter case they are usually made explicit by others and the Welfare State is an example of the institutionalization of rank-compensation.

There are probably countless examples of this kind of self-righteousness based on disequilibrium. One thinks of such cases as nations trying to equilibrate crowded territory to economic rank achieved by means of rapid industrialization (Germany, Japan) or to equilibrate territory to rank derived from a glorious past (Italy). In all these cases very explicit references were made to the perceived disequilibrium—it became a part of national ideology, so to speak. Or one may think of real or fictional cases of people who have felt that their high rank on one dimension has entitled them to deviance, that it has made legitimate what would have been illegitimate to the complete underdog. Thus, we would imagine that to many juvenile delinquents the world comprises a bitter discrepancy between high ranks in terms of some resources they possess, such as intelligence or muscular power or initiative, and low rank on more institutionalized dimensions such as age, income, position, education.[15] Obviously, one would have to use what sociologists refer to as 'informal status' in addition to institutionalized statuses to come closer to a sufficient explanatory basis.

To summarize: it is socially guaranteed, by the very structure of the system, that the disequilibrated is never left in peace with his disequilibrium unless he cuts out and closes down some interaction channels. In this unstable situation he has both the resources and the inner justification needed for acts of deviance. Nevertheless, we do not hypothesize aggression unless 1) other means of rectification have been tried and 2) the culture has some practice in aggression.

4. More About Rank-dimensions and Disequilibria

The time has now come to be more specific about the rank-dimensions. These are concerned with the most crucial things of life, the matters for which people live and die.[16] But they differ tremendously, and should be analyzed from at least three angles: 1) is it possible, both in theory and in practice, for one element to change position at all, 2) how does the change of one element affect the position of the other elements, and 3) what kinds of disequilibria are most important?

Where the first problem is concerned the traditional distinction made in sociology between ascribed and achieved dimensions is useful. The ascribed position is known at birth, the achieved position is what the individual himself makes out of his life-situation. However, this conceals the important distinction between dimensions that are *indelible* in the sense that the element cannot escape from it (age, sex, race, primogeniture, family, ethnicity) and perhaps even *visible* (age, sex, race)—and the 'delible' dimensions like nationhood or ecological background which the individual can move away from—even though they are known at his birth. Achievement may also be so conditioned by the matrix of ascribed dimensions, as in most societies today (skill is not known at birth, but the possibility or impossibility of demonstrating it if it exists is known), that mobility becomes illusory except for persons with the particular mixture of good and evil that makes for mobility. The most aggression-provoking case is probably the half-open dimension of unfulfilled promises, but the completely closed channel will also serve to accumulate aggression unless *all* channels are closed.

The second problem is more interesting. Imagine a system with two elements and one dimension only: we are interested in how the position of one affects the position of the other. In principle, there are three possibilities. The *units* may be *positively coupled* in the sense that if one rises so does the other, and that they will also follow each other on the way down. Then, again, they may be *negatively coupled:* the rise of one is the fall of the other.[17] And, thirdly, they may not be coupled at all. Different economic systems provide examples of all three. Concretely, the most dramatic example of negative coupling in the case of nations is the dimension of *area:* one nation's gain will have to be the loss of one or more other nations unless the game can be made 'variable-sum' through the exploration of outer space (or as it was in the period of the great discoveries). And the same applies to property at any given point of time: one person's loss is somebody else's gain, unless the game is changed through such factors as destruction or creation of property or is stretched out in time.

Correspondingly, the *dimensions* may be coupled positively, negatively, or not at all: the rising of a unit on one dimension may imply its rising on another dimension, or its fall, or it may imply nothing at all. More age means more power—at least the power to influence elections through voting, and so on.

In general it is obvious that dimensions with negative coupling between units are the dangerous ones, and this may lead one to speculate how many they actually are. With the concept of a nation tied to the idea of a territory, usually contiguous, international politics is dangerous precisely because of the simple metric quality of that dimension. Today national identity is linked to territory in a rigid way—but one can think away that condition even though only the Jews and some others have had long experience in territory-free national existence. Thus, one could imagine each

nation as consisting of a non-negotiable geographical core surrounded by a periphery that could be exchanged for other goods or even lost with no irreparable damage done to national integrity and identity. Or one could imagine a world where all nations were like the Jewish nation prior to the birth of Israel—with a central authority, but no territory—where the nations mix much like strata in a society.

But even though it may serve the prevention of aggression to reduce the salience of competitive dimensions and increase the importance of the cooperative dimensions an important *caveat* should be inserted here. World economy can probably be structured in such a way that wealth becomes a cooperative dimension so that no unit's loss can be another unit's gain (if in no other way, by the simple method of taxation of such gains). But even if nations rise together on a dimension of prosperity there is one aspect of this dimension that will remain competitive forever: not absolute prosperity, but relative prosperity. One nation's gain of the no. 1 position, regardless of the absolute value, is another nation's loss. And this gives rise to a major question that can only be decided on empirically. What matters most, absolute or relative position? What is most important to a competitive pupil, to improve his grades or his relative position? If he improves his grades but slides back in relative rank, how does he look at the net balance of his achievement? And what about the nation accustomed to a no. 1 position in military power that is bypassed by another nation even if it has also itself increased its military capability?

Probably absolute positions are of paramount importance only in systems with little or no interaction or in extreme cases (e.g. below subsistence level). With a high level of interaction we know of nothing in social science literature to disprove the idea that concern about relative position on a rank-dimension will increase, and since increase in interaction is a general trend in the world community this should make dimensions more, not less competitive, and conflicts for the reason we are discussing more, not less probable in the future.

Finally, we turn to the problem of distinguishing between disequilibria. To say that disequilibrium matters is not to say that all kinds of disequilibrium matter equally much. A typology of disequilibria is needed, and we shall discuss this from three angles, two of them formal and one of them substantive.

First of all, there is the obvious dimension of degree of disequilibrium. Imagine that we introduce a 'middledog,' call him M. We define 'degree' of disequilibrium as internal distance between the ranks, which would make TTM less disequilibrated than TTU. Generally, the experience based on data from persons in disequilibrium tend to show that the effects of disequilibrium do not show up unless there is a considerable amount of disequilibrium present.[18] The consequence is a tendency towards J-shaped relationships: deviation tendencies stay at the base level for equilibrium and low degrees of disequilibrium, and then rise quickly for high degrees of disequilibrium.

Secondly, there is the problem of disequilibrium *profile*. The sum of internal distances in the combinations TTU, UUT and TMU are the same, viz., 4, so we would expect more of an effect than for the combination TTM where the sum is 2. But do we expect the *same* effect with this crude measure of internal distance? *A priori,* one might argue that TTU is more desperate about his low status and UUT more proud about his high status, so that the former is the more aggressive, and then one might argue just the other way round.[19] One might say that TMU is exposed to a particularly deviation-generating mixture, and one may say that his aggression will be neutralized precisely because of the complex social structure in which he finds himself. In other words, one should leave this problem to the data; their richness, provided they are good, will probably by far outdo even a good theoretical imagination.

Thirdly, there is the problem of *which* dimensions. Obviously, not all disequilibria even with the same profile will have the same deviation-generating effect. The effect will depend on the salience of the dimensions and of the disequilibrium. There is also the important suggestion made by

Jackson[20] that the *achieved v. ascribed* distinction may be used here. Let us compare these two patterns with the same internal distance, based on three dimensions:

Dimension:	ascribed	achieved	ascribed
Pattern 1	high	low	high
Pattern 2	low	high	low

Of the three mechanisms we have mentioned in the section on 'how disequilibrium works' this distinction should affect the third mechanism, the norm about justice, in particular. The unit with the second pattern is an overachiever relative to his ascribed case; the unit in the first pattern is an underachiever, and the overachiever more than the underachiever will feel that he deserves a fairer deal, at least in an achievement-oriented culture.

According to Jackson one might predict extrapunitivity for the overachiever and intrapunitivity for the underachiever;[21] the overachiever will blame society for constraining him, the underachiever will blame himself for doing less than society or the system might expect from him. But the overachiever is in the difficult situation that he is low on ascribed dimensions where mobility, by definition, is impossible. Hence, he will have to fight like the educated Negro, not for white status, but for the elimination of race as a rank-dimension. Thus, outward aggression takes a form other than simple fight for mobility and scarce value; it may be a fight about the definition of value.

The underachiever, e.g. the white high-class who is low on education or income, might be more motivated to direct aggression to promote his own mobility. But just as likely is aggression due to a desire to keep what he has—perhaps precisely against the attacks of the overachiever. Thus, the two will be pitted against each other, probably with the strongest aggression potential for any possible pair of combinations. In more concrete terms, the underachiever may possibly be identified as a member of the extreme right and the overachiever as a member of the extreme left;[22] the former will keep his privileges since that is the high basis he has in the system, the latter will deny the system of privileges or change them to his own advantage. Thus, we disagree with Jackson that outwardly directed aggression should necessarily be less probable for the underachiever, only that it *may* come as a reaction to the aggression of the overachiever and be less spontaneous.

It is interesting in this connection to compare the state of the Negroes in the USA and in Brazil. Comparisons are very often to the effect that there is less discrimination or prejudice in Brazil, but statistical data do not appear to demonstrate this. Rather, the impression is that there are more Negroes in higher positions in the USA than in Brazil. We shall only suggest an interpretation in terms of the present theory. If we have a nation where race and position are equilibrated we would predict a very low level of aggression, and hence more of a tendency to express oneself in accordance with the predominant ideology of our time, the ideology of racial equality. Thus, there will be no laws prescribing segregation and little overt prejudice, for rank-equilibrium is built into the social structure.

On the other hand, imagine a nation where many Negroes are high in social position and many whites are low. In that case we would predict formal and informal barriers to secure segregation, and as a barrier against aggression resulting from the disequilibrium. In fact, the way to obtain 'racial equality' will be through the suppression of race as a dimension at all—and here as elsewhere the role of ideology and perception is probably tremendous. Thus, to the extent that these models are approximations to Brazilian and US reality the USA seems to be much further along the road towards racial equality than Brazil, only she is in a transitional period with tremendous potentials of aggression that Brazil has not yet really entered. The revolt of the Negroes in the USA is like the revolt of the colonies in this age of anti-colonialism: these are both efforts to eliminate dimensions, by making all citizens 'first class', or all nations 'independent'.

5. Methodology

The time has now come to look at the thesis from a methodological point of view.

We shall discuss first procedures for testing the hypothesis, secondly some other properties of the theory.

The hypothesis relates two variables that describe elements: degree of rank-disequilibrium on the one hand and degree of aggressiveness on the other. For individuals the former is relatively easily measured. A considerable part of social science ingenuity has been invested in the development of good indicators of basic rank-dimensions. Most authors that have made use of this kind of thinking have trichotomized the dimensions in 'high', 'medium' and 'low', tabulated them against each other and used the distance from the diagonal of agreement as the measure of disequilibrium. One can also use rank-order and perhaps get a more sensitive measure, but it is only meaningful in relatively limited systems with a high interaction pitch.

For nations it should be possible to do the same. Increasingly good statistics are available for most dimensions of interest.[23] Data are actually likely to be too good, not too bad—since only gross discriminations are necessary to test the theory. But the difficulty lies in finding which rank-dimensions to use. Obviously, this will vary with time and place. Christian or not, monarchy or not, socialist or not; such concepts may be meaningful and even clear rank-connotations in some periods and not in others. One procedure for finding which rank-dimensions to use would be to peruse the writings and speeches of leading statesmen to see what dimensions they make reference to, and more particularly what disequilibria they make explicit reference to. Another procedure for the contemporary world would be to make use of opinion polls where a sample could be introduced to a large variety of rank-criteria and asked to rank the criteria in terms of salience (for instance by means of paired comparisons or the technique of double alternatives). One could then pay particular attention to answers given by the elite.

As to aggressiveness there is a continuum from the idea of *change* in the structure of the system via the overt expression and propagation of such ideas and actions designed to change the social structure, to real aggression, i.e. efforts to pursue such ideas even against the will of other elements—and even at the expense of other elements. The extremes are, as mentioned, called *crime* in the individual case, *revolution* or *internal war* in the group case, and *external war* in the case of nations.

This means that there is a large variety of indicators. So far the only thing that has been explored systematically in the literature has been the individual case with attitudinal indicators, and the hypothesis has been well confirmed.[24] The logically next step would be to use behavioral indicators. Thus, the theory would predict disproportionately great rank-disequilibrium among radical politicians, among criminals (especially those who are engaged in crimes against property), among leading revolutionaries and leaders of change-oriented groups in general, and among very bellicose nations.

For nations attitudinal indicators could be based on national polls and aggregate measures, or on elite polls, or on what the elite has expressed without being solicited by social scientists, e.g. in articles and speeches. Thus, it should be possible to test the idea that there is a disproportionately great desire for change in disequilibrated nations. And the behavioral indicators should not be too difficult to find with the growing experience social science gains with 'statistics of deadly quarrels'.[25]

A major virtue of the hypothesis is that it should be valid both synchronically and diachronically. It should point out the likely aggressors at any given point in time, as was discussed in the introduction. But given one element, an individual or a nation and its history, the hypothesis should help us locate the periods of aggression in that history: the theory is dynamic. Thus, there is a piece of common folklore about radicalism and youth belonging together which gains in perspective if we apply this theory: the youth may be at the period of institutionalized disequilibrium with education high and most other dimensions low, the period of student riots and demonstrations. This is the age where change seems logical, inevitable and desirable and the attitude is known to taper off somewhat with age. The folklore interpretation is in terms of growing wisdom, 'he who is not a radical in his youth does not have a good heart, but he who is not a conservative when he becomes older does not have a good brain'. Our interpretation is in terms of growing equilibrium more than growing wisdom, and hence decrease in motivation due to decrease in relative deprivation.[26] The condition is that the society permits this equilibration, that there is structural provision for it—otherwise the result will be a society with pockets of accumulated disequilibrium that may one day burst and yield a revolution.

For diachronical tests of the theory the system could be observed through a period and the period divided into time-chunks of, say, from one to five years. For each time-chunk the elements should be rated according to degree of disequilibrium and degree of aggressiveness displayed. Since the theory does not predict overt aggression as an immediate outcome of disequilibrium (other alternatives are tried out first), the test of the hypothesis should provide for a time lag between disequilibrium and aggression, and more so for the behavioral and extreme forms than for the attitudinal and more tranquil forms. A great deal of experimentation with time cuts and lags will probably be necessary before a pattern can emerge.

In this process 'proof' by illustration should not be accepted. One can always 'prove' by the usual library hunt for ten cases in favor and one against (to show that one is not biased), but we have preferred to postpone the presentation of such data till they can be evaluated against a background provided by data amenable to statistical treatment.

One may ask: why not systematically study all wars during, for instance, the last one hundred and fifty years to find in how many cases the aggressing nation can be said to have been disequilibrated? There are two objections to this primitive procedure. First of all, a percentage of disequilibration among nations that aggress says nothing if it cannot be compared meaningfully with the corresponding percentage for nations that do not aggress. One is not interested in the percentage of belligerent nations that are disequilibrated, but in the percentage of disequilibrated nations that engage in aggressive acts. But apart from the trivial point about rules for percentaging there is another objection: the danger of running into a tautology. Given a war and an aggressor it is only a question of time and research imagination to dig up a rank-disequilibrium, for the number of dimensions along which a nation can be ranked is legion. Thus, the methodology will make the theory non-falsifiable in practice. Undoubtedly, a test of the theory will require much speculation about relevant disequilibria, but the strength of the theory will depend on the ratio between number of types of disequilibria and number of aggressive acts they can explain. The lower the ratio the more powerful the theory; if each aggressive act should be explained by its own kind of disequilibrium we would still have a disequilibrium theory, but a far less powerful one.

A major advantage of this theory, in addition to its dynamic character, is that the hypothesis is meaningful across different levels of social organization. Individuals as well as groups and nations can be ranked in terms of rank-dimensions and aggression, although there will be problems in connection with the choice of indicators.[27] Thus, the theory is a theory in general conflictology, not in any of the special fields concerned (social psychology, sociology, international relations, not to mention history).

There are three aspects of this cross-level nature of the theory.

First of all, the theory points to a basic *isomorphism* between different levels of social organization. Disequilibrium is relatively easily identifiable at all levels, and its consequences are spelt out in the hypothesis. The hypothesis is about systems of interacting units and three interpretations are given; to the extent that the hypothesis is verified these three levels of organization will have to be isomorphic.

Secondly, there is the possiblity of a *causal connection* between the levels. We shall not explore this, only indicate some possibilities. Disequilibrium at one level can lead to disequilibrium at another level:

a highly disequilibrated individual may become the leader of a completely underdog group and lead it into disequilibrium by giving it power, property or education. The group, in turn, may lead the nation into disequilibrium. But we are more interested in the cases where disequilibrium at one level expresses itself as aggression at another level, as perhaps may be argued to be a description of the case of Hitler and Nazi Germany.

Thirdly, there is the problem of *interaction*. Imagine that a disequilibrated person brings a disequilibrated group to power in a disequilibrated nation. Would one not expect the motivational energy stored in these disequilibria to multiply rather than to add up, and to result in a particularly spectacular form of aggression? Again the case of Hitler's Germany comes to mind, but also, perhaps, the case of Castro's Cuba, and in general, new nations high on economy and with a more or less revolutionary leadership.

The methodological implication of this is not only the necessity of independent tests at all levels as pointed out above, but, in addition, the need to explore patterns of causality and interaction.

6. Discussion

Let us now imagine that there is something to this reasoning, at least in the statistical sense that disequilibrium in rank accounts for a major part of the variation in aggressive behavior. We can probably do this with some justification partly because some excursions into data seem to corroborate the theory, and partly because the contrary idea of placing the peak of the probability distribution for aggressiveness *a priori* on the points of equilibrium seems to lack theoretical justification. The question is *what follows from this,* can anything be said in more concrete terms about specific arrangements of systems, specific structures. With no value-implication to the effect that aggressiveness is an absolute evil, it is both theoretically and practically important to know something about conditions that promote or do not promote aggressiveness. We shall try to spell out some implications of this kind, mainly for the international system, since this is our major concern.

a. *The Consequences of Economic Development*

Economic development is a major issue of our times, for most people on earth probably the major issue. The motives for giving technical assistance are interesting.[28] Economic and technical aid are defended (against the attacks from those who want to give less or nothing) on such diverse grounds as: 1) it buys us friends, who (a) will not attack us themselves (the direct insurance argument) and (b) will support us if somebody else attacks us (the indirect insurance argument); 2) it increases our military power by securing bases etc. in return; 3) it increases our political power by securing UN votes etc. in return; 4) it increases our economic power by tuning the market to our products or otherwise; 5) if we do not do it the others will do it and gain 1, 2, 3 and/or 4; 6) for humanitarian reasons, all human beings shall be guaranteed a minimum standard of living; 7) for reasons of justice: there is an equitable distribution of economic goods that should at least be approximated to; 8) because it promotes world peace. We are concerned with the last argument.

Some would say it follows directly from one or more of the first seven arguments, which may be true but is certainly not self-evident. Then it may be said that the transfer of technical economic assistance requires a kind of international cooperation and even superstructure that by itself will be conducive to a safer world community. But the argument is usually interpreted so as to mean something else: statesmen talk about the North-South conflict being of equal or even greater importance than the East-West conflict, alluding to the conflict between rich and poor nations. This may be true in more than one sense, but it does not follow that economic development is the remedy. Of course, it is a tautology to say that in a world where economic value has been evenly distributed

(if such a world is imaginable) there will be no conflict because of differences in wealth. That leaves us with the conflicts due to similarities in wealth: the desire to be high in a relative sense, not only an absolute one, and the highly important factor that equally rich nations are often nations in more or less similar stages of economic (and even social) growth and hence will be competing for exactly the same goals, the same values, the same markets, the same friends.

But the argument is rather that economic development will deter the poor from joining together to rob the rich, for when they receive aid they will be deprived of the motive. The argument rarely specifies how this is going to happen in detail, and one reason may be that the idea is probably wrong. Imagine a world with four salient rank-dimensions, (or three, or two for that matter) and that aid is given from TTTT nations to UUUU nations, developing some of them into TUUU nations. In all probability this would be a more, not a less dangerous world to live in—*ceteris paribus*. All theoretical reasons mentioned in the beginning of this article, the sense of self-righteousness, the access to resources of different kinds, the internal strains due to differential treatment in different interaction contexts would operate. As a matter of fact, the following development seems much more likely: that a group of TUUU nations join their newly gained forces and resources in making an organization for revolution in the international community. Another version of this would correspond to a pattern for revolutions discussed in the following section: one or a few heavily disequilibrated nations mobilize the complete underdog nations against the complete topdog nations according to the eight-point scheme to be presented below.[29]

In other words, and to put it bluntly: economic development *per se* will probably create more, not less rank-disequilibrium and hence be conducive to more, not less aggression. It is unnecessary to add that this does not imply that it cannot be justified on other bases, or that economic development and technical assistance in particular cannot have peace-building functions for other reasons, e.g. by contributing to international superstructure.

b. *The Conditions for Revolutions*

According to the theory presented the recipe for a revolution should be relatively clear. A revolution needs leaders and followers, and traditionally the leaders seem to come from somewhere high up in the tertiary sector of society whereas the followers come from somewhere low down in the primary and secondary sectors. Thus, what is needed is first of all a sufficient amount of built-in disequilibrium in these social positions. If the point of departure is a feudal system, for instance a newly independent, formerly colonial territory, then one way of arriving at this would be as follows: [30]

1. *Create universities* and other institutions of higher learning so as to turn out a sizeable number of intellectuals who feel they have a key—their high level of education--not only to their own well-being, but to the welfare of the whole society, e.g. economists, physicians.
2. *Make few positions available* so that the high educational staus will not be translated into the kind of instrumentality that gives power. Regardless of the economic situation, this intellectual proletariat is a proletariat in the sense of not having access to the machinery they know (or think they know) how to turn. They are forced into other positions, and these positions will call for subsidiary capacities (accounting, typing, low administration) and the disequilibrium is created.

It should be noticed how easily such an intellectual proletariat is created: in the age of technical assistance and international fellowships it takes little time to turn out university graduates, but it still takes much time to tune an administration to an efficient utilization of their skills. The intellectuals will probably oversell their products precisely because they are underbought and underdemanded, and they will be feared, envied and hated by their rank opposites, the powerful non-intellectuals. Both sides will develop ideologies that make symbiosis less likely, as is so easily observed in most countries in Latin America. Thus, a climate for the emergence of revolutionary leadership is created, unless the rulers are clever enough to co-opt the intellectual proletariat by giving them something that tastes of power, e.g. by paying them for writing recommendations.

The revolutionaries may be able to sway a sufficient number of followers to do the footwork for them, but we are concerned with the structural conditions for automatic supply, not with special conditions. Thus, one simple formula is to copy what is mentioned above lower down, and in the primary or secondary sectors of society:

3. *Institute mass education* with a compulsory base and easy access to educational follow-up institutions of various kinds especially so as to permit autodidactic leaders to emerge. The factor of self-righteousness will probably work more strongly for the autodidact than for the formally trained person, especially if he is high on what he has learnt himself and low on formal schooling. This contributes to an explanation of the role of typographers in social revolutions: their work brings them close to a source of rank-disequilibrium through studies.
4. *Make no other changes,* which means that the recent rise in education is not accompanied by any corresponding rise in economy or power.

Again, it should be noticed how easily this is done. Mass education, like mass medication, costs little compared to building dams or irrigation schemes or the creation of a sector of heavy industry. Also, like mass medication it can bring quick results and cause disequilibria. The disequilibrium caused by raising the hygienic standard without a corresponding rise in the economic basis is well known—to this can be added the effects of a free education market without a corresponding freedom in the markets of economics (goods) and politics (power). [31]

Let us then add to these four conditions four more, and we should have a relatively good set of predictors:

5. *A pattern of boom followed by depression or repression* as mentioned earlier —the pattern made explicit by Davies in his article.
6. *Contact* between the two (or more) disequilibrated groups, between the tertiary high and the primary or secondary low in disequilibrium. Urbanization provides the medium for such contacts, and is a rapidly increasing resource on the world level.
7. *An ideology* that does not have to explain the past or present nor to predict or prescribe the future, but has to provide a kind of semantic bridge over the social distances within the group urging change. This function of ideology, to provide a revolutionary group with emotive symbols that are easily applied and have the same reference for those who use them, is the more necessary the greater the social distance within the group.
8. *A charismatic leader.* The functions of personification and centralization are not easily satisfied without a leader. To say that he should have charisma is probably a tautology since the proof of his charisma lies in his ability to be a leader and sway people into action. But a personality with appeal across social distances is indispensable.

Any one of these conditions may serve as a spark to ignite the motivational energy stored in the disequilibrium mentioned in points 1–4—and all four together should be more than sufficient. We would, as mentioned, believe more in disequilibrated rank as a source of revolutions than in the Davies factor, for a completely balanced underdog group is so psychologically and ideologically conditioned as to absorb the vagaries of economic cycles. But it may also be argued that the two factors are rather similar. They are both themes of frustration, and more than that: a boom followed by a depression or repression is likely to create rapidly a high number of

disequilibria at critical points in the social structure. But disequilibria are also created by rapid economic growth, so the arguments in the preceding section about the consequences of economic development for external war can also be turned into arguments for internal war. In other words, there is little inspiration in our theory for anyone who might want to stop 'communism' nationally or internationally through a policy of technical assistance and economic aid. What is wrong with that theory is that it confuses the social situation in nations or groups equilibrated at the top with all the disequilibrium states they have to go through on their way up from a complete underdog situation.

c. *On the Number of Elements in a System*

All our reasoning so far has been with no reference whatsoever to the number, N, of elements in a system. This simple variable, number, is rarely used for other purposes than data analysis in social science; here we shall try to point out one theoretical implication of *number*. We choose a simple world: it is ranked according to two dimensions and in a random way so that 1/4 of the elements are TT, 1/4 are TU, 1/4 are UT and 1/4 are UU. The question is: what difference, if any, does it make if this world has 4, 40, 400, 4,000 or 4 million elements?

We expect the drastic demands for reallocations to come from the TU and UT positions. But there is a long distance between making a demand, a request and open aggression, and the probability of aggression will also depend on the number of alternatives. With increasing N the number of combinations for a given element increases very rapidly. There is no need to enter into the mathematics of the combinatorics since they reflect nothing of substantive interest except the extreme rapidity with which the number of subsystems that can be formed increases with N.

Some of these subsystems may be belligerent coalitions that increase the probability of aggression. But there is another kind of subsystem which is more important in this context. To discover it one only has to recognize one way in which tensions are alleviated for disequilibrated individuals in intra-national systems: they form subsystems that dissolve the disequilibrium. A group of 100 TUs isolating themselves from the rest of the system will no longer see themselves as TUs; the dimensions are negated in the homogeneity of the groups. Thus, one university professor may feel entitled to more power, to the power that corresponds to his wisdom—together with 99 others he may be more concerned with minute differences in wisdom within the group than gross differences between his position and other positions in the society.

If the idea is simply that people and groups and nations like feeling superior or at least not inferior, then the implications are equally simple. A TU for N = 4 will have one other element to associate with (UU), whereas the TU will have 19 others for N 40 (10 UU and the remaining 9 TU). The UT are excluded because their profiles lie over the profile for TU at one point. The gain in sources of gratification is conspicuous and continues: 1, 19, 199, 1,999, . . . On the other hand, as soon as these subsystems are formed they may serve to reduce effectively the number of elements until one has a supersystem of four elements, where the elements are complicated organizations, bearing the TT, TU, UT and UU characteristics.

Thus, the higher the number of elements, the higher the probability of finding some kind of organizational insulation against the strains produced by a disequilibrium position. The world with four elements throws the elements against each other mercilessly: all comparisons involve some element of strain, there is no refuge in the relaxed atmosphere of the complete peer, the real equal. With only two elements it would be still worse, especially if they were posited against each other in TU and UT positions, one being high in power and low in culture and the other one being just the opposite. It is easy enough to see where the difficulties disappear: only at the point where all elements have coalesced into one.

If there is stability of the kind under discussion in systems consisting of one element on the one hand and systems consisting of many (hundreds, thousands, millions) on the other hand, then some conclusions can be drawn. Nations owe their stability, if they have any, to 1) a large number of individuals, and 2) a sufficiently complicated social structure in terms of all kinds of rank-dimensions to prevent a simplification to a very low number of groups. Of course, stability is enhanced by obliterating the rank-dimensions, by making them irrelevant, as during a foreign occupation—but this is a rare occasion and when it does not obtain there is strength in number alone.

Similarly the international community should have its points of stability for the one world state as well as for a world consisting of a large number of nations. With the present trends the world is probably moving into the in-between region; for instance with two federations developing out of the NATO-alliance, (one North-American and one European), of the Warsaw alliance (Soviet and Eastern Europe), Asia (for or against China), Africa (Arab and bloc) and Latin America (Spanish and Portuguese) one is left with a dozen nations and all kinds of rank-profiles. Formal political union is not necessary for such effects to be demonstrable: even now European nations play a counterpoint to the US; Eastern European nations (singly more than combined) to the USSR; in Asia a China-non-China division is meaningful; in Africa the Sahara is a dividing region and in Latin America the poor could well be pitted against the rich.

d. *On the Number of Dimensions*

It looks as if one may use the same argument about the stability in one and many, but not in few, for the number of dimensions. Of course, the number of dimensions is a more volatile characteristic of the system than the number of elements. But it is not operationally meaningless, as indicated in the section on methodology. One will have to count the number of criteria of ranking on which there is a degree of consensus above a pre-established level.

Imagine that there is only one such dimension—for instance *per capita* income. This does not mean that conflicts and aggression will disappear, but that one source of aggressive behavior, arising from disequilibrium (e.g. with size of territory) does not exist. The 'haves' will be envied by the 'have-nots' but quite possibly be more safe in their topdog position than they would have been if there were some more dimensions available. For on these other dimensions the underdogs might rise and get into the web of disequilibrium. No doubt, there are exceptions to this. Topdogs have always and everywhere known the importance of stretching out a ladder of compensation to the underdogs, for instance in the form of an ideology that promises salvation in a transcendent existence (religion) or in this world ('die orgiastische Chiliasmus'). But these ladders are not rank-dimensions in the sense that they lead to identifiable positions where one is treated differently by the whole society. Thus, to institute mass education and give knowledge to the masses with the idea that 'this will satisfy them, they will think less of getting property' is both unpsychological and unsociological. Not much time will pass before the UT, high on education, starts wondering why he should be less well off than the TT, not to mention the TU—he may find comfort in his top position for a while, and then start worrying about his low position.

The question is now whether there is a limit to this kind of reasoning set by the number of dimensions. A world with a very high number of salient dimensions would permit more flexibility; the number would serve as a cushioning against the effects of disequilibrium. For each new dimension gives a possibility upwards, and hence a source of gratification, especially if different nations climb on different dimensions. To take an example: sports competitions and 'contests' as to which nation has the highest number of Nobel laureates both define positions that can be highly gratifying and compensating. Our hypothesis, then, is that a U position may loom high in the national conscience if it is surrounded by one or a couple of T positions but not if it is surrounded by very many such positions. Then it may even be turned into a point of pride: look at what we have been able to do in spite of that handicap (the national ethos of the small nations in North-West Europe, Norway for instance, illustrates the case).[32] Again, if the U is surrounded by nothing because the system is seen as one-dimensional, then the hypothesis is that an attitude of acquiescence will be more likely, for there is no disequilibrium present to provoke restlessness.

The consequence of this is a prediction of stability in extremely monolithic and extremely pluralistic cultures—in the former there will be one criterion, in the latter many, for pluralism is precisely a multi-faceted basis for evaluation. Again, it may look as if the world is presently moving towards the in-between region. Communications and international organization make greater areas relevant for each other—but at the same time the richness in total cultural variation is broken down. But what could be called the world consensus is probably richer today than the narrow military-economic basis of evaluation prevalent during the period of colonialism.

Combined with the preceding section this means roughly the following: the world is neither in the simple monolithic world-state, nor in a very pluralistic system of numerous and small nations—say a couple of thousand. The world is in-between and in a situation where there is considerably less than maximum protection to be found in the formation of subsystems. We are then thinking not only of the subsystems where nations that feel similar keep together, but also of cultural subsystems where a nation regards as salient only some dimensions. She may pick the dimensions where she ranks high—and receive gratification. But, undoubtedly, she may also pick precisely the dimensions that present her with a maximum internal disequilibrium—so richness and variety in number of dimensions give a potential for containment of aggression, not a fool-proof recipe.

*   *   *

In general, one may say that this perspective implies a number of connections between change and conflict, between the causes of disequilibria and their aggressive dissolution. Social change is structural; it may, for instance, introduce new and usually disequilibrated rank-combinations. Or it may distribute new resources more evenly, which is another way of saying that some complete or nearly-complete underdogs will rise on one or more dimensions due to mass education, prosperity, universal suffrage or, on the national level, to such factors as freedom from colonialism or economic development. The result is disequilibrium with consequent aggression until more equilibrated combinations of rank-sets are achieved—or a precarious balance between equilibrated and disequilibrated combinations as described by the criss-cross theory. And thus world history unfolds itself, and makes aggression as lasting as rank-disequilibrium, that is, as long as human society exists. But that does not imply, of course, that the forms of aggression will necessarily be as dangerous as is the case today, nor that social change will always cause as much rank-disequilibrium as it does today.

In a sense the whole theory is located somewhere between purely system-oriented theories of aggression (like the theories of Richardson processes) and purely element-oriented theories (attributing aggression to national character). According to the theory it is the rank-balance within a unit that counts, not the rank-balance between units. But this balance within is defined with reference to the balance between and is meaningless except in a system context. In fact, as indicated in the reasoning about the formation of subsystems, the system reference is indispensable if one is to decide whether an element is in equilibrium or not.

7. *Some Policy Implications*

Not much can be said in terms of policy implications of a principle so general as the principle under discussion, and not much should be said as long as the principle has not been confirmed for a variety of strategically placed tests. Nevertheless, it is interesting to speculate as if this had already been done and to look further at the implications.

First of all, the principle and a value premise against aggression are compatible with a large variety of possible worlds. Among these worlds should be mentioned, 1) *the feudal order* consisting of the complete topdog and the complete underdog alone, 2) *the pluralistic world* consisting of a large variety of nations, possibly several thousands or based on a large variety of criteria of ranking and achievement, and 3) *the unitary world* where independent national actors have disappeared from the scene or there is only one dimension of evaluation. In all other worlds, according to the theory, unbalanced configurations exist and are bound to harbor aggression —as long as one assumes the existence of rank-dimensions and values worthy of being pursued. In general ideological debate these three worlds are usually considered so disparate that one of them would exclude one or more of the others; the theory points to what they have in common.

Secondly, a general implication well known from debates on economic development is the following one: if change is one-dimensional only from the position of the complete underdog, aggression is likely to be its effect; for aggression to be avoided a necessary condition is multi-dimensional change. This calls for a tremendous amount of political ingenuity.[33] One nation leaps economically ahead of the others 'with whom it is natural to compare oneself.' The idea of compensation and egalitarian concepts of social justice would prescribe some kind of mobility to the other nations so that the first nation 'does not become too strong.' Thus, one maxim of statesmanship will have it that federal capitals should be placed in one of the poorer member States and State capitals at least not in the richest or biggest city of the State. Within a well-integrated nation this is probably non-consequential, the forces created are not unleashed because of the strong bonds between the constituent elements. But in a loosely integrated group of individuals or nations the principle would predict aggressive consequences unless the system generates enough value to permit mobility that is not at the expense of the others.

The prescription based on the principle would rather make increase in political influence an immediate concomitant of economic growth. This would be in agreement with achievement conceptions of social justice, but lest it should lead to a feudal world order that many people would rule out on the basis of other value premises, the principle should rather be interpreted negatively. That is, to take the most important example in the world just now, if a nation which is the world's largest in terms of population, one of the largest in terms of area and the most 'glorious' in terms of history undertakes the transition from a semi-colonial status to independence and autonomy through the catharsis of a revolution and then undergoes a dramatic socio-economic change that alters its economic status towards that of an industrial nation: if that nation is voted out of existence as a political entity by being denied membership in the club of nations and more particularly by being denied access to the club of great powers, then the hypothesis of this article would be very wrong if the predicted aggression did not occur within a reasonable time-span. Whether that nation adds to its territory or seeks *de facto* political control through other media the principle does not predict, but the principle would predict that if due political status is given to it before aggressive tendencies have had too much of a habit-forming effect, then its neighbors should have less to fear.

It is not difficult to look through national statistics and to discover disequilibria and make predictions about the future behavior of some nations in terms of aggressive behavior. A major formula of aggression will probably be precisely the nation favored by nature, culture, talent or an economic aid benefactor that makes a jump ahead of its neighbors so that all three mechanisms of disequilibrium are set into motion. This makes those economic policies to the effect that some nations should be developed first, as has been advocated by some,[34] particularly dubious from this point of view. And since parallel development of many nations on one dimension is also an implication of the principle one is not stuck with the elitist formula of parallel development of one nation on many dimensions.

Clearly, if aggression had less dangerous consequences, as it may have in a world where arms are controlled and alternative methods of conflict management better developed, one could focus on the positive aspect of aggression and leave the negative side of the coin, the damage done unto others, aside. For disequilibrium is a reservoir of initiative that serves evolution unless it is frustrated. But in the present world there are probably better theoretical reasons to favor some kind of equilibrium principle than the opposite principle, if economic development is to take place without too many deviations into war and warlike processes. And throughout the article a number of indications given should make it clear that the implications of an equilibrium principle are not necessarily on the 'conservative' side, or necessarily on the 'radical' side—whatever these terms may mean.

Summary

The article, which is completely theoretical with no attempts at empirical verification, develops a structural theory of aggression between individuals, groups and nations. The theory sees a social system as a system of units in interaction and multidimensionally stratified according to a number of rank-dimensions. The theory tries to locate the maximum probability of aggression against other units, and after exclusion of one-dimensional rank or the complete topdog and complete underdog positions and excluding one-dimensional downward and upward mobility as a suitable basis of explanation, settles for rank-disequilibrium as a (nearly) sufficient condition. The theoretical basis is the differential treatment and relative deprivation that follows from rank-disequilibrium, the resources that the high status provides the unit with to improve his low status, and the sense of self-righteousness that easily develops. A methodology for testing the theory is developed, and a number of implications for the theory of the consequences of economic development, the theory of revolutions, for the number of nations in the international system or the number of rank criteria used are examined. Three world orders are thought to be aggression-reducing: a feudal international order, a highly pluralistic system with many nations or rank criteria and a highly unitary system with a world-state or one rank-criterion. The importance of economic development in such a way that there is a multi-dimensional growth and a parallel development between nations is emphasized.

NOTES

[1] This is different from standard definitions in the field, e.g. the famous definition given by Dollard that aggression is any 'sequence of behavior, the goal-response to which is the injury of the person toward whom it is directed'. This definition is also used in the standard work by Berkowitz, L., *Aggression: A Social Psychological Analysis* (New York: McGraw-Hill, 1962). But we agree with Klineberg when he writes *(The Human Dimension of International Relations,* New York: Holt, Rinehart and Winston, 1964, p. 11) that 'The question of universality of aggression is further complicated by considerable difference in the definition of the term itself. One writer, for example, refers to the original meaning of aggression as a tendency to go forward or approach. This is regarded as instinctive, whereas the inborn or instinctive nature of *hostility* has never been demonstrated. Another describes it as the will to assert and to test our capacity to deal with external forces, and it it this, rather than hostility, that is a fundamental characteristic of all living beings' (p. 10). But universality or fundamentality still leaves us with the problem of where or for whom aggression in this broad sense is most pronounced, and with the problem of under what conditions aggression expresses itself as hostility. We use aggression somewhat in the sense of 'self-assertion', but only insofar as this self-assertion implies an effort to change social relations, i.e. no longer to comply with existing conditions.

[2] Klineberg, op. cit., pp. 7–17.

[3] For an analysis of the concept of interaction see Galtung, J., 'Expectations and Interaction Processes', *Inquiry,* 1959, pp. 213–34.

[4] See, for instance, the brilliant analysis in Tannenbaum, F., *Slave and Citizen, The Negro in the Americas* (New York: Knopf, 1947). It took many years before the rank-disequilibrium of some, and complete underdog status of most US Negroes led to the mutinies of the 19th century.

[5] See, for instance, the analysis in Barth, Fredrik, 'The System of Social Stratification in Swat, North Pakistan', in Leach, E. (Ed.), *Aspects of Caste in South India, Ceylon and North-West Pakistan* (Cambridge: Cambridge University Press, 1960), p. 113.

[6] Davies, J. C., 'Toward a Theory of Revolution', *American Sociological Review,* 1962, pp. 5–19.

[7] Op. cit., p. 6.

[8] Zawadzki, B. and Lazarsfeld, P. F., 'The Psychological Consequences of Unemployment,' *Journal of Social Psychology,* 1935, pp. 224–51.

[9] Davies, op. cit., p. 7.

[10] See, for instance, Ch. 5 in Arnold Rose, *Indagine sull'integrazione sociale in due quartieri di Roma* (Roma: Istituto di Statistica, 1959), pp. 60–69; or such classics as Angell, R. C., *The Family Encounters the Depression* (New York: Scribner, 1936) or Mirra Komalovsky, *The Unemployed Man and his Family* (New York: Dryden, 1940).

[11] Kogon, E., *The Theory and Practice of Hell* (New York: Berkley Medallion Books, 1958), Chapter 23, 'The Psychology of the Prisoners.' (Title of the original: *Der SS Staat*)

[12] Quoted from Davies, op. cit., pp. 5 ff.

[13] The condition of rank-disequilibrium is, of course, not a necessary condition for aggression. Aggression may arise for other reasons. And it is hardly a sufficient condition either—perfect relationships between variables are rarely if ever found in the social sciences—but we shall argue later that for high levels of disequilibrium aggression seems to be a very probable consequence.

[14] *Rank and Social Integration* (Oslo: Peace Research Institute, stencil 10–2, 1963), to be published in Berger, Zelditch, Anderson, *Sociological Theories in Progress* (Boston: Houghton Mifflin Co., 1965).

[15] Work is under way at the Peace Research Institute in Oslo to test this implication of the hypothesis. So far it is based on more intuitive impressions of delinquents, and some investigations purporting to show that juvenile delinquents more than others in comparable positions are marked by some of the characteristics of the *entrepreneur,* viz., initiative, intelligence, energy, ability to take risks and to see possibilities, etc.

[16] The following list may be useful as a reference. We have presented two sets of variables for nations, depending on whether the variables are 'analytic' (based on statistical information about individuals) or 'global,' i.e. *sui generis*.

INDIVIDUAL DIMENSIONS	NATIONS, ANALYTIC	NATIONS, GLOBAL
1. *Age* (adults *v.* adolescents and children)	population pyramid	*Age as a nation*
2. *Sex.* (men *v.* women)		
3. *Family* ('good' *v.* 'bad')		*Alliances* ('good' *v.* 'bad')
4. *Primogeniture* ('first born')		*Doyen* in a group of nations
5. *Race* (Caucasoid, Mongoloid, Negroid, etc.)	rates of racial composition	*Dominant culture*
6. *Ethnicity* (Gentiles *v.* Jews, emigrants *v.* immigrants)	rates of ethnical composition	*Dominant culture*
7. *Ecology* (urban *v.* rural)	*rate of urbanization*	
8. *Geography* (center *v.* periphery)		*Central v. peripheral nation*
9. *Nation* (for individuals only—all national variables relevant as context)		
10. *Education* (degree)	*rate of literacy*	*Educational structure*
11. Occupation, split into		*Occupational structure*
a. *sector* (tertiary, secondary, primary)	*1-rate in primary occupations*	
b. *position* (high *v.* low)	*1-rate of population in low occupations*	*Social structure*
12. *Ideology* ('right' *v.* 'wrong')	*rates of believers*	*Dominant ideology* *Stage of economic growth*
13. *Income, property* (rich *v.* poor-'dispossessed'; bourgeoisie *v.* proletariat)	*per capita income = per capita consumption + per capita investment standard of living*	*GNP* (development) *natural resources* *utilization of resources* (rate of growth)
14. *Power* (rulers *v.* subjects)	*rate of popular participation*	*Political structure* *International power*
15. *Legality* (law-abiding *v.* law-breaking)	*rates of criminality*	*Legality*
16. *Health* (well *v.* ill)	*rates of morbidity etc., life expectancy*	*Medical Structure*
17. *Knowledge* (those who know *v.* those who do not know)		*Cognitive culture*
18. *Skill* (those who can *v.* those who cannot)		*Technical culture*
19. *Conviction* (the 'true believers' *v.* the others)	*rates of true believers*	*Ethical culture*
20. *Taste* (artists *v.* laymen)		*Esthetic culture*

[17] This corresponds to the distinction made in game theory between cooperative and competitive games. Also see Schelling, T., *The Strategy of Conflict* (Cambridge: Harvard University Press, 1960), Chs. 2, 3 and 6.

[18] See Jackson (9, p. 473) or Galtung, J., *Members of Two Worlds, A Sociological Investigation of Three Villages in Western Sicily* (Oslo: PRIO publication no. 6–2, forthcoming), section 4.6.

[19] See Jackson, op. cit.

[20] Ibid., pp. 476 ff.

[21] Loc. cit.

[22] I am indebted to Tom Broch for this suggestion.

[23] For many of the nation variables indicated above, in note no. 16, *United Nations: Statistical Yearbook* and *United Nations Demographic Yearbook* will do. For other variables the excellent *World Handbook of Political and Social Indicators* prepared by the Political Data Program of Yale University will answer many questions. But this is for the contemporary scene; since the hypothesis should also be tested over time historical data are needed where cruder distinctions will have to be made.

[24] The main findings in the empirical investigations based on the ideas of rank-equivalence can be summarized as follows for this and other references:

Author	About the rank-equilibrated	About the rank-disequilibrated
Fenchel et al.	less so (4)	unstable self-images because of differential treatment
Adams	(1) 'less subject to discontents or compensatory behavior' *group* performance low *group* atmosphere 'harmonious, trusting cooperative'	'lack of congruency is an effective motivator of the individual' *group* performance high group atmosphere less harmonious
Lenski	(14) less radical	support Democrats more, have liberal and left views
Lenski	(16) less isolated more sociable in their motivation	'social isolates more numerous' 'less likely to report sociable motivations'—for social participation
Goffman	(6) less concerned about change of power distribution	'prefer extensive change of the distribution of power in society'—but only when 'experience opportunities for upward mobility are low'
Jackson	(9) less frustration less ambiguity	frustration leads to 1. *stress* (intrapunitive) if low status more achieved 2. *radicalism* (extrapunitive) if low status more ascribed
Landecker	(13) in general, more consciousness of class status	less so

The focus of the research has been on the persons with rank-differences. Unfortunately, only the very stimulating article by Adams has group data in addition to individual data, and this leads him to the important conclusion: 'it should be noted that there is an apparent antithesis between productivity and group euphoria, at least in settings such as the military organization' (ibid., p. 22). In general, it should be noticed that all findings reported by these authors are based on relatively small percentage differences. Hence, even though the phenomenon is too consistent to be written off in any way, it is probably of secondary importance to other factors.

[25] The science of peace research, when it gains momentum and perspective, will probably acknowledge its tremendous debts to the genius of Lewis F. Richardson even more clearly than is the case today. Regardless of the criticism that can be raised against his work, his courage in treating nations and wars like the physicists treat bodies in mechanics has been invaluable. It is to be hoped that there will be many follow-up studies such as Paul Smoker's work on the mathematical side (*JPR*, 1964, pp. 55–64) or J. D. Singer's forthcoming work on '150 years of conflict' on the statistical and theoretical side.

[26] Similarly, one can predict at what period in a woman's life the tendencies towards participation in emancipist movements will be most pronounced. She starts as a young girl with equilibrium between her low sex-status and her low age and probably also education, income, power (if only in the family), etc. But as she grows older she will grow into disequilibrium between her sex position and all the concomitants of age; hence, we would predict participation in radical movements at a much older

age than for men. Men gain equilibrium as they grow older, women lose it—hence the difference.

[27] The only author to our knowledge that has written consistently about the sociology of international relations from the point of view of international stratification is Lagos, Gustavo, *International Stratification and Underdeveloped Countries* (Chapel Hill: University of North Carolina Press. 1963). However, as pointed out by Amital Etzioni in his review of the book (*American Journal of Sociology*, 1964, pp. 114 f.) 'the potentially promising line of examining the consequences of status inconsistency, of a country rich but weak, poor but honest, etc., is not sufficiently developed.' For further comments see Appendix 2 in Galtung, 'Rank and Social Integration' in Berger, Zelditch, Anderson, op. cit.

[28] See article by Mari H. Ruge, 'Technical Assistance and Parliamentary Debates,' *JPR*, 1964, pp. 77–94.

[29] The role of China in the follow-up of the 1955 Bandoeng conferences can probably be studied under this perspective.

[30] A study of the Cuban revolution guided by this theoretical perspective is in process at the Peace Research Institute in Oslo. The reader may find it useful to test the ideas against standard knowledge of this revolution and of the life history of Fidel Castro.

[31] Thus, it is not surprising that turns towards the left have taken place where the rate of illiteracy is relatively low, as in Kerala in Southern India, Cuba or Chile, which stood a fair chance of electing into power a Marxist president, Senator Salvador Allende. The relation between the interplay of social indicators and the type of political system is probably

a good deal more complicated than the famous analysis by Seymour Lipset: 'Economic Development and Democracy,' in *Political Man* (New York: Doubleday, 1960), pp. 45–76.

[32] Norwegians love *per capita* statistics, for the simple reason that many indicators when divided by a small population will make Norway rank relatively high.

[33] Adoption is a system whereby a wholesale transition from (almost) complete underdog to (almost) complete topdog position can take place. The Japanese feudal system of bestowing on a servant 'who has proven himself' status as son of the family is a good example, and very functional for the preservation of the feudal order precisely because it preserves rank-equilibrium. Knighting in the middle ages probably had a similar function, whereas winning in the lottery does not, it may create gross disequilibria. However, since equilibration will be on other dimensions than property, aggression may not necessarily result from this type of disequilibrium.

[34] See, for instance, Shonfield, Andrew, *The Attack on World Poverty* (London: Chatto and Windus, 1961).

REFERENCES
On Rank-Disequilibrium

1. Adams, Stuart. 'Status Congruency as a Variable in Small Group Performance,' *Social Forces*, 1953, pp. 16–22.
2. Benoit-Smullyan, E. 'Status, Status Types and Status Interrelationships,' *ASR.*, 1944, pp 151–61.
3. Broom, L. 'Social Differentiation and Stratification,' in *Sociology Today*. (New York: Basic Books 1959) pp. 429–41.
4. Fenchel, G. H., Monderer, J. H. and Hartley, E. L. 'Subjective Status and the Equilibration Hypothesis,' *JASP*, 1951 pp. 476–79.
5. Freedman, R. *et al. Principles of Sociology*. (New York: Henry Holt, 1956) Chs. 7, 13.
6. Goffman, I. W. 'Status Inconsistency and Preference for Change in Power Distribution,' *ASR*, 1957, pp. 275–81.
7. Hodge. 'Status Consistency of Occupational Groups,' *ASR*, 1962, pp. 336–43.
8. Hughes, E. 'Dilemmas and Contradictions of Status,' *AJS*, 1944, pp. 353–57.
9. Jackson, E. F. 'Status Consistency and Symptoms of Stress,' *ASR*, 1962, pp. 469–80.
10. Kaufman, H. F. *et al.* 'Problems of Theory and Method in the Study of Social Stratification in Rural Society,' *Rural Sociology*, 1953. p. 15.
11. Kenkel, W. F. 'The Relationship Between Status Consistency and Politico-Economic Attitudes,' *ASR*, 1956, pp. 365–68.
12. Landecker, W. 'Class Crystallization and Its Urban Pattern,' *Social Research*, 1960, pp. 308–20.
13. Landecker, W. 'Class Crystallization and Class Consciousness,' *ASR*, 1963, pp. 219–29.
14. Lenski, G. 'Status Crystallization: A Non-Vertical Dimension of Social Status,' *ASR*, 1954, pp. 405–13.
15. Lenski, G. 'Comment on Kenkel's Communication,' *ASR*, 1956, pp. 368–69.
16. Lenski, G. 'Social Participation and Status Crystallization,' *ASR*, 1956, pp. 458–64.
17. Morris, R. T. and Murphy, R. J. 'The Situs Dimension in Occupational Structure,' *ASR*, 1959, pp. 231–39.
18. Ringer, B. B. and Sills, D. L. 'Political Extremists in Iran,' *POQ*, 1952/53, pp. 689–701.
19. Sorokin, P. *Society, Culture and Personality*. (New York: Harper, 1947) pp. 289–94.
20. Weber, Max, in Gerth, Mills. *From Max Weber: Essays in Sociology*. (New York: Oxford University Press, 1946) pp. 180–95.
21. Zaleznik, Christensen, Roethlisberger. *The Motivation, Productivity and Satisfaction of Workers*. (Boston: Harvard University Press. 1958) pp. 56–66.

IS THERE A MILITARY-INDUSTRIAL COMPLEX WHICH PREVENTS PEACE?: CONSENSUS AND COUNTERVAILING POWER IN PLURALISTIC SYSTEMS *†

MARC PILISUK and THOMAS HAYDEN

Introduction

The term "military-industrial complex" is very much in the literature. If its most sinister depictions are correct, then the peace researcher who works with the hope that his research may actually improve chances for world peace is wasting his time. A research finding, like a bit of knowledge, is always double-edged in what it portends for application. The project which tells us the surest steps to peace, tells us with equal certainty the steps which must be bypassed if peace is shunned. If there exists an omnipotent elite, committed to militarism, then there is simply no basis for hope that voices for peace have gotten, or can get, an influential channel into inner policy circles. If, on the other hand, the pluralist thesis can be said to apply in full even to basic policy directions of preparedness for war or for peace, then some influential decision makers must be eagerly awaiting the research findings on paths to peace with intentions to press for their immediate application.

* Research relevant to this paper was made possible by a series of small grants from the Chrisopher Reynolds Foundation, The Society for Psychological Study of Social Issue, The Institute for Policy Studies, and the University of Michigan Phoenix Memorial Project. Appreciation is also due to Michael Locker and Anatol Rapoport for review and assistance with the manuscript and to the University of Michigan's Mental Health Research Institute and Center for Research on Conflict Resolution for the use of facilities.

† Reprinted by permission of the authors and publisher from *Journal of Social Issues*, 1965, *21*, 67–117. Pages 99–112 are omitted. A fuller version of the article may be found in the original and in R. Perrucci and M. Pilisuk, *The Triple Revolution: Social Problems in Depth* (Boston: Little, Brown and Co., 1968).

Because we agree with neither of the above positions, because we believe that most research workers in this area tend either to ignore or to over-rate the potential consequences of their work to peace, and because we feel that consideration of the conditions which dictate major directions of policy is essential for an evaluation of any contribution to peace research, we are bringing the concept of the "military-industrial complex" to both the microscope and the scalpel. The implications of this inquiry point to a research approach which does have relevance to the decision process and to the most central agencies of social change, and resistance to change, within American society.

The New Concern

Not since the 30's has there been such a rash of attention to military-industrial power as there is today. Then, as now, the President himself raised the spectre of improper military influence. FDR, on the eve of a Senate investigation of the munitions industry, said flatly that the arms race was a "grave menace . . . due in no small measure to the uncontrolled activities of the manufacturers and merchants of the engines of destruction and it must be met by the concerted action of the people of all nations." (Raymond, 1964, p. 262; also Congressional Quarterly Weekly Report, 6, 1964, pp. 265–278.) While Dwight Eisenhower did not sound as militant as Roosevelt, and while he never adopted FDR's 1932 campaign pledge to "take the profits out of war," he did resume a popular tradition with his warning about the "unwarranted influence" of the military-industrial complex. It may be a significant measure of the times that one President could make such warnings in his very first campaign for office, while the other couched it among several other going-away remarks.

The 30's serve as a prelude to the 60's, too, in the area of congressional investigation of militarism. Then it was Senator Gerald P. Nye investigating the fabulous World War I profits of U.S. Steel and Hercules Powder and discovering, with horror, the instrumental role of munitions-makers and other commercial interests in beginning the war. Nye revealed, for example, that the American ambassador in London informed President Wilson in 1917 that probably "the only way of maintaining our pre-eminent trade position and averting a panic is by declaring war on Germany" (Raymond, p. 264). As Roosevelt was more aggressive than Eisenhower, so also were Nye, Borah and other popular Senators more aggressive than their present counterparts in the 60's. But, nevertheless, similar issues are now being raised in congressional committees. The most shocking of these may be found in the hearings of Senator John McClellen's committee on *Pyramiding of Profits and Costs in the Missile Procurement Program*. This report pointed out the likely danger that the government "can be placed in the unenviable position of reluctant acquiescence to the demands and conditions set by the contractor," and that "profits were pyramided on other profits without any relationship at all to the effort being expended by those making the profit." In what might have been front page scandal in any area but national defense, the committee documented two mechanisms by which millions upon millions of dollars of excess profit have been reaped by the defense industries. The mechanisms are: a) claiming profits on work subcontracted to other firms (which in turn subcontract portions of their work to others and charge a profit on the sub-subcontracted work, too), and b) overestimating the subcontracting costs (on incentive type contracts) thereby reaping huge profit rates by undercutting the original estimates. However, the contrast with the 30's is clear; Senator McClellen only wants to improve the efficiency of what he calls "these necessary monopolies." (U.S.

Senate, Committee on Government Operations, report of the Permanent Subcommittee on Investigations, *Pyramiding of Profits and Costs in the Missile Procurement Program*, March 31, 1964.) A more far-reaching investigation, under the direction of Senator Clark, deals with the convertibility of the defense empire to civilian job-creating tasks. He claims that 1) the new defense emphasis on electronics and on research and development, and the monopolization of defense by a few companies and geographic areas, considerably reduces the potential effect of defense as an economic stabilizer; and 2) that certain firms, especially those in the aerospace industry, are suffering an overcapacity crisis that spurs them to insist on more missiles than the nation needs. (U.S. Senate, Committee on Labor and Public Welfare, report of the Subcommittee on Employment and Manpower, *Convertibility of Space and Defense Resources to Civilian Needs: A Search for New Employment Potentials*, 88th Congress, 2d Session, 1964.) Senator Clark's hearings, too, are mild in contrast to the 30's. Even milder, however, was the recent survey report of Senator Hubert Humphrey, who says it is "nonsense" to believe American industry is opposed to disarmament. (U.S. Senate, Committee on Senate Foreign Relations, Subcommittee on Disarmament, *The Economic Impact of Arms Control Agreements*, Congressional Record, October 5, 1962, pp. 2139–2194.)

Another measure of interest in military-industrial power is the number of popular and technical books dealing with the subject. In the 30's, the widely read books were Davenport's *Zaharoff, High Priest of War*, Engelbrecht and Haneghen's *Merchants of Death* and Selde's *Iron, Blood and Profits*. Two decades then passed before the work of C. Wright Mills began to attract broad attention to the subject of organized militarism. Including Mills' pioneering books, there have been at least 21 major books published in this area during the past several years. Many of them are by journalists (Cook, Coffin, Raymond, Swomley, Wise and Ross); some by economists (Benoit, Boulding, Melman, Peck, Perlo, Scherer); sociologists (Etzioni, Horowitz, Janowitz,

Mills); political scientists (Meisel, Rogow); novelists (Bailey, Burdick, Knebel, Sutton); and at least one physical scientist (Lapp).

Whatever the objective referent, if any, of a "military-industrial complex" may be, it is undeniable that the concept occupies an important role in the political consciousness of many persons, on a scale without precedent since the 30's. It is a telling fact that the new literature, with the exceptions of Mills, Cook and Perlo, still lacks the bite of the old, and that the proposed solutions are quite "modest." In the 30's a typical popular solution, proposed by the Nye Committee but never implemented, was the nationalization of the munitions industries. By the 60's the reverse has happened; most military research, development, and production is done by private companies subsidized by the Federal government. The loci of military-political-industrial cooperation are so pervasive and frequent that it becomes a hair-splitting task to identify specifically any "merchants of death." Also, the scale of potential destruction has so increased, the nature of warfare strategy so changed, and the existence of the military in peacetime so accepted, that it seems quaint to associate defense contractors with bloody hands. Furthermore, the assumed threat of communist expansion has become the ultimate justification of the post-war military buildup, whereas in the past such buildups could be attributed more clearly to industrial profit and power motives. Probably reasons such as these explain both the long silence and the modest character of the current resurgence in discussion of these matters.

But these reasons account partially for the inadequacy of analysis as well. The question, "Does there exist a military-industrial complex which prevents peace?" at first seems debatable in straightforward yes-or-no terms. Indeed, it might have been answerable in the 20's or 30's but not in the post-war period. When there is permanent intermingling and coordination among military, industrial, and governmental elites, and whenever greater war-preparedness can be justified by reference to the communist movement, it becomes a much "stickier" question. Because it is sticky, the easiest con-

clusion to support is that a "complex" simply does not exist as an omnipresent obstacle to policy change. Indeed, this belief has become the accepted norm for "informed" discussion of interests vested in the perpetuation of military preparedness. The next most easily supported conclusion would be that we have become trapped in the hell-fires of militarism by a sinister but concealed elite of military-industrial leaders, which through its puppets, pulls the strings on every major policy decision. This latter theory is non-conformist, radical, and smacks too closely of classical conspiracy theory to be palatable to most scholars. Indeed, the dominant attitude (explicit or tacit) in most of the new literature is that there exists no military-industrial complex capable of preventing peace. It is claimed that the military-industrial complex operates as a sub-group within the limits of an essentially civilian society. In this view the complex is seen as making an interest-conscious equation of its own interests with those of the nation as a whole. But, it is argued, this tendency of power aggrandizement is checked by countervailing interest blocs in the society. Moreover, the "complex" is not seen as having a corrosive effect on democratic processes; even if it is conceded that military and technological expertise or well-financed public relations give the "complex" unusual privilege and visibility, this is no different, in principle, from certain other influential groups, all of which are limited by the web of constraints but comprise a pluralist society. Usually, it is added that the internal differences in the "complex" such as differences among the separate services or between the military and the industrial procurement sectors, tend to restrict further its ability to impose a policy "line" on the United States. These points of view appear in scattered form throughout the literature. A few examples are cited to demonstrate this.

Wise and Ross call their brilliantly-rich study of the CIA *The Invisible Government* without realizing the theoretical problems immediately raised by such a title. Does the CIA, and the broader "intelligence community" actually have the tools and, more importantly, the prerogatives of sovereignty (for its own operations) associated with the concept of "government"? If this is the case, then the conventional pluralist argument would be perforated decisively, because it rests on the assumption that no power centers are unaccountable to democratic review. The nature of the evidence used in the book, however, precludes an objective answer to this question. Using case studies primarily, although there also are chapters on the CIA structure, the authors are concerned with such issues as: the contradictions between sinister CIA practices and professed U.S. policy objectives; the tendency of the CIA to support only conservative or reactionary governments; the danger that the CIA can influence specific policy objectives of the U.S. government, as in the case of the U-2 interference with the 1960 Paris summit meetings; the progressive acceptance in America of subversive techniques as part of a "necessary Cold War strategy." But it is explicitly maintained that the "invisible government" is subordinate, at least so far, to the visible one in general as well as in nearly every specific case. At worst, it has an undefined "quasi-independent" status which should be brought under somewhat greater congressional and executive review (p. 352). Also, the authors suggest fewer statements of misinformation and "more discreet silence" by the government "in difficult circumstances" (p. 356). Accepting the broad lines of government policy, but realizing the dilemmas of such a stance, the authors conclude:

The secret intelligence machinery of the government can never be totally reconciled with the tradition of a free republic. But in a time of Cold War, the solution lies not in dismantling this machinery, but in bringing it under greater control. The resultant danger of exposure is far less than the danger of secret power. If we err as a society, let it be on the side of control (356).

New York Times reporter, Jack Raymond, is much less forboding in his *Power at the Pentagon,* but assumes the same framework of government control over the defense establishment. He goes further, however, to point out "the United States could embrace militarism under civilian as well as military

auspices." With the same popular democratic values as Wise and Ross (the better journalists remain pugnaciously committed to the civil liberties), he believes that the traditional arguments against military dominance must be broadened to challenge civilian, or bureaucratic, dominance as well.

The military apparatus must not be an automated juggernaut whose operations we take for granted. We ought to raise hell with it constantly, ask questions, demand truthful answers. (334)

This point of view is reflected also in periodic statements by political leaders as disparate as Dwight Eisenhower and Hubert Humphrey. Eisenhower's speech, as mentioned, was instrumental in spurring and legitimizing later discussions. His point of view was that the military-industrial complex might exercise "unwarranted influence":

In the councils of government, we must guard against the acquisition of unwarranted influence, whether sought or unsought, by the military-industrial complex. The potential for the disastrous rise of misplaced power exists and will persist. . . . Only an alert and knowledgeable citizenry can compel the proper meshing of the huge industrial and military machinery of defense with our peaceful methods and goals, so that security and liberty may prosper together. (Eisenhower's Farewell Address)

Humphrey's Subcommittee report claimed that by and large U.S. industries not only could, but would be delighted to shift to full peace-time production of goods and services.[1] According to Humphrey, the military-industrial complex that President Eisenhower warned against "is one which appears to be centered in a few hands and in a few key places." Where Raymond attempted to use fragmentary evidence, mostly personal interviews and citations of particular instances, and Eisenhower cited

[1] Senator Humphrey's investigation consisted of an inquiry sent by mail to a sample of major industrial defense contractors asking about their willingness to shift to non-defense areas if cutbacks were necessitated by progress toward arms reduction. For some unexplicable reason the results were classified but the Senator's statement indicated apparent readiness to make the shift.

no evidence at all, Humphrey is more like Wise and Ross in his attempt to generalize from studies of a "slice" of military-industrial organization. That is, even were we to accept his evidence as a valid representation of industrial reality, it still neglects the interrelation of industry with military and political interests. It isolates a part from the whole, then makes claims about the nature of the whole. While extremely interesting and useful, it takes the word of contractors as a valid measure of the desirability and feasibility of conversion. No doubt such words are critically important, but they constitute only a piece of objective reality. It is with such pieces that the existence of an obstructing elite is denied.

Disarmament and the American Economy, edited by Benoit and Boulding, is a collection of essays and studies by several separate individuals. That many of these individuals have connections in the worlds of defense, industry, and government probably reflects the degree to which these worlds command the intellectual resources of modern America. It is a book which received considerable attention in policy-making circles when it appeared last year. It is considerably more lenient in its interpretation of a military-industrial complex, merely pointing out that a few vested interests of long duration are among the structural obstacles to a disarmament pact. These obstacles, according to Emile Benoit, can be overcome rather easily by economic growth in sectors which could more lucratively employ those presently in defense-related work. Prosperity becomes the lubricant for change. But this approach glosses over the existence of propensities to place short-run security over long-run prosperity, and so avoids delineating the kind of political forces which might oppose economic change. As the authors themselves admit, their volume is abstracted from politics. In plainer fact, this abstracting process considerably dissolves any military-industrial complex which might exist. What is left is a pooh-poohing of the threat of a complex, plus the claim that increased overall demand, and therefore new employment opportunities, will make "structural adjustments" manageable:

[The massive defense complex] does not mean that disarmament is impossible or that the possibilities of peace are threatened by the vested interests of an holy alliance of generals and war contractors. It does mean that to redefine the content of many defense jobs will be a far easier and more constructive solution than to abolish them. (291)

While the authors address themselves only to the question of what the economy can do if disarmament should somehow come about, they are obviously aware of the potential socio-political consequences of removing the threat of the more foreboding economic consequences of disarmament which have sometimes been suggested. Perhaps the authors assume that *only* through a new consensus, sweetened by economic opportunities, can there be a chance for disarmament. That, however, is allowing the problem of social change to be defined by the hope for disarmament. Such an approach may well be a utopian one, and tends to the pole opposite Wise and Ross among the believers in civilian control.

Easily the most well-researched book of this kind is *The Weapons Acquisition Process* by Peck and Scherer, both at Harvard Business School. This book is by and for persons with a sophisticated business viewpoint. After several hundred pages of detailed data and analysis, it concludes that the weapons acquisition process is honest and efficient. However, it too is relatively "above" the politics of the defense economy. Much politics, they find, is ritualistic, with "little impact at the operating levels where the source selection decision is made" (382). Where they believe politics do enter, for instance when competing producers of the Bomarc and Nike-Hercules take out full-page advertisements, they defend its practice. While President Eisenhower warned against the "munitions lobby," in the Bomarc-Nike-Hercules case Peck and Scherer believe that "selling" the Government is symptomatic of a healthy tendency.

Both contractors and sponsoring agencies, which are often the contractors' allies, believe their weapons programs are essential to the national defense. If this sincerity does not come from pride in invention, it soon develops as a result of constantly living with the idea. This zeal serves a useful function, since it fortifies the participants' . . . personal contact with "the right people" and is an effective means of getting ideas accepted. Similarly, creating public demand for a program through advertising and feature articles is a way of winning over or by-passing balky decision-makers. (243)

This book thus explicitly defends the "advocates" who exaggerate their weapons' capabilities, "whatever the effect of this (military-industrial) complex upon grand strategy" (243).

Whether such salesmanship or advocacy is as ethical as it is effective is a question not raised in the Peck and Scherer book. One of our own interviews with the vice-president of a defense contracting firm specializing in Research and Development, sites the positive ethical value of developing and promoting strategic conceptions of military function (which include the use of the weapon system being worked upon). Such promotion is an absolutely essential buttress to the military services which are incapable of constructing their own strategic doctrines. The system manager concept, a concept used by some prime contractors to justify profit pyramiding, in testimony before the McClellen committee, seems to suggest that promotion of the concept of the entire weapon system is part of the contractor's service to the military and as such is not only ethical but deserving of compensation.

None of these denials of irresponsible military-industrial power marshall very significant evidence to support their views. There are examples given of specific conflicts between civilian and military groups which were lost by the military (e.g., the dropping of General Walker, the refusal to be first to break the moratorium on testing). There are examples given of heated divisions between the services over what military strategy should be pursued (the arguments over conventional warfare in the late 50's and the more recent RS 70 controversy). There are sociological studies which reveal underlying diversities within single corporations, between competing corporations, and within the demographic and institutional character of each branch of the

armed services.[2] And, throughout, there are citations of American pluralism as an automatic check system against any elite group.[3]

At a more general level, these fragments of evidence point toward three grounds for denying that a military-industrial complex prevents peace:

1) it is held that the *scope* of decisions made by any interest group is quite narrow and cannot be said to govern anything so broad as foreign policy.
2) it is held that the "complex" is not *monolithic, not self-conscious,* and *not coordinated,* the presumed attributes of a ruling elite.
3) it is held that the military-industrial complex does not wield power if the term "power" is defined as the ability to realize its will even against the resistance of others and regardless of external conditions.

These formulations, to repeat, are made neither explicitly nor consistently in the new literature. But they crystallize the basic questions about definition which the new literature raises. Moreover, they are quite definitely the major contentions made by academic criticisms of power elite theory. The more widely read of these academic critics include Daniel Bell, Robert Dahl, and Talcott Parsons. Since their critiques are mainly directed at the work of C. Wright Mills, it is with Mills that we will begin to analyze the theories which claim there *is* a military-industrial complex blocking peace.

The Thesis of Elite Control

Mills is by far the most formidable exponent of the theory of a power elite. In his

[2] See Janowitz for a good sociological study of interservice differences.

[3] For the thesis that a "peacefare state" counterweighs the "warfare state," see Klaus Knorr's review of Fred J. Cook in the *Journal of Conflict Resolution, VII, 4* (December, 1963). The "pluralist position," which usually is that the social system has semi-automatic checking mechanisms against tyranny, appears as basic in discussions not only of the military, but of economics and politics as well. See Robert Dahl, *Who Governs?*; John K. Galbraith, *American Capitalism;* Seymour Martin Lipset, *Political Man;* Talcott Parsons, *The Social System.*

view, the period in America since World War II has been dominated by the ascendance of corporation and military elites to positions of institutional power. These "commanding heights" allow them to exercise control over the trends of the business cycle and international relations. The Cold War set the conditions which legitimize this ascendance, and the decline and incorporation of significant left-liberal movements, such as the CIO, symbolizes the end of opposition forces. The power elite monopolizes sovereignty, in that political initiative and control stem mainly from the top hierarchical levels of position and influence. Through the communications system the elite facilitates the growth of a politically indifferent mass society below the powerful institutions. This, according to the Mills argument, would explain why an observer finds widespread apathy. Only a small minority believes in actual participation in the larger decisions which affect their existence and only the ritual forms of "popular democracy" are practiced by the vast majority. Mills' argument addresses itself to the terms of the three basic issues we have designated, i.e., scope of decision power, awareness of common interest, and the definition of power exerted.

By *scope*, we are referring to the sphere of society over which an elite is presumed to exercise power. Mills argues that the scope of this elite is general, embracing all the decisions which in any way could be called vital (slump and boom, peace and war, etc.). He does not argue that *each* decision is directly determined, but rather that the political alternatives from which the "Deciders" choose are shaped and limited by the elite through its possession of all the large-scale institutions. By this kind of argument, Mills avoids the need to demonstrate how his elite is at work during each decision. He speaks instead in terms of institutions and resources. But the problem is that his basic evidence is of a rather negative kind. No major decisions have been made for 20 years contrary to the policies of anti-communism and corporate or military aggrandizement; *therefore* a power elite must be prevailing. Mills might have

improved his claims about the scope of elite decisions by analyzing a series of actual decisions in terms of the premises which were *not* debated. This could point to the mechanisms (implicit or explicit) which led to the exclusion of these premises from debate. By this and other means he might have found more satisfying evidence of the common, though perhaps tacit, presuppositions of seemingly disparate institutions. He then might have developed a framework analyzing "scope" on different levels. The scope of the Joint Chiefs of Staff, for instance, could be seen as limited, while at the same time the Joint Chiefs could be placed in a larger elite context having larger scope. Whether this could be shown awaits research of this kind. Until it is done, however, Mills theory of scope remains open to attack, but, conversely, is not subject to refutation.

Mills' theory also eludes the traditional requirements for inferring monolithic structure, i.e., consciousness of elite status, and coordination. The modern tradition of viewing elites in this way began with Mosca's *The Ruling Class* in a period when family units and inheritance systems were the basic means of conferring power. Mills departs from this influential tradition precisely because of his emphasis on institutions at the basic elements. If the military, political, and economic *institutional orders* involve a high coincidence of interest, then the groups composing the institutional orders need not be monolithic, conscious, and coordinated, yet still they can exercise elite power.[4] This means specifically that a military-industrial complex could exist as an expression of a certain fixed ideology (reflecting common institutional needs), yet be "composed" of an endless shuffle of specific groups. For instance, our tables show 82 companies have dropped out of the list of 100 top defense contractors, and only 36 "durables" have remained on the list in the years since 1940. In terms of industry, the percentage of contracts going to the automobile industry dropped from 25 percent

[4] See James H. Meisel, *The Myth of the Ruling Class*, for the best available discussion of this innovation in theorizing about elites.

in World War II to 4 percent in the missile age. At the same time, the aircraft companies went from 34 to 54 percent of all contracts, and the electronics industry from 9 to 28 percent (Peck and Scherer, 1962). Mills' most central argument is that this ebb-and-flow is not necessarily evidence for the pluralists. His stress is on the unities which underlie the procession of competition and change. The decision to change the technology of warfare was one which enabled one group to "overcome" another in an overall system to which both are fundamentally committed. Moreover, the decision issued from the laboratories and planning boards of the defense establishment and only superficially involved any role for public opinion. The case studies of weapons development by Peck and Scherer, in which politics is described as a marginal ritual, would certainly buttress Mills' point of view.

Making this institution analysis enables Mills to make interesting comments on his human actors. The integration of institutions means that hundreds of individuals become familiar with several roles: General, politician, lobbyist, defense contractor. These men are the power elite, but they need not know it. They conspire, but conspiracy is not absolutely essential to their maintenance. They mix together easily, but can remain in power even if they are mostly anonymous to each other. They make decisions, big and small, sometimes with the knowledge of others and sometimes not, which ultimately control all the significant action and resources of society.

Where this approach tends to fall short, is in its unclarity about how discontinuities arise. Is the military-industrial complex a feature of American society which can disappear and still leave the general social structure intact? Horst Brand has suggested a tension between financial companies and the defense industries because of the relatively few investment markets created by defense (1962). Others are beginning to challenge the traditional view that defense spending stimulates high demand and employment. Their claim is that the concentration of contracts in a few states, the monopolization of defense and space

industry by the largest 75 or 100 corporations, the low multiplier effect of the new weapons, the declining numbers of blue-collar workers required, and other factors, make the defense economy more of a drag than a stimulant (Melman et al., 1963; Etzioni, 1964). Mills died before these trends became the subject of debate, but he might have pioneered in discussion of them if his analytic categories had differentiated more finely between various industries and interest groups in his power elite. His emphasis was almost entirely on the "need" for a "permanent war economy" just when that need was being questioned even among his elite.

However, this failure does not necessarily undermine the rest of Mills' analysis. His institutional analysis is still the best means of identifying a complex without calling it monolithic, conscious and coordinated. Had he differentiated more exactly he might have been able to describe various degrees of commitment to an arms race, a rightist ideology constricting the arena of meaningful debate, and other characteristics of a complex. This task remains to be done, and will be discussed at a later point.

Where Mills' theory is most awkward is in his assertions that the elite can, and does, make its decisions against the will of others and regardless of external conditions. This way of looking at power is inherited by Mills, and much of modern sociology, directly from Max Weber. What is attributed to the elite is a rather fantastic quality: literal omnipotence. Conversely, any group that is *not* able to realize its will even against the resistance of others is only "influential" but not an elite. Mills attempts to defend this viewpoint but, in essence, modifies it. He says he is describing a tendency, not a finalized state of affairs. This is a helpful device in explaining cracks in the monolith—for instance, the inability of the elite to establish a full corporate state against the will of small businessmen. However, it does not change the ultimate argument—that the power elite cannot become more than a tendency, cannot realize its actual self, unless it takes on the quality of omnipotence.

When power is defined as this kind of dominance, it is easily open to critical dispute. The conception of power depicts a vital and complex social system as essentially static, as having within it a set of stable governing components, with precharted interests which infiltrate and control every outpost of decision-authority. Thereby, internal accommodation is made necessary and significant change, aside from growth, becomes impossible. This conception goes beyond the idea of social or economic determinism. In fact, it defines a "closed social system." A "closed system" may be a dramatic image, but it is a forced one as well. Its defender sees events such as the rise of the labor movement essentially as a means of rationalizing modern capitalism. But true or false as this may be, did not the labor movement also constitute a "collective will" which the elite could not resist? An accommodation was reached, probably more on the side of capital than labor, but the very term "accommodation" implies the existence of more than one independent will. On a world scale, this becomes even more obvious. Certainly the rise of communism has not been through the will of capitalists, and Mills would be the first to agree. Nor does the elite fully control technological development; surely the process of invention has some independent, even if minor, place in the process of social change.

Mills' definition of power as dominance ironically serves the pluralist argument, rather than countering it. When power is defined so extremely, it becomes rather easy to claim that such power is curbed in the contemporary United States. The pluralists can say that Mills has conjured up a bogeyman to explain his own failure to realize his will. This is indeed what has been done in review after review of Mills' writings. A leading pluralist thinker, Edward Shils, says that Mills was too much influenced by Trotsky and Kafka:

Power, although concentrated, is not so concentrated so powerful, or so permeative as Professor Mills seems to believe. . . . There have been years in Western history, e.g. in Germany during the last years of the Weimer Republic and under the Nazis when reality approximated this picture more closely. . . . But as a picture of Western societies, and not just as an ideal type of extreme possibilities which might be realized if so much else that is vital were lacking, it will not do. (Shils, 1961)

But is Mills' definition the only suitable one here? If it is, then the pluralists have won the debate. But if there is a way to designate an irresponsible elite without giving it omnipotence, then the debate may be recast at least.

This fundamental question is not answered in the other major books which affirm the existence of a military-industrial complex. Cook's *The Warfare State* and Perlo's *Militarism and Industry* are good examples of this literature which is theoretically inferior to Mill's perplexing account.

Cook's volume has been pilloried severely by deniers of the military-industrial complex. At least it has the merit of creating discussion by being one of the few dissenting books distributed widely on a commercial basis. It suffers, however, from many of the same unclarities typical of the deniers. Its title assumes a "warfare state" while its evidence, although rich, is only a compilation of incidents, pronouncements, and trends, lacking any framework for weighing and measuring. From his writing several hypotheses can be extracted about the "face of the Warfare State," all of them suggestive but none of them conclusive: 1) the Department of Defense owns more property than any other organization in the world:[5] 2) between 60 and 70 percent of the national budget is consistently allocated to defense or defense related expenditures: 3) the Military and Big Business join in an inevitable meeting of minds over billions of dollars in contracts the one has to order and the other to fulfill: 4) the 100 top corporations monopolize three-fourths of the contracts, 85 percent of them being awarded without competition; 5) as much as one-third of all production and service indirectly depends on defense; 6) business and

[5] Swomley (1964) accounts for Department of Defense holdings equivalent in size to eight states of the U.S.A. Kenneth Boulding, including personnel as well as property criteria, calls the Department of Defense the world's third largest socialist state. (Personal discussion, 1963.)

other conservative groups, even though outside of the Defense establishment, benefit from the warfare emphasis because it keeps subordinate the welfare-state which is anathema to them (pages 20–24, 162–202).

Cook's work, much more than Mills' is open to the counter-argument that no monolithic semi-conspirational elite exists. Even his definitions of vested interests are crude and presumed. Moreover, he suffers far more than Mills from a failure to differentiate between groups. For instance, there is nothing in his book (written in 1962) which would explain the economic drag of defense spending, which Cook perceptively observed in a *Nation* article, "The Coming Politics of Disarmament" in 1963. One year he wrote that Big Business was being fattened off war contracts, but the next year the "prolonged arms race has started, at last, to commit a form of economic hara-kiri." "Hara-kiri" does not happen spontaneously; it is a culmination of long-developing abnormalties. That Cook could not diagnose them before they became common in congressional testimony illustrates the lack of refinement in his 1962 analysis. Cook's failure lies in visualizing a monolith, which obscures the strains which promote new trends and configurations.

It is in this attention to strains that Perlo's book is useful. He draws interesting connections between the largest industrial corporations and the defense economy, finding that defense accounts for 12 percent of the profits of the 25 largest firms. He adds the factor of foreign investment as one which creates a further propensity in favor of a large defense system, and he calculates that military business and foreign investments combined total 40 percent of the aggregate profits among the top 25. He draws deeper connections between companies and the major financial groups controlling their assets.

This kind of analysis begins to reveal important disunities within the business community. For instance, it can be seen that the Rockefellers are increasing their direct military investments while maintaining their largest foreign holdings in extremely volatile Middle Eastern and Latin American companies. The Morgans are involved in domestic industries of a rather easy-to-convert type, and their main foreign holdings are in the "safer" European countries, although they too have "unsafe" mining interests in Latin America and Africa. The First National City Bank, while having large holdings in Latin American sugar and fruit, has a more technical relation to its associated firms than the stock-owner relation. The Mellons have sizeable oil holdings on Kuwait, but on the whole are less involved in defense than the other groups. The DuPonts, traditionally the major munitions makers, are "diversified" into the booming aerospace and plutonium industries, but their overseas holdings are heavily in Europe. Certain other groups with financial holdings, such as Young and Eaton interests in Cleveland, have almost no profit stake in defense or foreign investments. On the other hand, some of the new wealth in Los Angeles is deeply committed to the aerospace industry.

Perlo makes several differentiations of this sort, including the use of foreign-policy statements by leading industrial groups. But he does not have a way to predict under what conditions a given company would actively support economic shifts away from the arms race. These and other gaps, however, are not nearly as grave as his lack of analysis of other components of the military-industrial complex.[6] There is no attempt to include politicians, military groups and other forces in a "map" of the military-industrial complex which Perlo believes exists. This may be partly because of the book's intent, which is to document profiteering by arms contractors, but for whatever reason, the book is not theoretically edifying about the question we are posing. Nor does it refute the pluralist case. In fact, it contains just the kind of evidence that pluralist arguments currently employ to demonstrate the absence of a monolith.

[6] In an earlier book, *The Empire of High Finance* (1957), he documented the close relations of the major financial groups and the political executive. He did not, however, carry this analysis to congressmen and senators, nor did he offer sufficient comparative evidence to demonstrate a long-term pattern.

Revising the Criteria for Inferring Power

After finding fault with so many books and divergent viewpoints, the most obvious conclusion is that current social theory is currently deficient in its explanation of power. We concur with one of Mills' severest critics, Daniel Bell, who at least agrees with Mills that most current analysis concentrates on the "intermediate sectors," e.g., parties, interest groups, formal structures, without attempting to view the underlying system of "renewable power independent of any momentary group of actors" (Bell, 1964). However, we have indicated that the only formidable analysis of the underlying system of renewable power, that of Mills, has profound shortcomings because of its definition of power. Therefore, before we can offer an answer of our own to the question, "Is there a military-industrial complex which blocks peace?", it is imperative to return to the question of power itself in American society.

We have agreed essentially with the pluralist claim that ruling-group models do not "fit" the American structure. We have classified Mills' model as that of a ruling-group because of his Weberian definition of power, but we have noted also that Mills successfully went beyond two traps common to elite theories, *viz.*, that the elite is total in the scope of its decisions, and that the elite is a coordinated monolith.

But we perhaps have not stressed sufficiently that the alternative case for pluralism is inadequate in its claim to describe the historical dynamics of American society. The point of our dissent from pluralism is over the doctrine of "counter-vailing power." This is the modern version of Adam Smith's economics and of the Madisonian or Federalism theory of checks-and-balances, adapted to the new circumstances of large-scale organization. Its evidence is composed of self-serving incidents and a faith in semi-mystical resources. For instance, in the sphere of political economy, it is argued that oligopoly contains automatic checking mechanisms against undue corporate growth, and that additionally, the factors of "public opinion" and "corporate conscience" are built-in limiting

forces.[7] We believe that evidence in the field, however, suggests that oligopoly is a means of stabilizing an industrial sphere either through tacit agreements to follow price leadership or rigged agreements in the case of custom-made goods; that "public opinion" tends much more to be manipulated and apathetic than independently critical; that "corporate conscience" is less suitable as a description than Reagan's terms, "corporate arrogance."

To take the more immediate example of the military sphere, the pluralist claim is that the military is subordinate to broader, civilian interests. The first problem with the statement is the ambiguity of "civilian." Is it clear that military men are more "militaristic" than civilian men? To say so would be to deny the increasing trend of "white-collar militarism." The top strategists in the Department of Defense, the Central Intelligence Agency and the key advisory positions often are Ph.D.'s. In fact, "civilians" including McGeorge Bundy, Robert Kennedy, James Rostow and Robert McNamara are mainly responsible for the development of the only remaining "heroic" form of combat: counter-insurgency operations in the jungles of the underdeveloped countries. If "militarism"[8] has permeated this deeply into the "civilian" sphere, then the distinction between the terms becomes largely nominal. Meisel's description is imaginative and alluring:

What we still honor with the name of peace is only the domestic aspect of a world-wide industrial mobilization let up at intervals by the explosions of a shooting war. . . . The industrial revolution in its class-struggle aspect is becoming externalized, projected upon the industrial field, that it is being relegated, so to speak, from barricade to barracks. . . . The armies, navies, and air forces of our time [are] the embodiment

---

[7] For this argument, see A. A. Berle, *The Twentieth Century Capitalist Revolution* and J. K. Galbraith, *American Capitalism*. For sound criticisms. but without sound alternatives, see Mills and Perlo's books. Also see Michael Reagan, *The Managed Economy* (1963) and Berland Nossiter, *The Mythmakers* (1964) for other refutations of the countervailing power thesis.

[8] We are defining the term as "primary reliance on coercive means, particularly violence or the threat of violence, to deal with social problems."

of the industrial revolution in its aggressive form (Meisel, 1962, pp. 157–158).

While the more traditional military men have not taken kindly to the takeover of military planning by civilian professors, the takeover has, none-the-less, gone far. More than 300 universities and non-profit research institutions supply civilian personnel to, and seek contracts from, the Department of Defense. Approximately half of these institutions were created specifically to do specialized strategic research. Probably the most influential of the lot of these civilian centers is the Rand Corporation.

Consistent with its Air Force origins, Rand's civilian army of almost 1,000 professional researchers and supporting personnel derives most of its support from Air Force Project Rand Studies. Rand charges the Air Force six percent of the estimated cost of the contracts which the Air Force farms out to private industry as a result of work done at Rand. This brings the Air Force contribution to Rand to over 80 percent where it has been for the past few years. When a large Ford Foundation Grant permitted Rand's reorganization in May of 1948, the organization was granted virtual autonomy from the Air Force and from Douglas Aviation which were its original parents. Such autonomy seemed necessary both to draw independent intellectuals into the establishment and to promote the image of objectivity in its research. The charter establishes a non-profit corporation to "further and promote scientific, educational and charitable purposes, all for the public welfare and security of the United States of America." The actual measure of Rand autonomy should not be taken solely from its dependence upon Air Force money. In actual practice, Rand scholars have differed with the Air Force and on issues quite important to the Air Force. The turns of the cold war strategies from massive retaliation through finite deterrence and limited war, through counter-force, and on into controlled response had never, until 1961 and 1962 involved major reductions in any type of weaponry other than the post Korean War automotive cutbacks. Automo-

tives were, however, a largely civilian market industry. The first place where the strategic innovations served not only to rationalize existing weaponry (in the more specialized defense industry) or to call for accelerated development in additional areas, but also to call for "cost effectiveness" or cutting back in a favored weapon area, came at the expense of the Air Force. In short order the Skybolt and the RS 70 met their demise. For a time, Harvard economist Charles Hitch (then with Rand, now Defense Department comptroller) and perhaps the entire battalion of systems analysts at Rand were personally unpopular with Air Force brass. The Air Force was particularly incensed over the inclination and ability of Rand personnel to consult directly with the Defense Department and bypass the Air Force. Rand, incidentally, maintains a permanent Washington office which facilitates such confrontation. This is not exactly what Air Force spokesmen intend when they see Rand serving the function of giving "prestige type support for favored Air Force proposals to the Department of Defense and the Congress" (Friedman, 1963). The controversy shows that there is obviously no monolithic influence in defense policy. It shows also that civilian and military factions are involved and that, in this instance, even the combined influential interests of traditional Air Force leaders and industrial aircraft contractors could not hold sway over the civilian analysts. The case also illustrates the weakness of the pluralist argument. The controversy, involving sums of money exceeding the total requested for President Johnson's war on poverty, did not threaten to starve either the Air Force or the aircraft industries. Indeed, it was a controversy among family members all sharing the same source of income and the same assumptions regarding the need for maximal military strength in the cold war. While Rand scientists played the role of civilian efficiency experts in this particular controversy, Rand experts have clearly played the role of military expansionists in civilian clothing at other times. Albert Wohlstetter and Herbert Dinerstein, Rand experts on military strategy and Soviet policy, deserve major credits for the creation of the mythical "missile gap" and for the equally unreal-preemptive war strategy for the Soviet Union during the period from Sputnik, in October of 1957, until the issue of inadequate military preparedness helped bring the New Frontier to Washington. Among the possible consequences of the U.S. missile buildup to overcome the mythical gap may well have been the Soviet resumption of nuclear tests in defiance of the moratorium, an act which completed a rung of the spiralling arms race which in turn nourishes all factions, civilian and military, who are engaged in military preparedness. We do not wish to labor the point that Rand experts have, at times, allowed the assumptions of their own ideology to form the basis of their rational analyses of Soviet capability and intentions. The point we wish to stress here is merely that the apparent flourishing of such civilian agencies as Rand (it earned over 20 million dollars in 1962 with all the earnings going into expansion and has already spawned the non-profit Systems Development Corporation with annual earnings exceeding 50 million dollars) is no reflection of countervailing power. The doctrine of controlled response under which the RS 70 fell was one which served the general aspirations of each of the separate services; of the Polaris and Minuteman stabile deterrent factions, of the brushfire or limited war proponents, guerilla war and para-military operations advocates, and of the counterforce adherents. It is a doctrine of versatility intended to leave the widest range of military options for retaliation and escalation in U.S. hands. It can hardly be claimed as victory against military thought. The fighting may have been intense but the area of consensus between military and civilian factions was great.

The process of "civilianizing" the military is not restricted to the level of attitudes but extends to the arena of social interaction. Traditionally, the military has been a semi-caste quite apart from the mainstream of American life. But that changed with World War II; as Mills points out:

Unless the military sat in on corporate decisions, they would not be sure that their programs would be carried out; and unless the corpora-

tion chieftains knew something of the war plans, they could not plan war production . . . the very organization of the economics of war made for the coincidence of interest and the political mingling among economic and military chiefs (Mills, 1965, p. 212).

One relatively early statement (January, 1944), by Charles E. Wilson, shows that the intermeshing of military and industrial leaders was, at least on the part of some, a self-conscious and policy-oriented enterprise. Wilson proposed a permanent war economy led by the Commander in Chief, and the War Department in cooperation with an industrial partner whose response and cooperation must be free from such political accusations as the "merchants of death" label. The program would not be a creature of emergency but rather an interminable measure to eliminate emergencies. "The role of Congress," Wilson added, "is limited to voting the funds" (Swomley, 1959). Now, twenty years later we can report a personal interview with a midwestern Congressman, a fourteen-year veteran, suggesting some truth to Wilson's projection.

It is not possible for a congressman to know, according to veteran Congressman George Meader, whether defense cutbacks are feasible. The whole area is very complicated and technical and Congress has very few military experts in its membership or on its research staffs. When budget time comes about the Department of Defense sends literally hundreds of experts to report before committee hearings. We have to take the word of the people who know. This paraphrased statement regarding the rubber stamping of more than 60 percent of the national budget was made by a congressman who claims a perfect record in opposition to the growth of governmental bureaucracy and to federal spending. If we were to examine the dozen or so congressional "experts" to whom Congressman Meader makes reference we find among them a number of high ranking reserve officers and a number representing districts or states economically dependent upon either military bases, or defense contracts, or both.

The same kind of planning requirements for modern war forced an overlapping of politicians with military and businessmen. There too, the very nature of world war, and especially cold war, integrated military, political and economic concepts of strategy, making the military officer much more than a cog. A variety of recent studies demonstrate the outcome of these developments. The 1959 hearings and survey by the House Armed Services Subcommittee disclosed that over 1400 retired officers with the rank of major or higher (including 261 of general or flag rank) were in the employ of the top 100 defense contractors (Hébert Subcommittee of the House Armed Services Committee, 1959). Coffin listed 74 Senators and Representatives with continuing status in the armed forces (Coffin, 1964). By 1957, 200 active (not reserve) generals or admirals were on assignment to "non-military" departments of the government or to international or interservice agencies. An added 1300 colonels or naval officers of comparable rank, and 6000 lower grade officers were similarly assigned (Swomley, 1959). Janowitz studied an historical sample of over 760 generals and admirals, administered questionnaires to about 600 current Pentagon staff officers, and interviewed 113 career officers. He found an "elite in transition" toward civilian and managerial habits: 1) the basis of authority and discipline is changing from authoritarian domination to greater reliance on manipulation, persuasion and group consensus; 2) the skill differential between civilians and soldiers is narrowing because of the need for technical specialties in the military; 3) officers are being recruited from a broader status and class base, reflecting the demand for more specialists; 4) the source of prestige recognition is shifting from military circles to the public at large; 5) this growth makes the officer define himself more and more as a political, rather than a technical, person with concerns about national security concepts and affairs (Janowitz, 1960, pp. 3–16, 442–452). These trends clearly demonstrate that the traditional American separation of military and civilian is outmoded. The new, blurred reality has not been successfully defined.

The main point here is that the pluralist argument relies on "counter-vailing forces" which are more mythical than real. The Wise and Ross book shows indisputably that at least during certain instances the Executive is not countervailing the CIA. Moreover, who is countervailing the "military-civilian" Executive centered in the Pentagon and the White House? What Knorr sees as a "peacefare state" countervailing the "warfare state" is merely its white-collar brother. The symbolic figure of the Arms Control and Disarmament Agency demonstrates this reality vividly. One side of the ACDA figure is a diplomat with tie and attaché case; the other side is a warrior dedicated to the pursuit of stabilizing control measures which might assure national advantages in a never ending cold war.

ACDA's narrow conception of its own role is as much a function of its internal quest for respectability as it is a matter of the prerogatives given it by a reluctant Congress. It has sought respectability not only in its apparent choice of essentially technical questions for study but also in its manner of study. One favored study technique is to collapse large socially significant questions into several questions answerable by short-term studies and suited for study by the grossly oversimplified techniques of policy appraisal employed by those same operations research corporations which serve, and live upon, defense contracts. These organizations have traditionally produced quick answers embedded in rationalistic models which ring with scientism and jargon. *Strategy and Conscience,* a powerfully written book by Anatol Rapoport, documents the manner in which the rationalist models employed in such strategic studies frequently conceal (often unknowingly) gross assumptions of the nature of the cold war. The point here is that if these are the same assumptions which necessitate a high level of military preparedness, then it matters little whether the studies are commissioned by civilian or military authorities.

Consensus

All that countervailing power refers to is the relationship between groups who fundamentally accept "the American system" but who compete for advantages within it.

The corporate executive wants higher profits, the laborer a higher wage. The President wants the final word on military strategies, the Chairman of the Joint Chiefs does not trust him with it. Boeing wants the contract, but General Dynamics is closer at the time to the Navy Secretary and the President, and so on: what is prevented by countervailing forces is the dominance of society by a group or clique or a party. But this process suggests a profoundly important point; that *the constant pattern in American society is the rise and fall of temporarily-irresponsible groups.* By temporary we mean that, outside of the largest industrial conglomerates,[9] the groups which wield significant power to influence policy decisions are not guaranteed stability. By irresponsible we mean that there are many activities within their scope which are essentially unaccountable in the democratic process. These groups are too uneven to be described with the shorthand term "class." Their personnel have many different characteristics (compare IBM executives and the Southern Dixiecrats) and their needs as groups are different enough to cause endless fights as, for example, small vs. big business.

[9] The term used in recent hearings by Senator Philip A. Hart refers to industrial organizations like Textron, which have holdings in every major sector of American industry.

No one group or coalition of several groups can tyrannize the rest as is demonstrated, for example, in the changing status of the major financial groups, particularly the fast-rising Bank of America which has been built from the financial needs of the previously-neglected small consumer.

However, it is clear that these groups exist within consensus relationships of a more general and durable kind than their conflict relationships. This is true, first of all, of their social characteristics. The tables which follow combine data from Suzanne Keller's compilation of military, economic, political and diplomatic elite survey materials in *Beyond the Ruling Class* (1963) and from an exhaustive study of American elites contained in Warner, et al., *The American Federal Executive* (1963). Data on elites vary slightly from study to study because of varying operational definitions of the elite population. However, the data selected here are fairly representative and refer exclusively to studies with major data collected within the decade of the fifties. (See Tables pp. 88–90.)

The relevant continuities represented in this data suggest an educated elite with an emphasis upon Protestant and business-oriented origins. Moreover, the data suggest inbreeding with businses orientation in backgrounds likely to have been at least

TABLE 1

SOCIAL CHARACTERISTICS OF AMERICAN ELITES

Elite	Nativity % Foreign Born	Rural-Urban % Urban Born[a]	Religion % Protestant	Education % College Grads.
Military	2%	30–40%[c]	90	73–98%[c]
Economic	6	65	85	61
Political	2	48	81	91
Diplomatic	4	66	60	81
U.S. Adult Males	7[b]	42[d]	65	7[b]

[a] Towns of 2,500 or more.
[b] 30 years of age and older.
[c] Taking the services separately.
[d] 1910 U.S. Population.

The majority of foreign-born and second-generation came from Northwestern Europe. The proportion of foreign-born from these areas is significantly lower for the general male population.

The difference between "political" and "diplomatic" and "economic" indicated that Congress, in the 1950's was more conservative—especially in its small business and non-integrationist attitudes—than the federal executive or the corporation leaders. The sharp difference between "military" and the rest lumps military policy-makers with lower level personnel, thus underemphasizing the new trend cited by Janowitz.

maintained, if not augmented, through marriage. The consistencies suggest orientations not unlike those which are to be found in examination of editorial content of major business newspapers and weeklies and in more directly sampled assessments of elite opinions.[10]

TABLE 2

FATHER'S OCCUPATION

	Civilian federal executives	Military executives	Business leader's	Total U.S. male pop. 1930
Unskilled Laborer	4%	2%	5%	33%
Skilled Labor	17	12	10	15
White-Collar (clerk or sales)	9	9	8	12
Foreman	5	5	3	2
Business Owner	15	19	26	7
Business Executive	15	15	23	3
Professional	19	18	14	4
Farm owner or manager	14	9	8	16
Farm tenant or worker	1	1	1	6
Other	1	1	2	2

The second evidence of consensus relationships, besides attitude and background data indicating a pro-business sympathy, would come from an examination of the *practice* of decision making. By analysis of such actual behavior we can understand which consensus attitudes are reflected in decision-making. Here, in retrospect, it is possible to discover the values and assumptions which are defended recurrently. This is at least a rough means of finding the boundaries of consensus relations. Often these boundaries are invisible because of the very infrequency with which they are tested. What are visible most of the time are the parameters of conflict relationships among different groups. These conflict rela-

[10] For some interesting work bearing upon the attitudes of business and military elites see (Angell, 1964; Bauer et al., 1963; Eells and Walton, 1961; and Singer, 1964).

tionships constitute the ingredients of experience which give individuals or groups their uniqueness and varieties, while the consensus relations constitute the common underpinnings of behavior. The tendency in social science has been to study decision-making in order to study group differences; we need to study decision-making also to understand group commonalities.

Were such studies done, our hypothesis would be that certain "core beliefs" are continuously unquestioned. One of these, undoubtedly, would be that efficacy is preferable to principle in foreign affairs. In practice, this means that violence is preferable to non-violence as a means of defense. A second is that private property is preferable to collective property. A third assumption is that the particular form of constitutional government, which is practiced within the United States is preferable to any other system of government. We refer to the preferred mode as limited parliamentary democracy, a system in which institutionalized forms of direct representation are carefully retained but with fundamental limitations placed upon the prerogatives of governing. Specifically included among the areas of limitation are many matters encroaching upon corporation property and state hegemony. While adherence to this form of government is conceivably the strongest of the domestic "core values," at least among business elites, it is probably the least strongly held of the three on the international scene. American relations with, and assistance for, authoritarian and semi-feudal regimes occurs exactly in those areas where the recipient regime is evaluated primarily upon the two former assumptions and given rather extensive leeway on the latter one.

The implications of these "core beliefs" for the social system are immense, for they justify the maintenance of our largest institutional structures: the military, the corporate economy, and a system of partisan politics which protects the concept of limited democracy. These institutions, in turn, may be seen as current agencies of the more basic social structure. We use the term "social structure" as Robert S. Lynd does as the stratification of people identified

TABLE 3
BUSINESS AND EXECUTIVE ORIGINS OF WIVES OF ELITES

Occupation	Political executives Father	Spouse's father	Foreign-service executives Father	Spouse's father	Military executives Father	Spouse's father	Civilian federal executives Father	Spouse's father	Business leaders Father	Spouse's father
Minor executive	10%	10%	11%	11%	15%	12%	11%	11%	11%	7%
Major executive	6	5	9	9	5	7	4	4	15	8
Business owner	21	25	19	24	19	22	20	23	26	28
Professional	24	19	25	23	18	19	19	16	14	15
Military executive					9	11				

according to kinship, sex, age, division of labor, race, religion, or other factors which differentiate them in terms of role, status, access to resources, and power. According to Lynd:

This structure established durable relations that hold groups of people together for certain purposes and separate them for others. Such social structures may persist over many generations. Its continuance depends upon its ability to cope with historical changes that involve absorption of new groupings and relations of men without fundamental change in the structure of the society of a kind that involves major transfer of power (Lynd, 1959).

The "renewable basis of power" in America at the present time underlies those institutional orders linked in consensus relationships: military defense of private property and parliamentary democracy. These institutional orders are not permanently secure, by definition. Their maintenance involves a continuous coping with new conditions, such as technological innovation and with the inherent instabilities of a social structure which arbitrarily classifies persons by role, status, access to resources, and power. The myriad groups composing these orders are even less secure because of their weak ability to command "coping resources," e.g., the service branches are less stable than the institution of the military, particular companies are less stable than the institutions of corporate property, political parties are less stable than the institution of parliamentary government.

In the United States there is no ruling group. Nor is there any easily discernible ruling institutional order, so meshed have the separate sources of elite power become. But there is a social structure which is organized to create and protect power centers with only partial accountability. In this definition of power we are avoiding the Weber-Mills meaning of *omnipotence* and the contrary pluralist definition of power as consistently *diffuse*. We are describing the current system as one of overall "minimal accountability" and "minimal consent." We mean that the role of democratic review, based on genuine popular consent, is made marginal and reactive. Elite groups are minimally accountable to publics and have a substantial, though by no means maximum, freedom to shape popular attitudes. The reverse of our system would be one in which democratic participation would be the orienting demand around which the social structure is organized.

Some will counter this case by saying that we are measuring "reality" against an "ideal," a technique which permits the conclusion that the social structure is undemocratic according to its distance from our utopian values. This is a convenient apology for the present system, of course. We think it possible, at least in theory, to develop measures of the undemocratic in democratic conditions, and place given social structures along a continuum. These measures, in rough form, might include such variables as economic security, education, legal guarantees, access to information, and participatory control over systems of economy, government, and jurisprudence.

The reasons for our concern with democratic process in an article questioning the power of a purported military-industrial complex are twofold. First, just as scientific method both legitimizes and promotes change in the world of knowledge, democratic method legitimizes and promotes change in the world of social institutions. Every society, regardless of how democratic, protects its core institutions in a web of widely shared values. But if the core institutions should be dictated by the requisites of military preparedness, then restrictions on the democratic process, i.e., restrictions in either mass opinion exchange (as by voluntary or imposed news management) or in decision-making bodies (as by selection of participants in a manner guaranteeing exclusion of certain positions), then such restrictions would be critical obstacles to peace.

Second, certain elements of democratic process are inimical to features of militarily oriented society, and the absence of these elements offers one type of evidence for a military-industrial complex even in the absence of a ruling elite. Secretary of Defense Robert McNamara made the point amply clear in his testimony in 1961 before the Senate Armed Services Committee:

Why should we tell Russia that the Zeus development may not be satisfactory? What we ought to be saying is that we have the most perfect anti-ICBM system that the human mind will ever devise. Instead the public domain is already full of statements that the Zeus may not be satisfactory, that it has deficiencies. I think it is absurd to release that level of information. (Military Procurement Authorization Fiscal Year 1962).

Under subsequent questioning McNamara attempted to clarify his statement that he only wished to delude Russian, not American, citizens about U.S. might. Just how this might be done was not explained.

A long established tradition exists for "executive privilege" which permits the President to refuse to release information when, in his opinion, it would be damaging to the national interest. Under modern conditions responsibility for handling information of a strategic nature is shared among military, industrial, and executive agencies. The discretion regarding when to withhold what information must also be shared. Moreover, the existence of a perpetual danger makes the justification, "in this time of national crisis" suitable to every occasion in which secrecy must be justified. McNamara's statement cited above referred not to a crisis in Cuba or Viet Nam but rather to the perpetual state of cold war crisis. And since the decision about what is to be released and when, is subject to just such management the media became dependent upon the agencies for timely leaks and major stories. This not only adds an aura of omniscience to the agencies, but gives these same agencies the power to reward "good" journalists and punish the critical ones.

The issues involved in the question of news management involve more than the elements of control available to the President, the State Department, the Department of Defense, the Central Intelligence Agency, the Atomic Energy Commission or any of the major prime contractors of defense contracts. Outright control of news flow is probably less pervasive than voluntary acquiescence to the objectives of these prominent institutions of our society. Nobody has to tell the wire services when to release a story on the bearded dictator of our hemisphere or the purported brutality of Ho Chi Minh. A frequent model, the personified devil image of an enemy, has become a press tradition. In addition to a sizeable quantity of radio and television programming and spot time purchased directly by the Pentagon, an amount of service, valued at $6 million by *Variety,* is donated annually by the networks and by public relations agencies for various military shows (Swomley, 1959). Again, the pluralistic shell of an independent press or broadcasting media is left hollow by the absence of a countervailing social force of any significant power.

The absence of a countervailing force for peace cannot, we have claimed, be demonstrated by an absence of conflicting interests among powerful sectors of American society. Indeed, such conflicts are ever-present examples of American pluralism. Demonstrating the absence of a discussion of the shared premises, among the most potent sectors of society, would go far in highlighting the area of forced or acquiescent consensus. But even the absence of debate could not complete the case unless we can show how the accepted premises are inconsistent with requisites of a viable peacetime social system. It is to this question: of the compatibility of the unquestioned assumptions of American society with conditions of peace, that we now turn. The "core beliefs" which we listed as unchallenged by any potent locus of institutionalized power are:

a) Efficacy is preferable to principle in foreign affairs (thus military means are chosen over non-violent means);

b) Private property is preferable to public property; and

c) Limited parliamentary democracy (see p. 41) is preferable to any other system of government.

What characteristics of a continuing world system devoid of military conflict fly in the face of these assumptions?

We identify three conditions for enduring peace which clash with one or more of the core beliefs. These are: 1) the requirements for programming an orderly transition and the subsequent maintenance of a non-defense economy within a highly automated and relatively affluent society; 2) the conditions for peaceful settlement of internal disputes within underdeveloped countries and between alien nations and commercial interests; and 3) the conditions under which disparities in living standards between have and have-not nations can be handled with minimum violence.

If one pools available projections regarding the offset programs, especially regional and local offset programs, necessary to maintain economic well-being in the face of disarmament in this country, the programs will highlight two important features. One is the lag time in industrial conversion. The second is the need for coordination in the timing and spacing of programs. One cannot reinvest in new home building in an area which has just been deserted by its major industry and left a ghost town. The short-term and long-term offset values of new hospitals and educational facilities will

differ in the building and the utilization stages and regional offset programs have demonstrable interregional effects (Reiner, 1964). Plans requiring worker mobility on a large scale will require a central bank for storing job information and a smooth system for its dissemination. Such coordination will require a degree of centralization of controls beyond the realm which our assumption regarding primacy of private property would permit.

Gross intransigence can be expected on this issue. Shortly after Sperry Rand on Long Island was forced to make major cutbacks of its professional and engineering staff to adapt to the termination of certain defense contracts, the union approached Sperry's management with the prospect of collaborating in efforts to commence contingency plans for diversification. The response, by Carl A. Frische, President of Sperry Gyroscope, a division of Sperry Rand, remains a classic. There must be no "government-controlled mechanisms under the hood of the economy." He suggested, with regard to such planning, that "we let Russia continue with that." (*Long Island Sunday Press,* February 23, 1964.) Sperry is an old-timer in defense production. Its board of directors average several years older than the more avant garde board of directors of, say, General Dynamics. But the prospect of contingency planning will be no more warmly welcomed in the newer aeroframe industry (which is only 60% convertible to needs of a peace-time society), (McDonagh and Zimmerman, 1964). Private planning, by an individual firm for its own future does occur, but, without coordinated plans, the time forecast for market conditions remains smaller than the lag time for major retooling. A lag time of from six to ten years would not be atypical before plans by a somewhat over-specialized defense contractor could result in retooling for production in a peace-time market. In the meantime, technological innovations, governmental fiscal or regulatory policies, shifts in consumer preferences, or the decisions by other firms to enter that same market could well make the market vanish. Moreover, the example of defense firms which have attempted even the smaller step toward diversification presents a picture which has not been entirely promising (Fearon and Hook, 1964). Indeed, one of several reasons for the failures in this endeavor has been that marketing skills necessary to compete in a private enterprise economy have been lost by those industrial giants who have been managing with a sales force of one or two retired generals to deal with the firm's only customer. Even if the path of successful conversion by some firms were to serve as the model for all individual attempts, the collective result would be poor. To avoid a financially disastrous glutting of limited markets some coordinated planning will be needed.

The intransigence regarding public or collaborative planning occurs against a backdrop of a soon-to-be increasing army of unemployed youth and aged, as well as regional armies of unemployed victims of automation. Whether one thinks of work in traditional job market terms or as anything worthwhile that a person can do with his life, work (and some means of livelihood) will have to be found for these people. There is much work to be done in community services, education, public health, and recreation, but this is people work, not product work. The lack of a countervailing force prevents the major reallocation of human and economic resources from the sector defined as preferable by the most potent institutions of society. One point must be stressed. We are not saying that limited planning to cushion the impact of arms reduction is impossible. Indeed, it is going on and with the apparent blessing of the Department of Defense (Barber, 1963). We are saying that the type of accommodation needed by a cutback of $9 billion in R & D and $16 billion in military procurement requires a type of preparation not consistent with the unchallenged assumptions.

Even the existence of facilities for coordinated planning does not, to be sure, guarantee the success of such planning. Bureaucratic institutions, designed as they may be for coordination and control, do set up internal resistance to the very coordination they seek to achieve. The mechanisms for handling these bureaucratic intransigencies

usually rely upon such techniques as bringing participants into the process of formulating the decisions which will affect their own behavior. We can conceive of no system of coordinated conversion planning which could function without full and motivated cooperation from the major corporations, the larger unions, and representatives of smaller business and industry. Unfortunately, it is just as difficult to conceive of a system which would assure this necessary level of participation and cooperation. This same argument cuts deeper still when we speak of the millions of separate individuals in the "other America" whose lives would be increasingly "administered" with the type of centralized planning needed to offset a defense economy. The job assignment which requires moving, the vocational retraining program, the development of housing projects to meet minimal standards, educational enrichment programs, all of the programs which are conceived by middle-class white America for racially mixed low income groups, face the same difficulty in execution of plans. Without direct participation in the formulation of the programs, the target populations are less likely to participate in the programs and more likely to continue feelings of alienation from the social system which looks upon them as an unfortunate problem rather than as contributing members. Considering the need for active participation in real decisions, every step of coordinated planning carries with it the responsibility for an equal step in the direction of participatory democracy. This means that the voice of the unemployed urban worker may have to be heard, not only on city council meetings which discuss policy on the control of rats in his dwelling, but also on decisions about where a particular major corporation will be relocated and where the major resource allocations of the country will be invested. That such decision participation would run counter to the consensus on the items of limited parliamentary democracy and private property is exactly the point we wish to make.

Just as the theoretical offset plans can be traced to the sources of power with which they conflict, so too can the theoretical plans for international governing and peace-keeping operations be shown to conflict with the unquestioned beliefs. U.S. consent to international jurisdiction in the settlement of claims deriving from the nationalization of American overseas holdings or the removal of U.S. military installations is almost inconceivable. Moreover, the mode of American relations to less-developed countries is so much a part of the operations of those American institutions which base their existence upon interminable conflict with Communism that the contingency in which the U.S. might have to face the question of international jurisdiction in these areas seems unreal. Offers to mediate, with Cuba by Mexico, with North Viet Nam by France, are bluntly rejected. Acceptance of such offers would have called into question not one but all three of the assumptions in the core system. International jurisdictional authority could institutionalize a means to call the beliefs into question. It is for this reason (but perhaps most directly because of our preference for forceful means) that American preoccupation in those negotiations regarding the extension of international control which have taken place, deal almost exclusively with controls in the area of weaponry and police operations and not at all in the areas of political or social justice.[11]

The acceptance of complete international authority even in the area of weaponry poses certain inconsistencies with the preferred "core beliefs." Non-violent settlement of Asian-African area conflicts would be slow and ineffective in protecting American interests. The elimination, however, of military preparedness, both for projected crises and for their potential escalation, requires a faith in alternate means of resolution. The phasing of the American plan for general and complete disarmament is one which says in effect: prove that the alternatives are as efficient as our arms in protection of our interests and then we disarm. In the short term, however, the effectiveness of force always looks greater.

The state of world peace contains certain conditions imposed by the fact that people now compare themselves with persons who have more of the benefits of industrialization than they themselves. Such comparative reference groups serve to increase the demand for rapid change. While modern communications heighten the pressures imposed by such comparisons, the actual disparities revealed in comparison speak for violence. Population growth rates, often as high as three percent, promise population doubling within a single generation in countries least able to provide for their members. The absolute number of illiterates as well as the absolute number of persons starving is greater now than ever before in history. Foreign aid barely offsets the disparity between declining prices paid for the prime commodities exported by underdeveloped countries and rising prices paid for the finished products imported into these countries (Horowitz, 1962). All schemes for tight centralized planning employed by these countries to accrue and disperse scarce capital by rational means are blocked by the unchallenged assumptions on private property and limited parliamentary democracy. A recent restatement of the principle came in the report of General Lucius Clay's committee on foreign aid. The report stated that the U.S. should not assist foreign governments "in projects establishing government owned industrial and commercial enterprises which compete with existing private endeavors." When Congressman Broomfield's amendment on foreign aid resulted in cancellation of a U.S. promise to India to build a steel mill in Bokaro, Broomfield stated the case succinctly: "The main issue is private enterprise vs. state socialism." (*The Atlantic*, September, 1964, p. 6.) Moreover, preference for forceful solutions assures that the capital now invested in preparedness will not be allocated in a gross way to the needs of underdeveloped countries. Instead, the manifest crises periodically erupting in violence justify further the need for reliance upon military preparedness.

We agree fully with an analysis by Lowi (1964) distinguishing types of decisions for which elite-like forces seem to appear

---

[11] An objective account of the major negotiations related to disarmament which have taken place may be found in Frye (1963).

and hold control (redistributive) and other types in which pluralist powers battle for their respective interests (distributive). In the latter type the pie is large and the fights are over who gets how much. Factional strife within and among military industrial and political forces in our country are largely of this nature. In redistributive decisions, the factions coalesce, for the pie itself is threatened. We have been arguing that the transition to peace is a process of redistributive decision.

REFERENCES

Angell, Robert C. A study of social values: content analysis of elite media. *The Journal of Conflict Resolution, VIII*, 1964, *4*, 329–85.

Bank Holding Companies: Scope of Operations and Stock Ownership. Committee on Banking and Currency. Washington: U.S. Government Printing Office, 1963.

Barber, Arthur. Some industrial aspects of arms control. *The Journal of Conflict Resolution, VII*, 1963, *3*, 491–95.

Bauer, Raymond A., Pool, I., and Dexter, L. *American business and public policy*. Alberton, New York, 1963.

Bell, Daniel. *The end of ideology*. Glencoe: Free Press, 1959.

Benoit, Emile, and Boulding, K. E. (Eds.) *Disarmament and the economy*. New York: Harper, 1963.

Berle, Adolph A. *The twentieth century capitalist revolution*. New York: Harcourt, 1954.

Bluestone, Irving. Problems of the worker in industrial conversion. *The Journal of Conflict Resolution, VII*, 1963, *3*, 495–502.

Brand, Horst. Disarmament and American capitalism. *Dissent*, Summer, 1962. 236–251.

Burdick, Eugene, and Wheeler, H. *Fail-safe*. New York: McGraw, 1962.

Burton, John. *Peace theory*. New York: Knopf, 1962.

Cartwright, Dorwin. Power: a neglected variable in social psychology, in Cartwright, D. (Ed.) *Studies in social power*. Ann Arbor: Research Center for Group Dynamics, 1959.

Catton, Bruce. *The war lords of Washington*. New York: Harcourt, 1948.

Coffin, Tristran. *The passion of the hawks*. New York: Macmillan, 1964.

Cohen, Bernard, C. *The press and foreign policy*. Princeton: Princeton University Press, 1963.

Convertibility of Space and Defense Resources to Civilian Needs, 88th Congress, 2d Session, Vol. 2, Subcommittee on Employment and Manpower. Washington: U.S. Government Printing Office, 1964.

Cook, Fred J. The coming politics of disarmament. *The Nation*. February 6, 1963.

———. *The warfare state*. New York: Macmillan, 1962.

Dahl, Robert A. *A modern political analysis*. New York: Prentice Hall, 1963.

———. *Who Governs?* New Haven: Yale University Press, 1961.

Dillon, W. *Little brother is watching*. Boston, Houghton Mifflin, 1962.

Economic impacts of disarmament. U.S. Arms Control and Disarmament Agency, Economic Series 1, Washington; U.S. Government Printing Office, 1962.

Eells, Richard, and Walton, C. *Conceptual foundations of business*. Homewood, Illinois; Irwin Press, 1961.

Etzioni, Amitai. *The hard way to peace*. New York: Collier, 1962.

———. *The moon doggle*. Garden City, New York: Doubleday, 1964.

Fearon, H. E., and Hook, R. C., Jr. The shift from military to industrial markets. *Business Topics*, Winter, 1964. 43–52.

Feingold, Eugene and Hayden, Thomas. What happened to democracy? *New University Thought*, Summer, 1964, *1*, 39–48.

Fisher, Roger (Ed.). *International conflict and behavioral science*. New York: Basic Books, 1964.

Fishman, Leslie. A note on disarmament and effective demand. *The Journal of Political Economy, LXX*, 1962, *2*, 183–186.

Foreign Assistance Act of 1964 (Parts VI and VII), Committee on Foreign Affairs. Hearings, 88th Congress, 2nd Session. Washington: U.S. Government Printing Office, 1964.

Friedman, S. The Rand Corporation and our Policy Makers, *Atlantic Monthly*, September, 1963, 61–68.

Frye, Wm. R. Characteristics of recent arms-control proposals and agreements. In Brennan, D. G. (Ed.), *Arms control, disarmament, and national security*. New York: Braziller, 1963.

Galbraith, J. K. *American Capitalism*. Boston: Houghton, 1956.

———. Poverty among nations. *The Atlantic Monthly*, October, 1962, 47–53.

Gans, Herbert J. Some proposals for government policy in an automating society. *The Correspondent*, 30, Jan.-Feb., 1964, 74–82.

Government Information Plans and Policies. Parts I-V, Hearings before a Sub-committee on Government Operations. 88th Congress, 1st Session, U.S. Govt. Printing Office: 1963.

Green, Philip. Alternative to overkill: dream and reality. *Bulletin of the Atomic Scientists*, November, 1963, 23-26.

Hayakawa, S. J. Formula for peace: listening. *N. Y. Times Magazine*, July 31, 1961.

Horowitz, David. World economic disparities: the haves and the have-nots. Center for Study of Democratic Institutions: Santa Barbara, 1962.

Horowitz, I. L. *The war game: studies of the new civilian militarists*. New York: Ballantine, 1963.

Humphrey, Hubert H. *The economic impact of*

arms control agreements. Congressional Record, October 5, 1962, 2139–94.

Impact of Military Supply and Service Activities on the Economy. 88th Congress, 2nd Session. Report to the Joint Economic Committee. Washington: U.S. Government Printing Office, 1963.

Isard, Walter, and Schooler, E. W. An economic analysis of local and regional impacts of reduction of military expenditures. *Papers Vol. 1, 1964 Peace Research Society International.* Chicago Conference, 1963.

Janowitz, Morris. Military elites and the study of war. *The Journal of Conflict Resolution, I,* 1957, *1,* 9–18.

——.*The professional soldier.* Glencoe, Ill.: The Free Press, 1960.

Keller, Suzanne. *Beyond the ruling class.* New York: Random House, 1963.

Knebel, Fletcher, and Bailey, C. *Seven days in May.* New York: Harper, 1962.

Knorr, Klaus. Warfare and peacefare states and the acts of transition. *The Journal of Conflict Resolution, VII,* 1963, *4,* 754–62.

Lapp, Ralph E. *Kill and overkill.* New York: Basic Books, Inc., 1962.

Larson, Arthur. *The internation rule of law.* A Report to the Committee on Research for Peace, Program of Research No. 3, Institute for International Order, 1961.

Lasswell, Harold. *Politics: Who gets what, when & how.* New York: Meridian, 1958.

Lipset, Seymour M. *Political man.* Garden City: Doubleday, 1959.

Long Island Sunday Press, The. February 23, 1964.

Lowi, Theodore J. "American Business, Public Policy, Case-Studies, and Political Theory," *World Politics,* July, 1964, 676–715.

Lumer, Hyman, *War economy and crisis.* New York: International Publishers, 1954.

Lynd, Robert S., and Merrill, Helen. *Middletown.* New York: Harcourt, 1959.

Mannheim, Karl. *Freedom, power, and democratic planning.* London: Routledge and Kegan Paul, 1956.

McDonagh, James J., and Zimmerman, Steven M. A program for civilian diversifications of the airplane industry. In *Convertibility of Space and Defense Resources to Civilian Needs.* Subcommittee on Employment and Manpower. U.S. Senate, 88th Congress. Washington: U.S. Government Printing Office, 1964.

McNamara, Robert S. Remarks of the Secretary of Defense before the Economic Club of New York. Department of Defense Office of Public Affairs, Washington, November 18, 1963.

Meisel, James H. *The fall of the republic.* Ann Arbor: University of Michigan Press, 1962.

——. *The myth of the ruling class.* Ann Arbor: University of Michigan Press, 1958.

Melman, Seymour (Ed.). *A Strategy for American Security,* New York: Lee Offset Inc., 1963.

——. *The peace race.* New York: Braziller, 1962.

Merbaum, R. Rand: technocrats and power, *New University Thought.* December-January, 1963-64, 45–57.

Michael, Donald. *Cybernation: the silent conquest.* Center for the Study of Democratic Institutions, Santa Barbara, 1962.

Milbrath, L. W. *The Washington lobbyists.* Chicago: Rand McNally, 1963.

Military Posture and Authorizing Appropriations for Aircraft, Missiles, and Naval Vessels. Hearings No. 36, 88th Congress, 2nd Session, U.S. Govt. Printing Office: 1964.

Military Procurement Authorization Fiscal Year 1962. Hearings before the Committee on Armed Services, U.S. Senate, 87th Congress, 1st Session, U.S. Govt. Printing Office: 1961.

Mills, C. Wright. *The causes of World War III.* New York: Simon & Schuster, 1958.

——. *The power elite.* New York: Oxford University Press, 1959.

Minnis, Jack. The care and feeding of power structures. *New University Thought V. 4,* Summer, 1964, *1,* 73–79.

Nossiter, Berland. *The Mythmakers: an essay on power and wealth.* Boston: Houghton, 1964.

Osgood, Charles E. *An alternative to war or surrender.* Urbana: University of Illinois Press, 1962.

Parsons, Talcott. *Structure and process in modern societies.* Glencoe: Free Press, 1959.

——. *The social system.* Glencoe: Free Press, 1951.

Paul, J., and Laulicht, J. Leaders' and voters' attitudes on defense and disarmament. *In Your Opinion,* V. 1, Canadian Peace Research Inst., Clarkson, Ontario, 1963.

Peck, M. J., and Scherer, F. M. *The weapons acquisition process.* Boston: Harvard University, 1962.

Perlo, Victor. *Militarism and industry.* New York: International Publishers, 1963.

Piel, Gerard. Consumers of abundance. Center for the Study of Democratic Institutions, Santa Barbara, 1961.

Pilisuk, Marc. Dominance of the Military. *Science,* January 18, 1963, 247–48.

——. The poor and the war on poverty, *The Correspondent,* Summer, 1965.

Pyramiding of Profits and Costs in the Missile Procurement Program, Parts 1, 2 and 3. Committee on Government Operations, U.S. Senate. Hearings, 87th Congress, 2nd Session. Washington: U.S. Govt. Printing Office, 1962.

Pyramiding of Profits and Costs in the Missile Procurement Program, Report, 88th Congress, 2nd Session, Report No. 970. Washington: U.S. Government Printing Office, 1964.

Rapoport, Anatol. *Fights, games, and debates.* Ann Arbor: University of Michigan Press, 1960.

——. *Strategy and conscience.* New York: Harper, 1964.

Raymond, Jack. *Power at the Pentagon.* New York: Harper, 1964.

Reagan, Michael. *The Managed Economy.* New York: Oxford, 1963.

Reiner, Thomas. Spatial criteria to offset military cutbacks. Paper presented at the Univ. of Chicago Peace Research Conference, Nov. 18, 1964.

Report on the world today. *The Atlantic*, September, 1964, 4–8.

Rogow, Arnold A. *James Forrestal*. New York: Macmillan, 1963.

Satellite communications, 1964. (Part 1) Committee on Government Operations, Hearings, 88th Congress, 2nd Session. Washington: U.S. Government Printing Office, 1964.

Scherer, Frederick. *The weapons acquisition process: economic incentives*. Cambridge: Harvard Business School, 1964.

Shils, Edward. Professor Mills on the calling of sociology. *World Politics, XIII*, 1961, 4.

Singer, J. David. A study of foreign policy attitudes. *The Journal of Conflict Resolution, VIII*, 1964, 4, 424–85.

_____. *Deterrence, arms control and disarmament*. Columbus: Ohio State University Press, 1962.

_____. (Ed.), Weapons management in world politics. *The Journal of Conflict Resolution, VII*, No. 3, and *Journal of Arms Control*, Vol. 1, No. 4.

Stachey, John. *On the prevention of war*. New York: St. Martin's Press, 1963.

Strauss, Lewis L. *Men and decisions*. Garden City: Doubleday, 1962.

Sutton, Jefferson. *The missile lords*. New York: Dell, 1963.

Swomley, J. M., Jr. The growing power of the military. *The Progressive*, January, 1959.

_____. *The military establishment*. Boston: Beacon Press, 1964.

Toward Full Employment: Proposals for a Comprehensive Employment and Man-power Policy in the U.S. A Report of the Committee on Labor and Public Welfare, United States Senate. Washington: U.S. Government Printing Office, 1964.

Toward world peace: a summary of U.S. disarmament efforts past and present. U.S. Arms Control and Disarmament Agency Publication 10: U.S. Government Printing Office, 1964.

Warner, Wm. Floyd, and Abegglen, J. D. *Big business leaders in America*. New York: Harper, 1955.

Warner, Wm. Floyd, Van Riper, P. P., Martin, N. H., and Collins, O. F. *The American federal executive*. New Haven: Yale University Press, 1963.

Watson-Watt, Sir Robert. *Man's means to his end*. London: Heinemann, 1962.

Westin, Alan. Anti-communism and the corporations. *Commentary Magazine*. December, 1963, 479–87.

Wise, David, and Ross, Thomas. *The invisible government*. New York: Random, 1964.

Wright, Quincy, Evans, Wm., and Deutsch, Morton (Eds.). *Preventing World War III: some proposals*. New York: Simon and Schuster, 1962.

E. Internation Conflict

1. Conflict Phenomena

ON THE CAUSES OF WAR AND
THE CONDITIONS OF PEACE* [1]

WERNER LEVI

One of man's fundamental problems is to live in peace with his fellow men. He cannot live alone. Yet, in coexistence with others, conflicts inevitably arise. It is therefore characteristic of individuals, alone or organized in groups, to seek power for the satisfaction of their interests. Lest this lead to an eternal state of war, men organize themselves to reap the greatest benefit from cooperation and to reduce as much as possible conflict and strife. In particular, it is the minimum goal of social organization that the satisfaction of vital interests—usually bodily integrity and survival—should not lead to violent conflict but should, rather, be assured by peaceful methods or, failing these, by the application of supreme coercive power which is socially organized and usually vested in a central authority.

The social organization of the state[2] is intended to provide adequate means for peaceful adjustment of conflicts and to obviate the need for individual violence. Even when the means prove inadequate, the state simply does not permit violence—except as a matter of self-defense. The individual's personal accumulation of power is limited to most kinds of power short of physical force. As a compensation the state guaran-

tees, as a minimum, the physical integrity and survival of the contestants in a conflict. This arrangement rests upon a habitual way of life and mental attitudes of the citizens indicating the existence of a community. The more complete the integration of the members into the community, the more successful.

In the international society, that loose association of states, the situation is basically different. Relations between states are ordered by routine practices and a vast network of international organizations promoting and regularizing the satisfaction of national interests. Much expedient cooperation exists between states, with well-established rules, regulations, and institutions. Innumerable conflicts of interest are resolved by accommodation and adjustment, either mutual or one-sided, depending upon the power relationship of the states involved. But this possibility is severely restricted because the society of states lacks an organized authority endowed with the legitimate supreme coercive power to guarantee the integrity and survival of each state, which is in turn merely an indication of the absence of any sense of solidarity among the peoples of the world. Every state is the guardian and guarantor of all its own interests. It must be ready to defend them at all times and for this purpose must possess power. In contrast to intrastate conditions, the possession of power cannot be limited to the non-physical kind because national interests may be threatened which a state wishes to defend by force. The time when such a vital threat may arrive is unpredictable, and the nature of the threat is unknown. Therefore, the quest for power becomes inevitably permanent, though not

* Reprinted by permission of the author and publisher from *Journal of Conflict Resolution*, 1960 *4*: 411–420.

[1] This article is a chapter in a forthcoming book, tentatively entitled *Principles of International Relations*.

[2] It should be understood throughout this article that "state" is used as a shorthand expression. It does not refer to any organism but rather, depending upon the context in which the word is used, to those making decisions on behalf of the people, those influencing these decisions, or all the citizens.

for this reason all consuming. It is conditioned by its relation to the goals the state pursues, by its relation to the power of other states, by the capabilities of the state, by the intensity of the state's will to survive integer, and by the results of the interrelations of these factors.

The quest for power becomes a major occupation of the state and a standard by which most aspects of its life and activities are measured, no matter how relative the magnitude of the desired power may be. It can be granted that, as states usually assert for the diplomatic record, they do not seek power for its own sake; they do so merely as a means to the end of satisfying their needs. For the nature of power, they can argue with cogency up to a point, like that of money, allows it to be accumulated and stored, to be expended for a great variety of unforeseeable ends at a time of need (25, p. 7). But whatever the end of the search for power and whatever its qualifications and limitations, the possibility remains that it can itself lead to violent conflict. States may become rivals in vying for elements of power or in one attempting to become more powerful than the other. The paradox here is that the search for power, even if only to have it available for a future conflict of interests, may itself become a source of violent conflict. This is an unending process because power as such has become a vital interest to some states. The search for it becomes necessary to guard against the consequences of this search.[3] Thus, until another way is found to guarantee satisfaction of a state's interest, especially those it considers vital (or until states disappear), the possibility of violent conflict is a built-in feature of the nation-state system in the modern world (16, 22).

This fact can easily enough explain the mutual suspicion among states and their potential hostility. Here is genuine conflict.

[3] The general ideas outlined here in regard to the role of power in international relations are old, although judging by recent debates raging around this subject, one may not think so. That states seek power to satisfy their interests was not discovered in the United States in the middle of the twentieth century. It was discussed in the pre-Christian era by such men as Kautilya in India and Mo Ti in China.

No amount of good will among nations, understanding among peoples, elimination of stereotypes, or clarification of semantic difficulties can obliterate it. Better knowledge of each other among peoples may gradually lead to greater integration on the way to a community and thereby reduce the chances of violence as a solution of conflict; but it cannot abolish conflict (4). It is therefore quite erroneous to assume, as has often been done, that states have violent conflicts because their citizens are aggressive, militaristic, and nationalistic. It is often the other way around: citizens assume these characteristics or are being prepared for warfare because there are real conflicts between states which may have to be solved with violence. The vicious circle is that a potential threat to their state makes citizens bellicose, and their bellicosity makes them appear as a threat to other states. Under the prevailing system the citizen must live in anticipation of violence and take the necessary precautions, including readiness for war. Polls in many European and some American states showed that anywhere from one-third to three-quarters of the people consulted did not think it was possible to live in peace (8, pp. 125–216, question 3a).

This expectation of war does not, however, have to lead to war in accord with the assertion that "expectations determine behavior" (9, p. 15). For the expectation may produce behavior which either leads to its fulfillment or to its frustration. History is full of proof that governments have genuinely tried to avoid wars, knowing their potential existence. One of the reasons why they have sometimes failed is that they did not or could not choose the right means to avoid it. In a nation-state system, with the close identification of the citizen with his state, the anticipation of violence regularly leads the citizen to turn to his own community for increased security rather than to attempt integration with the threatening state for the sake of reducing the chance of violence (15, p. 19).

There are relations between states to which this general description does not apply. Not all states are hostile to each other, or, at any rate, not all consider every other state a potential threat to vital interests. Albania and Honduras are not anticipating violent conflict, nor are Norway and Great Britain, nor Canada and the United States. Such states either are not rivals for interests or power; or there is enough sentiment of community between them to obviate violence; or they repress violence for the sake of unity against a common enemy. They may still have conflicts of interest, but for a variety of reasons, including possibly the technical inability to be violent with each other or much simultaneous cooperation, they do not consider the use of violence. Such reasons may change, of course, or new causes may produce violence. Colombia was engaged in violent conflict with North Korea under United Nations action in the name of collective security. There was no reason for this in the direct relations between the two states, but for reasons sufficient to the Colombian government the violent conflict between the two states existed nevertheless, and very likely North Korea as such had very little to do with these reasons. As peace becomes increasingly indivisible and as technical developments enable—in the future—even small states to possess weapons which can reach any point on the globe and wipe out any state in the world, the chances for violent conflict between two states hitherto geographically, politically, and in every other way remote from each other, increase; just as—a compensating virtue—the chances for their integration and growth into a community also become greater. With such a community come the patterns of behavior facilitating peaceful solution of conflict and making the application of coercive power by the supreme authority only one of the means of conflict solution and an increasingly rare one.

In the meantime, while states continue to fight each other, almost all conceivable and some inconceivable reasons have been given why they use violence in the solution of some of their conflicts. Supernatural powers, the state-system, social institutions, the character of groups, and the nature of man have been named as the causes of war (34, 5, 17, 33, 12, 7, 18). If supernatural causes are disregarded, the common denominator of the rest is, sooner or later in the argu-

ment, man. But whether, as the constitution of UNESCO asserts, it is the mind of man or some other part, is a matter of debate—so is whether it is man as an individual or a member of a group.

The number of natural traits held responsible as the cause of war is almost unlimited. As so often with psychological explanations of personal or social phenomena, any trait can somehow be made to serve as explanation. A man with an inferiority complex may either become a dictator or a mouse! There are many reasons for these kinds of alternatives: the same natural trait can find many different outlets, depending upon the opportunities which the environment offers; man is a complex of psychological factors from whose interaction behavior results, so that no one factor can be singled out; many psychological factors which appear mutually exclusive in the abstract can nevertheless in practice produce the same action. If the explanations of all psychologists are accepted as valid, the whole spectrum of natural traits of man is covered as cause of war—which is no explanation at all, for it is obvious that the nature of human beings is responsible for human actions. In most cases, therefore, only certain natural traits or psychological factors are singled out by various authors to account primarily for the existence of war.

One group of these factors can be classified as destructive: aggressiveness, hostility, rivalry, bias and prejudice, hatred, sadism, projection of one's own shortcomings upon the enemy. Another group contains factors calling for balancing or compensation, such as boredom, thirst for adventure, social frustration, insecurity, to which war offers the alternative of excitement and personal license. A third group refers to ego fulfillment: need for prestige, status, and recognition; desire to be wanted, wish for possessions. There is, finally, the not very frequently cited group of constructive factors allegedly causing people to go to war: sense of sacrifice, neighborly love, contribution to the community, sense of mission.

The protagonists of the theory that these psychological factors are the causes of war maintain that they can find particularly good expression in war and, without further ado, they jump to the conclusion that they are the cause. As one author put it, "eventually the growing hostility and the military preparation do lead to war, each side believing that the war was made necessary by the actions of the other" (13, p. 132). Unfortunately, things are not so simple. Even as a description of events this statement is not borne out by the facts, for there are innumerable instances in history of states being both hostile and militarily prepared without war breaking out between them. Things become even more complicated when the causes of war are sought in group conflict, regardless of one's concept of the group.[4]

Depending upon that concept, various explanations have been given to make the peculiar characteristics of the group responsible as the cause of war: in a group the individual loses the customary social restraints, so that he can act aggressively against the enemy as he would not against a fellow member of his community; or, in joining a group, the individual's destructive drives become magnified and war offers itself as an outlet. Tensions between states, which can exist in the absence of concrete conflicts, have been blamed for the outbreak of violence (24, pp. 427–30). Or, it has been claimed, tensions and conflicts within a state are externalized for the sake of maintaining the national community and war results. Psychoanalysts blame unconscious remnants of man's earliest past which survive in the group and perpetuate war as an institution.

Some value cannot be denied to these attempts at explaining wars through psychological factors since it is men who are making wars. But they are not the whole explanation. Indeed, they leave many crucial questions unanswered. When for instance, will certain natural traits or psychological

drives find outlets in war, and when in something more peaceful? Why did German fight German before the political unification of Germany, and why has such a contingency been practically unthinkable since? How are these traits and drives of millions of individual citizens suddenly crystallized into a state of war against a specific enemy at a given moment? What these explanations fail to do is to indicate how these human factors are translated into violent conflict involving all citizens, regardless of their individual nature, and performed through a highly complex machinery constructed over a period of years for just such purpose.

There is always the missing link in these fascinating speculations about the psychological causes of war between the fundamental nature of man and the outbreak of war. It is fairly easy to understand how a conflict of interest can lead to personal violence in a face-to-face situation between two or a very few people. But this situation is vastly different from conflict between two states, each possibly composed of hundreds of millions of individuals. It then becomes evident that the natural traits of the citizenry cannot, by themselves, directly be related to international violence and adequately explain the origin of wars. Even on the assumption that the cause of war lies somehow in the total population of a state, these explanations need qualifications and refinements and amplifications whose character becomes clearer when psychological factors are more closely related to the nature of modern wars and the citizen's role in them.

In this connection the distinction between the causes and the conditions of war is of relevance (22, p. 224; 32, epilogue). In practice such a distinction may not be easily feasible, and there is danger that its definition may deteriorate into semantics. Nevertheless, there is good purpose in separating, as has often been done, the circumstances which are necessary prerequisites for war (sometimes called the "deeper" or "underlying" causes) and those which are directly resulting in war. The possession of weapons, for instance, is an indispensable condition of modern war, but not necessarily its

---

[4] Some differing conceptions of the nature of groups are: a group is the sum total of its individuals, no more, no less; a group is something more than the sum total of its individual members, it becomes a new, independent creature (what Morris Cohen, opposed to this idea, called the "Communal Ghost"); the "group mind" is part of the psychic equipment of each individual (explains Edward Glover [14, p. 183]).

cause. The occupation of any enemy's territory, if the enemy resists, is a cause of war, and so is the enemy's resistance. Usually, the psychological factors and human traits can be classified as conditions of war more correctly than as causes.

The example of the invading enemy brings to mind another distinction which might be equally difficult to make in practice, but which nevertheless raises questions unanswered by the theories on psychological causes of war. There are aggressive wars and defensive wars. Regardless of what the parties themselves claim, it is objectively possible for a government to start a war in the conviction that its country is about to be attacked and that its action is truly defensive. It would seem that the differing motivation behind these two types of wars requires different psychological explanation, even though the wars will all look alike (27, pp. 43–47).

In fact, the failure of most psychological explanations of war to distinguish between different kinds of wars is another one of their weaknesses. Contrary to the usual assumption, wars are not always the same thing. In addition to being different regarding the aggressor and defender, wars can differ in regard to the kind of violence used, the weapons employed, the number and types of people involved, and several other things. Although the actual soldiers doing the fighting may have certain characteristics in common, from the standpoint of explaining on psychological grounds the origin of wars, it makes a basic difference whether Indian tribes fight, or armies hired by princes meet in battle, or the German people fight the French people in a total war.

The juxtaposition of these types of war shows clearly that each provides quite a different "environment," meaning: supplies quite different outlets for human traits and psychological drives. In modern wars there are never enough "aggressive" men flocking to the recruiting stations, while on the home front attractive salaries for war work seem to have greater attraction than the psychic rewards of a contribution to the war effort.[5]

Everywhere men are drafted into armies. Their and the general public's fighting spirit is aroused by government effort at great expense and not always successfully. How, for instance, can these explanations fit into their scheme Britain's war on Egypt in 1956 which had to be stopped because (among other reasons) a large section of the British public did not want to fight it? In some armies more than half the men who were supposed to shoot did not pull the trigger. At home from ten to twenty people are required in order to maintain one man at the front lines, most often continuing to do their routine work. In future push-button wars, any psychic satisfaction in war at the home front will be even further reduced. Usually, the mass at home has to be stirred up by an enormous propaganda campaign to become bellicose—after the war has started or is about to start—and the stimulus of revenge or defense of the fatherland soon has to be replaced by "war aims" conjuring up visions of a beautiful, peaceful future world. In brief: in the long run, the more effective appeals to keep people in a fighting spirit are not to aggressiveness and hatreds but to the desire for lasting peace and greater welfare. This is no conclusive argument against the possibility that people may yearn for war for other reasons. But, first, it is not likely that people switch their attitudes so radically from pro to con regarding war so quickly; second, it is, historically, extremely rare to find before modern wars appeals arousing sentiments designed directly to cause a war (19, p. 199; 27, p. 34); and third, when preparation for war is compared, chronologically, to warlike appeals to the public, it will be found that the appeals begin at a considerably later moment, if not after the outbreak of the war; just as stereotypes of one people about another are often adjusted to suit the demands of the war.[6]

The long and complex preparations needed for modern wars make it quite inconceivable that they result from some

---

[5] It must be recognized, though, that such psychic satisfactions exist. Fred Blum discovered among factory workers that they began to enjoy work, which they had found dull and monotonous, as soon as it contributed to the war effort (6).

[6] "How Nations See Each Other" is a very variable matter. This was strikingly demonstrated, for instance by the stories about the Soviet Union in the popular journals during World War II and after the war.

sudden, collective impulse of the state's citizenry. Whatever destructiveness and aggressiveness may be part of man's nature, "it is not a part of his native behavior to combine these into strategy and tactics, into armies and sea power and air forces, all controlled for the purposes of the State" (31, p. 254). This is all the more true as the majority of citizens, even in the best-educated countries, are notoriously uninterested in foreign affairs and uninformed about the course of international events. When polled, these citizens may express a phobia against foreigners in general or against a particular people, but there is no evidence that this has ever been strong enough to lead them to demand war or prepare for it. Indeed the relative insignificance of such phobias and stereotypes about other peoples as causes of war can best be discovered in the fact that a people has found itself allied with another people in war about which it had worse ideas than about the common enemy. A *Fortune* poll in 1939, for instance, showed that 6.9 per cent of American pollees considered themselves most friendly to the Germans, while only 0.9 per cent considered themselves friendly to the Russians (8, p. 117). Similarly, Great Britain was at war with Germany twice in modern times, although the British people consistently show a sentimental preference for Germans over Frenchmen.

The weaknesses in attempts to give individual psychological or natural traits as causes of war can be found, *mutatis mutandi,* in group psychology. Whatever the accepted theory about group behavior and group tensions, the need remains to explain how these characteristics of the group are organized and translated into war (27, p. 44; 28, p. 83). For it should be clear that, while man is endowed with certain psychological qualities, the environment of every individual man determines how these qualities become effective and what results they will produce. What may be said about psychological contributions to the outbreak of war, if "man in general" is considered, is that the institutionalization of war does indeed provide numerous and convenient outlets for psychological drives which might otherwise be channeled into different directions or be sublimated to produce different results. To some citizens the outbreak of war might thus become a pleasant prospect and lead to emotional readiness for it. But this is, essentially, a passive readiness, which is, besides, produced in almost every citizen in modern times by his civic training and his habitual way of life. This is an indispensable condition for war as long as it remains a mass war. Such readiness is, however, not the same thing as being a cause of war. It will be even less relevant when the perfection of missile warfare might conceivably lead to the ending of a war before anybody has had a chance to develop any feelings about it.

The relevance of psychological or natural traits upon war becomes greater with a better differentiation among groups and individuals in a state and the role they play in the shaping of the state's destiny (18, p. 47–50; 11, p. 32). Since obviously some citizens are more important than others in relation to the decision to make war, the failure to distinguish between them has led of necessity to such a generalization of explanations in psychological terms that they are not very fruitful. The nature of those making decisions within a state and of those prominently influencing these decisions is not only of importance in uncovering the origin of wars but may also be easier of investigation than the people as a whole. Even then, however, personal natural factors are likely to be only among the conditions of war. Even the most powerful dictator in a modern state cannot determine policy, least of all policy directed toward war, entirely according to his whims. Like all policymakers, he is dependent upon many conditions over which he has no or little control. He too is part of the environment in which he lives and which contributes to the shaping of his personal character, though he may not be very conscious of this, while consciously many elements of the situation in which he must make his decision will enter into his calculations.

This brings into focus a possible cause of war which has been too often neglected in the preoccupation with finding psychological reasons: the use of war deliberately as an instrument of foreign policy. It is true that anyone considering war today as a political means must be, in a manner of speaking, "insane." Yet historical evidence is convincing in demonstrating that modern wars did not result from emotional outbursts or accumulated frustrations by either decision-makers or the general public. Instead, they were preceded by long and cool-headed preparations and finally started after carefully calculated decisions. Mr. Anthony Eden's memoirs—to take only a very recent example—show quite clearly that military action against Egypt in the Suez crisis in 1956 was much discussed by the British cabinet and in contacts with the United States Department of State and was eventually undertaken on the basis of a fairly unemotional conclusion that British interests in the Suez Canal made it worthwhile.

It is quite possible that the motivations of those who wish to use war as a means to reach certain goals are irrational,[7] also that non- or irrationality affects the judgment of the instrumental usefulness of war in the particular situation. The decision-maker can hardly help seeing the world through his own eyes. This is natural and therefore unavoidable. But this is merely saying that there are limits to man's rationality and that these limits are among the conditions for peace and war which must be studied. Nevertheless, the decision to go to war has usually been made, as history shows, upon careful deliberation of the usefulness of war as an instrument and can largely be understood as such. Indeed, since usually many individuals contribute to the making of the war decision, the chances are very good that the variations and peculiarities of their natural traits have canceled out each other and that the decision has been arrived at upon the merits of war as a desirable instrument (1, 10). That decision-makers take war into their calculations at all will remain true as long as war remains as an institution. Only as the use of violence between contesting parties becomes suppressed as it has been, generally, within

many states, will this possibility change.

The fundamental difficulty in discovering the cause of war is that any fact, to be the cause, requires a particular conjunction of conditions not any one of which may itself be directed toward war. War is a social situation, a complex of relationships developing out of the interplay of a great many factors (27, p. 33; 34, II, p. 1284; 20, p. 45). This interplay is unique and many different variations can be responsible for some fact or facts becoming causes of war. Hence the impossibility of specifying what particular facts may cause wars. Hence, also, the experience that roughly similar historical situations may in one case end in war and in another not. One and the same factor in a number of situations will not always have the same result. The possession of weapons, for instance, is a condition always present in situations leading to war and may therefore appear as co-responsible. Yet, in other situations (Switzerland during World War II) it not only fails to lead to war but may contribute to the preservation of peace. Obviously the context in which the possession of weapons occurs is of decisive importance. The conclusion appears inevitable that no generally valid specifiable factor causes war but that, instead, only a particular constellation of factors can produce the conditions of war in which a factor or factors can become effective as causes. To overlook this nature of war has been a shortcoming in most of the attempts to look to the nature of man as the cause of wars. What most of these attempts have done is to search for all possible elements present in the situation to explain the origin of war. What they have usually not done is to try to discover whether there are missing elements whose presence would lead to the avoidance of the use of violence. Yet this discovery is not difficult when states are considered, in which the use of inter-group violence has become a rarity and the exception for the solution of conflicts. It will then be found that the relative peacefulness within states was not achieved by changing human nature, altering human psychology, or eliminating conflict. It was not even achieved by eliminating hatreds between groups, discrimination, false stereotypes,

[7] The concepts of rationality and irrationality have been avoided here as much as possible, mostly for methodological reasons. Where the concept is used, it should be understood according to the definition given to it by Felix B. Oppenheim (26).

prejudices, bias, rivalry, or competition—all of which continue in some of the most peaceful (internally) states with an intensity matching that of nationalism. Only the use of violence as a normal and accepted pattern of social relations has disappeared. To the extent that it has so disappeared, it did so by the addition of new behavior patterns, that is to say institutions, leading to the integration of hitherto separated groups into a community.[8]

Once a group has grown into a community (20, pp. 1–27; 2, pp. 205–06; 29, pp. 12–14; 23, p. 28), its members habitually act in conformity with a sense of solidarity, unity, and cohesion which normally excludes violence as a means for the solution of conflicts between them. An organization has evolved which reinforces from without the habit of peaceful relations originating in the attitudes within the members, with a continual interaction between the two. Thus a community possesses the ideological and material restraints necessary to make warfare among its members practically unthinkable. It provides outlets for personality factors in the great variety of its institutions, such as legislatures, public opinion media, plurality of interest groups with overlapping memberships, which in their totality guarantee peaceful change and perform fundamental peace-preserving functions. The monopoly of coercion by a central authority—i.e., force and violence—is largely a result of these institutions and exists primarily for emergency situations. But also, its existence provides the citizen with that sense of security which makes him trust in the success of these peace-preserving institutions. In a community, conflicts of interest are adjusted without violence for the sake of higher interests in the preservation of the community which the contestants share. The use of violence is simply not considered either because of a common higher loyalty to the community, or because of learned habitual behavior and inner compulsion of social responsibility, because of fear of effective sanction against

antisocial behavior made possible by the creation of the community or because of all these and possibly other reasons.

Unfortunately for the peace of the world, the growth of groups into such a community is a slow process. Many of the organizations calling themselves states in Asia and Africa today can hardly be described as communities in this sense, for they lack, above all, the peace-preserving plurality of interest groups which allows them to develop a common loyalty toward the state as such and therewith that sense of security which is one of the foundations of peaceful behavior (21, pp. 25–29.) The development of a community requires high frequency and great intensity of contact between its members, directly or indirectly through shared experiences of almost any kind. The more they have things spiritual and material in common, the greater is the chance that a community will develop (30, pp. 18–74). It is for this reason (and not for reasons of eliminating conflict) that all those enterprises undertaken for the sake of bringing about "better understanding" among nations may, in the long run, have the effect of diminishing the use of violence in international relations (3, p. 40). There may be a faster and less-complicated way to stop violence. The means of war may become such that their use will guarantee the destruction of the user as well as the enemy. Then the uselessness of war as an instrument might lead to the elimination of war.

---

[8] Among the first men to emphasize the nature of community and discover its relevance for peace were Confucius, Marcus Aurelius, and Jesus Christ.

REFERENCES

1. Abel, T. "The Element of Decision in the Pattern of War," *American Sociological Review,* VI (1941), 853–59.
2. Angell, Robert C. "Discovering Paths to Peace." In International Sociological Association, *The Nature of Conflict.* Paris: UNESCO (1957), 204–23.
3. _____. "Government and Peoples as Foci for Peace-Oriented Research," *Journal of Social Issues,* XI (1955), 36–41.
4. Bernard, Jessie. "The Sociological Study of Conflict." In International Sociological Association, *The Nature of Conflict.* Paris: UNESCO (1957), 33–117.
5. Bernard, L. L. *War and Its Causes.* New York: Henry Holt & Co., 1944.
6. Blum, Fred. *Toward a Democratic Work Order.* New York: Harper & Bros., 1953.

7. Bouthoul, G. *Les guerres, éléments de polémologie*. Paris: Payot, 1951.
8. Buchanan, William, and Cantril, Hadley. *How Nations See Each Other: A Study in Public Opinion*. Urbana: University of Illinois Press, 1953.
9. Cantril, Hadley (ed.). *Tensions that Cause Wars*. Urbana: University of Illinois Press, 1950.
10. Deutsch, Karl W. "Mass Communications and the Loss of Freedom in National Decision-making," *Conflict Resolution*, I (1957), 200–211.
11. Farber, Maurice L. "Psychoanalytic Hypothesis in the Study of War," *Journal of Social Issues*, XI (1955), 29–35.
12. *Findings of the Conference on the Cause and Cure of War*, Washington, D. C., 1925.
13. Gladstone, Arthur. "The Conception of the Enemy," *Conflict Resolution*, III (1959), 132–37.
14. Glover, Edward. *War, Sadism and Pacifism*. London: George Allen & Unwin, 1946.
15. Haas, Ernst B., and Whiting, Allen S., Jr. *Dynamics of International Relations*. New York: McGraw-Hill Book Co., 1956.
16. International Sociological Association. *The Nature of Conflict*. Paris: UNESCO, 1957.
17. Johnsen, Juli E. *Selected Articles on War—Cause and Cure*. New York: H. W. Wilson Co., 1926.
18. Kelman, Herbert C. "Societal, Attitudinal and Structural Factors in International Relations," *Journal of Social Issues*, XI (1955), 42–56.
19. Klineberg, Otto. *Tensions Affecting International Understanding*. New York: Social Science Research Council, 1950.
20. Levi, Werner. *Fundamentals of World Organization*. Minneapolis: University of Minnesota Press, 1950.
21. _____. "The Fate of Democracy in South and Southeast Asia," *Far Eastern Survey*, XXVIII (1959), 25–29.
22. Mack, Raymond W., and Snyder, Richard C. "The Analysis of Social Conflict—Toward an Overview and Synthesis," *Conflict Resolution*, I, (1957), 212–48.
23. May, Mark A. *A Psychology of War and Peace*. New Haven, Conn.: Yale University Press, 1943.
24. Morgenthau, Hans J. *Politics among Nations*. New York: Alfred A Knopf, 1960.
25. Nitze, Paul M. "Necessary and Sufficient Elements of a General Theory of International Relations." In William T. R. Fox, *Theoretical Aspects of International Relations*. Notre Dame: University of Notre Dame, 1959.
26. Oppenheim, Felix E. "Rational Choice," *Journal of Philosophy*, L (1953), 341–50.
27. Röpke, Wilhelm. *Internationale Ordnung*. Erlenbach-Zürich: Eugen Rentsch, 1945.
28. Rüstow, Alexander. "Zur soziologischen Ortsbestimmung des Krieges," *Friedenswarte*, XXXIX (1939), 81–94.
29. Schwarzenberger, Georg. *Power Politics*. London: Stevens & Sons, 1951.
30. Smend, Rudolf. *Verfassung und Verfassungsrecht*. München: Duncker & Humblot, 1928.
31. Stratton, George M. *Social Psychology of International Conduct*. New York: D. Appleton & Co., 1929.
32. Tolstoy, Leo. *War and Peace*.
33. Waltz, Kenneth N. *Man, the State, and War*. New York: Columbia University Press, 1959.
34. Wright, Quincy. *A Study of War*. Chicago: University of Chicago Press, 1942.

SOME PATTERNS IN THE
HISTORY OF VIOLENCE*

FRANK H. DENTON[1] and WARREN PHILLIPS

Introduction

This paper reports on progress made in a research project aimed at describing systematic trends in the violence between political groups. The report is in two parts. Part one describes the formulation of an empirical test for the existence of (1) a short-term (15–30 years) and (2) a long-term (80–120 years) periodic fluctuation in the historical occurrence of war. Although some background is given about why such a test should be made, the research described in part one is based, largely, on empirical rather than theoretical generalizations. That is, not much attention is given to the "why" of such patterns.

The tests tend to confirm the existence of the expected patterns. Obviously, it is desirable to go beyond the simple observation that an empirical regularity exists to some explanation of the forces leading to that regularity. The available data do provide clues as to possible explanations. The second part of the paper speculates about several possible reasons for these patterns. The explanations are consistent with the data, but their testing must await the collection of historical material broader in scope than that now available.

Transformations of the International System

Among the effects of the rise to prominence of general systems models in the social sciences, especially international re-

* Reprinted by permission of the authors and publisher from *Journal of Conflict Resolution*, 1968, *12*: 182–195.

[1] Any views expressed in this paper are those of the author. They should not be interpreted as reflecting the views of The RAND Corporation or the official opinion of any of its governmental or private research sponsors. Papers are reproduced by The RAND Corporation as a courtesy to members of its staff.

lations, has been the focusing of attention on transformations of the system. The idea of systematic analysis of changes in the system, although new in its particular form, is based on a long history of speculation about evolutionary or cyclical transformations in the social experience. Perhaps influenced by the unrest, violence, and (at times) chaos of this half-century, recent writers such as Spengler, Toynbee, and Sorokin have largely discarded evolutionary "development" in favor of large cyclic movements in history.

Data which would permit the empirical testing of these speculative theories about system changes are not always readily obtainable. In order to perform such tests, data are needed which cover extended periods of time and which are collected in a systematic manner. Records of the incidence of wars represent one of the few types of data meeting these requirements. Some previous research has been done in this area. Sorokin, for one, has attempted in a semi-systematic manner to test for cyclic patterns in war. He expresses a very negative view about the occurrence of cyclical patterns as a result of this examination (1957, pp. 534–604). Richard Rosecrance, in an excellent volume, examined patterns of diplomacy for system changes. Although he was apparently not looking for a cyclic pattern, his findings suggest such a pattern (1963).

Other collections of statistics on war have formed the basis for exploratory examinations for possible time-dependent patterns. Lewis Richardson investigated the possibility of a general trend toward a greater number of wars in the international system. He chose a run of 432 years, divided it in half, and demonstrated that no such trend existed in the data examined. His examination of the frequency of outbreak of war on an annual basis indicated a random

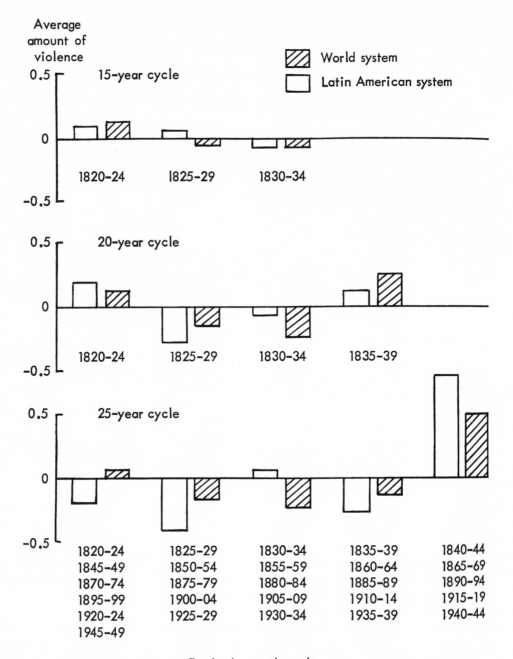

FIG. 1. A generation cycle.

fluctuation over time which could be well approximated by a Poisson distribution. Groupings of the data into longer periods (longer than one year and less than 230 years) do, however, indicate fluctuations which cannot be explained as random occurrences (1960, pp. 139–40).

J. E. Moyal (1949) reexamined Quincy Wright's list of wars in order to test two hypotheses. His first hypothesis states that the number of wars in a given period may be correlated with the number of wars in a past period, separated by a fixed interval. Moyal finds that, with time lags of five and 15 years, there is a distinctly significant autocorrelation in the *outbreak* of war.

Moyal's second hypothesis assumed a slow fluctuation in the probability of an outbreak of war. He averaged the number of outbreaks of war using a fifty-year running average. On plotting this running average against the central date, a marked periodic variation in the outbreak of wars was discernible, the half-life being about 100 years.

These findings, as well as those in previous research by one of the authors, suggest that periods of relative peacefulness tend to alternate with relatively warlike periods. Such a regular fluctuation in the intensity of war is of interest in itself; however, these earlier findings also suggest that violence in the international system is to a great extent a reflection of the political state of affairs of the system. More specifically, when the system is characterized by instability and intense political disputes it is also characterized by widespread and intense violence. Thus, to some extent, changes in the state of the international political system can be observed by observing changes in the amount and type of violence in the system. Again, more precisely, it is assumed that the data on war go beyond just indicating the amount of violence; these data reflect something about international politics as well. This assumption, critical to the "explanation" of the observed patterns, is discussed in the brief review of previous research in the next section.

Exploratory Analyses

Two exploratory analyses of systematic trends in violence generated findings which are felt to be relevant to the work reported upon in this analysis. The first study defined the spatial-temporal domain of interest as the internation system from 1820 until 1949 (Denton, 1966). The second study, also by Denton (unpublished), focused on Latin America between 1820 and 1949. The data for both of these studies were taken from Lewis F. Richardson's collection (1960).

In each case one goal of the analysis was to test the data for a periodic upswing in

violence every 15 to 30 years. Since the concept of "upswing in violence" could be represented by one or two large wars as well as by many small wars, the Richardson and Moyal measures of new outbreaks of war did not provide a satisfactory index. Rather a composite "amount of violence" index was formulated from the number of wars, the number of casualties, and the number of participants.[2]

Both studies indicated a definite tendency for a periodic increase in the level of violence about every 25 years.

The level of violence in each of the bars in Figure 1 is found by averaging the level of violence over five-year periods separated by intervals of 15, 20, or 25 years. Thus the first bar in Figure 1, for the 25-year cycle case, is the mean level of violence for the five-year periods: 1820–24, 1845–49, 1870–74, 1895–99, 1920–24, and 1945–49. A pattern with all averages near zero indicates that the amount of war was roughly uniform across time. If a recurring tendency exists for more war at a fixed interval, some averages should deviate significantly from zero. It is readily apparent that these two analyses indicate a tendency for violence to be relatively intense about every 25 years. These findings are surprisingly consistent with Richard Rosecrance's divisions of the temporal dimension of the international political system.[3]

A chi-square test assuming as a null hypothesis an equiprobable distribution of values above and below the mean for each of the five intervals indicated a deviation from equiprobability significant at the .15 level for the world system and at the .04 level for the Latin America system.

In addition to the 25-year cycle indicated above, a longer-term cyclical effect was suggested. Again, known historical pat-

---

[2] This index is a weighted composite of the three variables indicated. It is formed by a technique called concept mapping (Jones, 1966). Mathematically the index is similar to a "factor" in factor analysis. The values of this index are standardized. That is, the set of index values has a mean of zero and a variance of one.

[3] Denton (1966). This provides some support for the assumed correlation between international politics and international violence.

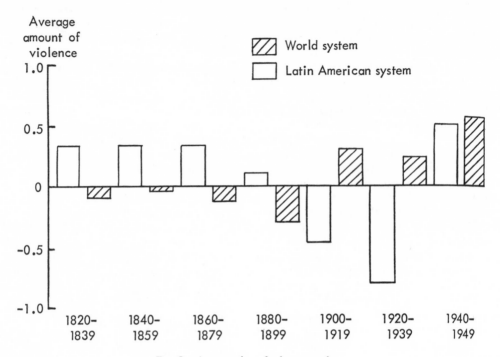

FIG. 2. A suggestion of a longer cycle.

terns are indicated by the trends in the data on war. The relatively turbulent times following the French revolution show a moderate amount of violence. The stable political situation usually associated with the latter part of the 19th century corresponds to a period of low violence in Figure 2. And finally, the 20th century, often referred to as a revolutionary time, is shown as a period of very intense violence.

While the data for this period covered by Richardson (1820–1949) provide a preliminary indication of a longer cyclic pattern, a test for a long-term rise and fall in overall intensity of violence requires a longer period to allow for more than one 80–120 year cycle. Quincy Wright provides a collection of statistics on violence covering the 420 years between 1480 and 1900 (Wright, 1942). This source of data is used for testing the two hypotheses suggested by the exploratory analyses. The remainder of this paper states the propositions which guide the work; delineates the empirical world; lays down the operational procedures; and presents the findings derived from these tasks.

Analysis of Wright's Data

Formulation of the Problem

The exploratory research reported on above suggests two cycles. The first cycle appears to have a period of about 25 years and to be superimposed on one of longer duration. The two hypotheses to be tested are: (1) There is a tendency for an upswing in the level of violence at about 25-year intervals. It might also be expected that the upswing will possess a gradual rise and decline, perhaps resembling a sine wave. (2) There is a tendency for an 80–120 year cycle in the violence level. This cycle may have a sine-wave pattern. However, a sharp reaction against extreme instability may result in a "saw tooth" effect. That is, the pattern may be a gradual rise followed by a sharp decline.

The data used for testing these hypotheses are taken from Quincy Wright's compilation covering the period 1480–1900. Wright's data include " . . . all hostilities involving members of the family of nations . . . which were recognized as states of war in the legal sense or which involved over

50,000 troops" (1942, p. 636). Thus, relatively small incidents of violence not involving a declaration of war are systematically excluded from the tables, contrary to the Richardson data used in the exploratory analysis. For each of his wars, Wright lists the start and end dates, the number of battles, and the primary participants.[4] Wright also divides wars into four *types:* (1) defense of civilization; (2) civil; (3) balance-of-power, and (4) imperial (1942, p. 641).

Criticisms have been justly leveled at both Richardson's and Wright's works for the lack of concreteness in the explanation of data-collecting procedures.[5] Work is now underway in an attempt to replicate and extend these data in at least two institutions.[6] This study is conceived of in an iterative sense. More detailed studies can check later on the "truth" of the findings. In any case, the errors in the two data collections are unknown and are probably small when patterns of this nature are being sought.

Two indices are formulated to test the above hypotheses. As in the exploratory studies, an index of the "size" or amount of violence in the system is required to test for the expected periodicities. Secondly, it is felt that the type of war prevalent in the system may be of some value in explaining fluctuations in intensity. Thus variables are included which indicate the relative frequency of the four types of war defined by Professor Wright (see above).

In order to reduce fluctuations caused by random or atypical events when very short time intervals are used, and in order to reduce the necessity for handling many small observations, the 420-year time interval is divided into 84 five-year periods.[7] Any war overlapping an interval for more than one year or totally contained in an interval is included in that interval. Thus, a war extending over 20 years might be counted four or five times (in successive intervals). The purpose in doing this is to include *all violence existing in the system at a given time,* rather than simply outbreaks of war during each period.

The following variables are included as potential indicators of size and type:

Size Indicators:
(1) Number of wars occurring within or overlapping the time period.
(2) The number of political groups having combat during the interval.[8]
(3) Number of groups from (2) divided by the number of nations listed in Wright's charts for that year. This normalizing factor is included to see if it might influence the results.
(4) The total number of *participant years* of war in the time interval.
(5) The number of battles fought in the time interval. Wright lists only the total battles for a war. For wars extending over more than one period the number of battles is allocated by the *percent of the war's participant years* which occurred in the given period.

Type Indicators. These indicators are "normalized" for size, since *predominance in the system* is the desired attribute. Thus the type of war variables are computed as the percent of wars in a time interval that are classified as a given type: (1) percent civil, (2) percent defense of civilization, (3) percent balance of power, and (4) percent imperial.

These items, observed for the 84 time periods, constitute the data for testing the hypotheses. The sample includes 375 wars, and 88 percent of the time periods include at least two wars. Thus, the data as aggregated are sufficiently well distributed to reduce somewhat the fluctuation which

[4] ". . . actual independence before or after the war rather than legal status under international law was the criterion used [for including a participant] . . . . Unsuccessful revolutionists, rebels, or insurgents which lacked even *de facto* status, except during the war itself, have not been so listed, and many of the small feudal principalities of the Holy Roman Empire have been ignored. . . ."

[5] See Singer, Small, and Kraft (1965) for a discussion of the merits of these works.

[6] Singer, Small, and Phillips at the University of Michigan, and Denton at the University of Southern California.

[7] This interval length results in four or five observations per period for the shortest cycle hypothesized.

[8] Contrary to Wright's formulation, revolutionary groups are included.

TABLE 1
DISTRIBUTION OF WARS OVER THE FIVE-YEAR PERIODS

Number of wars in the observation period	Number of periods with indicated number of wars
0	1
1	9
2	10
3	14
4	12
5	10
6	8
7	7
8	8
9	5
	84

might result from occasional atypical events (see Table 1).

Size or Amount of Violence Index

The primary need in this research is for a valid indicator of size or scope of war in the international system during each of the five-year periods. The five measures indicated above are all felt to be manifestations of the general concept *size of violence*. That is, a period with much violence can typi-

cally be expected to have many wars, many participants, many battles, etc. However, it also is possible to have few wars but still have much violence during a five-year period if a few large wars occur. Intense violence may also be manifested in many small wars during the period. For these reasons it is felt that no one of these variables is as good an index of "size" as is a combination of them.

An examination of the empirical record indicates that, with the exception of *number of battles,* these variables do correlate quite highly (Table 2). Since Wright often failed to list any battles for non-European conflicts, this variable was deemed of lower quality and is not used in the index. The high correlations indicate that the occurrence of a "few large" or "many small" wars is uncommon and that the number of belligerents is a reasonably good estimator of the others. However, an index can be formulated which is a still better predictor (has higher correlations). Two methods are used to obtain an index of size: (1) a principal component (factor analysis) fit to the data, and (2) a construct-mapping fit. The construct-mapping routine fits a factor between the four retained variables so that each variable is equidistant from that factor (Jones, 1966). Table 3 gives the correla-

TABLE 2
CORRELATION OF SIZE VARIABLES

	Variables				
	1	2	3	4	5
1. Number of battles	—				
2. Number of belligerents	.36	—			
3. Number of belligerents normalized	.25	.73	—		
4. Number of belligerent years	.35	.85	.69	—	
5. Number of wars	.05	.67	.53	.51	—

TABLE 3
INDEX FIT TO THE DATA

	Variables				
	2	3	4	5	6
6. Principal Component	.84	.85	.89	.79	—
7. Construct Mapping	.84	.84	.84	.84	.97

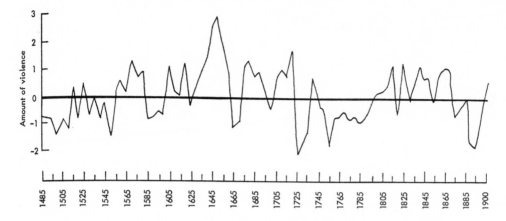

FIG. 3. Amount of violence (Wright's data).

tion of these two indices (or factors) with each of the original variables and with one another. The two fits are essentially the same (correlation of .97) and account for almost the same proportion of variance (71+ percent). They are each better predictors than the belligerent variable (67 percent of variance), and the construct-mapping index is arbitrarily chosen for this analysis.

Twenty-five Year Cycle

Figure 3 is a plot of this size-of-war index for the period 1480–1900. Visually it is difficult to note any outstanding trends. An examination of periods 20, 25, and 30 years apart provides little indication of a periodic upswing in violence when the size of conflict variable is divided into periods above and below its mean value (Table 4).

There is some tendency for periods of relatively low violence to occur every 30

years starting in 1490. The hypothesis is in terms of periods of relatively intense violence rather than periods of relative quiet, however.

Returning to Figure 3, the fluctuations do appear to be more rapid for the first half of the period than for the second. The two halves, taken separately, might show a trend which is cancelled out when both halves are combined. Such a periodicity could show some drift across a temporal domain of this length. For example, if the periodicity is explained in terms of a generation or a decision-maker "life time" effect, the increase in man's life span would lead to an expectation of a slower fluctuation in the latter part of the sample. Moreover, if such a cycle is considered as probabilistic rather than deterministic, a rare event of two violent periods exceptionally close together (or far apart) could result in a shift in the phase of the cycle, giving a cancel-

TABLE 4

TEST FOR A 25-YEAR CYCLE

		Number of periods when amount-of-war index is					
20-year	Above mean	11	8	12	11		
intervals	Below mean	10	13	9	10		
25-year	Above mean	9	10	7	8	8	
intervals	Below mean	8	7	10	9	8	
30-year	Above mean	7	3	8	8	8	8
intervals	Below mean	7	11	6	6	6	6
		1485	1490	1495	1500	1505	1510
				Initial Time Period			

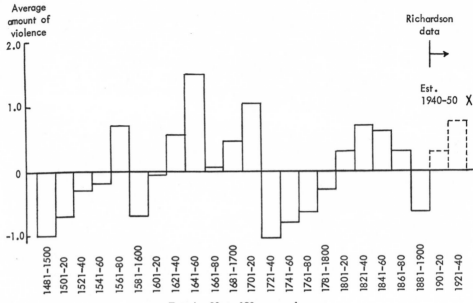

FIG. 4. 80- to 120-year cycle.

ling effect over a period of this length. To test for these possibilities the data are divided into pre-1680 and post-1680 groups.

TABLE 5
TWENTY-YEAR CYCLE—PRE-1680

	Number of periods			
Above mean	5	4	9	5
Below mean	6	7	2	6
	1485	1490	1495	1500
Average value of amount-of-war	.07	−.08	.30	.08

The data for the period prior to 1680 indicate an upswing in violence about every 20 years, starting with the period ending in 1495 (Table 5). After 1680 there is a history of relatively high violence about

every 30 years starting in the time period ending in 1690 (Table 6).

The data are generally supportive of the hypothesis that an upswing in violence occurs about once every generation to a generation and a half, if one assumes some change in the life spans making up the "generation."

80- to 120-year Cycle

While it is necessary to have a relatively short observation time to examine the data for the expected 25-year cycle, it is desirable to average out these fluctuations when examining the data for longer-term trends. Such an averaging makes visual observation easier; that is, short-term fluctuations are masked in order to give a more ordered appearance to the longer fluctuations. The amount-of-war index values are

TABLE 6
THIRTY-YEAR CYCLE—POST-1680

	Number of periods					
Above mean	5	6	3	1	3	4
Below mean	3	2	4	6	4	3
	1685	1690	1695	1700	1705	1710
Average value of amount-of-war	.04	.58	−.39	−.59	−.03	.09

averaged over four periods (20 years) in Figure 4.

A pattern similar to that postulated is exhibited by these data. Throughout the period of the data a consistent rise in the level of violence is exhibited for several years (a minimum of 60 years—a maximum of 120 years). A sharp decline is noted after each rise and the decline is in each case followed by another rise in violence. The dashed curve indicates an extrapolation using Richardson's data for the first half of the 20th century.

How significant, statistically, is this visually detectable pattern? That is, could a pattern of this nature result by random chance? The original hypothesis is formulated in nonoperational terms. The prime expected effect is that periods of high violence will be followed by a decrease in violence and that periods of low violence will be followed by an increase in violence. Operationally the hypothesis may be expressed by two statements:

(1) Periods of high violence in the system will be followed by a decrease in the level of violence.

(2) Periods of low systemic violence will be followed by an increase in violence.

These hypotheses imply a system in which conflict (manifested in violence) grows in scale until a reaction against violence *per se* occurs. This reaction results in lower conflict in the system until conditions permit the growth of new conflict.

The only remaining problem in operationalizing the hypothesis is to select a level above which violence will be considered high. The mean is one obvious "level" for this purpose. "High violence," on the other hand, intuitively implies a condition somewhat above average, that is, more than just barely above the mean. Two levels of "high" are tested to determine if the results differ depending on how high "high" is.

(1) In the first case, "high" violence is defined as above the *mean* (a 20-year average of the size index). Below the mean is defined as "low" violence.

(2) In the second case, "high" violence is defined as more than half a standard deviation above the mean. "Low" violence is below this value. This test is perhaps more consistent with the original hypoth-

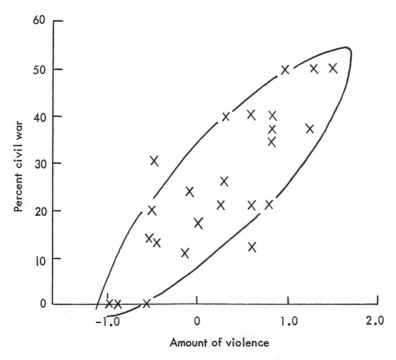

FIG. 5.   Percent of civil war versus amount of war (20-year averages).

esis. The cushion of half a standard deviation eliminates from the "high" violence category those time periods with *only slightly* greater than average violence.

For both definitions, as we see in Table 7, periods of high violence are usually followed by a decrease in violence and periods of low violence by an increase. The division of high at half a standard deviation above the mean gives a pattern with only two of 20 periods deviating from the expected trend.

Previous research indicated a correlation between high violence and the prevalence of civil conflict (Denton, 1966). Checking on these data it is found that, across the 84 five-year observations, the indicator involving the percent of wars that are civil wars correlates .39 with the size-of-war indicator. For 84 observations a product moment correlation of .39 (two-tailed test) is significant at about the .01 level. Figure 5 shows a plot of the 20-year average of percent civil war versus the amount-of-war values for the same intervals. The correlation is obviously even higher when the longer time periods are used. Thus, periods in which there is much war are quite consistently periods which exhibit a relatively high frequency of civil wars. In addition to supporting the hypothesis about a long-term cyclical trend in violence, the data also support the postulate that those periods of intense conflict are associated with social change or turmoil, as indicated by a concomitant relatively high frequency of civil conflict.

Summary and Conclusions

The primary purpose in this analysis is to test for the existence of two postulated cyclical trends in the historical record of violence. The data generally support the hypotheses. That is, evidence of cyclical patterns exists in the historical data.

Why such patterns and what are the theoretical implications? Some speculation about the "why" was made in the earlier formulation of the hypotheses. Although the data give few direct clues for going beyond the empirical *description* to an *explanation,* it does seem appropriate to dis-

TABLE 7

LEVELS OF VIOLENCE AND INCREASE OR DECREASE IN NEXT PERIOD

	Next Period	
1)		
Period with	*Increase in Violence*	*Decrease in Violence*
High Violence*	4	6
Low Violence	10	0

Fisher exact test Significance: $\approx$ .025

	Next Period	
2)		
Period with	*Increase in Violence*	*Decrease in Violence*
High Violence**	1	5
Low Violence	13	1

Fisher exact test Significance: $\approx$ .005

* "High" defined as above the *mean* (20-year average of size index).

** "High" defined as more than half a standard deviation above the mean.

cuss possible explanations which might be tested.

Hypothesis 1 suggested an upswing in the level of violence about every 25 years. The data support such a general trend with 20 years providing a "best" fit prior to 1680 and about 30 years thereafter.[9] Others have alluded to a generation effect in decision-making, or a fading into the past of the last war as a permissive condition for future war. Several conditions may be associated with such a periodic increase in violence:

(1) Immediately following an intense war the public remembrance of it is of the horrors, the human suffering, the dislocations. The "horror" remembrance may be reinforced by the memoirs, biographies, novels, or fireside stories written and told by first-hand participants while their own experiences are fresh. At the same time, the glory of defending the fatherland, the adventure, and the grim humor of war are themes which are often expressed. Perhaps,

[9] The process of grouping five-year intervals somewhat limits the accuracy of these statements.

through a defense against the distasteful, the "horror" is suppressed as memories age and as an increasing number of society's members have not had first-hand exposure to violence. On the other hand, the requirement[10] for ensuring willingness to defend the state or society against intruders motivates many to further glorify "dying for one's country." Thus the themes employed in the descriptions of the last great war shift from "horror"-dominant to "glory"-dominant.[11] This shift is then tied to the human life cycle of 20 to 30 years.

Such an hypothesis could be easily tested by examining the frequency of the above themes in the public literature at various times after major conflicts.

(2) Perhaps even more important would be the application of a similar thesis to decision-makers. Subjectively, it seems that major conflicts have created the next generation of decision-makers. Thus, for a number of years after major conflicts, the *system's* decision-makers have had first-hand experience with violence. Decision-makers seldom obtain power before they are 40 to 45 and seldom retain power beyond 65 to 70. A new, "unsullied" group of decision-makers gradually comes into power after the conflict. A generation's time sees almost a complete turnover.

By examining the records of the accession to office of decision-makers, and by comparing the attitudes of "war responsible" decision-makers toward the use of violence with those of the new generation without war responsibility, it would be possible to test such an explanation.

(3) Implicit in the above explanations is an assumption that the opportunities for employing violence are always present. The only condition necessary for violence is the willingness to become engaged. However, Richardson for one has shown that there is an indication of continuity in conflict. In fact, he goes on to explain this continuity in terms of a generation effect (1960, p. 200):

We may suppose that the generation who had not fought in the earlier war, but who were brought up on tales about its romance, heroism, and about the wickedness of the enemy, became influential 30 to 60 years after the war ended and so delayed the process of forgetting and forgiving [Richardson observed an increase in retaliatory and revenge wars 30 to 60 years after the original conflict].

Thus, a third effect of continuity of conflict and hatred may exacerbate the above trends. A planned research project will involve the investigation of continuity in alliance and conflict patterns.

The generation effect was *a priori* a "reasonable" explanation. The longer-term cycle is, in the minds of the authors, a pattern which is not as easily explained on intuitive grounds. It appears that one promising explanation is offered by an action-reaction process in political philosophy (taken in the broad sense to include the general attitude of the elites[12] toward the "correct" society). Man seems to strive both for a better society and for more security in those desirable aspects of the present society. As previously noted, periods of intense violence are typified without exception by a relatively high frequency of civil conflict. This would, of course, indicate dissatisfaction with the *form of society*. Moreover, periods of intense conflict are consistently followed by periods of low violence with a *very low* frequency of civil violence.

It seems logical to expect that philosophies of change are associated with periods of intense civil violence. The religious controversies of the 16th and 17th centuries, the French and European revolutions of the late 18th and early 19th centuries, and the Communist revolutions of this century are all associated with philosophies of change. A reasonable hypothesis could be made that, in a given society, the relative weight given to the desire for improving society as opposed to *maintaining* society is dependent on the conditions of (1) *rate of change* and (2) discrepancy between the *actual* and the *ideal* society.

Thus, first, conditions of rapid change, associated with high tensions and violence,

---

[10] Some might go further and say man's inherent evil.

[11] Today's TV programs on World War II seem rather "humor"-dominant.

[12] In the abstract sense, those who influence and/or make decisions.

induce philosophic positions emphasizing the importance of an *orderly* society and philosophies glorifying the *traditional* strengths of the established system. That is, insecurity leads to emphasizing the desire for maintenance of the good aspects of an idealized society of the past.[13]

Second, periods of stability reduce the *experience* and thus the fear of insecurity. Moreover, it seems intuitively true that there is almost always a *discrepancy* between the *real* and *ideal* form of society. It may even be true that periods of social stability (slow change) increase this discrepancy. That is, to use an old adage, "them that has gets." Philosophers, freed from the need to emphasize order in an already orderly society, concentrate on the need for reducing the discrepancy between the *real* and the *ideal.*

The result of these hypotheses is that change tends to be followed by stability, by change again, and so on. The period of the cycle (averaging about a century in length), while it is not intuitively obvious, does not seem unreasonable. Truths die slowly and perhaps the passage of several generations is needed to tilt the scales.

A systematic examination of themes in philosophic positions could provide a test of this hypothesis. These data provide one-half the objective situation, that of violence and social disruption. It might also be worthwhile to determine, as possible, if periods of slow change do increase the discrepancy between real and ideal.

Obviously the above explanations go beyond the data. However, it is believed that they are *consistent* with the patterns exhibited in the history of violence. Moreover, if the explanations are useful models

they provide a framework for a theoretical explanation of certain changes in the international (or perhaps more appropriately the interpolitical group) system.[14]

In addition to the limitations on our explanations, the assumption that violence reflects the political issues of the day may be questioned by some.[15] Beyond this, the data are not complete (there is some discrepancy between the Wright and Richardson data for the period in which they overlap). The possible effects of improved data are, of course, not known.

REFERENCES

Denton, Frank H. "Some Regularities in International Conflict, 1820–1949," *Background,* 9, 4 (Feb. 1966), 283–96.

Jones, Ronald D. *Construct Mapping.* Kansas City: University of Missouri, mimeographed, June 1966.

Moyal, J. E. "The Distribution of Wars in Time," *Journal of the Royal Statistical Society,* 112 (1949), 446–58.

Richardson, Lewis F. *Statistics of Deadly Quarrels.* Pittsburgh: Boxwood Press, 1960.

Rosecrance, Richard N. *Action and Reaction in World Politics.* Boston: Little, Brown, 1963.

Sabine, George H. *A History of Political Theory.* New York: Holt, Rinehart and Winston, 1961.

Singer, J. David, Melvin Small, and George L. Kraft. *The Frequency, Magnitude, and Severity of International War, 1815–1940.* Ann Arbor: Mental Health Research Institute Preprint 158, University of Michigan, July 1965.

Sorokin, Pitirim. *Social Change and Cultural Dynamics.* Boston: Porter Sargent, 1957.

Wright, Quincy. *A Study of War.* Chicago: University of Chicago Press, 1942.

[13] George Sabine in his *History of Political Theory* explicitly discusses philosophic reactions against violence, though not the reverse. Sabine states that Bodin's "divine right of kings" could be considered as a reaction against the instability and violence of the religious wars (p. 399). He also describes Burke's decision to codify his philosophy as ". . . the beginning of a shift . . . [in] social philosophy from attack to defense and . . . to an emphasis on the value of stability . . ." as the result of the French Revolution (p. 617). In our own time the conservative reaction to instability and change seems to gather greater strength with more change.

[14] In order to (try to) escape the label of "historical determinist" let us offer the following position statement. It is not felt that patterns in history absolutely determine the future. However, it is felt, because of historical learning, ongoing environmental factors, and certain regularities in man's behavioral structure, that he is partially a product of his past. While individually man may enjoy "free will," be "adaptive," etc., as a group he is conservative and not very adaptive, at least in the short run. Even if faced with the "truth" of a needed revision in beliefs he (and a number of his prophets) is perfectly capable of "rationally" showing that the old ways are best. And who is going to give him the truth? On the other hand, there is obviously a long-term learning process which may change such factors.

[15] The pattern of violence (Figure 4) does seem to reflect known historical trends, however.

2. *Economic Considerations*

DEMOGRAPHIC DIMENSIONS OF
WORLD POLITICS*

PHILIP M. HAUSER

Politics in general, as well as world politics, is a branch of engineering—social engineering—not of science. Yet the consideration of the demographic aspects of world politics is not an appropriate subject to be treated in this book. It is the purpose of this chapter to point to ways in which the findings of the science of demography illuminate various aspects of the world political scene.

There are various ways in which this subject can be developed, but I have arbitrarily chosen to discuss population factors in relation to politics, broadly conceived, on the global and on the international levels, respectively. By "global" problems I mean those that concern the earth as a whole; by "international" problems I mean those that arise among the various political subdivisions of the globe.

Global Considerations

There is no world government charged with the task of achieving world order and performing other civil governmental functions for the earth as a whole. This, however, does not mean that there are no political problems of a global, as distinguished from an international, character. Some such global problems are in fact dealt with by the United Nations and its specialized agencies, which are, of course, organizations of individual sovereign nations rather than organs of world government. Examples of global problems—problems which transcend and cannot be contained within national boundaries—include health, weather, fallout, and the newly emergent problems of outer space. It is easy to demonstrate that the contemporary rate of world population

growth also constitutes a global problem—one which would be of great concern to a world government if we had one, and one which is of increasing concern to various organs of the United Nations and the specialized agencies.

Although the first complete census of mankind has yet to be taken, it is possible to reconstruct, with reasonable accuracy, the history of world population growth. This history may be encapsulated in the following estimates of the population of the earth: at the end of the Neolithic period in Europe (8000 to 7000 B.C.) (*1*), perhaps 10 million; at the beginning of the Christian era, 200 to 300 million; at the beginning of the modern era (1650), 500 million; in 1950, 2.5 billion.

These four numbers constitute a measurement of one of the most dramatic aspects of man's existence on the globe, and they explain the purple language of the demographer in describing the changes in rates of population growth during the modern era as a "demographic revolution" or "population explosion" (2).

The demographer's concern is not based only on considerations of the past. It is even more justified by postwar developments in population growth.

Since the end of World War II the rate of population increase has continued to accelerate and has reached a level of about 1.7% per year. There is justification, indeed, for pointing to a new population explosion in the wake of World War II of a greater magnitude than that previously observed. At the rate of world population increase for the period 1800–1850, for example, the present population would double in 135 years; at the 1900–1950 rate, in 67 years; and at the postwar rate, in only 42 years.

* Reprinted from *Science* by permission of the author and publisher.

TABLE 1

POPULATION, INCOME, AND ENERGY CONSUMED PER CAPITA, BY CONTINENT, ABOUT 1950
SOURCE OF DATA: UNITED NATIONS, EXCEPT WHERE OTHERWISE INDICATED

Area	Total population		Aggregate income		Per capita income ($)	Energy consumed per capita (kw-hr) **
	No. (millions)	(%)	Dollars* (billions)	(%)		
World	2497	100.0	556	100.0	223	1676
Africa	199	8.0	15	2.7	75	686
Northern America***	219	3.8	241	43.3	1100	10,074
South America	112	4.5	19	3.4	170	741
Asia	1380	55.3	69	12.4	50	286
Europe (exclusive of U.S.S.R.)	393	15.7	149	26.8	380	3117
U.S.S.R.	181	7.2	56	10.1	310	1873
Oceania	13	0.5	7	1.3	560	3543

* See *(8, 9)*.   ** See *(33)*.   *** Central America included.

Projection of the post-World War II rate of increase gives a population of one person per square foot of the land surface of the earth in less than 800 years. It gives a population of 50 billions (the highest estimate of the population-carrying capacity of the globe ever calculated by a responsible scholar) in less than 200 years! This estimate, by geochemist Harrison Brown (3), is based on the assumptions that developments in the capturing of solar or nuclear energy will produce energy at a cost so low that it would be feasible to obtain all the "things" we need from rock, sea, and air, and that mankind would be content to subsist largely on food products from "algae farms and yeast factories!"

Moreover, the United Nations estimates of future world population indicate even further acceleration in the rate of world population growth during the remainder of this century. Between 1950 and 1975 the average annual percentage of increase, according to the United Nations "medium" assumptions, may be 2.1%, and between 1975 and 2000, almost 2.6% (4). Such rates of increase would double the population about every 33 and 27 years, respectively.

It is considerations of this type that would make it necessary for a world government to exercise forethought and planning, which constitute rational decision making, in facing the future. This, of course, is the purpose of the projections. The figures do not show what the future population of the world will be—for the world could not support such populations. They do demonstrate that man, as a culture-building animal, has created an environment in which the rhythm of his own reproduction has been modified in such a manner as to point to crisis possibilities.

Crisis Possibilities

The crisis possibilities are of several forms, each posing major world political problems. The first, we may note, is the ultimate crisis, which would result from the fact that the globe is finite (5) and that living space would be exhausted. Unless one is prepared to argue that future technological developments will enable man to colonize other globes (6), it is clear that present rates of population increase must come to a halt by reason of lack of space. No facts or hopes as to man's ability to increase his food production and to increase other types of goods and services can indefinitely increase man's *Lebensraum* (or could do so even if we accept the absurd assumption that man, at terrific cost, could burrow into the earth, live in man-made layers above it, or live on the seas).

In the short run, let us say to 1975 or to 2000, world population will be confined to much more manageable numbers. The United Nations projects, on the basis of its medium assumptions, a world population of about 3.8 billion by 1975 and 6.3 billion by 2000 (I, p. 23).

In the short run there is no problem of exhausting the space on the globe, nor is there reason to fear serious decreases in world per capita food supply, as is evidenced by projections of The Food and Agricultural Organization, and others concerning foodstuffs (7). But there is great reason to be pessimistic about the possibility of greatly increasing the average world level of living during the remainder of this century.

In 1950, world per capita income was estimated at $233 (8, 9). In North America, per capita income was $1100. Had each person on the globe enjoyed the North American level of living in 1950, as measured by per capita income, the aggregate world product in 1950 would have supported only 500 million persons, as contrasted with the actual world population of 2.5 billion. For average world income to have matched income in North America, aggregate income would have had to be increased about fivefold. To bring world per capita income by 1975 to the level enjoyed in North America in 1950 would require about a 7.5-fold increase of the 1950 level in 25 years. To do the same by 2000 would require a 12-fold increase in the 1950 world income within 50 years.

Even if the more modest income level of Europe ($380 per capita in 1950) were set as the target, great increases in productivity would be necessary, because of prospective rates of population increase, to raise average world income to the required level by 1975 or 2000. To achieve this goal by 1975, world income would have to be increased 2.5-fold over the 1950 level, and to achieve it by 2000, the required increase would be greater than fourfold. A decline in the rate of world population growth to that of the period 1800 to 1850—namely, to 0.5%—would decrease by three-fourths and four-fifths, respectively, the projected world-income requirements for attaining this goal by 1975 or 2000.

These considerations not only show the enormous difficulty of materially increasing the world level of living on the basis of present rates of population increase but indicate, also, the weakness of the argument that a solution to the population problem is to be found in more equitable distribution of the world's food supply or of goods and services in general (10). The equitable distribution of world income in 1950 would, to be sure, have raised the per capita income of Latin America by 31%; of Africa, almost threefold, and of Asia, four- to fivefold, but it would still have produced a per capita income per annum of $223, only one-fifth that in North America and only three-fifths that in Europe (exclusive of the U.S.S.R.). The miserably low level of living of most of the world's population is attributable not so much to maldistribution as to low aggregate product, the result of the low productivity of most of the world's peoples.

These political problems of a global character may perhaps be better understood through consideration of their international aspects, special attention being given to the plight of the two-thirds of the world's population resident in the underdeveloped areas of the world, in Asia, Africa, and Latin America.

International Considerations

The short-run implications of present rates of world population growth are manifest in specific forms and in varying degrees of intensity among the various regional and national subdivisions of the globe. The distribution of the world's population and of the world's utilized resources, manifest in differentials in levels of living, is the result, of course, of millenia of human history. The demographic dimensions of international politics may best be comprehended against the background of differences among peoples in levels of living and the significance of these differences at this juncture in world history (8, 11, 12) (Table 1).

To note the extremes, North America in 1950, with about 16% of the earth's land surface, contained less than 9% of the world's population but about 43% of the world's income. Asia, in contrast, with about the same proportion of the world's land surface (18%), had 55% of the world's population but only 12% of the world's income. Per capita income in Asia was at a level of about $50 per year as contrasted with a level of $1100 in North America. Despite the fact that such comparisons are subject to considerable error (13), there is no doubt that a tremendous difference in per capita income existed, of a magnitude perhaps as great as 20 to 1.

The major factor underlying this difference is indicated by the contrast in the difference in nonhuman energy consumed in North America and Asia, respectively— over 10,000 kilowatt-hours per capita per year for the former in contrast to less than 300 for the latter. The availability of nonhuman energy for the production of goods and services is perhaps the best single measurement available of differences in capital investment, know-how, and technology which account for the great differences in productivity and, consequently, in the size of the aggregate product available for distribution.

The other relatively underdeveloped continents of the world also had relatively low shares of world income as compared with their proportions of world population. Africa, with a per capita income of about $75 per year, and South America, with $170 were also well below not only the level for North America but also the levels for Europe (exclusive of the U.S.S.R.), the U.S.S.R. and Oceania. There is a high correlation among these areas between per capita income and amount of non-human energy consumed (Table 1).

These differences in levels of living, as it turns out, are in general inversely related to present and prospective rates of population increase. The populations of the relatively underdeveloped continents of the world are increasing at a more rapid rate than those of the economically advanced continents (4, 14). Between 1950 and 1975, to use the medium projections of the United Nations, while the population of Northern America is increasing at an average annual rate of 1.7% and that of Europe, at 1.2%, that of Asia will be growing at an average annual rate of 2.4%, that of Africa at 2.1%, and that of Latin America at 3.4%. Between 1975 and 2000, while the rate of increase for Northern America will average 1.2% per

year and that for Europe, 1.0%, the rate for Asia will be 3.0%, that for Africa 2.8%, and that for Latin America 3.8%, a rate at which the population would double about every 18 years.

As I have indicated above, rapid increase in world population imposes a severe burden on efforts to raise levels of living. It is easy to demonstrate that the burden would become an impossible one for the economically underdeveloped areas should their rates of population increase follow the trends indicated in the United Nations projections.

For example, Asia, merely to maintain her present low level of living, must increase her aggregate product by 60% between 1950 and 1975, and by an additional 75% between 1975 and 2000. To raise her per capita income to the European level for 1950 while continuing to experience her rapid population growth, Asia would have to increase her 1950 aggregate income 12-fold by 1975 and 21-fold by 2000. Africa, to do the same, must increase her aggregate income eight-fold by 1975 and 13-fold by 2000, and Latin America would have to increase her aggregate income four-fold by 1975 and eightfold by 2000 (15).

To achieve a per capita income equal to that of North America in 1950 while experiencing the projected population growth, Asia would have to increase her aggregate income 35-fold by 1975 and 62-fold by 2000. Africa, to achieve a similar goal, would require 22-fold and 38-fold increases, respectively, in aggregate income, and Latin America, 12-fold and 23-fold increases.

These considerations provide additional justification for the use by the demographer of the phrase *population explosion;* and they certainly indicate the hopeless task which confronts the underdeveloped areas in their efforts to achieve higher levels of living while experiencing rapid population growth. The control of rates of population growth would unquestionably decrease the magnitude of the task of achieving higher levels of living in the underdeveloped areas, especially in those with populations that are large relative to resources (16).

Increasingly large proportions of the population in the underdeveloped areas of

TABLE 2

SUMMARY OF PROJECTIONS OF URBAN POPULATION FOR THE WORLD
AND FOR ASIA, 1975 (18)

Cities (category)	Population (millions)			Estimate of increase in population 1950–1975 (millions)		Estimate of increase in population 1950–1975 (%)		Proportion of total population in cities	
	Projection for 1975		1950					Projection	
	Upper	Lower		Upper	Lower	Upper	Lower	1975*	1950
The World									
100,000 and over	745	488	314	431	174	138	55	19	13
20,000 and over	1155	779	502	653	277	130	55	30	21
Asia									
100,000 and over	340	176	106	234	70	222	66	15	8
20,000 and over	544	283	170	374	113	220	66	25	13

* Figures are based on the "upper" projection, which assumes urbanization of an increasing proportion of the population.

the world are becoming concentrated in urban places. The continued acceleration in the rate of world urbanization during the first half of this century was mainly attributable to urbanization in the underdeveloped areas, which proceeded at a pace considerably above that in the developed areas (17). I have had occasion to make projections of the urban population of the world and of Asia to 1975; these are presented in Table II as illustrative of what is in prospect in the underdeveloped areas of the globe (18). For the rate of urbanization in Latin America and Africa is, also, accelerating.

The projections for Asia indicate that in the 25 years between 1950 and 1975, in cities either of 100,000 and over or of 20,000 and over, urban population will increase by at least two-thirds and may perhaps triple. The lower projection is based on the assumption that the proportion of urban population in Asia will be the same in 1975 as it was in 1950. Under this assumption the projected increase would result from total population growth alone. But if it is assumed that the rate of urbanization in Asia will increase as it did between 1900 and 1950 while the total population continues to grow at the rate projected by the

United Nations, then tripling of Asia's urban population is indicated.

Thus, while the nations of Asia are attempting to improve their miserable urban living conditions, their urban populations will continue to increase explosively—perhaps to triple within a period of less than one generation.

In the economically more advanced nations of the world, urbanization is both an antecedent and a consequent of technological advance and of a high level of living—a symbol of man's mastery over nature. In the underdeveloped nations, however, urbanization represents instead the transfer of rural poverty from an over-populated and unsettled countryside to a mass urban setting. In the economically underdeveloped areas of the world, urbanization is outpacing economic development and the city is more a symbol of mass misery and political instability than of man's conquest of nature (17, 19).

The prospect for individual nations, while variable, is in general the same—one of explosive growth. Between 1955 and 1975, according to the United Nations medium projections, the population of China will increase by 294 million persons and that of India, by 177 million (4, 20). That of Pakistan will increase by 45 million persons, and that of Indonesia, by 40 million, in these 20 years. To confine our attention to the Far East for the moment, smaller countries with the most explosive increases include South Korea, Taiwan, and Ceylon. Each of these nations is faced with a task of tremendous proportions merely to maintain her present level of living, let alone to greatly increase it while continuing to grow at the projected rates.

Political Instability

What will happen if the underdeveloped areas in Asia are frustrated in their efforts to attain a higher standard of living?

Warren S. Thompson devotes his latest book to providing an answer to this question (21). The larger of these nations are not apt to remain hungry and frustrated without noting the relatively sparsely settled areas in their vicinities—the nations in the South-East Asian peninsula: Burma, Thailand, and the newly formed free countries of Indochina, Laos, Cambodia, and Vietnam. (Vietminh, that is North Vietnam, is already engulfed by Communist China). Even parts of thinly settled Africa may be subject to the aggressive action of the larger and hungrier nations as feelings of population pressure mount. Moreover, Communist China, the largest nation in the world by far, faced with the greatest absolute population increases to add to her already heavy burdens in striving for economic development, may not confine her attention only to the smaller nations within her reach. Her present actions relative to her boundaries with India and possible tensions over her boundaries with the U.S.S.R. contain explosive possibilities.

It is Thompson's conclusion that the larger nations in the Far East, including Japan, India, and Pakistan as well as China, may resort to force to achieve access to additional resources under sufficient population pressure. The smaller countries may not be able to resort to force but are almost certain to require outside aid to prevent chaos. Furthermore, Indonesia and the Philippines, under mounting population pressures, are likely to continue to experience growing internal political instability.

Population pressure as a factor in political instability is not confined to the Far East. Populations of the Middle East and North Africa—the Muslim area (exclusive of Pakistan)—may increase from 119 million in 1955 to 192 million by 1975, an increase of 73 million or 61% in 20 years (4). As Irene Taeuber has noted, this is an area "where internal instabilities and conflicts of religious and ethnic groups create recurrent crises for the region and world." Taeuber observes that the immediate political instabilities in this area are attributable more to "diversities among the peoples and the nations than to population pressure or population growth" (22). But she points to the importance, in the decades that lie ahead, of economic advances to lessen tension in this region and to the barrier that rapid population growth may contribute to that development.

Latin America, although in large part still a sparsely settled area of the world, is already experiencing problems associated with rapid population growth which give promise of worsening. For Latin America, as has been reported above, is faced with a population increase of 86% between 1950 and 1975 and of 95%, almost a doubling, between 1975 and 2000 (4, 23). Especially difficult in Latin America are the problems posed by accelerating rates of urbanization. Recent measurements of rate of urban growth in Latin America indicated that of 15 countries for which data were available, urban population in one, Venezuela, was increasing at 7% per year, a rate which produces a doubling about every 10 years; seven had growth rates which would double their population in less than 18 years; and only two (Chile and Bolivia) had rates of urban growth of less than 1% per year (19, 24). Growth rates (total and urban) of the magnitude which Latin America is experiencing are likely to add appreciably to the difficulty of raising living levels and are likely to worsen already existent political instabilities that threaten internal order and may affect world peace.

Finally, a fourth region of political instability to which the population factor is a contributing element, and one where it will be increasingly manifest, is sub-Saharan Africa (22, 25). Middle Africa is sparsely settled, but increasing knowledge about the area indicates high birth rates, decreasing death rates, and explosive growth. The United Nations projections indicate a population increase from 154 million in 1955 to about 202 million in 1975, or an increase of 31%. The familiar syndrome of under-developed areas—malnutrition, disease, and urban and rural squalor on the one hand and aspirations for independence and economic development on the other—are now emergent in this most primitive continent of the globe. And here, as in the other under-developed areas, rapid population growth is likely to intensify political unrest.

In southern Africa another type of population problem is also a major element in a political problem that has grave implications for world order as well as for the stability of the Republic of South Africa. This is the problem arising from the conflict between the indigenous people and European settlers manifest in apartheid. Rapid and differential rates of growth of native and European populations are likely to intensify rather than to allay conflict in southern Africa.

The tensions and political instabilities generated by explosive population growth in the economically underdeveloped nations have a special significance in the contemporary world, characterized by the bipolar conflict between the Western and Communist blocs and the efforts on the part of each to win the allegiance of the uncommitted nations of the world. This conflict has several demographic dimensions of importance.

The Western and Communist Blocs

The first of these dimensions is evident in the way in which population is distributed among the three political blocs into which the world is divided. For in 1955 each of these political groups—the Western nations, the Communist nations, and the uncommitted nations—had approximately the same population. The Western and the Communist blocs, respectively, each have much to gain in the struggle to win the allegiance of the uncommitted third of the world's people. This titanic competition is focused primarily on South and Southeast Asia at the present time, because the bulk of the world's politically uncommitted population is located there.

In this war for men's minds, the competition between Western-world and Communist ideologies, each of the contestants has powerful weapons. Apart from military power which I will leave out on the assumption that a nuclear stalemate exists, the key weapons of the Communists, as is daily attested to by their propaganda, are the exploitation of the wide gap between the levels of living of the "have" and "have-not" nations and the attribution of blame for the misery of the "have not" nations on the imperialistic and colonial practices of the "have" powers. Needless to say, the fire of this propaganda is effectively fed by the frustration of the underdeveloped areas in their efforts to advance their levels of living, or in their efforts to win independence from imperial powers, where this is not yet accomplished.

The Communist bloc, with relatively little, but with increasing, surplus product, is attempting more and more to help the uncommitted nations in economic development. The U.S.S.R. may perhaps be departing from its postwar cold-war policy of trying to persuade uncommitted nations to accept its ideology by means either of internal coups or direct external aggression.

The chief weapon of the western nations, apart from the example of their free way of life is, undoubtedly, the provision of assistance to the underdeveloped nations to help them achieve their economic goals.

Thus, the success or failure of underdeveloped areas to raise their levels of living has the most profound world political implications. The most important immediate international political question is the question of whether the Western-world approach or the Communist approach is the more effective one for achieving economic development.

It is to be emphasized that this is not a rhetorical or hypothetical question. It is being answered by the course of events, the definitive test of achievement. It is being answered by what may be regarded as the most important experiments of all time—experiments under way in each of the three blocs of nations. A great race is on among the economically underprivileged nations to attain higher living levels—some by relatively free, and some by totalitarian and Communist, methods. The contests involve nations within each of which both economically advanced and underdeveloped areas are to be found (26).

The greatest single race under way is undoubtedly the race between the leaders of the Western and Communist blocs, respectively—that is, the United States and the U.S.S.R. The U.S.S.R. has certainly served notice that, by its methods, it hopes to surpass the level of living attained by the United States, and in the not too distant future. Overshadowed only by the direct contest between the United States and the U.S.S.R. is the race between India and Communist China (27), a race of special and direct immediate interest to the underdeveloped areas. For these mammoth nations, the two largest in the world, are bending every effort to achieve higher living standards—one through the Communist approach and the other by democratic methods. The outcome of this race will be of great interest not only to the underdeveloped nations in the uncommitted bloc but also to those in the Western bloc—the underdeveloped nations in Latin America as well as those committed to the Western bloc in Asia and Africa.

The international political situation, then, as described above, gives a special significance to explosive population growth. For present and future rates of population growth may, indeed, prevent underdeveloped nations from raising their levels of living. Simon Kuznets' examination of the evidence indicates that the gap between "have" and "have-not" nations is increasing rather than decreasing (12). To the extent that underdeveloped nations are frustrated in their efforts to advance their living standards, they will, it may be presumed, be more open to the blandishments of the Communist bloc. Furthermore, if the underdeveloped Communist nations demonstrate

that they can achieve more rapid economic progress than the underdeveloped Western nations, the free way of life may well be doomed. Success or failure in this fateful contest may well hinge on the ability of the nations involved to decrease their rates of population growth (28).

The Alternatives

The "why" of the population increase, in an immediate sense, is readily identifiable. It is to be found in the great increase in "natural increase"—in the gap between fretility and mortality (1). Quite apart from the precise timing of changes in the relations between mortality and fertility, it is clear that explosive growth can be dampened only by decreasing natural increase. This is true for the world as a whole in the ultimate sense, with differences in timing for different parts of the world. For suggested solutions to the problems of present and prospective rates of population growth in the various subdivisions of the world through migration, foreign trade, redistribution of wealth, and similar means hold forth little promise, if any, even in the short run (21, chap. 18).

There are only three ways to decrease natural increase: (i) by increasing death rate; (ii) by decreasing birth rate; and (iii) by some combination of the two.

Although it is true that decreased death rates were largely responsible for the population explosion in the past and are foreseen to be a large factor in the future, the adoption of a policy to increase mortality, or to diminish efforts to increase longevity, is unthinkable. Unless one is prepared to debate this, two of the three ways of decreasing natural increase are ruled out. For two of them involve an increase in death rates.

If longevity gains are to be retained, then, the only way to reduce explosive population growth is to decrease the birth rate. That is, the "death control" mankind has achieved can be retained only if it is accompanied by birth control. This proposition, even though it flows directly from the demographic facts of life, in view of prevalent value systems provokes heated debate of the type manifest in the press. Birth control has recently, indeed, made the front pages of the world press.

What is important about the value controversy under way is that it definitely affects global and international policy and action on matters of population and, therefore, on the crucial political problems involved. The most significant thing about all the available methods of birth control—a fact mainly obscured in the present public controversy—is that they are by no means adequate to the task of slowing down explosive world population increase, especially that in the underdeveloped areas. The great mass of mankind in the economically less advanced nations which are faced with accelerating rates of growth fail to limit their birth rates not because of the factors at issue in the controversy we are witnessing but because they do not have the desire, the know-how, or the means to do so. The desire to control fertility, arising from recognition of the problem, is, however, increasing. Japan is already well down the road to controlling its birth rate, although by methods which are not enthusiastically endorsed either by the Japanese themselves or by other peoples. China, India, Pakistan, and Egypt (29) have population limitation programs under way or under serious consideration, and other underdeveloped areas are showing increasing interest in this problem (30). The changes in value systems which will create mass motivation to adopt methods of family limitation are not easily brought about (31), but they are at least under way.

Birth control methods in use in the economically more advanced nations are not, in the main, well adapted for use in the underdeveloped areas. But the results of increased research and experimentation with oral contraceptives are encouraging (32), and there may soon be a breakthrough on obtaining adequate means for the task of limiting population growth in the underdeveloped areas.

Conclusion

The demographer and the increasing number of his allies, in directing attention to the implications of world population growth, are in fact pointing to major global and international political problems—problems that cannot be ignored. Needless to say, the solution to the problems is not to be found in appeals to the traditions of the past, sacred or secular. The solution is to be found in the policies and actions which man himself, as a rational animal, must work out and implement. The mind of man, which has conceived remarkable methods for increasing life expectancy, is probably ingenious enough to devise methods by which the population explosion can be controlled within the framework of man's diverse value systems.

REFERENCES AND NOTES

1. *Determinants and Consequences of Population Trends* (United Nations, New York, 1953), chap. 2.
2. See the objection to this phrase in "Statement by Roman Catholic bishops of U.S. on birth control," New York *Times* (26 Nov. 1959).
3. H. Brown, *The Challenge of Man's Future* (Viking, New York, 1954).
4. *The Future Growth of World Population* (United Nations, New York, 1958).
5. This fact was ignored by Roman Catholic bishops [see New York *Times* (26 Nov. 1959)] and by the Pope [see "Pope denounces birth limitation," New York *Times* (15 Dec. 1959)].
6. The impracticability of colonizing other planets is considered by G. Hardin [*J. Heredity* 50, 2 (1959)].
7. W. H. Leonard, *Sci. Monthly* 85, 113 (1957).
8. "National and Per Capita Income of 70 Countries in 1949," *U.N. Statist. Papers, Ser. E, No. 1* (United Nations, New York, 1950).
9. The calculations were made by using United Nations per capita income figures for each continent applied to revised United Nations estimates of 1950 population of continents to obtain revised aggregate income by continent and for the world, as shown in Table I. A new world per capita figure of $223 was obtained, as compared with the published figure of $230.
10. For the Communist position see F. Lorimer, "Population policies and politics in the Communist world," in *Population and World Politics*, P. M. Hauser, Ed. (Free Press, Glencoe, Ill., 1958); for the Catholic position see "Pope denounces birth limitation," New York *Times* (15 Dec. 1959); for the Socialist position, see J. D. Bernal, "Population growth is no threat for a free society," *Natl. Guardian* (7 Dec. 1959) (extract from J. D. Bernal, *Science in History*).
11. W. S. Woytinsky & E. S. Woytinsky. *World Population and Production* (Twentieth Century Fund, New York, 1953).

12. S. Kuznets, "Regional economic trends and levels of living," in *Population and World Politics*, P. M. Hauser, Ed. (Free Press, Glencoe, Ill., 1958).

13. *Report on International Definition and Measurement of Standards and Levels of Living* (United Nations, New York, 1954).

14. Note the different definitions of area in Tables I and II. In Table II, which gives population projections to 1975 and 2000, "Northern America" includes only North America north of the Rio Grande; "Latin America" includes South America, Central America and North America south of the Rio Grande. For the rough comparisons made, no adjustment of the data was necessary.

15. Calculations were based on revised data, as explained in *(9)*. For Latin America the calculations were based on a comparison of estimated aggregate income for "Latin America" in 1950, per capita income for "South America" being used.

16. The "population problem" differs for areas with different ratios of population to resources; for example, see Political and Economic Planning, *World Population and Resources* (Essential Books, Fairlawn, N.J., 1955).

17. P. M. Hauser, "World and urbanization in relation to economic development and social change," in *Urbanization in Asia and Far East* (UNESCO, Calcutta, 1957), p. 57, based on work of K. Davis and H. Hertz.

18. _____, "Implications of population trends for regional and urban planning in Asia," UNESCO Working Paper No. 2, U.N. Seminar on Regional Planning, Tokyo, Japan (1958).

19. _____, Ed., "Urbanization in Latin America" (UNESCO, New York, in press).

20. "The Population of South Asia (Including Ceylon and China: Taiwan) 1950–1980," *U.N. Rept. No. 3 on Future Population Estimates by Sex and Age* (United Nations, New York, 1958).

21. W. S. Thompson, *Population and Progress in the Far East* (Univ. of Chicago Press, Chicago, 1959).

22. I. B. Taeuber, "Population and political instabilities in underdeveloped areas," in *Population and World Politics*, P. M. Hauser, Ed. (Free Press, Glencoe, Ill., 1958).

23. "The Population of Central America (Including Mexico), 1950–1980," *U.N. Rept. No. I on Future Population Estimates by Sex and Age* (United Nations, New York, 1954); "The Population of South America, 1950–1980," *U.N. Rept. No. 2 on Future Population Estimates by Sex and Age* (United Nations, New York, 1955).

24. "Demographic aspects of urbanization in Latin America," UNESCO Seminar on Urbanization Problems in Latin America, Santiago, Chile (1959).

25. *Social Implications of Industrialization in Africa South of the Sahara* (UNESCO, London, 1956).

26. K. Davis, "Population and power in the free world," in *Population and World Politics*, P. M. Hauser, Ed. (Free Press, Glencoe, Ill., 1958).

27. W. Lippmann, "China is No. 1 problem," Chicago *Sun-Times* (14 Dec. 1959); "To live India must change its way of life. . . .," Chicago *Sun-Times* (15 Dec. 1959).

28. Nor is population a factor in political instability only in the underdeveloped areas. There are many other demographic dimensions of world politics which cannot be treated here because of limitations of space. The authors of a recent symposium volume which it was my privilege to edit include further considerations of population as a factor in world politics. Especially pertinent are the articles by Kingsley Davis, Frank Lorimer, Irene Taeuber, and Quincy Wright, from which I have drawn material for this discussion.

29. "Japan's population miracle," *Population Bull.* 15, No. 7 (1959); "The race between people and resources—in the ECAFE region," pt. 1, *Population Bull.* 15, No. 5, 89 (1959).

30. *Asia and the Far East, Seminar on Population* (United Nations, New York, 1957).

31. E. W. Notestein, "Knowledge, action, people," *University—A Princeton magazine*, No. 2 (1959); P. Streit and P. Streit, "New light on India's worry," New York *Times Magazine* (13 Mar. 1960).

32. See, for example, G. Pincus *et al.*, *Science* 130, *81* (1959);—, "Field Trials with Norethynodrel as an Oral Contraceptive" (Worcester Foundation for Experimental Biology, Shrewsbury, Mass., in preparation).

33. Data are based on the following: J. J. Spengler, *Proc. Am. Phil. Soc.* 95, *53* (1951); original data (for 1937) from "Energy Resources of the World," *U.S. Dept. State Publ.* (Government Printing Office, Washington, D.C., 1949), p. 102 ff.

3. *Political Strategy and Decision-Processes*

THE ESCALATION OF INTERNATIONAL CONFLICTS*

QUINCY WRIGHT

This study suggests a method for judging the probability that international conflicts will escalate or terminate rapidly, and tests it by application to a number of conflicts since 1914. It suggests the relative importance of national interest, national power, and world opinion on the one hand, and international law and organization on the other, in influencing the course of these conflicts.

The relations of states may be studied from the viewpoint of the world as a whole by locating states in an analytic field of which the coordinates indicate their values and their capabilities. The location of states in the field determines the nature of the field, and the nature of the field, especially the images states have of it, influences the behavior of states and their movements in the field. These movements are also influenced by the changing relationship of forces within each state, and by the changing objective and subjective relationships of each pair of states (Wright, 1955, p. 543 ff.).

The field may present to some or all states the varied characters of a power equilibrium; a competitive, communicating, or co-operating community; a system of law; or an organized society. The states may be guided by government policy, national culture, constitutional prescriptions, or public opinion. Relations of conflict, competition, coexistence, or cooperation may exist in varying degrees between the members of a pair of states because of their changing objective and subjective distances from each other in the field (Wright, 1965, pp. 1241 ff., 1276 ff., 1466 ff., 1485 ff., 1493). The processes of conflict, competition, negotiation,

and administration continuously influence the behavior of states and their bilateral, regional, and universal relations.

Such analyses may deal with long periods, perhaps the entire life of a civilization, a group, or a state; or with a particular situation of dispute, conflict, crisis, intervention, or war of limited duration (Wright, 1965, p. 955 ff.). The present study is confined to particular conflicts; but we keep in mind that, in the contemporary world, the course of a particular conflict is in some degree influenced by the entire field of international relations.

1. Analyses of Conflict in the Broad Sense

Conflict is a particular relationship between states and may exist at all levels and in varied degrees. In the *broad sense* of the term it may be divided into four stages: (1) awareness of inconsistencies, (2) rising tensions, (3) pressures short of military force to resolve the inconsistencies, and (4) military intervention or war to dictate a solution (Wright, 1954, p. 142 ff.; 1957). The first two periods, in which conflict is latent, may be characterized by an arms race which tends to accelerate by a process of action and reaction, the anxiety of each party being augmented by perception of the increasing capability of the other. An equilibrium or balance of power may, however, bring the race to a halt because of the moderating influence of increasing costs, diminishing grievances, and fear of war. The course of arms races has been subjected to mathematical analysis, supported by empirical data, by Lewis F. Richardson (1960, p. 12 ff.; Wright 1965, p. 1482).

Richardson developed and applied the formulae:

* Reprinted by permission of the author and publisher from *Journal of Conflict Resolution*, 1965, 9: 434–449.

$$dx/dt = ky - ax + g$$

$$dy/dt = lx - by + h$$

This means that the military budget of state x will rise because of x's grievances (g) against state y, and that this rise will tend to accelerate as x's anxiety over y's military budget (ky) increases, but will be moderated by rising costs and internal pressures against rising taxes (ax). The same is true of y. The action-reaction pattern will, therefore, accelerate the arms race to infinity or the outbreak of war unless rising costs, diminution of grievances, and fear of war establish an equilibrium. Richardson analyzes the relative stability of such an equilibrium under conditions of bilateral and multilateral participation in the race. C. B. Joynt (1964) suggests other factors that may bring about an equilibrium, especially the relative size and character of armaments and of resources available to the parties.

2. Analyses of Conflict in the Narrow Sense

Conflict in a *narrow sense* refers to a situation in which the parties are taking action against each other, i.e., to the last two stages of conflict in the broad sense. The latent period of conflict in the broad sense may or may not involve an arms race or other domestic preparation, but conflict in the narrow sense does not exist unless international action is taken by one or both parties in the form of diplomatic protest, subversive intervention, retortionary or retaliatory economic measures, or military attack. Conflict in the narrow sense, therefore, implies that subjective hostility or tension (evidenced by domestic opinion and preparation) is objectively manifested in international relations by diplomatic, subversive, economic, or military hostilities. Richardson's analysis may be developed, I believe, to predict the probability of escalation, cease-fire, or settlement of such a conflict situation. I suggest the following equations:

$$dx/dt = (Nx + Fy) - (Cx + Wx) + \\ (Px - Py) - (Vx - Vy)$$

$$dy/dt = (Ny + Fx) - (Cy + Wy) + \\ (Py - Px) - (Vy - Vx)$$

These equations include the perception by the parties x and y of their national interests involved in the conflict (N), of the forces immediately available (F), of the costs of hostilities and preparations (C), of world pressures for peace (W), of potential military forces (P), and of vulnerability to destruction (V).

The magnitude of the positive or negative value of the growth rates of hostility $(dx/dt$ or $dy/dt)$ at a given moment indicates the degree of willingness of x and y respectively to escalate or to stop hostile activities. These equations imply that the course of a conflict, in the narrow sense, is influenced by the emergence of new considerations by the participants as it proceeds through four stages indicated by the parentheses. The formula does not attempt to predict the probable duration of these stages.

Once x takes action to solve the conflict, it will develop forces in readiness for further action at a rate (dx/dt) in proportion to the intensity of its national interest in the issue (Nx) and its apprehension of the obstacles presented to realization of its policy by y's preparation of forces to resist (Fy). In the second stage, x will consider the increasing costs of its preparations and, if hostilities are in progress, its losses in life and property (Cx); it will also consider the pressures of world opinion, including the intensity of opinion both at home and abroad demanding maintenance of peace or termination of hostilities, the effectiveness of the organization of that opinion, and the adequacy of the procedures which that opinion proposes in the particular situation (Wx). These considerations may induce willingness in one or both participants to accept a cease-fire and to negotiate or adjudicate. If, however, hostilities continue, x is likely to consider the long-run power position in military forces, economic capability, political morale, and potential allies of itself (Px) and its enemy

(Py), and to escalate or negotiate as that position seems favorable or unfavorable. If hostilities continue to the final stage, x will consider its vulnerability to destruction by the military resources available to its enemy (Vx), comparing this with what it perceives as its enemy's vulnerability to destruction by its own attack (Vy). It is assumed that the satisfaction of visiting huge destruction upon its enemy will seem sufficient compensation for its own heavy losses and that, therefore, the party most vulnerable will surrender—i.e., a state will surrender before its total destruction unless it has a good prospect of totally destroying its enemy. Unilateral suicide will be avoided, but mutual suicide may seem preferable to surrender.

Party y will progress through the same stages as those just described for x. Each stage may be terminated by escalation, cease-fire, negotiation, surrender, or protracted stalemate in which each awaits a favorable opportunity to renew hostilities.

Foresight about the later stages may influence behavior in the earlier stages. Thus x may have a lesser interest in the issues of the conflict than y, and may be behind in forces in readiness, but x may believe that y's economy will not permit of much escalation, that world opinion is going to turn against y, that in the long run it can gain allies and marshal much greater power than y, and that y will be vulnerable to total destruction by nuclear weapons which only its side (x) will possess. On the other hand, x may take a more pessimistic view of the future and seek a cease-fire while it still has an advantage; but governments are often unrealistically optimistic about the prospects of hostilities. If, at any stage, either side calculates that these ultimate developments will be favorable, it will be willing to escalate hostilities. If both sides see it this way—i.e., if the signs of both dx/dt and dy/dt are positive—the conflict will probably escalate.

It must be emphasized that these stages are not distinguished by the latency or the activity of the conflict—in all stages the conflict is active—but by the degree of attention likely to be directed to the future and to the ultimate outcome. Because of the tendency of governments to act mechanically and not rationally, attention is usually devoted at first to past grievances and present interests and capabilities. A conflict in which one or both of the parties has only a minor interest may not get beyond stage one (consideration of N and F). More serious conflicts in which armed forces have been employed are likely to direct the attention of the parties to the costs and to the development of national and world opinion, perhaps manifested in the national legislature or in regional or universal international organizations. Such reflection may bring hostilities to an end with a cease-fire at stage two. A conflict which each side believes involves its vital interests is likely to escalate until its costs, in economic resources and casualties, have been so great that each is emotionally affected and incapable of rational thought. Each side may then ignore losses, world opinion, international law, and even its future existence in its effort to destroy its enemy. Eventually, however, the probable destruction of one or both parties may become so obvious—if not to the government, then to the revolutionary regime which succeeds it—that the instinct of self-preservation induces an end to hostilities.

3. Measurement of Variables

The magnitudes attributed to the variables in each conflict listed in the accompanying tables (see pp. 443–49 below) are, in the main, subjective estimates on the scale of 100 based on the considerations indicated in the notes to Table 1. I recognize that my conclusions are subject to criticism because of the lack of objectivity in these measurements. They are educated guesses. The figures for immediately available and potential military forces (F and P) represent percentages of total military forces in the world at the time, but consideration was given not only to army, navy, and air personnel, which can be dealt with statistically,[1] but also to estimates of relative effi-

---

[1] The *Britannica Book of the Year* includes statistics of the "Armed Forces of the World" by states every year.

ciency and equipment, including planes, missiles, and nuclear weapons. The figures for costs (C) represent estimates of the percentage of the national budgets devoted to the conflict, with some consideration to costs in casualties and property destruction.

The figures given for the degree of national interest involved in the conflict (N) and world opinion about it (W) are subjective estimates which might be improved by detailed analyses of opinion polls, debates in national legislatures and international conferences, and content analysis of the press and official documents. A comparison of many expert opinions might also give greater objectivity to these estimates. The subjective estimates of vulnerability (V) of the parties might similarly be improved by detailed analyses of official and unofficial strategic studies. I have not made such studies; they would require elaborate research and perhaps a corps of computer analysts. Furthermore, I have assumed that the forces potentially available to each side (P) and the vulnerability of each to destruction (V) will be ascertained by each side with respect to itself and its enemy with sufficient objectivity so that the perceptions of each on these matters will not differ radically. This assumption is not entirely justifiable. Each side is likely to overestimate its own potential force and its defenses against destructive attack, and to underestimate the forces and defenses of the enemy.

It must be emphasized that the important variable in determining willingness to escalate or negotiate is the *perception* of the situation by the decision-making authority, not the objective reaility. Detailed analysis of the materials suggested might disclose the divergence of these perceptions on each side from each other and from any criterion of statistical reality. The figures in the tables are intended to represent psychological perceptions, not objective facts.

It must also be emphasized that the symbols are all variables which change as the conflict progresses. In early stages each side usually believes it is going to win very soon and so the influence of perceptions of ultimate power (P) and vulnerability (V) is practically zero. At a later stage these poten-

tialities may loom up as of major importance, although, as noted, they may be overshadowed by the emotional irrationality bred of hate and suffering.

4. Application of the Formula to Conflicts

The intent of the study is (1) to provide a rough measure of the probable motivations of the parties which induce them to escalate a given conflict, to urge a cease-fire, or to negotiate at a given stage; and (2) to test the formula which relates these motivations by applying it to estimates of the magnitude of the variables at successive stages of 45 conflicts beginning with World War I. Some of these conflicts did not involve military hostilities at all, and two of them escalated to general war.[2]

The positive or negative magnitude of the hostility of each party (dx/dt, dy/dt) at a given stage of each conflict should indicate the direction and vigor of each party's policy at that point in time. If both signs are negative, a cease-fire is likely. It is assumed that the considerations in the two final stages (P and V) will not usually be of much influence in the earlier stages because, as has been noted, governments are prone to act mechanically by established reaction patterns and to think wishfully, if they think at all, of the future. There may be evidence in a particular conflict that somewhat objective consideration of the future has been influential, with the result that all the factors represented by the cumulative figure at the end of the formula may have influenced policy at the beginning of the conflict situation. This is especially likely to be true if disparities in power and vulnerability are very great.

Of the 45 international conflicts analyzed in the tables, nine involved no military action, 20 resulted in conclusion of hostilities by an agreed or tacit cease-fire in less than a year (or longer if there were less than

---

[2] See Table 1. The 45 conflicts were selected from lists of 160 since World War I, 147 of which came before the League of Nations or the United Nations. Seventy conflicts during this period involved military hostilities, listed as "war" in 46 cases, all but 13 of which came before the League or the UN (Wright, 1965, pp. 646, 1429 ff., 1544 ff., 1552 ff.).

1,000 casualties), and 14 conflicts escalated for a longer time and with larger casualties, while only two went to the stage of general war.

A. *Conflicts with No Military Hostilities*

Part A of Table 1 (see below, p. 443) lists the nine conflicts settled without military hostilities. In these cases the national interest (N) of the less interested party to the conflict was relatively small (never rated over 30 and on the average less than 12), and world opinion demanding settlement (W) was relatively large (average rating, adding the two parties, over 41). In four cases, even though the pressure of organized world opinion was not great, the potential political power situation was roughly equal, suggesting a stalemate (Berlin blockade), or else the low interest level of the state resisting change induced a settlement without hostilities (Alexandretta, Morocco, Tunisia).

In all of these nine situations the formula, as shown in Part A of Table 2 (p. 447), gave a negative sign to the party that lost its contention and a positive sign, or negative in less degree, to the winning side, except in the two colonial cases (Morocco and Tunisia). In these two cases the formula gave a positive sign to both, suggesting the possibility of escalation, but the colonial power was positive in much less degree, and bowed to the demand for self-determination in spite of its superior power position and lesser vulnerability.

The signs for both of the parties were always positive in these situations at the end of the first stage, when national interest and the hope of gaining superiority over opposing forces were the main considerations.

In seven of the nine cases the sign was negative for one or both parties at the end of the second stage when potential costs, and especially world opinion, were influential, inducing at least one party to seek a settlement. In two situations (Morocco, Tunisia) the signs of both sides were positive at this stage, but the losing side in each case shows a much smaller value. In every case the indications at the end of the second stage were confirmed by the formula as a whole, which gave consideration to ultimate power positions and relative vulnerabilities.

B. *Conflicts in Which Military Hostilities Did Not Escalate*

When hostilities occurred but were soon ended by acceptance of a cease-fire or some termination tacitly agreed on, the less interested party of the two usually had a greater interest than was true in the cases where there were no hostilities at all (17 on the average, and never less than 10; see Part B of Table 1). The pressure of world opinion was about the same as when there were no hostilities (40 on the average) but this pressure, usually expressed by the League of Nations or the United Nations, was a major factor in ending hostilities in the second stage. The signs at the end of this stage were often negative for both parties and always for one party, with the exception of the Hyderabad, Quemoy-Matsu, and Goa situations. In these the signs of both parties were positive, indicating the probability of escalation at this stage. In none of the three exceptional cases was there a cease-fire. In the Quemoy-Matsu case, however, as in the Berlin blockade, consideration of potential power suggested a stalemate and hostilities were tacitly ended. In the Goa and Hyderabad situations the superiority of Indian power in the locality induced Portugal and Hyderabad, respectively, to acquiesce in—though not formally to accept—Indian acquisition of the disputed territory. The pressure of world opinion was divided in these two cases. Western opinion recognized the legal validity of Portugal's case, and to a lesser extent that of Hyderabad, but was unable to influence India by way of United Nations resolutions because the new states of Asia and Africa and the Communist states favored India on grounds of anti-colonialism.

In all of these 20 cases, the will to settle or at least to stop hostilities is indicated by the negative signs of one or both parties when the formula as a whole is applied. No final settlement has been reached in some of these situations, although supposedly temporary cease-fire arrangements are in effect. It is interesting to note that the greater positive or lesser negative magnitude of the sign at the end of the formula indicates the state which was, at least temporarily, successful.

C. Conflicts in Which Military Hostilities Escalated, Including World Wars

In all of the 16 situations which involved considerable hostilities, both parties had a strong national interest at the beginning of the conflict—never less than 20 (see Parts C and D of Table 1). The party with the lesser interest had an average national interest rating of 35, in contrast to the average of 12 for situations without hostilities and the average of 17 for situations where hostilities terminated early.

In seven of these 16 situations both parties had a positive or zero sign in the second stage of the conflict, indicating probable escalation in spite of considerable world opinion pressing for peace. In cases where the pressure of world opinion and the cost of hostilities gave one party a negative sign at this second stage (Bolivia in the Chaco, Japan in Manchuria, Italy in Ethiopia, the Soviet Union in Finland, Yugoslavia on the Greek frontier, North Korea, France in Algeria, Katanga in the Congo, and the Arabs in South Arabia), that party apparently believed its power potential to be such that it continued hostilities.

In all of these sixteen cases, application of the formula as a whole gave one or both parties a positive sign, indicating stalemate or a victory by one party after considerable escalation. In every case the side with greater positive magnitude was the victor when hostilities ended, or the probable victor in those cases where hostilities are still going on. In the two world wars, the side ultimately defeated did not recognize the consequences of the potential power of the enemy and its own vulnerability until, as indicated by the formula, its capacity to continue was very low.

Of hostilities active at this writing, application of the formula suggests the following results. Hostilities in Vietnam are likely to escalate for a time, but eventually South Vietnam and the United States will win unless mounting national and world opinion brings about a cease-fire, or unless entry of the Soviet Union or China, or both, initiates World War III.

The Malaysian conflict may escalate, but there is likely to be a termination of hostilities favorable to Malaysia because of the superior forces available to it as a result of British assistance.

The South Arabian conflict seems about to end with victory for the British side.

The conflict in Yemen is likely to end without further escalation by a compromise favorable to the Republican side supported by the United Arab Republic.

The situation in the Dominican Republic also seems unlikely to escalate seriously; it appears instead to be headed toward settlement by the United States and the Organization of American States.

5. Influence of International Law

This study has been in the realm of predictive science and throws little light on the normative science of international law, though the two are related because world opinion influences state behavior and international law influences world opinion. The tables throw some light on this relationship.

In 27 of the 45 situations included in this study, one of the parties seems to have made or resisted demands, or initiated hostilities, in violation of an international obligation. Such violation has been formally recognized by an international body in 10 of these cases,[3] but it was implied by such a

---

[3] The Versailles conference recognized the violation of legal obligation by Germany in initiating World War I and particularly in invading neutralized Belgium. The League of Nations recognized a violation by Greece for invading Bulgaria in 1925; by Peru for invading Leticia in 1932; by Japan for invading Manchuria in 1931; by Paraguay for refusal to withdraw from the Gran Chaco in 1934; by Italy for invading Ethiopia in 1935; and by the Soviet Union for invading Finland in 1939. The Nuremberg Tribunal recognized such violation by Germany for initiating World War II and invading various countries in 1939. The United Nations recognized such violation by North Korea and Communist China for invading South Korea in 1950, and by the Soviet Union for invading Hungary in 1956.

body in eight cases,[4] and in my opinion a violation probably occurred in nine other cases.[5] The violator lost in nine of these 27 situations,[6] won—at least temporarily—in ten,[7] and compromised in five.[8] Three of these conflicts are continuing at this writing.[9] In the remaining 18 situations, those in which violations of international law did not seem to be involved, the claims of one or both parties were political rather than legal in character, as in the claims for colonial self-determination[10] or territorial adjustment,[11] or the law was uncertain.[12] It seems clear that appraisals of national interest and world opinion and calculations of relative power and vulnerability had more influence in determining the course

[4] A special juridical commission implied the violation of legal obligation by Italy for invading Corfu in 1923. The UN implied such violation by Italy and Germany for intervening in the Spanish civil strife, 1936–38; by the Soviet Union in not promptly withdrawing its forces from Iran in 1946; by the Netherlands for renewing hostilities in Indonesia in 1947; by Yugoslavia and Bulgaria for permitting invasion of Greece by insurgents in 1947; by Israel for occupying territory in Palestine beyond that awarded by the UN, and by Egypt for closing the Suez Canal to Israel in 1949; by Israel, Great Britain, and France for invading the Suez area in 1956; and by Indonesia for invading Malaysia in 1964.

[5] By Germany for invading the Rhineland in 1935, and for demanding the Sudetenland in 1938; by Pakistan for invading Kashmir in 1948; by India for invading Goa in 1962; by China for invading India in 1962; by the United States for supporting a refugee invasion of Cuba in 1961 and conducting a blockade against Cuba in 1962; by the United States for intervening in Lebanon in 1958, and in Vietnam and the Dominican Republic in 1965.

[6] World War I, Leticia, Greece-Bulgaria, World War II, Iran, Indonesia, Greek frontier, Korea, Suez.

[7] Gran Chaco, Manchuria, Ethiopia, Rhineland, Sudetenland, Spain, Finland, Palestine partition, Hungary, Goa. Four of these situations—Manchuria, Ethiopia, Rhineland, Sudetenland—were rectified as a result of the defeat of the Axis powers in World War II.

[8] Corfu, Kashmir, Lebanon, Cuba, Indian frontier.

[9] Malaysia, Dominican Republic, Vietnam.

[10] Syria-Lebanon, 1946; Indochina, 1947–54; Morocco, 1952; Tunisia, 1952; Algeria, 1954–62; Congo, 1960–; West Irian, 1961–62.

[11] Aaland Islands, 1921; Saar Valley, 1935–37; Alexandretta, 1936–37; Indian partition, 1948–49.

[12] Hyderabad, 1948; Quemoy-Matsu, 1954–56; Berlin blockade, 1949; Tibet, 1959; South Arabia, 1963; Cyprus, 1963–64; Yemen, 1962–.

of these conflicts than did the requirements of international law. If that law is to be effective in predicting the outcome of international conflicts, it must be developed better to serve the interests of the members of the community of nations, especially their interest in world stability and peace; governments must become more convinced that observance of the law will serve their interests, and international organization must be developed better to improve and support the law.

Conclusion

It appears that the proposed formula had considerable predictive value when applied to situations which have come to an end, if my educated guesses at the magnitude of the variables are not far off. More precise estimates of these magnitudes and analysis of a larger number of cases are needed, finally to establish the value of the formula.

The study suggests that the factors *promoting* escalation of international conflicts are perceptions of vital national interests by both parties, relative equality in forces immediately available, and belief by each party that superior forces will eventually be available to it from its own efforts or from allies, rendering its opponent more vulnerable to unacceptable losses and costs.

The factors *militating against* escalation are the relative unimportance of the national interests which one or both parties perceive to be involved in a given conflict; obvious and great inequality of forces available to or anticipated by the parties or, alternatively, comparative equality and great capability for destruction; high costs in proportion to the state's economy; and particularly a strong world opinion, manifested in international organization, demanding a cease-fire, negotiation, or renunciation of its cause by one party.

Such world opinion is likely to develop against a party which is making demands or initiating hostilities in clear violation of its obligations under international law. International law, however, needs clarification, especially on what constitutes unlawful use of force and what constitutes unlawful intervention in the domestic affairs of other states. More effective sanctioning procedures by the community of nations are also needed. With such improvements, law might control force, right might prevail over might, and qualitative analysis of norms might serve better than quantitative analysis of forces to predict the outcome of international conflicts.

Violations of the rules of the road by fast-moving cars on a crowded highway are likely to result in lethal collisions. Similarly, under contemporary conditions, violations of the international law of peaceful coexistence of sovereign nations are likely to result in the escalation of international conflict to nuclear disaster.

REFERENCES

Coffey, Rosemary K. "The Heart of Deterrence," *Bulletin of the Atomic Scientists*, 21 (April 1965), 27 ff.

Joynt, C. R. "Arms Races and the Problems of Equilibrium," *Year Book of World Affairs* (London Institute of World Affairs), 8 (1964), 23 ff.

Morgenthau, Hans J. *Politics among Nations*. New York: Knopf, 1954.

Richardson, Lewis F. *Arms and Insecurity*. Pittsburgh, Pa.: Boxwood Press, 1960.

Russett, Bruce M. "The Calculus of Deterrence," *Journal of Conflict Resolution*, 7, 2 (June 1963), 97–109.

Stoessinger, John G. *The Might of Nations*. New York: Random House, 1965.

Van Dyke, Vernon. *Pride and Power: The Rationale of the Space Program*. Urbana: University of Illinois Press, 1964.

Webster, Charles K. *The Art and Practice of Diplomacy*. London: Chatto and Windus, 1961.

Wright, Quincy. *Problems of Stability and Progress in International Relations*. Berkeley: University of California Press, 1954.

_____. *The Study of International Relations*. New York: Appleton-Century-Crofts, 1955.

_____. "International Conflict and the United Nations," *World Politics*, 10 (Oct. 1957). 24 ff.

_____. *A Study of War*. 2nd edn. Chicago, Ill.: University of Chicago Press, 1965.

TABLE 1

ESTIMATES OF THE MAGNITUDE OF SIGNIFICANT FACTORS INDUCING THE ESCALATION OF INTERNATIONAL CONFLICTS

A. CONFLICTS WITH NO MILITARY HOSTILITIES

(x is the party named first)	N		F		C		W		P		V	
	x	y	x	y	x	y	x	y	x	y	x	y
Aaland Islands, 1921 Sweden—Finland	10	10	1	1	3	3	50	20	10	2	5	5
Saar Valley, 1935–37 Germany—France	20	15	5	10	5	5	30	40	6	7	10	5
Rhineland Occupation, 1936–37 Germany—France	20	5	5	10	5	5	30	30	6	7	10	5
Alexandretta, 1936–37 Turkey—France	20	3	2	2	3	3	15	15	2	7	2	1
Sudetenland, 1938 Germany—Czechoslovakia	30	30	5	3	5	5	20	40	6	13	15	50
Forces in Iran, 1946 Soviet Union—Iran	5	25	5	1	3	5	60	10	20	1	1	15
Berlin Blockade, 1949 Soviet Union—US, NATO	10	10	5	3	4	1	10	10	20	50	40	5
Morocco, 1952 Morocco—France	50	10	1	3	5	3	5	5	1	4	5	1
Tunisia, 1952 Tunisia—France	50	10	1	3	5	3	5	5	1	4	5	1

TABLE 1 *(continued)*

B. CONFLICTS IN WHICH MILITARY HOSTILITIES DID NOT ESCALATE

(x is the party named first)	N x	N y	F x	F y	C x	C y	W x	W y	P x	P y	V x	V y
Corfu, 1923 Italy—Greece	10	15	3	2	3	5	25	5	6	3	3	5
Demir Kapu, 1925 Greece—Bulgaria	10	10	1	1	3	3	40	30	3	2	1	3
Leticia, 1932–35 Peru—Colombia	10	10	1	1	3	3	40	20	2	1	1	1
Forces in Syria, 1946 France, UK—Syria, Lebanon	10	25	1	2	1	3	20	10	7	1	1	3
Indonesia, 1947–48 Netherlands—Indonesia	30	40	1	1	10	10	30	10	1	1	1	1
Indian Partition, 1948–49 Pakistan—India	30	20	2	3	20	20	10	10	2	3	10	10
Hyderabad, 1948 India—Hyderabad	50	20	2	1	2	5	5	5	3	1	1	20
Palestine Partition, 1948–49 Arabs—Israel	30	60	1	2	20	10	30	30	4	2	2	15
Kashmir, 1948 Pakistan—India	30	30	1	2	5	5	30	30	2	3	5	3
Quemoy—Matsu China—Taiwan, US	20	15	4	2	1	1	10	15	18	25	5	1
Suez, 1956 Israel, France, UK—Egypt, UN	15	20	1	1	5	5	50	10	8	20	15	15
Hungary, 1956 Soviet Union—Hungary	20	30	5	2	5	10	50	5	20	1	3	70
Lebanon, 1958 Chamoun, US—Lebanon, UAR	10	10	1	1	1	1	20	5	30	1	1	3
West Irian, 1961–62 Indonesia—Netherlands	30	10	1	1	5	5	5	15	1	1	1	1
Tibet, 1959 China—Tibet	20	40	5	1	5	30	40	5	18	1	1	70
Goa, 1961 India—Portugal	20	12	2	1	5	3	10	10	3	1	1	1
Cuba, 1961–62 Refugees, US—Castro, Soviet Union	20	40	1	1	3	5	20	20	30	20	20	50
Indian Frontier, 1962 China—India	20	40	3	2	5	15	40	5	18	3	1	15
Cyprus, 1962–64 Cyprus, Greece—Turkish Cypriots, Turkey	30	30	1	1	5	5	30	30	3	2	3	3
Dominican Republic, 1965 Rebels—Junta, US, OAS	10	10	1	1	3	3	10	20	1	30	10	3

358   *Conflict Resolution*

TABLE 1 *(continued)*

C. CONFLICTS IN WHICH MILITARY HOSTILITIES ESCALATED

(x is the party named first)	N x	N y	F x	F y	C x	C y	W x	W y	P x	P y	V x	V y
Gran Chaco, 1928–36 Bolivia—Paraguay	40	40	1	1	15	10	30	30	1	2	10	5
Manchuria, 1931–35 Japan—China	30	30	5	3	10	20	30	10	6	5	2	10
Ethiopia, 1935–38 Italy—Ethiopia	40	60	3	2	20	30	50	5	6	5	5	40
Spain, 1936–39 Franco, Mussolini, Hitler— Republic, Soviet Union	50	50	3	3	10	30	20	20	15	10	20	40
Finland, 1939–40 Soviet Union—Finland	20	50	5	2	3	10	60	10	10	3	3	40
Greek Frontier, 1946–48 Rebels, Yugoslavia, Bulgaria—Greece, US	20	30	2	1	3	10	40	5	15	30	5	30
Indochina, 1947–54 France—Vietnam	30	60	3	1	10	15	20	15	3	1	1	10
Korea, 1950–53 N. Korea, China—S. Korea, US	40	40	2	5	15	15	40	10	25	30	40	40
Algeria, 1954–62 Algeria—France	60	40	1	4	20	20	10	30	4	4	15	2
Congo, 1960–64 Congo, UN—Katanga	20	20	1	1	10	10	10	40	6	4	10	20
Vietnam, 1961–65 N. Vietnam, Viet Cong— S. Vietnam, US	60	50	1	1	20	20	20	30	30	40	70	60
South Arabia, 1962 South Arabia—UK	20	20	1	1	3	1	20	5	2	5	3	1
Yemen, 1962 Republic, UAR— Monarchy, Saudi Arabia	20	20	1	1	5	5	10	15	3	3	5	5
Malaysia, 1963 Indonesia—Malaysia, UK	25	40	1	1	2	2	20	10	5	15	5	3

D. WORLD WARS

	N x	N y	F x	F y	C x	C y	W x	W y	P x	P y	V x	V y
World War I, 1914–20 Germany, Central Powers— Allies, US	50	40	20	30	40	50	30	10	20	60	20	10
World War II, 1939–45 Axis—Allies, US	70	70	20	20	40	50	30	10	20	70	50	10

NOTES TO TABLE 1

N refers to the magnitude of the *national interest* which a party believes is at stake in the conflict, measured on a scale of 100. Richardson (1960) refers to this interest as a "grievance" or "ambition." It would appear, however, that the term "national interest" is more familiar in international politics. A grievance is a conviction that a national interest has been encroached upon or endangered; or that an ambition or a policy has been frustrated or threatened. National interests vary from minor to vital. They may be estimated from declarations of the government, from its behavior in accepting or rejecting compromises, and from assumptions about sovereign states. States seem to regard the spread of their ideologies; the observance of their commitments; the realization of their policies; the preservation of the national character; the gaining of prestige; the satisfaction of pride; the augmentation of power; the security of independence, territorial integrity, and continued existence as interests which usually increase in importance in somewhat this order. Often, subjective interests such as respect, reputation, pride, and prestige may be regarded more highly than objective interests such as wealth, territory, or even power (Stoessinger, 1965, p. 28ff.; Van Dyke, 1964, p. 119ff.; Morgenthau, 1954, p. 5ff.; Webster, 1961, p. 2ff.; Wright, 1955, p. 577). Russett (1963) has suggested the factors which establish a national interest in defending another state and making credible deterrent threats in its behalf.

The order of importance of national interests differs among states and changes with circumstances. A revolution may for a time put ideology ahead of territory or even state existence, but usually only for a short time. Nehru thought the major difference between the United States and the Soviet Union lay in the time which had elapsed since their respective revolutions, and General de Gaulle has attributed greater permanence to nationality than to ideology. It is clear that, even before the death of Lenin, Russia had become more interested in preserving its territory and national existence than in spreading communism. Power position may sometimes be put ahead of independence or territorial integrity, as when vulnerable territory is ceded or an alliance is made, but more often power is regarded as a means to preserve independence and territory, and the capacity to preserve them is regarded as evidence of power. It seems clear that the importance which a state attaches to a national interest involved in a conflict situation varies with the state of opinion, the character of the government, and the situation it faces. An appraisal of N can, therefore, be only a subjective judgment based on an understanding of the particular state and the particular situation. This rating is of major importance in the formula, but it seems unlikely that any statistical index can be devised to measure it other than comparison of the judgments of a number of qualified experts.

F refers to the *armed force* which the parties believe are actually engaged in the conflict or immediately available to them, expressed as a percentage of the total armed force in the world at that time. Since such force includes not only land, naval, and air personnel, but also their equipment in rifles, machine guns, artillery, war vessels, aircraft, missiles, nuclear warheads, and means of transport, and their morale and efficiency, precise statistical measurement is difficult if not impossible, especially when technology is changing rapidly. Furthermore, the figures given under the F heading are intended to refer to the perception of the effectiveness of available force, which may differ from the objective fact. In spite of these difficulties it is possible to utilize available statistical information about total military personnel in the world at the time and the forces which a state has mobilized in the conflict (*Britannica Book of the Year*, "Armies of the World"), with suitable modifications from knowledge of weaponry, morale, transport, etc., to arrive at figures which are comparable—with, it is true, a considerable margin of error.

C refers to the *cost of the hostilities* perceived by the parties at a given stage in the conflict—in budgetary expenditures, losses of military personnel and material, destruction of civilian life and property, and deterioration of national morale and standards, expressed as a percentage of national wealth in these values (Wright, 1965, pp. 219, 242ff., 675ff., 1503, 1561). Here again, no precise statistical measurement is possible, though the percentage of the national budget devoted to the conflict can be taken as a starting point with modifications from knowledge of material and moral losses.

W refers to the degree of pressure by *world opinion* demanding preservation of peace or cessation of hostilities as perceived by the parties, measured on a scale of 100. The effectiveness of opinion, national and international, because of its organization in national constitutions and international organizations, and its formulation as law, must be considered. Polls of opinion, comments in the press, declarations of government, resolutions in national and international assemblies, and the imposition of international sanctions may be useful as indices, but no precise statistical measure of this variable is likely to be found. The imposition of UN military sanctions against North Korea and Communist China in 1950 suggests that the pressure of world opinion upon these powers to end hostilities approached 100, while that upon South Korea and the US was 0; but—in view of the actual situation, in which the Soviet Union and some other states supported North Korea and only 14 states actually gave military support to South Korea, the US, and the UN—the figures $+40$ and $+10$ seemed a more realistic estimate of the probable perception by the parties of the pressure of world opinion.

P refers to the *military power* likely to be available to a party if the war escalates to the limit, measured as a percentage of the total military power in the world at the time. It includes all the elements of military force referred to under C, but also gives consideration to the productive and recruiting capacity of a party; its ability to acquire allies with arms-in-being and productive capacity; and its ability to conquer territory with military potential. While such statistical factors as military personnel, military budgets, and population of the nation and the world provide a starting point (see F above and Wright, 1955, p. 577), the possibility presented by potential allies and conquests makes the figure highly speculative. The military value of a state's forces are relative to the size of the enemy's forces; so each party must estimate both its own and its opponent's potential power.

The intelligence services of states are usually more reliable on the military capability of other states than on their political intentions, but there is likely to be a discrepancy between the state's own estimate of its potential power and the enemy's estimate. This possible discrepancy has been ignored, however, and a single figure is used for Px (and also for Py) as perceived by x and by y. The difficulty of estimating this important figure can be seen from the following questions. Could South Vietnam in July 1965 count on the support, if necessary, of the entire power of the United States with its nuclear capability? Could North Vietnam on that date count on the support of the Soviet Union with its nuclear capability, and of China with its huge land army? Would North and South Vietnam make the same calculations on these points? As a conflict escalates, calculations of this type become increasingly important in determining policy, but they are highly speculative for the parties and

no less so for the researcher trying to predict the outcome of the conflict.

V refers to the *vulnerability* foreseen by a party to the destruction of its armed forces, wealth, population, national unity, and culture in the event of an escalation of hostilities. It is expressed as a percentage of these national values as a whole. Vulnerability refers to *anticipated* losses, and so it is more speculative than costs, which refer to the present situation. It has been estimated that a nuclear war between the United States and the Soviet Union would rapidly eliminate a third of the population and most of the large cities of each party, but such estimates have little statistical accuracy. Numerous contingencies such as counterforce effectiveness, civilian defenses, and strategic policy are involved in the probability of such destruction and even more in the perception by the parties of their eventual vulnerability. If the parties are very unequal in military potential, their vulnerability will obviously be very different, and if both lack modern weaponry and are geographically separated the vulnerability of each may seem very small. The two sides may differ in their estimates of their own and the enemy's vulnerability but, as in the case of P, the same figure is used here to represent the perceptions of both sides.

The degree of destruction which will induce surrender, and the degree of anticipated destruction which will deter escalation, depend on many circumstances including the period of time during which destruction occurs or is anticipated. In a short nuclear war, anticipated vulnerability to losses of 50 percent would probably always be unacceptable, and the figure might be as low as 10 percent (Coffey, 1965).

TABLE 2
PROBABLE ESCALATION OF INTERNATIONAL CONFLICTS
A. CONFLICTS WITH NO MILITARY HOSTILITIES

$dx/dt =$ $dy/dt =$	$+ Nx + Fy$ $+ Ny + Fx$ Stage 1	$- Cx - Wx$ $- Cy - Wy$ Stage 2	$+ Px - Py$ $+ Py - Px$ Stage 3	$- Vx + Vy$ $- Vy + Vx$ Stage 4
Aaland Islands, 1921				
Sweden	+10 +1(+11)	–3 –50 (–42)	+10 –2 (–34)	–5 +5 (–34)
Finland	+10 +1(+11)	–3 –20 (–12)	+2 –10 (–20)	–5 +5 (–20)
Saar Valley, 1935–37				
Germany	+20+10+(30)	–5 –30 (–5)	+6 –7 (–6)	–10 +5 (–11)
France	+15 +5(+20)	–5 –40 (–25)	+7 –6 (–24)	–5+10 (–19)
Rhineland, 1935				
Germany	+20+10(+30)	–5 –30 (–5)	+6 –7 (–6)	–10 +5 (–11)
France	+5 +5(+10)	–5 –30 (–25)	+7 –6 (–24)	–5+10 (–19)
Alexandretta, 1936–37				
Turkey	+20 +2(+22)	–3 –15 (+4)	+2 –7 (–1)	–2 +1 (–2)
France	+3 +2 (+5)	–3 –15 (–13)	+7 –2 (–8)	–1 +2 (–7)
Sudetenland, 1938				
Germany	+30 +3(+33)	–5 –20 (+8)	+6 –13 (+1)	–15+50(+36)
Czechoslovakia	+30 +5(+35)	–5 –40 (–10)	+13 –6 (–3)	–50+15 (–38)

TABLE 2 *(continued)*

A. CONFLICTS WITH NO MILITARY HOSTILITIES *(continued)*

$dx/dt =$ $dy/dt =$	$+ Nx + Fy$ $+ Ny + Fx$ Stage 1	$- Cx - Wx$ $- Cy - Wy$ Stage 2	$+ Px - Py$ $+ Py - Px$ Stage 3	$- Vx + Vy$ $- Vy + Vx$ Stage 4
Iran, 1946				
Soviet Union	+5 +1 (+6)	–3 –60 (–57)	+20 –1 (–38)	–1+15 (–24)
Iran	+25 +5(+30)	–5 –10(+15)	+1 –20 (–4)	–15 +1 (–18)
Berlin Blockade, 1949				
Soviet Union	+10 +3(+13)	–4– 10 (–1)	+20 –50 (–31)	–40 +5 (–66)
US, NATO	+10 +5(+15)	–1 –10 (+4)	+50 –20(+34)	–5+40(+69)
Morocco, 1952				
Morocco	+50 +3(+53)	–5 –5(+43)	+1 –4(+40)	–5 +1(+36)
France	+10 +1(+11)	–3 –5 (+3)	+4 –1 (+6)	–1 +5(+10)
Tunisia, 1952				
Tunisia	+50 +3(+53)	–5 –5(+43)	+1 –4(+40)	–5 +1(+36)
France	+10 +1(+11)	–3 –5 (+3)	+4 –1 (+6)	–1 +5(+10)

B. CONFLICTS IN WHICH MILITARY HOSTILITIES DID NOT ESCALATE

	Stage 1	Stage 2	Stage 3	Stage 4
Corfu, 1923				
Italy	+10 +2(+12)	–3 –25 (–16)	+6 –3 (–13)	–3 +5 (–11)
Greece	+15 +3(+18)	–5 –5 (+8)	+3 –6 (+5)	–5 +3 (+3)
Demir Kapu, 1925				
Greece	+10 +1(+11)	–3 –40 (–32)	+3 –2 (–31)	–1 +3 (–29)
Bulgaria	+10 +1(+11)	–3 –30 (–22)	+2 –3 (–23)	–3 +1 (–25)
Leticia, 1932–35				
Peru	+10 +1(+11)	–3 –40 (–32)	+2 –1 (–31)	–1 +1 (–31)
Colombia	+10 +1(+11)	–3 –20 (–12)	+1 –2 (–13)	–1 +1 (–13)
Syria-Lebanon, 1946				
France, UK	+10 +2(+12)	–1 –20 (–9)	+7 –1 (–3)	–1 +3 (–1)
Syria, Lebanon	+25 +1(+26)	–3 –10(+13)	+1 –7 (+7)	–3 +1 (+5)
Indonesia, 1947–48				
Netherlands	+30 +1(+31)	–10 –30 (–9)	+1 –1 (–9)	–1 +1 (–9)
Indonesia	+40 +1(+41)	–10 –10(+21)	+1 –1(+21)	–1 +1(+21)
Indian Partition, 1948–49				
Pakistan	+30 +3(+33)	–20 –10 (+3)	+2 –3 (+2)	–10+10 (+2)
India	+20 +2(+22)	–20 –10 (–8)	+3 –2 (–7)	–10+10 (–7)
Hyderabad, 1948				
India	+50 +1(+51)	–2 –5(+44)	+3 –1(+46)	–1+20(+65)
Hyderabad	+20 +2(+22)	–5 –5(+12)	+1 –3(+10)	–20 +1 (–9)
Palestine Partition, 1948–49				
Arabs	+30 +2(+32)	–20 –30 (–18)	+4 –2 (–16)	–2+15 (–3)
Israel	+60 +1(+61)	–10 –30(+21)	+2 –4(+19)	–15 +2 (+6)
Kashmir, 1948				
Pakistan	+30 +2(+32)	–5 –30 (–3)	+2 –3 (–4)	–5 +3 (–6)
India	+30 +1(+31)	–5 –30 (–4)	+3 –2 (–3)	–3 +5 (–1)
Quemoy-Matsu, 1954–56				
China	+20 +2(+22)	–1 –10(+11)	+18 –25 (+4)	–5 +1 (0)
Taiwan, US	+15 +4(+19)	–1 –15 (+3)	+25 –18(+10)	–1 +5(+14)
Suez, 1956				
Israel, France, UK	+15 +1(+16)	–5 –50 (–39)	+8 –20 (–51)	–15+15 (–51)
Egypt, UN	+20 +1(+21)	–5 –10 (+6)	+20 –8(+18)	–15+15(+18)

TABLE 2 *(continued)*

B. CONFLICTS IN WHICH MILITARY HOSTILITIES DID NOT ESCALATE *(continued)*

$dx/dt =$ $dy/dt =$	$+ Nx + Fy$ $+ Ny + Fx$ Stage 1	$- Cx - Wx$ $- Cy - Wy$ Stage 2	$+ Px - Py$ $+ Py - Px$ Stage 3	$- Vx + Vy$ $- Vy + Vx$ Stage 4
Hungary, 1956				
Soviet Union	+20 +2(+22)	–5 –50 (–33)	+20 –1 (–14)	–3+70(+53)
Hungary	+30 +5(+35)	–10 –5(+20)	+1 –20 (+1)	–70 +3 (–66)
Lebanon, 1958				
Chamoun, US	+10 +1(+11)	–1 –20 (–10)	+30 –1(+19)	–1 +3(+21)
Lebanon, UAR	+10 +1(+11)	–1 –5 (+5)	+1 –30 (–24)	–3 +1 (–26)
West Irian, 1961–62				
Indonesia	+30 +1(+31)	–5 –5(+21)	+1 –1(+21)	–1 +1(+21)
Netherlands	+10 +1(+11)	–5 –15 (–9)	+1 –1 (–9)	–1 +1 (–9)
Tibet, 1954				
China	+20 +1(+21)	–5 –40 (–24)	+18 –1 (–7)	–1+70(+62)
Tibet	+40 +5(+45)	–30 –5(+10)	+1 –18 (–7)	–70 +1 (–76)
Goa, 1961				
India	+20 +1(+21)	–5 –10 (+6)	+3 –1 (+8)	–1 +1 (+8)
Portugal	+12 +2(+14)	–3 –10 (+1)	+1 –3 (–1)	–1 +1 (–1)
Cuba, 1961–62				
Refugees, US	+20 +1(+21)	–3 –20 (–2)	+30 –20 (+8)	–20+50(+38)
Castro, Soviet Union	+40 +1(+41)	–5 –20(+16)	+20 –30 (+6)	–50+20 (–24)
Indian Frontier, 1962				
China	+20 +2(+22)	–5 –40 (–23)	+18 –3 (–8)	–1+15 (+6)
India	+40 +3(+43)	–15 –5(+23)	+3 –18 (+8)	–15 +1 (–6)
Cyprus, 1962–64				
Cyprus, Greece	+30 +1(+31)	–5 –30 (–4)	+3 –2 (–3)	–3 +3 (–3)
Turkish Cypriots, Turkey	+30 +1(+31)	–5 –30 (–4)	+2 –3 (–5)	–3 +3 (–5)
Dominican Republic, 1965				
Rebels	+10 +1(+11)	–3 –10 (–2)	+1 –30 (–31)	–10 +3 (–38)
Junta, US, OAS	+10 +1(+11)	–3 –20 (–12)	+30 –1(+17)	–3+10(+24)

C. CONFLICTS IN WHICH MILITARY HOSTILITIES ESCALATED

Gran Chaco, 1928–36				
Bolivia	+40 +1(+41)	–15 –30 (–4)	+1 –2 (–5)	–10 +5 (–10)
Paraguay	+40 +1(+41)	–10 –30 (+1)	+2 –1 (+2)	–5+10 (+7)
Manchuria, 1931–33				
Japan	+30 +3(+33)	–10 –30 (–7)	+6 –5 (–6)	–2+10 (+2)
China	+30 +5(+35)	–20 –10 (+5)	+5 –6 (+4)	–10 +2 (–4)
Ethiopia, 1935–38				
Italy	+40 +2(+42)	–20 –50 (–28)	+6 –5 (–27)	–5+40 (+8)
Ethiopia	+60 +3(+63)	–30 –5(+28)	+5 –6(+27)	–40 +5 (–8)
Spain, 1936–39				
Franco, Mussolini, Hitler	+50 +3(+53)	–10 –20(+23)	+15 –10(+28)	–20+40(+48)
Republic, Soviet Union	+50 +3(+53)	–30 –20 (+3)	+10 –15 (–2)	–40+20 (–22)
Finland, 1939–40				
Soviet Union	+20 +2(+22)	–3 –60 (–41)	+10 –3 (–34)	–3+40 (+3)
Finland	+50 +5(+55)	–10 –10(+35)	+3 –10(+28)	–40 +3 (–9)
Greek Frontier, 1946–48				
Rebels, Yugoslavia,				
Bulgaria	+20 +1(+21)	–3 –40 (–22)	+15 –30 (–37)	–5+30 (–12)
Greece, US	+30 +2(+32)	–10 –5(+17)	+30 –15(+32)	–30 +5 (+7)

C. CONFLICTS IN WHICH MILITARY HOSTILITIES ESCALATED *(continued)*

$\begin{array}{l} dx/dt = \\ dy/dt = \end{array}$	$\begin{array}{l} + Nx + Fy \\ + Ny + Fx \end{array}$ Stage 1	$\begin{array}{l} - Cx - Wx \\ - Cy - Wy \end{array}$ Stage 2	$\begin{array}{l} + Px - Py \\ + Py - Px \end{array}$ Stage 3	$\begin{array}{l} - Vx + Vy \\ - Vy + Vx \end{array}$ Stage 4
Indochina, 1947–54				
France	+30 +1(+31)	−10 −20 (+1)	+3 −1 (+3)	−1+10(+12)
Vietnam	+60 +3(+63)	−15 −15(+33)	+1 −3(+31)	−10 +1(+22)
Korea, 1950–53				
N. Korea, China	+40 +5(+45)	−15 −40 (−10)	+25 −30 (−15)	−40+40 (−15)
S. Korea, US, UN	+40 +2(+42)	−15 −10(+17)	+30 −25(+22)	−40+40(+22)
Algeria, 1954–62				
Algeria	+60 +4(+64)	−20 −10(+34)	+4 −4(+34)	−15 +2(+21)
France	+40 +1(+41)	−20 −30 (−9)	+4 −4 (−9)	−2+15 (+4)
Congo, 1960–64				
Congo, UN	+20 +1(+21)	−10 −10 (+1)	+6 −4 (+3)	−10+20(+13)
Katanga	+20 +1(+21)	−10 −40 (−29)	+4 −6 (−31)	−20+10 (−41)
Vietnam, 1961–65				
N. Vietnam, Viet Cong	+60 +1(+61)	−20 −20(+21)	+30 −40(+11)	−70+60 (+1)
S. Vietnam, US	+50 +1(+51)	−20 −30 (+1)	+40 −30(+11)	−60+70(+21)
South Arabia, 1962				
South Arabia	+20 +1(+21)	−3 −20 (−2)	+2 −5 (−5)	−3 +1 (−7)
United Kingdom	+20 +1(+21)	−1 −5(+15)	+5 −2(+18)	−1 +3(+20)
Yemen, 1962				
Republic, UAR	+20 +1(+21)	−5 −10 (+6)	+3 −3 (+6)	−5 +5 (+6)
Monarchy, Saudi Arabia	+20 +1(+21)	−5 −15 (+1)	+3 −3 (+1)	−5 +5 (+1)
Malaysia, 1963				
Indonesia	+25 +1(+26)	−2 −20 (+4)	+5 −15 (−6)	−5 +3 (−8)
Malaysia, UK	+40 +1(+41)	−2 −10(+29)	+15 −5(+39)	−3 +5(+41)

D. WORLD WARS

	Stage 1	Stage 2	Stage 3	Stage 4
World War I, 1914–20				
Germany, Central Powers	+50+30(+80)	−40 −30(+10)	+20 −60 (−30)	−20+10 (−40)
Allies, US	+40+20(+60)	−50 −10 (0)	+60 −20(+40)	−10+20 (+50)
World War II, 1939–45				
Axis Powers	+70+20(+90)	−40 −30(+20)	+20 −70 (−30)	−50+10 (−70)
Allies, US	+70+20(+90)	−50 −10(+30)	+70 −20(+80)	−10+50(+120)

NOTES TO TABLE 2

In the above table, dx/dt and dy/dt refer respectively to the rate of escalation of hostilities (diplomatic, subversive, economic, or military) by x against y and by y against x at any moment of time.

The meaning of the other symbols, all of which refer to perceptions of x and y which may or may not correspond to objective facts, are explained in the notes to Table 1 above. The figures in parentheses at the end of each stage of the conflict situation, in Table 2, are cumulative. If they are positive (+) they indicate the degree of willingness of the party to escalate hostilities at that stage, and if negative, the degree of willingness to end hostilities. If the figures for both parties are positive,

escalation is probable, especially if one or both figures are of large magnitude. If both are negative, a cease-fire is probable.

In the Aaland Islands conflict of 1921, escalation after the first stage was very improbable; in the two world wars, on the other hand, escalation was probable in the first and second stages (though in World War I the Allies, because of heavy losses, seemed more willing than the Germans to end the war in stage two—a willingness perhaps suggested by Wilson's effort to initiate negotiations in December 1916). After American intervention in stage three of both wars (April 1917 and December 1941), the Allies were progressively more willing to escalate and the Germans more willing to negotiate.

AN ANALYTICAL STUDY OF THE BALANCE OF POWER THEORIES*

DINA A. ZINNES†

1. Introduction

Two very different studies of recent origin suggest and make possible a reappraisal of one of the oldest concepts in the literature of international relations: the balance of power. On the one hand, Claude's (1962) excellent analysis of the various dimensions along which the balance of power concept has been used allows us to disregard those discussions that have been principally polemical, and to concentrate instead on those which might explain certain international phenomena. On the other hand, Singer and Small (1967) have recently proposed what appears to be a new interpretation of the balance of power concept and, further, have collected data and performed a series of analyses that point in the direction of testing hypotheses concerning the functions of a balance of power. These two studies suggest that the time is appropriate to begin enumerating the various balance of power hypotheses and devote some concentrated attention, along the lines initiated by Singer and Small, to techniques and designs that will test these propositions. These are the joint purposes of the present paper.

2. The Variety of Uses of the Balance of Power Concept

Claude indicates that there are at least four quite different ways one might employ the concept 'balance of power'. It has been used in a prescriptive sense to indicate the type of policy a state is pursuing or ought

* Reprinted by permission of the author and publisher from *Journal of Peace Research*, 1967, *4*: 270–288.

† The author particularly wishes to thank J. David Singer, Rudolph Rummel, Dean Pruitt, Harold Guetzkow, Charles Hermann and Harold Sprout for their many useful comments and suggestions on an earlier draft of this paper, and Klaus Knorr and the Center for International Studies at Princeton for providing the facilities which made possible the writing of this article.

to pursue; as a symbol of what is either considered good or bad in international relations; and as a label describing a specific historical period, most notably the 18th and 19th centuries. More recently, Kaplan's (1957) analysis has generalized the label usage by providing abstract characteristics of what can now be called balance of power systems.

These are the three dimensions along which we will *not* venture. If I understand Claude correctly it is the fourth sense in which I wish to explore the balance of power concept, what Claude calls the usage of the balance of power to denote a situation: 'to indicate the character of a situation in which the power relationship between states or groups of states is one of rough or precise equality . . . Balance of power refers to a situation in which power is literally "balanced" by equivalent power'. (Claude 1960, pg. 13). Since it refers to a specific distribution of power Claude feels that this usage of the term is 'purely descriptive.' For our purposes, however, the use of the balance of power to denote a situation becomes more than just a description, it is a definition of the independent variable in hypotheses about the relations among nations.

3. The Dependent Variable: Peace or Status Quo?

What then are the balance of power hypotheses? Following the direction initiated by Haas (1953) some years ago and updating his extensive bibliography on the balance of power, I have isolated what appear to be seven reasonably distinct hypotheses which predict certain international consequences (the dependent variable) as a function of the independent variable, a balance of power. Since there is considerably greater agreement on the definition of the dependent variable it provides an obvious point of departure.

The consequences of a balance of power world appear to be principally two. Some writers, though probably a minority, claim that a true balance of power leads to international peace. While it is not the only avenue to peace, they feel that it is one workable solution to violent international conflict. The majority of writers, however, contend that the maintenance of peace is a possible but not necessary by-product of a balance of power. These writers argue that the critical consequence of a balance of power is that it holds all states in check; it does not allow any state to become overwhelmingly strong and therefore in a position to take over the territory of another state. Consequently, a balance of power preserves the status quo of the system and guarantees the independnece of every state, no matter how small. This may or may not involve war.

Thus we have two possible definitions of the dependent variable: (1) the balance of power preserves peace and/or (2) the status quo of the system. This discrepancy between the definitions of the dependent variable is troublesome but can be bypassed. We will assume that there are two sets of theories, one for each definition of the dependent variable.

4. The Independent Variable: Six Definitions of a 'Balance of Power'

The major difference in the balance of power theories, however, lies not in the definition of the dependent variable but in the definition of the independent variable, the concept 'balance of power.' This is the source of the seven different theories—one for each definition of the balance of power. Six of the seven definitions have been abstracted from the numerous balance of power discussions and as such share certain characteristics. We will therefore present them first and as a unit. The seventh definition, derived from the recent Singer-Small article, can then be compared with the six perhaps more traditional definitions.

Most discussions of the balance of power do not explicitly enumerate the necessary and sufficient conditions for the existence of a balance of power world. They provide instead a description of the key characteristic of a balance of power world, i.e. that characteristic without which a system would not qualify as a 'balance of power.' It is therefore possible to construct all those worlds (i.e. systems) which contain this central or key characteristic. In this sense, then, the first six definitions do not come directly from the literature. Rather, they represent plausible interpretations of balance of power worlds based on the discussions concerning the essential ingredient of a balance of power system.

What is this defining characteristic of a balance of power world and to what extent do writers agree on a single characteristic? Listed below, in as nearly a parallel fashion as possible, are a series of quotes in which this key characteristic is described. This survey covers several hundred years of writings on the balance of power and should highlight any similarity of thought among the writers. To provide parallelism, each quote is structured using the following format:

A balance of power is

1. '. . . an equal distribution of Power among the Princes of Europe as makes it impractical for the one to disturb the Repose of the other . . .' (Anonymous, 1741)
2. 'The doctrine of counterpoise among nations, in order to make the declaration of war, by any one, less alluring . . .' (Leckie, 1817)
3. '. . . action by a state to keep its neighbor from becoming too strong . . . because the aggrandizement of one nation beyond a certain limit changes the general system . . . (and) may mean the ruin and subjection of all the other neighbors . . . attention to the maintenance of a kind of equality and equilibrium between neighboring states . . .' (Fenelon, 1835)
4. '. . . an arrangement of affairs so that no State shall be in a position to have absolute mastery and dominate the others . . .' (Vattel, 1916)
5. '. . . an equilibrium . . . between the members of the family of nations . . . to prevent any member of the family . . . from becoming omnipotent . . .' (Oppenheim, 1920)
6. '. . . (in the simple case involving only two units) . . . two states or aggregations of power equally balanced . . . (and in the more complex case of) five Great Powers, acting independently . . . there was to be balance between the individual States . . . when combined . . . and the

unruly member against whom they united . . .
(Here) there was . . . no need of strict equality
and no necessary disturbance if one State grew
stronger than another so long as the growth was
not so great as to threaten the united strength
of the other four . . .' (Pollard, 1923)

7. '. . . such a "just equilibrium" in power
among the members of the family of nations as
will prevent any one of them from becoming
sufficiently strong to enforce its will upon
others . . .' (Fay, 1937)

8. '. . . "equilibrium" of the type represented by
a pair of scales. When the scales are equal, balance results . . . the balance of power assumes
that through shifting alliances and countervailing pressures no one power or combination of
powers will be allowed to grow so strong as to
threaten the security of the rest.' (Palmer and
Perkins, 1953)

9. '. . . the system of maintaining an equilibrium
among the powers . . .' (Herz, 1959)

10. '. . . the quest for safety expressed . . .
chiefly in a search for allies. The safety of all
was assured only if no one nation or group of
nations was permitted to achieve a preponderance of power—if, in other words, a rough balance was achieved.' (Stoessinger, 1961)

11. '. . . a maneuvering among the three or
several powers with one main objective in mind,
to prevent any one of them from dominating
the others . . .' (Kulski, 1964)

If we ignore differences in expression particularly evident from one historical period
to another, this list of 'definitions' illustrates, perhaps surprisingly, almost complete
agreement on the defining characteristic
of a balance of power world. These writers
agree that a 'balance of power' involves
a particular distribution of power among
the states of the system such that no
single state and no existing alliance has an
'overwhelming' or 'preponderant' amount
of power. As Pollard indicates, and others
imply, when there are only two states or
alliances of states in the system the basic requirement (no preponderance) can only be
met if there is an equality of power between
the two. But as you move away from this
simplest case, a variety of distributions of
power are permissable. In effect, any distribution is permissable as long as the power
of each unit—state or alliance of states—in
the system is less than the combined power
of all the remaining units.

Clearly, the defining characteristic of a
balance of power world, according to all
these writers, rests on two critical variables:
(1) the distribution of power among the
states of the system and (2) the alliance
configuration. If we assume that the power
of an alliance is a linear function of the
powers of the individual members (e.g. the
power of an alliance composed of A and
B = the power of A + the power of B), it is
possible to construct the following six balance of power systems based on a system of
five states which meet the requirement set
forth by the above writers, viz. that there
be no all-powerful, omnipotent unit in the
system.

A balance of power is a world in which:

(1) There are no alliances and all states
    have equal power. ($A = B = C = D = E$).
(2) All states belong to one of two alliances
    and the power of the two alliances is
    equal. ($A + B = C + D + E$).
(3) There are two alliances equal in power
    and one non-aligned state. ($A + B =
    C + D; E$).
(4) There are two alliances and a third non-
    aligned state, such that the power of
    either alliance plus the non-aligned state
    is greater than the power of the other
    alliance. ($A + B \neq C + D, E; A + B +
    E > C + D$ and $A + B < C + D + E$).
(5) There are no alliances, and the power
    of each state is less than the summed
    total power of all the remaining states.
    ($\sum_{i \neq j} X_i > X_j$ for $j = 1, \ldots, N$, where $N =$
    total number of nation states in the
    world).
(6) There is one state or alliance which is
    more powerful than any other unit in
    the system but such that condition (5)
    above is still met, ($\sum_{i \neq j} X_i > X_j$ for $j = 1,
    \ldots, N$, where $N =$ total number of states
    in the world and $A > B > C > D > E$).

This set of six definitions clearly does
not exhaust the possible permutations and
combinations that one might generate using the two variables and meeting the basic
requirement. These definitions are however, the more interesting ones and the ones
encountered most frequently in the balance

of power literature. The first two definitions are immediately derivable from the quotes given earlier. The third and fourth represent two plausible interpretations of those balance of power discussions that point to Britain's performance in the 18th and 19th centuries as a 'balancer.' The fifth definition most clearly resembles the notion of a collective security as attempted in the concert of Europe, the League, and United Nations; it is also, as discussed earlier, easily derivable from the quotes given above. The last definition has been included because of the number of discussions of the balance of power in which the writer indicates that a balance of power really means, on the order of a check account balance, a positive or a balance in favor of a particular state.

While the above six are different types of balances of power, note that they all meet the basic requirement of a balance of power world. This is perhaps where some of the confusion in the balance of power literature lies. One writer describes a balance of power via definition (1), another via definition (4), and there appears to be a lack of agreement on the use of the term. As can now be seen, the balance of power definitions have a common denominator, but they can be expressed in a variety of forms.

The differences and similarities between the six definitions can be graphically shown by examining a hypothetical world composed of five nations. If we construct all possible alliance configurations (designated by ABC/DE where the slash indicates an alliance between those nations on either side) and power distributions (i.e. rank ordering) for this world, we can demonstrate which alliance configuration and power distribution combination each definition chooses as a 'balance of power' world. Figure 1 is such a matrix. This matrix has been entitled a 'general' as opposed to a 'specific' matrix because each representation of an alliance configuration or a power distribution refers to a *pattern* and not to a *specific* alliance configuration or a *specific* power distribution. For example, the following alliance configurations and power distributions are here equal:

$$AB/C/D/E = AC/B/D/E = AD/B/C/E =$$
$$AD/B/C/E = BC/A/D/E \text{ etc.}$$
$$A>B>C>D>E = B>A>C>D>E =$$
$$C>A>B>D>E = D>A>B>C>E \text{ etc.}$$

In other words, the labels of the nations are unimportant. The relevant factors are the number of alliances of various sizes and the placing and number of power equalities and inequalities.[1]

Definitions (1) and (6), which are only a function of the distribution of power, pose no problems and are easily located in the matrix. Definition (1) is clearly more restrictive than definition (6); the latter definition, which only requires that there be one all powerful nation, allows for eight times as many systems (where each matrix cell is now considered to be a system).

Definitions (2), (3), (4), and (5) are not as easily located in the matrix. Even assuming, as noted earlier, that there is a linear relationship between the power of individual nations and the composite power of an alliance of those nations, without knowledge of the specific power of each nation we cannot, for these definitions, determine exactly whether a system is balanced. Does the following power distribution and alliance configuration represent a balance of power system using definition (2) (where the power of the two alliances must be equal): $A>B>C>D>E$, and AC/BDE? This can only be answered by knowing the actual amount of power possessed by each of the nations, or, what here amounts to the same thing, knowing the magnitude of the difference in power between the nations.

Thus, definitions (2), (3), (4), and (5) sometimes identify three, but more fre-

[1] A 'specific' matrix can easily be constructed by considering all permutations for each alliance configuration and each power distribution. This would increase the matrix by a factor of $(5!)^2 = 14,400$, and make it completely unwieldly. Note also that we have included all possible overlapping alliance configurations. It should be mentioned that no general formula exists for determining the number of alliance configurations for nations when one ignores labels and allows for overlapping. A solution, for example, does exist for finding the number of r-termed splittings of a given integer M. But in our case we are also interested in determining the number of ways in which m can be split.

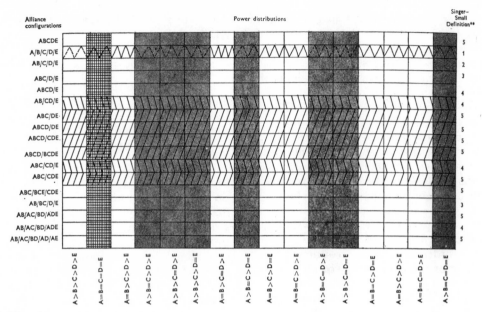

Definition: *

A balance of power is a world in which:

(1) There are no alliances and all states have equal power. ▦

(2) All states belong to one of two alliances and the power of the two alliances is equal. ▨

(3) There are two alliances equal in power and one non-aligned state. ⟋⟍

(4) There are two alliances and a third non-aligned state, such that the power of either alliance plus the non-aligned state is greater than the power of the other alliance. ⟋⟍

(5) There are no alliances, and the power of each state is less than the summed total power of all the remaining states. ⋀⋁   ⋀⋁

(6) There is one state or alliance which is more powerful than any other unit in the system but such that condition (5) above is still met. ▬

  * These definitions follow those given in the text.

  ** Numbering indicates the rank ordering of the systems from '1'—the most perfect balance of power system—to '5' the poorest representation of a balance of power system, under the Singer-Small definition.

quently only two, sets of systems. First, by a process of elimination, all four definitions identify those systems (i.e. matrix cells) that could *not* qualify as balance of power systems regardless of the specific power of each nation (within the restriction imposed by the particular power distribution under consideration).[2] Second, all four definitions permit the designation of those systems that *could be* but are not necessarily balance of power systems.[3] Only definition (5) designates the third set of systems, namely those which would be balance of power systems regardless of how one assigned power to the nations within the given power distribution restriction.

Since definition (5) is the easiest to locate in the matrix, the analysis can best begin with it. The requirement that there be no alliances immediately indicates that balance of power systems under this definition must fall somewhere in the second row of the matrix. Hence, by a process of elimination the first set of systems—those which could not qualify under any circumstances

[2] For example, using definition (2) regardless of the specific power of each nation the power configuration of $A = B = C = D = E$ would not be acceptable; whether the nations each had ten units of power, twenty, or thirty would be irrelevant since it is not possible to divide these nations into two equal alliances.

[3] The example given earlier illustrates this point: $A > B > C > D > E$ and AC/BDE could be a balance of power system for definition (2) if A's power is not that much greater than B's. In other words, according to definition (2) AC must equal BDE, and this is not ruled out by the power distribution of $A > B > C > D > E$.

—are pinpointed as all remaining cells in the matrix. The third set of systems designated by this definition—those systems which would be balance of power systems regardless of specific power differences—are all those systems (in the second row) in which the first, or most powerful, position is tied. Whenever there are two or more nations having equal superior power (and no alliances) a balance of power system results. This is shown in the matrix. The second set of systems—those which could be balance of power systems given specific power differences—consists of the eight remaining cells in the no-alliance row. These cells, where there exists one nation more powerful than each of the others, could be balance of power systems if the difference between the most powerful nation and the other nations is not too great, in particular, not greater than the sum of the remaining nations.

Definitions (2), (3), and (4) designate only the first two types of systems: by implication, those that are definitely not balance of power systems and those that could be balance of power systems. Recall that we are concerned here only with the *patterns* of alliance and power configuration and not with the specifics of who belongs to what alliance. Note also that the three definitions depend heavily on the *number* of nations in the system: specifically, whether the number of nations in the system is odd or even.

Definition (2)—there exist two and only two alliances equal in power—immediately chooses rows 7, 8, 9, 10, and 12. The remaining rows of the matrix therefore belong to the first class of systems: those which could under no circumstances qualify as balance of power systems. With three exceptions, however, it is not possible further to delineate balance of power matrix cells. For each matrix cell in rows 7, 8, 9, 10, and 12, with three exceptions, there exists at least one (and frequently more) *specific* alliance configuration and one *specific* power distribution which could meet definition (2) criteria. These cells therefore belong to the second class of systems—those that could be but are not always balance of power systems—and are shown in Fig. 1.

The exceptions concern the power distribution pattern where all the nations are equal. Here the three alliance configuration patterns ABC/DE, ABCD/CDE are not acceptable under definition(2) and therefore belong to the first class of systems indicated above.

Since definitions (3) and (4) differ only in the magnitude of the discrepancy between the power of the two alliances and the non-aligned nation, it is not surprising to find that these definitions coincide in the general (though obviously not in the specific) matrix. They both choose rows 6 and 11. Once again, for reasons just discussed we cannot delineate beyond this.

The matrix comparisons of the six definitions, then, show where the differences and congruencies occur. Note that definitions (1) and (6) do not overlap nor do definitions (2), (3), (4), and (5), but that the two sets of definitions do overlap. Definitions (1) and (6) share at least one common matrix cell with definitions (2), (3), (4), (5)—if we consider the matrix cells which could be but are not necessarily balance of power systems by definition (5). Hence there are a number of systems which meet the criteria of two definitions. The matrix also demonstrates what systems are not considered balance of power systems under any traditional definition.

5. The Independent Variable: The Seventh Definition of a Balance of Power

Singer's and Small's (1967) definition of a balance of power world provides an interesting contrast to the six described above. As was the case with the first six definitions, Singer and Small do not explicitly enumerate the defining characteristics of a balance of power system. However, on the basis of their discussion these features can be abstracted. The following excerpt should provide the rationale for the derived definition given below:

Without going into the quagmire of terminological and normative dispute which has characterized much of the theoretical literature on the balance of power, we can nevertheless note that its defense or justification clearly rests on the assumption that the stability of the international system can be maintained without reliance on superordinate political institutions . . . Central to this notion is the understanding that the invisible or unseen hand will function only to the extent that all nations are free to deal with all others as their national interests dictate. Thus, it is assumed that every dyadic relationship will be a mixture of the co-operative and the conflictful, with political, economic, ideological, and other issues all producing different interest configurations for each possible pair of nations. The net effect, it is believed, is such a welter of cross-cutting ties and such a shifting of friendships and hostilities that no single set of interests can create a self-aggravating and self-reinforcing division of cleavage among the nations; A and B may well have competitive economic interests in the Middle East, but harmonious strategic interests in the Caribbean, while B and C's political interests may coincide in regard to West Africa and clash in an international organization setting. It follows from this sort of a model that anything which restrains or inhibits free or vigorous pursuit of the separate national interests will limit the efficiency of the stabilizing mechanism. And among those arrangements seen as most likely to so inhibit that pursuit are formal alliances. Nations in the same alliance are less free to compete with their allies in such spheres of incompatibility, and less free to co-operate with outsiders in areas of overlapping interests.

Thus, a perfect (or at least precondition for) balance of power system for these authors appears to be one in which every state in the system has equal positive and negative sentiments towards every other state in the system. Since alliances are defined as obstacles which impede this balance between positive and negative ties, the operational measure of a perfect balance of power system is one in which no state belongs to an alliance.

How does this definition compare with those discussed above? First, the Singer-Small definition is not dichotomous as are the above definitions. The traditional definitions only allow for balance of power and non-balance of power systems. Using the Singer-Small definition one can gradually move away from the perfect system by increasing the number of nations having alliance commitments. Second, unlike the first six, the Singer-Small definition is not a function of power; it is solely a function of alliances. Third, there is a difference be-

tween the alliance configuration variable found in the first six definitions and the alliance variable in the Singer-Small definition. The initial six definitions are a function of the *number of alliances* in the system (two or none). The Singer-Small definition counts the *number of nations* having at least one alliance commitment. Only at the extreme end are the two formulations equivalent: if there are no alliances then there can be no nations having an alliance commitment, and vice-versa. Otherwise, there is no obvious relationship between the alliance configuration variable of the first six definitions and the number of alliances of this definition. Although the number of alliances in the system will always be less than the number of nations in the system having alliances, since a given nation may belong to more than one alliance, there is no simple way to determine the relationship between the number of alliances in the system and the number of nations *having at least* one alliance commitment.

Let us now attempt to place the Singer-Small definition in the matrix of Fig. 1. The perfect Singer-Small balance of power system clearly falls in the second row of the matrix. But since this definition allows for degrees of 'balance-of-powerness,' we have indicated, along the alliance column margin, the rank ordering of the systems from the 'best' (perfect balance of power) to the 'worst' balance of power system, using the Singer-Small operational definition (number of nations having at least one commitment). The large number of ties is due to the fact that the Singer-Small formulation does not separate overlapping alliance membership systems for non-overlapping ones.

How does the Singer-Small definition compare with the traditional definitions of the basis of the matrix? It is interesting that the perfect balance of power system for Singer and Small coincides with definition (5) in the matrix. But this overlap is due to the reason described earlier: if there are no alliance commitments then there can be no alliances. Thus, while the two definitions agree on this one point they are basically of a different character; one counts numbers of alliances and the other counts the number of nations having at least one alliance commitment.

The difference between the Singer-Small formulation and the traditional balance of power definitions is emphasized by the fact that systems which, according to Singer and Small, depart farthest from a balance of power frequently qualify under the traditional definitions. Furthermore, the second and third 'best' systems under the Singer-Small definition do not overlap any of the four definitions which consider alliance configuration. These second and third choices do overlap definitions (7) and (10), but this is because these definitions are solely a function of power, whereas the Singer-Small definition is solely a function of alliances. If the Singer-Small definition does not restrict systems on the basis of power distributions then it can easily permit those power distributions designated by definitions (7) and (10).

We conclude then that the Singer-Small definition is of a considerably different character than any of the traditional definitions. Systems which qualify under traditional definitions are considered by Singer-Small standards to be poor representations

results do not permit us to draw any conclusions concerning the validity of their balance of power model. However, their design does suggest modifications which would allow us to test directly their interpretation of the balance of power. Since they have begun the difficult task of testing the balance of power theories, it seems wise to pursue their initial attempts.

There are three basic problems inherent in the Singer and Small study: the operationalization of the independent and dependent variables and the assumptions involved in testing the relationship between the variables. We will analyze the study in this sequence. From our earlier discussion we recall that for Singer and Small a perfect balance of power world is one in which every state has equivalent positive and negative ties with every other state in the system. The crosspressures on each state, under this condition, are at a maximum; hence, they argue, the superimposition of friendly and hostile relations reduces the prospects for war. Alliances are then defined as obstacles which prevent the successful operation of crosspressures. The theory can be outlined as follows:

free, uncommitted nations⟶ cross-pressures⟶ peace.
(i.e. non-aligned nations)

of a balance of power, while the better Singer-Small representations are not considered balance of power systems by the traditional writers.

6. Testing a Balance of Power Theory

Combining the two dependent variables with each of the possible definitions of a balance of power we arrive at a potential set of fourteen hypotheses. Clearly the next step is to subject at least some of these propositions to empirical tests. Singer and Small (1967) have begun the pioneering work in this area. They derive an hypothesis from their balance of power model and test it for the 130 year period between 1815 and 1945.[4] Undoubtedly this is the first attempt empirically to verify any of the balance of power propositions. Unfortunately, due to difficulties in the operationalization of the variables and the execution of the analyses, the

On the basis of the theory the writers derive their central hypothesis:

'The greater the number of alliance commitments in the system, the more war the system will experience . . . '

A comparison of the hypothesis with the original theory shows that what was originally a one-way implication has now become an equivalence: the theory maintains that free and uncommitted nations implies cross-pressures, but the hypothesis indicates that the non-existence of alliances is *equivalent* to the existence of cross-pressures.

The validity of an equation between free, uncommitted nations and the existence of cross-pressures in the system depends heavily on the index used to measure the free-

---

[4] Half of the data on which this study is based can be found in Singer, J. David & Small, Melvin, 'Formal Alliances, 1815–1939,' *Journal of Peace Research*, 1966, Vol, I, pp. 1–32.

dom of the nations. The 'interaction-opportunity' ratio, designed to measure inversely the amount of freedom or 'uncommittedness' of nations in the system, is formed by counting the number of nations having *at least* one alliance, and dividing this number by the total number of nations in the system. The ratio necessarily varies between zero and one, where zero indicates the existence of no commitments and hence the maximum operation of crosspressures, and one indicates that all nations are in some alliance and crosspressures are non-existent. To what extent is the interaction-opportunity ratio an inverse measure of the amount of crosspressures existing in the system?

Suppose the world contained only five nations, A, B, C, D, and E, and consider the following possible alliance configurations:

(1) ABC/DE
(2) ABC/BCD/CDE/DEA
(3) AB/AC/AD/AE
(4) ABCDE

Using the interaction-opportunity ratio, the amount of crosspressures existing in each of the four international systems is the same, namely $5/5 = 1$. Accordingly, for each of these systems crosspressures are non-existent. In the first system this result is intuitively appealing. With all nations committed to one of two sides there is little likelihood that all pairs of nations have equal positive and negative ties. But what happens in systems two, three, and four? Could not one argue that in system two, A's, B's, and E's membership in two alliances and C's and D's membership in three alliances *produces* crosspressures? Are not some of these alliances *contributing* rather than diminishing crosspressures? In other words, the interaction-opportunity ratio is a valid measure of crosspressures if it can be assumed that nations belong to one and only one alliance. When multiple memberships occur, an index is required which not only considers the decrease in crosspressures as a consequence of committed nations but also accounts for the increase in crosspressures as the result of overlapping alliance membership.[5] Thus,

[5] The independent variable contains a second.

the principal difficulty with the interaction-opportunity ratio as an operational measure of the independent variable is that it assumes nations belong to only one alliance.

To what extent is the one-alliance-per-nation assumption met in the Singer-Small data? The number of alliance memberships held by each nation per year was determined and an 'overlap' index constructed by summing the number of multiple memberships held by each nation. For example, in 1833 Austria, Prussia, and

though less serious, difficulty. The independent variable of the theory is not necessarily equivalent to the one stated in the derived hypothesis. The number of free, uncommitted nations is not always equivalent to the number of alliance commitments; the same nation may have more than one commitment. This becomes particularly obvious in the use of the interaction-opportunity ratio as a measure of the independent variable. Since the ratio ignores multiple memberships it does not count the 'number of *alliance commitments*' but the number of *nations* which have *any alliance commitment*. If no multiple memberships occur then there is a perfect correlation between the two variables, and they can be used interchangeably.

Overlapping alliance memberships, however, destroy this correlation, as can be seen with reference to the above four hypothetical systems. The interaction-opportunity ratio for all four systems is one; yet, regardless of how the variable 'alliance commitment' is operationalized, the four systems yield different values. If we assume every nation in an alliance has a commitment to all other nations in that alliance and we count the number of commitments from the point of view of each nation—i.e. if we count all possible pairs of nations within each alliance—then the number of alliance commitments for the four systems would be: (1) 8, (2) 24, (3) 8, (4) 12. If we exclude repetitions across alliances, i.e. if we count BC once in system two even though it appears twice, then the results reduce to: (1) 8, (2) 21, (3) 8, (4) 12. This can be further reduced if we do not compute the number of commitments from the viewpoint of each nation, i.e. if we count only the number of *different* alliance commitments: (1) 4, (2) 9, (3) 4, (4) 10. In any case, however computed, when nations belong to more than one alliance a one-to-one correspondence does *not* exist between the number of free nations in the system (or the percentage thereof, as given by the ratio) and the number of alliance commitments.

This difference between the theory and the hypothesis is not, however, particularly serious. The main concern is to test the theory, and the interaction-opportunity ratio is a direct measure of the number of free, uncommitted nations in the system described in the theory. While the stated hypothesis is not directly derived from the theory, the hypothesis actually being tested can be deduced from the theory.

Russia each belonged to two alliances. The amount of overlap for that year would be $1 + 1 + 1 = 3$. If a nation belongs to four alliances in the same year it contributes three to the 'overlap' index. In general, the overlap index for a given year can be computed from the formula:

$$\text{Overlap} = \sum_{i=1}^{m} (n_i - 1)$$

where n = the number of alliances in which nation i holds membership, and m = the number of nations in the system belonging to any alliance.[6] Note that the index is only concerned with the set of nations having some alliance membership.[7]

The results of the analysis indicate that the one-alliance-per-nation assumption is only valid for 22 of the 130 years: from 1824 to 1832, 1849, 1860 to 1862, 1865, 1871 to 1876, 1879 to 1880. Only for these years is the interaction-opportunity ratio an adequate measure of the amount of crosspressures existing in the system.

There are, however, indications in the text that the authors were aware of the overlap problem, though perhaps from a different viewpoint.[8] In an attempt to measure structural characteristics of the alliance system they construct an additional index: a 'bipolarity' index. This is calculated for each year roughly as follows:

1. Determine all alliance memberships.
2. Determine the targets of these alliances.
3. Eliminate these two sets of nations (allied and targets) and count the number of nations remaining in the system: (the free, non-aligned nations).
4. The number of free nations is squared, since each nation can ally with all other free nations, and this result is added to the product of the number of free nations times the size of the largest alliance or the sum of the targets, whichever is bigger. The resulting figure is divided by the number of pairs theoretically possible as determined by $\dfrac{n\,(n-1)}{2}$ where n = the number of nations in the system.[9] The bipolarity indices can therefore be described by the two ratios:

$$\frac{(\text{number of free nations})^2 + (\text{number of free nations} \times \text{number of nations in largest alliance})}{\text{number of theoretically possible alliance pairs}}$$

or

$$\frac{(\text{number of free nations})^2 + (\text{number of free nations} \times \text{number of target nations})}{\text{number of theoretically possible alliance pairs}}$$

[6] Numerous other indices could be constructed. Two others considered were (1) count the number of nations belonging to more than one alliance—this was felt to be too conservative, it would mean that system three (above) would have only slightly more crosspressures than system one; (2) count the number of times in a given year all alliances overlapped —this produces a somewhat inflated figure: given alliances ABC, ADE, AFG this index would compare the first and second alliance, the first and third alliance and then the second and third alliance producing an overlap of three. The overlap index described in the text above seemed to be a reasonable compromise between these two extremes.

[7] A table giving the results of these tabulations can be obtained upon request. It indicates the number of alliances each nation belonged to in each year. The lower portion of the table gives the total number of nations having some alliance commitment, the number of nations in the system, and the amount of overlap for each year as measured by the index described above.

[8] For example: '. . . if the alliance configurations show less and less partial overlap, and they instead increasingly reinforce a tendency toward a very few (but large sized) coalitions, the system's loss of interaction opportunities becomes even more severe . . .'; and again: '. . . there should be a difference between the effects of a structure which reflects a crazy-quilt pattern of all sorts of overlapping alliance memberships and one in which only a very few easily distinguishable coalitions emerge.'

[9] There appears to be an error in the Singer-Small test. As they describe the index, the theoretical number of pairs would fall in the numerator: 'Once the number of feasible remaining defensive alliance links was ascertained, that number was divided *into* the original number that would have been possible in the absence of any such alliances, to give the percent of major power defensive alliance ties exhausted,' (italics are mine). Presumably they mean that the remaining number of possible alliance links was divided *by* the number of theoretical pairs. Otherwise the resulting index would not give the '*percent* . . . of alliance ties exhausted.'

These ratios again vary between zero—indicating complete bipolar cleavage in the system—and one—indicating the total absence of such cleavage.

The first significant feature of the two ratios is the important role played by the number of free nations in the system. One extreme, when there are no alliances and bipolarity is non-existent, is intuitively appealing. The other extreme, however, produces difficulties. If there are no free nations in the system then bipolarity, or cleavage, according to the index, is maximum. But compare the following two systems of five nations:

(1) ABC DE, where the target of one alliance is the other; and
(2) ABC, BCD, CDE, where the targets in order are D, E, and A.

Both systems, according to the bipolarity index, are maximally bipolar. Yet only the first would appear to be truly 'bipolar' as that term is commonly used. The difficulty does not occur only at the extreme. Compare the following three systems, each containing seven nations:

(3) ABC DEF G, where the target of one alliance is the other, and
(4) ABC BCD EF G, where the targets of the alliances in order are D, E, and A, and
(5) ABC BCD CDE DEF G, where the targets of the alliance in order are D, E, F, A.

The bipolarity index for all three systems is 3/21. Again, only the first would appear to be truly bipolar.

The bipolarity index, then, contains the same difficulty encountered in the interaction-opportunity index: systems having no overlapping membership are indistinguishable from systems in which considerable criss-crossing of alliance membership exists. Since this new index is specifically designed to measure the extent to which a system contains cleavages, the defect here would appear to be particularly serious.[10]

[10] The bipolarity index contains two additional problems. As pointed out to this author in correspondence with Dean Pruitt, the construction of the index assumes that already allied nations can-

Having examined the operational measure of the independent variable, we turn now to a consideration of the dependent variable. To restate the original hypothesis: 'The greater the number of alliance commitments in the system the *more war* the system will experience . . . ,' (italics mine). What is meant by 'more war?' The crosspressures balance of power theory would seem to dictate that 'more war' be defined as the probability that war breaks out. The fewer the alliance commitments, the greater the crosspressures in the system pulling each nation towards divergent goals, the less the probability that strong animosities will develop between nations, the less probable is war.[11]

But how does one measure the probability of war? Singer and Small propose three different operational measures for the dependent variable. Of the three, the one that would seem to be the best measure of the probability of war is the frequency or number of wars that began each year. This, however, is the index which the authors feel is the least instructive of the three, since it does not discriminate between large and small wars nor between long and short wars: 'Thus the correlation of alliance aggregation with mere war frequency would be of limited interest (if not downright

not form additional alliances. In other words, to discover how many alliances could still be concluded in the system after eliminating existing alliances, one only counts the number of possible alliances between free nations and others in the system. Alliances which cut across existing alliances are not considered; in system one above, for example A cannot ally with D or E.

The second difficulty with this index is that it does not measure a *bi*-polar cleavage in the system. As shown in the examples above (especially systems three and five), if two systems have the same number of free nations in the largest alliance (or set of targets) then the actual number of alliances in the system is irrelevant. System three above has two alliances and system five contains four alliances—yet the two systems have equal *bipolarity* indices.

[11] There are indications in the Singer-Small text that this was originally their meaning: '. . . our dependent variable: the incidence of war . . .'; 'Alliance Aggregation as a Predictor to War . . .'; 'as the system's interaction opportunities diminish wars will increase in frequency . . .'; and finally 'alliance aggregation *should* correlate with the onset of war . . .'

misleading) and further graduation is clearly necessary'. An examination of the war data, however, discloses a perhaps more serious defect with the use of this index: there are few instances in which more than one war breaks out in any given year. Necessarily, a correlation between this index and any measure of the independent variable will be, and in subsequent analyses is found to be, small. The low frequency of wars per year is partially alleviated by using three and five year periods. A count is made of the number of wars that began not in just the following year but in the following *three* and *five* years to obtain three different frequency measures (wars that broke out in one year, within three years, within five years). While this increases the frequency count somewhat, it adds a new problem for testing the hypothesis (to be discussed below).

It would seem that the difficulty here is that the dependent variable is actually dichotomous. Since wars can be of any size involving from two to all system nations, a simple count of the number of wars which began in each year would be inappropriate. If all nations were involved in a particular war, clearly only one war could begin that year. And, should the war last several years no wars could begin for as many years.

Two alternative measures might be suggested. The simplest expedient would be to treat war as a dichotomous variable: either wars began or did not begin in the system for any given year. A somewhat more complicated measure, but one which would discriminate between wars involving only two nations and wars involving all nations, would be to calculate—along the lines of the Singer-Small interaction-opportunity index—the number of dyads at war. The number of dyads at war divided by the number of possible dyads in the system could be interpreted as the probability of war for that year.

The other two measures used by Singer and Small were designed for the purposes of discriminating between wars of different size and severity. As they explain it:

Having identified those international wars which interest the student of international relations as he examines the effects of alliance patterns, the next point to note is that these wars differ markedly in their duration, magnitude, and intensity. Thus, the correlation of alliance aggregation with mere war frequency would be of limited interest (if not downright misleading) and further gradation is clearly necessary. This gradation is achieved in the first instance by use of the nations-months-of-war measure, so that the simple magnitude of each war is the sum of the months which all nations individually experienced as a participant in the war . . . In addition to nation-months as an index of the magnitude of war, at least one other factor seems to justify consideration. That fact we will call *severity* and it will be measured by the number of battle-connected deaths of military personnel sustained by all participants in any given war.

The purpose of these measures is presumably to provide probabilities of different types of war—wars of varying magnitudes and severity. Unfortunately, however, the use of these measures alters the hypothesis being tested. Compare the following two statements:

(1) Crosspressures lead to a lower probability of war,
(2) Crosspressures lead to smaller and less severe wars.

Only the first hypothesis can be deduced from the crosspressures balance of power theory. Yet the use of the magnitude and severity measures changes the first hypothesis into the second, and it is the second that is actually being tested. What is wanted is a technique which will hold constant the varying magnitudes and severity of war. Do alliance commitments and the probability of wars of a certain magnitude and severity correlate significantly?

We come now to an examination of the third aspect of the Singer-Small research design: testing the hypothesis. As the authors describe the analyses: 'the method to be employed is a trend analysis. After developing several different measures of alliance aggregation and several measures of the onset of war, we will examine the extent to which the two sets of variables rise and fall together, over time.' Correlations were computed using five variations of the operational measure for the dependent variable ('more war') and seven variations of the operational measure for the independent variable ('alliance aggregation'), namely:

The last technique—the use of three and five year lags—warrants special consideration. Here the measures of the two variables were summed and/or averaged, thus making the data non-independent. If we sum the nation-months for wars beginning in

Operational Measures of 'More War'	Operational Measures of 'Alliance Aggregation'
1. Number of months each nation participated in a given war.	1. Percentage of all nations in any alliance for a given year.
2. Number of months major nations participated in a given war (major is defined by a special list).	2. Percentage of all nations in a defensive alliance (a subset of all alliances) for a given year.
3. Total number of battle deaths for all nations involved in a given war.	3. Percentage of major nations in any alliance for a given year.
4. Total number of battle deaths for major nations involved in a given war.	4. Percentage of major nations in defensive alliances for a given year.
5. Number of wars in a given year.	5. Percentage of majors allied with minors.
	6. Bipolarity initial.
	7. Bipolarity alternate.

The measures for the dependent variable were always assigned to the year in which a war began.[12] The correlations were computed within three time periods, 1815–1945, 1815–1900, and 1900–1945, for the entire international system and for only part of that system, the central system (nations either located in Europe or deeply involved in relatively durable relationships with European nations) and using one, three, and five year lags.[13]

1815, 1816, and 1817 (or average over the three years for alliance aggregation), then sum over 1816, 1817, 1818, etc. the data become highly interdependent. As such, a Pearson product moment correlation (i.e. any significance test thereof) is inappropriate.[14] That this lack of independence is an important contributor to the results can be shown by a comparison of the one year lag condition with the three year lag condition for the severity and magnitude war measures.

[12] For example, if war broke out between two nations in 1827 and lasted for 18 months, the first measure would assign 2 nations × 18 months = 36 nation-months to the year 1827. The previous discussions analyzed only measures one, three and five for the dependent variable and measures one and six for the independent variable because the other measures produced consistently lower (and nonsignificant) correlations and did not appear to have any greater validity than the measures examined.

[13] A one year lag correlation was computed between the alliance aggregation measures and any of the 'more war' indicators for the following year. Thus, if war broke out in 1827, 1829, and 1834 the number of months all nations participated in each war would be calculated and assigned to these years; these measures would then be compared with the alliance aggregation measure for years 1826, 1828 and 1833 respectively. The three and five year lags were computed in a somewhat different fashion. A three year lag for the 'more war' variable involved *adding* the specific indicator over three year periods.

In other words, the number of nation-months for all wars beginning in a three year period are summed; for the above example, the number of nation-months for 1827, (1828 = 0), and 1829 are summed. Similarly, the five year lag means that the measures are summed over five years. The three and five year lags for the independent variable are computed slightly differently. Averages, rather than totals, are determined for the periods. The results reported in the body of the text are based on the three year lag for both variables; tables in their Appendix give results for all combinations of lags for both variables.

[14] A similar problem exists in the correlation reported between the various measures of the dependent variable and the various measures of the independent variable. A correlation, for example, between measures one and two for the dependent variable will necessarily be high since one measure is a subset of the other. A part-whole correlation is required here.

Table 1 shows that in all cases the three year lag condition is higher.[15]

A second difficulty in the conduct of the analyses was hinted at in the previous section. Since the magnitude and severity war measures alter the hypothesis being tested the correlation design should be appropriately amended. The revised hypothesis given above—crosspressures leads to smaller and less severe wars—should in fact more accurately read: the greater the crosspressures, *given that war has occurred,* the

of their theory? A number of suggestions were implied in the foregoing pages, and our purpose here will be to summarize these points.

With respect to the independent variable, two approaches can be suggested. First, since the interaction-opportunity index is appropriate for years in which no overlapping alliance membership occurs, a correlation could be computed using only the 22 years which meet the one-alliance-per-nation assumption. Second, during the

TABLE 1

A COMPARISON OF CORRELATIONS BETWEEN PERCENT OF ALLIANCE COMMITTED NATIONS
AND SEVERITY AND MAGNITUDE OF WAR FOR TWO LAGS

	Percentage of all nations in any alliance					
	Total system			Central system		
	1815–1945	1815–1900	1900–1945	1815–1945	1815–1900	1900–1945
Nation-months						
Three year lag	.30*	—.16	.53*	.33*	—.19	.45*
One year lag	.25*	.00	.37	.25*	—.09	.34
Battle deaths						
Three year lag	.34*	—.27	.56*	.35*	—.45*	.50*
One year lag	.25*	—.09	.37	.25*	—.18	.35

Taken from J. David Singer and Melvin Small, 'Alliance Aggregation and the Onset of War, 1815–1945,' in *Insights and Indicators in World Politics: Ten Quantitative Studies,* ed. J. David Singer (Glencoe, Ill.: Glencoe Free Press, in press).

* P $<$ .05, i.e. the null hypothesis can be rejected at the .05 level.

smaller and less severe the wars will be. A correlation should then be computed using only years in which wars began. Since there are 55 years during the total period in which no wars began, this difference could be significant. On purely intuitive grounds it would seem that this restriction would increase the correlations found since it will eliminate many years in which the dependent variable has a zero value, years which, by inspection, appear to have varying values for the independent measures.

7. A Retest of the Singer-Small Theory

What modifications could be made in the Singer-Small design to afford a closer test

[15] The authors seem to recognize this lack of independence in their data but their solution, which involves the Fischer exact test, does not remedy the difficulty. The solution would seem to lie in the elimination of the three and five year lags.

years in which overlapping occurs a multiple correlation could be computed using both the interaction-opportunity index and the overlap index as joint predictors of war. Since, as the interaction-opportunity index *increases,* the expectation is that the probabilities for war *increase;* whereas when overlapping *increases,* one would expect war probabilities to *decrease,* the interaction index must thus be modified. By simply reversing the interaction-opportunity index, i.e. by determining the percentage of nations having *no* commitments, both independent variables will predict in the same direction.

Two alternative measures for the dependent variable, probability of war, have already been described: (1) treat war as a dichotomous variable or (2) compute a 'probability of war' index by dividing the number of nation pairs at war by the number of possible pairs in the system. The use of the second index is straightforward, and the usual correlation can be computed against the alliance measures. If war is used as a dichotomous variable, a measure of association could be computed between it and a dichotomized or trichotomized interaction-opportunity index using simple chi-square formulae. Or, an appropriately modified correlation formula might be employed to compute correlations between the essentially continuous interaction index and the dichotomized war variable.

The combination of modified measures for the independent and dependent variables should provide results on the cross-pressures balance of power theory. While it is beyond the scope of this paper to carry out these various tests, the results of one small exploratory test might be mentioned. Fischer's Exact Test was applied to the data for the 22 years which met the one-alliance-per-nation assumption (i.e. years having no alliance overlap). The number of alliance commitments for those years were classified into two categories: low number of commitments and high number of commitments.[16] The cut-off point was determined by the mean number of commitments for those years (which was 8). War was treated as a dichotomous variable and of the 22 no-overlap years we determined how many years fell in each of the four categories:

TABLE 2

A Test of the Singer-Small Hypothesis

	war	no-war	marginal totals
low number of commitments	1	13	14
high number of commitments	4	4	8
marginal totals	5	17	22

Following the Singer-Small argument it was felt that low commitment years should

[16] Number of alliance commitments rather than percentage of commitments (over number of system nations) were used for ease of analysis. A separate test, however, was conducted using percentages and found to be almost identical.

coincide more frequently with no-war years, while high commitment years should tend to contain more war years. No lags were used in this calculation, since it was observed that alliances tended to endure for a number of years, and it seemed unnecessary to introduce lags to measure their effect on the outbreak of war (furthermore, an inspection of the data showed that there was little difference between one and no year lag conditions). The Fischer Exact Test is comparable to a chi-square analysis, except that exact probabilities are directly obtained. For the above analysis $p = .039$. In other words, we can reject the null hypothesis that the two variables are independent at the .039 significance level. Thus, for the no-overlap years the Singer-Small hypothesis can be accepted: *some relationship exists between the level of commitments in the system and the outbreak of war.*

A similar type of analysis was attempted for the overlap years, by holding the level of overlap constant. Separate tests were made for years in which there were few overlapping alliances and years in which there were many overlapping alliances. However, strictly speaking, this analysis is incorrect, since the overlap index and the alliance commitment index are not independent: if there are few alliance commitments there can only be a few overlaps, and if there are a large number of overlaps (particularly if the number of overlaps exceeds the number of nations in the system) there will probably be many commitments. Whether for this reason or others, the chi-square computed for these data were not significant.

8. Summary and Conclusion

There are, then, at least seven distinct balance of power theories. Six of these share a common concern, the seventh is of a considerably different character. Each of these should be subjected to empirical tests, and this is obviously the next stage in an analysis of the meaning and significance of the balance of power. An initial attempt in this direction has been made by Singer and Small. Taking their interpretation of the balance of power theory, they have derived and tested an hypothesis. We have examined this study and discovered that certain aspects of the research design mitigate against drawing any conclusions concerning the viability of their balance of power theory. However, these writers have presented us with some fascinating data and the first thrust towards testing any of the theories. Hopefully, the stimulus of their research and some of the suggestions made herein will bring forth a series of studies designed to evaluate the viability of the balance of power model.

Summary

This study examines the literature concerning the 'balance of power' concept, and abstracts from these discussions seven hypotheses which postulate the international consequences of a balance of power system. The dependent variable of these hypotheses is generally agreed to be either peace or the preservation of the system. Considerable variability, however, is found in the possible interpretations of the independent variable, a 'balance of power.' Seven different definitions of a balance of power are constructed from the literature and then compared. One of the hypotheses, proposed by Singer and Small, has been subjected to empirical tests. However, due to certain difficulties in their research design, the results of their study are not yet applicable to a further understanding of the validity of any of the balance of power theories. The present author examines some of the difficulties of this analysis and suggests where the problems lie and several alternative solutions, with the hope that this initial study will be further pursued to provide the needed tests of at least one of the balance of power theories.

REFERENCES

1. Anonymous, 'Europe's Catechism,' (London, 1741) pp. 11–12 quoted from Gulik, Edvard, *Europe's Classical Balance of Power*, (Ithaca: Cornell University Press), 1955, p. 2.
2. Claude, Inis L., Jr., *Power and International Relations* (New York: Random House, 1962).
3. Fay, Sidney B., 'Balance of Power,' *Encylopedia of the Social Sciences*, (1937), pp. 395–399.
4. Fenelon, *Oeuvres*, Vol. III (Paris 1835), p. 361.
5. Haas, E. B. 'The Balance of Power: Prescription, Concept or Propaganda?' *World Politics*, July 1953, Vol. 5, pp. 442–477.
6. Herz, John H., *International Politics in the Atomic Age* (New York: Columbia University Press), 1959, pp. 65–67.
7. Kaplan, Morton A., *System and Process in International Politics* (New York: John Wiley and Sons, Inc. 1957).
8. Kulski, W. W., *International Politics in a Revolutionary Age* (Lippincott, 1964), pp. 11–15.
9. Leckie, Gould F., *An Historical Research into the Notion of the Balance of Power in Europe* (London: Taylor and Hessey, Fleet Street, 1817), pp. 1–9.
10. Oppenheim, L., *International Law*, R. F. Roxburgh (ed.) (3d. ed.; London, 1920), Vol. I, sec. 51.
11. Organski, A. F. K., *World Politics* (New York: Alfred A. Knopf, 1958).
12. Palmer, Norman D. and Perkins, Howard C., *International Relations* (Boston: Houghton Mifflin Co., 1953), pp. 308–337.
13. Pollard, A. F., 'The Balance of Power,' *Journal of the British Institute of International Affairs* No. 2, Vol. II, March 1923, pp. 53–64.
14. Richardson, Lewis F., *Arms and Security* (Pittsburgh: Boxwood Press, 1960).
15. Singer, J. David & Small, Melvin, 'Formal Alliances, 1815–1939,' *Journal of Peace Research*, 1966, Vol. I, pp. 1–32.
16. Singer, J. David and Small, Melvin, 'Alliance Aggregation and the Onset of War,' in J. David Singer, ed., *Insights and Indicators in World Politics, International Yearbook of Political Behavior Research*, VI (New York: Free Press, 1966).
17. Stoessinger, John G., *The Might of Nations; World Politics in our Time* (New York: Random House, 1964), pp. 177–182.
18. Valtel, E. de, *The Law of Nations*, (Washington, 1916), Book III, chap. 3, sec. 47.

NATION STATE ESCALATION AND INTERNATIONAL INTEGRATION[*][†]

PAUL SMOKER

1. Introduction

In this paper we shall be dealing with international integration and nation state escalation. Escalation is defined here in a rather broad sense to include the phenomena of the run-away arms race.[1] It refers to an interactive situation where increases of tension become manifest through increasing national defense expenditures.[2] International integration here means transnational bonds that bring individuals in one country into direct cultural and social relations with individuals in another country. While international integration as defined here can be exhibited through national behavior, as in the case of joint governmental cultural agreements, this need not be the case. Integration can also take place through non-governmental activity, such as international scientific conferences or football matches.

To clarify the theoretical argument that follows, we must define what will be meant by the 'international' and the 'nation state' systems, terms that are used here in a particular way for the sake of the theoretical

argument. A nation state system is defined here as a system in which nations are the only actors, and, therefore, the nation is the only behavioral group[3] for the purpose of analysis. An international system, however, is defined to include a variety of actors, from individuals to nations to international organizations of both the governmental and non-governmental kinds.[4] Here there are many different behavioral groups, although one could, for example, take nations as the central actors and try to analyze behavior within the international context.[5]

2. The Three World Arms Races[6]

Richardson, in his analysis of arms races, worked within the nation state system framework. He assumed that in a two-nation arms race the rate at which the first nation arms depends upon the amount of armament the other nation has, the colossal costs of armaments, and the feelings toward the other nation (for instance, as expressed in treaties[7]). He expressed

[*] This research was supported by JWGA/ARPA/ NU project (Advanced Research Project Agency, SD 260) on Simulated International Processes conducted at Northwestern University, Evanston, Illinois, USA.

The author wishes to thank Professor Harold Guetzkow for his very helpful comments and suggestions during the execution of this study.

[†] Reprinted by permission of the author and publisher from *Journal of Peace Research*, 1967, 4: 61–75.

[1] In many instances a distinguishing characteristic of an escalation process is its exponential character. All three world arms races have exhibited this phenomenon.

[2] In the case of the present arms race, defense expenditures have to be corrected to allow for polarization using trade data if more than the two super-powers are included. Increase then refers to the corrected figures. For a description of this see Paul Smoker, 'Trade, Defense, and the Richardson Theory of Arms Races: A Seven Nation Study', *Journal of Peace Research*, 1965, 2, pp. 161–176.

[3] The term 'behavioral group' corresponds to the usual term 'behavior unit' and is used to avoid any misunderstanding of the word 'unit' as it is used in measurement.

[4] An international governmental organization is an international organization which is founded by treaty between at least two governments, and, as a rule, has as its members representatives of the governments involved. International nongovernmental organizations comprise all other international organizations.

[5] This is related to the classic level of analysis problem. See, for example, J. David Singer, 'The Level of Analysis Problem in International Relations,' in Knorr, K. E. and Verba, S. (eds.) *The International System: Theoretical Essays*. (Princeton, N. J.: Princeton University Press, 1961).

[6] The term 'world arms race' is used here for those arms races leading to the first two world wars and the present arms race.

[7] Lewis Richardson in *Arms and Insecurity* (Pittsburgh: The Boxwood Press, 1960), pp. 33–35, suggested that trade might be relevant also to the feelings between nations. This effect is now seen as related to the polarization phenomenon as explained in footnote 2.

these assumptions in mathematical form[8] and tested his mathematical model against the behavior of nations in the first and second world arms races.[9] Given the simplicity of his model and the many problems of measurement involved, the model was remarkably consistent with the facts. For the first world arms race, however, the agreement was better than for the second.[10]

For a two-nation nuclear arms race within the nation state context, Richardson argued that a submissiveness or fear factor should be included to allow for the mutual fear induced by nuclear weapons.[11] This submissiveness model, when applied to the present arms race, for the United States and the Soviet Union suggested the possibility that this fear factor was completely absent before 1952 but came into being quite suddenly during that year.[12] In terms of the Richardson models, this meant that the present arms race behaved in the same way as the previous two up to 1952, in that the growth of defense expenditure was exponential; and then after 1952 behaved in a way consistent with the assumptions of the submissiveness model.[13]

[8] See Richardson, op. cit., pp. 12–17.

[9] See Richardson, op. cit., chapters 2, 7, 9, 10, 19, and 20.

[10] See Richardson, op. cit., p. 89, pp. 205–209, and pp. 221–225.

[11] Richardson first suggested this possibility for a nuclear arms race in 'Could an Arms Race End Without Fighting', *Nature*, September 29, 1951.

[12] See Paul Smoker, 'Fear in the Arms Race: A Mathematical Study', *Journal of Peace Research*, No. 1, 1964, pp. 55–64.

[13] As pointed out in Paul Smoker, 'The Arms Race: A Wave Model', *Peace Research Society (International), PAPERS, Vol. IV.,* 1966, Cracow Conference, 1965, pp. 151–192, the decay of the arms race after 1952 is more consistent with an exponential decay process than with the Richardson submissiveness equations, which are not exponential decay in form. When seven nations are considered and allowance is made for polarization by the use of trade data, an exponential model gives a correlation of −.95 for the ten pairs of observations from 1952 to 1962, when the arms race accelerated once again, while the submissiveness model on the same data gives a correlation of −.72 and the unadapted submissiveness model a correlation of .4. Nevertheless, the argument here is not altered by a reinterpretation of the functional form of the submissiveness effect.

This paper relates this change in behavior to the possible change from a nation state type of system to a kind of international system, and suggests a possible functional relationship between escalation and integration in this type of international system.

3. The Theory

To begin with we shall take an interpretation of Talcott Parsons' theory of social systems[14] and consider its relevance to the possible movement of a nation state type of system toward an international type of system. The four basic functional requirements of a social system suggested by Parsons—namely, pattern maintenance, adaptation, goal attainment, and integration—can at the national and international levels of analysis be very roughly equated with specific subsystems.

Thus, at the national level the nation can be viewed as individuals and groups who are mainly responsible for pattern maintenance through such activities as practicing cultural values and providing labor; an economy which is mainly responsible for adaptation; a governmental subsystem which is mainly responsible for goal attainment of the nation; and a cultural subsystem that is responsible for integration.

In a nation state system, it can be argued, the interaction is primarily an interaction of the goal attainment subsystems of each of the participating nations. A classical interpretation of such goal attainment interaction is pure power politics. There is, by definition, no integrative subsystem working between nations in a nation state system; the situation resembles a zero sum game in that 'might is right.'

In an international system we can assume that:

(1) The pattern maintenance function may be characterized by individuals and families throughout that international sys-

[14] The interpretation used as a starting point is that of Karl Deutsch taken from *The Integration of Political Communities* edited by Philip Jacob and James Toscano. (New York: Lippincott, 1964).

tem. The individuals might be referred to as 'international man'[15] and may represent, at present, a tiny fraction of the world's population.

(2) The adaptation subsystem might be represented roughly by the international economic system, which includes international corporations.[16] In the world of the future these corporations may play an increasingly important role, as giants like General Motors, whose sales in 1965 were more than the gross national product of the Netherlands and well over a hundred other countries, become more common.

(3) The goal attainment subsystem might be represented by parts of the United Nations. Thus, some organs of the UN are concerned with world politics—for example, the General Assembly—while others are concerned with educational or cultural matters—such as UNESCO.[17] Thus, the General Assembly might be seen as characteristic of an international goal attainment subsystem.

(4) The international integrative subsystem can be characterized by the various international cultural activities and may be indexed approximately by international non-governmental organizations[18] and international conferences.[19] The nonpolitical aspects of the United

Nations and the family of international governmental organizations also might index the international integrative subsystem.[20]

Figure 1 illustrates a three-nation nation state system within the context of three national systems. Interactions between subsystems (as represented by squares) are shown by arrows. This system defines nation state interaction as motivated purely by the goal attainment subsystems of the particular nations as illustrated by the shaded areas.

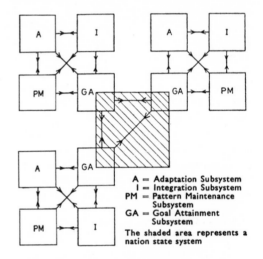

A = Adaptation Subsystem
I = Integration Subsystem
PM = Pattern Maintenance Subsystem
GA = Goal Attainment Subsystem
The shaded area represents a nation state system

FIG. 1. A nation state system.

Figure 2 illustrates an international system as defined. Here goal attainment, pattern maintenance, integration and adaptation are associated with international institutions and attitudes as defined above. Each of the four subsystems is represented by a circle, and the interactions between them by arrows.

Now, to put forward these two definitions is not to argue that such pure types exist or have existed in world affairs. However, it will be argued in the next section

---

[15] See, for example, Program 18 of the International Peace Research Institute, Oslo, *Working Program 1966–67*, Oslo, May 1966.

[16] For a theoretical discussion of the structure of International Corporations, see Howard Perlmutter, 'Social Architecture of the Multinational Firm', *The Journal of Social Issues* symposium on 'The Generation and Management of Conflict in the World Community, 1966'. It has been estimated that by 1975, through international mergers, overseas investment and assorted practices, 300 corporations will control more than 75 per cent of all industrial assets.

[17] I am grateful to Robert Beattie of the Comparative International Processes project at Northwestern University for making this observation. In an earlier study, 'A Preliminary Empirical Study of an International Integrative Subsystem in International Associations', November 1965, a political/nonpolitical continuum was constructed on page 642 using empirical data on membership of international nongovernmental organizations.

[18] The *Yearbook of International Associations* published by the Union of International Associations, Brussels, provides well-documented informa-

tion on both governmental and nongovernmental international organizations.

[19] The Union of International Associations published an annual Calendar also with details of international conferences and monthly supplements in their monthly publication, 'International Associations'.

[20] See footnote 17.

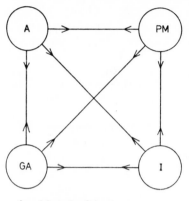

A = Adaptation Subsystem
I = Integration Subsystem
PM = Pattern Maintenance Subsystem
GM = Goal Attainment Subsystem

FIG. 2. An international system.

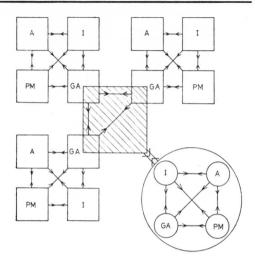

FIG. 3. The world system.

that there is evidence that world affairs are moving from a situation resembling that in Figure 1 toward a situation resembling that in Figure 2. It is not argued here that this gradual shift is as yet very great: on the contrary, the structure of the world society today is probably still like Figure 1 in many ways according to the theory presented here. It is not even argued that we will eventually reach the situation illustrated in Figure 2, the position of those who campaign for some kind of world government. Rather, it is suggested that the structure of the world community is likely to be an amalgam of both types as well as other major structural features, such as rank disequilibrium between nations and between international organizations as suggested by Galtung.[21]

For the purpose of this article it is sufficient to suggest that particularly since the Second World War, partly through the advent of modern communications, the international component of the world system has grown significantly. Here the world system is defined as the amalgam of the nation state and the international component parts and is illustrated in Figure 3. The relative importance of the nation state and the international components may change in time, it is suggested here, and

[21] See Johan Galtung, 'A Structural Theory of Aggression', *Journal of Peace Research*, 1964, 2, pp. 95–119.

such changes are likely to affect the relationships between variables in the world system.

This model of the world system, therefore, places considerable emphasis on the size of the two component parts. It is argued here, and subsequently investigated empirically, that as the international component grows in size, significant interactions between the international component and the nation state component become important in the analysis of the world system. Viewed in terms of levels of analysis, this is to suggest that there are now interactive links between the nation state and the international level. For the purposes of this article, it is argued that the types of interactions depicted in the shaded box in Figure 4 are of particular importance to the arms race in general and nation state escalation in particular.

This is not to argue that the complete nexus of interrelationships presented in Figure 3 should not be considered; a complete analysis would have to include all the linkages. Rather, it is to suggest that in exploring the theoretical model put forward here, the particular interrelationships shown in Figure 4 are of interest. The reader, therefore, should bear in mind the partial nature of the empirical testing and theoretical argument that follows.

Figure 4 depicts a situation in which a three-nation nation state system is linked

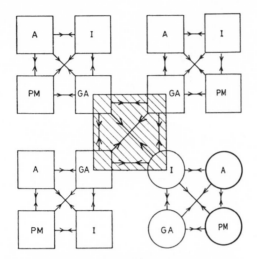

FIG. 4. The circular subsystems comprise an international system, the square subsystems national systems. The shaded area represents the escalation/integration space in which a nation state system interacts with an international integrative subsystem.

to an international system through the international system's integrative subsystem. While no integrative control operates within a nation state system, it is suggested here that the international integrative subsystem has increased in size and now exerts a controlling influence on both the international system *and* the nation state system. This is not to argue that the nation state system component (or nationalism) is necessarily weakening, but to suggest that the international integrative subsystem has a greater controlling influence because it is now operating at a significant level.

However, in the same way that the old equation 'hunger down equals war down'[22] does not take into account structural properties of the situation, so the equally popular proposition 'integration up, war down' fails to consider the nexus of interactions involved in structural relationships. When integration is operating at a low or zero level, as in the case of a nation state type of system, any increase in integration is likely to modify the power politics of simple goal attainment interaction. But when integration is operating at a relatively high level, as in the case of husband and wife, relatively high levels of tension become possi-

[22] See Galtung, op. cit.

ble. The fact that husbands and wives murder each other with high frequency relative to other groups of people, even allowing for the increased opportunities, is consistent with the assumption that for high levels of integration the relationship between integration and hostility or violence is more complex.[23]

Consider now the situation in Figure 4: suppose that the nation state interaction of the goal attainment subsystems has entered an escalation feed-back process. That is, the Richardson equations:

(1)
$$\frac{dx}{dt} = ky - ax + g \text{ and}$$

$$\frac{dy}{dt} = lx - by + h$$

become relevant in that increases in defenses seem necessary to each nation to counter the rising tension and protect its interests. In these equations, x and y represent defenses; k and l defense coefficients that indicate the sensitivity of each nation to changes in defenses of the other; a and b fatigue and expense coefficients that indicate the economic and other restraints on building defenses; and g and h are grievances that indicate the feelings for each nation about the other. The Richardson equations show how these increases in defenses lead to new increases designed to protect each nation's interests, and the tension continues to rise.[24]

Now, this is not necessarily a dangerous situation, for it could be that the increases in world tension due to an arms race are being matched by increases in the international integrative subsystem. This leads to a situation in which tension is rising, but where the system's ability to contain tension and avoid violence is increasing.

[23] Kenneth Boulding, for example, in 'Towards a Theory of Peace', in Fisher, Roger D. (ed.) *International Conflict and Behavioral Science: Craigville Papers* (New York: Basic Books, 1964, pp. 70–87), distinguishes between the threat system, the exchange system, and the integrative system, and argues for functional relationships between all three.

[24] The problem of measuring defenses is discussed elsewhere. See footnote 25.

The over-all strain on decision-makers may not, therefore, be increasing in proportion to the escalation process.

However, if a secondary feedback process is at work in which increases in tension adversely affect the growth of the integrative subsystem, then a drop in integration might occur, and, at the same time, the arms race escalation process may continue. From the point of view of actors within the system, the situation would have worsened; the strain would rise much faster than previously, and proportionately faster than the tension. The effect of such an increase in strain on decision-makers, where strain is defined as the tension in the system relative to the strength of the system, will, it is argued, depend to some extent on the structure of the world system. Three distinct types of situation can be identified:

(1) A world system which continues to contain a significant international integrative component.

(2) A world system in which a significant international integrative component has become negligible as a result of the feedback effects of the arms race on the international system.

(3) A world system in which the international integrative component was negligible even before the feedback process began.

This article argues that the three world arms races have, in some ways, produced each of these three types of situations. For the first world arms race, it is argued, the situation throughout resembled a nation state interaction process and the collapse of the insignificant international integrative subsystem was irrelevant to the outcome because the level of that subsystem was so low. For the second world arms race, it is argued, an international type of system collapsed into a nation state system; while for the present arms race during the period 1948–52 the drop in the integrative subsystem was not great enough to destroy the significant international component.

Of course, the argument presented here, and discussed in the light of empirical data below, ignores many important points and is based on a relatively simplistic theory. The question of alliances, for example, is not dealt with here in terms of our model. Nevertheless, the model put forward here is, in principle, susceptible to rigorous analysis and even in this simple form appears to be consistent with international

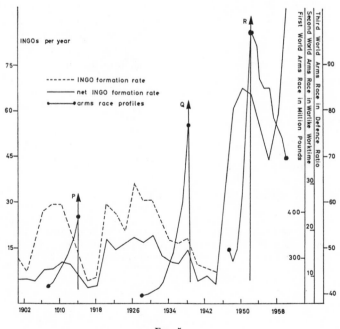

Fig. 5.

and nation state behavior during the period 1900 to 1960 considered below.

4. Comparing Theory and Data

(a) *Integration and Escalation*

Two types of indicators are used to compare the theory with data. The first type of indicator concerns nation state escalation, the second international integration.

For nation state escalation the well documented data on the three world arms races have been used.[25] Thus, for the first world arms race, the defense expenditures of the Triple Alliance and the Triple Entente have been used; for the second world arms race, when the value of money was not so stable,[26] defense expenditures for the ten nations, Germany, Russia, Japan, Italy, France, China, United Kingdom, United States, Poland, and Czechoslovakia, as calculated by Richardson in terms of defense hours worked in million person years per year, have been used; and for the present world arms race, defense expenditure for the United States and the Soviet Union in terms of Smoker's defense ratio have been used.[27]

In the case of defenses, the indicators used rest upon the justifications given by the authors[28] and their relative success in describing the escalation in each of the three arms races. Because this part of the paper is concerned with a time series trend type analysis, the problem of intercomparability of units does not arise. The escalation process is indexed clearly in each case, while the relative magnitude of the process is conveyed very approximately by means of the respective scales used in Figure 5. In line with the Parsonian framework, the integration indicator used is the growth rate of international nongovernmental organizations (INGO's).[29] Some comparative data on the number of international congresses is used as background data,[30] although for reasons discussed below the number of conferences is not suitable for our purposes here.

In the case of the integration measure, the need was for an indicator (1) relatively sensitive to short run fluctuations, and (2) relatively representative of over-all international trends. The number of international congresses per year does not seem to satisfy these criteria so well as the number of new INGO's formed per year. There are a number of studies which show that the number of international congresses show trends from decade to decade[31] not from year to year.[32] For example, in ten-year periods from 1840 to 1959 the number of international congresses held is 9, 22, 75, 149, 284, 469, 1,082, 974 (the period of the first world war), 2,913, 3,655, estimated 7,000, and estimated 9,600. However, year to year trends are often severely distorted by international exhibitions. From 1900 to 1960 there had been fifteen such international exhibitions.[33] In every single case the number of congresses in the year of the exhibition was more than the number in either the preceding or the following year. Further, the percentage of conferences held in the town of the international exhibition was always more than ten per cent, and sometimes as high as eighty or ninety per cent. Typical examples, however, are the two Brussels exhibitions of 1935 and 1958, which attracted thirty-three per cent and

---

[25] For the first two world arms races, the data have been collected from the studies of Richardson, op. cit. For the present arms race, the data are given in Paul Smoker, 'A Pilot Study of the Present Arms Race', *General Systems Yearbook*, Vol. VIII, 1963, pp. 61–76.

[26] See Richardson, op. cit., chapter 11.

[27] See footnote 12.

[28] See Richardson, op. cit., and Smoker, op. cit.

[29] Collected from the *Yearbook* of the Union of International Associations, see footnote 16.

[30] See footnote 19.

[31] For example, Genevieve Deville, 'Les Réunions Internationales en 1958', in *International Associations*, No. 6, 1959.

[32] See footnote 30 and the two monographs 'International Congresses, 1681 to 1899', and 'International Congresses, 1900–1919' published by the Union of International Associations, Brussels, 1960.

[33] They were held at Paris (1900), Glasgow (1901), Hanoi (1903), St. Louis (1904), Liège (1905), Milan (1906), Dublin (1907), Brussels (1910), Roubaix (1911), Gent (1913), Rio de Janeiro (1922), Barcelona (1929), Liège (1929), Brussels (1935 and again in 1958).

twenty per cent, respectively, of the total conference universes for the year.

Because of this influence, the second criteria, that of reflecting over-all international trends, also is less well satisfied by international congresses than by INGO formation over the short run.

The relative inadequacies of the number of international conferences as an indicator should not obscure the approximations involved in using the rate of formation of INGO's as an indicator of growth in the international integrative subsystem. The indicator used here does not distinguish between large and small or rich and poor organizations; the considerable variance on these matters could very well affect the interpretation of trends.[34] However, for our immediate purposes the indicator chosen, rate of formation of INGO's, is assumed to be adequate, partly because of the relatively large numbers involved. In future studies better indicators might be developed.

Before proceeding to Figure 5, however, one further difficulty should be mentioned concerning the measurement of the rate of formation of INGO's: many of the organizations formed go out of existence after a number of years. Thus, up to 1951, 1,409 INGO's had been established; at that time, 905 remained in existence. Thus the net growth of the international integrative structure might be taken as an indicator, or the number of organizations formed could be taken. Although new organizations are being formed every year, in some years the over-all total drops because the disbanding rate is higher than the formation rate.[35] Thus, two INGO indicators have been used to 1944, namely the number of new INGO's formed per year and the net number formed from the point of view of an observer in the late 1950's.[36] Because the fall-out rate becomes significant only after a number of years, only the INGO formation rate as recorded in the tenth edition of the *Yearbook of International Associations* has been recorded after 1944.

Figure 5 shows both sets of integration indicators, the lower profile being the net formation rate, together with the three escalation profiles, one for each arms race. As explained above, the escalation indicators are not comparable in quantitative terms; they simply indicate that each arms race has been considerably larger than the previous one. The arrow P marks the outbreak of World War I, Q the outbreak of World War II, and R the point at which submission, or the fear factor, can be assumed to have come into being.[37] We are able now to compare each of the three arms races with the theory suggested above.

For the first world arms race, the exponential escalation process began slowly in 1907, as shown by Richardson,[38] and led to war in 1914. The rate of formation of INGO's, and the net rate of formation both showed a general increasing tendency from about 1902 to 1910.[39] After 1910, however, while escalation continued, the international integrative subsystem collapsed. Also the profile of the rate of formation after rising sharply up to 1906 seems to show signs of weakening from 1907–08 onwards. This is consistent with the feedback effect of the nation state system on a very weak international integrative subsystem. The World War I profiles are consistent with the assumption that a nation state system was dominant throughout; the collapse of the international integrative subsystem had no visible effect on the escalation process, due to the relatively insignificant level at which it was operating.

[34] For example, the forty largest INGO's in 1951 had a joint membership of 719,954,442 members, while the smallest INGO's may have only ten or twenty numbers. Similarly, while the estimated total budget of all the INGO's in 1960 was $306,150,380, two INGO's jointly handle more than $110,000,000 a year and others get along on less than $200.

[35] For example, if all international organizations, governmental and nongovernmental, are considered in 1906 there were 160; 1912, 437; 1921, 321; 1926, 397; 1930, 524; 1938, 705; 1947, 416; 1948, 650; and 1951, 1020.

[36] The tenth edition has been used supplemented by data from 'The Development of the International Structure', in *International Associations*, June-July 1952.

[37] See Smoker, op. cit., footnote 12.

[38] See Richardson, op. cit., footnote 7.

[39] The year 1900 caused a certain disturbance in the rate of formation of INGO's because of its symbolic significance.

For the second world arms race, as mentioned above, Richardson did not get such a good agreement between his nation-state interaction theory and national behavior. In fact, he found it necessary to assume in his model that the second world arms race was in two parts, one up to 1932 and one from 1933 onwards.[40] After 1932 the acceleration was more marked and the escalation process typically run-away exponential.

The following assumption is consistent with the finding of Richardson described above, the theory presented in Section 3, and the integration and escalation profiles between 1926 and 1938 in Figure 5. That is, that the international integrative subsystem was operating at a significant level,[41] in that it was constraining the goal-seeking behavior to some extent; but then with the feedback process from the nation state escalation starting around 1930, the international control element became insignificant by the mid-1930's, and the national state interaction dominated. Certainly the collapse of the integrative subsystem is well marked in the Figure and to some extent reflected in such events as the decay of the League of Nations, which was in part a weak international goal-seeking subsystem.

As with World War I, the decay continued through World War II. Thus, even in 1947 there were fewer than 400 INGO's functioning as compared to about 600 in 1938. After the Second World War, however, the INGO profile shows a tremendous increase, such that by 1951 there were 905 INGO's, more than ever before.

However, the third world arms race had been under way since 1948;[42] and the feedback, according to our theory, first became visible in the over-all INGO growth rate during the period 1951–52. The effect is even more visible in trans-cold war INGO's —that is, INGO's who have members living in any of the NATO, SEATO, and CENTO countries and in any of the Warsaw Pact or Socialist countries.[43] Our concern here, however, is with the general phenomena in the whole international system and not so much with effects on particular parts of the system. Obviously, such effects could be very important for example, the tremendous integrative underdevelopment of South East Asia—but to consider them in this article would detract from the central point.[44]

As stated above, a previous article argued that a fear factor came into being during 1952, having been absent previously, and caused the arms race to slow.[45] According to the profiles in Figure 5, it was during the period 1951–52 that the rate of formation of INGO's first dropped while the escalation continued. The fear factor finding, the theory presented in Section 3, and the profiles in Figure 5 are consistent with the following assumption: the international integrative subsystem was operating at a significant level in 1952, but due to feedback effects of the arms race escalation its growth rate had dropped. Despite this drop, the integrative subsystem still continued to operate at a significant level; and the nation state and international systems remained functionally linked to each other. The increase in strain relative to the increase in tension caused submission to operate on decision-makers of both sides.

To escalate in a situation with no interdependencies is, in other words, qualitatively different from escalation between interdependent parties. In the 1952 case, it is argued, a decrease in integration, coupled with a still significant level of operation by the integrative subsystem, contributed to a decrease in escalation because of the relative levels of tension and strain.

(b) *Trade and Defense.*

The argument outlined in the preceding sections concerns structural change. It suggests that because of the increasing international system, the nation state and international components are becoming progressively more linked over time. This

---

[40] See Richardson, op. cit., p. 225, footnote 7.

[41] It must be remembered that the profiles show the rate of formation, not the number of INGO's in existence. By 1951 this was over 900.

[42] See Smoker, op. cit., footnote 12.

[43] See Paul Smoker, op. cit., footnote 17.

[44] The article by Genevieve Deville gives INGO membership for all nations for each year from 1950 to 1958. See footnote 31.

[45] See footnote 12.

increasing linkage is not, it is argued, a steady linear thing for during the three periods of nation state escalation considered feedback from the nation state escalation undermined the international integrative subsystem. However, it is suggested that the pre-World War I period, the pre-World War II period, and the post-World War II period will exhibit relatively increasing linkages between the nation state and the international systems.

In order to investigate in a preliminary fashion this possibility, it is of interest to compare the trade/defense relationships during each of these three periods. Trade can be conceived of as a part of the international adaptive subsystem to a first approximation, and has received increasing attention in the study of international relations.[46] One interpretation of international trade used Galtung's ideas on polarization[47] to construct a polarization index F_{mn} where:

$$(2) \qquad F_{mn} = \frac{1}{2} \left(\frac{t_{mn}}{T_m} + \frac{t_{mn}}{T_n} \right)$$

Here t_{mn} is the intertrade between the mth and n^{th} nation, while T_m and T_n represent the total trade of the mth and n^{th} nations. This index tries to record the relative importance of intertrade between two nations. In the study where this index was suggested,[48] it appeared to give a reasonable indicator of polarization during the period 1948–62. This index is used here, however, simply to index intertrade between two nations.

Defense is measured here using the ratio Defense Expenditure/Government Expenditure. During the 1950's and early '60's this ratio appears to correlate with threats,

accusations, and protests, while defense expenditure alone does not.[49]

The selection of nations for each period is as follows: For the first world arms race, Richardson's work suggested that the Triple Alliance and the Triple Entente were the dominant national actors. The six nations Germany, Austria-Hungary, Italy, France, Russia, and Britain have, therefore, been taken. For the pre-World War II period, five of these six nations (all but Austria-Hungary, which had ceased to exist) were taken, together with Japan and Italy. For the post-World War II period, the seven nations USA, USSR, UK, People's Republic of China, Federal Republic of Germany, People's Republic of Poland, and France were taken. The time periods taken are 1906–1913, 1929–1937, and 1952–1962, all inclusive.[50] Standard data sources are used.[51]

Table 1 shows the correlation by dyad of the trade ratio for the dyad against the sum of the defense ratios for the two nations in the dyad. The hypothesis concerning the increasing linkage between the nation state and the international systems is supported by this Table, for during the first period, 5 out of 15 dyads—or one third,—exhibit a significant relationship;[52] during the sec-

[46] For example, see Johan Galtung, 'East-West Interactions Patterns', *Journal of Peace Research*, 1966, No. 2, pp. 146–177; Steven J. Brams, 'Transaction Flows in the International System', American Political Science Review, LX, 4, December, 1966), pp. 880–898; I. Richard Savage and Karl W. Deutsch, 'A Statistical Model of the Gross Analysis of Transaction Flows', *Econometrica*, Vol. XXVIII (July, 1960), pp. 551–572.

[47] Johan Galtung, 'Summit Meetings and International Relations', *Journal of Peace Research*, 1 (1964), pp. 36–54.

[48] See Smoker, op. cit., footnote 12.

[49] See Rudolph Rummel, 'Some Dimensions of International Relations in the Mid 1950's', (New Haven, Connecticut: Yale University, Dimensionality of Nations Project, August 1964) (mimeo).

[50] For the present arms race, data problems for the period prior to 1952 prevented all the nations here being considered since 1948. However, for those nations for which data are available similar results were obtained over the whole period 1948–62.

[51] For the first world arms race the *Statesman's Year Book* was used. For the second world arms race the *League of Nations Armaments Year Book* and the *Statistical Year Book of the League of Nations* were used. The *Stateman's Year Book* compared favorably with these sources. For the present world arms race the *United Nations Statistical Year Book* and the *Series T Publication Direction of International Trade* were the main sources.

[52] 'Significant' is used here in the sense that such a correlation would be significant in a random population of statistics. While this condition is not satisfied, it is still possible to take the correlation coefficient as a guideline in the sense that it enables comparisons across similar populations of statistics to be made.

TABLE 1

COMPARATIVE TABLE OF TRADE/DEFENSE RELATIONSHIPS FOR THREE PERIODS IN HISTORY

(The left-hand column shows the probability of such values of r arising by change in an uncorrelated population of statistics. It merely serves as a method of comparing correlations from different sample sizes and should not be interpreted as a measure of significance.)

	1906–13 inclusive (N = 8)		1929–37 inclusive (N = 9)		1952–62 inclusive (N = 11)	
	Triple Alliance and *Triple Entente*		UK Japan		USA FGR	
	Germany	France	US Italy		USSR Poland	
	Austria-Hungary	Russia	Germany USSR		UK France	
	Italy	UK	France		China (Peoples Rep.)	
.001	Germany/Italy	−93	UK/Japan	−94	USSR/France	−95
					UK/China	−90
					UK/USA	−88
.01	Austria-Hungary/Italy	−85			Poland/FGR	−79
					USSR/Poland	+77*
					USA/FGR	−76
					Poland/UK	−76
.02			USSR/USA	+79*	France/China	−71
			USSR/Germany	−79	USSR/China	+68*
			UK/Italy	−76		
			UK/USSR	+75*		
			Germany/Italy	+75*		
.05	France/Italy	−73	USA/Japan	−71	USA/USSR	−67
			USSR/Italy	−69	USA/Poland	−67
					FGR/USSR	−65
					FGR/France	−60
.1	Germany/UK	−66	Japan/Italy	−64	USA/China	+59*
	France/UK	−62	France/USSR	+58*	FGR/China	−58
					USA/France	−56
Not significant in a random population of statistics.	Germany/Austria-Hungary	+55	France/Italy	−57	UK/FGR	−44
	France/Russia	+50	France/Germany	−53	UK/USSR	+08
	Italy/Russia	−46	Germany/UK	−52	UK/France	−17
	Germany/France	+39	France/UK	−52	Poland/France	+18
	Austria-Hungary/UK	−33	USA/Italy	−49	Poland/China	+05
	Germany/Russia	+27	Germany/Japan	−35		
	Italy/UK	−29	USA/France	+34		
	Russia/UK	+14	France/Japan	−29		
	Austria-Hungary/Russia	+08	USSR/Japan	+24		
	Austria-Hungary/France	+07	USA/UK	+06		
			USA/Germany	−05		

* indicates positive correlations.

ond period, 10 out of 21—roughly one half; while during the third period, 16 out of 21 —roughly three quarters—exhibit significant linkages.

A closer examination of Table 1 reveals that certain correlations, marked with an *, are positive. Before World War II, the USSR appears to have been improving its trading relations with the USA, UK, and France despite increasing nation state escalation. The same appears to be the case for Italy and Germany in their relations. For each of these dyads, trading relationships with eventual allies increased as the escalation increased. With the exception of the Japan/Italy dyad, all the other significant trade/defense relationships decreased as the nation state escalation increased and were associated with dyads comprising eventual adversaries. This is consistent with the assumption that those dyads that were operating under the constraints of the international system had trade/defense linkages consistent with the eventual alliance formation.

Since 1952, the USSR/Poland and the USSR/China dyads both show decreasing intertrade with de-escalation of the arms race, as does the USA/China dyad. To use Galtung's terms, this is consistent with the assumption that polarization within the Socialist nations has been decreasing as has polarization between the Socialist and Western nations, with the exception of USA/China, while polarization within the Western nations has been increasing with the following exceptions—the UK/FGR and UK/France dyads have not followed this trend within the Western nations, UK/USSR and Poland/France between the two alliances, and Poland/China within the Socialist nations.

The over-all trends support the Galtung hypothesis that during this period, the international system was moving from its highly polarized state into a new pattern.[53] The particular differences, however, argue that other factors may be relevant to the trade/defense relationship. That is to say, while it is obviously possible to interpret the deviants from the general trends in terms of political differences, it might also be possible to interpret them in terms of the over-all model presented in the early part of this paper.

For example, the international integrative subsystem is not, as observed above, uniformly distributed around the world. Such differential distribution is likely to influence linkages between trade and defense. Thus, in the case of the UK, the great increase in integration in Europe, other than the UK, is likely to influence such dyads as UK/FGR and UK/France.[54] Future work using the model presented above will investigate such possibilities.

[53] See Galtung, op. cit., footnote 47.
[54] See Smoker, op. cit., footnote 17.

5. Theoretical Implications

The first implication of this paper suggests that the classic analysis of international affairs, simply in terms of the nation state, is likely to be less valid in the future, as an international type of system develops in the way suggested above. Multilevel analysis using many behavior groups and individuals is likely to be of more value in such matters.

Of course, it could be that the present analysis is inadequate or incorrect due to theoretical methodological mistakes. It thus goes without saying that all the conclusions in this and the next section need further consideration before they can be regarded as valid in any sense. However, the findings here suggest that any analysis of escalation or de-escalation that does not include the integration dimension of human relations as a functional component is likely to run into difficulties in interpreting international relations. Similarly, any analysis of international integration which does not relate to international power politics is likely to be in error. On the research side, it would seem from this rather limited article that detailed studies of integration and its relationship to other variables are of some importance. For it can be argued that the simple formula 'integration down, war up' is not sufficient if we wish to understand the complex structural relationships involved.

6. Policy Implications

At the policy level this article, on a tentative basis, argues that the social context for escalation or de-escalation is important if control is to be retained. As mentioned, INGO indicators for certain areas of the world suggest a look at such international structures in these parts. Within such areas it might be argued that might equals right, but it is likely to be accompanied by force. Nor is it at this time clear how heterogeneous international integration, unevenly distributed around the world, will affect the functioning of the whole integrative subsystem.

At the world level, the possible success of the integrative system in 1952 might be interpreted as supporting evidence for a new brinkmanship. However, the eroding properties of feedback from the nation state system to the international system, as witnessed by the steady decline of INGO trans-cold-war bonding from 1952–59, should caution against such a view. It seems likely that increased integration, paradoxically enough, makes possible increased tension. Nuclear deterrence may only be able to function as a deterrent if the international integrative system is strong enough to contain and modify its power political use. But increased escalation decays the integrative subsystem and could in the not-too-long run lead to a dangerous situation. Any prolonged escalation, such as the Vietnam war, could do great damage in this respect.

On the positive side, the preventative approach to international conflict might be adopted on a large scale by governments through properly conceived technical assistance, cultural exchange, and exchange visitors. Besides this, those individuals whose professional or human concern lies in this area can contribute themselves to international integration by participation in activities of INGO's.[55]

A useful aid to those concerned with international integration might be the publishing of a monthly international integration index, together with a tension and strain index. Such information, even though crudely measured, might prove of value to those INGO's, peace groups, and politicians who are involved in action for peace.

[55] An earlier study, see footnote 17, suggests that the less political an INGO, the greater its integrative effect. Peace action INGO's are, therefore, less suited to this task.

Summary

A model of world affairs is defined which identifies two interacting systems. The first system is called a nation state system, in which nations are the only actors. The second system is called an international system, in which there are many actors, from individuals to nations to international organizations and corporations. The world system is defined as the amalgam of these two.

Within nations, the four functional requirements of Parsons are used to identify the economy as representative of the adaptation subsystem, the culture as representative of the integrative subsystem, individuals and families as representative of the pattern maintenance subsystem, and government as representative of the goal attainment subsystem. An internation system is then specifically defined as interaction between the goal attainment subsystems of nations. A similar procedure is adopted for the international system.

The three world arms races are then interpreted in the light of the model using the idea that the international component has been greater in each arms race than in the previous one. In this way it is possible to interpret the differences in behavior in each of the arms races in terms of the model. It is also found that the linkage between trade and defense has increased in each successive arms race.

It is suggested that future analysis of world affairs should take into account other actors, such as international organizations and international corporations, as well as nations. Further, the importance of the integrative system is stressed and some suggestions for strengthening it are put forward.

UNCONVENTIONAL WARFARE*

J. K. ZAWODNY

In the third century B.C. in the city of Argos, Pyrrhus of Epirus, known as the Red King, was killed by a chamber pot thrown from a roof top by an elderly lady. The basic elements of what is today known as "unconventional warfare" were embodied in her action: there was surprise, and an unusual—if not extraordinary—weapon; the object of attack was strategically important; the attack was successful; and it was performed by a nonprofessional warrior. The performer, not the technique, is the significant element of this episode.

The outstanding feature of unconventional warfare is that it is carried out by people of all ages and backgrounds and of both sexes. It is a "People's Warfare." A warfare of masses who have lost patience, it is an unremittingly violent way of saying to the enemy by all possible means: "We hate you; we are everywhere; we will destroy you!" Unconventional warfare is the effective weapon of the weaker adversary; and, strange as it may sound, the United States is as vulnerable to this sort of warfare as Cuba. It is, furthermore, an extremely cheap weapon—at least, monetarily. . . .

Unconventional warfare is that part of "Special Warfare" that employs violence. It can be broadly classified as offensive and defensive. It is offensive when one government promotes the overthrow of a foreign government or a change of its political elite. In these circumstances, organization, manipulation and assistance are carried into another territory; the recent affair with Cuba is an example. It is defensive when a frustrated political group structures itself into a disciplined organization to apply violence against the government of its own nation or when a people fight the occupational forces of an invading army. This classification does not preclude both types from being (and they usually are) *strategically and tactically* offensive.

There seem to be three prerequisites for initiating unconventional warfare. First, an organization must be created to support those who will carry the violence directly to the enemy. Leadership, supplies and money are indispensable for the inception and survival of the underground. Guerrilla and saboteur units are only a small part of the structure; also included are Headquarters, Intelligence, Communications, Propaganda, Cadres in Reserve and Training, and Logistics.

The second ingredient essential for the initiation of unconventional warfare is a culture that allows or promotes violence, and the effectiveness of the organization usually depends on the degree to which the cultural values and traditions of a people condition them to use violence. . . .

The third prerequisite for unconventional warfare is the volunteer, the guerrilla and saboteur, who carries violence to the enemy. Any movement aimed at using violence gathers to its ranks those who are threatened and/or dissatisfied. In the Polish underground movement between 1939 and 1945, the resentment against the cruelty and oppression of the German and Soviet occupation, the absence of formal channels for voicing grievances and the lack of opportunities to change conditions caused the people to band together. Such at least were the usual explanations. Many men were unable to articulate the reasons why they fought. But they did believe that it was the only way they could "do something" about their problems. The messenger of a company in the Uprising of Warsaw (1944) was eight years old. No one knew why he was there; but the boy wanted to fight and was dependable. In one of the actions a sergeant who had been a university professor was fighting because it was "his moral duty to uphold justice."

Women, following precedents in Polish history, were splendid unconventional fighters and did men's jobs, including manning street barricades and shooting. In fact it

* Reprinted by permission of the author and publisher from *American Scholar*, 1962, 31: 384–394.

appeared to this writer that when prolonged and steady physical effort was necessary, women, particularly peasant women, had more stamina and resilience than men. Like the men, they were of all ages and from all social classes. Women with high levels of intelligence worked themselves up into the policy-making levels of the underground (and of the enemy). Nor were they lacking in heroism. A beautiful Polish girl, who was a superb linguist in the movement's Intelligence, was captured and tortured by the Gestapo in a most sadistic fashion. When she could no longer stand it, she asked for poison through a bribed guard. She revealed no information.

It should be emphasized, however, that not only the noblest are attracted by this kind of fighting. Because its participants spring from a very broad cross-section of the population, unconventional forces are also a cesspool of killers and people with aberrations looking for a formalized excuse to use violence. There was many a man ready and willing to kill a prisoner to get "even" for some real or imaginary reason known only to himself. Many kinds of men can be found, particularly among guerrillas. To idealize them is self-destructive.

Guerrillas and saboteurs are the true "unconventional fighters" for they carry violence directly to the enemy. It seems that, irrespective of culture and country, the people who are close to the soil and nature are the main stock of guerrilla units. These are not, on the whole, rich peasants; the well-to-do tend to stay out of the fighting. The guerrillas' pattern of living requires stamina, physical endurance and a rather philosophical acceptance of hardship. The greatest hardship, other than physical, is the lack of women. Pleasures are scarce. . . . Mobility is one of the guerrilla's greatest assets: yet, the men tend to get overequipped, particularly with heavy weapons when they are available. Such weapons provide them with some feeling of security. Another painful problem is the lack of identity. In many societies it appears that men would rather fight in uniforms and be identified as a military unit rather than a guerrilla band.

Their lives are largely regulated by the degree of support given by the indigenous population, and also by the climatic conditions and the terrain. While valleys are avoided because they might become deadly traps, guerrillas can operate in literally any terrain so long as the distance between their hideouts and the targets is relatively short. When in danger of being encircled by the enemy, the guerrilla units will try to "evaporate" by disbanding and reassembling at a predetermined point. This is not a difficult task if the climate and terrain are favorable.

When possible, the members of the group try to live within communities among the peasants, and to assemble only when necessary for action. The Chinese Communist guerrillas during the revolutionary war tried to be self-sustaining and in some instances even operated cooperatives helping peasants produce food and the necessities of daily life; at the same time they carried on very intense political indoctrination. This kind of approach has two direct gains: first, it conserves energy which can be utilized at the time of action; second, it cements the relationship between the guerrillas and the local population.

Guerrilla fighting has no rules. For security reasons it might be necessary to shoot one's own wounded—an act practically unheard-of in conventional forces. Participants usually do not wear uniforms; thus captives in many instances are treated as "bandits" and shot. Tactics are basically offensive in spirit. Hit-and-run fighting is practiced. Mobility, surprise and dispersions are necessary. Ideally guerrillas follow the principle of "Move while attacking; attack while moving." (Han Wu-ti, 140 B.C.) It would be this writer's axiom that if the enemy has a chance to reload his weapon, the guerrilla action was poorly planned or executed and should be abandoned.

The smaller the groups, the more active they seem to be in searching out and hitting the enemy. The greater the imagination of the leader, the more enterprising and unusual are the actions of the group. In July 1950, four Koreans in a jeep rode into an American post and wanted their gas tank filled. After this was done they rode away, spraying the Americans with automatic fire. Successful action to some extent seems to depend upon determination and a cool head.

Guerrillas are not after territorial gains. Their effectiveness lies rather in binding the enemy forces, killing and spreading terror, destroying elements that are of strategic and tactical importance. Furthermore, they preserve and protect to a considerable degree the economic wealth and structure of a community.

In regard to the destruction of tactically and militarily important objectives, one can point to the techniques of French guerrillas dealing with German transportation. The range of their activities was broad: faking, changing and turning the directional signs; felling roadside trees; spreading spikes on the roads; burning wooden bridges; mining roads; attacking telephone lines; blocking inland waterways.

Needless to say, picking off a high-ranking officer or a member of the political elite is considered a coup by any guerrilla. Soviet partisans poisoned at least one German general and carried another out of his own headquarters wrapped in a carpet.

In many instances guerrillas in Italy and the Soviet Union acted as protectors of the local industry, at the last moment preventing the German dismantling effort. One of the techniques by which guerrillas may preserve the integrity of the plants is to synchronize with their activities public riots and general strikes. Both of these weapons were used in China, Italy and the Soviet Union.

One final facet of guerrilla activities worth mentioning here is the organization of evasion. This term may encompass attempts to evacuate allied prisoners, airmen shot down or sympathizers. It can also refer to the establishment of an underground railroad facilitating the escape of ablebodied men or specialists to join guerrillas or their supporters abroad. As many as two thousand French volunteers to the Free French forces were entering England monthly in the late summer of 1940, in spite of the fact that the Vichy Government and the Germans were trying to stop them.

Troublesome as they may be to the enemy, guerrillas at certain times become as troublesome to their own political leadership. This happens when the country is liberated or when the political leadership feels obliged to set forth a concrete political program. Political leaders try to avoid specific pronouncements at the inception of the organization. By remaining vague they are able to accommodate individual aspirations and thus increase their ranks. When the elite feels strong enough to seize power officially, however, or when, for one reason or another, they are compelled to state their political objectives, they prefer to do so when the guerrillas have been disarmed. Hence a gentle, and sometimes not so gentle, tug-of-war arises between the political leadership and the guerrillas. "Give us the weapons and we will give you the political program." "Give us the political program and we will give you the weapons." If the leaders have a label of legality and have the territory under control, the usual practice is to incorporate the guerrillas into the conventional military forces. Thus the guerrillas retain the weapons but they have little to say about the direction and content of political programs. Any successful guerrilla movement, however, carries within it the seeds of violent opposition to its own political leadership.

If guerrilla fighters are the artisans in violence, those who are engaged in sabotage are the artists. They are the "surgeons of violence" by profession: they deal with the nerves, heart and brain of the enemy. They hit power stations, transformers, high tension lines and all possible centers of communication. They work themselves into the industrial network of the enemy, causing stoppages, faulty production, delays and physical destruction of anything that might be of value.

The ingenuity with which sabotage men choose and attack their targets is boundless. There was one instance when even condoms produced for the German army were punctured. (How this was supposed to contribute to Allied victory is not clear.) They might put sugar in gas tanks, cause faulty execution of aircraft engine parts, spike oil wells and change the labels on freight cars. This latter procedure was used by the Polish underground in diverting precious metals used in the production of high-grade steel from Berlin to a small town in southern Greece. It took three months for this transport to reach Berlin, part of it having been blown up by Greek saboteurs.

If these groups really want to get a man, there is practically no chance for him to survive. The German general who commanded the security police in Warsaw rode to and from his office by different routes every day with an escort of armored cars. Nonetheless he was ambushed and killed.

There is no logistics problem with the members of sabotage units as there is in the case of guerrillas. They live "ordinary" lives and maintain themselves. The Polish experience showed that to pass information to the members of the group took about ten hours in a large city; to get them ready and assembled at the point of action took an additional six to ten hours. Outside of their time in action, they are responsible for their own maintenance and their own lives.

It must be emphasized that as effective as is the guerrilla and sabotage units' tactical and strategic contribution to defeating the enemy, this does not adequately explain their value in the struggle for political power. Here, *the greatest contribution of guerrillas and saboteurs lies in catalyzing and intensifying counterterror which further alienates the enemy from the local population.* The enemy as a rule will relegate the responsibility for dealing with unconventional fighters to military forces or security agencies. These groups deal with the fighters by using the only methods available to them—those involving force. Because the guerrillas are elusive and the saboteurs even more so, the frustration of the pursuers results in counterviolence, which falls on the lifeline and source of manpower of these units—the local population. Reprisals begin.

This is what sophisticated political leaders of guerrillas may expect. There is no better way to alienate a regime in power from the population than to incite it to apply nonselective terror. Guerrillas and saboteurs serve this purpose eminently. The ebb and flow of membership in these units is not related to the number of tactical victories, to their losses or even to their prospects for success. The rate of recruitment

is directly related to the intensity of terror applied by the enemy in suppressing the movement. Any counterterror by the enemy brings to the ranks of the unconventional fighters new recruits who are escaping from the reprisals or who wish revenge. In this way the movement perpetuates itself. Unless the guerrillas are also using terror against the population, the more terror the enemy applies, the more fighters he produces, provided, of course, that the cultural values permit violence. (Certainly Quakers would react to counterterror differently from Catholic Poles.)

The existence of an underground and its result—unconventional warfare—is evidence of the breakdown of social order. When this occurs, there is a considerable alteration of the operational values and social mores of the society. What was a crime before the struggle can become exemplary behavior during strife. Killing, destroying property that may be of use to the enemy and slowing production become not only respectable, but also moral obligations. This modification of values affects the process of socialization of the generation growing up while the underground activities are in progress. Violence becomes an acceptable means and part of solving problems for that generation. Polish underground authorities were aware of this and established a special "Pedagogical Council" to see that the boys would not become one-track killers, but would continue with the acquisition of education and the development of moral values necessary for existence in a normal democratic society. A man who grows up in the Judaic-Christian tradition of compassion and love has to go through intellectual calisthenics to rationalize his participation in the ruthless operation of unconventional warfare. This is not the case with the Communists, where all activities of this kind can be explained and justified in terms of class struggle.

In terms of American cultural values, it seems that to engage in unconventional warfare we would have to abandon two rules in our code of manly conduct—waiting for the enemy to reach for his gun first and face-to-face combat. These two ideals are the very antithesis of unconventional fighting.

Mass movements using unconventional

warfare exist at this time in at least eleven countries: Algeria, South Africa, Angola, Burma, China, Vietnam, South Korea, Kenya, Laos, Venezuela and Guatemala. There are also "dormant" underground movements in at least ten countries in East Central Europe now within the sphere of Soviet influence. In the years since the end of World War II, the political elites and forms of governments in six countries have been changed through the application or with the assistance of the techniques of unconventional warfare: China, Israel, Vietnam, Iraq, Cuba and Laos. Such techniques for gaining political power will be used frequently by technologically backward people because they are cheap and effective.

Our political leadership ought to face this question squarely: Is unconventional warfare an instrument of foreign policy to be applied in international relations as an element of power and pressure, or is it merely an infantry combat technique to be used in wartime? If the latter is what we have in mind, then we are really using "unconventional warfare" in the most "conventional" fashion. On the other hand, *if* we intend to enter the game of systematically initiating, manipulating and fostering political mass movements in order to help peoples realize their political objectives through violence, then we must understand and clearly distinguish between the prerequisites, the techniques and the objectives of unconventional warfare.

If such a definition takes place, then the aspirations and expectations of the indigenous people with whom we plan to work ought to be given paramount attention and faced squarely and honestly! Otherwise we shall fail as we did in Cuba.

This is even more important when we try to fight guerrillas, as we are doing now in Southeast Asia. True, in some situations it is necessary to deal with guerrillas in the most stern and unyielding manner. (Seek them out and put such pressure on them that the guerrilla will not have a chance to stop behind a bush to relieve himself. . . .) But this is a short-term tactical answer; the final solution should not rest at this. For a long-range consideration, it is necessary that a basic question be asked: "Why did guerrillas emerge and what are their values, goals and grievances?"

You cannot expect a starved peasant in an underdeveloped country to fight on behalf of "free enterprise"—he has experienced it already from his landlord. Neither does the word "freedom" mean much to him—freedom to do what? Behind a guerrilla's gun is a man; that man shoots in the direction from which there is no hope. He shoots because he does not believe that for him justice and satisfaction can be achieved in any other way. In the long run, therefore, he should be met on the level of his expectations and hopes, and not with a rifle. "For a partisan may be completely wrong on what he is fighting *for,* but is not likely to be nearly so wrong on what he is fighting *against.*"

ISOLATION AND COLLABORATION:
A PARTIAL THEORY OF
INTER-NATION RELATIONS[*][1]

HAROLD GUETZKOW

Résumé

This paper develops a theory of how groups meet their members' demands. It is argued that the members of social units obtain satisfaction of their economic, cultural, and political needs through participation in social groups, including states or nations. It posits that changing environmental conditions may give rise to new needs or demands on the part of the members of groups. It argues that these new demands may be realizable either through self-reliant policies pursued in isolation or through relations with other political and social units. The theory is concerned particularly with national behaviors—be they individual or group, official or unofficial—which constitute the external responses of peoples comprising nation-states.

[*] Reprinted by permission of the author and publisher from *Journal of Conflict Resolution*, 1957, *1:* 46–68

[1] The essay is an outcome of work and discussion at the Center for Research on World Political Institutions at Princeton University. Its director, Dr. R. W. Van Wagenen, helped me formulate my problem; members of the center's 1952 summer conference on "Expanding Community"—Drs. Werner Levi, Harold Engle, Melvin Tumin, Ralph Ross, George Belknap—influenced its development. The criticisms and suggestions of Professors James Coleman, of Columbia University; Karl W. Deutsch, of Massachusetts Institute of Technology; Alfred O. Hero, of the World Peace Foundation; Alfred J. Hotz, of Western Reserve University; Richard C. Synder, of Northwestern University; and Paul L. Ward, of Carnegie Institute of Technology, are much appreciated. The manuscript was reworked into its final version by Jane Applebaum Jacobs, formerly of the Fletcher School of Law and Diplomacy and London School of Economics.

This piece is the more general essay deriving from my summers' appointment as Research Associate at Princeton; the more specific work is my *Multiple Loyalties: Theoretical Approach to a Problem in International Organization* (Princeton: Princeton University Press, 1955).

The model essentially consists of the opposition of the two sets of factors. The direction of behavior of a group is schematized as the resultant balance between the strength of factors driving and/or attracting behavior inward and the strength of those factors pushing and/or pulling toward collaboration. The paper discusses factors influencing the choice in each of the two directions and predicts that the individual's and group's behaviors at any given time will be determined by the balance between these factors. The direction of behavior of the group is hypothesized to be conditioned upon such past history and current realities as the following:

1.1 and 1.2. The satisfactoriness or unsatisfactoriness of the group's experiences with its self-reliance versus its experiences with collaborative measures.

2.1 and 2.2. The degree to which the ideologies of the group's members are isolationist or collaborative.

3.1 and 3.2. The extent to which self-reliant means seem practical and advantageous versus the extent to which collaborative means seem feasible and advantageous.

3.3. The extent to which the group's task requires interdependence on other groups or allows the group to pursue its goal in isolation.

4.1. The degree to which the group's leadership perceives isolation or collaboration as supporting or destroying its elite positions.

4.2. The extent to which the members of the group think of collaborative relations as interfering with successful self-reliance.

In addition to factors which give directionality to the behavior of groups, the model hypothesizes that there are auxiliary factors, which may facilitate or hinder the extent to which the group achieves isolation or collaboration, such as:

5.1. The extent to which the groups which interact have common and congruent, rather than contradictory and conflictful, elements in their cultural backgrounds and language-thought processes.

After a discussion of the model's general characteristics and its inadequacies and limitations, brief illustrations are given of its use in the analysis of current policy issues in international affairs. For example, the theory indicates that regional collaboration, whether it is successful or unsuccessful, will tend to make universal collaboration less likely. On the issue of the number of functions which should be encompassed by a supra-group organization, the model predicts that single-purpose collaboration will tend to be extinguished, while multifunctionalism generates further collaboration.

Orientation

My attempt to construct a theory of internation behavior stems from a belief that methods and propositions of the basic social sciences may be useful in developing theories of international relations (32). Nations are a special and particularly powerful kind of group, but they are groups. Thus it becomes relevant to explore the value of propositions from social psychology and sociology in interpreting and predicting their behavior. The focus is upon how the behavior of individuals and groups within the nation determines the isolationistic or collaborative tendencies of its external relations.

As the history of the development of models in economics and psychology indicates, early hypothetical systems are generally crude. They may omit many important features of the phenomena. Often they distort features of the process itself. My set of propositions may have all these limitations. But models advance a discipline by this very process of artificially reducing complexity. Perhaps even more important, model-building requires the scholar to define his factors more adequately and eventually leads to more precise empirical testing of the system he formulates (2). My formulations should therefore be "open game" for other scholars, so that the behavioral

approach to problems of international politics may become more adequate.

The exposition of the model consists of two parts: first, a brief description of the kinds of demands that members may make upon their groups; then an investigation of some of the factors which determine whether groups turn toward isolation or toward collaboration in attempting to meet those demands. No claims are made to originality in the choice of the variables of the system—or to exhaustiveness. I hope those chosen, however, are of import.

A Theory of Intergroup Relations

Kinds Of Demands

Groups in general are organized to meet human needs; their structures and processes are in part molded by these needs. In the case of a relatively comprehensive and broad-based group, there may be a great range and variety of needs which its members look upon it to fulfill. We can distinguish three basic areas of needs or demands at the level of the nation: (1) economic needs, from the simplest, most fundamental needs for food, clothing, and shelter, to those needs expressed through complex economic relationships, such as access to raw materials, maintenance of high levels of employment and investment, and the like; (2) social-cultural needs, such as intellectual-artistic activities, religious institutions, satisfactory customs for the regulation of primary and secondary group relations, etc.; and (3) political needs. Because of my special interest in this third area, political demands will be broken into three subgroups:

a) Security needs, including protection against coercion by other members of the group itself and by other groups.

b) Group loyalty needs, including the need to identify with and belong to a social unity.

c) Prestige needs, including those satisfied by wielding power.

These needs are universal, although their intensity varies among persons and groups from nation to nation. As empirical work in this area develops, it will be profitable to specify them in more detail with some exactness.

Factors Which Determine How Demands Will Be Met

The basic hypotheses of the model follow:

1. If new demands arise or members believe their existing demands are not being met satisfactorily, one or both of the following responses may occur: (*a*) members may try to satisfy their demands self-reliantly by making internal changes in the group itself, acting in isolation from other groups; and/or (*b*) members may try to satisfy their demands through co-operation with other, external groups by collaboration. Should neither of these alternatives succeed, the demands themselves might be changed, restructuring the alternative responses.

2. If the needs of group members are relatively constant and relatively well satisfied, there will not be any significant impulse for change.

When members of the group are self-reliant, they may seek fulfillment of their demands through the central institutions of the group itself or in a decentralized way through the institutions of its subgroups. For example, in a depression, needs might be met by setting welfare and redevelopment agencies at the national and/or at the local level. When, on the other hand, group members are motivated toward collaboration, they also may seek fulfillment of their demands in a variety of ways. At the local, individual level, for example, citizens may leave the group as emigrants when employment levels are low. Action may also be taken at the institutional level, as when the government, in the very process of making emigration arrangements, initiates interstate co-operation. Or members of different national units may have relations with one another through non-governmental organizations, such as trading companies, professional societies for the exchange of scientific information, and the like.

It should not be especially difficult to categorize particular acts of particular states as "self-reliant" and "collaborative." There will be borderline cases, of course. However, the huge mass of empirical evidence available should make conclusive testing

possible. For example, in the late spring of 1954 officials of the United States Department of Agriculture were attempting to handle farm-commodity surpluses. They made many suggestions as to where to seek solutions. Some of the officials looked to Congress, hoping for more flexibility in farm price-support legislation. Others wished to approach the FAO with suggestions for a special international committee to help market the surpluses. Other clear-cut examples may be found. The more difficult, though surmountable, problem will be selecting a field of events to submit to the classification process. One can work with such universes of events as congressional acts for preliminary empirical work, until one focuses more exactly the type of events one wishes to sample.

Whether the unit turns toward self-help or toward interstate relations depends upon many factors. The essay now enumerates some of these factors, with attention to the underlying sociopsychological mechanisms involved in each.

Past Experience Factors

The first set of factors is concerned with the impact of past occurrences upon a group's internal and external relationships. The effect of these past occurrences is exerted by means of learning mechanisms which have been under investigation by psychologists for a number of years.

1.1 Self-reliant experience hypothesis: Other things being equal, *the more consistently and the more fully members' needs have been satisfied through internal or self-reliant measures, the greater the tendency for members to seek solutions to their new needs in isolation.*

This tendency to continue using self-reliant devices arises because members are conditioned by a successful past to expect that the state, or non-governmental institutions within the state, will meet their needs in the future. This is the "transfer" or "generalization" mechanism at work (15). Thus when the group has been functioning well, there are likely to be strong tendencies toward self-reliant behavior. When, on the other hand, members have had unsatisfactory experiences with their group, they are considerably less likely to turn toward their own institutions for the achievement of their demands.

1.2. Collaborative experience hypothesis: Other things being equal, *the more satisfactorily group members have been able to solve their past problems through inter-group relations, the more likely they are to collaborate with other groups when new needs arise.*

This proposition involves the same sociopsychological mechanism as does Hypothesis 1.1. In this case, if members of states succeed in satisfying some of their demands through relations with other states, the satisfaction will be generalized or transferred to expectations regarding future relations. If, on the other hand, the group's past experience with other groups has been unsatisfactory, then its members will tend to avoid such relations in the future. This phase of the hypothesis is particularly important, for it invalidates the widespread notion that sheer contact between nations necessarily produces collaboration. The contact must be satisfying to the parties concerned in order to increase the likelihood of its being attempted again. For example, Mitrany holds that one of the benefits to be derived from functional international organizations such as WHO and ILO is the satisfactoriness of the experience that members of different states gain in working together (24).

Note that in any given situation both these variables are operating simultaneously. It is possible that the self-reliance variable (1.1) might be weak, while the collaboration variable (1.2) is strong, as is illustrated by the receptivity of Japan to United States aid after World War II. Or, contrariwise, the experience with internal measures might be positive and with external relations negative, as some contend was the case in Stalinist Russia. Or both factors might be relatively strong, with conflicts arising because of the contradictory pressures felt by the citizenry, as in France during its first decade after World War II. This simultaneous operation of factors is

an integral feature of the model, as will be evident in the remainder of the essay.

Empirical work on these two hypotheses might be carried through by coding successes and failures in the major historical experiences of a group over an extended period of time. The coding procedures now being developed in the social sciences (3, 6) could be adapted to indicate the extent and intensity of a nation's successes and failures in solving its economic, cultural, and political problems. Classifying the events into those dependent upon self-reliant behavior and those involving interstate relations would then yield a crude measure of the two factors.[2]

Ideological Factors

But past occurrences are not the sole conditioners of the behavior of groups. Members develop "sets-of-mind" not only on the basis of past experience but also partly from independently operating ideological factors —religious, philosophical, cultural. An important pair of hypotheses is to be derived from the *ideological* attitudes of a society toward self-reliance and collaboration:

2.1 Self-reliant ideology hypothesis: Other things being equal, *the more widespread the general ideological conviction that the group ought to meet its needs through its own efforts, the greater the tendency to rely on the group alone for solutions.*

This faith in group isolation may spring from a variety of non-rational sources. Often it stems from a virile nationalism, such as is sweeping the newly free Asian countries today. Traditional hostility toward potential collaborators may turn a group toward self-reliant, rather than collaborative, measures. Or a deep-seated suspicion of "entangling alliances" can become

---

[2] Deutsch (11) has gone far in the pioneering of the measurement of factors in the relations among nations; see especially his discussions of the measurement of communication, pp. 64–70, the quantification of national assimilation, pp. 130–36, and his chap. vi of case examples on "National Assimilation and Differentiation," along with its technical appendixes.

so strong that it outlives its usefulness to the nation, producing old responses which do not take changed conditions into consideration. Such an ideology "provides the standards by which a man determines, measures and then justifies his acts" (20).

A particularly significant source of an isolationist or anticollaborative ideology may be the strong sense of attachment to the group which is found in members of especially cohesive groups. We might state this particular relationship as follows:

2.11. End-value hypothesis: Other things **being** equal, *the greater value that membership in the group has for its members, the greater their tendency to use the group in isolation as a means to their ends.*

There is widespread agreement among students of social behavior that groups are generally organized to meet human needs (12). Their initial value is as an *instrument* by which members expect to achieve their goals. But what began as a means to an end may become an end in itself; an object which once served directly to satisfy needs may become a need-arouser (25). Thus a group which at first served only to satisfy its members' demands now becomes a need, a good in itself, regardless of the instrumental value that the group has or may have had. As Curti noted in his study of loyalty in the United States, at first the union of states was a means to maintain freedom from the interference of the mother country, England. Later, its continuation became a goal in its own right (10). Then members take pride in the unique identity of their group and are highly sensitive to any arrangements that seem to submerge or threaten it. In their relations at the group level, members will choose to act through their own group to the exclusion of other groups because such instrumental value will again enhance the group's value as an end.

Groups are sometimes found taking paradoxical positions as a result of the operation of these attachments by their members. They may fail to join forces with other organizations having the same goals for fear of losing their identity in the larger effort, even when the very nature of the

common problem seems to necessitate cooperation. Consider the case of a local group which organized and ran an unusually successful fund-raising campaign for UNICEF in an American city. The success of the experience welded its members so closely together and gave them such attachment to their group that they chose not to affiliate with the state and national levels of the same organization but to carry on their activity autonomously. Another example, less extreme, is found in the policy of the United States when the nations, after World War II, faced the problem of raising living standards and productivity in underdeveloped areas. The United States government chose to offer technological aid not through the UN but unilaterally, through agencies of its own. Feeling for the group as an end in itself was so strong, especially where American technology was involved, that the essential identity of the United States could not be submerged in the joint effort. Corbett notes how international service agencies have learned to increase their effectiveness by stimulating the "development of resourceful and devoted native organs" within the countries in which the agency operates. "Conducted in this way, the more successful an international service agency proves, the more it would seem to focus the loyalty of its beneficiaries upon their states rather than upon any supranational society" (9).

However, there may be a quite different kind of ideological context within which the member's loyalty to his group may not necessarily be at odds with the seeking of collaborative solutions. The ideology which contrasts with the self-reliant one may be stated as follows:

2.2 Collaborative ideology hypothesis: Other things being equal, *the more widespread the general ideological conviction that the group can satisfy its needs through collaboration with other groups, the greater the tendency toward co-operative intergroup relations.*

Perhaps the strongest non-rational source of an outward-oriented ideology has been the religious or philosophical belief in the brotherhood of man. The Hellenists, with their concept of a commonwealth of mankind inherited from the Stoics; the Middle Ages, with its sense of unification under the church; and many small religious or humanistically based groups in present-day Western societies all share some aspects of this belief. Once such ideological convictions are held, they are as effective in determining the direction of a group's activities as its past experiences are. Indeed, they may even contradict the lessons of the past and force an interpretation of those experiences so as to make them reinforce, rather than oppose, a fervently held collaborative ideology.

Hypotheses 2.1 and 2.2 are a pair and operate simultaneously, as do 1.1 and 1.2. If both are simultaneously strong, there will be conflict among the members of the group, which in extreme cases may even fragment it into subgroups. The end-value mechanism (Hypothesis 2.11) gives a "multiplier" effect, depending upon the group to which the attachment is made. If it is made with the individual's own national group, as is usually the case, the factor serves to increase the impact of the tendency toward isolation. If, however, an international organization has become an end value to its members and is the target of the attachment, the tendency will be to induce collaboration among the national units.

Ideological factors are essentially all-encompassing attitudes and hence may be appraised by the appropriate interviewing techniques being developed in the social sciences (5). The foregoing hypotheses could then be tested by comparing the ideology of a number of groups with the direction of their policies over a period of time. Patton (27) has already developed a method of describing ideology which would be directly applicable to the isolation versus collaboration distinction.

Perceptions of the Short Run

The experiences and ideology hypotheses deal with general attitudes toward isolation and collaboration per se. Although these factors are powerful in molding action in the long run, responses to the immediate are often influenced by members' perception of the short-run situation. One of the basic propositions in the psychology of social perception is: "Objects or events that are close to each other in space or time, or resemble each other, tend to be apprehended as parts of a common structure."[3] The pair of propositions which follow postulate tendencies toward isolation and collaboration from the perceptual characteristics of short-run situations.

3.1 Proximity hypothesis: Other things being equal, *members of groups tend to use self-reliant means to their goals when such intra-group measures are more proximate.*

Indigenous techniques for inducing change tend to be structured into short-run situations. Citizens of a nation often feel there are no real alternatives in such remote procedures as collaboration within an international organization or participation in multilateral arrangements with other states. Corbett implicitly used this hypothesis in explaining how international service agencies have learned that "the best means of achieving the common object in each country is to stimulate the development of resourceful and devoted native organs" (9). Internal procedures are familiar procedures. Citizens often can perceive more clearly the structure of the initiation, control, and results of intra-group means. Their executive departments can be expected to implement the group's goals in a range of familiar ways.

But these same factors in the structuring of immediate perceptions also operate in determining the short-run reactions of citizens to the advantages and disadvantages of collaboration, as is asserted in the following hypothesis:

3.2. Advantages hypothesis: Other things being equal, *the more adequately the members of a group envision the techniques of intergroup collaboration as means to their ends, the greater the tendency to move toward collaboration.*

If the advantages to be derived from collaboration are vivid and concretely tied to

[3] Krech (17, pp. 76–146); quotation from p. 108; note especially chaps. iii, "Perceiving the World," and iv, "Reorganizing Our Perceptions."

clearly formulated means, they are likely to be more adequately perceived. When the gains of collaboration are thought of as indirect and marginal, there is little tendency toward intergroup relations. When the fruits of co-operation are remote in time, increasing only after a considerable period of marginal returns, the probability of any initial action is low. This hypothesis predicts, for example, that a nation seeking to control local epidemics would probably be more interested in co-operating with WHO if it offered a short-term medical program of mass inoculation than if it offered a long-range public sanitation program—even if both programs were to have the same cost. An information campaign which makes the long-range or indirect benefits of inter-nation activity seem more concrete and more tangible is predicted to increase collaboration.

Because these hypotheses are directly concerned with the immediate perceptions of group members, data for testing them could be obtained through the various techniques for measuring attitudes. For example, Roper has surveyed attitudes toward world organization among citizens of the United States. He found some individuals who felt that world organizations were ineffective because other countries want only to "take our money and give nothing in return." Others considered the UN to be valuable—a potential agency for further collaboration—because it was "the only way to handle Russia" (29). The quality of the perceptions as to the usefulness of international collaboration in achieving American goals would seem to play a powerful part in shaping the behavior of the United States on the international scene. Almond has already studied some of the effects of such perceptions on foreign-policy formulation (1).

But it is not sufficient to confine our attention only to the perceived advantages and disadvantages in an immediate situation; it is important to recognize that the actual physical, economic, and social realities underlying these perceptions also influence the direction in which the group moves. The following hypothesis attempts to formalize the impact of these factors:

3.3. Nature of the task hypothesis: Other things being equal, *by their very nature the group's unsatisfied demands may or may not necessitate relations with other groups for their realization.*

The nature of the task confronted when meeting a group's demand may impose powerful constraints upon the behaviors of the members of a group. This factor classically has been treated in terms of the group's limitations of the natural resources. There are also non-material demands which, by their very content, direct the energies of a group inward or outward. For example, if there exists within group members a strong need to convert disbelievers in the outgroup to their own form of salvation, they must necessarily turn outward in attempting to fulfil it. Needs of this kind may be essentially religious, as in Asoka's early peaceful penetrations to propagate Hinduism. Or they may be more secular, as in the imperialisms witnessed by the nineteenth and twentieth centuries.

There may be economic or military problems which, by their very nature, require or rule out relations with other groups. A small state with neither the quantities nor the range of raw materials to supply its own needs will seek trading relations with other units far more often than will a large continental power with a wide variety of resources within its own borders. In the military sphere, it has recently become necessary for a nation to extend its security borders by collective defense arrangements with others, since technological developments have made defense areas global. In preindustrial ages these security needs could often be met best by a turning inward to consolidate the domestic defenses.

Internal Group Factors

But experience and ideology, even as they interact with the citizens' perception of the immediate task situation, do not work alone in determining whether the behaviors of groups are collaborative or isolationistic. The following hypotheses are concerned with some effects of the internal structure and functioning of the group, and the effects of intergroup collaboration upon internal group functioning. Other features of group life may be as important, but, for the time being, my effort is limited to these aspects of the group's structure.[4]

4.1. Leadership hypothesis: Other things being equal, *the more leaders believe that a self-reliant or collaborative policy will reinforce their elite position, the greater will be their tendency to pursue such a policy.*

It now becomes relevant to distinguish between the leadership elements of groups and the rank and file of the memberships. The unsatisfied need which motivates action may be felt by the followers, or it may be shared by the leadership as well. In either case the leaders have another purpose, or need, of their own: to maintain and consolidate their own positions as leaders. Leaders tend to view their problems in these terms. In cases where the citizens' demands need to be fulfilled through some specific program, leaders may comply willingly if they see this program as supportive of their own leadership role. Where the membership demands that a need be fulfilled but does not specify, or cannot agree upon, a method, leaders are likely to seek or select that solution which seems also to strengthen their own positions.

For example, if a political and military threat from the outside produces widespread insecurity in a national public, its leaders, other things being equal, may judge it best to respond with an inward-directed program for increasing the nation's military strength. Such a program, like others which expand governmental activity, increases the political and economic patronage that can be distributed by those in power. It also provides the psychological atmosphere and the symbols for building personal attachments. Indeed, to reap these very benefits, leaders sometimes set in motion a massive rearmament program even when it is not directly relevant to the fulfillment of the country's existing needs. The

history of modern dictatorship abounds in instances of leaders who reinforced their own power with military programs aimed at enemies.

There also are circumstances in which leadership maintains its power through the very mechanism of co-operating with external groups. Throughout the period of European colonization in the Near East and Asia, there were many native elites which managed to consolidate their power locally either by collaborating with the colonizers or by joining forces with another European power against the would-be colonizers of their own state. The rulers of some princely states in India, for example, secured from the English the right to defend their country themselves and, in the process of making defense arrangements, confirmed their own local leadership.

Although leaders have their vested interests to protect, it must be remembered that the followers, too, gain considerably from the group. Thus the following hypothesis:

4.2. Expectations of internal interference hypothesis: Other things being equal, *the more interference with need-satisfying internal activities that is predicted to arise from collaboration with other groups, the greater will be the tendency for members to avoid such collaboration.*

A well-functioning, cohesive group has undoubtedly developed practices and behavior patterns for satisfying many of its members' needs. It came into being for this purpose, and in its development, as suggested earlier (Hypothesis 2.11), it probably generated end-value needs for itself, while simultaneously fulfilling others. Hence, if potential collaborating groups or a supranational organization are thought likely to demand changes in these practices which have been need-satisfying in the past, they will be avoided as dangerous, and "national sovereignty" and other arguments may be called in to resist them.

Auxiliary Factors

There may also be factors which play no role in the original determination of the direction of the groups' behavior but which

---

[4] See Cartwright and Zander (7) and Hare *et al.* (13), two excellent collections of basic propositions in the gradually emerging field of group processes.

either facilitate or hinder behavior, once it has been decided upon. One important factor is hypothesized below:

5.1 Cultural background hypothesis: Other things being equal, *the greater the similarity of language, customs, and ideology among nations, the more easily will their members collaborate with one another.*

If the play of forces within a nation results in a period of collaborative policies, the way will be smoother and the chances of success greater if potential collaborators have similar cultural backgrounds. Use of a common language reduces the chance for misunderstandings which on occasion produce needless conflict. As Newcomb states it: "Two individuals can communicate successfully only to the extent that they are using similar frames of reference" (25). The possession of related cultural heritages provides common norms, so that problems and approaches to problem-solving are likely to be similarly conceived.

Mead has developed a method to appraise empirically the degree to which concepts are shared by two cultures (22). Cattell's efforts to isolate the dimensions along which cultures vary may give us another framework with which to make empirical approaches to this problem (8). Although both these methodologies are in need of further development, it would not seem impossible to measure the similarity of cultures. We could then test the foregoing hypothesis by comparing the extent of collaboration between similar and dissimilar cultures, other things being equal.

One can cite a number of other auxiliary factors which help to influence the success or failure of policy, once its direction has been determined. For example, the possession of adequate, smoothly functioning governmental machinery might be an important enabling factor for a nation choosing self-reliant measures. Similarly, well-developed channels for communication and action at the international level are likely to make collaborative behavior easier and more fruitful. At either of these political levels, on the other hand, cumbersome, ineffective machinery might render action almost impossible. In that case the initial

decision in favor of self-reliant or collaborative courses of action would need to be remade. Instead of being merely auxiliary factors which facilitated or hindered group action, such factors as government machinery and communication channels would become prime in altering the very direction of the group's behavior. In such a case, they would operate as experience (1. or 3.) or internal group (4.1) factors, which have already been discussed.

The Model as an Operating System

Characteristics Of The Model As A Whole

The hypotheses just presented constitute a model whose central feature is the opposition of factors which, by their relative strengths, determine the direction of behavior. These factors may operate simultaneously with varying intensity upon different segments of the group. For example, an elite may believe that its demands can be achieved through collaboration with external groups, while the peasantry of the same nation may feel that its interests lie in internal changes. Or the factors may operate differently with respect to different coexisting needs. Security needs may be handled through relations with other nations, perhaps through collective-security pacts, while cultural needs may be satisfied internally. Given this variation in needs and these subgroups within nations, the model predicts much variation in behavior and considerable inconsistency and ambivalence as well.

The extent to which the behavior of group members tends in one direction rather than in another depends upon the relative strengths of the different variables. We might have a relatively simple situation, with factors 1.1, 2.1, and 3.1 strong and their complements (1.2, 2.2, and 3.2), driving behavior outward, weak. If the other factors play no significant part, there will be a strong tendency toward self-reliant measures and much general agreement among group members on the appropriateness of isolation.

However, the model also predicts that the picture at times will be quite mixed, as, for example, when 1.1 and 3.1 are strong simultaneously with a strong 2.2 and a leadership

(4.1) looking to intergroup relations to reinforce its position. Here the outcome might depend on the relative *strengths* of these opposing factors, or it might depend on how another factor might overbalance the opposition of forces toward isolation. In either case, with strong tendencies in both directions, we might expect considerable conflict among group members, perhaps even within some individual members, as to which direction ought to be pursued.

The model also predicts two types of stalemates within the group, wherein there is approximately the same balance between opposing sets of factors but at different levels of strength. When the balance is achieved between weak forces, there will be inaction—but little conflict. When the balance is achieved between strong opposing forces, there will be stalemate with inaction, but it will be accompanied by much internal conflict (21).

Since the same direction of behavior may occur because of quite different driving factors, the model assumes that there is an adding of forces, the one to the other. The citizens of one nation might seek external relations because of a strong collaborative ideology (2.2) and, in addition, a widespread perception of collaboration as an advantageous direct route to the solution of their problems (3.2). Those of another nation might encourage their government to be active internationally because of highly successful past experiences in this area (1.2) and because the very nature of their task seems to require it (3.3). In these cases, the direction of the behavior will be the same—collaboration. However, the scholar and the practitioner attempting to reinforce or change the directional tendencies must know the sources of the forces, not only the resultant.

Quincy Wright (33) has developed an "analytic field" theory in which one of his dimensions would seem to approximate closely the one upon which my model focuses: "co-operation-isolation." His model differs from mine in that he conceives of the dimension as consisting only of forces toward co-operation, with the "capability" for "participating in effective international institutions" as depending, "on the one

hand, upon relative necessity to cooperate arising from economic and military interdependency, and on the other hand, upon a disposition to cooperate, manifested by attitudes, opinions, acts, and policies." Does the conceptualization given the dimension in my essay represent the very real conflict between collaboration and isolation which exists in the inter-nation affairs more adequately than is done by Wright's model?

Methods of Producing Change in the Direction of Group Behavior

Our model represents a system of factors, constantly interacting and in flux, which by their relative strengths at any given moment are determining the over-all direction of national policy. In the natural operation of this system, the direction of policy may change as a result of a change in strength of any of these factors. However, if we are concerned with the manipulation of the system to bring about a change thought to be desirable, there are at least two general considerations which might determine our approach.

First, as policy-makers, we would be concerned with ease of change, the relative maneuverability of the specific factors involved. For example, whereas past experience factors (1.1 and 1.2) and the inherent task implications of a newly arisen need (3.3) might be virtually unalterable, there might be long-range advantages in collaboration (3.2) which could be made more meaningful to the public through a propaganda campaign. Or, whereas ideological factors (2.1 and 2.2) might be very difficult to influence, leaders might be shown or induced to find new ways to reinforce their roles (4.1) by moving in the new direction. In each case the specific forces operating within the group at the time would need to be explored, their strength estimated, and their susceptibility to change judged, by whatever tools of analysis and measurement were available.

The second criterion is the degree of tension in the system. When there are pulls in both directions, the stronger they are, the greater the conflict or tension among group members. In extreme cases this might fragment and destroy the group. For example,

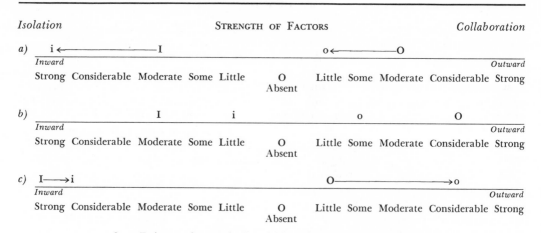

STRENGTH OF FACTORS

Isolation   *Collaboration*

O, o: Estimate of strength of variables orienting behavior Outward
I, i: Estimate of strength of variables orienting behavior Inward

FIG. 1—Graphic representation of resultants of factors driving group behaviors inward or outward.

consider a nation with strong antithetical forces, with the balance just slightly in favor of self-reliance. Its policy might consist of frequent, sporadic measures first in one direction and then in the other (with the swing toward collaboration occurring slightly more frequently), or it might be crippled almost completely by the conflict.

Suppose that the practitioner is distressed both by this deadlock and by the potential trend toward collaboration rather than self-reliance. He may attempt either to decrease collaboration-directing factors or to increase isolation-directing factors, or to do both simultaneously. He proceeds to analyze the maneuverability of the factors involved and finds that it would be easiest to increase the strength of the isolation-directed factors. However, unless his impact upon the situation is large, he may succeed only in equalizing the strengths of the opposing factors. This may increase tension to unbearable levels and induce fragmentation of the very group he tries to manipulate. In the face of this possibility, he may attempt to decrease the strength of the collaboration-directing factors instead, even if this is a far more difficult and expensive task.

We might diagram some different ways in which changes in the direction of behavior could occur. Suppose we represent the strength of the factors operating in a given group at a given time as being continuous on a line, as illustrated in Figure 1, *a*. The extreme left end of this line symbolizes the state of affairs when the tendency inward toward self-reliant isolated behavior is very strong. The extreme right end of the line represents conditions in which tendencies outward toward intergroup collaboration are very strong. When pressures in both directions are moderate and roughly equal, we might place the symbols *I* (inward-directing factors) and *O* (outward-directing factors) in the middle of each half of the continuum. An abrupt swing of behavior inward would be brought about by a simultaneous decrease in the strength of the *O* factors and an increase in the strength of the *I* factors, as is illustrated by the displacement of *i* and *o* in Figure 1, *a*, as indicated by the arrows.

In this model the same predominance of *O* over *I* (or vice versa) might come about at different levels of strength. In the hypothetical cases illustrated in Figure 1, *b*, the tendency for collaboration dominates the internal factors to the same extent in both situations (in *O* and *I*, as in *o* and *i*); yet in the one situation (*O, I*) there will be more intra-group tension, with occasional "inconsistent" (internally directed) behavior.

The model is useful in speculating as to what configuration of factors exists for different periods in the history of the United States. Figure 1, *c*, illustrates my estimates of the difference between the balance of factors in the United States around 1910

(*I* and *O*) and in 1950 (*i* and *o*). I have used arrows again in this example to illustrate the changes.

Is the Model Tautological?

When one encounters models in the social sciences, one at first may feel that the hypotheses they incorporate are somewhat tautological. For example, Hypothesis 2.1 might seem to be saying simply that if the ideology of a people is anticollaborative, then they will not collaborate. However, closer examination of the relationships between attitudes and behavior dispels this initial impression. There are tremendous differences between ideology and behavior. When attempts are made to measure the variables involved, these differences become evident. Suppose we measure attitudes toward intergroup collaboration by interviewing the elite of one of the nations concerned as to how useful they felt a particular regional development, such as the Colombo plan, to be. The resulting index of social perception could then be used to predict the extensiveness of measures taken by that nation in implementing the plan. When the variables are thus redefined in the terms of the actual testing operation, the distinction between one of the driving factors and its consequence (in this example, between 3.2 and *o*) becomes clear.[5]

The Group as the Basic Unit

The model has focused upon the internal functioning of groups,[6] and therein the model may be but a partial description of reality. It may be argued that when one deals with behavior that is outward-oriented, particularly if it involves more than unilateral actions toward, or bilateral relations with, other groups, there may be new supra-unit characteristics which should be taken into consideration.

An example of circular effects from inter-unit relations may be found in the studies of Robert T. Holt (14) on coalitions, using French cabinet collaborations as his empirical data. Holt argues that, once collaboration begins, there may be increases in *I* because of increases in *O,* as when a political party gains internal strength through the patronage it receives by having collaborated with other parties in forming a national government. But, at this glance, it seems that the principal features of internation behavior may be accounted for through the internal characteristics of the group.

When ILO enacts a set of international labor standards, it establishes a new norm to which citizens can appeal in pressing for reforms within their nation and to which governments can refer in instituting such reforms. Here is a new element in the situation, a new code of conduct arising out of and given sanction by the transnational organization. However, even these transgroup factors exercise their influence through the internal functioning of the groups themselves. In the ILO case, any changes which occur in national labor policies are due to pressures from internal subgroups, or to the initiative of national leaders. Hence these transgroup factors, too, can be dealt with adequately in terms of the group as the basic unit.

In describing the internal functioning of this basic unit—the group—I have tended to stress the importance of the group member's perception of the social reality within which he functions as citizen or official. This reflects the fundamental, widely accepted assumption of social behaviorists that realities do not affect behavior until they have been experienced and translated into perceptions. Of course, over time the underlying realities influence the perceptions; for, if policies repeatedly fail, experience and ideologies are re-examined and sometimes altered in light of the vivid evidence presented by the environment. It is interesting to note the Sherifs (30)—two scholars who have placed tremendous emphasis upon social perception—taking a most balanced view of the importance of the factual consequences of intergroup relations. They state: "The limiting factor in determining favorable and unfavorable

---

[5] Drs. M. F. Millikan and I. deS. Pool, of the Center for International Studies at Massachusetts Institute of Technology, already have studies in progress which aim to understand the effect of the elites upon foreign-policy formation (23).

[6] In this way my approach differs from the psychologists, who emphasize the behavior of the individual, as exemplified by Klineberg (16).

intergroup attitudes is the nature of the functional relations between the groups. In large group units, these relations may not be perceived directly by all individual members. Thus their conceptions may be dependent on communication from others, which may or may not reflect the actual state of affairs."[7] It is difficult for me to agree that the realities are any more limiting than the perceptions: both are of fundamental importance in determining the behavior of states.

The Model Applied to Nations

There will be those who question the validity of my interchanging the terms "group" and "nation" and of applying concepts developed in the study of groups to nation-states. It has sometimes been argued that the sovereignty (4) of nation-states is a unique characteristic, not possessed by other groups. This "sovereignty," runs the argument, invests nations with unlimited power and with some mystical existence of their own, independent of their citizens, which places them in a category by themselves. Such assertions seem to me to be overstatements, resulting from careless conceptualization and the extravagant nurturing of the original sovereignty concept by eighteenth- and nineteenth-century nationalisms. The facts of international life indicate that states, like other groups, are circumscribed in their behavior by political, social, cultural, and economic realities both within themselves and in their external environment. The leaders of nations, just like the leaders of other groups, are dependent for their very positions upon a complex structure of power within the group. For the realization of their aims they depend upon internal and external conditions over which they as leaders exercise only a very partial control.

In this sense, nations share common features with less comprehensive and less powerful groups. Just as the family might dictate children's eating habits but not be able

to control their emotions; just as unions might secure benefits from management by force but not be able to prevent scabbing in their own membership; just as city councils might seize land by eminent domain but might not be able to cope with industrial unemployment, so a nation might totally regiment its economy but still be unable to withstand a prolonged military struggle. As in innumerable other instances, a nation's supposed "sovereignty" does not uniquely distinguish it from other groups.

Thus it is not unreasonable to explore hypotheses about the behavior of members in groups to see whether and how they extend to the behavior of citizens in nation-states. In the study of politics, the historian and the traditional political scientist have worked in isolation, removed from the sociologist, anthropologist, and social psychologist. My model endeavors to help cross these artificial academic barriers by developing a general theory of intergroup relations applicable to nations. Even as the model applies concepts about groups to nations, it, in turn, should be applicable not only to nations but to all groups. It should thus be useful in explaining and predicting the behavior of social and community groups, political parties, cities, states, and both regional and international organizations. By identifying a basic similarity among all these units, it may help to refocus thinking and research in them all.

Limitations of the Model

Additional Variables

The model does not enumerate all the factors which play an important part in determining the direction of national behavior. For example, I have not explicitly traced the influence of a possible reduction in prestige at home which might occur when a government shifts from self-reliance to international collaboration. To some extent I have purposely limited the factors to be considered, in the belief that the model's usefulness, in part, lies in its simplicity. To a much larger extent, the limitations arise from my own limited experience in applying the model to specific cases. There can be no doubt that, as particular instances of

---

[7] Their chap. ix on "Intergroup Relations" reports the first attempt to experiment in a laboratory-type situation with intergroup relations, conceiving the group as their basic unit.

national behavior are analyzed in terms of the model, many additional factors will come to light and should be given their place in the system.

Nor can I claim that those I have enumerated will, in the long run, necessarily prove to be the most important ones. They are merely factors which appear to be particularly significant in our own national history and in current world developments. If they are useful as a framework for empirical testing, they have served their initial purpose.

Analysis of the Underlying Mechanisms

There is also a need to refine our concepts concerning the various psychological and sociological mechanisms through which the factors operate. An attempt was made, in the paragraphs expanding each hypothesis, to sketch something of the processes underlying it, but the full import of the model will be realizable only after these mechanisms have been delineated more adequately.

For example, someone must sketch out the details of the processes underlying an armaments race. Although Richardson (28) has developed a formal model of the mechanism, it needs supplementation. The members of a group feel unprotected when faced with an external threat. They increase their arms, which is perceived as a tremendous "absolute" increase in security. But the reality indicates that their armament has induced the potential enemy to increase his protection threefold, thus leaving the first group less well protected, despite its felt satisfaction of its security demands. Just how do the "felt" and "real" factors interrelate to produce the interaction? The work involved in refining the underlying mechanisms promises to be a task of considerable dimensions.

Generality of the Model

One of the difficulties with the model is that in its present form it is concerned only with the *direction* of group policy: whether the group will turn inward toward self-help or outward toward collaboration with others. It does not predict the *form* which behavior in either direction might take; yet

the latter is often one of the most significant features of national behavior. Will the pressures directing action inward bring about changes in the procedures and objectives of the government, or will they result in an overthrow of the present regime? If the group moves outward, will it be in terms of private, non-governmental organizations or through the official foreign-relations apparatus? If the governmental machinery is brought into action, will it seek bilateral treaty arrangements or some form of multilateral international organization with permanent machinery? Landecker has begun the work of spelling out some of these important details, both in his doctoral dissertation (18) and in his more recent research outline for UNESCO (19). The model of the essay, as it now stands, may be able to predict the general trends in group behavior. But without much further amplification, it cannot predict these most important aspects of the trends.

This brief discussion indicates that the present model has painful shortcomings. But perhaps it will stimulate others to make better formulations or to explore empirical data for use in recasting it. The basic ideas in the model are not new—many of its propositions are implicit in the writings of historians and political scientists. Its contribution lies, I hope, in making the implicit more explicit, so that it may be submitted to empirical testing, refined, and made more adequate.

Application of the Model to Policy Issues in the Organization of International Affairs

The productiveness of a theory is tested as much by its relevance to problems in the field as by its accuracy in mirroring the phenomena as "they really exist." And one of the tests of the fruitfulness of this particular theory of inter-nation relations is its ability to give insight into problems of international organization of practical importance. This section is devoted to a brief analysis of three such problems in terms of the variables and relationships embodied in the model.

Universal Against Regional Organizations

One of the issues confronting foreign-policy planners is whether regional inter-state organizations which include only a few states aid or hinder the development of "universal" organizations which encompass many or all states. The model of this essay predicts that the development of partially inclusive groups would tend to delay the growth of more inclusive, universal organizations, to the extent that partial arrangements are successful in meeting the members' goals.

There are two alternate ways in which regional groupings are thought to pave the way for an ultimate, all-inclusive organization. It has been argued that the regional experience makes it easier for individual nations to participate eventually in a universal organization. It has also been thought that it would be easier eventually to weld several regional groups into a universal organization than to join together a larger number of individual nations. Let us examine the two alternatives in terms of the theory of inter-nation behavior developed in this essay.

The first argument suggests that the recurrent satisfaction obtained by fulfilling needs through *regional* collaboration would be generalized (via the mechanism of Hypothesis 1.2) into expectations concerning future *universal* collaboration. Closer examination of the generalization mechanism suggests that this is not necessarily the case. Satisfactions arising from collaboration with nations A, B, C, . . . to K are more likely to be interpreted by members as related specifically to this particular region (via mechanism of Hypothesis 3.1) and not to collaboration with nations L, M, N, . . . to T (another regional unit) or even with nations A, B, C, . . . K, L, M, N, . . . through Z, jointly. Unless some very special circumstances structure the immediate perceptions of the proximate regional organization as prototypic of a universal organization, intensive participation in a regional unit is likely to generate support for that regional organization, not support for a more comprehensive international organization. To the extent that a regional orga-

nization is successful, the model predicts that chances for establishment of a wider organization are reduced. The very fact that the regional grouping successfully meets some of the needs of its constituents means that these needs no longer would serve as instigators for broader collaboration. And if a regional community actually becomes an end in itself for its members (Hypothesis 2.11), it has created another in-group which may delay collaboration in a wider world community.

But what of the second argument, that these regional organizations can eventually be joined together, possibly more easily than could their individual member states, in a comprehensive, world-wide organization? Note that these regional, interstate organizations are also groups. Whereas the participating nations' behaviors will be collaborative (toward one another), the behavior of the regional unit itself will be determined by the same hypotheses as the region's sub-units, the nations. The model predicts that the more successfully their needs are met, the more exclusively member states will direct their energies inward and the more isolationist the behavior of the regional organization itself will be. Hence it is only when new needs begin to arise which cannot be satisfied within the regional framework that one predicts a collaborative trend in the behavior of the regional organization. These needs might be essentially national, pertaining to member nations in the regional structure, or they might be essentially regional. In any event, however, to the extent that regional collaboration is effective in meeting needs, the regional groupings would be *more* difficult to join together than nations, not less.

In both cases, then, the formation of regional institutions would seem to decrease rather than enlarge the probabilities of an eventual, comprehensive, world-wide organization.

Single-function Against Multi-function Collaboration

In practical planning for international organization, should one begin with a limited, single-function organization or with one having many functions? Given the existing unmet or partially met needs of nations, how extensively should an international organization attempt to fulfil them? Should it attempt to cope directly and single-mindedly with the most compelling problem of the times, or should it be designed so as to operate in a larger number of areas over the long run, instead?

This problem has been discussed often in terms of military security as the most compelling need of national units. One "minimalist" view is that security from military attack is the most immediate goal and can be achieved by measures designed to deal with unprovoked attack directly and forcefully. Such measures are usually judged to involve the enforcement of international law and morality by an international police force. This position holds that co-operation at other, less immediate and less threatening, levels is too indirect to meet the security need.

The "maximalists," on the other hand, feel that effective maintenance of a "rule of law," particularly if this must be done through police power, depends upon building a community among nations and that this feeling can best be developed by co-operation in many areas. This type of thinking suggested that the specialized agencies be planned and made integral parts of the United Nations: to provide opportunities for collaboration in many problem areas which would weld a firm mesh of overlapping interests among the nations.

Let us look, in terms of our model, at each of these positions as a practical proposal for establishing international collaboration. If several states develop strong security needs which cannot be met through their own resources in isolation, a single-functioned defense arrangement might be agreed upon among them. The model predicts that when the situation giving rise to the security needs has passed, such a collaborative effort will lose its *raison d'être* and is likely to fade away. The experience becomes part of the nations' past (Hypothesis 1.2), however, and remains as a dormant tendency toward collaboration whenever new needs arise which cannot be satisfied internally. But, in the main, the collaborative effort arises and passes away as the

intensity of the need changes—it does not possess within itself any strong self-reinforcing factors.

On the other hand, when a number of important needs exist simultaneously within a number of national publics, the model predicts multifunctioned collaboration, which tends to become more or less permanent and self-reinforcing. Its relative permanence arises because it is unlikely that a number of needs in different areas will all cease to exist simultaneously. Should international tensions relax and security demands be less keenly felt, there probably would still be needs for trade, for exchange of industrial know-how, for joint attacks on disease and poverty. Hence any one or several of the common problems may be resolved or may cease to exist, still leaving the organization with other functions to perform.

Other self-reinforcements arise from the operation of the generalization mechanism (Hypothesis 1.2). Suppose needs 5, 12, 23, 28, and 46 are all being met successfully within the universal organization—say, 5 through the General Assembly, 12 and 23 in UNESCO, 28 in the ILO, and 46 in WHO. Each need fulfilment takes place within a set of specific conditions, but all are perceived as occurring within a common framework. Satisfactions thus experienced will generalize to expectations about the future potentialities not only of each specific agency but of the multifunctioned international organization itself and of international collaboration in general. In the regional organization, collaboration is focused in the regional unit as the source of need satisfaction. In the single-purpose universal organization, the international organization is perceived as capable of satisfying but one specific need. When the need is satisfied, the collaboration (or alliance) ceases. The simultaneous fulfilment of multiple needs makes not only for relative permanence in the inter-nation relations but also for a network of related satisfactions which reinforce each other and produce generalized support for universal collaboration among the nations. As Cordell Hull thought of it, "particular acts of cooperation can gradually take form as a larger pattern of law and orderly international process" (26).

Conditions of modern technology may require an organization, originally conceived as single-purposed, to expand its functions, simply to achieve the purpose for which it was initiated. Take as an example an inter-state security organization, set up in strictly military terms, to protect its members against some immediate threat of war. When and if the attack actually comes, the very nature of total war may force the organization to respond with total mobilization. This may necessitate its rapid, informal penetration into areas of members' activities previously not thought of as directly related to security—especially economic areas, such as production, distribution, and transportation. So that, even if single-functioned collaboration is determined upon at first, the nature of the task itself (Hypothesis 3.3) may dictate that it become multifunctioned in order to gain its end.

It is difficult to find data which may be used to check the predictions with respect to the regional versus universal and single-function versus multifunction organizational problems. At the level of opinion, the 1953 Roper survey of attitudes of United States residents toward international organizations provides results which can test an aspect of the model's prediction (29). The pollers asked their respondents what purposes they felt international organizations should serve. Those persons favoring the continuation or strengthening of the United Nations, in the majority of cases, conceived of its functions as security-oriented—as a way to "handle Russia" or to bring about disarmament. This singleness of purpose contrasts with the many purposes of those who wanted federated regional organizations (as "Atlantic Union") or "one world government for all nations." The regionalists and the world-government advocates tended to emphasize many functions as appropriate in international collaboration—they wanted solutions to health, education, and economic problems as well as peace and security. This evidence confirms the model's predictions. Those who felt unmet needs in many areas

favored stronger inter-nation organizations of greater scope. Those who saw but one need—security—supported continuation and reinforcement of a relatively limited form of collaboration.

Institutions First Against Consensus First

Another subject of much controversy among policy-makers is how much public support must be evidenced before formal international institutions are launched. Should the creation of an international organization await a large degree of consensus among potential members, or can it be established with the minimum of support, in the expectation that it will build members' confidence and co-operation as it operates?

The model provides no general prediction in the instance of this question. It may be used, however, to approach policy in terms of specific conditions. To the extent that the institutional formalities of any proposal seem to provide concrete, direct means to members' goals, they are useful in inducing collaborative behaviors (Hypothesis 3.2) and thus will help to create the degree of support initially needed. And if, when it begins to operate, the organization is able to live up to its promise and genuinely to provide direct and satisfactory channels for need fulfilment, it will build enough consensus to insure its continuation (Hypotheses 1.2 and 2.11). If, on the other hand, the institutional formalities are regarded as interference in the internal affairs of member states, as the Human Rights declarations are viewed by some in the United States at present, they will tend to increase isolationist behaviors (Hypothesis 4.2). Such an increase in isolationism, in extreme cases, may be enough to disrupt initial plans for the institution's creation or to make impossible an insitution's creation or to render ineffectual an institution that has already begun to operate.

The model offers no answer to this issue *in general*. If applied in each specific instance, however, it has two contributions to make to the policy-maker. It provides a framework for assessing and predicting the possibilities of success, and it suggests emphases, in planning the institution and campaigning for support, which may help to enlarge those possibilities.

It is hoped that the model developed in this essay is provocative and will encourage further development of basic behavioral theory directed toward application in the field of international relations.

REFERENCES

1. Almond, G. A. *The American People and Foreign Policy,* chap. ii. New York: Harcourt, Brace & Co., 1950.
2. Arrow, K. J. "Mathematical Models in the Social Sciences." In Lerner, D., and Lasswell, H. D. (eds.), *The Policy Sciences,* pp. 124–54. Stanford, Calif.: Stanford University Press, 1951.
3. Berelson, B. *Content Analysis in Communication Research.* Glencoe, Ill.: Fress Press, 1952.
4. Brierly, J. L. *The Law of Nations,* pp. 46–49. Oxford: Clarendon Press, 1949.
5. Cantril, H. *Gauging Public Opinion.* Princeton: Princeton University Press, 1944.
6. Cartwright, D. "Analysis of Qualitative Material." In Festinger, L., and Katz, D. (eds.), *Research Method in the Behavioral Sciences,* chap. x. New York: Dryden Press, 1953.
7. Cartwright, D., and Zander, A. F. (eds.), *Group Dynamics: Research and Theory.* Evanston, Ill.: Row, Peterson & Co., 1953.
8. Cattell, R. B. "The Dimensions of Culture Patterns by Factorization of National Characters," *Journal of Abnormal and Social Psychology,* XLIV (1949), 443–69.
9. Corbett, P. E. *The Individual and World Society,* p. 57. ("Publications of the Center for Research on World Political Institutions," No. 2.) Princeton: Princeton University Press, 1953.
10. Curti, M. *The Roots of American Loyalty,* New York: Columbia University Press, 1946.
11. Deutsch, Karl W. *Nationalism and Social Communication.* New York: John Wiley & Sons, 1953.
12. Festinger, L. "Informal Social Communication," *Psychological Review,* LVII (1950), 271–82.
13. Hare, P., Borgatta, E. F., and Bales, R. F. *Small Groups: Studies in Social Interaction.* New York: A. A. Knopf, 1955.
14. Holt, R. T. Personal communication.
15. Hovland, C. I. "Human Learning and Retention," pp. 659–75. In Stevens, S. S. (ed.), *Handbook of Experimental Psychology,* chap. xvii. New York: John Wiley & Sons, 1951.
16. Klineberg, Otto. *Tensions Affecting International Understanding.* New York: Social Science Research Council, 1950.
17. Krech, D., and Crutchfield, R. S. *Theory and Problems in Social Psychology.* New York: McGraw-Hill Book Co., 1948.
18. Landecker, W. S. "Integration and Organization in Federal Aggregates." Ph.D. thesis, University of Michigan, 1947.
19. _____. "The Dynamics of Political Integration in Federal Systems," *International Social Science Bulletin,* IV (1952), 55–70.
20. Levi, W. *Fundamentals of World Organization,* p. 167. Minneapolis: University of Minnesota Press, 1950.
21. Lewin, K. "Frontiers in Group Dynamics." In Lewin, K., *Field Theory in Social Science,* ed. D. Cartwright, chap. ix. New York: Harper & Bros., 1951.
22. Mead, M. "A Case History in Cross-national Communications." In Bryson, L. (ed.), *The Communication of Ideas,* pp. 209–29. New York: Harper & Bros., 1948.
23. Millikan, M. F., and deS. Pool, I. "What Foreign Trade Policy Does American Business Want?" p. 12. Center for International Studies, MIT, 1955 (multilithed).
24. Mitrany, D. *A Working Peace System: An Argument for the Functional Development of International Organization.* London: Royal Institute of International Affairs, 1943.
25. Newcomb, T. N. *Social Psychology,* pp. 122–26 and 291. New York: Dryden Press, 1950.
26. Owens, John W. *Baltimore Sun,* December 20, 1943.
27. Patton, H. R. "A Study of Ideologies Relating to World Peace," Ph.D. thesis, University of Pittsburgh, 1952.
28. Richardson, L. F. "Generalized Foreign Politics," *British Journal of Psychology* (Monograph Suppl. No. 23), 1939.
29. Roper, E. "American Attitudes on World Organization," *Public Opinion Quarterly,* XVII (1953–54), 405, 442, Tables 5, 6, 7, and 8.
30. Sherif, M., and Sherif, C. W. *An Outline of Social Psychology,* p. 329. Rev. ed. New York: Harper & Bros., 1956.
31. Snyder, R. C., Bruck, H. W., and Sapin, B. *Decision-making as an Approach to the Study of International Politics,* p. 120. ("Foreign Policy Analysis Series," No. 3.) Princeton: Princeton University Press, 1954.
32. Van Wagenen, R. W. *Research in the International Organization Field.* Princeton: Princeton University Press, 1952.
33. Wright, Q. *The Study of International Relations,* pp. 543–53 and 593–99. New York: Appleton-Century-Crofts, 1955.

4. Social Psychological Processes

NATIONALISM AND STRATEGIES OF INTERNATIONAL CONFLICT RESOLUTION* †

DANIEL KATZ

The major concern of this chapter is an analysis of the strategies for dealing with international conflict. In this analysis we shall examine how conflicts arise, the forms they assume, and the methods by which they are resolved. The background for approaching these problems is to be found in a study of the functions of the national state and its integrating ideology of nationalism. Nation states and their nationalistic ideologies are not of a piece, and different forms of nationalism have different consequences for international conflict. One type of nation state will behave differently from another both as an active agent in the international scene and as the reactive recipient of external influences.

Our approach will be social-psychological in that we will consider both the nature of the social systems, national and international, and the nature of the psychological variables involved. Thus we are interested both in the people, whose many partial, parallel, and interdependent acts comprise national behavior, and in the social settings in which these actions take place. We are not so much concerned with the national leader as a personality but as a person operating in the role of decision-maker with all the constraints and pressures this implies. In contrast, the individual-psychological, or personality, approach attempts

to explain the events at the macroscopic level by postulating a parallel process at the microscopic level. For example, nations take belligerent actions and it is assumed that this is a function of the aggressive warlike character of their peoples, as if social processes consisted of the summation of individuals acting in parallel rather than of complex patterns of interaction. The facts are, however, that a declaration of war by a national state is the outcome of many interdependent cycles and subcycles of behavior within which personal aggressiveness may be an inconsequential variable.

A social-psychological approach differs not only from the individual or personality approach but also from the conventional point of view of social science. Political science and history, for example, are more concerned with the global description of social structures, products, or outcomes and the interactions of complex systems. Collective structures are seen as independent of people. These structures comprise the walls of the human maze and so determine behavior rather than being determined by human beings. The approach of social psychology, however, is to inquire into the walls of the human maze, since after all these walls are made up of people playing their roles in predictable fashion. In other words, the social system does not consist of a physical structure like an automobile, which exists even when it is not functioning. A social system ceases to exist the moment it stops functioning, because its systemic character consists in the relationships between acts of people.

The personality theorist, in looking at belligerent national action, would see people showing aggression; the political scientist would see nations at war; and the social psychologist would see people playing their

* The author is heavily indebted to his colleagues Herbert C. Kelman and Richard Flacks for the discussion of nationalism in this chapter. His collaboration with them on a research project on nationalism is the source of much of the present discussion. Neither Dr. Kelman nor Dr. Flacks, however, is responsible for any errors or misconceptions that may appear in this formulation.

† Reprinted by permission of the author and publisher from Kelman, H. (Editor), *International Behavior* (New York: Holt, Rinehart, and Winston), 1965, *10*: 354–390.

various roles in the national structure in relation to their needs and the social constraints of the situation. Each approach would seek different causal variables: the personality theorist would look to the frustrations in the child-rearing practices of the society; the political scientist might seek for the informational input of a threatening nature coming from another nation; and the social psychologist would search for the reasons why citizens can be mobilized into military roles in playing their parts in the system, and why national leaders behave as they do in their capacities as decision-makers.

An example of the basic thesis to be developed in these pages is the observation that the tactics and strategies employed by national decision-makers are a function of the forces and constraints affecting them as the incumbents of positions in a given structure. Though ideal models of rational decision-making can be argued upon these leaders by mathematicians, the fact remains that the models they will employ in practice will be limited by the system constraints in which they operate. Organizational variables impose limits on leadership behavior in that (a) they set the range of choices outside of which no decision can be made and (b) they present a hierarchy of alternatives or a priority of choices. Thus March and Simon (1958) have pointed out in their analysis of the cognitive limits of rationality in organization decision-making that the approach to problem-solving is through a limited and simplified model of the real situation. The way in which the situation is simplified and defined is partly in terms of *givens* of the organizational structure and its immediately preceding history. Typically, there will not be a thorough search to find all the alternative possible answers to a problem, nor will there be an adequate assessment of the risk and certainty of consequences attached to each alternative, nor will there be a complete utility ordering of the consequences of all possible alternatives. For each of these processes there will be a short-circuiting, simplification, and distortion based upon existing organizational variables.

Our general procedure will be to start at the system level to find the relevant variables that affect people as members of their nation. The major systems to be considered are the nation state and the international system. We shall then turn to the ways in which people become involved in national roles and the conditions for arousing their behavior as nationals. Finally, we shall use these considerations in discussing the strategies employed by nations for dealing with international conflict.

The Nation State and Its Ideology

In viewing the nation state as the critical unit at the social system level, we shall first call attention to its major functions and then to the part played by nationalism or the ideology of the nation state in its functioning.

Functions of the Nation State

Three major functions of the political state can be identified:

1. *Internal Integration.* The state as the source of political decisions is the final arbiter of the allocation of resources, the final arbiter of conflicts within the society, and an important mechanism for providing common services to the society. In most of the societies with which we are familiar the state has a monopoly on the use of organized physical force for the implementation of its decisions. When organized force is employed by any subgroup we have a society in rebellion. Even conservative Southerners in the United States will not countenance organized force in opposition to desegregation. Intrasystem conflict within the nation is generally resolved, compromised, or muted by the hierarchical authority structure of the political state.

2. *The Maximization of a Favorable Input—Output Ratio for the Society.* The state, like other systems, functions to provide effective utilization of resources both within its borders and in its dealings with the outside world. Thus, there are moves to acquire territory, resources, and markets. There are also moves to control such resources when they cannot be directly acquired. The primitive method is conquest

and confiscation. We tend to neglect this aspect of the development of national states though much of history is the story of one group moving in on another and subjugating it (Oppenheimer, 1914). The United States too had this origin but it is neglected because the native inhabitants were too weak and too sparse a population to put up much of a fight. The resort to force in the American Revolution led to the creation of the American state. Though this primitive means for maximizing systemic resources has been replaced in part by economic forms of domination, the basic point is that social systems do move toward a favorable input—output ratio of resources.

This maximizing dynamic generally pushes in the direction of growth and expansion. It is, moreover, accelerated or decelerated by the type of dominant institutions of the society. The mode of its expression is similarly determined by these major subsystems of the society. The Marxians saw the socio-economic institutions, the ownership of the means of production, or the social relations of production, as the key institution. Today we give greater emphasis to technology and to bureaucratic structure. While there are those like Kardiner (1945) who regard the socializing process of the family as the key institution, we would argue that, at the very least, technology and bureacracy contribute heavily to the maximizing dynamic of modern, industrialized nations. It is this dynamic that has the heaviest implications for international conflict and cooperation. Maximization of the operations of the system does not necessarily benefit all members of the system or even a majority of them. It is the system that is being advanced, not its individual members.

3. Survival and Protection against External Enemies. This function is the counterpart of the expanding dynamic in that a nation not only moves to extend its control and influence internationally but in turn is the object of influences and sometimes aggression from other nations. Self-preservation and survival can be as strong forces at the group as at the individual level. National security is a central value reflecting the emphasis upon survival. Its potency is such that it can be invoked even in the absence of realistic threats to the nation.

Since the state is the guardian of the national interest, and since it represents the organization of the forces of the society for this purpose, it moves to acquire power in relation to other states. Any danger to its survival or any threat from without leads to attempts to increase the power of the national state.

The problem of peace is one of identifying those forces and institutions within interrelated societies that are expansionist or overly defensive in nature and of determining the ways in which their dynamics can be handled without military conflict. Nationalism is part of this problem in that, as a system ideology, it not only reflects the functions of the system but also contributes to systemic functioning.

Nationalism, the Ideology of the Nation State

Nationalism as a property of the nation state is the ideology that both reflects and sustains the major functions of the state. As a value system it not only justifies and glorifies the major activities of the state, but it also helps to give direction to them. It is both an effect and a cause of the functions of the state. In speaking of nationalism as a system ideology we refer to the integrated set of values and beliefs that represent a coherent pattern for the collectivity. Individual members of the system may show varying degrees of acceptance of these beliefs and values; the leaders will have a more articulated belief pattern, and official pronouncements and documents may contain specific elaborations. There is no simple one-to-one relationship between system ideology and the sum of the attitudes of individual members. Individuals will show, however, modal acceptance of certain selected beliefs.

Three types of nationalistic ideology can be distinguished. All three of these value systems are generally represented by the ideology of the nation state.

1. Statism. One type of nationalistic ideology centers around the political state itself; we shall refer to it as statism, for want of a better term. It includes the doctrine of national sovereignty, the doctrine that the authority of the state is absolute and supreme, that the state is the legitimate source for decisions affecting the political system as a whole, that allegiance to the state and its legitimately made decisions is the duty of all citizens. It also includes the belief that the state functions to protect national security and to advance national interests that are valued in themselves. Related to this ideology of the national state are the symbols that reify its existence, the offices of its titular head, the King, President, and so on.

Value systems about the nation state can vary in terms of reification of the state as opposed to a realistic differentiated conception of it. Reified belief systems, for example, would center values around an entity standing above the people. More realistic beliefs would see the state as the collective instrument for compromising and solving common problems.

3. Institutional Nationalism. Another type of nationalistic ideology would center around certain societal institutions as the embodiment of national purpose and national goals. Thus, American nationalism may consist in part of belief systems about the political institution of democracy, and the economic institution of free enterprise and the related institution of technology as expressions of American national purpose. Value systems centering around these institutions can exist independently of values about the national state itself, but they are often linked to one another or even fused. Thus, nationalism has an input from the dominant institutions of the society. Advancing national interests means extending these institutions.

The interaction of value systems about the state and about the dominant institutions of a society has interesting implications for international behavior. On the one hand this linkage may result in policies of aggressive nationalistic expansion. On the other hand, the institutional values may outweigh the values of the political state for some subgroupings of society and make for international cooperation. For some of the owning and privileged groups in Europe during the Hitler era the values of the socio-economic institutions were more important than values of the political state. In this case national values were deserted in favor of institutional values. It may also happen, however, that two or more nations with similar institutions have a basis for cooperation because their nationalisms embrace common value systems based upon similar social structures. Conflict, of course, can still result when similarly structured societies are competing for the same common objects, in other words, when there is a realistic basis for conflict. John Paul's example (1963) of twelve men stranded on a desert island with Elizabeth Taylor may be relevant here. They have the same common values, the same goal, and hence plenty of conflict. Where there is little to be gained from conflict, however, cooperation is a real possibility between systems sharing common institutions, as we have seen in the development of the European community.

3. Cultural Identity. A third type of national ideology consists of the values centering around the character of a people, the common cultural heritage, the language, the way of life of a people, in short the *cultural identity* supposedly shared by the members of the nation state. At the individual level we speak of consciousness of kind of fellow nationals. In extreme form this is often called ethnocentrism or racism. These values can exist without linkage to a national state, as with the Jewish group in the United States. When a nation state does exist, however, it quickly links together the ideology of the state with the cultural identity of the people.

Generic Dimensions of Nationalism: Affective Symbolic Codes vs. Pragmatic Reality Codes

We have distinguished among three components of nationalism with respect to substantive belief areas. Another fundamental distinction concerns the generic psychological basis of nationalistic values. Two dimensions are of relevance to the role of these values in national and international problems. The first is the symbolic or reality-oriented character of the value or belief. By symbolic we do not mean that the value stands for something it is not, as in language symbols, but rather that the symbol is accepted as the essential reality. The beliefs are reified and have little in the way of an objective referent. They are what Thurman Arnold (1935) referred to when he spoke of symbols of government, or what some of the semanticists have in mind when they speak of polarized concepts. The doctrine of national sovereignty has much of this character. In contrast to such symbolic codes are the empirically oriented belief systems, which have objective referents. The symbolic codes are closed to everyday experience, the reality codes are not. Thus, when people believe in the majesty of the law as if it were a supernatural force, they will accept the idea that the law must take its course even if in a given case the accused are not guilty. Others, however, may see the law as a set of rules for accomplishing human objectives that can be changed to accord with new problems. In the former case we are dealing with a symbolic belief, in the latter with a reality-oriented belief.

A second dimension is the amount of emotional investment in the belief. Some beliefs have a heavy affective loading. Others are held with little emotional feeling. Though there is not a perfect correlation between the symbolic-reality dimension and the amount of affective loading, the symbolic values in general tend to have much more emotional loading than do the reality beliefs.

The integration of people into a group, organization, or larger system can occur at two levels. At the one level they are tied into the structure through their emotional investment in system symbols. These sacred values are accepted without question and generally have to do with the nobility of the system and its mission. Leaders can invoke these symbols to hold people in the system, to excommunicate deviants, to mobilize followers for emergency action. At another level people are integrated into the system through their functional interde-

pendence in their everyday activities and their empirically oriented beliefs about these interdependent activities. Durkheim's profound analysis (1933) of the nature of societal solidarity called attention to these two types of integration. In societies characterized by a slight division of labor, with people performing the same types of tasks, the integrating factor was a collective moral conscience. Deviations from moral norms led to an outraged public feeling that was the basis of criminal law. In societies characterized by a great deal of division of labor the integrating factor became the functional interdependence of people and their acceptance of civil codes governing their relations with one another. Though our use of affective symbolic codes as against empirical belief systems is not an exact reiteration of the Durkheim analysis, it is similar in pointing to two different bases of social integration. Our contention is that either or both methods can be operating in any given social structure and, further, that the strategies for dealing with conflict must take account of the differences between these two kinds of integration and the two kinds of values systems they reflect. We shall return to this problem, but for the present purpose of exposition let us merely call attention to an example of the operation of these two belief codes. The experienced leader will often avoid conflict within a structure by introducing change in such a way that none of the symbolic values of the system is made salient. The change will be presented as dealing with practical problems in terms of empirical belief systems. The less experienced leader will unwittingly touch off some of the sacred symbols and be in difficulty.

Dynamics of National Systems

Nations are not only integrated by the various types of national value systems but also by more objective factors: specifically, the functional interdependence of the substructures within the nation, and the common fate and common rewards accruing to its members. Nations will differ with respect to internal structure and institutions. Where there is a high degree of commonality of reward and of functional interdependence there is also a high degree of objective integration and hence less need for a heavy emphasis upon national ideology of a symbolic affective kind. National leaders can use symbolic integration to achieve more objective integration, as did Hitler and his fellow Nazi leaders. Though the Nazis succeeded in destroying most of the organized substructures within Germany that were relatively independent of the state, they never achieved as much economic integration as the totalitarian state implies.

In addition to the differences in social structure it is also important to take into account the inputs into the national system, both from its own internal resources and from its relations with other nations. The United States, as a developing nation with a continent of natural resources available to it, presents a pattern different from that of Germany, arriving as a latecomer to the international scene with the world resources already staked out by other nations. If we take into account both the social structure of the nation and its available inputs we can distinguish among four patterns: (1) the revolutionary society, characterized by the development of a nation as the expression of new institutions replacing or overthrowing old institutions, (2) the empire-building society, characterized by the extension of national power on an exploitive basis, (3) the bureaucratic technological society, either of a capitalistic or of a socialist type, and (4) the declining society, in which the state or its subsystems are blocked, threatened, or losing power. This is not intended as a comprehensive typology of national states but as an illustration of how differing social structures with differing inputs will move toward different patterns of nationalism.

1. The revolutionary society would be illustrated by the development of national states in overthrowing feudal institutions. This is the classic picture of nationalism in the writings of Carleton Hayes (1926). There are some similarities here with the growing nationalism in underdeveloped countries that have successfully revolted against colonialism. The older institutions in both of these instances were exploitive

in character and the revolt is fostered by groups who seek a more advantageous position. These groups develop national ideology as a weapon in the struggle and in so doing they broaden the ideological base of the conflict to include all the people of the society. The hypothesis here is that there is a close linkage and even an integration between all three types of national ideology: the political doctrines about the new state, the values centering about new institutions, and the ethnocentrism of the people. The new nation state is the people's state—that is, people of that nationality; it stands for new institutions and a new and better way of life. Such an integrated ideology has real advantages in mobilizing people on a mass basis behind national leaders. And it has some reality basis in that most of the people have a common fate in throwing out the oppressors, especially if they are foreigners.

The fusion of these elements may make for more potential conflict with other nations. Not only are other nations seen as rivals, if there is competition for scarce resources, but they are also seen as threats, if they represent either different institutions or different cultural values.

2. The empire-building period is one of direct power moves to maximize the input—output ratio for the dominant institutions of society. Expansionist power is accompanied by an ideology that attempts a continued integration of the three components of nationalism. Integration becomes more difficult, however, in that the commonality of interests of all subgroups in the nation and of all nationals against other nations and other nationals is less clear. Certain privileged subgroups benefit much more from expansionist power moves than do others. To maintain the integration of the society, the ethnocentrism doctrine moves toward the extreme of racism—for example, toward the doctrine of the white man's burden (now reversed among some African nationals) as a type of extreme aggressive ethnocentrism. At the psychological level, some of the motivational basis of nationalism shifts from identification based upon consciousness of kind to compensatory

mechanisms of identification with power symbols.

3. With the rise of such economic institutions as the market place and with the accumulation of investment capital and the increasing division of labor, nations move toward becoming technological bureaucratic societies. This form of social organization has certain characteristics that have implications for nationalism. Some of these characteristics are: (a) the divorce of organizational forms from traditional, personal, and nonfunctional elements, thus permitting flexibility and rapid growth; (b) the development of role readiness as part of childhood socialization (the ability of people to move into any role so long as it is legitimized); (c) a value orientation that is geared to pragmatic outcomes rather than absolute, sacred symbols (hence the development of technology is favored—in fact technology is often the leading subsystem of the total society); (d) an increase in the standard of living for all people because of the efficiencies of the system; and (e) the development of a maximization or growth dynamic.

The maximization dynamic of the technological bureaucratic system derives from many sources. Bureaucratic technological structures call for a high degree of specialization of labor and of function. To operate effectively the system requires great chunks of physical and social space, as well as large numbers of mobile people to allow for specialization of function. Thus, in the United States, with all our anti-trust laws, there is a continuing problem of holding down the size of organizations. Another source of maximization is the tendency to acquire control over the inputs into the system, either by direct acquisition of input sources or indirect mechanisms for tying them into the system. An industrial firm, for example, may acquire title to its sources of supply or may develop control over satellite companies that furnish it raw or semi-processed materials. Moreover, anticipatory mechanisms develop, such as research and development departments in industrial organizations, for more complete exploitation of the system's potential in dealing with its environment. Growth, then, becomes inevitable until checked by powerful forces external to the system.

In bureaucratic society the linkage between the political aspects of nationalism and the cultural identification with nationality becomes further weakened. As the nation state becomes more bureaucratized the ethnocentrist element is no longer closely tied to statism. The national identity of people is now more a matter of their bureaucratic roles and less a matter of the distinctive culture of the nation. What ties the citizen to the nation state is less the affective symbol codes than the ideology of the state as the source of bureaucratic authority.

If this analysis is correct, then it would follow that ethnocentrism or identification with cultural identity is a minor factor in promoting or otherwise affecting international conflict between bureaucratic states. Attempts to minimize conflict by intercultural contact, by trying to develop tolerance and understanding of other nationals, are exaggerated as a means of preventing war. Differentiated cultural identities of peoples can facilitate militant propaganda once a conflict is under way, but the fact of cultural differences does not in itself generate international conflict. We do not engage in war against another nation because they possess a different culture or a different set of customs. Otherwise the United States would have fought France rather than Germany in 1916 and in 1941. In fact American soldiers in both wars had something of this naive conception and wondered why they were fighting the Germans rather than the French. The facts are, however, that they were fighting against Germany since wars are clashes between political states, not between peoples of different cultures. It may help the cause of peace if we can get individuals from one culture to understand individuals from another culture, but this is not the major means for bringing about a peaceful world.

4. When the state or its subsystems become blocked in expansion and threatened with loss of power, a retreatist or revivalist nationalism is fostered. The power expansion may be blocked by the superior power of other nations or by other constraints in

the external environment. This may lead to a redefinition of nationalism, which narrows the nationality definition with respect to the types of people and the kinds of values considered truly patriotic. There is a restriction in what is considered genuinely national and in those who qualify as true nationals. More attention may be given to internal enemies than to external. The state no longer receives unquestioning allegiance, but it, too, is redefined in terms of old traditions.

Often this type of nationalism is represented by groups within the population who are losing power or are threatened with the loss of power. Hence they narrow the concept of the national to include only those like themselves. The radical right in the United States may reflect some of this psychology.

The Arousal of Nationalism and the Assumption of National Roles

In spite of the state's priority over other social structures, the role systems comprising the national state are often latent rather than active in the national population. The life of the ordinary citizen is devoted to his roles as a member of his occupation, of his family, his church, his union, and so forth. His national roles may make few demands in times of peace. He does vote on occasion and may even take part in the political process more actively. He pays his taxes and obeys national laws. He gives customary compliance to national rituals, such as standing when the national anthem is played. Yet his national involvement does not occupy much of his psychological life space. When the nation is at war, however, the situation changes radically. More national roles are specified for him and many of his peace time roles become national roles, for example, his peace time role as a worker in a plant now becomes that of a defense worker for the nation.

Forces and Conditions Basic to the Arousal of Nationalism

What, then, are the latent forces in the individual that can be aroused for his assumption of national roles and what are the conditions for the arousal of these forces? Four types of forces can be distinguished: (1) emotional and behavioral conditioning to national symbols, (2) the sense of personal identity as a national, (3) compensatory and defensive identification with militant nationalism, and (4) instrumental involvement in the national structure.

1. *Emotional and Behavioral Conditioning to National Symbols.* Part of the socialization process in many countries includes the conditioning of the behavior of children in the observance of national rituals. In the United States, for example, school children pledge allegiance to the flag in unison, rise together in singing the national anthem, and at a more complex level are encouraged to worship national heroes and detest traitors. This conditioning includes an acceptance of national authorities such as the President or the Supreme Court speaking in their appropriate legitimate roles. The depth of the emotional affect that becomes tied to national symbols in this fashion will vary depending upon the intensity of the experience and the amount of repetition. The depth of the affective conditioning is not always great because of the mechanical nature of the process, akin in some instances to a class repeating aloud the German prepositions governing the accusative case. National states vary in the intensity of this type of training. What is always potent, however, is the social reinforcement in the process. The ritual is observed by everyone and no deviations are tolerated. Not many learning experiences of the child have this unanimity of social reinforcement.

The emotional and social conditioning in itself does not provide an adequate basis for the generalization of responses to many of the complex situations in which the individual is expected to play a national role. The basic arousal condition is the appearance of the old stimulus of the flag or some other symbol to which the individual shows respect. Another arousal condition is the perceived unanimity of others following a supposedly patriotic course of action. This is consistent with early training in which no deviations were permitted in the observance of national rituals. This respect and compliance can generalize to the acceptance of a specific directive from national authority, as in the case of the presidential letter asking the person to join the armed forces. But it provides little basis for the citizen in peacetime engaging in activities supportive of a national policy supposedly representing national interests. In other words, emotional conditioning does lay the foundation for the belief in patriotism as a positive value, but it does not specify how patriotism can be expressed beyond respecting national symbols, complying with orders from national authorities, and conforming to the patriotic practices of the overwhelming majority.

2. *The Formation of the Self Concept as Inclusive of National Identity.* A significant aspect of the socialization process is the development of the individual's perception of himself as a national, as an Englishman, a Frenchman, an Algerian, and so on. The growing child establishes his self identity not only as a unique personality but as an individual belonging to an in-group showing the same values and orientations in contrast to foreign out-groups. This group identification develops readily around immediate local groupings, but extends to people embraced by the national structure with a common fate, history, and culture. National identity, thus, is an anchoring frame for the individual's conception of himself. Many Englishmen living in the United States will not change their citizenship and cannot understand how any Englishman could make such a change. It would be tantamount to rejecting his self image.

The factors conducive to the development of a sense of national identity also have implications for the arousal conditions in adult life that lead to national role taking. They have to do with the simplicity of cognitive structuring in terms of in-group vs. out-group under circumstances of competition and conflict. Thus, a people possessing a homogeneous culture with a perceived common fate in competitive contact with other nations can readily internalize a sense of national identification.

We called attention earlier to the possible fusion of statism, institutional ideology, and cultural identity. Where it occurs we generally find a high incidence of people whose self concepts include a feeling of national identity.

Even though an individual includes his national identity as part of his self concept it is latent in most situations. It becomes manifest under conditions of confrontation at two levels. At the level of personal experience it is aroused by direct contact with other nationals either through travel abroad or through the presence of foreigners in one's own country. Its arousal is further facilitated and the feeling maintained if the confrontation with other nationals entails some degree of conflict, competition, or even comparison. Thus, programs of cultural exchange designed to improve international understanding are not necessarily successful in changing attitudes toward other nationals in a favorable direction. (See, for example, Selltiz and Cook, 1962.) The visiting foreigner is made aware of his foreignness and is stimulated to compare his nation with the host nation. This may have a variety of consequences. Much depends upon the type of experience, the expectations of the person, and his personality characteristics. (See Chapters 4 and 15 in this volume.)

At the secondary level of the world created by the mass media and communications from leaders, the sense of national identity is aroused by perceived matters of *national interest* and *national security* in relation to other nations. Again the closeness of the problem to the citizens is an important variable. The Cuban situation was more potent in arousing American nationalism than the situation in Viet Nam.

3. *Compensatory Identification.* We have been describing a positive extension of the individual's self image to include people like himself with the same values and interests. In addition there is a type of national identification that is based not so much on the individual's attraction by the advantages of group belongingness as on his attempts to solve his own internal conflicts and insecurities. In general this is referred

to as defensive or compensatory identification. Here the motivation stems from the individual's own inadequacy and his attempts to be part of a powerful group from which he can derive a vicarious sense of power. This is basically the authoritarian syndrome as described by Adorno, Frenkel-Brunswik, Levinson, and Sanford (1950). It has been demonstrated that individuals who have met their childhood conflicts through repression of their hostilities can readily project their hatreds on the out-group. Thus ethnocentrism, anti-Semitism, and chauvinism have been found to have some degree of relationship with personality insecurity. Moreover, attitudes of emotional rejection of minority out-groups are correlated with attitudes highly critical of international cooperation (Levinson, 1957). Similarly, a study of Norwegian nationalism reports that power-oriented nationalism is related to the authoritarianism syndrome, whereas a people-oriented nationalism is not (Bay, Gullväg, Ofstad, & Tønnessen, 1950). We are postulating, then, a defense mechanism of compensatory identification with the nation as an intervening variable which links the person's initial mode of handling conflict with certain types of nationalism.

Germany after World War 1 presents an example of the conditions making for the development of this type of defensive identification. Young people reared in fairly authoritarian families, made even more insecure by conditions of economic deprivation, readily sought psychic compensation in identifying with the power of their nation. The situation was aggravated by the fact that the nation had been defeated in a war and that its signs of power such as a large military force had been stripped away. The needs of the people were such, however, that they refused to face their military defeat in World War I and instead accepted the notion that the army had been betrayed by traitors at home (Fried, 1942). The Nazis, by providing a rationale for their needs and by furnishing through their marching storm troops, their uniforms, and their military slogans a visible indication of German strength, built something of a mass basis for their final coming to power.

The basis, then, for compensatory identification is the repressed hostility of a people stemming from early frustrations. The conditions for its arousal are similar frustrations and threats to security in the present. Since we are dealing here primarily with problems internal to individuals, it is not so much the actual threat from outside forces that triggers them off. Any event can be seized upon by leaders, as an insult to national honor and a threat to national power, to exploit this type of identification and arouse people to assume national roles. Even if the duly constituted national leadership takes a responsible position in minimizing possible external threats, the danger is that leaders seeking power will seize upon incidents to rally people to the defense of the nation and to indict the present leaders. Whereas national interest is the more common means for arousing the positive types of national identification, appeals about national honor and national power are more effective for eliciting defensive identification.

4. *Instrumental Involvement in the National Structure.* National involvement also has a firm basis in all the instrumental rewards that accrue to the loyal citizen in playing his part in society. People often assume their national roles in large measure because their way of life and their means of livelihood are tied into the national structure. To refuse to accept the legitimate demands of the nation is to reject the system. There is an all-or-none quality about the matter (Allport, 1962). One is either a loyal citizen or he is not. The realistic alternatives to rejecting the system are forbidding and vary from imprisonment and exile to virtual ostracism. Hence people will pay their taxes, testify before the House Committee on Un-American Activities, and support their national leaders because they want to remain in the system. And the greater the rewards accruing from system membership, the less will individuals consider the prospects of deserting the system.

In describing the forces of emotional conditioning and of positive and of compensatory identification we were calling attention to the internalized factors that make the expression of nationalism rewarding in and of itself. But we are now recognizing the fact that for many people and at many times the assumption of a national role may be an instrumental act which is motivated by its consequences rather than by the intrinsic satisfactions from performing it. And it has been our general thesis that in large bureaucratic societies such instrumental involvement may be relatively more important than in newly emerging national states. There is a common belief that the conduct of modern total war requires that the masses of people be stirred to action by a hate propaganda against the enemy. The facts are, however, that the war effort of the United States in World War II was accomplished with no concerted governmental campaign of an emotional or ideological character. The domestic propaganda efforts were limited to specific practical programs, such as buying bonds, saving scarce materials, observing the ration rules, and following suggestions with respect to security of information. There was a marked absence of parades, of beating of drums, and of emotional arousal. Whatever emotional dynamics existed arose largely from the conflict itself and not from a planned program of indoctrination.

The arousal condition for instrumental national involvement is the appearance of the legitimate symbols of national authority. This can be at the specific level, where either the symbol or legal directive calls for some particular act of compliance; or at the general level, where a national leader attempts to secure support for a program of action. At the specific level the critical issue is the legitimacy and appropriateness of the demand, in other words, whether it comes from duly constituted authority speaking in their realms of jurisdiction. For example, some of the Southern states in the United States attempted to create a con-conflict over symbols by asserting the supremacy of state rather than federal laws in areas of civil rights. Where actual resistance to national authority was threatened the federal government nationalized the state militia and made clear the priority of legal symbols, so that governors had

to step aside and acknowledge federal authority. At the general level the national leader must speak as a national figure and not as the representative of a specific party or group. At the general level, moreover, national symbols such as the Constitution or polarized concepts such as national security may be employed to encourage a course of action through appeals to national involvement. Such appeals, which are directed at the basic membership character of belonging to the national structure, are most effective in emergency situations or circumstances in which people see their way of life being threatened by internal or external enemies.

For purposes of exposition we have presented these four sources of motivational support for the assumption of national roles as if they were alternative and independent bases for action. In practice, however, the general finding would be that a number of these motive patterns reinforce one another. The conditioning to national symbols, even if not accompanied by intense affective experience, does make clear to the individual the things he must observe to protect his instrumental national involvement. And the fusion of a sense of personal identity as a national with the instrumental involvement in the structure provides a combination of motive forces that may operate in a multiplicative rather than a simple additive manner. The great energizing fire of nationalism in the newly emerging nation states in the seventeenth and eighteenth centuries was a fusion of such motives. The rising middle classes found increasing instrumental returns from the expansion of their nations and at the same time derived psychic satisfactions from their new national identities.

The Relationship between Psychological Sources of National Role-Taking and the Nature of the Nation State

Though there is some combination of the forces basic to national role-taking in all nations, the relative emphasis upon a given factor will vary according to the nature of the nation state. We have already indicated that the revolutionary and newly emerging nation tends to integrate both instrumental rewards and satisfactions from personal identification as a national for key groups in the society; and that the nation preserving some of its basic institutions through counter-revolution relies heavily upon compensatory identification with power symbols. Many nation states today, however, are well-developed bureaucratic structures representative of an advanced technological society. There are certain elements that are common to such large technological bureaucratic societies with respect to nationalistic ideology and the taking of national roles by leaders and citizens. Specifically, in these types of nations (1) there is some tendency toward divorcing the cultural identity of the people and doctrines of statism, (2) people are tied into the national state more through their functional involvement in the structure of the society than through their ideological commitment to its symbols and (3) bureaucratic functioning creates a task orientation in which leaders learn to deal with problems at the reality rather than the symbol level.

1. The divorce between the cultural identity and doctrines of statism means that the people of a country can still identify with one another and with their way of life without a concurrent commitment to the symbols of government. Americans can derive major satisfactions from being Americans without loving their government. There is even a question as to whether the English crown symbolizes the British political state as much as it does the cultural identity of the English people. Certainly since Winston Churchill there has been no British political leader who has integrated in his own personality the cultural as well as the political ideals of the British.

This shift away from the marriage of political and cultural symbols has profound implications for international conflict and cooperation. It means in effect that there is a popular basis in certain nations for political cooperation and for the peaceful settlement of international disputes, providing people can retain their cultural identity.

2. The affective conditioning to national symbols still takes place in the socialization process but it has become more of a routine matter in the bureaucratic state. In the

smaller and newer states, and in an earlier day in the older states, this conditioning was accompanied by the development of personalized beliefs about the symbols. But these symbols have lost some of their potency in arousing deep feelings in a bureaucratic society. A reported insult to the American flag is not as widely perceived as a sense of personal outrage as was once the case. People still assume their national roles but more on the basis of their functional involvement in the national structure.

This change from emotional commitment to national symbols to involvement in functional roles also has important consequences for international conflict. Warlike sentiment is not so easily aroused throughout the population of the nation by the news of international incidents or insults to national honor. The mass media have carried stories about scores of American soldiers being killed in Viet Nam without an outburst of patriotic emotion in the nation. National leadership now has an increased scope in defining international situations for the people and perhaps a more difficult task in justifying an actual declaration of war.

3. National leaders in a bureaucratic society cannot escape the influence of the organizational training of the society. To be an effective organizational leader the individual has to acquire skills in building and maintaining a structure and in increasing its effectiveness and productivity. All this requires a heavy task orientation and an assessment of objective and social realities. The leader who spends his time in flying flags, getting embroiled in symbolic fights, is often left behind in the competition for higher positions.

International Systems and Types of Conflict

Nation states are not self-contained as the proponents of isolation assume. Systems of economic exchange and other forms of cooperative activity are more common than is generally recognized. In addition to formal organizations such as the United Nations, UNESCO, the World Court, the World Health Organization, international scientific, professional, religious, and business organizations, there are many other international systems. These range from cooperative arrangements for communication, news, travel, copyrights, the control of criminal activity, and the exchange of students and specialized personnel to international cartels. Some of the clearest forms of such international systems are regional in nature, such as the European Common Market, or the Scandinavian Union in which the passport from one Scandinavian country is recognized by any other Scandinavian country as the equivalent of its own passport for many purposes. Every nation is involved with many other nations through treaty arrangements covering a wide range of problems. In September 1963, for example, the United States had 622 treaties in force governing its relations with other nations.

A number of these international arrangements may actually increase the potential for conflict in that they organize the world into opposing camps such as NATO, the Comintern, SEATO, or the European Community. The effect of these arrangements, however, is probably to increase the magnitude of the disaster if it should come rather than to make its occurrence more likely. A major alliance can exert a controlling influence on its more belligerent members.

In his theory of internation relations, Guetzkow (1957) maintains that regional associations of nations will tend to delay a world organization to the extent that such regional groupings successfully meet the needs of members. If the needs can be satisfied within the regional structure there is less motivation toward broader international collaboration and more turning inward to the regional structure. Though Guetzkow does acknowledge that regional isolation could be breached by needs not provided for by the regional organization, he does not believe that successful collaboration will generalize beyond the nation states collaborating. From the short-run point of view this theory has much merit but it may overlook the long-range consequences of the impairment of national sovereignty, and the undermining of the linkage of cultural identity to statism. Nationalistic doctrines

of this type constitute a major barrier to the acceptance of a World Court and an enforceable system of international law. The fact of regional association will not in itself produce a world order and is thus not a *positive* force in this direction, but it will help to undermine such *negative* forces against world cooperation as national sovereignty.

Another weakness in international systems that Guetzkow describes is the singleness of function in many cooperative arrangements. An international labor association has the one objective of cooperation with respect to workers' interests. When that goal is met or recedes in importance relative to other needs the international organization loses significance. On the other hand, international associations that could fulfill multiple needs would be a potent factor in producing generalized support for world cooperation. Hence some writers have stressed the fact that the hope for the United Nations is to assume more functions and thus develop a greater amount of interconnection among nations in many fields of endeavor.

The growth of international systems has been accompanied by a tremendous increase in cross-national communication, travel, and contact. The number of days of American tourist stay in Europe in 1957, for example, was 33 million, or triple the volume of that before the war. This shrinking of the physical and psychological universe and the breakdown of national barriers has fostered the development of world opinion as a factor in international relations. In fact the prestige of America abroad became one of the campaign issues in the 1960 election.

The problem is, however, that the involvement of people in the international system is not as wide or as deep as involvement in the national system. In the first place only a small minority of nationals are directly involved in international systems. The growth of tourism and of international exchange of students does not necessarily mean an increase in the number of people who actually play an international role. Many political and industrial leaders do become members of international systems but the primary membership of the political leader is in his own nation state. It is possible, of course, that the exchange of students and of specialized personnel has some effect in that these people may be more supportive of their own national leaders when these officials assume a cooperative international position. It is doubtful that the same effect holds for the tourist group.

Implications of National System Analysis for Strategies in Dealing with International Conflict

It is our contention that national decision-making is neither a rational process in the objective, mathematical sense nor dominantly the expression of the personalities of a few national leaders. Rather it represents the subjective rationality of the national system. The economic and social structure of the nation, the current valence of different types of national ideology, and the inputs from internal and external sources define the limits within which leaders formulate policy and take action. Not all alternatives for action are explored, and the weights assigned to possible consequences are heavily affected by system forces. The different patterns of national systems we have described not only have historical reference but they have contemporary relevance: not all nation states are of a piece and hence each will follow its own subjective patterns of rationality in taking actions that increase or decrease international tension.

Political leaders are the centers of networks of decision-making about national policy. Although they are just one link in the total chain and although their degrees of freedom in making choices are very limited, they are *key* links and they are commonly perceived as playing the role of advancing national interest and protecting national security. They can be challenged by competitors for their leadership roles on the basis of their actions, their pronouncements, and their stance with respect to national prestige, national advantage or disadvantage, and national security. The challenge will be open and public in a democracy and covert and implicit in a totalitarian state. They cannot be seen as less patriotic, less protective of national interest than their competitors.

In a sense national officials also play roles as members of international systems. Here they must be responsive to the demands of the international system if they are to negotiate successfully for their own country, and thus they are impelled toward a longer-range point of view of national interest and of the common goals of many countries than would be true of the rank-and-file of their own nation. These dual roles often place them in a position of conflict in that the agreement that makes sense for the international system may not be one they can defend as patriotic representatives of their country. Part of the art of diplomacy is to evolve formulas for the settlement of a dispute that will be palatable to the people of the contending nations. Where the leader gives primary consideration to his international role he is likely to experience rejection of his efforts from his own people, as was the case with Woodrow Wilson in his contributions toward the development of the League of Nations. The dominant forces playing upon the national leader, save perhaps for small powerless nations, are the internal subgroups of his own country, especially the rival political factions, which interpret his moves from the point of view of a narrow nationalism. Exceptions do occur; for example, domestic business interests will sometimes push for agreements with foreign business interests. In general, however, the forces from within the nation are more immediate and more potent and more shortsighted concerning national interests than are the forces in the international system. Domestic organizations that theoretically could counter these national pressures, such as the Friends of the United Nations or the Foreign Policy Association, are too weak to be of much help. And the chances of such organizations gaining real power are remote because they are built around men of good will and of intellectual understanding and have little functional basis.

Sources of International Conflict

The international system reflects not

only the cooperative interconnectedness of nation states and their subgroupings, but also the competitive and conflictual strivings of their subsystems. The types of conflict are not capricious in character but are rooted in the type of nation state involved and the dominant functions it is carrying out.

In discussing the nature of national systems we have already described the dynamic sources of conflict between nations. The maximization dynamic according to which systems push toward completion—toward realizing more of their basic character—often results in expansionistic moves. The nation may attempt to extend its title or control over resources, territory, and markets. It may attempt to extend its institutions and ideology beyond its borders. Conflict results either from encroachment on another nation or its preserves, or from competition with a similar expanding system. The sources for expansion may be of two types: the first is a genuine push toward maximizing the return to the system and the second is a compensatory move to cover over the failure of internal integration. In this second case the internal conflicts of the nation state may not have been resolved by the political system. These unresolved conflicts are then projected outward upon other nations. Since the symbols of the state can be used to rally the nation against external threat, elite groups may maximize the external conflicts to create internal unity. In so doing they may link their own enemies within the nation to the enemies without—a technique utilized effectively by Hitler but not unique to him. Externalization of internal conflict is an ancient but not anachronistic cause of tension and war.

A more indirect form of the external solution of internal problems occurs in the building up of an industrial-military complex to maintain the economy of a nation. In the United States some of the motivation behind the fifty billion dollars spent on defense, comprising over half the national budget, is to meet domestic problems of full employment and economic growth.

These generic causes of struggle take different forms of expression depending on the type of nationalism and nation state,

as we have already suggested. Economic conflicts arise over competition for scarce resources and markets. But even in the economic sphere different objectives may be sought at different developmental stages. At one period colonization and the subjugation of other peoples was the answer, at another point ownership of their essential resources backed up by military force was sufficient, and more recently control through bureaucratic devices has been effective.

In addition to the economic manifestation of the maximization dynamic we need to take account of its *ideological expression*. In the newly emerging state or in the expanding national system the justification of the way of life and the institutions of the society in a nationalistic ideology create conditions of conflict. The struggle between the East and the West in its ideological form is between value systems centering not merely around social institutions but around nationalistically conceived social institutions. Ideological conflict is not limited, however, to the confrontation of different national value systems of expanding structures. The doctrine of statism and national sovereignty of any country is always a potential source of incompatibility with that of other countries, as are value systems about the essential rightness of its institutions and the superiority of its culture. These ideologies make possible the mobilization of the people around concepts of national honor, national purpose, or national security. In general the ideological basis for conflict is greatest when all three types of nationalism (statism, cultural identity, and beliefs in national institutions) are tightly integrated and when these belief systems are more symbolically than empirically oriented.

Since nation states are in good part systems for dealing with power relationships, the most general form that conflicts between nations assume is one of a *power* struggle. Political power is utilized to support both economic and ideological interests. But power is not only a means for securing economic advantage or ideological maximization, it is also a source of conflict in its own right. It is a measure of the strength of a national system in general and, since this measure is relative to the power of other nations, it constitutes a continuing potential for conflict. Werner Levi (1960) expresses this as follows:

The quest for power becomes a major occupation of the state and a standard by which most aspects of its life and activities are measured, no matter how relative the magnitude of the desired power may be. It can be granted that, as states usually assert for the diplomatic record, they do not seek power for its own sake; they do so merely as a means to the end of satisfying their needs. . . . But whatever the end of the search for power and whatever the qualifications and limitations, the possibility remains that it can itself lead to violent conflict. States may become rivals in vying for elements of power or in one attempting to become more powerful than the other. The paradox here is that the search for power, even if only to have it available for a future conflict of interests, may itself become a source of violent conflict (pp. 411–420).

As Singer (1965) has pointed out, the international system of two nations in potential conflict has a built-in mechanism for intensifying the conflict. The political elite of country A may assume a hostile stance toward country B. This elite group receives positive feedback from its own citizens in moving toward a position of strength. In country B, however, the political elite responds with similar hostile moves. This gives added justification to country A for its actions and for increasing the severity of those actions. A similar process is, however, going on in the antagonist nation, B. There is thus reinforcement for the political elites in both countries, both from their own citizenry and from the behavior of the other nation. Hence the interaction between the states makes it difficult to reverse the self-perpetuating and self-enhancing cycles of militant preparations within the nation state.

Though many international conflicts are rooted in more than a single source, there are disputes that are basically economic, others that are in good part ideological, and still others that are dominantly power-oriented. Different types of struggles will show some differences with respect to the strategies appropriate to their causal basis.

For example, labor-management conflicts in the United States have sometimes represented economic disputes and sometimes ideological differences. The American Federation of Labor assumed that the basic conflict was one of immediate economic interest and accordingly followed bread-and-butter unionism in which they accepted the business ethic of the culture. Though their leaders might drive a hard bargain, the disagreements were negotiable at the conference table. In contrast, radical unions like the I.W.W., committed to a certain type of Marxism, assumed that the differences were ideological. Hence these matters were not amenable to the same type of bargaining process.

Many conflicts of course are mixtures of economic, ideological, and power differences, and their resulting strategies and modes of resolution may shift as one or the other basic source becomes salient. Hence the following analysis of conflict strategies will make reference to their relevance to given sources of conflict.

Methods and Strategies for Dealing with Conflict

Though parties to a conflict may utilize a wide range of specific methods for advancing their cause, for living with tensions, or for bringing an end to the conflict, these techniques can be subsumed under six broad classes. At the one extreme, to utilize H. Shepard's (1961) analysis, would be the primitive methods of force and violence and destruction that imply the annihilation of the opponent, and at the other extreme would be the methods of integrative solution involving problem-solving. Intermediate between these extremes would be the recognition of an involuntary interdependence with bargaining and limited warfare as its expression. More specifically, we shall use the following categories for our analysis: (1) the use of force, threats, counterthreats, and deterrence, (2) conflict denial, (3) conflict restriction and containment, (4) nonviolence and ideological conversion, (5) bargaining and compromise, and (6) problem-solving and creative integration. A number of these methods may of course appear in progression or combination. Thus, attempts to negotiate a compromise settlement may follow the use of threats so that a nation tries to bargain from a position of assumed strength. These methods and their combinations need to be considered with respect to their outcomes, that is, to whether they produce an intensification of conflict, a continuation, a reduction, or a genuine solution.

The Use of Force, Threats, and Deterrence

Traditionally, nations have relied upon force or threats of force as the ultimate means of securing their objectives or of resisting agressor nations. The logic is that there is no answer to force but superior force. The nations that have not built up their armaments have been those either too weak or too well protected geographically to need armies. The United States, in a fortunate strategic position, did little to build up its armed might until its international involvement in an atomic age. It is to be expected that fascist nations with their glorification of physical force would give the highest priority to military armament. But communist nations, accepting socialistic doctrines of the common humanity of mankind, have also proceeded to develop their military might. Democracies have proved no exception. Even India, despite its greater acceptance of an ideology of non-violence than the Western nations, reacted to the Chinese attacks upon its northern border by dismissing its defense minister and by seriously moving to build up its armed forces. It must be remembered that the very nature of the state makes this type of development logical. The state as the organization that holds a monopoly of organized force within the nation is so constituted as to turn to military means when threatened from without.

The threatened nation generally reacts to threats and a show of force by countermeasures of the same type. Very weak and powerless nations may capitulate and attempt to appease the superior power, although in 1939 Poland, despite its relative weakness, mobilized its strength against Hitler's threats. In the main, when a nation has some prospect of power parity, its response to threat is reactive in nature—it counters by mobilizing its strength and presenting counter-threats. In such a situation the armaments race proceeds apace. Russia and the United States have both developed their atomic arsenals with the objective of attaining an overkill capability.

The argument for counter-threat and deterrence is to make the prospect of successful outcome of aggression by the other side unlikely or at least so costly that it will not be attempted. Though the ability to muster force against threats has on occasion discouraged aggression, it is no guarantee of security or peace. The opposing side may perceive a point of advantage in striking at a particular time whether or not it has correctly assessed the situation. And the logic of utilizing force as the means of handling conflict would justify a preventive war by one's own side based on the assessment of a favorable set of circumstances. In addition to these hard-headed considerations, account must be taken of the psychology of the reliance upon force. A psychology of threat and deterrence leads to a situation in both nations in which there is a perceived magnification of the belligerence and intransigence of the other side and to resulting actions of a belligerent character. A spiraling process develops that limits the role of national leaders to their specific function as protectors of national security. In this situation the perceptions of the actions of the other side are subjected to a coding process in the mass media that makes for simplification and distortion. The temporal dimension of the spiraling process becomes all important, for if it proceeds too rapidly there is no opportunity for other system forces to cut through the cycle before war breaks out. R. North, R. A. Brody, and O. Holsti (1964) have shown that such a cycle developed rapidly in 1914 after the assassination of the Austrian Archduke. The rapid spiral of events precipitated a war that many of the important leaders on both sides did not want.

Resort to force creates four specific dynamics within a national system making for war. (1) It builds up an elite group of military specialists who think in terms of overkill capacity, preventive war, and a gaming psychology in which millions of human lives are weighted in terms of tactical costs rather than in human terms. (2) It fosters a military-economic complex, to use Eisenhower's term, the power of which is geared to ever-increasing armament. The facts are that this complex is aided and abetted by local groups throughout the country who fight vigorously for their share of defense contracts. (3) It creates mechanisms for international destruction that can be triggered into action by events other than the warlike moves of an enemy. (4) It leads to a climate of opinion that equates national security and strength with the relative nuclear striking power of the country. Within this climate, national leaders are under constraints not to appear to do anything that could be interpreted as appeasement of the other side.

Though reliance upon force and deterrence does not ordinarily create specific system forces making for peace, the prospect of nuclear warfare does present a special case. The use of force at the level of nuclear weapons is no solution of the power struggle. Both sides are decimated if not destroyed by the nature of the conflict. Hence there are forces within the national system, both East and West, that are pushing against nuclear conflict. The elites of the West are not eager to have the economic empires in which they are involved blown to bits. The Russian leaders, who have developed their institutions through a long, difficult period, do not wish to see their chance for further development destroyed by a nuclear holocaust. In the strategy of military planning there is no percentage in a war in which both sides will lose.

The Hegelian dialectic which postulates antithesis or reaction formation at the social level may find a curious confirmation in that the development of organized force creates a dynamic for peace. Pacifists have long cherished the belief that armed weapons will become so terrible that no nation will dare to go to war. The military-minded share some of this belief, and their strategy of deterrence is based upon it. In the past this type of belief has proved to be wishful thinking on the part of the pacifists and militarists alike. We have reached the point, however, where it is increasingly clear that the nations involved in the Cold War have more in common in maintaining peace than in destroying it. Such a perception of common fate was extremely difficult before the development of nuclear weapons. And of course even this perception today will not guarantee peace. The perception does not extend to all groups. Certain types of military specialists do not share it. Nor do extremist groups who may come to power if the responsible authorities are not seen as coping adequately with national problems. Moreover, the functioning social system of a nation is a complex matter and is not governed primarily by a common perception of the means for survival. Nevertheless, the recognition of mutual dependence in controlling a nuclear disaster is growing and is a force to be reckoned with in assessing the chances for peace.

Limitations of Threat in Dealing with Revolutionary States. Threats of force against the newly emerging revolutionary state by older nations often do not have the desired effects. The national leaders of the young government, representing as they do the new institutions, would jeopardize their positions of leadership if they appeared to betray the revolution. Hence they will risk destruction by the external enemy rather than play a submissive role. The common belief that these revolutionary leaders only understand toughness and force overlooks the roles they play in their own system and the dynamics of that system. Hence these leaders are more likely to recognize a show of force if this technique is accompanied by offers of negotiation that make their own internal position tenable.

Diplomatic recognition is critical for the new government in its early stages. Recognition is first of all the necessary condition for any attempts to negotiate with the new state. Failure to recognize its existence means that important channels of communication are closed, that other nations are not prepared to accept it in the family of nations. It is not only a blow to the psychological pride of the country but is also interpreted as an action bordering on war. The older nations, however, are sometimes reluctant to grant recognition because they do not want to give their moral support to a regime inimical to their own interests and ideological principles. Withholding of recognition is part of a campaign to undermine the new government and is often accompanied by economic sanctions and tariff embargoes and even by support to counter-revolutionary forces. The major problem with these attempts at overthrowing the new government is that they do not necessarily work. The philosophy of punishment, threat, and force is used, but generally in a fairly feeble manner. The older countries believe that the new regime will not last and that minor support to its enemies and moral chastisement will bring about its downfall. This is in part due to the fact that the information sources utilized generally represent the older power structure rather than the forces of change. Hence the assessment of new governments by the established powers has been repeatedly in error, whether the new regime was in Russia, China, Africa, or Cuba. It is not so much that diplomats and legislators are incapable of learning from experience in the international field as that they are captives of their own closed informational system.

A critical determinant of the outcome of a policy of nonrecognition, threats, and sanctions toward a new government is the extent to which the new regime represents a newly developing set of institutions within the society. If a revolution is a palace revolution or a coup d'état in which the only change is the replacement of one set of rulers by another, then a hostile international climate may be enough to overthrow it. If, however, the revolutionary government reflects changed internal institutions, it is not likely to be changed from without save by crushing sanctions and organized force. Historically the error has often been made, as we have just noted, of regarding a new revolutionary regime as a new group of adventurous leaders without the support of changed institutions within their own borders.

Finally it should be noted that the use of force, of threats, and of deterrence is no solution for ideological conflicts. Religious and political ideologies have with-stood military might throughout history. The Nazi conquest of Europe did not insure the success of Nazi doctrines nor did the Nazi defeat guarantee the success of democratic beliefs. It is true that a military triumph and subsequent totalitarian control over generations can produce ideological changes. Even in this case, however, it is more the teaching of the new generation in a different context that leads to change than the imposition of the ideology through force.

Conflict Denial

At the individual level we recognize the doctrine that it takes two to make a fight. If a person ignores the insults and belligerent attitude of an aggressor he may avert a struggle. Within an organized group the top leadership will sometimes refuse to recognize intragroup feuding in the hope that it will go away or at least remain below threshold. At the national level the same policy is on occasion followed toward the actions of other nations. There is a large area of national and international incidents that can be perceived as threatening or aggressive actions on the one hand or as innocuous or trivial behavior on the other.

Denial of conflict at the national level is not so much a matter of blocked perceptions, as is the case at the individual level, but a matter of interpretation of the actions of other nations. Four conditions make for conflict denial. In the first place, the nationalism of the well-established bureaucratic state is not as sensitive to insults to its symbols as is the revolutionary nationalism of the newly developing state or the regressive nationalism of the counter-revolutionary state.

In the second place, the national state that is functioning satisfactorily and has few internal problems will minimize the potentially aggressive actions of other nations. Both leaders and masses are not eager to jeopardize the satisfactory state of affairs.

In the third place, some degree of involvement in international systems can lead to interpretation of national policies and practices as non-warlike in character. Some elements in the upper classes in Britain and France were involved in the preservation of conservative social structure in Germany to such an extent that they refused to credit Hitler's regime with warlike intentions. They thought they could do business with Hitler. Similarly, the identification of some of the ruling group in India with Communist China's struggle against white colonialism blinded them to China's aggressive policies until India was actually invaded.

In the fourth place, the weak, powerless nation may refuse to acknowledge the true meaning of hostile acts against itself by a powerful neighbor in the hope of avoiding a disastrous conflict.

Relation of Denial to Types of Nationalism. The interaction of the two conditions of symbol sensitivity and internal conflict has implications for international relations. The belligerence and flexing of muscles of a newly emerging national state can be ignored for a period in the hope that its development and expansionism will not assume a military form. The newly developing nation need not resort to force against other countries if it can make progress through internal growth and external economic expansion. But the regressive type of nationalism, if it captures the state, can rarely succed without the resort to military aggressiveness or war. The very reason for the revival of the patriotism of the past is the failure of internal institutions to meet the problems of the present. Instead of the development of new institutions there is an attempt to anticipate revolutionary change by a reactionary counter-revolution. This is accomplished by internal repression and the use of the machinery of the state to resurrect old institutions utilizing emotional chauvinism. There is a narrowing of national norms and any form of deviation is labeled as treasonable. The nation is thus on a military footing to combat internal evil and external threat. The dynamic is one of war. To maintain power the elite groups, moreover, must make societal institutions work better than they did before the counter-revolution took over and one method is that of external conquest and confiscation. The internal stresses and strains are projected outward. This externalization of internal conflict occurs in other types of

nation states but regressive nationalism is the example par excellence of this process.

Thus conflict denial is not a satisfactory technique for dealing with a nation whose outward belligerence is determined not so much by its relations with other powers as by its own internal conflictual dynamics.

Consequences of Denial. The outcome of the denial method of dealing with conflict can lead either to its minimization or its aggravation. We have suggested some of the factors that will predispose toward one or the other of these types of outcome. At the level of tactics the problem becomes one of the realistic assessment of the nature of conflictual tendencies in the other party. If an action by another nation appears aggressive or can be interpreted as belligerent, there are criteria for evaluating its underlying meaning. We have already noted that the most important assessment relates to an understanding of the internal institutions and the character of the nationalism of the state in question. In addition, the following practical criteria are often employed. If the incident is the outcome of a deliberate official policy of the nation it can be interpreted in terms of that official policy. The actions of individuals, even though they hold official positions, such as American congressmen, are not necessarily representative of national policy. A second criterion is the purpose of the course of action that may have aggressive implications. Its objective may be for internal consumption rather than to serve as a blueprint for foreign policy. It may be a move by the moderate group in power to undercut the extremist group and so can be discounted in part by the other nation. Sometimes the party in power may espouse a belligerent nationalism during an election campaign, which is intended to affect the election outcome and not to affect international relations. Such a line of conduct may get out of hand and take on a logic of its own. Often, however, the professional diplomats are sufficiently informed about the meaning of national actions to be able to discount the sabre-rattling that is intended for domestic rather than foreign consumption. A third criterion is the consistent and cumulative character of aggressive or potentially aggressive actions. As the pattern of *Mein Kampf* (rearmament, militant nationalism and racism, and aggression to secure German domination) became translated into action it became increasingly clear that other nations could not negotiate with Hitler. The strategy of nations seeking peace thus may follow a pattern of not imputing belligerent intentions to other nations on the basis of one or two incidents but of waiting and testing the objectives of the other side.

Conflict Restriction and Control: Limited War

Another strategy of conflict reduction, not necessarily coordinate with or independent of negotiation and deterrence, is the localization and containment of overt conflict. The Cold War has been marked by armed clashes that have been successfully confined to the locality in which they occurred. Geographical restriction and psychological definition have been employed for this purpose so that even the Korean struggle was viewed as a police action rather than a war. The containment of conflict is an interesting aspect of national policy in that it reflects the reluctance of the major powers to follow through on the logical consequences of force and deterrence to an all-out war. Thus it often reflects the difficulties described by T. C. Schelling (1957) with respect to the coordination of the mutual expectancies of each side toward the anticipations of the other. On the one hand the use of force in itself logically implies a breakdown in negotiation, but on the other hand restriction on the force to be employed calls for some degree of agreement. Thus, for limited war there must be agreement or acquiescence about the limits in situations where communication is greatly restricted. In his analysis Schelling argues that implicit agreements can be reached to restrict the conduct of a war but they must be about *qualitatively* distinctive courses of action and not about *matters of degree*. Both sides refrained from using poison gas in World War II, but such an agreement on the basis of tacit understanding could not have occurred with respect to some *lim-ited degree* of the use of poison gas. With incomplete communication the situation itself defines the accepted practice and hence must provide a *clear anchoring point*. In Korea both sides refrained from atomic weapons of all sorts, tactical and strategic, clean and unclean. In fact the Chinese did not use conventional bombs against the major American supply base of Pusan with the tacit understanding that the United States would not use atomic weapons, according to subsequent press reports. A Soviet diplomat was reported to have leaked information to the West that atomic bombing of Manchurian bases would result in Chinese bombing of South Korean supply centers and even of Japan. Whatever the factual details, both sides followed the line of not violating mutual expectations based upon limited communication.

Prior announcement of intentions by one side in advance of conflict (Schelling suggests), even though not formally agreed to by the other, can help to set up limitations in the struggle if the proposal is qualitatively clear and of an all-or-none character. In an actual emergency the prior announcement could serve to crystallize expectations and guide courses of action. For example, the statement by a nuclear power that it will not resort to atomic weapons in the protection of its interests in the Near East might help to confine the conflict to the use of conventional weapons by both sides even if war broke out.

Nonviolence and Ideological Conversion

The pacifist doctrines of nonviolence are sometimes seen as techniques of denial and appeasement. The nonviolent Gandhian philosophy, however, is not of this character. It is pacifist only in method. In a sense it is militant in its moral objectives and permits no departure from its ethical principles. The central norm of the system, according to A. Naess (1958), is "act in a group struggle and act, moreover, in a way conducive to long term reduction of violence." The emphasis is upon action and not passivity, and not only upon refraining from violence oneself but on behaving so that violence in others will be reduced. To attain that objective the person must avoid actions that would have the effect of humiliating the rival group, attempt to achieve a high degree of empathy with respect to the values of members of the opposing group, adopt a consistent attitude of trust toward the rival group, including an open statement of one's own plans and intentions, and initiate friendly interactions with opponents. In addition one must make visible sacrifices for one's cause and maintain a consistent set of positive activities which are an attempt at the explicit realization of the goals of the group.

Janis and Katz (1959) have called attention to some of the psychological mechanisms that are called into play with the use of violence and that distort its good objectives. The guilt associated with the use of violence leads to justification through the attribution of evil to the target. Participating in violent action may lead to a weakening of superego controls. The social sanctioning of violence, which is normally seen as antisocial, can lead to all types of excesses in its use, for now primitive impulses receive social approval.

Mutual Understanding and Nonviolence. The logic of the pacifist methods is that threat, force, and violence are evil and that they can not be used to secure good outcomes. There is a rejection of the separation of means from ends and a repudiation of the notion that the end justifies the means. The assumption is that unethical means will corrupt a good objective. The pacifist argument is that arming to the teeth will not necessarily deter an opponent but will change the nation resorting to armament and threats into the same evil warlike character as the opponent. The logic of handling conflicts through force readily countenances a preventive war even by the side originally seeking to protect itself rather than to aggress against others. The nonviolent rationale, on the other hand, assumes that the readiness to use force, violence, and preventive war is self-defeating. The possible success of force against an opponent is only temporary, for the opponent or other opponents will rise again. Moreover, the nation enjoying temporary success is corrupted in its way of life because it has taken on the character of an executioner.

Not all methods or all advocates of peaceful policy reflect this philosophy in complete or ideal form. Nonetheless, it was the major tactic in winning the independence of India from British rule. It was moreover, employed by the early Christians in establishing the Church within the Roman empire. Nonviolence, though not always approximating the Gandhian ideal, has been a major weapon of the Negroes in fighting the battle of civil rights in the United States. Where this tactic has been employed it creates real problems for the opposition. Since it is tied to moral principles or humanitarian goals, and since it pleads for the oppressor as well as for the oppressed, it defies the traditional coping behavior of force and authority. Organized force is rationalized as necessary in dealing with illegality but the use of nonviolence creates a reversal of norms in which the legal authorities appear brutal and immoral.

The tactic of nonviolent moral persuasion has seen little use at the international level. It has been primarily a strategy for revolutionary movements within a national structure. Nonetheless, some of its precepts, such as empathy and understanding and positive nonviolent actions toward moral goals, have application for the behavior of nations. The mutual trust emphasized in this doctrine is one basis of treaties and international agreements. Though many treaties have been broken or maintained by force, many have also resided on trust. Moreover, the nonviolence philosophy cuts through the reactive cumulative character of suspicion, threat, and counter-threat and its ascending cycle of tension.

Pacifist and religious groups embracing the doctrine of nonviolence tend to remain outside the national system with respect to decision-making. The philosophy is important, not because these splinter groups are likely to become critical actors within the national system, but because their ideas may have some impact over time on decision-makers. We shall turn, then, to consider methods of negotiation and compromise which assume that some degree of conflict

Bargaining and Compromise

A common complement of the use of threat is the resort to negotiation to reach a compromise settlement. After the threat of a strike by organized labor, or during a strike, the representatives of the union and of management will sit down at the bargaining table to attempt to reach some agreement about the dispute. Negotiations are possible only if each side is prepared to give up something in order to gain some of its objectives. In other words, the contending parties must be ready to accept a compromise rather than to seek for a final solution of all their differences.

The logic of bargaining and compromise is well suited for reaching agreement about economic and power differences, but it is scarcely appropriate for the settlement of ideological differences of a symbolic character. Workers can settle their dispute with management over wages and fringe benefits by accepting a compromise, such as half the wage increase they wanted, without compromising their ethical standards. They cannot, however, bargain an ideological principle without compromising their moral position. For example, they cannot allow the company to appoint the union stewards in the foundry in return for fringe benefits without sacrificing the ideological principle of having their own independent union, any more than the company can allow the union to name the manager who is to run the foundry.

There is an all-or-none quality to moral principles. We consider the mother of a single illegitimate child as immoral as the mother of illegitimate twins or triplets. Hence ethical standards as such are not the proper subject matter of bargaining and compromise, though the means for achieving them may be. This simple principle has not been grasped by the majority of the white people in the United States with respect to the civil rights of Negroes. The majority position has been one of gradualism, of delay, and of compromise. The intensity of the Negro reaction has come as a surprise. But to the Negroes a moral issue

is at stake, which is not subject to bargaining. If their children are entitled to equality of opportunity in public education as the Supreme Court has ruled, then a compromise which would permit integrated schooling up to fifth grade only is unacceptable.

In controversies, then, there should be clarity about the points of difference and the methods for dealing with them. To prevent the two types of difference from getting confused both sides may send to the bargaining table task-oriented representatives, rather than ideologues. One function of the umpire or arbiter in labor disputes is to keep the negotiations centered around bread-and-butter issues rather than around ideological principles.

In international relations the same logic applies. Trade agreements can be negotiated between Communist and capitalist countries if the discussions are about trade and not about ideology. The major difficulty in the use of bargaining at the international level is that the countries involved have a nationalistic ideology to uphold which can exacerbate their differences and make a compromise impossible. Much as Berlin has been a source of controversy, the United States cannot offer to trade it to the Soviet Union for some other city, because of moral commitments and ideological considerations.

The problem at the international level is one of the needless contamination of economic and power differences with nationalistic ideology. Such confusion hampers the negotiation process in areas where it might prove useful. A major criticism of former Secretary of State John Foster Dulles was his use of moralistic symbols in describing American and Russian policies. He saw controversies between the East and West as differences in basic morality. By moving to the plane of ideological symbols, he contributed to placing issues on a level where bargaining and compromise were impossible.

In general, however, there seems to be an increasing tendency for large bureaucratic nations to select leaders who are pragmatic, task-oriented men with some system perspective and understanding of the nature of national and international structure. The ideologues like Churchill were products of an older order. Hence we may find greater willingness and ability at negotiation and compromise among the younger leaders of the large bureaucratic societies.

Another confusion of moral principles and pragmatic issues can be seen in the United States policy with respect to the diplomatic recognition of other nations. Diplomatic recognition can be used pragmatically in two ways. It can be withheld in the hope of undermining a new government, or it can be bestowed to encourage it and maintain channels of communication. But it can also be used as a moral weapon; that is, the refusal to recognize the new government is supported by the rationale that the new regime is illegitimate and evil. This was the American rationale for not recognizing Soviet Russia for the first fifteen years of its existence. The difficulty with this policy was that the United States finally had to recognize the Soviet Union even though its character had not changed. The long period of diplomatic and other forms of boycott may have contributed to the Stalin era of international distrust and irresponsibility. Moreover, the confusion of moral and practical issues inherent in American policy is apparent when the United States recognizes dictatorial and reactionary regimes, so that among some groups outside the United States the American government is seen as endorsing undemocratic governments. The recent agreement about a "hot line" of direct telephonic communication between the Kremlin and Washington to avert an accidental war shows how far the United States has moved from its earlier moral position of not communicating with an opponent regarded as unclean. Nevertheless, the old ideological principle is still invoked against the government of Communist China and against its admission to the United Nations and the family of nations. The United States is one of the few nations that still refuse to grant recognition to the government of some 600,000,000 Chinese people. And this tough policy toward China does not seem to have made it less militant.

Often it is difficult to achieve successful negotiation of differences because disagreements about present problems of conflicting interests have taken on a moral cast and a win-lose character. Nations have committed themselves to a position from which it is difficult to withdraw. J. D. Singer (1958) points out, therefore, that negotiations should start on procedures for handling future events, rather than on immediately pressing issues. Success in such areas may prepare the way for other types of negotiations.

The outcome of the process of negotiation over pragmatic matters is not necessarily successful in achieving compromise even if ideological issues do not confuse the bargaining. There is a tendency to move toward a deadlock in that each side wants to drive as hard a bargain as possible and thus starts with as high a level of demands as possible. Hence there is the problem of knowing what the other side will really settle for and the reluctance to yield on any essential before the antagonist does. Real movement in negotiation may therefore never get very far and may sometimes not even get started. The intensity of the need, by either or both of the parties, for some settlement is one factor facilitating movement. Another factor is the ingenuity in finding a concession valued by the other side, but not of much value to one's own group.

Where an umpire or arbiter is utilized in labor-management conflict, part of his role is to ascertain the realistic as against the stated positions of both contending parties. He can then suggest proposals in the intermediate area of the realistic demands of the two groups or leak information to each side about what the other group will settle for. He can assess the reality basis of the threats of either side to leave the negotiation table and resort to force. He can then communicate his assessment to the other side.

In international disputes similar devices of arbitration are employed to help in the negotiation process. The services of the larger nations are often employed in disputes between smaller powers. International commissions are accepted even by the more powerful nations in some areas of disagreement. The symbolic principle of national sovereignty serves as a serious obstacle for the big powers in accepting the services of an international arbiter for issues deemed important. Neither Russia nor the United States is willing to utilize either the United Nations or the World Court for the arbitration of their basic differences.

As modern nation states take on more and more of the form of large technological bureaucratic structures, they are likely to depart from adherence to absolutistic dogmas of national sovereignty. A major function of leadership in such structures is negotiation, compromise, and adjudication to maintain the balance of the component subsystems. Hence more carry-over to the international system of the negotiation principle is possible and even probable.

Negotiation and bargaining are not necessarily used in isolation as the only method for conflict reduction. They often follow the use of threats and the mobilization of force so that one or both sides are negotiating from a position of strength. One area of empirical research that has not been exploited is the examination of the validity of the argument that negotiation from a position of strength is the most effective basis for bargaining. Case studies of international conferences resulting in agreement or deadlock could explore the types of conditions leading to given outcomes.

The difficulty with the compromise outcome, however, is that the basic problem may not be solved and may continue to be a source of tension. Fundamental political settlements, it is often contended, must come before bargaining about specific issues. On the other hand, a genuine solution of differences in interests and ideology may be impossible of accomplishment and in fact may not be necessary for the preservation of the peace. Getting down to basic issues often means the invoking of affective ideological symbols, whereas more may be attained by negotiations in which emphasis is upon securing procedural agreements.

Shifting from a Strategy of Deterrence to One of Negotiation. We have already commented on the common notion that if negotiations are to be effective for a given party it must bargain from a position of strength. This point of view generally is a one-sided appraisal of the struggle and

overlooks the two-sided nature of conflict, which could logically result in deadlock and even war if both sides accepted this philosophy. A radically different strategy has been enunciated by Charles Osgood (1959) in his doctrine of graduated unilateral disengagement. Osgood argues that the way to reverse the tensions-arms-race spiral would be to take a unilateral step towards disarmament. Such a unilateral act, to be effective in inducing the enemy to reciprocate, "(1) should, in terms of *military aggression*, be clearly disadvantageous to the side making it, yet not cripplingly so; (2) should be such as to be clearly perceived by the enemy as reducing his external threat; (3) should not increase the enemy's threat to *our* heartland; (4) should be such that reciprocal action by the enemy is available and clearly indicated; (5) should be announced in advance and widely publicized to ally, neutral and enemy countries —as regards the nature of the act, its purpose as part of a consistent policy, and the expected reciprocation; (6) but should not demand prior commitment to reciprocation by the enemy as a condition for its commission" (p. 316).

The major problem in Osgood's proposal is not the probable effectiveness of the unilateral act but the difficulty of any nation taking the first step. The graduated unilateral disengagement has the advantage, however, of pointing to the key problem of cutting the cycle of the arms race, in which tension leads to more armament and more armament to more tension. A negotiated mutual move toward slowing this race could have some of the effects of the Osgood proposal. At least this has been the hope in the treaty between the United States and Russia banning nuclear testing in the atmosphere. In fact, President Kennedy's 1963 speech at American University suggested that he appreciated the merit of the Osgood analysis.

The test-ban agreement was preceded by moves that also reduced the threat-arms spiral. Specifically there has been a shift away from intensifying the perception of threat by both sides in changing the emphasis from first-strike capability to second-strike retaliatory power. The first-strike capability aimed at the military demolition of the opponent is interpreted as more threatening than a retaliatory second strike because it is more offensive than defensive in nature. It is predicated upon the success of beating the enemy to the punch and its build-up implies aggression. Its weapons and their disposition could not survive a retaliatory strike if it failed in the initial round. Hence a well-developed first-strike capability may create some feeling of security to the side possessing it, but resulting insecurity to the other side in that it is geared to going first, to aggression and offense. Thus, Soviet Russia regarded United States weapons in Turkey and at other points close to its borders as part of our first-strike capability, useful to the United States for aggressive purposes only. In the same fashion the United States regarded atomic weapons in Cuba as part of a first-strike capability and hence as offensive weapons. Both sides have moved in the direction of giving greater emphasis to retaliatory strikes with some lessening of the tension between them. To reduce the tension still further there would have to be more pulling back of atomic bases and less concern with a weapons system geared to a first-strike capability.

Problem Solving and Creative Integration

Mary P. Follett in her *Creative Experience* (1924) applied to social disputes the distinction between compromise and genuine solution, which Edwin B. Holt (1915) conceptualized at the level of individual conflict. Holt pointed out that the individual can meet his internal conflicts by alternate concessions to both sets of conflicting impulses or he can, through discriminating analysis, discover an integration or solution. Follett used the term "creative experience" to describe the same problem-solving process in social disagreements in which a discriminating course of conduct could permit each individual to achieve his central purpose. More recently Anatol Rapoport (1961) has called attention to the same need for deeper analysis of problems with which Holt and Follett were concerned. Many problems are not capable of solution with the usual approach and take on the char-

acter of dilemmas. To solve them requires a new frame of reference. They are like puzzles that continue to baffle us as long as we remain in the usual set and apply the usual techniques. It is only when we shift our approach and utilize a radically different set of assumptions that the dilemma can be solved.

In a recent volume entitled *Preventing World War III* (Wright, Evan, & Deutsch, 1962) scholars and scientists from many disciplines have discarded the conventional assumptions of policy makers and have set forth imaginative proposals for more integrative solutions of the conflict between the East and West. They include, for example, the following suggestions:

1. An extension of the United Nations to include a forum of supranational communities (the unit of membership would not be a nation state but a regional entity) and a forum of infranational entities where the membership consists of nongovernmental or private organizations (Evan, 1962).

2. The development of a community of international interest through cooperation among nations to employ world-wide technology for improving the climate by transporting great masses of water, by directing ocean currents, and by modifying the reflective properties of the earth's surface (C. Pokrovsky, 1962).

3. The diversification of the areas of international competition for prestige. If there are many different types of repeated contests, from the exploration of outer space to the conquest of diseases in underdeveloped areas, a defeat by one nation in the prestige competition is not total or necessarily irreversible (Etzioni, 1962).

4. Unilateral moves in areas other than those of immediate obvious tension. The proposal of C. Osgood for a graduated program of tension reduction through a unilateral step toward disarmament has already been discussed. D. Riesman (1962) points out that similar unilateral moves could be made in other ways and has illustrated his point by the "Nylon War"—a satirical example in which American consumer goods are dumped throughout Russia without charge.

5. Internationalizing military force. The

problem of national security is now met by national military forces and generally by alliances between nations for the cooperative use of their armies and weapons. This cooperative arrangement could be extended by setting up a new international institution to which nations would contribute their armaments and armed forces. Countries would maintain their national identities in every other respect, but would turn to this international force for protection against attack. The essence of this proposal is that it means a change in commitment to means rather than to goals. Thus it emphasizes a pragmatic solution through a new institutional arrangement rather than a restructuring of value systems concerning national identity and nonviolence (Kelman, 1962).

6. *Economic steps toward peace.* The industrial-military complex with its pressures toward maintaining and increasing the armament build-up is not an inevitable development. It is socially determined and hence can be changed through social planning. E. Benoit (1962) gives specifications for how the economic consequences of disarmament can be handled without major disruption of the economy. They include (a) allocating some stated proportion of the cut in the national military budget to nonmilitary programs, (b) encouraging defense contractors to budget as a deductible cost some percentage of their contracts to programs for handling their reconversion problems, (c) tax reductions for companies engaged in innovation and risk-taking, and (d) across the board tax cuts on personal income.

The many proposals offered by social scientists who have approached the dilemma of international tension from a problem-solving point of view differ in theoretical merit and practical utility. They can be dismissed as too academic and too remote from the practical operations of the national system. Such a blanket rejection, however, is in itself unrealistic in that the national system is not without adaptive features. These adaptive features of the modern technological bureaucracy, which is empirically oriented, make possible the acceptance of innovative ideas under given

system conditions. For example, the Kennedy administration, confronted with the dilemma of the survival of our national system in its present form, showed interest in the Osgood proposals for reducing international tensions and made progress in its treaties banning atmospheric testing and prohibiting atomic weapons in space. The Benoit proposals for economic steps toward peace are sufficiently close to current measures to cut taxes and to guide the national economy in given directions so that they are not outside the system. In summary, creative ideas of a problem-solving type can gain acceptance if they are adaptable to the functioning of the national system in which they are made.

Finally, the development of the European community is an interesting case study of a creative solution to some of the age-old conflicts among European nations. The bitter memories of past wars and the deep antagonisms between some of the countries would have prevented the most optimistic internationalists of a preceding generation from predicting a unified Europe. But the economic and technological forces of the competing bureaucratic systems pushed toward integration. Haas (1958) has written about this development as follows: "The 'good' Europeans are not the main creators of the regional community that is growing up; the process of community formation is dominated by nationally constituted groups with specific interests and aims, willing and able to adjust their aspirations by turning to supranational means when the course appears profitable" (p. xiv). Trade union members and businessmen both saw the advantages of a more rational organization of industrial and political life. Haas names four conditions as critical to European integration: (a) industrialized nations already heavily involved in international trade and finance, (b) the organization of the masses in these countries in interest groups and political parties, (c) the leadership of these groups by elites competing for influence, and (d) the influence of traditions and assumptions of political democracy upon these elites.

The European integrative process can,

moreover, be described within the framework of our social-psychological analysis of nation states. We had specified that the assumption of national roles depended upon the arousal of one or more of four types of factors: emotional conditioning to national symbols, sense of national identity, compensatory identification, and instrumental rewards. Moreover, we had assumed that with the growth of technological bureaucracy the instrumental involvement becomes more important than emotional conditioning to symbols and that the sense of national identity no longer has to be tied to national symbols. In the European nations the interest groups pushing for regional unity were more concerned with instrumental rewards than with symbols and they saw clearly that their way of life could be enriched by extending the subsystems to which they belonged across national boundaries. At the same time they could maintain their national identity in non-economic sectors of life. In short, the nation state, in spite of its dominant role during the past two centuries, is not the final organizational arrangement of human lives. The increasing interdependence of all parts of the world in the space age may be productive of the further growth of international systems.

The European development has interesting implications for the sociological position that a peaceful world order is dependent upon consensus with respect to a common set of values. Thus Talcott Parsons (1962) argues that "every effort be made to promulgate carefully considered statements of value commitments which may provide a basis for consensus among both have and have-not nations" (p. 318). There is, however, a grave danger in an emphasis upon ideological agreement. Once discussion begins at this level the symbolic character of values involving absolutistic, finalistic, affective, and moral qualities may precipitate conflict rather than debate. It would seem wiser to emphasize common practical interests, as in European integration, and to seek agreement on ideological values as a later step in the process. Parsons himself recognizes this problem in part when he speaks of downgrading some issues

that formerly have been treated as fundamental moral issues. Such downgrading, however, can occur more readily in a context of task solution of empirical problems than in a discussion of values per se. Finally Parsons does note the significance of establishing consensus at the procedural level. Again, it seems wiser to attempt to gain acceptance of procedures for solving problems and for institutionalizing specific norms than of general value codes. Both Communist and capitalist societies already have some common norms about specific practices, and integration can be achieved at this procedural normative level more readily than at the level of ideological goals. Bureaucratic expansion as in the developing European community has proceeded in this fashion. The surplus meanings and the irrelevant emotions associated with the ideological symbols of a system are more functional for mobilizing that system against a competing system than for reaching consensus across systems.

REFERENCES

Adorno, T. W., Frenkel-Brunswik, Else, Levinson, D. J., & Sanford, N. *The authoritarian personality.* New York: Harper, 1950.

Allport, F. H. A structuronomic conception of behavior. *J. abnorm. soc. Psychol.,* 1962, *64,* 3–30.

Arnold, T. *Symbols of government.* New Haven: Yale Univer. Press, 1935.

Bay, C., Gullväg, I., Ofstad, H., & Tønnessen, H. *Nationalism: A study of identification with people and power.* Oslo: Institute of Social Research, 1950. (Mimeographed)

Benoit, E. Economic steps towards peace. In Q. Wright, W. M. Evan, & M. Deutsch (Eds.). *Preventing World War III.* New York: Simon & Schuster, 1962. Pp. 136–154.

Durkheim, E. *The division of labor.* Translated by G. Simpson. New York: Macmillan, 1933.

Etzioni, A. International prestige and peaceful competition. In Q. Wright, W. M. Evan, & M. Deutsch (Eds.). *Preventing World War III.* New York: Simon & Schuster, 1962. Pp. 226–245.

Evan, W. M. Transnational forums for peace. In Q. Wright, W. M. Evan, & M. Deutsch (Eds.), *Preventing World War III.* New York: Simon & Schuster, 1962. Pp. 393–409.

Follett, Mary. *Creative experience.* New York: Longmans, Green, 1924.

Fried, H. E. *The guilt of the German army.* New York: Macmillan, 1942.

Guetzkow, H. Isolation and collaboration: A partial

theory of international relations. *J. Confl. Resol.*, 1957, *1*, 48–68.

Haas, E. B. *The uniting of Europe.* Stanford: Stanford Univer. Press, 1958.

Hayes, C. J. H. *Essays on nationalism.* New York: Macmillan, 1926.

Holt, E. B. *The Freudian wish.* New York: Holt, Rinehart and Winston, 1915.

Janis, I. L., & Katz, D. The reduction of intergroup hostility. *J. Confl. Resol.*, 1959, *3*, 85–100.

Kardiner, A., et al. *The psychological frontiers of society.* New York: Columbia Univer. Press, 1945.

Kelman, H. C. Internationalizing military force. In Q. Wright, W. M. Evan, & M. Deutsch (Eds.), *Preventing World War III.* New York: Simon & Schuster, 1962. Pp. 106–122.

Levi, W. On the causes of war and the conditions of peace. *J. Confl. Resol.*, 1960, *4*, 411–420.

Levinson, D. J. Authoritarian personality and foreign policy. *J. Confl. Resol.*, 1957, *1*, 37–47.

March, J. G., & Simon, H. A. *Organizations.* New York: Wiley, 1958.

Naess, A. A systematization of Gandhian ethics of conflict resolution. *J. Confl. Resol.*, 1958, *2*, 140–155.

North, R. C., Brody, R. A., and Holsti, O. R. Some empirical data on the conflict spiral. *Peace Research Society (International) Papers*, 1964, *1*, 1–14.

Oppenheimer, F. *The state.* Indianapolis: Bobbs-Merrill, 1914.

Osgood, C. E. Suggestions for winning the real war with communism. *J. Confl. Resol.*, 1959, *3*, 295–325.

Parsons, T. Polarization of the world and international order. In Q. Wright, W. M. Evan, & M. Deutsch (Eds.), *Preventing World War III.* New York: Simon & Schuster, 1962. Pp. 310–331.

Paul, J. *Research for peace.* Canadian Peace Research Institute, 1963. (Mimeographed)

Pokrovsky, G. I. Improving the world. In Q. Wright, W. M. Evan, & M. Deutsch (Eds.), *Preventing World War III.* New York: Simon & Schuster, 1962. Pp. 278–288.

Rapoport, A. A new logic for the test ban. *The Nation,* April 1, 1961.

Riesman, D. The nylon war. In Q. Wright, W. M. Evan, & M. Deutsch (Eds.), *Preventing World War III.* New York: Simon & Schuster, 1962. Pp. 213–225.

Schelling, T. C. Bargaining, communication and limited war. *J. Confl Resol.*, 1957, *1*, 19–36.

Selltiz, Claire, & Cook, S. W. Factors influencing attitudes of foreign students toward the host country. *J. soc. Issues*, 1962, *18*(1), 7–23.

Shepard, H. A. Responses to situations of competition and conflict. In Elise Boulding (Ed.). *Conflict management in organizations.* Ann Arbor, Mich.: Foundation for Research on Human Behavior, 1961. Pp. 33–41.

Singer, J. D. Threat-perception and the armament-tension dilemma. *J. Confl. Resol.*, 1958, *2*, 90–105.

Singer, J. D. The political science of human conflict. In E. B. McNeil (Ed.), *The nature of human conflict.* Englewood Cliffs, N.J.: Prentice-Hall, 1965. Pp. 139–154.

Wright, Q., Evan, W. M., & Deutsch, M. (Eds.), *Preventing World War III.* New York: Simon & Schuster, 1962.

SOCIETAL, ATTITUDINAL AND STRUCTURAL FACTORS IN INTERNATIONAL RELATIONS[*][1]

HERBERT C. KELMAN

In classifying research approaches to the problems of war and peace, Angell distinguishes between those who do research in terms of governments and those who do research in terms of peoples. It is possible to make another distinction which overlaps to some degree with that made by Angell. This is a distinction between those who approach the problem in terms of macroscopic units, such as the nation, and those who essentially use the individual as their unit of analysis. Of the papers in this issue, Cottrell's comes closest to the first type of emphasis. Operational research and regulatory research, as discussed by Wright, would also fall in this category. The papers of Gladstone, Farber and Angell represent pretty much the second type of approach.

Along with this difference in terms of the units of analysis used in the two approaches, there appears also to be a difference in the assumption about the nature of the phenomenon of war.

War as a Deviation and War as an Instrument of Policy

Those who deal with the individual tend to conceive of war as a deviation: essentially, it occurs because of some failure in the mechanisms of maintaining peace. The extreme of this position is represented by the psychoanalytic approach, as described by Farber. According to this approach, war is an aspect of irrational behavior, related to irrelevant, personal motivations, usually traceable to childhood experiences. According to the approach presented by Gladstone, war is related to the typical ways in which individuals react to threat. It is assumed that certain kinds of attitudes in the face of provocation or perceived threat are likely to interfere with a peaceful settlement of conflict. For Angell, one of the determinants of war is a lack of adequate cultural bridges which would promote international understanding and prevent the outbreak of war when conflicts arise. It follows, from the conception of war as a phenomenon of deviant behavior, that war could be prevented by changing the people (their attitudes, motivations, understanding) and by placing individuals of a certain type into leadership positions.

Farber, Gladstone and Angell do not claim, by any means, that the variables they discuss encompass the whole range of causes of war, and that war should be treated exclusively as a deviation. To do so would be to neglect the social, economic and political conditions which provide the context for international relations. Out of these conditions very real conflicts of interest among nations may arise, which in turn will have important effects on the probability of war. Attitudes and motivations of the kinds described by Farber, Gladstone and Angell may affect the extent to which nations are able to resolve their conflicts without recourse to war, but these attitudes are meaningful only in relation to the actual social conditions and may in part be determined by them. That these "societal" factors may outweigh the importance of personal motivations and attitudes is suggested by the fact that "peace-loving" nations engage in war as often as "war-like"

[*] Reprinted by permission of the author and publisher from *Journal of Social Issues*, 1955, *11:* 42–56.

[1] Many of the ideas presented in this article were originally developed at the 1953 summer workshop of the Research Exchange on the Prevention of War by William Barth, Arthur Gladstone, Dean Pruitt and the author (6). The writer is very grateful to Robert Agger, Kenneth Boulding, Arthur Gladstone and Robert Hefner for many helpful suggestions concerning the manuscript.

445

nations; that a nation may follow a fairly consistent foreign policy over a period of time despite decisive changes in its leadership; that the same elite may be highly belligerent towards one nation, yet highly conciliatory towards another; and that nations may establish alliances with each other despite the existence of negative attitudes and misunderstandings (cf. 8).

Those who deal with more macroscopic units tend to conceive of war as an instrument of policy. According to this view it is possible that war will occur even if the elite of a nation is not particularly subject to war-like motivations and attitudes and even if there is considerable understanding among the nations concerned. In fact, an elite may decide on war without any substantial provocation or threat. War in this view is one of many means used by an elite in the pursuit of its ends. An elite may decide "cold-bloodedly" that war is necessary, or it may follow policies which are likely to result in war, in order that it may achieve certain ends that are important to it. Cottrell is quite explicit about this assumption. He conceptualizes war as a consequence of human choice and an outcome of an elite's normal pursuit of its ends. War will be selected if the elite considers it the course of action most likely to maximize its values. It follows from this view, as Cottrell points out, that to prevent war it would be necessary to show to the elite in a convincing way that war is not the best way to maximize their particular values, that it is actually more costly than other means available to them.

The conception of war as an instrument of policy seems to rest on the further assumption that the choices made by the elite are essentially "rational." Cottrell indicates that these choices may be determined by myths, prejudices and hunches, but he implies that they would be rational if the elite had all the necessary facts. They would choose peace if it could be demonstrated convincingly that peace would make more likely the maximization of their values. This, however, is precisely one of the major difficulties in war prevention. How *can* it be made clear and convincing to an elite that war is not the best means

available to them? There have certainly been occasions when, to the objective observer, it seemed clear that war was not a desirable course of action, and yet, the elite resisted this evidence. Their perceptions were distorted, either because of some particular investment in the method of war as such, unrelated to the rational, conscious ends that they were pursuing; or because of some strong resistance to the alternative means that were available. In such cases it would do little good to demonstrate that the elite's ends could be served best by peaceful means, because the real problem would be to persuade the elite to accept the diagnosis. If it is true, as Cottrell suspects, that all the necessary conditions for his Model Five of a peaceful world exist except the condition that it be clearly manifest to all elites that war is inferior to peace in the pursuit of their values, then perhaps a major focus of research might be: how can this be made clearly manifest? It is here that the kinds of variables discussed by Gladstone, Farber and Angell may become of primary importance. Perhaps there is something in the basic values and character patterns of a nation and its elite or in their traditional attitudes towards the other nations concerned which predisposes them towards perceiving situations as requiring war and towards resisting alternative means.

In short, we have tried to point out that while personal attitudes and motivations may be of great importance in the conduct of internatonal relations, "societal" factors set very stringent limits on their operation; and while war and peace may be instruments of policy, selected by the elite in line with their goals, "attitudinal" factors predispose them towards one or the other course of action. The study of war and peace inevitably, therefore—as recent writers are increasingly pointing out—requires us to pay attention to both societal and attitudinal factors and to the interaction between the two.

Societal Factors

It is probably clear from the preceding comments what we mean by societal factors. In the most general terms this refers to those variables which describe characteristics of the society as a whole. Societal factors relate to macroscopic units—usually nations, but sometimes also large segments of a nation, or certain groupings of nations. Some of these factors represent aggregations of actions on a part of a large number of individuals, or products of such actions. In these cases the individual behavior is abstracted via concepts which refer to the aggregations or the products as such.

There is a wide variety of societal factors that are likely to affect the probability of war and peace. For example, there are such "natural" factors as the geographic position of the country and the basic resources that it has available. Probably of great importance are the economic conditions of the country, including the kind of productive activities on which its economy is based, the point in the business cycle in which it finds itself, and the general standard of living of the population. Closely related are the technological conditons, whose relationship to war and peace is described in detail by Cottrell. (See especially 2). Population factors may be related to tendencies towards geographic or economic expansion, and also determine the manpower resources and hence the productive capacity and the military potential of a nation. Other military factors and strategic considerations are also likely to enter into the picture. And there are political conditions, such as the nature of the regime, the stability of the government, and the existence of internal political conflict. Finally, there are factors relating to international politics and diplomacy, such as the existence of power blocs and alliances, the maintenance of balance of power, and the many other factors which are the traditional domain of the students of international relations.

It can be assumed that societal factors determine to a great extent the policies followed by the decision-making elite, since they affect the goals towards which the decision-makers are striving and the means that are available to them. For example, if nation A has a poorly developed technology, it is likely that its elite will pursue a policy of peaceful cooperation vis-a-vis its more advanced neighbor B, both because

the elite may desire technical and economic assistance from B and because it lacks the means for effective military resistance to B. Attitudinal factors may modify the effects of such societal factors, but the latter will surely set limits on the policies pursued by the elite. The decisions of the elite will be affected not only by the conditions in their own country, but also by the conditions in other countries and the resulting goals and means of these other elites. For example, if the conditions in nation C are such that the elite of C is bent on territorial expansion, and if C has the necessary resources to carry this program through, then the elite of A may decide to increase its own arms production and to enter into military alliances with other nations. Of course, here again, other factors enter into the picture: A's perception of the goals and resources of C may be distorted because of certain attitudes on the part of the elite of A, or because of certain flaws in the communication process.

The study of societal factors is important both in the analysis of a specific international situation, and in the derivation of general laws about international relations. In a specific situation, determination of such factors helps predict the probability of war or peace. It may also point to the specific conditions that would have to be changed in order to reduce the probability of war; and it may help to convince the elite—as Cottrell suggests—that war would not be the most effective means for maximizing their values. As far as general laws are concerned, it might be useful to establish two kinds of relationships. On the one hand, one could attempt to derive laws which link societal factors to certain broad social outcomes: in these types of law, in other words, both the independent and dependent variables would refer to macroscopic units (as they do in modern economic theory). On the other hand, one could attempt to derive laws which link societal factors to the decision-making processes. When we are dealing with laws of the first kind, it is possible to ignore the attitudes and motivations of the individuals who determine the final outcome, and to seek relationships completely on the macroscopic level. When dealing with laws of the second kind, however, the importance of the attitudes and motivations of the decision-makers, and of all those who influence their decisions, becomes particularly apparent.

Attitudinal Factors

When speaking of "attitudinal" factors we refer, in a general way, to those variables which describe characteristics of individuals. More specifically, we want to deal with attitudes, values and motivations which are part of the individual's general outlook on the world and which determine his reactions to important social events. The individual—whether he be a member of the elite or of the public-at-large—brings these attitudes and motivations into situations which require decision and action relevant to international affairs. We might also speak of these variables as "predispositional" factors, in that they tend to predispose the person towards one kind of perception, decision and action as over against another.

Attitudinal factors relevant to international relations may be unique to the individual involved, or (and these are probably more important in international relations) they may be typical for the culture as a whole. The source of these attitudes may be in the past history of the individual (as Farber suggests), in the immediate social conditions of his society, or in previous interactions between his and other nations (as suggested by Angell). When their source is the life history of the individual, then we may speak of these attitudes as products of individual personality or national character—particularly if they are rooted in the process of socialization: we can then proceed, as Farber does, to relate attitudes to personality factors. When their source is interaction with the other nation, then they may take on the character of stereotypes and social distance scales (8). Regardless of the source, these factors constitute readinesses or tendencies to prefer certain kinds of goals over others, to choose or accept certain courses of action as over against others, to perceive and interpret the actions of other groups and nations in certain ways rather than in others.

Examples of attitudinal factors that might affect international relations are attitudes toward other nations (often based on traditions of long standing); attitudes towards internationalism in general (as discussed by Wright, for example), international organization, specific international bodies; attitudes towards one's own nation, its destiny, its honor, its sovereignty; general attitudes relating to the perception of threat (as discussed by Gladstone); values or ideologies regarding war and violence, regarding alternative ways of resolving conflicts; expectations about war and assumptions about its inevitability; images of war and military life (such as the glamorization of war as an exciting experience, or as a test of heroism). As far as the general public is concerned, the kinds of attitudes that are particularly important are those which determine the extent to which people will *accept* the policies of the elite and the enthusiasm with which they will help to carry them out. Included here, for example, would be attitudes towards the government in general and values regarding political action and individual responsibility. The acceptance and morale of the public is always a factor in foreign policy, although there are differences in the amount and kind of influence which public opinion exerts, depending on the political structure (5).

It would be possible to ignore attitudinal factors and to deal completely on the level of societal factors if we could make two assumptions: (1) that the goals of decision-makers (and opinion-makers) are, within broad limits, geared to some sort of "objective needs" of the society, and (2) that the actions of the decision-makers are, by and large, rational, in the sense that they are chosen so as to maximize their conscious goals. In the field of international relations, however, it seems hardly possible to make these assumptions. First of all, the decisions are made and influenced by a large number of individuals and groups, each of whom brings into the picture a wide variety and a complex constellation of goals, many of which are only indirectly related to the international situation as such. The relation of this complex array of goals to the needs of the society is certainly not a simple one. Secondly, even some of the goals and values relating to war and peace which are generally shared in the society are not produced by the needs of the society in any objective sense, but rather by the dominant ideology and ethos. Thirdly, there appear to be preferences, in every society, for certain kinds of policies and actions, even if these do not lead to a maximization of conscious goals; and aversions to certain alternative policies which might actually be more profitable. These preferences become especially important since the ambiguities faced by decision-makers in the area of international relations make "rational" choices extremely difficult: the goals towards which they are striving are often not clear-cut, particularly when they aim for goals which are incompatible with each other and when some important goals are not verbalized; and frequently they have little objective basis for evaluating the consequences of various courses of action, particularly when these evaluations depend on guesses about the goals, plans and reactions of other nations. For all these reasons, then, it seems to be necessary to supplement the study of societal factors with a study of attitudinal factors, and particularly to deal with the interaction between the two.

The study of attitudinal factors, just like the study of societal factors, is important both in the analysis of a specific international situation and in the derivation of general laws. It is necessary to establish the exact nature of the attitudes that underlie foreign policy, as well as public opinion on international affairs. Without this information, programs designed for attitude change may be ineffective since they may not be aimed at the relevant issues.

Structural Factors

The attempt to deal with the interaction between societal and attitudinal factors raises the question of *whose* attitudes have to be studied. One could arbitrarily limit oneself to the official decision-makers. In doing so, however, a great deal of informa-

tion would be lost, since they are not the only ones who have a hand in formulating policy. Their decisions are influenced by various individuals and groups, official and unofficial, within their own nation as well as outside it. Within a given country, the list of influential groups would include, for example, governmental agencies, legislative bodies, military agencies, economic groupings, various pressure groups, and the communications industry. Outside of the nation it would include the elites of other nations with whom this particular nation is in alliance or who are co-members in certain regional groupings, international organizations (such as the U. N.) and less official international bodies (such as churches and labor organizations). To varying degrees, the actions of decision-makers are also determined by public opinion and public sentiment. If we want to take into account the effects of these different influences, we have to deal with the problem of how the attitudes and actions of the different groups and individuals are aggregated so as to produce national policy and action. In other words, we have to identify the individuals and groups who are able to exert influence, and to determine the degree to which they are influential, the issues over which they have some control, and the way in which they exert their influence.

The need for dealing with this problem of aggregation brings into focus a third set of factors that have to be studied: structural factors, including the power structure and the communication structure of the nations in question. Study of the power structure would reveal which groups have control over foreign policy decisions (or, more probably, over particular areas of foreign policy) and under what conditions and in what ways they can make their influence felt. Study of the communication structure would reveal which groups have access to the information enabling them to play a role in foreign policy and to communication channels enabling them to exert influence. The distinction between power structure and communication structure is, of course, only a formal one, since in actuality power depends on a central position in the communication structure, and vice versa.

Structural factors represent a level of analysis different from that of either societal or attitudinal factors. As we have seen, societal factors typically describe characteristics of nations; attitudinal factors refer to characteristics of individuals. In the study of structural factors, however, the units of analysis are formal or informal structures, or machineries for aggregating the values of a variety of individuals and groups (cf. 1). Structural factors refer to the characteristics of such structures or machineries. These factors are of great importance since they determine the way in which societal and attitudinal factors are channelled into decisions and actions. The nature of this channelling process in itself may have decisive effects on the probability of war and peace. It is quite conceivable that two situations in which societal and attitudinal factors are alike will have different effects depending on the power and communication structures through which decisions are made.

Since decisions are affected by groups and individuals within and outside the nation, it is important to study both the national and international structures. The national structure will affect, among other things, the amount and kind of influence exerted by public opinion. On the one hand, it will determine the extent to which the public is able to make its "will" felt, i.e., how much information is available to the citizens, how much power they have to influence policy, and how much opportunity is given them to communicate their wishes to the decision-makers. One might assume, for example, that there would be considerable differences in this respect between democracies and dictatorships, although these differences are by no means simple, since in the area of foreign relations dictatorships also consider the public will in order to be sure of morale and support, and democracies also ignore and manipulate the public will in determining policy. On the other hand, structural factors will largely determine the actual content of public opinion, by affecting the kinds of information that will be communicated *to* the public. A totalitarian regime, for example, is in a better position to manipulate public opinion since it has almost sole control over the mass media of communication.

In studying the international structure, we would have to consider the alliances and groupings to which a nation belongs. Elites of allied nations will be in a position to exert influence on this nation's policies, depending on the degree to which it needs their support and the extent to which channels of communication are available. If two nations involved in a potential conflict are themselves allies or co-members of a group of nations, certain additional channels for mutual influence and resolution of the conflict would be available; and also, both would be more receptive to influence from other allies. An international organization would be in a position to exert influence on a given nation depending on its power, the place of the nation within the structure of the international organization, the availability of institutionalized ways of dealing with conflicts between nations, and the extent to which it provides open channels of communication among its member-nations. International communication structures, formal and informal, will be of decisive importance, since they will determine to a large extent the way in which one nation will interpret the intentions and estimate the capacities of other nations.

In the analysis of a specific international situation, one would want to identify the different positions in the power and communication structures and determine the amount and manner of influence exerted by each. While this appears to be a huge task, it may actually turn out that the number of people that have decisive influence on international relations is fairly small (cf. 4). This kind of analysis would point to the groups that are influential and upon whom attempts at changing attitudes should be concentrated; and to possible changes in the structure (e.g., increasing the power or information of certain groups) which might produce changes in foreign policy. On the level of general laws, we would want to establish relationships between particular kinds of structures and the probability of war and peace. The derivation of such laws would be greatly facilitated if we had concepts that provide summary descriptions of complex structures (such as democratic vs. totalitarian). The development of such concepts is a difficult task, and it is here that a great deal of creative imagination is needed.

The Process of Interaction Between Nations

In our attempt to provide a preliminary kind of mapping or framework for research on international relations we have, so far, distinguished three types of variables which may affect the probability of war and peace. Up to this point this framework is essentially static. We have discussed relationships between these variables and the probability of war or peace at a given moment in time, but have not presented the variables in the context of continuing interactions between nations. The interaction between nations, of course, involves an ever-changing succession of events. An action of the part of one nation, as Gladstone points out, will be communicated to another, and produce a reaction which in turn will be communicated to the first nation, and so on. It is very likely that the effects of our three types of factors will change in relation to this flow of events. For example, if nations A and B mutually distrust each other but are both disarmed, the chances of war are probably low; as these two nations become engaged, however, in the mutual stimulation of an armaments race (7), the effect of attitudes of distrust on the probability of war is likely to become more noticeable. To be sure, it may happen that there are forces so strong that they will determine war or peace almost regardless of particular events in the relations between two nations: for example, a nation may initiate war without provocation, or keep out of war no matter how extreme the provocation. In general, however, societal, attitudinal and structural factors will operate with reference to specific events in the process of interaction, and a useful framework must, therefore, include consideration of these events.

In line with this requirement, we would state the problem with which the framework deals as follows: when a particular event, or situation of interaction, occurs, what is the probability that its outcome will be peace or war, and how is this probability affected by societal, attitudinal and structural factors? By situation of interaction is meant any action on the part of A which is communicated to B and which B deems relevant to its own interests. Selecting a specific situation of interaction and trying to determine its outcome is, of course, an abstraction from the real situation made for purposes of exposition. In actuality, especially in present-day international relations, there are always a series of situations of interaction occurring simultaneously and it is impossible to trace the effects of one of them without taking into account the whole set of events that are occurring. Perhaps, eventually, this gulf will be bridged by the development of indices which stand for a whole set of simultaneous events, such as Richardson's index of arms expenditures (7).

A situation of interaction, or a series of such situations is, however, not the proper starting-point for our analysis. Each situation of interaction occurs in the context of the general *level of interaction* that exists between two nations. Level of interaction refers to the nature of the relationship as it extends over a period of time. Examples of such levels are all-out war, limited war, armed peace, stable compromise, peaceful cooperation, and federation. The level of interaction is, of course, never completely stable. There will always be fluctuations in it due to forces pushing it one way or the other. We can say, however, that a given level of interaction exists between two nations, as long as, despite minor fluctuations, the relationship will tend towards an equilibrium over a period of time. It is this level of interaction, then, that should be used as the starting-point for analysis, and the effects of a specific situation of interaction must be evaluated in relation to this general level. We might restate the problem with which the framework deals as follows: when a particular situation of interaction occurs, what is the probability that the sequence of events initiated by it will produce a change in a given level of interaction, or that—despite minor fluctuations

—the level will remain stable and return to its equilibrium; and how is this probability affected by societal, attitudinal and structural factors?[2]

If we want to design research that will help us answer this question, it would be useful to have some way of spelling out the sequence of events that leads from a particular situation of interaction (or set of such situations) to a final outcome (i.e., change of or return to the initial level of interaction). This kind of detailed analysis of the sequence will give us a picture of exactly how a given outcome is produced. When we know this process we are in a much better position to evaluate the effects of different societal, attitudinal and structural factors on this outcome. The usefulness of a detailed analysis is particularly clear when we are interested in producing change: we may be unable to change a situation of interaction which initiates a sequence, but we might be able to change the final outcome by affecting one or another step in the sequence.

Steps in the Sequence of Events

We shall illustrate the kind of analysis we have in mind by suggesting a distinction among five steps in the sequence of events that is initiated by a given situation of interaction. These steps refer to the sequence of events within a single nation only. Actually, of course, a situation of interaction will initiate a sequence in every nation that is involved in the interaction. Moreover,

---

[2] It is likely that the factors that determine changes in the level of interaction will turn out to be the most significant variables in his area. In general there seem to be forces, as Wright has pointed out in his discussion of regulatory research, towards the maintenance of a stable equilibrium in international relations. If this equilibrium breaks down and a new level of interaction is achieved, such as the outbreak of war, then it must mean that some kind of turning-point has been reached which caused a reversal in the direction of the forces that usually maintain the equilibrium. The same would be true if the relationship between two nations has been one of intermittent war and armed peace for a period of time, and then it turns into one of friendly cooperation. An understanding of the characteristics of such turning-points and the factors that affect them would be a great advance in our knowledge.

events occurring in one nation will produce reactions in other nations, which in turn will initiate new sequences of events. The final outcome of a situation of interaction depends, therefore, on a number of sequences occurring simultaneously or successively in different nations. We shall restrict ourselves, however, to an analysis of a single sequence in one nation, keeping in mind that it represents only a small part of the flow of events. The steps are merely illustrative, and may not at all represent the best way of slicing the process.

(1) *Communication about the situation to the elite and other segments of the population:* What is the content of the information that is communicated? How much distortion has entered into it and what is the direction of the distortion?

(2) *Definition of the situation and perception of choices:* Is there a perception of threat or provocation? Is the situation defined as one of conflict or harmony? As a matter of central importance to the nation or one of peripheral interest? What courses of action are seen as available to the policy-makers and other influential groups? Do they see the choices as limited to the use of violent force or do they consider other alternatives?

(3) *Development of a climate or state of readiness for certain actions:* Is the general climate favorable to violence or to compromise? Is the atmosphere characterized by military preparations, threat, expectations of attack and war, anxiety and hysteria—or is it characterized by calm, confidence, faith in existing mechanisms for adjusting conflict, disarmament, and conciliatory gestures?

(4) *Commission of specific acts relevant to the interests of the other nation:* What specific actions are taken by the government or by other official or unofficial groups or individuals? Are actions of a hostile nature taken, such as border incidents, blockades, etc.? Actions of a friendly or conciliatory nature?

(5) *Achievement of a new level of interaction or return to the initial equilibrium:*

Does the situation of interaction which initiated the sequence of steps represent only a temporary fluctuation in the level of interaction between the nations, or does it lead to a general change in the level of interaction? If a new level develops, what is its nature?

Research can be done on the relationships among these five steps, and particularly on the relationship between each step and the final outcome of the sequence. For example, we might study whether certain kinds of climate are conducive to certain kinds of specific actions; or whether certain definitions of the situation are more likely to result in war than others. In general, it can be assumed that the sequence of steps we have outlined represents a cumulative process, at least to some extent: a particular situation of interaction is likely to be communicated in a particular way; this communication, in turn, is likely to produce a particular definition of the situation, and so on.

The chain reaction which is implied here, however, is by no means inevitable—and that is precisely where societal, attitudinal and structural factors enter the picture. The way in which a given sequence develops towards a final outcome depends on a large number of factors of these three types. A given factor may affect any or all of the steps in the sequence, and in this way alter the probability of a given outcome: it may enhance the probability that the sequence will take its "natural course" or it may help to reverse the course of events. For example, let us say nation A has taken an action which appears threatening to nation B, but A and B are actually allies and very dependent on each other because of the existence of a common enemy. This fact is likely to affect the way in which the event is communicated, such that the threat will be minimized; even if it happens that the event is communicated with its full impact, it is likely that the situation will be redefined so as to reduce that impact. In every stage of the process it is likely that forces will be created in the direction of maintaining the existing level of interaction, and that the "natural" sequence will

be reversed. On the other hand, let us say again that nation A has taken an action which appears threatening to nation B, but this time the elite of B is an oligarchy which is in danger of losing its power and therefore eager to create a climate of external threat. In this case, forces will be created to enhance the impact of the communication of the threatening event, the definition of the situation as one of imminent danger, and the creation of a climate of anxiety and hysteria.

Spelling out the steps in the sequence of events that lead to a final outcome is likely to suggest hypotheses about various societal, attitudinal and structural factors that may affect the probability of war or peace. There are many such factors which affect final outcomes by virtue of the fact that they influence particularly one or another of the steps in the sequence, e.g., the kinds of choices that are perceived or the kind of climate that is developed. Some of these factors are only indirectly related to the international situation as such. It is quite possible that factors of this sort would not come into consideration if we deal only with final outcomes, and not with the detailed processes whereby these outcomes are produced.

Let us look as some examples. We might hypothesize that a climate favorable to war would develop as a function of such factors as economic recession, general feelings of insecurity and instability of values, and a central role in the communication structure on the part of veterans' organizations and "patriotic" groups. Some relatively harmless situation of interaction may occur, to which these factors may have no particular relevance. Yet, by enhancing the development of a climate of war-preparation, they may have profound effects on the final outcome. To take another example, we might hypothesize that nation A will commit isolated acts of a hostile nature against nation B, even though the elite wants to stay out of war, if nation B has a low military potential and hence little capacity to retaliate; if the people of A believe in the effectiveness of violence and the threat of violence; and if certain pressure groups have the power to influence specific actions even though these go counter to the government's over-all policy. It seems to us that, in general, it would be fruitful to formulate hypotheses relating societal, attitudinal and structural factors to individual steps in the sequence.

Spelling out the steps in the sequence has another advantage in that it greatly increases the range of researchable problems. It is usually difficult to do research in which certain factors are related to final outcomes, but it is much simpler to relate these factors to some of the steps in the sequence that leads to the final outcome. For example, if we wanted to establish the relationship between attitudes of internationalism and the frequency of war, we would be restricted to historical research in which our indices of attitudes would not be very trustworthy. If, however, we wanted to relate attitudes of internationalism to the way in which situations of interaction are defined, then we could set up a wide variety of empirical researches and might even be able to design appropriate experimental models (3). Of course, we could also have to establish the kind of relationship that exists between the definition of a situation and the final outcome of a sequence of events that this situation initiates.

Summary and Conclusions

We have presented a framework for research on war and peace designed to answer the following question: Given a particular level of interaction between two nations, what is the probability that the sequence of events initiated by a given situation of interaction will produce war or peace, or some other final outcome? The framework suggests a breakdown of the sequence of events into five steps: communication of the event, definition of the situation, development of a climate, commission of specific actions, and achievement of a new level of interaction (or return to the initial equilibrium). It suggests, further, a distinction among three types of factors which are likely to affect each step in the sequence and hence the final outcome of the interaction: societal, attitudinal and structural factors. These three types of factors differ in terms

of the units of analysis and levels of theorizing to which they refer: societal factors describe characteristics of nations, attitudinal factors characteristics of individuals, and structural factors characteristics of structures or aggregating machineries. Societal factors set limits on international relations; attitudinal factors determine predispositions towards certain decisions and actions and thus modify the effects of societal factors; and structural factors determine who influences decisions and how this influence is exerted and thus prescribe the way in which societal and attitudinal factors are channelled into action. It is assumed that factors of each of these three types are important in determining the final outcome of interactions between nations, and that their effects—and particularly the effects of interaction between them—should be explored.

The framework is applicable not only to *existing* societal, attitudinal and structural conditions, and the effects that they might have on one or more of the steps in the sequence of events, but also to *potential* conditions. In other words, we could ask the question: What sets of conditions would have to exist (or be created) in order that the sequence of events would have a particular desired outcome? This is, of course, the question with which most of us are really concerned, since we are afraid that the existing conditions in the world will lead to war, and want to discover conditions which would increase the chances for peace. Research oriented to this question would explore alternatives to the techniques used by the great powers today for the resolution of international conflicts; and ways of changing societal conditions, attitudes and social structure so that they would favor the chances for peace.

The framework can be visualized, essentially, as a matrix consisting of fifteen cells. Each of these cells poses special questions of its own, which need to be subjected to research. Similarly, relations among the cells have to be investigated. The framework is not intended to be a theory as such: it does not propose a set of concepts, definitions and propositions and does not postulate relationships between specific variables or derive hypotheses for research. It is intended to be preliminary to the steps of theorizing and hypothesis-testing. It is at best the scaffolding within which theories may be built. Essentially, it is designed to call attention to the types of variables that may be important and to help us determine relevant questions for research. In short, it is simply a more systematic way of asking questions which can then be subjected to empirical tests. As research is done on a given question, it is hoped that creative theories will be developed to deal with it. The kinds of research that are needed and the kinds of theoretical models that will prove useful will differ for the different questions. Eventually it may be possible to build a coordinated theory with a unified set of concepts to handle the entire framework, but for the present it will probably be most fruitful to use separate concepts and miniature theories for the different questions, which are most suited to their particular requirements.

It is not very likely that anyone will use the framework as the basis for a research program. Theories and research do not usually develop out of such a formal mapping of the problems of a field, but rather out of substantive interest in a small part of the field. And, indeed, this is probably the most productive method of operating. What is the potential value, then, of a framework such as this?

This can be answered only in the light of the present status of research on war and peace. Among many social scientists there is a pronounced feeling of pessimism about this area. They feel that the problems are so complex and so much in need of a sophisticated interdisciplinary attack, that social science today is not capable of handling them. They are not at all encouraged by the one-sided theories of war and peace that claim to offer complete explanations, when in actual fact they neglect some of the most obvious variables, nor are they encouraged by isolated researches which appear to be related to war and peace, but whose relevance is not at all established. In this atmosphere it is particularly important for those who are concerned with research in this area to get their bearings: to gain a clearer conception of the limits of the field, and of the relation of different research approaches to one another. If we can find this kind of orientation, we may be less likely to despair and consider the problem unmanageable, and more likely to proceed with research on the assumption that our limited and partial approaches will eventually add up to something and fit into a larger picture. It seems to us that the potential contribution of a mapping of the field, such as is attempted in the framework we have described and in this issue as a whole, is precisely that it can help provide orientation and perspective.

REFERENCES

1. Arrow, K. J. *Social Choice and Individual Values.* New York: John Wiley and Sons, 1951.
2. Cottrell, W. F. "Men cry peace." In *Research for Peace,* Essays by Q. Wright, W. F. Cottrell and Ch. Boasson. Published for the Institute for Social Research, Oslo. Amsterdam: North-Holland Publishing Company, 1954. Pp. 95–162.
3. Gladstone, A. I. "Can the prevention of war be studied experimentally?", *Bulletin of the Research Exchange on the Prevention of War,* 1953, *1*(2), 1-3.
4. Hunter, F. *Community Power Structure.* Chapel Hill: University of North Carolina Press, 1953.
5. Kelman, H. C. "Public opinion and foreign policy decisions," *Bulletin of the Research Exchange on the Prevention of War,* 1954 *2*(4), 2-8.
6. Kelman, H. C. "A proposed framework for the study of war and peace," *Bulletin of the Research Exchange on the Prevention of War,* 1954, *2*(6), 3-13.
7. Richardson, L. F. "Threats and security." In *Psychological Factors of Peace and War,* edited by T. H. Pear. London: Hutchinson, 1950. Ch. 10.
8. Sherif, M. and Sherif, Carolyn W. *Groups in Harmony and Tension.* New York: Harper, 1953.

Part Three

The Resolution of International Conflict:
Approaches, Strategies, and Policy
Recommendations

PREDICTING THE TERMINATION OF WAR: BATTLE CASUALTIES AND POPULATION LOSSES [*][1]

FRANK L. KLINGBERG

Introduction

One of the major factors expected to induce the surrender of a belligerent in war, or bring about a mutually desired armistice, is the number of deaths incurred. This paper is concerned with the possibility of attempting to predict the end of a war from a knowledge of the casualties and population losses sustained. The first object of war, according to Clausewitz, is to conquer and destroy the enemy's armed forces, and similarly, strategies of defense are designed largely to *prevent* heavy casualties. However, deterrence of attack or aggression is believed to depend upon the expectation of retaliatory destructive blows designed to incur such heavy casualties as to be "unacceptable" (Singer, 1962, p. 31). Mutual fear of enormous numbers of casualties in the nuclear age may well be the factor which eventually leads the nations to disarmament, and helps bring the Cold War to an end.

In the summer of 1945, the Japanese were still fighting with suicidal fury, and were still in possession of a great part of their vast territorial conquests, particularly on the Chinese mainland. Japan's battle casualties were extremely high—very few Japanese soldiers surrendered. What should American strategy be to bring the war to

and end? Very few knew of the atomic bomb, and no one could be completely assured of its successful use.

Dr. William B. Shockley (later a joint winner of the Nobel Prize for his work in developing transistors) was an expert consultant to the Secretary of War, engaged in part in gathering and organizing information bearing on the problem of casualties in the Pacific war. He believed that historical studies of casualties might be helpful "for consideration in connection with the total casualties to be expected in the Japanese war, the rate at which land invasion should be expected in the Japanese war, the rate at which land invasion should be pushed ahead in Japan or held back while attrition by air and blockade proceeds, and the relative apportionment of effort between the Army Air forces and the Army Ground Forces and within each Force."[2] It was recognized that "the big cost to the nation in this war will be dead and disabled Americans," so that "in evaluating one plan or another, the expected casualties should be estimated as accurately as possible."

"The most basic problem in the Japanese war," Dr. Shockley continued, "is the establishment of what is necessary to cause Japan to capitulate." Studies were being made by intelligence units of the casualty ratios between Japanese and American troops in battle. The Japanese battle casualties in America's recovery of the Pacific islands were very high, and fairly accurately known. Dr. Shockley felt the need of a historical study of casualties "to determine to what extent the behavior of a nation in a war can be predicted from the behavior of her troops in individual battles."

He discussed the problem with Professor

* Reprinted by permission of the author and publisher from *Journal of Conflict Resolution*, 1966, *10*: 129–171. Pages 155–166 are omitted.

[1] This study was originally undertaken in the summer of 1945, in an effort to help understand the conditions under which the Japanese might be induced to surrender. The writer wishes to express his appreciation to W. B. Shockley, Expert Consultant to the Secretary of War (1944–45), for making the main part of the study possible at the Pentagon in the summer of 1945; to Quincy Wright for suggesting the formulation of the original hypotheses and appropriate procedures; and to J. David Singer for his current interest in the study.

[2] Quotations from Dr. Shockley are taken from a memorandum which he prepared for Edward L. Bowles, advisor to Secretary of War Henry L. Stimson.

Quincy Wright, and found that no such historical study had apparently been made. Professor Wright was asked to prepare an outline to be used as a basis for such a project, and the present writer was brought to Washington to undertake the study. In the midst of its preparation Japan surrendered, but the study was completed in a provisional way in the two months allotted to it. This paper describes the procedures followed and the results secured at that time, along with some additional figures and comments.

With the sudden ending of the war with Japan in the two great atomic blasts of August 6 and 9, there was a widespread feeling that war may have been outmoded in human behavior and might not recur at any early date. However, within five years a major war had begun in Korea, followed by major hostilities in Indochina, Algeria, and most recently in Vietnam. The problem of attempting to predict the end of war or hostilities therefore remains with us, along with a need to evaluate the major factors involved. This study will be confined to the possible role of battle casualties and population losses in bringing about the defeat of a nation or people in war, or an end to the hostilities.

Two major hypotheses were considered, without any opinion by the proposers as to whether the study would support them: (1) that there might be a constant ratio for defeated nations between battle casualties and population losses, before surrender, particularly in certain types of wars; and (2) that certain trends in battle casualties throughout a specific war might be useful in helping to predict the end of that war. The procedure and results will be analyzed for each hypothesis, respectively, in Parts I and II.

A basic problem for the research was that of obtaining the figures for battle casualties and population losses. Although the statistics of casualties and war losses are notably unreliable, particularly for more remote wars, much data have been compiled for certain modern wars. This study was confined to wars of the relatively modern period—since 1618. The wars among nation-states since this date are somewhat comparable, as being in the same general

historical period (including, we might expect, World War II).

Deaths from epidemics related to wars add a special complication in obtaining statistics on population losses. During the Thirty Years' War (1618–48), the great depopulation of Germany is attributed chiefly to severe epidemics of typhus fever and bubonic plague. Similarly, there were very heavy losses from epidemics during the French Revolutionary and Napoleonic wars. Particularly severe was a great typhus fever epidemic in central Europe, 1812–14, following Napoleon's Russian campaign (Prinzing, 1916). Not until World War II had medical science and sanitation advanced to such a point that deaths from disease were decisively minimized.

In interpreting the results, different types of historical periods would also have to be kept in mind. A study of casualties over the past three centuries demonstrates periods of very high war intensity—as during the Thirty Years' War, the French Revolutionary and Napoleonic wars, and World War I (the coalition wars against Louis XIV were also of high, but secondary, intensity) (Wright, 1941, Vol. I, pp. 658, 660). Wars tended to become "unlimited" and total during times of great ideological struggle (as over religion in the early seventeenth century or "democracy" in the Napoleonic period). At other times they were usually "limited" to specific objectives, and tended to be shorter and less costly. Among the most destructive wars in the past have been "civil wars," particularly when moral issues have been at stake (as in the American Civil War). Under the absolute kings of the eighteenth and late seventeenth century, wars were quite limited, and employed many mercenary troops. The French Revolution signaled the return of unlimited war, with "mass armies" used first by the French and then by the belligerents against France (see Fuller, 1961, pp. 15–41). The more limited wars of the nineteenth century were again followed by the "totalitarian" wars of the twentieth.

In relation to the specific problem of Japan in 1945, the "unlimited" character of the war was supported by a number of considerations: (1) the violent revolutionary character of the times, analogous to that following the French Revolution; (2) the high degree of hatred exhibited by both sides; (3) the desperate fighting of the Japanese, with very high casualties in battle before surrender; (4) the decision of the Allies in 1943 to demand the "unconditional surrender" of the Axis powers; and (5) the expected invasion and probable occupation of the Japanese home islands before surrender.

Part I: Ratios of Battle Casualties and Population Losses

Hypothesis and Assumptions

Professor Wright proposed a hypothesis to be tested by historical study, and suggested a plan of procedure. The aim was to study "casualties of past battles and wars in order to throw light upon the probable time and cost in American lives of Japan's unconditional surrender and the influence upon that time and cost of alternative strategies."[3]

The hypothesis for investigation was "that the average proportion of battle losses to forces engaged for a defeated belligerent before giving up *battles* in a given war may have a fixed relation to the proportion of population losses to total population of that belligerent before giving up the *war*." If the hypothesis were found to be true, it "would provide a basis for estimating from the known data concerning Japanese *battle* losses, the *population* losses which it would be necessary to inflict upon Japan before that country would surrender."

This hypothesis assumed, Professor Wright continued, (a) that the factors inducing the officers and soldiers to give up a battle are similar to the factors inducing the government and people to give up a war, and (b) that among these factors human losses are of outstanding importance. Professor Wright discussed the role of military and civilian losses; the factors which seem to have influenced the behavior of armies in battle and of a nation in war; the

[3] Quotations are from Professor Wright's memorandum for Dr. Shockley and the writer, summer 1945.

rise of "public opinion" as an important factor in war, especially after the mid-nineteenth century; and the significance of war mechanization.

To clarify the hypothesis, it might be helpful to give a hypothetical example. Let us assume that a historical study showed that a certain nation, which suffered average *battle* casualties of 20 percent in a given war, surrendered when five percent of its *population* had been destroyed (with the ratio of battle casualty percentages to population loss percentages thus 4:1); that the nation at another period in its history fought with less determination—showing battle casualties of 10 percent and a population loss before surrender of 2.5 percent (still a ratio of 4:1); that another nation was defeated after losing 10 percent of its population, when its battle casualties averaged 40 percent (ratio of 4:1); and that this ratio was supported by evidence from all wars. Then, one could predict with some assurance that if Japan's battle casualties were averaging 60 percent, Japan would be likely to suffer a loss of about 15 percent of her total population before she would surrender.

Professor Wright's first assumption—that the factors influencing the behavior of officers and soldiers might be similar to those for a government and its people—would appear to be logical for wars of the nineteenth and twentieth centuries, at least, for armies have been recruited more and more since 1792 from the ordinary citizenry. For a long period before 1792, when wars were fought mainly by mercenary troops, there would be little reason to assume much correlation between the behavior of the army and the behavior of the population as a whole. On the other hand, there might be some correlation between the behavior of a mercenary army and the behavior of a monarchical government. The king needed to keep the support both of his army and of his population, which supplied the money and raw materials and equipment necessary, yet neither the army nor the population as a whole had much direct influence over the government. With the rise of democratic governments and mass citizen-armies, attitudes of the population as a whole were reflected more and more in the behavior of the troops and also of the government.

The second assumption—that human losses are of outstanding importance as a factor in determining surrender in battle or war— is supported by the behavior of almost all men, with their concern for human life in their own families and communities and nations (with variations of degree among peoples). Lewis F. Richardson, in his mathematical study of "deadly quarrels," classified wars on a scale of the magnitudes of the numbers of "quarrel-dead," and stated that "the amount of suffering at the time of defeat can be crudely expressed by reckoning the war-dead as a percentage of the prewar population" (1960, p. 298). A study in World War II of "fear of battle" by enlisted American infantrymen after a year in Mediterranean fighting showed that "battle fighting" became more frightening for them the more they saw of it.[4] The maximum number (6–9) of "fear symptoms" in battle were reported by 54 percent who were in companies suffering high casualties, who saw one or more of their best friends killed, and who witnessed an enemy atrocity; with low casualties, only 20 percent suffered this number of symptoms (Stouffer *et al.*, 1949–50, Vol. II, p. 81). These figures lend weight to the common observation that the number and types of casualties (particularly deaths) have a powerful psychological impact on soldiers.

A quick glance at certain wars adds further plausibility to the hypothesis. For example, France fought doggedly in World War I. She suffered over 800,000 casualties in 1916, mostly in the successful defense of Verdun; her war losses were high, yet she did not give up. In 1940, her battle casualties were much less, and the nation surrendered with only a small population loss. One of the most notable wars in modern history, from this point of view, was

the Lopez War (1865–1870, a war of the Triple Alliance of Argentina, Brazil, and Uruguay against Paraguay), in which President Lopez led Paraguay through a bitter struggle which ended in surrender only after nearly every male, including Lopez, had been killed. In battle, similarly, the Paraguayans often fought practically to the last man.

Three possible results could emerge from a detailed historical study of casualties: (1) support for the theory of a constant ratio between battle casualties and population losses; (2) no support for the theory; and (3) evidence for different constant ratios for different types of wars. Some wars have been initiated, for example, to impose more or less unlimited servitude upon another people. Others have been entered upon for strictly limited objectives, such as the acquisition of a certain piece of territory. It is reasonable to suppose that the psychological factors involved in these types of war would be considerably different. And, after all, the decision to surrender appears to be a matter of psychology—of feelings, attitudes, and beliefs. The hypothesis formulated above merely emphasizes the importance of human losses in inducing the decision to surrender.

Other considerations might cast doubt on the validity of the hypothesis. But the question would still remain—what do the figures of history for battle casualties and population losses show?

Procedures

The chief source of casualty data used in this section of the study was Gaston Bodart's *Militär-historisches Kriegs-Lexikon, 1618–1905* (1908), which lists in chronological order the absolute and relative losses for both sides in 1,700 important battles. Official sources were used for World War I battle casualties, and figures for population losses were secured from Samuel Dumas and K. O. Vedel-Peterson's *Losses of Life Caused by War* (1923) and Friedrich Prinzing's *Epidemics Resulting from Wars* (1916). Other sources, including those for the various charts, are listed in footnotes and the references at the end of this paper.

---

[4] Of the enlisted men, 74 percent found continued fighting more frightening, while 12 percent regarded it as frightening all the time; the corresponding figures for company grade officers were 28 percent and 27 percent. In the Pacific area, where there was less prolonged combat, the percentages were 34 and 31 for enlisted men, and nine and 21 for officers (Stouffer *et al.*, 1949–50, Vol. II, p. 71).

TABLE 1
CASUALTY-LOSS RATIOS FOR EIGHT WARS

War	Date	Defeated nation	Casualty percent	Pop. loss percent	Ratio
Thirty Years	1618–48	Austria	23.1	50.0	0.5
Spanish Succession	1702–13	France	14.2	12.1	1.2
Seven Years	1756–63	Prussia	17.0	11.1	1.5
Fr. Rev. and Nap.	1792–1815	France	14.7	12.7	1.2
US Civil	1861–65	Confederacy	15.4	3.9	4.0
Seven Weeks	1866	Austria	6.3	0.8	8.0
Franco-Prussian	1870–71	France	9.1	2.0	4.5
World War I	1914–18	Germany	22.5	3.9	5.8

Sources: See footnote 5.

Total military *and civilian* losses attributable to war could be determined for only eight major wars during the entire period. These losses were calculated as a percentage of the defeated nation's total population at the beginning of the war. While a high birth rate in these nations might have compensated to some extent for these war losses, this numerical consideration was disregarded, since the losses among the living (particularly the adults) would be expected to have much greater military and psychological effects than would the number of births. Then, for these eight wars, calculations were made of the average casualties for the troops of the defeated nation in battles which they lost. Bodart's figures were often divided into only two categories: dead-wounded and prisoners-missing; casualty percentages, for the purpose of this comparison, were limited to those in the dead-wounded category, since the majority of the prisoners in wars were probably captured after the morale of the troops had broken. The assumption is that the percentage of dead and wounded before defeat in battle has occurred is somewhat comparable to the proportion of dead in the nation before surrender of the nation in war; the wounded in battle are effectively lost to the army for purposes of fighting in that engagement, just as the dead are lost to the nation as a whole.

Bar graphs were then drawn to illustrate the comparative percentages, and the figures were also plotted on a scatter diagram to show the degree of correlation (for perfect correlation, the points would of course appear in a straight line, at the appropriate angle). The next step was to determine comparative ratios for the other wars in which total population losses were *not* available. This was done by comparing battle casualty percentages with military deaths, expressed as a percentage of the population; estimates of *military* losses were available for most of the wars. Finally, a general comparison of casualty figures for the different major nations was made, with notice taken of the difference in casualty percentages in victorious and lost wars.

Results

Casualty-Loss Ratios for Defeated Nations. Calculations for the eight wars for which full data were available are shown in chronological order in Table 1.[5] For the nation which was defeated in the war, battle casualties (dead and wounded) were calculated, for each (major) battle lost, as a percentage of the total number of that nation's troops engaged in the battle. These figures were then averaged for the whole

[5] In Table 1, the battle casualty percentage for Germany in World War I (for lost battles) was calculated by averaging German casualties in five major campaigns which may be regarded as German defeats—the opening campaign in 1914; Verdun; Somme; the offensive in the spring of 1918; and the retreat in the summer and fall of 1918. Other battle casualties were obtained by averaging Bodart's (1908) figures for the separate battles. Population losses were found mainly in Dumas and Vedel-Peterson (1923), Prinzing (1916), and Bodart (1916).

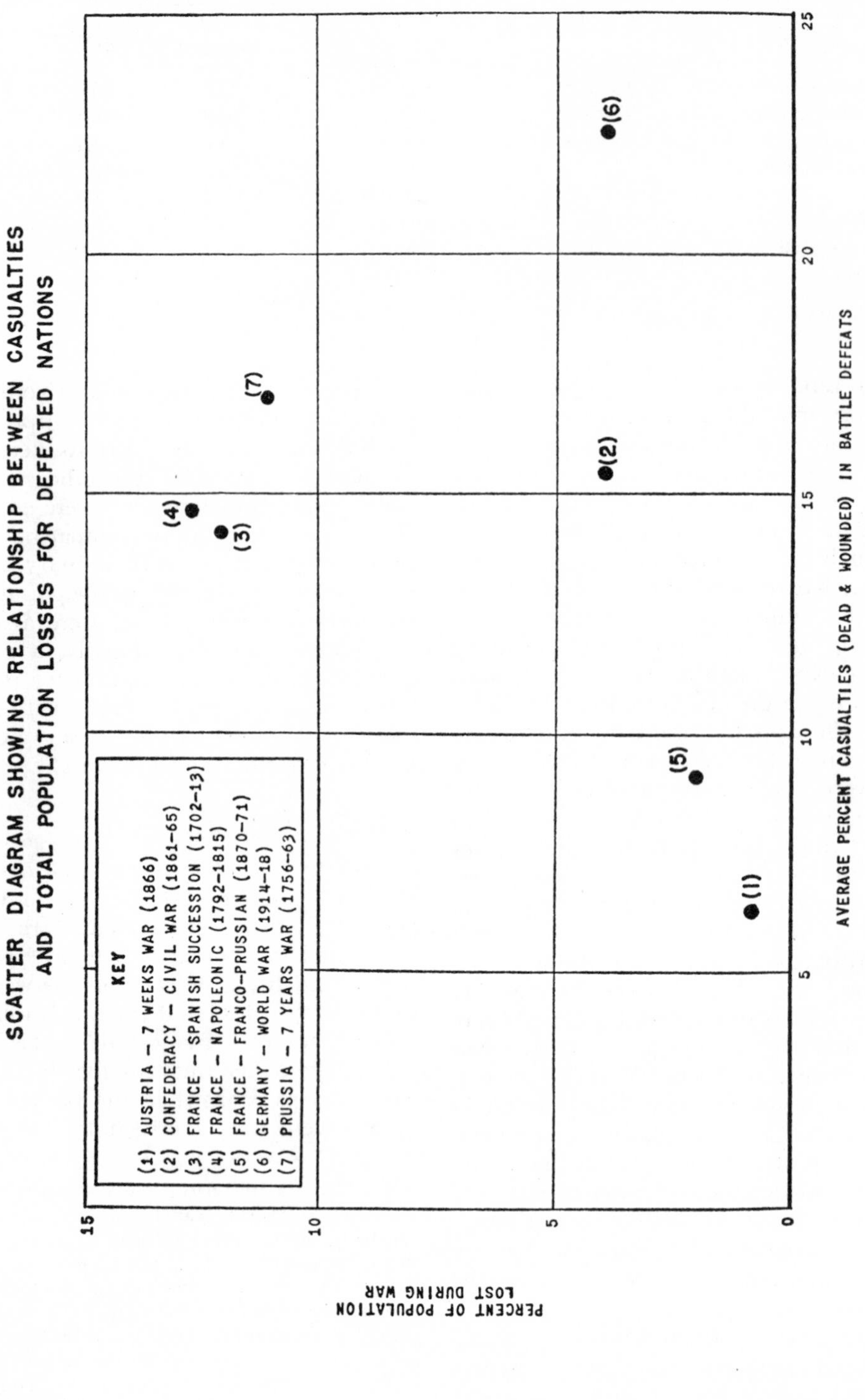
SCATTER DIAGRAM SHOWING RELATIONSHIP BETWEEN CASUALTIES AND TOTAL POPULATION LOSSES FOR DEFEATED NATIONS
KEY
(1) AUSTRIA – 7 WEEKS WAR (1866)
(2) CONFEDERACY – CIVIL WAR (1861–65)
(3) FRANCE – SPANISH SUCCESSION (1702–13)
(4) FRANCE – NAPOLEONIC (1792–1815)
(5) FRANCE – FRANCO-PRUSSIAN (1870–71)
(6) GERMANY – WORLD WAR (1914–18)
(7) PRUSSIA – 7 YEARS WAR (1756–63)
AVERAGE PERCENT CASUALTIES (DEAD & WOUNDED) IN BATTLE DEFEATS
PERCENT OF POPULATION LOST DURING WAR
0
5
10
15
20
25
(1)
(2)
(3)
(4)
(5)
(6)
(7)

Fig. 1.

war, and the averages appear in the table under "Casualty percent." The total population losses (military and civilian) during the war were figured as a percentage of the population of the defeated nation at the beginning of the war. The percentage of casualties divided by the percentage of population loss is shown as the ratio.

There is no constant ratio, it is clear—with a spread from 0.5 to 8.0. There are some marked similarities, however, within different historical periods, as from 1702 to 1815 (average of 1.3) and again from 1861 to 1918 (average of 5.6). Two of the wars between 1861 and 1871 (US Civil War and Franco-Prussian War) show ratios not far apart; the third one (Seven Weeks) was unusually short, with the Prussian objectives limited and the offer of peace terms exceptionally reasonable. The marked length of the earlier wars, along with epidemics, accounted in part for the high population losses and thus the lower ratios. It may be significant that the two modern wars quite comparable in length and intensity (the Civil War and World War I) both ended with a population loss of 3.9 percent for the defeated nations; the high casualty percent for Germany is partly attributable to the unusually long battles during the World War. Finally, one is led to speculate that the rise of democracy in the nineteenth and twentieth centuries was perhaps an important factor in helping to reduce the population loss which a nation was willing to suffer before ending a war.

The casualty and population loss percentages (except for the unique Thirty Years' War, in which the huge population loss has been variously estimated) are also plotted as a scatter diagram in Figure 1, to help show the degree of correlation. Considering the wars as a whole, little correlation is evident. But the chart does demonstrate that the short wars (in 1866 and 1870) had rather low casualty rates as well as low population losses. The moderately long wars (four years) show heavy casualties and relatively low population losses, while both indices are quite high for the long wars.

One war of modern times stands in a class by itself, and shows to what lengths a disciplined, fanatic nation can go in war. In the Lopez War (1865–70), one estimate is that Paraguay's population decreased from 1,337,000 to 221,000, a loss of 83.5 percent.[6] Of these 221,000, only 29,000 (2.2 percent) were men; 106,000 (7.9 percent) were women over 15, and 86,000 (6.4 percent) were children. Another author estimates that only three percent of the men were left at the end of the war, and less than 14 percent of the women (Washburne, 1871, p. 594). Battle casualties were of the same order of magnitude. In August 1865 a Paraguayan army of 2,500 is supposed to have fought to the last man against a Brazilian army of 13,000, which likewise suffered 2,500 casualties. In May 1866 a Paraguayan army of 25,000 lost 13,000 (52 percent) dead and wounded, and only 350 prisoners—all wounded—were taken, while the Allied army of 40,000 lost 8,000. One of the last major battles was fought in December 1868, the battle of Avay; the Paraguayan army of 4,000 lost 3,100 dead and wounded (78 percent) and 700 "sound" prisoners (18 percent), while the Brazilians lost 4,000 (Thompson, 1869). During this war Paraguay was a potential Prussia, with great designs for conquest; in response to the threat, Argentina, Brazil, and Uruguay had signed a treaty of alliance against Paraguay in 1865. Its publication in 1866, revealing territorial designs against Paraguay, went far to convince the Guarani people of Paraguay that their national existence was at stake. This factor plus the disciplined, religious training of the Paraguayans for generations, and the absolute dictatorship of Lopez, probably kept the nation at war until Lopez himself was killed in 1870 (Box, 1927, pp. 179, 270–73, 289). In the summer of 1945 one could well wonder, with the Paraguayan example in mind, about the ultimate extent of Japanese resistance.

Casualty-Loss Ratios with Battle Deaths as Military Loss. Since only eight wars have been considered thus far, the next step is to determine ratios for other wars in which

[6] *Encyclopaedia Britannica* (11th edn.), article on Paraguay.

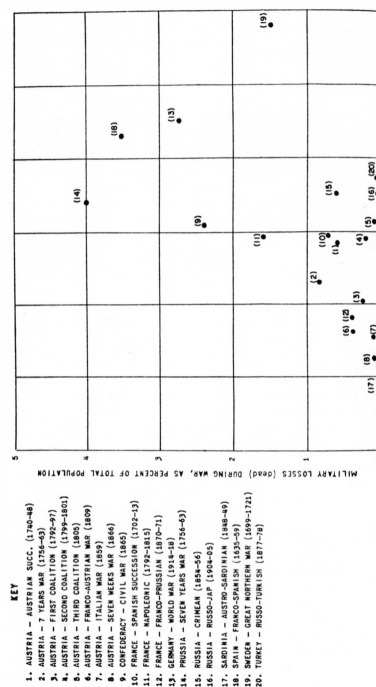

SCATTER DIAGRAM SHOWING RELATIONSHIP BETWEEN CASUALTIES
AND MILITARY LOSSES (AS PERCENT OF POPULATION) FOR DEFEATED NATIONS

KEY

1. AUSTRIA — AUSTRIAN SUCC. (1740-48)
2. AUSTRIA — 7 YEARS WAR (1756-63)
3. AUSTRIA — FIRST COALITION (1792-97)
4. AUSTRIA — SECOND COALITION (1799-1801)
5. AUSTRIA — THIRD COALITION (1805)
6. AUSTRIA — FRANCO-AUSTRIAN WAR (1809)
7. AUSTRIA — ITALIAN WAR (1859)
8. AUSTRIA — SEVEN WEEKS WAR (1866)
9. CONFEDERACY — CIVIL WAR (1865)
10. FRANCE — SPANISH SUCCESSION (1702-13)
11. FRANCE — NAPOLEONIC (1792-1815)
12. FRANCE — FRANCO-PRUSSIAN (1870-71)
13. GERMANY — WORLD WAR (1914-18)
14. PRUSSIA — SEVEN YEARS WAR (1756-63)
15. RUSSIA — CRIMEAN (1854-56)
16. RUSSIA — RUSSO-JAP (1904-05)
17. SARDINIA — AUSTRO-SARDINIAN (1848-49)
18. SPAIN — FRANCO-SPANISH (1635-59)
19. SWEDEN — GREAT NORTHERN WAR (1699-1721)
20. TURKEY — RUSSO-TURKISH (1877-78)

Fig. 2.

TABLE 2

MILITARY LOSSES (AS PERCENT OF POPULATION) IN DIFFERENT CASUALTY RANGES

% Casualties	No. of wars	Av. % mil. loss	Range of % mil. loss	Range of ratios
4.9– 9.9	5	0.19	0.02–0.38	21–306
10.0–14.9	6	0.71	0.2 –1.6	14– 73
15.0–19.9	6	1.19	0.03–4.0	4.3–416
20.0–24.9	2	3.11	2.73–3.5	6.1–7.9
25.0–29.9	1	1.55		(19)

total population (military and civilian) losses were not available. This was done by comparing battle casualty percentages with military deaths expressed as a percentage of the population. Estimates of military losses were available for most of the wars; calculations were also included for a number of the wars listed above. The scatter diagram in Figure 2 illustrates the general degree of correlation.[7] A certain amount of correlation (for some of the wars) is evident at a glance: for example, the low casualty percentages are again associated with the small military losses, and long, hard wars with a large military loss are associated with high

casualties. But the reverse does not hold true, since high casualty percentages may be associated with low military losses and short wars (note, for example, the Russo-Turkish War of 1878 and the Russo-Japanese War of 1905). Table 2 also helps show the degree of correlation.

The correlation is fairly high in the casualty ranges from 4.9 to 14.9 percent. It is extremely low in the range from 15.0 to 19.9, as shown by the wide range in the percentage of military loss, and it is again high from 20.0 to 24.9.

Table 3 gives the figures for those wars which were fought to gain major strategic objectives. Correlation is shown as high only for the first period (ratios from 19 to 21), and as fairly high for the wars since 1792 (ratios of 6.4 to 9.2, if the Franco-Prussian War is omitted as a relatively short war, in which Prussian aims were rather limited, while the French effort was reduced by the overthrow of Napoleon III's empire). In other words, there are again some similarities for major wars *within* periods, as well as marked differences *among* the periods.

Five of the wars (all fought between 1854 and 1905) can be readily placed in the class

TABLE 3

CASUALTY- (MILITARY) LOSS RATIOS FOR MAJOR WARS

Period	Defeated nation	War	Casualty percent	Mil. loss percent	Ratio
1702–48	France	Spanish Succession	14.2	0.71	20
	Sweden	Great Northern	29.0	1.55	19
	Austria	Austrian Succession	14.2	0.67	21
1756–1815	Austria*	Seven Years	11.6	0.85	14
	Prussia*	Seven Years	17.0	4.0	4.3
	France	Napoleonic	14.7	1.6	9.2
1860–71	Confederacy	Civil War	15.4	2.4	6.4
	France	Franco-Prussian	9.1	0.38	24
1914–18	Germany	World War	22.5	2.7	7.9

* Note: Austria and Prussia are both included under the Seven Years War, since Austria was defeated by Prussia, and since Prussia doubtless would have been defeated had not the opposing alliance split in the latter part of the war.

[7] Populations of the nations at different times were found in a variety of sources. For example: Hassel (1809); Quetelet (1865); US Bureau of Statistics, census figures for 1860; Brachelli (1907); Woytinsky (1925); Huber (1937); Gini (1930).

of "limited" strategic objectives. Their characteristics are shown in Table 4, where the outstanding feature is the lack of correlation. For example, the casualty percentages

TABLE 4

CASUALTY- (MILITARY) LOSS RATIOS FOR
LIMITED WARS, 1854–1905

Defeated nation	War	Casualty percent	Mil. loss percent	Ratio
Russia	Crimean War	17.6	0.6	29
Austria	Italian War	7.8	0.05	156
Austria	Seven Weeks	6.3	0.077	82
Turkey	Russo-Turkish	18.7	0.045	416
Russia	Russo-Japanese	17.6	0.036	489

for Russia remained constant for her two lost wars, while the Russian military loss was over thirteen times greater in the Crimean War than in the Russo-Japanese War. The armies apparently fought with the same determination, but the nation surrendered as soon as military defeats convinced the government that the limited aims for which it went to war could not be achieved, except possibly by an enormous effort not worth the cost. (An obvious difference between the two wars was the region of combat: in the Russo-Japanese War, the battle area was so far from European Russia and the transportation facilities were so poor, especially after the destruction of the Russian navy, that only less limited aims on the part of the Japanese could have induced the Russians to continue the war, especially in view of the Russian uprisings.) Thus it appears that for a "limited war," at least, the factors influencing the nation in its decision to end the war are not the same as the factors which bring about the defeat of an army. Military defeat and the casualties suffered therein constitute only one set of factors to be considered in determining a nation's war policy in such cases.[8]

Finally, some comparative statistics should be given of the losses of the defeated nations in World War II. It is difficult to secure authentic figures for German and Japanese losses in this war, but the following estimates of battle dead and missing,

and of civilian deaths (mostly from bombing), illustrate the relatively high losses:[9]

(1) Germany—Estimated population in 1939, 65,000,000; battle dead and missing, 3,250,000; civilian deaths, 800,000; total loss, 4,050,000; loss as percent of population, 6.23.

(2) Japan—Population in 1940, 73,114,-000; battle dead and missing, 2,566,000; civilian deaths, 600,000; total loss, 3,166,-000; loss as percent of population, 4.33.

The very high percentage loss for Germany may well be related to the demand for unconditional surrender, along with the complete military occupation of the country. However, the estimates for Japan may be much too high, for Richardson uses figures showing only 1.2 percent of the population lost.[10]

Comparison of Casualties for Different Nations, Victorious and Defeated. The identical figures for Russia's casualty percentages in the lost Crimean and Japanese wars lead one to wonder whether different nations demonstrate such identities, and whether there are marked differences among nations. Figure 3 shows the average casualty percentages for all wars, won or lost (including battle victories and defeats), engaged in by six nations. Separate bar graphs are shown for wars from 1618 to 1905, and for World War I, since these periods are only partially comparable: the World War was virtually one continuous battle on the various fronts.[11]

[8] For a discussion of how the morale of a nation may be raised by the "stimulus of blows" (especially defeats), see Toynbee, Vol. II (1934, pp. 100–12).

[9] Battle deaths for Germany from *Information Please Almanac*, 1958, p. 415; for Japan, from Enock (1951). Civilian deaths were estimated by Enock; most of the civilian deaths were caused by bombing. The US Strategic Bombing Survey, *Civilian Defense Division Final Report* (2nd edn., Jan. 1947), estimated German civilians killed by Allied air raids at 499,750.

[10] Richardson (1960, p. 299) gives the war dead (note that the number "dead and missing" was used in this paper) for Germany as 4 percent of the population in World War II, while his figure for Japan is only 1.2 percent. His source was *Keesing's Contemporary Archives* (London and Bristol), pp. 7508 and 7837. These figures suggest a major discrepancy for Japan.

[11] For Figs. 3, 4, and 6, World War casualties were obtained from a number of sources: *Statistisches*

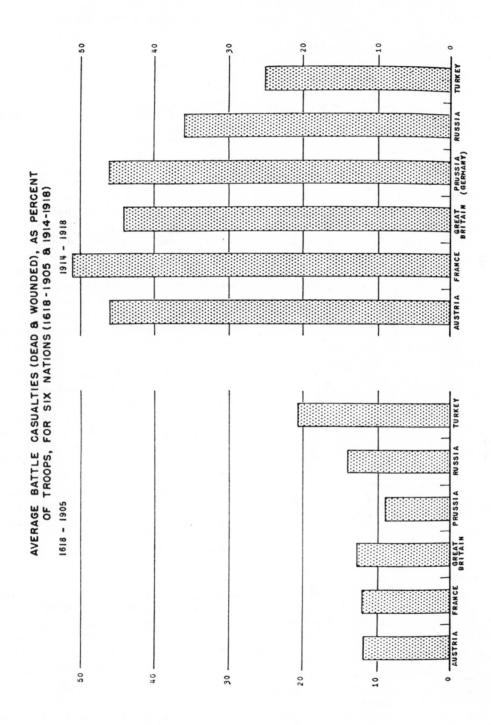

FIG. 3.

These graphs, covering all wars, make no allowance for victory or defeat, except where this is known in World War I. Turkey stands out as suffering the highest casualties before the World War, and the lowest during that war (perhaps because the hostilities in the Middle East, in 1914 and after, were more mobile). It can be seen that, among the great powers, Prussia suffered least before 1905, while France, without surrendering, experienced the heaviest casualties in World War I. French morale was doubtless renewed in 1917 and 1918 by the increasing support of the United States. Russia had a lower percentage of casualties than the others in World War I, but, unlike France, had no fresh allies on the eastern front in her year of despair (1916–17). It would appear that the differences in casualty percentages among the nations are often a function of the particular war and its circumstances. There is also considerable variation for any one nation in different wars: for example, the Russian average percentage was about 14 before 1905, so that the identical figures of 17.6 percent for two wars is somewhat misleading.

That a nation normally suffers somewhat heavier casualties in lost wars, as compared to victorious wars, is shown in Table 5 (covering wars from 1618 to 1905). Only Prussia shows a slightly lower percentage in a lost war. The significance of the average differences, however, is considerably diminished by the wide *range* of casualty percentages, once again suggesting the importance of the circumstances of each particular war.

The possible influence of different historical periods on casualties is shown by the bar graphs in Figure 4. From 1815 to 1905, a period of generally limited war, there was a steady drop in the percentages

Jahrbuch für das Deutsche Reich, 1921–22, p. 29; Der Heeres-Sanitätsinspektion (1934, Vol. III, p. 5); Chambre des Deputés, Session de 1920, Report No. 633, pp. 24, 173–74; Larcher (1934, p. 198); War Department (1924, pp. 7–9, 19); War Office (1922, p. 64); *Der Grosse Brockhaus,* 1935, Vol. 20, article "Weltkrieg," p. 193; Kohn (1932); Golovine (1931).

TABLE 5
AVERAGE PERCENT OF BATTLE CASUALTIES BY NATIONS (1618–1905)

Nation	WARS WON		WARS LOST		Range of casualty %
	No.	Cas. %	No.	Cas. %	
Austria	4	11.4	11	12.0	3.9–18.8
France	9	11.7	5	12.6	6.9–22.3
Great Britain	3	10.8	1	18.8	6.9–18.8
Prussia	4	9.2	1	9.1	2.9–13.5
Russia	6	12.4	3	17.3	9.1–22.3
Turkey	0		8	20.8	14.7–33.9

for the victorious nations, but a rise for the defeated ones. Charts (not reproduced here) were also prepared for all the wars from 1618 to 1905, so that the average battle casualty percentages and average size of armies (in battles) for the victorious and defeated powers could be compared. In most cases, the casualty percentages for the defeated nations were considerably higher. The ratios (both of casualties and of number of troops) between the victorious and the defeated nations seemed to have considerable significance in indicating the relative effort of the two nations. For example, in the Austro-French Wars of Napoleon's time, Austria was defeated in 1805 by considerably smaller French armies, and with a relatively low casualty rate. (It should be noted that casualty percentages *tend* naturally to decline as armies increase in size, for a smaller proportion of a larger army would ordinarily be engaged in active, front-line fighting.) In 1809, Austria put forth a much greater effort, as shown by the increase in the average size of her armies, by the willingness of her troops to suffer greater casualties, and by the greater effort required of the French to defeat them (shown particularly in the increase in the size of the French armies).

In Figure 5, a comparison is made between the victorious and defeated nations as to battle casualties and military losses in five wars for which data could be readily obtained. For the two major wars shown there is a marked similarity in the ratios of military losses. In the Civil War, the military losses of the Confederacy amounted to

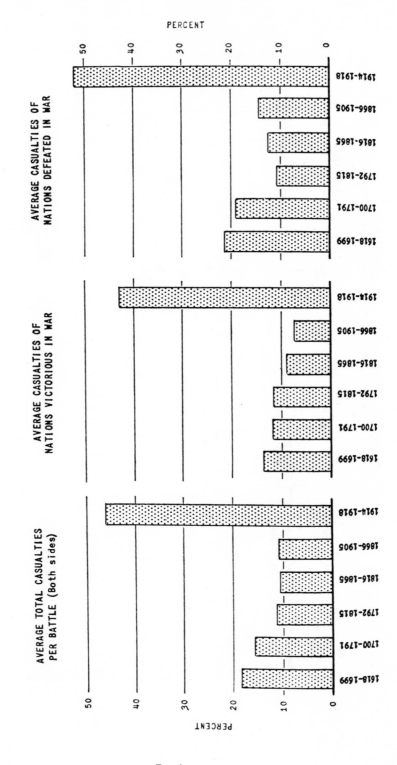

FIG. 4.

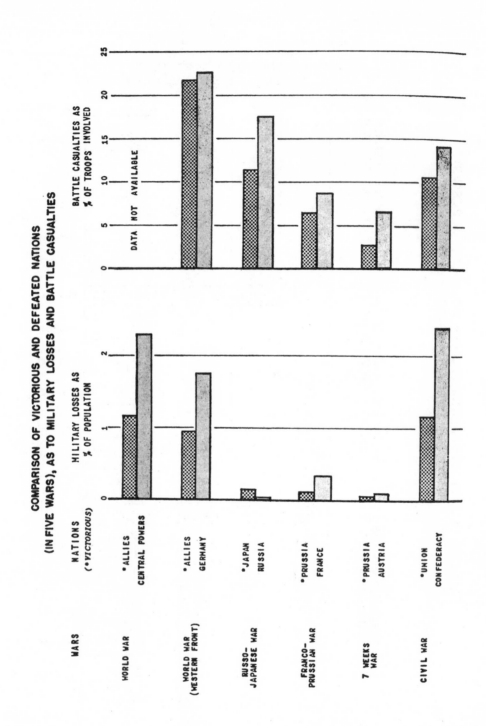

COMPARISON OF VICTORIOUS AND DEFEATED NATIONS
(IN FIVE WARS), AS TO MILITARY LOSSES AND BATTLE CASUALTIES

Fig. 5.

2.40 percent of the population, and of the Union, 1.19 percent (ratio of 2:1). In the World War, the Central Powers lost 2.30 percent and the Allies 1.16 percent (ratio of 2:1). This similarity of ratios may result in part from the similar population ratios: the South had 35 percent as much population as the North, while the Central Powers had 37 percent as much as the Allied powers. Nearly the same ratio of military losses is found when the war on the Western Front (1914–18) is considered separately (Germany, 1.79 percent loss; Western Allies, 0.98 percent loss). In most cases, however, battle casualty percentages were only fractionally more for the defeated nations.

The graphs for the three "limited wars" in Figure 5 show the unusual case of Russia's smaller population losses in the Russo-Japanese War, but this is partially explained by Russia's larger population, the heavy losses suffered by the Japanese in their capture of Port Arthur, and by the 1905 "revolution" in Russia.

Interpretation of Results

Reliability of Figures. The difficulty of securing reliable figures must be mentioned again. Certain comparisons and conclusions made above were based on only a small number of wars for which fairly reliable data could be had. Only during the latter half of the nineteenth century did many nations begin to collect accurate population statistics and reasonably accurate estimates of war casualties. Accurate battle statistics are particularly hard to find (see Wright, 1942, Vol. I, p. 218; also Dumas and Vedel-Peterson, 1916, ch. 1). However, it is probably reasonable to assume that the averages of these figures, especially after 1850, are fairly accurate and that errors would often tend to cancel each other out.

Magnitude of Wars. Richardson classifies all "deadly quarrels" from 1820 to 1949 (300 of them) on the basis of the number of total casualties per quarrel, using as an index "the logarithm to the base ten of the number of people who died because of that quarrel" (Richardson, 1960, p. 6 and *passim*). (These logs were rounded off to one decimal place.) Two wars were of the first magnitude, with logs between $7\frac{1}{2}$ and $6\frac{1}{2}$:

World War II, 7.3 (20,000,000 deaths); World War I, 7.2 (15,800,000). Seven had a magnitude from $5\frac{1}{2}$ to $6\frac{1}{2}$: Taiping Rebellion (1851–64), 6.3 (2,000,000); the Spanish Civil War (1936–39), 6.3 (2,000,-000); the First Chinese Communist War (1927–36), 6.1 (1,250,000); the Great War in La Plata (the Lopez War, 1865–70), 6.0 (1,000,000); communal riots in the Indian peninsula (1946–48), 5.9 (795,000); the North American Civil War (1861–65), 5.8 (630,000); and the sequel to the Bolshevik Revolution (1918–20), 5.7 (501,000). Among the wars from $4\frac{1}{2}$ to $5\frac{1}{2}$ were: Russo-Turkish War (1877–78), 5.4 (250,-000); the Crimean War, 5.4; the Franco-Prussian War, 5.4; the Spanish-American War, 5.3 (200,000); the Russo-Japanese War, 5.1 (123,000); the First Balkan War, 4.8 (63,000); and the Seven Weeks War, 4.6 (40,000). Wars of the next magnitude, $3\frac{1}{2}$ to $4\frac{1}{2}$, vary in deaths from 3,200 to 32,000.

These total casualty figures remind us of one way of distinguishing what we have called "unlimited" and "limited" wars, on a scale of magnitude. They also stress the importance of civil wars and rebellions (in this study only the American Civil War was used).

Wide Variation in Battle Casualties in the Same War. It is also important to note that the percentage of battle casualties for a given nation in a given war varies widely from battle to battle, so that it is difficult to determine the degree of significance which should be attached to the average. To illustrate the variation, one may take nine major French defeats of the Franco-Prussian War. The average French casualties (dead and wounded) were 11.1 percent, with a mean deviation of 4.3 (which amounts to 39 percent of the average) and a range from 4.7 to 19.8. In the same battles, Prussia's average was 9.6, with a mean deviation of 4.2 (44 percent) and a range from 2.4 to 23.7.

Table 6 further illustrates (for the American Civil War) the great differences in battles. The distribution in Table 6 is bimodal, and the variation is probably due to differences in military circumstances of

TABLE 6

Number of Confederate Defeats in the
Civil War, by Casualty Percentages

Casualty percent	Number of battles
2.5– 4.9	3
5.0– 7.4	4
7.5– 9.9	4
10.0–12.4	5
12.5–14.9	0
15.0–17.4	3
17.5–19.9	0
20.0–22.4	2
22.5–25.0	4
37.5–40.0	1

the battles. For example, a certain important strategic point may be attacked and defended with great zeal, while an army may give up an unimportant area without much resistance. The morale of the troops may vary widely in different phases or campaigns of the war. The existence of these wide variations does not invalidate the significance of an average figure—for an average casualty percentage of, say, 20 is very high as compared to 10, even though the range may be nearly the same for both armies. But these variations do suggest that there may be *trends* in casualty figures during a war which are as significant as the *average* figures.

Rate of Losses and Length of Wars. A special factor affecting a nation's decision to surrender might be the *rate* of losses suffered. Annual rates of losses were calculated for the wars studied. The annual rate for the Confederacy, for example, was

0.6 percent (2.4 divided by 4 years); for Austria in the Seven Weeks War, it was 0.54 (.077 multiplied by 7). No higher correlation was obtained for these figures with casualty percentages than for military or population losses for the whole war. One would expect the length of the war to be very important also; to obtain a figure which would include both rate and length of the war, a scatter diagram was drawn using the higher figure for percentage loss (that is, using the total loss if the war lasted over a year, and the "annual rate" if it lasted under a year). Again there was no higher correlation with the casualty percentages. It is quite possible that the rate of loss is an extremely important factor, regardless of its relation to casualty percentages. However, this rate of loss usually changes during a war, and one would expect the changing trends to exert more influence.

The intensity of a war might be measured by the average number of deaths per day. This rate of deaths, in relation to the length of the war, should be a significant factor for both sides. Ernest L. Bogart (1919, p. 270) gives the length in days and the number of dead in wars from 1790 to 1913, as shown in Table 7 (the average daily rate of deaths is added). Table 8 shows similar estimates for World Wars I and II, along with the rates for the major defeated nations. These daily death rates dramatize the relative enormity of the casualties for the two great wars of the twentieth century, and help explain mutinies, collapses, and the final termination of the war after four or five years of such bloodletting.

TABLE 7

Average Number of Battle Deaths per Day in Certain Wars (1790–1913)

War and dates	Duration in days	Dead	Average deaths per day
Napoleonic (1790–1815)	9,000	2,000,000	233
Crimean (1854–56)	730	785,000	1,075
Seven Weeks War (1866)	40	15,000	375
American Civil (1861–65)	1,350	700,000	519
Franco-Prussian (1870–71)	210	184,000	887
English-Boer (1899–1902)	995	9,800	98
Russo-Japanese (1904–05)	548	160,000	293
Balkan (1912–13)	238	462,000	1,941

TABLE 8

AVERAGE NUMBER OF BATTLE DEATHS PER DAY IN WORLD WARS I AND II

War-Nation (population)	Duration in days	Dead	Average deaths per day
WORLD WAR I	1,567	8,538,000	5,449
Austria-Hungary (61 m.)	1,567	1,200,000	766
Germany (68 m.)	1,567	1,773,700	1,132
Russia (178 m.)	1,188 (to Nov. 1, 1917)	1,700,000	1,431
WORLD WAR II (dead and missing)	2,175	16,830,000	7,738
Germany (65 m.) (including civilians)	2,077	4,150,000	1,999
Japan (73 m.) (including civilians)	2,936 (from Aug. 1937)	3,165,880	1,071
	1,346 (from Dec. 7, 1941)		2,352

Other Factors. The great variations in casualty percentages and in population losses before the end of wars remind us that many other possible influences need also to be considered. The material capacity to carry on the war would be important; for example, Enock (1951, p. 108) has estimated the damages on land in World War II for Germany at 85 billion dollars, and for Japan at 20 billions. The location of the area of hostilities for the different belligerents and the possibility of vital help from present or potential allies might affect decisions.

The importance of the strategic purpose served by a battle to the end, or by retreat, would affect the scale of fighting. The expected treatment of prisoners would be another factor. Similarly, a nation's decision might depend upon the leniency or severity of peace offers and the expected consequences of surrender.

Conclusions (Part I)

On the basis of the figures analyzed in this study, there is little evidence to support the general hypothesis of a fixed ratio between average casualty percentages in lost battles and the proportion of population losses in lost wars. Although such support was scarcely to be expected, the possibility needed to be checked by actual calculations.

Furthermore, limited wars showed extremely large variations in these ratios.

On the other hand, there is some evidence of a tendency toward relatively fixed casualty/loss ratios for nations fighting for major or unlimited strategic objectives during a given historical period. The ratio was 4.0 for the Confederacy (1861–65), 4.5 for France (1870–71), and 5.8 for Germany (1914–18). The rough figures for the Lopez War (1865–70) suggest a ratio of around 1.3—with Paraguayan battle casualties varying between 52 and 78 percent, while the population loss was estimated as over 80 percent. Although such unusual wars as the Lopez War indicate that the hypothesis could not be used for predictive purposes with high assurance, the ratio figures between 4 and 6 for major modern wars do offer some guidelines. If a ratio between 4 and 6 had been applied to Japan in 1945, the population loss to be expected before surrender would have been very high indeed.

When a comparison was made between casualty percentages and military losses (expressed as a percentage of the total population), the ratios were naturally somewhat higher. For the Confederacy, the ratio was 15.4:2.4 (6.4), and for Germany (1914–18), 22.5:2.7 (7.9). This would suggest a possible ratio for Japan in 1945 in the range from 6 to 8.

It is possible to look upon national losses alone (without regard to casualties in battle) as a significant factor in bringing about the defeat of a nation. Since 1850, with the exception of the Lopez War, defeated nations have not suffered extremely high military or population losses in war. The Confederacy's military losses in the Civil War were 2.4 percent and her total losses perhaps 3.9 percent. In World War I, the corresponding figures for Germany were 2.7 (2.3 for the Central Powers) and 3.9; for Russia, about 1.0 and perhaps 3.0. In more limited wars, the military losses ranged from 0.016 (little Sardina's defeat in her lone war against Austria in 1848–49) to 0.6 percent (Russia's loss in the Crimean War). In short wars, where it is possible for one nation to deliver a knock-out blow early in the war or where the war aims are strictly limited, population losses will be low (although the "annual rate" of losses may be high). Population losses may well assume great significance in long wars (i.e., three or more years) for the nation which is being pushed toward defeat. It would appear from the figures above that when population losses approach three or four percent, a critical period may have been reached in the nation's morale. Other factors affecting a nation's fighting power must also be considered: its control and production of raw materials; its production of weapons; its control of strategic areas; the military position of its allies or potential allies; and the like. If one assumes that the given nation is losing productive power by steady attrition (as in the case of the Confederacy, Germany, and Russia) and has lost hope of aid from other nations, then there may be a critical figure in population loss beyond which the nation will not go without surrendering.

It would be important in this connection to determine German and Japanese casualties and losses in World War II as accurately as possible, and to calculate their percentages as in this study. The results should throw further light on relative ratios and critical loss percentages.

According to the unreliable estimates of German losses in World War II, the figure was over six percent, as compared to 3.9

percent in 1918. If true, this significant difference might be ascribed largely to the changed Allied approach to Germany in World War II (partly as a response to Hitler), with the demands for "unconditional surrender" and military occupation. However, Richardson's figure of four percent for World War II may suggest that this figure is close to a "critical loss" percentage for unlimited wars in the past hundred years.

The atomic bomb introduced a new factor in the case of Japan, for even if Japanese losses were only one percent before the atomic bombs were dropped (Richardson's figure for total losses was 1.2 percent), the Japanese could quickly calculate the enormous losses to be expected from many more such bombs dropped on Tokyo or other cities. This "astronomical" rate of loss was apparently "unthinkable" under the circumstances of the war against Japan in 1945.

Part II: Trends in Battle Casualties during Wars

The general aim of this project was to study the relation of casualties and population losses to the defeat of a nation in war. Part I compared different wars as wholes— using an average battle casualty percentage and total population loss for an entire war. But the fact, noted in Part I, that battle casualty percentages differ widely throughout a war suggests the existence of significant trends in battle casualties throughout a war. These trends were analyzed to see if they could be used in helping to predict the end of a given war in progress.

Casualties are closely related to the size of the armies engaged and to the victories gained or defeats suffered. Therefore, it was logical that trends in these factors be studied at the same time. Such trends were first clearly suggested by graphs drawn for the statistics of World War I.

Procedures

In studying the progress of individual wars, each war was divided into logical periods such as years (for very long wars), or quarters (as in the four-year Civil War), or months (for short wars, or for the World

War when the figures were available by months). For these periods, the size of the armies and the number of casualties of the defeated nation were shown on graphs, and they were compared with the corresponding figures for the victorious nation. This latter comparison was regarded as particularly important because war, after all, is a struggle between two opposing parties, and it is relative strength which determines the outcome. Not only were the trends in total casualties analyzed, but the casualty figures were also broken down into subcategories where possible.

Results

Relative Size of Armies and Percentage of Casualties in Individual Wars. In order to compare the armed strength of the opposing forces in a given war, the size of forces of the defeated nation was expressed as a percentage of the forces of the victorious nation for each period. If the forces were of equal strength, the percentage was 100; if the forces of the defeated nation were twice as large, the percentage was 200. Any percentage below 100 may ordinarily be regarded as a factor negatively affecting the chances of the nation which was defeated.

To compare casualties, the average casualty percentage of the *victorious* nation was expressed as a percent of the average casualty percentage of the *defeated* nation. Again, a percentage below 100 could be regarded as unfavorable to the defeated nation. For example, if Germany's casualties in a certain month were 10 percent and Allied casualties five percent, the resulting ratio is 5:10, or 50 percent. If the Allies were suffering greater casualties than Germany—say 15 percent—then the ratio is 15:10, or 150 percent (favorable to Germany). Such a comparison is charted for armies and casualties on the Western Front (1914–18) in the upper part of Figure 6.[12] On all such charts, the horizontal line at 100 percent can be regarded as a threshold: if the graph is above the line, the ratio tends to be favorable to the defeated nation, and if below, unfavorable.

It is impossible to judge these trends logically without also knowing the general course of the war. It would not have been very unfavorable to Germany had the casualty ratio in Figure 6 been 50 percent during a given month, if only 100 Germans had been killed during the whole month (as compared to 50 Allied soldiers). Therefore, it is important to know how intensive the fighting is at any given time. This is shown in a separate graph in the lower part of Figure 6, depicting the average monthly casualties for both sides (total). Thus, for example, the army and casualty ratios are significantly unfavorable to Germany in the early fall of 1916 when the intensity of battle had reached a peak.

Furthermore, one needs to know which side, if any, is winning the battles during the period. Germany did not begin losing definitely, or was not forced to retreat on a big scale, until the summer of 1918. For this period the figure shows a new peak of intensive fighting, with both army and casualty ratios dropping to more unfavorable positions. The German army had dropped to a low of 53 percent of the Allied armies, German casualties were increasing relatively, and the army was retreating rapidly. Germany was defeated unless she could quickly reverse one or more of the three unfavorable trends. She was unable to do this, and surrendered, since there was no hope of increasing her strength nor of securing aid (in fact Germany's allies were dropping out of the war, one by one) and, at the same time, the Allies offered peace terms which appeared acceptable. The alternative was invasion of German territory and ultimate defeat anyway. There is much evidence that a nation will ordinarily surrender when its strength is ebbing, when the opponent presses the war with increasing fury (particularly against the nation's own homeland), and when a peace is offered the terms of which appear preferable to a continuation of the war (which will be lost anyway).[13]

The importance of Germany's relative decline in armed strength is given further support in the following statement from

[12] Sources for Fig. 6 are given in footnote 11.

[13] For a discussion of "what makes the loser quit," see Calahan (1944), ch. 6.

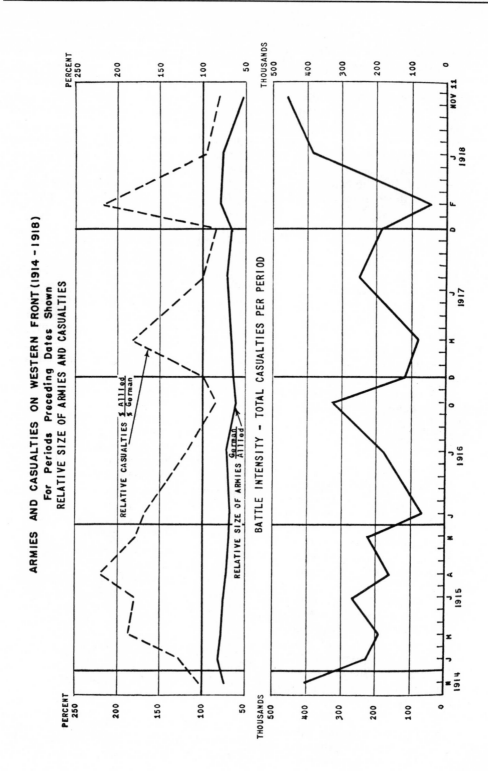

Fig. 6.

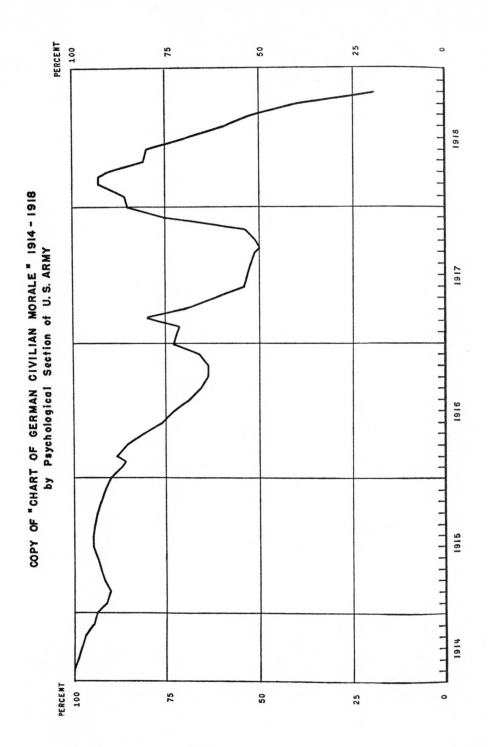

FIG. 7. *Source:* Bruntz (1938), p. 192.

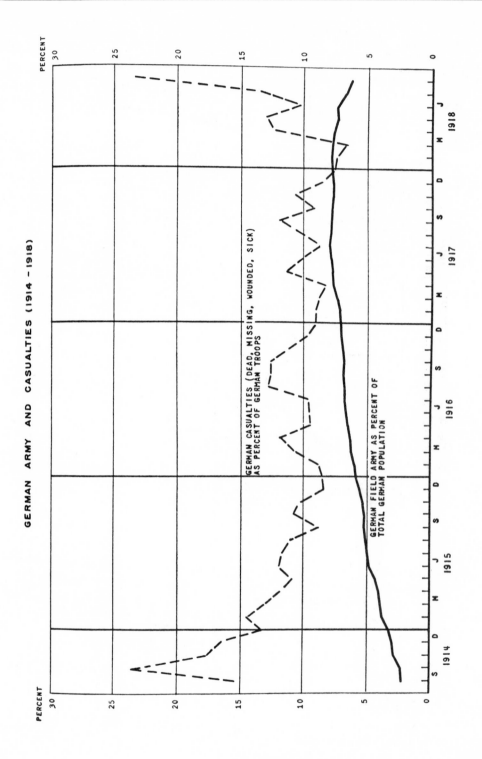

Fig. 8.

the German Reichstag's official postwar report concerning Germany's defeat:

> The offensive, which in March, April, and May resulted in great tactical successes but no strategic decision, came to a standstill in July, 1918, not owing to any failure on the part of the troops but because the forces of the opponents at the front steadily increased while our own were decreasing [see Lutz, 1934, p. 7].

A counterpart of Figure 6 could logically have been used in the summer of 1918 to predict with some assurance the end of the war before winter, if the Allies continued to increase their relative strength and maintain their pressure on the Western Front, and, at the same time, offered peace terms. This chart may lead the reader to wonder why the war did not seem to be nearing its end in the fall of 1916 or 1917, when the casualty and army ratios were both unfavorable to Germany. In the first place, Germany was not retreating on a large scale at either time, and she was able to stop the retreat after only relatively small Allied gains. In the second place, the chart shows that Germany was able to reverse the downward trends during the next period. In the spring of 1918, the trends were unfavorable: the theory is that Germany was doomed unless she could reverse one or more of these trends in the next period. This she was unable to do. The war ended at a time when many were predicting that Germany would fight far on into 1919.

It is interesting to compare Figure 6 with Figure 7, a chart of German civilian morale based on many trends (such as the military situation, submarine sinkings, food, interviews and letters from German prisoners, and the like). The periods of low morale shown in Figure 7 in 1916 and 1917 correspond to the critical points in Figure 6. The situation on both charts looks particularly favorable early in 1918, when the German army had reached its highest relative strength since the early part of the war. Figure 8, which gives army and casualty figures for Germany only, demonstrates even more clearly the unfavorable position of Germany by July 1918 (the monthly figures for this chart stopped at July).[14] The German army, which had only a few months before reached a peak of strength, was decreasing rapidly and casualties were mounting. Figure 9 shows more exactly when the peak of German strength was passed, using the figures for rifle strength on both sides.

One must remember that the proper interpretation of charts like these, during a war, would require the fullest possible knowledge of all important factors related to the war. Some of these factors could also be presented graphically—most notably the figures for the estimated economic power of the enemy, particularly in so-called "bottlenecks" (as oil or transportation). If these were known, graphs like those shown here could be helpful in determining critical points in the enemy's war effort—even though one must recognize that it is harder to get such information during a war than after it.

*   *   *   *   *

Conclusions (Part II)

Part II was concerned chiefly with studying various indices which might be used in detecting the approaching surrender of a nation at war. It appeared that most wars end within a fairly short time after certain significant shifts in trends occur. Such shifts often appear immediately after a final great effort of the nation has ended in failure, like the great German drive in the spring of 1918.

Perhaps the most important index is the relative decrease in size of armies (which is often associated with a decline in *matériel*). All the indices should be held in mind, however, when an appraisal of the progress of a war is being made, including shifts in casualty ratios (as compared to the opponent), proportion of military defeats (in battles or campaigns), possible increase in the percentage of prisoners and sick, and the like.

It is impossible to predict accurately

[14] The graphs in Figure 8 are plotted on a monthly basis. Sources were Der Heeres-Sanitätsinspektion (1934), pp. 8, 140–43; and Dumas and Vedel-Peterson (1923), pp. 167–76.

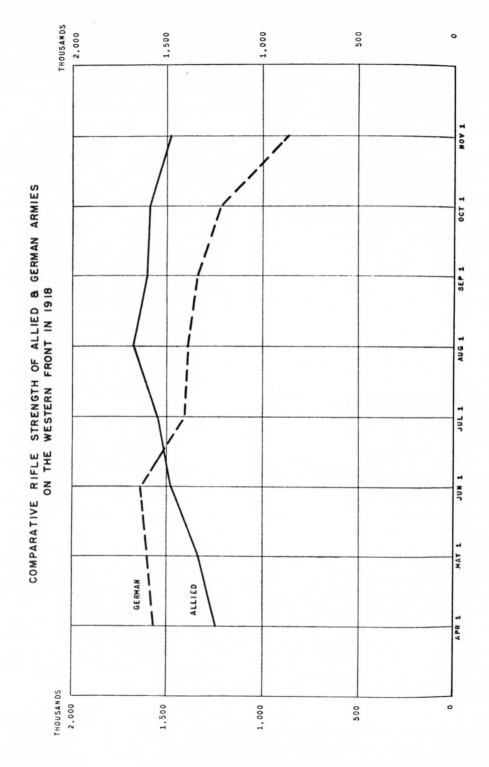

FIG. 9.   *Source:* McEntee (1937), p. 497.

during a war how long the war will last. There is some evidence, however, that periods of intensive warfare do not last over four or five years (see Wright, 1942, Vol. I, p. 226). The major wars of the twentieth century have been of this length—1914–18, 1940–45 (Germany, little active fighting of the Great Powers before 1940), 1941–45 (Japan).

In the past, with the opposing belligerents rather evenly matched at the beginning of a war (or so situated that neither could deliver a knock-out blow early in the war), one could safely predict a fairly long war (i.e., three to five years). Close study of the various military trends referred to might enable one to detect the approaching end of a war with some degree of accuracy many months before the surrender. It is particularly important to detect signs of definite weakening of the enemy as early as possible, so that a great psychological offensive can be started at that time. Propaganda for surrender is of little importance unless the enemy is beginning to weaken.

Summary and General Conclusions

Historical-statistical data from 1618 to 1918 were used in this study to test the hypothesis that a fixed relationship might exist between a nation's casualties in battle defeats and its population losses in lost wars. The results show that there is no general ratio between casualties and population losses, but that there is a marked similarity in these ratios for some major wars at certain historical periods, with a tendency for the ratio to be higher in more recent times. The ratio for the Confederacy (1861–65) was 4.0; for France (1870–71), 4.5; and for Germany (1914–18), 5.8. Short wars, in general, show little correlation.

There is some evidence that nations in modern times will tend to surrender before they have suffered population losses greater than three or four percent. Both the Confederacy and Germany (1918) had lost about 3.9 percent of their population. But in the Lopez War (1865–70), little Paraguay may have lost as much as 80 percent of its whole population.

A study of statistical trends during long wars indicates that certain shifts in these trends might be used to help predict the approaching surrender of a nation. Four indices which proved particularly significant, when viewed as a whole, were casualty percentage ratios between the opposing belligerents, army-size ratios, proportion of battle defeats, and intensity of fighting. When these indices showed unfavorable trends for two successive periods (as campaign periods), the end of the war was ordinarily at hand. Another trend of importance was the abnormal increase in the number of prisoners or sick which sometimes preceded the surrender by some months.

An increase in the rate of relative casualties for the defeated nation (as compared to the victor) was also noted near the end of long wars. The atomic bomb gave the United States an opportunity in 1945 to step up the rate of Japanese losses suddenly to catastrophic proportions. The very heavy casualties suffered by the Japanese in lost battles doubtless suggested to American analysts that, under normal conditions, Japan would have to suffer a heavy population loss before she would surrender. It had been estimated, according to President Truman (1955, pp. 416–17), that an invasion of Japan would probably require until the late fall of 1946 to defeat the Japanese, with an expected loss of half a million American lives. It was apparently believed that the Japanese would put up a desperate fight on their own home islands (possibly like the Paraguayans). The ratio of Japanese killed to Americans killed in the recapture of Pacific islands had varied between 4 (Iwo Jima) and 22 (Leyte), with Okinawa at 14.5.[17] The average Japanese casualty percentages in lost battles are not known to the writer, but let us assume that they may have measured around 50 percent. Using a casualty-loss ratio between 4 and 6, as suggested in Part I, the expected population loss before surrender might vary between eight and 12 percent (that is, between 5.8 million and 8.8 million people). An alternative to such a holocaust

[17] Memorandum from W. B. Shockley, *loc. cit.*

would lie in a sudden, unprecedented increase in the rate of Japanese losses.

The successful atomic test in New Mexico took place on July 16, 1945. At Potsdam on July 26, the United States, Britain, and China called for the "unconditional surrender of the Japanese armed forces," and warned that "the alternative for Japan is prompt and utter destruction" (Wilcox and Kalijarvi, 1952, p. 39). On August 6, the atomic bomb on Hiroshima killed approximately 80,000, and injured another 80,000 to 100,000.[18] This daily *rate* of deaths was beyond man's previous imagination, but the Japanese remained silent until the second bomb fell on Nagasaki on August 9 (45,000 deaths, 50,000 to 60,000 injuries). American experts calculated that atomic bombings of Japan's five largest cities would produce 2,375,000 deaths and 3,225,000 injuries. On August 10, Japan agreed to accept the ultimatum, provided this did not prejudice the prerogative of the Emperor as a sovereign ruler. The Allies accepted the Emperor on the understanding that he would be subject to the Supreme Command of the Allies. Under the circumstances, it would have been unbelievable for the Japanese not to surrender. Casualties—past, present, and expected—appear to have been the decisive factor.

In 1898, Jean de Bloch (1903, ch. 7) forecast that the advance of weapons technology had already made major strategic war too costly in casualties to be used. Whether or not this was true in 1914 or 1941, it appears to be a logical conclusion in 1965, when Secretary of Defense Robert McNamara estimated that between 120 and 150 million Americans might be killed in a Soviet missile attack on American cities (based on a 1970 population of 210 million). He estimated that the United States, after absorbing a first strike, could cause more than 100 million fatalities in Russia with missiles alone, and destroy about 80

percent of Russia's industrial capacity.[19]

Yet limited wars—international, and revolutionary or subversive—*have* occurred in the atomic age. The problem of bringing such wars to a successful conclusion still remains—and, once again, casualties play a significant role. The US Military Assistance Command in Vietnam reported on February 3, 1965, that South Vietnamese troops killed 2,210 Vietcong guerrillas in January.[20] Late in March 1965 it was reported that the Vietcong rate of desertion was increasing: the average monthly desertion rate from 1962 through 1964 was 188, while during the most recent four months the monthly average was 350. Early in April, reports also showed a trend favorable to the government in the relative ratio of casualties between the opposing forces: in February, 1,730 Vietcong dead to 870 government troops (ratio of 2:1); in March there were 2,000 Vietcong dead to 730 government troops (ratio of 2.7:1).[21]

This study has suggested how such statistics can be used to graph the course of a war in terms of casualties and all other major factors which affect the morale and fighting strength of the opposition. In terms of the world of the future, it might also be well to consider all possible means of ending such wars successfully with the lowest possible loss of life on both sides. Many people in all countries must be yearning for an end to the current "age of violence," in which unlimited wars and threats of catastrophe have been the rule. In the past such violent "revolutionary" periods have normally ended within fifty years (as from 1776 to 1824). If the world should soon enter upon an era of the controlled and limited use of military power, the study of

[19] *Congressional Quarterly Weekly Report*, 23, 9 (Feb. 26, 1965), p. 314.

[20] *New York Times*, Feb. 4, 1965.

[21] It may be of some significance in this connection that many successful "wars of liberation" have lasted about seven years (as compared to the four- or five-year span for major international hostilities): the American Revolution, 1775–82 (year in which fighting ended); the Greek War of Independence, 1821–29; Indochinese Revolution, 1947–54; Algerian War, 1955–62.

[18] These atomic bombing figures and estimates are given in US Strategic Bombing Survey (March 1947), pp. 84–86.

casualty data might help achieve limited objectives with the minimum expenditure of human life.

REFERENCES

de Bloch, Jean. *The Future of War.* (6th vol. of original study, translated by R. C. Long.) Boston: Ginn, 1903.

Bodart, Gaston. *Militär-historisches Kriegs-Lexikon, 1618–1905.* Vienna, 1908.

_____. *Losses of Life in Modern Wars.* Oxford: Clarendon, 1916.

Bogart, Ernest L. *Direct and Indirect Costs of the Great World War.* New York: Oxford University Press, 1919.

Box, Pelham Horton. "The Origins of the Paraguayan War," *University of Illinois Studies in the Social Sciences,* 15 (1927).

Brachelli, H. F. *Die Staaten Europas.* Leipzig, 1907.

Bruntz, George G. *Allied Propaganda and the Collapse of the German Empire—1918.* Stanford, Calif.: Stanford University Press, 1938.

Calahan, H. A. *What Makes a War End?* New York: Vanguard Press, 1944.

Dumas, S., and K. O. Vedel-Peterson. *Losses of Life Caused by War.* London: Milford, 1923.

Enock, Arthur Guy. *This War Business.* London, 1951.

Fuller, J. F. C. *The Conduct of War, 1789–1961.* New Brunswick, N.J.; Rutgers University Press, 1961.

Gini, Corrado. *Demografia.* Turin, 1930.

Golovine, Nicholas N. *The Russian Army in the World War.* New Haven: Yale University Press, 1931.

Hassel, G. *Statistische Übersichts, Tabellen der sammtlichen Europäischen . . . Staaten.* Gottingen, 1809.

Der Heeres-Sanitätsinspektion des Reichsministeriums. *Sanitätsbericht über das Deutsche Heer im Weltkriege, 1914/1918.* Berlin, 1934.

Huber, Michel. *La Population de la France.* Paris: Hachette, 1937.

Kohn, Stanislaus. *The Cost of the War to Russia.* New Haven: Yale University Press, 1932.

Larcher, Lt. Col. "Données Statistiques sur les Forces Françaises, 1914–1918," *Revue Militaire Française,* 52 (1934).

Lutz, Ralph H. (ed.) *The Causes of the German Collapse in 1918.* Stanford, Calif.: Stanford University Press, 1934.

McEntee, Girard L. *Military History of the World War.* New York, 1937.

Prinzing, Friedrich. *Epidemics Resulting from Wars.* Oxford: Clarendon, 1916.

Quetelet, A. *Statistique Internationale.* Brussels, 1865.

Richardson, Lewis F. *Statistics of Deadly Quarrels.* Pittsburgh, Pa.: Boxwood Press, 1960.

Singer, J. David. *Deterrence, Arms Control and Disarmament.* Columbus: Ohio State University Press, 1962.

Stouffer, Samuel A., *et al. Studies in Social Psychology in World War II.* Vol. II, *The American Soldier: Combat and Its Aftermath.* Princeton, N.J.: Princeton University Press, 1949–50.

Thompson, George. *The War in Paraguay.* London, 1869.

Toynbee, Arnold J. *A Study of History,* Vol. II. London: Oxford University Press, 1934.

Truman, Harry S. *Memoirs by Harry S. Truman,* Vol. I. Garden City, N.Y.: Doubleday, 1955.

United States Strategic Bombing Survey. *Civilian Defense Division Final Report.* 2nd edn. Washington, D.C., Jan. 1947.

_____. *The Effect of Atomic Bombs on Health and Medical Services in Hiroshima and Nagasaki.* Washington, D.C., March 1947.

United States War Department, Statistics Branch, General Staff. *Special Report No. 178* (Feb. 25, 1924).

War Office. *Statistics of the Military Effort of the British Empire during the Great War, 1914–1920.* London, 1922.

Washburne, Charles A. *The History of Paraguay,* Vol. II, Boston, 1871.

Wilcox, Francis O., and T. V. Kalijarvi. *Recent American Foreign Policy: Basic Documents, 1941–1951.* New York: Appleton-Century-Crofts, 1952.

Woytinsky, Wladimir S. *Die Welt in Zahlen,* Vol. I. Berlin, 1925.

Wright, Quincy. *A Study of War,* 1st edn. Chicago: University of Chicago Press, 1942.

THE TERMINATION OF CONFLICT*

LEWIS A. COSER[1]

Certain social processes are finite, i.e., they are defined by their transitory character and the manner of their termination is institutionally prescribed. Courtship ends when union with the beloved has been attained in marriage; formal education ends when the educational goal has been reached and examinations or commencement exercises mark completion of the process. Other social processes, however, such as friendship or love, have no precise termination point. They follow a law of social inertia insofar as they continue to operate if no explicit provision for stopping their course is made by the participants. Social conflict is such a process. While in a game, for example, the rules for the process include rules for its ending, in social conflict explicit provisions for its termination must be made by the contenders. If no mutual agreements are made at some time during the struggle, it "ceaseth only in death" or in total destruction of at least one of the antagonists. The termination of conflict hence presents problems that do not arise in finite processes.

Various types of conflicts can be classified according to the degree of their normative regulation. Fully institutionalized conflicts, such as duels, may be said to constitute one extreme of a continuum while absolute conflicts, in which the goal is the total destruction of the enemy rather than a mutually agreed-upon settlement fall at the other extreme. In the second type, agreement is reduced to a minimum; the struggle ceases only upon the extermination of one or both of the contenders. As Hans Speier has said, "peace terminating an absolute war is established *without* the enemy" (9, p. 223).

It stands to reason that conflicts of this kind—at least between contenders with a rough equality of strength—are exceedingly costly and exhausting. If the contenders wish to prevent their struggle from becoming a zero sum game in which the outcome can only be a total defeat or total victory, they have a common interest in establishing mechanisms which can lead to an agreed-upon termination of the struggle. The fact is that most conflicts do indeed end long before the defeated has been totally crushed. "Resistance to the last man" is almost always a phrase. As long as one belligerent survives in one's camp further resistance is always possible; yet combat usually ceases long before this point is reached. This is so because both parties agree upon norms for the termination of the conflict.

While absolute conflicts allow practically no agreements as to their termination, certain types of highly institutionalized conflicts have built-in termination points. Trials by ordeal, duels and other agonistic struggles are centered upon symbolic endings which give them game-like features and determine the outcome automatically. A score is kept, a goal line established, maximum injury is conventionally fixed. When the score adds up to a certain number, when a certain type of injury has been established, or the goal line has been crossed, the conflict is over and the loser as well as the winner can easily perceive the outcome of the contention.

In conflicts not fully institutionalized, assessment of relative strength is not an easy matter so that the loser may not in fact concede that he has lost, nor may he even be aware of it. Therefore, it is to the interest of both contenders that the point at which victory is attained or the point beyond which no more gains can be anticipated, be marked as clearly as possible so as to avoid unnecessary exertions on both sides. Termination of conflict becomes a problem to be solved by both parties.

The termination of conflict is a social

* Reprinted by permission of the author and publisher from *Journal of Conflict Resolution*, 1961, 5: 347–353.

[1] This paper was written while the author was carrying out research at the Institute for Social Research, Oslo, Norway, under a Fulbright grant.

process dependent upon, but not directly deducible from its pursuits. It is, as Georg Simmel has noted, "a specific enterprise. It belongs neither to war nor to peace, just as a bridge is different from either bank it connects" (8, p. 110). To be sure, the outcome of a conflict is related to the goals of the antagonists and to the means by which it is fought; its duration and intensity will depend on objectives and available resources plus the time and effort required to achieve a decision. But the termination of the conflict, that is agreement as to what constitutes a true decision, highlights some factors which are not deducible from its pursuit and must hence be studied separately.

For all except absolute conflict, termination involves a reciprocal activity and cannot be understood simply as an unilateral imposition of the will of the stronger on the weaker. Therefore, contrary to what common sense might suggest, not only the potential victor but also the potential vanquished makes crucial contributions to the termination. As a military commentator has pointed out, "war is pressed by the victor, but peace is made by the vanquished. Therefore, to determine the causes of peace, it is always necessary to take the vanquished's point of view. Until the vanquished quits, the war goes on" (1, p. 18). Victory, in other words, involves the yielding of the vanquished. By the very act of declaring himself beaten, he achieves a last assertion of power. With this act, as Georg Simmel has said, "he actually makes a gift to the victor" (8, p. 114). The capacity of making gifts is a measure of autonomy.

If both victor and vanquished are to make a contribution to the termination of their conflict they must arrive at some agreement. Thomas Schelling has recently argued persuasively that "limited war requires limits . . . but limits require agreement or at least some kind of mutual recognition and acquiescence" (7, p. 53). This applies not only to the conduct but also to the termination of conflicts. In order to end a conflict the parties must agree upon rules and norms allowing them to assess their respective power position in the struggle. Their common interest leads them to accept rules which enhance their mutual dependence in the very pursuit of their antagonistic goals. Such agreements make their conflict, so to speak, self-liquidating. To the degree that such rules are provided, the conflict is partly institutionalized and acquires some of the features of the agonistic struggle alluded to earlier.

Agreements as to goals and determination of outcome shorten the conflict. Once a goal has been reached by one of the parties and this accepted as a clue to the acceptance of defeat by the other, the conflict is ended. The more restricted the object of contention and the more visible for both parties the clues to victory, the higher the chances that the conflict be limited in time and extension. Emile Durkheim's dictum concerning human needs, "The more one has, the more one wants, since satisfaction received only stimulates instead of filling needs" is applicable in this connection. Agreed-upon limits upon the "appetites" of the contenders place normative restrictions upon a process which does not inherently contain self-limiting properties. The history of trade unionism provides interesting examples.

Struggles engaged in by business unionism, given its limited goals, provide for the contending parties an opportunity for settlement and furnishes them at the same time with recognizable signals as to the opportune moment for ending a conflict. Revolutionary syndicalism, on the other hand, has always been plagued by the problem of ending strike action. Since its goal is the overthrow of the capitalist order rather than improvements within it, it cannot accept as the end of the conflict outcomes which would constitute victories from the point of view of business unionism. Revolutionary syndicalism is faced with the dilemma that no outcome of a strike, short of the overthrow of capitalism, can be considered an acceptable form of conflict resolution so that its strategy is foredoomed to failure. Not sensitized to clues which would allow them to conclude that a victory has been reached, unable to recognize peace overtures or concessions from the adversary, revolutionary syndicalists are not in a position to take advantage of partial gains. Paradoxically, in this case, those who are under ordinary conditions the *weaker* party demand "unconditional surrender" of the stronger so that they make it inevitable that the struggle can cease only upon total exhaustion.

The above examples illustrate how closely specific outcomes are related to the aims of the contenders. The smaller the sacrifice a party demands from the opponent, the more limited the aims, the higher the chances that the potential loser will be ready to give up battle. The loser must be led to decide that peace is more attractive than the continuation of the conflict; such a decision will be powerfully enhanced if the demands made upon him are not exorbitant (1, p. 253 *et passim*). When the war aims of the winning side are limited as, say, in the Spanish-American war or the Russo-Japanese conflict of 1905, the making of peace is relatively easy. Once the Japanese war aims—the stopping of Russian penetration into the Far East—had been reached, Japan could afford to make the first move for peace by appealing to Theodore Roosevelt to act as a mediator. Once Cuba was liberated and the Spanish fleet defeated, American war aims were attained and the United States had no interest in continuing the war through an attack upon the Spanish mainland.

It remains, however, that no matter how the activities of the potential winner have facilitated an early termination of the conflict, the final decision to end the war remains with the potential loser. How, then, is the loser moved to decide that he has, in fact, lost? Not only the objective situation but the perception of the situation is crucially important since only the latter will bring forth the requisite admission of defeat. "If an opponent," writes Clausewitz, "is to be made to comply with our will, we must place him in a situation which is more oppressive to him than the sacrifice we demand" (2, vol. 1, p. 5). This elegantly phrased dictum is, however, meaningless unless the criteria be specified that determine how the antagonist will in fact assess the situation. Different contenders might arrive at variant estimates as to the degree of oppressiveness of a situation and of the

value of the sacrifice demanded. Since such assessments are difficult to make and do not depend on rational calculations alone, they are greatly facilitated by the availability of symbolic signposts.

Whenever wars have been strictly limited, as in eighteenth-century warfare, some visible event, such as the taking of a particular fortress, the reaching of some natural barrier and the like, symbolized to both parties that the desired objective has been reached by one of them and that the conflict could now be considered solved through the subsequent acquiescence of the loser. When such mutually acceptable symbolic clues are not available, the resolution of the conflict will be more difficult.

The nature of such symbolic clues may vary considerably[2] and it is hence important that the potential winner ascertain which clues will be accepted by the potential loser as symbols of defeat. If in the common consciousness of the citizens, the capital symbolizes the very existence of the nation, then its fall will be perceived as defeat and will lead to the acceptance of the terms of the victor. The Fall of Paris in 1871 and 1940 symbolized to the bulk of Frenchmen the end of the war despite the fact that Gambetta had rallied significant numbers of undefeated troops in the provinces, and that de Gaulle appealed for the continuation of the war from London. Only a relatively small number of Frenchmen refused to accept the Fall of Paris as a symbol of defeat. In less centralized nations, however, where the capital has no such symbolic significance, its fall is not perceived as a decisive event. Pretoria and Bloemfontein fell to the British in 1900, yet Boer resistance, rather to the surprise of the British, continued for two more years. The British failed to understand that, to the rural Boers, the vast countryside rather than the cities symbolized the nation; to them the war ended only when want of forage, capture, and overwork decimated the Boer horses. In a country in which men

---

[2] One must further distinguish between purely symbolic events, such as the capture of a flag, and events which, as in the examples that follow, have realistic as well as symbolic significance.

were bred in the saddle, the decimation of horses symbolized defeat (1, p. 114). Similarly, the sacking of Washington in 1812 did not signal defeat to Americans for whom the open spaces of the country rather than the federal capital symbolized national independence. In other situations the capture of charismatic war lords rather than any taking of a locality will symbolize defeat.

The structure of the opposing camp furnishes clues as to meaningful symbols of defeat and victory. It is hence of the utmost importance for both sides to have as much knowledge as possible about the characteristic features of their respective structure and symbols. When ignorant armies clash at night, their pluralistic ignorance militates against their ability to come to terms short of mutual exhaustion.

The contenders' ability to make use of one another's symbols of defeat and victory does not only depend on their awareness of the structure of the opposing camp, but also on the dynamics within each camp. Internal struggles may be waged over what set of events may be considered a decisive symbol of defeat. A minority may consider that resistance can be continued even though the majority has accepted defeat. Subgroups may consider that the decision-makers have betrayed the cause by agreeing to end the conflict. Peace terms provide ample material for internal conflict within each of the contending camps. These terms are, moreover, likely to be defined and redefined in the course of the conflict in tune with the fortunes of battle. Different parties may disagree violently on whether a given event is to be considered decisive or of only incidental significance. Such contentions are likely to be the more deepgoing the less integrated the social structure. In integrated structures internal contentions may vitalize and strengthen the groups' energies, but if divergencies as to appropriate action affect the basic layers of common belief, symbolizations of victory and defeat are also likely to be basically divergent (3, pp. 72–80). In highly polarized social systems where a number of internal conflicts of different sorts are superimposed upon one another, there exists hardly any common definition of the situation binding all members of the society to commonly held perceptions (3, p. 76 ff., 4, pp. 213 ff.). To the extent that a society or group is rent into rival camps so that there is no community of ends between the parties, if one party is not willing to accept the definition of the situation which the other propounds, the making of peace becomes an almost impossible enterprise. In such situations a prior settlement of scores within, an unambiguous definition or redefinition of the balance of power between contending groups, may be the precondition for concluding peace without. The Russian provisional government after the March 1917 revolution being continuously goaded and challenged by the growing Bolshevik Party, was unable either to wage war effectively or to conclude peace; once the Bolsheviks had seized power their definition of the situation prevailed and peace could be concluded at Brest Litowsk.

Even when such deep going fissures are not present in a social structure, the ever-present divergencies between the perspectives of the leaders and the led, between those in authority and those submitted to it (4, ch. 5), require considerable effort on the part of the leaders to make the led accept their definition of the situation. Just as at the beginning of the struggle the leaders must convince the led that the sacrifice demanded of them will redound to their benefit and that the conflict concerns wide interests of all rather than the narrow interests of the top stratum, so the leaders must also be able to convince the led that the acceptance of defeat is warranted and even desirable from the point of view of the total system rather than in terms of special leadership interests. To make defeat palatable may require as much effort as to make war desirable.

Leaders will typically differ from the led not only in terms of social perspectives but also in regard to their cognitive horizon so that leaders may be able to assess consequences and relative advantages more rationally than the led. A leader foreseeing a defeat which is not as yet visible to his followers must adjust his strategy to the need of convincing the followers. In such an effort it might be advantageous to him to construe partial defeat in such a way as to make it appear as at least a partial victory. Often the led, like the mark in a con game, might have to be cooled out by being told that what they experience as a loss is "really" a partial victory (5).

Contentions within enemy camps as to the proper definition of the situation once again highlight the importance of symbolizations. The leader will have to rely on his ability to manipulate the symbolic system by which the led define the situations if he is to soften the blow that defeat implies. In labor-management conflicts, for example, events which may appear to an outsider as having only peripheral importance may in fact have highly charged emotional significance to the participants. The return to work of a few strikers or, alternatively, the success of a demonstration or the support of public officials or the reactions of an organ of public opinion, may be invested by the rank and file with high symbolic significance and trigger off a return to work or a revival of the will to victory. This is why it is important for the leaders to manage the symbols that structure the perception of the led. The strike leader must know how to end a strike at the opportune moment, but his knowledge would serve him but little if he did not also have the ability to communicate his knowledge to the led. This may often involve the highlighting for the rank and file of a partially attained victory in order to divert attention from a partially suffered defeat.

This is the stuff of which compromises are made. Often seen by the rank and file as a "betrayal" by the leaders, they actually derive from the structural circumstance that the leaders' position allows them a view of the total situation which is denied to the led. Moreover, leadership roles require to so manage intragroup tensions as to keep the group united in adversity even though this might entail certain sacrifices insofar as the attainment of the group's goals are concerned. "System maintenance," to use Parsons' terminology, may sometimes require lowered task performance.

Indeed, most conflicts end in compromises in which it is often quite hard to specify which side has gained relative advantage. Hence, one must distinguish between the will to make peace and the will to accept defeat. Quite often the former may be present although the latter is not. The parties to the conflict may be willing to cease the battle when they recognize that their aims cannot be attained or that they can be attained only at a price which they are not willing to pay, or, more generally, when they conclude that continuation of the conflict is less attractive than the making of peace. In neither of these cases would they be willing to accept defeat although they are willing to stop short of victory. In such situations they may be impelled to explore the chances for a compromise. The willingness to negotiate a compromise, that is to stop chasing the mirage of victory, will, of course, depend on correct assessment of the situation and such assessment, just as in the cases discussed earlier, will be facilitated by the availability of indices of relative standing in the battle. It is one of the key functions of the mediator to make such indices readily available to both parties. To the extent that the contenders share a common system of symbols allowing them to arrive at a common assessment, to that extent they will be able to negotiate. Symbols of defeat and victory thus turn out to be of relevance in order to stop short of either.

Relative appraisal of power is difficult before the contenders have measured their respective strength in conflict. But accommodation may be reached once such an assessment has been achieved. Such redefinitions in the course of a struggle often bring to the fore elements which remained hidden during its onset. Accomodation is facilitated if criteria are available which allow the contenders to gauge the situation. The chance of attaining peace without victory depends on the possibility of achieving consensus as to relative strength and on the ability to make this new definition "stick" within each camp. When the United States chose the neck of Korea as their symbolic standing place in the Korean war, they succeeded in conveying to the other side as well as to the American people their determination to hold it. When enough blood had been let and it became clear to both sides that the other could be beaten only at a cost that neither was willing to incur, negotiations got down to a compromise that took into account the real balance of political and military power and proved acceptable at home. "Peace through stalemate," writes B. H. Liddell-Hart, "based on a coincident recognition by each side of the opponent's strength, is at least preferable to peace through common exhaustion" (6, p. 370).

Although it is true that in many cases an assessment of the relative strength of the opponents is possible only in conflict, it is also true that their travail may be shortened if clear symbolizations of outcome and relative strength are readily available. When recourse to such measures of success or failure has been highly institutionalized, the duration of the conflict can be shortened and its intensity limited. In this sense, research directed toward an understanding of those symbols which move men to accept compromise or even defeat might be as valuable as research to uncover symbols which incite to war.

REFERENCES

1. Calahan, H. A. *What Makes a War End*. New York: Vanguard Press, 1944.
2. Clausewitz, Karl von. *On War*. London: Routledge and Kegan Paul, 1956.
3. Coser, Lewis A. *The Functions of Social Conflict*. Glencoe, Ill.: Free Press, 1956.
4. Dahrendorf, Ralf. *Class and Class Conflict in Industrial Society*. Stanford, Calif.: Stanford University Press, 1959.
5. Goffman, Erving. "On Cooling the Mark Out," *Psychiatry*, 15 (November, 1952), 451–63.
6. Liddell-Hart, B. H. *Strategy, the Indirect Approach*. London: Faber and Faber, 1955.
7. Schelling, Thomas C. *The Strategy of Conflict*. Cambridge, Mass.: Harvard University Press, 1960.
8. Simmel, Georg. *Conflict*. Trans. Kurt H. Wolff. Glencoe, Ill.: Free Press, 1955.
9. Speier, Hans. *Social Order and the Risks of War*. New York: George W. Stewart, 1952.

THE PREVENTION OF WORLD WAR III*

KENNETH E. BOULDING

When we talk about preventing something we imply two things. We imply, first, that there is a dynamic system which is now proceeding that, if allowed to proceed unchanged, will result in an event which is regarded as undesirable and which, therefore, we want to prevent. We imply also that it is possible to change the dynamic system in question and replace it by another dynamic system in which the unwanted event does not occur. Thus, suppose we find ourselves driving towards a railroad crossing and suddenly we see the red lights flashing and a train approaching. Our dynamic system at the moment consists simply of velocity and direction. We are proceeding, say at 50 miles per hour, towards the crossing. The distant early warning system of our eyes informs us the crossing is dangerous. The knowledge which we have of our existing dynamic system informs us that if it continues we will arrive at the crossing at the precise moment when the train is there. The combination of a distant information system coupled with the simple dynamics of automobiles enables us, however, to prevent the disaster. We do this by putting on the brakes long before we get to the crossing. This in effect changes the dynamic system under which we have been operating. It introduces a new variable into it, indeed a new dimension, deceleration. Because of this, we are able to prevent the disaster, as we are able to avoid simultaneous occupancy of the crossing by ourselves and the train.

We must be careful, of course, in applying the analogy of a simple psycho-mechanical system like a man driving a car to the enormous complexities and uncertainties of the international system. However, the international system is still a system, even though it has important random elements in it. Because it is not entirely ran-

* Reprinted by permission of the author and publisher from *The Virginia Quarterly Review*, 1962, 38: 2–12.

dom, it has elements of predictability. One of the greatest difficulties lies precisely in the stochastic nature of the system. We are driving a car, as it were, that may or may not respond to brakes according to whether dice held by the driver indicate "respond" or "fail." The situation is made all the more difficult by the fact that we face here a stochastic system with a very small universe, that is, a very small number of cases. Stochastic systems with a large number of cases can be treated by the theory of probability. We have a pretty fair idea, for instance, how many people are going to die in automobile accidents next year, although we do not know exactly who they are.

The problem of reducing the total number of automobile accidents is a very different kind of problem from the one that faces the driver of the preceding paragraph. Nevertheless, even with our present knowledge it would not be difficult to design an automobile and a road system which would kill, let us say, 20,000 people a year instead of 40,000. What we would be doing here would be to reduce the probability of disaster on the part of a single individual. It is by no means impossible to think of the international system in a rather similar way, and to talk about the things we can do to reduce the probability of disaster. What we mean by this is that if we had a very large number of planets roughly identical with our own we could postulate changes in the system which would reduce the number of cases in which disaster occurred. This would be the analogue of treating road deaths as a public health problem and seeking to reduce their probability. As far as we know, however, we do not have a large number of planets like ours and for our purposes at least there is only one. Hence, reducing the probability of disaster does us very little good if the disaster actually occurs. The problem of stochastic systems with a small number of cases has received insufficient attention in the theoretical literature. It is precisely this kind of system, however, with which we have to deal in international affairs.

I believe the present international system to be one which has a significant probability built into it of irretrievable disaster for the human race. The longer the number of years we contemplate such a system operating, the larger this probability becomes. I do not know whether in any one year it is one per cent, ten per cent, or even fifty per cent. I feel pretty sure, however, that it is of this order of magnitude, not, shall we say, of the order of magnitude of .01 per cent. The problem of system change, therefore, is urgent and desperate, and we are all in terrible danger. This is largely because of a quantitative change in the parameters of the international system under which we now live. This is still essentially the system of unilateral national defense in spite of the development of the United Nations and certain international organizations. Unilateral national defense is workable only if each nation can be stronger than its potential enemies in its home territory. This is possible under two circumstances. The first is that the nations must be far enough away from each other, and the extent to which their power declines as they operate further away from their own home bases must be sufficiently great. Then each nation can be stronger than the other *at home* with on-the-spot forces because of the fact that in a nation's home territory the enemy operates at a certain disadvantage. There is a second condition, however, which is that each nation must be able to dominate an area around its home base equal in depth to the range of the deadly missile. Because of quantitative changes in these conditions even in the last few years the system of unilateral national defense has become infeasible on a world scale. No nation is now far enough away from potential enemies to be sure that it can dominate even its own territory. Furthermore, the range of the deadly missile is rapidly reaching 12,500 miles, which means that the second condition cannot possibly be fulfilled. The condition which unilateral national defense attempts to establish, therefore, which I call *unconditional viability,* is now no longer possible.

The urgent and desperate nature of the present situation is created by the universality of the disaster with which we are threatened. The system of unilateral national defense has never given permanent security. The rise and fall of nations and empires is a testament to this fact. Indeed, looking with a large historical eye, one may say that unconditional viability has never existed except perhaps for brief periods and the best that unilateral national defense could do for any society was to postpone disaster. The situation of the individual society, that is, is rather analogous to that of the individual, whose life, on this earth at any rate, must also end in irretrievable disaster, that is, in death. Where we have a large number of individuals, however, death for the individual is not death for the race. In fact death for the individual is necessary if the race is to survive. Where the number of individuals becomes smaller and smaller, however, there comes to be a critical point where death for the individual is also death for the race and the irretrievable disaster which the individual suffers is likewise irretrievable disaster for the species. The unilaterally defended national state now seems to me to have got to this state in its development. It is no longer appropriate as a form of organization for the kind of technical society in which we live. Its death throes, however, may destroy the whole human race. The age of civilization out of which we are passing was characterized by a large number of nation-states or independent political organizations practicing unilateral national defense. Because of the large number of these organizations there were always some being born and always some ready to rise into the places of those which suffered disaster. With the number of effectively independent nation-states now reduced to two or perhaps at most three, the possibilities of irretrievable disaster become much greater.

The problem which we face, therefore, is how to effect a system change in the international order, or perhaps we should say the world political order, sufficient to lower the probability of disaster to a tolerable level. The critical problem here might be described as that of "system perception." To revert again to the analogy of the car and the railroad crossing, if the driver of the car does not see that he is approaching the crossing, if the warning lights are not working, and if he cannot see the train approaching, he will naturally not take any steps to avert the disaster. The world problem here is perhaps psychological rather than mechanical. There is a fairly widespread sense abroad of impending doom. The doom, however, is so large that we do not really believe it and we go about our daily actions as if it did not exist. This is the mechanism, as Jerome Frank has pointed out, known to the psychologists as "denial." Up to a point this is actually healthy. We all know that we are going to die sometime and we may die tomorrow; but we act pretty much as if we are going to live forever. We do not spend much time in taking tearful farewells and in writing our last wills and testaments. We plan ahead for months and even for years, in spite of the fact that these plans may never come to fruition. This perfectly legitimate response to uncertainty becomes pathological when it prevents us from taking steps which would postpone disaster or make it less likely. The man who is afraid that he has cancer but who will not go to a doctor because he might find out that he has one is a good example. Where the prospect of disaster, therefore, is so vague or so uncertain that it merely results in pathological denial, it is necessary to bring the actor to a more realistic appraisal of the system within which he is acting.

If the problem of "denial" is to be overcome, it is necessary to do more than merely scare people with horrendous pictures of the possible future. Indeed, the more horrendous the picture which is drawn, the more it is likely to result in denial and pathological inactivity. The future which faced our driver at the railroad crossing was also horrendous, but instead of denying this and continuing on his way he presumably applied the brakes, that is, initiated a system change. The problem in the international system is that we seem to have no brakes. That is, it is hard for people to visualize the nature of the system change which is necessary for survival. This, then,

is one of the major tasks today of the political scientist, the philosopher, the journalist, and the prophet: to give the people an image of changes in the international system which seems small enough to be feasible yet large enough to be successful. It is not useful to picture Utopias which seem utterly unattainable—this perhaps is the main difficulty with the World Federationists—even though the function of Utopias in providing a constant driving force in social dynamics should not be underestimated. The present situation, however, calls not for Utopia, but for political solutions. Indeed, one of our great difficulties today is that we have too many Utopias. We need to think, therefore, in terms of a world social contract: that is, a minimum bargain between the contending parties which will give the world a sufficient system change to relieve it from the intolerable burden which it now bears. This social contract does not even have to be explicit or contractual. It can begin by being tacit; indeed, one can argue that a world social contract already exists in a tacit embryo form. We can visualize perhaps the following five stages of development.

I. The stage of tacit contract. In systems which have an inherent instability, such as duopoly in the relations of firms, or a bipolar system of mutual deterrence in the relations of states, it is often possible to maintain a quasi-stable position for a long time through tacit contract: that is, through mutually consistent unilateral behavior on the part of each party. A quasi-stable position is like that of an egg on a golf-tee—it is stable for small disturbances but not for large. For considerable periods of time, however, the disturbances may be small enough so that Humpty-Dumpty does not fall. Comes a slightly larger disturbance, however, and all the King's horses and men cannot put him together again. The international system under the Eisenhower administration exhibited this kind of quasi-stability. An important element in that stability was a tacit agreement between the United States and the Soviet Union to do nothing effective about civil defense. We agreed, in effect, that our civilian populations should be mutually exchanged as hostages, for we each had the power to destroy large numbers—at least half—of each other's civilians. This meant that the chance of deliberate nuclear war was very small, though the chance of accidental war was appreciable; indeed, the missiles almost went off on at least two occasions. A natural accident, such as a large meteor, or an electronic breakdown, or a social accident, such as a mad pilot, or a political accident, such as an unwise commitment to an irresponsible third party, could under these circumstances easily set off a mutual exchange of nuclear weapons, so that the system could not be regarded as more than a temporary expedient.

Another example of tacit contract was the mutual suspension of nuclear tests, recently broken by the Soviet Union. Here the fear, perhaps, of world opinion, and the fear also of the technical consequences of an uncontrolled race for technical development of weapons, created a temporary tacit agreement. We have had similar tacit agreements in regard to spheres of influence and intervention in third-party quarrels. The United States did not interfere in Hungary, nor the Soviet Union in Egypt during the Suez crisis. The Russians allowed themselves to be thrown out of the Congo, and are not threatening to be more than a nuisance in Cuba. The conflicts in Korea and Viet Nam were temporarily settled by latitudinal partitions. The Arab-Israeli conflict does not become an arena of the cold war. All these represent systems of mutuality of conduct which might be classified as tacit agreement.

II. The fate of the tacit agreement on nuclear testing, and what looks like the impending fate of the tacit agreement on civil defense, is a testimony to the inherent instability of the tacit agreement in the long run. It is something like the gentleman's agreement in economic competition, which suffers from the defect that not all people are gentlemen. The danger is that in the absence of organization between contending parties their only means of communication is by a "threat system." A threat system, which is characteristic of unilateral national defense, is based on the proposi-

tion, "If you do something bad to me I will do something bad to you," by contrast with an exchange system, which is based on "If you do something good to me I will do something good to you." Both systems tend to lead to consummation, but whereas the consummation of exchange is an increase of goods, the consummation of threats is an increase of "bads." War is mainly the result of the depreciation in the credibility of threats in the absence of their consummation, and hence a threat system has a basic instability built into it, which tacit contract may postpone but cannot ultimately avoid. The great problem, therefore, is how to get rid of threat systems. This, I suspect, happens historically mainly by their being overlaid with other systems of relationship —trade, communication, organization—until they fall so much to the bottom of the pile that they are no longer significant.

The essential instability of threat systems and the weakness of tacit agreements, therefore, make it highly desirable to pass into the second stage of formalized agreement, and the building of what might be called "peace-defending" organizational structures. The first of these obviously is an arms control organization designed at first perhaps only to limit the present arms race but capable of the ultimate hope of policing genuine disarmament. We could begin, perhaps, with an organization for the prevention of accidental war. This will be a joint organization of the major armed forces of the world. Once this has been accomplished, a major system change is under way. It is the organizational disunity of the armed forces of the world which constitutes the real threat to humanity. If they were united they might threaten us with a great many disagreeable consequences but they would not threaten us with extinction. An arms control organization, therefore, would be the beginning of a very powerful social change. It would constitute the formal recognition of the fact that unilateral national defense is no longer possible. Once this initial break is made, system change may be expected to take place quite rapidly. It may be that we shall have to look forward to a substantial separation of the armed forces organization from the states which they are supposed to defend, and which they can no longer defend. Just as we solved the problem of religious wars by the separation of church and state, so we may be able to solve the problem of nuclear war by the separation of the armed forces from the state. The plain fact is that today the threat which the armed forces of the world present to their own civilian populations is much greater than any conflict among the nations. Arms control will be the beginning of the recognition of this social fact.

III. Arms control must move fairly rapidly into disarmament; otherwise it will be unstable. The organization of the world armed forces will be a loose and unstable one at first, and it will always threaten to break up. It may be, of course, that the major pressure towards disarmament will come from the economic side. Once the threat of war is removed by arms control and by organizational unity of the world armed forces, the economic burden of maintaining these monstrous establishments will seem intolerable, especially in view of the fact that it is the arms burden (equal to the total income of the poorest half of the human race!) which perhaps prevents the world from really tackling the problem of economic development and which condemns hundreds of millions of people and their descendants to live in misery. One looks forward, therefore, to the third stage of rapid and total disarmament, under the arms control organization. There are many difficult problems involved in this which have not been worked out and on which research desperately needs to be done. One research program is on the way at the moment on the broad problems of the economics of disarmament, conducted by Professor Emile Benoit of Columbia University. The United Nations is about to inaugurate a similar study. However, the organizational and social-psychological problems involved are very great and quite unprecedented. Growth is always much easier than decline and the problems of adjustment involved in a rapid decline in the world's armed forces still have to be faced. These problems, however, are difficult rather than insoluble.

IV. Even universal total disarmament, however, is not enough, for this too is likely to be unstable even though disarmament itself will reduce many of the sources of conflict, especially those which arise out of strategic considerations. It will not eliminate all conflicts by any means. In a world as divided as this, ideologically and economically, we may expect serious conflicts continually to arise. These conflicts will constantly present the temptation to the losing side to resort to violence and to redevelop organized armed forces. If disarmament is to be stable, therefore, there must be a system of conflict control. Conflict control is one of the essential functions of government. It is not, however, the only function. In thinking of world government, this is probably where we ought to begin. In the early stages it is more important to establish conflict control than to establish justice or to solve all social problems. Conflict control as a function of government has been inadequately studied and identified. This is perhaps because the study of conflict systems themselves is still in its infancy. However, this is a rapidly developing body of social science and one hopes that it may be possible in the not-too-distant future to develop a substantial body of knowledge on the identification and control of conflict systems. The problem, of course, is the identification of conflict processes in early stages before they become pathological. There are very difficult problems here in the definition of the pathology of conflict, as this, of course, goes very deep into our value systems. Conflict which is regarded as pathological by one person may not be so regarded by another. If, however, we regard violence as generally a sign of pathological conflict, we may be able to identify the processes of social dynamics which lead towards it, and we may therefore be able to interpose counterweights which will correct these processes. We may revert once more to the analogy of the car at the crossing. We need to develop both perception of dangers ahead and also organizations which can act as brakes. These processes have been fairly well worked out in industrial relations, where a whole profession of mediators and conciliators and personnel experts has come to being. There is no reason why these principles should not be applied in other fields of social life and especially to the conflict of states.

V. The last stage, of course, is true world government, capable not only of controlling conflict but of expressing and developing the common concerns and aims of mankind. At the moment this seems to be a long way off. Fortunately, the prevention of war does not depend, I think, on the establishment of full world government. If the stages of development which I have outlined can be pursued rapidly enough, war may be postponed for longer and longer periods until the postponement becomes indefinite by the establishment of a true world government. We must therefore find half-way houses and quarter-way houses which are moderately habitable. We must not allow Utopian longings to deprive us of political bargains.

The actual negotiation of the world social contract is going to be a long and arduous business. We need to put many more resources into this than we are now doing. Nevertheless, there is something here which can be done. There is a road which leads somewhere. If we are to break out of the apathy, irrationality, and despair which beset us, we must gain a vision of that road of escape and make at least one step along it. This is the great significance of the growing movement for peace research. Just as we no longer accept depressions as "acts of God," wholly unpredictable and uncontrollable, so we need no longer accept mass violence as unpredictable and uncontrollable. The fact that we cannot yet predict or control it should stir us to a great intellectual effort in this direction, for this way lies hope. The only unforgivable sin in the present crisis of mankind is despair.

SOME PROBLEMS OF DISARMAMENT RESEARCH*

I. GLAGOLEV and M. GORYAINOV

The necessity of scientific research of the problems connected with the safeguarding and strengthening of peace has won international recognition. In a number of countries peace research institutes have been established. Some organizations are studying questions on armament control and the theory of solving international conflicts.

In the Soviet Union many institutes and public organizations are studying different aspects of the strengthening of peace, for instance the Pugwash Committee of Scientists, the Soviet Committee for Securing Peace, the Institute for World Economy and International Relations, the Historical Institute of the Academy of Sciences, and other institutes. A characteristic feature of the Soviet research is that the problem of disarmament occupies the first place among them. All the above-mentioned institutes have a special section or a permanent commission dealing with disarmament. Some books and a great many articles are being published yearly on some aspects of disarmament or other (besides a huge number of articles and books on general questions concerning the strengthening of peace and international security).

Soviet scientists are each year taking part in international conferences on disarmament and are systematically convening their own conferences on this problem.

One of these Soviet conferences on disarmament questions and international security was convened at the end of 1962 in Moscow. Explicit reports from this conference appeared in the Soviet Press. The greater part of them will appear in an international publication on disarmament. A new conference of this kind was convened in Moscow from 3–8 August 1964. The main theme there was disarmament and economic cooperation. The aim of the first

part of this conference was to give an extensive analysis of the theoretical and practical problems in connection with the reduction of military expenses and general and complete disarmament. Special attention was paid to the international importance of the Moscow Treaty on test ban in three spheres, the decision of the Soviet Union to reduce the military budget and numerical strength of the armed forces, the decision of the Soviet Union, the USA and Great Britain to reduce the production of fission materials, and other concrete steps toward disarmament. Practical possibilities of employing human reserves, financial means, military techniques in the production of power and scientific institutes for peaceful development, will be indicated.

The aim of the second part of the conference was to give an extensive analysis of questions of economic cooperation in connection with problems of peaceful coexistence and problems of economic development in the Asian, African and Latin-American countries. Special problems and perspectives were indicated regarding commercial and other forms of relations between the socialist countries and between the socialist and capitalist countries. Factors promoting and preventing international and economic cooperation were also discussed. Twenty-four lectures by specialists from the Soviet Academy of Sciences, the Moscow State University and other scientific institutes were given and discussed.

Facts show that at the majority of western institutes the study of disarmament problems is either pushed into the background or not dealt with at all. In the USA the Peace Research Institute in Washington has been closed and merged into another institute not dealing explicitly with such a subject. On the other hand, an Armament Control Institute has been opened at Ann Arbor.

* Reprinted by permission of the authors and publisher from *Journal of Peace Research*, 1964, *1*: 150–154.

This does not imply that research of disarmament problems in the western countries is non-existent. But its extent in no way corresponds to the importance of the disarmament problems, inseparably connected as they are with the question of safeguarding life in the world.

In the Soviet Union the study of disarmament problems will be systematically increased, developing at the same time cooperation with scientists in other countries on this subject on a level with the Pugwash movement, UNESCO, etc. We intend to increase the exchange of material, oral and written discussions, exchange of specialists on disarmament questions, international conferences and organization of scientific team-work.

Disarmament is in reality an international problem. Therefore cooperation between scientists from different countries is especially important.

In our opinion research on disarmament problems must include the question of the interest among peoples and states in preventing mutual destruction through the abolishing of armaments.

If we proceed from the opposite presupposition—from an alleged interest among the peoples in an endless arms race—the researchers will have to accept fantastic demands in the field of control, aimed at forcing the peoples to disarm. They will have to accept conclusions about the precariousness of disarmament or even the complete unfeasibility of this idea. Of course, the degree of interest in disarmament is not the same in the different governments, among the different classes and groupings. One can surely find governments and groupings which due to narrow egoistical considerations are supporters of arms races. But this does not alter the cardinal, objectively existing fact that humanity is interested in the elimination of armaments.

Thanks to the fact that there does exist an interest in stopping the arms race it has been possible to conclude agreements on banning tests with atomic weapons in three spheres, on banning the launching of missiles with weapons of mass-destruction into space, on peaceful utilization of the Antarctic, and a number of other agreements.

On this basis it is possible to reach—and in some cases it has been practically realized—a policy of mutual example regarding the reduction of military expenses and limitation of the arms race. The Soviet Union, for instance, reduced her military expenses by 4.5% in 1964, then followed the USA's decision to reduce the military grants for 1964/65 by 1.5%.

These measures go to show that there are great possibilities in using so-called national means of control on disarmament. There is a huge quantity of such means available for any economically developed state. Among such are the use of different scientific methods, the study of information published on a large scale all over the world, etc. At diplomatic negotiations on disarmament representatives from some western countries often forget these possibilities and demand anew a system of control which creates difficulties of a political, technical and economic character.

Scientific research of the disarmament problems must reveal the full spectrum of the control methods already available now. They must point out the degree of accuracy of these methods and define the necessary supplements in those cases where the degree of accuracy is not high enough. It is of course necessary to bear in mind that absolutely accurate methods do not exist in this world. But absolute accuracy is not compulsory if we take into consideration the great effect of the interest in disarmament and the different additional guarantees for maintenance of the disarmament, agreed upon by the states.

The question of additional guarantees must also be examined. One of these guarantees which has already been acknowledged by scientists both in the East and the West is the rocket-nuclear umbrella. The securing of a limited quantity of rockets in the USA and the Soviet Union during the whole period of disarmament would obviate efforts to conceal some rockets or bombers from destruction.

Everybody knows that the process of disarmament will take a certain time—even some years. When determining the succession of the measures leading to disarmament and the stages of the disarmament itself it is necessary to take into consideration the special urgency of some of the measures. One example is the test ban on atomic weapons. It is no accident that the first step toward disarmament was taken in this very field. As a result of the atomic explosions begun by the USA in 1943, the radio-activity in the atmosphere increased to a level inadmissable for human health. Further nuclear tests in the atmosphere are intolerable. Even a single series would lead to the destruction of many people. And resumption of the nuclear test-race which might follow such a series would lead to the deaths of millions of people and would seriously affect the health of not only the present but also the next generation. In this respect we must especially consider the tests of atomic weapons now being prepared by the French government in the Pacific. The problem of banning these tests is especially urgent and acute, both from a medical and a moral point of view.

The necessity of a quick solution of such questions as the banning of tests with atomic weapons and the beginning of disarmament is objectively based on the fact that the stock of weapons of mass-destruction has reached an exorbitant level from all points of view. Thus, according to an estimate by the Soviet Government made in 1962 the TNT equivalent of the stock of atomic weapons reached 80 tons per individual in the world. The use of such a quantity of weapons would, besides destruction of whole nations from the very beginning of the war, result in a continuous poisoning of the world's atmosphere by radio-active elements.

Now we would like to turn to the outlining of a concrete program for the study of different aspects regarding disarmament, prevention of war and the strengthening of peace.

The first problem indissolubly connected with the main aim of disarmament is an objective estimation of the probable consequences of a thermo-nuclear war. Individual scientists have made their estimates. Linus Pauling is, for instance, often referred to,

more seldom other specialists. It would have been very important if an authoritative commission of scientists from the East and the West worked out a coordinated point of view on this question. Then a definite and, of course, a negative reply would be given to the admissability of a nuclear war.

Further we hold that every second year or so a supplement and corrections be worked out if the arms race does not stop.

The question about materials and information may arise. Here it is, in our opinion, not necessary to reveal any state secrets. General information about the mining of uranium ore, the production of fission materials, the storing of bombs and their means of delivery, already available from the international Press, will be sufficient for working out a report.

The second problem is the urgency of disarmament, especially of nuclear rockets. On the basis of new information it is important to point out the growing necessity of a rapid disarmament and to carry out measures leading toward general and complete disarmament. After the states in principle have agreed to a general and complete disarmament, the question of the first efficient steps has acquired an immense and fundamental importance. And the sooner the realization of these principles begin the better.

The third problem is a discussion of the conditions which would prevent production of weapons—especially nuclear ones— after disarmament. This is a future theme, but it is not difficult to see that it is important also from the present point of view. Our generation is facing the most serious peace problem in order to save the earth from a nuclear catastrophe. It is obliged to do its utmost in order that the next generation shall not be faced with the same problem.

The fourth problem: Recommendation ought to be given to limit the spreading of reactors producing fission materials used in nuclear weapons. In this field important steps have been taken by the three big powers, but much still remains to be done. The number of nuclear reactors has increased extremely quickly during the last years. Hundreds of them are now in action. Among them there are reactors of great and some of extremely great power. On account of the dense net of reactors in the world the danger of utilizing their produce for aggressive aims will not be avoided if we do not see to it beforehand. In our opinion there are at least two solutions to this problem, a political one and a technical one. The technical problem obviously concerns the scientists and the engineers. This problem is important both at present and in the future, especially in the near future because more and more states are now getting their own reactors.

In connection with this it would be advisable to have in view also ways of saving humanity from the terrible effects of the by-products of nuclear industry and reduce them to an acceptable minimum, if such a minimum exists.

Problems concerning the by-products of nuclear industry ought to worry us more and more. Up to now there have existed no international regulations limiting the disposal of the by-products in the ocean or other places of deposit. Scientists ought not to wait until the quantity of such by-products increases so much that everybody sees the danger. Something must be done in time, that is now, because the by-products from this industry may bring harm to the flora and fauna of the world, not to speak of mankind.

The fifth problem concerns the development of confidence. Of course there exists a certain degree of confidence among people already today. In time of peace this confidence is naturally higher. But humanity today is in need of a higher degree of confidence than ever before. Finding ways and giving recommendations for developing a higher degree of confidence are necessary in order to solve the disarmament problems. A very important and responsible task is here facing the scientists, politicians and public personages. Scientists ought also to do their best to solve this problem.

The sixth problem concerns the 'nuclear umbrella'. This proposal has been approved by many governments. Practically, the idea

of this 'umbrella' has obtained a foundation for its adoption and it will secure the interests of all people. This idea can play an important role in strengthening confidence and in hurrying on disarmament.

The seventh problem is connected with the economic aspects of disarmament. A responsible task is now facing the economists, namely to point out the stimulating influence of disarmament on the economy and the possibility of using the extra resources, and to work out in good time compensating programs for peaceful development—inclusive help programs—for the Asian and African countries.

The eighth problem is the task of attracting people's attention to the control of disarmament. This problem is closely connected with the problem of confidence, but it has also its own theoretical significance and technical particularity.

The ninth problem: working out of recommendations on a system of measures to ensure against the weakening or dissolving of the Moscow Treaty on the banning of nuclear tests in three spheres and the agreement about banning the launching into space of objects with weapons of mass-destruction. We hold that scientists must not refrain from strengthening the position already reached as shown in the above-mentioned agreement.

Scientists may offer useful recommendations for the widening and strengthening of the importance of the agreements already signed. This is so much the more necessary in so far as such international agreements may be subject to attack from different sides. In our opinion such activity on the part of scientists is especially important now when the French Government is preparing to carry out tests with nuclear and thermo-nuclear weapons, in the atmosphere as well.

The tenth problem is connected with measures to prevent violation of the disarmament. The importance of this problem is determined by the changes of the political life in the different states. A scientific study of this question might point out the conditions restricting the influence of these processes on disarmament.

The eleventh problem: Sanctions against possible violators of the disarmament agreements. We find that this problem has many facets which involve a great number of acute questions. Life compels us to deal with this problem. Even a preliminary treatment of it might, in our opinion, be of indubitable advantage.

The twelfth problem: To create a solid system for international security. This theme might include the question of developing international cooperation, the activity of international organizations, the creation of international security forces and others.

The thirteenth problem is connected with a disarmed world. Many aspects of a disarmed world are not seen clearly today. In this desirable world, dictated by the historical development of mankind, there will —together with bright sides—probably be some gloomy ones, some difficulties which

we are obliged to overcome. Research on economic, political, national, cultural and other problems in a disarmed world is important also from the situation of today. Such research work will help us to deal rationally with the problems which are now worrying mankind.

The problems put forth by us in methodological order are in pursuit of the following aims: hastening the conclusion of an agreement about general and complete disarmament, and if possible making the very process of disarmament more effective. In discussing one methodological problem or another it is important to avoid conflicts about the main ones. It is important that the conclusion of an agreement on general and complete disarmament as soon as possible should not be hampered by additional study of methodological problems. The conclusion of an agreement is an inevitable demand of our time. The necessity to conclude an agreement has grown so ripe that the more it is opposed the more mankind must suffer.

UNITED NATIONS USE OF
MILITARY FORCE*

INIS L. CLAUDE, JR.

There are two possible ways of approaching the question of the purposes of the United Nations. One is to concentrate on the Charter—to treat this formal constitutional document as an authoritative and meaningful expression of the goals which the world organization seeks to achieve and toward which it must be presumed to be working. The Charter, of course, was not handed down from on high, but was formulated by states. Thus, this approach appears to suggest that the Charter was, in 1945, a valid statement of a real consensus among the original members as to what the UN should be and do. As for the present, it suggests that the same conception of the UN is held by the expanded membership of the organization—that the consensus has been widened but not substantively altered —or, alternatively, that the UN is an entity sufficiently autonomous to function in accordance with the original consensus, whether or not that consensus, or *any* consensus, still prevails among its members.

The second approach is to focus upon the political interests and purposes of the members of the UN—to proceed upon the assumption that the words of the Charter are less determinative than the policies of the states. Following this approach, we may expect to find that the purposes of the organization are not fixed, but are continuously redefined as states develop new agreements among themselves as to what ends they wish or expect the UN to serve. Moreover, we may expect to find that the organization's purposes are as ambiguous as they are mutable, for it is altogether unlikely that the members have ever been, are now, or ever will be in full agreement concerning the uses to which this international instrument should be put. In these terms,

the explorer of the UN's purpose must wrestle with change and conflict, renouncing the expectation of finding the purposes of the organization conveniently spelled out for him.

Adopting the first course, we may ask what the Charter says with respect to the use of military force. What are the purposes to which 51 states ostensibly subscribed in 1945 and which they, along with 59 additional states, now purport to regard as appropriate and acceptable? The UN is intended to discourage the irresponsible, national use of military force—aggression, in short. It recognizes the legitimacy of defensive action by victims of attack and by other states which may wish to join in that reaction to aggression, but it undertakes to make such defense unnecessary by making offensive action unlikely. In a variety of ways, the UN undertakes to prevent aggression. Its purpose is to deprive states of anything to fight *about*—by inhibiting the development of, and promoting the elimination of, conditions that might make for conflict, and by facilitating the settlement of difficulties that have reached the critical "dispute" stage. By promoting disarmament negotiations, the organization expresses the urge to deprive themselves and each other of anything to fight *with*. Thus far, this analysis suggests that the UN is concerned with the use of force by states, acting on their own. The Charter goes on, however, to say something about the use of force by the UN, or, more accurately, by states acting under its auspices. The two subjects are closely interrelated; provisions calling for the use of force by or on behalf of the UN are integral parts of the scheme for inhibiting aggressive national action and thereby reducing the necessity for individual or collective defensive action. The Charter purports to classify the national use of force under three headings: that

* Reprinted by permission of the author and publisher from *Journal of Conflict Resolution*, 1963, 7: 117–129.

which is required, that which is prohibited, and that which is permitted. Insofar as it requires members to provide coercive support for the world organization, the Charter adopts the view that the responsible use of force for international purposes is the ultimate antidote for the irresponsible use of force for national purposes.

The Charter does not in fact go very far in this direction. It pays lip service to the ideal of erecting a collective security system, which would promise to cope with any prohibited use of force by invoking the requirement of collective resistance. But it does not attempt to provide for the actual creation or operation of such a system. At most, it contains a plan for developing a system under which the UN may mobilize collective action against *minor* aggressors in circumstances which find the major powers unanimously disposed to support or at least to tolerate such action. The crucial provisions pertinent to this scheme, Articles 43 and 45, which contemplate agreements on military contingents to be placed at the disposal of the Security Council by states, have become dead letters but have not been formally erased. The Charter does *not,* it should be emphasized, either provide or promise a system for UN action or UN-sponsored action to repress aggression launched or supported by any of the major powers. The famous veto clause of Article 27 expresses the founding fathers' rejection of the attempt to require member states to join forces under the UN banner for resistance to great-power aggression; the "individual or collective self-defense" clause of Article 51, a permissive clause, expresses the judgment of the founding fathers as to what can and must be done under such circumstances. The Charter, in short, prohibits but does not purport to prevent the most dangerous sort of aggression—that undertaken by or under the auspices of a major power.

We might summarize this reading of the Charter by saying that it speaks much more decisively about the use of force by states than about the use of force by the UN. The purpose of the UN is to discourage the irresponsible, disruptive use of force by states. The organization itself is to use, or to sponsor the use of, force only when—or if—the great powers concur in the implementation of Articles 43 and 45 and subsequently in Security Council decisions regarding particular cases.

Shifting to the second of the approaches to analysis of the purposes of the UN discussed at the beginning, which stresses the policies of states rather than the words of the Charter, one may express doubt as to whether the statesmen who drafted the Charter were as unanimously and as unreservedly dedicated to the creation of an effective peace-preserving organization as they said they were. Equally, one may doubt whether the purposes stated in the Charter are in fact the purposes which all or most member states now wish the UN to pursue and hope that it may realize. There is conflict over the purposes for which the organization is to be used—conflict deriving not from differing interpretations of the Charter but from differing national interests, or conceptions of national interests.

There is no difficulty in securing general condemnation of aggression in the abstract, and agreement that the UN should discourage, if not effectively prevent or suppress, aggression. In concrete terms, however, one state's aggression is always another state's "legitimate use of force to defend vital national interests." What states really want is the imposition of effective international restraint upon the military ventures of "others," not of themselves or of states intimately associated with themselves. It can hardly be imagined that the Soviet Union wishes the UN to be capable of inhibiting Communist conquest of Laos. India presumably does not regret that the organization failed to protect Goa against Indian invasion. The United Arab Republic does not aspire to make the UN an effective guarantor of the integrity of Israel. The United States would have limited enthusiasm for the project of making the UN a bulwark against any possible American attack upon Cuba. With respect to its own resorts to force, actual or potential, every state wants to secure at least the tolerance of the UN, even better the blessing of the UN, and at best such substantial support and reinforcement as the organization might provide.

States vary, of course, in their ability and disposition to use force for the promotion or protection of their interests as they see them. They vary also in the degree to which they conceive their interests as compatible with a stable world order in which respect for the territorial integrity and political independence of all states is enshrined and effectuated as a basic principle. I would argue, for instance, that Washington's view of the national interest of the United States is much more compatible with and conducive to that kind of global system than Moscow's view of the interests and purposes which Soviet policy is to serve. I do not suggest that all states are equally bellicose and aggressive. Nevertheless, it seems to me quite clear that every state has to contemplate the possibility that it might, under some circumstances, feel impelled to take military action that would seem to it absolutely necessary for the protection of vital national interests but might not be regarded as legitimate by the political organs of the UN. States *do* contemplate this possibility; consequently, they do not genuinely commit themselves without reservation to the proposition that they will never resort to force in the face of international disapproval expressed through the UN; consequently, they are not ultimately dedicated to the purpose of enabling the UN— that is, its member states—to control the unilateral resort to military action by any and all states, including themselves.

If I am correct in attributing this attitude to states, then it follows that states must have reservations about conferring upon the UN an extensive legal competence and actual capability to exercise a coercive function. One does not fully endorse the principle of the international use of force unless one fully repudiates the policy of the national use of force, for it must be presumed that a militarily effective UN might frustrate one's state in its efforts to safeguard its vital interests—interests which the state may regard as justifying the national use of force but which a sufficient number of the

members of a UN political organ might not so regard.

I submit that this is the actual situation today. We must resist the temptation to take too seriously the simple proposition that the world is divided into two groups of states, one of which (including, most prominently, the Soviet Union) opposes the strengthening of the UN, and the other of which (led by the United States) favors the development of that organization as an international respository of coercive authority and power.

It is easy enought to demonstrate that the Soviets oppose that development. It is perhaps less self-evident that the United States does not favor that development. I would argue, however, that the record shows that the United States favors a UN which can give permissive endorsement and lend moral and perhaps more tangible varieties of support to military actions which we regard as necessary and legitimate; I look in vain for evidence that the United States wishes to equip the UN with either the formal competence of the effective capability to prevent this country and its allies from fighting whenever we may feel it necessary to fight, or to require us to fight when we are not diposed to do so. In the case of Korea, the UN gave an international blessing to, and stimulated the mobilization of multilateral support for, a military reaction to Communist aggression which we felt impelled to undertake. We valued this marginal assistance, and attempted, in the Uniting for Peace plan, to maximize the possibility that such internatonal aid might be rendered to upholders of similarly worthy causes in the future. This was, however, a far cry from endorsing the actual creation of, or expressing the willingness to accept the onerous obligations of, a fullfledged collective security system. The United States has subsequently supported the quasi-military interventions of the UN in the Middle East and the Congo, but these can hardly be characterized as manifestations of, or even as preliminary approaches to, the establishment of a UN capacity to use international military force to squelch illicit national resorts to force.

It might be noted that the United States has, since 1960, stated for the public international record that it regards an effective international coercive mechanism as an essential part of a world system characterized by general and complete disarmament. Perhaps I may be forgiven if I choose to treat this more as an exercise in logic than as a statement of policy. It seems to say that the United States advocates the establishment of a world government—but it should be noted that President Kennedy, in his State of the Union address in January, 1962, described our goal for the future as "a peaceful world community of free and independent states" or "a free community of nations, independent but interdependent" (Kennedy, 1962, pp. 159, 163). Moreover, another spokesman for the Administration declared that: "The ultimate question at issue is whether this small planet is to be organized on the principles of the Communist bloc or on the basis of voluntary cooperation among independent nation-states. . . . We expect this planet to organize itself in time on the principles of voluntary cooperation among independent nation-states . . ." (Rostow, 1962, pp. 835, 838). These statements seem to belie the proposition that American policy is dedicated to the creation of a global governmental authority entrusted with supreme coercive power. In any case, the completely disarmed world to which this proposition is linked is not our world. In dealing with the world as it is, and with the UN as it is and seems to be becoming, the United States betrays little enthusiasm for making the use of military force by the UN the central element in plans for the safeguarding of American security and the maintenance of world peace.

The purpose of this paper is not to speculate about what the world would be like if it were utterly different from what it is. Focusing on the existing situation and the existing global institution, let us ask what role can reasonably be assigned to the UN in the military-security field.

First, there is the question of the possible use of the UN as a military instrument for dealing with great-power aggression; in our terms, this refers to the possibility of the

organization's serving as a defensive bulwark against aggressive action launched by, or supported by, the Soviet Union or Communist China. My response to this is quite negative. We rely, quite properly in my judgment, upon our national power and our alliances for security against this threat. The UN was not designed to cope with this sort of problem, and I see no point in criticizing the organization for not doing what it was not supposed to do, or in regretting its inability to do what it was, from the start, constitutionally debarred from attempting to do. Nor do I see any point in trying to transform the UN into an organization appropriate for this role. The UN is not a NATO, and if we undertake to make it a kind of super-NATO, we may sacrifice its values as a global institution without in fact succeeding in making it a valuable free-world institution. We need not choose between global and free-world organizations. We have both kinds, and we need both kinds, to perform different types of functions. If NATO is defective, the answer is to improve NATO, not to attempt to convert the UN into a NATO-like institution.

I am arguing, in short, that the task of providing a military deterrent against Communist expansionism is a task for a coalition of allies, not for a general international organization that includes Communist states and uncommitted states among its members. The usefulness, actual and potential, of the UN lies in other realms. Conceivably, of course, the UN may lend helpful support to the Western coalition, as it did in the case of Korea. We cannot count on this, however, given the increasing numerical strength of the uncommitted states in the UN. Moreover, I have serious doubts as to whether it would be, on balance, advantageous to the West to have the UN function as a reliable endorser of our position in contests with the Soviet bloc. Insofar as the UN habitually plays that role, it tends to take on the appearance of a pro-Western institution, thereby endangering its potential usefulness as neutral ground, or an impartial instrument, in the Cold War. I shall return to this point later.

Secondly, we might ask whether the UN has a significant capability for dealing militarily with clashes between states which lie outside the alignments of the Cold War and the spheres of interest of the major Cold War antagonists. This is precisely what the UN was intended to have, as is indicated by the plan for making national units available for use by the Security Council, stated in Article 43 of the Charter. The question, then, is whether this plan can or should be revived, or a different scheme be substituted for it. The outlook is not encouraging. The early negotiations regarding the implementation of Article 43 indicated that neither the Western powers nor the Soviet Union trusted the other to participate loyally, without ulterior motives, in a collective UN force (Claude, 1962, pp. 175–90). Since this mutual distrust has become stronger rather than weaker, it seems perfectly evident that any anti-aggression force assembled by the UN would have to exclude units from the major powers and their most intimate allies. This observation suggests a major limiting factor—the pervasiveness of the Cold War. It is extremely difficult to conceive of an international conflict in our time which the Western and Soviet blocs would not regard as at least potentially related to their competitive struggle; in virtually any case that can readily be imagined, UN military action against an aggressive state would be likely to evoke conflicting reactions from the Soviet Union and the United States. Even though these powers might be excluded from participation in the action, they might well find themselves at odds concerning the propriety of the action, the identity of aggressor and victim, and the nature of the political result which the UN should endeavor to promote. The world is too small to provide a wide zone of indifference between the major contestants. In short, an attempt by the UN to deal coercively with almost any conflict would probably be assimilated to an attempt to deal coercively with great-power struggles.

Thus, I see little scope for UN military action in defending one small state divorced from Cold War blocs against another one. Moreover, I see little evidence that the neutralist members of the UN are prepared to institute and effectuate a collective security arrangement among themselves, even assuming that the major powers would be willing to stand dispassionately aside. I would not be willing to advise the leader of any state to base his security policy upon the expectation that a UN force might be mobilized to defend his country against aggression.

What if the UN were equipped with a permanent military force of its own, a force designed to defeat aggressors, and thus ceased to be dependent upon the willingness of states to contribute, or to permit others to contribute, military contingents for UN actions? This possibility seems to me to have no relevance to the problem of restraining great powers. Military power must rest upon a base—a territorial, demographic, social, political, economic, industrial, scientific base. The only base capable of producing and sustaining a military establishment able to match that of a great power is another great power. Concretely, only the United States—or, more broadly, the Western coalition—is able to generate the force required to balance that possessed by the Sino-Soviet bloc. The United States, or the Western coalition, might be rechristened the United Nations, but the change would be both literally and figuratively nominal. The UN is not a New World which can be called in to redress the balance of the old.

Might such a UN force be relevant to the problem of restraining minor aggressors? Possibly—but let us note again how little is really changed by the device of switching from national contingents to an international military organization. Assume that enlistments from major powers are forbidden, so that the question of the force's being internally subverted to the service of one or another of the major powers does not arise. Nevertheless, the critical political issues remain: Who will control the force? Against what state will it be used in a given situation? For what purpose will it fight? Toward what political result will it press? Neither great nor small powers will be indifferent to such issues, or be satisfied with the simple-minded answer that the UN will exercise policy direction and will use the force to achieve the purposes stipulated in the Charter. The retort to this answer is, of course, that the UN is owned and operated by states. Which states will control the UN policy organs that direct the force? The documentary purposes of the Charter are less important than the political purposes of the states which dominate the policy process. There is nothing in the nature of an international military force that makes its use a less contentious issue in a world of political conflict than the use of an assemblage of national units.

More generally, I think we must be on guard against the illusion that a UN fighting force would somehow enable us to escape from national states—from their quarrels and conflicting policies and purposes, from their power. As I have suggested, such a force would not be any less an instrument of states for being labeled an instrument of the UN, for states constitute the UN and their rivalries permeate the policy process of the organization. Moreover, a force which is sustained by the UN is in fact dependent upon states for its sustenance. This is true not only in the general sense that financial support of the UN and its various activities is derived predominantly from states, but also in the more specific sense that the supplies and equipment necessary for transforming a group of men into an effective military unit must come from states. We are back again to the problem of the power base. An army without a country generates no more military power than a country without an army. A UN armed force must be based upon thin air unless it is grounded in dependence upon the very states over which it is supposed to exercise independent authority. Whatever power a UN force might wield would be, in effect, borrowed national power. This is to say that the establishment of a UN force for countering aggression would not in any real sense represent the creation of an autonomous central authority, emancipated from dependence upon the support and cooperation of states and able to function coercively without regard to the policies and attitudes of states.

It might be argued that, given the new technology of warfare which enhances the significance of ready striking power, the problem of the power base has lost, or is losing, its importance. Thus, the UN might gain an impressive military status simply by acquiring a stock of missiles and nuclear warheads, without the necessity of developing the supportive foundations traditionally required by a military establishment. Leaving aside the question of the willingness of states to endow the UN with such a striking force, I think it is clear that this suggestion reflects an exaggerated notion as to the military significance of a finished and finite supply of weapons and delivery vehicles, divorced from the resources and facilities implicit in the concept of the power base. It relies upon a static conception of military force, at precisely the moment in history when military technology has become unprecedentedly dynamic, when the rate of obsolescence has been dramatically accelerated. The current arms race is not primarily a competition in quantitative accumulation, but in qualitative development of military means; national leaders are not intent upon expanding "over-kill" capacity, but upon keeping up or getting ahead in the quest for innovations that may alter the relative significance of existing weapons. In this setting, a static UN striking force, inherently vulnerable because of the impossibility of maintaining secrecy concerning its vital details, would soon become a negligible factor in the global political-military situation. The problem of keeping the UN force up to date, thus eliminating its tendency toward diminishing significance, brings us right back to the issue of the power base.

Moreover, the project of equipping the UN with a self-contained nuclear striking force involves imposing upon the organization all the difficulties and dilemmas associated with the doctrine of massive retaliation. It would be ironical if the United States escaped from the snares of reliance upon massive retaliation, only to saddle the UN with that strategic concept. It is hardly credible that such a political body as the UN would resort to thermonuclear attack whenever international aggression occurred or threatened—or desirable that it should do so. An international military establishment designed to maintain peace and security would require military versatility, the capacity for flexible and graduated response, to the same degree that a major national force requires it. To assert this is to deny that the problem of the power base can be circumvented by providing the UN with a stock of ready-made instruments of thermonuclear destruction, and to reaffirm the dependence of the UN upon its member states. A permanent UN military force for combating aggression is not a substitute for the willing collaboration of states, but simply one of the possible vehicles for such collaboration.

Thus far, my position regarding the possibilities of the use of military force by the UN has been essentially negative. I do not see the task of organizing an effective defense against Soviet aggression as one which can appropriately be assigned to the United Nations. This is a function of a coalition—and of institutions which comprise those states that are willing to associate themselves with the coalition and to contribute whatever they can to its strength. I am doubtful that there is a major role for the UN to play in mobilizing power— whether by pulling together national military contingents or by operating a permanent armed force under its direct authority —for the suppression of aggression outside the framework of the Cold War struggle. What then, if anything, is left as a military function for the UN?

We might find some clues in a perusal of the record of the organization. I think we can set aside the Korean case. Here, the UN endorsed and encouraged joint action against Communist aggression, and came to be clearly associated with one side in what was obviously a major episode of the East-West conflict. The initial enthusiasm for putting the UN into this kind of role, so sharply at variance with the original conception of the UN expressed in the Charter, quickly died away. By the end of the Korean War, the UN was being pushed— by the United States, among other members —into the position of a third party, disengaged from the conflict. It has been vigorously pulled in that direction in subsequent years, as its neutralist members have grown in numbers and matured in their understanding that their neutralism would be violated and endangered if they adhered to an international organization that entered— and brought them with it—into the vortex of Cold War disputes. Korea was an aberration, the expression of an ephemeral urge to make the UN an instrument of collective security in cases falling well within the scope of the Cold War. There is little sentiment among members of the organization for reviving this conception of the UN's function, and it is doubtful that the West can realistically expect or usefully attempt to bring about a development of the UN along these functional lines.

More promising clues are to be found in the string of cases which have involved the use of military personnel under UN auspices for purposes other than doing battle with aggressors—for supervising truces, patrolling borders or armistice lines, observing the degree to which rival parties respect agreed arrangements for stabilizing their relationships, and the like. These cases include UN interventions in the Palestine and Kashmir cases, in Lebanon, and—most notably—in the Suez and Congo crises. These are peace-stabilizing, or peace-keeping, or peace-restoring operations, efforts to aid disputant states in the implementation of political resolves to avoid the outbreak or the renewal of military conflict; they are not measures for the international defeat of determined acts of aggression. We may take UNEF and the military operation in the Congo as the outstanding instances of this sort of UN enterprise.

The late Secretary-General of the UN, Dag Hammarskjöld, functioned in this realm not only as a man of action but also as a man of thought. Having responded to critical needs and grasped opportunities for making the UN significantly useful in emergency situations, by creative improvisation of the UNEF and Congo forces, he turned to the articulation of a most perceptive theoretical analysis of the international political role which the UN had thus assumed. Hammarskjöld's classic statement of what he chose to call the concept of "preventive diplomacy" is contained in his Introduction to the Annual Report submitted to the Fifteenth Session of the General Assembly in 1960 (Hammarskjöld, 1960).

In this essay, the Secretary-General brushed aside the idea that the UN could usefully or safely intervene in "problems which are clearly and definitely within the orbit of present day conflicts between power blocs." The effort to put the UN effectively into such situations would, he feared, be not only futile but dangerous as well—dangerous to the continuing usefulness of the organization in general and of its chief officer in particular. From this, he drew the conclusion that "the main field of useful activity of the United Nations in its efforts to prevent conflicts or to solve conflicts" should be defined as that of taking action to fill vacuums in areas of conflict outside of, or marginal to, the zones already clearly involved in the Cold War struggle, so as to minimize the tendency of—or to diminish the incentive for—great powers to move competitively into those situations. Thus, he hoped that the organization might prevent the widening and aggravation of the bloc conflicts. In these terms, the major political potentiality of the UN is to promote the stabilization of the Cold War, to help the great powers avoid or back away from confrontations that might have disastrous results for themselves and all the rest of the world. It is evident that Hammarskjöld was not engaging in armchair theorizing, but was stating an interpretation of what the UN had been doing, and was doing, in the Middle East and the Congo, and was projecting this same role into the future.

Two points are crucial to the theory of preventive diplomacy:

1. The kind of operation which is envisaged, designed to seal off a zone of trouble from the competitive intrusions of the East and the West, is dependent upon the active or the passive consent of both the major contestants in the Cold War. Hammarskjöld acknowledged this—perhaps not quite explicitly—when he described the UN's role as that of "providing for solutions whenever the interests of all parties in a localization of conflict can be mobilized in favour of its efforts." He hoped that

the major powers would tolerate or even support UN ventures in preventive diplomacy because each would recognize its own interest in avoiding new confrontations that might disrupt their delicate relationships. The theory rests upon the assumption that conflict of interest breeds a limited community of interest, particularly in the thermonuclear era. Rival parties have a common interest in preventing their conflict from degenerating into uncontrollable violence. This common interest does not suggest that the conflict is unreal, or is not fundamental and deep-seated, or is diminishing in intensity. Quite to the contrary, it arises precisely because the conflict is a basic one; the community or mutuality of interest is a function of the intensity of the conflict of interest.

It is one thing to assert that the United States and the Soviet Union both *have* a stake in the avoidance of a military showdown, and thus in the encouragement of preventive diplomacy by the UN. It is another thing to assume that both great powers are *aware* of this common interest and prepared to act on the basis of that awareness. Putting Hammarskjöld's point negatively, we can say that the UN cannot hope to develop the function of preventive diplomacy successfully if the major powers do not share the conviction that their own interests would be served thereby. A UNEF or ONUC intervention is something that the UN can do *for* the great powers; it is not something that the UN can reliably do *against* the great powers, or either of them.

This immediately limits the field. It should be recalled that Hammarskjöld spoke of the possibilities of preventive diplomacy in areas *outside* of, or *marginal* to, the well-defined zones of the Cold War. He assumed, realistically, that neither of the major antagonists would look favorably upon UN intervention of the type under discussion within its own sphere of influence. Preventive diplomacy is applicable to the no-man's-land of the Cold War, the in-between area where both contestants may, on grounds of self-interest, give greater weight to the value of avoiding mutual confrontation than to the hope of winning a competitive encounter.

2. The function of preventive diplomacy is essentially *neutralist* in character. It does not involve neutral mediation in disputes and conflicts between the Cold War blocs —that is also an important political potentiality of the UN, but it falls under a different heading, and it calls for diplomatic or legal techniques rather than military or quasi-military instrumentalities. Rather, preventive diplomacy as such involves neutral interposition between contestants, using military personnel under UN direction as agents for achieving the neutralization of a trouble spot—i.e., for insulating the area against the intrusion of Cold War competition.

Preventive diplomacy is neutralist in method as well as design. It promises to fill a vacuum with forces contributed by relatively uncommitted states; note that the exclusion of military units from the major powers or the states most intimately aligned with them has been a cardinal principle in the constitution of UNEF and ONUC. Thus, it treats neutralist states as the members of the organization uniquely eligible for service as agents of the UN in the performance of its neutralizing function. Preventive diplomacy provides the relatively uncommitted states (I use the qualification in recognition that neutralism is never absolute) with an opportunity and a challenge to make their neutralism positive and constructive; it invites them to use their limited military forces, on behalf of the UN, to do something for the great powers that the latter could not do for themselves, and thereby to promote their own interest in the survival of civilization. Preventive diplomacy, in short, places the major active responsibility for the military function of the UN upon the smaller and less involved states. The great powers must *permit* the UN to play the neutral role; the states that stand most aloof from Cold War alignments must *enable* the UN to play that role.

It might be argued that the UN should develop, for the performance of this role, a standing international force, conceived as a continuously available UNEF, an instrument of preventive diplomacy rather than an army dedicated to the defeat of aggressors. Thus equipped, the organization would presumably be emancipated from dependence upon the uncertain willingness of neutralist states to provide units for exercises in preventive diplomacy. I am not convinced that such a development is either necessary or desirable. Thus far, the record indicates an impressive willingness on the part of the uncommitted states to do the jobs which preventive diplomacy requires of them. Moreover, there is substantial doubt that a standing international force would necessarily turn out to be the most appropriate or most acceptable instrument for dealing with particular cases that might arise; it may be that every case will be so distinctive as to require a tailor-made UN force. In practical terms, a permanent force might be inordinately expensive, given the budgetary realities of the UN. In any case, I suggest that the UN will be able to carry out successful operations of preventive diplomacy only if and when there is widespread willingness among its uncommitted members to undertake the military burden, and there is little point in attempting to evade the implications of this reality.

Up to this point, at least, the major difficulty has had to do not with the willingness of neutralist states to serve, but with the willingness of the great powers to be served. The problem of securing the necessary consent of the great antagonists is intimately connected with the issue of the neutral character of the UN in its practice of preventive diplomacy. The great powers will tolerate or support UN action in this realm only if they *want* the neutralization of a given trouble spot and if they *believe* in the neutral character of the UN's activity.

Let us look first at the question of the will of the great powers. In the major cases that have arisen—UNEF and ONUC—the United States has welcomed neutralization. The American stake in the avoidance of new confrontations that might disturb the Cold War situation has been amply recognized. Nevertheless, it is not at all clear that either our public or our government is prepared to accept the general proposition that the UN can best serve us—or the world—by operating as a neutral force in global politics. We have valued the UN primarily as an instrument whereby Western victories have been won—or, at least, as a stage upon which Western triumphs have been enacted—and it is not easy to shift to the view that its value to us may be increased as our control over its operations diminishes. Yet, the point stands that the United States has approved and supported the neutralizing function of the UN in the Middle East and Congo cases.

The attitude of the Soviet Union has been different. In the case of UNEF, Soviet disapproval has taken the mild form of passive opposition—refusal to contribute financial support. One might make a case that this is really passive acquiescence. The Congo, of course, makes a much more interesting story. Why did the Soviet Union, after initially supporting the Congo operation, turn against it? A plausible answer is that the USSR did not want the UN to achieve the neutralization of the Congo, but preferred to have a free hand in undertaking to achieve the Communization of the Congo. The Soviet Union supported the UN initiative in the hope that it would contribute to the de-Westernization of the Congo—notably by ousting the Belgians—and then moved to enter its own Soviet elements into the situation. This analysis would suggest that the Soviets did not want to avoid the intrusion of the Cold War competition into the Congo, but welcomed such a competition in the expectation that they would win.

The second problem is that of great-power confidence in the impartial character of the UN: can the organization be trusted to function neutrally in the no-man's-land of the Cold War? The experience of the United States presents no difficulties for us. With considerable reason, we have normally regarded the UN as a pro-Western institution; at worst, it has appeared to function, or to be likely to function, neutrally. Again, the Soviet case is quite different. Starting with a deep-rooted conviction that it confronts a hostile world, the Soviet Union has had a virtually unrelieved experience as a perpetual minority in the UN; from the Soviet vantage point, the UN might, at best—but most improbably—function with genuine impar-

tiality as between East and West. Note that the constant theme of the Soviet attack upon the conduct of the Congo operation is that ONUC is only spuriously neutral, that the whole affair represents the prostitution of the UN to the service of the Western powers. I am in no position to judge the sincerity of the Soviet assertions, although I must admit to some difficulty in believing that a Russian would not have serious doubts about the impartiality of the UN. We have not helped matters by our inveterate declarations that the UN does, and assertions that it should, serve the anti-Soviet cause—interspersed occasionally with appeals to the Soviets to recognize the "obvious" fact that the UN presides with majestic impartiality over the affairs of all the nations.

Indeed, the Soviets are not alone in interpreting the Congo operation as a move favorable to the West. Note what Ambassador Adlai Stevenson said in an address at Hofstra College on June 5, 1961:

The Belgian withdrawal was followed by anarchy with which on the one hand the Belgians stepped back and on the other the Russians began to step in. In these circumstances, any direct intervention by the West would have been interpreted as an attempt to reimpose colonialism. Local opinion would have swung over to support the Communists, and the West would have been left in the impossible position of fighting a guerrilla war against a background of implacable local hostility . . . direct Western interventions tend of their very nature to produce a revulsion of local feeling which threatens the effectiveness of the intervention. . . . The result is that in situations such as the Congo, the Western World would be almost powerless if there were no United Nations force available to restore order, [and] check a takeover by an outside power. . . . Direct Western action would only hasten a communist takeover.

Mr. Stevenson went on to say explicitly that the UN had frustrated the Soviet plan to establish control over the Congo, and that the UN is "the only instrument by which the end of the Western system of colonialism can be prevented from opening the doors to the new imperialism of the East" (Stevenson, 1961, p. 70).

I do not mean to be critical of the UN's

giving the West a victory which, according to Mr. Stevenson, the West could not have won for itself. My point is that if an official American spokesman can regard the UN's Congo operation as an intervention justified less by its helping both blocs to avoid the dangers of a confrontation than by its helping the West to contain the expansionist thrust of the Communist bloc, it is plausible that a Soviet spokesman should regard the operation as an instance of unneutral, pro-Western, UN activity. Moreover, if we regard the Congo action as a defeat inflicted by the UN upon the Soviet Union, it hardly makes sense for us to expect that the Soviets will refrain from opposing that action, or will help to pay for it, or will be inspired to assist in equipping the UN to act similarly in future contingencies.

The Congo operation has not yet been concluded, although it now appears likely to be brought to a successful conclusion. This possibility might be taken as an indication that preventive diplomacy can, after all, be effectively performed in the face of great-power opposition. Perhaps the Soviet attack upon the operation was never as determined as it was made to appear, or the Soviet hostility was mollified by the alterations of UN policy and personnel which occurred in the course of the operation. In any event, the Soviet Union refrained from carrying out the threat to wreck the organization because of its activity in the Congo. While the outcome of the Congo case may suggest the wisdom of testing the limits of Soviet toleration for operations of this kind, rather than surrendering to announced opposition, it ought not to simulate the confident assumption that the UN can be regularly used to carry out the function of preventive diplomacy, with or without the support or acquiescence of such a power as the Soviet Union. The extreme difficulties which the Soviet reaction against the Congo operation posed, and the grave risks which the UN encountered in conducting that operation under the political circumstances which developed, should be taken as a warning against adopting that assumption. Regardless of the outcome of the Congo case, it seems, on balance, to confirm the general proposition that the UN can effectively perform the quasi-military role attributed to it under the theory of preventive diplomacy only if, and insofar as, the major powers are impelled by their perceptions of their own interests to welcome UN interposition as a means of helping them to avoid dangerous confrontations, and are convinced that the UN can be relied upon to act in a neutral manner in the exercise of this function.

It appears that the only significant military function which may reasonably be attributed to the UN is that suggested by the theory of preventive diplomacy—the conduct of operations, analogous to UNEF and ONUC, designed to assist the great powers in keeping the Cold War cold. This can be done for the great powers only if they are agreed in wanting it to be done, and only if each of them is confident that the UN will genuinely promote the neutralization of trouble spots, not act in the interest of the other. The outlook for the continuation and development of this role by the UN is discouraging, primarily because of the disaffection of the USSR. If the Soviet Union is not persuaded that it has more to gain from the containment of the Cold War, the prevention of its spreading into new and dangerously explosive situations, than from the waging of the Cold War competition wherever it may spread—and if the Soviet Union is not persuaded that the UN is capable of serving with genuine neutrality as an agent of preventive diplomacy—then it seems to me that it is a major task of American policy, inside and outside of the UN, to promote these convictions on the part of the Soviet Union. If the United States and the Soviet Union can join in accepting and even in valuing the performance of this role by the UN, it seems to me that the organization may contribute significantly to the stabilization of the global situation. If they cannot, the UN may yet contribute valuable services in other realms, but I see no important role for it with respect to the use of military force under international auspices.

REFERENCES

Claude, Inis L., Jr. *Power and International Relations.* New York: Random House, 1962.

Hammarskjöld, Dag. Introduction to the Annual Report of the Secretary-General on the Work of the Organization, 16 June 1959–15 June 1960. General Assembly, Official Records: Fifteenth Session, Supplement No. 1A, United Nations, New York, 1960.

Kennedy, John F. "The State of the Union," *Department of State Bulletin,* 46 (1962), 159–63.

Rostow, Walt W. "The Domestic Base of Foreign Policy," *ibid.,* 46 (1962), 833–9.

Stevenson, Adlai E. "The United Nations, First Step Toward a World Under Law," *ibid.,* 45 (1961), 68–71.

GRADUATED UNILATERAL INITIATIVES FOR PEACE*

CHARLES E. OSGOOD

There are many paradoxes about the nuclear age in which we live. I shall delineate four of them which provide a framework for this paper.

PARADOX I. *The greater the destructive capacity of the weapons in our hands, the less concern most people seem to have about the problem.* I have heard it estimated that if all of the energy in weapons now stockpiled were to be transformed into its measuring unit—that is, every ten-megaton bomb into ten million tons of TNT and so forth—and then spread evenly over the area of our country, we would be wading around in TNT well above our ankles! Be that as it may, it is certainly true that never before in human history have so few been able to destroy so many and so much in so short a time. Yet how many intellectuals have fully committed themselves to working on this problem? How much attention have our mass media given to the search for fresh alternatives? How much success have we had in disarmament negotiations?

PARADOX II. *While feverishly engaged in a nuclear arms race, all sides express peaceful intentions and fervent hopes that these weapons never will be used.* I believe these hopes and intentions are sincere, yet roughly half the national budgets of the two polar powers go into military preparations. Surely, future generations will look back upon these years as the Age of Unreason.

PARADOX III. *The more nations spend for what they call "defense," the less real security they seem to have.* The basic reason for this is that, in terms of military technology, offensive capability has far outstripped defensive capability. Policy-makers are fond of talking about great defensive "shields"

or "umbrellas," but these defenses are more in men's minds than in their weapons.

PARADOX IV. *The greater a nation's military power, the less rather than greater seems to be its freedom of initiative in foreign policy.* Witness the squashing of the Suez situation, the attempts on all sides to neutralize Laos, or the actions of the United States with respect to little Cuba. Quite apart from fears of retaliation, the mere possession of nuclear weapons has a sobering, restraining effect. For rational men, at least, possession of power brings with it a sense of responsibility. And so we find the nuclear age characterized by a Great Freeze on initiative along traditional lines.

If a psychologist or psychiatrist were faced with an individual human being so full of irrational paradoxes in his thinking, he would probably recommend that he be institutionalized. Unfortunately, there are no institutions for nations. However, the psychologist or psychiatrist would also realize that this individual's behavior seems paradoxical only because the dynamics of his case are not understood. Therefore *the first purpose of this paper will be to explore the dynamics of the cold war mentality.* We will be looking for psychological sources of the sense of inevitability which most people feel about war and which blocks serious consideration of other alternatives.

But, you may object, the fact is that we are concerned with the behavior of nations, not individuals, so of what relevance is a psychological analysis? By way of answer I would say, first, that the problems we face are primarily matters of human nature and human relationships; there is nothing about nuclear science that automatically produces bombs and nothing about space science that automatically produces missiles; it takes human decisions based upon human fears and aggressions to produce these things.

* Reprinted by permission of the author and publisher from Wright, Q., *et al.* (Editors), *Preventing World War III* (New York: Simon and Schuster, 1962), 161–177.

Second, I would say that, in the absence of any real science of international relations, what we do know about the principles of individual behavior may provide a model and at least a set of hypotheses about the behavior of nations. And finally I would point out that the extraordinary development of the media of mass communication during this century has done much to bridge the gap between publics and elites. The greater the communality of stimuli, the greater the communality of responses.

This poses the second problem for this paper. Novel situations usually demand novel solutions. As the paradoxes of our time indicate, we certainly face a novel situation today. Yet relations among nations are still being governed by traditional policies that are felt to be realistic primarily because they are habitual. Recent technological developments in communications, transportation, and other forms of human interdependence—to say nothing of weaponry—have not merely made some kind of world government feasible, they have made it essential if our civilization is to survive. But the problem is to get from here to there, to somehow bridge the great cultural lag between our technology and our form of political organization. We find ourselves at the crest of nationalism at a time when our technology requires one world under common law. *The second purpose of this paper will be to suggest a kind of international behavior, based on behavioral science considerations, that may be more appropriate to this nuclear age.* But first we must look into some of the dynamics of the cold war mentality.

Dynamics of the Cold War Mentality

Denial. When faced with overwhelming danger, but having no acceptable way of handling it, the typical human reaction is to deny its existence, that is, repress it. This mechanism underlies public apathy about civilian defense. It leads people to avoid exposing themselves to information which revives the danger and to seek out information which promises security, however illusory. Once unconscious acceptance of the danger has been repressed, the unconscious

anxiety is free to produce symptoms. A typical symptom is what Edgar Allan Poe has called "the Imp of the Perverse." This is the irrational compulsion to flirt with the threatening situation—to play with fire, to lean out over the edge of a cliff, or to press that critical button. The more one denies the seriousness of the danger intellectually, the less the restraint on the compulsion. The way out of this dilemma is to have some acceptable solution which will channel the fear into constructive action. One of the troubles with pacifist approaches to this problem has been that they frighten the living daylights out of people with threats of nuclear fire and brimstone without providing any acceptable solution—acceptable, that is, under present conditions of competing national sovereignties.

The meaninglessness of abstract terms. Most of the words we use to talk about nuclear war are abstract terms that get their meanings indirectly through association with other words rather than directly through association with real objects and events. Words like "intercontinental ballistic missiles," "megatons," and "thirty million casualties" just simply do not have the emotional, gut meanings of words like "blood," "bread," and "mother." Furthermore, one cannot directly sense the potential danger of a nuclear missile five thousand miles away as he can the danger in a man seen holding a gun or knife; we require special gadgets to tell us that we are exposed to even lethal doses of radiation, and it takes a truly magnificent feat of imagination to comprehend the significance of "thirty million casualties." I am told that most Russians seem more concerned about the dangers of a "hot" nuclear war than most Americans. Perhaps it is because they have lost many millions under conditions of ordinary war well within the memory of present adults.

Psycho-logic. Over the past two decades a great deal of social psychological research has been converging on a conclusion about human thinking that common sense had already isolated as "the consistency of little minds." Whenever cognitively inconsistent elements are brought together in assertions, stress toward mental consistency is produced; psycho-logic resolves this stress along the lines of least resistance, in such a way as to retain the simplest possible cognitive structure. Thus if Our Revered Leader praises some obscure diplomat, it is cognitively consistent for us to feel more favorably inclined toward this man ourselves; but if The Enemy says this same diplomat's ideas are sound, we find ourselves suspecting him.

Psycho-logic is the lowest common denominator of human thinking. It contributes to the oversimplified "two-valued orientation" stressed by the general semanticists. It runs rampant into the area of international relations, where the usual corrective process of reality-testing is difficult to apply, and it forces all shades of gray toward absolute blacks and whites. Psycho-logic has made bogeymen of the opponents in every human conflict: If WE are *good, kind, fair,* and so on—as most of us are in everyday relationships—then psycho-logic dictates that THEY (the enemy) must be equally *bad, cruel, unfair,* and so on throughout the opposites of all traits we attribute to ourselves.

Once this fundamental evaluative polarity has been established, psycho-logic operates subtly but continuously on the interpretation of all subsequent incoming information. One effect is to push both sides in a conflict down opposite paths of *self-delusion.* Observe the alacrity and near-universality with which American media people jumped on the "Blame It All on Khrushchev" bandwagon even before the dust of the Paris Summit fiasco had settled—at the expense of some healthy self-criticism. Another effect is the setting up of *double standards of national morality.* Exactly the same behavior is moral if the WEs do it but immoral if the THEYs do it. Why? Because different motives are attributed to WE and to THEY in keeping with psycho-logic. Witness the debate in the United Nations over the U-2 spy-plane incident: Americans, knowing themselves to be peaceful in intent but being afraid of treacherous surprise attack, viewed this as a legitimate defensive operation; Russians, knowing themselves to be peace-loving, not treach-

erous, but suspecting treachery from the other side, viewed this as an illegitimate aggressive operation.

Many American travelers to Russia, including statesmen, scientists, and scholars, have been impressed by the "mirror image" of their own attitudes they find there. I have no information about it, but I strongly suspect that the same observation has been made by Russians visiting the United States. Each group blames the other for the mutually aggressive relation. Each sees the other as untrustworthy and not sincerely desirous of peace; each sees the other as warlike, but itself as peace-loving. If—as is certainly true—each can recognize the falsity of the other's image of him, can he not admit the probability of bias in his own image of the other? The mutual bogeyman images certainly can be cut down to more realistic size and shape. By so doing, we open the doors to mutually acceptable alternatives; by taking the bogeyman images at their face value, we close the doors to anything other than mutual annihilation.

The relativity of human judgment. "Man is the measure of all things," it has been said—but surely this is true only to the extent that his science is primitive. One can trace in the development of science a progressive freeing of man's measurements from the arbitrary platform of his own senses. Social judgments are also made relative to one's own position as observer. What a person perceives as "neutral" or "normal" on any dimension of judgment depends upon the particular range of relevant objects or events to which he happens to have been exposed. These norms, taken together, constitute his "frame of reference" for judging subsequent objects and events. Consistent shifts in the range of stimuli produce a gradual drift in one's norms. Stimuli which deviate only slightly from a norm tend to assimilate with it, and real differences are minimized; stimuli which deviate a great deal produce a contrast effect, and real differences are exaggerated.

We are seldom aware of our own norms. They are projected outward as the natural design of the universe. When Ego unconsciously assumes that Alter shares his frame of reference, it is natural for him to think of Alter as somehow dishonest, evil, or at least abnormal in some way when he calls "straight" what to Ego is obviously crooked and calls "tasty" what to Ego is obviously distasteful. It is a quite sophisticated Ego who recognizes the relativity of Alter's frame of reference; this produces a more humane approach, a "forgive *them* for they know not what they do" kind of attitude. But it is the unusually sophisticated—or civilized, if you will—Ego who realizes the equally relativistic nature of his own norms, who will accept his own judgments on the tasty-distasteful or even moral-immoral scales as being as arbitrary as those of the Mexican or Hindu. Social relativity does *not* mean that there are no external criteria for distinguishing good from evil; quite the reverse, it means that we must search for dependable external criteria just because social judgments are so liable to bias.

To fully appreciate the arbitrariness of one's own norms it helps to get outside the pervasive frame of reference provided by one's own culture, including its mass media. Foreign travel is a great help, particularly if you can escape from the protective "bubble" of your own culture. During the past few years I have spent considerable time outside the United States, in connection with some cross-cultural research on the generality of meaning systems. I read foreign newspapers as avidly as my linguistic talents would permit me, and I found them full of refreshing heresy—at least as far as East-West relations were concerned—to the extent that I was moved to wish with Robert Burns:

> O wad some Pow'r the giftie gi'e us
> To see oursels as ithers see us!

The admonition of many religious teachers to "Know Thyself" seems *a propos* here; only to the extent that we understand the dynamics of our own minds can we hope to understand others.

Possibilistic decision-making. The tendency to make decisions in terms of mere possibilities rather than in terms of estimated probabilities is seen most clearly in paranoid schizophrenics, but it also colors the judgments of normal people under stress. The fact that there is a general cor-

relation between what people wish (or fear) would happen and how strongly they believe it actually will happen is well known to psychologists—but I think I should also mention, somewhat ruefully, that in one study this correlation turned out to be highest for professional gamblers and social scientists! If the paranoid knows it is *possible* that his doctor belongs to the secret society that is persecuting him, he leaps to the conclusion that he *does* belong and acts accordingly. Similarly in the international arena, if the WEs know that the THEYs *could* be cheating, lying, or planning a surprise attack, it is easy for the WEs to conclude that the THEYs *are* doing these immoral things—and then, driven by psycho-logic, the WEs are liable to do the same immoral things *first* in order to protect themselves, firmly proclaiming their motives benign.

Cognitive stereotypy. The basic psychological notion here is that, beyond some optimal level, increasing emotion serves not only to further energize the organism but also to reduce its capacity to select among alternatives. The multiplicative relation between drive and habit strength means that the most probable responses become even more so relatively while the less probable become even less so. Since the behavioral system seems to be organized throughout in hierarchies of alternatives, heightened motivation or emotion serves to produce stereotypy in perceiving, in associating, and in interpreting as well as in overt behavior.

One effect of drive-produced stereotypy is that it *reduces capacity to solve problems.* Problem situations are more or less defined by the fact that the dominant, habitual responses don't work—if they did, there obviously wouldn't be any problem. The raccoon is a pretty intelligent little animal; in a situation where it must discover which of several doors to food is open, it will flexibly try one after the other; but if we then put it under a stinging shower it will persistently bang its head against a locked door that *used to be open,* completely ignoring free passageways to left and right. In analogous fashion, nations today are lumbering down the one habitual path to "security"—bigger and better weapons—gathering as they go tensions which make it less and less possible to conceive of any other alternatives. Being the habitual response to external threat, this course is felt to be "realistic." Unfortunately, anthropologists are familiar with cultures that, through blind adherence to practices that once were realistic, have gradually committed suicide. I think that we are in exactly the same spot: We are continuing to practice rites and rituals of international relations that were developed in and appropriate to the past—firmly believing them to be realistic—in a nuclear present that renders them suicidal.

Another effect of heightened motivation is *foreshortening of perspective*. In general, as we trace the course of evolution and particularly the development of the cortex, we find higher species capable of maintaining longer delays, employing more extended foresight, and striving for more remote goals. But emotion has the effect of primitivizing this capacity. The motivational conditions of controversy, e.g., our present tensions/arms-race dilemma, are precisely those designed to restrict perspective. Thus we find that the truly magnificent achievements of human science—achievements that soon may free us from earthly bondage and catapult us toward the stars—seem to have significance only within the petty framework of the cold war; the only question we ask is, who's ahead? We seem fixated on the immediate goal of passing our opponent in total military power—without asking whether being able to annihilate an enemy ten or a hundred times over deters him much more than being able to annihilate him just once. And no one in the mad scramble pauses to even consider the obvious next question: *when and how does this end?* Surely a policy of nuclear deterrence that, at best, can offer us nothing more than a world continually poised for mutual destruction, held together by nothing more than fragile psychological needs of mutual fear, must not be the last word.

Arms Control and Tension Control

The combination of nationalism, cold-war thinking, and the paradoxes of the nuclear age—particularly the imbalance between offensive and defensive capabilities—is forcing nations inexorably toward the policy of mutual nuclear deterrence. This combination of factors has simultaneously been forcing policy-makers toward serious consideration of the stability of such deterrence. Just because we have a phrase, "stabilized deterrence," which seems to imply that there must be some solid, protective technological system, does not mean that such a referent really exists.

Deterrence is more a psychological question than a technological answer. An opponent is assumed to be deterred from initiating a nuclear attack by his expectation of unacceptable retaliation. But if the opponent is not deterred, if he makes a wrong decision—whether due to fear, to overconfidence, to misinformation, or even to some accident—then the invulnerability of one's retaliatory capacity and the certainty of its delivery does nothing whatsoever to defend one's own civilian population. This is why discussions of stabilized deterrence inevitably involve matters like the "credibility" of retaliation and the "rationality" of human decisions, which are also psychological problems. So let us now confront some of the assumptions of stabilized deterrence with some of the facts of human decision-making under stress that we have just been analyzing.

The credibility of deterrence assumes full appreciation of the dangers of nuclear war on all sides; but the mechanism of denial, the perverse attractiveness of denied dangers, and the essential meaninglessness of the words with which we talk about it all prevent such full appreciation. Stability of deterrence assumes objective evaluation of the intentions of an opponent and objective interpretation of world events; but both psycho-logic and the relativity of social judgment hinder such objectivity and transform the complexities of international relations into an over-simplified contest between the Good Guys and the Bad Guys. Stability requires that decisions be based on accurate determination of probabilities rather than emotional reaction to mere possibilities; but the wishful-fearful thinking characteristic of schizophrenics also affects the decisions of normals under stress, and they become prone to deciding in terms of their wishes (over-confidence) or their fears (underconfidence). Maintaining stable deterrence in a world where situations change with bewildering speed and complexity demands great flexibility of means yet consistency of ends; but cognitive stereotypy both restricts the range of alternatives and shortens perspective, substituting blind reactions to immediate pressures for long-range persistence toward ultimate goals.

It is true that men can be rational, and often are, but it is also true that they can be nonrational, and these are merely some of the mechanisms of nonrationality. These are some of the ways in which humans reach decisions without the benefit of logic and without even maximizing their own self-interest in the game-theoretic sense, and yet these ways of thinking are lawful in that they conform to and are predictable from the principles of human behavior. In a situation where the consequences of wrong decisions are so awesome, where a single bit of irrationality can set a whole chain of traumatic events in motion, I do not think that we can be satisfied with the assurance that "most people behave rationally most of the time."

What are the conditions that strengthen and exaggerate these nonrational mechanisms in human decision-making? What conditions make normal people appear irrational? And we must add, what conditions make truly irrational people appear normal, because under analysis it seems that the same conditions which make normals seem irrational make irrationals seem normal: To a population driven into nonrationality, a fanatic may seem not only normal but ideal. There are two general sets of conditions that magnify nonrationality: The first concerns *information*—its availability, bias, and overload in the human decision system; the second, and the one I wish to emphasize here, is *tension-level*.

We have already seen that, beyond some optimal level, further increases in tension serve to restrict the range of perceived alternatives, thereby limiting the flexibility and creativity of human problem-solving. It is also certainly true that increases in tension, beyond some optimal level, serve to magnify the ratio of nonrational to rational alternatives. Under stress men are more

likely to act irrationally, to strike out blindly or even to freeze into stupid immobility. In other words, both flexibility and rationality "ride on the back" of tension-level.

World events may have either a tension-increasing or a tension-decreasing impact upon the international system. *The real stability of the system depends upon its capacity to absorb such event-shocks, and this in turn depends upon the absolute level of tension*. If the system is at a relatively low level of tension, it can absorb a succession of event-shocks, such as a revolution in Latin America, the demonstration of a new weapon, or the accidental explosion of an old one, without being moved far from an optimum level of flexibility and rationality. But if the system is already functioning at a relatively high level of tension, then the same set of event-shocks may push it over into the region of rigidity and irrationality.

It is important to realize that while tension cumulates across various sources, its effect upon flexibility and rationality is independent of source. Equally important for the remainder of my argument is the fact that reduction in tension-level is independent of its sources. In other words, tension is something like money in a bank account; its amount can be increased by "deposits" from a variety of sources and decreased by "withdrawals" for a variety of uses.

If my analysis of the relation between what is called "stability of the military environment" and tension-level is valid, then it puts a premium on the development and application of *techniques of tension control*. Stability is a dynamic concept, not a static one, and we need to create and maintain a dynamic, shock-absorbing "cushion" for the international system. But tension control cannot be entirely a unilateral affair, so we must look for techniques which are likely to induce reciprocation.

The traditional, if seldom successful, method of reducing international tensions is through mutual-disarmament negotiations. We have behind us a long and dismal history of unsuccessful negotiations. It is perhaps another paradox that the greater the need for negotiated agreements, the more difficult they are to obtain. It is easy for each side to blame these failures on the intractability and insincerity of the other, but the same mechanisms operate on both sides. One is what I call *biased perception of the equable:* Given their quite different national life-histories, both sides approach negotiations with different sets of meanings; "inspection" means espionage for one but elimination of secrecy for the other, "The United Nations" means a biased tool to one but an unbiased international body to the other, "overseas bases" mean aggressive intent to one but defensive intent to the other, and so on. Another mechanism is *the self-fulfilling prophecy:* Prior to any negotiation, the press on each side predicts that the other is insincere and merely using the discussions for propaganda purposes; each side then behaves in such a way as to counteract what it expects of the other; nothing is accomplished, and both sides go away saying, "I told you so!" And then there is the plain, ordinary matter of *mutual distrust:* Under the impetus of psychologic, each side expects the other to cheat, and one even hears it said that treaties with THEM are not worth the paper they're written on.

The conclusion we seem driven to is this: *Negotiated agreements require commitment prior to action, and under the conditions of the cold war mentality commitments of any significance are difficult to obtain; thus neither side is able to take the initiative as long as it remains chained to the requirement of prior commitment by the other.* Clearly, some other approach is needed if we are ever to break out of this impasse.

Initiative Through Unilateral Action

In the remainder of this paper I would like to explore with you the possibilities that may lie in unilateral action of a particular type. For several years I have been trying to develop and justify an approach to international relations which I call *Graduated Reciprocation in Tension-Reduction.* The essence of the idea is that the tensions/arms-race spiral may provide the model for its own reversal. As a type of

international behavior, *the arms race is a case of graduated and reciprocated unilateral action.* It is unilateral in that the nation developing a new weapon, increasing its stockpile, or setting up a new military base does not make its action contingent upon any prior agreement with the other side. It is reciprocal, however, because each increment in military power by one side provides the stimulus for the other to try to catch up and get ahead. It is necessarily graduated, first by the irregular and somewhat unpredictable occurrences of technological break-through and second by the oscillating nature of the threat stimulus itself.

But the arms race is obviously a *tension-increasing* system. One can readily conceive of a graduated and reciprocated, unilaterally initiated system that is *tension-reducing* in nature. The question is whether or not it is feasible under present conditions. I will try to demonstrate that, given anything like the dedication and energy now being thrown into the arms race, it would be feasible, even though by no means magically simple.

This approach must be sharply distinguished from the kind of abject and complete unilateral disarmament sponsored by pacifist groups. To the contrary, what I am proposing is a flexible, self-regulating procedure in which the participants continually monitor their own actions on the basis of their evaluation of the reciprocating actions taken by the other side. It involves some risk, to be sure, but the risk is limited; merely going on doing what we are now doing involves infinitely greater risk! It is broader than disarmament, or even disengagement as usually conceived, since it would include programs of graduated unilateral actions of a tension-reducing nature in the areas of science and secrecy, social, economic, and cultural exchange, Communist China and the United Nations, controls and inspection, and so forth, as well as actual military and disarmament steps. It may be viewed as a kind of international (rather than interpersonal) communicating and learning situation, where the communication is more by deeds than by words and where what is learned is mutual understanding and trust.

However, being both unconventional and conciliatory in nature, this procedure is liable to suspicion abroad and resistance at home, particularly under conditions of the cold war mentality. Therefore it needs to be spelled out in detail, critically evaluated, and even tried out under both laboratory and field conditions. Specifically, it is necessary to indicate the characteristics that unilateral actions in such a program should have in order to maintain adequate felt security while nevertheless inducing reciprocation from an opponent; furthermore, we need to clarify the criteria for both determining the substance of unilateral initiatives and evaluating the bonafideness and significance of unilateral reciprocations. In other words, while admittedly idealistic in purpose, this rather novel approach must be shown to be realistic and feasible within the existing situation of competing sovereign states.

In the following analysis I will be speaking from the viewpoint of a nation which initiates such a policy of graduated reciprocation in tension-reduction. This is necessary to maintain a consistent orientation. But I want it understood that I have no particular nation in mind as the initiator—it could be either of the two polar nuclear powers, the United States or the USSR, or it could very well be some other nation or group of nations, present or future. Furthermore, just as with an arms race, once this kind of international behavior were underway, the distinction between initiation and reciprocation would become as meaningless as the distinction between stimulus and response within the central nervous system.

Maintaining Security

1. *Unilateral actions should not reduce a nation's capacity to inflict unacceptable nuclear retaliation on an opponent should it be attacked.* I would be the first to agree that nuclear deterrence does not provide any real security over the long haul, but on the other hand, highly invulnerable second-strike forces will exist in the near future, if not already, and under present levels of tension they are not likely to be given up. Particularly if their retaliatory nature is made explicit, and moral prohibition against their first use is accepted by all sides, nuclear weapons can be viewed not only as a deterrent *but also as a security base from which limited risks can be taken.* I am assuming that since there is no necessary correlation between the tension-reducing impacts of actions and their military significance, a program of graduated reciprocation in tension-reduction could produce an atmosphere of mutual trust in which the nuclear deterrents themselves could ultimately be eliminated by negotiated agreement.

2. *Unilateral actions should be graduated in risk potential according to the degree of reciprocation obtained.* This is the essential self-regulating characteristic of the proposal. The magnitude of a unilateral step taken at a particular time would depend upon that nation's evaluation of the reciprocative behavior of the other. The process can be slowed down or speeded up, as conditions require, but it should be kept going.

3. *Unilateral actions should be diversified in nature so as not to weaken a nation progressively in any one sphere.* Diversity in areas of action both provides an essential flexibility of approach and prevents the unstabilizing effect of too large steps in a single sphere. The only common property of the actions envisaged in this proposal is their tension-reducing nature. This, as I pointed out earlier, can be cumulative over a highly diversified range of actions, e.g., student exchanges, sharing of scientific information, reducing trade barriers, diplomatic recognition, elimination of bases, and so on.

4. *Prior to announcement, unilateral actions should be unpredictable by an opponent as to their nature, locus, and time of execution.* This is to minimize the likelihood of encroachment. I submit that, psychologically, an opponent is much less likely to encroach aggressively in an area after public announcement of intent by another than prior to it, and he is certainly less likely to gain world support if he does.

However, if encroachments do occur they must be resisted just as firmly as if this policy were not in operation. Yet, this resistance should be pinpointed to the area of encroachment and the program of tension-reducing moves continued flexibly in other areas. This is clearly a different approach than the traditional, monolithic reaction of nations to tension-increasing events, but it is an approach that seems necessary in a nuclear age. Under conditions of nuclear deterrence, encroachments are likely to be tentative and probing in nature, and therefore can constitute a learning experience on all sides—learning that graduated reciprocation in reducing tensions is not synonymous with surrender.

Inducing Reciprocation

1. *Unilateral actions should be announced publicly at some reasonable interval prior to their execution and identified as part of a deliberate policy of reducing tensions.* Announcement prior to action is suggested as a means of augmenting pressure toward reciprocation, of avoiding the unstabilizing effect of unexpected moves, of providing time for preparing reciprocation, and, particularly, of influencing the interpretation of the action when it comes. Public announcement makes it possible to enlist pressures of world opinion toward reciprocation, and identification of each act as part of a deliberate policy is designed to make the pressures toward reciprocation cumulative.

2. *In their announcement, unilateral actions should include explicit invitation to reciprocation in some form.* Initiation and reciprocation need not be the same in kind nor even equal in quantity. There are some unilateral actions that could not be reciprocated in kind (e.g., if the United States were to denuclearize some Pacific base, the Chinese Communists could not reciprocate in kind) and the burden of the same rule may be quite different in two countries (e.g., absolute amounts of inspection permitted). On the other hand, the fact that reciprocation in some form is expected must be made explicit. The isolated unilateral gestures that have occasionally been made in the past have been largely abor-

tive, in part because they did not call for reciprocation.

3. *Unilateral actions that have been announced must be executed on schedule regardless of prior commitment by the opponent to reciprocate.* This is the characteristic that distinguishes this policy from traditional bargaining and negotiating procedures; it is the characteristic that provides an increased degree of freedom on all sides for taking the initiative. Of course, if no reciprocation is forthcoming, or attempts are made to take advantage of the initiator, then the process slows down or stops. In this sense, reciprocation can be viewed as a kind of postcommitment that enables the policy to continue.

4. *Unilateral actions should be planned in graded series and continued over a considerable period regardless of immediate reciprocation or police action elsewhere.* Given the tense atmosphere in which such a strategy must begin, it is likely that initial actions would be greeted by cries of "cold war trick!"; but the bonafideness of the intent becomes more and more difficult to deny and rationalize as action follows announced action. Furthermore, the pressure toward reciprocation should cumulate over such a period of continued action. Here again we have a kind of international learning situation—in this case, unlearning the bogeyman image of the opponent, since the psycho-logic expectations and prophesies being made about him are being repeatedly denied.

5. *As far as possible, unilateral actions should be overt deeds rather than either positive or negative sanctions and should be as unambiguous and as susceptible to verification as possible.* Overt acts have the obvious advantage of bonafideness, particularly if the announced action includes invitation to observe and inspect. Sanctions, on the other hand, have no visible execution or test until their failure—the unilaterally imposed bans on nuclear testing are a case in point. This emphasizes another difference between this kind of policy and ordinary negotiations, a difference well expressed by the homely saying, "actions speak louder than words."

What about the problem of *evaluating*

reciprocations (and, for that matter, the problem an opponent has in evaluating one's unilateral initiations)? There are two rather different questions here: One concerns the bonafideness of actions, which seems to come down to the adequacy of intelligence in the military sense; the other concerns the significance of actions, and this seems to be a matter for strategic analysis. To enhance *bonafideness,* both the initiator's unilateral acts and the reciprocations requested should be as unambiguous and susceptible to verification as possible; provisions for adequate inspection may be included in both initiations and requested reciprocations. As a matter of fact, it might be possible to get around the apparent deadlock on inspection by introducing it in small, manageable and perhaps palatable packages under such a program as this; if one side accepts an invitation to unilaterally inspect some specific action of the other, it becomes psychologically difficult to deny him the same privilege. As to the *significance* of reciprocations, two criteria would have to be kept in mind: first, that the risk potential in the unilateral actions by one party should be roughly balanced by the increased security gained through the reciprocations of the other party; second, that tension-decreasing steps in one area must be balanced against the total level of tension-increasing and tension-decreasing events in all areas. I realize that these estimations are not easy, but they involve the sort of strategic analysis that is going on all the time anyhow.

Finally, there are some additional criteria for selecting actions that should be mentioned. First, it is probably wisest to begin such a program with actions in areas other than the critical military and disarmament spheres, moving in toward these matters only when the general level of tension has been sufficiently reduced. Second, particularly in the early phases, unilateral initiatives should involve areas in which both parties in the conflict are known to be ready to move, in which restraints may already have been reciprocally self-imposed, and in which both are likely to see issues of human welfare rather than national security. Again, we have here a kind of learn-

ing situation on all sides, and it is important that the probabilities of reinforcement be high at first. And since we would wish the substance of our actions to be consistent with our long-term goals as well as our immediate needs to control tensions, they should be designed to gradually shape the world of tomorrow; therefore, unilateral initiatives and reciprocations should involve gradual transfer of sovereignty from national to international auspices, gradual lessening of the imbalance between "have" and "have not" countries, and gradual shifting of scientific research onto an international basis on the model of the IGY, particularly research having military implications where scientific breakthroughs have an unstabilizing impact.

Despite the unilateral initiative which characterizes this proposal, it should be apparent that the two parties in conflict are really dependent on each other for its success. This is because on each side there are competing factions spread over the spectrum of policy alternatives. If President Kennedy, exercising administrative initiative, were to announce and execute a carefully planned series of tension-reducing moves, opposition groups in the United States government, in its mass media, and in its public would become increasingly critical. The only way to quiet this opposition and keep the policy moving, in the long run, would be to receive reciprocation from the opponent. I am sure that much the same situation would hold in the case of Soviet initiation. Now it is true that the leadership of a nation would be risking its position by initiating such a policy and that an opponent might assist in the demise by withholding reciprocation—*but in doing so the opponent should be fully aware of the fact that he is strengthening forces more violently antagonistic to him and more likely to act inflexibly and irrationally in future relations.* Thus it would be to the advantage of both sides to be on the alert for tension-reducing probes from the other and to be prepared for reciprocations that will allow the process to continue.

Could the initiator of such a policy expect to obtain bonafide and significant reciprocation under present conditions? I cannot give an unqualified "yes" to this question. Here, obviously, lies the risk—but as I pointed out earlier, merely going on as we are involves even greater risk. And surely it would be cause for cosmic irony if two human groups in conflict were to bring their world down in destruction because of their threatening images of each other without ever testing the validity of these images. Despite the differences between us, there are many things we share; we share common modes of thinking and feeling, we share a common technology that is rapidly transforming us into one world whether we like it or not, and above all we share a common desire to get out of this dangerous situation and go on living. If my basic assumption about the contemporary motivation of international behavior is right—that it is based more on fear and insecurity than on any urge toward national aggrandizement —then I think reciprocation would be forthcoming, if not for reasons of good will then for reasons of good sense. And here another psychological principle applies: If two people are forced to keep on behaving *as if* they trusted each other, their beliefs and attitudes tend to fall in line with their behaviors. I think the same applies to nations.

Conclusion

The preservation of peace is the biggest problem of our time, and I have no illusions about my own capacity to comprehend it all. Although the problem has important psychological components, much more than psychology is involved—political science, economics, international law, communications, nuclear and space technology, diplomacy, and the military, to call only part of the roll. And no one as aware as I am of the strength of the contrary forces, of the deeply ingrained mechanisms of the cold war mentality, could be very sanguine about our chances of escaping from this situation unscathed.

On the other hand, I have convinced myself, at least, that such a policy of graduated reciprocation in tension control is feasible for our time. True, it would require extraordinary sensitivity, flexibility, and restraint from leadership on all sides, as well as high-level strategic planning and execution, but this could be viewed as a challenge rather than a flaw. If it were successfully initiated, such a policy could, over the short term, increase the stability of the military environment and perhaps create an atmosphere in which more significant steps toward disarmament could be taken; over the long term, it might offer a model for international relations that is more appropriate to this age of nuclear technology. I can do no better than close with a quotation from Albert Einstein that might have been written today: "The unleashed power of the atom has changed everything except our ways of thinking. Thus we are drifting toward a catastrophe beyond comparison. We shall require a substantially new manner of thinking if mankind is to survive."

THE CASE FOR UNILATERAL DISARMAMENT*

ERICH FROMM

There is little doubt that the proposal for a unilateral disarmament—in the broad sense of the unconditional dismantling of a country's military establishment—will be acceptable neither to the United States nor to the Soviet Union in the immediate future. Hence, inasmuch as this paper is concerned with *practical* suggestions for arms control, it proposes another and very limited concept of unilateral disarmament, one which has been called by Charles Osgood *"graduated unilateral action (or disengagement)"* or which might be called *unilateral initiative in taking practical steps toward disarmament.* The basic idea underlying this concept is that of a radical change of our method of negotiating multilateral disarmament. This change implies that we give up the present method of bargaining in which every concession we make is dependent on a corresponding and guaranteed concession on the part of the Russians; that, instead, we take, unilaterally, gradual steps toward disarmament in the expectation that the Russians will reciprocate and that, thus, the present deadlock in the negotiations for universal disarmament can be broken through.

In order to describe the nature of this policy of unilateral steps, I cannot improve on the following description by Osgood, who as far as I know was the first one to express this idea, in two brilliant and profound articles.[1] "To be maximally effective," he writes, "in inducing the enemy to reciprocate, a unilateral act (1) should, in terms of *military aggression,* be clearly disadvantageous to the side making it, yet not cripplingly so; (2) should be such as to be clearly perceived by the enemy as reducing his external threat; (3) should not increase the enemy's threat to our heartland;[2] (4) should be such that reciprocal action by the enemy is clearly available and clearly indicated; (5) should be announced in advance and widely publicized to ally, neutral, and enemy countries—as regards the nature of the act, its purpose as part of a consistent policy, and the expected reciprocation; but (6) should not demand prior commitment to reciprocation by the enemy as a condition for its commission."[3]

As to the specific steps which should be taken in this fashion, it would require a great deal of further thought, aided by competent specialists. But in order to give at least an idea of the concrete steps this policy would envisage, I want to mention the following (some of them in agreement with Osgood): sharing of scientific information; stopping of atomic tests; troop reductions; evacuation of one or more military bases; discontinuation of German rearmament; etc. The expectation is that the Russians are as willing as we are to avoid war, hence that they will begin to reciprocate and that once the course of mutual suspicion has been reversed, bigger steps can be taken which may lead to complete bilateral disarmament. Furthermore, I believe that disarmament negotiations should be paralleled by *political* negotiations, which aim essentially at mutual noninterference on the basis of the recognition of the *status quo.* Here, too (and again in essential agreement with Osgood's position), unilat-

* Reprinted by permission of the author and publisher from Wright, Q., *et al.* (Editors), *Preventing World War III* (New York: Simon and Schuster, 1962) pp. 178–191.

[1] Charles E. Osgood, "Suggestions for Winning the Real War with Communism," *Conflict Resolution,* III, No. 4 (December 1959), p. 131, and also "A Case for Graduated Unilateral Disarmament," *Bulletin of the Atomic Scientists,* XVI, No. 4, pp. 127 ff.

[2] This condition is in my opinion to be taken only as an optimal *desideratum,* since any weakening of one power's aggressive potential means strategically some increase in the opponent's aggressive potential.

[3] Osgood, "Suggestions for Winning the Real War with Communism," p. 316.

eral steps such as the recognition of the Oder-Neisse line and admission of China to the United Nations would be taken in the expectation of reciprocation by the Russians (i.e., curbing of Chinese aggression, noninterference in the Middle and Far East).

What are the premises underlying the proposition for unilateral steps toward disarmament? (At this point I shall mention only some fundamental ones, while others will be discussed in the second part of this paper which presents the argument for total unilateral disarmament.) They are briefly: (1) that, as indicated before, the present method of negotiations does not seem to lead to the goal of bilateral disarmament because of the deeply ingrained mutual suspicions and fears; (2) that without achieving *complete* disarmament, the armament race will continue and lead to the destruction of our civilization as well as that of the Russians or, even without the outbreak of a war, will slowly undermine and eventually destroy the values in defense of which we are risking our physical existence; (3) that while unilateral steps constitute a definite risk (and must do so by the very nature of the idea), the risk at every step is not a crippling one and is infinitely smaller than the danger we run by the continuation of the arms race.

Even though the broader concept of complete—rather than graduated—unilateral disarmament is, as stated before, not a practical possibility in the near future, as far as the United States and the USSR are concerned, I believe it worth while to present the arguments for this position, not primarily because the editors of this volume asked me to present this position nor even because I share it with a small minority of others who believe that the risks in the continuation of the armament race are far greater than the very serious risks of unilateral disarmament. While both reasons might not be sufficient to justify the following presentation, I do believe that it is not only justified but important for another reason: Thinking through the arguments for a radical—even though practically unacceptable—position contributes to breaking through the thought barrier

which prevents us now from getting out of the dangerous circle of seeking peace by means of threat and counterthreat. Taking seriously the reasoning which supports the unpopular position of complete unilateral disarmament can open up new approaches and viewpoints which are important even if our practical aim is that of graduated unilateral action or even only that of negotiated bilateral disarmament. I believe that the difficulty of arriving at complete disarmament lies to a large extent in the frozen stereotypes of feelings and thought habits on both sides and that any attempt at unfreezing these patterns and of rethinking the whole problem can be of importance in finding a way out of the present dangerous impasse.

The proposal for complete unilateral disarmament has been advocated from a religious, moral, or pacifist position by such men as Victor Gollancz, Lewis Mumford, and some Quakers. It has also been supported by men like Bertrand Russell, Stephen King-Hall, and C. W. Mills, who are not opposed to the use of force under all or any circumstances, yet who are uncompromisingly opposed both to thermonuclear war and to all and any preparation for it. This writer finds himself somewhat between the position of the strict pacifists and men like Bertrand Russell and Stephen King-Hall.[4]

The difference between these two groups, however, is not as fundamental as it may seem. They are united by their critical attitude toward the irrational aspects of international politics and by their deep rever-

[4] See Bertrand Russell, *Common Sense and Nuclear Warfare*, (London: Allen & Unwin, 1959); Stephen King-Hall, *Defense in the Nuclear Age* (Nyack, N.Y.: Fellowship Publications, 1959); Jerome Davis and General H. B. Hester, *On the Brink* (New York: Lyle Stuart, 1959); Lewis Mumford, *The Human Way Out* (Pendell Hill Pamphlet No. 97, 1958); C. W. Mills, *The Causes of World War Three* (New York: Simon and Schuster, 1959); George F. Kennan, "Foreign Policy and Christian Conscience," *The Atlantic Monthly*, (May, 1959); Richard B. Gregg, *The Power of Nonviolence* (Nyack, N.Y.: Fellowship Publications, 1959); and American Friends Service Committee, *Speak Truth to Power, Quaker Search for an Alternative to Balance* (Philadelphia, Pa.: American Friends Service Committee, 1955).

ence 'for life. They share the conviction of the oneness of the human race and faith in the spiritual and intellectual potentialities of man. They follow the dictates of their conscience in refusing to have any "part in making millions of women and children and noncombatants hostages for the behavior of their own governments."[5] Whether they think in theistic terms or in those of non-theistic humanism (in the sense of the philosophic continuum from Stoic to eighteenth-century Enlightenment philosophy), they all are rooted in the same spiritual tradition and are unwilling to compromise with its principles. They are united by their uncompromising opposition to any kind of idolatry, including the idolatry of the state. While their opposition to the Soviet system is rooted precisely in this attitude against idolatry, they are critical of idolatry whenever it appears in the Western world whether it is in the name of God or of democracy.

While there is no proponent of unilateral disarmament who does not believe that the individual must be willing to give his life for the sake of his supreme values, if such an ultimate necessity arises, they are all equally convinced that to risk the life of the human race, or even the results of its best efforts in the last five thousand years, is immoral and irresponsible. As warfare becomes at once more senseless and more devastating, the convergence between religious pacifist, humanist, and pragmatic opponents to nuclear armament grows.

From the standpoint of the proponents of unilateral disarmament, to continue the armament race is catastrophic, *whether the deterrent works or not.* In the first place, they have little faith that the deterrent will prevent the outbreak of a thermonuclear war.[6] They believe that the results of a ther-

monuclear war would be such that in the very "best" case they completely belie the idea that we ought to fight such a war in order to save our democratic way of life. There is no need to enter the guessing game as to whether one-third or two-thirds of the population of the two opponents and what proportion of the neutral world (depending on how the wind blows) will be destroyed. This is a guessing game that verges on madness; for to consider the possibility of the destruction of 30 percent, 60 percent, or 90 percent of one's own and the enemy's population as an acceptable (although, of course, most undesirable) result of one's policy is indeed approaching pathology. The increasing split between intellect and affect, which is so characteristic of our Western development in the last centuries, has reached its dangerous, schizoid peak in the calm and allegedly rational way in which we can discuss possible world destruction as a result of our own action. It does not take much imagination to visualize that sudden destruction and the threat of slow death to a large part of the American population, or the Russian popula-

[5] George F. Kennan, *op. cit.,* pp. 44 ff.

[6] This premise is shared by the report of the National Planning Association of America: *1970 Without Arms Control; Implications of Modern Weapons Technology* (by NPA Special Project Committee on Security through Arms Control; Planning Pamphlet No. 104, May 1958, Washington, D.C.), which states: "Not only does the danger of war remain a possibility, but the probability totalled over time increases, becoming a certainty if sufficient time elapses without succeeding in finding alterna-

tives." Or, E. Finley Carter, president of the Stanford Research Institute, writes: "In the search for security through the application of technology to weapons for destruction, the Soviet bloc and the Western allies have created a mortal common enemy —the threat of accidental nuclear war" *(SRI Journal,* Stanford Research Institute, Fourth Quarter, III (1959), p. 198). Herman Kahn also concludes, "It is most unlikely that the world can live with an uncontrolled arms race lasting for several decades" *(ibid.,* p. 139). He emphasizes that it is unrealistic to believe that war has become impossible because of its extremely destructive character.

The advisor on Science and Technology of the Democratic Advisory Council on 27 December 1959 declared: "All-out nuclear war seems not only possible but probable as long as we pursue our present military policies and fail to achieve international agreements of broad scope designed to alleviate this unstable situation. The triggering of a nuclear war by mistake, by misadventure or by miscalculation is a constant danger." It must be stressed that the danger lies not only in technical errors, but equally in the blundering decision-making by political and military leaders. If one remembers the political and military blunders committed by many of the leaders in the conduct of the wars of 1914 and 1939, it is not difficult to visualize that, given present-day weapons, the same type of leaders will blow the world to pieces, in spite of good intentions.

tion, or large parts of the world, will create such a panic, fury, and despair as could only be compared with the mass psychosis resulting from the Black Death in the Middle Ages. The traumatic effects of such a catastrophe would lead to a new form of primitive barbarism, to the resurgence of the most archaic elements, which are still potentialities in every man and of which we have had ample evidence in the terror systems of Hitler and Stalin. It would sound most unlikely to many students of human nature and psychopathology that human beings could cherish freedom, respect for life, or love after having witnessed and participated in the unlimited cruelty of man against man which thermonuclear war would mean. It is a psychological fact that acts of brutality have a brutalizing effect on the participants and lead to more brutality.

But What If the Deterrent Works?

What is the likely future of the social character of man in a bilateral or multilateral armed world, where, no matter how complex the problems or how full the satisfactions of any particular society,[7] the biggest and most pervasive reality in any man's life is the poised missile, the humming data processor connected to it, the waiting radiation counters and seismographs, the over-all technocratic perfection (overlying the nagging but impotent fear of its imperfection) of the mechanism of holocaust? To live for any length of time under the constant threat of destruction creates certain psychological effects in most human beings—fright, hostility, callousness, a hardening of the heart, and a resulting indifference to all the values we cherish. Such conditions will transform us into barbarians—though barbarians equipped with the most complicated machines. If we are serious in claiming that our aim is to preserve freedom (that is, to prevent the subordination of the individual under an all-powerful state), we must admit that this freedom will be lost, whether the deterrent works or does not work.

[7] For a detailed analysis of modern society see my *The Sane Society* (New York: Rinehart, 1955).

Aside from these psychological facts, the continuation of the arms race constitutes a particular threat to Western culture. In the process of conquering nature, producing and consuming have become Western man's main preoccupation—the goal of his life. We have transformed means into ends. We manufacture machines which are like men, and we produce men who are like machines. In his work, the individual is managed as a part of a production team. During his leisure time, he is manipulated as a consumer who likes what he is told to like and yet has the illusion that he follows his own taste. In centering his life around the production of things, man himself is in danger of becoming a thing, worshipping the idols of the production machine and the state while he is under the illusion of worshipping God. "Things are in the saddle and ride mankind," as Emerson has put it. Circumstances which we created have consolidated themselves into powers which rule over us. The technical and bureaucratic system we have built tells us what to do; it decides for us. We may not be in danger of becoming slaves, but we are in danger of becoming robots, and the human values of our tradition are threatened—integrity, individuality, responsibility, reason, and love. Talking about these values more and more becomes an empty ritual.

This trend toward a world of impotent men directed by virile machines (both in the United States and in the Soviet Union) —brought about by technological and demographic factors, and by the increasing centralization and bureaucracy in big corporations and government—will reach the point of no return if we continue the arms race. Dangerous as our present situation is, we still have a chance to put man back into the saddle, to effect a renaissance of the spiritual values of the great humanistic tradition. Unless such a renaissance occurs, unless we can achieve a radical revitalization of the spirit on which our culture is founded, we shall lose the vitality necessary for survival and we shall decay, just as many other great powers have decayed in history. The real threat to our existence is not Communist ideology, it is not even the Communist military power—it is the hol-

lowness of our beliefs, the fact that freedom, individuality, and faith have become
empty formulas, that God has become an
idol, that our vitality is sapped because we
have no vision except that of having more
of the same. It seems that a great deal of the
hatred of Communism is, in the last analysis, based on a deep disbelief in the spiritual values of democracy. Hence, instead of
experiencing love of what we are *for,* we
experience hate of what we are *against.* If
we continue to live in fear of extinction
and to plan mass destruction of others, the
last chance for a revival of our humanist-
spiritual tradition will be lost.

Benefits and Dangers of
Unilateral Disarmament

If these are the dangers of the policy of
the deterrent, what do the proponents of
unilateral disarmament consider to be the
benefits—and the dangers—of their policy?

The most likely result of unilateral disarmament—whether it be undertaken by
the United States or by the Soviet Union—
is that it would prevent war. The main reason which could impel either the Soviet
Union or the United States to atomic war is
the constant fear of being attacked and pul-
verized by the opponent. This position
is succinctly expressed by Herman Kahn,
who is in no way a proponent of unilateral
disarmament. Kahn states that, "aside from
the ideological differences and the problem
of security itself, there does not seem to be
any objective quarrel between the United
States and Russia that justifies the risks and
costs that we subject each other to. The
big thing that the Soviet Union and the
United States have to fear from each other
is fear itself."[8] If, indeed, the main cause of
war lies in mutual fear, then the disarmament of either the Soviet Union or the
United States would most likely do away
with this major cause and, thus, with the
probability of war.

But are there motives other than fear
which could prompt the Soviet Union to
try for world conquest? One such motive
could be economic interest in expansion,

which was a basic motivation for the initiation of war in the nineteenth century
and also for the first two World Wars. Exactly here we see the difference between the
nature of the conflicts in 1914 or 1939 and
the present situation. In World War I, Germany threatened British markets and the
French sources of coal and iron; in 1939,
Hitler needed territorial conquest for the
economic expansion he wanted. Today,
neither the Soviet Union nor the United
States has overriding economic interests in
the conquest of markets and supplies, since
a 2 or 3 percent rise in the level of national
productivity would bring a greater advantage than would any military conquest, and,
morever, each has the capital, raw material,
supplies, and population for a constant
increase in its general productivity.[9]

The more serious possible motive is
found in the fear, widely held in the
United States, that the Soviet Union is out
to conquer the world for Communism and
that, if the United States disarmed, Russia
would be all the more eager to achieve her
wish for world domination. This idea of
Russian intentions is based on an erroneous appreciation of the nature of the present-day Soviet Union. It is true that under
Lenin and Trotsky the Russian Revolution
was aimed at conquering the capitalistic
world (or at least, Europe) for Communism, partly because the Communist leaders
were convinced that there was no possibility
of success for Communist Russia unless the
highly industrialized states of Europe (or
at least Germany) joined their system, and
partly because they were prompted by the
belief that the victory of the Communist
revolution in the world would bring about

[8] Kahn, *SRI Journal,* III (1959), 140.

[9] For the very same reasons, there is a real chance
for the future abolition of war, a chance which
never existed in the past. In most of man's history,
the improvement of his material situation required
an increase in human energy (slaves), additional land
for cattle-raising or agriculture, or new sources of
raw materials. The techniques of the present and of
the future will permit an increase in material wealth
by an increased industrial and—indirectly—an agricultural productivity, without the need of enslaving
or robbing others. At present and in the future, war
would have as its only "rationale" the irrationality
of human desire for power and conquest.

the fulfillment of their secular-messianic hopes.

The failure of these hopes and the ensuing victory of Stalin brought about a complete change in the nature of Soviet Communism. The annihilation of almost all the old Bolsheviks was only a symbolic act for the destruction of the old revolutionary idea. Stalin's slogan of "socialism in one country" covered one simple aim—the rapid industrialization of Russia, which the Czarist system had not accomplished. Russia repeated the same process of accumulating capital which Western capitalism had gone through in the eighteenth and nineteenth centuries. The essential difference is that, while in these centuries in the West the sanctions were purely economic, the Stalinist system now developed political sanctions of direct terror; in addition, it employed socialist ideology to sugar-coat the exploitation of the masses. The Stalinist system was neither a socialist nor a revolutionary system, but a state capitalism based on ruthless methods of planning and economic centralization.

The period of Khrushchevism is characterized by the fact that capital accumulation has succeeded to a point where the population can enjoy a great deal more consumption and is less forced to make sacrifices; as a result, the political terror can be greatly reduced.

But Khrushchevism has by no means changed the basic character of Soviet society in one essential respect: it is not a revolutionary nor a socialist regime, but one of the most conservative, class-ridden regimes anywhere in the Western world, humanly coercive, economically effective. While the aim of democratic socialism was the emancipation of man, the overcoming of his alienation, and the eventual abolition of the state, the "socialist" slogans used in Soviet Russia reflect empty ideologies, and the social reality is the very opposite of true socialism. The ruling class of the Soviet Union is no more revolutionary than the Renaissance popes were followers of the teachings of Christ. To try to explain Khrushchev by quoting Marx, Lenin, or Trotzky shows an utter failure to understand the historical development which has

taken place in the Soviet Union and an incapacity to appreciate the difference between facts and ideologies. It should be added that our attitude is the best propaganda service the Russians could wish for. Against the facts, they try to convince the workers of Western Europe and the peasants in Asia that they represent the ideas of socialism, of a classless society, etc. The Western attitude, of falling for this propaganda, does exactly what the Russians want: to confirm these claims. (Unfortunately, very few people except democratic socialists have sufficient knowledge of the difference between socialism and its distorted and corrupt form which calls itself Soviet socialism.)

The role of Russia is still more emphasized by the fact that Russia feels threatened by a potentially expansionist China. Russia one day might be in the same position with regard to China as we believe we are in relation to Russia. If the threat to Russia from the United States were to disappear, Russia could devote her energy to coping with the threat from China, unless by universal disarmament this threat would cease to exist.

The above-mentioned considerations indicate that the dangers which might arise if the Soviet Union were not to give up its armaments are more remote than they seem to many. Would the Soviet Union use her military superiority to try to occupy the United States or Western Europe? Aside from the fact that it would be exceedingly difficult, to say the least, for the Soviet Union's agents to run the economic and political machines of the United States or Western Europe, and aside from the fact that there is no vital need for Russia to conquer these territories, it would be most inconvenient to try to do so—and for a reason which is generally not sufficiently appreciated. Even the pro-Communist workers in the West have no idea of the degree of coercion to which they would have to submit under a Soviet System. They, as well as non-Communist workers, would oppose the new authorities, who would be forced to use tanks and machine guns against the protesting workers. This would encourage revolutionary tendencies in the satellite states, or even within the Soviet Union, and be most undesirable to the Soviet rulers; it would especially endanger Khrushchev's policy of liberalization, and hence his whole political position.

Eventually the Soviet Union might try to exploit its military superiority for the penetration of Asia and Africa. This is possible, but, with our present policy of the deterrent, it is doubtful whether the United States would really be willing to start a thermonuclear war in order to prevent the Russians from gaining certain advantages in the world outside of Europe and the Americas.

All these assumptions may be wrong. The position of the proponents of unilateral disarmament is that the chance that they are wrong is much smaller than the chance that the continuation of the arms race will finish civilization as we cherish it.

Some Psychological Considerations

One cannot discuss the question of what might happen as a result of unilateral disarmament—or, for that matter, of any mutual disarmament—without examining some psychological arguments. The most popular one is that "the Russians cannot be trusted." If "trust" is meant in a moral sense, it is unfortunately true that political leaders can rarely be trusted. The reason lies in the split between private and public morals: the state, having become an idol, justifies any immorality if committed in its interest, while the very same political leaders would not commit the same acts if they were acting in behalf of their own private interests. However, there is another meaning to "trust in people," a meaning which is much more relevant to the problem of politics: the trust that they are sane and rational beings, and that they will act accordingly. If I deal with an opponent in whose sanity I trust, I can appreciate his motivations and to some extent predict them, because there are certain rules and aims, like that of survival or that of commensurateness between aims and means, which are common to all sane people. Hitler could not be trusted because he was lacking in sanity, and this very lack destroyed both

him and his regime. It seems quite clear that the Russian leaders of today are sane and rational people; therefore it is important not only to know what they are capable of, but also to predict what they might be motivated to do.[10]

This question of the leaders' and the people's sanity leads to another consideration which affects us as much as it does the Russians. In the current discussion on armament control, many arguments are based on the question of what is *possible*, rather than on what is *probable*. The difference between these two modes of thinking is precisely the difference between *paranoid* and *sane* thinking. The paranoiac's unshakable conviction in the validity of his delusion rests upon the fact that it is logically possible, and, so, unassailable. It is logically possible that his wife, children, and colleagues hate him and are conspiring to kill him. The patient cannot be convinced that his delusion is *impossible;* he can only be told that it is exceedingly *unlikely*. While the latter position requires an examination and evaluation of the facts and also a certain amount of faith in life, the paranoid position can satisfy itself with the possibility alone. I submit that our political thinking suffers from such paranoid trends. We should be concerned, not with the possibilities, but rather with the probabilities. This is the only sane and realistic way of conducting the affairs of national as well as of individual life.

Again on the psychological plane, there are certain misunderstandings of the radical disarmament position which occur in many of the discussions. First of all, the po-

[10] Whether or not political leaders are sane is not a matter of historical accident. Any government which has set out to do the impossible—for instance, to achieve equality and justice when the requisite material conditions are lacking—will produce fanatical and irrational leaders. This was the case with Robespierre, as it was with Stalin. Or, a government which tries to reconcile the interests of the most backward social class (the lower middle class) with those of the economically progressive classes (workers and businessmen) as the Nazi government did, again will produce fanatical and irrational leaders. The Soviet Union today is on the road toward solving its economic problems successfully; hence it is not surprising that her leaders are realistic men of common sense.

sition of unilateral disarmament has been understood as one of submission and resignation. On the contrary, the pacifists as well as the humanist pragmatists believe that unilateral disarmament is possible only as an expression of a deep spiritual and moral change within ourselves: it is an act of courage and resistance—not one of cowardice or surrender. Forms of resistance differ in accordance with the respective viewpoints. On the other hand, Gandhists and men like King-Hall advocate nonviolent resistance, which undoubtedly requires the maximum of courage and faith; they refer to the example of Indian resistance against Britain or Norwegian resistance against the Nazis. This point of view is succinctly expressed in *Speak Truth to Power:*

> Thus, we dissociate ourselves from the basically selfish attitude that has been miscalled pacifism, but that might be more accurately described as a kind of irresponsible antimilitarism. We dissociate ourselves also from utopianism. Though the choice of nonviolence involves a radical change in men, it does not require perfection. . . . We have tried to make it clear that readiness to accept suffering—rather than inflict it on others—is the essence of the nonviolent life, and that we must be prepared if called upon to pay the ultimate price. Obviously, if men are willing to spend billions of treasure and countless lives in war, they cannot dismiss the case for nonviolence by saying that in a nonviolent struggle people might be killed! It is equally clear that where commitment and the readiness to sacrifice are lacking, nonviolent resistance cannot be effective. On the contrary, it demands greater discipline, more arduous training, and more courage than its violent counterpart.[11]

Some think of armed resistance, of men and women defending their lives and their freedom with rifles, pistols, or knives. It is not unrealistic to think that both forms of resistance, nonviolent or violent, might deter an aggressor from attacking. At least, it is more realistic than to think that the use of thermonuclear weapons could lead to a "victory for democracy."

The proponents of "security by armament" sometimes accuse us of having an unrealistic, flatly optimistic picture of the nature of man. They remind us that this "perverse human being has a dark, illogical, irrational side."[12] They even go so far as to say that "the paradox of nuclear deterrence is a variant of the fundamental Christian paradox. In order to *live,* we must express our willingness to kill and to die."[13] Apart from this crude falsification of Christian teaching, we are by no means oblivious of the potential evil within man and of the tragic aspect of life. Indeed, there are situations in which man must be willing to die in order to live. In the sacrifices necessary for violent or nonviolent resistance, I can see an expression of the acceptance of tragedy and sacrifice. But, there is no tragedy or sacrifice in irresponsibility and carelessness: there is no meaning or dignity in the idea of the destruction of mankind and of civilization. Man has in himself a potential for evil; his whole existence is beset by dichotomies rooted in the very conditions of his existence. But these truly tragic aspects must not be confused with the results of stupidity and lack of imagination, with the willingness to stake the future of mankind on a gamble.

Finally, to take up one last criticism, directed against the position of unilateral disarmament: that it is "soft" on Communism. Our position is precisely based on the negation of the Soviet principle of the omnipotence of the state. Just because the spokesmen for unilateral disarmament are drastically opposed to the supremacy of the state, they do not want to grant the state the ever-increasing power which is unavoidable in the arms race, and they deny the right of the state to make decisions which can lead to the destruction of a great part of humanity and can doom future generations. If the basic conflict between the Soviet system and the democratic world is the question of the defense of the individual against the encroachment of an omnipotent state, then, indeed, the position for unilateral disarmament is the one which is

---

[11] American Friends Service Committee, *op. cit.,* pp. 52 and 65.

[12] Peter B. Young, "The Renunciationists," *Airpower,* Air Force Historical Foundation, VII, No. 1, p. 33.

[13] *Ibid.*

most radically opposed to the Soviet principle.

Having discussed the case for unilateral disarmament (in the broad sense), I want to return to the practical proposition of unilateral steps toward disarmament. I do not deny that there are risks involved in this limited form of unilateral action but, considering the fact that the present method of negotiations has produced no results and that the chances that they will in the future are rather slim, considering furthermore the grave risk involved in the continuation of the arms race, I believe that it is practically and morally justified to take this risk. At present we are caught in a position with little chance for survival, unless we want to take refuge in hopes. *If* we have enough shelters, if there is enough time for a warning and strategic evacuation of cities, *if* the "United States' active offenses and active defenses can gain control of the military situation after only a few exchanges,"[14] we might have only five, or twenty-five, or seventy million killed. However, if these conditions do not materialize, "an enemy could, by repeated strikes, reach almost any level of death and destruction he wished."[15] (And, I assume, the same threat exists for the Soviet Union.) In such a situation, "when nations are poised at the last moment when an agreement appears possible to end the risk of horrifying war, unleashed by fanatics, lunatics or men of ambition,"[16] it is imperative to shake off the inertia of our accustomed thinking, to seek for new approaches to the problem, and above all, to see new alternatives to the present choices that confront us.

[14] Herman Kahn, *Report on a Study of Non-Military Defense* (New York: Rand Corporation, 1958), p. 13.

[15] *Ibid.*

[16] General de Gaulle, in a speech in April, 1960.

GUIDE LINES FOR RESEARCH IN INTERNATIONAL CO-OPERATION*

GORDON W. ALLPORT

Confronted with the cheerless spectacle of the modern world, an increasing number of today's prophets are saying that our international troubles are wholly *moral*. Technical progress, they point out, brought in its wake a perilous secularization of life. Among its macabre consequences we reckon technological unemployment, technological warfare, and now the black portent of atomic destruction. The present century, in spite of its unexampled inventiveness, has been the bloodiest century on record in terms of international, civil, and criminal violence.

Secularization, these prophets continue, led mankind to forget the Commandments of Moses, the ethics of Confucius, the self-discipline of Krishna, and the vision of Christian Brotherhood. It were better now, they say, for each man to look to his own salvation. Let religion revive. Let character be restored. Only then may we expect human relations to improve.

Can one doubt that these advocates of moral reformation are right in arguing that the great moral creeds of the world, *if taken in their purity,* would help control the ravages of technology? Were men to backtrack from the present gulf of secularization, were they to start practising their creeds, peace on earth would be more readily achieved.

* * *

But the manifest difficulty in accepting this seemingly simple counsel lies not in the falseness or inapplicability of our creeds, but in their sheer antiquity. Many, perhaps most, inhabitants of the earth would recognize "Love thy neighbour as thyself"

* From Gordon W. Allport, "Guide Lines for Research in International Cooperation." *Psychological Factors of Peace and War,* edited by T. H. Pear (New York: The Philosophical Library, 1950), pp. 141–157. Reprinted by permission of the author and the publisher.

as a worthy imperative but this commandment tells twentieth-century man very little about how he may translate his affectionate purposes into action. How, in an age of giant industries, bureaucracy, instant communication, and atomic energy, shall one effectively love one's neighbour?

* * *

Perhaps my ethical views are in the modern vein. I may prefer to be guided by the insights of Kropotkin, Lenin, or Dewey. But so long as my moral standards are meliorative and not pejorative, I am confronted always with the need for knowledge in order to implement my belief.

Sound moral purpose is by no means lacking in the world. It still flows from the great creedal literature of past ages, even while it is being reinterpreted in the light of modern conditions. The present chasm between technology and morals, as reflected by the bloody twentieth century, has formed chiefly because physical engineering has outstripped social engineering, because physical science has been allowed to outdistance social science. The worship of technological efficiency, for its own sake, is an almost universally recognized evil; but its control through moral efficiency awaits knowledge and instrument.

Policy, Research and Operations

Perhaps the most heartening event of our times is the establishment of the Economic and Social Council of the United Nations, its dependent specialized agencies, particularly UNESCO. The last of these in the Preamble to its Charter, strikes the keynote of a new era. "Since wars begin in the minds of men it is in the minds of men that the defences of peace must be constructed." The implications are crystal clear: man's moral sense condemns war; let us therefore study scientifically the sources of this evil in

535

men's minds and scientifically remove them.

But it is here that an initial misgiving arises. Can research into the causes of war be translated effectively into operation? During the past five years a certain pessimism has descended upon many of the world's most active social scientists. Aiming to improve morale in wartime, industrial relations in peacetime, amity between races, they have pressed ahead with research and have proffered solutions. For the most part their findings have been disregarded, and their zeal correspondingly dampened. Political expediency, power politics, selfish national purposes have conspired to overlook, to 'place on file,' their counsel. . . .

The situation can be remedied in three ways: (1) Boldness in taking risks is called for. Everyone knows there are serious inherent limitations in social research. It is likely that social investigation can never attain an exactness equivalent to that of physical technology whose ravages it aims to control. Unlike physical and chemical research, social studies are infrequently additive, and their powers of generalization are limited. But just what the inherent limitations of social science may be we cannot tell until an opportunity of adequate scope is given it. The possible imperfectibility of social engineering is no excuse for failing to encourage its growth, or to employ its aid wherever practicable.

* * * *

The United States alone spent two billion dollars on the invention of the atomic bomb. What is there absurd in spending an equivalent sum, if necessary, on the discovery of means for its control? And, as the Preamble to the UNESCO Charter states, it is undoubtedly in the minds of men that the defences of peace must be sought. Success cannot be guaranteed; it is entirely possible that social engineering may fail to implement the moral sense of mankind and that mankind may go under. But we shall never know the potential value of social science unless the risk is taken.

(2) Policy makers (I speak of the Department of State as well as of the highest policy authorities in the United Nations) can and should open their minds continually to the documented advice of social scientists. When it is good, they should follow it. Publicity given to relevant research, to the recommendations of social scientists, and to the policies finally adopted, will reveal the extent to which international practices are determined by selfishness and momentary expediency, and to what extent they conform to the best social knowledge available.

(3) Let social scientists continually strive to attain a standard in research that merits respect. Too often in the past their findings have been trivial or incompetent. Equally often they have failed to make even the soundest of their principles intelligible, or their applicability clear. Psychologists, sociologists, anthropologists, economists have *much* to learn about practical orientation of their studies, and about effective means for communicating their results to policy makers.[1]

If developments move in the direction of the three suggestions just offered the integration between policy bodies and social scientists will be greatly improved. Much encouragement comes from the knowledge that during recent years beneficial coordination has already been achieved. In numerous instances social science gave indispensable aid to the war effort. In spite of resistance and some hostility social science scored triumphs, notably in the areas of psychological warfare, personnel selection, morale building, effective communication between the government and the public.[2] The scope of these successes is sufficiently great to raise our hopes high for the potential results of team-work between social scientists and administrators in the area of international co-operation.

[1] Suggestions for bridging the chasm in communication and for improving the relevance of social research are made by A. H. Leighton, *The Governing of Men* (Princeton University Press, 1945), esp. pp. 390–7; and G. W. Allport, "The Psychology of Participation," *Psychological Review*, 1945, 53, esp. pp. 128–30.

[2] Although a record of the successful wartime applications of social science to administrative policy has not yet been completely compiled, some indication of their variety and nature can be obtained from D. Cartwright, "American Social Psychology and the War," *Journal of Consulting Psychology*, 1946, 10, 67–72.

Social research must be international.
While the natural scientist or the medical
scientist operating alone in his individual
laboratory may do significant research, of
importance to the entire world, it is safe
to say that almost no social research of international significance can be successfully
carried forward in this manner. Even if a
whole nation should concentrate its energy
upon social investigations it is unlikely that
it could accomplish much of *world* significance. A single nation's culture-bound outlook is restrictive. True, in the past social
scientists of one nation occasionally trav-
elled abroad in their quest for data, but
their reports have seldom been broad-
gauged enough and free enough from provincialism to serve as a guide to international policy of any type whatsoever.

At the present time barriers of language,
of inadequate facilities (especially in
smaller and poorer countries), meagreness
of intercommunication, and lack of incentive to focus upon common problems, conspire to separate and segregate the social
scientists of the world. As yet the resources
of their knowledge and skill, as well as
their eagerness to aid, have not been
tapped in the interests of world peace.

To obtain the concerted effort of the
world's social scientists, even in regard to
limited and special topics, we now need
international stimulation, facilities, and
co-ordination. Thousands of highly skilled
physical scientists worked in collaboration
on a *national* scale for the production of
the destructive atom bomb. The control of
its destructive potential, and the realization
of its latent benefits, will require equally
many, and equally able minds co-operating
on an *international* scale.

What Is Known and What Is Needed

International social research need not
start at scratch. Already much initial work
has been done. Even now a sufficient number of general principles are known, and
widely enough agreed upon, to set the guide
lines for urgently needed investigations.
What is more important, these principles
might *immediately* be applied with im-

mense profit to the conduct of international
relations if the proper officials were so
disposed.

In examining these principles and their
usefulness as guides to concrete research
and policy, two limitations should be held
in mind. First, they are offered as illustrations rather than as final system. An adequate survey should, of course, have the
benefit of wide discussion and concerted
approval by a large number of social scientists assembled from many nations.[3]

Secondly, the discussion is limited largely
to psychological principles, with some bor-
rowing from social anthropology and sociology. The potential contributions of economics, geography, political science, and
history are unquestionably large. But these
disciplines fall outside the range of the
present survey.

Trends toward Collective Security. Perhaps the first principle to which the social
scientist would call attention is the unidirectional historical trend towards the formation of a world government. From the cave-
man to the twentieth century human beings
have formed larger and larger working and
living groups. At some time in the dim past
families became clans, clans turned into
tribes and states. Federations followed. Empires had their day. Commonwealth and
regional unions have flourished. During
the past century non-political international
organizations have sprung up in bewildering numbers, especially among scientific,
professional, and recreational groups. The
League of Nations, followed by Hitler's sinister and abortive New Order, were chapters
in the same saga. The United Nations is
the latest and best hope mankind has devised, though it is not necessarily the final
effort. Even now it is unclear whether one
world is the next step in the series, or
whether mankind is doomed first to live
through a divided period, a pro- and anti-
Russian world.

* * * *

[3] The list of principles here offered is not, however, quite as individual and arbitrary as may appear. Several of them are contained in "Human
Nature and the Peace," a statement subscribed to
by 2,058 American psychologists, all members of the
American Psychological Association.

Participation in Own Destiny. Various lines of research in recent years have demonstrated the inescapable importance of personal participation in matters affecting one's own welfare. People almost always want to solve their problems for themselves, or at least feel that they play an important part in the process of achieving a solution. International relief organizations have learned that charitable hand-outs seldom strengthen the recipient or win his gratitude. Apathy, boot-licking, or resentment may accompany 'benevolence' of any sort, whether it be alms or an imposed political system. On the other hand, personal efforts at upbuilding and rehabilitation are usually undertaken with joy by a person who feels that the product he achieves will be his own and not suffer destruction or expropriation.

* * * *

Economic and Social Insecurity. Persons who feel that their livelihood or safety is threatened generally make poor citizens— of a town, a nation, or of the world. They tend to be defensive, restless, suspicious. Now, since poverty is well-nigh universal, and social insecurity widely prevalent, it becomes imperative to determine the types of provisions, guarantees, and reassurances that are most needed to allay fear and unrest. What are the standards of security and well-being below which no people can fall without social disaster ensuing? Up to now these standards have been guessed at through intuition and in terms of expediency, but only the results of an objective investigation will serve.

While certain minimum guarantees against starvation and disease may be a legitimate objective for all nations acting in concert we repeat that human interests are best served when people themselves are consulted and permitted to play an active part in providing for their own security. Just what sorts of self-help can be encouraged, and in what order of priority, are subjects for research not speculation.

* * * *

International Conference Procedure. At the root of much of the vagueness and inconsistency of international decisions lie the human failings that come to light in the work of committees and assemblies. Men, even trained statesmen, do not know how to deliberate efficiently. Up to now in social science only a bare beginning has been made in the study of the processes of discussion, group criticism, and decision.

We may expect much basic work to be done in the future even without international support. But so essential is it for international groups to learn how to employ the most effective conference procedures, that money and time would be well invested in additional investigations.

* * * *

Focusing on Children. Social scientists know that in a single generation it is theoretically possible to have a world language, to build universal loyalty to a world state, and to eliminate most racial and national prejudices. They know equally well that the goal cannot be achieved in practice, for it is from their parents that children chiefly learn their social attitudes. The older generation unfortunately inclines to be firmly set in its bitterness and in its blindness. Although children, with their almost limitless plasticity, will acquire much of this burden, they still constitute the best possible focus for our internationalizing efforts. Children can readily identify with symbols of world unity, even while holding inviolate their loyalty to family, neighbourhood or nation. Multiple loyalties are not necessarily incompatible. Wendel Willkie was no less a Hoosier or an American because he acclaimed One World.

To overlook children is to be stupidly inefficient from the standpoint of social engineering. Twenty-five years is not too long to await results in the perspective of social evolution. Social scientists might reasonably advise that adults be largely disregarded in favour of children. The establishment of health centres, nutritional standards, curricular standards, welfare stations, model schools, a children's village, research in social attitudes, social training, and symbols, might well hold the centre of the stage. The children of today are the custodians of the United Nations of tomorrow. The problems we cannot solve they will inherit, and their ability to cope with these problems will exceed ours only if their loyalties are stronger and their initial training sounder.

* * * *

The Common Ground of Human Nature. To teach children the ways of peace requires, among other things, a factual knowledge of the peoples of the world. What, up to now, have anthropologists given us? And what have the schools been teaching? Broadly speaking, both have accented the *differences* that divide the families of mankind. Even though there has been little malice in the practice, the results have often been harmful. The American child, for example, learns with horror about headhunters, about infanticide; and he learns to laugh at the Dutch who clop in wooden shoes, and at the quaint observances of Easter among adherents to the Orthodox faith. The implication of inferiority is a usual by-product of our present method of teaching cultural and national differences. Less dramatic, but far sounder, would be the teaching of the common considerations of justice and morality that are identical over vast areas of the earth. Practices that may *seem* to differ dramatically often indicate common aspirations and common values. The prayer wheels of Tibet and the silent Quaker meeting have virtually identical functional significance; so too the initiation rites of the Pawnee and the American high school commencement.

* * * *

The desires and opinions of the common man. It is not merely the enduring uniformities and equivalences in culture that need to be known, but likewise the *current* state of world needs and world opinion at successive periods of time. Here too internationally sponsored social research is indispensable.

* * * *

. . . To focus on matters that are of *prior* importance to the citizenry would often bring a re-definition of the issues and disclose unexpected solutions. For the root desires of two people are seldom incompatible with one another. When they con-

front each other with the basic *desires,* cooperation can usually satisfy both sets of interests.

* * * *

Communications. A reciprocal research service is required in order to achieve effective communication to the public of all lands. How may radio, motion pictures, television, books, news services, periodicals, lecturers be best employed in order that people everywhere may be informed in affairs of international import?

* * * *

Condescension and its Perils. A principle upon which social scientists almost unanimously agree is that human relations founded upon an attitude of condescension are perilous. So far as is known no group of people is content to think of itself as inferior to any other group, nor is any single individual normally willing to regard himself as of less worth or merit than another. In spite of periods of history when slavery or feudalism seemed to lead a temporarily peaceful existence, it may be safely asserted that policies based on condescension will sooner or later lead to violence. In the world today the unrest of citizens formerly regarded as second-class is manifest. Dark-skinned people are moving ahead towards independence. The white-skinned third of the world's population cannot prevent the movement. The English-speaking tenth certainly cannot do so. It is for this reason that an attempt to preserve the older imperial and colonial systems is doomed to breed violence and war.

* * * *

Summary

Our plea is for an accelerated development of social engineering based on social research, to the end that we may overtake and control the ravages of a rampant and amoral technology.

The argument assumes that the basic moral sense of mankind is sufficiently established in direction and in motive power to employ with profit the principles and instruments that the nascent science of human relations has already developed and will continue to develop at a rapid rate if adequate support is given.

The principles stated in this paper derive from psychology, sociology, and anthropology. In all probability they would be endorsed by most specialists in these disciplines. Yet a completer list of principles and fuller account of the applications would result if many social scientists were to work in concert upon the problems here treated. Such concerted action should be instigated on an international scale.

Should any 'hard-headed' statesman scorn the guide lines here offered as an expression of futile idealism, he himself would stand revealed as the most impractical of men. For scientific facts in the social field, as in any field, can be disregarded only with peril. The Einsteinian equation, $E = MC^2$, was once dismissed as pedantry. The formula led to the release of atomic energy. The 'pedantry' of social science might even now contribute enormously to the establishment of peace and international co-operation were its applications understood and employed by policy makers.

Yet it is true that social science has as yet by no means realized its potential power as a welder of international relations. Nor will it do so until adequate support is given on both a national and international scale. Since its most needed discoveries pertain to world-wide problems, it is international support that is most acutely needed. The co-operation of social scientists all over the world, as yet non-existent, would not be difficult to achieve.

Though some of the research required for international policy is of an *ad hoc* and momentary character, often statistical in nature, the pivotal investigations that are needed for long-range planning fall for the most part in the areas this paper has surveyed.

In all cases the research here recommended is intimately related to basic principles of social science. These principles, so far as they are now known, and as rapidly as new ones are formulated inductively with the aid of research, should be allowed to direct policy.

There follows a brief re-listing of the essential areas of research mentioned in this paper. Though manifestly incomplete, the topics are both accessible and important. They are intended to serve as a starting point for discussion among interested groups of social scientists and policy makers.

1. Prepare an historical survey of the trend towards larger and larger units of collective security.
2. Determine the conditions for democratic mass participation.
   (a) The conditions required for a sense of freedom to build.
   (b) The conditions for linking self-interest to the techniques of mutual aid.
   (c) The conditions for widening the individual's circle of co-operative enterprise.
3. Determine the effects of economic and psychological insecurity.
   (a) Under what circumstances, and in what degree, does insecurity serve as an incentive?
   (b) Under what circumstances, and beyond what point, does insecurity engender morbid and anti-social reactions?
   (c) Study especially the relation between childhood insecurity and the formation of delinquent and hostile attitudes.
   (d) What forms of insecurity lead to national unrest and to warlike sentiments?
   (e) What international policies, if consistently maintained, would lead to an optimum sense of security?
4. Investigate international conference procedures.
   (a) What are the requirements of effective deliberation and group decision in large assemblies? In committees?
   (b) How are these requirements modified when participants are of different cultural and linguistic backgrounds?
5. Direct main efforts upon children.
   (a) How are multiple loyalties created without mental conflict?
   (b) Explore the possibilities of a Children's Village for war orphans or stateless children.
   (c) Prepare international standards for health and nutrition.

(d) Investigate the conditions for the formation of attitudes.

(e) Devise model curricula for the elimination of ethnic prejudice and for the explanation of the interdependence of nations.

(f) Determine on world-wide scale parental aspirations for children.

(g) Devise methods for keeping policy bodies aware of children and their needs.

(h) Explore methods for the installation of child training projects in all countries.

6. Determine objectively the common ground of mankind.

(a) Prepare an encyclopedia of the uniformities and similarities of cultures.

(b) Interpret cultural difference in terms of functional equivalences.

(c) Explore in detail the conception of national character.

7. Ascertain current opinion.

(a) Establish a continuing operation for revealing the state of men's needs, aspirations, opinions; commence in countries where machinery is already available.

(b) Centre attention upon common needs rather than upon divisive demands.

(c) Translate findings into implications for policy.

8. Investigate channels of communication.

(a) Study the merits of all media in respect to their value for international co-operation.

(b) Experiment with programmes and determine their effectiveness.

(c) Determine the strategy and tactics of propaganda, and methods for building immunity.

(d) Trace the dissemination of ideas through rumour, through illicit and authoritative channels.

(e) Explore continually the problems of polylingualism and the conditions for a world language.

9. Clarify the problem of race.

(a) Solve the problem of indentities and differences in racial abilities and temperament.

(b) Prepare authoritative ethnographic maps.

(c) Examine the psychological effects of policies of condescension.

(d) Estimate in advance the probable effects of proposed policies respecting bases, trusteeships.

(e) Determine the causes of xenophobia.

(f) Determine the conditions for mutual understanding between individuals of diverse backgrounds.

10. Develop symbols of international co-operation.

(a) What symbols appeal to diverse groups?

(b) Pre-test plans for world centres, flag, music, parks, universities, and other symbols of unity.

(c) Determine means for encouraging the development of effective symbols.

STRATEGIC MODELS FOR A DE-POLARIZING WORLD*

AMITAI ETZIONI

1. Introduction

It is becoming commonplace to state that a Western strategy that assumes or seeks to foster a bi-polar world is obsolescent. The four models on which the combination of containment and deterrence that characterizes the prevailing Western strategy, and upon which this strategy draws, are increasingly viewed as inadequate. The two integrated camps, which the *bi-polar balance of power* which underlies containment assumes, are disappearing from international reality; the *balance-of-terror* image, which underlies deterrence, according to which two nuclear giants check each other, is facing the proliferation of nuclear dwarfs; the *zero-sum notions,* borrowed from game-theory, are seen as having declining relevance by more and more strategists; and the *psychology of frustration,* on which containment draws, has been shown to be too narrow. To put it differently, every component of the Western strategic formula has changed since it was formed in the late 40s—the technology of weapons, the cohesion of the super-blocs, the nature of the USSR, and the composition of the UN.

While the need for a basic strategic revision is recognized, actual policies are slow to change, and postures implemented after years of staff work, production of the necessary hardware, and negotiations with allies, are not readily replaced like numbers in a mathematics mode. A few measures taken indicate experimentation with new conceptions—such as the emergency communication link between the White House and the Kremlin, the 1963 Nuclear Test Ban Treaty, simultaneous US and USSR assistance to India under Chinese attack, and the unanimous General Assembly reso-

† Reprinted by permission of the author and publisher from *Journal of Peace Research,* 1965, 2: 136–150.

* This article was written in June 1964. Ed.

lution banning the orbiting of weapons of mass destruction. But, by and large, the policies of the United States (and, for the most part, those of the USSR) are still under the spell of old conceptions. Instead of accepting polycentrism in the West as a fact of the next decade, the US is engaged in a maneuver to restore the unity to the Western alliance by offering the Europeans a joint nuclear force, and playing up West Germany to exert pressure on de Gaulle's France. The full import of the Sino-Soviet rift is only slowly becoming recognized, and policies that take the split into account are only gradually evolving. Arms control, not to mention arms reduction, is still a goal not actively pursued, in part because the USSR keeps insisting that it is interested only in more radical measures than the US is willing to discuss, and in part because some of the most effective steps which could be taken would upset America's ally Germany, and hence are not advanced in this period in which efforts to cement NATO are considered of primary importance.

While many strategic writings are long on criticisms of the present models, conceptions and policies, they are short on spelling out alternative conceptions. The importance of formulating alternatives should not be underestimated. At best, changing one's strategy is psychologically and politically strenuous, and economically costly. Without a clear conception of what might follow such a shift in outlook, continued adherence to obsolescent conceptions, patching-up rather than redesigning, is almost inevitable.

The alternative model we seek to explore is one that substitutes a dynamic, *peaceful competition* for static, *peaceful coexistence.* The most basic tenet of this model is that the time is now ripe for the institutionalization of a set of rules that would effectively curb the use of arms, while accepting a continued, even intensified, contest among the world powers, but with non-military means, such as aid, trade and propaganda. This strategy advocates a more free use of power to stimulate development of a global institutional framework, without, however, providing an opening for other contestants to advance their military blocs or weakening Western security. It aims, on the one hand, at building up the rules of the competition and the machinery necessary to enforce these rules, and on the other, at maintaining if not strengthening the West in that very competition. More specifically, we examine a balance-of-power model that is multi-polar and which has 'N' nuclear countries rather than two, which borrows notions from non-zero-sum models, and from the psychology of sublimation rather than extinction.

2. The De-polarizing World

The parallelism between the Sino-Soviet and Franco-American rifts can be readily overdrawn. The West has not been as monolithic as the East, nor did American hegemony remotely approach the iron fist with which Stalin ran the Soviet bloc. The ideological rifts of the East are unmatched in the West, while China's rivalry with Russia cannot compare with the economic competition the European Common Market poses for the US. But there are two critically important parallels: *whatever ups and downs the two grand alliances experience over the next decade,* neither a return to the state of the higher bloc unity of the early 50s, nor the *rival of even a semblance of a bi-polar world, is at all likely.* The underlying reason is that in addition to ideological splits, differences of economic interests, differences in diplomatic style, etc., nationalism is too strong and the danger of nuclear war too great for these blocs to be as united as they were.

With the mass deployment of invulnerable long range missiles in the USSR, which is expected in the next few years, the US might have to put all its major cities on the line for the defense of every slice of Western Europe the Soviets might try for. The US might be willing to take such a risk, but the Europeans simply cannot be expected

to rely upon it. This is not just a question of credibility of the American promise to commit suicide for Europe's defense, which is not beyond doubt, but the need to agree on the conditions under which the US would push what button.

Similarly, a full reconciliation between the USSR and, Communist China would involve finding a formula to determine which advances in the non-Communist world are 'too risky' and which would not seriously risk triggering a nuclear war. Such an agreement would require either that China toe the line pronounced in Moscow or that Russia allow, at least under some conditions, China to trigger Russia's involvement in a world war. Neither of these Sino-Soviet accommodations seems even remotely likely, aside from all the forces that divide the two Communist powers, which seem hard to reverse.

The world, it is often stressed, is de-polarizing. Attempts to patch up the existing alliances will, I believe, ultimately fail. Yet, to a large degree, American strategy still assumes bi-polarity, if not in the under-developed world, at least among the big powers. Cooperation among the Western allies is taken for granted in containing Communist expansion. Conversely, it is assumed that the US cannot count on members of the opposite bloc for help in this task; it is incompatible with this rigid two-camp outlook to imagine some Communists helping the West to contain other Communists. Yet in the real world of many centers of power, there are many new possibilities—including this seemingly absurd one. Developments in Southeast Asia illustrate this point. The US does not recognize Communist China, and expects no help from the USSR in stemming Chinese aggression within this area. Actually, there is no evidence that the USSR provided arms to the Communist forces either in Laos or South Vietnam (although the North Vietnamese are reported to have used some old transport planes that the USSR sold to China during the Korean War); in fact there is reason to believe that the USSR is interested in the neutralization of the region, as a counter to expanding Chinese influence. Moreover, a strong case can be made that the Russians would be as concerned as the West if India should fall under Chinese control, following a Chinese takeover of Southeast Asia. The US did not try to maintain neutrality in the region in collaboration with the USSR.

To illustrate further the wide range of new combinations that emerge in the new pluralistic era, the *French* neutralization plan, if underwritten by the US military force (on the model of Austrian neutrality) would help the *Russian* efforts to contain Communist China!

Similarly, the US should expect cross-bloc 'deals' in Europe and not be fooled by the 'tougher' line either Bonn or Paris demands of the US in its negotiations with the Russians. The French have already indicated their willingness to recognize the Oder-Niesse line between East Germany and Poland, which helps them score points in Poland (points which the US gave up to please the Germans). The West Germans, who denounce the US for slightly increasing its trade with the USSR in 1963, have increased their trade in the same year to a much larger degree.

The lessons that emerge are many. First of all, in a de-polarizing world American diplomacy will be more difficult than in the bi-polar world, as there will be many more possible combinations, trade-offs, and avenues of maneuver. Above all, the Western flank is no longer 'safe', nor is that of the other side impregnable except to the extent of US inability to see that it is no longer so.

Secondly, those matters that can be settled through direct American-Russian negotiations can be agreed upon without the need for either side to fear that the 'thaw' in the Cold War, which such accomodations will bring about, will break the ideological glue that holds the blocs together; this glue—which is presumably helped by defining one side as virtuous and the other as evil, is already shattered. For the US to inhibit inter-bloc accommodations because of the fear of weakening bonds that have already been badly damaged, seems less than effective policy-making.

Thirdly, universal arrangements—to bind all the big powers—can no longer be de-

cided in Moscow and Washington; it is necessary to win the consent of Paris and Peking, and soon Bonn and London, if the arrangements are to be heeded. The American-Russian attempt to draft a test ban treaty that would bind all the bloc members illustrates this new situation. The treaty binds the US and the USSR, but neither China nor France. (Germany finally acceded to it, but only after much American pressure.)

'But are we not consulting our allies all the time?' many an American will ask. The answer lies in part in the politics of alliances in the nuclear age; and in part in clarifying the semantics. First, the US often does not consult its allies, or even inform them ahead of time of planned moves. For instance, if the Cuban blockade had triggered a nuclear war, Western Europe might well have been wiped out. (The majority of the Soviet missiles are aimed at Western Europe because the US is beyond their range: Western Europe thus serves as a hostage.) Still, the US established the blockade without consulting or informing (before the act) its NATO allies, as Britain and France failed to inform the US in 1956, when their national interests were considered to be at stake in the Suez crisis.

In other cases, US consultation is largely perfunctory. The Europeans are free to advise, and their advice is taken into account, but frequently only as long as they agree with US policy. This is not due to some arbitrary desire always to have the last word, but because the US believes that it understands nuclear strategy and the Communist danger better than do its European allies. Also, the US pays for most of the global Western commitments, and has more military power than all the European allies combined.

One reason the US does not fully realize the limitations of maintaining a united-bloc front through consultation is that it is reluctant to acknowledge the genuine differences between American and European interests; for instance, that a limited nuclear war—as defined by the US—might be a total war as viewed by West Germany (because all of Germany might be wiped out). Similarly, the Europeans have fewer interests in Asia and Latin America than does the US, and are less willing to risk their cities for the defense of Laos or Quemoy and Matsu. As the Europeans' power continues to grow, and their estimates of the Soviet danger continue to decline, these allies will act more and more as independent centers of power—without necessarily dropping their NATO affiliations. They will have to be *genuinely* consulted, that is, their consent must be won through give and take as if they were not bloc-members.

While it appears likely that the world of tomorrow will see an increased importance of capitals other than Washington and Moscow, it does not follow that there will be four or more big powers where yesterday there were two, as is implied in many statements about the shift from a bi-polar to a multi-polar world. For at least the next ten years there will be considerable differences in the power of the various big powers. There will be only two super-powers (or nuclear giants) and several big powers (or nuclear dwarfs). Thus, what is emerging is not a multi-polar world of equal powers, but one in which there will be two grades of big powers. Nuclear protection from one of the nuclear giants will continue to affect the relations of all big powers with the other nuclear giant. Thus, France would be most adventurous to allow its defense bond with the US (via NATO) to lapse; or China to renounce its defense alliance with the USSR. The US and the USSR, on the other hand, will seek to use this residue of power-superiority to gain support for policies they favor, especially to prevent their allies from pursuing policies that might engulf them in nuclear war with each other.

Power is thus 'sliced' in the following way: each big power can follow a foreign policy of its own on any matter except the most important ones. China can refuse to follow Soviet policy in Laos, threaten Formosa, perhaps even split the Communist movement, but if it were to attack Formosa, or invade India proper, without prior Russian consent, the Kremlin might use the 'hot-line' to inform the US that it is folding the nuclear umbrella—i.e. withdrawing the nuclear protection—under which Chinese conventional forces are advancing. While the US might still not bomb the Chinese forces, China cannot but find it risky to rely on such US self-restraint.

Similarly, if France were to use its nuclear sting to annoy Russia, or West Germany were to rush with its growing militia to help an uprising in East Germany in an effort to reunify Germany by force—counting on American nuclear protection—the same 'hot-line' might carry the same message in the opposite direction.

'Folding the nuclear umbrella' is an exercise of power that can be used only sparingly. It cannot even be threatened too often, because it is not credible for less than crucial issues, and would be detrimental to the interests of the super-powers as over-use of this threat would tend to encourage big powers to build their own nuclear forces. Thus, the edge of super-over big powers is not large, and the residue of bi-polarity is limited.

This residue would further shrink for any big power that does not believe that the USSR has aggressive military intentions toward it (let us say, France) or that a small number of nuclear weapons will suffice to deter whatever aggressive intentions the USSR still might have, or that the USSR will respect neutrality (as Britain might hope, or West Germany, trading neutrality for reunification). Or, if China has decided to rely on indigenous uprisings in neighboring countries rather than outright invasion (despite pronouncements to the contrary, which are useful propaganda in the Communist movement), it might feel that it does not need the protection of the Soviet umbrella.

If this situation should develop, it is not inconceivable that the super-powers will become more assertive in their policies toward each other's allies, to demonstrate the need for their respective nuclear umbrellas, and to maintain whatever remains of the bi-polar world and the special status they once enjoyed (American warlike acts against North Vietnam would be a case in point).*

---

* The points made here are elaborated in my *Winning Without War* (Garden City: Doubleday, 1964).

Or, surely safer for mankind, the super-powers—each too weak on its own—might collaborate in imposing 'rules' on third countries. Neutralization pacts underwritten by the US and USSR (perhaps using the UN machinery) in areas where China and France have interests, would be a case in point. A USSR-US agreement to limit arms in Central Europe is another possibility.

Further decline in the superiority of the two nuclear giants seems hard to prevent, that is, it seems impossible to imagine a way to stop the spread of nuclear arms, short of general and complete disarmament and the founding of a world government—two developments that cannot be expected in the practicable future. At best, after the present attempts to patch up alliances have proven futile, the US and the USSR might agree that neither will provide nuclear arms or technical know-how to any third country. Such an agreement would not prevent these countries from gaining nuclear arms, but would *slow down* the process, keeping them—at least for the next decade—as nuclear dwarfs among nuclear giants, rather than helping them to become giants in short order. If these countries themselves would become parties to the test ban treaty, this might slow down the birth of additional nuclear dwarfs and avert future nuclear chaos. (We do not *favor* even the limited spread of nuclear arms, but to refrain from cooperating with France to halt further proliferation because the French already have nuclear weapons is an unfortunate line of policy, which ignores the feasible in favor of the unattainable.)

The bi-polar model is to be replaced by a multi-polar one that recognizes gradations of power. The stalemate conception that underlies the division of the world into two spheres of influence, the basis of containment, is to be replaced by a much more complicated conception, one of a new world which contains many new dangers as well as opportunities. At worst, the more aggressive big powers will make the deals while the US and USSR will seek vainly to make reality conform to a bi-polar image: at best, the US and USSR—sometimes bi-laterally, hopefully often in cooperation with all powers—will advance a new world order, through neutralized zones, limitations on the spread of nuclear arms, arms reduction and strengthening the UN. To put it more formally, as pluralism increases, the interests of the super-powers, and, to a somewhat lesser degree, of all the powers, might well become clad in universal rules, backed up by a growingly effective international machinery aimed above all at limiting the multi-faceted competition to non-military means.

3. Beyond the Balance of Terror

The traditional balance-of-power image appears twice in the strategic thinking that governs current American policy: first in the concept of *containment,* according to which the West is to 'balance' the East and ensure peaceful coexistence by generating a global stalemate; and second, in the concept of strategic *deterrence* (or 'balance of terror') according to which the threat implicit in the military power of each nuclear giant not so much prevents the gradual expansion of the other side (against which counter-subversion measures, conventional forces, and political and economic stabilization are used more than the threat of nuclear arms), but deters the sides from a major war which would risk mutual annihilation. In addition to containment, at the line separating the blocs, the present strategy sees a nuclear ceiling that prevents the sides from leaping at each other. It is widely believed that this balance of terror can be stabilized.

But authorities as different as C. P. Snow and Herman Kahn, Bertrand Russell and John F. Kennedy, have repeatedly pointed out that this balance *might* be upset, unintentionally, because of a technological break-through or a miscalculation. All previous balance-of-power systems, it must be emphasized, have occasionally been unbalanced and led to war. Even if the probability of a major blow-up in the balance of terror is slight, the scope of disaster in the event of such an occurrence is so large as to make the system most unsatisfactory.

The major argument of the supporters of arms control is that more comprehensive measures would involve prerequisites that, they believe, cannot be met. The question is whether there are any circumstances under which the implementation of more far-reaching measures of arms reduction can be attained. It seems to me that while a world government cannot be established just because it is needed, nor can universal disarmament be brought about because there is a danger of nuclear war, under the changed circumstances the hope for some progress beyond arms-control is not utopian, and the probability that it will come about can be increased if it is more thoroughly pursued.

Part of the problem is psychological. As long as either the West or the Communist bloc maintains that it is involved in a holy war to eradicate evil from the earth, little progress toward a safer world can be expected. But the situation eases with the appearance of gray shades in what was a black-and-white conception. The decline of bi-polarity as a conception, generates a considerable degree of psychological disarmament in the Cold War, and creates the domestic backdrop for the acceptance of many international accommodations that only yesterday would have been considered heresy.

Second, the evolution of large, invulnerable, second-strike forces allows the arrest of the strategic arms race. Whatever the outcome of the numerical build-up of long range bombers and missiles, most experts agree that the US and the USSR are moving rapidly toward *strategic* parity in nuclear weapons. For the next decade, whatever France and China build could hardly compete with the more than 40,000 owned by the US, and whatever the Russians have amassed. If the arms race could be kept from outer space, the anti-missile and civil defense race from taking off, the domestic forces that wish to order more hardware because of irrational fears or the economic and political hay they expect to make could be curbed, the main US-USSR strategic arms race might be brought to a halt.

This might be followed by considerable bi-lateral US-USSR arms reductions, since the two nuclear giants are so much ahead of everybody else that even if they cut their nuclear forces by 50 per cent they would still command ten times more strategic forces than all other countries *combined*. Such reductions, especially if the numeri-

cal differences were adjusted in the process so as to cement the strategic parity, would make a first-strike by either side less feared. And whatever the saved funds were used for—be it improving the standard of living or of education, or for foreign aid—they would contribute more toward a safer and better world than their investment in an upward spiralling arms race.

Reductions of these magnitudes, which still leave the US and the USSR with fully effective retaliatory forces, could, as several studies have shown, be safely undertaken without inspection, through various other verification devices such as destruction of missiles in neutral spots, and turning over fissionable material to atoms-for-peace programs. Further reduction could be attained through reciprocal inspection of limited parts of the USSR and the US, thus delaying the difficult problems raised by plans to form an international inspection authority and international police force.

Many of these ideas, which yesterday seemed little more realistic than general and complete disarmament, are today supported by studies by such federal agencies as the Institute of Defense Analysis, and by key men in the Pentagon and the Department of Defense.[1] If the world continues to evolve along the pluralistic lines suggested above, and American and Soviet strategies evolve to favor peaceful competition, the interests of the super-powers might be increasingly expressed through the development of international machinery for the peaceful settlement of disputes, prevention of armed intervention in third countries and pacification of wars among them. Soviet spokesmen early in 1964 stated, for the first time, that they see the need for a global authority if disarmament is to be implemented; this is a point the US has insisted on, but which many observers believed the USSR would not concede. The assumption that the UN will provide 'collective security,' which many Americans made in 1945, was rather illusory. But the change in the composition of the UN, with the admission of many non-aligned countries, and the loosening of the blocs, as well as the search

[1] See Statement of Secretary of Defense Robert McNamara before the House Armed Services Committee on 30 January 1963.

of the super-powers—and some big powers—
for universal institutions to facilitate their
accommodations, might bring a new reality
to the UN and provide for the first time a
power-politics basis for the noble ideas expressed in its Charter. This firm basis is
required if there is to be world peace under
world law.

4. Non-zero-sum 'games'

The USSR, it is said, might temporarily
agree to world-wide peaceful competition,
especially as its influence in East Europe
is large enough to make defections from
the Soviet bloc unlikely (the USSR has
already removed the Red Army from most
'satellites'), and as countries in the Soviet
sphere of influence are several times fewer
than those in America's. But once the Soviets discover that the US is doing better
in the peaceful competition, would they
not, long before such options disappear,
choose to revive armed efforts at expansion?
Others ask, if the US found that it was
doing poorly in the peaceful competition,
would the US not resort to force rather than
lose out?

Underlying these criticisms is the notion
of a zero-sum relationship, wherein Western success spells Soviet loss, and vice versa.
Actually, peaceful competition, under effectively enforced rules, brings into focus some
shared and some compatible interests which
the US and the USSR do have. The list of
these interests is hardly new, but their significance for the stabilization of peaceful
competition, once it is established, has not
been fully recognized. Avoiding nuclear
war, and conventional wars that might escalate into nuclear wars, is a shared interest
that has already limited the use of arms
by both sides in numerous confrontations,
from Berlin in 1948 to South Vietnam in
1964. Many situations that might have
generated major wars in the pre-nuclear
age, have resulted—at most—in limited conventional clashes, and, more commonly,
with the exchange of bitter diplomatic
notes. Ruling out arms altogether in such
confrontations—let us say through an effectively guarded neutralization of areas of
contention—would be only one step removed from the present situation. Once the

rule of 'non-armed contests only' had been
established, it would not readily be reversed,
because a reversal might escalate further
than either side desires, and because experience has shown to the USSR since 1949
that no more gains are to be had through
use of military force. In short, the factors
which deter both nuclear war and conventional aggression are effective forces which
would support peaceful competition once
established.

But what about USSR insistence that
it will support 'wars of national liberation'? The main question is not whether
Russia will or will not support indigenous
uprisings, but by what means support will
be granted. Armed support could lead to
the subjugation of a country and must be
ruled out. Statements made by the Soviet
Premier at the beginning of 1964 would
suggest that he might be willing to limit
himself to non-armed support, if the US
would also limit itself to non-armed support of the governments of these countries.
This is an accommodation the West ought
to accept, not only because this is a way
of preventing dangerous armed confrontations between the USSR and US in third
countries, but because if forces of social
change in third countries are allowed to
run their course, these countries would be
more likely to move toward development
and to evolve responsive governments. This
would constitute another gain for both the
US and the USSR.

The division of the world into 'have'
and 'have-not' countries—with the USSR
and the US classed as 'have' countries—
endangers the world order. A country with
nothing to lose but its chains might be so
desperate as to push the brinkmanship of
nuclear blackmail to the point where it will
either trigger a pre-emptive strike, or wipe
out some cities in the Western sphere of
influence (e.g. Saigon) to demonstrate its
resolve, thus unleashing an international
disaster. Hence, all 'have' powers, while
they quarrel among themselves over the
global distribution of spheres of influence,
will recognize—as the Cold War dust settles
—that increasing the stakes of 'have-not'
countries in the world order, by assisting
them to meet their most basic needs, is in
the deepest interest of all 'have' countries.

The US-USSR competition, which is largely geared to advancing their positions *vis-à-vis* each other, has a most productive 'side effect,' which benefits both powers: it is the major lever that shifts some resources from the rich to the poor countries. Under conditions of peaceful competition the importance of this 'side effect' will grow, and will encourage the continuation of the competition, even if the primary goals of advancing the position of one's bloc were to be curtailed.

Finally, the game-theoreticians emphasize that there are not just win-lose or lose-win situations, but also win-win or lose-lose ones.[2] But they often fail to mention those outcomes in which *none* of the 'players' gains *or* loses, a state which peaceful competition might approximate. The USSR and the US were seeking, for a while, to 'attach' countries; the USSR to expand the Communist bloc, and the US to attract countries to its counter-alliances—to SEATO, CENTO, and NATO. But both sides have already lost most of their taste for these kinds of payoffs as they have found the 'game' costly, frustrating, and dangerous. Increasingly, both super-powers seek to maintain the non-alignment of third countries rather than induce them to join their respective blocs, which means, no-gains and no-losses of members, but still a state of affairs which can satisfy—or at least be 'lived with'—by both sides simultaneously.

Surprisingly, in the nuclear age, this point might be applied not only to third countries but also to allies. The image of a rigid bi-polar world is defunct not only because the third countries cannot be nicely 'divided' as Africa was in the late 19th century between the European powers, but also because those already in the two super-blocs cannot be tied to the super-powers' apron strings, nor are the 'losses' incurred when an ally breaks away even remotely as detrimental as the super-powers make it sound, in this 'the alliance must be saved' stage. To take a rather extreme example: if France, West Germany, and Britain should suddenly become non-aligned and their non-alignment maintained, US

security in this age of inter-continental missiles could not be much affected, and the breaking away of China probably improves rather than undermines the security of the USSR, whatever status and 'political' setbacks it might create. In short, there is nothing in game theory to suggest that peaceful competition is not as acceptable a strategy as the conception of bi-polarity which underlies the strategies of yesterday. Nor is the distribution of power in the world which this conception assumes available.

5. The Psychology of Competition

Psychologically, peaceful competition adds 'do's' to 'don'ts,' and rewards to sanctions. Thus while Western countries will not tolerate the expansion of the Communist bloc, by armed subversion of third countries, they nevertheless welcome the Soviet-led camp to participation in the world community, by peaceful means such as foreign aid, technical assistance, and trade concessions. As long as effective procedures ensure that peaceful contacts are not used for armed expansion—e.g. that technicians are really working at development and not military training—no efforts are made to keep Communist countries out of the competition; on the contrary, pains are taken to draw them in. Thus, under a strategy of peaceful competition, the US would cease the pressure now put on Latin American countries not to trade with Russia, on the assumptions that trade accelerates the development of Latin America, which is desirable; that trade provides a test of quality and prices of products—and by implication, that of technological and economic systems—which America has no reason to fear; and that if the USSR attempted to use its trade for political blackmail, the US could step in and provide—at world market prices—whatever Russia is threatening to cut off. Similarly, the US would cease to object to any country—be it Ghana, Egypt, or Indonesia—receiving Soviet foreign aid, since, as has been seen time and time again, aid cannot be used to subvert a country. None of the 22 countries that received Soviet aid over the last decade have been converted to Communism, and

[2] This point was made by J. David Singer, 'The Return to Multilateral Diplomacy', *Yale Review*, Vol. LIII (1963), pp. 36–48.

the 23rd—Cuba—received Soviet aid only after it had turned Communist.[3]

The model of peaceful competition draws on sublimation psychology, which suggests that it is much easier for an expansionist power to accept a half-blocked, half-open passage—where competition by some means is permitted although other means are disallowed—than to accept complete frustration of its deep-seated drive to bring its way of life to other people. Since the USSR recognizes the increased dangers of escalation involved in even small scale use of arms, and firmly believes in the efficacy of its economic and ideological appeal, there seems to be reason to believe the USSR might agree to limit its expansionist ambitions to peaceful contests, and to the procedures that would ensure that these contests remain limited. (To push the psychological analogy a step further, one might suggest that containment seeks *suppression* of a drive, while peaceful competition seeks its *sublimation,* and the transfer of part of the energy to 'control-functions', to international equivalents of ego and super-ego functions.) Positive rewards can be generated, on the international level, to the degree the disposition of countries toward global welfare will be measured by the amount of genuine foreign aid they grant, the interest rate they charge on loans they extend, and the number of technical assistants they send, etc.

Nor will Western countries continue to be limited by the bars of containments. The containment stalemate, it should be stressed, frustrates not only the USSR but also the keen desire of the West to spread the values it believes in to all people, including those behind the Iron Curtain. In line with a newly invigorated endeavor to build a world community, which would be signalled by the new strategy of peaceful competition, the US would renounce any tacit or implicit recognition of the limitation of our peaceful contacts with members of the Communist bloc. The US should favor increased Western trade with Poland, Romania, Outer Mongolia and

any other Communist country. While the US should not call for the overthrow of any government by force, it should absolutely refuse to limit broadcasts of ideas and information to countries of the Communist bloc.

In short, psychologically speaking, peaceful competition allows for more legitimate assertion of both sides, involves less suppression and frustration, and hence provides healthier foundations for the patterns of conduct advocated.

There is one other model, not explicitly discussed here, which underlies much of the analysis: the assumption that when competition is effectively limited to peaceful means, more than favoring any one participant it advances values that the competition supports and binds them closer together. This is just another way of saying that it advances social justice and political freedom (e.g. by favoring development and keeping armed intervention out of the third world) and stabilizes peace by peaceful engagement of the sides in a world community.

Summary

An analysis of de-polarization draws on four analytical models. The traditional balance-of-power analysis suggests that as the level of integration of the two blocs (East and West) declines, the number of possible political combinations increases, foreign policy gains in the number of political options, the probability of a military showdown declines, and the ideological fervor is expected to be reduced. The balance-of-terror, the model behind deterrence, is weakened by the appearance of an increasing number of small nuclear powers, and it is expected to be further undermined by more nuclear powers with a growing nuclear capability. This is an unbalancing trend. Game-theory is used to point out the non-zero-sum characteristics of the depolarizing system and the payoffs it offers to all sides. Psychological analysis is employed to suggest that bi-polarity is frustrating for both blocs, while a competition limited by rules would allow some expression to the legitimate drives of all sides.

[3] H. J. P. Arnold, *Aid for Developing Countries* (Chester Springs, Pa: Dufour Editions, 1962).

INDEX-BIBLIOGRAPHY

ALLPORT, GORDON W. "Guide Lines for Research in International Co-operation," in T. H. Pear (Editor), *Psychological Factors in Peace and War.* New York: The Philosophical Library, 1950, pp. 141–157.

BOULDING, KENNETH E. "The Prevention of World War III," *The Virginia Quarterly Review,* 1962, *38*: 11.

BROWN, JUDSON S. "Principles of Intrapersonal Conflict," *Journal of Conflict Resolution,* 1957, *1*: 135–153.

CLAUDE, INIS L., JR. "United Nations Use of Military Force," *Journal of Conflict Resolution,* 1963, *7*: 117–129.

COSER, LEWIS A. "Social Conflict and the Theory of Social Change," *The British Journal of Sociology,* 1957, *8*: 197–207.

COSER, LEWIS A. "The Termination of Conflict," *Journal of Conflict Resolution,* 1961, *5*: 347–353.

DENTON, FRANK H. "Some Patterns in the History of Violence," *Journal of Conflict Resolution,* 1968, *12*: 182–195.

DEUTSCH, MORTON. "Conflict and Its Resolution," Presidential Address to the American Psychological Association, 1965, 20 pp.

DYNES, RUSSELL R. "The Absence of Community Conflict in the Early Phases of Natural Disasters," American Sociological Association Meeting Paper, San Francisco, Sept., 1969, 16 pp.

ETZIONI, AMITAI. "Strategic Models for a De-Polarizing World," *Journal of Peace Research,* 1965, *2*: 136–150.

FISHER, ROGER. "Fractionating Conflict," in Roger Fisher (Editor), *International Conflict and Behavioral Sciences: The Craigville Papers.* New York: Basic Books, 1964, pp. 91–110.

FROMM, ERICH. "The Case for Unilateral Disarmament," in Q. Wright *et al.* (Editors), *Preventing World War III.* New York: Simon & Schuster, 1962, pp. 161–177.

GALTUNG, JOHAN. "A Structural Theory of Aggression," *Journal of Peace Research,* 1964, *1*: 95–119.

GAMSON, WILLIAM A. "A Theory of Coalition Formation," *American Sociological Review,* 1961, *26*: 373–382.

GLAGOLEV, I. "Some Problems of Disarmament Research," *Journal of Peace Research,* 1964, *1*: 150–154.

GORYAINOV, M. "Some Problems of Disarmament Research," *Journal of Peace Research,* 1964, *1*: 150–154.

GUETZKOW, HAROLD. "Isolation and Collaboration: A Partial Theory of Internation Relations," *Journal of Conflict Resolution,* 1957, *1*: 46–68.

HAUSER, PHILIP M. "Demographic Dimensions of World Politics," *Science.*

HAYDEN, THOMAS. "Is There a Military-Industrial Complex Which Prevents Peace?: Consensus and Countervailing Power in Pluralistic Systems," *Journal of Social Issues,* 1965, *21*: 67–117.

HIMES, JOSEPH S. "The Functions of Racial Conflict," *Journal of Social Forces,* 1966, *45*: 1–10.

HOROWITZ, IRVING LOUIS. "Consensus, Conflict and Cooperation: A Sociological Inventory," *Social Forces,* 1962, *41*: 177–188.

JANIS, IRVING L. "The Reduction of Intergroup Hostility: Research Problems and Hypotheses," *Journal of Conflict Resolution,* 1959, *3*: 85–100.

JANIS, IRVING L. "Problems of Theory in the Analysis of Stress Behavior," *Journal of Social Issues,* 1954, *10*: 12–25.

JEFFRIES, VINCENT. "Class Conflict: Forget It!" *Sociology and Social Research,* 1970, *54*: 306–320.

KATZ, DANIEL. "Current and Needed Psychological Research in International Relations," *Journal of Social Issues,* 1961, *17*: 69–78.

KATZ, DANIEL. "Group Process and Social Integration: A System Analysis of Two Movements of Social Protest," *Journal of Social Issues,* 1967, *23*: 3–22.

KATZ, DANIEL. "Nationalism and Strategies of International Conflict Resolution," in H. Kelman (Editor), *International Behavior.* New York: Holt, Rinehart, & Winston, 1965, *10*: 354–390.

KATZ, DANIEL. "The Reduction of Intergroup Hostility: Research Problems and Hypotheses," *Journal of Conflict Resolution,* 1959, *3*: 85–100.

KELMAN, HERBERT C. "Societal, Attitudinal and Structural Factors in International Relations," *Journal of Social Issues,* 1955, *11*: 42–56.

KLINGBERG, FRANK L. "Predicting the Termination of War: Battle Casualties and Population Losses," *Journal of Conflict Resolution,* 1966, *10*:129–171.

LEVI, WERNER. "On the Causes of War and the Conditions of Peace," *Journal of Conflict Resolution,* 1960, *4*: 411–420.

MACK, RAYMOND W. "The Analysis of Social Conflict—Toward an Overview and Synthesis," *Journal of Conflict Resolution,* 1957, *1*: 212–248.

MORRIS, RICHARD T. "Class Conflict: Forget It!" *Sociology and Social Research,* 1970, *54*: 306–320.

OSGOOD, CHARLES E. "Graduated Unilaterial Initiatives for Peace," in Q. Wright *et al.* (Editors), *Preventing World War III.* New York: Simon & Schuster, 1962, pp. 161–177.

PATCHEN, MARTIN. "Decision Theory in the Study of National Action: Problems and a Proposal," *Journal of Conflict Resolution,* 1965, *9*: 164–176.

PETTIGREW, THOMAS F. "Social Psychology and Desegregation Research," *American Psychologist,* 1961, *16*: 105–112.

PHILLIPS, WARREN. "Some Patterns in the History of Violence," *Journal of Conflict Resolution,* 1968, *12*: 182–195.

PILISUK, MARC. "Is There a Military-Industrial Complex Which Prevents Peace?: Consensus and Countervailing Power in Pluralistic Systems," *Journal of Social Issues,* 1965, *21*: 67–117.

QUARANTELLI, E. L. "The Absence of Community Conflict in the Early Phases of Natural Disasters," American Sociological Association Meeting Paper, San Francisco, Sept., 1969, 16 pp.

RUMMEL, R. J. "Dimensions of Conflict Behavior Within Nations, 1946–59," *Journal of Conflict Resolution,* 1966, *10*: 65–73.

SCHURMANN, FRANZ. "On Revolutionary Conflict," *Journal of International Affairs,* 1969, *23*: 36–53.

SHUBIK, MARTIN. "On the Study of Disarmament and Escalation," *Journal of Conflict Resolution,* 1968, *12*: 83–101.

SMOKER, PAUL. "Nation State Escalation and International Integration," *Journal of Peace Research,* 1967, *4*: 61–75.

SNYDER, ROBERT C. "The Analysis of Social Conflict—Toward an Overview and Synthesis," *Journal of Conflict Resolution,* 1957, *1*: 212–248.

STAGNER, ROSS. "Personality Dynamics and Social Conflict," *Journal of Social Issues,* 1961, *17*: 28–44.

TANTER, RAYMOND. "Dimensions of Conflict Behavior Within and Between Nations, 1958–60," *Journal of Conflict Resolution,* 1966, *10*: 41–64.

WRIGHT, QUINCY. "The Escalation of International Conflicts," *Journal of Conflict Resolution,* 1965, *9*: 434–449.

ZAWODNY, J. K. "Unconventional Warfare," *American Scholar,* 1962, *31*: 384-394.

ZINNES, DINA A. "An Analytical Study of the Balance of Power Theories." *Journal of Peace Research,* 1967, *4*: 270–288.